861 preaching as Sacrament
877 preaching as concrete

THEOLOGICAL DIMENSIONS
OF THE LITURGY

THEOLOGICAL DIMENSIONS OF THE LITURGY

A General Treatise
on the
Theology of the Liturgy

by

CYPRIAN VAGAGGINI, O.S.B.

translated by
Leonard J. Doyle
and
W. A. Jurgens

From the Fourth Italian Edition
Revised and Augmented by the Author

THE LITURGICAL PRESS

COLLEGEVILLE   MINNESOTA

THEOLOGICAL DIMENSIONS OF THE LITURGY is the authorized English version of *Il senso teologico della liturgia* — quarta edizione notevolmente riveduta ed aggiornata dall'Autore, Dom Cipriano Vagaggini, O.S.B.; published by Edizioni Paoline, Rome, Italy.

Nihil obstat: William G. Heidt, O.S.B., S.T.D., *Censor deputatus*. *Imprimatur*: † George H. Speltz, D.D., Bishop of St. Cloud. September 28, 1976.

ISBN 0-8146-0928-7

CONTENTS

PART ONE

THE NATURE OF LITURGY

CHAPTER 1

THE GENERAL BACKGROUND OF THE LITURGY:
REVELATION AS SACRED HISTORY

CHAPTER 2

THE LITURGY AS A COMPLEXUS OF SENSIBLE SIGNS

CHAPTER 3

THE LITURGY AS A COMPLEXUS OF EFFICACIOUS SENSIBLE SIGNS

CHAPTER 4

THE LITURGY AS A COMPLEXUS OF SENSIBLE EFFICACIOUS SIGNS OF THE CHURCH'S SANCTIFICATION AND WORSHIP

CHAPTER 5

THE NOTION OF THE LITURGY AND THE MASS AS REALIZATION AND SYNTHETIC EXPRESSION OF THE WHOLE LITURGICAL COMPLEXUS

PART TWO

THE LITURGY AND THE GENERAL LAWS OF THE DIVINE ECONOMY IN THE WORLD

CHAPTER 6

THE LITURGY AND THE LAW OF OBJECTIVITY

CHAPTER 7

FROM THE FATHER, THROUGH CHRIST, IN THE HOLY SPIRIT, TO THE FATHER: THE LITURGY AND THE CHRISTOLOGICAL-TRINITARIAN ACTIVITY IN THE DIVINE PLAN

CHAPTER 8

THE KYRIOS — THE PASCHAL MYSTERY:
THE ONE LITURGIST AND THE ONE LITURGY

CHAPTER 9

THE LITURGY AND THE LAW OF SALVATION IN COMMUNITY

CHAPTER 10

THE LITURGY AND THE LAW OF THE INCARNATION

CHAPTER 11

THE LITURGY AND THE LAW OF THE COSMIC UNIVERSALITY OF THE KINGDOM OF GOD
1. LITURGY, MAN, AND THE INFRAHUMAN WORLD

CHAPTER 12

THE LITURGY AND THE LAW OF THE COSMIC UNIVERSALITY OF THE KINGDOM OF GOD
II. LITURGY, SAINTS AND ANGELS

CHAPTER 13

THE TWO CITIES: THE LITURGY AND THE STRUGGLE AGAINST SATAN

PART THREE

LITURGY AND BIBLE

CHAPTER 14

HOW THE LITURGY MAKES USE OF SCRIPTURE

CHAPTER 15

REMARKS ON THE CENTRAL THEMES OF THE INDIVIDUAL PSALMS AND THEIR REFERENCE TO THE MYSTERY OF CHRIST IN THE LITURGY

PART FOUR

LITURGY, FAITH, AND THEOLOGY

CHAPTER 16

LITURGY AND FAITH

CHAPTER 17

POSITIVE-SCHOLASTIC THEOLOGY AND LITURGY

CHAPTER 18

THEOLOGY AND LITURGY IN SAINT THOMAS

CHAPTER 19

THEOLOGY AND LITURGY IN THE FATHERS

CHAPTER 20

SUGGESTIONS FOR THE SYSTEMATIC INCLUSION OF THE LITURGICAL-THEOLOGICAL ASPECT IN THE INDIVIDUAL QUESTIONS OF GENERAL SYNTHETIC THEOLOGY

PART FIVE

LITURGY AND LIFE

CHAPTER 21

LITURGY AND SPIRITUALITY

CHAPTER 22

THE EXAMPLE OF A MYSTIC: ST. GERTRUDE AND LITURGICAL SPIRITUALITY

CHAPTER 23
LITURGY AND PASTORAL: THE PRINCIPLES

CHAPTER 24

HINTS ON THE MEANS OF LITURGICAL PASTORAL: IN PARTICULAR, PREACHING AND LITURGY, CATECHISM AND LITURGY

PREFACE

Although the liturgy does not comprise the Church's whole activity, still it is the summit toward which the Church's spiritual life as well as her pastoral life is directed, and at the same time the fount from which all her power flows.[1] Whoever concurs in this judgment of the Second Vatican Council must agree that the Constitution on the Liturgy promulgated by the council marks a memorable date not only in the history of the liturgy but also in the entire life of the Church.

The object of the Constitution is directly pastoral. But its secret strength lies in the fact that it views the pastoral goal, and the liturgical reform which serves as a means of attaining that goal, in the framework of an integral concept of the liturgy. In this concept the theological aspect of the liturgical reality is central and essential, the historical aspect is presupposed and the spiritual, pastoral and juridical aspects are derivative.

As a result, the general structure of the exposition as set forth in the Constitution rests on an accurate analysis of the nature and theological properties of the liturgy in the framework of the history of salvation, of Christology and of soteriology, as well as of ecclesiology and of a theology of the sacraments in general.[2] Moreover, the general and particular practical norms for liturgicas pastoral and for liturgical reform[3] are continually projected against the background of the theological principles which govern them.

This concern of the council, to inculcate at every opportunity an integral concept of the liturgy based on its theological value, appears also in the norms proposed for teaching the liturgy. It is to be taught, says the council, both under its theological and historical aspects and under its spiritual, pastoral and juridical aspects.[4]

[1] CL, art. 10.
[2] *Ibid.*, art. 2; 5-13.
[3] *Ibid.*, art. 14-46 and chapters 2-7.

[4] *Ibid.*, art. 16. See also art. 23 on the general norms for reform.

The concept of liturgy hereby acquires a completeness and maturity never achieved in the past. Until about 1920–1930 the liturgy was commonly considered as the whole body of ceremonies of the Church's public worship and the complexus of Church laws regulating that worship. Liturgical science was treated as a part of canon law, in which history, theological speculation and the pastoral art were involved only in so far as they contributed toward a knowledge of the rubrical laws of worship. The textbooks of "liturgy" were based on this conception.

This idea of the liturgy has been a hard one to stamp out, and no one would dare deny that some trace of it still survives.[5]

About the year 1920, however, a strong reaction set in against this arbitrary limitation of the liturgical reality. The reaction was twofold.

First of all the object considered in liturgical science was broadened. Thus it was found desirable to treat under "liturgy" not only the ceremonies and the rubrics but the liturgical actions or rites themselves, the liturgical formularies, the buildings destined for worship, the altar, the sacred vessels, the liturgical insignia, Gregorian chant; and not only the Mass, the breviary, the sacraments and the sacramentals, but also the feasts and the liturgical year — in short, all the elements that have some relation to worship. Moreover, the ideal was to consider all this not only in the Roman liturgy but also in the other liturgies, and to make a comparative study of them (comparative liturgy).

In the second place, it became the practice to give all this material a predominantly historical treatment. The ideal pursued was to trace the historical development of the objects listed above, which constitute the liturgy, from their origin to the present day, and this, if possible, not only in the Roman liturgy but in all the liturgies, obsolete or current.

If formerly liturgical science had been considered essentially as a matter of learning rubrics, from that time on, in almost all cases, it was considered essentially as mere history. There were indeed hints at the theological content or the ascetico-spiritual and pastoral value of the liturgy, but for the most part these were only hints, often very brief. The essential preoccupation was with the historical aspect, the successive steps in the formation of the liturgy we have today. Thus the effort in liturgical instruction was to make a synthesis of the historical inquiries into the liturgy which had their scientific beginnings with the great liturgical historians of the seventeenth century,[6] and

---

[5] MD expressed clear disapproval of a similar concept of the liturgy: "It is an error consequently and a mistake to think of the sacred liturgy as merely the outward or visible part of divine worship or as an ornamental ceremonial. No less erroneous is the notion that it consists solely in a list of laws and prescriptions according to which the ecclesiastical hierarchy orders the sacred rites to be performed" (n. 25).

[6] See, e.g., the list of them given by Righetti, I, 70 ff. These studies have had their encyclopedia, unfortunately not free from defects, since, after the first volume, it was compiled almost completely by one editor: Henri Leclercq, *Dictionnaire d'archéologie chrétienne et de liturgie* (Paris: Letouzey, starting from 1907).

have made extraordinary progress from about the beginning of the present century. In Germany the outstanding textbook of this type of liturgy seems to have been that of Ludwig Eisenhofer.[7] In Italy we now have Mario Righett's fine compendium in four volumes,[8] which offers an excellent general introduction to the history of the individual liturgical objects and elements considered separately.

Even from the purely historical point of view, however, both Righetti and Eisenhofer, who divide their works into general liturgy and special liturgy, lack a panoramic view of the development of the liturgy in all its constituent elements according to the different epochs. They lack a vision in which we might see for each great epoch the reflections of the dominant cultural-religious and ethnical tendencies in the whole liturgical field, something which is of supreme importance for a true understanding of the liturgy, be it only from the historical viewpoint.[9]

Obviously, the historical method of considering the liturgy marked a vast improvement over the rubricist method. A knowledge of the historical origin of the liturgical complexus, under all its aspects, leads to a much more substantial understanding of the liturgy which we have today.

From this it follows, in the first place, that these studies are obviously indispensable: they must be continued and perfected. It follows moreover that the results of the historical research must always be kept accurately in mind for the further probing of the liturgy. They are a necessary foundation for liturgical pastoral, for the reform of the liturgy and for the study of liturgical law. And without this foundation it would be foolish to construct further explanations, even theological and mystical, of the liturgy.

Granted this much, after the Second World War there seemed to be a further obvious and urgent need in the study of the liturgy. This was the need: while basing oneself always on historical research whenever the matter is susceptible

---

[7] *Handbuch der katholischen Liturgik*, 2 vols. (Freiburg i. B.: Herder, 1932, 2nd printing 1941-42). The author himself made a compendium of it, *Grundriss der katholischen Liturgik*, now replaced by *The Liturgy of the Roman Rite* by Ludwig Eisenhofer and Joseph Lechner (New York: Herder and Herder, 1961).

[8] *Storia liturgica*, 4 vols. (Milan: Ancora, 1945-53, followed by later editions of the various volumes). I. General introduction; II. The liturgical year; the breviary; III. The Eucharist; IV. Sacraments and sacramentals.

[9] With the aim of supplying for this defect there is now a first worthwhile attempt, worthy of every encouragement, in E. Cattaneo's *Introduzione alla storia della liturgie occidentale* (Rome, 1962). Among the previous works see: Anton Baumstark, *Vom geschichtlichen Werden der Liturgie* (Freiburg i. B.: Herder,

1923); the excellent work of the Anglican Gregory Dix, *The Shape of the Liturgy* (Westminster [London]: Dacre Press, 1945, reprint 1954). In 1949 Theodore Klauser wrote an informative panoramic article on the same subject: *Abendländische Liturgiegeschichte*, published in English translation under the title *A Brief History of Liturgy* (Collegeville, Minn.: Liturgical Press, 1953). Josef A. Jungmann in his *The Mass of the Roman Rite* gives the same question a substantial treatment, but with respect to the Mass in particular (New York: Benziger, 1950-55), I, 7-167. There is a good panorama of the general development of the liturgy by epochs also, but in the Lutheran interpretation, in Rudolf Staehlin's "Die Geschichte des christlichen Gottesdienstes von der Urkirche bis zur Gegenwart," *Leiturgia*, I (Kassel: Stauda, 1954), pp. 1-81.

of it, to go beyond the stage of purely historical, or even predominantly historical interest.

The liturgical movement, while itself being a powerful stimulus to historical inquiry into the liturgy, from which inquiry in turn it received a very strong impetus, tended at the same time to surpass that historical stage in three directions: in an ascetical direction which led beyond mere historical understanding to the point where the liturgy became a source of doctrine and a ferment of the spiritual life; in a pastoral direction which was concerned further with the means best suited for bringing the Christian people back to the liturgy and the liturgy to the Christian people; in a third direction more properly theological which probed the liturgy in the light of the ultimate synthesis of thought which alone can yield the general synthetic theology now called dogmatic.

During that time there was a striking growth of interest in the liturgy from the pastoral viewpoint. "Liturgical pastoral," a pastoral art based on the liturgy, became the great dynamic force of the liturgical movement. Beyond doubt, it was this interest that made it a truly worldwide movement, which even before the Second Vatican Council was of profound interest not only to large groups among the Christian people but to an ever increasing number of members of the hierarchy and of priests in charge of souls, both in the countries where the faith is of long standing and in the missions. Pastoral concern, again, was the decisive force which led Pius XII to promulgate the first liturgical reforms of the present period, reforms which were spectacular for their time.

It cannot be said, on the other hand, that the investigation of the theological aspect of the liturgy during the same period was commensurate with its real importance, nor even adequate to provide a solid foundation and a balance for the pastoral concern and the work of reform. I do not mean that nothing was accomplished at all in this field. The liturgical movement had indeed achieved results by its theological inquiries during the past century or so; and the best of these results were nicely summed up in the encyclical *Mediator Dei* along with the fruits of liturgical research from other viewpoints. Moreover, there were essays and monographs of definite importance.[10] But much remained to be done.

[10] The most thought-provoking essays into the theological-liturgical field seem to have been the efforts of Odo Casel towards a theology of the mystery. Aside from Casel's specific theory of the re-presentation of Christ's historical redemptive actions, these efforts, even by the opposition they have aroused, have been the occasion for a more precise determination and a better appreciation of a certain number of worthwhile ideas.

Dom Lambert Beauduin, inaugurator of the liturgical center of the abbey of Mont César at Louvain, Belgium, also showed interest in the theological aspect of the liturgy, an interest which was subsequently continued in the publications of that group, especially in *Les questions liturgiques et paroissiales* and in the *Cours et conférences des semaines liturgiques* (since 1912).

The "Centre de pastorale liturgique" of Paris took care not to neglect this aspect either, as is apparent from the periodical *La maison Dieu* and the collection *Lex orandi*.

The collection *Ecclesia orans* and the reviews

A more notable awakening of interest in the properly theological investigation of the liturgy began only a few years before the council. At any rate, in the council itself, the theological consideration of the liturgy, even if it is not explicit, appears everywhere as the source which casts light on the pastoral norms and the rules for reform in the framework of an integral concept of the liturgical reality.

And it is normal that this should be so. It is also necessary; this we must not tire of repeating, even today, after the council, while the full exuberance of the reforms is with us. How calamitous it would be to forget that these reforms, however important they may be, cannot be anything but an instrument — and not even the most decisive one — in helping attain the aim of liturgical pastoral.

If the aim of liturgical pastoral is to bring the liturgy and, in the liturgy, Christ Himself, back to the people and to bring the people to the liturgy and thus to Christ, the decisive means will always be an understanding, or rather a vital penetration, of the soul of the liturgical world.

The reform of structure, of language, of chant, the very creation of new liturgical forms cannot be anything more than an aid, important though it may be, toward introducing the people into the world of the liturgy. A certain French priest showed that he did not overestimate the effectiveness of this aid when he observed, in a discussion about the liturgical language, "Whether the liturgy is done in Latin or in French, for my people it will always be in Hebrew!"

And even today, after the council, with the liturgy happily almost all in the vernacular, it remains substantially "in Hebrew," not only for the people but also for the clergy. And if the clergy do not first master this Hebrew and then explain it to the people, the liturgical reform will not have done much toward christianizing the world.

The Hebrew here means: the theological study of the liturgy, not separated, of course, from biblical and spiritual thinking. Only a theology of the liturgy, by considering the liturgical reality in the light of its ultimate principles, in the framework of the view of the world given by revelation and studied by general theology, will penetrate to the marrow of the liturgical

Jahrbuch für Liturgiewissenschaft (1921-41) and *Archiv für Liturgiewissenschaft* (since 1950) of Maria Laach must also be noted in this connection.

More recently, Jean Daniélou and Louis Bouyer saw the importance of a more decisively theological grounding in the study of the liturgy. Cardinal Daniélou engaged in an effort of critical rehabilitation of the biblical and patristic typology, especially in his two works *From Shadows to Reality: Studies in the Biblical Typology of the Fathers* (Westminister, Md.: Newman Press, 1960) and *The Bible and*

the Liturgy (Notre Dame, 1956). Notable works of Louis Bouyer are *The Paschal Mystery* (Chicago: Regnery, 1950) and *Liturgical Piety* (Notre Dame, 1955).

Besides these, there are a certain number of individual essays, to which we shall refer in the course of this study.

All in all, with regard to liturgical theology, one gets the impression that, very often, rather than getting down to technical and systematic research, the necessary basis of any work in depth, the authors have been content with essays that are sporadic and popular in character thought. Such a theology of the liturgy, therefore, is the only solid basis for a liturgical spirituality as well as for a liturgical pastoral.

Hopefully, then, theologians will begin to concern themselves more and more with the liturgy, while liturgists will become more and more concerned with theology. Should this in fact come about in any notable degree, it will result in great gain not only to liturgy and the liturgical movement, but even to theology itself.

However much attention be devoted to systematic instruction in the liturgy, to expect to achieve successfully the purpose of opening the way even to an initial discovery of the vast world of the liturgy will remain but a vain hope unless first there is a defining of the principles of this introduction in order to establish a synthetic liturgico-theological overview, so as to make evident the position of the liturgy in the general plan of salvation.

Theological liturgy defines the study of liturgy in a theological context by bringing to the historical inquiry about liturgical action the importance of what has been the subject of prior research, and by introducing the results and consequences thereof into the elaboration of its spiritual, pastoral and juridic content.

General theological liturgy, while concentrating on the theological point of view, studies the elements common to the individual parts of the liturgy. Special theological liturgy studies in the same way the elements which are peculiar to these same individual parts: the Mass, the other sacraments, the sacramentals, and the liturgical year.

The aim of this present treatise on general theological liturgy is to shed some light upon the nature of liturgy, the place which it occupies in the general plan of salvation in connection with the general laws which govern this plan, and its relationship to the Bible, to theology, and to the spiritual and pastoral life.

I shall consider myself happy if with this essay I can help some readers more easily to quench their thirst at the majestic fountain of the liturgy, a fountain of living water which gushes forth unto life eternal. And the fountain is Christ.

PREFACE TO THE FOURTH EDITION

The production of a new edition of this work, the fourth since it first appeared in 1957, necessitated some updating; but at the same time any substantial change of viewpoint was neither possible nor desirable.

The promulgation of the Constitution on the Sacred Liturgy by the Second Vatican Council proved to be a source of particular satisfaction to the author, inasmuch as in the conciliar document the basic positions which this book had adopted already in 1957, in its conception of the nature and function of the liturgy in the Church, have now been widely accepted and solemnly confirmed by the supreme authority.

Thus, in addition to an updating of the bibliography, a few occasional revisions have been sufficient. First of all, wherever possible, the idea elaborated upon has been supported by explicit references to the conciliar texts and to sources emanating even more recently from the Apostolic See. Furthermore, it was necessary to take into account the change in the practical status of the liturgy, in consequence of recent reforms. Even in chapter 24, however, it seemed more advisable to hold fast to the theological character of our work, and not to engage in particular suggestions in regard to the reforms in the structure, in the language and in the singing of the liturgy. Such suggestions were of some utility, I think, before the council; but by this time the principles of such reforms have been established and we are already in the period of their full implementation.

Finally, a more searching consideration has prompted the statement or development of a series of questions. These we have set down for the most part in reference to the definition of the liturgy, the efficacious use of signs in the liturgy, the *opus operantis Ecclesiae*, the nature and importance of the paschal mystery, and in reference to the problem of the relationship between liturgy and mystical prayer.

Dom Cyprian Vagaggini, O.S.B.

PREFACE OF THE TRANSLATOR

Already in 1959 The Liturgical Press published Mr. Leonard J. Doyle's translation of the first edition of Dom Cyprian Vagaggini's *Theological Dimensions of the Liturgy*. The English edition of 1959 was a book of only 242 pages. The present volume is, even by its size, an eloquent testimonial to the growth of interest in the liturgy in the last two decades.

Mr. Doyle's work of translating the present volume was interrupted in the midst of chapter four by his untimely death. The Liturgical Press then requested that I take the work in hand, along with Mr. Doyle's notes, and bring it to completion.

What Dom Cyprian stated in his preface of 1965 can be said also of the present translation, produced some ten years later: remarkably few changes in the text have been necessitated by the passage of years. The Council was already over when the fourth Italian edition was published ten years ago; and in translating that fourth edition I have had to make only a very few changes in Dom Cyprian's text, changes occasioned by the implementation of more recent liturgical reforms, in order to make the text conform to present liturgical usage.

The portion of the work completed by Mr. Doyle and his abundant notes on further chapters were an immense help to me in completing this translation. For the present volume much credit is due Mr. Doyle; but of course, for the accuracy of translation throughout, and for any inadvertent errors which may be present, I must take full responsibility myself.

W. A. Jurgens, H.E.D.

Bratenahl, Ohio
September 23, 1976

KEY TO ABBREVIATIONS

CL   Concilium Vaticanum II, *Constitutio de Sacra Liturgia*. Our quotations from this and other documents of Vatican II are according to the translation in *Vatican Council II: The Conciliar and Post Conciliar Documents*, edited by Austin Flannery, O.P. (Collegeville, Minn.: The Liturgical Press, 1975).

Dz   *Enchiridion symbolorum* of H. Denzinger, C. Bannwart, I. Umberg, K. Rahner, and (thirty-second edition) A. Schönmetzer. The numbering is given first according to the new system, followed in parentheses by that of former editions.

MD   Encyclical *Mediator Dei*. Quotations and numbering of paragraphs are according to the Vatican Library translation (Washington: National Catholic Welfare Conference). The numbering marked "Lat." is according to the Latin text in *Documenta pontificia ad instaurationem liturgicam spectantia (1903–1953)*, edited by Annibale Bugnini, C.M., (Rome: Edizioni Liturgiche, 1953), pp. 95 ff.

PG   Migne, *Patrologiae cursus completus . . . series graeca.*

PL   Migne, *Patrologiae cursus completus . . . series latina.*

Righetti   Mario Righetti, *Storia liturgica*, 4 volumes (Milan: Ancora, 1945 ff). The first volume is cited from the second edition, *ibid.*, 1950.

Jurgens   W. A. Jurgens, *The Faith of the Early Fathers* (Collegeville, Minn.: The Liturgical Press, 1970). Numbers are paragraph references.

PART 1 THE NATURE OF LITURGY

1 THE GENERAL BACKGROUND

OF THE LITURGY:

REVELATION AS SACRED HISTORY

In order to penetrate the world of the liturgy we must penetrate the world of revelation and consider things in that over-all view of its own in which revelation, especially the Scripture, considers them. The liturgy, as a matter of fact, is nothing else than a certain phase of revelation, a certain way in which the meaning of revelation is realized in us. For this reason it is imperative to consider the liturgy always against the general background of sacred history, because sacred history is precisely the over-all view in which revelation considers everything.

1. Revelation Takes the Form Primarily of a Sacred History

Among human sciences, metaphysical speculation has its own way of considering things, which can be called entitative or ontological, because it is concerned primarily with determining the position of anything in the ladder of being, of entity. Thus, for example, if I consider in analyzing this man, George, that he is a being, a substance, an animal, but a rational one and therefore with the capacity for such things as laughter and study, that he is social, that he can be religious, and the like, I am considering in George the entitative or ontological aspect primarily.

3

Christian revelation, especially in the Scripture, is not presented to us *primarily* as a system explanatory of things seen under their entitative aspect, after the manner of a metaphysical explanation of being. The primary and predominant aspect under which revelation is presented to us is not a kind of revealed metaphysics.

I do not mean to say, be it understood, that there is not in revelation, and even in the Scripture itself, a more or less considerable number of statements of entitative and metaphysical value, quite important objectively. On the contrary, it is clear that there are such statements.

Here is what I do mean to say. First, statements of this kind are relatively rare and sporadic. Second, they cannot be spoken of as a *system* of entitative or metaphysical explanation of the cosmos, but at most as parts or principles which, further developed and completed, could serve for the construction of such a system. In the third place and principally, these statements, however important they may be in themselves, are not in the foreground of attention, interest and concern in revelation. They are rather like presuppositions accepted as a matter of course; the Scripture merely alludes to them now and again, without making them, for the most part, an object of primary concern and attention.

It would not be accurate to say, either, that revelation, especially in the Scriptures, is presented to us primarily as a practical rule of life, as a collection of directives and moral precepts. The Scripture is this, too, of course; in fact this aspect is everywhere very explicit and is quite essential. But it would not be accurate to say that this ensemble of directives and moral precepts is primary, as if it were the first thing to be seen in the Scripture, which in this interpretation would take the form *primarily* of a rule of life, a moral code. This, I say, is not accurate, because the moral law, though strongly explicit and emphatic in the Scripture, is proposed there always as an immediate consequence of something else, as a natural and inevitable derivation from another element from which everything is immediately derived and which itself occupies the foreground.

Revelation, especially in the Scripture, is presented rather, *first of all*, as a history; as a history always in the making; as a sacred history always in the making. This sacred history presupposes, and from time to time affirms, in its background, a certain metaphysics; and from this sacred history is immediately derived and sharply accentuated a rule of life, a morality. It is the sacred history, always in the making, of God's interventions in the world, to draw His rational creatures to Him, to communicate His divine life to them, and thus to bring about His universal reign; as well as the history, always in the making, of the response of these creatures. This is the predominant, specific view under which revelation presents everything of which it speaks. It is not metaphysics or morality, then, that predominates, but history, with a metaphysical background and a moral derivation which is powerfully brought out.

In all this there is more than a mere nuance of language. This distinctive note of being primarily a sacred history always in the making, with a metaphysical background and the vigorous presentation of a moral code, gives Judeo-Christian revelation its specific physiognomy, which distinguishes it profoundly and immediately from any merely philosophical or ethical system.

For example: there are views of the world essentially philosophical, which are only incidentally the source for a practical rule of life: Platonism, Aristotelianism, Plotinism, Kantism, Hegelianism. On the other hand, there are systems which are primarily a rule of life, a morality: Confucianism, and also, it seems, the original Buddhism, as an experience of life. Again, the following are primarily historical events: the conquest of Asia by Alexander the Great, the discovery of America by Christopher Columbus, the barbarian invasions of the Roman Empire, etc. Caesar's *Gallic War* relates a historical event; it is first of all a history.

Now Christian revelation too is presented first of all as a phenomenon in the order of historical events: the story of the continuing intervention of a concrete person, God, in space and time to approach concrete persons, men, who have been placed in existence and are maintained in existence by God Himself, but from whom He wants their free cooperation in order that He may fulfill His plan of universal dominion over them. This is the primary picture of Christian revelation.

If there is a metaphysical background in this picture, that is simply because no story can be without one. Thus also in the *Gallic War* there is a certain background of affirmations of metaphysical value, however general they may be. For it is clear that a reader would miss completely the historical import itself of the *Gallic War* if he did not admit from the beginning the objective value of, for example, the concepts of man, Roman Empire, Celts, war, human freedom, responsibility, time, space, etc. If these and similar concepts are denied, the historical event which the *Gallic War* seeks to narrate, and the book itself, will not make sense. It follows from this that the author, who certainly does not intend to occupy himself with metaphysics, nevertheless cannot help presupposing, and perhaps also stating explicitly from time to time, a certain number of concepts of properly metaphysical import.

But it is no less obvious that in a historical narrative like the *Gallic War* metaphysics enters only as a background, as something naturally presupposed and occasionally, perhaps, more or less explicitly affirmed, but always in the service of the story; that is, to whatever extent is necessary to safeguard the value of the story and make it understood. Likewise in Christian revelation the metaphysics in the background of the picture is there as an object of affirmation only to whatever extent is necessary to safeguard and make understandable the import of the history, always in the making, of God's interventions in the world. Such is the function of the metaphysical background, no more and no less.

The fact that in Christian revelation the moral rule of life is brought out strongly, comes from the very nature of the story which revelation tells. It is a sacred story, which, by the nature of Him who is its principal actor, God, and by the purposes which He is pursuing, encounters and involves directly the life and the activity of man, his rights and his duties, in their deepest roots.

In Christian revelation, then, there is always question of a morality which in its concrete and proper form is derived *immediately* from a story and not simply from a metaphysics. For, if man accepts things as presented in revelation, he is to act in this or that way not simply and solely for metaphysical reasons or out of other considerations but, immediately, because God, a real person, has intervened and is intervening concretely and freely in Christ, in the Spirit, in this or that way in the history of the world, in the history of man, of every man — in your history. Christian revelation says to man, "God freely has acted and is acting and will act thus and so with men, with you; *therefore* it is your duty to act thus and so."

This rule can be exemplified first of all from the Old Testament. It is characteristic of the Old Testament to derive the motive for the moral law immediately and concretely from the pact which God has entered into with Israel. This is seen, for example, in Exod. 20:2 ff., where the Ten Commandments are given. To the first commandment, "You shall not have other gods besides Me," is prefaced as immediate motivation, "I am the Lord, your God, who brought you out of the land of Egypt, out of the slave house" (v. 2). The second commandment, "You shall not make any carvings or images . . . you shall not bow down before them," is followed by the motivation, "For I, the Lord your God, am a jealous God . . ." (v. 5). To the commandment of the observance of the Sabbath is given as motivation, "For in six days the Lord made the heavens and the earth, the sea and all that is in them, and on the seventh day He rested. Therefore the Lord blessed the Sabbath day and made it holy" (v. 11). To the same effect see Deut. 4:2, 7-9, 15, 16, 32-40; 5:6; 7:6-11; 10:12–11:9.

Quite characteristic among these texts is that in which the motive is given for the supreme commandment to love God above all things: "And now, Israel, what does the Lord, your God, ask of you, if not that you fear the Lord, your God, and walk in all His ways, love and serve the Lord, your God, with your whole heart and your whole soul, keeping the commandments and statutes of the Lord which I enjoin on you today for your own good? Consider! The heavens, even the highest heavens, belong to the Lord, your God; the earth and everything on it. *Yet* the Lord became attached only to your fathers, in His love for them; and after them He has preferred you, their descendants, to all other peoples, and He does to this day. *Circumcise, therefore*, your uncircumcised hearts, and be no longer stiff-necked . . ." (Deut. 10:12-16). See also the motive for the precept of love of the alien dwelling among the Israelites: "For the Lord, your God, is the God of gods . . . who has no favorites, accepts no bribes . . . and befriends the alien, giving him food and clothing. *So you too must befriend* the alien, for you were once aliens your-selves in the land of Egypt" (*Ibid.*, vv. 17-19).

The prophets too saw everything in this perspective. From God's way of dealing with Israel in history, His way of acting as Father and as Spouse, but also as revenging Judge, the duties of Israel to God are deduced and the gravity of Israel's sins is measured. Hence arises, for example, the great prophetic theme of the love of God, the Bridegroom, for Israel, His bride; of the unfaithfulness of the wife toward the husband and of the complaints of God the husband against the unfaithful wife, as well as the endless tribulations the wife will encounter through her infidelity — a theme dramatically devel-oped by Hosea (1:2; 2; 3:1-5; 4:10-19; 5-10; 14:2 ff.).

The very concept of creation and of God the Creator, which is so important in the Old Testament as motivating the relations between the world and God, is not considered so much in its metaphysical import as in its relations with history, especially in the more ancient texts. Creation is seen there primarily as the beginning of history.

In all this the same phenomenon always appears: the moral law is derived immediately and concretely from a story and not simply from a metaphysics, still less from some human need that is merely practical and hedonistic.

In this as in so many other points the New Testament is the heir and the con-tinuation of the Old. Here, however, that divine activity from which the moral code is immediately deduced, is a story much more striking than that which the ancient Israelites had known. And this story is summed up in the fact that, in the person of Christ, God Himself has come among us and has lived with us, and "after having spoken of old to our fathers through the prophets at different times and in various ways, in these last times God has spoken to us through His Son" (Heb. 1:1 ff.). "For God so loved the world as to give His only-begotten Son, that whoever believes in Him may not perish, but may have life everlasting" (John 3:16).

Then Christ after leaving this world sent His Spirit from His place at the Father's side. And the Spirit is always present in the faithful and effects the divine sonship in them, transforming them and configuring them to the in-carnate Word, who died and rose again, in order to lead them to the ultimate goal: the glorious resurrection into the life of blessedness with Christ (see, e.g., John 14:15-21, 25-31; Rom. 8).

The specifically Christian motivation for action is now deduced from this extraordinary intervention of God in the world through Christ, through the Spirit. Consider some examples.

Here is how St. John justifies the necessity of loving God and one's neigh-bor: "He who does not love does not know God; for God is love.[1] In this has

---

[1] This is not a metaphysical definition of God; and neither, for that matter, is the "I am who am" of Exod. 3:14, whatever some au-thors may have said of it. St. John's meaning is: God's whole action towards the world in sacred history has as its origin and its form the gratuitous love of God. The context is clear.

God's love for us been shown, that God sent His only-begotten Son into the world that we may live through Him. In this is the love, that without our having loved God, He has first loved us, and has sent His Son as a propitiation for our sins. Beloved, *if God has so loved us, we also should love one another.* No one has ever seen God. If we love one another, God abides in us and His love is perfected in us. From this we know that we abide in Him and He in us, by the fact that He has made a gift of His Spirit to us. And we have seen, and we testify, that the Father has sent His Son to be Savior of the world. . . . Let us love God, therefore, because He has first loved us" (1 John 4:8 ff.). "From this we know His love: from the fact that He sacrificed His life for us; and we likewise ought to sacrifice our lives for the brethren" (*Ibid.* 3:16).

Why is fornication forbidden? "Do you not know that your bodies are members of Christ? Shall I then make the members of Christ members of a prostitute? By no means! . . . Flee fornication. . . . Or do you not know that your body is a temple of the Holy Spirit, who is in you, whom you have from God, and that you are not your own because you have been bought at a great price? Glorify God, then, in your body" (1 Cor. 6:15, 18, 19-20).

Why may not the brethren be scandalized? ". . . And through your 'knowledge' the weak one will be ruined, the brother for whom Christ died. Thus when you sin against the brethren, and wound their weak conscience, you are sinning against Christ. For this very reason, if food scandalizes my brother, I will eat meat no more forever, that I may not scandalize my brother" (1 Cor. 8:11 ff.).

And here, finally, is the source from which St. Paul deduces immediately and concretely the specifically Christian rule for every withdrawal from sin, for every ascetical practice and every tendency to ultimate perfection: "By sending His Son in the likeness of sinful flesh as a sin-offering, God has condemned sin in the flesh. . . . Those who are carnal cannot please God. You, however, are not carnal but spiritual, if indeed the Spirit of God dwells in you. For if anyone does not have the Spirit of Christ, he does not belong to Christ. But if Christ is in you, the body, it is true, is dead by reason of sin, but the spirit is life by reason of justification. If, then, the Spirit of Him who raised Jesus from the dead dwells in you, He who raised Jesus from the dead will also bring to life your mortal bodies, through His Spirit who dwells in you. *Therefore*, brethren, we are debtors, not to the flesh, that we should live according to the flesh, for if you live according to the flesh, you are on the way to death; but if by the spirit you put to death the deeds of the flesh, you will live. For whoever are led by the Spirit of God, they are the sons of God. . . . But if we are sons, we are heirs also: heirs of God and joint heirs with Christ, provided, however, we suffer with Him that we may also be glorified with Him. Why, I count the sufferings of the present time as not worthy to be compared with the glory to come that will be revealed in us" (Rom. 8:3 ff.).

Even without entering into the particulars of this text which is so packed with thought, we can see its general movement: The coming of the Son of God has shattered by right the dominion of sin (of the flesh); having communicated His Spirit to us, God frees each one of us from that dominion; *therefore* it is not permissible for us to live by sin (according to the flesh), but we must live as sons of God, docile to the motions of the Spirit who is in us; by suffering now for Christ we shall be glorified together with Him when the Spirit who dwells in us makes us also rise gloriously.

When we turn from Scripture to dogmatic tradition and the ordinary teaching of the Church, we must observe that here also revelation is presented first of all as a sacred history, just as it is in the Scripture. A first proof of this is the fact that dogmatic tradition and the ordinary *magisterium* propose to the faithful the Scripture itself first of all, since the message of the Scripture constitutes the principal object of their own message. Another proof, no less convincing, is the "symbol" of the faith, the creed, proposed by tradition and by the ordinary *magisterium* as a short, easy summary of revelation.

This concept was not only a very ancient one, common in the tradition of the Fathers[2] and of the liturgy,[3] but persisted in the scholastic tradition,[4] which, as we know, did give its greatest attention to considering revelation from the entitative point of view. It is easy to see that the dominant perspective in constructing the symbol of the faith, especially in its most ancient form, that expressed by the Apostles' Creed, is the sacred history of God's interventions in the world. The accentuation of the entitative aspect for some points of doctrine in the formulas of the symbol itself was, as we know, the work of the extraordinary *magisterium* intervening by way of a polemic against heretical deviations.[5]

In short, the conclusion is always the same: the whole Judeo-Christian revelation rests on a history and is presented first of all as a history, a history always in the making, which has a long past and will be completed only in

---

[2] Cf. D. van den Eynde, *Les normes de l'enseignement chrétien dans la littérature patristique des trois premiers siècles* (Gembloux, 1933). See, e.g., Irenaeus, *Adv. Haer.*, I, 10, 1-2; Tertullian, *De Praescript.*, 13; Origen, *De Princ.*, prologue. From the fourth century on, the idea is common; see, e.g., Jerome, *Contra Ioan.*, 28; Rufinus, *Com. in symb. apost.*, 2; Augustine, *De symb. ad catech.*, 1.

[3] We are concerned with the *Traditio symboli*, the handing-on of the creed, to the catechumens, in which the symbol was considered as the summary of the whole Christian faith (see, e.g., Righetti, IV, 36 ff.; see also the *Sacramentarium Gelasianum*, ed. Leo Cunibert Mohlberg (Rome: Herder, 1960), p. 48, n. 310. Even in most ancient times there was the rite of the profession of the faith, after the manner of a symbol, in the very act of baptism (see Righetti, IV, 65 f., and the text of the

Traditio Apostolica of Hippolytus of Rome, 21).

[4] It was a common doctrine in scholasticism that the whole faith is contained in the articles of the Apostles' Creed. For the scholastics, those points of the faith not directly contained in the creed can be reduced to one that is contained in it, either as presupposition or as consequence. See, e.g., Alexander of Hales, *Summa*, III, q. 69, ed. Quaracchi, IV, nn. 698 ff.; Bonaventure, in III *Librum Sententiarum*, d. 25, a. 1, q. 1.

[5] A typical case: the modifications which the Council of Nicaea introduced into the symbol to defend the orthodox teaching against the Arians. The so-called Athanasian Creed also, with its strong insistence on the entitative aspect of the Trinity and of the incarnation, is a clearly polemical composition.

the future, the history of God's free and loving interventions in the world and of the free response of creatures.

2. The Great Phases of This History

What, more concretely, is this history? In summary the essential phases of it may be observed in the following outline:

ETERNITY: God (the Father by appropriation) freely, out of love, decides to share His inmost life with creatures in order to develop that life into a single, spiritual, cosmic kingdom (under the primacy of Christ), which will be realized fully in the heavenly Jerusalem. Predestination (of Christ and) of the elect (under His primacy). Creation of the angels before time; the drama in the angelic world: faithful angels and unfaithful angels.

TIME: Execution of the aforesaid plan in the visible world and in time:

FIRST PHASE: IN ADAM: tending, that is, to the execution of the plan with the inclusion of Adam as spiritual head of the human race (whether with subordination to Christ or not): creation, elevation, condition in Paradise; cosmic unity; commandment; temptation by the fallen angels; fall; rupture of cosmic unity; rise of the two cities: of God and of the devil, in continuous dramatic struggle; failure of the first phase; promise of the Redeemer.

SECOND PHASE: IN CHRIST THE SECOND ADAM: resumption of the execution of the plan in Christ the Redeemer:

The preparation of the ages for Christ the Redeemer:

— From Adam to Abraham: Sethites; Cainites; Noah; the flood; the Semites.
— From Abraham to Moses: the patriarchs: Abraham, Isaac, Jacob; the people in Egypt.
— From Moses to Christ: the theocracy of Israel:
Moses; liberation; exodus, covenant; wandering in the desert.
Entrance into the promised land.
The judges; the kings, in particular David, Solomon; the temple, the worship.
The prophets.
The exile.
Messianism.
The restoration: the synagogue.
John the Baptist.
Mary.

The fullness of time: the last times, still unfolding:

— The full and final communication and manifestation of God in the person of Christ the Redeemer:
Mary, the incarnation; nativity, epiphany; hidden life.
Public ministry of Jesus.
The paschal mysteries of Jesus: institution of the Eucharist and of the priesthood; Passion; death on the Cross; burial; descent into hell; resurrection; the forty days with the disciples; ascension; the sitting at the Father's right hand.

— Participation in the fullness of Christ the Redeemer, priest, dead and risen, brought about in individual souls, in the Church, in the time extending from the ascension to the parousia:

Coming of the Spirit sent by Christ from His place at the Father's side: Pentecost.

Effects of the presence of the Spirit (salvation *in Spiritu*):

Birth of the visible Church with hierarchical structure as full communal manifestation on earth of the divine life in Christ in the Spirit (mystical body).

Growth of the Church, body of Christ, until the parousia:

Essentially and in the first place through the liturgical way: sacrifice; sacraments; sacramentals; liturgical prayer.

For which all the other activities in the Church prepare and from which they follow:

Hierarchical activities: teaching; governing; apostolate of the hierarchy and participation in it.

Private activity of individuals:

Ascetico-mystical moral correspondence of individuals with the liturgical realities.

Temporal activities ordained to the spiritual level.

Terminal realization (final eschatology):

Individual: death; saints in heaven; faithful in purgatory.

Cosmic: parousia; universal judgment; general resurrection.

ETERNITY: Eternal punishment of the damned and final establishment of the Kingdom of God (Father by appropriation) in Christ in the one city of faithful angels and redeemed men in an eternal cosmic liturgy of praise and thanksgiving.

This in brief, then, is sacred history in the essential phases of its development; this is the specific world of the liturgy, just as it is the specific world of the Scripture and of Christian revelation in general. This is also by right, and should be in fact, the specific world of theology. Theology's task, that is to say, must be precisely to explain this world of sacred history under all the aspects in which scientific research can help us to understand it better. The explanation, of course, must never lose sight of the fact, either in the general view or in the individual details, that in this world there is question first of all of a history, even though it be against the background of a metaphysics, and though the moral consequences be made clearly and forcefully explicit.[6]

[6] During the sessions of the Second Vatican Council, there was good reason for the repeated demand that the perspective of sacred history or of the history of salvation be given once more the prominence which belongs to it in theology. With this perspective theology can find again the better balance for which everyone is hoping today. The differences which became evident in the debates on the liturgy and on the Church had their origin, largely, in different ways of conceiving theology, giving more importance or less importance to the history of salvation in the general plan of theology. See Cyprian Vagaggini's "Lo spirito della Costituzione sulla liturgia," *Riv. Lit.* 51 (1964), 8-30.

3. Explanatory Observations

For the end which we are here pursuing, which is to situate the liturgy in this general picture of sacred history, outside of which it is incomprehensible, it will suffice for the time being to make some explanatory observations on the outline proposed above. It will be the task of the following chapters to take up some of these points again and probe them in more detail.

Sacred history is biblical

Any fairly attentive reader of the Bible, especially of St. Paul's letters and of the Apocalypse, will recognize readily in this outline a simple schematization of the essential ideas underlying the whole Scripture, ideas which St. Paul has made explicit and has developed, though fragmentarily and in scattered passages of his letters, and which the Apocalypse has brought out with much force.[7] For the proof of this statement, recourse to the following texts will suffice.

For the general picture: Eph. 1–3; Col. 1:9-23; 1 Tim. 3:16. For the general meaning of the relations of the Old Testament with the new economy in Christ: 1 Cor. 10:1-5; Rom. 9–11; Heb. 7:1-10, 18; and also Mark 1:15; Gal. 4:4. For the idea that the growth of the Church, Christ's body, takes place essentially and primarily by way of the sacraments, see, for example, what St. Paul says in Rom. 6:1-12 about the role of baptism in the Christian life; for the role of the Eucharist: 1 Cor. 11:23-30; 10:16 ff.; John 6:32-59. For the heavenly Jerusalem and the cosmic liturgy: Heb. 12:22-24; Apoc. 5:8-14; 21:1–22:5.

It is a theology of history

Sacred history presents itself as a theology of history, because it reveals the ultimate meaning of history, namely the meaning which time and history have in the eyes of God. For, although God is inexpressibly immanent and involved, as it were, in history, still He transcends it beyond measure, and therefore sets it in motion, directs it, gives it a meaning.

This history is linear, because it gets its impetus from a single point of departure, the counsel of God in eternity, which is followed by the creation of the angels before time and of all the rest in time, and unfolds successively and irreversibly toward a point of arrival at which it has been aimed from the very beginning and in which, fulfilling and realizing itself, it attains its end.

This history is unitary, because in its unfolding toward its point of arrival the successive phases are directed infallibly by a unique and all-powerful stage manager, God, in a well determined direction with a view to the attainment of a preestablished end. For this reason the successive phases are intrinsically

---

[7] See, e.g., L. Tondelli, *Il disegno di Dio nella storia* (Turin, 1947); Suzanne de Dietrich, *God's Unfolding Purpose* (Philadelphia: Westminster Press, 1960); Ceslaus Spicq, *L'épître aux hébreux* (Bible de Jerusalem, Paris: Cerf, 1950), pp. 25-33; Henri Oster, *Le grand dessin de Dieu dans la pastorale et la prédication* (Paris: Cerf, 1955).

connected with one another, the preceding ones preparing for those that follow and being already a first imperfect fulfillment, which, however, surpasses itself in the next phase and is realized perfectly only in the final phase.

This history is marked by a profound eschatological dynamism. The antecedent phases all tend to the subsequent ones, and all together tend to the ultimate. All the times tend to the ultimate times (*ta eschata*), which thus exercise an intrinsic force of attraction on all and each of the individual phases of
the process, imparting momentum to them and giving them an intelligible
meaning.

This history is not simply a necessary cosmological process, but rather a
dramatic development, because the protagonists — God, the angels, men — are
free persons, and the angels and men, free and fallible creatures, have in this
process the free choice of going against the designs of God or of conforming
to them. As a matter of fact, some of the angels and some of the men have
freely accepted and seconded those designs, and these are the elect; but the rest
of the angels and, at their instigation, some of the men have rejected and im-
peded those designs. This division in the free creatures makes the whole of
temporal history a dramatic struggle between two cities: on the one hand the
angels rebellious against God with the men who are their satellites; on the
other hand the faithful angels with the elect of mankind. Dominating this
drama is God; its theater is the cosmos: earth and heaven.

It is the "mystery," the mystery of Christ, the paschal mystery

This whole history, in so far as it is sacred history, has a meaning in God's
eyes which only He knows by nature, but which now, in the "last times," He
has revealed to the followers of Christ, chiefly in the very person of Christ.
St. Paul calls this whole history, in the meaning which it has in God's eyes,
"the mystery" (e.g., Rom. 16:25; 1 Cor. 2:7; Eph. 5:32; Col. 1:26-27), "the
mystery of the will of God" (Eph. 1:9), "the mystery which has been hidden
from eternity in God" (Eph. 3:9; Col. 1:26). There is now general agreement
in recognizing [8] that this way of conceiving things in St. Paul owes nothing
to the idea of the pagan mysteries but is simply the development, from the
Christian point of view, of a concept of the Old Testament (e.g., Dan. 2:20-
30). According to this concept, the unfolding of history and its true profound
meaning, which can only be a religious meaning, is known naturally only by
God, by the wisdom of God, is a secret, a mystery, a hidden thing of His wisdom, and if men succeed in knowing it, this can only be because God reveals it.

But this sacred history, this mystery, is wholly centered in Christ. This fact
stands out still more strikingly if we accept a theory held by many theologians.
According to this theory, God from eternity willed Christ and constituted Him
the head of all creation; and this decree was, from the logical point of view,

[8] Contrary to the opinion of Odo Casel.

prior to and independent of the foreknowledge of Adam's sin. Thus according to the divine plan the Word would still have become incarnate in any hypothesis, even if Adam had not sinned. — But the matter is disputed, and for that reason I have put it in parentheses in the outline.[9]

At any rate, the whole of sacred history is divided clearly into two parts: before Christ and after Christ. Before Christ, at least beginning with Adam's sin, everything tends to Him, and after Christ everything derives from Him. For that reason this story, this mystery, can be called simply in the Pauline spirit "the mystery of Christ."

It is true that St. Paul himself with the expression "mystery of Christ" (Col. 2:2; 4:3; Eph. 3:4), strictly speaking, means only the calling of the gentiles, together with the Jews, to salvation, by means of Christ, in the one body of Christ Himself, which is the Church. Yet in the context of all the passages referred to above, where sacred history is spoken of as mystery, mystery of God, it is clear that St. Paul's attention is focussed on Christ as center of the divine plans. That is why St. Paul clearly has in mind this whole perspective of sacred history centered in Christ when he speaks simply of the mystery which "refers to Christ and to the Church" (Eph. 5:32); "the mystery of the gospel" (Eph. 6:19); "the mystery of faith" (1 Tim. 3:9); "the mystery of piety" (1 Tim. 3:16). In fact, in 1 Tim. 3:16 (and in Col. 2:2 according to the variant reading which apparently should be preferred), "mystery" means simply Christ Himself and everything that He signifies, by God's will, for the world.

Christ's role as Man-God, Redeemer and High Priest of the human race, accounts for the place He holds in God's plans and in their realization. Those plans are realized both in Himself and with respect to the other creatures whose relations with God constitute the sacred history which is still in the making. If we use the expression "mystery of Christ" to refer simply to everything that Christ stands for in those divine plans and in their realization, we shall be showing respect for the teaching and the mind of St. Paul. Hence we can equate "sacred history," "mystery," "mystery of Christ," because we are concerned with a single reality, in as much as the very center of this sacred history, this mystery, is Christ Himself.[10]

---

[9] This is the famous dispute between Scotistic and Thomistic theologians. In the Scotist theory, now accepted by many, even in case Adam had not sinned the Word would have become incarnate; but even then Adam would have been spiritual head of the human race, though under the supreme head, Christ, who would thus have been supreme Head and Mediator, but not Redeemer. The question is extended also to the angels. The data of Scripture and of tradition do not suffice to solve it. It seems undeniable, however, that the tendency and, as it were, the secret development of St. Paul's thought is in this direction (Col. 1:15-20). But St. Paul himself has not made this explicit. This way of looking at things gives the divine plan and all of sacred history a much greater unity.

[10] For the concept of mystery in St. Paul see, e.g., D. Deden, "Le 'mystère' paulinien," *Eph. theol. lov.*, 1936, pp. 405 ff.; Gottlieb Söhngen, *Der Wesensaufbau des Mysteriums* (Bonn: Peter Hanstein, 1938); John T. Trinidad, "The Mystery Hidden in God," *Biblica*, 31 (1950), 1 ff.

Thus the time before Christ, at least beginning with Adam's sin, has the essential significance of being a preparation for Christ the Redeemer, Mediator, Priest, gloriously reigning Lord, and, as it were, a series of sketches of the reality which is completed in Christ. And the time after Christ has no other meaning than this: to bring about in the creatures who appear on the world's stage until the end of time, the participation and assimilation of those realities of divine life which exist in the dead and risen Christ and which Christ communicates to them. The time between the Lord's ascension and His glorious return in the parousia is nothing but the interval in which Christ wants to communicate His own being and His own activity to the men who appear successively in history, drawing them thus into His mystery, into the fullness of the divine life which superabounds in Him.

All this is true because the purpose intended by God in setting history into motion and directing it—to communicate His inner life to creatures—is realized in the person of Christ in an absolutely full and final way. In Christ, especially after His resurrection, the communication of the divine life to the creature reaches its culmination and its absolute epiphany. After Him nothing substantially new is to be expected which is not already wholly present in His person. The only thing to be expected is the sharing and extension of those realities from Christ to other creatures, and the glorious, cosmic revelation of these transformations which have their full realization in Christ, a revelation which will take place at His glorious return, in the resurrection of bodies. Thus the time from the ascension to the parousia has this meaning: to reproduce in individuals the fact of Christ, the mystery of Christ, to enter into this mystery, to be absorbed by it.

Christ's appearance on earth, and in a very special way His resurrection, marks the beginning of the last times, the *eschata*, precisely because in Christ the meaning of time and of history is realized fully. These *eschata* are already going on, having started with that moment when Christ appeared. The time from the ascension to the parousia, in which we are living, forms a part of these *eschata*; it is the eschatological time which will close with the glorious return of the Lord and the passage from time into the eternity that is without time.

To enter into the world of the liturgy, it is most important to understand that the whole of sacred history is the mystery of Christ, that in sacred history everything before Him tends to Him, or more precisely to His death and resurrection, and that after Him everything derives from Him; to understand that after His death and resurrection nothing radically new is to be expected, but only that His mystery is to be reproduced in creatures until the end of time, the mystery of the Son of God who became man, who died and who rose; to understand that creatures are to share in this mystery and to quench their thirst in its fullness.

The liturgy, in fact, is nothing but a certain way in which Christ, in the present intermediate time which extends from Pentecost to the parousia, in this eschatological time already going on, communicates the fullness of His divine life to individual souls, reproduces His mystery in them, draws them into His mystery.

It is the mystery of the Church

This intermediate time from Pentecost to the parousia — a time in which everything is already substantially and radically realized and in which we are only waiting until the number of the brethren is complete (cf. Apoc. 6:11) to whom the divine reality brought by Christ is to be communicated — is the specifically ecclesial time, the time of the Church. In the Church, Christ, Son of God, incarnate, dead and risen, visibly gives His mandate to the Apostles and their successors in the hierarchy, fortifying them with specific powers to sanctify, to teach and to govern. At the same time, invisibly, He sends the Holy Spirit, who inwardly gives life to their work. Thus He brings the reality of His mystery into souls and so fulfills the meaning of history.

The Church is the human and divine, visible and invisible, spiritual and yet socially structured framework of life which was brought into being by the will of Christ. By Him also it is constantly maintained in existence and in vital strength, through the Spirit which He communicates to it. It is the means which He has chosen to make irreplaceable, for communicating the fullness of the life of which He Himself is full, to the men who appear, one after another, in the time from Pentecost to the parousia.

The Church, again, is the messianic community of the last times composed of a great number of gentiles and a little remnant of faithful Jews; that community foretold by the prophets (cf. Rom. 9:27-29) and called together by God around the Messiah, Jesus Christ, as an actuation on earth of the whole influx of divine life which spreads out from Christ, and as a preparation for the final summons to the glory of the heavenly Jerusalem (cf. Heb. 12:18-24).

The Church is that holy people, chosen and loved by God, whom God had the aim of purchasing for Himself when He set history into motion and guided it (cf. 1 Peter 2:9-10). What is made real in this people is precisely that mystery of Christ of which we are speaking, that sharing by men in the fullness of Christ (cf. John 1:16), Christ's drawing to Himself of all the men (cf. John 12:32) whom the Father has given Him (cf. John 10:27-29) before gathering them all into the heavenly Jerusalem.

We can make the following comparison. Christ realizes and expresses in His own person the meaning of history because He is the incarnate expression of God, His full and exhaustive image, since in Christ "dwells bodily all the fullness of the Divinity" (Col. 2:9; cf. John 14:9-11; 2 Cor. 4:4, 6; Heb. 1:3; Col. 1:15). So also the Church expresses and realizes in herself the meaning of history because she is the complete human-divine expression on earth of the existence and activity of Christ. (We must recognize, of course, the distinction that between Christ and the Church there is not a physical personal union, and recognize all the consequences that flow from that distinction.) By the Spirit which He communicates to her, Christ gives life inwardly to the Church, so that she can be compared in this respect to a body; for the body is the visible expression of the invisible soul which intrinsically gives it life, it is the soul's complete and concrete sphere of vital outward action (cf. Eph. 1:23).

Finally, another parallel may be drawn. Whatever there is of divine life in the world is found wholly in Christ, Man and God, and no one is saved unless he is really and currently united to Christ through grace, participating through Him in the fullness of the divine life. So also, after Christ, whatever there is of Christ-life and divine life in the world is found wholly in the Church, human and divine, visible and invisible at the same time, and no one is saved except in real and current union, at least invisible,[11] with that same Church.

For the Holy Spirit is contained wholly in the Church "as in a good vessel containing a precious treasure which is perennially young and communicates its perennial youth to the vessel in which it is contained. . . . (For which reason) God has placed in the Church Apostles, prophets, teachers (cf. 1 Cor. 12:28) and all the other working of the Spirit. Anyone who does not belong to the Church does not share in that Spirit, but deprives himself of life by erroneous doctrine and bad conduct. For where the Church is, there is the Spirit of God, and where the Spirit of God is, there is the Church and every grace; and the Spirit is truth. Therefore those who do not share in the Spirit are not nursed by the maternal breasts and do not drink of the limpid spring which flows from the body of Christ."[12]

It is thus that on this earth from Pentecost to the parousia, the Church, true new Eve of the true new Adam, is the mother of all those who live with the divine life; the one spouse, immaculate spouse (cf. Eph. 5:24-27), who bears children to Christ. Only she "assigns to the Kingdom the children whom she has borne. Whoever (is) separated from the Church . . . is a stranger, is profane, is an enemy. He who has not the Church for a mother cannot have God for a Father."[13]

Now it is all this—her being human and divine like Christ, the concrete and total expression of Him in the world, His body, the living vessel containing entirely the eternal youth of the Spirit; her being the new people of God, announced by the prophets, composed of many gentiles and a little remnant of faithful Jews; her being the fulfillment of the previous history (cf. 1 Cor.

[11] Every man of good faith who lives rightly according to his conscience, adheres by that very fact, at least implicitly, to whatever the divine will desires of him, ready to do whatever that divine will demands as soon as he knows it. Thus he has at least the implicit desire to adhere visibly to the Church, such being now the will of God for every man. For this desire the man of good faith receives the grace of God, and this grace makes him a member really and currently, though still invisibly, of the one true Church which is also visible; and this much suffices for salvation.

[12] Irenaeus, *Adv. Haer.*, III, 24, 1.

[13] Cyprian, *De cath. eccl. unitate*, 6.

10:11) and the preparation for the heavenly Jerusalem (cf. Gal. 4:25 ff., Heb. 12:18-24; Apoc. 21:9–22:2), the mother of all the living and the one spouse of Christ — it is all this, I say, that constitutes "the mystery of the Church," that mystery which is "great in reference to Christ and to the Church" (Eph. 5:32); that "cosmic mystery of the Church" of which the *Didache* speaks; [14] the "wondrous sacrament of the whole Church." [15]

Thus sacred history, mystery, mystery of Christ, mystery of the Church are indivisible, are even a single reality, so that we could actually speak of a single concept given different shadings by these various expressions.[16] We shall use them one for another without differentiation.

All this should by no means be taken for lyrical flights of fancy, but as a perfectly sober expression of the plain reality. To explain its particulars in more detail belongs to a "theology of the Church," and we also will do it for certain points in one of the following chapters.

Here we have offered a broad vista to show that the liturgy is incomprehensible if it is not related to the Church, just as the Church is incomprehensible if it is not related to Christ, and Christ is incomprehensible if He is not related to the general plan of God in sacred history.

From this it follows that the liturgy cannot be understood unless it is seen against the background of sacred history, mystery, mystery of Christ, mystery of the Church. Not without reason does the Second Vatican Council [17] explain the nature of the liturgy in just this perspective.

---

[14] II, II.

[15] Roman Missal, Holy Saturday, collect after the second prophecy when there were still twelve. The expression is quoted by CL, art. 5. The same prayer, modifying only this one phrase to "the sacrament of the whole Church," is now found in the sacramentary, as the first of three alternative prayers after the seventh reading of the Easter Vigil.

[16] The Second Vatican Council also uses them in this profoundly unified perspective. See CL, articles 2, 5, 35:2, and the *Constitution on the Church*, ch. 1.

[17] CL, art. 5-8. See also the important art. 16 on this point.

2 THE LITURGY AS A COMPLEXUS

OF SENSIBLE SIGNS

The liturgy, concretely, is made up of: the seven sacraments, with the Eucharist a sacrifice and a sacrament at the same time; the sacramentals; the prayers and the ceremonies with which the Church clothes, so to speak, the celebration of the sacrifice, the sacraments and the sacramentals; and the Divine Office of the canonical hours.

Is not all this a heterogeneous collection? What is the element that unites it in the concept of liturgy? The question before us now is the true definition of the liturgy and the explanation of the individual elements that go to make it up.

1. The General Definition of the Liturgy

Unanimity has not yet been achieved among the liturgists themselves concerning the true, technical, precise definition of the liturgy.[1]

[1] We know that the word "liturgy" as used to indicate the particular ensemble of things which we now indicate by it, goes back to the humanists and the learned liturgists of the seventeenth century. The ancients spoke of *ministerium divinum, ministerium ecclesiasticum, officia divina.*

The word "liturgy," from the Greek *leitourgia, leiton ergon*, indicates a work which concerns the whole people in the sense that it is undertaken in the interests and for the welfare of all, and thus: public work, originally of a political and technical nature, then also of a religious and cultual nature.

A moot question

It is certain that the encyclical *Mediator Dei* did not mean to settle this question.[2] It is equally certain that the Second Vatican Council did not intend to resolve it. From the Acts of the Council and from repeated oral statements it is clear that the council's intention was to leave open for discussion by the experts the problem of the definition strictly so called, the perfect definition, of the liturgy, and to give only a description by means of characteristic notes which all theologians recognize as present in the liturgy.

This description is as follows: "The liturgy, then, is rightly seen as an exercise of the priestly office of Jesus Christ. It involves the presentation of man's sanctification under the guise of signs perceptible by the senses and its accomplishment in ways appropriate to each of these signs. In it full public worship is performed by the Mystical Body of Jesus Christ, that is, by the Head and his members." [3]

It is in this religious-cultual sense that the word is used in the Septuagint to indicate the religious service of the priests in the temple (cf. Num. 4:33; Exod. 28:35, 43; 1 Chron. 23:28). This sense is known also in the New Testament (e.g., Luke 1:23; Heb. 9:21; 10:11), which, in addition, carries the word over to signify the ministry of worship of Christ's priesthood (Heb. 8:2, *leitourgos*; 8:6); St. Paul's apostolic ministry which permits him to offer as a sacrifice to God the faithful (Rom. 15:16) and their faith (Phil. 2:17); the offering which the faithful make to God as a sacrifice when they make charitable donations (Rom. 15:26-28; 2 Cor. 9:12 f., to be connected with Phil. 4:18; Heb. 13:16); probably also the Christians' cultual liturgical actions properly so called (Acts 13:2).

Very soon "liturgy" as a term of Christian worship became synonymous in the East with sacrifice or with Mass (perhaps this was true as early as the *Didache*, 15, 1, and 1 *Clem.*, 41, 1 ff.; starting with the fourth century it was common). This is only to be expected if we consider that theologically, and also in liturgical language, especially that of ancient times, the Mass is truly the summing up and the center of the whole of Christian worship, a fact of which the ancients were vividly aware. On all this see, e.g., E. Raitz von Frentz, "Der Weg des Wortes 'Liturgie' in der Geschichte," *Eph. Lit.*, 55 (1941), 74 ff.; Antonino Romeo, "Il termino 'leitourgia' nella grecità biblica," *Miscellanea liturgica in honorem L. Cuniberti Mohlberg*, II (Rome: Ed. Liturgiche, 1949), 467 ff.

[2] At the end of a passage which develops the

concept that in the Church and especially in the liturgy it is Christ Himself who honors the Father, and that the Church honors the Father only by associating herself with Christ and acting through Him, the encyclical says, "The sacred liturgy is consequently the public worship which our Redeemer as Head of the Church renders to the Father as well as the worship which the community of the faithful renders to its Founder, and through Him to the heavenly Father. It is, in short, the worship rendered by the mystical body of Christ in the entirety of its Head and members" (n. 20). Here the encyclical intends only to make the point that the liturgy, *in as much as it is worship rendered to God*, is the worship of the whole mystical body of Jesus Christ, Head and members.

The same encyclical, moreover, with the intention of clarifying as perfectly as possible the nature of the liturgy, presents other definitions of it, or other rough drafts of definitions (see also the edition of Roguet, p. VII), e.g., n. 22: ". . . since the liturgy is nothing more nor less than the exercise of this priestly function of Jesus Christ" (cf. also n. 3); especially in n. 171 (Lat. 169): "Such is the nature and the object of the sacred liturgy: it treats of the Mass, the sacraments, the Divine Office; it aims at uniting our souls with Christ and sanctifying them through the divine Redeemer in order that Christ be honored and, through Him and in Him, the most holy Trinity." Here in a special way the aspect of sanctification is more strongly emphasized.

[3] CL, art. 7.

Practically all the elements of this description are taken from *Mediator Dei*. But in two points the council makes noteworthy progress by comparison with the encyclical:

1) It emphasizes strongly the importance of sign in the liturgy, to the extent that its structuration in a system of signs perceptible to the senses appears as a central fact of the liturgy. The council does not consider the liturgy simply as the exercise of Christ's priesthood (this is a poor interpretation which has been given by someone), but as a certain specific exercise of Christ's priesthood. Among other things, this exercise has this special note about it that it takes place through signs perceptible to the senses.

2) These signs perceptible to the senses, as well as Christ's priesthood itself which is exercised through them in the liturgy, are referred by the council not only to worship, but to sanctification and worship together. The double movement of the liturgy, from God down to man and from man up to God, is much more clearly marked in the very notion of the liturgy as expressed by the council than it was in the encyclical.

The notion of the liturgy given by the council contains precious elements, therefore, which will have to be taken into account. And yet it cannot be the technical definition which liturgical science needs. Why? Or rather, in the first place, does liturgical science really need a strict technical definition of the liturgy?

Why a strict technical definition?
What this requires

An examination of what has been written in this field even by experienced liturgists shows that there is something lacking. In my humble opinion, what is lacking in many cases is the fundamental notions themselves — yes, the philosophical notions — concerning the necessity and the particular requirements of a strict definition of the object in any science whatsoever. I beg the reader's indulgence for presuming to list those requirements here.

To begin with, the search for a strict technical definition of the object of a science is not just a question of terminology, or a pedantic fussiness. Rather, it is the problem of the precise determination of that one among all the necessary properties of the object of the science, which is the root and the ultimate *raison d'être* of all the other properties.

In every science the orientation of the inquiry and of the exposition depends on this determination, expressed precisely by the definition of the object of the science. For, in the science of anything whatsoever, the property which is the ultimate root of all the others is necessarily the first principle of intelligibility of that thing, to which must be referred or from which must be deduced whatever is affirmed of that thing. To have scientific knowledge of an object means precisely, in the last analysis, to know this relation between its first principle of intelligibility and everything else that can be said about the thing. Thus we can see how much the whole science of the liturgy depends on the correct technical definition of the liturgy.

Here, then, is how we arrive at the technical definition of a thing.

In the first place we must consider this thing as a whole. The reason for this is that the technical definition of an object must be coextensive with the object; that is, it must be applicable to the whole object, without omitting any one of its parts, and it must be applicable only to the object, to the exclusion of others. Otherwise it would not be a "definition," that is, a determination and distinction with respect to other things. As we have said, the elements that belong to the liturgy are concretely, in their wholeness: the seven sacraments, with the Eucharist a sacrifice and a sacrament; the sacramentals; the prayers and ceremonies with which the Church accompanies the actual celebration of the sacrifice, the sacraments and the sacramentals; the Divine Office of the canonical hours.

In the second place we must seek the essential characteristic notes in which all these elements agree, leaving aside those notes which are proper to some elements of the object but not to all, and for that reason cannot belong to the object as such.

In the third place, among the essential notes themselves we must look for that one on which all the rest depend and which explains them as their ultimate root, because only this note is the true principle of intelligibility of everything else in the object under consideration. Thus a technical definition must not only be clear, brief, coextensive with the object and containing only essential notes; it must also exclude the notes which are merely presupposed or derived from other objects. This is the classical way of seeking the definition of the object in any science.[4]

Description of the liturgy by its essential notes

The first observation is that all the elements which go to make up the liturgy, concretely — sacrifice, sacraments, sacramentals, prayers, ceremonies, Divine Office — as they actually exist in the liturgy, agree in one common essential concept, that of *sensible sign*.

("Sensible sign" means a sign that can be perceived by the senses. The reader should disregard the meaning of "sensible" which has now become common in English as in the expression "the sensible thing to do," and remember that "sensible" will be used hereinafter in its original meaning, "perceptible to the senses.")

They are all sensible signs of sacred, spiritual, invisible things: realities which do not fall directly under the senses.

The sacrifice of the Mass, while it is an exterior sacrifice too, has the formal value of sacrifice only as sensible sign of an invisible sacrifice in the soul. This invisible sacrifice is in the soul of Christ Himself, as far as His sacrifice is con-

---

[4] See, e.g., Aristotle, *II Post. Analyt.*, ch. 13 and 14.

cerned. It is in the souls of the faithful who share in His sacrifice, in as much as the sacrifice they offer *is* Christ's sacrifice, which they have made their own. St. Augustine observed this fact perfectly: "The visible sacrifice, therefore, is *sacramentum*, that is, sacred sign, of the invisible sacrifice." [5]

For the seven sacraments, the doctrine of St. Thomas is well known: "that is properly called a sacrament which is a sign of some sacred thing pertaining to men; so that 'sacrament' is properly used, in the sense in which we are now speaking of sacraments, when it is predicated of 'a sign of a sacred thing, in as much as it sanctifies men.'" [6]

The sacramentals too are signs of invisible, spiritual things; in this they do not differ from the sacraments. The same may be said of the rites and ceremonies of all kinds which the Council of Trent calls precisely "visible signs of religion and of piety." [7]

Finally, since liturgical prayer is also by its nature external and vocal, it too falls under the concept of sign: speech is by definition a conventional sign of interior concepts and emotions.

Thus all the elements which make up the liturgy agree in the concept of sensible sign of sacred, spiritual, invisible things. Peculiar to these sensible signs in the liturgy is the fact that they were instituted either by Christ Himself — the substance of the sacrifice and of the seven sacraments — or by the Church — sacramentals, ceremonies, prayers.

In the second place, sacrifice, sacraments, sacramentals, ceremonies and canonical prayer have an efficacy all their own with respect to the end for which they were instituted. This efficacy follows strictly from their other qualities: they are sensible signs of spiritual, invisible things, and they belong not to just any man or any society, but to Christ and to the Church because they were instituted by Christ and by the Church and are employed as instruments by Christ and by the Church. These *signs* are always *efficacious* with respect to that which they signify. [8]

But this efficacy is of different kinds, according to whether there is question of the sacrifice and the seven sacraments, instituted by Christ and instruments of Christ (which operate primarily *ex opere operato*, as the expression goes, literally "from the work wrought"), or of the other signs, instituted by the Church and instruments of the Church (which operate primarily *ex opere operantis Ecclesiae*, literally "from the work of the Church working").

In the third place, those invisible, spiritual, sacred realities to which the signs of the liturgy refer, as well as the ends themselves for which these signs were instituted and are continually employed, look on the one side to the sanctification of the Church by God and on the other side to the worship which the Church as such renders to God. Through the use of these signs God sanctifies

---

[5] *De Civ. Dei*, X, 5.
[6] *Summa*, III, q. 60, a. 2.
[7] *Sess. XXII*, ch. 5. Dz 1746 (943).

[8] For the precise meaning of this expression with respect to sanctification and worship see below, pp. 96 ff.

the Church and the Church renders its public worship to God. These two aspects are inseparable.

God, however, sanctifies always by means of Christ, God and Man. At least after Adam's sin, there is no grace and sanctification which is not grace and sanctification of Christ and in Christ, that is, merited by Christ, effecting real union with Christ, and, since the incarnation, effected, caused by Christ's humanity itself as conjoint instrument with His divinity.

In the same way, any worship rendered by the Church to God is always in Christ, that is, in union with Christ and through Christ as Head of the Church. Rather, more properly, the Church's worship is nothing but the participation of the Church in the worship which Christ the Head renders to God. Therefore it is the worship of Christ the Head rendered to God, and the priesthood of Christ, continued in the Church, by the Church and with the Church, His body.[9]

In the liturgy, therefore, the sanctification of the Church by God and the worship of God by the Church are "in Christ."

If they are "in Christ" they are "in the Spirit." For, according to the general teaching of the New Testament, the action of Christ and the action of the Spirit are inseparable, and there is no union with Christ except in the presence and in the possession of His Spirit. Hence worship "in Christ" is necessarily worship "in the Spirit." Not only is baptism "in the Spirit"[10] and not only is the Spirit received in confirmation, in penance, in the Eucharist and in holy orders,[11] but every Christian sacrifice and every Christian prayer is sacrifice and prayer in the Spirit.[12]

In this precise sense Christian worship is "spiritual,"[13] and Christians, being "in Christ," are a holy temple of the Lord, in whom they are being "built together to form a dwelling place for God in the Spirit" (Eph. 2:22). Of them it is to be said, with the comprehensive Pauline formula, showing precisely the nature of the worship they practice, that "through Him (Christ) they have access in the Spirit to the Father"[14]: The Father (by appropriation), the source from whom worship originates and the end to whom it is directed; Christ, the sole mediator of this worship; the Spirit, the One who with His presence renders "the oblation . . . acceptable, sanctified" (Rom. 15:16).

---

[9] See CL, art. 7; MD, nn. 2, 3, 20, 22.

[10] See, e.g., 1 Cor. 12:13.

[11] See, e.g., Acts 8:15 ff.; John 20:23; 1 Tim. 4:6-14; Acts 20:28.

[12] See Rom. 15:15 ff.; cf. also Heb. 9:14 with the variant reading *hagiou*; Rom. 8:26 f.; Gal. 4:6; Eph. 6:18; Jude 20.

[13] Cf. Phil. 3:3, directly in the reading *Theo*, indirectly in the reading *Theou*. Christian worship is "spiritual worship" not by exclusion of the worship which is also exterior and sensible, but because, even if it is exterior and sensible, it is rendered *in Spiritu*.

[14] This is almost literally the formula of St. Paul: Eph. 2:18. Note that the idea of "having access" (*prosagogen*) to God (cf. also 1 Peter 3:18) and also the idea of drawing near, being near (*eggizo, eggus; erchomai, proserchomai*: cf. Eph. 2:11-13; Heb. 4:14-16; 7:19; 10:19-22) refer to worship. See, e.g., Karl L. Schmidt, "Prosago, prosagoge," *Theol. Wört. zum NT*, I, 131 ff.; Herbert Preisker, "Eggus, eggizo," *ibid.*, II, 330, 21; Johannes Schneider, "Erchomai, proserchomai," *ibid.*, II, 663, 50 ff.; 681, 9 ff.; 682, 3 ff.

If all these elements are put together, the following concept of the liturgy is obtained: *The liturgy is the complexus of the sensible signs of things sacred, spiritual, invisible, instituted by Christ or by the Church; signs which are efficacious, each in its own way, of that which they signify; by which signs God (the Father by appropriation), through Christ the Head and Priest, and in the presence of the Holy Spirit, sanctifies the Church, and the Church as a body, in the presence of the Holy Spirit, uniting herself to Christ her Head and Priest, through Him renders her worship to God (the Father by appropriation).*

At this point let us recall the three articles of doctrine explained above with reference to sacred history:

1) the meaning of sacred history is simply the communication of divine life to men;

2) this meaning is realized wholly within the mystery of Christ, which mystery consists in the fact that God, pouring into Christ the fullness of the divine life, unites men to Himself in Christ, in as much as Christ communicates to them the divine life with which He is filled;

3) finally, the meaning of sacred history and of the mystery of Christ, for the time from Pentecost to the parousia, is realized in the mystery of the Church as a human-divine entity, instituted as the only port of salvation, in which and through which is realized that communion of divine life which Christ transmits to men, giving them the Spirit and thus uniting them with Himself and with the Father.

If these points are kept in mind, it will be easy to acknowledge that the liturgy is nothing but a manner *sui generis*, that is, under the veil of sensible signs, sacred and efficacious, in which the meaning of sacred history — mystery of Christ, mystery of the Church — is realized from Pentecost to the parousia.

The strict technical definition of the liturgy

The above description of the liturgy is obtained simply by adding up its most characteristic essential properties. Now we want to determine which of these properties constitutes the very essence of the liturgy and thus formulate a strict technical definition of the liturgy by proximate genus and specific difference. We can do this if we merely eliminate from the above description those expressions which follow from and explain the other expressions contained therein without really adding anything new for anyone who grasps the full force of these other expressions in the light of general theology.

Thus, in the first part, the words "of things sacred, spiritual, invisible" will be eliminated. For these sacred, spiritual, invisible things to which the signs of the liturgy refer are concretely: sanctifying grace, more or less immediately signified in the various liturgical signs; the Author of this grace, Christ; its end, the glory to come; and the interior worship which the Church renders to God, which also is more or less immediately signified in the various signs. It suffices to say, therefore, that the liturgy is a complexus of signs of the sanctification of the Church by God and of the worship of God by the Church.

It is not necessary, either, to say that those signs have been instituted by Christ or by the Church. If we say that the signs are efficacious of sanctification and of public worship, we include in that very concept the fact that they have been instituted by Christ or by the Church; for only signs that are Christ's own or the Church's own, and therefore instituted by Christ or by the Church and employed by Christ or by the Church, can effect what these signs signify.

After "efficacious" it is not necessary to add "each in its own way of that which they signify"; for the efficacy of the sign, as sign, is necessarily related to that which it signifies, and, when the concern is with a complexus of signs, it is obvious that the different signs will have their effects in different ways. It will be sufficient, therefore, to distinguish the various signs that make up the complexus when we come to the explanation of "complexus of signs." The different kind of efficacy of each sign will follow from the different nature of each one.

In a definition of the liturgy by proximate genus and specific difference it is not necessary, either, to mention explicitly that all sanctification comes from the Father (by appropriation) through Christ the Head and Priest, in the presence of the Holy Spirit, and that all worship of the Church is directed to God (the Father by appropriation) in the presence of the Holy Spirit through Christ the Head and Priest. It is not necessary because this is simply the general theological doctrine of the way in which every good comes to us from God and the way in which every return of ours to God is made (though I would not presume to say that this doctrine is much heeded or much understood, still less that it is effectively lived).

In this "from God and to God" the progress always has to be from the Father, through Christ the incarnate Son, in the possession of the Holy Spirit, to the Father. He who states, therefore, that the liturgy is the complexus of the signs of the sanctification of the Church by God and of the worship of God by the Church, has already sufficiently stated, for anyone who understands the general doctrine of theology, that this process takes place necessarily from the Father, through Christ the incarnate Son, our High Priest, in the possession of the Holy Spirit, to the Father. For the same reason, it is not necessary to specify that the liturgy is an exercise of Christ's priesthood.

It is not necessary to say, either, that the Church's worship is rendered to God. This is already included in the very idea of the Church's worship. Nor is it necessary to say that the sanctification of the Church comes from God, because this is already included in the idea of sanctification.

Finally, in a strict definition it is not necessary to say explicitly that the Church's worship of God in the liturgy is done as a body, officially, publicly. Actually "Church," understood formally as Church, necessarily implies all this.

Thus, among all the essential properties which constitute the liturgical complexus, we arrive at that which is the root of all the others and, as such, includes them, constitutes the essence of the liturgy and therefore its definition by proximate genus and specific difference. The liturgy is: *the complexus of the sensible, efficacious signs of the Church's sanctification and of her worship.*[15]

The liturgy, then, is in the proximate genus of sensible signs. The specific difference which distinguishes liturgical signs from all other sensible signs is that they signify, and really effect, *ex opere operato* or else *ex opere operantis Ecclesiae,* the sanctification of the Church by God and the worship of God by the Church.

This definition includes all the elements of the liturgy and applies to them only. For it includes not only that in the liturgy which is action of the Church toward God, namely worship, but also that which is a work more properly of God toward the Church, namely the sanctification of the Church which God effects. And all this holds in its own way not only of the ceremonies and prayers instituted by the Church, but also of the seven sacraments and of the sacrifice of the Mass itself in that central essence of them which is of divine institution.

Observations on other "definitions"

The other definitions[16] violate, in our opinion, some essential rule of definition properly so called.

Many of them are, at best, more or less apt descriptions, but not strict definitions, because they do not take the trouble to distinguish, among the notes to which they call attention, that one which is the root of all the rest, and thus to eliminate those which are only secondary and derived.[17] Even the notion of the liturgy simply as "exercise of the priesthood of Jesus Christ" cannot be admitted as a strict definition because, among other things, it defines the liturgy by a note which is not primary, but derived, as has been said above.

Other notions violate the rule that a strict definition must be coextensive with the object defined. The definition of the liturgy as "exercise of the priesthood of Jesus Christ" offends against this rule also. For even purely interior and private worship, as well as pious exercises of every kind, is an exercise of the priesthood of Jesus Christ, through which Christ continues His

---

[15] A substantially equivalent definition would be had by simply inverting the terms: the liturgy is the sanctification and the worship of the Church actualized in sensible and efficacious signs.

[16] No purpose is served, I think, in reporting even the principal ones among those proposed. A long exposition of them may be found in Herman A. P. Schmidt's *Introductio in liturgiam occidentalem* (Herder, 1960), pp. 47-86. Lambert Beauduin's definition of the liturgy as "the Church's worship," meaning her public, official worship, was widely accepted. See, e.g.,

his "Essai de manuel fondamental de liturgie," *Les quest. lit. (et parois.),* 3 (1913), 56-66; Emmanuel Caronti, "Per una definizione della liturgia," *Riv. lit.,* 8 (1921), 4 ff.; Alois Stenzel, *Cultus publicus. Ein Beitrag zum Begriff und ekklesiologischen Ort der Liturgie,* thesis of the Gregorianum (Innsbruck, 1953).

[17] This is the case, for example, with the definitions proposed by J. H. Miller, Alois Stenzel and Herman Schmidt. See Herman A. P. Schmidt's *Introductio in liturgiam occidentalem,* pp. 57, 59, 64.

work of sanctification and of worship in the Church, so that this notion by itself is not enough to characterize the liturgy.

Offending in a special way against the rule of coextension with the object defined is the definition of the liturgy as worship alone, even when public and integral worship is specified; for example, the definition which says: the liturgy is the public and integral worship of the mystical body of Jesus Christ. This notion leaves out everything in the liturgy that is directly and primarily sanctification of man, that is, the very essence of the sacraments and of some sacramentals, such as exorcisms.

Whoever accepts that notion as a strict definition is thereby compelled to consider the primary and essential aspect of the sacred actions of the sacraments and of some sacramentals as not belonging to the essence of the liturgy, but, at most, as a condition or a derivative of the liturgy. Now it is absolutely certain that, for example, the Eucharist as a sacrament transforming man, or baptism as an action sanctifying man, are not mere presuppositions or derivatives of the liturgy, but coessential parts of it; just as the body, for instance, is a coessential part of man and not a presupposition or a derivative of man.

To include in the definition of the liturgy only the aspect of worship is to make an arbitrary selection among the elements of the concrete liturgical reality. This reality includes in its essence not only a certain attitude, a certain action of the Church towards God, but also an attitude, an action of God towards the Church. The liturgy is not a monologue, but a dialogue between God and the Church, in which, moreover, the initiative is always God's. The liturgy is a point of contact and of encounter between God and the Church. Its concrete reality involves an inseparable compenetration of the action of God sanctifying the Church and the response of the Church rendering her public worship to God.

And, since the action of God in sanctifying the Church is realized only through Christ and in Him, and the worshipful response of the Church is made only through Christ and in Him, the liturgy is, under the veil of sensible, efficacious signs, the point of encounter, in Christ, of God who sanctifies the Church and the Church who responds by rendering her worship to God.

Not without reason does the Second Vatican Council insist everywhere on viewing both the work of Christ and the liturgy which continues that work on earth under the twofold indivisible aspect of sanctification and worship.[18] It is to be hoped that henceforth this point will remain solidly established.[19]

---

[18] Besides article 7 of CL, see articles 5, 6, 10, 33, 48, 59, 61, 83. See also MD, nn. 3, 171 (Lat. 169), 205 (Lat. 203).

[19] So much the more are those definitions of the liturgy to be rejected which not only consider the aspect of worship alone but further limit themselves to that which is of ecclesiastical institution in worship, without including that which is of properly divine institution. Thus, for example, Camillus Callewaert, *Liturgicae institutiones—De S. Liturgia universim* (Brussels, 1911), p. 5, defined the liturgy as "the ecclesiastical arrangement of public worship," "public worship in so far as it is ordained by ecclesiastical authority."

Can the definition proposed by Odo Casel be

Definition of the liturgy and *sacramentum*

It will surely be noticed that the proposed definition of the liturgy is basically no more than a broadening of the classical definition of the seven sacraments in general, which, according to St. Thomas, are defined as *sensible signs effecting (ex opere operato) the grace which they signify.*

The extension occurs in two essential points. First of all, by efficacious signs are understood not only those which are efficacious *ex opere operato,* but also those which are efficacious *ex opere operantis Ecclesiae.* In the second place, by sensible signs are understood not only those which signify directly and produce the grace through which God sanctifies men, and signify only indirectly the worship which men render to God, but also those which signify directly the worship which men render to God and only indirectly the grace through which God sanctifies men. Moreover, it is explicitly stated that the direct subject of the sanctification which God effects and of the worship which is rendered to Him, is the Church as such.

A thing no less notable is that the aforesaid broadening which the concept of sacrament is made to undergo in order to include the whole of the liturgy simply brings us back to the concept of *mystérion, mysterium, sacramentum* (or, in the plural, *mysteria, sacramenta*) with which the ancient patristic and liturgical tradition designated just those elements which we today commonly call "liturgy." And there is nothing surprising in this if we consider that historically what the scholastics, and St. Thomas in particular, did, when they set limits to the familiar concept of sacrament in general, was precisely the reverse of what we are doing. They restricted the ancient concept of the *sacramenta* or *mysteria,* which had traditionally applied to all the liturgical rites in general, so as to make the concept of *sacramentum* signify only the essential characteristics of the seven major rites which we today call sacraments.

Another section of this chapter will deal more explicitly with the ancient concept of *mystérion, mysterium, sacramentum.* Here it is enough to recall that the ancients included the whole liturgical reality under this concept of *mystérion, mysteria; mysterium, mysteria; sacramentum, sacramenta.*

For example, St. Augustine used the term *sacramentum, sacramenta* not only for the doctrines, the mysteries, the figures and prefigurations of the Old Testament, the Bible itself, but also for baptism, confirmation, the Eu-

accepted as a strict technical definition of the liturgy? He defines the liturgy thus: "The liturgy is the worship-mystery of Christ and of the Church" ("Mysteriengegenwart," *Jahrbuch für Liturgiewissenschaft,* 8 [1928], 212); or: "The liturgy is the ritual action of Christ's work of salvation in the Church and for the Church; that is, it is the presence of the divine work of redemption under the veil of symbols" (*ibid.,* p. 145). In my opinion, two criticisms must be made of this definition. *a)* Left unexplained are the expressions "worship-mystery," "ritual action," "presence of the work." A definition should be clear. *b)* Actually, Casel intended "worship-mystery" and "presence" not only in the general sense of mystery explained by us above, but in the exact sense of a re-presentation of Christ's redemptive actions in their numerical individuality. This, I think, is something that cannot be accepted (see below, pp. 106 f.). If, on the other hand, the concept of "mystery" were understood without this specification, only the first criticism would apply against the definition.

charist, the Apostles' Creed, the Lord's Prayer, exorcisms, fasting, all the ceremonies and prayers of the Mass, the liturgical feast of Easter, etc.[20]

This was possible because *mystérion, mysterium, sacramentum* was understood in a very broad sense simply as: signs which have reference to the sacred things of God's economy in the world and which at the same time manifest these sacred realities to one who understands the sign and hide them from one who does not understand it.[21] For the ancients the *sacramenta* of the rites, moreover, really contain in some way the realities which they signify.[22]

But does all this have any real objective importance beyond purely historical

---

[20] All these meanings are met with, e.g., in *Sermo* 228, 3; 227; *Ep.* 98, nn. 9-10. That is, Augustine uses the word *sacramentum* for our sacraments, our sacramentals, the whole of the Church's language and actions in the liturgy: "temporal *sacramenta* . . . all those things about which we are speaking to you, those things which are heard and which take place, whatever is done temporally in the Church," as: the preaching and the recitation of the Gospel, the imposition of hands by the bishop, etc. (see *In Ps.* 146, 8). On the *sacramentum* of the feast of Easter in St. Augustine see *Ep.* 55, 2. The *Indiculus*, in the same sentence which contains the celebrated formula "Let the rule for prayer determine the rule of belief," calls the Church's liturgical prayers themselves *sacramenta*: "Let us look also to the *sacramenta* of the priestly supplications" (Dz 246 [139]). See: H. Feret, " 'Sacramentum' dans le language théologique de S. Augustin," *Rev. des sciences phil. et théol.*, 1940, pp. 218 ff.; C. Couturier, " 'Sacramentum' et 'mysterium' dans l'oeuvre de S. Augustin," *Etudes augustiniennes* (Paris: Aubier, 1953), pp. 163-332.

For the concept of *sacramentum* in the Ante-Nicenes see: Joseph de Ghellinck, *Pour l'histoire du mot "Sacramentum." I. Les anténicéens* (Louvain, 1924); Odo Casel, "Zum Worte Sacramentum," *Jahrb. für Liturgiewis.*, 8 (1928), 225 ff.

[21] ". . . of the signs which, since they pertain to divine things, are called *sacramenta*" (Augustine, *Ep.* 138, n. 7). "These (bread and wine) are called *sacramenta* because in them one thing is seen and another understood" (Augustine, *Sermo* 272). The concept of *mystérion* in the Greek Fathers is essentially the same, as will be demonstrated in more detail in its own place. The *mystérion* is always a representation of supersensible sacred things by means of sensible signs. Theodore of Mopsuestia says, "Every *mystérion* is an indication in sensible signs of invisible and inexpressible things" (*Catech.*,

XII, 2). And St. John Chrysostom: "It is called *mystérion* when we do not consider" (according to the alternative reading in PG) "what we see, but see one set of things and consider another" with regard to sacred things (see the "one thing is seen and another understood" of Augustine). ". . . Here the judgment of the believer is one thing, while that of the unbeliever is another. For myself, I hear that Christ has been crucified, and at once I marvel at His love for men; he who does not believe hears the same thing said and thinks that it is folly. . . . The unbeliever, hearing of a bath" (of baptism), "thinks it is only water; I, on the other hand, consider not only what is seen, but the purification of the soul by the Holy Spirit" (*In ep.* 1 *Cor. Hom.* 1, n. 7). For the Pseudo-Dionysius see, e.g., *Hier. eccl.*, I, 5; II, 1; II, 3, 1; II, 3, 2. Thus for the Greek Fathers also *mysterion*, said of things related to worship, has a very broad meaning. The Pseudo-Dionysius, for example, indicates by this word not only our sacraments but also the consecration of the chrism and of the altar, the rite of monastic profession and that of burial. Simeon of Salonika, in the fourteenth century, under the same word explicitly enumerates also the dedication of a church, the consecration of the emperor, the recitation of the Pater Noster, the canonical hours, the funeral office, etc. For all this see, e.g., A. Michel, "Sacramentaux," *Dict. de théol. cath.*, XIV, 1 (1939), 468 ff.; Gerhard Fittkau, *Der Begriff des Mysteriums bei Johannes Chrysostomus* (Bonn: P. Hanstein, 1953); René Roques, *L'univers dionysien* (Paris: Montaigne, 1954). The same situation obtains in the Syrian Fathers; see: Wilhelm de Vries, *Sakramententheologie bei den syrischen Monophysiten* (Rome: Pont. inst. orient. stud., 1940), pp. 29-37.

[22] See the concept of *res* in St. Augustine. He applies it also to the *sacramenta* of the feasts, at least to Easter (cf. *Ep.* 55 and *Ep.* 98, 9) and to the *sacramenta* of the liturgy of the

interest? Yes, enormously so. It means the rediscovery that "sacramentality" does not apply exclusively to the seven major rites which we today call sacraments, as if to say sacraments *par excellence*. Except for those aspects of sacramentality which are proper to these seven rites — their divine institution and their special efficacy *ex opere operato* — sacramentality is common to the whole liturgy.

In fact, the vision grows broader, and the discovery is made that structuration in a "sacrament" system is common to the whole Church, which is therefore the "wonderful sacrament of Your whole Church," and that the Church is a sacrament because it is nothing but the expression and the continuation on earth of the first and original "Sacrament" who is Christ the Lord.[23]

Thus we begin to see the whole liturgy as that point at which the sacramental flow of divine life from Christ, in the Church, reaches us. And we begin to surmise that precisely in the liturgy is the very heart of the Church, her most perfect expression, her epiphany *par excellence*. The liturgy is the point in which the Church appears most clearly as the pure instrument, perceptible to the senses, which the divine life uses to manifest itself and transmit itself to men who are properly disposed.

These are not idle fancies. It is just this general picture of *sacramentum* into which the Second Vatican Council itself fits the concept of liturgy.[24]

As we have explained above, the liturgy is nothing but the realization from Pentecost to the parousia of the meaning of sacred history under the veil of the sensible and efficacious signs of sanctification and of worship. We see now that this specific mode of realization was called *sacramentum, mysterium* by the ancients. Hence if we want to preserve the terminology of the ancients, we can say that the liturgy is simply the carrying out *in sacramento* or *in mysterio* of sacred history from Pentecost to the parousia.[25]

Mass and of the part which the faithful take in it (cf. *Sermo* 227). The *res* of the Eucharist is the unity in the body of Christ; the *res* of the *sacramentum* of exorcism and of fasting is a certain spiritual maceration; the *res* of confirmation is receiving the Holy Spirit; the *res* of the *sacramentum* by which the words "Lift up your hearts; we lift them up to the Lord" are said in the Mass, is the fact that what is meant is that Christ is in heaven and that He gives us the grace of having our heart in heaven and not on earth. The *res* of the *sacramentum* of the sacrifice is our own sacrifice: ". . . He wanted us to be His sacrifice ourselves . . . we also are God's sacrifice, that is, the sign of the thing which we are." The *res* of the kiss of peace is peace of conscience; the fact that the heart is united to one's brother. For all this see *Sermo* 227.

[23] For further explanation of this point see below, pp. 61-62.

[24] CL, art. 5-7 and art. 2 and 41.

[25] This manner of understanding the expression *sacramentum* and *mysterium*, definitely the traditional way and widely preserved in the liturgy itself, does not imply in any way the personal theory of Odo Casel on the mystery, in so far as that theory is specifically his own: the re-production or re-presentation through a sacred sign, above all the Eucharistic sign, of Christ's historical redemptive actions, especially His Passion, in their numerical individuality though in a supra-temporal manner. It would be ridiculous to hold suspect the doctrine expressed by the words *sacramentum* and *mysterium*, so well founded in patristic and liturgical tradition, for the simple reason that one does not agree with the personal theory which Casel tried to attach to these words. It would be no less truly unjust to deny that the credit for having rediscovered a very rich vein of authentic traditional theology belongs to Casel, always aside from his own specific theory.

Since the whole liturgical economy, therefore, falls under the concept of sign, the first thing to be explained is this concept itself and its precise meaning in the liturgy.

2. Sign

Notion

The following observations may suffice for our purpose.[26]

St. Augustine explains perfectly what the concept of sign involves: "A sign is a thing which, besides the species it impresses on the senses, leads to the knowledge of something other than itself. Thus, seeing the footprint of an animal, we know that the animal which made the track has passed this way; seeing smoke, we know that there is a fire from which it is rising; hearing the voice of a living being, we know its feelings; soldiers at the sound of a trumpet know whether they are to advance or retreat or do anything else in battle." [27]

"Sign" thus defined is an instrument [28] which makes some other thing present to the cognitive faculty through the relation it has to the other thing, by the mere fact of being known in that relation. Towards the cognitive power the sign in some way acts as a substitute for this other thing, which is absent or hidden. For that very reason the sign must be distinct from that thing, and, in so far as it is a sign, it must depend on that thing and therefore be less perfect than it. But, as far as the knower is concerned, the sign must be better known than the thing it signifies, since the knower has to arrive at the knowledge of the thing signified from the knowledge of the sign.

Thus the sign, a sensible thing which makes present to the mind something else whose place it takes, must have the following characteristics. It must be: distinct from the thing signified; in a relation of dependence on the thing and therefore less perfect than it; not only like it but also unlike it; more known than the thing.

The sign, therefore, at the same time and under different aspects, reveals

---

[26] For more ample particulars and especially for a metaphysical analysis of the concept of sign, see: John of St. Thomas, *Logica*, II, qq. 21 and 22, ed. Reiser, I (Turin: Marietti, 1930), 646-722; Jacques Maritain, "Signe et symbole," *Rev. thom.*, 44 (1938), 299-330; A. M. Roguet, "Les sacrements," *S. Thomas d'Aquin, La somme théologique*, ed. de la revue des jeunes (Paris: Desclée, 1945), pp. 269 ff.; Eugène Masure, *Le signe: psychologie, histoire, mystère* (Paris: Bloud et Gay, 1953); Karl Rahner, "Zur Theologie des Symbols," *Cor Jesu* (Herder, 1959), I, 463-505; on pp. 465-66 a further bibliography on recent studies. *Filosofia e simbolismo* (*Archivio di filosofia*, Padua, 1956); *Le symbolisme* (*Recherches et débats*, n. 29, Dec. 1959).

[27] *De doctr. christiana*, II, 1. See also Origen, *In R. Co.* (PG 14, 968 A). I see no solid basis for the criticism of Augustine's concept made by Masure in the work mentioned in the preceding footnote, pp. 15, 188.

[28] In scholastic terminology, we are concerned with an *instrumental* sign so called to distinguish it from a *purely formal* sign. An instrumental sign leads to the knowledge of another thing *through* the knowledge of itself, noticed and conscious in the one who knows. A purely formal sign, the *species expressa*, is a perfectly translucid sign, *in which* (and not by means of which), without knowing and noticing the sign itself in any way, the mind knows only the thing which the sign serves to make known.

the thing signified and hides the thing signified. It reveals it; for it is like a bridge between the thing signified and the cognitive power. It hides it; for in the instrumental sign the thing signified does not appear immediately in itself but only through a thing distinct from itself and expressing it imperfectly.

Every sign is expressive and impressive, because it is the expression of a hidden thing which it signifies, and, by impressing it on the cognitive power, it renders present to that power the thing which it expresses and signifies.

The instrumental sign is not perfectly translucid, but offers a resistance, as it were, to the knowledge of the thing signified; one must pass through the sign to arrive at the thing signified. The sign is like a veil, though transparent; for the eyes that do not know how to penetrate the veil, the sign is a screen. To penetrate the veil means to grasp the sign precisely in its value as signifying the thing. Hence for one who does not grasp its value the sign acts as a screen; for one who does grasp it, on the other hand, the sign acts as a bridge and informant.

When the thing signified is immediately, and therefore openly, present to the cognitive power, the sign has no more reason for being; the value of the sign is limited wholly to the time during which the thing signified remains hidden. Therefore a system of signs makes sense only as a bridge between two worlds hidden from each other, but not foreign to each other. The instrumental sign is like a sensible bridge by which the human spirit, spiritual principle of ideas and affections, communicates through matter with the invisible world, or at any rate the world not present to it, and expresses itself in the visible world.

Division

Since the value of the sign for making something known depends essentially on its relation to the thing it signifies, signs are divided essentially according to the relation which each one has to the thing signified. Thus among instrumental signs there are two great categories: real signs and signs of pure reason. The real signs in turn can be either not-free, that is, natural, or free.

In *real signs* the relation between sign and thing signified is real because there is between them a relation of effect and cause: thus smoke is a real sign of fire because it is the effect of fire; in the same way, when someone chooses to bow down to express his respect for another, the bow is a real sign of his feeling of respect. Real signs really contain in some way the thing signified, and therefore really express it and signify it, as the effect really contains in some way something of the cause and expresses it.

Real signs which are natural or not free are those in which the relation between sign and thing signified does not depend on a free decision of man, but is established by nature as a law of necessity. Thus smoke is a natural sign of fire, the track of an ox is a natural sign of the passage of the ox, certain cries are natural signs of pain, the acorn is a natural sign of the oak, the rough cast is a natural sign of a statue; even a portrait or a photograph is, under this aspect, a natural sign of the one whom it represents. Such signs are common and understandable to all men. To understand them, it is enough to know the nature of which they are the expression.

Real signs which are free are sensible objects, actions or gestures made freely by man as signs of things which do not fall, at least concurrently, under the senses, and with which the signs have no necessary relation by nature. Here free will creates real sensible expressions. Thus: flag – country; spoken word – concept; writing – spoken word; plus sign to signify addition in arithmetic; bow to signify reverence; emblems of every kind.

It should be noted that, even in this case, the relation between sign and thing signified is real, and that even here the sign really contains, in its own way, the thing signified as the effect contains the cause. It is not in really containing or not containing in its own way the thing signified that real signs that are free differ from real signs that are natural, but in the way in which each of the two types contains the thing signified.

In real signs that are natural the thing signified is contained directly in the sign by virtue of nature; in real signs that are free the thing signified is contained in the sign by virtue of a free determination and by virtue of man's free creative power. It is for this reason that natural signs are common to all men and a knowledge of nature is enough for an understanding of them, while for understanding free signs it is necessary to know the free will which has determined them as signs and as the kind of signs they are.

Real signs that are free are therefore, as such, real sensible effects which depend on free will as their efficient cause; and it is the determination of this free will which they contain, express and signify by themselves and immediately, as the effect does its cause. It is only by means of this free determination of the will that real signs which are free contain, express and signify the concept or emotion signified.

Thus, for example, a flag contains, expresses and signifies the concept of country only because this manufactured object is the effect of the free determination and creativity of the man who has made it to express his concept of country. Thus the flag expresses and signifies, as an effect expresses and signifies its cause, first of all and immediately that free determination, and by means of it the concept of country. The concept of country has moved the will as object and as end, and through the will it has moved the other faculties to make the flag, acting as efficient causes. Thus the flag, being the effect of the concept of country and of the feeling for country, really contains in itself in some way this concept and this volition. For this reason the flag can also manifest the concept of country to anyone who is aware of the connection formed between that object and that concept by a free decision.

In the same way, the bow made to express respect truly contains, as an effect contains its cause, this feeling of respect, and thus it expresses the sentiment and signifies it to anyone who understands the motive for the bow.

Hence real signs that are free are free creations of man in which he incarnates and makes sensible his invisible concepts and sentiments, and through which it is possible for another person to become aware of these concepts and sentiments.

Signs of pure reason are not only signs that are free and not natural, but they are in no way creations of man and therefore are not real effects of his will and of his concepts and emotions. They are external objects not created or modified by man, but taken by him, in a conventional way, of his own choice, as signs of something else. Thus, for example, two men might wish to take, not just an emblem of the rainbow, but the rainbow itself in the sky, as a sign of their reconciliation.

Sign, image and symbol

Among the concepts very close to that of sign, the concepts of image and symbol are rather important in the liturgy. They are often used today as synonymous, but, strictly speaking, image and symbol are particular species of signs.

Image, in the meaning we give it today, is a natural real sign which involves a relation of likeness according to species between the sign and the thing signified, or at least likeness according to a characteristic note of the species, especially according to extrinsic configuration.[29] For this reason we do not say that smoke is the image of fire, or that the track of an ox is the image of the ox (unless perhaps we say this of the footprint and the foot), nor do we say that the acorn is the image of the oak; while we do say that the rough cast is the image of the statue, and the statue the image of the one it represents, and the son the image of his father, and we speak of man as the image of God.

It is much harder to fix the limits of the modern concept of symbol.[30] Every symbol is a sign; that much we can say. But not all signs are symbols. Thus we do not say that smoke is a symbol of fire, but its sign, its indication. We do not say that a portrait is the symbol of the one it represents, but his image. Nor do we say that a cry is the symbol of the pain it expresses. Symbol is not identified, therefore, either with sign in general or with image in particular.

Symbol seems rather to indicate for us today a free sign, whether real or of pure reason, as distinguished from a natural sign. Thus for us emblems are symbols. We use the term symbol also of many things made by us with the precise intention of signifying something, therefore of real signs which are free; thus: crosier – episcopal power; scepter – royal power; scales – justice. And we speak of symbolic gestures and actions and of mathematical symbols.

[29] Cf. St. Thomas, *Summa*, I, q. 93, aa. 1 and 2. The notion of image, *eikon*, in the ancient Greek was broader: everything which leads to the knowledge of another was called *eikon*.

[30] From the Greek *symbolon*, from *syn ballo*, that is, identifying tally formed by a part of an object which must be reunited to the missing part, thus forming the entire object again.

We apply the concept of symbol also to many signs of pure reason, such as: sun – Christ; salt – wisdom; incense – prayer; etc.

Very often, too, the symbols, being signs freely chosen, whether real or of pure reason, have superadded a certain analogy of being or of action between the symbol and the thing symbolized, thus becoming a sort of sensible metaphor; e.g., sun–Christ (illuminates, warms, gives life: as the sun illuminates, warms and gives life in the natural order, so Christ in the supernatural order); salt – wisdom (preserves); incense – prayer (rises to heaven); eagle – St. John (flies high, looks straight at the sun, etc.); keys – papal power (to open and close); crosier – episcopal power (directs the flock); etc.

Again, the symbol, whether real or of pure reason, often superadds a real or supposed relation between the symbol and the thing symbolized, as a relation of belonging, of origin or of likeness to the thing or to the name, to facts that are memorable or at any rate characteristic; thus, e.g., wolf – Rome; bear – Russia; cross – Christianity; crossed hammers – Adrian Hamers Company; ἰχθύς, fish – Christ; Constantinian monogram XP – Christ. The iconographic symbols of the saints are also of this category, as: sword – St. Paul; keys – St. Peter.

The ancients' way of thinking and the moderns' way of thinking about sign, image, symbol and related concepts

The concepts of sign, image, symbol (to which must be associated, for the ancients, the concepts of *eikon, symbolon, mystérion, typos, imago, species, figura, sacramentum, mysterium,* among others), since they all agree in the general concept of sign, necessarily involve a twofold antithetical relation toward the thing to which they refer and which they signify.

First of all they involve an aspect of identity, by which the sign, in some way, agrees really with the thing signified, contains it in itself, is really the thing signified. From this it follows that the sign can manifest the thing signified; and, when a person knows the sign, the image, the symbol, he will know the thing signified, represented, symbolized.

This identity *sui generis* between sign and thing signified is evident in the case of all real signs, whether natural or free. For in these signs the relation between sign and thing signified is always based on the relation of cause and effect, according to all the various types of causality: material; formal, whether intrinsic or extrinsic, that is, exemplary; efficient; final. And the effect always contains the cause in some way, because it really has in itself something of the cause, it participates in the cause, in as much as the cause really leaves a sort of imprint of itself in the effect.

But a similar, though partial, identity between sign and thing signified must also be affirmed for signs of pure reason, at least for very many of them. This is the case with all those which have been freely chosen by man because of a certain real analogy of being and of action between the sign and the thing signified; as: the sun is called a sign, a symbol of Christ because, just as the sun illuminates, warms and gives life in the physical order, so Christ illuminates, warms and gives life in the supernatural order. In fact, one who speaks of analogy, be it only metaphorical, between two things, affirms not only a certain dissimilarity but also a certain identity between these things.

The fact, therefore, that the sign involves an aspect of a certain real identity with the thing signified is so general that we may well ask whether there can be a sign which forms an exception to this rule.

The other aspect of the relation between sign and thing signified, no less real than the aspect of identity although its antithesis, is the otherness of that thing: the sign is distinct from the thing signified. And on this aspect there is no need to insist, because it is too evident.

There is real identity, then, under one aspect, real diversity under the other. This is inevitable because the sign is a reality which is a bridge between two worlds hidden from each other and a transparent veil which at the same time shows and hides that which it signifies.

Hence arises the possibility that in the consideration of the concepts of sign, image, symbol, the accent may be put now on the aspect of real unity and identity between sign and thing signified, now on the aspect of diversity. In these concepts the ancients paid attention primarily to the unity and identity between sign and thing signified, though being conscious of the aspect of real diversity. The moderns, on the other hand, without being ignorant of the aspect of unity — which, however, remains rather in the background in their psychology — pay attention above all to the aspect of real distinction and diversity.

As early as the beginning of this century Harnack was making this fundamental observation, à propos of the doctrine of the Eucharist in Christian antiquity. Concerning the body and blood of Christ in the Eucharist, "as far as we can judge," he says, "no one saw a problem here (that is, whether it was real or symbolic). The symbol was a mystery, and mystery was not conceived of without symbol. What we understand by 'symbol' today is a thing which is not what it signifies; at that time 'symbol' denoted a thing which, in some real way, is what it signifies. Besides, for the ancient way of thinking, the heavenly reality was always present in the form or under the form in which it is manifested, without, however, being identified completely with it on this earth. For this reason we must reject completely the distinction between a symbolic concept and a realistic concept of the Eucharist"[31] in order to understand the thinking of the ancients.

He means, in other words, that we are putting a false question if we ask whether this way of thinking held that Christ's body is present really in the Eucharist or whether it held that His body is present symbolically. The question, that is, presupposes the modern idea that what is symbolic is not real.

[31] *Dogmengeschichte,* I (4th ed., 1909), 476.

Recent historical inquiries, for example about the concepts of *eikon, symbolon, mystérion, typos, signum, imago, figura, species, sacramentum, mysterium* among the ancients,[32] have confirmed fully the truth of Harnack's observation. The matter is highly important, both historically and currently, in the general theological field and in the liturgical field.

Dependent upon this observation in general theology are: the exact understanding of the scriptural and patristic theme of Christ the image of the invisible God;[33] the correct evaluation of the so-called allegorism or typologism of the Bible and the Fathers, including both the Old Testament typology of New Testament subjects, whether the types be of Christ or of His followers, and the New Testament typology of the future eschatological realities;[34] the understanding of the whole patristic sacramental theology and especially of the patristic theology of the Eucharist;[35] finally, the understanding of the theological bases of the struggle of the Greek Fathers in the seventh and eighth centuries against the iconoclasts.[36]

As far as the liturgy is concerned, only from the ancient approach to the concept of sign and related concepts can the true thinking of the Fathers be grasped when they speak of the liturgical realities, as they so often do, in terms of *mysterium, sacramentum, imago, species*, etc.; that is, only on this condition will the profoundly realistic aspect of the thinking inherent in these expressions be perceived.

Hence only this mentality will enable a person to grasp the precise meaning of many ancient liturgical texts still in use such as or similar to the following:

Aeternae pignus vitae capientes humiliter imploramus ut apostolicis fulti patrociniis quod in imagine	Receiving the pledge of eternal life, we humbly implore that under the patronage of the Apostles we may

---

[32] For a first general orientation in this matter see: Tommaso Cammelot, "Simbolo e simbolismo," *Enciclopedia cattolica*, 11 (1953), cols. 611-16, with bibliography. To be noted further among other works see: H. Willms, *Eikon. Eine begriffgeschichtliche Untersuchung zum Platonismus* (Münster, 1935); the article "Bild" in the *Reallexikon für Antike und Christentum* of Theodor Klauser, written by H. E. Killy and M. Höpfner for the Greek and Roman idea, and by J. Kollwitz for the Christian; this last especially from 336 to 341; Lucas Koch, "Zur Theologie der Christusikone," *Benediktinische Monatschrift*, 19 (1937), 375-87; 20 (1938), 32-47; 168-75; 281-88; 437-52; H. Menges, *Die Bildlehre des hl. Joannes von Damaskus* (Münster, 1937); Hermann Kleinknecht, "Der griechische Sprachgebrauch von 'eikon,'" *Theol. Wört. zum NT*, II, 386 f.; Hugo Rahner, *Greek Myths and Christian Mystery* (New York: Harper & Row, 1963); Walter

Dürig, *Imago. Ein Beitrag zur Terminologie und Theologie der römischen Liturgie* (Munich: Karl Zink, 1952).

[33] See Col. 1:15. Cf. Kleinknecht in *Theol. Wört. zum NT*, II, 386 f. In patristic thought the concept returns in the struggle against Arianism and again in the Christological arguments.

[34] See, e.g., Jean Daniélou, *Origen* (New York: Sheed & Ward, 1955); *From Shadows to Reality*; Henri de Lubac, *Histoire et esprit* (Paris: Aubier, 1950); Celestin Charlier, *The Christian Approach to the Bible* (Westminster, Md.: Newman, 1958), pp. 248-80.

[35] See, e.g., a brief exposition of the question in Tommaso Cammelot's "Simbolo e simbolismo," *Enciclopedia cattolica*, 11, cols. 611-16.

[36] Among the works cited above in note 32, see in this regard those of Koch, Menges, Kollwitz.

gerimus sacramenti manifesta percep-
tione sumamus.[37]

Perficiant in nobis, Domine, quae-
sumus, tua sacramenta quod con-
tinent, ut quae nunc specie gerimus,
rerum veritate capiamus.[38]

Quorum oblationem benedictam
ratam acceptabilemque facere di-
gneris, quae est imago et similitudo
corporis et sanguinis Iesu Christi filii
tui ac redemptoris nostri.[39]

consume with full knowledge what
we consecrate in a sacramental image.

May Your Sacraments, O Lord, we
pray, effect in us what they contain,
that what we now do in appearance,
we may obtain in reality.

And may You see fit to make the
oblation of these things blessed, ratified and acceptable — this oblation,
the image and likeness of the body
and blood of Jesus Christ, Your Son
and our Redeemer.

But we are interested in bringing out especially the general consequence for
the understanding of the whole of the liturgy and of what we may call the
liturgical style, resulting from the ancients' and the moderns' respective ways
of thinking about the aforesaid concepts.

We have said that the liturgy is a complexus of sensible signs; that under
the veil of these signs and through them is fulfilled in us, today, the meaning
of sacred history as God's communication of the divine life to all of us through
Christ and as our response in Christ to God's action. If this is so, it is easy to see
what consequences will follow for the manner of penetrating and living the
liturgy from the frame of mind with which the world of signs is approached.

We must accept the ancients' view: that under the veil of the sign, of any
sign, the reality of the thing signified is reached, and that the reality reaches
us through this sensible veil because there is a certain real, though partial,
identity between the sign and the reality signified. We must understand that
the sign is the bridge over which our encounter is made with the invisible
reality and this reality is made present to us, even if that encounter and that
presence are always very imperfect because the sign can never contain and
transmit all the wealth of the invisible reality which is expressed in it. Only
if we have a lively sense of all this are we predisposed for entering the world
of the liturgy.

The contrary view would be to think on principle that, since the sign is not
the thing signified, the sign and the thing signified are basically two foreign
worlds linked only artificially to each other. Such a view, pushed to its logical
conclusion, will undervalue the real force of any sign and the reality of its
content and lead us to see in the liturgy a purely arbitrary game, like children's

[37] *Sacramentarium Leonianum*, ed. Mohlberg (*Sacram. Veronense*), n. 335.

[38] *Sacramentarium Gelasianum*, ed. Mohlberg (*Liber sacramentorum romanae ecclesiae
ordinis anni circuli*), n. 1051, p. 161 (this was
also the text of the postcommunion for Ember

Saturday in September, until the promulgation
of the new Roman Missal of Pope Paul VI).

[39] Mozarabic liturgy, *Liber ordinum*, ed.
Férotin, col. 322 (see also Johannes Quasten's
Monumenta eucharistica et liturgica vetustissima
[Bonn: P. Hanstein, 1936], p. 160).

play: a game of empty signs. There will be a psychological difficulty in admitting that God can, or at any rate will, fulfill the mystery of Christ in us through signs; that in signs man renders his true worship to God, expressing effectively in them his interior and spiritual worship; that thus it is precisely sensible signs, in the present economy, that are the primary and connatural point of encounter between God and man.

There is no denying that the ancients were greatly helped by the Platonic-Neoplatonic mentality in admitting much more easily than we do, this economy of signs, images, symbols, etc.

Platonism distinguished sharply between the spiritual, supersensible, eternal world as the true world which alone was full of being, and the sensible world as shadow and image of the supersensible world. The value of the sensible world was supposed to consist wholly in its being a participation and expression of that higher world and a stairway for man to return by way of the sensible to the eternal world which transcends the senses.

Neoplatonism strongly emphasized the concept of the degrees of being, emanating from the supreme degree uninterruptedly in a descending scale, by which every form impressed its own image and likeness on the lower grade and every being was connected with the higher degree by that which was highest in it and with the lower degree by that which was lowest in it.

Characteristic of this whole tradition of thought, Platonism and Neoplatonism, was its contemplation of the profound unity of the whole cosmos. Thus the minds of the ancients were habituated to reading in each individual being the bonds with the whole universe, and in the sensible world in particular the bonds with the spiritual and supersensible world.[40]

In the pagan thinkers this mentality has serious flaws: the deficiency of their concept of God; their idea of analogy conceived almost entirely as a quantitative descent, which does not safeguard the specific distinction of beings; especially their ignorance of the concept of creation, resulting in a tendency, with repercussions on the notion of image and related concepts, to think of the participation from the highest grade to the lowest as a mere emanation of the same form. These defects give the pagan mentality a strong monistic flavor, heightened by the religious and mystical afflatus which was present in Neoplatonism itself and in the undiscriminating gnostic tendencies of the age.

We grant these defects in the pagan thinkers. We grant that ancient Christian authors such as Clement of Alexandria, Origen, Gregory of Nyssa, the Pseudo-Dionysius, Ambrose and Augustine were imbued with Platonic-Neoplatonic thought. We grant that their philosophical formation helped them to conceive the Christian economy realistically in terms of signs, images and symbols. All this does not shake the fact that these Christian thinkers do not depend on that which is perishable in Platonism-Neoplatonism, or even

---

[40] See, e.g., H. Willms, *Eikon*. See also Plotinus, *Enneads*, III, 6, 11-14.

on that which is of erroneous tendency, for the essence of their attitude. The bases of their attitude are quite sound independently.

The first of these bases is the metaphysical truth of the gradations of being, of the analogical unity of all these degrees, of the participation of being. This truth, the vital core of the Platonic and Neoplatonic intuition, St. Thomas was later to vindicate, having purified it of the dross with which it was covered in pagan Greek thought.[41] The metaphysics of participation, sign and image, everything that is true in the Platonic intuition, is perfectly capable of preservation and deserving of preservation in the Christian system. It can be preserved even in the Aristotelian-Thomistic metaphysics, where the doctrine of creation, the specific distinction in beings, the analogy of being, the production by efficient causality are taught, with the negation of all monism and emanationism.

The production of an effect by efficient causality is always accompanied by a sharing of form from cause to effect. Every being acts by its form and *omne agens agit sibi simile.* Hence the effect is a real sign of the efficient cause in whose form it participates. This is because there is no efficient causality in the world which does not involve the directive action of an intellect and therefore of an idea and of an exemplary causality. Every efficient causality involves at least the directive action of the divine intellect and idea. In specifically human causality, the human intellect and idea is also involved; it is an exemplary formal cause of the action and of the thing done.

Thus in every effect of efficient causality, there is always an exemplary causality at work also. This means that there is always in the effect a participation of the form of the agent, who is first of all God Himself.

It is for this reason that all things are necessarily real signs, vestiges, images of God; they really partake of Him, and He is really present in them. And in making a statement like this, we do not have to fall into monism, pantheism, or even an unsound mysticism, nor need we adopt in its entirety the metaphysics which was historically that of Platonism and Neoplatonism.

Next, all things, in as much as they act upon one another, and especially in as much as they are made and directed by the supreme intellect according to a unitary plan in which they are all in some way connected and consolidated with one another, are, in some real way, similar to one another and signs of one another; from one can come knowledge of another. And this is the nucleus of truth in the great stoic and gnostic theme of universal harmony and *sympathy.*

Finally, man in a special way expresses himself really and, as it were, imprints something of himself really in his outward sensible actions and in the works which he produces as an artificer.

Hence a phenomenon which has general value is that of the artist who

[41] Cf. *Summa,* III, q. 60, aa. 2 and 3; Cornelio Fabro, *La nozione metafisica della partecipazione secondo San Tommaso d'A.* (2nd ed.; Milan, 1950).

really expresses himself in his work of art, who imprints and incarnates in it his ideas, his desires, his sentiments, his whole personality, in such a way that the work of art of this whole person is really a sharing and that anyone can see and find this whole person in the work of art, provided he knows how to read it. This phenomenon is reproduced in its own way in every causality that occurs in the world. As the artist leaves his stamp on the canvas, God imprints Himself on every being; man imprints himself on all his gestures and all his works; things imprint themselves on one another in as much as they act upon one another.

Universal exemplarism is no mere fancy, therefore. The principle itself, held by the ancients, is valid from the point of view of sound philosophy.

On the other hand, the validity of the principle provides no justification in fact for the way in which the ancients, and especially their less distinguished medieval successors, often interpreted this universal exemplarism in detail. Even in a canvas, although everything there reveals the artist, a person must know how to read the individual details correctly in order to specify in what way they really reveal the artist and not to indulge in arbitrary and subjective statements.

The second foundation on which ancient Christian exemplarism rests is revelation. Here a series of themes contained in Scripture and tradition have great importance: the theme of the unity of sacred history and of the divine plan of salvation, in which the antecedent phases prepare, in rough draft, for the subsequent ones, which in their turn are the realization of the antecedent phases, while all the phases tend to the ultimate one of the heavenly Jerusalem, which includes all in itself; the theme of the unity of the cosmos, infrahuman, human, angelic and divine; the theme of man the image of God, substantial unity of matter and spirit, who expresses himself in the sensible, and through the sensible rises to God; the theme of the ability to know God even by means of sensible and material things; the theme of the incarnation and of Christ, the perfect image of the Father, in whose countenance the Father can be contemplated, "that, while recognizing God in visible form, we may be carried away by Him to the love of things invisible."[42] Later we shall have to return more at length to these themes and their importance for understanding the liturgy.

Our present purpose is achieved by having merely hinted at them. Now when our contemporary liturgists (and not only the liturgists) invite our positivistic minds to a more impartial consideration of the real import of sign, image and symbol, and when they hope that we can reacquire something of the realistic sense these concepts had for the ancients, we shall understand what they mean. We shall have no cause to become frightened immediately at the danger of an unsound, nebulous mysticism; rather, we shall know that it is really worth the trouble to examine the question with calm objectivity.

---

[42] Preface I of Christmas, "De Christo luce."

3. Sign in the Liturgy

The signs in the Catholic liturgy have, of course, a religious value. They are sacred signs; they concern the relations between God and man; more precisely, the relations between God and man in the Christian regime, and, still more explicitly, in the Catholic regime.

The first thing to be observed is that everything in the liturgy is done under the veil of sensible signs and through their mediation. Hence the whole liturgy and each of its parts has the value of a sign; always in the liturgy "one thing is seen and another understood."[43] Even the mere presence of a community of the faithful in a church for the liturgical celebration has the value of a sign. It is a sensible expression of those secret, invisible relations which obtain between God and mankind in the regime of grace in Christ. It is not just any assembly, but, for one who knows how to see through the veil of the sign, it is a convocation, an *ekklesia*, of God in Christ Jesus,[44] an assembling "in the name" of Christ.[45] Everything that is seen, done or said here is in its own way a sensible sign of this invisible situation. Can there be any intention here of bringing the modern man back to the arbitrary and naive medieval liturgical pansymbolism of an Amalarius or a Durandus?

The criterion of its existence and interpretation

Although everything in the liturgy has the value of a sign, the sign does not signify just anything. We are not in fact left without guidance, to form arbitrary and fanciful judgments in determining the existence and the precise meaning of the individual signs.

Let us note first of all that the liturgical sign is never simply a natural sign. In the liturgy we are always concerned with signs that are free, that is, determined by the free and positive will of God or of the Church to signify the things they do signify.

The invisible realities of which the signs are the sensible expression in the liturgy are supernatural realities: the divine life which God communicates to the Church and the supernatural and Christian worship which the Church renders to God as a participation in the worship which Christ Himself renders to God.

Now no sensible thing is a simply natural sign of such realities, as smoke is a sign of fire or a certain cry is a sign of pain, because the supernatural realities transcend the order of the sensible. The immersion in water and the emersion from water is a disappearance and a reappearance, but does not signify naturally the death to sin and the resurrection to the supernatural life in Christ. The washing with water does indeed signify naturally a physical purification, but not the purification from sin. An assembly does not signify naturally the

---

[43] Augustine, *Sermo* 272.
[44] Cf., e.g., 1 Thess. 1:1; 2 Thess. 1:1.
[45] Matthew, 18:20. See in Robert Will's *Le culte*, II (Paris: Alcan, 1929), 47, a phenomenological description of what is aroused in the believer by the fact of a religious assembly.

convocation of God in Christ Jesus, a gathering "in the name" of Christ. An embrace does not signify naturally the brotherly love in Christ. A bow does not signify naturally the worship of God in Christ.

In all this, therefore, the free positive will of God or of the Church must always intervene, the free will which wants to express with just these signs certain precise realities and no other.

One man or even several men as private persons have no authority to determine the existence and the meaning of liturgical signs. They lack this authority not only when there is question of the sacrifice and the seven sacraments in their substance, but also when there is question of the remaining liturgical signs. In the former case the only one competent is God, because the seven sacraments are primarily instruments of God. In the latter case the only competent one is the Church, and not by delegation of men but by authority received from God, in her authoritative hierarchical structure. Such competence never belongs to a private person as such. And this is so because the liturgy as worship is an action by the Church, and therefore the signs in which liturgical worship is sensibly expressed are the Church's signs and not any private person's.

This does not mean that the liturgical signs are or can be unrelated to individuals — the question here concerns the relation between individual and Church in worship, which will be treated in its own place — but that for the individual to render true and personal worship to God in Christ in the liturgy involves necessarily his making his own, personally, the Church's signs and the realities which the Church expresses through the signs; it involves his "tuning in" on those signs and those realities.[46]

Still these signs do have meanings, either naturally or by a more or less general convention in the society in which the Church has actually developed or is developing. To ignore those pre-existent meanings when choosing liturgical signs to signify the Christian supernatural realities would be an arbitrary procedure. And of course God Himself and the Church have not proceeded and do not proceed in an arbitrary way in their free choice of the liturgical signs.

Rather, the contrary is to be affirmed. Water was freely chosen by Christ as a sign of the washing away of sin and of the rebirth to a new supernatural life, either by reason of its previous use in Hebrew society, for example in the baptism by John, or by reason of its natural signification. Because of their natural signification and their use in Hebrew society, for example in the paschal banquet, bread and wine were used by Christ as signs of His sacrifice in the Eucharist. The laying-on of hands and anointings were signs known and used in Judaism. Practically all the liturgical signs chosen for the worship of the ancient Church were, as we know, known and used, whether in religious or in profane context, by the synagogue or the Hellenistic and Roman world. And

<hr />

[46] See also St. Thomas, *Summa*, III, q. 60, a. 5.

the same holds, with respect to the medieval Germanic world, for the liturgical signs introduced into the liturgy in the Middle Ages.[47]

The various liturgical signs have been freely chosen, therefore, by Christ and by the Church to signify supernatural spiritual realities which they did not signify by their own natural power or by a purely human convention; but not without taking into account a certain analogy between their natural or conventional signification and the new Christian supernatural realities which they were destined to express in the liturgy from that time on.

From all this is deduced the general criterion for determining in particular cases the existence and the precise meaning of the individual signs in the liturgy. *This existence and this precise meaning depend essentially on the free positive will of God and of the Church.*

The will of God is made known to us by revelation and can be determined according to the general criteria of theology, as in the theological determination of the matter and form of the sacraments.

The will of the Church is known to us in the first place through all the authentic documents in which the Church makes her intention clear; for example, the liturgical words which accompany the placing of the sign and also determine its precise meaning.

Thus, in the rite of pouring a drop of water into the wine in the chalice at the offertory of the Mass, the fact of the symbol (*mysterium*) and its meaning is established by the accompanying prayer: "*Per huius aquae et vini mysterium* . . . By the mystery of this water and wine may we come to share in the divinity of Christ, who humbled himself to share in our humanity." The symbolic significance of the incensation of the altar is explained by a prayer which formerly accompanied the rite: "May my prayer, O Lord, arise as incense in your sight." The symbolic penitential meaning of the imposition of ashes on Ash Wednesday is explained by the invitation to prayer which now begins the ceremony of blessing and imposition: ". . . that these ashes which we place on our heads for the sake of penance. . . ."[48]

The significance of the procession with palms on Palm Sunday used to be explained thus by the fifth prayer of the blessing: ". . . that the devoted hearts of Your faithful may understand to their benefit the mystery alluded to in the act of the multitude (*quid mystice designet in facto*) who today, inspired by a heavenly illumination, went out to meet the Savior and strewed His path with branches of palm and olive. The palm branches signify His triumph over the

[47] See, e.g., the bibliography of Josef Löw's "Simbolo e simbolismo liturgico," *Enciclopedia cattolica*, 11, col. 621, as also the individual words in the *Dict. d'archéologie chrétienne et de lit.* and, now, in Klauser's *Reallexikon für Antike und Christentum*, where the individual liturgical signs and rites are explained, when such an explanation is in order — and it almost always is — from the use of similar rites in the synagogue or in the Roman-Hellenistic world or in the Germanic medieval world. See also the six volumes of *Antike und Christentum* edited by Franz Dölger (Münster: Aschendorff, 1929-50).

[48] Roman Missal, at the beginning of the rite "*Benedictio et impositio cinerum.*"

prince of death, while the sprigs of olive proclaim in a way the coming of Him in whom there is spiritual unction. . . . And we, in fervent faith retaining both the ceremony and its signification (*factum et significatum retinentes*) . . ."

It often happens that the exact symbolic meaning of a rite has become obscured in the present form of the liturgy. This happens sometimes because the texts now in use do not explain the meaning; for example, the drawing with ashes of a great cross on the floor of the nave in the rite of consecration of a church. In other cases it happens because the symbolic rite itself has been so reduced materially that it can now be perceived only with difficulty as a symbolic rite; for example: the fact that the priest in the administration of penance raises his hands slightly toward the penitent at the moment of absolution; the full symbolism of the rite of baptism, recognizable only with difficulty in the present common rite of pouring a little water on the head of the baptized;[49] the same may be said of the full symbolism of the table in some of our present altars.

In view of these examples, *it must be stated as a practical general rule that, for an exact knowledge of the liturgical signs and their signification according to the precise will of the Church which has adopted them and determined them*, especially in the cases where the texts themselves do not explain the Church's will explicitly, *the historical study of the origin and development of the rites is indispensable.*

At any rate, it is never permissible to indulge in subjective fancies of interpretation. It is never private authority that determines the meaning of liturgical signs. Nor is the private opinion of a Father of the Church enough in this matter. One must always see whether the mind of the Church herself has really been such, at least in the sense that the Church has later accepted this symbolism by sanctioning it with her authority and thus making it an expression of her worship. Any liturgical symbolism not documented in this way is to be rejected as arbitrary and unfounded.

Thus we can pass judgment on the hypersymbolistic fancies indulged in by a good number of medieval interpreters beginning with Amalarius of Metz.[50] Their fault lay in a lack of sufficient concern with reporting the mind of the Church. Instead they proposed too many personal opinions, which were often founded, moreover, on very extravagant analogies. By the reaction they aroused, these exaggerations were the principal cause of the undeserved disrepute into which even the true symbolic sense of the liturgy fell in the following age, beginning with the Renaissance. We know that some of these inventions of liturgical symbolism of the Middle Ages, with no other foundation, have survived even in certain modern books of devotion, for instance the

[49] See Louis Bouyer, "Le symbolisme des rites baptismaux," *La maison Dieu*, n. 32 (1952), 5-17.
[50] Died in 850. On the principal medieval allegorists and their works see Righetti, I, 45-48, 65-68. On pages 46-47 can be found some examples of this allegorism.

attempt to see signified in the parts of the Mass the various episodes of Christ's Passion and in the decorations of the priest's chasuble the instruments of the Passion.

The principal groups of liturgical signs

To go over the individual signs of which the liturgy is constituted, explain their meaning, examine the problems raised about their correct use, their efficacy, the understanding of them — this is one of the essential tasks of special liturgy.[51] Here a brief account of the principal groups will suffice. Considering both the signs instituted by God and those instituted by the Church, it seems that we can reduce these principal groups to five.

Speech as sign. Speech is the first and greatest sign employed by the liturgy, whether it be the liturgy instituted by God or that instituted by the Church.

In the very substance of the sacraments, speech is the coefficient which determines (as form) the meaning of the element which serves as determinable matter.

Thus immersion into water and emersion from it do not of themselves signify a supernatural reality. Still less do they signify participation in Christ's death and resurrection. On the other hand, the words "I baptize you in the name of the Father . . ." give these gestures this meaning: that the baptized participates in Christ's death and resurrection. And similarly with all the other sacraments.

Through the coefficient of speech the determinable element is raised to the determinate signification of the spiritual reality proper to the particular sacrament. The determinable element and the determining factor of speech constitute together, in a moral unity of signification, the single sacramental sign, consisting precisely of things and words, *rebus et verbis*, as the theologians say.[52]

As early a writer as St. Augustine set down, *à propos* of baptism, a formula which has become famous: "Take away the words and what is the water but just water? Add the words to the element and you have a sacrament (*accedit verbum ad elementum et fit sacramentum*), which itself is like a visible word."[53]

Thus, if we think of the importance of the sacramental life in the plan concretely willed and observed by God to communicate the divine life in Christ from Pentecost until the parousia, we see at once the importance of speech as sign in the realization of the meaning of sacred history, mystery of Christ,

---

[51] See in general A. G. Martimort, *L'Église en prière* (Tournai: Desclée, 1961), pp. 150-78.

[52] Cf. St. Thomas, *Summa*, III, q. 60, aa. 4-8. For example: "In the sacraments a single thing is somehow made out of words and things, as out of form and matter, that is, in as much as the signification of the things is completed by the words" (*ibid.*, a. 6 ad 2).

[53] *In Io. tract.* 80, 3.

mystery of the Church, in this intermediate time preparatory to the Lord's coming.

Drawing a parallel between the spoken word and the Word who is second Person of the Blessed Trinity, St. Thomas actually compares the dignity of the word in the sacraments to the dignity of the Word in the incarnation, and conceives of the sacrament as a sort of word made flesh: "It is also common to all (the sacraments) to consist in words and corporeal things, just as in Christ, the Author of the sacraments, the Word is made flesh. And just as the flesh of Christ is sanctified and has the power of sanctifying by the Word which is united to it, so also the sacramental elements are sanctified and have the power of sanctifying by the words which are pronounced over them. And for that reason Augustine says, 'Add the words to the element and you have a sacrament.' For this reason the words by which the sacramental elements are sanctified are called forms of the sacraments, and the sanctified elements are called their matter, as water is the matter of baptism and chrism is the matter of confirmation."[54]

In the sacraments, under incarnate form, God transmits life to men in Christ and through Christ. Here speech is the sensible manifestation of the intention and the positive will of God and of Christ: "one thing is seen and another understood." The word fills a role like that of Christ Himself, who, because He is the Word made flesh, is the personal and substantial manifestation in the world of God's intentions and wishes concerning men.[55] In both cases we see in operation the economy of sign, of *sacramentum* or *mysterium* as the ancients would have said. Speech as sign is therefore essential in God's sanctification of the Church in the liturgy.

Speech in this function is the instrument of God and of Christ. Hence, as far as its meaning in the substance of the sacraments is concerned, it is instituted by Him.

Speech also takes first place among the signs in the liturgy instituted by the Church. It is the greatest instrumental sign which incarnates and expresses, more directly than any other, the Church's reply to its sanctification by God, that is, the Church's inner worship. This inner worship is incarnated more directly in the speech that is prayer, in all its forms: adoration, thanksgiving, expiation, petition or impetration, with all the shadings and subspecies. The same inner worship is incarnated more indirectly in the speech that proclaims and teaches, which, in proximate connection with the liturgical action, is an instrumental sign of the Church to dispose the faithful immediately for receiving God's sanctifying action in the liturgy and for participating through the liturgy in Christ's worship.

[54] *De articulis fidei et ecclesiae sacramentis,* n. 614, *Opuscula theologica,* ed. Verardo (Turin: Marietti, 1954), I, 148.

[55] Cf. Heb. 1:1 ff.: "After having spoken at many times and in various ways through the prophets, now in these last days God has spoken through the Son, whom He has appointed heir of all things and through whom He created the universe. He, being the splendor of His glory and the image of His substance . . . ."

The sign which is speech, as expression of the Church's interior prayer of impetration, dominates also the whole economy of the sacramentals properly so called, whether the concern is with sacramental things (like holy water) or with sacramental actions (consecrations, simple blessings, exorcisms). For in the sacramentals, constructed in the likeness of the sacraments, speech — the Church's petition — is the coefficient which determines the nature of the thing or action as a sign. The sign in this case signifies the invisible realities which God, hearing the Church's prayer, grants to the person who uses the sacramental with the proper dispositions.

Thus it is clear beyond doubt that, among the sacred signs of the liturgy (*signa rei sacrae, sacramenta*), speech occupies first place, though in intimate union with the signs which are gestures and elements.[56] It was God's will to give highest importance to the sensible word as a bridge between Himself and men in the supernatural economy in Christ.

This fact by itself shows how profoundly social is this economy in Christ, not a merely spiritual and interior affair. It shows also how much God has taken account of the most natural tendencies of human nature in this whole matter, since speech among men is the natural vehicle for the specifically human communication of thoughts and affections.[57]

When the liturgy makes use of metaphor and extensive imagery in its language, as it very frequently does, speech becomes a sort of sign in the second degree: a sign as vehicle of other signs.

Finally, it is obviously of the highest importance that a good balance be maintained in the liturgy between gestures, things, elements as signs and speech as sign. If speech predominates too much, an exaggerated conceptualism will result. If the function of speech is too much suppressed because there is not enough of it or because it has become a sign no longer understood, then the liturgy will become a psychologically ineffective dumb-show of the other signs.

Gestures, attitudes and movements as signs. The importance of gestures, attitudes and movements as signs, whether they be of individuals, of groups, or of the whole Christian community, arises from the fact that they express in the whole body the interior thoughts and emotions of worship; and this expression, in turn, influences the interior thoughts and emotions, thus tending to complete the tuning-in of the whole person with the liturgical reality.

This is true, for example, of inclinations, genuflections, prostrations, holding the hands extended or joined, making the sign of the Cross either on the breast or in the form of a blessing, striking the breast, standing, the laying-on of hands in many sacraments, insufflations, finally the ordered movements of more than one person together, whether of the sacred ministers or even of the whole assembly, as in processions.

[56] See Louis Bouyer's observations on this intimate union in his *Rite and Man* (Notre Dame, 1963), pp. 53-62.

[57] See Augustine, *De doctr. christ.*, II, 4.

A rite, especially a sacramental rite, lacking gesture or unduly restricting its role, is abnormal and badly constructed psychologically.[58]

Elements and objects as signs. Natural elements are also instrumental liturgical signs of the sacred realities of sanctification and worship. Thus there are bread, wine, water, chrism, oil, incense, salt, light, darkness, time: day, night, week, year. Likewise to be classed as signs and hence as possessing symbolic value are the church edifice itself, especially the altar (see, for example, the liturgy of the consecration of a church or of an altar); the sacred vestments (see, for example, the prayers the priest used to recite while vesting); and also, today, their color (each color reserved to express one particular senti-ment rather than another).

To this great category of signs which are objects belong also the signs which are figures: decorations, pictures, statues.

Art as sign in the liturgy. Art is another facet of the liturgy[59] which appeals to the senses. Art itself has the function of a sign, and it may (but does not have to) embellish the other liturgical signs: speech first of all, and then also manufactured objects, the gestures of persons and their attitudes and movements. In practice the whole action and environment of worship are clothed with the splendors of art: art of speech and of song, instrumental music, architecture, painting, plastic art, choreography, the goldsmith's craft, and other lesser arts.

The liturgy reinforces other signs by superimposing artistic form on them. It gives them, as signs, a power to express and to impress, on a level to which only art, among the human means of expression and of communication, can attain.

Among all the arts, those reinforcing the sign which is speech have particular importance in the liturgy: rhetoric, poetry, and especially song, while instrumental music may be considered as a development of song which has become autonomous. Song, more than any other artistic means of expression, is intimately connected with the nature of the liturgy, as the means *par excellence* for expressing and creating the communitarian sense, uniting the singers as it does in the very undulation of their voices.[60]

Speech, objects, etc., precisely because they are signs, are admitted into the

---

[58] See Righetti, I, 296-341; Hélène Lubien-ska de Lenval, *The Whole Man at Worship* (New York: Desclée, 1962).

[59] See, e.g., CL, ch. 6-7; MD, nn. 195 f. (Lat. 193 f.); *Musicae sacrae disciplina*, especially nn. II and III; see in *Liturgia* under the direction of R. Aigrain (Paris: Bloud et Gay, 1947), pp. 1016 ff.; Pie-Raymond Régamey, *Art sacré au XX siècle?* (2nd ed.; Paris: Cerf, 1957); Msgr. Johannes Wagner, "Liturgical Art and the Care of Souls," *The*

Assisi Papers (Collegeville, Minn.: Liturgical Press, 1957), pp. 57-73.

[60] It is vital to investigate thoroughly the theological dimension of liturgical song. See starting points in: Oskar Söhngen (Protestant), "Theologische Grundlagen der Kirchen-musik" *Leiturgia* IV (1961), 1-267, with bibliography; Joseph Gelineau, *Voices and Instruments in Christian Worship* (Collegeville, Minn.: Liturgical Press, 1964). See also below, p. 56, note 71.

liturgy only to serve the invisible realities which the Church wants to express through them and which are summed up in the actualization here and now of the mystery of Christ, sacred history, as the Church's sanctification and worship.

With greater reason, the art which reinforces those signs is not an independent mistress in the liturgy, as if it were admitted there in consideration of its own value alone and by reason of some intrinsic and specific purpose which it has when considered in itself and for no other end (art for art's sake!).

On the contrary, art in the liturgy is a noble lady in the service of a mistress greater than herself. The end of art is at the service of a higher end, the liturgy's own end: the Church's sanctification and worship in Christ. Art, in its own way, must help the liturgy's end to be better expressed and better realized, by disposing souls to that sanctification and worship.

In order to understand how and under what conditions this can take place, it would be necessary to analyze the nature of art in general (in fact, of the individual arts, especially vocal music, architecture and painting), that of religious or sacred art in particular, and to show the possible relations between the proper end of art and the proper end of the liturgy, thus delimiting the concept of liturgical art. But this would be an extensive task, for the ideas of art and religious art are highly controversial.[61] For our purpose let the following remarks suffice.

Art. The concept of art (understood of the fine arts) must be defined in relation to the beautiful.[62] But the beautiful can be defined only in relation to that specific pleasure which it has the power of producing, called esthetic pleasure. Hence art can be defined as the aptitude for perceiving and expressing sensibly in things the quality by which they are able to cause esthetic pleasure.[63]

In its turn, the definition of esthetic pleasure — something more easily known by experience than analyzed in concepts — presupposes a doctrine of

[61] See, e.g., Adriano Prandi, "Arte," *Enciclopedia cattolica*, 2 (1949), 33-44, with bibliography of previous writings, *ibid.*, 43 f. To be noted among the previous authors are: Jacques Maritain, *Art and Scholasticism* (New York: Scribner, 1946); *Id.*, *Creative Intuition in Art and Poetry* (New York: Pantheon, 1953); A. Carlini, *La religiosità dell'arte e della filosofia* (Florence, 1934); P.-M. Léonard, "Art et spiritualité," *Dictionnaire de spiritualité*, I (1932), 899-934; G. van der Leeuw, *Vom Heiligen in der Kunst* (Gütersloh, 1957).

[62] The concept of creativity alone is not enough, because, among other things, this concept does not distinguish art sufficiently from technology or from science. Even the concepts of expressiveness, of incarnation of the spirit in matter, etc., do not distinguish art sufficiently from technology. The related ideas of sublime, graceful, dramatic, etc., must be understood as something like species of the beautiful.

[63] Art — and therefore the concept of artist — in its wholeness includes both the aptitude for perception and the aptitude for sensible expression. One who has the first and lacks the second can be called an artist in spirit only. In the Aristotelian tradition, however, the ability to perceive things as capable of arousing esthetic pleasure was considered the essential note in the concept of art and of artist. The aptitude for expression was considered as connected with technical ability of a more material order.

psychology. In terms of Aristotelian-Thomistic psychology, esthetic pleasure is the enjoyment of the human elicited appetite in the very actuation of the cognitive powers in a certain proportion conformably to their innate or acquired dispositions (conformably to their innate appetite). Esthetic pleasure occurs especially when the powers of sight, hearing and imagination are actuated,[64] and principally if there is more or less simultaneous actuation.

This enjoyment is distinguished from all other enjoyment by the fact that it is disinterested. It does not proceed from (and does not tend to) the physical or material possession of the thing. It proceeds from the mere contemplative possession of the thing when this possession is achieved in conformity with the dispositions of the cognitive faculties.

Esthetic pleasure is calming and stimulating at the same time because, affecting us as a secret harmony between the being and the activity of our faculties, in fact of different faculties, it gives the impression that the fullness of being and of acting has been reached.

The artistic quality is not in things — real or imagined or thought — considered absolutely in themselves, but considered according to a certain relation they have to the cognitive faculties. Art therefore comprises an objective and a subjective aspect, because it is realized in a certain harmony between things and faculties.

The human cognitive faculties in their fundamental structure are the same in all men; but they admit of a wide margin of diversity in the innate or acquired dispositions, not only from one epoch to another, from one group to another, from one individual to another, but also in the same individual at different times and under different circumstances. Hence taste, that is, the aptitude of each one to thrill in esthetic enjoyment at his harmony with certain particular things, admits of wide margins of variability and is subject to education.

The esthetic perception is an instinctive or intuitive type of perception precisely because it involves a certain harmony of connaturality between the object perceived and the dispositions of the perceiving subject's cognitive faculties. Thus the esthetic perception is not analytic but synthetic. And it is not communicable directly and discursively, in the way in which a theorem of geome-

---

[64] The actuation of the intellect is also included as an essential part of the esthetic phenomenon. But as long as we stop at the mere esthetic enjoyment by contemplation and do not pass on to the external sensible execution of the work, we are not dealing with a discursive activity, but with an intuitive actuation. It is intuitive not in the sense that, while we are still in this life, our intellect can terminate directly at the singular sensible thing, at which our external senses terminate intuitively. Such intuitive termination of the intellect, in Thomistic psychology and noetics — which we presume here — is impossible, because the formal and proper object of the intellect in this life is the *abstracted* quiddity of sensible things. But when the intellect itself is in act in a more or less ordinary discursive way, it can indirectly, *in obliquo*, perceive itself and the whole *ego*, actuated in such and such a way conformably to its own nature or not, and this by an intuitive and not a discursive perception. This is precisely what happens also in the esthetic perception. Here also the intellect perceives the *ego* intuitively, with its senses actuated in conformity to the appetite innate in them.

try is communicated to a student, but only by an indirect method. That is, the artist must seek by certain sensible means to induce in another person the dispositions which he found in himself, in such a way that the other person, placed before the same object, will have the same esthetic experience.

The intrinsically specific end of art (the end of the work, as the scholastics say) is therefore simply to actuate the cognitive faculties in such a way as to bring about esthetic enjoyment in the subject, and nothing else. This esthetic enjoyment is morally indifferent, as is scientific knowledge or technical knowledge.[65] It becomes good or bad action if the one who seeks it does so for a further good or bad end (for the end of the agent, in scholastic terminology).

Thus it is possible to embellish morally bad objects or actions with the quality of art, provided they be considered and represented in such a way as to stimulate esthetic pleasure. By the same token, it is not enough that an object or an action be morally good, or that the artist have a morally right intention, in order for the result to be esthetic.

Still, since artists, and in general those who enjoy an esthetic experience, are men and not only artists, they are obliged to subordinate their act to the morality which derives from the relation of every concrete act to the last end of man. For the good which is art is, for man, a particular good — a certain good of his cognitive faculties — and not the total and simply ultimate good.

If he is to act in an ordered way, therefore, every time a person seeks or enjoys esthetic pleasure, he must subject this act to his ultimate total good, which is the moral good. Thus, as far as the end of the agent is concerned, art must be subordinated to morality.

Religious art. It is here that religious or sacred art comes in. For when art, while remaining art according to the intrinsic requirements of its nature, submits itself, besides, to the specific end of religion,[66] by this very fact it becomes religious, sacred, exhibiting simultaneously the twofold quality of artistic and religious.

How does this come about?

The end of religion is to produce in man that substantially interior attitude

---

[65] For the independence of every art and every science from morality, in virtue of the end itself of the work, see St. Thomas, *Summa*, I-II, q. 57, aa. 2-4.

[66] There are degrees to this submission. Among others, there is a submission which can be called material, of content only. It is that which consists in taking as subject of an artistic composition a religious subject: putting religious words to music, painting a Madonna, building a church, etc. But, artistically speaking, it is possible to treat a religious subject in a *way* (in a form) anything but religious, even if truly artistic. Many painted or sculptured Madonnas are truly artistic, but the artistic quality or form does not bear on the subject "Madonna" but on the subject "mother," for which the Madonna simply gives a pretext. For the Madonna is not just any mother, but a mother who is very special in a religious sense; so that, in executing a Madonna, to treat artistically of the theme "mother" does not at all mean to have made sacred art, unless in a purely material sense. Only if the artistic form bears on that which is peculiar to the Madonna in a religious sense will there be formally sacred art, as there is, for example, in the Madonnas of Fra Angelico.

When we speak here of submission of art to religion, we mean formal submission.

which is made up of submission, admiration, prayer, faith, hope and especially love, towards God.

Art, remaining art, submits itself formally at the same time to the end of religion whenever the esthetic enjoyment which is its own end is concretely not opposed to, but rather positively directed and subjected to the higher end of the religious attitude (in the artist who has the esthetic enjoyment to begin with; then in the sensible means by which he wants to transmit it to others; and in those others who, through these sensible means, reproduce it in themselves). Then there is fusion and formal union between art and religion, esthetic attitude and religious attitude.

But this fusion and this union also admit of degrees and of various forms of concrete expression, just as there are degrees and various forms of concrete expression in the esthetic quality itself and in the religious attitude.

The marriage between art and religion is possible. This is proved above all from psychological experience and from examples of works recognized by all as religious art: Gregorian chant, the works of Fra Angelico, the sculptures of the portals of the cathedral of Chartres, the ancient Christian basilical architecture.[67] There is also the historical fact of the marriage of art and religion in general.[68]

The possibility of this marriage derives in the last analysis from the nature of the esthetic attitude and of the religious attitude. The esthetic process of knowledge-enjoyment has something in common with the religious and mystical attitude and can serve as psychological preparation for it without detriment to their essentially diverse natures, if certain precautions are observed.

In spirituality the devices of more or less remote psychological preparation for meditation, prayer, mental prayer, etc., are well known. Among them are some devices of a simply physico-psychic nature which serve to create a general psychological atmosphere, propitious for disposing the senses, and through the senses the attention and the whole person, to the desired activity.

St. Ignatius, for example, advises one to close the window and to stand in the dark or with a dim light for meditating; to say certain prayers by pronouncing the words slowly to the rhythm of inhalation and exhalation; to take certain bodily attitudes, for example placing the hand to the breast, keeping the eyes fixed in one position or on some object.[69]

The function of these attitudes is to create the sensitivo-psychological atmos-

---

[67] These examples are by no means exclusive. Just as there are various embodiments of authentic art and of authentic religious sensibility, so also are there various embodiments of authentic religious art. I do not mean to present these examples, therefore, as models outside of which there cannot be any authentic religious art.

[68] Which, be it noted, holds abundantly also of the Old Testament for the arts of speech, song, music, architecture.

[69] See, e.g., *Exercises*, First Week, Daily Particular Examination of Conscience, first additional direction (see *The Spiritual Exercises of St. Ignatius*, translated by Louis J. Puhl [Westminster, Md.: Newman, 1951], p. 16); additional directions at the end of the fifth exercise, nn. 6-9, *ed. cit.*, pp. 36-37; Fourth Week, the Three Methods of Prayer, second and third methods, *ed. cit.*, pp. 110, 112.

phere of a certain recollection of the senses. This atmosphere can then cooperate in its way in bringing about the attitude of meditation properly so called and of prayer in general properly so called. The physico-psychic recollection alone is obviously not prayer itself; still less is it mystical union; but it can contribute to preparing the subject for them. In the framework of this physico-psychic disposition, it will be possible to produce prayer properly so called in the subject, even prayer of a mystical order.

The root of all this lies in the nature of man: substantial unity of matter and spirit, with mysterious but real reciprocal influence of one part on the other.

The esthetic experience can, under certain aspects and in certain conditions, fulfill a role somewhat similar. This is true fundamentally[70] because the esthetic perception-enjoyment, which takes place by an attuning of two natures (the same kind of attuning as that in which the mother instinctively "knows" her son), involves a kind of activity of the senses and of the intellect itself which is completely unique, superior to their ordinary way of acting. It is not the conceptual and discursive activity of the intellect, but rather intuitive, synthetic, without painful and searching effort. The impression is given that the soul leaves its ordinary surface activity and enters into immediate contact with the most profound depths of itself and of things. In the esthetic attitude there is, as it were, a suspension of the common and superficial action of the senses and of the understanding, their concentration in a simpler and more inward sphere of life, and a manner of behavior toward external things which is at the same time more distant, more elevated and more penetrating.

These features are the result of a purely natural physico-psychic procedure. Suppose now that the moral conditions of the subject are favorable. Then the esthetic experience may be a fertile ground in which, with the intervention of the necessary supernatural factors, prayer properly so called, and even mystical union properly so called, may develop, just as those physico-psychic devices recommended by the spiritual authors, which we mentioned above, can be an excellent approach to the same end.

The reason is fundamentally the same too. In virtue of the substantial physico-psychic spiritual unity of man with reciprocal influence of one part on the other, prayer, and union with God in general, implies a certain surpassing of the common surface activity of the senses and of the soul. And the deeper the prayer or union with God, the more it surpasses the common activity. From this fact arise certain physico-psychic features common to the esthetic experience and the mystical experience.

But just as those physico-psychic expedients recommended by the spiritual authors as preparatory to prayer must be used with discretion in order to serve their purpose, so, in fact with greater reason, the esthetic sentiment and art can serve the religious attitude only under well determined conditions. I say with

[70] See, e.g., P.-M. Léonard, "Art et spiritualité," *Dict. de spir.*, I, 925 ff.; Henri Brémond, *Prayer and Poetry* (London: Burns Oates & Washbourne, 1927).

greater reason, because there may be greater danger of confining onself simply to the play of the faculties acting on the sensible, without rising to God, in virtue of the powerful pleasure of esthetic perception brought about by this knowledge-enjoyment activity of the faculties.

One who takes the means for the end will be prone to this danger, which we call esthetism, a greater or lesser danger according to the dispositions of the subject and the strength of his spiritual life in overcoming sensuality. This danger of esthetism is reflected in the very means of expression of the work of art if, for want of being adequately spiritualized, they rivet the attention on the sensible.[71]

[71] Delicacy is certainly required in maintaining the objective and subjective balance which makes art a truly profitable means for raising the mind to God. There was sometimes real provocation in the history of the Church for the repeated reactions of the spiritual-minded against the invasion into the sanctuary of an art which monopolized the attention and enticed the senses too much.

St. Augustine, certainly predisposed by nature to sensuality and to esthetism, has excellently described in himself, in connection with singing in the church, the dangers and the advantages of art in raising one to God:

"The pleasures of hearing had held me more closely in bondage and subjection, but You broke the bonds and set me free. At present I do admittedly take some pleasure in the music to which Your words are set, when it is sung with a sweet and well trained voice; not to the extent of being captivated by the music, but so that I can rise above it when I wish. Yet that music, together with the thoughts which give it life, seeks a place of some importance in my heart, and I find difficulty in giving it just the proper place.

"For sometimes I feel that the flame of piety is kindled in our minds by those holy words with more devotion and ardor when they are so sung than it would be if they were not so sung, and that all the stirrings of our spirit have their corresponding moods in voice and song, being roused by some secret affinity with the music. And then I seem to give the music a place of greater honor than it deserves. But the bodily pleasure, which should not be allowed to enervate the mind, often deceives me, when the senses are not content to accompany the reason as followers, but, once admitted for the sake of the reason, try to run ahead and lead it. Thus in this matter I sin before I realize it, but later become aware of my fault.

"Sometimes, on the other hand, but very rarely, becoming too anxious to avoid this deception, I err on the side of excessive severity, to the point of wishing that the whole music of the sweet chants to which David's Psalter is sung should no longer sound in my ears or in those of the Church herself. Then the safer course seems to me to be that of Bishop Athanasius of Alexandria: I remember having been told often that he had the reader of the psalm modulate his voice so little that his delivery was closer to a recitation than to a song.

"Yet when I remember the tears that I shed over the chants of Your Church just after I had recovered my faith, and consider how I am moved now, not by the singing but by the things that are sung, provided the chant is clear and well modulated, I recognize again the great usefulness of ecclesiastical chant.

"Thus I fluctuate between the peril of sensual indulgence and the experience of real benefits; and I am more inclined — though not, indeed, offering this as an irrevocable opinion — to favor the custom of singing in the church, since it raises up the rather weak spirit to sentiments of piety by pleasing the ear. Still, when it happens that the singing affects me more than the content of the song, then I confess that I am sinning in a manner that deserves punishment, and I would rather not hear the singing.

"Look at my plight! Weep with me, and weep for me, you who have some good interior dispositions from which good works proceed. (These considerations will leave you cold if you have no such stirrings.) And You, O Lord my God, listen to me! Look on me, see me, have mercy and heal me! In Your eyes I have become uncertain of myself, and that is my weakness" (Confessions, X, 33).

For the complete position of Augustine and of the Church Fathers on singing see, e.g.: H. Edelstein, Die Musikanschauung Augustins nach seiner Schrift "De musica" (Freiburg, 1929); Th. Gerold, Les Pères de l'Église et la musique (Paris, 1931); Henri Davenson,

So much for religious art in general. Only one who is at the same time sincerely religious and a true artist will be able to produce authentic religious art.

Liturgical art. But not all religious art is liturgical art. Liturgical art requires not only that the work be beautiful and the enjoyment which it arouses be directed to the religious attitude in general, but also that it serve to actuate that particular type of piety which is proper to the liturgy.

Now liturgical piety, compared to piety in general, has a certain number of characteristics, which will be better explained in subsequent chapters of this book. Among other things: the liturgy is essentially an action; it is a communitarian action of the whole assembly present and hierarchically structured in which each one has his own active part without leveling or confusion; it is a communitarian action centered in the sacrifice of the Mass and in the sacraments; it is an action in which the whole of dogma is lived under the dominating vision of the mystery of Christ, sacred history always in the making, with its own way of propounding dogmas in a certain hierarchy and its own way of stimulating the various faculties in man.[72]

This is the particular religious world which art in the liturgy must not only respect but, in its way, express and positively help to realize. While keeping its own necessary characteristics as art, liturgical art must direct into this religious world the esthetic pleasure which it has the task of arousing.

From this it is seen that the artist besides being an authentic artist must be vitally penetrated not only with piety in general but with that liturgical world in particular, or he will never be able to produce works of authentic liturgical art.

The practical consequences of all this are innumerable for all the branches of art which find a place in the liturgy, especially for the arts of singing and instrumental music, for architecture and for painting. From these principles can be deduced a series of rules governing religious art and liturgical art in particular.[73]

Traité de la musique selon l'esprit de St. Augustin (Neuchâtel: Baconnière, 1942); Ambrosius Dohmes, "Der pneumatische Charakter des Kultgesanges nach frühchristlichen Zeugnissen," *Vom christlichen Mysterium* (Düsseldorf: Patmos, 1951), pp. 35-53.

[72] The proper characteristics of liturgical piety are a determining item in the concept of liturgical art. This whole book aims at explaining what these characteristics are. See especially the second section of chapter 21: notion and general characteristics of liturgical spirituality.

[73] This is just what the Church's authority does. See *Mediator Dei*, nn. 195 f. (Lat. 193 f.); *Musicae sacrae disciplina* in its entirety; the *Instruction on Sacred Music and the Sacred Liturgy* according to these two encyclical letters,

English translation in *Worship*, 32 (1958), 590 ff.; *Istruzione sull'arte sacra della Suprema Sacra Congregazione del S. Ufficio diretta ai Vescovi di tutto il mondo*, June 30, 1952 (see, e.g., in *Enciclopedia liturgica* under the direction of R. Aigrain, Italian ed. [Rome: Paoline, 1957], pp. 1016-19); Cardinal Celso and Monsignor Giovanni Costantini, *L'Istruzione del S. Ufficio sull'arte sacra*, text and commentary (Rome, 1952); G. Mariani, *La legislazione ecclesiastica in materia d'arte sacra* (Rome, 1945); see also *Enciclopedia cattolica*, 2, cols. 44 f.).

For the liturgical requirements of sacred architecture see Theodor Klauser, "Directives for the Building of a Church," and His Eminence Giacomo Cardinal Lercaro, "The Christian Church," *Documents for Sacred Archi-*

On condition that these rules be observed, the liturgy opens the door wide to art. It has done so from the very beginning: at first principally to the art of speech and of song; then, beginning from the third-fourth century, to monumental architecture, to mosaics, to painting, to choreography, to the lesser arts; later still to statuary and to polyphonic and instrumental music.

As has been said, art and artistic taste include also a noteworthy subjective aspect, changing from one person to another, one place to another, one time to another — something which keeps making new embodiments of the esthetic world possible. Recognizing this fact, the liturgy has generously admitted the most varied manifestations of taste and of style, just as it grants today's artists the right to feel their way also in liturgical art.[74] This is so much the more proper because not only the artistic sensibility but also the religious sensibility itself is quite variable. By religious sensibility I mean the way in which the various natural sensibilities react to the religious phenomenon properly so called.

tecture (Collegeville, Minn.: Liturgical Press, 1957); G. Bevilacqua, "La chiesa nella città," report to the Congress of Bologna of 1955, *Dieci anni di architettura sacra in Italia 1945-55*, Acts of the Congress (Bologna, 1956), pp. 25-27; T. Costermanelli, *Architettura sacra* (Milan, 1956).

For the liturgical requirements of the architecture of the altar in particular, see: Pie-Raymond Régamey, "Architecture de l'autel et exigences liturgiques," *La maison Dieu*, n. 29 (1952), 71-87. The same number carries several other theological, historical and liturgical-architectural notices about the altar.

For all this matter see also *Enciclopedia liturgica*, pp. 96-279 with bibliography.

[74] The principle has been solemnly proclaimed by the Second Vatican Council, which says concerning music and song: "The Church approves of all forms of true art which have the requisite qualities, and admits them into divine worship" (CL, art. 112). The same principle is accepted for art in general: "The Church has not adopted any particular style of art as her own. She has admitted styles from every period, in keeping with the natural characteristics and conditions of peoples and the needs of the various rites. Thus in the course of the centuries she has brought into existence a treasury of art which must be preserved with every care. The art of our own times from every race and country shall also be given free scope in the Church, provided it bring to the task the reverence and honor due to the sacred buildings and rites" (*ibid.*, art. 123).

On the same subject, the discourse of Pope Paul VI to artists, delivered May 7, 1964, is worthy of note for its expression of the Church's attitude toward modern art in general.

Mediator Dei, n. 195 (Lat. 193), had already expressed the same ideas, on the whole.

The situation existing lately in Italy has been described as a cold war between clergy and modern artists. Very interesting in this connection were the reactions of the architects to the congress of Bologna of 1955. In the discourse mentioned above, Paul VI recognized this unwelcome state of affairs as well as the faults of the clergy in this regard.

Among the Italian works which seek to contribute to solving the problem of sacred art in general are: Cardinal Celso and Monsignor Giovanni Costantini, *Fede e arte. Manuale per gli artisti*, 3 vols. (Rome: Tumminelli, 1945 ff.); L. Bartoli, *L'arte nella casa di Dio* (Turin, 1950); A. Raule, *L'arte nella chiesa* (Bologna, 1953); periodicals: *Arte cristiana* from 1913 (Milan: Scuola Beato Angelico); *Fede e arte* from 1953 of the Central Pontifical Commission for Sacred Art, Rome; *Chiesa e quartiere* (Bologna, since 1957).

For France see Joseph Pichard's *L'art sacré moderne* for the period 1914-53 (Paris: B. Arthaud, 1953); periodicals: *L'Art d'église*, successor in 1950 to *L'Artisan liturgique* which was published since 1932 (Bruges, Belgium: Abbaye de S. André); *L'Art sacré* (Paris, beginning with 1946).

A quarterly periodical in English is *Liturgical Arts*, published by Liturgical Arts Society, Inc., 521 Fifth Ave., New York, N.Y. 10017.

But, just as there is no denying the dangers in the relations between art and religion in general, so also the dangers in the relations between art and liturgy in particular cannot be denied. There is not only the common peril of esthetism when the esthetic function is sought by itself and not directed to the religious attitude, but also the specific peril that that function — even if directed to religion in general — will not serve the peculiar needs of the liturgy, especially its communitarian needs.

Particular arts which have often failed on this score are song, instrumental music and architecture.

Under the pretext of producing works of art as perfect as possible esthetically, the liturgical chants which by their nature belong to the people have been given forms which are perhaps very beautiful esthetically and even truly religious, but difficult or even practically impossible for the people themselves to sing. As a result, these chants have been taken away from the people and reserved to a group of specialists.

In a similar way, churches have been built which are perhaps very beautiful esthetically and whose architecture is even pervaded with a deep feeling for religion in general, but in which most of the congregation are far removed from the altar, so that they can neither see it easily nor participate actively in what is being done there.

And the altar itself, when relegated to the far end of the church, away from the people, was transformed into a splendid setting for exposition and made to look like the back of an immense throne, something in which it was hard to recognize the table of the Eucharistic banquet and sacrifice normally surrounded by all those present.

It would be only too easy to multiply similar examples. They all have their root in forgetfulness of the fact that art in the liturgy has not just a general esthetic-religious function, but an esthetic-liturgical function. It is a liturgical sign, and every sign is essentially functional with respect to that which it is to express and in some way to make real. For this reason, whoever uses art as a sign in the liturgy must first be permeated with the liturgical religious realities which that sign is called upon to express and to realize in its way, and must submit himself to their requirements.

Persons as signs. As we said above, the whole Christian assembly as such has the value of sign in the liturgy in as much as it is the convocation of God in Christ Jesus, the gathering "in the name" of Christ, the gathering of the "people of God." Thus it fulfills in itself the *ekklesia* of God (*Qᵉhal Yahweh*) of the Old Testament; it is the maximum expression of the local community and of the universal Church; and it is already a sort of first sketch, a foreshadowing, of the perfect cosmic liturgy of the heavenly Jerusalem described in the Apocalypse.

With still more reason, the hierarchical ministers of the liturgy have the value of sign, and the dictum "one thing is seen and another understood" holds in a special way for them, because they are special representatives and delegates of Christ.

It was a profound sense of the significative value of the persons who take part in the liturgy that enabled the Fathers to write as did St. Ignatius of Antioch to the Magnesians: "I advise you: be zealous to do all things in the peace of God, the bishop presiding in the place of God and the priests in the place of the Apostolic college, and my beloved deacons being entrusted with the ministry of Jesus Christ. . . . Just as the Lord, therefore, did nothing of Himself or through His Apostles without the Father, to whom He was united, so also do you do nothing without the bishop and the priests. . . . Let there be one prayer, one supplication, one mind, one hope in charity and in the innocent joy which is Jesus Christ, the unsurpassed. Hasten all of you together as to one temple of God, to one altar, to one Jesus Christ, who came forth from one Father, existed in the unity of one Father and returned to Him." [75]

If we consider the sensible signs of the liturgy from the point of view of the different senses to which they are immediately directed, we see how hearing and sight are predominantly affected. There is nothing extraordinary in this, since these two senses, because of their greater spirituality, predominate in the whole field of human communications and expressions.

St. Augustine in early times had already made this observation: "Among the signs, therefore, by which men communicate their thoughts and feelings to one another, some are directed to the sense of sight, most to the sense of hearing, very few to the other senses.

"When we nod, for example, to communicate our will, we are giving a sign only to the eyes of the one to whom the nod is directed. There are people who indicate practically everything with movements of their hands. Actors make signs, for the initiated, with all sorts of movements, and they practically speak with their eyes. Military flags and standards communicate the will of the commanders by means of the eyes. All these things are like visible words.

"The signs which pertain to hearing are, as I said, most numerous; and they consist especially in words. To be sure, the trumpet, the flute and the cithara also make sounds which for the most part are not only pleasing but also meaningful. But all these signs are very few in comparison to words. Words have obtained absolute primacy among men for signifying every concept and affection that anyone wants to make known.

---

[75] *Magnes.*, 6:1–7:2. On the theology of the liturgical assembly see P. Massi, *L'assemblea del popolo di Dio* I (Ascoli Piceno, 1962), with ample bibliography. Another point worth mentioning is the value of sign attributed to certain numbers by the liturgy according to the custom of the whole ancient tradition, both Hebrew and Hellenistic. This point is evident mostly in the liturgical language, whether biblical or of ecclesiastical composition; but there is no lack of examples in the rites, aside from the language (such as the twelve crosses in the consecration of a church, for the twelve Apostles and the twelve gates of the heavenly Jerusalem).

"True, the Lord did give a sign in the odor of the ointment with which His feet were perfumed; by taste also He signified what He intended, in giving the sacrament of His body and blood; again, He expressed something in the fact that the woman who touched the tassel of His cloak was cured.

"Nevertheless, the overwhelming majority of the signs with which men make their thoughts known is made up of words. In fact, I have been able to express in words all the other signs I have briefly mentioned, but I could never explain the words by means of those signs." [76]

Rite as a complexus of liturgical signs. Let us note, finally, the concept of *rite*. A rite is the employment of the whole combination of signs (words, songs, gestures, attitudes and movements, employed, moreover, with regard to certain definite objects by specified persons) by which a liturgical action is performed. Thus we speak of the rite of baptism, the rite of the Mass, the rite of the consecration of a church, the rite of Vespers, etc. The Roman, the Byzantine, the Ambrosian rite signifies the whole of the liturgical rites in the Roman, the Byzantine, the Ambrosian arrangements and practice; and so for the other particular rites also.

Why is the encounter between God and men in a regime of signs?

At this point the question spontaneously arises: Why, after all, must the encounter between God and men, the actualization in individuals of the mystery of Christ, the transmission to individuals of the life in Christ, be made in a regime of symbols, under their veil and, so to speak, through their mediation? This question is a really disturbing one for the modern man. By reason of many circumstances of environment and education, he immediately fears in this introduction of sensible signs between the individual person and God a materialization and an impediment to religious spontaneity and sincerity. The problem will be examined further in subsequent chapters. Meanwhile let the following observations suffice.

The positive will of God: the "sacramental" regime of salvation. The ultimate satisfactory answer to the question can be found only in the free will of God, who has willed and does will such a regime in the relations between Himself and men. Absolutely speaking, such a regime is not necessary. God could have adopted an order of things in which religion would be a purely individual and interior affair without any mediation either of other men or of outside things.

But the great law that dominates the liturgy, and to which we shall have to return in the following pages, is the law of objectivity: the very way by which we can and must go to God is not left to our free choice, still less to our caprice; it is prescribed for us by God Himself. Our salvation can be

[76] *De doctr. christ.*, II, 4.

achieved only in following this way objectively shown to us, accepting it, tuning ourselves in to it.

Now this way is an incarnate way: it is through men and things, even sensible and material things, that God communicates Himself to men and men go to God.

The prototype of this law is Christ Himself, God and Man, who is the unique way for going to the Father. In Christ, in an absolutely plenary fashion, the divine has descended into the human and the human has encountered the divine.

A continuation, expression and instrument of Christ, constructed wholly on the incarnate model which is verified in Christ Himself, is the Church, divine and human, invisible and social-visible, through which and in which Christ, from Pentecost to the parousia, communicates His divine life to men, and mankind renders its perfect worship to God.

An instrument of Christ and of the Church, constructed on the same incarnate model, through which and in which God by means of Christ sanctifies the Church, and the Church through Christ and in Christ renders her worship to God — this is the whole system of signs which constitutes the liturgy.

Law of objectivity, law of incarnation, law of salvation in community or more precisely in the Church, this is the ultimate basis on which to explain why the encounter between God and men takes place in a system of signs — *in sacramento, in sacramentis*, the ancients would say. From the great and original *sacramentum* which is Christ, is derived the general *sacramentum* which is the Church; and this finds expression chiefly in the *sacramenta* which constitute the liturgy: first of all in its seven major rites, the seven sacraments properly so called, and in a very special way in the most holy sacrament *par excellence*, the Eucharistic mystery.[77] In all these phases the transmission of the divine life to men and the return of men to God takes place by an incarnate route in a regime of signs, in *sacramentis*, where "one thing is seen and another understood."

Furthermore, sacred Scripture itself is based wholly on the concept of sign, both the sign which is speech and the sign which is things or persons. For, because of the profound unity of sacred history and because of reasons which

[77] This is the concept explicitly pointed out by the Second Vatican Council, CL., art. 5-7. See also Cyprian Vagaggini, "Lo spirito della Costituzione sulla liturgia," *Riv. Lit.,* 51 (1964), 8-16; P. Visentin, "Il mistero di Cristo nella liturgia secondo la Costituzione liturgica," *ibid.,* 55-62. See also St. Augustine, *Ep.* 187, 34: "Now the sacrament of our regeneration . . . was . . . something hidden to people of Old Testament times. . . . For there is no other mystery of God but Christ"; as well as St. Leo the Great, *Sermo* 74, 2: "That which was visible in Christ passed over into sacraments of the Church." See also E. H. Schillebeeckx, *Christ the Sacrament of the Encounter with God* (New York: Sheed and Ward, 1963); P. Broutin, *Mysterium Ecclesiae* (Paris, 1947); Otto Semmelroth, *Die Kirche als Ursakrament* (Frankfurt: J. Knecht, 1955); *Id., Vom Sinn der Sakramente* (Frankfurt: J. Knecht, 1960); Karl Rahner, *The Church and the Sacraments* (New York: Herder and Herder, 1963).

we shall have to explain later, the very things and persons about whom the words of Scripture are written have intrinsic reference also, in the designs of God, to other sacred realities. If we consider these facts, we shall see that we can repeat as a general principle for all the phases of the supernatural relations between God and men which constitute sacred history, what Origen said with regard to the story of Abraham: "Everything that is done, is done *in sacramentis*." [78]

In fact, not only was the Mosaic law based on a great number of rites which were *sacramenta*, but we know that in the natural religions also, both before and after the Mosaic law, rites which can be called *sacramenta* in their own way were of use and are of use to God for the salvation of men. [79]

Thus has God disposed; and what He wills has no other reason, in the last analysis, than His free will. There is nothing for man to do but ascertain what the divine will is and accept it.

Human nature. Still, we can get a glimpse of the profound wisdom of God's course of action in this whole plan. He is merely treating man as man, exactly as human nature requires. For man is a substantial unity of soul and body, of spirituality and materiality. His spiritual soul gains knowledge, and therefore perfects itself, through the body and sensible things, and, in turn, expresses and manifests itself in the body and in sensible things, impressing on them something of itself. To such a nature, spirit incarnated, the incarnate way and the regime of signs is supremely suited.

The ancient ecclesiastical writers did not fail to observe this, precisely in connection with the *sacramenta* and especially our seven sacraments.

St. John Chrysostom, for example, observes concerning the Eucharist and baptism: "Since the Word says, 'This is My body,' let us assent and believe and consider Him in this sacrament with spiritual eyes. Actually what Christ has given us is not anything perceptible to the senses. Rather, the realities given are wholly spiritual, though clothed in sensible things. The same holds for baptism: the gift is given through a sensible thing, water; the spiritual reality accomplished is birth and renewal. If you had been incorporeal, He would have given you bare, incorporeal gifts; but since the soul is united to the body, He offers you spiritual realities clothed in sensible things." [80]

"Divine wisdom," observes St. Thomas in his turn, "provides for everything according to the manner proper to each one, and hence it is said that wisdom 'disposes all things sweetly' (Wis. 8:1). . . . Now it is natural for man to rise to the knowledge of the intelligible through the sensible. But a sign is the thing by means of which one arrives at the knowledge of something else. Therefore, since the sacred realities signified by the sacraments are the spiritual

---

[78] *In Gen. Hom.* 9, 1.
[79] See, e.g., St. Thomas, *Summa*, III, q. 61, a. 3.

[80] *In Matthaeum hom.* 82, 4; this passage used to be read at the second nocturn of Matins on the second Sunday after Pentecost.

and intelligible goods by means of which man is sanctified, it follows that the sacramental signs consist in sensible things." [81]

This general reason for a regime of signs, the agreement of the sign with human nature itself, can be greatly particularized and probed from the psychological point of view. The process required will be a minute descriptive analysis of the manner and the effectiveness with which the process of religious knowledge and expression takes place in the individual liturgical signs and the whole liturgical action.

In ancient times, St. Augustine already saw deeply into this vital psychological efficacy of the sign and of the symbolic allegorical expression in general: "All these things brought home to us in figures have the aim of feeding and somehow fanning the flame of love which, like a sort of specific gravity, carries us above or within ourselves until we come to rest. Thus proposed, these realities move and enkindle love more than if they were set forth in a starkly intellectual way and not as *sacramenta*. It is hard to say why this should be so. But it is certain that anything expressed by way of allegory is more moving, more pleasing and better heeded than if it were said outright in the most appropriate words. I think the soul is slower to catch fire as long as it is involved in mere earthly things; while if it is directed to bodily symbols (*similitudines*) and from the symbols to the spiritual realities expressed by them in figure, this very process enlivens it, enkindles it like a waving torch and draws it with more ardent love to its resting-place." [82]

What Augustine had surmised as a psychological aim of signs, the moderns, with the instrument of phenomenological psychological analysis, have attempted to describe in detail in the sphere of worship. Among the Catholics, Romano Guardini has shown particular interest in this aspect of the liturgy.[83] Among the Protestants a noteworthy work is that of Robert Will, *Le culte*, in three volumes,[84] the second of which is concerned wholly with the phenomenology of worship, including Catholic worship. He deals with the subject very minutely, striving to penetrate into the psychological process of the religious efficacy which worship has, in its simple or complex sensible elements, for bringing about the encounter between God and man. Apart, of course, from certain defects congenital to the mentality of a Protestant when he speaks of Catholic worship, many of Will's observations on the psychological necessity and efficacy of the liturgy in its structure as a complexus of signs are quite

[81] *Summa*, III, q. 60, a. 4. In III, q. 61, a. 1, St. Thomas specifies exactly: "Thus through the institution of the sacraments man is instructed, consistently with his nature, through sensible things; he is humbled, having to acknowledge himself subject to bodily things, since he is helped by them; and he is preserved from sinful actions" (i.e., recourse to superstitious rites) "through the salutary frequenting of the sacraments." See also the excellent, long text in

C. Gent., III, 119.
[82] *Ep.* 55, n. 21.
[83] Especially in *The Spirit of the Liturgy* (New York: Benziger, 1931); *Sacred Signs* (St. Louis: Pio Decimo Press, 1956); *Liturgische Bildung* (Mainz, 1923); *Die Sinne und die religiöse Erkenntnis* (Würzburg: Werkbund, 1950).
[84] Paris: Alcan. The second volume was published in 1929.

justified; and some of his eloquent passages on this subject can, with a few changes, be fully approved by a Catholic.

Thus, for example, on the psychological necessity of a worship embodied in signs: "All worship demands expressive forms: images, sounds, words, gestures, rites, persons. These forms, interposed between God and the faithful, serve as commutators for the currents of life which connect the subjective pole to the objective pole or vice versa. They give concrete expression to the soul's aspirations and raise them up. In the other direction, they make concrete the graces descending from on high and channel them into souls. Thus phenomena in the sphere of worship, placing themselves at the service both of the religious subject and of the divine object, respond to a twofold necessity, the one being of the psychological order, the other of the metaphysical order. In other words, the nature of man demands phenomena and the essence of revelation also requires them." [85]

Again: "The rites of worship appear, therefore, as means designed to preserve the objective values of religion, because they are considered as translating into phenomena the supersensible data of divine revelation. Without this translation into figures, religion, purely subjective, would run the risk of deteriorating into mystical states, cold ideologies or moralizations. . . . The religion which has no interest in worship wastes away in the rarefied atmosphere of an excessive spiritualism.[86] . . . In short, there is no more justification for denying to transcendental inspiration a representation by figures perceptible to the senses than there is for denying such representation to the soul's aspirations. The translation of the transcendental realities into the sensible world is a postulate of the divine essence in communication with the world [87] as the concrete figuration of the data of religious consciousness is a postulate of human nature." [88]

Or again this observation on private religious life and worship: "The worship-experience will be an empirical prolongation and a concrete enlargement of the religious experience. The encounter with God in worship will be the end result and the combination of all the experiences provided us by our previous contact with God, by our faith and by our prayer. The divine reality of the faith feeds the dynamic forces of our subjective faith, which overflow into worship. In virtue of the generative action of the Spirit, therefore, worship is like a superabundant prayer, springing from personal prayer, but of a better channeled and more copious flow, a sensible and collective prayer." [89]

"In short, worship, prolongation of the mediating action of Christ, is the religious symbol *par excellence*. Forming the bridge which leads from tran-

[85] P. 13. This "requires" means: requires them in order to be communicated to man in accordance with his nature.

[86] Or, as the author said above, of a cold ideologism or an exaggerated moralism.

[87] More precisely: it is the act of a positive free will of God in His communicating Himself to the world, which, though it is a free act, corresponds wonderfully to the very nature of man.

[88] Pp. 26 f.

[89] P. 38.

scendence to immanence, it has the mission of helping the whole world to be penetrated with the divine presence."[90]

A Catholic will be pleased to see these and similar observations by a Protestant as proof that, even considering the matter solely from the psychological point of view, it is supremely effective, agreeable to the nature of man, even morally necessary, for the encounter between God and man to take place in a regime of cultual signs. He will understand better that worship cannot occur outside of a system of signs if the right psychological equilibrium of the religious life is to be always observed; if the subjective and the objective are to be balanced in equitable measure; and if certain dangers are to be avoided: an uncontrolled subjectivism, an excessive introspectionism and psychologism, an ideologism without vital efficacy; a moralism which does not distinguish sufficiently between the Christian religion and a mere philosophical ethics.

All these dangers Protestantism has been unable to avoid, largely because of its almost complete opposition to the incarnated forms of Catholic worship. Only Anglicanism, with its eclectic character, is a certain exception. Catholicism, on the other hand, thanks to its incarnated worship, has been able to preserve a psychological balance; and Robert Will himself does not hesitate to recognize the superiority of the Catholic equilibrium.

"It is a fact," says Will, "that the Protestant churches, and especially reformed Puritanism, have tipped the balance of the two hemispheres — the external and the internal — in favor of the internal. The spiritual impoverishment resulting from this imbalance does not respond to the demands of our dualist nature or to the needs of popular piety or to the trends of our generation so eager for reality, objectivity and intense life."[91]

This observation, a just one from the psychological point of view, acquires its full weight when we add that such an imbalance fails above all to respond to the positive will of God and of Christ because, besides ignoring the laws of psychology, it ignores also the laws of sacred history which God has chosen to observe in His relations with men: law of objectivity; law of incarnation; law of salvation in community, in which God saves men by means of other men.

Thus it is understandable that the discovery of the liturgy, even if the occasion be only its psychological utility, as it is today with the Protestants,[92] carries with it in germ the recognition of values which, logically developed, might lead to the discovery of Catholicism.

In recognizing that the divine will was supremely wise when it decreed that the encounter between man and God should be achieved essentially in a system of signs that are not merely intelligible but sensible, these observations appeal to the nature of man considered first of all as an individual. To these observations is added another consideration, to which our generation is particularly

[90] P. 25.
[91] P. 9.
[92] We know that for the last thirty years there has been a notable liturgical movement among Protestants. See chapter 22, section 2, on liturgy and ecumenism.

sensitive: the social nature of man and of all the manifestations, even the deepest, of his life and activity, therefore the social nature of religion also.

Sociality of religion and system of sensible signs are things inseparably connected. For society implies unity, unification, in as much as it implies relations between individuals in the communication of thoughts and desires and of the accompanying affections, for the attainment of common ends in the use of common means and in reciprocal aid. If, moreover, the society in question does not actually include all men, this implies not only unity and unification, but also distinction. Society unites and distinguishes.

Now all this, among individuals who are spirits substantially united to bodies, is established only through the exterior and the sensible, as expression of thoughts, desires and affections which of their nature do not fall under the senses. It is established, therefore, through sensible signs in which such thoughts, desires and affections are embodied. Sensible signs, in a society, are precisely the expression and the cause of union of all its members and of distinction from all other persons.

Hence there is no society or social life without a very extensive use of sensible signs: meetings, festivities, hierarchical uniforms and insignia, emblems, songs, ceremonies and external rites. The rites are performed in community, and their distinctive parts are assigned to the various groups of which society is made up, especially to anyone who holds authority in some way. The phenomenon of "communist rites" is well known. The role of the sensible sign in social life is therefore essential.

The positive fact that God has freely willed that the encounter between Himself and man in Christ take place in a regime of sensible signs appears thus as a natural consequence of the other positive fact that He has willed that the same encounter have a social and communitarian character; and the one and the other respond to the deepest tendencies of human nature.

Thus the structured religious system of sensible signs, which is precisely the liturgical system, appears as a protection and guarantee not only of objectivity and incarnationism against the danger of a subjectivism which withdraws into abstract concepts and of a disembodied spiritualism, but also as a protection and guarantee of a sound communitarian sense against the dangers of an exaggerated individualism. Anyone who has discovered the value of the communitarian aspect of religion and of Christian piety not only has no fear of liturgical symbolism but feels at ease with it, because his communitarian sense makes him see at once the social value of the liturgical sign.[93]

Of course many and serious consequences follow from the fact that the liturgical sign has, among other things, an essentially communitarian and social value. We shall have to return to these consequences later. For the present, let it suffice to mention one: that the liturgical sign is made for the

---

[93] The social aspect of the liturgical sign is brought out particularly by Jean C.-M. Travers, *Valeur sociale de la liturgie d'après S. Thomas d'Aquin* (Paris: Cerf, 1946), e.g., pp. 313-17.

community and must be understood by the community under pain of losing its psychological effectiveness. This simple observation gets the whole liturgical pastoral art started on a very definite path.

New proof: rite and religion. What has been said above about the relations between rite and human nature is amply confirmed today by the latest developments in two relatively new sciences: the comparative history of religions, and depth psychology as applied to the study of the religious phenomenon.[94]

The material brought to light by these two sciences can make a considerable contribution toward understanding better the solidly human roots of the liturgy's structuration in a system of signs perceptible to the senses and the correspondence of this structure to the most firmly established laws of religious psychology.

Many of our contemporaries have to rediscover this fundamental fact. The rediscovery is made the more necessary for them in the measure in which their thinking has been influenced by certain developments: the way in which theology developed after the thirteenth century;[95] Protestant anti-ritualism; the purely interior and individualistic experimentalism of certain spiritual currents; the abstract conceptualism of the seventeenth- and eighteenth-century Enlightenment, which has left so many traces even in ourselves in the religious field; finally, today's widespread technico-mechanical way of thinking. All these developments conspire to hide from our contemporaries the demands of concrete human nature in this field of liturgy.[96] We can see symptoms of a healthy reaction leading to a more wholesome balance, but these symptoms are still far from constituting a common mentality.

From these studies can arise also a better understanding of the dangers that threaten the liturgy if a proper balance is not preserved between speech and the other kinds of sign; if the signs, made precisely to mean something, are no longer perceived in their meaning, and therefore, in fact, no longer mean anything; if, worse still, liturgical speech, which to a great extent has precisely the function of determining the meaning of the other signs, is itself no

---

[94] See, e.g., Nicola Turchi, "Simbolo e simbolismo nelle religioni non cristiane," *Enciclopedia cattolica*, II, cols. 609 f., with bibliography. Particularly important in the field of the comparative history of religions are: under this aspect, the works of Mircea Eliade, especially *Patterns in Comparative Religion* (New York: Sheed and Ward, 1958), *Images and Symbols* (*ibid.*, 1961), *Myths, Dreams and Mysteries* (New York: Harper, 1960); under various aspects, the works of G. van der Leeuw, principally his work on the essence of religion and its manifestations; see the French translation, *La religion dans son essence et ses manifestations* (Paris, 1955). Valuable in the field of religious

psychology are many of the observations made by C. G. Jung; see, for example: *The Archetypes and the Collective Unconscious* (New York: Pantheon, 1959), pp. 3-41; "Mind and Earth" and "The Spiritual Problem of Modern Man," *Civilization in Transition* (*ibid.*, 1964), pp. 29 ff. and 74 ff.; *Psychology and Religion* (*ibid.*, 1958).

[95] To understand how a profound change in theological thinking took place at that time, see M. D. Chenu's *La théologie au XIIe siècle* (Paris, 1957), pp. 159-220.

[96] See F. W. Dillistone's *Christianity and Symbolism* (Philadelphia: Westminster Press, 1955), with bibliography.

longer understood; if, finally, the whole system stagnates in an unchangeable tradition which no longer corresponds to anything in life.

Unfortunately, the liturgical movement up to now has not given anywhere nearly enough attention to this kind of studies either for the liturgy in general or for its individual parts in particular.[97]

4. The Things Signified by Signs in the Liturgy

Having explained the concept of sign in general and having observed the universal dominion of signs in the liturgy, we must determine more particularly what are the invisible sacred realities signified by the liturgical signs — realities which concern the relations between God and man.

The four dimensions of the liturgical sign in general

We know that the liturgy is the complexus of sensible signs by means of which God, in Christ and through Christ, in the Church and through the Church, sanctifies man, and man, in Christ and through Christ, in the Church and through the Church, renders his worship to God. Thus the liturgical sign, in the system effectively willed by God, is the meeting place between God and man, where God descends to man and man rises to God.

The realities signified by the liturgical signs are therefore those which constitute the encounter between man and God: the sanctification of the Church by God in Christ and the worship which the Church renders in Christ to God. Sanctification and worship, as we shall explain more fully in what follows, are two things which necessarily call for each other and are inseparable in the liturgical reality. Hence they are always signified in every liturgical sign.

But they are signified on different levels as befits each case. For when we consider the individual liturgical signs, we see that in some of them sanctification is primary and will therefore be signified directly, while worship is secondary and will be signified indirectly; in the other liturgical signs, the contrary takes place: worship, being primary, will be signified directly, while sanctification, being secondary, will be signified only indirectly.

At any rate, every liturgical sign will always signify those supersensible, spiritual, sacred realities in which God's sanctification of the Church in Christ and the Church's worship of God in Christ consist.

* * *

What, more precisely, are these realities? Under various aspects, many different elements concur in their makeup. The liturgical signs referring in one way or another to such things signify them under various titles. We can get an idea of what these realities are exactly, by analyzing the various

[97] See: *La maison Dieu*, n. 22 (1950), on the theme of the lasting value of symbolism;   Louis Bouyer, *Rite and Man.*

spiritual, supersensible elements which are somehow involved in sanctification and worship according to the different orders of causality.

The *intrinsic formal cause* of sanctification is sanctifying grace with all the infused virtues that accompany it.

The intrinsic formal cause of worship is the interior attitude of reverence towards God based on the recognition of His pre-eminence. This attitude is made up of admiration, esteem, honor, entreaty, as well as humility and avowal of submission, which includes repentance and the will to make satisfaction in case of sin. The whole is an expression of the virtue of religion with all its implications, a virtue which makes us render to God whatever is due Him precisely as first Principle, Creator and Governor of all things.

To the order of invisible *material causality* in Christian sanctification and in Christian worship belongs, in the first place, the soul as supersensible subject of sanctification. But, let it be noted carefully, this is never the individual soul considered apart from the Church as the fellowship of those who believe in Christ — a society that is invisible in so far as it is based on an invisible situation. Rather, the subject of sanctification is the soul *in* the Church. In this sense we say that it is the Church which is sanctified in the liturgy, while individual souls are sanctified in the Church and through the Church.

In the second place in the order of invisible material causality of the liturgy belong the moral dispositions necessary in the soul to make it a fit subject to receive sanctification and to render Christian worship to God. And on this point we must dwell.

In the adult it is a fully human act, therefore free and moral, to receive sanctification and to render worship to God. It is never a purely mechanical act. When we say that the seven sacraments give grace *ex opere operato*, we mean always that they give it in this way to one who interposes no obstacle of the moral order. The obstacle would be a lack of the prerequisite human and free moral dispositions. Without these dispositions, grace does not take effect.

It is for this reason that, against all the Protestant and rationalist misunderstandings in this field, Catholic theology keeps repeating that the process by which sanctification takes place in these seven sacraments, while immeasurably transcending the possibilities of the moral power of man alone, has nothing to do with magic.

In magic it is man who, by a physico-mechanical process, thinks to force a divine power to put itself at his disposal, and this independently of his moral dispositions toward that power.

In the sacraments, on the other hand, man submits himself morally to the will of God, who has decided to communicate the divine life in this sacramental way, and man accepts this way; so that the effect of the communication of grace in the adult is always dependent on his moral dispositions. Moreover, the preservation in the adult of the sanctification received in the sacrament is likewise dependent on these moral dispositions. As long as he is living here on earth, there remains the possibility of a downfall by the introduction of contrary moral dispositions.

To be numbered among the moral dispositions of sanctification is THE MORAL OBLIGATION FOR THE FUTURE of living in a way that corresponds to the requirements of the new mode of being received in the sanctifying act. This obligation is always more or less explicit in the adult who receives sanctification, precisely because sanctification always involves the moral order of free cooperation. In this precise sense every sacrament is for the adult recipient an OATH.

This holds also for worship. In worship we recognize the pre-eminence of God and we profess our submission to Him. The disposition of soul in which interior worship consists is not conceivable without the obligation, at least implicit, of living in the future as God's pre-eminence and our submission require. Every liturgical act, therefore, in which man receives sanctification and renders his worship to God, involves an engagement, an obligation freely assumed for the future, an implied oath; and the Christian sinner, in breaking the pacts sworn with God, is necessarily a traitor.

Faith also must be noted among the moral dispositions which are always indispensable if the soul is to receive sanctification fruitfully and to render worship. Every liturgical action presupposes and expresses the faith of anyone who takes part in it. Hence not only are the seven sacraments *sacramenta fidei*, sacraments of faith, but the whole liturgy is in an eminent degree a *protestatio fidei*, a profession of faith.

The invisible principal *efficient cause* of sanctification is God.

Christ in His humanity is the invisible instrumental efficient cause, because the divinity uses His humanity as a conjoint instrument for sanctification.

The meritorious efficient cause of the same sanctification is the saving actions of Christ in His mortal life, especially His Passion and death on the Cross.

The principal supersensible efficient cause of the worship which the Church renders to God is Christ Himself, because the Church's worship is nothing but the worship which Christ renders to God through the Church, making the Church participate in His worship. Hence the Church's spiritual dispositions are an instrument which Christ uses and a participation in Christ's dispositions.

Proper *final cause* of sanctification (the final cause common to all things is always God's glory) is the future glory of the beatific vision to which grace is intrinsically ordained as the seed is intrinsically ordained to the tree.

Proper final cause of the worship rendered here below is the eternal, cosmic worship of God in the heavenly Jerusalem.

Under one aspect, the *exemplary cause* of the sanctification effected and the worship offered in our liturgy is Christ Himself, in whose sanctification and in whose worship we participate and are formed in the liturgy.

Under another aspect, all the sanctification and all the worship which took place on earth before Christ, at least after Adam's sin, especially in the history of the people of God, have a relation of exemplarity with respect to the sanctification and the worship in our liturgy; for they were nothing but first imperfect rough casts of the sanctification and the worship which was fulfilled first in Christ Himself and is fulfilled now in our liturgy in Christ.

Under a third aspect, the exemplary cause of the sanctification effected and the worship offered in our liturgy is the perfect sanctification and the perfect worship of the heavenly Jerusalem: our sanctification and our worship are but rough casts and sketches, still imperfect, of that sanctification and that worship, tending to them as the supreme ideal in which they will find perfect fulfillment.

These, therefore, are the supersensible spiritual realities implied by the sanctification and the worship in the liturgy; and these realities are signified, in their own way, by the liturgical signs. It is all this that is "understood" in the liturgical signs, in which "one thing is seen and another understood."

*   *   *

There is a certain order, however, according to which these realities are signified by the liturgical signs. The order is determined by the relation of each of these realities to the intrinsic formal element of our sanctification and our worship, which is sanctifying grace and the disposition of soul in which our worship consists. This is the central and primary element which the liturgical signs signify immediately and primarily.

They signify all the other elements in so far as these have a necessary and intrinsic relation to the primary and central element on which the significative and representative function of the liturgical sign bears first of all.

Our sanctification and our worship presuppose, among other things, our moral dispositions, especially faith and the moral obligation for the future. Hence the liturgical signs, signifying directly our sanctification and our worship, signify also our dispositions, in particular our faith and our obligation for the future. They are moral and obligating signs.

Further: our grace comes from God, but it comes through Christ the Redeemer; He has merited it for us, especially in His Passion; He transmits it to us by sharing with us the holiness or divine life which He has in abundance. The worship we render to God is the worship Christ rendered on earth and continues to render to God, in which He associates us. Thus the liturgical sign, signifying first of all our sanctification and our worship, signifies as a result God acting in us, and Christ and His sanctity and His Passion and His worship.

Then, since our sanctification and our worship are directed to future glory and to the worship of the heavenly Jerusalem, the glory and the heavenly Jerusalem will also be signified in the liturgical sign.

Again, given the fact that our sanctification and our worship fulfill in themselves, as the more perfect statue fulfills the rough cast, whatever there was in the world, after Adam's sin and before Christ, of sanctification and of worship acceptable to God, especially in the Old Testament, so, necessarily, the liturgical signs will signify also that sanctification and that worship before the time of Christ.

Thus we perceive, noting these invisible sacred realities signified by the liturgical signs under the aspect of the present, the past and the future, that the liturgical signs have a significative relation to the whole of sacred history, present, past and future.

They signify, in the first place, a series of supersensible sacred realities as present here and now in the sacred action: sanctifying grace with the infused virtues, in which consists formally the sanctification denoted by the signs; the worshipful disposition of the soul as expression of the virtue of religion in its various aspects, in which consists formally the worship signified by the same signs; the presupposed moral dispositions, especially faith and the obligation for the future; God operating at present as principal efficient cause of sanctification and as ultimate object of worship; Christ also in His humanity as exemplary and instrumental cause of sanctification and principal efficient and exemplary cause of worship; the Church as people of God in her invisible aspect, object of sanctification and instrumental cause of the worship which Christ renders to God through her.

A second series of invisible sacred realities signified by the liturgical signs are realities of the past: the saving actions of Christ in His earthly life, especially in His Passion and death, which are the meritorious cause of the grace signified by the liturgical signs and which constituted the beginning of that worship of God which Christ now continues in the liturgy; the sanctification and the worship which took place on earth after Adam's sin, the foreshadowings and imperfect rough casts in whose fulfillment our liturgy approaches much nearer to final perfection.

Finally, a third series of realities signified by the liturgical signs are realities of the future, namely the glory and the worship of the heavenly Jerusalem. These are the end and the perfect exemplar to which the sanctification and the worship in the liturgy here below tend, looking to them as their intrinsic perfection.

Thus every liturgical sign looks to the present, the past and the future. But as sign of the present the liturgical sign has two functions which should be carefully distinguished.

On the one hand, many of these present realities are indicated by the liturgical sign as simply present: sanctifying grace and the dispositions in which interior worship formally consists; God effecting the sanctification and object of the worship; Christ instrumental and exemplary cause of the sanctification as well as principal efficient cause and exemplary cause of the worship; the Church object of the sanctification and instrumental cause of the worship.

On the other hand there is a reality which the liturgical sign does indeed indicate as present but which intrinsically looks to future actions in this life. This reality is the disposition prerequisite in the soul of one who receives the sanctification or renders the worship, by which he obligates himself now to live for the future in conformity with the requirements of the sanctification received and the interior worship manifested.

Thus the obligating sign is both sign of the present and sign of the future. It is of the highest importance. On the one side, in the free cooperation and the good moral life which it strictly demands, it shows how deep the liturgical life goes. On the other side, it shows how the moral and ascetical life outside of the liturgical action is not something merely parallel and unconnected to the liturgical life, but a connatural derivation of it demanded in germ by every liturgical ceremony.

*   *   *

In conclusion, therefore, the liturgical sign has four dimensions. It is a sign demonstrative of the present invisible sacred realities: primarily of sanctifying grace and interior worship; then of God effecting sanctification and being object of worship; of Christ, instrumental and exemplary cause of sanctification, and principal and exemplary cause, as well as object, of worship; of the Church, object of sanctification and instrumental cause of worship. *It is a moral sign obligating* even now in the present to the future actions in the life of him who receives the sanctification and renders the worship. *It is a sign commemorative* of Christ's saving actions, especially of His Passion and death, as well as of the worship and sanctification which took place in the world after Adam's sin and before Christ. *It is a sign portending or prophetic* of the heavenly glory and of the worship in the future Jerusalem.

It should be observed, however, that the realities of the past and those of the future are not signified in the liturgical signs as purely past or future, but in some way also as present.

The question how this presentness of the past sacred reality in the current liturgical action should be conceived of, when the concern is with the saving actions of Christ in His mortal life, and especially with the Passion, will be examined separately because of its special difficulty.

But it is clear even from what we have said so far that the sanctification and the worship which took place before Christ are signified in the liturgical signs also as present. For the liturgical sign signifies Christian sanctification and worship as present; and Christian sanctification and worship fulfills in itself and renders present in an eminent way the acts of sanctification and worship before Christ, just as the more perfect statue fulfills in itself and renders present the rough cast which has preceded it.

On the other hand, the future glory and the worship of the heavenly Jerusalem are signified in the liturgical sign also as present. For the grace of sanctification and the worship signified in the liturgy are really the seed and the first rough cast of the glory to come and of the heavenly worship. And the seed and the rough cast signify as present and, in their way, make already present the thing of which they are the seed and the rough cast.

The past and the future are signified in the liturgical signs, therefore, as in a supratemporal present, because the invisible sacred realities signified under one aspect as past or future are signified under another aspect as concentrated in the present reality. Thus the liturgical signs, in their own way, gather into one place the whole reality of sacred history, present, past and future.

It will be observed that in all this I have done nothing but to complete and adapt to the liturgical realities in all their aspects what St. Thomas had asserted of the seven sacraments in particular, as far as the meaning of sacred signs is concerned, when he saw in them a threefold signification.

"That is properly called a sacrament," the holy doctor had observed, restricting the old concept of *sacramentum* to the seven sacraments only, "which is ordained to signify our sanctification.[98] In this sanctification three things can be considered: the cause itself of our sanctification, which is the Passion of Christ; the form of our sanctification, which consists in grace and the virtues; and the ultimate end of our sanctification, which is eternal life. And all these are signified by the sacraments. Hence a sacrament is a sign commemorative of that which preceded, namely Christ's Passion; a sign demonstrative of that which is effected in us by Christ's Passion, namely grace; and a sign prophetic, that is, foretelling the future glory."[99]

The broadening of St. Thomas' concept to the whole complexus of the signs constituting the liturgy is legitimate and necessary. For it is the relation between sanctification and the various causes on which it depends that justifies St. Thomas in saying that the signs of the seven sacraments have three

[98] St. Thomas means that it is ordained immediately (and not only mediately) to signify our sanctification as a thing which is realized at present, *hic et nunc*. Thus St. Thomas excludes from the concept of *sacramentum* what we now call the sacramentals, because in them the sign does not signify sanctity directly in itself, but only mediately, since immediately it signifies only a disposition to sanctity; thus also he excludes from the *sacramentum* all that which is immediately ordained to signify the worship of God, for example the Divine Office and even the sacrifice of the Mass (hence St. Thomas in the Eucharist distinguishes the *sacramentum* from the sacrifice).

[99] *Summa*, III, q. 60, a. 3.

dimensions of signification. And this same basis holds, in its way, for all the signs which constitute the liturgy, as I have explained above.

Further, the reality of the moral obligating sign in the order of dispositive causality is no less evident than that of the demonstrative, commemorative and prophetic sign in the order of efficient, formal and final causality.

This broadening from sacramental sign to general liturgical sign not only restores to us the old patristic concept of *sacramentum, mysterium*. It recovers for us more particularly the whole force of the meaning of that concept, a stimulating intuition — one which had been, for example, the great incentive of Origen.[100]

When we come to examining in detail this property of four-dimensional signification which belongs to the individual liturgical signs, we have to distinguish between liturgical signs instituted by God and those instituted by the Church. Although this examination belongs more properly to special liturgy, a rapid glance will be very useful at this point also, to show more vividly this fourfold dimension of signification of the liturgical signs, a very necessary thing if we are to penetrate effectively into the world of the liturgy.

The fourfold dimension of the liturgical signs instituted by God

The concern is with the seven sacraments and the sacrifice of the Mass in that which pertains to their substance and is of divine institution. The examination of the fourfold dimensionality of signification of these signs has this special advantage that, with regard to the two fundamental sacraments of baptism and the Eucharist, it shows how this doctrine is already expressed clearly in the Scripture.

Baptism. When he says that by baptism we die to sin, St. Paul affirms that the baptismal rite is a sign demonstrative of Christ's grace in which the believer participates by means of baptism: "We died to sin . . . when we were baptized into Christ Jesus . . . our old humanity was crucified with Him in order that the body of sin might be destroyed, that we might no longer be slaves to sin" (Rom. 6:2 ff.); or when he says that baptism is "a bath of regeneration and renewal by the Holy Spirit" (Tit. 3:5; see Eph. 5:26; John 3:5).

That baptism is an obligating sign in which the believer binds himself to live all the rest of his life as his new status demands, is the explicit theme of chapter 6 of the letter to the Romans: "What shall I say, then? Shall we remain in sin that grace may abound? By no means! How shall we who are dead to sin still live in it? Do you not know that all of us who have been baptized into Christ Jesus have been baptized into His death? We were buried together with Him, therefore, by baptism into death, that, as Christ

---

[100] Cf. Hans Urs von Balthasar, "Le 'my-sterion' d'Origène," *Rech. de sc. rel.*, 26 (1936),   513 ff.; 27 (1937), 38 ff.

has risen by the glory of the Father, so we also may walk in newness of life. . . . Our old humanity has been crucified with Him in order that the body of sin might be destroyed, that we might no longer be slaves to sin. For he who is dead is acquitted of sin. . . . So also you consider yourselves as dead to sin, but as alive to God in Christ Jesus. See to it, therefore, that sin no longer reigns in your mortal body so that you obey its lusts. And do not offer your members to sin as weapons of iniquity, but present yourselves to God as men who have come to life from the dead and your members as weapons of justice for God. . . . But now, set free from sin and become slaves of God, you have your reward in sanctification . . ." (Rom. 6:1 ff.; see also Col. 3:1-4:5).

This explains how Tertullian[101] and several Latin ecclesiastical writers after him[102] were expressing a profoundly scriptural thought when, with the same idea of *sacramentum* in mind, they likened baptism to the *sacramentum militiae*, which in ancient times was simultaneously a military oath and a rite of religious initiation and consecration.[103] This is so much the more understandable since the rite of initiation into the pagan mysteries was often considered also as an oath and an initiation into a sacred militia,[104] and since, moreover, the ancient baptismal rite itself already included the explicit renunciation of Satan and all his pomps and his angels,[105] something which has the value of a real oath. Thus Tertullian could say, "We have been called to the militia of God . . . when we reply in the words of the *sacramentum*;"[106] and St. Cyprian has this protestation made to the confessor of the faith: "I did want to fight bravely; mindful of my *sacramentum*, I took up the arms of *devotio* and of the faith."[107] Thus every grave sin committed by a Christian was considered as an attempt to "obtain a discharge from the *sacramenta benedictionis*," that is, from the obligations of the oath blessed in baptism.[108]

Baptism is a sign "commemorative" of the past redemptive action of Christ, that is, of His death: "Or do you not know that all of us who have been baptized into Christ Jesus have been baptized into His death? For we were buried with Him by means of baptism into death. . . . If we have indeed grown to be one with Him in the likeness of His death . . ." (Rom. 6:3 ff.).

The way in which baptism is also a sign "commemorative" of past sacred history before Christ can be seen, for example, in 1 Cor. 10:1-11: the baptism

---

[101] See Joseph de Ghellinck's *Pour l'histoire du mot "sacramentum,"* I, 66-113.

[102] See Albert Blaise's *Dictionnaire latin-français des auteurs chrétiens* (Strasbourg: Le Latin chrétien, 1954) at the word "Sacramentum," where he quotes, e.g., St. Cyprian, Arnobius, Optatus of Milevis, St. Hilary.

[108] Cf. Franz Dölger, *Antike und Christentum* (1930), p. 280; *Jahrb. für Liturgiewis.*, 1928,

p. 227; Odo Casel in *Theologische Revue*, 1925, p. 41.

[104] Cf. Tertullian, *De corona*, 15, à propos of the Mithraic initiation.

[105] See Tertullian's *De spectac.*, 4.

[106] *Ad martyr.*, 3.

[107] *De lapsis*, 13.

[108] Tertullian, *De pudic.*, 14.

of the Israelites "in Moses, in the cloud and in the sea. . . . Now these facts have become types for us. . . . All these things happened to them as a type, and were written for our correction, upon whom the final age of the world has come." See also 1 Peter 3:20 ff.: ". . . in the days when Noah was building the ark, in which a few, that is, eight souls, were saved through water. The antitype, which now saves us also, is baptism."

St. Paul teaches how baptism is a prophetic sign of future glory in the same text to the Romans 6:2-11: ". . . If we have indeed grown to be one (with Christ) in the likeness of His death, we shall be so in the likeness of His resurrection also. . . . If we have died with Christ, we believe that we shall also live with Him." [109]

The Eucharist. Read the narrative of the institution in the synoptics: Matthew 26:17-29; Mark 14:12-25; Luke 22:7-20; the reflections of St. Paul: 1 Cor. 10:16-21; 11:23-30; the Eucharistic discourse in the sixth chapter of St. John.

The Eucharist is a sign demonstrative first of all of Christ's body and blood here present: "This is My body . . . this is my Blood" (words of the institution); "The bread which I shall give is My flesh given for the life of the world. . . . Unless you eat the flesh of the Son of Man and drink His blood. . . . He who eats My flesh and drinks My blood . . ." (John 6:51 ff.); "The cup of blessing which we bless, is it not the communion of Christ's blood? The bread that we break, is it not the communion of Christ's body?" (1 Cor. 10:16).

Further: the Eucharist is a sign demonstrative of the divine life and of the grace of union with Christ and among ourselves: "He who eats My flesh and drinks My blood abides in Me and I in him. . . . He who eats Me, he also shall live because of Me" (John 6:56 f.; cf. 6:50-52). "Because the bread is one, we who are many are but one body, for we all partake of the one bread" (1 Cor. 10:17).

Of the Eucharist as a sign obligating to a corresponding life St. Paul speaks explicitly in 1 Cor. 10:14-22 to make the Christians understand the obligation to flee idolatry: "Therefore, my beloved, flee from idolatry. I speak as one speaks to persons of intelligence. Judge for yourselves what I say. The cup of blessing which we bless, is it not the communion of Christ's blood? The bread that we break, is it not the communion of Christ's body? . . . What the gentiles sacrifice, they sacrifice to demons and not to God. And I do not want you to be in communion with demons. You cannot drink the cup of the Lord and the cup of demons; you cannot partake of the table of the Lord and the table of demons. Or are we provoking the Lord to jealousy? Are we stronger than He?"

---

[109] Cf. also Tit. 3:5-7. This fourfold significa- affirmed in the ancient rite of baptism by im-
tion of baptism was much more expressively   mersion. See Righetti, IV, 65, 68 f.

The concept of the Eucharist as a sign obligating to a certain kind of life and to a way of behaving towards God is included in the concept of a new pact, a new alliance in the blood of Christ (Matthew 26:28; Mark 14:24; Luke 22:20; 1 Cor. 11:25). This recalls the concept of pact and alliance of the Old Testament with its strong emphasis on the consecration and the irrevocable obligation involved for man, who receives the alliance from God. The obligation was consecrated in the blood of the victim and in the sacred banquet before God (cf. Exod. 24; Deut. 29–30).[110]

The concept of the Eucharist as a sign "commemorative" of the Last Supper and of Golgotha is contained in the following texts: "The Lord . . . took bread, gave thanks, broke it and said, 'This is My body, which is for you; do this in memory of Me.' In the same way also the chalice, after He had finished supper, saying, 'This chalice is the new pact in My blood; do this every time you drink of it, in remembrance of Me.' In fact, every time you eat this bread and drink the chalice, you keep proclaiming the death of the Lord" (1 Cor. 11:23 ff.).

The reference of the Eucharist to previous sacred history is expressed in the words "This chalice is the new pact in My blood" (1 Cor. 11:25; cf. Matthew 26:28; Mark 14:24; Luke 22:20). These words allude to the old pact at the foot of Sinai in the blood of the lamb (Exod. 24:8) and to the prophecies of the future pact which God would make with the new people in the time of the Messiah (cf. Jer. 31:31; Zach. 9:11). Then there is a connection between the Eucharist and the manna in the desert: "Your fathers ate the manna in the desert and they died. This is the bread that comes down from heaven, so that he who eats of it will not die. I am the living bread that has come down from heaven . . . and the bread which I shall give is My flesh given for the life of the world" (John 6:49 ff.; cf. 6:32 ff., 59. See also 1 Cor. 10:1-4).

The eschatological meaning of the Eucharist and, therefore, the Eucharist as a sign prophetic of the future glory, is also a concept that recurs in the texts: "Every time you eat this bread and drink the chalice, you keep proclaiming the death of the Lord, until He comes" (1 Cor. 11:26). "It has been My heart's desire to eat this paschal supper with you before I suffer; for I tell you that I shall not eat it again until it is celebrated in the kingdom of God . . . for I tell you that I shall not drink again of the fruit of the vine until the kingdom of God has come" (Luke 22:15 ff.). The spiritual connection of the Last Supper celebrated by Christ with the paschal banquet of the Jews is certain; no less certain is the eschatological meaning of the Jewish paschal

---

[110] For the connection of the concepts "sacrifice—sacred banquet—alliance—obligation," see, e.g., D. Walther Eichrodt, *Theologie des AT*, I (Berlin: Evangelische verlagsanstalt, 1948), 69-70, and in the *Theol. Wört. zum NT* the words *diatheke*, II, 106 ff., and *koinonos*, III, 802, 805 f.

feast; so that the eschatological meaning of the Last Supper can be seen even from this verse.

Again, the connection of the Eucharist with the resurrection and the glory to come appears, for example, in the following texts of St. John: "He who eats My flesh and drinks My blood has life everlasting, and I will raise him up on the last day . . . not as your fathers ate the manna, and died: he who eats this bread shall live forever" (6:55, 59).

For baptism and the Eucharist the fourfold dimension of signification of the respective signs is affirmed quite clearly in the Scripture. For the other sacraments, however, the point must be deduced by reasoning from the general theology of each one.

Confirmation. Confirmation is a sign demonstrative of grace as a full outpouring of the Spirit which occurs in the believer at the moment of the liturgical rite.

It is a sign obligating for the rest of one's life as seal, character of belonging, consecration to Christ and deputation to His militia.

It is a sign commemorative of the Passion, because the full outpouring of the Spirit is the effect of the Passion of Christ, who on the Cross merited the communication of the Spirit to the faithful. It is also a sign commemorative of the communications and effusions of the Spirit of God in the Old Testament, which were rough casts and prefigurations of His full communication in the New Testament.

Confirmation is, finally, a sign prophetic of the fullness of the Spirit in the heavenly glory when this fullness will be such as to revive and transform the very bodies of the faithful to the likeness of Christ's glorified body.[111]

Penance. The very fact that a penitent, detesting his own sins, confesses them and submits them to the judicial power of the Church, makes his resolution for the future, and receives absolution from his sins, is a sign of the aforesaid fourfold signification.

It is a sign demonstrative of the reconciliation with God and with the Church by which the believer, in the rite of penance, passes once more from death to life. This new life is grace and the Holy Spirit, which God restores to the penitent, as participation in the fullness of the divine life of Christ.

---

[111] Cf. Rom. 8:11 ff. In the history of the liturgical rite of confirmation and in its present state it is easy to find the four significations. The laying-on of the hands with the epicletic invocation of the Holy Spirit shows confirmation as a sign demonstrative of the full and perfective outpouring of the Spirit. The *consignatio*, that is, the sign of the Cross on the forehead, which already in the ancient rites often accompanied the laying-on of hands (see, e.g., Righetti, IV, 91 f.) and in the modern rite has become the formula of the sacrament ("Be sealed with the Gift of the Holy Spirit"), indicates how confirmation is a sign commemorative also of the Passion of Christ, as well as an obligating sign, a sort of mark of belonging to Christ. An example of a formula which indicated explicitly the eschatological meaning of confirmation was the formula of the Gelasian Sacramentary: "The sign of Christ unto life everlasting."

The value of obligating sign in penance is unmistakably expressed in the resolution to sin no more.

Its value as sign commemorative of Christ's Passion is based on the fact that from the Passion, as from a meritorious cause, comes the possibility of reconciliation with God and with the Church, the efficacy of the Church's power to remit sins and the supernatural usefulness of the penitent's dispositions. For the penitent's detestation, confession and resolution are vital acts for obtaining reconciliation in so far as they are a participation in the dispositions with which Christ, especially in His Passion, was animated toward the sins of men.

Penance is a sign prophetic of the future glory and of the happy life because the grace reacquired in penance is the seed which naturally requires to flower in glory.[112]

The anointing of the sick. The anointing of the sick, says St. Thomas Aquinas, "is the sacrament which in some way brings to a conclusion the whole process of spiritual healing, and through which man is prepared, as it were" (he means: immediately) "to participate in glory." [113]

Through the devil's influence, not yet completely eliminated, a spiritual weakness results from original and habitual sin, even though the sins be already forgiven. The anointing of the sick is a sign demonstrative of sanctifying grace as strengthening against that weakness.[114]

It is a sign obligating to the future acts that may still remain in life, because there is no cure from sin that does not imply a resolution of this kind in the recipient.

It is a sign commemorative of Christ's Passion, which is the meritorious cause of such healing.

It is a sign prophetic of the future glory which is the one natural consequence of this healing.[115]

Holy orders. Holy orders is a sign demonstrative of grace and of the priestly character as a very special participation in the priesthood of Christ.

---

[112] In the formulas and the rites of penance, whether historical or present-day, the various significations are abundantly expressed. For example, in the present rite there is a prayer after the formula of absolution: "May the Passion of our Lord Jesus Christ, . . . heal your sins, help you to grow in holiness, and reward you with eternal life."

In the ancient public penance all this was expressed still more strikingly. See, e.g., in the Roman Pontifical the preface for the reconciliation of penitents on Holy Thursday; for the history of this formula see Righetti, IV, 195 f. See also the formula of absolution, *ibid.*, at the end of the rite: "May the Lord Jesus Christ . . . ."

[113] C. Gent., IV, 73. See also "L'onction des malades" by Bernard Botte, La maison Dieu, n. 15 (1948), 91-97.

[114] See St. Thomas, *Summa*, III, suppl., q. 30, a. 1.

[115] In the present rites of holy anointing the value of sign demonstrative of healing and of strengthening the soul is especially expressed (see, e.g., the Collectio Rituum for the United States of America, n. 10; the rite of anointing; the prayer Respice at n. 13).

It is a sign obligating the life of the priest himself to the service of Christ according to the requirements of the priestly ministry.

It is a sign commemorative of the saving acts of Christ and especially of His Passion, because it is in these acts, and principally in His Passion, that Christ exercised the priesthood in which His priestly ministers now participate, and it is in these acts that He merited the sharing with them of the priestly grace with all that it implies. Holy orders is also a sign commemorative of all the priesthoods of history before Christ, especially those of the Old Testament, which were but a rough cast of the priesthood of Christ and of the participation which He now grants in that priesthood to His ministers.

It is a sign prophetic of future glory as full fruit of the priesthood of Christ and of His ministers.[116]

Matrimony. Matrimony is a sign demonstrative of sanctifying grace as grace of union between the two partners in marriage with a view to the procreation and education of children who are to be members of the Church and citizens of the heavenly city, the whole as participation in the grace of Christ, who in the Church and through the Church begets children to God.

It is a sign obligating the future life of the partners according to the requirements of Christian marriage.

It is a sign commemorative of Christ's Passion, where He acquired the Church as spouse (Eph. 5:25 ff.) and thus acquired the right to sanctify men and to make them, by various titles, cooperators in His action of begetting divine life. It is at the same time a sign commemorative of all the marriages as grace of union before Christ because they were first rough casts of the grace of matrimonial union in Christ.

It is a sign prophetic of future glory conceived, as the Apocalypse would have it (19:7; 21:2, 9), as the perfect and definitive nuptials of the Lamb.[117]

The fourfold dimension of the liturgical signs instituted by the Church

The liturgical signs instituted by the Church may be distinguished into three groups.

The first group comprises the ceremonies or gestures, attitudes, movements, with which the Church accompanies and, so to speak, clothes the essential nucleus which is of divine institution in the celebration of the Mass and in the administration of the seven sacraments, and with which also she accompanies the recitation of the canonical hours.

[116] In the various prefaces of ordination of the present rites great emphasis is put on the concept of the grace of the priesthood through the infusion of the Spirit, the concept of sign commemorative of the priesthood, etc., of the Old Testament, and the concept of sign obligating for the rest of the life of the one ordained.

[117] The present ceremonies of the Roman Ritual for the blessing of matrimony are very sober, not to say impoverished. The Byzantine ritual, for example, is much more developed.

The second group comprises the prayers instituted by the Church: those which are said in the celebration of the Mass and in the administration of the seven sacraments, and especially those which make up the Office of the canonical hours.

The third group comprises the sacramentals, understood in the present strict sense.

It is not necessary, for the purpose we are here pursuing, to discuss the questions which might be raised by such a grouping of the liturgical signs instituted by the Church.

Although even in the liturgy instituted by the Church, worship and sanctification are realities which cannot be dissociated, still in this liturgy, including, as it seems, even the sacramentals, the aspect of worship is primary and predominates over the aspect of sanctification. It is therefore the reality of worship that these signs will signify first of all; but even in the signification of this reality the fourfold dimension of the liturgical sign will be found, in its own way: demonstrative of the present; moral and obligating for the rest of one's life; commemorative of the past; portending or prophetic of the future.

The present invisible reality of which the liturgical sign is demonstrative will be here, first of all, the interior disposition of the Church in which liturgical worship formally consists; it will be also the disposition of Christ in which His worship of God consists and of which the Church's worship is merely a participation and an instrument.

The present reality of which worship is a moral and obligating sign will be the moral life of the believer.

The past reality of which worship is a commemorative sign will be first of all the worship which Christ rendered to God on earth, chiefly in His Passion, in which He inaugurated the worship which continues today in the Church and earned for the Church the privilege of participating in that worship. Then it will be also all that worship which was rendered to God after Adam's sin and before Christ, which was simply a rough cast and foreshadowing of the worship of Christ and of the Church.

Finally, the future reality of which worship is a prophetic sign will be the perfect worship of the heavenly Jerusalem in glory.

To understand with what proper shadings this fourfold signification is found in each sign instituted by the Church, we must examine more closely the three groups of signs listed above.

Ceremonies. Every gesture, attitude, movement, in which the ceremonies consist, has the purpose of expressing, and at the same time creating, in the one who performs it and in those who see it, various interior dispositions. These interior dispositions — such as adoration, veneration, humility, compunction, prayer — formally constitute the interior worship which the

Church renders to God. Hence every gesture, attitude or movement of the ceremonies will be in its own way a sign of the fourfold dimension explained above.

A simple genuflection before the Blessed Sacrament, for example, is a sign demonstrative of the sentiment of reverence and adoration which the Church has for Jesus Christ; and in this sentiment she does not separate Christ from the Father and the Holy Spirit.[118] It is also a sign demonstrative of Christ's interior worship of God, of which the Church's worship of God is but a participation and an instrument.

The genuflection is also a sign obligating for the moral life of the one who makes it. For, if the one who makes the genuflection did not have, in a more or less explicit way, this disposition obligating for the future, but intended, for instance, to reserve for himself the freedom to sin, he certainly would not be performing an act of worship, but rather committing an offense against God. An act of worship necessarily implies a moral obligation for the future.[119]

The genuflection is also a sign commemorative of the past. First of all, being made before the Blessed Sacrament, it proclaims that the Word was made flesh, died and arose again, ascended to heaven to the right hand of the Father and is now sacramentally present in the Eucharist. It recognizes also that that disposition in which the worship of veneration and adoration expressed in the outward gesture consists, would not be possible if Christ had not merited it in His Passion. It recognizes that, in as much as that worship of veneration and adoration is directed to God, it is nothing else but the participation in the worship which Christ rendered to God in His earthly life, especially on the Cross. The genuflection is a commemorative sign also of the worship that was rendered to God before Christ, at least after Adam's sin, because that worship was nothing but a foreshadowing and a rough cast of the future worship which the Church in Christ would render to God.

Finally, the genuflection is also a sign prophetic of the future veneration and adoration which we shall render to God and to Christ in the heavenly Jerusalem, since our adoration here below is already really, though imperfectly and *sub signis*, our future adoration in heaven.

An analogous reasoning could be made about every liturgical gesture or movement, taking into account the nature and the proper object of each one of them. Thus it would hold of a simple bow before the altar or before the cross. It would hold also of the liturgical gestures of respect expressed to

---

[118] Father and Spirit also, as we know, are present in the Eucharist by mediate concomitance, as it is called technically; that is, by reason of their unity of nature with the Son, who is present in the Eucharist in virtue of His hypostatic union with humanity in Christ.

[119] The ancients, mistakenly explaining the etymology of the word "religion" from *re-*

ligare, had nevertheless grasped the idea that in every act of worship man binds himself to God. "The worship of God," says St. Thomas, "is called religion because through these acts man in some way binds himself to God so as not to stray away from Him and also because, by a certain natural instinct, he feels himself obligated toward God" (*C. Gent.*, III, 119).

persons, as, for instance, to the bishop, to the priest, to the assembly of the faithful itself; because with these gestures the Church honors, in the said persons, their invisible spiritual character; here also the "one thing is seen and another understood" holds good, and therefore it is always to God, to Christ and to His redemptive work that such gestures, as liturgical signs, are directed; they also are an act of worship.

Prayers. These prayers, in all their forms — adoration, thanksgiving, impetration, expiation — are the chief means, among the signs instituted by the Church, through which the Church, in Christ, renders her worship to God. They are the chief means in virtue of the predominance of speech as sign over the other sensible signs in the communication between God and men. These signs of prayer also have the usual fourfold dimension.

The liturgical prayers are a sign demonstrative directly of the Church's dispositions which constitute her interior prayer of adoration, thanksgiving, impetration, expiation. Hence they are signs also of the corresponding dispositions in Christ Himself, now glorious at the right hand of the Father, since the Church's prayer is nothing else than Christ's prayer to God, in which the Church associates herself, or rather, in which Christ associates the Church.

The Church's prayer is an obligating sign for the one who recites it, making it also his personal prayer, always for the same reason that no act of worship, and hence no prayer, is an act of worship if the one who performs it does not bind himself in some way for the future.

The Church's prayer is a sign commemorative of the worship by prayer which Christ rendered to the Father in His earthly life, chiefly in His Passion. By His worship, Christ inaugurated Christian prayer, of which the Church's prayer is but the continuation. The Church's prayer is also a sign commemorative of all the prayers offered to God from Adam's sin to the time of Christ, since they were nothing but a first imperfect rough cast which had its fulfillment in Christ's prayer, in which He now associates His Church.

Finally, the Church's prayer is a sign prophetic of the perfect and eternal prayer of adoration, thanksgiving and praise in the heavenly Jerusalem together with the angels, just as the seed already contains in itself and portends the perfect tree (cf. Apoc. 5:8-14).

Sacramentals. Ideas about the sacramentals are often not very clear.[120] In order to give a precise account, therefore, of the way in which the four dimensions of signification of the liturgical signs are found in the sacramentals also, it is necessary first to recall certain notions about them, among those accepted for the most part today by the theologians, and to define some other notions exactly.

---

[120] See, e.g., A. Michel, "Sacramentaux," Dict. de. théol. cath., XIV, 1, 465-82; Antonio Gaboardi, "Sacramentali," Enciclopedia cattolica, 10 (1953), 1555-58.

Notion. The tendency today is to exclude from the sacramentals the mere ceremonies which accompany the celebration of the Mass and the administration of the seven sacraments, as well as the works of piety and the whole canonical prayer of the Church. Instead, the tendency is to reserve the notion of sacramental to certain rites, instituted by the Church, which in themselves do not form part of the celebration of the Mass and of the administration of the seven sacraments, but are of a structure similar to that of the sacraments and which the Church is accustomed to use for obtaining with her impetration effects that are principally spiritual.[121]

The distinction is generally made between the sacramentals that are things and the sacramentals that are actions.

The sacramentals that are things are those which remain even after the action has taken place, such as holy water, blessed candles, blessed olive or palm branches, the ashes of Ash Wednesday.

The sacramentals that are actions are those which pass with the action itself with which they have been constituted. They are distinguished into three classes.

The first class comprises the consecrations which, by a blessing called constitutive, separate definitely from profane use and reserve to God, deputing it permanently to His service, the thing or the person to which they are applied; for example: the consecration of a church, of an altar, of a chalice; the clericature; the blessing of an abbot; the consecration of a virgin; the monastic or religious profession.

To the second class belong the simple invocatory blessings of things or persons to bring down upon them the divine protection and benefits; for example: the nuptial blessing, the blessing of children, of the sick, of all the people with the Blessed Sacrament, of fields, of tools.

The third class is formed by the exorcisms for driving away the diabolical influence from the thing or the person over which they are performed.

The sacramentals consist immediately and primarily in a prayer of impetration which the Church directs to God, and only secondarily and mediately, that is, by the mediation of this prayer, in a sanctification. The sanctifica-

---

[121] Cf. CL, art. 60; *Codex Iuris Canonici*, canon 1144; Michel and Gaboardi, the articles cited in the preceding footnote. The extension to be given to the concept of sacramental, and therefore its precise definition, has undergone several variations throughout history. Around the thirteenth century a division was made in the old concept of *sacramentum*. The aim was to achieve a better distinction between the proper characteristics of our present seven sacraments and all the other rites which had been included in the concept of *sacramentum*. These latter began to be called *sacramentalia*, that is, little *sacramenta*. At that time these sacramentalia still included not only all the accessory rites in the celebration of the seven sacraments but also the mere ceremonies in the celebration of the sacraments and of the Mass, as well as many ceremonies (and objects) used on other occasions; some prayers, like the Our Father; all the canonical prayers; some works of piety such as almsgiving, fasting, etc. It was only in more recent times, starting with Bellarmine, that there appeared among some theologians the tendency to restrict further the concept of sacramental by excluding the mere ceremonies, the works of piety and the whole canonical Office of the Church.

tion of persons or of things is what the Church asks and obtains from God through these rites.

Here the concept of sanctification obviously does not have the same meaning when applied to persons and when applied to things. Only the person, and immediately the soul, is a subject fit to receive sanctification as a formal participation in the divine life. With regard to bodies and external things we may speak of participation in the divine life, that is, sanctification, in three different kinds of cases, of which only the third is verified in the sacramentals.

In a first way we may speak of sanctification of bodies and of external things when God uses them as instruments to transmit the divine life to men. St. Thomas holds, rightly, that in Christ the body itself is the conjoint instrument, holy and sanctifying, of which the divinity makes use to transmit grace to men.[122] The sacraments also, according to St. Thomas,[123] are the separate physical instrument of Christ, by means of which the divinity transmits the divine life to men.

In a second way we may speak of sanctification of bodies and of external things when, without being destroyed in their nature, they are nevertheless profoundly perfected and elevated in their qualities by the influx of the divine life with the aim of cooperating more perfectly with the life of the spirit. This will happen perfectly and permanently in the glorious resurrection of bodies and in the transformation of the cosmos after the parousia, when there will be a new heaven and a new earth. This already happened, in some way, in paradise, before sin, by means of the preternatural gifts. This happens, even now on earth in the ascetical life of every Christian, but only tendentially and very imperfectly. This happens also, in its way, in the obedience of things to the transitory miraculous influence of God and of those to whom God sometimes grants the charism of miracles.

The third way in which the body and infrahuman things in general can receive the influx of the divine life is the way proper to the sacramentals. Here the things are not made true instrumental causes of grace, nor are they perfected or elevated in their natural qualities. Still, in consideration of the Church's impetrative prayer, they are taken under the special divine protection or acceptance for the spiritual good of whoever possesses them or uses them with the proper dispositions.

This special protection of God is shown in His protecting or freeing the things in question from the possible influence of the devil in answer to the plea which the Church makes for them in an exorcism. It is shown, again, in His protecting them, through a special providence and at least for a certain time or on a certain occasion, from natural corruption or the natural impedi-

[122] See, e.g., *Summa*, III, q. 8, a. 1 ad 1; q. 2, a. 6, arg. 4 et ad 4; q. 43, a. 2; q. 49, a. 6 ad 1. This is the common teaching of the Greek Fathers.

[123] This seems certainly to be the mind of St. Thomas, although some authors have tried to cast doubt on the matter. Cf. *Summa*, III, q. 62; A. M. Roguet, "Les sacrements," *S. Thomas d'A., La somme*, ed. rev. des jeunes, pp. 353 ff.

ments of other second causes, in order that whoever possesses them or uses them with the proper dispositions may have occasion to effect his salvation better. God does this in consideration of the Church's impetration in the rites of the action-sacramentals through simple invocatory blessings, as in the blessing of the sick, of fields, of tools.

God's special acceptance of certain things takes place in two ways.

The first way applies to such things as holy water, blessed candles, blessed ashes. The Church makes impetration for such objects in the rites which make sacramentals out of things with a simple blessing. In consideration of the Church's prayer, God agrees to give special graces on the occasions when the faithful use these things with the proper dispositions.

The second way applies to such objects as a consecrated chalice, a consecrated church, a consecrated virgin, a monk at his solemn profession. The Church makes impetration for such objects in the rites which make sacramentals out of things with constitutive blessings or consecrations. In consideration of the Church's prayer, God accepts these things, or even these persons, including their bodies, as reserved exclusively to Himself.

The acceptance of things or persons consecrated as specially reserved brings it about that whoever, culpably, would alienate them from the use to which they have been reserved, would be committing not only a sin, but a sacrilege. When the concern is with consecrated things, that same acceptance by God implies also that He will give special graces to those who use them with the proper dispositions. And, when the concern is with consecrated persons, the acceptance implies in these persons a moral title with God to obtain at the right time the graces of their state necessary to discharge the duties which that permanent consecration carries with it.

In short, a sacramental, in today's restricted sense, consists immediately in a prayer of impetration by the Church and, by means of that prayer, in a sanctification. When the concern is with the soul, this is a formal sanctification. When the concern, on the other hand, is with the body or with exterior things, it is a special protection or divine acceptance for the spiritual good of whoever possesses or uses these things with the right dispositions.

The formal sanctification of the soul implies, in the last analysis, sanctifying grace. But the general opinion is tnat in the sacramentals there are actual graces which the Church implores and obtains immediately for the person in question, such as contrition for sins, acts of faith, hope and charity, which will be dispositions favorable to the good use of the sacraments or to acts of perfect charity. And it is held that God has chosen to give sanctifying grace or its increase immediately only when the sacraments are used or an act of perfect charity is made.

It is seen also that when a sacramental (exorcism, simple blessing or consecration) has for its object a thing, that special divine protection or acceptance which the Church obtains for it by means of the rite and in which consists its sanctification, implies, basically, an initial and still imperfect, but real, reintegration of this thing to the service of the divine life. This integration had been a fact in the earthly paradise before original sin and will be achieved perfectly in the heavenly Jerusalem with the resurrection of bodies and a new heaven and a new earth.

The fourfold dimension of the sign in the sacramentals. It can be understood now in what sense the fourfold signification of the liturgical signs in general is found also in the sacramentals.

Every sacramental, involving primarily and immediately a prayer of impetration by the Church, is, like all the liturgical prayers instituted by the Church in general, first of all a sign demonstrative of this prayer. It is demonstrative also of the prayer of Christ at the right hand of the Father, that prayer of which the Church's is but a participation.

Then it is an obligating sign for the one who recites or receives this prayer as his own.

It is a sign commemorative of Christ's impetrations in His earthly life, chiefly in His Passion, as well as of the impetrations directed to God after Adam's sin and before Christ, which foreshadowed Christ's impetrations and those of the Church. Finally, it is a sign prophetic of the prayer of the heavenly Jerusalem when the impetration will be changed into the cosmic and eternal praise, the perfect goal to which it tends.

Every sacramental, involving secondarily a sanctification in the manner explained above, will also be a sign demonstrative of this sanctification.

When the concern is with the sacramentals which have for immediate object the sanctification of the soul, to be obtained by the Church's impetration, they will be immediately signs demonstrative of the actual graces which the Church seeks in the rite and which dispose the believer to habitual grace or its increase. By means of these actual graces, those sacramentals will be signs demonstrative also of the habitual grace.

When the concern, on the other hand, is with sacramentals which seek immediately the special protection or acceptance of God over the body or over exterior things, they will be signs demonstrative of this protection and acceptance with everything that they imply as the case may be: protection or liberation from the possible influence of the devil, in the exorcisms; protection from natural corruption or natural impediments, in the sacramentals which are actions; graces to be granted in the use with the proper dispositions of the sacramentals which are things constituted by simple blessing; special deputation and reservation for the divine use of the persons and things in the consecratory sacramentals.

All the sacramentals which have for immediate object the body and external things are, moreover, signs demonstrative of the initial but real reintegration of material things to the service of the divine life.

Every sacramental, even if it be only the simple blessing of a house or of a tool, or a mere sign of the Cross, in as much as it involves a sanctification, is, for the one who asks for it or makes use of it with the proper moral dispositions, a sign professing these dispositions and obligating for the rest of his life. Obviously, this holds in a special way for the persons who receive the consecratory sacramentals such as the consecration of a virgin, the clericature, the religious profession.

All the sacramentals, in as much as they involve a sanctification, are also signs commemorative of Christ's Passion as meritorious cause of this sanctification. They are commemorative also of the sanctifications which took place before Christ and after Adam's sin, in as much as these were foreshadowings and first sketches of the sanctifications which now take place in the Church in Christ.

Finally, the sacramentals, in as much as they involve a sanctification, are also signs prophetic of the future glory, where there will be perfect sanctification and perfect reintegration of the cosmos to the service of the divine life, of which the sanctifications and the reintegrations which are taking place now in the sacramentals are but shadows and imperfect rough casts.

Feasts and liturgical cycles. If the sacrifice of the Mass, the seven sacraments, the sacramentals, the ceremonies and prayers of the Church are all liturgical signs of the fourfold dimension explained above, the same must be said of the liturgical feasts and the liturgical cycles. For a feast is really a compound of sacrifice, sacraments, sacramentals, ceremonies and prayers of the Church; while a liturgical cycle is a grouping of feasts or, at any rate, of liturgical days, under an idea that applies to them all.

This means that the key to the understanding of these feasts and these cycles will have to be the understanding of their special object and its consideration under the fourfold dimension proper to every liturgical sign.

To explain just how this occurs is an object of that part of the theology of the liturgy which treats of the liturgical year.

For example, the object of the liturgical cycle of Advent-Epiphany is the mystery of Christ as the manifested coming of the Lord. This manifested coming will be considered according to the aforesaid four dimensions. As demonstrative sign this liturgical cycle will indicate the Lord's manifested coming as presently realized in every Mass and in every soul. As commemorative sign it will indicate the same manifested coming realized historically at one time in Palestine and prepared for, desired, announced, prefigured, etc., still earlier in the Old Testament. As obligating sign the Advent-Epiphany cycle will indicate the requirements of moral living which the Lord's coming imposes on the faithful as preparation for being made worthy of it and as consequence for having received it. As sign prophetic of the future this cycle will speak of the same coming, which will be perfectly and definitively fulfilled in the parousia.

A similar reasoning must be gone through for the Septuagesima-Pentecost cycle, whose object is the mystery of Christ as redemption. The concern will be with the redemption made necessary, announced, prefigured, prepared for in the Old Testament and realized historically in Christ Himself in Palestine, especially in the mysteries of His Passion, death, resurrection and ascension. The concern will be also with the redemption being realized every year by men: by means of the Mass and the sacraments for the catechumens admitted to the Christian initiation; in reconciliation for the penitents; for the ordinary faithful, in the increase of their life through participation in the paschal mysteries every year. The moral aspect will be emphasized as preparation for the worthy reception of this redemption and as requirements following upon the same. The eschatological aspect (to tell the truth, less effectively developed in this cycle of the Roman liturgy than it is in the Advent-Epiphany cycle) will be the consideration of the full redemption which will take place with the parousia, the resurrection of bodies and the beatific vision.

* * *

In concluding this chapter, it is easy to notice how the liturgy, thanks to its structuration in a regime of signs, is like an extraordinary mirror. In this mirror are reflected and gathered as real and present all the relations between God and man, rather between God and the world in general, which constitute sacred history, mystery of Christ, mystery of the Church, in its past, future, and present reality: as God's descent in Christ among men, always going on, and men's ascent to God in Christ, always going on.

It is not by any idle play of the imagination, then, that we can state that the liturgy has cosmic perspectives and dimensions, as does sacred history, mystery of Christ, mystery of the Church. For under the veil of signs, *in sacramentis, in mysteriis*, the liturgy does concentrate in itself the whole meaning of sacred history.

Every liturgical assembly in particular, by the very fact of being an assembly "in My name," in which "one thing is seen and another understood," proclaims to the eyes of faith the *ekklesia* in act, the assembling, of men, effected by God the Father in Christ Jesus (cf. 1 Thess. 1:1; 2 Thess. 1:1; Deut. 4:9-13; 9:10; 18:15-18; Heb. 12:18 ff.), the ever actual and vivifying presence of Christ among men, the unity of the faithful with the Father through Christ in the presence of the Spirit and the unity of the faithful among themselves in one body in Christ.

Every liturgical assembly proclaims also the pact and the obligation of the Church to follow God in Christ, to walk in Christ's footsteps, something which involves the whole extraliturgical Christian life.

It proclaims in the third place the intervention of God in history, the unity of this sacred history directed by Him, the full and substantial manifestation of God in Christ, "in the last times," Christ's death and resurrection, His sitting gloriously at the right hand of the Father.

And finally, it proclaims, announces, hopes for, calls for, His glorious return as Judge and the future glory of the blessed city when God will be all in all.

All this is perceptible only to the eyes of faith. Here neither a purely philosophical or ethical view of the world nor a mere retreat of psychological introspection will suffice, but the "mind of Christ," the *sensus Christi*, is required. In fact, I do not think a Christian mind in general will be enough. We need to have been dazzled by that reality which is the mystery of Christ as St. Paul explains it, precisely because the concern here is with the process, always going on, of making real, under the veil of signs, the mystery of Christ, of history and of the Church. The concern here is with the wisdom of which St. Paul spoke "among the mature . . . wisdom of God in mystery (*in mysterio*), hidden wisdom, which God preordained before all ages for our glory, and which none of the rulers of this world has known. . . . To us, however, He revealed it through the Spirit . . . we have not received the spirit of the world, but the Spirit which is from God, that we may know the things that have been given us by God. . . . But the natural man does not grasp the things of the Spirit of God; for they are folly to him, and he cannot understand them because they are judged according to the teachings of the Spirit . . . we have the mind of Christ" (1 Cor. 2:6 ff.).

We cannot repeat too often that, outside of this perspective, the liturgy cannot be understood, and still less can it be effectively lived, in all its fullness. Conversely, there is no means more efficacious than the liturgy for understanding and especially for living this perspective, which is the very substance of the biblical doctrine, and the Pauline doctrine in particular, of the mystery of Christ.

In particular, outside of this perspective it is impossible to grasp the true import of the liturgical texts. It will be seen in another chapter how the meaning which the biblical texts take when they are used in the liturgy depends wholly on the fourfold dimension of the liturgical sign. And the same thing holds, essentially, also of the liturgical texts composed by the Church. Not in the sense that the entire scheme of the four dimensions explained above will be found explicitly in every individual text; but in the sense that that scheme is always presupposed as the common background against which every action and every thought of the liturgy moves, and then in the sense that every liturgical text expresses also, explicitly and in a more or less direct manner, one or more aspects of that fourfold dimension. Here are a few examples taken at random from the missal.

The collect of the Mass of Christmas *in Vigilia* is the following:

> You gladden us, O Lord, with the annual expectation of our redemption. Joyfully do we welcome Your only-begotten Son as

> Redeemer. Grant that we may welcome Him also with a tranquil
> conscience when He comes as Judge. Through our Lord Jesus Christ,
> Your Son, who lives and reigns with You . . . .

In this collect the vigil of our Lord's Nativity is considered as a sign
in which is expressed our worshipful disposition of expecting the increase
of the redemption in ourselves, and as a sign of that coming of Christ
into us as Redeemer which is realized in this liturgical celebration and in
that of the morrow, chiefly in the Mass itself.

The tranquil conscience which is implored of God for the judgment to
come, makes allusion to the function of obligating sign with regard to the
corresponding moral life which this Mass *in Vigilia* has for those who take
part in it. The moral life consists of the good works into which we are
obliged to translate our participation in the liturgical action, good works
which alone will be able to give us the tranquil conscience for the future
judgment and which therefore we ask God to grant us the grace to perform.

The concept of the annual expectation of our redemption alludes also to
the value of the present liturgical feast as a sign commemorative of the
historical coming of Christ on earth.

The thought of the future coming of Christ as Judge expresses the meaning of the feast as a sign prophetic of the parousia and of the future glory.

The postcommunion of the midnight Mass of Christmas was formerly as
follows:

> It is our joy, O Lord our God, to celebrate in mysteries the birth of
> our Lord Jesus Christ. Grant, we pray You, that by living worthily we
> may become fit to be His companions.

Here the liturgical celebration of the birth of our Lord is considered as a
sign ("in mysteries") of our interior celebration of joy and of grace ("It is
our joy to celebrate in mysteries the birth of our Lord"). The worthy life
alludes to the obligating function of the sign. Its commemorative function is
included in the concept of the celebration of the historical birth of our Lord.
Its prophetic value is included in the concept of the future fellowship in glory
with Christ, to which we shall attain by means of a holy life with the help of
grace.

The collect of the dawn Mass of Christmas says:

> We have been flooded, O God all powerful, by the new light of Your
> incarnate Word. Grant, we pray You, that the light which shines by
> faith in our mind may sparkle in our deeds.

The new light of the incarnate Word which floods us is the reality of the
grace of which the liturgical celebration is a demonstrative sign. The translation of this reality into deeds is indicated by the same celebration as an
obligating sign.

Characteristic also, from the point of view with which we are concerned, is the postcommunion of the daytime Mass of Christmas:

> Grant, we pray You, God all merciful, that as the Savior of the world, born today, is the author of our divine regeneration, so also He may be the donor of immortality.

"The Savior born today, author of our regeneration" indicates in the liturgical celebration the sign demonstrative of the grace granted to us in this celebration: today in the Mass, regeneration is born anew in us and fulfilled anew in us. It indicates also the sign commemorative of the historical occurrence of the birth of Jesus: "born today, as author of our regeneration" must be understood also in the sense of "born on that day whose anniversary we commemorate today." The hope that the same Savior will be for us also some day the giver of immortality expresses the value of the same celebration as prophetic sign.

In the collect of the Mass of the Paschal Vigil are expressed the demonstrative, commemorative and obligating aspects of the liturgical celebration of the resurrection, without explicit allusion to the prophetic aspect of future glory:

> O God, You have brightened this most holy night with the glory of the Lord's resurrection (*commemorative and also demonstrative aspect*). Arouse (*obligating aspect*) in Your Church the spirit of adoption (*allusion to the newly baptized: demonstrative aspect*). Renewed in body and in spirit (*demonstrative aspect*), may they offer You an immaculate service (*obligating aspect*).

All four aspects, on the other hand, are perfectly expressed in the epistle of the same Mass: "All of us who have been baptized into Christ Jesus were baptized into His death. We were buried therefore with Him by baptism into death, so that as Christ was raised from the dead by the glory of the Father, we too might walk in newness of life. For if we have been united with Him in a death like His, we shall certainly be united with Him in a resurrection like His. We know that our old self was crucified with Him so that the sinful body might be destroyed, and we might no longer be enslaved to sin. For he who has died is freed from sin. But if we have died with Christ, we believe that we shall also live with Him. For we know that Christ being raised from the dead will never die again; death no longer has dominion over Him. The death He died He died to sin, once for all, but the life He lives He lives to God. So you also must consider yourselves dead to sin and alive to God in Christ Jesus" (Rom. 6:3-11).

I do not think it necessary to dwell on this point, it is so obvious if one merely reads the texts with a little attention. It is true, therefore, that the liturgy, in virtue of the import of the signs, is like an extraordinary mirror in which is reflected and concentrated the mystery of Christ, of the Church, of history, in its present, past and future.

It is reflected and concentrated; but not in a solely and purely psycho-logico-intentional manner, by way of knowledge, recollection and affection; rather in a much more profound and real way. The signs of the liturgy are, in their own way, efficacious signs.

3   THE LITURGY AS A COMPLEXUS

OF EFFICACIOUS SENSIBLE SIGNS

In the definition of the liturgy we speak of *efficacious* signs of the Church's sanctification and of her worship. Now we must explain the general meaning of this efficacy and describe the particular ways in which it operates, both in the liturgy instituted by God Himself and in that instituted by the Church.

1. What Does It Mean to Say in General that the Signs in the Liturgy Effect the Church's Sanctification and Her Worship?

The sign, formally, as a sign, cannot have an efficient causality. Its proper causality is in the order of representation: the sign, as a sign, only brings about knowledge. The causality in question, therefore, is one of exemplarity, what the scholastic philosophers call an extrinsic formal cause.

Nevertheless, the theologians rightly say that the seven sacraments not only signify grace, but also cause the grace that they signify; that in the sacraments, in fact, there is a close connection between signifying grace and causing grace: *significando causant.*

It is in the same sense — allowing for the difference between sacraments and sacramentals — that it is stated in the definition of the liturgy that the signs in the liturgy are efficacious of the Church's sanctification. What precisely is this sense?

When we say that the sign in the liturgy effects the sanctification which it

96

signifies, we mean that God, as principal efficient cause, has freely decided to produce such sanctification every time the conditions He lays down are fulfilled. We mean that He produces this sanctification in reference to the placing of the sign and to its meaning and, as it were, in dependence on the placing of the sign and on its meaning. (The further determinations of this dependence are a subject of discussion among the theologians.)

But can it be said that the signs in the liturgy are efficacious also of the Church's worship which they signify?

Certainly the efficacy of the liturgical sign with regard to the Church's worship must be understood in a sense somewhat different from the efficacy which the sign has with regard to the sanctification of the Church.[1] That is why we said above[2] that every liturgical sign is efficacious *in its own way* of the Church's sanctification and of her worship.

Granted this, the fact remains that the liturgical sign is efficacious not only of the Church's sanctification but also of her worship which it signifies. In what sense?

Substantially, in the precise sense that the Mystical Body (Head and members), at every due placing of the liturgical sign, actuates or produces, in the manner signified by the sign itself and in dependence on it, an act of worship of God, because the Mystical Body has freely decided to do so whenever the sign is so placed. The better to explain this statement, let us distinguish the sacrifice in its essence from the other liturgical signs.

As far as the consecration of the Mass is concerned, to say that the liturgical sign effects the worship it signifies means two things:

1. When the sign (matter and form of the sacrifice) is placed and the conditions are fulfilled, God has decided to bring about, each time, the transubstantiation by which Christ is made present in the act of perpetuating, in an unbloody and mysterious but real way, His own sacrifice which He offered in a bloody way on Golgotha, and therefore in the act of rendering, as Head of the Church, His supreme worship to God. And since, by His own free decision, it is in infallible connection with the placing of the sign and with its meaning, and in dependence on them, that Christ the Head here exercises His worship every time in the aforesaid way, it is rightly said that in the Mass the liturgical sign not only signifies but also produces worship.

2. The Church has decided that every time an authorized minister places this sign under the required conditions, she intends to affirm, precisely in connection with the sign and in dependence on it and on its meaning, her will to offer the divine Victim in supreme worship to God, to adore that Victim

---

[1] To draw attention to this fact in some way, the Second Vatican Council, CL, art. 7, uses different expressions to indicate the efficacy of the liturgical signs with respect to sanctification and with respect to worship. Through the liturgical sign, it says, the sanctification of man is effected (*efficitur*) and worship is performed (*exercetur*).

[2] Pp. 25 f.

and to offer herself together with Him. And God Himself in the placing of
the sign sees and accepts all this. Thus the essential sign of the Mass not only
signifies but also causes the Church's worship.

A similar line of reasoning is to be followed with regard to the other liturgical signs which in some way signify the Church's worship. To say that they
also effect the worship which they signify means that the Church (Mystical
Body, Head and members) has freely decided to intend, affirm and renew, at
every placing of the sign under the required conditions and in dependence
on the sign and on its meaning, her will to offer her worship to God in the
manner signified by the sign. And God so understands the signs and accepts
them. Thus it is always proper to say that the placing of the sign actuates the
Church's worship each time.

With regard to the kind of efficacy and the degree of efficacy proper to the
liturgical signs, the Second Vatican Council, in a sentence following immediately its proposed concept of liturgy, expresses itself thus: "From this it
follows that every liturgical celebration, because it is an action of Christ the
priest and of His body which is the Church, is a sacred action surpassing all
others; no other action of the Church can equal its efficacy by the same title
and to the same degree."[3]

This sentence is certainly concise; in fact, so concise that it leaves something to be desired in clarity. Somewhat helpful for a better understanding
of it is this passage a little further on in the same conciliar document: "From
the liturgy, therefore, and especially from the Eucharist, as from a fount, grace
is poured forth upon us; and the sanctification of men in Christ and the glorification of God, to which all other activities of the Church are directed as
towards their end, is achieved in the most efficacious possible way."[4]

For further clarity, however, we must turn to the official explanation of
the language of article 7 given by the relator. He says that the efficacy of the
sacrifice of the Mass and of the sacraments is *ex opere operato*, while the efficacy of the Church's public prayer and of the sacramentals is *ex opere operantis
Ecclesiae*. And he observes that this efficacy is described in the documents of
the *magisterium* as being of the highest order, and is distinguished from the
effect of other actions, whether of the Church herself or of her members, on
just this ground, the objective efficacy of the actions, aside from their subjective merit, which is another way of looking at the same actions.

The distinction between *opus operatum* and *opus operantis Ecclesiae*, which
does not enter into the text itself of the constitution,[5] goes back evidently to
Mediator Dei, the first official document to codify it. The text in the encyclical
is as follows:

[3] CL, art. 7.
[4] *Ibid.*, art. 10.
[5] To understand how this came about, see
Cyprian Vagaggini's "Lo spirito della Costitu-

zione sulla liturgia," *Riv. lit.*, 51 (1964), 46-
47. On this point, unfortunately, the constitution takes a step backward in comparison with
Mediator Dei.

"The worship rendered to God by the Church in union with her divine Head is the most efficacious means of achieving sanctity. This efficacy, where there is question of the Eucharistic sacrifice and the sacraments, derives first of all and principally from the act itself (*ex opere operato*).

"But if one considers the part which the immaculate Spouse of Jesus Christ takes in the action, embellishing the sacrifice and sacraments with prayer and sacred ceremonies, or if one refers to the 'sacramentals' and the other rites instituted by the hierarchy of the Church, then its effectiveness is due rather to the action of the Church (*ex opere operantis Ecclesiae*), in as much as she is holy and acts always in closest union with her Head."[6]

We see, therefore, that the liturgical signs, with respect to their efficacy, are distinguished into signs instituted by God — the substance of the Mass and of the sacraments — whose efficacy is above all and before all *ex opere operato*, and signs instituted by the Church — ceremonies, prayers and sacramentals — whose efficacy is primarily *ex opere operantis Ecclesiae*. Let us explain both kinds of efficacy.

2. The Efficacy of the Liturgical Signs Instituted by God

Obviously we do not intend to explain the classical Catholic doctrine of the *opus operatum* here in this book as it should be explained in a general theological treatise on the sacraments. For our purpose it will be enough to recall briefly its general meaning and, in particular, to bring out some of the major consequences of liturgical interest.

The *opus operatum* and some characteristics of the liturgy

The efficacy of the liturgical signs instituted by God does not proceed from the *opus operatum* exclusively, but does proceed from it primarily and above all. As we know, it is a doctrine of the Catholic faith that the seven sacraments confer *ex opere operato* the grace which they signify, supposing the proper faculties, intentions and actions on the part of the minister, and provided the subject who is to receive the sacraments does not freely place any impediment of intention or any impediment of a moral order in their way.[7]

When we say that the sacraments confer grace we mean, of course, that God confers it as principal cause, but that He confers it in connection with the sacramental rite and in consideration of the sacramental rite. The Council of Trent says: "by means of these sacraments."[8] The same council defines explicitly for baptism that the "by means of" signifies the instrumental cause.[9] There is no reason for doubting that the council considered all the other sacra-

---

[6] Nn. 26-27.
[7] Defined explicitly by the Council of Trent against the denials of the Protestants. See Dz 1606-08 (849-51).

[8] Dz 1607 (850).
[9] *Ibid.*, 1529 (799).

ments also as instrumental causes which God uses to confer grace. Hence this is the doctrine accepted today by all theologians.

We know, on the other hand, that there is still a diversity of opinion today as to the precise way in which the instrumental causality of the sacraments is to be understood with regard to the grace they confer.

Some speak of physical instrumentality, meaning that the sacramental rite has a real and direct influence, though only as God's instrument, on the grace which is conferred through it by God.

Others have recourse to the concept of a moral instrumentality, meaning that God's will, the only true efficient cause, allows itself, so to speak, to be moved psychologically through the sacramental rite to confer the sacramental grace, and that in this conferral of grace the sacramental rite is only a moral instrumental cause which moves God.

A third group, finally, have recourse to the concept of intentional instrumentality. They say that the sacrament is God's instrument in as much as it is a mere sign which signifies God's will to give the sacramental grace; hence it is a sign such that, by divine disposition, it entitles the person who receives the sacrament to an infusion of grace by God, on the supposition, of course, that there are no impediments.

The sacraments do confer grace, then. When we add that they confer grace *ex opere operato*, we mean that the sacramental rites as instruments of God produce this effect simply by the fact that the sacramental sign has been validly placed (this is what *opus operatum* means), and not by the moral merits either of the minister or of the one who receives the sacrament.

On the part of the minister the only requirement is that he have faculties and that he freely lend his instrumental work to Christ and to the Church, agreeing to do what the Church wants done in this rite.

For the recipient it is required only that he be a proper subject to receive the sacrament validly and that he do not willingly put any impediment in the way of the action by which God will give him grace.

But these dispositions, in the minister and, according to the common explanation, in the recipient also, are simply conditions required that the grace of the sacrament be infallibly granted. In speaking of the dispositions, we have not yet come to the causes of this grace. These are known facts; there is no need to insist on them.

There *is* need, however, to bring out explicitly right now certain characteristics which the liturgy and the liturgical life of the Christian receive from the *opus operatum*, although the concepts in question will have to be specified exactly later on.

The seven sacraments, with the Eucharist a sacrifice and a sacrament at the same time, are the central nucleus of the liturgy. Hence it is clear that, in virtue of the *opus operatum*, there is a strong emphasis on the fact that something is given objectively and received objectively when the mystery of Christ, of the Church and of history is realized in souls in the liturgical action.

We do not mean, be it understood, that this actualization can be achieved, and we especially do not mean that it can be fully achieved, in individual souls without their cooperation, their involvement, their moral tuning-in. We do mean that this actualization, supposing the prerequisite moral tuning-in and even when achieved in the interior of individual souls, transcends immeasurably, in its quality and its intensity, the purely psychological subjective and experimentable plane of these individual souls. It is not measured simply by the extent to which they are tuned in or by their moral merits, still less by the moral merits of the minister.

As has already been observed, the *opus operatum* has nothing to do with magic. Still, it cannot be denied that the *opus operatum*, and, still more, the usual way of explaining the need for the moral tuning-in of the subject to the *opus operatum* only as a condition prerequisite to the conferral of grace on God's part,[10] shows the Catholic liturgy as immeasurably superior to the mere moralism and psychologism of the Protestants, which never gives the liturgical rite any value beyond that of an exhortation and a sermon.

If in the Catholic liturgy the believer, even without ever feeling himself dispensed from moral obligation and moral tuning-in of his life, knows that his encounter with God takes place on a rock much more solid than the shifting, treacherous sands of his own subjectivism and his own puny moral forces, this is due above all to the *opus operatum*.

Hence we begin to see — and later on we shall have to go into it in more detail — in what way the liturgy achieves the balance of the binomial subject-object, man-God. For this will follow from the *opus operatum*: not only that it will not be for the subject to determine the object, or for man to determine God, but that these two quantities cannot be conceived, either, as two parallel data, placed next to each other or simply coordinate, but must be considered in a relationship of subordination: it is up to the subject to accept the object, to vibrate in unison with it; it is up to man to accept God and His gift.

In the liturgical realization, it is God who actualizes in souls the mystery of Christ, mystery of the Church, of history: He gives the mystery to man, shares it with him, draws him to it. Man's salvation lies first of all in not obstructing God's work, then in responding to His action, tuning himself in to the object which God objectively presents to him: the mystery of Christ; letting himself be dominated by its majesty, letting himself be attracted by it.

Man, of course, may never reduce himself to an attitude of heterodox quiet-

---

[10] I do not deny the need, to be sure, for probing more deeply than is done in the common explanation, into the relationship between the sacramental rite and the faith of the recipient with respect to the grace which God confers in the sacrament. But, in any hypothesis, the *opus operatum* must remain intact, and, with it, the transcendence of the liturgy over psychologism or mere moralism.

ism. This fact always bears repetition and rephrasing. But it cannot be denied that in the liturgy, especially in that of the sacraments, precisely because of the *opus operatum*, there is a real and psychological triumph on the first level of the majesty of the object, the mystery of Christ realized by God and not by human power, under the veil of the signs; and a triumph of the majesty of God, who works all in all.

Hence in the liturgy the encounter between man and God will not be organized by a procedure in which introversion and psychological analysis predominate. For man's concern in the liturgy is not so much to concentrate on himself in order to analyze himself and discover the psychological reactions of his own ego confronted with the mystery of Christ. Rather, it is much more to watch and to listen outside of himself, to get out of himself, so to speak, and immerse himself in the present object in order to forget himself in it, if possible.

The liturgy, like every way of going to God, requires interiority, much interiority. The ideal, to which it tends and for which it sets out, is an interiority so dominated by the object — God and the mystery of Christ realized under the veil of the signs — that it tends to be unaware of itself, so strong is the stamp of the *opus operatum* in the structure of the liturgy.

The *opus operatum* gives a stamp of objectivism, of God-centeredness, therefore of realism, to the liturgy. The liturgical signs of the sacraments are efficacious not only because they really actualize in the believer the knowledge, the remembrance, the love and the desire of the mystery of Christ, of history and of the Church on all its levels. They are efficacious because in the actualization of this mystery, as instruments of God they reach and transform the interior of souls at a point much more radical and profound than the mere level of psychology, and for that very reason of a different order. While this different order is strictly spiritual, the theologians call it physical, to distinguish it precisely from the psychological spiritual order; and it might be called transphysical or hyperphysical, to avoid any possibility of misunderstanding "physical" in a gross material sense.

Finally, the *opus operatum* offers a grand view onto that other essential character of the liturgy — which is also to be further analyzed and described later on — that it is primarily an action not of the Church, her ministers or her faithful, but of Christ; that the Church, her ministers and her faithful are object and instrument of Christ's action in the liturgy and that they cannot actively perform the liturgy except in so far as they associate themselves actively with Christ's action and take part in it. The *opus operatum* demonstrates in the highest degree how the minister and the believer are nothing in the liturgy without Christ, and, on the other hand, how great they are before the Father when, by keeping closely united to Christ, they receive His influx, share in His being and His activity.

The *opus operatum* and the real presentness of the spiritual realities signified by the sacramental sign, especially in its commemorative dimension

In virtue of the realism introduced by the *opus operatum*, it is relatively easy to understand in what sense the liturgical sign in the seven sacraments really involves the actualization of those spiritual realities which it signifies as a demonstrative, obligating and prophetic sign and also as a commemorative sign with respect to sacred history before Christ. On the other hand, special difficulties arise in connection with the question as to how the sacramental liturgical sign actualizes Christ's historical redemptive actions in His mortal life.

The presentness of the spiritual realities signified by the sacramental sign. In the case of the sacraments, the sign refers immediately to sanctification and only mediately to worship. We have said above that when we are concerned with a sign of this kind, the liturgical sign as demonstrative signifies immediately sanctifying grace, and mediately the other realities, namely: the worshipful dispositions; God present and operating as principal cause of the sanctification and ultimate object of the worship; Christ even in His humanity as instrumental cause of the sanctification and principal cause and also object of the worship; the Church as object of the sanctification and instrumental cause of the worship which Christ renders to God.

Now in the liturgical signs of the seven sacraments, the valid and fruitful placing of the sign makes these realities present, each in its own way but in a very effective way; it actualizes them presentially, as it were; and this in virtue of the *opus operatum*. For it is by the placing of the sign that sanctifying grace is produced by the divinity and applied through the humanity of Christ as conjoint instrument, in the invisible interior of souls in as much as they are members of the Church, Christ's mystical body. At the same time, the valid and fruitful placing of the sacramental sign involves as realities presentially actualized, the spiritual dispositions of the one who receives the sacrament. These dispositions formally constitute the worship which he renders to God through Jesus Christ, Head of the Church, His mystical body.

It is easy to understand also how the valid and fruitful placing of the sacramental sign involves, as a reality made present and actual, that invisible spiritual reality which is signified by the sacramental sign as an obligating sign. That reality is nothing else than the spiritual disposition of the one who receives the sacrament, which obligates him for the future. In fact, without this disposition there is no fruitful placing of the sign.

The invisible spiritual realities signified by the liturgical sign in the seven sacraments as prophetic sign are the glory and the perfect worship of the heavenly Jerusalem. In virtue of the *opus operatum* these realities, in their own way, are actualized as already present here and now, in the same way that the acorn renders the oak already really present — really, that is, in seed — and in the way that the rough cast makes the future statue really present, though inchoatively.

Quite similar to this last way, but reversing the order of the terms, so to speak, is the efficacy of the sacramental sign in making present those spiritual realities of sanctification and of worship which took place in sacred history after Adam's sin and before Christ, especially the sanctification and the worship of the Old Testament liturgy. In virtue of the *opus operatum* these realities, to which the sacrament refers as commemorative sign, are actualized by the sacramental sign as the statue actualizes and makes present the rough cast which it realizes and from which it was prepared.

As we have seen, in virtue of the *opus operatum* the efficacy of the liturgical sign in the seven sacraments and its power to make really present the spiritual realities signified must not be limited to grace alone, but must be extended, in its own way, to all the aforesaid realities according to the various kinds of signification. In this there is no special difficulty.

The presential actualization in the sacramental sign of the historical redemptive actions of Christ's mortal life. Greater difficulty is presented by the question of the exact sense in which we can say that the sacramental sign, as a commemorative sign efficacious *ex opere operato*, actualizes and makes really present in the liturgical actions the saving works which Christ performed in His earthly life, and above all His Passion and death. How should we understand precisely and with respect to all the sacraments the words "the memory of His Passion is recalled" of the antiphon "O sacred banquet"?

In 1922 the Rev. Odo Casel began a controversy among the theologians on this matter which is still going on. For the sake of information, here are the points which I consider essential in his personal theory on the "mystery," in that which is peculiar to his theory with regard to the concept of mystery explained above.[11]

According to Casel, there is rendered objectively present in the sacramental act of worship not only the *effect* of Christ's historical redemptive actions and especially of the Passion; in other words, there is made objectively present not only grace; but also the past redemptive action itself, in particular the Passion on Golgotha, not indeed in all the least circumstances of persons and

---

[11] Cf. above, pp. 13-18 and 29-32. For Casel's theory see: *Jahrb. für Liturgiewis.*, 6 (1926), 113-204; 8 (1928), 145-224; *Das christliche Kultmysterium* (Regensburg: Pustet, 1935); Theodor Filthaut, *Die Kontroverse über die Mysterienlehre* (Warendorf: Schnell, 1947).   See also the studies *Vom christlichen Mysterium* edited by Anton Mayer (Düsseldorf: Patmos, 1951); Louis Bouyer, *La vie de la liturgie* (Paris: Cerf, 1956), pp. 115-31, 220-29; Polycarp Wegenaer, *Heilsgegenwart* (Münster i. W.: Aschendorff, 1958).

environment, but, as he says, in what was essential in that action, in its substance.

Thus, according to Casel, in the rite which in the liturgy is performed in space and in time, Christ's historical redemptive actions on earth and especially the Passion are "commemorated" in the sense of being rendered objectively present, re-presented, and, be it noted, numerically the same, although — and this also must be carefully noted in Casel's position — in a way of their own completely unique.

This way of their own, according to Casel, transcends space and time, while the liturgical rite itself is performed in space and in time; and he calls it a "mysterious" way, a "mystery." Thus he gives the traditional expression "mystery" in connection with the liturgy this specific meaning of a rite of worship which, under the veil of the signs and in a manner transcending space and time, would render objectively present even Christ's past historical redemptive action itself, in its numerical individuality, above all the Passion. This is properly a new meaning for "mystery," although Casel thought he could demonstrate this meaning in the use which the Fathers made of "mystery" in connection with the liturgy and in the very usage of the liturgical texts.

In the Eucharist particularly, for Casel, there is made present in the aforesaid manner not only Christ who suffered on Golgotha and is now glorious at the Father's right hand, but also the past historical action itself of the Passion, and in this precise sense not only Christ who suffered but Christ's suffering itself.

Casel not only tried to base these explanations of his on the texts of the Fathers and of the liturgy. He believed also that the concept of Christian mystery in worship, in the exact sense in which he understood it, had been historically speaking the Christian response, true and transcendental, to those general religious aspirations of mankind which were manifested in ancient times in the aberrations of the pagan mystery cults.

In these pagan ritual mysteries, thought Casel, under the symbol of the rite of worship, representing the historical vicissitudes of a divinity supposed to be a savior, above all his death and resurrection (e.g., Mithras, Isis and Osiris), the initiate was persuaded to relive in himself, by way of worship and through a mysterious assimilation, those same vicissitudes of the god, above all his death and resurrection, and thus to obtain *soteria*, salvation.

It is not my intention to enter into the particulars of the controversy aroused by this theory and into the attempts at correction and adaptation made by some theologians. A few observations will suffice for our purpose.

First of all, the historical inquiries occasioned by Casel's theory have established definitively, it may now be said, three points of capital importance, on which there tends to be unanimous agreement among scholars.

The first point is that Casel's theory of numerical re-presentation cannot

identify itself with the concept of *mystérion* in the New Testament and specifically in St. Paul. We have already spoken in our first chapter of the *mystérion*
in St. Paul, and we have seen that the concept connected with this expression
is not explicitly extended by St. Paul himself to worship but is predicated
simply of sacred history in general. So much the less can the idea of numerical
re-presentation be found in St. Paul.

The second point is that Casel, under the influence of Reitzenstein, has
exaggerated the true significance of the pagan mystery cults. He has not
brought out sufficiently their foundation in nature as mere symbolism of the
cycle of vegetation in its successive stages. This symbolism is far removed
indeed, especially in the most ancient times, from the idea of an historical, or
supposedly historical, personage who is a redeemer by means of his death and
resurrection.

Moreover, Casel is quite inaccurate in his conception of the relations of
Christian tradition, especially the most ancient, before the fourth century,
with the pagan ritual mysteries it confronted. As a matter of fact, the pagan
mystery cults had no influence on the historical makeup of the essence of
Christian worship.

Patristic theology does see Christian worship against the background of the
concepts of *mystérion, mysterium, sacramentum*. But this explanation of worship is developed essentially out of the concept and the scriptural reality of
sacred history. It sees the facts, texts and persons of the Old Testament as
allegories and types. If there is any contact with paganism, it is with the general mentality of Platonic tradition, which saw primarily in the realities of
this world images and symbols of the ultramundane world.[12]

The third point on which there is now ever-increasing agreement is this:
The concept of mystery in worship, understood of Christian worship in the
sense of numerical re-presentation which Casel gives it, is unknown either
to the Fathers or to the liturgies.[13]

When these speak of *mystérion, mysterium, sacramentum* with regard to
Christian worship, they do so simply in the sense — which we have briefly
explained in its place and to which we shall return again — of sensible sign

[12] See chapter 19 below, which considers theology and liturgy in the Fathers.

[13] See, e.g., the studies of Gottlieb Söhngen,
Der Wesensaufbau des Mysteriums; H. Marsh,
"The Use of *Mysterion* in the Writings of
Clement of Alexandria," *Journal of Theological Studies*, 1936, pp. 64 ff.; Hans Urs von
Balthasar, "Le 'mysterion' d'Origène," *Rech.
de sc. rel.*, 26 (1936), 513 ff.; 27 (1937), 38
ff.; Gerhard Fittkau, *Der Begriff des Mysteriums bei Johannes Chrysostomus*. Johannes Betz
in his work *Die Eucharistie in der Zeit der
griechischen Väter*, Band I/1: *Die Aktualprä-*

*senz der Person und des Heilswerkes Jesu im
Abendmahl nach der vorephesinischen griechischen Patristik* (Freiburg: Herder, 1955), de-
fends Casel's historical thesis, though trying to
explain in a different way the re-presentation
of Christ's redemptive work. See the review of
his work by J. Barbel in *Theologische Revue*,
53 (1957), 61-71, the severity of which, in
my opinion, is substantially justified. Bernard
de Soos, *Le mystère liturgique d'après saint
Léon le grand* (Münster i. W.: Aschendorff,
1958).

which signifies a sacred thing in relation to the transmission of the divine life in Christ to the world, and which, *in some way*, contains and transmits this sacred reality. But to specify that way as Casel does is to go far beyond the thinking of the Fathers.

Nevertheless, it is perfectly legitimate to try to supply better theological explanations in this field than those which can be found in Scripture or in patristic tradition. But, even considered under this aspect, Casel's theory does not appear satisfactory.

We must indeed admit as legitimate the ultimate end which Casel apparently wants to reach. He wants to prove that the bond between sacramental grace and Christ is not simply a psychological reminder. He wants to vindicate strongly the reality of the bond which links the sacramental grace signified and produced by the sacramental rite not only to Christ in a generic way but also to Christ's historical redemptive action, to that which Christ did and suffered in the flesh, above all on Golgotha. This action is properly the cause in Christ of the grace that is given us. It is right, therefore, to make the faithful more clearly aware that in the sacramental rite they are placed, in some real way, in the presence of that historical redemptive action and in contact with it.

But there are two elements that can be considered in Christ's historical redemptive actions. The first is of a non-permanent nature: the actions themselves in their numerical individuality, which passed on with the placing of the act. The other element is of a permanent nature: the permanent spiritual disposition, in other words the operative habit from which the individual redemptive actions in Christ's whole earthly existence emanated as from a stable psychological root.

Since we are concerned with knowing whether in the sacramental rite the individual actions are made really and numerically present in themselves, as Casel would have it, we must analyze metaphysically the nature of action and discover the source of the individualization of actions, to see whether such numerical re-presentation is possible, even by a miracle.

Let it suffice to note that action in itself is an entity of a non-permanent, and, in this precise sense, successive, nature, which, as far as its efficient cause is concerned, is an act of an operative faculty; an entity which exists in a determinate moment of time and ceases to exist with the interruption of the actual efficient influx of the faculty. And let it be noted that this holds of every human action performed in this life, including the properly spiritual actions of understanding and volition. The exercise of these spiritual powers is connected with bodily organs and depends on them in this life. In virtue of this connection and dependence, mysterious but real, these spiritual actions also fall under time, come into being in a determinate moment of time and cease to exist with the interruption in time of the actual efficient influx of the faculty.

Because of the non-permanent nature of action, the element of time enters into its individuation in an essential way. The interruption in time of an interior act, or an exterior one, distinguishes it numerically from any antecedent or subsequent act of the same species. Hence for the individuation of any single action, in as much as it is a non-permanent entity, it is decisive that it have been done without interruption in this space of time and not in another.[14]

From this it follows that it is metaphysically impossible, therefore impossible even by a miracle because it is self-contradictory, that an action be reproduced or re-presented numerically the same after an interruption of time, in a succeeding period of time. It is therefore impossible to speak of Christ's Passion, and in general of Christ's historical redemptive action, as an entity of a non-permanent nature re-presented objectively in itself numerically the same in a successive time. If it is performed in a period of time, distinct by interruption from the original period, by that very fact it is no longer numerically the same, but a new action.

It does not help to say that, although it is precisely the past historical action which in its numerical singularity is made present in the liturgical rite performed in space and time, still the action is made present in a way of its own which transcends space and time. For the answer is that just this way, in the present case, involves a contradiction with the nature of individual action as such; therefore, whoever makes such a statement still has to explain how an entity of non-permanent nature, individuated in its singularity by the time in which it was done, can be preserved, even by a miracle, to be re-presented later in its numerical singularity, if this previous time was ever interrupted and fell into nothingness.

Thus the answer is given also to Casel's statement when he says that Christ's historical redemptive action is re-presented in the sacramental liturgy numerically the same, not in its details of space and time, but in its substance. From what has been said above, it is evident that precisely the element of time belongs to the substance of a numerically individual historical action, because time is one of its individuating elements. It is contradictory, therefore, to say that the action is re-presented in its substance numerically individual but without the circumstance of time.

It is no help at all to reject the metaphysical conceptual analysis which distinguishes between permanent entity and non-permanent entity and determines the manner of individuation of the one and the other, and take refuge in a vitalist and anti-intellectualist intuitionism, for two reasons. First, to deny the demands of conceptual reason and of metaphysical reasoning is not to resolve the questions which they inevitably pose. Second, this would mean questioning fundamental principles of philosophy without which faith itself and theology as such cannot exist.

---

[14] See, e.g., St. Thomas, *Quodlib.* IV, q. 3, III, q. 12, a. 1 (ed. Reiser, II, pp. 636 ff.). a. 5; John of St. Thomas, *Philos. nat.*, part

Among the difficulties which can rightly be laid to Casel's theory, we cannot pass over this one either: If the Passion of Golgotha were re-presented in the Mass in its numerical individuality, the Mass would be a bloody sacrifice and Christ would merit anew in it.

We must say, therefore, that the sacramental rite does not make present objectively in themselves Christ's historical redemptive actions considered as non-permanent acts, individuated numerically by the time in which they were performed.

Yet those actions, now past and not re-presentable in their numerical individuality, continue to have their influence in the grace which is granted us, of which they are always instrumental efficient, meritorious and exemplary cause.

It is the constant teaching of St. Thomas that all of Christ's historical actions, all the things He did and suffered in His mortal life, continue to exercise an influx of efficient instrumental causality on all the graces by means of which salvation is applied to men in all places and at all times. This is so because they were not simply human actions — for, as such, they were of limited effect even in space and in time — but theandric, human-divine actions. Through their human element itself, as through an instrument, the divine power was at work, "which by its presence is in touch with all places and times."[15] And thus those same actions, limited in their human element, in space and in time, reach to all places and all times in their total effect.[16]

Moreover, they continue to have an influence as meritorious cause on the grace that is given us. For, being present by way of intention in the divine acceptance, they have their influence, so to speak, morally, on the will of God, who grants the grace out of regard for these actions.

Finally, they are also exemplary cause of our sanctification and of our wor-

---

[15] *Summa*, III, q. 56, a. 1 ad 3.

[16] The doctrine of St. Thomas on this point is set forth by Polycarp Wegenaer, *Heilsgegenwart*. Among the texts of St. Thomas, note the following:

General statements: "All Christ's actions and sufferings operate instrumentally in virtue of His divinity for the salvation of men" (*Summa*, III, q. 48, a. 6 c.). "Just as all other things which Christ did and endured . . . are profitable to our salvation through the power of His divinity, . . . so also is Christ's resurrection the efficient cause of ours through the divine power, . . . which power by its presence is in touch with all places and times" (*Ibid.*, III, q. 56, a. 1 ad 3). "The things that were done by the humanity of Christ were done not only by reason of human power, but by the power of the divinity joined to His humanity. Hence, just as His touch cured the leper in as much as it was an instrument of the divinity, so also is Christ's resurrection the cause of our resurrection" (*In 1 Thess.*, IV, *lect.* 2). "Owing to Christ's infinite power, just as through contact with His flesh the regenerative power entered not only into the waters which came into contact with Christ, but into all waters throughout the whole world and during all future ages, so likewise from Christ's uttering these words" (of the institution) "they derived their consecrating power, by whatever priest they be uttered, as if Christ present were saying them" (*Summa*, q. 78, a. 5 c. See a. 4 c.).

For the Passion of Christ as efficient, exemplary and meritorious cause, see *Summa*, III, q. 48, a. 6 c.; *ibid.*, ad 2 and ad 3; q. 56, a. 1 ad 4; a. 2 ad 4. For the resurrection of Christ as efficient and exemplary cause of our resurrection, see *Summa*, III, q. 56, a. 1 c. and ad 3, ad 4; a. 2 ad 4; *In 1 Thess.*, IV, *lect.* 2; *In 4 Sent.*, d. 43, q. 1, a. 2, sol. 1.

ship. For our sanctification is nothing but a participation in Christ's sanctity, of which those actions were the fruit. And our liturgical worship is but the continuation of the worship which Christ rendered to God in those same actions.

Thus Christ's redemptive actions, even in their numerical individuality already now past and not reproducible, are rendered really present in the liturgical rite in the manner in which the living image makes present the prototype which it represents and re-presents because it really participates in the prototype.

Hence, even when we consider Christ's redemptive actions as non-permanent entities not reproducible in their numerical individuality, the "commemoration" of these actions in the liturgical rites is never reduced to a mere remembrance of things past. In the liturgical rite they are really present in their ontological effects; and they are really present because, through the divine power which brings about these effects in instrumental dependence on these actions, the faithful are placed in real contact of power not only with Christ in a generic way, but with that which Christ did and suffered in the flesh.[17]

If in Christ's historical redemptive actions we consider, on the other hand, the permanent spiritual disposition or the habit from which they issued, it is undeniable that in the sacramental rite the faithful are put into contact with them and put into their presentness in a still deeper way. For that disposition of Christ, of which the redemptive actions in His earthly life were but the individual and successive expressions, was not itself a successive entity, but permanent in its nature. Never interrupted or even diminished from the first moment of His existence, it remained always numerically the same until the last breath of His earthly life, and continues so in Christ, now glorious at the right hand of the Father.

In the Eucharist, where the very person of Christ, and not only His supernatural power, is really present in His divinity and in His full, glorious humanity — body, soul, intellect, will — the objective presentness of that permanent disposition of His soul is of a nature altogether special by reason of its force and realism. We call it personal presentness, in as much as it is bound up with the real presence of Christ's very person in the Eucharist.

In the other sacraments that presentness is of power and not of person, and the believer is put into real objective contact of power with that permanent disposition of the soul of Christ. But that presence and that real contact of

[17] The encyclical *Mediator Dei* in a passage where it speaks of the rites of the liturgical year makes an unfavorable allusion to Casel's tentative explanation: "These mysteries are ever present and active not in a vague and uncertain way as some modern writers hold, but in the way that Catholic doctrine teaches us. According to the doctors of the Church, they are shining examples of Christian perfection, as well as sources of divine grace, due to the merit and prayers of Christ; they still influence us because each mystery brings its own special grace for our salvation" (n. 165 [Lat. 163]).

power is not a mere remembrance or a mere knowledge or emotion in the believer. It is of an order which the theologians, to distinguish it precisely from the order of mere knowledge, affection or remembrance, call physical. For every transmission of grace in the sacraments is caused by Christ's full humanity as a living instrument of the divinity. And Christ's full humanity, now glorious, includes His dispositions of soul, from which the individual redemptive acts flowed in His earthly life.

Let us note in conclusion that Christ's historical redemptive actions in His earthly life were many, because they began with the first instant of the incarnation of the Word and ended with Christ's last breath on the Cross. Moreover, every one of them was, by itself, quite sufficient to redeem us. Nevertheless, in the order effectively willed by the Father and freely accepted by Christ, they all concurred as partial causes to form the total single cause of our salvation, which is achieved, in its wholeness, only with Christ's last breath on the Cross.

All of Christ's redemptive actions in His mortal life tended, therefore, to the Cross as their fulfillment, took their meaning from the Cross; and only on the Cross did Christian worship in its integrity, as a complete thing, begin. The Cross, then, sums up and fulfills in itself all the preceding redemptive actions of Christ's life. It is for this reason that the individual redemptive mysteries of Christ's life all involved the mystery of the Cross. In fact, Christ's whole earthly life is but one redemptive mystery which is fulfilled on the Cross.

It must also be observed that the resurrection and the ascension, with the sitting at the Father's right hand and Christ's subsequent sending of the Holy Spirit, were not meritorious acts and in this sense redemptive, just as Christ's second coming will not be a meritorious act and in this sense redemptive.

Nevertheless, in the sacramental rite, rather in the liturgical celebration in general, just as the presential actualization, in the manner described above, of the individual historical mysteries of Christ's life is never separated from the presential actualization of the mystery of the Cross, so also this actualization of the mystery of the Cross is never separated from the efficacious, commemorative, presential actualization of the resurrection, the ascension, the sitting at the Father's right hand and the sending of the Spirit. Nor is this actualization of the mystery of the Cross ever separated from the prophetic, efficacious, presential actualization of the future second coming of the Lord.

All this is true because all the phases of the Lord's historical and meta-historical life, to His second coming inclusive, are so closely knit together that they form only one single great mystery: the mystery of Christ Redeemer. From the incarnation to the death on the Cross, everything tended to Golgotha as a peak and fulfillment, from which all the rest took its meaning. But Golgotha itself tended with all its momentum to the resurrection, ascension, sitting at the Father's right hand and sending of the Spirit at Pentecost, because only with the resurrection, the ascension, the sitting at the Father's right hand and Pentecost did Christ gather for Himself and for us the fruits of Golgotha and communicate them to us.

These fruits are summed up for us in the Spirit which Christ communicates to us with all that the Spirit and His presence among us and in us involves: Church, sacraments, grace, virtues, gifts. Finally, the fruit of the Spirit is meaningful only in view of the definitive cosmic restoration of the kingdom of God which will take place in the parousia.

This means that every sacramental sign, as effective "commemorative" sign of Christ's historical redemptive actions, actualizes presentially, in the sense explained above, not only one of these actions but all the mysteries of Christ's life from the incarnation to the Cross to the resurrection and to Pentecost; and as prophetic sign it effectively actualizes the future second coming. Thus the sacramental sign effectively actualizes *ex opere operato* the mystery of Christ in its fullness as a single whole, though in different ways and according to its different aspects.

3. The Efficacy of the Liturgical Signs Instituted by the Church

With regard to the proper efficacy of the liturgical signs instituted by the hierarchy of the Church, the encyclical *Mediator Dei* says, as we have mentioned, that it "is due rather to the action of the Church (*ex opere operantis Ecclesiae*), in as much as she is holy and acts always in closest union with her Head."

It says "is due *rather* (*potius*) to the action of the Church" because the efficacy does not depend exclusively on that action. The allusion here is first of all to the fact that, when God grants favors in view of the rites instituted by the Church, He has regard also, secondarily, to the moral dignity, the worthiness and the holiness of life of the one who receives these rites or of the one who performs them, granting greater actual graces in view of these qualities. Besides, according to the opinion of some theologians, in the rites instituted by the Church some effects are also obtained infallibly by the objective performance of the rite, and therefore by a certain *opus operatum*, as it were.

Certain spiritual effects are obtained infallibly by the mere performance of a rite or the mere recitation of a prayer instituted by the hierarchy, provided they are done by persons authorized by the hierarchy for this purpose and with the intention and according to the rules established by the hierarchy.

The effect is first of all the very impetration of the Church. That is just what the liturgical signs instituted by the Church have as their immediate aim to signify. This means that in the ceremonies, prayers or sacramentals instituted by the hierarchy, once the rite is performed or the prayer is recited by authorized persons, with the intention and in the manner prescribed by the Church for their validity, the impetration itself of the Church signified in them is infallibly realized, apart from the moral dignity or personal sanctity of the one whom the Church uses to lift up her impetration to God at this time.

Thus, for example, in the prayer of the canonical hours, recited by persons expressly delegated by the hierarchy to fulfill this office in the name of the Church, provided the rules laid down for its validity be observed, there is always and infallibly realized the prayer of the Church, spouse of Christ, apart from the personal sanctity of the one who offers it in her name.

Another effect infallibly obtained in the rites instituted by the Church, in virtue of the objective and valid performance of the rite or of its objective and valid reception, is the consecration of things or persons in the sacramentals instituted by the hierarchy for this purpose, such as religious profession, the consecration of virgins, the consecration of a church, of altars, of chalices. In cases like these it is certain that the objective and valid performance of the rite produces infallibly the spiritual effect, which consists in the fact that God accepts the object or person as reserved for His exclusive use.

The other effects connected efficaciously to the liturgy instituted by the Church are granted by God at the Church's prayer which is said in those rites, and this is done according to the general laws which regulate the hearing of prayer. These effects are particularly:

1) every kind of actual grace for persons, such as sentiments of faith, hope, charity, repentance, etc., and, by means of these actual graces, the recovery or increase of sanctifying grace;

2) the prevention of diabolical influence on persons or things, the effect sought in exorcisms;

3) temporal graces granted by God with a view to spiritual good.

All this, therefore, is granted by God in the liturgy instituted by the Church, chiefly out of regard for the *opus operantis Ecclesiae*. It is the first time, if I am not mistaken, that an official document of the *magisterium* has systematized this concept introduced by the liturgists not so very long ago.[18] It is this concept which we must now strive to clarify, so much the more, it seems to me, because it is anything but clearly defined by the very ones who have had recourse to it up to now.

The notion of the *opus operantis Ecclesiae*

It is a well known fact that the expression *ex opere operantis* as distinguished from *ex opere operato* signifies in general that the spiritual effect which follows upon the religious action is produced by God not simply through the rite and out of regard for the rite, objectively and duly performed,

---

[18] But the thing is already found in St. Thomas. See *Summa*, III, q. 82, a. 6 c.: in the parts of the liturgy instituted by God (the substance of the sacraments and of the sacrifice) the minister acts "in the person of Christ"; in those instituted by the Church he acts "in the person of the Church." In either case the action obtains its effect even if the minister is unworthy. See also *Summa*, III, q. 82, a. 7 ad 3; II-II, q. 83, a. 12; *In 4 Sent.*, d. 5, q. 2, a. 2, qla. 2 ad 2; *In 4 Sent.*, d. 15, q. 4, a. 1 ad 3 q.

but out of regard for the moral dignity of the active contribution by the man who performs the rite or receives it.

The spiritual effect of the *opus operantis* is not simply the fruit of man's effort or dignity, but is an effect produced by God which transcends man's power. Yet in producing a certain quality or intensity in the effect, God has regard to the moral dignity of the act produced by man. Thus the action itself of the man who performs the rite or receives it has the value, with regard to the spiritual effect which God produces, of moral and intentional cause which is impetratory, satisfactory, meritorious: God produces a spiritual effect of such and such a nature and intensity in response to the prayer, the power of satisfaction and of merit which is expressed in the religious action of the man who performs the rite or receives it.

The question is to determine accurately the various degrees or types which can be distinguished further in the same *opus operantis*. Generally the distinction is proposed of *opus operantis* of the minister of the rite or of the subject who receives it, and *opus operantis* of the Church.

To determine the notion further in its particulars, I propose the following division and terminology. I distinguish between the *opus operantis* of the minister of the rite or of the one who receives it in the Church, and the *opus operantis* of the Church herself. I further subdistinguish the *opus operantis* of the Church into liturgical (public and official) *opus operantis* of the Church and non-liturgical (public but not official) *opus operantis* of the Church.

With this division and terminology I mean to point out first of all that every *opus operantis*, of any individual whomsoever, which has for effect a spiritual fruit, takes place always in the pale of the Church; that in every such action the Church is always expressed and acts in some way, and that in the eyes of God no action has any supernatural value or dignity without the real and actual union with the Church.

But, notwithstanding this, there is a difference between the *opus operantis* of an individual or a group of individuals *in* the Church and the *opus operantis* which is *of* the Church herself.

Secondly, I mean to point out that not all the *opera operantis* of the Church, even when these actions have for their object prayers and rites externally similar in all things to the liturgical actions, are necessarily for that reason liturgical actions. For example, the public and solemn recitation of the rosary in a parish under the direction of the pastor, advised or actually imposed by the authority of the hierarchy, bishop or pope, is a public action of the Church herself and not only of the individual private believers or of a private group of believers in the Church.

It must be concluded, therefore, that there is a difference between the nature and force of the *opus operantis* of the Church in the liturgy (let us call it public and official *opus operantis Ecclesiae*) and the nature and force of the *opus operantis* of the Church outside of the liturgy (let us call it public but not official *opus operantis Ecclesiae*).

All this, as can be seen, is intended to specify in their nature and in their respective efficacy the various degrees of the Church's intervention in her intercession with God, something which is necessary, I believe, in order to grasp the proper nature and efficacy of the liturgy created by the Church.

For the sake of greater clarity let the following be noted. In a certain sense it is quite true that when a lay person prays, be it only in private and only mentally, if he is united to the Church, that is, to the hierarchy and through them to the rest of the faithful, in this prayer of his before God he is never an isolated individual, performing an action which is of interest to him alone, nor does God consider him separately from the whole Church. Rather, God considers him only as a member of the Church, and thus as united to Christ and a member of Christ.

Thus in a certain sense it is quite true that when this believer prays, it is the Church that prays in this believer and through this believer, just as it is true that Christ prays in this believer and through this believer. Every action of supernatural value by any man, as it is always an action "in Christ," is always also an action "in the Church," outside of which there is no union with Christ and no salvation.[19] Therefore, in every supernatural good work, in every prayer, the Church herself is in act in some real way, doing this work and offering this prayer.

With greater reason it must be said that the Church is in act, praying, when several believers gather to pray together, even in a non-religious place, as in a private house, and without the direction of a member of the hierarchy: "for if two of you unite your voices on earth to ask for anything whatsoever, it will be granted you by My Father who is in heaven; for wherever two or three are gathered in My name, I am in the midst of them" (Matthew 18:19-20).

Nevertheless, it is true that the Church is actualized in a higher way when the actions in question are not only those of believers united in a general way to their pastors, but are done under the actual conduct of the pastors in virtue of the powers received by them not from the faithful but from Christ. The pastor is then acting as Christ's agent and representative, and he heads the faithful and represents them before God only as a result of the fact that Christ is their Head before God.

In such an action, for example in a prayer offered under such conditions, the Church as such is much more engaged formally than in the first example.

[19] We know that for salvation a real and present union with the visible Church is certainly required, but it is enough that this union be invisible, by means of the grace which God gives to whoever lives according to his conscience, has the disposition to do what God wants of him as soon as he knows God's will, and thus has also the implicit desire of baptism and of visible union, not merely invisible union, with the visible Church. See: Cyprian Vagaggini, "L'unione alla Chiesa e la salvezza," *L'Osservatore Romano*, May 14-15, 1962, p. 5.

The individual seems to be relegated more to second place as member of a society which transcends him; and the action seems more like the action of that society, which, although made up of individuals, transcends the individuals.

In fact, that action is the direct action of Christ Himself, Head of His members and operating through His special visible representatives and agents, to whom He gave a special investiture for that purpose, which the rest of the faithful do not have. Therefore Christ Himself considers such action in a very special way His own action, which, through His visible hierarchical agents, He fulfills before God as Head of His members, in other words as Head of His Church. In this action Christ is immeasurably more engaged before God, so to speak, than He was in the first example.

Such action has a much greater spiritual efficacy before God than the private action of a lay person even though the private action be done in union with Christ and with the Church. With good reason, therefore, the liturgists have recourse, to specify this action, to the concept of *opus operantis Ecclesiae*.

We already have the *opus operantis Ecclesiae* in a certain degree when the faithful recite the rosary in a parish under the direction of the pastor. For the pastor, as a member of the hierarchy, has received through legitimate organs the special mandate from Christ to be His representative and agent in the public prayer which the faithful offer to God, or rather, which Christ Himself, as Head of the faithful, offers to God with the faithful and for the faithful.

But the rosary in its formulas and its rites, though approved by the hierarchy, is not, at least as yet, approved as *official* prayer of the Church. The hierarchy alone by Christ's special mandate are competent to judge what is official, namely the prayer which the Church, or rather Christ, considers in all respects as His own, in which, so to speak, He considers Himself wholly engaged before God. Hence the *opus operantis Ecclesiae* is not yet exemplified in the highest degree possible when the rosary is said.

The highest actualization of the *opus operantis Ecclesiae* will be found in the liturgical rites and prayers properly so called which are instituted by the Church. Here Christ as Head of His members assumes responsibility before God, so to speak, for the performance of the prayer and the rite which He by special mandate has given power to the hierarchy to institute and to perform in His name as Head of the Church. These rites and prayers are not rites and prayers of Christ acting through His ministers by the same title as the sacraments which operate *ex opere operato*, but they are such by a title superior to that of the supernatural actions and prayers which lay people, united to Christ and in the Church, offer to God as private individuals.

For what reason are the rites and prayers instituted by the hierarchy of the Church rites and prayers of Christ by a title inferior to that which holds for the substance of the sacraments? Why, in the sacraments, does God produce the spiritual effect infallibly without making it depend on the moral dignity of men as on a cause, provided everything is in order as it is supposed to be, while in the rites and prayers instituted by the hierarchy He links the effect to the moral dignity of the Church? The only adequate answer is God's positive will, known through the revelation set forth by the Church.

Through this revelation it is known that Christ has not given the Church the power to institute rites and prayers to the mere performance of which, *ex opere operato*, He attaches the conferral of grace on the one who does not put any impediment in the way.

On the other hand, He has given the hierarchy the power to institute and perform rites and prayers which, even though performed by men determined by the hierarchy, still would not be rites and prayers of these men by title of a private individual, but prayers and rites of the Church itself, shepherds and flock, as body of which Christ is Head or as spouse of which Christ is Spouse. To these rites and prayers God has granted the benefits requested, not *ex opere operato* in virtue of the mere performance of the rite duly carried out, but on the other hand not only according to the private moral dignity of those individuals who perform or are object of those rites and those prayers, but according to the moral dignity of the Church as spouse intimately united to Christ her Spouse, or body intimately united to Christ its Head.

The individuals who perform those rites and those prayers are merely the agents of this Church, authentically delegated as such by the hierarchy, which has from Christ the power to do this, and therefore authentically accepted as such by Christ and by God.

The *opus operantis Ecclesiae* and the distinction between liturgy and "devotions"

The ideas set forth above, concerning the *opus operantis Ecclesiae*, are the theological foundation for the distinction between liturgy and "devotions," as well as for the distinction within devotions themselves between those conducted by order of the hierarchical authority (first the authority of the Apostolic See and then the authority of the local bishops) and those conducted by free choice of individuals (first as a group and then singly), even if these latter are in forms approved, at least in general, by the competent hierarchy.

These distinctions are now made by the official documents. The "Instruction" of 1958 distinguishes the liturgy from devotions in this way: " 'Liturgical services' (*actiones liturgicae*) are those sacred services which, by institution of Jesus Christ or the Church and in their name, are performed according to the liturgical books approved by the Holy See by persons lawfully deputed for this function, in order to give due worship to God and the saints and blessed (cf. canon 1256). Any other sacred services, whether performed in church or outside of church, even with a priest present or conducting them, are called 'devotions' or 'devotional services' (*pia exercitia*)."[20]

Accepting this distinction, the Second Vatican Council further determines certain aspects of it: "Popular devotions of the Christian people, provided they conform to the laws and norms of the Church, are to be highly recommended, especially where they are ordered by the Apostolic See. Devotions proper to individual churches also have a special dignity if they are undertaken by order of the bishops according to customs or books lawfully approved."[21] Here the devotions themselves are distinguished according to their dignity into two categories: those which are held not only with the approval, but also by order, of the hierarchy (first by order of the Apostolic See, then by order of the local bishops), and those which are held without any such order.

In keeping with what has been said above, we must distinguish further in this last category between devotions held in common by groups and those performed by a person alone.

Thus we obtain the following outline:

Sacred services:
  I. Efficacious *ex opere operato*:
     liturgy instituted by God.
 II. Efficacious *ex opere operantis*:
     A. *Ex opere operantis* of the Church:
        1. with public and official authority:
           liturgy instituted by the Church;
        2. with public but not official authority:
           devotions held by order of the hierarchy:
           a. by order of the Apostolic See:
              devotions of apostolic authority;
           b. by order of the local bishops:
              devotions of episcopal authority.
     B. *Ex opere operantis* of individuals in the Church:
        1. acting in a group: private group devotions;
        2. acting as individuals: private individual devotions.

(Liturgy brace spanning items I through A.1; Devotions brace spanning items A.2 through B.2)

The theological basis of these distinctions is always the different degrees of objective efficacy of the individual actions (aside from the question of personal merit, as has been said), arising from the different degrees of involvement of Christ Himself and of the Church in each of the actions.

This makes it obvious why the Second Vatican Council was able to say that "every liturgical celebration, because it is an action of Christ the Priest and of His Body which is the Church, is a sacred action surpassing all others. No

[20] *September 1958 Decree on Participation in the Mass* (Collegeville, Minn.: Liturgical Press, 1958), n. 1; Latin in *AAS* 50 (1958), 632.
[21] CL, art. 13.

other action of the Church can equal its efficacy by the same title and to the same degree."[22]

And it explains also why a prayer, whatever its structure, thought-content and the like, can never be liturgy unless it is approved as such by the Church, and why the Church here means the hierarchy under the primacy of the Roman Pontiff. For the liturgy always involves the authority of Christ and of the Church by a special title which does not belong to any other action and which implies the exercise of the threefold power of sanctifying, teaching and governing.

Have the bishops sufficient authority to create liturgy, or to make a sacred celebration liturgical, at least within their own territory? To answer this question, we must make the following observations.

By virtue of the episcopal consecration itself, the bishop receives directly from God all the powers necessary for conducting to their supernatural end the people whose shepherd he is, as long as he remains within the unity of the Church. This is the doctrine clearly set forth in the Second Vatican Council. Certainly included among these powers is the power of determining and regulating the liturgy in his diocese.

The pope, however, has the particular responsibility for the unity and the common good of the whole Church. By virtue of his universal primacy and this responsibility which goes with it, the pope has the right to reserve to himself the exercise of certain powers for as long as he judges this to be advisable. And among these powers is that of creating and regulating the liturgy, even in the individual dioceses, a power which is inherent *per se* in the dignity of each bishop.

To know whether the Roman Pontiff in fact has reserved or still reserves such power to himself is a simple question of history.

Actually, while the liturgy up to the sixteenth century had been commonly under episcopal jurisdiction, from that time on the Holy See has reserved solely to itself the power to "regulate the liturgy and approve the liturgical books,"[23] even for the particular Churches.

As long as this right lasts, therefore, there cannot be a liturgy of any kind unless it has been approved as such by the Holy See.[24] The Second Vatican Council has certainly left a considerably greater margin to the regional episcopal authority, as well as to the individual bishops, for determining and regulating the liturgy within their own jurisdiction.[25] But "their decrees" must be "approved, that is, confirmed,"[26] or, as it is said elsewhere, "reviewed,"[27]

---

[22] *Ibid.*, art. 7.

[23] *Code of Canon Law*, can. 1257.

[24] Hence there does not seem to be any basis for the opinion that the bishops at the present time have the power to give the character of true diocesan liturgy to a rite or a prayer of their own creation, even without the approval of the Holy See. See: Josef A. Jungmann,

"Liturgie und *pia exercitia*," *Liturgisches Jahrbuch*, 9 (1959), 79-86.

[25] See CL, art. 36, sections 3 and 4; 39; 54; 63; 77; 120; 55; 57; 64; 68; 71; 76; 79; 97; 101, sections 1 and 2; 124-130.

[26] *Ibid.*, art. 36, section 3.

[27] *Ibid.*, art. 63 b.

by the Apostolic See. In practice, therefore, even now there is no liturgy, be it only diocesan in extent, which does not have to be approved as such by the Holy See.

The basis of the efficacy of the liturgy *ex opere operantis Ecclesiae*

Some find it hard to conceive of the *opus operantis Ecclesiae* as a reality distinct from and more efficacious than the mere *opus operantis* of one of the faithful or of a group of the faithful. The root of this difficulty lies in the fact that they can hardly conceive of the Church as something more than the mere sum of the private persons of the faithful who believe in Christ. Thus they see in the personality of the Church nothing more than a juridical concept, perhaps even a juridical fiction. Hence they cannot understand how the moral dignity of the Church can be greater than the sum of the moral dignity of the private individuals which make it up, and the prayer of the Church can be, before God, more efficacious than the mere prayer of the individuals who recite it in her name.

If they add further what we have observed above, that even the private and mental prayer of any believer within the Church is, in a certain very real sense, the prayer of the Church, they do not see just why the "official" prayer should be more effective than the unofficial, conditions being equal. And some perhaps will think that when the liturgists magnify the Church and the transcendental efficacy of the Church's prayer over merely private prayer and similar things, they are not far from falling actually into the error which some Protestants impute to the Catholics: making the Church a kind of hypostatized Platonic entity.

Yet the concept of *opus operantis Ecclesiae* is undeniably theological and right, as is proved by its official consecration by the *magisterium*. Besides, the same encyclical *Mediator Dei*, when it explains the relations between liturgical prayer and private prayer, has this sentence: "Unquestionably liturgical prayer, being the public supplication of the illustrious spouse of Jesus Christ, is superior in excellence to private prayers."[28] We have to suppose, therefore, that the aforesaid prejudices against the *opus operantis Ecclesiae* proceed from the forgetfulness of some important point of Catholic doctrine.

The doctrine forgotten is nothing less than this, that the Church is not a society like others, not even like other religious societies. In the other societies, civil and religious, the organization of the society, its constitution, as well as

[28] N. 37. On the special efficacy of the prayer of the Church as such, surpassing the efficacy of private prayer, see also the text of St. Ambrose, *In Luc.* V, n. 11: "Great is the Lord. The merit of some leads Him to forgive others; pleased with the former, He relieves the latter of their sins. Why do you deny your fellow man any influence over you, when the Lord grants a slave the right to intervene and to obtain what he asks for? . . . If you have no hope of pardon for grave sins, have recourse to those who pray, have recourse to the Church, who will plead for you. Out of regard for the Church, the Lord will grant you the forgiveness that He might have denied to you."

the designation of the individuals who will hold authority in it, though the authority be from God, depends immediately on men, who, with the same powers by which they constituted it, can also change it as they see fit for a good reason pertaining to the common good.

The Church, on the other hand, is formed by the fact that Christ gathers men to Himself, transforming them intrinsically by the communication to them of divine life in a manner and order well determined. He makes some men His representatives and intermediaries with the rest and gives them special powers. These powers, not only juridical but real, are powers of sanctifying, of teaching and of governing. All other men must submit to their mediation, which is real and not just purely juridical, in order to obtain, preserve and increase the real union with Christ and, through Christ, with God.

Those powers do include, as a basis, an authentic mandate which is also of juridical value, but they surpass in their nature the juridical level of the purely human civil and religious societies. For Christ, with that authentic mandate which has also the force of human juridical mandates, transmits to His special representatives and agents a supernatural reality which no human juridical mandate can transmit: the character of holy orders and the special assistance of the Spirit. This spiritual reality really affects the being and the power of action of these men in their activity as intermediaries representing Christ with other men.

The corollary is that these other men, because Christ has so willed it, depend on these intermediaries and their powers, not by a mere juridical fiction, nor only in the line of mere moral causality of affection or of knowledge, but in the line of physical causality, or, if you will, to avoid misunderstanding "physical" in a material sense, transphysical or superphysical causality. This means that only he who is in contact with those realities and those powers obtains divine life, is really associated with Christ and therefore united to God;[29] is really, in the order of the divine life, gathered and united with the other brothers in Christ by a bond much more profound and real than a juridical or merely moral one.

From all this it follows that the Church is not simply the sum or the human organization of the private individuals who are in its pale, but a very special entity, more profound and immeasurably more real than any purely human juridical or moral aggregate there might be.

Without Christ there is no Church; without hierarchy there is no Church; without the character of holy orders and the assistance of the Spirit with powers of governing, teaching and sanctifying, there is no Church. In the Church the hierarchical structure has an irreplaceable role; in it resides a being and powers which transcend the being and the powers of any private

[29] As we have said in note 19, p. 115 above, invisible contact is sufficient.

person, including the hierarchy themselves as private persons, and on which depends the birth, subsistence and growth of the faithful in Christ.

Yet the hierarchy alone is not the Church. Still less can it be said that the individual faithful as private persons are the Church. The Church is the indissoluble whole which results from: Christ the Head; the hierarchy as human-divine mediating structure, agent and representative of Christ and by His will irreplaceable; and the people who are united through the hierarchy to Christ the Head.[30] The Church is the sum of these elements. Hence it can be seen how the Church transcends the sum of the men who, as individuals, make it up.

When we speak, therefore, of the *opus operantis Ecclesiae* as transcending the *opus operantis* of a mere private individual or of a group of private individuals, it is of the Church described above that we must think. We are concerned with the "people united to the bishop, and the flock gathered under its shepherd,"[31] and people and bishop both united to Christ as the body to the head or as the wife to the husband. And although, as we have said, even in the prayer of a private lay person in the Church it is somehow the Church who prays, still this actualization of the Church as such reaches its maximum of reality and intensity in the liturgical action.

The liturgical action is that which the hierarchy, in virtue of the special powers it has received from Christ for this purpose, determines to be in the highest degree the prayer of the Church as mystical body of Christ, that is, of the Christian people informed by the hierarchy, as a whole intimately united to Christ.

The powers given by Christ to the hierarchy as His representative and agent are real and efficacious in the sight of God, not fictitious powers. Because they are real, efficacious powers, the performance of the rite or the recitation of the prayer determined by the hierarchy as eminently the rite and prayer of the Church as such, really puts into motion before God, so to speak, the faithful people informed by the hierarchy and united to Christ. Their union with Christ is a spiritual and mysterious one, not merely a moral union, still less a fictitious one, but a real union, just as the mystical body of Christ, which is the Church, is something real, not just a moral entity or a fictitious one.

This, I think, makes it easier to understand why *Mediator Dei* says that in the liturgical rites instituted by the hierarchy the efficacy "is due rather to the action of the Church (*ex opere operantis Ecclesiae*)[32] in as much as she is

---

[30] St. Cyprian expresses it perfectly: "They are the Church: the people united to the bishop, and the flock gathered under its shepherd. Hence you should know that the bishop is in the Church and the Church in the bishop, and that if anyone is not with the bishop, he is not in the Church" (*Ep.* 66, 8). See also CL, art. 26.

[31] St. Cyprian, *loc. cit.*

[32] The teaching on the *opus operantis Ecclesiae* as set forth here has been contradicted by Karl Rahner in his "Thesen über das Gebet 'im Namen der Kirche,'" *Zeitschr. für kath. Theol.*, 83 (1961), 307-24. His essential thesis is this: the intrinsic dignity of a prayer and its efficacy with God depends solely on the

holy and acts always in closest union with her Head" and that "liturgical prayer, being the public supplication of the illustrious spouse of Jesus Christ, is superior in excellence to private prayers." It is against this background also that the statement of the Second Vatican Council must be understood, that the liturgy has an efficacy which no other action of the Church can equal by the same title and to the same degree.

personal devotion of the one who offers it or the one who listens to it. Hence even the fact that the prayer in question is a liturgical prayer, recited by order of the Church, "does not confer on it greater dignity before God" (p. 317) or greater efficacy than it already has from the personal devotion of the priest who is saying it or of the believer for whom it is being said. In liturgical prayer the Church's intervention helps only in as much as it fosters this personal attitude in some way, for example by obliging the priest to pray (obligation of the breviary) and by regulating the celebration (see pp. 310-12; 317-18; 321). The proof for such statements? The proof, answers Rahner (see, for example, pp. 311-12) is that the dignity and efficacy of a prayer depends solely on the grace with which it is said.

It is easy to see how such a thesis involves the negation of the distinction, as far as dignity and efficacy are concerned, between liturgical prayer and purely private prayer, in as much as the distinction is reduced to a purely external arrangement made by the Church, without intrinsic efficacy *per se* before God. Besides, adds Rahner, is not every prayer a prayer of the mystical body of Christ?

But such reasoning is based on a sophism. For it can be said that the intrinsic dignity and the efficacy of a prayer before God depends on the grace with which the prayer is offered. But in liturgical prayer we must distinguish: 1) the grace of Christ as Head of the mystical body; 2) the grace of the "Church," that is, of all the members of the mystical body, hierarchically structured and united to their divine Head, in as much as they constitute among themselves, together with their Head, that unity *sui generis* which is called precisely the mystical body of Christ; 3) the personal grace of the minister; 4) the personal grace of the individual believer who is assisting at the liturgical prayer or for whom it is being said.

Rahner's sophism consists in this, that when he is appraising the dignity and the efficacy even of liturgical prayer, he still considers only the personal grace of the minister or of the in-

dividual believer. But that which is proper to liturgical prayer as compared with prayers that are not liturgical is precisely this, that while liturgical prayer *is* the personal prayer of the minister or of the individual believer, it is never *only* that, nor principally that. For:

1. When the concern is with the form of the sacrament or of the sacrifice, liturgical prayer is above all the prayer and action of Christ Himself as Head of the mystical body. Thus, for example, the deprecative form of the sacramental absolution in the Byzantine rite is by no means primarily the personal prayer of the priest or of the individual believer; nor is it primarily the prayer of the Church; it is the prayer of Christ Himself, using the priest as instrument. The priest in this instance acts primarily "in the person of Christ." Hence the dignity and efficacy of this prayer depends primarily on the grace of Christ, Head of the mystical body, and not on the grace of His members, even as united to Him, still less on the grace of the minister alone or of the individual believer. It is efficacy *ex opere operato*.

2. On the other hand, when the concern is with liturgical prayers instituted by the Church, they are primarily prayers not of Christ the Head alone, nor of the minister or the individual believer, but of the Church, as has been explained above; and their dignity and efficacy depends primarily on the grace of all the members of the mystical body as the unity *sui generis* described above. These prayers are said by the minister primarily "in the person of the Church." Nor does this imply an undue hypostatization of the Church in the Platonic sense, but simply the doctrine of the mystical body as a unity *sui generis*, but real. And it is true that, in a certain sense, the entire mystical body is involved in every prayer, just as Christ Himself is involved, but in varying degrees and therefore with varying efficacy.

All this is the teaching of *Mediator Dei* (see n. 27; 36), and is clearly the teaching of St. Thomas (*Summa*, III, q. 82, a. 6 c.), whose position is in direct contradiction to Rahner's statements.

4 THE LITURGY AS A COMPLEXUS OF SENSIBLE, EFFICACIOUS SIGNS OF THE CHURCH'S SANCTIFICATION AND WORSHIP

We have defined the liturgy as: THE COMPLEXUS OF THE SENSIBLE, EFFICACIOUS SIGNS OF THE CHURCH'S SANCTIFICATION AND OF HER WORSHIP. We have explained the concept of sign and its efficacy; it remains for us to explain the concept of sanctification and of worship in the liturgy. The concern is with the proximate specific end of the liturgy; the common and remote end is always and only, as for everything else, the glory of God.

On God's part, this specific end is our sanctification, which, in as much as it is effected in us within the Church and as members of the Church, is precisely the sanctification of the Church. On our part, in other words on the part of the Church, the end is the public and official worship of God. Thus the liturgy is seen as the privileged place of encounter between man and God; under the veil of the signs, God descends toward man, man rises to God.

1. Sanctification and Worship in the Liturgy in General

In the concrete liturgical reality, the action of God who sanctifies and the response of the Church who renders her worship to God are closely intertwined and cannot in fact be separated, being like two correlative and indivisible aspects of one and the same reality. The ultimate reason for this is the intimate compenetration of the divine action and the human response in the work of man's sanctification and of worship. In this work the divine action can never be received by an adult in an inert and mechanical way, but is received vitally and freely.

Thus every receipt of the sanctifying action of God is, in the adult, a conscious and free acceptance, and implies, as something to which God has a right, the conscious and free recognition of the divine excellence and of man's subjection to God. Now such recognition is the very soul of worship. Every receipt of the sanctifying action of God therefore implies, in the adult, an act of worship.

Vice versa, any act of Christian worship directed to God, being a supernatural and meritorious work, is impossible for man without a profound sanctifying action of God in man which gives or maintains or increases the state of grace and precedes and accompanies the act of worship.

It is for this reason that St. Thomas, in connection with the sacraments, insists strongly on the indivisibility of God's sanctification of man and man's worship of God. The act of religion, he says, is performed "either by offering something to God or by receiving something divine." [1] For St. Thomas, to receive the sacraments is an outward, and not merely implied, act of *latria*. [2]

Consequently, in the treatise on the sacraments it is a basic principle of his proposed explanation that the specific end for which the sacraments of the New Law have been instituted is twofold: to sanctify man by cleansing him from sin, and to bring it about that he renders to God the worship due Him: "The sacraments of the New Law are ordained for a twofold purpose, namely, as a remedy for sin, and for the worship of God"; [3] "in the use of the sacraments two things may be considered, namely, the worship of God, and the sanctification of man; the first pertains to man as referred to God, while the second pertains to God in reference to man." [4] It is clear that all this holds, in its own way, not only of the sacraments but of the whole concrete liturgical complexus.

Still, though in the concrete liturgy God's sanctifying action and the worship which the Church renders to God are indivisible, it is just as clear that some aspects and some parts of the liturgy bring out more sharply the sanctifying action of God, while some bring out more sharply the worship which the Church renders to God.

---

[1] *Summa*, II-II, q. 81, a. 3 ad 2.
[2] See II-II, q. 89, prologue.

[3] III, q. 63, a. 6 c.
[4] III, q. 60, a. 5 c.

Thus, for example, it is evident that in the sacrament of penance the aspect of the sanctification of man predominates and is consequently brought out more sharply in its outward expression, especially in the modern rite. The same may be said of the anointing of the sick if, as St. Thomas holds, its immediate purpose is the strengthening of the sick person against that languor which is a vestige of sin.

Still, even in penance and the anointing of the sick the aspect of worship is very real. The sinner in submitting to penance proclaims the sovereign majesty of God, His right to our subjection; what is more, he subjects himself effectively to God. All these are acts which constitute the quintessence of worship. Moreover, it is with a view to sharing fully and fruitfully in the worship of the Church together with the brethren, that is, in the Eucharistic worship, that the sinner submits to penance; this sacrament rehabilitates him precisely in order that he may participate fully in that supreme act of worship.

We may reason similarly about many other parts of the liturgy; for example, about parts instituted by the Church, some of the sacramentals and the exorcisms, in which the aspect of sanctification predominates.

On the other hand, parts of the liturgy where the aspect of worship clearly predominates — though even here the aspect of sanctification is never absent — are, for example, the prayers of the Church: those with which she accompanies the administration of the sacraments and the sacramentals, and, chiefly, the prayer of the canonical hours.

The Eucharist, as sacrament and sacrifice, unites the two aspects in the highest degree. For God's sanctification of men through Christ is found in the highest degree in the Eucharist as sacrament, provided it is received with the proper dispositions. And the summit of the Church's worship of God in Christ is found in the Eucharist as sacrifice. It is for this reason, as we shall have occasion to explain more fully, that the Mass is the center of the whole liturgy and its greatest expression.

From all this we can understand once more how inadequate it is to define the liturgy solely as worship, and how necessary it is to define it also as God's sanctifying action.

This is not the place to go into a fuller explanation of the aspect of sanctification in the liturgy. Let it be recalled only that in Catholic doctrine the sanctification of souls which takes place in the sacraments through sanctifying grace is conceived as something profoundly real, transcending immeasurably the mere psychological level of knowledge and affection because it goes to the very roots of man's being and activity.

In sanctifying grace we are speaking of a true, though accidental and mysterious, participation of the divine nature; of participation in the Incarnation and of conformity to Christ, which includes the indwelling within us of the divine Persons and which will lead us even to the glory of the beatific vision as its natural fulfillment.

From all this follows the seriousness and the *tremendum* of the liturgical action. Even the actual graces (the immediate purpose of the rites instituted by the Church is to obtain such grace for us), in so far as they flow from sanctifying rites, are directed to the recovery or increase of sanctifying grace in us. In fact, this holds also for the graces of the temporal order which some of these rites instituted by the Church have the immediate end of obtaining for us from God, since the Church requests these temporal graces, and God grants them, only in so far as they can help us the better to achieve our salvation.

Finally, when the concern is with the sanctification of the body or of objects exterior to us, which some of the rites instituted by the Church are intended to obtain for us, the sanctification, as we have explained above, is understood as a special protection or divine acceptance of those things, for the spiritual good of whoever possesses or uses them with the proper dispositions.

We must now turn our attention to explaining the relations between liturgy and worship.

2. Religion and "Devotio"

Worship is an expression of the virtue of religion. An eminent fruit of the virtue of religion in general and of worship in particular, worthy of special consideration in the study of the liturgy, is that disposition which the ancients called *devotio*. In order to penetrate better into the world of the liturgy as a complexus of signs by means of which the Church renders her public and official worship to God, I think it is time to clarify some essential points of these concepts of religion and *devotio*.

Religion

Scholastic theological tradition, principally following St. Thomas, who in his turn follows the usage of previous theologians which is tied in with a concept of Cicero's, explains the concept of the virtue of religion in connection with the concept of justice. This justice was conceived by the scholastics, after the Greek tradition, in the scheme of the four cardinal virtues, with notable hesitations and indecisions about the very manner of defining it.[5]

Thus the virtue of religion is held to be a justice, namely, that virtue of justice which makes us render to God what is due to Him precisely in so far as He is first principle, Creator, Governor and end of all things.[6] It is

[5] For all this see Odon Lottin's *Psychologie et Morale aux XII⁰ et XIII⁰ siècles*, III (Louvain: Abbaye du Mont Cesar, 1949), 313-26; and his "Vertu de religion et vertus théologales," *Dominican Studies*, 1 (1948), 212 ff.

[6] For St. Thomas cf. *Summa*, II-II, q. 81, a. 3 c. and a. 5 ad 2.

impossible, however, for man to render to God what is due Him in an exact measure of equality, as the concept of strict justice would require, demanding as it does the equality of the parties confronting each other. Hence it is said that religion is not properly a species of the genus justice but a virtue annexed to justice strictly so called, of which it is a certain imperfect participation. This is what is meant by saying in technical language that religion is a "potential part" of justice.[7]

Recently, serious doubts have been raised by some theologians about this incorporation of the virtue of religion into the general scheme of the four cardinal virtues of the Greek tradition as annexed to justice.[8] Historical reasons — the knowledge we now have of the way in which these schemes of systematization of the virtues originated and of the way in which they entered into the tradition of the school and are maintained there — as well as theoretical reasons on the relations of the virtue of religion with the moral virtues and the theological virtues, certainly oblige us to consider seriously a rethinking of this whole question.

Nevertheless, for our purpose it is not opportune to enter into the heart of this discussion, since all the authors are agreed on three fundamental points which are the key to understanding the relation between liturgy and religion: (a) the general meaning of the virtue of religion in the Christian life as man's recognition of his deep debt to God the author and end of all existence; (b) the fact that the virtue of religion transcends the other moral virtues; (c) the fact that the virtue of religion is in such intimate connection and proximity with the theological virtues that these are like the matter which the virtue of religion uses — maintaining at the same time that the theological virtues are the source of the virtue of religion and that this virtue in its turn is an excellent soil in which the theological virtues prosper and develop.

Because being is one, it is a natural law that every effect return in some way to its cause. This return to God takes place in all creatures. In man, it is achieved through the virtue of religion, in as much as man is a knowing, conscious and loving effect of God, totally dependent on Him in his being and his activity. Man therefore knows this total dependence of his. Placed before the transcendent majesty of the divine Being,[9] he conceives a feeling of admiration, fear, reverence and subjection before that *tremendum* which transcends him and overwhelms him; he is already adoring, in the original spontaneous sense of adoration.

Then, coming back reflectively to this sentiment, man freely approves it as just and necessary, as the most primary and most inevitable of the debts

---

[7] Cf. St. Thomas, *Summa*, II-II, q. 80.

[8] See Odon Lottin's *Morale fondamentale* (Tournai: Desclée, 1954), pp. 350-63, with a résumé of the arguments that have been advanced, and a bibliography on p. 363, note 1.

[9] See Lottin, *ibid.*

he owes the supreme Being. It is the free response of man to the vision of the primordial obligation of dependence which he has toward the Being who is first principle and last end, Creator and Governor of all beings. Thus man accepts and proclaims God's excellence and his own subjection to and dependence on God. He praises God, thanks Him and, being unable to do anything better, puts himself wholly at God's disposal.

Understanding, moreover, that God is his supreme personal good also, he loves Him, desires to possess Him, and asks God to give Himself to him and to grant him all that is necessary in order to attain that supreme end. What is more, he strives to live in his daily existence a moral life which will be acceptable to God.

Thus admiration, reverential fear, protestation and free acceptance of one's own subjection, adoration, love, praise, thanksgiving, desire, petition, will to live in conformity with what pleases God and other related sentiments are all dispositions which proceed from a single fundamental attitude. This attitude may be called the total response of man felt as a strict debt which he owes God as the supreme Creator, Governor and ultimate end of all things.

This attitude is the religious attitude. We see at once how deeply it involves man's whole life and somehow carries in its train all the other virtues, in a definite direction. That is, religion directs the other virtues toward satisfying, in the manner proper to man and according to his powers, the profound obligation he feels toward God as supreme Creator, Governor and end of all things.

For this reason all theologians, in comparing the virtue of religion with the other moral virtues, agree in giving it an eminent place which surpasses all the rest.

Those who do accept the concept of religion as annexed to the cardinal virtue of justice do not fail to exalt it above all the other moral virtues. These other moral virtues, so the reasoning goes, regulate acts which refer to a created thing not immediately ordained to God — fortitude, for example, regulates our acts where dangers are concerned — while religion regulates our acts with regard to things that refer directly and immediately to God in as much as we render Him that which is due Him as supreme Creator and Governor. "Religion," observes St. Thomas, "comes closer to God than the other moral virtues, in as much as its actions are directly and immediately ordered to the honor of God. Hence religion excels among the moral virtues." [10]

The theologians who do not accept the concept of religion as annexed to the virtue of justice are led to their conclusion, from the theoretical point of view, precisely from the evident transcendence of the virtue of religion with

[10] *Summa*, II-II, q. 81, a. 6 c.

respect to all the other moral virtues. They hold that this transcendence is not sufficiently protected by relegating the virtue of religion to a place among the mere adjuncts of justice.

One of these theologians, Père Lottin, proposes the general distribution of the moral virtues into five classes: 1) the virtues which regulate our behavior toward ourselves: temperance and fortitude; 2) those which regulate our behavior toward our equals: benevolence and justice; 3) those which regulate our behavior toward the creatures superior to us, such as parents, teachers, country: submission to authority; 4) the virtue which regulates our behavior toward God: religion; 5) the whole directed by right reason: prudence. In this distribution also, the eminent dignity of the virtue of religion is evident. Since it alone has God for its object, it is superior to all the others, which refer immediately to created things; and it marks the summit of the moral life.[11]

Just as all theologians agree in giving religion a pre-eminent place among the moral virtues, so they are equally in agreement when they affirm the intimate connection between the virtue of religion and the theological virtues.

St. Thomas characterizes the theological virtues as those which have God Himself for their immediate object, and holds that this is the case only for faith, hope and charity, while it is not the case for the virtue of religion. This virtue, according to the angelic doctor, does indeed have God as the *end* to which it refers its acts immediately and directly, and for this reason it is superior to the other moral virtues; but it does not have God for its immediate *object* as do the theological virtues; and this for St. Thomas explains why religion is inferior to faith, to hope and especially to charity, the uncontested queen of all the virtues.[12]

Still, even for St. Thomas, the connection between the virtue of religion and the theological virtues is supreme and singular. He holds in the first place that the theological virtues are the root of the supernatural virtue of religion: "by their command (*suo imperio*) they cause the act of religion"; [13] for it is presupposed, if we are to honor God supernaturally in the act of religion, that we believe that God is Creator, Governor and last end of all things,[14] that we have the hope that God will accept our homage; charity, in the one who possesses it, is in a special way "the principle of religion." [15]

But then St. Thomas recognizes with the other theologians that the virtue of religion is also a general virtue which makes use of all the other virtues, including the theological virtues, to fulfill itself, offering the acts of these other virtues in homage due to God as supreme Creator, Governor and end

[11] Odon Lottin, "La definition classique de la vertu de religion," *Ephemerides theologicae lovanienses*, 24 (1948), 350.

[12] Cf. *Summa*, II-II, q. 81, a. 5.

[13] *Ibid.*, ad 1.

[14] Cf. *In Boethii de Trinitate*, lect. 1, q. 1, a. 2.

[15] *Summa*, II-II, q. 82, a. 2 ad 1.

of things. Thus the other virtues are like the matter of which the virtue of religion makes use: "Religion itself . . . has . . . for its matter, as it were, all the acts of faith or of another virtue, which it offers to God as His due." [16]

Finally, by a reciprocal influence, the virtue of religion, which under one aspect arises out of the theological virtues and especially charity, under another aspect nurtures the theological virtues and charity: "Charity causes devotion . . . but charity is also nourished by devotion, just as any friendship is preserved and increased by the practice and consideration of friendly deeds"; [17] and the same may be said of faith and of hope.

The connection between the virtue of religion and the theological virtues is such that there have even been theologians who hold that, theoretically speaking, the virtue of religion has all the required characteristics to be classified as a fourth theological virtue,[18] or as the general synthesis of the theological virtues. [19]

At any rate, the domain of the virtue of religion in the Christian life is quantitatively and qualitatively most profound.

Beginning with a contemplative admiration of the excellence of God, supreme Creator, Governor and end of all things, religion arouses in the soul the reflective and free sentiment of complaisance and of reverential submission which is translated into interior adoration. This interior disposition of the will, soul of all worship, finds outward expression connaturally in attitudes, gestures and words, because the interior will expresses itself by mobilizing and commanding the exterior powers. It commands also the intellect, which it bends to attention and even to prolonged and difficult contemplation, and, of course, the imagination and the other interior faculties which concur in the act of religion.

In short, this interior disposition of the will commands the whole person and goes so far as to offer it to God in perfect submission, to place it, so to speak, at the Creator's discretion and disposal, even to the point of destruction, if He consider this opportune.

This offering is the interior sacrifice, the supreme expression of religion of which the outward sacrifices are externalizations and the things offered outwardly are substitutions. The maximum expression of the interior sacrifice of one's own person even to the point of destruction, if the Creator judges this to be opportune, is martyrdom, for which the religious life in all its forms and virginity consecrated to God are substitutes. All these are acts of the virtue of religion or its expression.

Let us recall further that religion makes use of the acts of the other virtues,

---

[16] *In Boeth. de Trin.*, lect. 1, q. 1, a. 2.
[17] *Summa*, II-II, q. 81, a. 2 ad 2.
[18] R. Hourcade, "La vertu de religion," *Bulletin de litt. eccl.* of Toulouse, 1944, pp. 181-219.

[19] A. Martinet, *Institutionum theologicarum quarta pars seu theologia moralis* (Paris, 1867), I, 355 (quoted by Lottin, *Morale fondamentale*, p. 354).

especially — when the concern is with supernatural religion — of faith, hope and charity, as matter which it offers God by way of expressing itself. Then we shall readily agree with Lottin's observation [20] that the virtue of religion is the general bond which unifies the whole moral life, in fact, when we treat of the supernatural virtue of religion, the whole supernatural life of the Christian. It connects all the good actions of contemplative life and of active life in the supernatural life of the Christian, gathering them for the one general purpose of due homage to be rendered to God as supreme Creator, Governor and end of all things.

Devotio

Among the acts of the virtue of religion St. Thomas considers prayer and *devotio* in a special way. This concept of *devotio* is of special interest in the study of the liturgy.

Today our word "devotion" suggests rather a certain inclination, especially of a sentient nature, to religious things in general — and in this sense we say of someone that "he is devout" — and, still more precisely, a certain personal inclination to particular considerations or aspects of religious doctrine or to particular religious practices — thus we say: to have devotion to the Sacred Heart, to the Passion of our Lord, to St. Joseph.

The ancient concept of *devotio* is something much more profound. "*Devotio*," says St. Thomas, "is derived from *devovere*" (to devote oneself to, to give oneself entirely to . . . even unto death); "therefore those are called *devoti* who in some way devote themselves to God so as to be entirely subject to Him. For this reason the pagans in ancient times called those people *devoti* who vowed to their idols to suffer death for the safety of their army, as Titus Livius says (VIII, 9; X, 28) of the two Decii. Hence *devotio* is seen to be just this: a certain ready will to give oneself to whatever concerns the service of God." [21] "*Devotio* is an act of the will whereby a man offers himself to God to serve Him.[22]

Thus *devotio* is a certain decision of the will by which it puts itself into an attitude of being basically always ready for the service of God. It is a total vowing of oneself to God, in which a man directs his own wishes and desires toward the sole aim of God's service, always ready to engage himself in whatever concerns God's honor. It is therefore a calm and virile attitude of the will, the fruit of a reflective decision.

Devotio is, as it were, the first, basic psychological attitude which is the fruit of the virtue of religion and permeates one's life, giving orientation and form to the subsequent acts in which this service is realized.[23] "Devotions"

---

[20] Odon Lottin, *Morale fondamentale*, p. 362.
[21] *Summa*, II-II, q. 82, a. 1 c.
[22] *Ibid.*, ad 1.

[23] Cf. *Summa*, II-II, q. 82, a. 1 ad 1. On the concept of *devotio* in general see Jean Chatillon in *Dict. de spir.*, III (1957), 702-16; Augustine Daniels, "*Devotio*," *Jahrb. für Liturgiewis.*, 1 (1921), 40-60.

can be of value only as means of nurturing and expressing *devotio*. In the last analysis, therefore, they must be directed to God. *Devotio* is like the immediate soil in which worship buds and flowers.

3. Worship in General

It is necessary at this point to review briefly the general notion of worship and its great divisions.[24]

Notion

The Latin word for worship, *cultus*, comes from *colere*, "to care for, to cultivate" in a very broad sense. Worship is veneration for a being, based on the sentiment of its excellence and of one's own inferiority and subjection in the face of that being. It is therefore, radically, a certain interior attitude, made up not only of admiration, esteem and honor but also of humility and of a protestation of submission.[24a]

This attitude can be expressed in very different acts, but only an act which has for its direct object the being to whom the worship is directed is held to be an act of worship properly so called.

Thus the act by which a son applies himself to his studies in order to honor his parents, or the citizen is well-behaved outwardly in order to honor his country, or a believer gives an alms or takes care of a sick person for love of God, will not be called worship or veneration of parents, of country or of God except in a broad sense, because in these cases the study does not have the parents for its direct object, nor does the good behavior have one's country for its direct object, nor does the alms or the care of the sick person have God for its direct object.

On the other hand, the act of veneration of the flag, since it does not have for direct object that piece of cloth but the country of which the piece of cloth is only the symbol and, so to speak, the substitute, will be an act of homage to the fatherland. The same may be said of prayer or sacrifice offered to God; these are acts of worship in the strict sense.

[24] Joseph Lécuyer treats of worship in the theology of St. Thomas, "Réflexions sur la théologie du culte selon S. Thomas," *Rev. thomiste*, 55 (1955), 339 ff.

[24a] Translator's note: The same meaning is found in the derivation of the English word "worship" from "worth-ship." The Oxford English Dictionary, which gives this derivation, also has the following definitions under "cult":

1) worship; reverential homage rendered to a divine being or beings (obsolete except as in sense 2);

2) a particular form or system of religious worship; especially in reference to its external rites and ceremonies;

3) by transference, devotion or homage to a particular person or thing, now especially as paid by a body of professed adherents or admirers.

Since the Italian *culto* has all these meanings, I shall render it by "worship" or "veneration" or "homage" or "cult" as the context demands.

Divisions

Various divisions of the concept of worship are possible according to the basis on which they are made.

On the objective basis of excellence. Since the excellence of the being which is venerated in worship is the objective basis of the worship or cult, there will be as many different kinds of worship or cult as there are different kinds of excellence.

Here is an outline:

Worship or cult
- profane
- religious
  - natural
  - supernatural
    - Jewish
    - Christian
      - absolute: latria, hyperdulia, dulia
      - relative

In profane worship or cult, for example, in the cult of ancestors, of fatherland, of the arts, of the philosophers, the excellence considered is of a profane nature. In religious worship it is of a religious nature, that is, having a relation to God and to the moral life.

True religious excellence, in the last analysis, is always God Himself, the divine life, in itself or shared with creatures. Religious worship, therefore, can refer only to God; it can refer to the creature only in so far as the creature shares the divine life in some way. That which is by participation, though being really something in itself, is always referred, in the last analysis, to that which is of itself, and is reduced to it. Just so, religious worship or veneration of any created being may be a real veneration also of this being and not only of God, by reason of the real excellence of the divine life present in this being; and yet, in the last analysis, the worship or veneration is always referred to God, ultimate cause of that excellence.

In a hypothetical purely natural order, the divine excellence, objective basis of worship, would be formally the divine life in itself or shared only in so far as God is Author of the natural order, and thus there would be a purely natural religious worship.

In the supernatural order, on the other hand, the objective basis of worship is formally the divine life in itself or shared in so far as God is Author of the supernatural order. Supernatural worship presupposes, therefore, a supernatural revelation and presupposes in us the faith by which we assent to this revelation, because the supernatural divine life is known to us only through that revelation to which we assent in theological faith.

Jewish worship in the Old Testament was already a supernatural religious worship because it was based on a supernatural revelation and on faith. God was honored in it with acts having for direct object God Himself as supreme Creator, Author and Giver of the covenant to Israel, His chosen people, with a view to the establishment of His supernatural kingdom in the world.

But the Old Testament, seen in the ensemble of the divine plans unfolding in sacred history, has only a sense of beginning and preparation: it is a first embodiment, temporary and imperfect, of that divine idea which God was to realize fully and wanted to realize fully in Christ and in the Christian economy, and which will be manifested and fulfilled perfectly in the Jerusalem to come. The worship in the Old Testament must be considered in this general perspective, which determines its deepest sense. It was therefore a first rough draft, a first figure and a first sketch of that worship which Christ would inaugurate in His mortal life, of which Christian worship is but the continuation under the veil of signs and symbols, and of which the worship of the future heavenly Jerusalem will be the perfect fulfillment in glory. This idea is one of the major themes of the Epistle to the Hebrews.[25]

Christian worship is the worship of God initiated by Christ in His mortal life, chiefly on Golgotha, as Redeemer and Head of redeemed humanity which was to be formed into His Church, His body and His spouse, the expression of Himself and the continuation of His work in the world until His glorious return. It is therefore the worship of God in Christ and through Christ: begun by Christ, continued invisibly by Him in us, through us and for our benefit, that is, in His Church by means of His Church and for the benefit of His Church, who simply takes part and associates herself in His worship. The proper excellence of the divine life on which Christian worship is formally based is therefore the divine life manifested in Christ.

Only an intellectual nature, a person, has formally in himself a religious excellence which makes him worthy of veneration and therefore of "cult." Thus the person can be the object of cult in himself, which cult of a person, for this reason and in this sense, is called absolute cult.

Objects, on the other hand, if they have any excellence in relation to the divine life, cannot have it formally in themselves, but only by some connection they have with a person, in as much as they belong to him in some way. Hence if there is any cult of objects, this must all go to the person. This cult is therefore called *relative*, that is, relative to the person.

Thus, for example, the cult with which honor is given the objects that have some connection with the person of the saints, such as their relics and their images, is merely relative. The relics and the images of the saints have no religious excellence through any value of divine life inhering in

[25] See: Ceslaus Spicq, *L'Épître aux hébreux*, I (Paris: Gabalda, 1952), 280-83, 291 ff., 311-24.

them. Their religious excellence comes only from the connection established mentally between them and the person of the saints by the one who venerates them. Thus the cult with which they are venerated goes wholly to the saints, in as much as the saints share in the divine life.

Again: there is a great difference, in the sphere of absolute cult itself, between that which is rendered to God and that which is rendered to creatures, however holy they be. The supreme worship offered to the divine nature itself, which is the worship of adoration, in which man professes his total servitude to God, is called worship of *latria* (Greek *latreia* — service). It is due only to the most holy Trinity and to the individual Persons, including Jesus Christ even in His humanity. In Christ, even under the sacramental species, the humanity is adored together with the divinity with a single act of adoration, in virtue of the hypostatic union.

The religious excellence of the angels and the saints is derived entirely from the fact that they are faithful servants of God. Hence the cult offered them is called cult of *dulia* (Greek *douleia* — slavery). And the most holy Mary, who has a most privileged post among all the servants of God, is the object of a cult which, though essentially different from that of *latria* and inferior to it, is none the less superior to that of all the other saints and the angels, and is therefore called *hyperdulia*.

Since the religious excellence of the saints is through participation, because it consists in the fact that with God's grace they participate in an eminent degree of divine life, the cult of the saints, while going really to them, because they do share in the divine life, still goes always to God in the last analysis, because the saints are *only* sharers in His life.

On the basis of the subject who renders the worship. The subject who renders worship is man. But man can be considered under various aspects. For example: man can be considered in as much as he is a composite of soul and body, and from this point of view worship will be distinguished into mere interior worship and worship which is interior and exterior at the same time; he can be considered in as much as he is a social being, and from this point of view his worship will be distinguished into public worship and private worship.

Worship is essentially and principally interior. This is so, first of all, because worship is a homage rendered to God; and honor is formally in the spirit of the one who renders it, being formally an attitude of spirit, especially of the will. Worship is interior also because God is spirit and it is principally by the spirit that contact is made with Him. Finally, it is interior because in man, although he is a composite of spirit and body, it is nevertheless the spirit which is the determining and more noble substantial part, giving to outward expressions all their properly human, hence moral, meaning and value.

Worship consists essentially and principally, therefore, in those acts and dispositions of the spirit, chiefly of the will, in which, relating directly to God, man recognizes the divine excellence and protests his inferiority and subjection to God. Without this interior spirit, any outward expression of worship is nothing but empty show.

Nevertheless, since man is not a pure spirit but a composite of soul and body and a social being, it is not only connatural and spontaneous but also obligatory, that is, really owed to God, that man's interior worship be expressed outwardly, at the proper time and in the proper measure. This is so for three reasons:

1) because it is the whole man, in his substantial union of soul and body, who should honor God, recognizing the divine excellence as his integral composite nature demands, and professing before God in the same way his own inferiority and his subjection;

2) because not only does the soul have an influence on the body, but, psychologically, the body's expression also re-affects in some way the attitudes and sentiments of the soul and nourishes them, both in us and in the others who see us, and thus the very perfection of the interior acts of worship requires, up to a certain point, their exteriorization; [26]

3) because man is a social being and also as such must render to God the worship that is His due; and without exteriorization of worship there is no social worship.

The connatural structure of worship as man's response to God, consisting of an interior spirit and its outward embodiment, corresponds perfectly, therefore, to the connatural structure of sanctification as descent of God into

[26] These two reasons are expressed by St. Thomas in the following passage: "Thus, therefore, religion consists in the act by which man renders worship to God, subjecting himself to God. Now this act must be adapted both to the One to whom the worship is rendered and to the one who renders it. But since the One to whom worship is rendered is a Spirit, He cannot be attained with the body only but with the mind; it is for this reason that the worship rendered Him consists principally in the spiritual acts through which our mind is ordered to God, which acts are principally those of the theological virtues. It is in this sense that Augustine (*Enchiridion*, 3) says that worship is rendered to God with faith, hope and charity. To these are added the acts of the gifts of the Holy Spirit which order us to God, such as wisdom and fear of the Lord. "But because we who render worship to God are corporeal and our knowledge begins with the senses, bodily acts too are required on our part for the aforesaid worship, both in order to serve God with all that we are and in order to arouse ourselves and others through these bodily acts to spiritual acts ordered to God.

"Hence Augustine in the book *On the Care That Should Be Taken for the Dead* (n. 7) says: 'Those who pray express their feelings of supplication with the members of their body when they kneel, when they extend their hands, or when they prostrate themselves on the ground or do any other similar outward act. It is true that their interior will and the intention of their heart are known to God, and that He has no need of these signs to know the human soul. But by such means man excites himself to pray and to groan with more humility and with more fervor' " (St. Thomas, *In Boeth. de Trin.*, lect. 1, q. 1, a. 2 c.; in Mandonnet edition, q. 3, a. 2 c. Cf. also *Summa*, II-II, q. 81, a. 7 c.; q. 83, a. 12 c. and ad 1; q. 84, a. 2 c.).

man consisting of divine life communicated to man through material and sensible things. It is always the law of incarnation that presides over the encounter between man and God.

In the interior worship of God there is no possibility of sinning by excess; on the contrary, whatever man does in this regard will always be less than what he should do in equity toward God as his supreme Creator, Governor and end. For the excellence of God, to whom homage is rendered in worship, exceeds all measure, and therefore the creature will never be able to honor Him as much as He is worthy of being honored.

The exterior acts of worship, on the other hand, are regulated by prudence. This means that, in these acts, there can be sin not only of defect but also of excess or of imbalance in the circumstances of manner, quantity, time. True, in the supernatural public worship regulated by the Church, there can be no sin by excess in the performance of those external acts which the Church imposes as obligatory. But in the external acts of worship approved by the Church but not imposed as obligatory, prudence must intervene in each man in order that he observe a just measure according to the circumstances of person, place and time. This observation has definite value as far as the relations between liturgy and spirituality, liturgy and pastoral are concerned.

Considering man as a social being, his worship is divided into private worship and public worship. Private worship may be either interior only, or interior and exterior at the same time. There is no true worship which is exterior only. Public worship is interior and exterior at the same time, since man communicates with other men only by means of the external.

Official public worship is that rendered by society as such, in other words by men in so far as they are a social body structured in hierarchy. Now men are a social body formally in so far as the individuals, in that which concerns the purpose of the society, depend on the authority which informs them, directs them, represents them and acts in their name. Therefore, official public worship is only that which is recognized by the legitimate authority as the society's worship, ordered and rendered by that authority as form and representative of the whole social body.

The legitimacy, rather the necessity, of a public worship for man in general stems from his social nature, by reason of which he is born, subsists, develops and reaches his perfection, under any aspect, only in society as member of a body structured by an authority. Therefore, in some way, man must render his worship to God also as a social being and a member of a body socially structured, and this implies that the society as such, socially structured through its legitimate authority, must intervene in this worship.

Beyond this general necessity, the degree and the specific concrete manner of sociality of Christian worship depends on the free positive will of God, who has decided to communicate with men only in Christ and in that society which is the Church, with her determinate means of sanctification and with her determinate hierarchical powers of governing and teaching. This last thought will be further explained in another chapter.

By making these distinctions among the different kinds of worship, we see that Catholic liturgy as worship is the Church's religious, supernatural, Christian worship, principally interior but also essentially exterior, public and official.

4. The Sacramental Characters and Christian Worship

One of the major characteristics of the theological explanation of the sacraments proposed by St. Thomas is the intimate connection he establishes between sacraments and Christian worship. Although we cannot say that St. Thomas' explanation in this field must be held as a dogma of faith, or as the only explanation possible, especially in all its details, still, as a whole, it is not only a very satisfactory explanation of the data of revelation but also one of indisputable grandeur. In fact, as far as the relation between baptismal character and Christian worship is concerned, it is generally accepted by the theologians and even cited by the second Vatican Council.[27] I shall therefore set forth a summary of it, followed by some observations of liturgical interest.

As we know, for St. Thomas the proper end of the Christian sacraments is twofold: to sanctify man by cleansing him of sin and to fit him for Christian worship: "Sacramental grace is ordained principally to two ends: 1) to take away the defects consequent on past sins, in so far as they are transitory in act but endure in guilt; 2) to perfect the soul in things pertaining to the worship of God according to the religion of the Christian life."[28]

With regard to worship as a specific end of the Christian sacraments, it should be noted that the concern is with perfecting the believer by means of the sacraments not just for any worship of God but for specifically Christian worship. We know that Christian worship is the worship which Christ rendered to God in His mortal life, especially on Golgotha, and which He keeps on rendering now. We know also that for St. Thomas, although all the sacraments qualify their recipients for the Christian worship of God, and in fact every sacrament received is already an exercise of Christian worship, still not all the sacraments are directed to worship in the same way or in equal measure.

St. Thomas connects baptism, confirmation and holy orders in a very special way with the cultual aspect of the sacraments, and this because of the indelible character which these three sacraments, and they alone, imprint on the one who receives them. The special relation between these three sacraments and the divine worship consists in the fact that the proper end of the indelible character is precisely to empower directly for Christian worship.

The character of baptism and of confirmation, for St. Thomas, empowers

---

[27] *Constitution on the Church*, art. 11. See also MD, nn. 88 (Lat. 87) and 104 (Lat. 103), as well as CL, art. 14.
[28] *Summa*, III, q. 62, a. 5 c.

directly for Christian divine worship in as much as this worship consists in participating actively in the other sacraments and above all in the Eucharist, in receiving them, but not in a purely passive way.[29]

The character of holy orders, on the other hand, empowers for Christian worship in as much as it empowers a person to give the sacraments to others.[30]

As we have often repeated, Christian worship is nothing else but Christ's own worship of God, which He initiated in His earthly life, especially on Golgotha, and which He always continues as supreme Priest, Mediator between God and men and Head of His mystical body which is the Church. The sacramental character which empowers precisely for Christian worship can do nothing else, therefore, than empower man to participate in the worship which Christ as Head of the Church, His mystical body, renders to God. Every sacramental character is therefore a participation in the priesthood of Christ.

"The character, properly speaking," says St. Thomas, "is a certain mark (*signaculum*) with which a thing is marked as being ordained to some determined end. Thus a coin is marked for use in commerce, and soldiers are marked as belonging to the army. Now the believer is deputed to two things: first of all and principally to the enjoyment of glory; and to this end he is signed with the mark of grace. . . . Secondly, each of the faithful is deputed to receive or to give to others things which pertain to the worship of God. This is the proper end which the sacramental character has in view. Now the whole rite of the Christian religion derives from the priesthood of Christ. It is therefore clear that the sacramental character is in a special way the character of Christ, configuring the faithful to His priesthood. The sacramental characters are nothing but certain participations in Christ's priesthood, derived from Christ Himself."[31]

Through the sacramental character which He imprints in the faithful by sharing His priesthood with them, Christ exercises His own priesthood, just as the principal cause exercises its action by means of the instrument and the instrumental power which it imparts to the instrument.[32]

---

[29] For baptism there is no difficulty; in fact, the point is strongly emphasized by liturgical practice: only the baptized may receive the sacraments, and, in ancient times, only the baptized could assist at the sacrifice of the Mass. For confirmation a certain difficulty arises by reason of the way in which it is commonly conceived today (thus also in St. Thomas, who says it is ordered to the Eucharist, "so that a person will not abstain from this sacrament out of fear," *Summa*, III, q. 65, a. 3. Likewise in St. Thomas there are hesitations about the proper finality of the character of confirmation; cf. *Summa*, III, q. 72, a. 5).

In the ancient usage, on the other hand, this difficulty seems not to exist, since confirmation was always received after baptism and before communion (e.g., on Holy Saturday night; consider also the custom still prevalent among the Greeks of confirming infants). Thus in antiquity confirmation really appeared as an essential part of the initiation and therefore of the Christian empowerment for the divine worship of the Eucharist.

[30] Cf. *Summa*, III, q. 63, a. 6.

[31] *Summa*, III, q. 63, a. 3 c.

[32] Cf. *Summa*, III, q. 63, a. 5 ad 1 et ad 2.

By means of any sacrament, man in some way shares in Christ's priesthood, at least in so far as he shares in its effects and, in receiving the sacraments, offers an act of worship to God. But in the three sacraments of baptism, confirmation and holy orders this participation is much more intimate and profound, precisely by means of the character which they imprint. For by that character a person is deputed to do or receive actively something which is proper to the priesthood of Christ.[33]

The character is thus a certain objective consecration in as much as it is a separation from profane use and a reservation for use in divine worship. "Man is sanctified through all the sacraments, in as much as sanctification involves purification from sin, which is effected through grace. But in a special way some sacraments, those which imprint the character, sanctify man by a certain consecration, deputing him for the divine worship; just as we say also of inanimate objects that they are sanctified by being designated for divine worship." [34]   •

St. Thomas thinks that the character resides in the faculties of the soul and more exactly in the cognitive faculty.[35]

From all this St. Thomas derives the explanation why the sacramental character is indelible. The subject in which it resides, the soul or intellect, is in itself indelible and perpetual, as long as God does not wish to annihilate it. And the priesthood of Christ, of which the character is a participation, is eternal. Hence that which is consecrated by a participation in this priesthood remains always consecrated, as long as it is not destroyed.[36] "Although exterior worship does not remain after this life, the end of that worship does remain. For this reason the character also remains after this life, in the good for their glory, in the wicked for their ignominy; just as the military character remains in soldiers after victory, both in those who win, for their glory, and in those who are defeated, for their punishment." [37]

In connection with the sacramental character, therefore, St. Thomas is able to propose a grand synthesizing perspective. First of all, the whole sacramental economy here appears as ordained in the first place and essentially to the Christian worship of God as its specific end, Christian worship as the prolongation in us of Christ's worship of God. The other essential end of the sacraments, the sanctification of man, appears as itself ordained to worship.

This fact must be noted well: the sanctification of man is ordained to the adoration, the glory to be given to God in Christian worship, and not vice versa. The two inseparable ends of the liturgy, sanctification and worship, are not parallel or independent aims, but one subordinated to the other: sanctification looks to worship.

[33] Cf. *Summa*, III, q. 63, a. 6 ad 1.
[34] *Ibid.*, ad 2.
[35] See *Summa*, III, q. 63, a. 4 et ad 2 et ad 3.

[36] Cf. *Summa*, III, q. 63, a. 5.
[37] *Summa*, III, q. 63, a. 5 ad 3.

It is evident that the whole sacramental economy, in fact the whole liturgy, derives from this fact a strongly theocentric coloring: in the liturgy everything, including the sanctification of man, is ordained to the homage to be given to God.

There is all the more reason to consider as strictly subordinate to the end of adoration and worship everything in the liturgy that has the immediate purpose of admonishing and instructing, such as readings, sermons, incidental explanations. The didactic and moralizing aim of the liturgy is subordinate to the aim of worship. It is for this reason that the didactic and exhortatory aspect in the liturgy must be regulated in such a way that the precise end to which it is immediately ordained is never lost sight of.

If we consider further that the sacraments and, with more reason, the liturgy instituted by the Church, are ordained to the Eucharist, as St. Thomas teaches [38] and as we also are going to bring out in the next chapter, we can understand how the whole work of sanctification, and a fortiori the whole work of teaching and governing in the Church, is ordained to the Christian worship of God in the sacrifice of the Mass. Thus we get some idea, once more, of how everything in the liturgy and in the Christian life, theocentrically conceived and lived, has for its center and sun the sacrifice of the Mass.

Moreover, through this doctrine of the sacramental characters, the whole system of sanctification of man and worship of God appears centered on the priesthood of Christ and on the worship which Christ renders to God. Hence it depends on the present participation and extension of Christ's priesthood and worship to the whole Church, primarily and in a singular way to the hierarchy through the character of holy orders, but also, in a different way indeed, but a very real way, to every one of the faithful, through the character of baptism and of confirmation. The Church's worship is the worship of Christ, the Head of the Church, who shares His worship with the whole body. The Church's priesthood is the priesthood of Christ, the Head of the Church, who shares His priesthood with the whole body.

From this is seen the specific character of Christian worship as prolongation and participation of Christ's worship of God, without parallel in anything that man could ever think of or achieve. We can see how far are mere philosophy, history of religions or religious psychology from being able even to suspect such depths, and how superficial is the idea which these sciences can form of Christian worship by their own lights alone.[39]

---

[38] *Summa*, III, q. 65, a. 3.

[39] That is why the Catholic theologian, though admiring in some cases a great number of interesting phenomenological observations of religious psychology, cannot help noticing how empty are the writings of non-Catholics when they speak of Christian worship; they can only scratch the surface of this reality. This is true, e.g., of William James, Pettazzoni, Jung, Otto. The observation is still more valid for the works of modernists like Tyrell and Buonaiuti.

We can see also how only he who is signed with the baptismal character is capable of a Christian worship and can take a real part in the liturgy, especially in the sacrifice of the Mass. This explains the ancient discipline which did not admit the unbaptized even to mere attendance at Mass.

5. The Priesthood of Christ and the Priesthood of All the Faithful

The doctrine of the sacramental character as "character of Christ, to whose priesthood the faithful are configured according to the sacramental characters, which are nothing but certain participations in the priesthood of Christ, derived from Christ Himself" [40] — this doctrine gives its exact meaning, neither exaggerated nor minimized, to the notion of the universal priesthood of the faithful, and thus enables us to understand in what it is that their active participation in the liturgical action and especially in the Mass consists.

The question

Some decades ago the question of the universal priesthood of the faithful once more claimed the attention of theologians, who set to work to study it anew in the Scriptures, in patristic, liturgical and theological tradition and in its theoretical aspects.[41] There were two incentives for this study: the liturgical renewal, bringing with it a desire to clarify better the theoretical aspect and to arrive at a better practical understanding of the active role of the faithful in the liturgical action, and more precise reflections in regard to the position of the laity in the Church.

First of all, from the theological point of view, every investigation in this matter must take the following fact as its starting point: Scripture, liturgical tradition and patristic thought as well as theologians both medieval and modern, attribute to all the faithful the character of *priests;* and they employ the term *sacrifice* in connection with an extraordinarily large number of actions and situations. Thus, they speak of the priesthood and of the sacrifice of all the faithful in connection with their prayer, especially that of praise; with their mortification; with virginity and the monastic and religious life in general; with martyrdom; with the fulfillment of the duties of their state in life; with the apostolic ministry; with doctrinal instruction; with the par-

---

[40] *Summa*, III, q. 63, a. 3 c.

[41] One of the more recent studies and, it seems to me, one of the best from the theoretical point of view, is that of Yves Congar, *Lay People in the Church: A Study for a Theology of the Laity* (Westminster, Md.: Newman Press, 1957), pp. 112-257. See also A. Piolanti, "Il sacerdozio dei fedeli," in *Enciclopedia del sacerdozio,* Florentine edition, 1953, pp. 715-

31, with its extensive bibliography. Among the other studies especially noteworthy are: P. Dabin, *Le sacerdoce royal des fidèles dans la tradition ancienne et moderne* (Brussels and Paris: Desclée, De Brouwer & Cie, 1950); Joseph Lécuyer, "*Essai sur le sacerdoce des fidèles chez les Pères,*" in *La maison Dieu,* 27 (1951-53), pp. 7-50.

ticipation of all the faithful in the Eucharistic sacrifice; with the fact that husband and wife administer the sacrament of matrimony to each other; with the life of fathers and mothers of families; with the administration of certain sacramentals; with Catholic Action. In all, about thirteen different expressions. Besides this, there are many explicit general affirmations of the existence of a special kind of priesthood which belongs to all the faithful.

These aspects have been made explicit in the history of theology not all together and at the same time, but successively. The outline of the historical development of these various points can be sketched approximately as follows.

Already found explicitly in the Scriptures is: first of all, the general affirmation of the priesthood of all the baptized (1 Peter 2:4-10; Apoc. 1:5-6; 5:9-10; 20:6). To these texts which use the very word *priesthood* in reference to all the faithful must be added: second, the texts in which it is said that now, in Christ, we draw near (*proserchomai*) to God (Heb. 4:14-16; 7:19; 10:19-22); or that in Christ we approach (*prosago*) or have access (*prosagoge*) to God (Eph. 2:18-22; see also Eph. 3:12; Rom. 5:2; 1 Peter 3:18). This theme of drawing near or of having access has indisputably a meaning of priestly worship: [42] one draws near to God to perform an act of worship, and it is mostly the priests who draw near and have access to Him (see the Septuagint, Num. 18:2-7; Exod. 29:10; Lev. 4:14; 7:6; Jer. 7:16; see also Clement of Rome, [*First Letter*] *To the Corinthians*, 31:3; and the anonymous *Letter to Diognetus*, 3:2). In the third place, there is in Scripture the explicit concept that the faithful offer worship and sacrifice to God: Phil. 3:3 (worship in general); Phil. 4:18 (sacrifice by way of financial assistance to missionaries); Rom. 12:1 (the sacrifice of their own bodies; see also Phil. 2:17 and 2 Tim. 4:6); Heb. 13:15-16 (sacrifice of praise and of charity to one's neighbor); Rom. 15:16 (St. Paul offering in sacrifice the gentiles as fruit of his own particular apostolate).

Besides the points already expressed directly in Scripture, patristic tradition [43] makes explicit the concepts especially of sacrifice and priesthood in martyrdom and virginity; and we find there also the concepts of sacrifice and priesthood in preaching and in the role of fathers and mothers of families. [44]

The Middle Ages make especially clear the concept of the Eucharistic priesthood and sacrifice even of the laity, with explicit reference to the sacramental character of baptism and of confirmation. The concepts, however, of sacrifice and universal priesthood in the administration of the sacrament of matrimony, in the use of sacramentals and in the apostolate of Catholic Action are ideas brought into prominence by modern theologians.

---

[42] See Karl L. Schmidt, "Prosago, prosagoge," in *Theol. Wört. zum NT*, I, 131-134; and Johannes Schneider, "Proserchomai," *ibid.*, II, 680-682.

[43] In this regard see especially the works of Dabin and Lécuyer cited above in note 41.

[44] See, for example, the texts of Justin Martyr, Irenaeus, John Chrysostom, and Leo the Great cited in A. Piolanti, *op. cit.*, p. 717 ff.

The question posed by theologians in regard to this terminology of Scripture, of patristic and theological tradition is simply this: How is this data to be organized in a unified speculative system in explanation of the common priesthood of all the faithful? What is to be the principle governing theological speculation in this matter?

The attempts at explanation have been many and various. We shall not speak of the frankly heretical deviations in this field from Tertullian the Montanist to Luther, which deny any kind of essential distinction between the hierarchical priesthood and that priesthood which is common to all the faithful.[45] Among Catholics themselves opinion ranges all the way from the minimalist position which understands the word priesthood in a metaphorical or even equivocal sense,[46] to positions diametrically opposed, which exaggerate to such a degree the reality of the priesthood common to all the faithful that they risk bringing to the fore a latent tendency which does not sufficiently protect its essential distinction from the hierarchical priesthood. This is the reason why the magisterial authority of the Church has recently insisted upon such an essential distinction.[47]

Attempt at systematization of the concept of the priesthood of Christ

Taking into account the observations made recently by theologians in this field, we propose the following summary outline which is concerned with the concept of the priesthood of Christ, and of the sharing therein of Christians. The purpose of this outline is to clarify the concept of the universal priesthood of the faithful as it is variously understood in Scripture and in tradition, including it in the general concept of the Christian priesthood and showing thereby its position in respect to the priesthood of Christ and in reference to the hierarchical priesthood.

PRIESTHOOD OF CHRIST

I. In itself;

II. Shared with Christians:

    A. Through the character of holy orders (=hierarchical priesthood)

        1. To offer *in persona Christi* the Eucharistic sacrifice itself;

        2. To offer it in its presuppositions and consequences:

            a. With regard to the faithful:

                i. In the presuppositions and consequences of a liturgical nature:

                    a. Administration of the other sacraments;

                    β. Institution and use of sacramentals, ceremonies, prayer and divine praise.

---

[45] The Protestant error was condemned by Trent; see Dz. 1767-78 (960-68).

[46] This is virtually the case with B. Capelle and the periodical *Les questions liturgiques et paroissiales*, in numerous articles and reviews.

[47] See the Second Vatican Council's *Constitution on the Church*, art. 10; MD, nn. 82-84 (Lat. 81-83).

      ii. In the presuppositions and consequences of an extraliturgical
         nature:
         α. Governing of the Church;
         β. Teaching of doctrine.
    b. With regard to unbelievers: missionary apostolate.
B. Through the character of baptism and confirmation (=priesthood
   common to all the faithful)
   1. To participate actively in the Eucharistic sacrifice;
   2. To participate in it in its presuppositions and consequences:
     a. Of a liturgical nature:
       i. Sacramental:
         α. To receive penance, anointing of the sick and holy orders;
         β. To administer to themselves and to live Christian
           matrimony.
       ii. Non-sacramental:
         α. To receive the sacramentals and to administer some of
           them;
         β. To take part in liturgical prayer.
     b. Of an extraliturgical nature:
       i. Holiness of life:
         α. Mortification;
         β. Virginity and religious life;
         γ. Duties of one's state;
         δ. Practice of charity towards one's neighbor;
         ε. Private prayer.
       ii. Apostolate, especially in Catholic Action.
      iii. Confession of one's faith, even unto death if the occasion
        arises.
A series of notations will serve to explain the meaning of the outline.

On the concept of priesthood. The first question which gives rise to different opinions among theologians about the priesthood common to all the
faithful is the very concept of priesthood in general. And first of all: Does
mediation enter in an essential manner into the concept of priesthood? In
such a way, indeed, that if there were no mediation, there would, by that
very fact, be no priesthood either? Were this the case, the "priesthood" common to all the faithful would be without analogy, not even metaphorical,
with the priesthood of Christ and of the hierarchy, because in the "priesthood" of the ordinary faithful mediation is lacking.[48] If this were in fact the

---

[48] At most, one might speak of the mediation which the layman exercises by his prayers
of praise and intercession between God on the
one hand and other men and infrahuman
creatures on the other. But it does not seem
that Scripture or even tradition speaks of any
such "priesthood" — certainly in no notable
degree. The Second Vatican Council's *Consti-*

case, to speak of general "priesthood" along with "priesthood" of Christ and of the hierarchy or even of the Old Testament would be to use an ambiguous expression.

Scripture, however, when it speaks of the "priesthood" of all the faithful, certainly intends to point out an analogy between the priesthood of the faithful and the priesthood of the Old Testament. This analogy consists in the offering of victims (*thysia*) and therefore of sacrifice:[49] "You also, as living stones, are built up as a spiritual (*pneumatikos*) edifice in view of a holy priesthood, to offer spiritual victims (*pneumatikas thysias*) acceptable to God through Jesus Christ" (1 Peter 2:5).

A relation is thereby established between the priesthood of the faithful and the offering of victims. The *tertium comparationis* between the priesthood of the Old Testament and the universal priesthood of all the faithful is none other than the offering of a sacrifice: the faithful of the New Testament are all priests, analogously to the priesthood of the Old Testament, because even the faithful of the New Testament offer victims.[50] The universal priesthood of all the faithful is therefore defined in relation to the offering of victims in sacrifice.

On the concept of sacrifice. But what is the precise notion of sacrifice that must be adopted? This question too is much discussed among theologians. Without entering into the details of discussion, we can propose the following notion: sacrifice, in the broadest sense, is the internal act of placing something at the complete disposal, even to the point of total destruction if necessary, of another person or another subject, in recognition of his superiority over the one who places the thing at his disposal. Thus it is possible to speak of sacrificing a sum of money to someone or something; of sacrificing our career or reputation for someone or something; and, especially, of sacrificing to someone or something a person or a living thing, which can then be termed quite precisely a victim.

The concept of sacrifice includes, therefore: 1) the concept of oblation: of offering something, putting it at someone's disposal; 2) the concept of destruction, at least potentially, of the thing offered; and such a destruction, if the object sacrificed is a living being, or victim, is called an immolation. But the destruction agreed to in advance by the one making the offering need not actually take place at all; what is essential is that it be agreed to in advance,

tution on the Church hints at such notions (art. 31; 34; 36) in connection with the idea of the consecration of the world; but the idea is not developed.

[49] *Thysia*, victim, is a sacrificial term in the Old Testament.

[50] The text of Heb. 5:1, which puts the idea of mediation in the foreground, does not in-

tend to define the priesthood in general, but speaks of the high priesthood of the line of Aaron: "Every high priest, in fact, who is raised up from among men, is ordained for the advantage of men in their relations with God, that he may offer gifts and sacrifices for sins."

if the circumstances should require it; 3) the concept of acknowledging the superiority of the thing or person to whom the sacrifice is offered.

In religious sacrifice, man places at the disposition of the divinity his own person or some of his goods, even to the point, if necessary, of their destruction, in order to acknowledge the sovereign dominion of the divinity over his goods or himself. In religious sacrifice, made by one who has a right concept of the divinity, the thing offered must always include in some way the life and the whole person of the one making the offering; otherwise, there would be no real acknowledgment of the effective dominion and superiority of the divinity, because this dominion extends to the life itself and to the whole personality of the man. One who would intend to exclude from the sacrificial act this acknowledgment of the dominion of the divinity over his proper life and person would certainly be offering to the divinity not sacrifice but offense.

Because the concept of religious sacrifice necessarily includes, as the matter offered, the whole person, other things cannot be the material of religious sacrifice except insofar as they have some relation to the person, either symbolically (symbolic matter), or as effect and manifestation of the person (such as well-being, recreation, honor, gladness), or as objects which he possesses (money, land, fields).

With this line of reasoning, then, it is easily seen that the concept of religious sacrifice contains an analogy of attribution and is concerned first of all with the sacrifice of the person, while the sacrifice of other things is only subordinate, inasmuch as they have some relationship to the person as a symbol or manifestation of him, or as an object possessed by him.

In the intrinsic constitution of sacrifice it is necessary to distinguish that which serves as its matter and that which serves as form. The form of the sacrifice is the internal disposition, the will, the intention of the one who is making the sacrifice, whether the thing offered is himself or something else, in order to recognize the superiority and the dominion of the person or thing to whom sacrifice is being made. The matter is the thing itself which is being offered, which is being placed at the disposal of the one to whom sacrifice is being made. This matter of the sacrifice can be distinguished as in the following outline:

MATTER OF THE SACRIFICE

I. *Real matter*: the very things which are offered for disposition:
   A. Intrinsic to the person of the one who offers:
      1. Total and primary: the whole person, his very life;
      2. Partial and secondary: the quite varied manifestations of the person, of his life (such as well-being, labor, honor, etc.).
   B. Extrinsic: whatever goods are extrinsic to the person (such as money and other property).

II. *Symbolic matter*: not the thing itself which is offered for disposition, but something else which takes its place as a symbol (such as an animal as a symbol of one's own life).

The sacrifice can remain purely internal or it can be externalized; and if the latter, it may be done imperfectly (e.g., with words alone of adoration, praise, thanksgiving, expiation, etc.), or perfectly (external sacrificial actions properly so called).

We know that the absolute ends of religious sacrifice are adoration, praise, thanksgiving; expiation, however, is a hypothetical end, and has its place when an offense has previously been committed. It is in sacrifice that religion, and devotion in particular, achieve their highest stature.

On the priesthood of Christ. Christ is essentially our Head and Mediator because He is constituted as such by the free will of God, who establishes His solidarity with us and ours with Him. In Christ, therefore, the priesthood is essentially a priesthood of Head and Mediator, and His sacrifice is essentially a sacrifice of Head and Mediator.

For that reason, in Christ, the sacrifice is formally the act and the disposition of His own will by which, as responsible Head and Mediator of all mankind, from the very first moment of His existence, He has placed at God's disposal His own person, even to the total destruction of His own life, such being the Father's will, in order to acknowledge the absolute sovereign dominion of God over Himself and over all mankind.[51]

The sacrifice of Christ, and therefore His priesthood, extends to the whole of His existence, because He offers that sacrifice from the very first moment of His existence. All the acts of His life were sacrificial because all the manifestations of His life were offered by Him to the Father as intrinsic matter, partial and secondary, of sacrifice. But this sacrifice was such only in reference to the sacrifice of the intrinsic matter, total and primary, that is to say, of His own life. And this last sacrifice, though it begins at the very first instant of Christ's existence, was completed only on Golgotha, because it was there that the effective destruction of the life offered actually took place, the destruction demanded by the Father. Thus, in Christ, all His sacrificial acts and therefore the whole of His priesthood are referred to Golgotha as to the sacrificial and sacerdotal act to which all His other acts are directed and from which they derive.

The sacrifice of the Last Supper was such in reference to Golgotha, of which it was a sacramental anticipation. The sacrifice of the Mass is such in reference to Golgotha, of which it is an unbloody sacramental actualization. In what precise sense? This, of course, is one of the questions much discussed among theologians. It seems to me that, in brief, the Mass is an un-

[51] There is an effective expression of these ideas in C. Spicq, *L'épître aux hébreux*, Vol. 1, pp. 291-324; Vol. 2, pp. 136 ff.; 303 ff.

bloody sacramental actualization of the sacrifice of the Cross, because it makes present in person Christ Himself, now glorious, but who suffered and died and is situated always in the disposition of mind numerically identical to that which formally constituted His sacrifice of the Cross and has now become eternal in Him with His passing over to the other life.

By this disposition, in continuation of the offering of Himself which He made on Golgotha, He places His own life at the complete disposition of God (the Father, by appropriation), in order to acknowledge God's sovereign dominion over Himself as man and over all mankind of which He is the Head, accepting that which the paternal will had willed from all eternity in regard to the eventual effective destruction of this particular life.

Thus, the sacrifice of the Cross and the sacrifice which Christ now makes of Himself in the Mass are entirely the same identical sacrifice insofar as the formal aspect (the disposition of mind) is concerned. In regard to the material aspect, they differ, on the contrary, in one respect: the offering which Christ made of His own life on the Cross was effected there with the shedding of His blood, in accord with the Father's will; while the continuation of this offering which now takes place in heaven and in the Mass is not effected in blood, because this the Father does not will. And the exercise of Christ's priesthood at the right hand of His Father is in fact a priestly exercise in reference to the sacrifice of Golgotha. The Cross of Golgotha therefore dominates the whole figure and life of Christ, as it dominates the whole Church and all history.

On the priesthood of Christians. From the sin of Adam henceforward, every sacrifice and every priesthood accepted by God, even among the pagans, was not and is not accepted save through reference to the priesthood and sacrifice of Christ on Golgotha; just as every grace given by God, it was always in reference to Christ, it was the grace of Christ and participation in the fullness of His grace. With even greater reason, then, the priesthood and the sacrifice of the Old Testament had an essential and intrinsic relation to the priesthood of Christ and to the sacrifice of Golgotha.

So much the more, then, among Christians, are the terms priesthood and sacrifice, in whatever sense they are employed, to be understood in reference to the priesthood and sacrifice of Christ and therefore in reference to Golgotha, which is, therefore, the principal analogical point to which every Christian priesthood and sacrifice is referred, and from which it derives, participating in it and receiving its designation from it.

The concept of sacrifice and of priesthood, whether applied to that of Christ Himself or to that which is found among Christians, is a concept, therefore, which involves an analogy of attribution: it is applied first of all to the sacrifice and priesthood of Christ and only derivatively to the priesthood and sacrifice of Christians.

In Christ Himself priesthood and sacrifice are realized first of all in the priesthood and sacrifice of Golgotha, and only derivatively in the sacrifice and priesthood of His whole life, at the Last Supper, at Mass, in heaven.

Among Christians priesthood and sacrifice mean primarily the hierarchical priesthood and the sacrifice of the Mass, and only derivatively and dependently on these, the priesthood common to all the faithful and sacrifices other than that of the Mass.

In the hierarchical priesthood, priesthood and sacrifice are verified first of all in the Eucharistic priesthood and sacrifice, and only derivatively, as preparation and consequence, in non-Eucharistic priesthood and sacrifice, such as the governing of the Church, the teaching of doctrine, the apostolate to unbelievers.

Among the laity, priesthood and sacrifice refer primarily to their priesthood and sacrifice in respect to the Eucharist in the Mass, and only derivatively to their priesthood and sacrifice in respect to other things such as holiness of life, martyrdom, apostolic action; for this second aspect of their priesthood and sacrifice is such only as presupposition and consequence of the first.

Since the sacrifice of the Mass is referred entirely to the sacrifice of Christ on Golgotha, it is clear that the sacrifice of the faithful in their holiness of life, in their virginity, in martyrdom, etc., is such only in reference to the sacrifice of Golgotha through the sacrifice of the Mass. Just as Christ is priest essentially on Golgotha, and throughout the rest of His life He is priest in reference to Golgotha as preparation and consequence thereto, so also the hierarchical priesthood is such essentially in the Mass, while in the other affairs and activities of life it is a priesthood in reference to the Mass as preparation and consequence; and thus too the priesthood common to all the faithful is such essentially in the Mass, but in the rest of life's activities only insofar as these activities are preparation and consequence of the Mass.

On the nature of the hierarchical priesthood and how it differs from the priesthood common to all the faithful. The hierarchical priesthood, like every priesthood among Christians, is a participation in the priesthood of Christ; but it is a participation of a degree and nature essentially different from that which is found in the priesthood common to all the faithful. This special participation is based on a special sacrament and on a special character: holy orders. In the exercise of his priesthood the hierarchical minister acts as representative and as direct and special instrument of Christ. This is what we mean when we say that he acts directly *in persona Christi* and not directly *in persona fidelium.* He represents the faithful only inasmuch as he directly represents Christ, Head of the Church, Head of that body which is ever inseparable from Him.

Such is the doctrine of the Second Vatican Council,[52] already forcefully inculcated in the encyclical *Mediator Dei*, against some expressions or directly against some ambiguous tendencies which, in this field, were being manifested in certain quarters.[53] "But we deem it necessary to recall that the [hierarchical] priest acts for the people only because he represents Jesus Christ, who is Head of all His members and offers Himself in their stead. Hence he goes to the altar as the minister of Christ, inferior to Christ but superior to the people."[54] "The unbloody immolation at the words of consecration, when Christ is made present upon the altar in the state of a victim, is performed by the [hierarchical] priest and by him alone, as the representative of Christ and not as the representative of the faithful."[55]

Among the ordinary faithful there is no priesthood and no sacrifice except in dependence upon the hierarchical priesthood; and in the last analysis, in union with the hierarchical priesthood exercised in the Mass. This is because among the ordinary faithful all their sacerdotal acts except those which they exercise by participating in the Mass are in fact sacerdotal acts only as presuppositions or consequences of the Eucharistic sacrifice. Moreover, the exercise of the priesthood of the faithful in the Mass itself necessarily implies a union with and a dependence upon the priesthood which Christ exercises in the Mass by means of the hierarchical priesthood.

In the Mass the faithful, by virtue of their baptismal character, offer a sacrifice of Christian dispensation, and thus they exercise a priesthood of Christian dispensation, which, in view of the concepts defined above, is such not just equivocally, nor merely metaphorically, but in fact is a real Christian priesthood. This is truly the case by reason of the fact that they offer as their own sacrifice, including in it the offering of themselves even to the point of destruction should God desire it, the sacrifice which Christ offers through the instrumentality of the hierarchical priesthood.

Although it is only the hierarchical priests who can be the instruments of Christ in effecting the consecration of the Eucharistic species, still and all, anyone among the faithful, armed with the baptismal character, is, in a proper sense, able to perform that sacrifice, is able to offer Christ, the victim, together with the hierarchical priest and through his instrumentality;[56] or rather, what is much more, together with Christ Himself and by means of Him, and (a condition essential to what we are predicating) is able to include therein the offering of his own life.

Such an exercise of priesthood common to all the faithful differs from the exercise of the properly hierarchical priesthood in the Mass, because to be a

[52] *Constitution on the Church*, art. 10: "Though they differ essentially and not only in degree, the common priesthood of the faithful and the ministerial or hierarchical priesthood are none the less ordered one to another."

[53] MD, nn. 80-104 (Lat. 79-103).
[54] *Ibid.*, n. 84 (Lat. 83).
[55] *Ibid.*, n. 92 (Lat. 91).
[56] CL, art. 48.

hierarchical priest consists, in virtue of the character of sacerdotal orders, in one's being the living instrument and the only living instrument by means of which Christ accomplishes in an unbloody fashion the offering of the actual sacrifice. The proper sacerdotal act of the hierarchical priesthood in the Mass does not include of necessity, for the validity or reality of the completion of the sacrifice which Christ makes sacramentally of Himself, the offering of the priest's own life.

On the contrary, this offering of the priest's own life, united to the offering of the victim which is Christ, becomes necessary for the hierarchical priest, just as for any other of the faithful, if he is to make personally his own the sacrifice which Christ makes of Himself through His intermediary; and in this way he is able to exercise in the Mass, apart from his own hierarchical priesthood, even that priesthood which he has in common with all the faithful.

"Now it is clear," the encyclical *Mediator Dei* explains, "that the faithful offer the Sacrifice by the hands of the priest from the fact that the minister at the altar in offering a Sacrifice in the name of all His members represents Christ, the Head of the Mystical Body. Hence the whole Church can rightly be said to offer up the Victim through Christ. But the conclusion that the people offer the Sacrifice with the priest himself is not based on the fact that, being members of the Church no less than the priest himself, they perform a visible liturgical rite; for this is the privilege only of the minister who has been divinely appointed to this office: rather, it is based on the fact that the people unite their hearts in praise, impetration, expiation and thanksgiving with the prayers or intention of the priest, even of the High Priest Himself, so that in the one and same offering of the Victim and according to a visible sacerdotal rite, they may be presented to God the Father. It is obviously necessary that the external sacrificial rite should, of its very nature, signify the internal worship of the heart. Now the Sacrifice of the New Law signifies that supreme worship by which the principal Offerer Himself, who is Christ, and in union with Him and through Him all the members of the Mystical Body, pay God the honor and reverence that are due to Him." [57]

The believer makes the sacrifice of the Mass his own only insofar as, together with the priest, he offers himself, his whole life, in union with Christ and by means of Christ on Golgotha; for it is only the life of the one who makes the offering that is real intrinsic matter, total and primary, of sacrifice to God. The rest has value as personal sacrifice only insofar as it includes or manifests his own life. If the believer were to completely exclude from the Mass this total offering of himself, he would not be participating in any way in the Mass, would not be making the Mass in any way his own

[57] MD, n. 93 (Lat. 93).

sacrifice. Contrariwise, the more this offering of himself is conscious, real, perfect, the more is his participation in the Mass real and perfect.

"In order that the oblation by which the faithful offer the divine Victim in this Sacrifice to the Heavenly Father may have its full effect, it is necessary that the people add something else, namely the offering of themselves as a victim. This offering in fact is not confined merely to the liturgical Sacrifice. . . . While we stand before the altar, then, it is our duty so to transform our hearts that every trace of sin may be completely blotted out, while whatever promotes supernatural life through Christ, may be zealously fostered and strengthened even to the extent that, in union with the Immaculate Victim, we become a victim acceptable to the Eternal Father. . . . For in the Sacrament of the altar, as . . . St. Augustine has it, the Church is made to see that in what she offers she herself is offered. Let the faithful, therefore, consider to what a high dignity they are raised by the Sacrament of Baptism. They should not think it enough to participate in the Eucharistic Sacrifice with that general intention which befits members of Christ and children of the Church, but let them further, in keeping with the spirit of the sacred Liturgy, be most closely united with the High Priest and His earthly minister, at the time the consecration of the divine Victim is effected, and at that time especially when those solemn words are pronounced: 'Through Him, with Him, in Him, in the unity of the Holy Spirit, all glory and honor is yours, almighty Father, for ever and ever'; to these words in fact the people answer: 'Amen'. Nor should Christians forget to offer themselves, their cares, their sorrows, their distress and their necessities in union with their Divine Savior upon the Cross." [58] Thus the whole life of the Church, by focusing on the notion of priesthood and of sacrifice, by that very fact converges and centers upon the Mass and on Golgotha.

In conclusion, our proposed theological explanation of the priesthood of all Christians can be summarized in the following propositions:

a) The priesthood in general is defined as a power to offer sacrifice.

b) Religious sacrifice is formally defined as the internal act of placing at the complete disposal of God, in recognition of His supreme dominion, one's own life, even to the point of its total effective destruction, if He so demand, either really in itself and therefore totally, or, still really, but in its partial manifestations; or, by means of a symbol in its stead.

c) The sacrifice of Christ is formally the act of His will by which, as Head of mankind with which God had joined Him, He placed His own life at the total disposition of God even to the point of its total effective destruction as willed by the Father, in order to acknowledge the latter's sovereign do-

[58] MD, nn. 98-104 (Lat. 97-103). See also CL, art. 48.

minion over the whole of mankind. This sacrifice begins with the first moment of His life and is completed on Golgotha.

d) Sacrifice and priesthood among Christians is their participation in the sacrifice and priesthood of Christ on Golgotha, actualized sacramentally and in an unbloody manner in the Mass.

e) The hierarchical priesthood among Christians is an enabling by means of the character of holy orders to be the instrument by means of which Christ actualizes sacramentally and in an unbloody manner in the consecration of the Mass the sacrifice which He made on Golgotha. The other specifically hierarchical sacerdotal acts, whether liturgical or extraliturgical, are such because they are preparation or consequence of the sacerdotal act in the Mass.

f) The priesthood common to all faithful Christians is an enabling by means of the character of baptism and confirmation which allows each one to make personally his own the sacrifice of Golgotha, which Christ, by means of the hierarchical priesthood alone, actualizes sacramentally in the Mass; and thus do they participate in the sacrifice and priesthood of Christ, the Head of mankind. This active participation by which every Christian, in an action which is really and not merely metaphorically sacerdotal, makes his own the sacrifice of Christ, takes place when, in the Mass, he unites himself with the will of Christ in the sacrificial sacerdotal act and offers to God, together with Christ, his own proper life, in order to acknowledge, united always with Christ, God's sovereign dominion.

The other actions, liturgical and extraliturgical, which Scripture and tradition call sacerdotal and sacrificial, common to Christians, (mortifications, virginity and the religious life, obligations of one's own state in life, charity toward one's neighbor, private prayer, apostolate, martyrdom, giving of one's goods), are such because they are either directed to the sacerdotal action of the Mass, or they are its effects and manifestations. In the same way a medicine is healthy or an atmosphere is healthy because it is disposed to the health of the organism; and the color of one's face is healthy because it is an effect of the health of the organism and manifests that health.

g) The concept of Christian priesthood and, with it, of sacrifice, in the various forms which are encountered in Scripture, in patristic and theological tradition, is an analogical concept. In view of the various possibilities concretely treated, this analogy is, to use scholastic terminology, an analogy of proper proportion, including at the same time also an analogy of attribution; or, as it may be, solely an analogy of attribution. When the same expressions are used in regard to sacrifice of praise and offering of spiritual victims which are the praises raised up to God, these are not equivocal and certainly not merely metaphorical expressions, because the praise of God, in its conscious and fullest sense, is none other than a consequence and a manifestation of the internal act by which a man places his own life at the complete disposition of God, even to the point of its total effective destruction, if God so demand, in recognition of the sovereign dominion of the Creator and Provider of all things.

h) The nature of the hierarchical priesthood, as is the case with every instrumental entity, is comprehensible only in reference to the principal cause, that is, the priesthood of Christ, on which all else depends; it is reduced entirely to the same genus and the same species. It is true enough, in a certain sense, that every Christian priesthood, even that which is common to all the faithful, is the instrument of Christ. But this is true in a different sense with the hierarchical priesthood than with the priesthood common to all the faithful. The hierarchical priesthood can be said to be a purely instrumental priesthood of Christ. So much is this the case that a Mass could be validly celebrated by a priest — and in it the unbloody sacrifice of Christ would be really and fully actualized — without there being any kind of personal sacrifice on the part of the priest celebrating. This is what happens when a priest celebrates while in a state of mortal sin. And such is the case analogously also with regard to the other sacraments.

i) The priesthood common to all the faithful, in reference to the priesthood of Christ, is analogously a priesthood, by an analogy of proper proportionality, although it is specifically different and includes, over and above, an analogy of attribution. In fact, in both cases priesthood means the ability to offer in sacrifice one's own life in order to acknowledge the supreme dominion of God. They are specifically different because in Christ sacrifice and priesthood are sacrifice and priesthood of the Head and they include the *gratia capitis*. An analogy of attribution is included because the sacrifice and priesthood of Christ are the prime analogates. After Adam's sin no man has the power to offer himself to God, except in reference to the sacrifice of Christ.

j) In respect to the purely instrumental priesthood and sacrifice proper to the hierarchy, the priesthood common to all the faithful is a priesthood only by analogy of attribution, because the priesthood common to all the faithful is an effect of that purely instrumental priesthood of the hierarchy.

5 THE NOTION OF THE LITURGY

AND THE MASS AS REALIZATION

AND SYNTHETIC EXPRESSION OF THE

WHOLE LITURGICAL COMPLEXUS

It will have been apparent to the reader that our primary concern in the preceding chapters has been to clarify the concept of the liturgy by referring it to its natural setting in the general panorama of salvation history. Thus, the liturgy has been seen as that specific means by which, from Pentecost to the parousia of the Lord, the mystery of Christ is actualized; the specific means which is employed in the sanctification which, under the veil and through the channel of efficacious sensible signs, God, in Christ, provides for man; the specific means which is employed in the worship which, under and through the same signs, man, in Christ, renders to God.

At this point it would seem to be advantageous, as if to provide something of a confirmation of the accuracy and fruitfulness of the concept of the liturgy explained above, to demonstrate how, with this concept as a starting point, an account of the real scope of one of the truths of the liturgical science can easily be rendered through other principles more generally recognized: to wit, that the Mass is the center and the radiant sun of the whole liturgical complexus.

If, in fact, the liturgy is nothing other than the expression, under the veil of sacred efficacious signs, of the mystery of salvation history, by which God sanctifies men in Christ and by which men in Christ render their worship to God, it must also be affirmed as a general principle that in every Mass, under the veil of the sacred efficacious signs, the liturgy achieves its object in its entirety, but in a manner foreshortened and condensed. To such a degree is this true that the rest of the liturgy is but preparation or consequence of this essential act and serves but to bring into relief, in various ways and successively, one or the other aspects of that unique mystery expressed and realized perfectly and synthetically in every Mass.

The basic thrust of this affirmation is that the Mass is, at one and the same time, both sacrament and sacrifice; and that as sacrament it contains and communicates, to those who receive it, Christ in person: divinity and humanity; body and soul; ultimate Author, as God, of all sanctification; while, as sacrifice, it is the sacrifice of Christ Himself, the primary source, highest expression, and point of reference of all worship which men render to God. The Mass is the sacrifice which Christ Himself, through the ministry of His priest, offers to God, and which the whole Church makes its own as the ultimate expression of its worship, inasmuch as it makes its offering with the priest conjointly with Christ and offers itself in sacrifice conjointly with Him.

Thus in the Mass, under the veil of the efficacious signs, there is realized to the highest possible degree the sanctification by God, in Christ, of the Church; and the worship which the Church, in Christ, renders to God; in other words, the whole dimension of the liturgy. The Mass, therefore, is the first and greatest of the efficacious sacred signs under the veil of which, from Pentecost to parousia, the encounter between man and God is effected.

1. How the Quadruple Dimension of the Liturgical Signs Has Its Highest Degree of Expression and Efficacy in the Mass

In the Mass the liturgical sign achieves its highest degree of expression and efficacy in regard to the spiritual realities which are signified and efficaciously realized therein as demonstratively present. These realities are: first of all Christ Himself, who, in the Eucharistic species, is really signified as present in person and not only in power, and is really made present as such. The Mass also signifies and actually realizes to the highest degree the union between God and man in Christ, because in it there is established between the person of Christ and the one communicating a union which is not only a moral union and one of grace, but a sacramental physical union which, consequently, is also a moral union and one of grace. It is also in the Mass that the union in Christ among men achieves its highest degree, because it is here that all communicate in a single principle of spiritual life, eating the one only bread and drinking the one only chalice; and receiving, therefore, in a sacramental manner, the same Christ, the one only indivisible principle of supernatural life.

It is likewise in the Mass that the reality of worship is presently signified and actually realized in the highest degree, because sacrifice is the supreme act of worship; and the sacrifice of Christ on Golgotha, of which that in the Mass is the unbloody extension, is the source and point of reference of all Christian worship and sacrifice. Most especially in communion does Christ unite to His sacrifice all the faithful, together with the priest and with Himself, the High Priest, who are offering the sacred Victim to the Father and who are offering themselves together with Him in sacrifice to the Father. Thus do they make the sacrifice of Christ their own sacrifice, they impart to their whole life a meaning of sacrificial worship offered to God in Christ, and they realize to the fullest the sacerdotal power, which they received in baptism, participating to the fullest in the worship and sacrifice of Christ.

The Mass is likewise the greatest of the obligating signs of the whole of Christian worship, by the very fact that it is the greatest and the most efficacious of the signs of sanctification which man freely receives and of the worship which he freely offers to God. Among all Christian acts, the Mass is *par excellence* the new covenant, the new alliance, in the blood of Christ (cf. Luke 22:20 and its parallels). Whoever participates in the Mass, especially in communion, accepts this covenant and makes it solemnly his own. And a covenant involves obligation. That is why St. Paul says: "You cannot drink the cup of the Lord and the cup of demons; you cannot be partakers of the table of the Lord and of the table of devils" (1 Cor. 10:21).

And for that reason too he adds: "Whoever eats this bread or drinks the cup of the Lord unworthily, will be guilty of the body and the blood of the Lord. Let every man, therefore, examine himself; and thus let him eat of that bread and drink of the cup: for whoever eats and drinks, if he does not perceive the body, eats and drinks unto his own condemnation" (1 Cor 11:27-29).[1]

---

[1] The first Christians were vividly aware of the obligation inherent in every act of worship and especially in the Eucharist. We have evidence of this, for example, in the famous letter in which Pliny the Younger, governor of Bithynia, informs Trajan about the liturgical gatherings — most likely Eucharistic assemblies — of the Christians: "And they asserted that this had been the whole of their guilt or error, that it was their custom to assemble be-fore sunrise on a fixed day, and in antiphonal style to sing a hymn to Christ as to a god, and *to bind themselves by a sacramentum* not to any crime, but that they would not commit any fraud, theft or adultery, that they would not deceive, that they would not deny a trust when called upon to deliver it up" (cf. Loeb Classical Library edition, book 10, letter 96). In the same way St. Hippolytus in *The Apostolic Tradition* 23, after having spoken of the

The Mass is the most highly expressive and efficacious among all the liturgical signs also in respect to that past reality to which it relates as a commemorative sign. In fact, it is in the Mass that *"recolitur memoria passionis eius"* in the highest degree, because it is none other than the very sacrifice of Golgotha that is continued in an unbloody manner in the sacrament. In the Mass there is re-actualized, then, in the highest degree, the priesthood of Christ and the worship of Christ in His mortal life, along with all the sacrifices, all the acts of sanctification and of worship accepted by God from the time of Adam's sin until Christ Himself, which were but figures and shadows of the sacrifice of Golgotha now re-actualized in the sacrament.

Thus the sacral reality which is fulfilled in every Mass is really the terminus toward which an immense succession of lines of force converge, and toward which, since creation, they tended as to their realization and as the reason for their existence. In fact, in the mystery of Christ, which is sacred history, all the phases of the historical preparation of the Old Testament lead to the phases of the historical realization in the earthly life of Christ: incarnation, redemptive Passion and death, resurrection and ascension.

In its own historical time the life of Jesus, up to his glorification, was directed intrinsically toward the inspiring of men; its meaning was realized in the life of the soul by communicating to men that divine life, by bestowing upon them that life which was the Word made incarnate. Now in our own time this is achieved first of all in the Mass. Thus it is clear that the sacral reality of the Mass is the point of convergence of all previous cosmic history, because, in the designs of God, all this history converged upon the historical Golgotha, while the historical Golgotha tended toward the mystical Golgotha of the Mass.

As an efficacious sign portending the future, and therefore as prophetic action, the Mass holds first place in the liturgy. In the Mass, under the veil of signs, there is really a new epiphany of the incarnate Word in person, and not in power only; of the same Word made flesh, immolated, raised up, transfigured. The Mass is already the return or parousia of the Lord, differing in substance from His definitive parousia only because that which takes place in the Mass is done under the veil of signs and not in a form unveiled and glorious. The Mass is already the banquet of messianic times awaited in the Old Testament, differing essentially from the definitive banquet *in regno Patris mei* (Matthew 26:29) only because it is not yet in its glorious form.

And it is for this reason that there is inherent in the Mass a meaning profoundly eschatological: it announces, proclaims and calls out, so to speak,

participation in the Eucharist, last act of the Christian initiation, adds: "And when these things are completed let each hasten to do good works and to please God and to live justly, devoting himself to the Church, practicing what he has learned, and advancing in the service of God" (cf. Jurgens, no. 394 i, p. 171).

with every fiber of its being, the glorious return of the Lord and the banquet in glory *in regno Patris*; for an action veiled in sensible symbols tends naturally, with all its strength, toward the reality unveiled and without symbols. Therefore, "every time you eat this bread and drink the cup, you proclaim the death of the Lord until He comes" (1 Cor. 11:26).

The simple act of participating in the Eucharistic body and blood of Christ is a proclaiming before the world of the redemptive death of the Lord, who is now glorious but hidden, a death which the Eucharist "commemorates" and, in its own way, proffers in an unbloody manner *in sacramento*. This mystery-proclamation of the redemptive death of Christ is the specific manner of proclaiming it which is proper to this present time between the ascension and the Lord's glorious second coming or parousia: when at last He is presented to all the world in the splendor of His glory, the Eucharist will have an end, because the mystery will cease when it is fulfilled and when that reality which is now proclaimed beneath the veils is made apparent in full light and without veiling symbols. Then the messianic banquet will continue openly and unveiled.

The eschatological significance of every Mass was felt strongly by the first Christians. This is the sense of a prayer of thanksgiving after the Eucharist, as it is reported in the *Didache*:

> "Remember, O Lord, your Church. Deliver it from every evil and perfect it in your love. Gather it from the four winds, sanctified for your kingdom, which you have prepared for it. For yours is the power and the glory forever. Let grace come, and let this world pass away. Marana Tha. Amen: Come thou, O Lord! So be it!" [2]

In short, the Mass, the supreme act of sanctification and of worship, in an eminent manner, more real and more profound than any other liturgical act, belongs to this time intermediate between the first and the second coming of the Lord, the central point in which, under the veil of sacred and efficacious signs, all the phases of the mystery of Christ, sacred salvation history, the mystery of the Church, have their life and toward which they converge. It is the great terminus in which the past finds its fulfillment and the present is fully realized; a reaching out toward that future which it prophesies, announces, actually begins, and toward which the whole of it is directed:

> "O sacred banquet, in which Christ is consumed,
> The memory of His Passion is renewed,

<hr>

[2] *Didache* 10, 5-6 (Jurgens, no. 7, with note no. 26 on p. 5). In a Coptic papyrus, probably of the fifth century, which reports an interpolated text of the *Didache* with some variants, the *Marana Tha* (imperative; or perhaps *Maran Atha*, present) of the *Didache* 10, 6 is translated as a past tense: "The Lord came. Amen." See G. Horner, "The New Papyrus Fragment of the *Didache* in Coptic," in the *Journal of Theological Studies*, Vol. 25 (1924), pp. 225-231.

The mind is filled with grace,
And a pledge of future glory is given us!"[3]

2. The Liturgical Expression of the Mystery of Christ as Seen in the Anaphoras

So profoundly pervasive is the general idea of the Mass as a summing up of the whole history of salvation and of the whole mystery of Christ that in every formulary of the Mass, even in the variable parts, the following four ideas, more or less clearly expressed, are found constantly recurring:

1) The Old Testament and the realities spoken of therein were preparation and figure of that which is realized in the life of Christ and which in its own proper way is realized continuously in the souls of the faithful in the liturgical action, especially of sacrifice, but also in that of the sacraments and sacramentals.

2) In the present sacrifice our redemption is completed.

3) Participation in the Mass presupposes certain moral dispositions and is a solemn pledge of life for the future. By means of this participation the faithful pray God that He may dispose their minds, granting it by his grace, that they will act in conformity with this pledge.

4) We expect, we desire, we pray that the present sacrifice in which we participate will lead us to glory.

These ideas, expressed in a manner more or less explicit, constitute, in particular, some of the fundamental themes of the postcommunion prayer of the Roman Mass.

This same general idea of the Mass, as a summary and synthetic expression of the whole mystery of Christ, is demonstrated essentially in the liturgy also by the fact that it is always present, more or less forcefully and clearly expressed, in that central part of the whole Mass which is called the anaphora, canon, or Eucharistic prayer. The anaphoral formularies are quite diverse in the various Christian liturgies. All of them, however, take the form of a great prayer to the Father in thanksgiving for the benefits which

[3] It is interesting to see how a Protestant, G. Harbsmeier (*Das wir die Predigt und sein Wort nicht verachten*, Munich 1958, pp. 161-162), profoundly hostile to the liturgy by reason of the dogmatics of his own confession, has understood so well that, in the logic of Catholic dogmatics, the Mass is necessarily the central point and the epitome of the mystery of salvation in action, and that it reveals a perspective of prodigious grandeur. "The Eucharist," he writes, "is not celebrated simply in memory of that night on which the Savior was delivered up and betrayed. This also it does. But along with this . . . it represents ritually, in symbol, in gesture, in word, in song, just about the sum total of what the Scriptures contain. Those who perform this representation introduce there the sum of all that the world knows about the act of religion. . . . There is presented to our gaze a vast translation into worship of the salvation event: a work complete and perfect. . . . Here it is understood that if worship can possibly serve as the realization of the mystery, such a realization ought to be total. In this sense the Eucharist is truly catholic, because it translates into worship really and in a global manner the totality of the mystery of salvation. As interpretation it is a marvelous realization."

He has given — the Eucharist is thanksgiving *par excellence* — chiefly through the mediation of Christ. The redemptive plan for the world in Christ, that is to say, the mystery of Christ, the center of sacred salvation history, is always recalled expressly in the anaphoras, with more or less detail.

All or virtually all the known formulas recall explicitly the mystery of Christ in its phase of historical realization during His earthly life, at least from the Last Supper — and it is here that the words of the institution of the Eucharist are inserted — to the ascension.

In the explicit expression of the other particulars of the mystery of Christ there is great variation. Sometimes they are scarcely alluded to, sometimes they are considerably developed; and sometimes they are merely implied in such a general expression that it includes in a generic way the whole mystery of Christ which is realized synthetically in the Mass.

The most ancient text of an anaphora that has been preserved is that of *The Apostolic Tradition* of St. Hippolytus. But this is perhaps an outline of an anaphora rather than an anaphora fully developed. At any rate, one of the characteristics of the text of Hippolytus is its great sobriety. The theme of God the Creator is scarcely alluded to, and that of the providence of God in the economy of the Old Testament as preparatory to the coming of Christ is only barely recognizable. Yet we know, from the allusions of Justin the Martyr for example, that these themes were common in the tradition of antiquity. They have been better preserved in the tradition of the Eastern anaphoras than in the Roman Canon of the West.[4]

The Eastern Anaphoras

Be that as it may, in the Eastern tradition the anaphoras exhibited a very ample development at least as early as the end of the fourth century. And although in several instances there may be a prolixity and a rhetorical redundancy in clean contrast to the sobriety and sharply lapidary character that marks the literary product of ancient Rome, it must nevertheless be admitted that in comparison to our present Roman Canon they have two great advantages: they are constructed according to a logical, coherent plan; and they develop, for the most part in a harmonious manner, all the great theological and liturgical themes of the most ancient and magnificent Eucharistic prayer, as they are known from tradition.

Thus, the Eastern anaphoras are much closer to that tradition. That is why, if we wish to see how the fourfold dimension of the Mass, in the sense outlined above, is expressed, we must turn first of all to the Eastern anaphoras.

Among the Eastern anaphoras we may direct our attention to the Greek

---

[4] In regard to the remark on St. Justin, see his *Dialogue with Trypho*, 41 (Jurgens, no. 135). The Hippolytan anaphora seems to have served somewhat as a model for the Second Canon of the present Pauline Roman Missal (see Jurgens, no. 394 a).

anaphora of St. Basil the Great, as one which is well-adapted to our purpose and which may justly be considered as particularly representative.[5]

The Greek Anaphora of St. Basil

Priest: "The grace of our Lord Jesus Christ, and the love of our God and Father, and the communion of the Holy Spirit be with you all."

People: "And with your spirit."

Priest: "Lift up your hearts."

People: "We have raised them to the Lord."

Priest: "Let us give thanks to the Lord."

People: "It is right and just to worship Father, Son, and Holy Spirit, the consubstantial and undivided Trinity."

Trinitarian theme.

Priest: "Immutable Being, Master, Lord God, adorable Father almighty, it is truly right and just and proper in view of the magnificence of Your holiness, to praise You, to bless You, to worship You, to give thanks to You, to glorify You, who are the one only true God, and to offer to You, with contrite hearts and in a spirit of humility, this our rational adoration, because it is You who have given us the knowledge of Your Truth. Who is able to tell of Your powerful deeds, proclaim all Your praises or explain all the wonders which You have performed in every age? Master of all things, Lord of heaven and of earth and of all creation, visible and invisible: You who are seated on a throne of glory and look down upon the depths below; You who are without beginning, invisible, incomprehensible, boundless, immutable; the Father of our Lord Jesus Christ, of our great God and Savior, of our Hope; of Him who is the image of Your goodness, the seal of Your likeness, who in Himself is the revelation of You, the Father; who is the living Word, true God, eternal

[5] Louis Bouyer, *Liturgical Piety*, Notre Dame Press 1954, pp. 132-137, also refers to the same anaphora, but from another point of view.

Wisdom, Life, Sanctification, Power, the true Light, from whom the Holy Spirit shines forth, who is the Spirit of Truth, the Spirit of adoption in sonship, the Pledge of future inheritance, the First-fruits of eternal benefits, the life-giving Power, the Source of sanctification, by whom every creature, rational and intellectual, is enabled to adore You and to extol You with eternal glorification; for all creation serves You. Angels praise You, Archangels, Thrones, Dominations, Principalities, Powers, Virtues, and the many-eyed Cherubim; the Seraphim stand round about You, six wings to each and every one; and with two they cover up their faces, with two their feet, and with two they fly, the while they cry aloud to each other, with voices unceasing, Your never silent praises. . . ."

People: "Holy, holy holy, ..."

Christologic theme: mystery of Christ.

Priest: "Together with this blessed company, Master and Lover of mankind, we sinners too cry aloud and say: truly holy are You, and all-holy; nor is there any limit to the magnificence of Your holiness, and You are holy in all Your works because all that You do is done in justice and in true judgment.

I. God's original plan: the nature thereof:

"For You shaped man, taking soil of the earth, and honoring him with Your image, You placed him in the paradise of delights, promising him immortality of life and enjoyment of eternal benefits, if he would but keep Your commandments.

its frustration:

"But he disobeyed You, the true God who created him, and when he succumbed to the deceit of the serpent and by his transgressions sentenced himself to death, You, O God, in Your just judgment, drove him out of paradise into this world, and made him return again to the earth from which he had been taken,

promise of a
Redeemer:

"while disposing that by means of a new birth he should obtain salvation again, salvation in Your Christ.

II. Renewal in
Christ the
Redeemer:

"For You, good Creator, did not reject forever the creature whom You had made, nor did You forget the work of Your hands; but in Your mercy You visited him in many ways.

A. Preparation
in the Old
Testament:

"You sent the prophets; You worked wonders through Your saints, who were pleasing to You in every generation; You spoke to us by the mouth of Your servants, the prophets, foreannouncing to us the future salvation; You gave us the Law to help us; You assigned angels to guard us.

B. Realization
in the life
of Christ:

"Then when the fullness of time had come, You spoke to us in Your own Son, through whom also You created the world. He, being the brightness of Your glory and the imprint of Your substance, and sustaining all things by the word of His power, did not think it a thing to be clung to, to be equal to You, who are God and Father;

1. First coming:

"but, remaining eternal God, He appeared on the earth and went about among men;

a. Incarnation:

and having taken flesh from the Virgin, He lowered Himself, taking the form of a slave, made in like form to the body of our lowliness, in order that He might make us in like form to the image of His glory. For since through a man sin had come into the world, and, through sin, death, Your only-begotten Son, who is in the bosom of You, God and Father, being born of a woman, the holy *Theotokos* and Ever-Virgin Mary, and being born under the Law, was pleased to condemn sin in His own flesh, so that those who had died in Adam might be brought to life in Him, Your Christ.

b. Life:

"And having become a citizen of this world, He gave us the precepts of salvation, set us free from the seduction of idols and brought us to the knowledge of You, the true God and Father, acquiring us for Himself as a chosen people, a royal priesthood, a holy nation;

c. Death: "and purifying us in water and sanctifying us in the Holy Spirit, He gave Himself in our place to the death into whose power we had been sold because of sin.

d. Resurrection: "And having descended, by means of the Cross, into hell, so that He might fulfill all things in Himself, He loosed the painful bonds of death; and on the third day He rose again, and opened to all flesh the way of the resurrection from the dead. Since it was not possible for the Author of life to be overcome by corruption, He became the first fruits of those who have been laid to rest, the first-born from among the dead, so that He might hold first place in all things.

e. Ascension: "And ascending to heaven, He sat at the right of Your majesty on high.

2. Second coming: "And He will come again to render to each one according to his works.

C. Sacramental Realization in the Eucharist: "And He left us these memorials of His redemptive suffering which we have now brought forward in accord with His command.

1. Institution and present renewal: "For, about to go to His voluntary and celebrated and life-giving death, on the night when He surrendered Himself for the life of the world, taking bread into His holy and immaculate hands, and lifting it up to You, God and Father, giving thanks, blessing it, sanctifying it, breaking it, He gave it to His holy disciples and Apostles, saying: 'Take, eat, this is My Body, broken for you unto the remission of sins.'"
People: "Amen."

Priest: "In like manner also, taking the cup of the fruit of the vine, tempering it, giving thanks, blessing it, sanctifying it, He gave it to His holy disciples and Apostles, saying: 'Drink of this, all of you, this is My Blood, that of the new covenant, shed for you and for many unto the remission of sins.' "

People: "Amen."

2. *Its value as efficacious and prophetic memorial:*

Priest: " 'Do this in memory of me. For every time that you eat this Bread and drink this Chalice, you will be proclaiming My death and confessing My resurrection.'

"We too, Master, calling to mind, therefore, the redemptive sufferings accomplished through the life-giving Cross, the three days in the tomb, the resurrection from the dead, the ascension into heaven, Your being seated at the right of Your God and Father, and Your glorious and fearsome parousia — we offer to You from Your gifts that which belongs to You absolutely and completely." [6]

To understand how in this anaphora the Mass truly appears as the center of all the phases of the unfolding mystery of Christ, let us read also the following prayers, which are recited shortly after the parts referred to above, and in which there is expressed the union of the faithful celebrating the Mass with the saints in heaven, with the dead, and with all those still living on earth in the midst of their various needs, as well as the import of the communion of the priest and of the faithful in this sacrifice and its value as an obligating sign:

> *Priest*: "Now that we have partaken of the one Bread and of the one Chalice, unite us to each other in the communion of the one Holy Spirit; and do not let any of us partake of the holy Body and Blood of Your Christ unto our own judgment or condemnation, but let us rather find mercy and grace together with all Your saints who have been pleasing to You from the beginning of the world, protoparents, forefathers, patriarchs, prophets, apostles, preachers, evangelists, martyrs, confessors, doctors, and all the spirits of the just who have fallen asleep in the faith, especially our all-holy, immaculate, blessed above all, glorious Lady, *Theotokos* and Ever-Virgin Mary." (The com-

[6] The Greek text from which Vagaggini has translated into Italian seems to be that of the *Hieratikon*, Rome 1950, pp. 189-195. We have translated into English with our brown eye on Vagaggini and our blue one on the *Hieratikon* (translator's note).

memoration of the saints and the prayers for the living and for the dead continue at some length.)

"O our God, God of our salvation, teach us to give thanks to You worthily for the benefits which You have granted and do yet grant us. Do You, our God, who have received these gifts, purify us of every stain, carnal and spiritual; and teach us to achieve our sanctification in fear of You, so that, receiving the particle of the gifts sanctified by You in the testimony of a pure conscience, we may be united to the holy Body and Blood of Your Christ; and, receiving them worthily, we may have Christ dwelling in our hearts and may become temples of the Holy Spirit. Yes, O our God, do not let any of us offend against Your awful and celestial mysteries, or become weak in soul and body through participating in them unworthily. But grant us even to our very last breath to receive worthily the particle of Your sanctified gifts, as Viaticum for eternal life, as an acceptable defense before the dread tribunal of Your Christ; and thus we too, with all the saints who have been pleasing to You from the beginning of the world, may become partakers of Your eternal good things which You have prepared, O Lord, for those who love You."[7]

The Roman Canon

All these ideas are found also in the Roman Canon, for centuries the sole canon of the Roman rite Mass, and now the first of the four canons or Eucharistic Prayers of the present Roman Missal. We shall make our observations primarily or solely in regard to the older Roman Canon, though much the same kind of analysis might be made also of the other three Eucharistic Prayers of the Roman rite.

But even if these same ideas as are found in the Eastern anaphoras and in the anaphora of St. Basil in particular are found also in the Roman Canon, they are, nevertheless, more widely dispersed in the Roman Canon and less developed, so that at first glance it is rather difficult to recognize them.

Actually, in the Roman Canon, many of these ideas are expressed in the first section, which is variable and which is called the preface. The changing of the preface for every Mass was considered the ordinary rule at Rome in ancient times. The Leonine Sacramentary, of which the first four months of the year are as yet lacking, had 267 prefaces for the last eight months of the year; the Gelasian still kept 54; the Gregorian Sacramentary reduced the number to 14; more recent Roman Missals had 15; and now, under a tendency to vary the preface more frequently, the present Pauline Roman Missal has revised the number of prefaces to 82.

[7] For the Greek, see the *Hieratikon*, Rome 1950, pp. 196-197, and 203-204. It is interesting to note that the Greek term *ephodion* and the corresponding Latin-English *viaticum* are of identical etymological significance: *provisions for the road*, which is to say, *provisions for a journey*.

It can be said that at Rome it has been customary for the most part to divide the expression of the various aspects of the mystery of Christ, which is realized in the Mass, among the different prefaces, the variable part of the canon, while, for example, in the Greek anaphora of St. Basil, they are all expressed together in every Mass, in a more logical and synthetic manner.

In reading the various prefaces of the present Roman Missal it is easy to see how the more notable aspects of the mystery of Christ are expressed separately, while in the Greek anaphora of St. Basil they are found all together. For example, by comparing the various seasonal prefaces for Advent, Christmas, Epiphany, Lent, Passiontide, Easter, Ascension, Pentecost, etc., and those for the various feasts of the Lord, we find expressed therein the various aspects of the mystery of Christ in the phases of its historical realization in the earthly life of Jesus.

In the fixed part of the Roman Canon, or Eucharistic Prayer I, the mystery of Christ being realized in the Mass is expressed, for example, from the *Qui pridie* through the *Unde et memores*: it is the phase of the real, mystical, liturgical realization of the mystery of Christ; the effective commemoration *in sacramento* of the institution of the Eucharist, of the sacred Passion, death, resurrection and ascension of Christ.

In the prayer *Supra quae propitio ac sereno* the mystery of Christ is expressed in the aspect of the historical preparation for it in the Old Testament: the sacrifice of Abel, of Abraham, of Melchisedech, types prefiguring the sacrifice of Christ on the Cross, now actualized in the Mass.

The *Nobis quoque peccatoribus*, asking for our admittance into the society of the saints, expresses the union of the sacrifice of the Mass with the heavenly Jerusalem, a union which had already found more explicit expression in the *Communicantes*, and is now only repeated in the *Nobis quoque*.

The union with all the living is expressed in the *Memento* for the living; and the union with the faithful departed is expressed in the *Memento* for the dead.

The eschatological phase of the mystery of Christ is frequently pointed out in various formulas, such as the *Haec commixtio Corporis et Sanguinis Domini nostri Iesu Christi fiat accipientibus nobis in vitam aeternam*, or the *Corpus [Sanguis] Christi custodiat me in vitam aeternam* of the communion rite. Perhaps it is hinted at in the *Beati qui ad cenam Agni vocati sunt*.

The version of the Roman Canon known as that of Moelcaich in the Irish missal of Stowe, of the eighth or ninth century, brings into splendid relief the eschatological thinking of the Mass when, immediately after the words of consecration, at the sentence *Haec quotiescumque feceritis, in mei memoriam facietis* [*Hoc facite in meam commemorationem* in the new Pauline Roman Missal], it adds the words *Passionem meam praedicabitis, resurrectionem meam adnuntiabitis, adventum meum sperabitis donec iterum veniam ad vos de coelis.*[8]

3. In the Liturgy Everything is Ordained to the Mass

If the concept of the liturgy as we have explained it in the preceding chapters helps us to understand that it is in the Mass that the liturgy necessarily achieves its summit of realization and of expression, then it will easily be understood that in the liturgy everything is ordained to the Mass.

Theological affirmation

The intrinsic ordering of all the other sacraments toward the Eucharist, as is well known, is taught quite forcefully by St. Thomas. He declares that the Eucharist is the greatest among all the sacraments not only because the other sacraments contain only an instrumental power derived from Christ, while in the Eucharist Christ Himself is contained substantially and in person, but also because of the reciprocal relationship among the sacraments themselves.

> "In fact," writes St. Thomas, "all the other sacraments are ordained to this sacrament as their end. It is obvious that the sacrament of holy orders is ordained to the consecration of the Eucharist. The sacrament of baptism is ordained to the reception of the Eucharist. Such also is the orientation of confirmation, so that a person will not abstain from the Eucharist out of fear. Again, through penance and the sacrament of the ill a man is made ready to receive worthily the body of Christ. Matrimony too is referred to this sacrament, at least by its symbolism, inasmuch as it represents the union of Christ and the Church, of which the sacrament of the Eucharist is a figure."[9]

In regard to the relation of matrimony to the Eucharist, it can also be added that the immediate and specific end of marriage is to bring forth for God, by the begetting of children, the subjects who are to become members of the Church and children of God in Christ, a thing which takes place already here on earth in a basic way in baptism and more perfectly in communion at the Eucharistic sacrifice. Thus matrimony is ordered toward the Eucharist, through the means of the procreation of children and of their baptism. It is, therefore, from the fact that the children, inasmuch as they are to be admitted to celestial glory and are already admitted here on earth to participation in the Eucharist in the sacrifice of the Mass, that the mar-

[8] Cf. Leo Eizenhöfer, *Canon missae romanae*, Rome 1954, p. 33. Consider also the similar formula of the Ambrosian liturgy: *Mortem meam praedicabitis, resurrectionem meam annuntiabitis, adventum meum sperabitis.*

For other formulas of a similar kind, see J. A. Jungmann, *The Mass of the Roman Rite*, New York 1951-1955, Vol. II, pp. 218-223.

[9] *Summa,* III, q. 65, a. 3 c.

riage of the parents achieves the fullness of perfection in all its purposes. This indicates, incidentally, what significance the first communion and the later communions of their children should have for parents.

Moreover, not only are all the other sacraments ordered toward the Eucharist, but they produce their proper grace only in virtue of their relationship to the Eucharist. The Eucharist alone has of itself the power to confer grace, while the other sacraments confer grace only in virtue of the desire which their recipients have of receiving the Eucharist also.

Basically, this was already the teaching of the Pseudo-Dionysius. It was his doctrine and that of his Greek commentators or followers that was revived and perfected by St. Thomas, repeated afterwards by numerous theologians, and finally incorporated explicitly in the Catechism of the Council of Trent.[10] The Pseudo-Dionysius had already said that the Eucharist "is the perfection of all perfections.[11] . . . We can say, therefore, that participation in the other hierarchical symbols reaches its fulfillment by means of the divine and perfective gifts of the Eucharist. For scarcely is any hierarchical sacrament fulfilled unless the most divine Eucharist, as crown of every rite, realizes the union of the initiate with the One and consummates his communion with God through the gift of the divine perfective mysteries. Therefore every other sacramental initiation of the hierarchy, being imperfect in itself and not carrying to its fulfillment our union and communion with the One, is deprived, by this lack within itself, of the character of a perfect initiation. And since the end and crown of the whole initiation is the communication of the divine mysteries to the initiate, hierarchical science has rightly taken from the reality itself this proper name (i.e., communion or *synaxis*) for the Eucharist." [12]

St. Thomas is aware of these thoughts of the Pseudo-Dionysius [13] and he develops them in the *Summa*: "This sacrament (of the Eucharist) has in itself the power to confer grace. No one has grace before receiving this sacrament except by a certain desire (*votum*) to receive it, the person's own desire in the case of an adult, or the Church's desire in the case of infants, as has been said above. The fact, therefore, that even from the mere desire to receive this sacrament there may proceed the grace which gives spiritual life,

---

[10] See, for example, M. de la Taille, *Mysterium fidei*, Paris 1921, pp. 573-587, which summarizes the whole teaching in two propositions: the other sacraments do not produce grace except by their being ordered to the Eucharist; the Eucharist itself does not produce grace without the other sacraments. The end of the other sacraments is to dispose toward the Eucharist.

[11] *Teleton telete:* which might be rendered *perfection of perfections*, or *sacrament of sacraments*, or *perfection of sacraments*. In any

case, the notion is clear: the Eucharist is supreme among the sacraments. The phrase may or may not have within itself the germ of the notion that the Eucharist somehow perfects the other sacraments since it is that to which they are directed; but, in any case, this notion too is developed as the Pseudo-Dionysius continues his treatise.

[12] *De ecclesiastica hierarchia* III, 1 (PG 3, 424-425).

[13] See *In sent.*, 4, d. 8, q. 1, a. 1 (ed. Moos, p. 308, n. 19; 310, n. 34).

follows from the efficacy of the power of this sacrament. Hence, when this sacrament is actually received, grace is increased and the spiritual life is perfected. . . . It is by this sacrament that grace is increased and the spiritual life is perfected, in order that man may be made perfect in himself through his being conjoined to God." [14]

This teaching is the foundation for the recommendation made by the Catechism of the Council of Trent to pastors of souls, when it obliges them to explain to the faithful what an abundance of riches is included in the mystery of the Eucharist. "This they will in some degree accomplish, if, having explained the efficacy and nature of all the sacraments, they compare the Eucharist to a fountain, the other sacraments to rivulets. For the Holy Eucharist is truly and necessarily to be called *the fountain of all graces*, containing as it does, after an admirable manner, the fountain itself of celestial gifts and graces, and the author of all the sacraments, Christ our Lord, from whom, as from its source, is derived whatever of goodness and perfection the other sacraments possess." [15] This, of course, takes for granted the power, contained in the other sacraments, of worship rendered to God. It is in this perspective that the words of our Lord in St. John are to be understood: "Unless you eat the flesh of the Son of Man and drink His blood, you shall not have life in you" (John 6:54).

It must be noted that, if it is true that the other sacraments are ordained to the sacrifice of the Mass and that they derive from it their sanctifying power and their value as worship rendered to God, with even greater reason is it true that everything else in the Church that is outside the strictly liturgical area has its sanctifying power and its value as glory rendered to God, whether in the private life, the ascetical and mystical life of each individual, or in the public life of administration, apostolate, teaching, only in reference to the sacrifice of the Mass, either as preparation thereto or consequence thereof, and through a certain desire for the sacrifice of the Mass. This observation is of capital importance for the solution to the question of the relationship between liturgy and spirituality, and between liturgy and pastoral.

The ultimate theological reason for the fact that all the sacraments are ordained to the Eucharist and that all the other sacraments derive their sanctifying power from the Eucharist is that the end of the sacraments is the sanctification of man and the tendering of worship to God in Christ. Golgotha, however, is the source of every sanctification which God works on man in Christ, and of every act of worship which man in Christ renders to God. Thus man is not sanctified and does not render worship to God except inasmuch as he is placed in contact with Golgotha and participates in Gol-

[14] *Summa*, III, q. 79, a. 1 ad 1. See also III, q. 73, a. 3, and parallel passages.
[15] Part 2, ch. 4, n. 47; in the translation by John A. McHugh and Charles J. Callan (*Catechism of the Council of Trent*, New York 1934), pp. 241-242.

gotha.[16] The Mass, however, is the sacramental extension of Golgotha in which man participates fully through the reception of communion. It is the Eucharist, therefore, sacrament and sacrifice, which realizes to the fullest the common notion and end of all the sacraments.

Liturgical expression

This ordering of all the sacraments to the Mass found its natural expression in the logical practice of antiquity, a practice which is being revived to some extent today, of administering and receiving all the sacraments in immediate connection with the Mass. This is a practice which made it possible for the faithful, by the very nature of the thing, to carry the sanctification received in the other sacraments and in the act of worship immediately to its natural fulfillment by participating in the Eucharistic sacrifice and in the reception of communion to which the other sacraments are precisely directed.

We know that baptism, confirmation and communion in the beginnings of ancient Christianity formed a single homogeneous rite begun at the baptismal font and completed in first communion at the Eucharistic sacrifice. Even the reconciliation of penitents took place normally in connection with the Mass of Holy Thursday: "So that, receiving the nuptial garment, they may be fit to partake of the royal table from which they had been kept away." [17] Even today the rite which prepares the sick for celestial glory is begun with the anointing of the sick and is completed with the reception of Viaticum. All those ordained in the sacrament of holy orders, in whatever degree, are normally ordained during a Mass; and they are to participate in the communion of that sacrifice. The Pseudo-Dionysius, in a text cited by St. Thomas, had already observed: "No one is perfected in a hierarchical order except by the most divine Eucharist." [18]

Finally, the celebration of marriage normally takes place during the Mass, or at least in immediate connection therewith; and the very nature of things demands no less peremptorily that the spouses seal their union by participating together in the Eucharistic sacrifice.

Thus, while certainly it remains true that the administration of the sacraments in immediate union with the Mass is not required for the validity of any of them, nevertheless, their connection with communion in the Eucharistic sacrifice is so close that the profound mind of the liturgy and, so to speak, its natural bent, lends itself to the expression of this even in the rites. It follows from this that everyone, insofar as it depends upon himself, ought to guard against frustrating the mind of the liturgy, lest he deprive the people of opportunity to perceive and live its profound significance. What is

[16] St. Thomas, *De veritate*, q. 27, a. 4. The humanity of Christ is the instrumental cause of justification.
[17] *Pontificale romanum*, last prayer of the rite of reconciliation.
[18] *De eccl. hier.* III, 1 (PG 3, 424); cited by St. Thomas in *Summa*, II, q. 65, a. 3 *sed contra*.

at stake is the understanding of the mystery of Christ and its practical efficacy in the lives of Christian people.

All that has been said of the sacraments, that they are ordained to the Eucharistic sacrifice, can be said with even greater reason about all those rites in the liturgy which are of ecclesiastical institution: ceremonies, sacramentals, prayers, and especially the divine office. The basic reason is the same: we know that all these liturgical rites of ecclesiastical origin have no other aim than divine worship in Christ and the sanctification of man in Christ. Moreover, both of these categories exist only as participation in the sacrifice of Golgotha and as derivations from it, a sacrifice which is continued sacramentally in the Mass. It is, therefore, only in the fact that they are dispositions, more or less immediate, to communion in the Eucharistic sacrifice, that all these rites have a significance.

And it is after all only natural that a sense of propriety has led the Church to celebrate even those rites which she herself instituted, in a special way the divine office and the sacramentals and in particular the more important among the various blessings and consecrations, in intimate connection with the sacrifice of the Mass.

Thus it is, for example, that the ideal toward which the liturgy tends is that the celebration of the Mass, at least of the conventual Mass, take place immediately after the recitation of a part of the office; that the more important blessings and consecrations (blessing of an abbot, consecration of a church, of a virgin, monastic profession) take place in the course of a Mass; that the obsequies of the dead be performed in connection with the Mass and by the same priest who has celebrated the Mass.

To be noted also is the frequent custom of blessing a great variety of objects (water, milk, honey, oil for the sick, and especially foods of every sort: grapes, beans, eggs, paschal lambs, bread, wine, fruit) in the very course of Mass, at the end of the canon at the formula: "... *per quem haec omnia*. . . ."[19] The same structure of the divine office was solidly affixed to the Mass of the day, for example, by the simple expedient of reciting the same oration in both.

4. The Meaning of the Liturgical Feasts and of the Liturgical Cycles

Given the fact that in the Mass under the veil of sensible and efficacious signs all the phases of the mystery of Christ, the past, present and future of salvation history, live and are highly condensed therein; and that all the other parts of the liturgy are ordered toward the Mass as to their center, finally we are able to understand the meaning of the liturgical feasts and of the liturgical cycle. If, in fact, in the Mass all the phases of the mystery of

[19] See J. A. Jungmann, *The Mass of the Roman Rite*, Vol. II, pp. 259 ff.

Christ are concentrated sacramentally and liturgically with the highest degree of expression and of efficacy, it must be said that every Mass is Advent, Christmas, Epiphany, Holy Thursday, Good Friday, Easter, Ascension, Pentecost, Christ the King, and All Saints. A liturgical feast cannot be anything that is not already really contained in each and every Mass.

What then is the precise relationship between each and every Mass and such a liturgical feast? Theologically and liturgically, every Mass expresses synthetically and, in its own way, realizes efficaciously the whole mystery of Christ. But we, limited as we are in our psychological capacity, are not able to penetrate all at one time the riches of grace of the mystery of Christ, which is expressed and synthetically realized in each Mass in a single point of space and time. Hence it is necessary that we have this mystery brought close to us successively, taken apart and analyzed, as it were, in its various aspects, always wholly and simultaneously present, so that we can concentrate successively, with a calm and sufficiently effective psychology, our attention directed now to one aspect and now to another; and thus we can arrive, very quietly, at a point where we can penetrate gradually and more deeply into the full meaning of each individual Mass. This bringing liturgically into prominence now one and now another of the various aspects of the one mystery of Christ which is realized simultaneously in all its aspects in every Mass is precisely what we mean when we speak of celebrating a liturgical feast.[20]

Generally feasts are organized liturgically in cycles of feasts, that is, in organic units of periodic recurrence. A detailed explanation of the historical formation and of the theological liturgical content of the individual liturgical cycles would require, of course, a special treatise of its own. Here it will be sufficient to emphasize their generic significance in reference to the general liturgical expression of the mystery of Christ, salvation history.

As was said above in Chapter 2,[21] the key to understanding the significance of every feast or liturgical cycle is in the consideration of its proper object, against the background of salvation history, according to the four significant levels of every liturgical sign: the demonstrative, commemorative, morally obligating, and eschatological levels.

There is the temporal cycle and the sanctoral cycle. In the Roman liturgy the festive cycle of time or temporal cycle comprises the period of the Advent-Epiphany feasts and the period of the Quadragesima-Pentecost feasts. The festive Advent-Epiphany period expresses the whole mystery of Christ, but under the aspect of the *manifested coming* (that is, the *adventual-epiphanic* aspect) of the Lord. In this period the manifested coming of the Lord is considered continuously and variously according to all the diverse

---

[20] See Odo Casel, "*Zur Idee der liturgischen Festfeier*," in *Mysterium. Gesammelte Arbeiten*   *laacher Mönche*, Münster 1926, pp. 53-61.   [21] Pp. 90-91.

levels or phases in which the mystery of Christ is unfolded: the level of the historical preparation for the coming of the Lord (the Old Testament considered as a straining toward preparation, annunciation, prefiguration of the manifested coming of the Lord); the level of the historical realization of the coming of the Lord in His birth and manifestation on earth (Christmas, Epiphany); the level of its mystical realization in the present period, which realization is liturgical in the sacrifice and in the sacraments and in the sacramentals, and extraliturgical but preparative to the liturgy and derivative from it in the private moral-ascetical transformation of individual souls as a morally obligatory response to the liturgical coming of the Lord; and finally, the level of the eschatological coming of the Lord, now already announced, prefigured, and initiated in His mystical coming and still to be perfectly accomplished in His second coming, which is proclaimed and awaited. The Lord was expected to come; the Lord came; the Lord comes every day to individual souls in a sacramental way, especially in the Mass, and in a moral way, in the moral life of each one; the Lord will come: and there we have the essential themes of this liturgical cycle. This is evident enough by merely glancing at the missal or breviary for this period, with these themes in mind.

The whole of the Quadragesima-Pentecost cycle is understood in an analogous way. Here it is once more the whole mystery of Christ that is treated, but against the background of the redemption. First, there is redemption made necessary, announced, prepared, and prefigured in the Old Testament; second, there is redemption historically realized in the life of Christ and principally in His Passion, death, descent into hell, resurrection, ascension, and His being seated in glory at the right of the Father; third, there is redemption realized and in the continuing process of realization in the Church, from its beginning on Pentecost, primarily by means of Christ's communication of the Holy Spirit to the Church as also by means of the visible foundation of this Church as a unique social institution for salvation (feast of Pentecost); and afterwards its subsequent and continuing realization in individual souls.

This subsequent realization in individual souls is achieved by liturgical and by extraliturgical means. By liturgical means, for the most part in the sacrifice and in the sacraments: the sacraments of Christian initiation given officially in the Paschal Vigil, and, according to former usage, in the Mass of the vigil of Pentecost; and again according to former usages, the sacrament of penance in the reconciliation of penitents on Holy Thursday, the sacrament of orders conferred on the ember days. By extraliturgical means, but as preparation for the liturgy and derivation therefrom: in the moral and ascetical life of each of the faithful, particularly in fasting, penance, almsgiving, good works, all the things that are especially emphasized in Lent, the quadragesimal period. Fourth and finally, there is redemption that is full, future, and eschatological in the glorious resurrection and in beatific glory, for which we are prepared by the gradually more perfect realization of the redemption made in us already in this life, in the aforementioned manner.

It is easy to see how the two grand temporal festive cycles in the Roman liturgy are thus perfectly adapted, each in its own way, to bring psychologically into prominent relief and to analyze successively, by placing more easily within our grasp, a reality of which the various aspects are in fact to be found integrally and simultaneously in each individual Mass.

In an analogous way the Marian feasts, the feasts of the angels, the feasts of the saints simply bring into prominence each of the aspects of the mystery of Christ, such as are already present in every Mass. Those of our Lady bring into particular prominence the position which, by divine pleasure, Mary occupied in this same mystery: the marvels which God accomplished in Mary, already in some way prepared for and prefigured in the Old Testament, to fit her to play the part which He had assigned to her in the realization of the mystery of Christ on its various levels; the effective action of Mary in this same realization, both in her earthly life and now in glory. Thus in the liturgy alongside the mystery of Christ there develops in a parallel way, but in a very broad sense and in a sense that subordinates it wholly to the mystery of Christ of which it forms a part, the mystery of Mary: prepared for in the Old Testament, historically realized in her earthly life, and now operative mystically in souls by disposing them to receive and live the mystery of Christ.

The feasts of the angels take into account the part played by the angels in the same sacred history, the mystery of Christ, on its various levels, from the beginning of the world to the triumph of the Apocalypse. In fact, as we shall have to explain more closely in a further chapter, salvation history, the mystery of Christ, even in its liturgical expression, is a cosmic totality in which the angels too are included.

The feasts of the saints bring into prominence as instructive models the fruits which Christ's redemptive actions have borne among men. The mystery of Christ always in action among men, operates in each individual with special shadings. No one realizes perfectly and in all its aspects this mystery which is to be a reproduction in himself of the characteristics of Christ; each one reproduces in himself in a special way some particular feature, and thus each one has his own proper physiognomy and a particular place assigned to him by God in the general realization of this mystery among men.

The feast of All Saints brings out forcefully the final, triumphal, eschatological phase of the mystery of Christ: the heavenly Jerusalem, the ultimate end of this mystery, of all sacred salvation history, the mystery of the Church, and therefore of the whole liturgy. Obviously all these things are already present synthetically in every Mass.

In this perspective it is readily seen that all the feasts are always celebrated in essence with the one same Mass. The diverse formularies by which it, though always the same, is adorned, so to speak, on diverse occasions, function simply and precisely to bring into greater prominence now one and now another of the aspects always present and which constitute the single and integral mystery of Christ.[22]

*   *   *

In concluding these chapters on the concept of the liturgy as based on sacred salvation history, it would not seem rash to assert anew the cosmic dimensions, spatial and temporal, of the liturgy under its humble appearances as a complexus of efficacious sensible signs by means of which God sanctifies the Church and the Church renders her worship to God.

In the light of the mystery of Christ lived in the liturgy so understood, it is surprising what a profound unity and simplicity attends the cosmos, all history and the Christian life. It is a reflection of the unity and simplicity which all things have in the eyes of God in Christ Jesus.

God's intention, His plan in creating the world and in guiding its history is extremely simple and unified: "Jesus Christ, the same yesterday and today and forever" (Heb. 13:8). The liturgy is nothing else but the constant and continuous actualization of this truth under the veil of efficacious sensible signs, an actualization fully realized in communion in the mystic sacrifice of Golgotha, prepared for in the other sacraments, in the sacramentals and ceremonies, contemplated and acclaimed in divine praise *donec veniat* — until He comes again.

[22] On the meaning of the feasts of our Lady and of the saints in the framework of the celebration of the mystery of Christ, see also CL, art. 103-104.

PART 2 THE LITURGY AND THE GENERAL LAWS OF THE DIVINE ECONOMY IN THE WORLD

6 THE LITURGY

AND THE LAW OF OBJECTIVITY

To understand correctly the nature and function of the liturgy in the Christian economy, it is indispensable to have a clear view of it in relation to the grand perspectives of Christian revelation. That is why in explaining the concept of liturgy we have been most careful to show that its natural basis is sacred history; we have presented a concept of the liturgy that views sacred history as perfectly synthesizing the framework of God's economy in regard to creatures and of the response of creatures to God in the Christian vision of the cosmos.

But up to now we have been able to show this framework only in a very general way. We have only hinted at the points of contact between the liturgy and those absolutes, the grand laws which effectively govern the relations between God and His creatures. Now it is necessary for us to go back and analyze more leisurely at least the principal aspects of the relationship between liturgy and these laws. The principal points which will be of greater interest to the concept of liturgy can be reduced, I believe, to six:

1. The law of objectivity.
2. The Christological-Trinitarian movement of salvation.
3. The law of the single liturgist and of the single liturgy, which further explains the Christological-Trinitarian motion.

4. The communitarian law of salvation.

5. The law of incarnation.

6. The law of the cosmic universality of salvation.

By analyzing these sublime laws which, by the very nature of things and by the positive will of God, govern the relations between God and His creatures in the economy which He has effectively willed, we shall be in a better position to see how the liturgy is but a particular instance within these general perspectives which express the quintessence of the Christian view of the world. Moreover we shall see that it is precisely in the liturgy that these laws achieve, in our regard, their maximum determination and application.

1. Objectivism, Subjectivism and Liturgy

We call the first law the law of objectivity. By this term we intend to express the fact that the way by which God is communicated to us and by which man reaches to God as his end, and hence attains to his own salvation, is not left to man's caprice and in no way to his own free choice. On the contrary, in the final analysis, it is objectively imposed upon him not only by his own nature, and therefore by God as Author of that nature, but also by the positive free will of God. Man, if he wishes to be saved, cannot do otherwise than to accept freely this objective route mapped out by God, submitting himself to it as to a given fact.

Of course, our own self and our freedom come into play also. First of all, it is precisely our own self, our own free personality, that God demands of us. But our subjective self cannot be developed, cannot be fulfilled, cannot be fully itself, cannot be saved, except in the free acceptance of these realities and in free submission thereto — realities which are objectively proposed, distinct from one's subjective self and independent therefrom. The subject has value only if it is governed and measured, as it were, by the object.

This normative reality, imposed upon us by God as the means and the measure of our approaching Him, is Christ the incarnate Son of God; it is the Scriptures; the sacraments; the Church, the people of God, outside of which there is no salvation; the people of God organized in such and such a hierarchical manner, under legitimate pastors, with the Pope at their head; the interpretive and determinative norms of the magisterium. The whole liturgy, as the medium of our relations with God, is characterized by this law of objectivity. The liturgy is but one particular case of this supreme law.

From this, one of the reasons why the liturgy is so distasteful to a certain type of modern mentality and why there are those who view it always with a jaundiced eye will immediately be apparent. If the ways of God are governed by the law of objectivity, the ways of modern man are, nevertheless, entirely concentrated upon the law of subjectivity; and, outside the Church, they end up in the most exasperating kind of subjectivism. We are accustomed to hear that the subject is one of the conquests of modern man. In fact, it is said to be the greatest of his conquests, because all the others are contained within this one. The modern world is interested only in research into subjective experience; and to this alone does it accord any value. And if the whole truth be told, this experience is not even considered as the reflection and product of the subject in contact with the object, but as a thing worthwhile in itself and of itself, independently of the object.

In its more radical forms, this tendency regards the object as a secondary and negligible thing, a mere reflection of the subject, which creates it, as they say, by objectifying its own ego. And they draw certain conclusions from this: life is absolute freedom in never-ending conquest over itself; God is an objectified creation of this same freedom; every aspect of religion in life represents a still unrefined stage and expression of inevitable creative spontaneity; all religions are equally good because they all result from subjective, religious experience.

It is easily perceived that when the subjectivist mentality has reached this point of development, it has arrived at the antipodes of the mentality which forms the world of the liturgy. The latter is in fact entirely a world of objectivity, placed there by God, and to which we cannot do otherwise than adapt ourselves.

The liturgical reality is Christ; Christ, who was immolated and is now glorious, is present; Christ, who transmits His own divine life, really and objectively; Christ, who exercises His mediation in a defined manner, under the veil of things sensible and symbolic. And there is a people officially present, the Church, a hierarchically constituted representative, which accepts Christ, His reality, His action, His mediation under this veil of sensible and symbolic things; and it is by subjecting itself to this reality, by its acceptance of Christ and by its submission to Him, that it communicates with God and realizes its life.

We hold that the individual subject is present and active in the liturgical reality. And we affirm that without this receptivity of the individual subject, this reality would produce no effect in him, would not save him, because in that event, insofar as the subject is concerned, all would be reduced to pure externalism and mechanics.

At the same time, however, we do not regard subjectivity in the liturgical action as a *deus ex machina* which creates the whole. The liturgical action is a reality which is completed only in dependence upon an objective reality, in which it finds its impetus and its norms. The world of the liturgy strongly affirms the axiom that for man there is neither creativity nor conquest if there has been no previous submission, not only to the laws of being in general and of nature, but also to the norms freely and positively determined by God, norms which surpass the laws of nature but never contradict them.

For an idealist who follows Kant or Gentile or Croce, for a vitalist and intuitionist like Bergson, or for an existentialist of the ilk of Jaspers, Heidegger or Sartre, what can these things mean: to unite oneself to the reality of Christ present in the sacrifice under the veil of things sensible and symbolic; to be saved through the reception of the sacraments working *ex opere operato*; to pray with the people of God? All this, in the idealist hypothesis, if it has any meaning and value at all, has such only as an external stimulus, primitive and unrefined, to thoughts of doctrine and movements of the will; no more than a stimulus to internal freedom and experience. Here we are worlds apart from the objectivity of the liturgy in which union with Christ signifies infinitely more than a mere union of thought and of will. It is a question of the whole reality of grace as physical elevation to the divine order and of the place of the sacraments in the transmission of this grace.

It is impossible, therefore, to enter into the world of the liturgy without an objectivist mentality, or, if you prefer, without a realist mentality, in which the values of subjectivity and of that which is internal are realized only by the correspondence of the subject to an object distinct from itself and independent of it. Thus, in respect to a particular point, the liturgy, we reconfirm the profound unity of the whole Catholic view of the world, fundamentally realistic and objectivist in all its ramifications.

There is a specifically Catholic balance in the pairing of subject and object; a balance which affirms quite forcefully not only the reality and the distinction of the two poles without permitting the suppression of one of the terms in favor of the other, but at the same time safeguards the individuality of each, even though the one be strictly subordinated to the other. Specifically, it is the subject which is subordinated to the object and governed by it.

The object and the objective norm in Catholicism means: God, Christ; the Church with its powers of sanctifying, governing and of teaching; the sacraments, the sacramentals, prayers, ceremonies. The individual and inward reaction of the subject means: man. The subordination of the subject to the object means: man's being confronted by the Christian, ecclesial, and liturgical reality, his becoming identified with it and his acceptance of its rule.

The maintenance of this balance is much more difficult than one might at first be inclined to suppose. Any change, be it ever so slight, in one's internal attitude and in the emphasis placed on various factors, will not be without its repercussions in the area of one's idea of the liturgy and of its function in Christian life. Such would be the case, for example, if any strong emphasis were to be placed on introspection, self-analysis, psychological experience of one's own internal status and of the reactions of one's own faculty of knowing, of willing and of perceiving, be it even in the consciousness of the presence of God and of Christ, but with the more or less conscious tendency of ending at this personal experience, at these personal psychological reactions, at these personal psychic acts, at this personal fruitional state, as if they were the important thing and the thing most to be sought after in our relations with God, instead of considering that the essential and primary thing is, quite simply, God Himself and Christ Himself: in fact, it is He and He alone who is the object of our acts.

An upsetting of this balance no less disastrous to an understanding of the liturgy and of its efficacy could also come about, of course, through fixing too exclusively upon the object and through placing such an importance upon the extrinsic data of the object, that no thought is any longer given to the fact that there must be a certain harmonious relationship between subject and object, demanding of the subject an effort toward interiorization.

A fruitless concentration on what is extrinsic unaccompanied by inward and vital reaction in the subject, and an interiorist and individualist psychologism of egocentric tendency — these are the two great enemies of the liturgy.

2. Gradations of Diverse, Possible Attitudes and the Full Efficacy of the Liturgy

The liturgy can have its full effect only in a climate in which the transcendent majesty of the object strongly dominates the psychology of the subject, and the subject interiorizes the object by responding vitally to its objective norms.

But in this matter of the balance to be observed between objectivity and subjectivity, between that which is normative and that which is personal, there can be, even among Catholics and within the limits of unimpeachable orthodoxy, a certain diversity and gradation in general attitudes; and these attitudes will not all be equally favorable to the full understanding and the full efficacy of the liturgy. Among Catholics, of course, there cannot be question of anything deeper than gradations in the safeguarding of the essential and immutable points. In the Catholic camp there is not and cannot be a piety or spirituality which is not in some basic way objectivist and therefore sacrificial, sacramental, ecclesial — that is to say, liturgical. No more can there be a liturgical spirit and piety that is truly Catholic, if it does not allow an essential place for the vital cooperation and correspondence, individual and personal, of the subject in respect to the objective, liturgical, sacrificial, sacramental and ecclesial reality.

The encyclical *Mediator Dei* and even more recently the second Vatican Council have called attention to this point, which must be absolutely clear to everyone.[1] Undoubtedly the warning was directed against the nebulous mentality of those who were making themselves the paladins of a certain self-styled "objective" piety, which they identified with liturgical piety and opposed to a "subjective" piety, whereas in reality what they were proposing was, as one author has quite correctly stated, nothing but "a caricature of piety which would transform the liturgy into a kind of magic."[2]

We shall have to return to this question in a later chapter, where we will treat explicitly of liturgical spirituality. Then it will be seen how, in practice, the very efficacy of the liturgy requires that the faithful be armed with a strong interior, spiritual life which is not simply limited to the very moments when they assist at the liturgy, but which pervades their whole lives, even in extraliturgical areas; a strong interiorization formulated, however, always in preparation for the liturgical action and as its consequence, and therefore in proximate and not merely remote connection with it.

Even while admitting, therefore, that the differences which can come about among Catholics in this area are concerned solely with certain gradations which from the viewpoint of faith and of orthodoxy, must be regarded only as secondary questions, it cannot be denied, it seems to me, that these same gradations of general attitude in regard to the subject-object relationship, from the viewpoint of the comprehension and of the full efficacy of the liturgy, have a real importance of their own. There can exist in a Catholic, then, fully protected within the bounds of orthodoxy, a mentality of such a kind that, in the face of the subject-object pair, it is particularly dedicated to the subject aspect, to the individual, to personal psychological experience, to self-determination, to an awareness of one's own psychological acts rather than to the object aspect, the sacrificial reality, the sacramentals, things communitarian and ecclesial; and this will have a tendency to diminish somewhat and perhaps even to reduce to an indispensable minimum his contact with the world of the liturgy. He will prefer to take refuge in a more individual form of piety, extraliturgical at best, having only a somewhat tenuous and remote connection with the liturgy itself.

This more individualized and extraliturgical piety will seem to such a Catholic to impose fewer restrictions on his liberty and on his individual spiritual creativity and to satisfy in a greater degree his strong preoccupation with self-determination, psychological introspection, self-analysis, and self-awareness of his own psychic acts; while a less parsimonious contact with the liturgy will seem to him to be less efficacious, a hindrance, or at least a distraction from the aim which he has in mind.

For one who wants to penetrate the world of the liturgy to its depths and to draw as much spiritual profit from it as possible, the attitude we have

---

[1] Cl, art. 12; 14. MD, nn. 26-32.   [2] A. M. Roguet, in his edition of *Mediator Dei*, p. 15, note 28.

been describing is not at all appropriate. In point of fact, the liturgy places a strong emphasis on the objective norm of salvation as given independently to the subject; it is concerned with leading the subject to his decisions, to his personal acts and to his individual psychological situation as he perceives it; but this whole subjective aspect is strongly conceived as the required response of the subject to the objective norm which God has set before him, as an attuning of the subject to the liturgical reality, always on the primary level of consciousness, as an accepting of this reality, as a participating in it.

It is a source of deep concern to us that in this liturgical world the activities of the subject, his personal psychological experiences in this encounter in Christ which takes place between God and man, even when the essential minimum is preserved, must not be erroneously regarded as if they had a salvational value of their own, independently of the object, which is the Christic, sacrificial, sacramental and ecclesial reality. Thus the liturgy is not so much concerned with constant psychological introspection and the analyzing of one's own psychic status, as with directing its attention and its gaze to God and the objective reality: Christ, the mystery of Christ, redemption, Church.

It is not, if I may repeat, that the subject is not to be concerned with himself; rather, for the most part, he will discover himself indirectly, much in the manner of one who, in a limited visual area where there are many objects, fixes his gaze steadfastly on one of them. Assuredly, he sees the others also; but they are somewhat vague and do not occupy the first level of his consciousness, because the object upon which his gaze is fixed reigns supreme. The therapy of the liturgy consists not so much in having the subject turn back on himself as in his concentrating more directly upon the object.[3]

These observations will help us to understand one of the reasons, probably one of the more profound, why among the same Catholics, even though they be fervent and desirous of a deeply spiritual life, their varied outlooks have not in the past nor do they even today lead them to an equally profound appreciation of the liturgy and to a fruition of its benefits equally

[3] Henri Brémond, who has an enviable knowledge of modern mystical literature, after having analyzed the prayers of Duguet, a contemporary of Fénelon, and having turned then to a current of spirituality of the liturgical sort, expresses it thus: "The contrast we have just indicated between Duguet and Fénelon — bourgeois Christianity, mystical Christianity — is found again between the formulas of meditation and the liturgical formulas. One of the advantages of the latter, one of their glories, is precisely this, that they cut short these passionate introspections, of which Du- guet's prayers offer us an example so pathetic and at the same time so disconcerting. The liturgy not only precludes the expression, and hence the exaggeration, of this rather morbid timidity, but even heals it, so to say, in radice. By keeping us from thinking so much about ourselves, the liturgy makes us live, effortlessly and unwittingly, the highest form of religion, which is disinterested adoration and pure love" (Histoire littéraire du sentiment religieux en France, Vol. 10, Paris 1932, p. 288, note 2).

abundant and efficacious in their lives.[4] Nor would it seem to be mere chance that in our day, among Catholics who feel and express better than others the needs of their generation, there is an ardent desire to rediscover the world of the liturgy. They are, for the most part, the same people who feel the need for a better balance in their lives, who desire among else, that a greater importance be attributed to that which is objective, realist and communitarian, than has been given it for some time past, yet without denying or foregoing any of the progress achieved in the domain of the subjective and individual.

In conclusion, we may say that the foregoing remarks will help us to understand that the basic problem confronting the liturgy today is this: how to lead Christians to a renewed vigor; how their personal and individual subjectivity is to relate to the objectivity of the liturgical reality: a Christic, sacrificial, sacramental, communitarian, ecclesial reality; how they are to make the liturgical world of this reality their own interior world, while safeguarding at the same time the harmony of the subject and object, and the primacy of the object as the determining and regulating element.

[4] For more details on this question, one may refer to the historical remarks, unfortunately too brief, of Jungmann in *The Mass of the Roman Rite*, Vol. I, pp. 103-132 and 141-151. See also the controversy to which I. Mennessier alludes in *S. Thomas d'A., Somme théologique, ed. rev. des jeunes*, in *La religion*, Vol. 1, Paris 1932, p. 327.

7 FROM THE FATHER, THROUGH CHRIST, IN THE HOLY SPIRIT, TO THE FATHER: THE LITURGY AND THE CHRISTOLOGICAL-TRINITARIAN ACTIVITY IN THE DIVINE PLAN

The way by which God comes to us and we go to God is left neither to our whim nor to our choice, but is positively pointed out for us by God Himself. It is the law of objectivity, the primary basis of the liturgy.

God has made manifest to us through His revelation, and in a quite detailed manner, how we are to approach this way of communion between God and men. Revelation teaches us, in the first place, that the God to whom we must go is God in three persons: Father, Son, and Holy Spirit. In the second place this same revelation, the better to illuminate our path, discloses to us a wonderful beam of light which rests upon the whole cycle of relations between that Trinitarian God and each one of us.

To describe this cycle in brief: every good gift comes to us from the

Father, through the medium of Jesus Christ His incarnate Son, in the presence of the Holy Spirit; and likewise, it is in the presence of the Holy Spirit, through the medium of Jesus Christ the incarnate Son, that everything must return to the Father and be reunited to its end, the most blessed Trinity. This is the Christological-Trinitarian activity of the sacred history of salvation, of the plan of God in the world. The whole structure of the liturgy presupposes this activity, without which the liturgy were incomprehensible. And therefore, the reality of which we treat being a thing unfortunately too little known today, it is necessary that we digress a little more than usual to show in some detail that this reality is authentic indeed and that it effectively saturates the whole liturgy.

1. Two Ways of Considering the Trinity:
The Way of the New Testament and of Most Ancient Tradition

It is relatively easy to understand that in the absence of the Christological sense it were impossible to penetrate the world of the liturgy. But to many people it will seem much less apparent that in order to enter into the liturgy in an intimate way, this Christological sense must be coupled to a Trinitarian sense. This is so much the more true today because so many Christians, even the fervent and sincere, are accustomed to regard the Trinity not only as the most august and impenetrable mystery of our faith, but also as the reality metaphysically most abstract of all our beliefs; and for the latter reason it has been regarded as the mystery farthest removed from the concrete affairs of our daily lives and one of those which, effectively, penetrates less deeply into our everyday experiences of religious psychology. Nor can it be denied that today the Trinitarian dimension is much weakened. For many people, God is the God of the philosophers or, perhaps, the God of the Jews rather than the Christian God: Father, Son, and Holy Spirit.

From the unity of divine nature to the trinity of Persons;
and from the trinity of Persons to the unity of divine nature

To me it seems that this state of affairs arises principally from two mental attitudes. First of all, there is the attitude which considers the mystery of the unity of the divine nature and of the trinity of Persons by starting from the divine unity and adjoining to it afterwards only mentally, in a second psychological instance, the trinity of Persons. And then there is the accustomed mental attitude of considering this same mystery of the Trinity primarily from the ontological and intratrinitarian metaphysical point of view. To account for these two facts and their consequences it may be necessary to call attention to the following points.

The dogma of the Trinity has two terms: numerical unity of nature, and a trinity of persons really distinct. The mystery, properly speaking, is in how to reconcile these two terms. But precisely because it comprises two antithetical terms, the unity of nature and the trinity of persons really distinct, this dogma can be correctly formulated in two ways, the one as perfectly orthodox as the other: but between the two there is an important diversity of psychological gradations in the various ways in which this mystery will be approached and in how it will become a part of our lives. As early as 1892 the Rev. Théodore de Régnon called the attention of theologians to this point which is so important even for the liturgy.[1]

In fact, in formulating this mystery, it is possible to start psychologically from the unity of nature and mentally subjoin to it afterwards, almost as a correction to the first affirmation, the trinity of Persons really distinct. Thus I might say: in God the nature is numerically one, although faith assures me that in this unity of nature there subsist three Persons really distinct. For one who so considers and so formulates the mystery of the Trinity, it is the unity of God's nature which occupies the first level of his psychological attention. It constitutes the basis for his point of departure, and admits of no debate; a basis which seems clear and certain enough because it is within the grasp of philosophical reasoning. At the same time, however, the trinity of persons really distinct, in the psychological attention of one who proceeds in this fashion, will be relegated to a secondary level, almost like an appendix or a mere correction to the clear and psychologically preponderant affirmation of the unity of the divine nature. It will be as if he were to say: a unity of divine nature, but of such kind that it does not impede the trinity of persons really distinct.

In this manner of considering the Trinity, the difficulty in the argument will not be one of saving in God the unity of the divine nature, because this is clear from the start and is stipulated as the point of departure. On the contrary, the difficulty will be one of saving the real distinction of the three Persons.

The problem will be: how, in a nature numerically one, is it possible for three Persons, really distinct, to subsist? Rationally this is a blind-alley, and it does not seem possible, with a nature numerically one, to still preserve a trinity of persons really distinct.[2] The God of the philosophers and, if you will, the God of the Old Testament, is kept safe and loudly affirmed in the living psychology of the believer; but what about the real distinction of the three Persons, Father, Son, and Holy Spirit? The psychological danger which threatens anyone who adopts this manner of viewing the mystery of

---

[1] Théodore de Régnon, *Études de théologie positive sur la Sainte Trinité*, 4 volumes, Paris 1892-1898.

[2] The explanatory and so-called psychological theory of the Trinity, which was proposed by St. Augustine rather as an intuitive psycho-logical description, transferred later by St. Anselm to a metaphysical level, and which was still later perfected by St. Thomas, is precisely an attempt to show how it is possible that the plurality of Persons is not incompatible with the unity of nature.

the Trinity is that he may not take seriously enough, from a vital point of view, the real distinction of the three Persons in God; and in thinking of God, he may take refuge in a psychology common to a philosopher or to a Jew, so much so that Father, Son, and Holy Spirit, and especially the Father and the Holy Spirit,[3] may not be accorded a sufficiently vivid reality in his religious psychology.

In the West, after St. Augustine, this manner of approaching the mystery of the Trinity prevailed.[4] This had profound effects, both advantageous and disadvantageous, not only on the manner in which we will be constrained to explain theologically the doctrine of the Trinity and describe the whole problem of God, but even in the manner in which the Trinity has been presented in catechisms and in preaching.

Certainly this manner of viewing the Trinity, if we may repeat ourselves, even though perfectly legitimate from the theological point of view — and from this point of view it presents certain advantages, not the least of which is that it forestalls the danger of Arianism right from the start — and even though from the point of view of the faith it is certainly orthodox, it is, nevertheless, not the primary viewpoint of Scripture in presenting the Trinity; and consequently it is not that which we are accustomed to find in the liturgy. It is, therefore, but a poor preparation for one who would penetrate the depths of the real trinitarian dimensions of the Christian view of the world and of life, as they are found in the New Testament and in the liturgy.

There is, in fact, another possible way of formulating this same mystery of the Trinity, which does not take as its mental starting point the unity of

[3] As far as the Son is concerned, He will always hold a conspicuous place in the believer's mind insofar as He is the incarnate Son, insofar as He is the Christ. But the awareness of the Father and the Holy Spirit as distinct Persons will be very tenuous. In practice, the faithful will scarcely think of anyone but God — a God who will be the God of the philosophers or, at best, the God of the Old Testament — and Christ. In theology there will be a treatise *On the One God* — strongly resembling, whatever anyone may say, a philosophical theodicy crammed with texts from Scripture and the Fathers — and a Christology. As for the treatise *On the Trinity*, it is much to be feared that its importance will not be seen.

[4] This was especially accentuated in St. Anselm, who exercised a major influence on later theologians in their manner of considering the unity and trinity in God. St. Thomas (see A. Malet, *Personne et amour dans la théologie*

trinitaire de S. Thomas d'A., Paris 1956), by defining the ontological concept of the person in God as subsistent relation and by distinguishing, in the question of the processions, the principle which produces (*principium quod:* the person) and the principle by means of which it is produced (*principium quo:* the common nature), was able to accentuate the "personalist" aspect of the Augustinian and Anselmian tradition. But these distinctions are in respect to the intratrinitarian metaphysical aspect of the divine life and do not change the general psychology in the manner of viewing the Trinity in the West, where the problem remains of how to proceed from *one* in order to arrive at *three*, and where the mystery is concentrated on the *three*. See Cyprian Vagaggini, "La hantise des rationes necessariae de St. Anselme dans la théologie des processions de S. Thomas," in *Spicilegium Beccense*, Vol. I, 1959, pp. 103-139.

nature, only to subjoin to it afterwards in a second psychological instant the trinity of Persons really distinct; on the contrary, it follows the inverse process, begins with the trinity of Persons really distinct, Father, Son, and Holy Spirit, and, in a second psychological instant, afterwards subjoins the notion that these three Persons, while really distinct, subsist in a nature that is numerically one. In accord with this manner of approaching the Trinity, the distinction of the three Persons is at the primary level of the believer's consciousness, while the unity of nature is relegated, so to speak, to a second level, almost like a corrective to the affirmation of the real distinction of the three Persons.

Here the problem which presents itself to the process of theological reasoning will be: how, in the face of the real distinction of the three Persons, to save the numerical unity of their nature, how to reduce the Trinity to a unity.[5] The specific danger which will have to be assiduously guarded against by those who approach the Trinity in this fashion will be of insisting so strongly upon the real distinction of the three Persons, Father, Son, and Holy Spirit, that the unity of nature is left too much in the shadowy area of consciousness and that their absolute equality in respect to eternity, power, knowledge, wisdom, etc., is effectively forgotten. Anyone who approaches the Trinity in this fashion will have an extremely strong and lively trinitarian consciousness. His God will not be purely and simply the God of the philosophers or of the Old Testament, but most specifically the Christian God, Father, Son, and Holy Spirit. Nevertheless, he will have to guard carefully against the danger of Arianism or Subordinationism.[6]

It is easy to see, therefore, that each of these two ways has its advantages and its dangers. And because it is necessary to choose either one or the other, it is needful to point out also that whichever of the two methods is followed, there must be a constant vigilance to affirm forcefully the antithetical term which one's choice has necessarily left somewhat in the shadows, and to bring it into a more vivid area of religious consciousness. This situation is quite unavoidable in view of the fact that the Trinity is a mystery having two antithetical terms, through which, whatever point of view one chooses in his consideration of the Trinity, one must always and necessarily end up

[5] The Greek Fathers, and the Latin Fathers before St. Augustine, who considered the Trinity in this second way, tried to solve the problem by affirming strongly, after the real distinction of the Persons, their inseparability and their unity of eternity, power, wisdom, action, etc. They had recourse, moreover, to helpful metaphors: the sun, its rays and its heat; a spring, the brook which flows from it and the lake which is formed by it; etc.

[6] And it was just so that some apologists of the second century and writers of the second and third centuries, like Tertullian, St. Hippolytus, Novatian, Origen and his school, came to give the Trinity a subordinationist explanation — which was an error, but an error on the level of the theological explanation of the faith and not on the level of the trinitarian faith itself, in which they were all perfectly orthodox. By paying attention too exclusively to the distinction of the Persons, they emphasized that distinction at the expense of the unity of the nature. Subsequently, the Arians transformed this error into a heresy.

back at the mystery. This does not mean, however, that the choice of one or the other point of view is a matter of simple indifference and without its consequences for the manner in which one will live the mystery.

It is indeed a fact that the trinitarian consciousness is psychologically more vivid in those who choose the second way, taking for their point of departure the distinction of Persons and placing this on the primary psychological level of affirmation. It is a fact also that in Scripture, in the Greek Fathers and in the pre-Augustinian Latin Fathers, in the liturgy and especially in the Roman liturgy, the second way of thinking about the Trinity, the personalist way in which the distinction of Persons is on the primary level, has been far and away the more prevalent. It follows, then, that to understand the trinitarian structure of the view of the world as proposed in the New Testament, in all the Greek Fathers, in nearly all the older Latin Fathers and in the liturgy, it is necessary to start with the second way and not the first.

The second way is, so to speak, closer to the source and more irenic, because it is that in which the trinitarian message was first presented to the simple faith of believers and in which, for the most part, it is still today presented to that same simple faith and, viewed on the practical level, in the liturgy.

The first way is, historically, a derived and primarily apologetic method. It made its appearance for the sake of an apologetic defense of the faith against the rationalist objections of Arianism, and it is in this perspective that it developed.

**The primarily entitative intratrinitarian point of view
and the primarily extratrinitarian point of view in the
intervention of the Persons of the Trinity in the world**

But this is not all. Besides this first matter of considering the Trinity by beginning with the distinction of Persons, a matter evidently common to Scripture and to the liturgy, there is a second matter in Scripture itself, which constitutes the point of departure for an understanding of another aspect of the manner in which the liturgy considers the Trinity, even if in this second matter the liturgy, in its historical development, is not satisfied to cling slavishly to the Scriptures. This second matter can be formulated thus: in considering the Trinity, Scripture is not really concerned in a primary way with what the Trinity is, from the ontological point of view, nor even with the internal metaphysical structure of the Trinity; rather, its primary preoccupation is with knowing what are the Trinity's relations with the world, what is the practical significance which Father, Son, and Holy Spirit have for the history of the world and for our own personal moral living.

Between these two concerns there is, of course, a most important difference in emphasis. Truly, there are intimate connections between the internal nature of a thing on the one hand, that is to say, that which it means in itself, the intrinsic ontological and constituent structure of this thing considered in itself independently of its circumstantial relationships with other things, and, on the other hand, the relations of this same thing with other things distinct from it, its importance for others, which is its practical significance for others. And in any case, there is a great difference between the primary and foremost concern of knowing what the internal structure of a thing is, and, contrariwise, a foremost concern with knowing what a thing is and what its practical significance is for other things, for ourselves for example.

It is generally agreed that, among the sciences, metaphysics occupies a primary position, whereas history and the experimental sciences, which are concerned almost entirely with establishing a quantitative relationship, occupy a secondary position. It is possible for one who is concerned primarily with knowing the relationships of one thing with others, and thereby, with its practical importance, to disregard, sometimes without even any notable detriment to the aim which he is pursuing, the intrinsic ontological constitution of the thing itself with which he is concerned, or, if you will, to be satisfied with knowing it very imperfectly. Thus it is not necessary to be a great philosopher and to know a great deal about the intrinsic constitution of man in order to write a good history, for example, of Julius Caesar. It is enough, if you will, to have a certain intuition about the psychological reactions of Caesar in the face of the circumstances of his life. Nor is it necessary to be able to define electricity in terms of its metaphysical structure in order to be an eminent electrical engineer.

Let us now point out that in its contemplation of the Trinity, Scripture not only considers the distinct Persons, Father, Son, and Holy Spirit, always *in recto*, but more than that, it considers these same Persons not with the primary concern of coming to know what they are ontologically in themselves and not even with a concern for their intratrinitarian life, but much more with a concern for learning what their practical significance is for us; what their real importance is and what their specific role in the history of the relations of God with the world and even of our personal relations with God. It is not the intratrinitarian aspect of the divine Persons that is at the first level of the trinitarian concerns of Scripture, but the extratrinitarian aspect, the relations of the divine Persons *ad extra*; we might say, the relationships of the divine Persons with sacred salvation history, the mystery of Christ, the mystery of the Church — whatever the concept being clarified in a specific passage.

This does not mean, of course, that affirmations of an intratrinitarian metaphysical order in regard to the Persons of the Trinity are not in fact to be found in Scripture; [7] still less that a certain number of such affirmations cannot be legitimately deduced from that which Scripture does directly and explicitly affirm.[8]

It must be noted in the first place, however, that these affirmations of an intratrinitarian metaphysical order in regard to the Persons of the Trinity, though they may be found in the Scriptures, are relatively rare and sporadic, and are not at the first psychological level of its interest, even though they may very well be of considerable importance in themselves and for theology. And in the second place, the deduction of such concepts, made from what Scripture does directly affirm, even if fully legitimate and, if you will, of great importance for theology, is not made by Scripture itself. The concerns of theological reasoning may be one thing, while the concerns of Scripture are something else; and here it has simply been our intention to insist that in order to understand Scripture, it is indispensable that we take Scripture's point of view.

The recapitulatory formula in the New Testament: *a, per, in, ad*

If we may be permitted to particularize: an attentive reader of the New Testament and especially of St. Paul and St. John will easily perceive that that which we can refer to almost as the specific role of the individual Persons of the Trinity in the sacred salvation history of the relations of God with the world and of our relations with God is formulated according to a certain scheme which is neither rigid nor absolute, but which is always present whenever sacred salvation history is discussed in its relationship to the divine Persons.

This scheme, expressed sometimes in its entirety, sometimes only in part while the rest is but implied, is formulated as follows: every good thing comes to us from the Father, through the mediation of His incarnate Son, Jesus Christ, by means of the presence in us of the Holy Spirit; and likewise, it is by means of the presence of the Holy Spirit, through the mediation of the incarnate Son, Jesus Christ, that everything returns to the Father. *A Patre, per Filium eius, Iesum Christum, in Spiritu Sancto, ad Patrem* — such is the primordial and predominant aspect under which the New Testament speaks of the Trinity.

[7] For example, the preëxistence of the Son, His true divinity, the nature of the Son prior to the incarnation, etc.

[8] Theological tradition has always and quite correctly deduced a most important series of such affirmations by presupposing or even by explicitly stating the principle that from the manner in which the single Persons of the Trinity manifest themselves *ad extra* and, so to speak, from the specific role which each, according to the Scriptures, seems to have in the history of the world and of salvation, it is possible legitimately to deduce the relationships which these same Persons bear to each other in their intratrinitarian life, saving always the monotheistic principle and the unity of the divine nature.

There the mystery of the Trinity is presented primarily with the point of departure being the real distinction of the Persons; and these same Persons are considered primarily in their relations with the world, in a movement descending from God to the world, whereby every existing being and every good thing derives ultimately from God; and in the ascending movement by which creatures return to God. In this broad perspective of sacred history of the *exitus a Deo* and of the *reditus ad Deum*, the Father appears primarily as the one *a quo* and *ad quem*, the Son as the one *per quem* and the Holy Spirit as the one *in quo*.

It must also be carefully noted that in this manner of considering the Trinity, the Son is primarily and in the first instance the incarnate Son Jesus Christ, viewed in the incarnation itself and in His works in the world, or at least, in relation to the incarnation and to the work of redemption.[9] Thus it can be said that there is a Trinitarian-Christological perspective which dominates the Scriptural view of the world and of history.

It would be much too lengthy a process to analyze here even a part of the New Testament texts that might be used to document our point. For an expression of the scheme in its complete form the enquirer may wish to read, with this point of view in mind, the beginning of the Epistle to the Ephesians:

> "Blessed be the *God and Father* of our Lord Jesus Christ, who has blessed us with every spiritual blessing on high in Christ. . . . By His love He predestined us to be His adopted sons *through Jesus Christ*, in accord with the good pleasure of His will, to the praise of the glorious manifestation of His grace; . . . predestined us to contribute to the praise of His glory . . . in whom (Christ) you too . . . have believed and have received *the seal of the Holy Spirit*, who is the pledge of our inheritance . . . *to the praise of His glory*" (1:3-14).

> "But *God*, who is rich in mercy, by reason of the great love with which He has loved us, has recalled us to life *in Christ* . . . through whom we have both (Jews and Gentiles) obtained access *in one Spirit to the Father*. Therefore . . . you are citizens with the saints and in the family of God, an edifice built upon the foundation of the apostles and prophets, the cornerstone of which is the same *Jesus Christ*; *on whom the whole edifice is* firmly constructed and *built up* into a holy temple of the Lord; and you too are part of this structure *which has become a dwelling-place of God in the Spirit*" (2:4-5, 18-22).

The interested may wish to read also the following passages:

[9] Certainly this is true also of St. John's conception of the Word. See Jacques Dupont, *Essais sur la christologie de S. Jean*, Brugge [Bruges] 1951, pp. 9-58.

"God, by sending His Son in the likeness of sinful flesh, has condemned sin in the flesh. . . . You are not in the flesh but in the Spirit, if the Spirit of God dwells in you. . . . As many as are led by the Spirit of God, they are the sons of God. You have in no way received the spirit of bondage, but the Spirit of adoption as sons, by virtue of which we cry, 'Abba! Father!' The Spirit Himself gives testimony to our spirit, that we are sons of God. And if sons, we are heirs also, heirs of God, joint heirs with Christ" (Rom. 8:3-17).

"But when the fullness of time came, God sent His Son, born of a woman, born under the Law, that He might redeem those who were under the Law, that we might receive the adoption of sons. And because you are sons, God has sent the Spirit of His Son into our hearts, crying 'Abba! Father!' " (Gal. 4:4-6).

"Or do you not know that your body is a temple of the Holy Spirit who is in you, whom you have from God? You are not your own, because you have been purchased at a great price. Glorify God, therefore, in your body" (1 Cor. 6:19-20).

No less frequent are those passages in which the scheme is found with only three terms, *a*, *per*, and *in* (see, for example, Eph. 4:4-7; Rom. 8:3-4; 15:15-19; 1 Cor. 12:4-6; 2 Cor. 1:21-22; 13:13). Even more frequent, of course, are passages in which two or even only one member of the *a*, *per*, *in*, *ad* formula is expressed. Such, for example, is the case in a context which speaks of only the First Person, whether under the name of Father or under the name of God — in accord with a tendency noted in the New Testament of reserving the name of God to the First Person [10] — presenting Him either as source or as ultimate end of the whole economy *ad extra*; [11] or of the incarnate Son as the one *per quem*, and the Holy Spirit as the *in quo*.

In the passages cited St. Paul writes these formulas incidentally and without any explanation, a fact which tends to demonstrate how clear and common the Trinitarian-Christological perspective was for the primitive faithful, even before the Gospels were written. And this is a fact confirmed by the primitive catechesis, as it is reported in the Acts of the Apostles (see, for example, Acts 2:32-33; 5:30-32; 15:7-11).

Obviously, and we repeat it, this manner of viewing matters poses a series of rather difficult questions to subsequent theological reflection. It would be naïve indeed to suppose that it would be sufficient for us simply to adopt the New Testament viewpoint, in order to solve the difficulties of the mystery without the bother of discursive reasoning.

To point out something of the difficulty: it surely does not seem necessary,

---

[10] See, for example, Col. 3:16-17; compare 1 Tim. 2:5 with 1 Cor. 8:4-6; compare Rom. 1:8-10; 8:14ff; 8:35 with 1 John 2:1 and with Heb. 7:25. See also Gal. 4:6; 1 Cor. 1:3; Col. 1:3; 1 Peter 1:3.

[11] See, for example, Rom. 3:21-26; 5:8-11; 8:26-30; 2 Cor. 5:18-19; Gal. 4:4-7; Eph. 1:3-14; 2:4-10; Titus 2:11-14.

theologically speaking, to explain the formula *a*, *per*, *in*, *ad* by reducing it purely and simply to that which in trinitarian theology is called an appropriation. Many theologians believe that this must be done;[12] but to us it seems that they have been too hasty. We can be content to interpret the formula in a purely appropriative sense only as a convenient means of expressing the efficient causality of the Persons in the world.

On the other hand it is possible to preserve a broadly personalist value in what looks to the kind of relations—always real insofar as creatures are concerned, but purely rational on the part of the divine Persons—of formal causality, whether intrinsic (through the Second Person only in regard to the human nature assumed by Him in the incarnation) or extrinsic, that is, exemplary. In this line of exemplary causality, or assimilation, it is possible to believe that in the formula *a*, *per*, *in*, *ad* there is expression of the special relation which creatures have even with that which the single Persons of the Trinity have in proper respect to each other, or, as theologians would say, with the *propria* (properties) of the individual Persons. But it is perfectly clear that as soon as an attempt is made to determine more precisely the intimate nature of the property of each individual Person, as expressed in the aforementioned formula by the prepositions *a*, *per*, *in*, *ad*, we must of necessity be confronted by the mystery.

But this necessity in no way diminishes the simple fact that it is truly and primarily in the perspective of the *a*, *per*, *in*, *ad* formula that the New Testament instructs the faithful in regard to the reality of the Trinity; that it is also in the perspective of this formula that it conceives in a concrete way the trinitarian life of the faithful and exhorts them to live it. It is through this formula that the New Testament constantly reminds us that each of the good gifts heaped upon us derives from the pure bounty of the Father; and that Jesus Christ, the incarnate Son of God, is the great and indispensable Mediator without whom no one can receive anything from the Father, nor even approach Him in any way; while without the Holy Spirit, merited for us by Christ and sent to us by the Father, present and dwelling in us, personally and with His gifts, no one would be united to Christ, nor would anyone be able to attain to his ultimate end, which is his return to the Father through the medium of Christ.

For the New Testament this reality, presented under this precise aspect, is something which has a profound influence in the concrete religious life of the faithful. It is this grand Christological-Trinitarian perspective *a Patre*, *per Filium eius*, *Iesum Christum*, *in Spiritu Sancto*, *ad Patrem* that animates their faith, hope, and charity, as will easily be seen by reading again, with this point of view in mind, the eighth chapter of the Epistle to the Romans.

[12] For example, P. Galtier, *Le S. Esprit en nous d'après les Pères grecs*, Rome 1946; and his *L'habitation en nous des trois personnes divines*, 2nd ed., Rome 1950.

202 THEOLOGICAL DIMENSIONS OF THE LITURGY

Again, this perspective is the inexhaustible source of their adoration, admiration, and gratitude to God, as is evident in the first three chapters of the Epistle to the Ephesians, especially 1:3-14; 2:11-21; and 3 in its entirety. And it is this also which determines their style of praying.

In fact, the explicit theory and actual practice of St. Paul is that the prayer of Christians, especially their prayer of thanksgiving, is made to the Father through His Son, Jesus Christ, with the consciousness that it is not possible to do this without the active presence in us of the Holy Spirit.[18] And it is always in the living consciousness that everything comes from the Father, through the mediation of His Son, Jesus Christ, in the presence of the Holy Spirit, and that similarly everything returns and must return to the Father, that the Christian finds the stronger and deeper specific motives which determine his moral conduct in the various circumstances of life and in his struggle for the good; that the obligation of living in accord with the exigencies of the Christian life in general is treated (see, for example, Rom. 8:8-18), or, in particular, of being kind and merciful (see, for example, Eph. 4:30-5:2), of being solicitous to preserve unity among the brethren (Eph. 4:1-16), or even more in particular, of fleeing adultery and immodesty.

It will be worthwhile, by way of example, to transcribe fully the reasoning of St. Paul on this last point:

> "Neither the effeminate, nor sodomites, nor thieves, nor the covetous, nor drunkards, nor the evil-tongued, nor the greedy will inherit the kingdom of God (— ad Patrem). And some of you were such; but you have been washed, you have been sanctified, you have been justified in the name of the Lord Jesus Christ (— per Christum) and in the Spirit of our God (— in Spiritu). . . . The body is not for immorality, but for the Lord, and the Lord for the body; and God, who raised up the Lord, will also raise us up by His power. Do you not know that your bodies are members of Christ? Now then, am I to make the members of Christ members of a harlot? By no means! . . . Or do you not know that your body is a temple of the Holy Spirit who is in you (— in Spiritu), whom you have from God (— a Patre), and that you are not your own because you have been bought at a great price (— per. Christum). Give glory to God (— ad Patrem), therefore, in your body" (1 Cor. 6:10-20).

These few indications will suffice, I think, to show us that even if the perspective of the relations of the creature with God expressed in the formula a, per, in, ad constitute, basically, a great mystery, this does not in any way prevent, according to the mind of the New Testament, the consciousness of these relations in this perspective from giving to the everyday affairs of Christian life an incomparable impetus and depth.

[18] See, for example, Col. 3:17; Eph. 5:18ff; Eph. 1:3-14; 5:20; 1 Tim. 1:2; Rom. 8:26ff. 6:18; Rom. 6:25-27; 7:25; 1 Cor. 1:4; 15:57;

The formula *a, per, in, ad* in ancient tradition

It is this same formula and the same great Christological-Trinitarian perspective of sacred salvation history that put its stamp so deeply upon the religious consciousness of the first Christian generations. It was in these terms and around the year 80 A.D., when St. Clement of Rome described for the Corinthians the establishment of the Church in the world:

> "The Apostles received the gospel for us from the Lord Jesus Christ (— *per Christum*); and Jesus Christ was sent from God (— *a Patre*). Christ, therefore, is from God, and the Apostles are from Christ. Both of these orderly arrangements, then, are by God's will. Receiving their instructions and being full of confidence on account of the resurrection of our Lord Jesus Christ, and confirmed· in faith by the word of God, they went forth in the complete assurance of the Holy Spirit (— *in Spiritu*), preaching the good news that the Kingdom of God (— *ad Patrem*) is coming. Through countryside and city they preached; and they appointed their earliest converts, testing them by the spirit, to be the bishops and deacons of future believers."[14]

Re-echoing the Pauline themes, the same St. Clement of Rome was able to exhort the Corinthians to unity in these words:

> "Why are there contentions among you, passions, dissensions, schisms and wars? Do we not have one God, one Christ, and one Spirit of Grace poured out upon us? And is there not one calling in Christ?"[15]

St. Ignatius of Antioch, writing about the year 110 A.D., was able to summarize for the Ephesians the meaning of the Christian life:

> "You are like stones for a temple of the Father, prepared for the edifice of God the Father (— *ad Patrem*), hoisted to the heights by the crane of Jesus Christ, which is the Cross (— *per Christum*), using for a rope the Holy Spirit (— *in Spiritu*). Your faith is what pulls you up, and love is what leads you to God (— *ad Patrem*)."[16]

Certainly for Ignatius this is no idle formula deprived of any vital force. In the enthusiasm of his approaching martyrdom he has not conceived the profound significance and worth of his coming immolation otherwise than in terms of the familiar Christological-Trinitarian perspective, in which everything comes from the Father, through Jesus Christ His Son, in the Holy Spirit, and returns then to the Father. Thus he wrote to the Romans:

> "After many prayers to God I have been permitted to see your holy faces. In fact, I have received more than I asked; for I hope to be in

---

[14] St. Clement of Rome, *Letter to the Corinthians* 42, 1-5 (Jurgens, no. 20).

[15] *Ibid.*, 46, 5-6 (Jurgens, no. 23).

[16] St. Ignatius of Antioch, *Letter to the Ephesians* 9, 1 (Jurgens, no. 40).

chains for Christ Jesus when I greet you, if the will of God considers
me worthy to reach the goal. The beginning is good: may I obtain the grace (—*a Patre*) to reach my inheritance without hindrance. . . . Let me imitate the Passion of my God (— *per Christum*).
. . . My earthly longings have been crucified; there is no longer in
me any desire for things material. The living water (— *in Spiritu;
see John 7:38ff*) murmurs within me and says 'Come to the Father'
(—*ad Patrem*)." [17]

Likewise, it is not possible to read without emotion, because of the
Christological-Trinitarian meaning which pervades it, the prayer which, in
155 or 156 A.D., St. Polycarp of Smyrna uttered in the face of the funeral
pyre at which he was about to suffer martyrdom, a prayer which certainly
re-echoes something of the great eucharist [thanksgiving] which the saintly
bishop was accustomed to pronounce in the Mass in the presence of the
assembled faithful:

> "Lord, God almighty, Father of Jesus Christ, Your beloved and
> blessed Son, through whom we have received the knowledge of
> You, . . . I bless You because You have esteemed me worthy of this
> day and of this hour, and of having a share among the number of
> the martyrs in the chalice of Your Christ, for the resurrection to life
> eternal of both soul and body, in the incorruptibility of the Holy
> Spirit. . . . In this way and for all things I do praise You, I do
> glorify You through the eternal and heavenly High Priest, Jesus
> Christ, Your beloved Child: through whom be glory to You with
> Him and with the Holy Spirit, both now and through ages yet to
> come. Amen." [18]

Between 180 and 199 A.D., St. Irenaeus of Lyons formulated the law of the
universal return to the Father in this way:

> "This is the order and the plan for those who are saved . . . ; they
> advance by these steps: through the Holy Spirit they arrive at the
> Son and through the Son they rise to the Father." [19]

From these texts, which could in fact be multiplied, it can easily be
understood how the Christological-Trinitarian consciousness in the scriptural
perspective of the formula *a, per, in, ad* operated efficaciously in the religious
psychology of the earliest Christian generations.

Neither was this viewpoint forgotten in the fourth and fifth centuries, even
if, by reason of the necessity of the anti-Arian polemic, the Fathers were
now obliged to interpret this same formula more explicitly of the intratrinitarian life of the individual divine Persons and to direct their attention more

---

[17] St. Ignatius of Antioch, *Letter to the Romans* 1, 1ff; 6, 3; 7. 2.

[18] *The Martyrdom of Polycarp* 14, 1-3 (Jurgens, no. 80).

[19] *Adversus haereses* 5, 36, 2.

to the eternal Word than to Christ. Here, for example, is how St. Athanasius and St. Gregory of Nyssa formulate the trinitarian law of the intervention of God in the world, one in terms quite general, the other much more precisely:

> "The Father does all things through the Word in the Holy Spirit." [20]

> "Whatever operation passes from God to the creature . . . takes its origin from the Father, is continued by the Son, and is brought to completion in the Holy Spirit." [21]

In the struggle which the Church had at that time to carry on against those who were denying the divinity of the Holy Spirit, it was once more to the familiar scriptural perspective that the Fathers had recourse in their defense of the faith. The Holy Spirit is truly God, they argue: and in fact, it is because the Holy Spirit is present in us that we are conformed to the Word and, through the Word, to the Father; and it is precisely in this conformity that our deification consists; but this deification of ourselves, our participation in the divine nature could not be accomplished by one who were himself a creature.

> "The Holy Spirit is the ointment and the seal with which the Word anoints and signs everything. . . . Thus signed, we rightly become partakers of the divine nature, as Peter says (2 Peter 1:4), and thus the creature becomes a sharer of the Word in the Spirit, and by the Spirit we are partakers of God. . . . Every time we say that we are partakers of Christ and partakers of God we mean that that unction and that seal which is in us is not of a created nature, but is of the Son, who joins us to the Father by the Spirit who is in Him. . . . If the Holy Spirit were a creature, there could be no communion of God with us through Him. On the contrary, we would be joined to a
> · creature, and we would be foreign to the divine nature, as having nothing in common with it. . . . But if by participation in the Spirit we are made partakers in the divine nature, it is insanity for anyone to say that the Spirit has a created nature and not the nature of God. Indeed, this it is whereby those in whom He is, are made divine; and if He makes men divine, it cannot be doubted that His is the nature of God." [22]

This reasoning is common among the Fathers of that era; it is not necessary to belabor the point. Enough only to observe that in those centuries the scriptural manner of considering the matter was so profoundly fixed in the minds of their contemporaries, so natural to their way of thinking, that

[20] St. Athanasius, *Four Letters to Serapion of Thmuis* 1, 28 (Jurgens, no. 782).

[21] St. Gregory of Nyssa, *Quod non sint tres dii*, PG 45, col. 125.

[22] St. Athanasius, *Four Letters to Serapion of Thmuis* 1, 23-24 (Jurgens, no. 780).

the Fathers were able to start out from it as from a principle already known and readily admitted by all, in their refutations of the errors of heretics.

Yet, even if it does seem to belabor the point, we must nevertheless insist that when we say that the perspective of sacred salvation history typified in the formula *a, per, in, ad* in Scripture and in ancient tradition has a profound influence on the Christian view of the world and of life, we do not mean to say that this formula is to be found always and everywhere in its entirety, whenever there is mention in the New Testament or in tradition of the relations between God and man, of the benefits bestowed by God, of prayer, etc. It would be easy to cite texts in which the author seems to refer only to God in general, or else to God the Father and to Christ, or again, to Christ alone, or to the Father alone, or to the Spirit alone.

We mean to say only that when these authors wish to consider the complete synthesis of the relations between God and man in the sacred history of those relations according to the specifically Christian viewpoint of the world and of life, this synthesis is always concretized by them according to the scheme indicated. Christ, the Spirit, the Father, considered separately, are for them only elements of that complete synthesis, which is always at least presupposed and in the subconscious, as is evidenced by the fact that they do state it explicitly when they intend to set forth the entire cycle of the *exitus* of the creature *a Deo* and of the creature's *reditus ad Deum.*[23]

[23] Let it be noted that this way which ancient tradition has of presenting the Trinity, *as long as it is limited to considering the divine Persons in their extratrinitarian relations* and to *expressing them in the formula* A, PER, IN, AD, does not yet constitute a particular theological theory for explaining the Trinitarian faith, but is simply the statement of this faith as it is made by Scripture, nothing more and nothing less. That which Père de Régnon has called the Greek explanatory theory of the Trinitarian belief, as opposed to the Latin theory, has its precise starting point when, going beyond the simple affirmations of Scripture and of the faith, and taking as basis the principle — and this part is certainly quite accurate, even if the distinction between Greek and Latin theory is not to the point — that from the extratrinitarian manifestations of the individual Persons it is possible to conclude to their intratrinitarian relations, the extratrinitarian scriptural scheme *a, per, in, ad* is translated to the intratrinitarian life and we attempt, insofar as it is possible, to explain this intratrinitarian life in the terms of this same scheme. It was along these lines, in the very core of the "Greek" theory, that the explanatory theory called "economical" developed. It is so called because it concludes from the "economy" of the Persons *ad extra* to their modes of existence *ad intra.* This theory was developed by the third-century teachers, like Tertullian, St. Hippolytus, Novatian and, in the main, Origen and those of his school. These teachers, however, were not entirely successful in escaping subordinationism in their theological explanations.

Be that as it may — and this is what presently concerns us — when the liturgy employs the *a, per, in, ad* scheme, applying it only to the extratrinitarian relations (and this is, to the best of my knowledge, almost always the case in the Roman liturgy, while the Eastern liturgical compositions, especially those of later date, not infrequently transfer the scheme to the intratrinitarian life), it does not depend at all upon the "Greek" explanatory theory and still less upon the "economical" explanation of the Trinitarian belief, but is simply content to assume the scriptural perspective. This is not sufficiently clear, it seems to me, in the observations which Dom M. Cappuyns has made in this area, in his article *"Liturgie et théologie,"* in *Le vrai visage de la liturgie, Cours et conférences des semaines liturgiques,* Vol. 14, Louvain 1938, pp. 194-209.

2. The General Christological-Trinitarian Perspective in the Liturgy

The first part of the present chapter sets forth the data which is indispensable to anyone who wishes to understand how the liturgy is permeated by the Christological-Trinitarian perspective of the world. Here, in fact, as in so many areas, the liturgy simply brings into play, in its own particular way, Scripture and most ancient tradition.

The first point to be noted is that the God of the liturgy is not simply the God of the synagogue, nor is He the God of the philosophers; rather, He is the specifically Christian God, the God in Three Persons. We do not mean, of course, that consideration of the unity of the divine nature in the sense of an unequivocal affirmation of monotheism is absent from the liturgy; for this, first of all, is always specifically present in the affirmation of unity conjointly with the trinity and through the use which the liturgy makes of Old Testament texts which speak of God. This use in particular prevents the loss in the liturgy of anything of the incomparable richness of the Old Testament concept of God as the transcendent God, the Creator, Lord, Judge, supreme and infallible Director of the world and of individuals.

But the liturgy never lets us forget, even on the practical level, that this same God who revealed Himself in the Old Testament in the unity of His nature is, in reality, a God in whose numerical unity of nature there subsist Three Persons really distinct. The context of the liturgy, whether remote or proximate, always interprets in a Christian and Trinitarian way the Old Testament texts which speak of God. In the Roman liturgy, for example, at least since the fourth century, the psalms have been immediately and explicitly Christianized by means of the doxology in the *Gloria Patri*. But even when this usage was not yet the custom, the liturgical context, with its Trinitarian viewpoint expressed in ternary or even in binary formulas, as will be seen below, always sufficed to achieve the same result. It is precisely in this sense that it is possible to say that in the liturgy the worship of the one God does not exist.

A second point, in the nature of a premise: in accord with the scriptural manner of considering the Trinity, the liturgy, like the most ancient patristic tradition, simply adopts the viewpoint which consists in placing the real distinction of Persons on the first level of conscious attention, and in affirming their unity of nature only in a second moment of psychological reflection.

In comparison to Scripture, which, in matters Trinitarian, considers the Persons themselves primarily in their extratrinitarian relations to sacred salvation history according to the *a, per, in, ad* scheme, we can see that the liturgy, in its historical development, permits itself to indulge various gradations of this same scheme. In texts of more ancient origin it is more squarely in the scriptural camp, and it has an enormous preference for the consideration of the divine Persons in their extratrinitarian relations to the sacred history of salvation in accord with the *a, per, in, ad* scheme. In these texts, therefore, the Christological-Trinitarian perspective is frankly dominant. It can be said, in fact, that this perspective constitutes the general basis for the liturgy's view of the world; and this is especially the case with the Roman liturgy.

Nevertheless, in regard to this matter, the anti-Arian controversies were the occasion of a certain shift of emphasis in the liturgy. It is precisely in view of Arianism that the liturgies, even while preserving always in basis the extratrinitarian consideration of the Persons in accord with the *a, per, in, ad* formula, and with it the Christological-Trinitarian perspective, begin to be preoccupied with a notable multiplication of affirmations, made in a second psychological instant, of the intratrinitarian equality of the Persons themselves, an equality advanced precisely as a denial of the Arian heresy. Thus it happens that attention is distracted from the level of the extratrinitarian relations of the Persons according to the *a, per, in, ad* scheme, and begins to be concentrated, in a degree considerably more pronounced than that which is directly encountered in the Scriptures, on the ontological and intratrinitarian level of the numerical unity of the divine substance and of the equality of the divine Persons.

In this way a whole series of affirmations which consider the Persons of the Trinity in themselves in the unity and equality of their divine nature and in a perspective that is more purely and directly Trinitarian comes to be juxtaposed to or even superimposed upon the ancient liturgical foundation of the Christological-Trinitarian perspective in which the relations of the Father, of Christ, and of the Holy Spirit with salvation history are treated directly. After having affirmed as heretofore, in various manners and gradations, that every good thing comes to us from the Father through Christ, His incarnate Son and our Head and Redeemer, in the presence in us of the Holy Spirit, and that in the same way everything returns to the Father, the liturgies now suddenly add, in a manner more or less explicit, that the Father, the Son, considered independently of His incarnation, and the Holy Spirit, viewed in their intratrinitarian life, are one single and equal Godhead. It might be said, therefore, that from the time of the Arian controversy, the complete formula in the liturgy becomes: *a Patre, per Christum Filium eius, in Spiritu ad Patrem, beata Trinitas unus Deus*.

It must be acknowledged, however, that this anti-Arian concern, all things considered, seems to be much less strong in the Roman liturgy than it is in the other liturgies, especially the Eastern ones; and yet, it is quite strong in the Spanish and Gallican liturgies, where also the anti-Arian polemics left a very deep impression. Practically speaking, this anti-Arian concern is evident in the Roman liturgy only in certain more highly developed liturgical prayer conclusions and in the doxology, where it is not very intrusive; in the Nicene-Constantinopolitan and Athanasian creeds; in the preface for the Feast of the Most Holy Trinity, which until quite recently was sung on all the ordinary Sundays of the year, and which was found already in the Gelasian Sacramentary toward the end of the ninth century; [24] especially on the feast itself, in the office and Mass of the Most Holy Trinity, which is of medieval Frankish origin — the work, essentially, of Alcuin, who died in 804, and of Stephen, Bishop of Liége from 903 to 920 — and the acceptance of which was for a long time opposed at Rome. Even some prayers addressed directly to the Trinity, and found in the Roman liturgy, are of Frankish origin, such as the *Suscipe Sancta Trinitas* and the *Placeat Tibi Sancta Trinitas*, which were introduced into the Mass between the ninth and eleventh centuries and remained in the Roman Missal until the current reform.

In regard to the Trinitarian theological speculations more properly so called, whether that which Père de Régnon refers to as the Greek theory of the Trinity or that which he called the Latin theory, and the latter whether in its Augustinian form or, *a fortiori*, in its scholastic form, their traces in the Roman liturgy are practically non-existent.[25]

In support of all this it will be enough to pass in review the collects, the doxologies, the liturgical cycles, the sacramentals, the sacraments — attaching to baptism our study of the professions of faith and of the creeds — and the Mass; and our review will be directed primarily to the Roman liturgy.

The orations

To put it briefly, in both the introduction and in the body of the liturgical orations or collects the predominant structural element is the Christological-Trinitarian, according to the usual perspective of the scheme *a, per, in, ad* expressed more or less integrally and referred directly to the relations of the Persons with salvation history. This holds true also for the conclusion of the orations of more ancient origin. Only from the time of the anti-Arian struggle is there an increasing number of conclusions which affirm the equality of Persons from a more directly intratrinitarian viewpoint. And only since the Middle Ages, and especially in even more recent times, has the Roman liturgy been infiltrated by some orations, very few indeed, of an entirely different sort.

[24] Mohlberg ed., n. 680, p. 105. See also J. Jungmann, "*Die Abwehr des germanischen Arianismus und der Umbruch der religiösen Kultur im frühen Mittelalter*," reprinted in the collection *Liturgisches Erbe und pastorale Gegenwart*, Innsbruck 1960, pp. 3-86, and especially pp. 30-52.

[25] Insofar as the Roman liturgy is concerned, we may say, in fact, that such anti-Arian polemicism as is to be found there does not have apologetic reasoning for its basis, but simply affirms a correct belief in the nature of the Persons and their equality.

The general rule quite well observed in more ancient times is that the liturgical orations are directed to the Father through the mediation of Jesus Christ, our mediator supreme. The force of this rule in antiquity was such that in 393 A.D. the Council of Hippo, at which Augustine, then still a simple priest, assisted, formulated the following rule in a universal and absolute manner, in spite of the danger of Arianism, a heresy to which this rule could easily provide the pretext for an attack upon the Catholic faith: [26]

> "In services at the altar, the collect is always to be directed to the Father." [27]

This rule is based not only on ancient tradition but ultimately upon the explicit exhortations of St. Paul, who wrote:

> "Let the word of Christ dwell in you abundantly in all wisdom, teaching and admonishing one another by psalms, hymns and spiritual songs, singing sweetly to God in your hearts; and whatever you do in word or in deed, do everything in the name of the Lord Jesus, giving thanks to God the Father through Him" (Col. 3:16-17).

> "Be filled with the Holy Spirit, speaking to one another in psalms, hymns and spiritual songs, singing and making melody in your hearts to the Lord, giving thanks always for all things in the name of our Lord Jesus Christ to God the Father" (Eph. 5:18-20).

St. Paul's own practice is in accord with his theorization.[28]

From this we understand the ancient structure of the liturgical prayer. The one who is praying addresses himself first of all to the Father, whom, most frequently in the very first words, he calls upon directly as Father, God, Lord, Lord God, etc.; and then he calls attention, in a more or less ample and insistent manner, to some of His attributes or to some of His interventions on our behalf, such as: Almighty, Eternal, Creator, who sent to us Your Son; who in the Old Testament worked such and such wonders or set in order such and such arrangements; who in this saint operated with such and such power; who now can grant us this benefit, or permit us such and such an activity. And therefore, right from the beginning, the prayer recalls a moment of salvation history, with the Father *ut a quo omnia.*

It must be noted in this regard that the One to whom the liturgical action is addressed is truly the Father, the First Person of the Trinity, and not simply God, the Three Persons together. This is true not only when He is called upon under the name Father and in a context which speaks of His

---

[26] That the Arians of the fourth and fifth centuries were able to argue from these Catholic liturgical phrases against Catholics themselves is demonstrated by the fragment of an Arian author of the period, edited by G. Mercati in *Studi e Testi* 7, Rome 1902, pp. 47-56. See also the text of the *Sacramentarium*

Veronense, Mohlberg ed., pp. 201-202.

[27] *Cum altari assistitur, semper ad Patrem dirigatur oratio.* Mansi 3, 884.

[28] See, for example, Rom. 1:8-10; 8:34; and in general the beginning of his letters, such as 1 Cor. 1:4-9; 2 Cor. 1:3-6; Gal. 1:3-5; Eph. 1:3ff; Col. 1:3ff; 1 Thess. 1:2-3.

special intratrinitarian relations with the Son (*Hyiós, Filius*) and with the Spirit (*Pneúma, Spiritus*), but even when He is called upon simply under the name God or Lord (*Déspota*), our Father, with attributes or operations that are in themselves common to all Three Persons, such as Almighty, Creator, Judge, and when Christ is then mentioned as His Servant (*Pais, Puer*), a specifically Messianic title; and this even when no mention whatever is made afterwards of the Holy Spirit. The reason for this is that by so doing the liturgy is simply conforming itself to primitive Christian usage as it is known to us from the Scriptures.

It is to be noted, in fact, that in the New Testament, although it is not the Father only, but, its rigid monotheism notwithstanding, the Son also, Jesus Christ, who is truly and properly regarded as God, while the same holds true also of the Holy Spirit,[29] there is, nevertheless, a strong tendency therein:

1) to reserve the name of God to the Father only;[30]
2) to call by the title "our Father" not the Triune God, but the Father only, the First Person of the Trinity, whose Son (*Hyiós*) is Jesus Christ; and of whom even we are the adoptive sons;[31]
3) to consider as said of the Father, the First Person of the Trinity, those things which the Old Testament said simply of God.[32]

It is certainly a thing most notable that the plans of the Christian doxologies in the New Testament, particularly in St. Paul, and the prayers as well, especially the great Eucharistic prayer of the Mass, are structured on the same lines as Jewish prayers, which are addressed to God, enumerating His attributes and operations; for example, omnipotence, creation, judgment, providence, and fatherhood over Israel. It is also to be noted, therefore, that the New Testament and earliest Christian tradition Christianized these plans by the very fact that in their context they apply the name God more or less explicitly to the Father, not simply the God who is our Father, but precisely to the First Person of the Trinity; and this is clear because mention is always made of the Son, and of the Father's having been revealed in Him.

This Christianization is real even if the Son is simply called Servant (*Pais, Puer*), Christ, Messiah. Indeed, in the New Testament, the revelation of the plurality of Persons in God was made from the outset not in an abstract but in a concrete way. When the Apostles were given to understand

---

[29] See, for example, Matthew 11:27; 28:18ff; John 1:14; 20:28; Rom. 9:5; Titus 2:13; Phil. 2:5ff; Col. 1:19; 2:9. All the properly divine operations which take place in us can be accomplished only through the Holy Spirit, to whom they are attributed.

[30] See, for example, Col. 1:3; 3:16ff; Rom. 1:8-10; Gal. 4:6; 1 Cor. 1:3; 1 Peter 1:3. Compare 1 Tim. 2:5 with 1 Cor. 8:4-6; and Rom. 8:5-35 with 1 John 2:1 and Heb. 7:25.

[31] In St. Paul the actual identification of our Father with the First Person of the Trinity, the Father of our Lord Jesus Christ, who is the Father's Son (*Hyiós*), is so frequent that even in those texts where it is not explicit it must be supposed. See, for example, Rom. 1:1-9; 1 Cor. 1:3-9; 2 Cor. 1:2ff; Gal. 1:1-16; 2:19-21; 4:4-7; Eph. 1:1-3; Col. 1:2ff; 1 Thess. 1:1-10. See also 1 John 1:12-14.

[32] See, for example, Heb. 1:7.

that that Man, the Messiah, the Servant of Yahweh, Jesus, was called Son of God by a most special right, then they understood that God, the God of the Old Testament, was indeed our Father; but even more, that by a title most special He was Father of Christ. No wonder, then, that the ancient texts which speak of the Father and of the Son remain strongly in this perspective of the God of the Old Testament and of His Servant, the Messiah.

Indeed, it is in this perspective and from this starting point that a plurality of Persons in God is revealed to the Apostles in a good pedagogical manner, gradually and always with greater clarity. So too, it was only when they began to have some concrete experience of the Holy Spirit that they were able the better to understand the existence of a Third Person in God. For these reasons, prayers which at first glance would appear to be addressed simply to God in general or even to our Father are in reality directed by Christians to Him whom they know as the Father of Jesus Christ, that is, to the First Person of the Trinity; and this is in accord with the well-known exhortation of St. Paul. That this is the case is shown by such a passage as Acts 4:24-31, which is clearly Trinitarian when it records the prayer which the Christians offered after the return of the Apostles from prison; and it is shown also by the introduction of such a form of address into so clearly a Trinitarian passage as that of St. Clement of Rome in his *Letter to the Corinthians*, ch. 58-61 (see also the same, 46, 6).

It seems to me that the *Didache* passages 9, 2-4 and 10, 2-5, notwithstanding the fact that they are verbally addressed to "our Father" and to "holy Father," are in reality no more nor less than a putting into practice of the rule laid down by St. Paul: ". . . giving thanks always in the name of our Lord Jesus Christ to God the Father."

In view of the themes mentioned above and in view also of the ancient and rigid ecclesiastical rule restated in the Council of Hippo of 393 A.D., there is even stronger reason to say that indubitably the *Deus* to whom, without any additional Trinitarian indication, so many of the liturgical orations are addressed, whether ancient — as is the case with almost all of those in the Leonine Sacramentary, along with a large part of the Gelasian — or modern, and which end with the simple conclusion *per Christum Dominum nostrum*, is in fact the Father, the First Person of the Trinity.

Following upon the introduction, the body of the ancient collect constitutes an expression of adoration, of thanksgiving, of compunction, of petitions for protection or for new graces. The most frequent of these, perhaps, are thanksgiving and petition. This adoration, thanksgiving, compunction, or petition is then very easily elaborated upon in a manner more or less ample; and the one who is praying shows why he wishes to adore, to give thanks, to repent, or to make a request. And here, most frequently, some point of salvation history is newly recited.

For example, thanksgiving is made to the Father for the benefits He has bestowed upon us, usually with the explicit mention of the fact that such benefits have come to us through the mediation of Jesus Christ, or by sending us the Holy Spirit; or it may provide occasion to take note of present benefits in a thankful manner, for example, such benefits as those of participating in the mysteries of the Mass, of celebrating a feast; or there may be a petition for new graces, temporal or spiritual; for the Church, that it might be effective in accomplishing its mission; for all Christian people, that they might attain happily to their end, which is their return to the Father in life eternal; for a specific individual, that God might grant him the graces of the sacrament which he is receiving — and here often enough mention is made of the Holy Spirit, who beseeches the Father to grant that which is desired — or of the sacramental which is being imparted. In all of this the Christological-Trinitarian perspective always predominates, with its consideration of the Persons *ad extra* in the scheme *a, per, in, ad*.

Finally, the collect has a conclusion. As Father Jungmann has rightly pointed out,[33] and whose conclusions on this point often provide us with the bases of our study, it is in the historical development of the conclusions of the orations (and of the doxologies) that, in the ancient era, there is manifested especially in the liturgy that progressive accentuation of the affirmation of the equality of the Persons of the Trinity, an anti-Arian reaction to which we have previously referred.

In the Eastern tradition the conclusion of the orations almost always contains a doxology; in the Latin Roman liturgy, however, this is not the case. In both traditions, however, the conclusion always contains some mention of Christ as Mediator.[34] The simplest of these conclusions is the Roman formula *Per Christum Dominum nostrum*, which in the Leonine Sacramentary served as the exclusive conclusion for collect, secret prayer, and postcommunion, and which in our present Pauline Roman Missal has now been restored as the conclusion for the secret or *super oblata* prayer and for the postcommunion prayer.

It now finds other usage also, as for example throughout the present Roman Ritual. The meaning of the formula is obvious enough: Father, we thank You, we worship You, we implore You *through Christ our Lord*, thereby associating ourselves with Him, in union with Him, in His name, through His intercession, who is our Head. It is simply the putting into practice of the frequently reiterated admonition of St. Paul, and of the teaching

[33] Josef A. Jungmann, *Die Stellung Christi im liturgischen Gebet*, Münster im W. 1925 (2nd ed., 1962). This is the work which, for the most part, cleared the ground in the area which presently interests us.

[34] In the prayers reported in the *Didache*, chapters 9 and 10, the mention of Christ as Mediator is found not properly in the conclusion of the prayer, but immediately before the conclusion. To the best of my knowledge, this is the only instance of such an arrangement that can be cited.

of the New Testament that Christ is our intercessor with the Father (1 John 2:1; Rom. 8:34; Heb. 7:25; John 14:16; 16:23).

The meaning of this *per Christum Dominum nostrum* is made explicit in a magnificent way in the conclusion of the great prayer of St. Clement of Rome in his *Letter to the Corinthians*, a prayer which is modelled on liturgical prayer, and which concludes as follows:

> "To You, who alone have the power to do these good things and others far greater for us, we give thanks *through the High Priest and Patron of our souls, Jesus Christ*, through whom be glory and majesty to You, both now and from generation to generation and in the ages of ages. Amen." [35]

The same formula is repeated in chapter 64 of St. Clement's *Letter to the Corinthians*, and it is found substantially in the same way in *The Martyrdom of Saint Polycarp*.[36] The same St. Clement of Rome illustrates the meaning of this formula when he explains what Christ's mediation means for us:

> "This is the way, beloved, in which we found our salvation, Jesus Christ, the High Priest of our offerings, the defender and helper of our weakness. Through Him we fix our gaze on the heights of heaven; through Him we see the reflection of the faultless and lofty countenance of God; through Him the eyes of our heart have been opened; through Him our foolish and darkened understanding shoots up to the light; through Him the Master willed that we should taste of deathless knowledge; who, being the brightness of His majesty, is as much greater than the angels as the more glorious name which He has inherited." [37]

The conclusion *through Christ our Lord*, or even more so, *through Christ our High Priest*, suggests the idea, therefore, that liturgical prayer is not possible, has no meaning or value, unless it unites the prayer of the Church to the prayer of Christ, now glorious at the side of the Father, our Head and Intercessor at the Father's side. Liturgical prayer has meaning and value, then, insofar as it is the prayer of Christ, active and present in the Church. We are able to present ourselves to the Father only inasmuch as we are hidden in Christ. As we proceed, we shall be obliged to return to this idea.

---

[35] St. Clement of Rome, *Letter to the Corinthians* 61, 3.

[36] *The Martyrdom of Saint Polycarp* 14, 3 (Jurgens, no. 80). Jungmann, in *Die Stellung Christi im liturgischen Gebet*, pp. 127ff., points out the same formula in the fragment of a prayer, probably liturgical, of a second- or third-century papyrus, and notes the same idea in Tertullian's *Against Marcion* 4, 9. See also

St. Clement of Alexandria's *Stromateis* 2, 9, 45, 6; 2, 22, 134, 2; and his *Protreptikos* 12, p. 84 in Otto Stählin's edition. These are all indications that in the second and third centuries the formula must have been quite common.

[37] St. Clement of Rome, *Letter to the Corinthians* 36, 1-2 (Jurgens, no. 18).

It is clear, however, that, up to the present time, the orations which have this conclusion, even without mention of the Holy Spirit, are, by reason of that conclusion, invariably in the Christological-Trinitarian tradition which views the Persons *ad extra* according to the scheme *a, per, in, ad*. They are all based on the consideration of the Father as the origin *a quo* and the end *ad quem* of the *ad extra* economy, and of the incarnate Son, now glorious beside the Father, as the *per quem* of the same economy.

A further development of the conclusion of the liturgical orations takes place with the joining of the Holy Spirit to the mention of Christ the Mediator. The Greek language texts can be studied from this point of view at the same time as the doxologies, because in the Greek tradition the orations conclude with a doxology in which mention of the Holy Spirit was added only at a later time.

In the conclusion of the Latin Roman orations, the mention of the Holy Spirit was introduced by means of an amplification of the ancient simple conclusion *per Christum Dominum nostrum*. This amplification finally led to the most fully developed conclusion of all: *Per Dominum nostrum Iesum Christum (Filium tuum), qui tecum vivit et regnat in unitate Spiritus Sancti (Deus) per omnia saecula saeculorum*. There is some discussion of the precise meaning of the phrase *in unitate Spiritus Sancti*, which, as you know, recurs in the final doxology in the Roman Canon, the *Per ipsum*.

Even if not everything has yet been clarified on this point,[38] for the orations it seems that the most probable explanation is to be found along the lines of what has been proposed by Dom Botte: the amplification of the old conclusion into its longer form was occasioned by a concern for the anti-Arian controversy. We have seen that the liturgical orations in their most ancient structure not only considered the divine Persons primarily from the perspective of their being really distinct from each other, but likewise that this was accomplished by viewing them first and foremost in their relations *ad extra* according to the scheme *a, per, in, ad*. And in this same regard, these liturgical orations fixed their attention for the most part on the Father alone, and always made mention of the incarnate Son also; but similar mention was not always made of the Holy Spirit.

In the struggle against the Arian heresy, without changing anything of the ancient tradition about the introduction and the body of the oration, the conclusion was amplified by naming there the Three Persons, transferring attention from the directly extratrinitarian level to that of the intratrinitarian life and realm, and from the level on which the distinction of Persons is predominant to that on which their unity and equality predomi-

---

[38] See the discussion in Jungmann, *Die Stellung Christi im liturgischen Gebet*, pp. 179ff.; or, in the 2nd edition, pp. xvi*-xvii*. Also Jungmann's *The Mass of the Roman Rite*, Vol. II, pp. 264-268. B. Botte, *L'ordinaire de la messe*, Paris and Louvain 1953, pp. 133ff.

nate. Thus, after the traditional words *per Christum Dominum nostrum* or *per Dominum nostrum Iesum Christum*, a formula was subjoined which expressed the idea that Christ, the Son of the Father, lives (lives and reigns) eternally together with the Father and the Holy Spirit. The formulas by which this was expressed were varied in their particulars. However, it seems certain that the expression *cum Spiritu Sancto* preceded that which reads *in unitate Spiritus Sancti*; and that the change from the former to the latter began about the year 420 or 430 A.D., the latter spreading more rapidly during the second half of the fifth century, by which time it was accepted almost everywhere in the West, except in Spain.

From all this, in spite of the difficulty about the phrase *in unitate Spiritus Sancti*, the precise meaning of which was no longer understood from the beginning of the sixth century, it seems that the significance of the amplified formula in its totality is: "Through our Lord Jesus Christ, Your Son, who lives and reigns with You in the unity of the divine nature which You and He have together with the Holy Spirit, through the ages of ages." In particular the resemblance to certain prayer conclusions which recur in Arnobius the Younger, who lived in Rome and died there about the year 450 A.D., confirms the interpretation here proposed.[39]

Be that as it may, this increased emphasis of the anti-Arian point of view in the conclusions of a certain number of the Roman liturgical orations does not deprive them of their dominant characteristic provided by their having been conceived against the background of the Christological-Trinitarian perspective of salvation history in accord with the *a, per, in, ad* scheme; only, the new conclusion subjoins to the ancient Christological-Trinitarian another perspective that is more simply and directly Trinitarian.

Thus the aforementioned Christological-Trinitarian character of the orations was preserved in antiquity, as long as the ancient rule was observed, that the liturgical orations were to be addressed to the Father through the mediation of Jesus Christ. When the rule was ignored, however, and some orations were addressed directly to Christ or to the Son, these, of course, had of necessity to take on a somewhat different character.[40] To these, the ancient conclusion was no longer adaptable. The new conclusion was *qui vivis et regnas. . . .* It begins to make its appearance already in the later recensions of the Gregorian Sacramentary, in a series of orations for the Masses of

[39] Texts of Arnobius the Younger cited by Botte, *op. cit.*, p. 136, are: *"Per ipsum Dominum nostrum Iesum Christum, qui regnat in unitate Patris et Spiritus Sancti in saecula saeculorum"*; and, *"Qui regnat cum Patre et Spiritu Sancto, in unitate deitatis."* There is nothing, however, which authorizes us to see in the phrase *in unitate Spiritus Sancti* the specifically Augustinian theory that in the

Trinity the Holy Spirit is the unity between the Father and the Son.

[40] In liturgical texts in the Greek language, the earliest examples are to be found in the liturgy of the *Apostolic Constitutions* 8, 43; and 8, 7; a compilation which is generally dated as belonging to the end of the fourth and beginning of the fifth centuries.

Advent addressed to *Domine* or *Deus,* which terms, however, are intended to designate no longer the Father but the Son. In the Middle Ages a series of new orations was composed, addressed quite clearly to the Son; and from the beginning of the fifteenth century, there are some that begin *Domine Iesu Christe.*

Even further removed from ancient tradition are those medieval orations which are addressed directly to the Trinity. They are, however, relatively few. Of the approximately one thousand collects, secret prayers (*super oblata*), and postcommunion prayers of the Roman Missal in use until the introduction of the present Pauline Roman Missal, Father Jungmann [41] was able to count only sixty-four of the new type. And of these sixty-four, moreover, seventeen are actually ancient orations of the usual type, addressed in the accustomed way to the Father, but which were misunderstood at a later time as being addressed to the Son.

The doxologies

The doxologies of the liturgy depend upon those of the New Testament, and these in turn have close connections with the doxologies of the Old Testament and of later Jewish tradition. [42]

In the New Testament a number of doxologies are addressed to the Father alone (*God,* or *our God and Father:* Rom. 11:36; Gal. 1:5; Phil. 4:20; 1 Tim. 1:17; 6:16; 1 Peter 5:11; Apoc. 4:9-11; 7:12). There are three addressed to the Father *through Christ:* Rom. 16:27; 1 Peter 4:11; Jude 25. Four are certainly addressed to Christ alone: 2 Tim. 4:18; Heb. 13:21; 2 Peter 3:18; Apoc. 1:6; and probably also a fifth: Rom. 9:5. One is addressed to God and to Christ, Apoc. 7:10; and one is addressed to the Father *in* the Church and *in* Christ, Eph. 3:21. The proximate occasion of these doxologies is the consideration of God's attributes (1 Tim. 6:16), of His operations in creation (e.g., Apoc. 4:11), and especially in salvation history and the history of redemption.

It is against this background that the doxologies of the liturgy are born. They have always been especially abundant in the Greek tradition, which was accustomed to conclude with a doxology not only the great Eucharistic prayer of the Mass, but every liturgical prayer, in accord with the usual Jewish practice. Very soon there were doxologies created as separate entities independent in themselves.

The Latin Roman tradition has not followed the custom of terminating every liturgical prayer with a doxology; but it has at least retained the universal custom of concluding with a doxology the canons of the Mass; and it has borrowed a certain number of the separately created doxologies from

[41] Jungmann, *Die Stellung Christi im liturgischen Gebet,* p. 103.

[42] See A. Stuiber, article "*Doxologie,*" in the *Reallexikon für Antike und Christentum,* Vol. IV (1959), pp. 210-222.

Greek tradition, in particular the *Gloria Patri*, the *Gloria in excelsis*, the *Te decet laus*, to which may be added the *Te Deum*, itself of Western origin; and it has ended its hymns with their own proper doxologies.

Even the doxologies themselves are constructed in the Christological-Trinitarian perspective, but in varying degrees. In the liturgical texts that have come down to us there are but few traces of the doxologies addressed solely to the Father.[43] All the others are either binary (referring to Father-God-Lord and Christ-Son) or ternary (Father, Christ-Son, Holy Spirit).

Naturally the anti-Arian struggle is reflected even in the doxologies, yes, first of all in the doxologies. Already in antiquity and even before the advent of Arianism, there were doxologies in which the Persons were named with simple coördinating conjunctions: *and . . . and*. Thus, for example, in the ancient Vesper hymn of the second or third century:

> Joyous light of the holy glory
>   Of the immortal Father,
> Heavenly, holy, blessed:
>   Jesus Christ.
>
> Having come to the setting of the sun,
>   Seeing the evening light,
> We praise the Father *and* the Son
>   *And* the Holy Spirit of God.
>   (Jurgens, no. 108).

St. Basil, who, in chapter 29 of his work *On the Holy Spirit*, reminds the Arians of this fact, is able to cite in addition a number of ancient authors who used similar doxologies, among whom are St. Dionysius of Alexandria, Julius Africanus, and St. Gregory the Thaumaturge.

This type of doxology, in which the equality of Persons is actually emphasized by their simply being connected by a coördinate conjunction, which takes Them in an absolute manner on the intratrinitarian level as the single object of the glory rendered Them, seems to derive from the baptismal formula of Matthew 28:19. Nevertheless, in the earliest times they were rare enough. We know that at Antioch in the year 350 A.D., they chanted the formula: "Glory be to the Father *and* to the Son *and* to the Holy Spirit, now and always and in the ages of ages. Amen"; and it was understood precisely in an anti-Arian sense. It is a formula that made history. About that same time St. Basil, with a distinctly anti-Arian purpose, introduced a new formula of the same type: "Glory be to God and Father . . . with (*metà*) the Son and with (*syn*) the Holy Spirit."

---

[43] *Didache* 9; 10 (Jurgens, nos. 6 and 7). See also the end of the prayer of the faithful in the papyrus of Dêr-Balyzeh, I verso, 10; ed. Quasten, in *Monumenta eucharistica et liturgica vetustissima*, Vol. I, p. 40.

These coordinating formulas were multiplied throughout all the East in the fourth and fifth centuries. Among the more frequently used were: ". . . with whom (*meth' hou*) You are blessed together with the Holy Spirit"; "Glory be to the Father and to the Son and to the Holy Spirit both now and always and in the ages of ages"; "Praise is due You, song is due You, glory is due You, Father and Son and Holy Spirit."

Contrariwise, before the Arian controversy, the much more frequent type of doxology was that in which the Persons were named in a correlative fashion with the prepositions *through* and *in*. Traces are found of ancient binary doxologies in which glory is rendered to the Father through Christ the Son, without naming the Holy Spirit at all.[44]

Other formulas, ternary in construction, render glory to the Father through (*dià*) the mediation of the Son and through the mediation of the Holy Spirit. Thus St. Justin the Martyr writes in a general way:

> "For everything that has been given to our use, we praise the Creator of all through (*dià*) His Son Jesus Christ";

and specifically in regard to the great Eucharist of the Mass:

> "Then there is brought to the president of the brethren bread and a cup of water and watered wine; and taking them, he gives praise and glory to the Father of all, through (*dià*) the name of the Son and of the Holy Spirit." [45]

And St. Clement of Alexandria writes:

> "To whom (*the Father*) be glory through His Servant (*pais*) Jesus Christ, Lord of the living and dead, and through the Holy Spirit." [46]

[44] *Didache* 9, 4; St. Clement of Rome, *Letter to the Corinthians* 58, 2; 61, 3; 64 (Jurgens, nos. 6, 28, 29a); fragments of the anaphora of St. Mark (Quasten's edition, in *Monumenta eucharistica et liturgica vetustissima*, Vol. I, p. 49); prayers for the blessing of fruits in *The Apostolic Tradition* of St. Hippolytus, according to the critical edition of Dom Botte, p. 76; or of Dom Dix, p. 54. A much discussed point is the primitive form of the *Gloria in excelsis Deo* (see Jungmann, *Die Stellung Christi im liturgischen Gebet*, pp. 144ff.; Capelle, "*Le texte du Gloria in excelsis*," in *Rev. d'histoire éccl.*, Vol. 44 (1949), pp. 439-457). The text in the *Apostolic Constitutions* 8, 47 has certainly been reworked from the Arian point of view. According to Dom Bernard Capelle, it is certainly the text of the Codex Alexandrinus that has preserved the substantially more authentic text of the *Gloria*. Nevertheless, it is probable that even in this recension the mention of the Holy Spirit (*kai hágion pneúma*), inserted into the midst of the acclamations to Christ, and without any development, is a later anti-Arian addition.

[45] St. Justin the Martyr, *First Apology* 67; 65 (Jurgens, nos. 129, 128).

[46] St. Clement of Alexandria, *Quis dives salvetur* 42, 20. The authenticity of the doxology in *The Martyrdom of Saint Polycarp* 14 (Jurgens, no. 80), in its present form, is extremely dubious (see, for example, J. A. Robinson, "The Apostolic Anaphora and the Prayer of St. Polycarp," in the *Journal of Theological Studies*, 1920, pp. 97-105; J. W. Tyrer, "The Prayer of St. Polycarp and Its Concluding Doxology," *ibid.*, 1922, pp. 390-392). It combines the very ancient binary formula, to the Father through Christ His Servant, with a ternary formula of the well-known type: "O God, . . . I do glorify You through the eternal and heavenly High Priest, Jesus Christ, Your beloved Servant (*pais*):

In the East, however, even before the struggle against the Arian heresy, the ordinary form of the doxology was that which linked Christ the Son and the Holy Spirit to the glory of the Father, by means of the prepositions *through* and *in*. Thus Origen explicitly recommends that prayer be concluded "by praising the Father of all things *through* Jesus Christ *in* the Holy Spirit." [47]

The ordinary conclusion of the orations in the Sacramentary of Serapion is: "We give You thanks, we beseech You . . . through Christ, (through Your Christ, through Christ our hope, etc."; and only rarely, "through Your only-begotten Jesus Christ), in the Holy Spirit, through whom be glory and power to You both now and in all the ages of ages. Amen." In the liturgical orations in Book VIII of the *Apostolic Constitutions* the conclusion, with some variation, is: ". . . through Christ our God and Savior, through whom be glory and veneration to You in the Holy Spirit, now and always and in the ages of ages. Amen." The oldest text of the *Te decet laus*, which likewise is to be found in the *Apostolic Constitutions*,[48] is: "Praise is due You, song is due You, glory is due You, God and Father, through the Son, in the Holy Spirit, in the ages of ages. Amen." [49]

The meaning of these formulas is clear enough to anyone who refers to the Christological-Trinitarian scheme, *a, per, in, ad*, of the Scriptures, which consider the Persons primarily in their extratrinitarian relations to salvation history: Father, we thank You, we beseech You, we glorify You through Jesus Christ, Your incarnate Son, our High Priest, Head and Mediator; and we do this in virtue of the Holy Spirit present in us, who gives us the power to do this. The doxology "through . . . in . . .", therefore, is the one that corresponds best to the full Christological-Trinitarian perspective of the New Testament, as well as to the explicit teaching and recommendations of St. Paul in regard to the manner in which Christian prayer should be offered.[50]

---

through whom be glory to You with Him and with the Holy Spirit, both now and through ages yet to come. Amen." To this group, intermediate between the correlative and the coördinative types of doxologies, belong also those formulas which are of rather frequent occurrence after the beginning of the Arian controversy: . . . through whom and with whom (*di' hou kai meth' hou*). In fact, it is for this reason that the present text of Polycarp's doxology is suspect. In the same *Martyrdom of Polycarp* a binary formula preserved in chapters 19 and 20 is certainly ancient; while a ternary formula found in chapter 22 and in the old Latin version, is undoubtedly of later origin.

[47] *On Prayer* 33 (PG 11, 561).

[48] Book VII, 48, 3; Funk ed., Vol. I, pp. 456-458.

[49] It does not seem to me to be sufficient simply to observe that the doxology in the *Apostolic Constitutions* is of the *a, per, in* type, and to suspect on that account, since the *a, per, in* formula is ancient, that in the particular case, as some have suggested, there has been an Arian reworking of the lines in question, even though it is certain enough that the author of the *Constitutions* was possessed of certain Arian tendencies.

[50] There is a noteworthy peculiarity to the final doxology of the anaphora of St. Hippolytus: ". . . giving praise through Your Servant Jesus Christ, through whom be glory and power to You, to the Father and the Son with

That this doxology in the period immediately prior to the Arian controversy was effectively more common in the East is demonstrated by the position which it occupied in the struggle between Arians and Catholics, a glimpse of which comes to our view in St. Basil's work *On the Holy Spirit*, written in 375 A.D. The doxology *per . . . in . . .*, precisely because it does no more than recapture the Christological-Trinitarian perspective proper to the Scriptures by directing to the first level of attention the real distinction of the Divine Persons and by considering it primarily in their relations to salvation history, by means of the *a, per, in, ad* formula, had inherent in itself the danger, as was explained above, that the faithful might not keep sufficiently in mind the unity of nature and the equality of the Divine Persons viewed on the intratrinitarian level. This danger was not an urgent one as long as the belief in this unity and equality was passively accepted and not the subject of discussion, and was not expounded upon. But it came much to the fore when Arian propaganda began to make its direct denial of this unity and equality, and to rage against it.

The Arians understood the traditional doxology as if the prepositions *per . . . in . . .* necessarily implied an essential subordination of substance of the Son and of the Holy Spirit in respect to the Father. Catholics explained that the prepositions *a . . . per . . . in . . .* were used primarily in view of considering the Divine Persons in their relations with the world. With these prepositions they wished only to say that every benefit comes to us from the Father, through the incarnate Son as Mediator, in the presence of the Holy Spirit; and this without in any way denying the unity of nature of these Persons, which is clearly expressed elsewhere.[51]

But inasmuch as the danger of Arianism was so pressing during the fourth and fifth centuries, it was thought better at that time to abandon

the Holy Spirit, in the Holy Church, both now and in the ages of ages." Mention of the Church may at first seem strange. Jungmann, however, in *Die Stellung Christi im liturgischen Gebet*, pp. 132ff., has cited various liturgical remains which allow us to suppose that such mention of the Church in the doxologies was not especially rare in antiquity. See also J. M. Hanssens, *La liturgie d'Hippolyte*, Rome 1959, pp. 343-370. Consider also St. Paul's remark in Eph. 3:21, ". . . to Him be glory in the Church and in Christ Jesus down through all generations forever and ever. Amen." It is a way of emphasizing that the Church, since it is the Body of Christ and the only place where the Spirit dwells in this world, is the only place where God the Father is glorified on earth. St. Irenaeus says in his *Adversus haereses* 3, 24, 1: "Where the

Church is, there is the Spirit of God; and where the Spirit of God, there the Church and every grace" (Jurgens, no. 226). And as St. Cyril of Alexandria says, "We are not made perfect in any other way but by being acceptable to God the Father, in the Church, Christ offering us, inasmuch as He is Priest" (*De adoratione et cultu in spiritu et veritate* 16 [PG 68, 1016A]). Undoubtedly this associating of the Church with the Holy Spirit in the glory which we give to the Father through Christ was an idea very dear to Hippolytus. It is found also in the doxologies of his *Apostolic Tradition* (no. 6, ed. Botte, p. 19; Jurgens, nos. 394a, 394b, 394c, 394i) and in his other writings.

[51] See St. Basil, *De Spiritu Sancto*, chapters 4-8 (PG 32, 77-105).

in practice the old formula for the doxology and to substitute for it that in which the Catholic and anti-Arian position was expressed more directly. Thus circumstances occasioned by strife and by apologetic defense brought it about that from early in the fourth century the Christological-Trinitarian and Scriptural perspective expressed by the prepositions *a, per, in, ad* was relegated to a position of much less prominence in the doxologies of the Eastern liturgy.

It is necessary to take all of this into account if we are to gain an understanding of the status of the doxology in the Roman liturgy as it is today. The ancient Latin Roman liturgy, in this area, accepted the form and frequently very nearly the text itself of the Greek doxologies of a directly anti-Arian character or even those of the more ancient type, but afterwards modified to take on an anti-Arian meaning. Specifically, this is the case with the *Gloria Patri*, with the clause *sicut erat in principio* [52] joined to the Greek text, the clause emphasizing again its polemical anti-Arian import. Thus, too, with the *Te decet laus*, with its coördinate conjunctions, the liturgical use of which had already been prescribed by St. Benedict for his monks (see the *Regula*, ch. 11). Such, too, is the case with the *Gloria in excelsis Deo*, in its Alexandrian recension, in which there is clear and direct affirmation of the divinity of Christ and explicit mention of the Holy Spirit.

The *Te Deum*, on the other hand, is of Western origin; but its authorship and the development of its text remain shrouded in obscurity. Its present text is certainly the result of successive reworkings and amplifications, more a patchwork than an original piece. The first part, much developed, is devoted to the Father; the second, likewise much developed, to Christ, the Son; the Holy Spirit is introduced in a lesser doxology, wedged between the first and second parts, which doxology in fact names all three Persons: *Patrem immensae maiestatis; venerandum tuum verum et unicum Filium, sanctum quoque paraclitum Spiritum.* One has the impression that this directly Trinitarian doxology is an anti-Arian addition to the primitive text.

Even the great final doxology of the Roman Canon is to be explained in the light of the historical framework described in the foregoing remarks. After referring to the fact that all good things come to us through Christ (a point of reference that holds true also for Eucharistic Prayers III and IV, as well as for the Roman Canon properly so-called), the doxology reads:

> "Through Him, with Him, in Him,
> in the unity of the Holy Spirit,
> all glory and honor is Yours,
> almighty Father, for ever and ever."

[52] For the history of the *Gloria Patri* in the West see Henri Leclercq, in the *Dict. d'arch. chrét. et liturgie*, Vol. 5, pp. 1525-1528; and Petrus Siffrin, in the *Enciclopedia cattolica*, Vol. 6 (1951), pp. 869ff.

In its attitude toward Father and Son the doxology is clearly of the ancient type. The Father is considered as the source of all good things, because it is He who creates, sanctifies, blesses all these things, and then gives them to us; and as the end of all things, all the honor goes to Him. Christ, our Lord, is considered as the great Mediator through whom the Father accomplishes everything. He it is who creates, sanctifies, vivifies, and blesses every good thing and gives it to men; it is Christ through whom, together with whom, and in union with whom, as our Head — and here we have the concept of Christ the High Priest — we return all glory to the Father. Father and Son are considered first of all as distinct; and in their relations with creatures they are considered according to the *a, per, ad* scheme of salvation history. How is the phrase "in the unity of the Holy Spirit" to be understood? According to an observation made by Jungmann [53] there would be no reason to explain it otherwise than as "in the unity which effects the presence of the Holy Spirit among believers." In fact, he notes, in the canon the phrase is tied to the *Per ipsum*, which is certainly older than the Arian controversy.

The Western doxologies of medieval origin, which are especially numerous in the concluding stanzas of hymns, were always Trinitarian in their directly anti-Arian perspective. Even more, especially in Spain and Gaul, this perspective became so exclusive that it is precisely at this time that those doxological compositions appear which are addressed directly to the Trinity as such, as can still be seen specifically in the modern office of the Feast of the Most Holy Trinity. Nevertheless, these last remain quite restricted as to their numbers in the modern Roman liturgy, in which the more ancient doxologies of the clearly anti-Arian Trinitarian type predominate.

The sacrifice of the Mass

That the sacrifice of the Mass, as is evident in the liturgy, is structured essentially on the Christological-Trinitarian perspective according to the scheme *a, per, in, ad*, and primarily in the extratrinitarian sense, as we have already stated so often, can be seen from the essential form of its central part, called the anaphora, canon, or Eucharistic prayer.

Whether, in fact, the most ancient records of the great Eucharistic prayers be considered, or whether one examines those anaphoras still in use, it is evident that their structure was always and still is essentially — and this is true of the Roman Canon also, even if in a manner less perfect and less evidently recognizable — the well-known Christological-Trinitarian structure in the scheme *a, per, in, ad*. The Father appears there as the *principium a quo* and the *terminus ad quem* of the Eucharistic action. Christ, the incarnate

---

[53] *Die Stellung Christi im liturgischen Gebet*, 2nd ed., p. xvii*, with reference to texts of Augustine, Chrysostom, and Basil, to show that the idea was common enough even in the fourth and fifth centuries.

Son, appears there as the High Priest, *through* whom we perform the same priestly action. The Holy Spirit appears there as the *in quo*, He in whose presence this same action is completed *hic et nunc*.[54] Essentially it is again the perspective of the Divine Persons in their relations with salvation history. And here again, the greater emphasis on affirming the unity and equality of the Persons themselves and of the intratrinitarian perspective will come only with the beginning of the Arian controversy.

The most ancient complete text of an anaphora that has come down to us is that of Hippolytus. It will be worth the trouble of transcribing it in its entirety, for the sake of the testimony that it brings to bear on the question that interests us:[55]

"The Lord be with you.
And with your spirit.

Hearts aloft!
We keep them with the Lord.

Let us give thanks to the Lord.
It is right and just.

"We give You thanks, O God, through Your beloved Son Jesus Christ, whom in these last days You have sent to us as Savior and Redeemer and as the angel of Your will; He that is Your inseparable Word, through whom You made all things, and who is well-pleasing to You; whom You sent from heaven into the womb of a Virgin, and who, dwelling within her, was made flesh and was manifested as Your Son, born of the Holy Spirit and of the Virgin; who, fulfilling Your will and winning for Himself a holy people, extended His hands when it was time for Him to suffer, so that by His suffering He might set free those who believed in You; who also, when He was betrayed to His voluntary suffering, in order that He might destroy death and break the bonds of the devil and trample hell underfoot and enlighten the just and set a boundary and show forth His resurrection, took bread and gave thanks [i.e., *made Eucharist*] to You, saying: 'Take, eat: this is My Body, which is broken for you.' Likewise with the cup too, saying: 'This is My Blood, which is poured out for you. Whenever you do this, you do it in My memory [i.e., *you do My anamnesis*].'

[54] The idea that the sacrifice is brought to completion *in Spiritu* is biblical. St. Paul supposes it in Rom. 15:15ff. It is also expressed in Heb. 9:14, certainly in the reading *pneúmatos hagíou*, but still clearly enough in the more probable reading *pneúmatos aioníou*, because in the Epistle to the Hebrews "*aiónios*" means not only 'without end' or 'of infinite duration,'" but also "one who has divine powers and abilities'" (Ceslaus Spicq, *L'épître aux hébreux*, Vol. I, Paris 1952, p. 296 n. 1), even if afterwards the same Spicq (*op. cit.*, Vol. II, p. 258ff) sees in *pneúmatos aioníou* reference to the divine nature of Jesus. See also St. Basil, *De Spiritu Sancto* 26, PG 32, 184ff.

[55] See B. Botte, *La tradition apostolique de Saint Hippolyte*, Münster im W., 1963, pp. 12-17 (Jurgens, no. 394a).

"Remembering, therefore [i.e., *doing the anamnesis of*], His death and resurrection, we offer to You the bread and the cup, giving thanks [i.e., *Eucharisting*] to You, because of Your having accounted us as worthy to stand before You and minister to You. And we pray that You might send Your Holy Spirit upon the offering of the holy Church. Gather as one in the fullness of the Holy Spirit Your saints who participate; and confirm their faith in truth so that we may praise and glorify You through Your Son Jesus Christ, through whom be glory and honor to You, to the Father and the Son with the Holy Spirit, in Your holy Church, both now and through the ages of ages. Amen."

This anaphora is not without certain textual problems, particularly in regard to the words of the so-called epiclesis for the coming of the Holy Spirit. But, by this time, the critics (Botte included) admit the authenticity of the passage. Be that as it may, without stopping to point out the particulars peculiar to the document, it is clear enough that it is structured in the Christological-Trinitarian scheme of the *a, per, in, ad* with which we are familiar.

The action that is carried out in this great prayer, the Eucharist, is conceived as *anamnesis*, i.e., an action which brings into God's presence in a real manner an event that took place in the past but in such manner that its consequences work their effect in the present.[56] Here the *anamnesis* is that of the death and resurrection of the Lord, which death and resurrection frees us from the devil, from hell and death, and enlightens the just in view of the resurrection. This *anamnesis*, in accord with the ordinance set by the Lord Himself, is done with the repetition of the Eucharist [thanksgiving] to the Father done by Jesus at the Last Supper. It comprises the prayer of thanksgiving to God for the redemption, with the offering of bread and of the chalice, and the request for the coming of the Spirit or, in any case, the request to be filled with the Holy Spirit as a spiritual effect of participating in the Holy Gifts.

In all this, the prayer is addressed to the Father, the *terminus ad quem* of the prayer and of the praise, as the first cause *a quo* of all the benefits that come to us, both past, such as redemption, and present, such as our being accounted worthy of standing before Him and of performing this priestly ministry. It is the Father who is both the end and the beginning of the benefits which we now request, to wit, His sending the Holy Spirit upon the oblation and upon His faithful who participate in the Holy Gifts.

The great Mediator is always Christ. It is through His mediation that we give thanks to the Father and render praise and glory to Him, because it is through His mediation that the Father has been gracious to us; and in the

[56] See Dom Gregory Dix, *The Treatise on the Apostolic Tradition of St. Hippolytus of Rome*, London 1937, pp. 7-9.

present "eucharistic" action what we are doing is simply the *anamnesis* of His death and resurrection, by repeating what He did at the Last Supper, in accord with His own command.

The Holy Spirit appears there as He in whose presence and with whose presence the oblation of the Church is made; or at least as He whom the faithful receive in their participation in the Holy Gifts and with the presence of whom they are able to praise and glorify the Father through Christ. That the mention of the Holy Spirit in the anaphora, apart from the question of its being fixed in a consecratory epiclesis, is of most ancient origin, is demonstrated by the allusions made to it in St. Justin the Martyr.[57]

This basic plan of the anaphora, with some variations and amplifications of greater or lesser importance — in particular, the much broader mention of the Father's work of creation, of Old Testament history, and the insertion of the *Sanctus* — constitutes the skeletal structure upon which, saving always the individuality of each, the oriental anaphoras of the liturgy fill out in their development. This in itself stands as an incontrovertible sign of the essentially traditional character of the Christological-Trinitarian schema as proposed by St. Hippolytus.

The full development of this schema can be seen in an Egyptian example in the anaphora of Serapion (fourth century), in a Syrian example of the liturgy from Book VIII of the *Apostolic Constitutions* (end of the fourth century), and in a Byzantine example in the anaphora of St. Basil (probably also from the second half of the fourth century), which we quoted at considerable length in chapter five, above. Naturally, the Arian controversy has left its mark on the Christological-Trinitarian perspective of a good many of the oriental anaphoras in a more or less notable degree, in the form of a greater emphasis on the intratrinitarian unity and equality of the Persons. Noteworthy in this respect is, for example, the anaphora of St. John Chrysostom, where traces, sometimes important ones, of theological speculations on the Trinity, particularly in regard to the Word, have insinuated themselves here and there. But the background remains predominantly the ancient perspective.

It cannot be denied that the Roman Canon in its present state, lacking as it does the linear logic and simplicity of the ancient scheme of the anaphora and having something of the appearance of a patchwork of prayers related

[57] *First Apology* 65; 67 (Jurgens, nos. 128; 129): "The president of the brethren . . . gives praise and glory to the Father of all, through the name of the Son *and of the Holy Spirit*"; "For everything that has been given to our use, we praise the Creator of all through His Son Jesus Christ *and through the Holy Spirit*." There are, however, numerous arguments tending toward a suspicion that the mention of the Holy Spirit in the anaphora was not formalized into a consecratory epiclesis properly so-called until quite late, perhaps at the end of the third or beginning of the fourth century (see Dix, *The Shape of the Liturgy*, London 1954, pp. 277ff). Nevertheless, there was always some misapprehension that in the Eucharist the faithful received the Holy Spirit (see Dix, *ibid.*, pp. 266ff).

to Eucharistic action, the internal connection of which is, at first glance, difficult to perceive, compares unfavorably with the oriental anaphoras in the matter of the general Christological-Trinitarian perspective. The usual problem of the Roman Canon is reflected even here. Nevertheless, an attentive eye will be able to discover even in the Roman Canon, and without any extreme difficulty, the presence of the traditional Christological-Trinitarian perspective. The following texts will help to make this clear:

> "The Lord be with you. . . . Let us give thanks to the Lord our God. . . .

> "Father, all-powerful and ever-living God, we do well always and everywhere to give You thanks through Jesus Christ our Lord. . . . (*At this point the various prefaces concentrate on one or the other aspects of the redemptive work of the Father accomplished through Christ.*) . . . Through Him the choirs of angels and all the powers of heaven praise and worship Your glory. . . .

We come to you, Father,
with praise and thanksgiving,
through Jesus Christ your Son.
Through him we ask you to accept
 and bless
these gifts we offer you in sacrifice. . . .
Bless and approve our offering;
make it acceptable to you,
an offering in spirit and in truth.
Let it become for us
the body and blood of Jesus Christ,
your only Son, our Lord.
The day before he suffered
he took bread in his sacred hands
and looking up to heaven. . . .
When supper was ended,
he took the cup. . . .
Do this in memory of me.
Father, we celebrate the memory of
 Christ, your Son.
We, your people and your ministers,
recall his passion,
his resurrection form the dead,
and his ascension into glory;
and from the many gifts you have
 given us
we offer to you, God of glory and
 majesty,

his holy and perfect sacrifice:
the bread of life
and the cup of eternal salvation.
Look with favor on these offerings
and accept them as once you
 accepted
the gifts of your servant, Abel,
the sacrifice of Abraham, our father
 in faith,
and the bread and wine offered by
 your priest Melchisedech.
Almighty God,
we pray that your angel may take
 this sacrifice
to your altar in heaven.
Then, as we receive from this altar
the sacred body and blood of your
 Son,
let us be filled with every grace and
 blessing.
(Through Christ our Lord. Amen.)
Through Christ our Lord
you give us all these gifts.
You fill them with life and goodness,
you bless them and make them holy.
Through him,
with him,
in him,

in the unity of the Holy Spirit,   for ever and ever. Amen (Copyright
all glory and honor is yours,   1969, International Committee on Eng-
almighty Father,   lish in the Liturgy, Inc.)

It is evident from the above that, in regard to the Father and to Christ,
the Christological-Trinitarian perspective expressed by the *a, per, ad* schema,
in its view of salvation history, is not less evident than it is in the anaphora
of Hippolytus or in the oriental anaphoras. The same, too, can be said of
the other three canons or Eucharistic prayers of the present Roman liturgy.
There is this difficulty, however: whereas the Eucharistic Prayers II, III,
and IV have an actual epiclesis, after the manner of the Eastern anaphoras,
in the present text of the Roman Canon, or Eucharistic Prayer I, the Holy
Spirit is mentioned only in the final doxology with the formula "in the unity
of the Holy Spirit."

If, as noted above, this phrase is interpreted in the sense of "in the unity
which is created by the presence of the Holy Spirit among us," the Christological-Trinitarian plan is clear enough, even if it is necessary to admit
that it is not so brilliantly apparent as it is in the Eastern anaphoras. So much
for the present text. But is this, historically speaking, the only mention in
the Roman Canon, of the part played, if we may so express it, by the Holy
Spirit in the carrying out of the Eucharistic action?

The point at issue is the question of whether or not there was an epiclesis
for the coming of the Holy Spirit in the ancient Roman Canon. The question,
of course, is much discussed by liturgists.[58] It seems to me that those who
deny that such an epiclesis ever existed in the Roman Canon, besides involving themselves in other minor difficulties, will be unable to offer a
satisfactory explanation for the peremptory testimony of Pope Gelasius
(492-496). This Pope, to demonstrate the necessity that any priest preparing
to celebrate the Eucharistic action do so with a pure conscience said:

> "How will the heavenly Spirit, invoked to consecrate the divine
> mystery — how will He come, if the priest who beseeches Him to
> come is reprobate before God because of his criminal perform-
> ance?" [59]

Jungmann, who endorses the thesis that it is not possible to conclude
from this text to the existence in the ancient Roman Canon of a consecratory
epiclesis of the Holy Spirit, concedes at the same time that "Gelasius . . .
could conceive of the calling down of the Holy Ghost as being presented
throughout the canon with its many petitions, for blessing, without any

[58] Tending toward a negative answer, there
is Jungmann, *The Mass of the Roman Rite*,
Vol. II, pp. 191-194; and towards an affirmative answer, S. Salaville, "Épiclèse," in the
Dict. de théol. cath., Vol. V (1939), pp. 218ff.,

and Righetti, Vol. III, pp. 320ff.
[59] Letter of Pope Gelasius to Bishop Elpidius
of Volterra, in Thiel, *Epistolae Romanorum
pontificium genuinae*, Vol. I, p. 484. Other
texts in Righetti, *loc. cit.*

express invocation of the third Divine Person." [60] It is difficult to see how such an explanation can truly account for the sense of the actual text of Gelasius (. . . *quomodo ad divini mysterii consecrationem coelestis Spiritus invocatus adveniet* . . .); and the difficulty of the explanation is only increased when we remember how general was the epiclesis in the various liturgies of the same period.

But even if Jungmann's explanation were correct, it would only demonstrate that at Rome, whatever arguments one may adopt, the great prayer and Eucharistic action was not conceivable apart from the proper role played in it, so to speak, by the Holy Spirit; and we suggest, therefore, that the prayer *Quam oblationem* or the *Supplices te rogamus* would be interpreted in this sense. Even Righetti, in his attempted reconstruction of the ancient Roman Canon,[61] introduces therein a mention of the Holy Spirit in two places: once where the *Quam oblationem* now stands, and again where the *Supplices* is presently found.

It is not necessary, for the sake of further illustration of our subject, the Christological-Trinitarian structure of the anaphoras, to delay for very long with the Gallican and Mozarabic liturgies. Enough in this regard to state two facts: the first is that these liturgies, in respect to the basic structure of the anaphora, are essentially like the Roman liturgy, except only in certain notable particulars. Among these latter peculiarities there is, in an especially noteworthy degree, a greater adaptability of the individual parts of the anaphora to various feasts and circumstances, and therefore a greater mutability through each Mass, similar in nature to the great variation in the numerous prefaces of the Roman Mass, observable in times past in the Leonine Sacramentary and again at the present time in the current Pauline Roman Missal.

The second fact is that the ancient Gallican and Mozarabic liturgies regularly had an epiclesis of the Holy Spirit, which is to be found, it seems, mostly in one of the variable prayers, called *Post mysterium, Post secreta,* and *Post pridie,* even if the precise form of the epiclesis in the Mozarabic liturgy was modeled after the oriental examples. Salaville affirms that only after the beginning of the sixth century and in an era in which it is difficult to make a more precise determination, was the epiclesis in some Masses in these

[60] *The Mass of the Roman Rite,* Vol. II, p. 194, note 37. [Since Vagaggini wrote the present work, the Pauline Roman Missal has been promulgated; and we must note that it is probably under an at least remote influence of Jungmann that the Roman Missal now describes the whole of the Eucharistic Prayer, from immediately after the *Sanctus* up to the narration of institution, and consecration, as

an epiclesis. See in the Roman Missal the section *Institutio generalis Missalis Romani,* ch. II, n. 55c. But of course Jungmann, Righetti, and Vagaggini are dealing with a historical question, and the present usage of the Pauline Roman Missal cannot be construed as a canonization of any particular historical view].

[61] Righetti, Vol. III, pp. 386ff.

liturgies altered, attenuated, or even suppressed. In the *Liber mozarabicus sacramentorum* edited by Férotin it is still quite prevalent.[62]

In the history of the Canon of the Ambrosian Mass, which, as you know, is in all respects almost the same as the Roman Canon, it is more difficult to offer a positive demonstration of a mention of the part played by the Holy Spirit in the Eucharistic action.[63]

In the modern text, the Holy Spirit is mentioned only in the final doxology with the phrase *"in unitate Spiritus Sancti,"* just as in the Roman Canon. Nevertheless, it is certain that St. Ambrose knew of an invocation of the Holy Spirit in the Mass. He remarks, in fact:

> "How can it be said, then, that the Holy Spirit does not possess entirely the divine nature, He who, together with the Father and the Son, is named by the priest in baptism, *is invoked in the oblations,* is celebrated together with the Father and the Son by the Seraphim in the heavens; who, together with the Father and the Son, dwells in the saints, is infused in the righteous and inspired in the prophets?" [64]

The sacraments

The Christological-Trinitarian dimension in the liturgy of the sacraments is very strong.

Baptism; the baptismal profession of faith; the rule of faith; the credal formulas of faith. For the task that we are pursuing it will be well for us to examine, along with baptism, also the baptismal profession of faith, the rule of faith, the credal formulas of the faith, and this for the obvious reason that in liturgical practice all of these elements are intimately connected.

Among the documents which assist in leading us to a knowledge of the Christological-Trinitarian dimension, in accord with the *a, per, in, ad* scheme, which the ancient Church invested in baptism, one of the more notable and more important is of St. Irenaeus, his *Presentation of the Apostolic Preaching*, written between about 190 and 200 A.D., in which he says:

> "Here is what the faith attests for us, according to what the ancients, the disciples of the Apostles, have transmitted to us. First of all it obliges us to recall that we have received baptism for the remission of sins in the name of God the Father, and in the name of Jesus Christ, the Son of God . . . and in the Holy Spirit of God. . . . Therefore the baptism which regenerates us is conferred

[62] See for example S. Salaville, *"Épiclèse,"* in the *Dict. de théol. cath.*, Vol. 5 (1939), pp. 216ff.; S. Portier, "The Mozarabic Post Pridie," in the *Journal of Theological Studies*, 1943, pp. 182ff.

[63] See S. Salaville, *op. cit.*, p. 218; and P. Borella, in Righetti, Vol. III, pp. 557ff.

[64] St. Ambrose, *De Spiritu Sancto* 3, 16, 22. See also Gaudentius of Brescia (d. 410), *Tractatus* 2, 15.

on us through these three articles[65] and guarantees our rebirth in God the Father, through His Son, by the Holy Spirit. For those who receive the Spirit of God are led to the Word, that is, to the Son; but the Son receives them and presents them to the Father, and the Father confers incorruptibility on them. Thus without the Spirit no one can see the Word of God, and without the Son no one can approach the Father; for the Son is the knowledge of the Father, but the knowledge of the Son is had through the Spirit. But it is the Son who, according to the Father's good pleasure, distributes the Spirit as a gift, as the Father wishes Him to, and to those to whom He wishes Him to give the Spirit." [66]

There is no clearer, no more profound way in which we might state how perfectly the ancient Church viewed baptism against the Christological-Trinitarian background in the *a, per, in, ad* schema.

It is certain also that the origin of the symbol, whatever be the numerous and difficult specific questions which are posed in this regard, is intimately connected with baptismal practice. In fact, in connection with baptism, there was exacted of the catechumen a solemn profession of faith, in regard to which, in the very ceremony of the conferring of the sacrament, he was officially and solemnly interrogated. This baptismal profession of faith is either to be identified with the creed itself at its beginning, or at least with something very similar, connected, moreover, with that which in antiquity was known as the rule of faith: a short formula in which the essential articles of the Christian faith were condensed.

Now, that baptismal profession of faith was essentially of a Christological-Trinitarian import couched in the usual *a, per, in, ad* scheme. And since that profession, in actual liturgical practice, was intimately connected with the act itself of conferring baptism, naturally this act received from it a very marked Christological-Trinitarian character. The clearest possible evidence of this is to be found in the ceremony of the conferral of baptism, as described by St. Hippolytus in *The Apostolic Tradition*:

> "When the one being baptized goes down into the water, the one baptizing him shall put his hand on him and speak thus: 'Do you believe in God, the Father Almighty?' And he that is being baptized shall say: 'I believe.' Then, having his hand imposed upon the head of the one to be baptized, he shall baptize him once.

> "And then he shall say: 'Do you believe in Christ Jesus, the Son of God, who was born of the Holy Spirit, of the Virgin Mary, and was crucified under Pontius Pilate and died and was buried, and rose up again on the third day, alive from the dead, and ascended into heav-

---

[65] In the context just preceding St. Irenaeus speaks of three articles of the creed, professing belief first in God the Father, second in Jesus Christ and third in the Holy Spirit.

[66] St. Irenaeus, *Presentation of the Apostolic Preaching* 3; 7.

en, and sat at the right of the Father, about to come to judge the living and the dead?' And when he says: 'I believe,' he is baptized again.

"And again he shall say: 'Do you believe in the Holy Spirit and the holy Church [67] and the resurrection of flesh?' The one being baptized then says: 'I believe.' And so he is baptized a third time." [68]

It is not necessary to dwell upon the Christological-Trinitarian structure of this baptismal profession of faith, nor on the Christological-Trinitarian dimension which it imparts to a baptism conferred according to this rite. Specifically the Holy Spirit is considered in relation to His presence in the Church and in relation to His operation therein, which is the very actualization of redemption with its ultimate conclusion: the resurrection of the flesh.[69]

This triple interrogation in regard to the three parts of the symbol, followed by the triple response of the one being baptized and by the triple immersion made without any other formula — at least there are no traces of any other formula in the texts — was the only form of baptism in Christian antiquity.[70] It is attested also by Irenaeus, by Ambrose, and it is likewise that of the Roman rite as found in the ancient Gelasian Sacramentary.[71] Even in the East there are no traces of any other usage before about the middle of the fourth century. Beginning about 341-360 A.D., or at the latest about 390 A.D., this formula is found there: "*N.* is baptized in the name of the Father, and of the Son, and of the Holy Spirit." The *Canons of Hippolytus*, the origins of which some would date as early as 341-360 A.D., add a formula to each of the three immersions which, in accord with ancient usage, follow upon the triple interrogation:

[67] For the reading *and in the holy Church*, see P. Nautin, *Je crois à l'Esprit Saint dans la Sainte Église pour la résurrection de la chair*, Paris 1947, pp. 13-27. Certainly the papyrus of Dêr-Balyzeh, at the third article of its baptismal profession of faith, has: ". . . I believe . . . and in the Holy Spirit and in the resurrection of the flesh and in the holy Catholic Church." See also C. H. Roberts and B. Capelle, *An Early Euchologium*, Louvain 1949, pp. 32ff.; 60ff.

[68] St. Hippolytus, *The Apostolic Tradition* 21; Jurgens, no. 394i; Botte ed., pp. 49-51. The same rite is presupposed by St. Ambrose, *De sacramentis* 2, 6, 16; 2, 7, 20-22; 6, 2, 5-8.

[69] The special connection between Holy Spirit and Church in the work of salvation is evidenced in all the credal formulas, even in the fact that the mention of the Church follows almost always immediately upon the mention of the Spirit.

[70] See A. Stenzel, *Il battesimo*, Alba 1962, pp. 129-145.

[71] St. Irenaeus, *Presentation of the Apostolic Preaching* 7. F. Sagnard (*La gnose valentinienne et le témoignage de St. Irénée*, Paris 1947, pp. 229-239), referring to that which the same Irenaeus (*Adv. haer.* 1, 21, 3) says about the usage of certain gnostics who in baptizing pronounce such formulas as "*In the name of the unknown Father, of the Truth, Mother of all, of Him who descended into Jesus; in the name of the union, of the redemption and of the unity of all the powers,*" is of a mind that these presuppose the pronouncing of a formula in the orthodox baptismal practice: "*In the name, etc.*" But this remains to be proven. See St. Ambrose, *De sacramentis* 2, 7, 20; Gelasian Sacramentary, ed. Mohlberg, n. 449, p. 74. For the East before the fourth century, see Stenzel, *loc. cit.*

"Ego te baptizo in nomine Patris et Filii et Spiritus Sancti qui aequalis est." [72]

The polemical anti-Arian intent is clear, as well as the fact that this formula is the result of an unhappy amalgamation. The ancient form of baptism which considered the three Persons of the Trinity in their relations with the world, employing the *a, per, in, ad* schema, was capable of abuse in its interpretation, and could be taken in a subordinationist or Arian sense. St. Ambrose was already concerned with rejecting such an interpretation. The new formula, which obviated this danger, penetrated to the West in the eighth century. [73]

In the context of the ancient form of baptism it will be easy to recognize the Christological-Trinitarian structure of the ancient Roman symbol, the symbol called the Apostles' Creed, whether it be in its more ancient form, [74] or in the more recent form in which it is now usually recited. The creed is divided into three parts which treat respectively of the Father; of Christ our Lord, the incarnate Son of God; and of the Holy Spirit. Each of the Three Persons is considered in His relations with sacred salvation history according to the proper role, so to speak, of each, which is explained in immediate connection with their individual names: for the Father, creation; for Christ, the incarnate Son, His incarnation, redemptive life and death on earth, His present state, now glorious with the Father, and His future parousia; for the Holy Spirit, the Church with her means of sanctification, looking to the resurrection of the flesh and to the final completion of the whole process of the *exitus* and *reditus* into life eternal. St. Irenaeus already expounded the rule of faith in substantially this same way. [75]

This Christological-Trinitarian structure remains substantially unchanged even in later creeds, such as the Nicene [76] and the so-called Nicene-Constantinopolitan, which latter is the creed recited in the Mass. These creeds merely enlarge upon certain points, in view of the anti-Arian struggle, within the ancient structure of the symbols in order to defend the divinity of the Son and of the Holy Spirit. Only the so-called Athanasian Creed, the *Quicumque*, belonging to the fifth century, and which until recent years had a rather

---

[72] See the text in L. Duchesne, *Les origines du culte chrétien*, 4th ed., Paris 1908, p. 540. In regard to the age of these canons, see B. Botte, "L'origine des canons d'Hippolyte," in *Mélanges Andrieu*, Strasbourg 1956, pp. 53-63. For the appearance in the East of the formula "N. is baptized in the name of the Father, etc.," see A. Stenzel, *op. cit.*, pp. 138-142. See also Jurgens, *The Faith of the Early Fathers*, Collegeville 1970, p. 171, n. 18, where it is pointed out that what is required for a baptismal form is a distinct expression of God, One and Three, and that this ex-

pression is contained in fact within the ceremony that St. Hippolytus describes, without the addition of any other words for a form: "Do you believe in God, the Father Almighty, . . . in Christ Jesus, the Son of God, . . . in the Holy Spirit? I believe!"
[73] St. Ambrose, *De sacr.* 6, 2, 5-8. Righetti, Vol. IV, pp. 68ff.
[74] Dz 11 (2).
[75] St. Irenaeus, *Presentation of the Apostolic Preaching* 6.
[76] Dz 125 (54).

prominent place in the liturgy of the Divine Office in the Roman rite, is composed in a quite different way, conceived with a view to affirming polemically the Catholic faith against the Trinitarian and Christological heresies.[77]

If the present-day ritual of baptism contains numerous texts which emphasize the unity and equality of the Persons, and hence the ontological Trinitarian view with its anti-Arian polemical dimension, still, it remains faithful in many points to the more ancient Christological-Trinitarian point of view, in accord with the *a, per, in, ad* schema. In the newly revised rite of baptism for children this is particularly evident in the exorcism prayers at n. 49, in the blessing at n. 54, in the interrogation on the creed at n. 58; and in general in the prayers addressed to the Father.

Confirmation. The Christological-Trinitarian dimension of confirmation is the result essentially of its intimate connection with baptism. Confirmation was always regarded as a sacramental rite granting a special infusion of the Holy Spirit for the purpose of carrying on to perfection and to strengthen and affix a seal to the work of God in the newly baptized. It is from this that it takes its name: seal, sign, consignation, confirmation. Hence, there is the implied concept that it is by means of a special presence of the Holy Spirit that the faithful attain to their fulfillment, to their perfection, and mature as adults in Christian life. It is, therefore, the sacrament which instills in a special manner the special role in Christian life, appropriated to the Holy Spirit, as the ultimate seal of God's gifts, in whom every Christian perfection is realized. It is a putting into liturgical action of the biblical concept that considers the Holy Spirit as the one *in quo*.

That is why St. Ambrose, repeating the concept of all ancient tradition,[78] was able to say:

> "Then comes the spiritual sign (*signaculum*), about which you have heard the reading today, because after the font there still remains the reception of perfection (*post fontem superest ut perfectio fiat*) when, at the invocation of the priest, the Holy Spirit is infused." [79]

St. Cyprian had already laid down the rule that

> "those who are baptized in the Church are then brought to the prelates of the Church; and through our prayer and the imposition of hands, they receive the Holy Spirit and are perfected with the seal of the Lord (*signaculo Dominico consummentur*)." [80]

Basically it is the idea already expressed in St. Paul:

[77] Dz 75-76 (39-40).
[78] See Righetti, Vol. IV, pp. 89ff.
[79] *De sacr.* 3, 2, 8.

[80] *Letter of Cyprian to Jubaianus, a Bishop in Mauretania* 73, 9 (Jurgens, no. 595).

"Whatever God has promised finds its 'Yes' in Him (Christ); and for that reason we say our 'Amen' through Him to God's glory. But the one who has established us firmly along with you in communion with Christ, and who has anointed us, is God, who also stamped us with His seal and gave us the Spirit as a pledge in our hearts" (2 Cor. 1:20-22).

The anointing of which St. Paul speaks is almost certainly the baptism to which God has called us and by which He has established us and given us a firm stability in Christ. For a greater guarantee and security, like a seal placed on an envelope containing precious things, God has added to this first gift the gift of the Spirit — almost certainly it is confirmation that is meant — which is the pledge of the total gift that He will give us in the life to come. For St. Paul, of course, the Spirit is the Spirit of Christ: "That you are sons (is clear from the fact) that God has sent the Spirit of His Son into our hearts, crying, 'Abba, Father!' " (Gal. 4:6; see also Rom. 8:5-18, a parallel and explanatory text). It is easy to recognize in these texts the Christological-Trinitarian perspective of the *a, per, in, ad* schema. And it is this Pauline theology that is at the basis of the liturgy of confirmation.

St. Ambrose was able to point out to the neophytes the Christological-Trinitarian significance of the rite of confirmation:

> "Remember, then, that you have received the spiritual sign, the Spirit of wisdom and of understanding. . . . Guard that which you have received. God the Father has signed you, Christ has confirmed you, sending into your hearts the pledge of the Spirit, just as you have heard in the reading of the Apostle." [81]

The liturgical formulas for the administration of confirmation have varied in the course of centuries. In the ancient Latin Roman liturgy, the formula, reported in the ancient Gelasian Sacramentary [82] and referred to by St. Ambrose,[83] is essentially the epicletic prayer, which, until the revision of the Roman Pontifical now in progress, was said at the beginning of the rite, and much the same as that which will now immediately precede the conferral of the sacrament:

> "All-powerful, eternal God, who have seen fit to regenerate these Your servants through water and the Holy Spirit and have granted them the remission of all their sins, send them from heaven Your septiform Holy Spirit, the Comforter: the Spirit of wisdom and understanding; the Spirit of counsel and fortitude; the Spirit of knowledge and piety. Fill them with the Spirit of the fear of the Lord and,

[81] St. Ambrose, *De mysteriis* 7, 42.
[82] Mohlberg ed., no. 451, p. 74.
[83] St. Ambrose, *De mysteriis* 7, 42; *De sacra-* mentis 2, 2, 8, and for the first part of the formula, *De sacr.* 2, 7, 24 in relation to the post-baptismal anointing.

in Your kindness, sign them with the Cross of Christ for life eternal." [84]

In the formula in use for the anointing from the beginning of the thirteenth century up to the promulgation of the present formula in 1971, "I sign you with the sign of the Cross and I confirm you with the chrism of salvation," the Christological-Trinitarian viewpoint seems to have been lost. As for the phrase "in the name of the Father and of the Son and of the Holy Spirit," which many theologians held was not an essential part of the form but merely an appendage thereto, it emphasizes as usual the ontological aspect of the Trinity.

The new form, promulgated in August 1971, to be adopted no later than January 1, 1973, is: *"Accipe signaculum Doni Spiritus Sancti."* At first glance it seems to have preserved the Christological-Trinitarian viewpoint no better than the previous formula; but upon more mature theological reflection the Christological-Trinitarian aspects begin to show themselves. The *Donum* is the Holy Spirit Himself; and it is the Father who promises the Holy Spirit (Luke 24:49; Acts 1:4) and does actually send Him (Acts 2:33); and it is through Christ that He is sent (John 14:26; 15:26). In fact, the Son's active sending of the Holy Spirit is implicit throughout the whole rite. Theologically, the *a, per, in, ad* consideration is intact, even if not explicitly stated, in the actual form of the sacrament.

Penance. In the present form in which the rite of penance has developed in the Roman liturgy, it is difficult to discover any traces of the Christological-Trinitarian conception of this sacrament. In the rites of the ancient liturgy, however, this dimension was very much in evidence.

In truth, the ancient liturgy brought into strong relief the fact that the reconciliation of the penitent was accomplished essentially by means of the imposition of hands and the imploring of the coming of the Holy Spirit, in accord with the biblical concept which sees an intimate connection between the remission of sins and the presence of the Holy Spirit (see John 20:22-23). The ancient concept was that sin ejects the Holy Spirit from the soul, and reconciliation of the sinner is accomplished by means of the return of the Spirit into the same. It is for the sake of the coming of the Spirit that hands were imposed and prayers recited in the rite of reconciliation. The Fathers not infrequently allude to this.

St. Jerome says:

> "The priest offers his oblation for the layman, lays his hand upon him when submissive, invokes the return of the Holy Spirit, and thus reconciles to the altar the one who had been consigned to Satan for the death of the flesh, so that the spirit might be saved." [85]

[84] This last phrase is an addition dating from the tenth century.

[85] *Dial. adv. lucif.* 5 (PL 23, 159).

St. Ambrose, though with a less clear allusion to the liturgical rite and with a greater emphasis on the invocation of the Three Persons of the Trinity in an ontological and anti-Arian perspective, suggests in a manner clear enough that the Holy Spirit has a rather more special role in the remission of sins through the ministry of priests:

> "You see, therefore, that it is through the Holy Spirit that sins are pardoned. In the remission of sins, men are only His instruments, and they exercise no power in their own name, but in the name of the Father and of the Son and of the Holy Spirit." [86]

The text from St. Jerome proves in peremptory fashion the presence in the ancient liturgy of an epicletic invocation of the Holy Spirit in conjunction with the imposition of hands in the public reconciliation of penitents. This fact suffices to situate the rite in the traditional Christological-Trinitarian perspective.

This perspective is no longer found, as far as I can see, in the later formulas of penance, whether public or private.

In the *Ordo Paenitentiae*, the new rite for the administration of the sacrament of penance promulgated by Pope Paul VI, we find the following enlightening perspective:

> "After the penitent has made his act of contrition . . . the priest then extends his hands, or at least his right hand, over the head of the penitent, and pronounces the formula of absolution, in which the essential words are: *"Ego te absólvo a peccátis tuis, in nómine Patris, et Fílii, et Spíritus Sancti."* While he pronounces these last words, the priest makes the sign of the Cross over the penitent. The formula of absolution points out that the reconciliation of the penitent comes forth from the mercy of the Father. It shows the connection between the reconciliation of the sinner and the paschal mystery of Christ. It extols the function of the Holy Spirit in the forgiveness of sins. And at the same time it focuses upon the ecclesial aspect of the sacrament, inasmuch as reconciliation with God is sought and granted through the ministry of the Church" (no. 19).

Holy orders. It is primarily in the consecratory prefaces in the ordination of deacons, priests, and bishops that the liturgy shows how the sacrament of holy orders is fitted into the Christological-Trinitarian framework. Indeed here there are true and proper epicleses for the coming of the Holy Spirit, accompanied by the usual imposition of hands.

These consecratory epicleses of deacons, priests, and bishops have remained in the Roman tradition from the time of Hippolytus to the present-day rite, in spite of certain changes. The tidiest formula, from the point of view with which we are concerning ourselves, is still that of Hippolytus'

[86] *De Spiritu Sancto* 3, 18, 137 (PL 16, 808-809).

Apostolic Tradition, because later rearrangements of the texts have made a little less obvious the Christological-Trinitarian character of the consecratory prefaces for priests and bishops.

Here is the text from *The Apostolic Tradition* of St. Hippolytus, for the ordination of bishops:

> "God and Father of our Lord Jesus Christ . . . You that have given ordinances to Your Church through Your Word of grace (cf. Acts 20:32). . . . pour forth now that power which comes from You, from Your Royal Spirit, which You gave to Your Beloved Son Jesus Christ and which He bestowed upon His holy Apostles, who established in every place the Church of Your sanctification for the glory and unceasing praise of Your name. You that know the hearts of all, grant to this Your servant, whom You have chosen for the episcopate, to feed Your holy flock and to serve without blame as Your high priest, ministering night and day to propitiate unceasingly before Your face; and to offer to You the gifts of Your holy Church; and by the Spirit of the high-priesthood to have the authority to forgive sins, in accord with Your command; and to assign lots (cf. Acts 1: 26), in accord with the authority which You gave to the Apostles; and to please You in meekness and purity of heart, offering to You an odor of sweetness: through Your Son, Jesus Christ our Lord, through whom be glory, might, and honor to You, [to the Father and the Son] with the Holy Spirit, both now and through the ages of ages." [87]

From the Christological-Trinitarian point of view, the formulas for the ordination of priests and of deacons are in every respect similar to that cited immediately above, for bishops.[88] The same structure, moreover, is found throughout antiquity, as can be seen from the Sacramentary of Serapion,[89] and in the *Apostolic Constitutions*.[90] Here, for example, you may see how the *a, per, in, ad* schema appears in the Sacramentary of Serapion, in respect to the ordination of priests:

> "Lord, Father of Your Only-begotten, we pray that the Spirit of truth may come upon this man . . . that he may rule Your people and dispense Your divine word and reconcile Your people to You, uncreated God . . . You who by the spirit of Moses granted the Holy Spirit to those who had been chosen, give this man also the Holy Spirit by the Spirit of the Only-begotten in the gift of wisdom, of knowledge and of right faith, that he may serve You with a pure conscience through Your Only-begotten Jesus Christ, through whom

[87] St. Hippolytus, *The Apostolic Tradition* 3; ed. Botte, pp. 6-11; Jurgens, no. 394a.

[88] *Ibid.*, 8-9; ed. Botte, pp. 6-11; Jurgens, nos. 394b-394c.

[89] Nos. 26-28; Funk ed., Vol. II, pp. 188-190.

[90] *Apostolic Constitutions* 8, 5, 3-7; 8, 16, 3-5; 8, 18.

be glory and empire to You in the Holy Spirit now and for all ages, world without end. Amen." [91]

Anointing of the sick. In the rite of the administration of the sacrament of anointing the ill, the Christological-Trinitarian theme appears only rarely it seems to me, in the form of the sacrament, which, as is well-known, has changed considerably in the course of time.[92] On the other hand, it appears very clearly in the epicletic prayers for the blessing of the oil of the infirm both in the present-day Roman rite and in the Gelasian Sacramentary.[93]

Matrimony. It does not seem to me that the Christological-Trinitarian perspective is in evidence in the sacrament of matrimony.

The sacramentals

For the question which concerns us here, there is no need to undertake a long study of the sacramentals. The situation with these is very much the same as that with the seven sacraments: among the most ancient and most important formulas of the sacramentals, many have preserved even to the present time a very markedly Christological-Trinitarian structure, epicletic in form.

Among the more notable in this regard we may mention the blessing of the baptismal font and of baptismal water, in the Eastern rites as well as in the Roman, in which latter the Christological-Trinitarian structure is most evident in the great preface which is found already in the Gelasian Sacramentary; [94] the blessing of the oil of the infirm, the epicletic oration of which is already found in the same sacramentary; [95] and among the Greeks, the consecration of the *myron*; the consecration of an altar or of a church; the consecration of virgins; the *commendatio animae*, in which the beginning of the prayer *Proficiscere* is especially noteworthy:

> "Take your leave, O Christian soul, of this world, in the name of God the Father all-powerful who created you, in the name of Jesus Christ, Son of the living God, who suffered for you, in the name of the Holy Spirit who has been poured out in you."

And when in the Middle Ages it became the established custom to give every blessing and to commence every important sacred action by making the sign of the Cross either on oneself or over the objects to be blessed, while reciting the formula, "In the name of the Father and of the Son and of the Holy Spirit," even if the Christological-Trinitarian aspect was obliged to take a secondary place in view of the greater prominence given to the more purely Trinitarian, it was not completely lost. Indeed, such blessings, made with the sign of the Cross and an invocation of the Trinity, signify

[91] No. 27; Funk ed., Vol. II, pp. 188-190.
[92] See Righetti, Vol. IV, p. 243.
[93] Mohlberg ed., no. 382, p. 61.
[94] *Ibid.*, nos. 445-448, pp. 72-74.
[95] *Ibid.*, no. 382, p. 61.

that we are commencing the sacred action in the strength which, through the means of the Cross of the Lord, comes to us from the Father, from the Son, and from the Holy Spirit, three distinct Persons in but a single nature. That is to say, we bless, we consecrate this object by means of the power which, through the Cross of the Lord, we have from the Father, from the Son, and from the Holy Spirit, three distinct Persons in a single nature.

The liturgical cycles

The same state of affairs that we have hitherto encountered, in which the fundamentals of the liturgy are grounded directly on the Christological-Trinitarian viewpoint, but to which a later superstructure has been added, which emphasizes in a notable degree, or in some particular sections even makes predominant, the direct affirmation of the unity of nature of the Persons in an ontological and anti-Arian dimension, is found also in the feasts and in the liturgical cycles. We shall confine ourselves to a quick glance at the Roman liturgy in its present state.

The most ancient cycle is that of Easter, which formerly embraced the period from Septuagesima until Pentecost. This cycle attained its full development towards the end of the seventh century. In the present structure of the liturgical year, with the promulgation of the Pauline Roman Missal, this cycle comprises the Lenten and Paschal periods, the former extending from Ash Wednesday until Holy Thursday, the latter from Easter to Pentecost, along with the sacred Paschal Triduum of the Holy Thursday evening Mass, Good Friday, and the Paschal Vigil of Holy Saturday intervening.

We will stress heavily the point that the object of this Easter or Lenten-Paschal cycle is the whole of salvation history, the mystery of Christ, the mystery of the Church, but under the aspect of redemption; redemption made necessary, prepared for, prefigured, initiated in the Old Testament; redemption radically realized in history through the coming, life, Passion, death, resurrection and ascension of Christ; redemption applied in the world after the ascension of Christ, by the Holy Spirit merited by Christ, sent by Him from His place at the Father's side, who animates the Church and gives spiritual life to every man through the sacraments and the ascetical and mystical moral life.

Now, looking toward the Divinity, this whole perspective in the liturgy is dominated by the Christological-Trinitarian viewpoint in the usual *a, per, in, ad* schema. Liturgically, in fact, we may view the Lenten-Paschal cycle as being divided rather neatly into three parts, the first embracing the period from Quadragesima to Holy Week, the second from Holy Week to the Ascension; and the third from the Ascension to Pentecost.

In the present-day Roman liturgy this first part brings into relief the presuppositions and the necessity of the redemption, and its preparation and prefiguration in the Old Testament up to Moses. In this period, to some extent in the Mass readings but perhaps even more notably in the breviary, the history of mankind is told, from creation until Moses and God's dealings with man through him. At the same time, however, the liturgy brings into prominence the actualization of the redemption for each of the faithful through their moral and ascetical life. The baptized faithful, in the state of grace, prepare themselves to receive an ever greater increase of redemption by means of the ascetical and liturgical life; the baptized who have sinned prepare themselves for reconciliation through penance; the catechumens prepare themselves for entry into the Church by means of the sacraments of Christian initiation.

In this initial period of the Lenten-Paschal cycle it is the Father who occupies the first level of attention in the liturgy. He appears there in the usual way, as the *a quo* and the *ad quem*. It is He who created the world and man, who elevated Adam and made him the religious head of the human race. He it is whom Adam offended by sin, and whom we have offended in Adam, thereby delivering ourselves to Satan, and meriting God's wrath and the miseries which have fallen upon us. And it is He who, in spite of all these things, promised us a Redeemer and prepared our redemption in the Old Testament. It is to the Father that we must return, and it is to Him that we must make satisfaction through penance, fasting, prayer, good works and almsgiving.

Christ, the Son, appears only at the second level of our attention, and especially in the various readings and in the Gospel pericopes of the Mass, primarily as the Teacher who, by His doctrine and example, imparts to us the precepts of moral life, of penance, of prayer, and of good works.

With the second part of the cycle, from Palm Sunday of the Passion of the Lord to the Feast of the Ascension, the perspective changes. Now it is the realization of the redemption that is brought to us by Christ in His *mysteria paschalia* that is in the foreground: and these paschal mysteries are His Passion, death, resurrection and ascension. The liturgy concentrates its attention on the Old Testament prophetic utterances about His Passion in Isaias and Jeremias; on the Passion, death, resurrection and ascension of Christ, the Redeemer, as historical events; and the present application of the fruits of redemption to the faithful: for it is in this period that the catechumens are initiated into the Christian life, penitents are reconciled, and the rest of the faithful are perfected.

Now, in all this it is Christ, the incarnate Son, our Redeemer and Head, in His Passion and in His glory, who occupies the first level of attention in the liturgy. Nevertheless, the Father too is constantly present, as the one from whom, in the final analysis, the sacred history of the suffering and glorified Christ takes its origin. It is a history which the Father has willed to be as it is, and which He directs infallibly to His own glory. It is the Father who has preordained the hour of Jesus; and the sacrifice is one which Jesus makes of Himself to the Father, in order to make satisfaction on our behalf and to reconcile us to the Father. It is the Father who has delivered up His own Son, Jesus, to the Passion, by reason of the infinite charity with which He has loved us.

And again, it is the Father who helps Jesus in His Passion: indeed, in this period the whole liturgy is full of the prayers which Jesus addresses to the Father. It is the Father who raises Him up; and in the Masses of the Easter octave, it is always the Father who is seen as the beginning and end of the whole paschal mystery of the regeneration of men to a new life through baptism. In the period of the ascension it is again the Father who is seen as the end of all things: for, in the ascension, it is the Father who glorifies the Son definitively, and makes Him to sit at His right in glory, while Christ, from on high, simply intercedes for us with the Father; He prays that the Holy Spirit may be sent to us, and prepares for us a place near to Himself.

In the last phase of the cycle, from Ascension to Pentecost, finally, it is the Holy Spirit who occupies the first level of our attention. Now the liturgy begins to develop the notion that the whole work of realizing the redemption of Christ in individual men, from the moment when Christ is taken up to the right of the Father in glory, is accomplished *in Spiritu*, with the presence and the operation of the Holy Spirit, who animates the Church and vivifies her means of sanctification, of teaching, and of government. In this phase, Christ is seen primarily as the one who has merited the Holy Spirit for us, and has vivified us by giving us the Holy Spirit. The Father is the one who, at Christ's intercession, sends us the Spirit, and back to whom the Spirit must, in accord with His mission, lead us.

There is no need to enter into details to illustrate these concepts liturgically, and to show that effectively they constitute the ideological framework of the whole cycle from Quadragesima to Pentecost. On the other hand, it is opportune to point out once more how the liturgy, in its principal cycle, looks upon the Persons of the Trinity primarily in the perspective of their real distinction and by considering them in the proper relations, so to speak, of each to the sacred history of our salvation: i.e., in the appropriate role that each has in salvation history. It is in relation to the events of this salvation history that the liturgical feasts look to the Father, to Christ, the incarnate Son, our Redeemer and Head, and to the Holy Spirit.

Historically speaking, the liturgical cycle from Quadragesima to Pentecost has had a gradual growth and has required long centuries to reach its present state. It can nevertheless be seen how, in the formation of the cycle, the Church was guided by a basic instinct for simplicity and by an intuition leading to unification. The Church put into practice in the liturgy the idea that St. Paul expressed in an almost completely synthetic way in his Epistle to the Romans, in a passage which formerly was read on Ember Saturday of Pentecost week, and which offered a very satisfactory conclusion to the whole cycle:

> "Having been justified, therefore, by faith, let us have peace with God through our Lord Jesus Christ, through whom, by faith, we have had access to this grace in which we stand; and we exult in the hope of the glory (of the sons) of God. . . . And this hope does not lead to disappointment because the love of God is poured forth in our hearts by the Holy Spirit who has been given us" (Rom. 5:1-5).

Thus the perspective *a, per, in, ad* is seen even in the structural framework of the cycle itself, its formation having been directed from the very beginning, as it were, by a profound spirit of the liturgy, an instinct for what were liturgically proper.[96]

And here we have the key to an understanding of why, in the ancient liturgy not only was there no feast dedicated to the Father in His intratrinitarian life,[97] nor was there any feast of the Son and Word, nor a feast of the Holy Spirit, each viewed in their own proper intratrinitarian life independently of their interventions in salvation history, but there was not even a feast of the Trinity as such, viewed directly and primarily in the unity of the divine nature. This feast begins to appear in Gaul only in the eighth century, and gains a firm hold in that same region in the course of the tenth century. Its introduction corresponds, in the area of liturgical feasts, to that phenomenon encountered also in all the other parts of the liturgy, which makes it evident how there developed in the Church, in reaction to the Arian heresy, the psychological necessity of joining to the ancient Christological-Trinitarian perspective of the *a, per, in, ad* schema an explicit and direct affirmation of the unity of the divine nature in the Blessed Trinity considered directly in its very self in a perspective which transcends time and history.

[96] The second great temporal cycle of the Roman liturgy, that which runs from Advent to Epiphany, is likewise constructed on the Christological-Trinitarian perspective, although in this cycle the role of the Holy Spirit is less emphasized. The concept of this cycle is the whole of salvation history, the whole mystery of Christ, but under the aspect of the manifested coming of the Lord: an advent prepared for and announced in the Old Testament, realized historically in the birth and life of Jesus, realized sacramentally and mystically every day in every soul, and still hoped for in the parousia of the Lord. In this sequence the Roman liturgy puts a primary emphasis on the parts played by the Father and by the incarnate Son.

[97] More than once, and again in recent times, attempts have been made to secure the introduction into the liturgical cycles of a feast of the Father. But Rome has always refused. See Benedict XIV, *De servorum Dei beatificatione*, book 4, part 2, chapter 31; M. Caillat, *"La dévotion à Dieu le Père: une discussion au XVII.ᵉ siècle,"* in *Rev. d'asc. et de myst.*, Vol. 20 (1939), pp. 35-49; 136-157.

Was this the effect of a lack of liturgical spirit? I think not. No more would I be prepared to say that it was a lack of liturgical spirit that allowed the development in the conclusions of the orations and in the doxologies, alongside the ancient Christological-Trinitarian stratum, of a more recent perspective in which the ontological-Trinitarian aspect of the unity of the divine nature among the Three Persons was more directly affirmed. It must be remembered that, as we stated at the beginning of this chapter, the Trinity being a mystery comprising two antithetical terms, any way of formulating it necessarily has its own inconveniences and its own dangers from the point of view of psychological efficacy. All things considered, it would seem that there is only one sure solution: after having affirmed very clearly and concretely the real distinction of the Persons, we must take care to bring out their unity of nature in a way sufficiently precise so that the believer will not forget it.

And just as the liturgy did this in the conclusions of the collects and in the doxologies, so too it has done it in its feasts. This is what has led the liturgy to institute, at the end of the Lenten-Paschal cycle, a feast in which, as if to recapitulate and complete in a psychologically efficacious way the whole Christian perspective of the world and of salvation history that unfolds itself in this period in accord with the ancient *a, per, in, ad* schema, the attention and affection of the believer is concentrated explicitly on the unity of the Trinity considered in itself.

In creating this feast, therefore, the liturgy seeks only to respond to the concern, inevitable in consequence of the Arian heresy, of presenting to Christian people in a balanced manner the vision of their relations with God. This concern already finds expression in St. Ambrose:

> "In all that we have done we have respected the mystery of the Trinity. Everywhere are found the Father, the Son, and the Holy Spirit; one operation, one sanctifying action, even if there be, as it seems, something special for each. . . . You have this that is special: it is God who has called you; while in baptism in a special way you have been crucified with Christ; and then, when you receive in a special way the sign of the Spirit, you see that there is a distinction of Persons, but that the whole mystery of the Trinity is bound up together." [98]

The Mozarabic liturgy, in an analogous dimension, prays thus on the day of Pentecost:

> "Untiringly we pray Your omnipotence, O God, holy Father all-powerful, that You might fill us with the gift of Your Only-begotten . . . and of His Holy Spirit: so that You may see fit to lead to perfection through the Holy Spirit those whom You first created and

[98] St. Ambrose, *De sacr.* 6, 2, 5-8 (PL 16, 455).

afterwards redeemed through Your Son. Not, indeed, that the operation of Your Trinity is separate or dissimilar, but so that the unconfused equality of the distinct Persons in the one Godhead may appear obvious." [99]

Rome, notwithstanding the earnest solicitations which began already in the eighth century, remained opposed through fully six centuries to the introduction of a feast of the Trinity into the liturgy. This was because the traditional instinct was always strongest at Rome, i.e., the ancient understanding that a liturgical feast is not to have for its object simply an abstract idea, but rather a historical event pertaining to our salvation, or, if you will, an idea perhaps, but one that has been concretized in one or more of the historical events of salvation history.

Thus, the hesitations of Rome in former times, when she was entreated to make an exception to this fundamental rule of tradition, are understandable. Indeed, the multiplication of similar exceptions would result in the grave disadvantage of proposing abstract notions, without much permanent effect, to the piety of Christian people. In particular, it would cause this people to forget the grand biblical and liturgical perspective of the salvation history that is to be identified with the mystery of Christ, with the mystery of the Church, with the mystery in which all things come *from* the Father, *through* Christ, *in* the Holy Spirit, all returning *to* the Father: the mystery that constitutes the connatural perspective outside of which the Bible is not understood and the liturgy is not lived.

What the discovery and the zealous safeguarding of this mystery can mean for doctrine and for the practical spiritual life is described for us, after many others before him, by St. Cyril of Alexandria. The best modern authority on the spiritual doctrine of St. Cyril is able to say:

> "The destiny of the Christian is to become, in the anointing and through the anointing of the Holy Spirit, conformed to the image of the Son, the only Mediator, who leads us back to the Father; such is the dominant motif of the spiritual doctrine of St. Cyril. His ascetical doctrine and his mystical theology appear to us, if we may repeat it, essentially Trinitarian. The Father sends His Christ; together with Christ and through Him, He sends the Holy Spirit; and it is in the Holy Spirit, through the Son, that our ascensional return to the Father is accomplished." [100]

Cyril himself wrote:

> "To sanctify has (in Scripture) the accustomed meaning of consecrating and of offering; and thus we say that the Son sanctifies

[99] *Liber mozarb. sacr.*, Férotin edition, Paris 1912, no. 785.
[100] Hubert du Manoir, "*Cyrille d'Alexandrie*," in the *Dict. de spiritualité*, Vol. II, part 2, col. 2682. The same author explains his conclusions at greater length in his work *Dogme et spiritualité chez S. Cyrille d'Alexandrie*, Paris 1944.

Himself for us (cf. John 17:19). Indeed, that Sacrifice and that Holy Victim is offered to God and Father, reconciling the world to Him and recalling to His friendship those who had lost it, that is, the human race. 'He, indeed, is our peace,' as we find written (Eph. 2:14). Our return to God which is made through Christ the Savior takes place only through the participation and the sanctification of the Holy Spirit. The one who joins us and, so to speak, unites us to God, is the Spirit. In receiving the Spirit, we become participants and sharers in the divine nature; we receive Him through the Son, and in the Son we receive the Father." [101]

The liturgy, if we know how to understand it and live it, is the best means of all for making us penetrate these marvelous realities and for keeping ourselves attuned to them.

[101] *Commentarium in Ioannis Evangelium* 11, 10 (PG 74, 544-545).

8   THE KYRIOS--THE PASCHAL

MYSTERY: THE ONE LITURGIST

AND THE ONE LITURGY

The perspective "from the Father, through Christ, in the Holy Spirit, to the Father" gives us the complete cycle of the descent of God among men and of the return of men to God. But even after all we said of this in the preceding chapter, it is still necessary to define with greater precision the role and proper part in the liturgy which belongs, in this perspective, to Christ, through whom, in the Spirit, everything comes from the Father and returns to the Father.

What precisely does the liturgy mean when it says *Per Christum Dominum nostrum*?

1. The Kyrios

Primarily, the Christ of *per Christum Dominum nostrum* is the *Kyrios*. This is precisely what is meant by the subjoining of *Dominum* to *Christum*. But what is meant by *Kyrios*? And why do we suddenly introduce this Greek word which is translated *Dominus* in Latin, *Signore* in Italian, and *Lord* in English? Because for us today the word *Signore* in Italian, the word *Herr* in German, and, no doubt to a lesser degree but still to a considerable extent, the term *Lord* in English, can have a great many extraneous overtones that the term *Kyrios* did not have for primitive Christians, and conse-

quently these terms fail to evoke the tremendous content of meaning that is
to be found in the word *Kyrios*.[1]

And we have an urgent need to recover that very content. Why? In the
one Person of Jesus Christ there is God and there is man. In regard to the
man we might consider the historical man who was born, lived, suffered
and died in Palestine, and the resurrected man who henceforward is seated
in glory at the right hand of the Father, and is present and operative invisibly in His Church. Catholic piety never dares forget any one of these
aspects; and it is easy to demonstrate that in fact, in the course of its
history, orthodox piety has forgotten none of them.

Nevertheless, owing to the objectively inexhaustible riches of the mystery
of Christ, in whom are all the treasures both of humanity and of divinity,
and owing also to the limitations of human psychology and to the exigencies
of the mind in response to diverse graces and temperaments, in diverse eras
and cultures, in the formation of mental conceptions of Jesus it is possible
to place the emphasis now on one of these aspects and now on another. Thus
the features of this single Person can be psychologically coördinated either
from the point of view of His humanity. In this latter case, in the synthesis
which the believer forms of it, it is possible to start with the historical man
as He was in Palestine, or from the risen Savior, henceforward in the state of
glory, in the full exercise of His sovereign lordship over the living and the
dead, over the whole cosmos: in a word, to start with the *Kyrios*, the Lord
Jesus. Each of these three principal types of the image of Jesus will be able
to be realized afterwards, colored in various degrees, sometimes even in a
quite high degree, by the influence, more or less emphasized, of one or both
of the other two.

We are not speaking simply of abstract possibilities. It is a fact that in the
history of spirituality it is possible to speak of various images of Jesus corresponding directly to the observations made above. Indeed, recent detailed
studies, particularly in regard to patristic spirituality,[2] call upon us to guard
against every over-simplification and rigid schematization of a reality which
is not infrequently quite complex. The fact remains, however, that in the
attention and viewpoint of the New Testament, and in the general effect of
the patristic age up to the fourth century, it is the glorified man, the *Kyrios*,
who clearly predominates. This is the Jesus who, with the Paschal events as
point of departure, is disclosed vitally and has actual existence as God, even

---

[1] Cf. F. X. Durrwell, *La résurrection de
Jésus mystère de salut*, Paris 1963; V. Taylor,
The Names of Jesus, London 1954; O. Cull-
mann, *Christologie du Nouveau Testament*,
Paris-Neuchâtel 1958; David M. Stanley,
Christ's Resurrection in Pauline Soteriology,
Rome 1961; L. Sabourin, *Les noms et les ti-
tres de Jésus*, Desclée de Brouwer 1963, trans-
lated into English by Maurice Carroll: *The
Names and Titles of Jesus, Themes of Biblical
Theology*, New York 1967.

[2] Cf. M. Balsavich, *The Witness of St. Gregory the Great to the Place of Christ in Prayer*,
Rome 1959, pp. 17-24, with bibliography on
pp. 9-16.

in the episodes and sensibilities of His earthly life in Palestine, from His birth to His Passion and death.

From the fourth century onwards, in a reaction to Arianism, there takes place, especially in the East, a parallel emphasizing of the direct consideration of Jesus as God in the unity of nature with the Father and with the Holy Spirit; but all things considered, the image of the resurrected one, the *Kyrios*, is still that which occupies the first level of attention. In Western spirituality this continues largely until the twelfth century.

At this time a change of emphasis in the West, discernible since the eleventh century, while it preserves a strong and direct consciousness of Jesus as God, begins to concentrate more and more upon the historical man Jesus, prior to His resurrection, centering upon the episodes and sensibilities of His earthly life, especially on His birth and His Passion.

The man henceforth in His state of glory, the *Kyrios*, the importance which He has of Himself for our individual and social history, and for all creation, the Paschal events and His resurrection, are realities which must never be forgotten; but they may be relegated psychologically to a background position. The spiritual life of the faithful finds nourishment in the consideration of the episodes and sentiments of the earthly life of Jesus in Palestine, and knows no necessity of finishing each time by explicitly adverting to the fact that there is, nevertheless, but one Jesus, the *Kyrios*, who is in glory, our High Priest at the side of the Father, and that it is to this state of the Lord in glory that all the episodes and sentiments of this earthly life reach out with all their might, and from it alone do they draw their full significance.

Crucifixes representing the man of sorrows torn on the Cross, Christmas cribs, the way of the Cross, portrayals of the *Ecce Homo*; the phenomena of the stigmata, visions of the infant Jesus, devotion to the Sacred Heart or sacred wounds, like that of St. Margaret Mary, are, along with many others, typical expressions of this religious sensibility which adverts foremost to the humanity of Jesus. Hence it is possible to speak, in particular, of a devotion to the Passion of Jesus separated, as it were, from His resurrection — or separated, at least, in the attention which the faithful give it. In general, this is consistently the sensibility of modern piety.

Noting this sensibility or sensitivity, of course, does not in any way in itself raise the question of the legitimacy of such devotion nor of its salutary fruits. Here we wish only to point out that it is not the only possibility, nor is it, in fact, that which predominates in the New Testament and in the patristic age. Neither is it (apart from a few compositions of medieval or modern origin) the religious sensibility exhibited by the liturgy which, in this as in so many other points, simply follows the biblical and patristic point of view, concentrating its attention on the *Kyrios* and, with Him as starting point, adverting again and again to the divinity of Jesus and to His historical life. Our intention, therefore, is simply to point out that in order to penetrate and live to its fullest the image of Jesus in the liturgy, it is necessary to take the *Kyrios* as starting point.[3]

2. The Paschal Mystery and Its Central Position in the Plan of Salvation

With the *Kyrios* as point of departure, we can arrive at some understanding of the paschal mystery in the whole of its extension and simplicity, as the focal point of the plan of salvation in Christ, as it is found in the Bible, in patristic tradition, and in the liturgy.

What is the paschal mystery, in the dimension under discussion? A very complex reality, and at the same time a reality quite simple and unified, which transcends by far the bare and simple fact of the resurrection of Jesus, taken simply as an apologetic argument for His divine mission.

The paschal mystery is the fact that Jesus is not only the incarnate Son of God, but incarnate and revealed *in forma servi*, and, what is more, dead and risen, the *Kyrios*. More precisely it is the fact that He, as *Kyrios*, is now seated at the right of the Father, in the continuous and glorious exercise, always as man, of His mediation as High Priest; and that, by means of His humanity, comprised in His glorious body, He communicates to us the divine life with which that body is not only full but even resplendent, the sole dispenser of divine life, allowing us primarily through the liturgy — and not only us but in some way the whole world — to pass over from spiritual and physical death to total life in God. The ultimate end of this process activated by Him is to make us, body and soul, like Himself in death and resurrection, so that, having communicated insofar as is possible His same form of existence and of action to everyone who sincerely follows Him, and having instituted a new heaven and a new earth, He might be able to offer everything together with Himself to the Father, and that finally God might be all in all.

It is this, in the totality and in the inseparability of its elements, that constitutes the paschal mystery, as the liturgy understands it; and not only the liturgy, but likewise ancient tradition and Scripture itself.[4]

[3] By this time, a broadly documented fact. See C. Vagaggini, "*Liturgia e pensiero teologico recente*," in the booklet of the same title, Rome 1961, pp. 51-53, with bibliography. Also, M. Shepherd, *The Paschal Liturgy and the Apocalypse*, London 1960; J. Gaillard, "*Le mystère paschal dans le renouveau liturgique. Essai de bilan*," in *La maison Dieu*, Vol. 67 (1961), pp. 31-87.

[4] See Odo Casel, "*Art und Sinn der ältesten*

christlichen Ostfeier," in *Jahrbuch für Liturgiewissenschaft*, Vol. 14 (1934), pp. 1-78; S. Czerwik, *Homilia paschalis apud patres usque ad saeculum quintum*, Rome 1961, with bibliography on pp. 7-11; C. Vagaggini, "*Fulget Crucis mysterium*," in *Pont. Instit. Regina Mundi*, no. 12 (1960), pp. 3-14; also of Vagaggini, "*Pasqua la festa christiana*," in *L'Osservatore Romano*, issue of April 22, 1962, p. 3; B. Fischer, "*Der verherrlichte Mensch Chri-*

This mystery, understood thus in its whole extension, is the great good news of the New Testament, the grand announcement of joy to mankind. The Apostles are witnesses thereto (Luke 24:28). This is the great mystery in which salvation history (cf. Apoc. 5:21; Heb. 10:12-21; 12:18-24), the mystery of Christ (cf. 1 Tim. 3:16; Phil. 2:5-11; Col. 1:15-20), in particular the mystery of His priesthood (cf. Heb. 9; 10:12-20; 12:18-24), as well as the mystery of the Church (cf. Eph. 1:3-3:20; 1 Peter 1:3-2:10), and consequently the mystery of the liturgy (Rom. 6; John 6) are made practical and concrete.

This mystery of life-death, therefore, in Jesus, in ourselves, in the world at large, is ultimately the primary object of the Apostolic catechesis, since it constitutes the concrete and synthetic point of view which effectively summarizes the various aspects of the *euaggélion*.[5] It is seen everywhere, whether it be in panoramic summations more or less complete, or in one or the other of its particular features.

Here, then, are some examples:

1. Death-life in Christ Himself: Phil. 2:6-11; Col. 1:15-20; 1 Tim. 3:16.

2. Death-life of Jesus which must become our form of existing and of acting:

 a. In general: 2 Cor. 5:12-21.

 b. In particular, in baptism: Rom. 6; Col. 2:8-15.

 c. In the Eucharist: concept developed in a special way in John 6; see also the narratives of the institution of the Eucharist and 1 Cor. 11:23-24.

 d. In the moral life: Rom. 4:24-8:39; 14:9; Phil. 1:27-2:11; 3:7-24; Col. 2:6-4:6; 1 Peter 1:1-2; 3:13-4:19.

 e. In the apostolate: 2 Cor. 4:7-5:5.

 f. In eschatology: 2 Cor. 5:1-15.

3. Death-life of Jesus in the whole of the cosmos: Rom. 8:9-23; 2 Peter 3:13; Apoc. 21:1-8; 2:28.

It is particularly obvious that the moral element in the teaching of Jesus, in the preaching of the Apostles and in the propositions of the liturgy cannot be in any way separated or, as it were, eradicated from this outline of the paschal mystery without degenerating into a form of moralism that is purely ethical and natural, which would amount to its utter perversion. That overview of sacred salvation history, from which, as pointed out above,[6] the specific nature of the Christian system of morality, the proximate motivation

stus und die Liturgie," in *Lit. Jahrbuch,* Vol. 8 (1958), pp. 205-217. For scriptural references see the works cited above in note 1 of the present chapter.

[5] See O. Cullmann, *Le prime confessioni di fede christiana,* Rome 1949; J. Schmitt, *Jésus*

réssuscité dans la prédication apostolique, Paris 1949; H. Schürmann, *Aufbau und Struktur der neutestamentlichen Verkündigung,* Paderborn 1949; and also the work of Stanley, cited above in note 1 of the present chapter.

[6] Pp. 6ff.

of Christian action, is derived, is, in the New Testament, the Jesus who is
dead and risen again, and who now communicates to us the divine life of
which He is filled: the paschal vision. This is easily verified from the passages
cited above.

The total and integral figure of the New Testament Jesus is that of the
Jesus of the paschal mystery: incarnate Son of God, born and become visible
in forma servi, dead, risen, and now in glory, in continuous act of communicating to the world the divine life of which He is the perfect and solitary
dispenser. To stop at the notion of a Jesus who is dead — or even worse, at
that of a teacher, however sweet and amiable, who wandered through Galilee
and Judea, or at that of a visionary voicing the Sermon on the Mount, or
at that of the *Gesù Bambino* — without having at the same time a clear consciousness of the fact that there is, after all, but one Jesus, the *Kyrios*, dead and
risen, who now transmits to us His own divine life, principally in the sacraments, is to run the very real risk of seeing in Jesus no more than a very
compassionate and profound teacher, whose only value is in the example
which he gave and in the ethics which he taught.

It may be only such a Jesus as this that will satisfy the naturalism current
today. But is this not perhaps because too often it is precisely such a Jesus
that we present to the world? And is this not perhaps the real reason why a
world which accepts that kind of a Jesus is not at all prepared to admit His
presence and His transforming action in the Church and does not know
what to make of the sacraments and of the resurrection of the body?

This, however, is not the Jesus of St. Paul, nor of St. John, nor of the
Catholic Epistles. And in actual fact, it is not even the Jesus of the synoptics;
for, quite obviously, they are treating of the words and deeds, the figure
of Jesus, always with the clear consciousness of His resurrection which had
already taken place, and which had been proven by themselves. And most
certainly, it is not the Jesus who was the object of the faith of the first
Christians and who turned the ancient world topsy-turvy.[7]

3. Why It Is Difficult for Us Today to Understand
That the Paschal Mystery Is Central

There are certain mental attitudes in theology, in spirituality, and in pastoral practice which make it difficult for us today, unfortunately, to appreciate the fact that basically the paschal mystery is at the center of Christian
life, even though this is evident enough in Scripture, in tradition, and in the
liturgy.

There is the positivist-historical mentality, which makes us consider the
resurrection of Christ separately from His Passion, His Passion and death

[7] See the works already referred to in notes 1 and 5 of the present chapter.

separately from His resurrection, and both of them separately from the sacraments.

Prevalent also is the juridic mentality which makes us consider salvation almost exclusively in categories of ransom, satisfaction, and merit; and the resurrection of Christ, in the totality of our salvation, is thereby reduced to an apologetic argument which proves His divine mission.

Then too there is the mentality of abstract and disembodied spiritualism which tends unconsciously to identify the man with his soul. Thus the role and value of the body in our salvation is no longer understood; and therefore there is no understanding either of the place and value of the incarnation, of the glorious resurrection of the body of Christ and of our own bodies nor of the sacraments, nor of the teaching about a new heaven and a new earth.[8]

And more particularly, there is the theological mentality generally impregnated by abstract conceptualism. Under the influence of this mentality, when we make theological judgments of things, persons, and events, we are limited to the abstract consideration of essences and perhaps of those properties which are always and necessarily connected with essences; everything else we relegate to a place among "the non-essential accidents." Thus, we no longer have eyes for the concrete historical aspects involved. In this perspective, many will no longer apprehend the capital importance, for Christ and for the world, of His resurrection from the dead.

One such good "Thomistic" theologian has said: "Why insist so much upon the resurrection of Christ? The great event of history is not the resurrection but, if you will, the incarnation of the Son of God. After the incarnation, the resurrection is but a simple episode." He concluded without delay, therefore, that the great feast is not Easter but the Annunciation.

Such affirmations, filled as they are with ambiguities, are only too characteristic of a widespread mentality that is quite incapable of encompassing the world of Scripture and of the liturgy. Who is there who would not sense immediately the ambiguity in such a statement as this: For Giovanni Battista Montini the great event is the birth of the man, while his election as Pope, the fact that he is now Pope Paul VI, is but a simple episode?

Certainly insofar as the essence of the man is concerned, the fact of his being Pope is a "non-essential accident." Metaphysically speaking, it is more basic and important to be a man than it is to be Pope. Nevertheless, in the history of this person and in the history of the world, and therefore, concretely speaking, the decisive and important fact is not that Giovanni Battista Montini is a man, but that that man is the Pope.

[8] See Cyprian Vagaggini, "*Riflessioni sul senso teologico del mistero pasquale,*" in *Riv. di pastorale liturgica,* Vol. 2 (1964), pp. 102-112.

And St. Thomas, following Aristotle, if I do not err, distinguishes a two-fold perfection:

> "The first looks to the essence of the thing, the second to its operation; and this second perfection is greater than the first. Therefore, to put it simply, we call a thing perfect which attains to perfection in its operation, which is the second area of perfection." [9]

This shows that many of our problems come not really from metaphysical theology (a necessary and beneficial thing under certain aspects), but from the mentality of certain champions of metaphysical theology who have lost their sense of the real and of history, and therefore of salvation history, and with it, of the Bible and of liturgy. The consequences of this for pastoral are all too obvious.

4. The Heavenly Priesthood of Christ

Only against the background of the *Kyrios* and of the paschal mystery is it possible to recover an integral concept of the present priesthood of Christ and of its vital significance to the life of the world, to understand the topsy-turvy figure of "Jesus Christ, the High Priest of our offerings, the defender and helper of our weakness," according to an expression of St. Clement of Rome (Jurgens, no. 18).

The presence of Christ in the liturgy. To determine the nature of the liturgy the Second Vatican Council deals with the notion, justifiably, not only of Christ Himself and of the Church as continuator of Christ's work, but more precisely, of the very special presence of Christ, now reigning in glory beside the Father, in the Church and particularly in liturgical action.[10]

Indeed, in our liturgy the part played by Christ is thus so real, so vivid, so present and preponderant, that in the final analysis there is in the world but one liturgist, Christ, and but one liturgy, Christ's liturgy.

In treating of the action and of the presence of Christ in His Church, and in the liturgy in particular, the danger is this: that we think more or less consciously of that activity as something which happened once and for all in the earthly life of Jesus from His incarnation to His death on the Cross, and which is now no longer present except in the purely psychological area of knowledge and feelings. Again, there is the danger of panpsychologism and of panmoralism. Basically, it is an attempt to conceive of Jesus as no more than a great teacher who has confided to us a wonderful moral teaching

---

[9] *Super ep. ad Gal. expos.* 5, 6. See also the *Summa*, I, q. 73, a. 1 c: "Indeed, the first perfection is that by which a thing is perfect in respect to its substance. . . . The second perfection, however, is in regard to the end. End, however, is either operation, in the sense

that the end of a guitarist is guitaring; or it is something that is arrived at through operation, in the sense that the end of a builder is the house which he builds."

[10] CL, art. 7.

to assist us in reaching God; as a wonderful model for our imitation. Perhaps it comes finally to a matter of not forgetting that Jesus is the one who voluntarily agreed to make expiation for us on the Cross, and in that way gave us once and for all the possibility of obtaining from God the necessary graces for our attaining to glory, where He awaits us.

But if the meaning of Christ for our lives be limited to these aspects alone, basically He would be no more than a great saint and in that way alone our teacher and model. His presence and present action in our midst, in the Church, would be of a kind no different from that of the presence and action of a great philosopher among his disciples, of a great and holy man among his devotees; or, we may suggest, that of a great founder among the members of his order. Christ, however, His action and His presence, is, for the Church, something immensely profound. He differs entirely from these others and is on an entirely different level. The action and presence of the ancient teachers or of the saints among their disciples is entirely of the moral or psychological order. The action and presence of Christ in His Church is first of all of the physical order, and then, by way of consequence thereof, also of the moral order.

To achieve an understanding of the action and presence of Christ in His Church, and particularly in the liturgy, we must start all over again with the great syntheses of history and of the Christian life set forth in the Epistle to the Hebrews.[11]

The heavenly priesthood of Christ. The author of the Epistle to the Hebrews, thinking of the ultimate meaning of all history and of all life, does not merely include this, as do all the New Testament authors, in the grand circular panorama by which all things come from the Father, through Christ, in the Spirit, and then return to the Father — a panorama which he takes for granted, even if he does not insist very much on the person of the Spirit,[12] but what is more, he considers this under the aspect of sanctification and worship. Salvation history and the Christian life are considered, in effect, as a liturgy which the author presents to us.

The Epistle to the Hebrews is an exhortation and an encouragement directly intended for a group of Hebrew priests and levites converted to Christ and who, in the midst of the trials of persecution, were tempted to look back with some regrets to the sanctifying efficacy and adorational splendor of the Jewish temple liturgy, when confronted by what must have seemed to them to be the bare spiritualism of the new religion. That is why the author is so anxious to demonstrate and illustrate the immense transcendency

---

[11] See Ceslaus Spicq, *L'épître aux hébreux*, 2 volumes, Paris 1953-1954, especially volume I at pages 286-329.

[12] *Ibid.*, Vol. I, pp. 147ff. The author of the Epistle speaks of the Father most often simply as God; see *Dieu* and *Esprit Saint* in the analytical index of the same work, Vol. II, p. 446.

that the Christian life has, as sanctification and worship, over the liturgy of the Old Testament.[13]

To do this presupposes that the whole life of the faithful, in the presence of God and on this earth, is basically nothing else but an immense liturgical procession of pilgrims advancing to the sanctuary where God dwells, in order to be admitted into His presence for the purpose of seeing Him, of praising Him, and of offering sacrifices to Him. Hence, the well-known fundamental themes of the Epistle: the people of God as pilgrims; the people of God as a community of worship; Christ the Son of God, the Redeemer High Priest (because of sin which had preceded), the Sanctifier, Head and Guide of this community of wandering worshipers; the moral life of Christians as both presupposition and consequence of their participation in the sanctifying and worshiping activity of Christ, their Head; the sanctification and worship of the Old Testament as figure and shadow of the sanctification and worship of Christ and in Christ; the presential actuality, henceforth without end, of the heavenly liturgy of the glorified Christ at the right of the Father in the liturgical and jubilant assembly (*panégyris*) of the angels and of the just who have already attained to their end, an assembly in which Christians take a real part even while they are still here below, in a relation of faith, still on their pilgrimage.

At the center of this whole perspective is the concept of the priesthood of Jesus Christ, the Son of God. His is the true, perfect, and eternal priesthood, of which all the others were nought but shadows and figures. It is a priesthood begun in the incarnation, carried on in the whole earthly life of Christ, and especially on Calvary; a priesthood joined to the final and eternal phase of perfection and efficacy in heaven, at the right of the Father, and which is reflected continuously and efficaciously on this earth by means of those who adhere to Him in the Christian faith and life. This is the principal and summational point (*kephálaion*, Heb. 8:1) of all this lofty doctrine (cf. Heb. 5:11) which the author wants to explain to his correspondents:

> "Now the main point in what we are saying is this. We have such
> a High Priest, who has taken His seat at the right of the throne of
> the Majesty in the heavens, a liturgist of the sanctuary and of the
> true tabernacle, which the Lord has erected and not man" (Heb.
> 8:1-2).

A priest who,

> "because He remains forever, has a priesthood that is not transitory;
> and therefore He is at all times able to save those who come to God

---

[13] All the basic and characteristic terminology of the Epistle is specifically liturgical: to approach to, to draw near to, to present one- self, to offer, to sanctify, to expiate, to purify, altar, priest, etc.

> through Him, since He lives always to make intercession for them. It was fitting, in fact, that we should have such a High Priest: holy, innocent, undefiled, set apart from sinners and elevated above the heavens. He has no need, as did the other priests, of offering sacrifices every day, first for His own sins and afterwards for those of the people; for this latter He did once and for all when He offered up Himself" (Heb. 7:24-27).

In the Epistle to the Hebrews this whole perspective of the celestial priesthood of Jesus and of His liturgy is strongly concentrated on the paschal mystery.

One of the principal themes is precisely the affirmation that it is through His own death and His own blood that Jesus, having become the Mediator and High Priest of the new covenant, has entered into the heavenly sanctuary and has taken His seat at the right of the Father, ready always to intercede for us.

It is directly the theme of the whole of chapter 9, with the central verses 11-15:

> "Christ, however, the High Priest of the good things to come, through the greater and more perfect tabernacle, not made by hands (that is, not of this creation), nor again by virtue of blood of goats and calves, but by virtue of His own blood, entered once and for all into the sanctuary, having obtained an eternal redemption. For if the blood of goats and bulls and the sprinkled ashes of a heifer sanctify the unclean unto cleansing of the flesh, how much more will the blood of Christ, who by virtue of His eternal Spirit offered Himself unblemished to God, purify your conscience from dead works to serve the living God! And this is why He is Mediator of a new covenant. . . ."

Moreover, the author of the Epistle to the Hebrews even explains explicitly why God has very wisely willed that the priesthood of Christ should be that of a mediator Son of God, incarnate, dead, and risen. Such is the content of chapter 2, verses 10-18, with the three concluding verses as follows: "For, of course, it is not angels to whose assistance He comes; rather, He comes to the aid of the offspring of Abraham. Therefore it was necessary that He should in all things be made like unto His brethren, that He might become a merciful and faithful High Priest in the things that look to God, for the purpose of expiating the sins of the people. Precisely because He Himself has suffered in having been put to the test, He is pleased to assist those who are being tried."

The High Priest of the Epistle to the Hebrews is squarely the *Kyrios*, dead, risen in glory, and sympathetic to His task of universal mediation in the business of leading men to God, even if in the Epistle the relationship between this mediation and the sacraments is not much developed.

Priesthood of Christ and Christian life. What does adherence to the faith and to the Christian life mean in this perspective? The author of the Epistle answers the question in a text which summarizes just about all the great themes to which we have been alluding. He tells Christians that they have not *approached* (again, a liturgical term) the Mount Sinai to which the Hebrews approached at the time of the covenant, in that well-known scene of majesty and terror; rather, "you have come near to Mount Sion and to the city of the living God, the heavenly Jerusalem, to myriads of angels, to a joyous liturgical celebration (*panegýrei*) and an assembly (*ekklesía*) of the firstborn enrolled in heaven, and to God, the Judge of all, and to the spirits of the just who have been brought to perfection, and to Jesus, the Mediator of the new covenant, and to a sprinkling of blood which speaks better than that of Abel" (Heb. 12:22-24) .

It is easy to see, from the point of view that is of interest to us, how it is possible to rediscover effectively in this text and in those few already cited, the great themes that we have been enunciating.

The Christian life is a liturgical procession of pilgrims whose purpose is, by arriving at a goal of perfection (*teleíosis*), to draw near to God in the sanctuary and to appear before Him. The sanctuary in this context is the sanctuary of heaven, where the myriads of angels and those men who are justified, already having arrived at the perfection to which they were called by God, through having arrived at the goal of their journey (*teteleioménon*), are gathered about God in a festive assembly (*panegýrei*).

Christians, by embracing the new faith and the new life, have already attained in some measure the goal of their liturgical pilgrimage; and in a very real way, even if not yet the perfect way, they have drawn near in a liturgical act to that holy Jerusalem and to that sanctuary in heaven. This has been made possible and remains possible for them, thanks to the High Priest, the Mediator of the new covenant, Jesus. He it is, who has sprinkled them with His blood; and by thus purifying them of their sins, He has introduced them, in a real way even now, into the sanctuary of the holy Sion. In a real way even now He has united them to the liturgical assembly of the angels and of the just, in which He is the eternal High Priest at the right of the Father, the liturgist of the sanctuary and of the true tabernacle, living always to intercede on behalf of those who are His own.

The worship, the sanctifications, the whole liturgy and the priesthood of the Old Testament were nought but shadow and figure (Heb. 8:5; 10:1) of this true priesthood, of this true worship and this true sanctification of which Christ is the liturgist and of which Christians now are really participants. Thus, the ancient priestly economy, sanctificative and cultic in the Old Testament is henceforth abolished, and there no longer exists any sanctificative and cultic priestly economy except that of Christ, in which Christians

already have a real share. It is obvious, then, how immensely the lot of
these latter transcends that of the Hebrews.

All this, therefore, can be recapitulated in the following summarization:
Christ, the one and perfect priest, after having fulfilled on earth His liturgy
of sanctification and of praise to the Father, principally on Golgotha, is now
ever-living and glorious at the right of the Father; and there in the one
sanctuary this one liturgist continues in intercessory action the one liturgy of
sanctification and of praise which He initiated already here below; and to
it He invites and really admits even those of His faithful who are still on
their pilgrimage, while he gives them the firm hope of arriving, through
perseverance in leading a good life, at their goal of perfection in the celestial
sanctuary.

5. Celestial Liturgy and Terrestrial Liturgy

In this general perspective what is the liturgical role, properly assigned to
Christians, which they are to fulfill here below? The author of the Epistle
to the Hebrews, completely occupied with his vision of the celestial liturgy,
does not develop the relationship which the terrestrial liturgy of Christians
has with it. Probably, however, he does make some allusions to this earthly
liturgy. It is in this sense that many commentators interpret the following
text:

> "Since, therefore, we have glad confidence to enter the sanctuary,
> in virtue of the blood of Jesus, an entry which He has opened up for
> us, a new and living way through the veil, that is, His flesh, and since
> we have a High Priest in charge of the house of God, let us draw
> near with a sincere heart, in fullness of faith, our hearts sprinkled
> and cleansed from an evil conscience and our bodies washed with
> pure water. Let us hold fast to the unwavering profession of our
> hope — for He who has given the promise is faithful — and let us
> take care to incite one another to charity and good works, not forsak-
> ing our own assembly, as is the custom with some; but rather let us
> exhort one another; and this all the more as you see the day drawing
> near" (Heb. 10:19-25).

In the assembly (*episynagogè*) which Christians are exhorted not to for-
sake, many commentators see the liturgical assembly. If this interpretation
corresponds in fact to the author's intention, perhaps it can be said that for
him the liturgical assembly is the natural place where Christians, their
hearts sprinkled and purified of an evil conscience and their bodies washed
in the pure water of baptism, draw near to God even now under the aegis
of the High Priest, Jesus, who has obtained so great a favor for us with His
blood, while in virtue of that same blood, He gives us a firm confidence of
being able one day to enter into the heavenly sanctuary, the ultimate end of
our pilgrimage, whither He has gone before us; all this on condition that we

preserve intact our faith and our hope, and that we translate them into good works.

Various commentators believe also that the author of the Epistle has made some allusions to the Eucharist (Heb. 13:10; 6:4).

But even if the Epistle to the Hebrews does not indicate precisely the relationship between the heavenly liturgy and the earthly liturgy of Christians, it does at least establish the basic principles according to which it is possible to determine this relationship, a determination which later patristic and liturgical tradition has actually made.

The basic principle is that already explained above and strongly inculcated in the Epistle itself: that there is one liturgist, who is Christ, and one liturgy, which is that of Christ, now glorious at the right of the Father. As complementary principle, either expressed or implied, there is the idea that the true and definitive world is the heavenly one, while the world here below is only its shadow, its figure, its imitation.[14]

It is true that the author of the Epistle develops this exemplarist viewpoint primarily to illustrate the interconnections between Mosaic worship and Christ's heavenly worship. In this matter it will not be tiresome to repeat once more that the Mosaic cult was but a pallid shadow, a weak imitation of the perfect worship of the future, that of Christ (Heb. 10:1; 8:2-5; 9:11-24). Nevertheless, it does not seem to me to be possible to demonstrate that the author, with a viewpoint in which certainly he is thinking primarily of the heavenly worship of Christ, has also in mind the worship of Christians here on earth.

It was inevitable, however, that in this perspective Christians should posit a direct question as to the meaning of terrestrial Christian worship in relation to celestial worship and to the worship of the Old Testament. And the answer was equally inevitable, in view of the principles of the Epistle: if the liturgy of the Old Testament was but shadow and figure of the heavenly liturgy of Christ, then the earthly liturgy of Christians is also shadow and figure of the celestial liturgy of Christ. With one grand difference however: the concept of figure and shadow applied to the earthly liturgy of Christians in reference to its relationship to the heavenly liturgy has a meaning immensely more profound and real, even realistic, than it has when it is applied to the liturgy of the Old Testament in respect to its relationship to the same heavenly liturgy.

The profound reason is that among Christians, even on this earth, there is but one sanctification, that which is continuously effected in them by Christ; and there is but one worship, that which is offered uninterrupt-

---

[14] In regard to this principle see Ceslaus Spicq, *L'épître aux hébreux*, Vol. I, pp. 72-76. The author of the Epistle, in the matter under consideration, takes his cue from the Platonic-Alexandrian tradition, an exemplarist doctrine.

edly through them and with them and by Christ; and therefore there is but the one liturgist: Christ Himself. If the earthly liturgy is true sanctification and true worship, it can be such only insofar as it brings about in a different way the same sanctification and performs the same worship as Christ does, now glorious in heaven; insofar as in the earthly rites there is repeated, or better, manifested, like something being visibly reduplicated, that which Christ Himself does in heaven. The earthly liturgy of Christians is possible under the veil of rites and symbols of the heavenly liturgy of Christ. It is the manifestation on earth of the heavenly liturgy, enclosed in an earthly wrapping. The earthly liturgy and the heavenly liturgy are one and the same reality, and between them there is a difference only of fullness and of visibility, such as there was in the ancient concept of the image and the reality which it manifests.

These ideas, easily developed from the principles of the Epistle to the Hebrews, have been employed to the best advantage in patristic and liturgical tradition. This tradition was deeply concerned with showing that in our earthly liturgy it is always and everywhere Christ Himself who acts under the veil of the rites and through the instrument of the human ministers; in such a way, in fact, that it is always and everywhere Christ Himself who is the principal minister of the whole liturgical action in all its forms, whether Mass, sacraments, sacramentals, or divine office.[15]

On the notion that it is Christ Himself who, as principal minister, offers the Eucharistic sacrifice, Dom Dix [16] is able to state:

> "I believe that with the exception of three series of Origen's *Homilies* I have read every sentence of every Christian author extant from the period before Nicaea, most of it probably eight or a dozen times or oftener. It is difficult to prove a negative from so vast and disparate a mass of material, but I have paid particular attention to this point for some years. I think I can state as a fact that (with two apparent exceptions which I will deal with in a footnote) there is *no* pre-Nicene author Eastern or Western whose Eucharistic doctrine is at all fully stated, who does not regard the offering and consecration of the Eucharist as the present action of our Lord Himself, the second Person of the Trinity. And in the overwhelming majority of writers it is made clear that their whole conception revolves around the figure of the High Priest at the altar in heaven.[17] This certainly is the conception of the early liturgical prayers. . . .
>
> "The important thing to notice from our immediate standpoint is

[15] Some hints in this regard will be found in Ph. Oppenheim, *Notiones liturgiae fundamentales*, Marietti 1941, pp. 109-132, with bibliography on p. 109.

[16] *The Shape of the Liturgy*, London 1954 (reprint), pp. 253-254.

[17] Among others, Dix cites Clement of Rome, Justin the Martyr, Irenaeus, Tertullian, Clement of Alexandria, Origen, Cyprian, and uncertainly, Polycarp. Afterwards he adds: "It is not necessary to multiply the citations."

that when the pre-Nicene Church thought and spoke of the Eucharist as an action, as something 'done', it conceived it primarily as an action of *Christ Himself*, perpetually offering through and in His body the Church His 'Flesh for the life of the world.' It is the perpetuation in time by way of anamnesis of His eternally accepted and complete redeeming act."

The Church has always believed that the Mass is really a certain way by which there is made present on earth that which was revealed to John in the Apocalypse when he saw "in the midst, where the throne was and the four living creatures and the elders, a lamb standing upright yet as if slain" (Apoc. 5:6); and the lamb is none other than that "High Priest who is seated at the right of the throne of the Majesty in the heavens, that liturgist of the sanctuary and of the true tabernacle" (Heb. 8:1-2), our "advocate with the Father" (1 John 2:1), who "lives always to make intercession" (Heb. 7:25) for us.

This concept of the Mass as action of Christ Himself now glorious at the right of the Father, who operates under the veil of the rites and through human ministers, is continued even after Nicaea in patristic and liturgical tradition. This is nonetheless true even if, in a certain respect, it is here and there somewhat weakened by reason of a strong emphasis placed, in the East and from the beginning of the fourth century, on the role of the Holy Spirit in the carrying out of the Eucharistic sacrifice.[18] By emphasizing the role of the Holy Spirit, it became possible for St. Cyril of Jerusalem, for example, to speak of Christ as if He were passive at the critical moment of the fulfillment of the sacrifice.[19] But even in those liturgies where, by means of a consecratory epiclesis, there is a stress laid upon the idea of the role of the Spirit in the Mass, the other concept, that Christ is actively operative at the critical moment of the sacrifice, is always preserved as well. And this is the case even if it is not explained how the two ideas can be mutually reconciled. Thus the Byzantine liturgy of St. Basil (and that of St. John Chrysostom), while having quite clearly a prayer for the coming of the Holy Spirit, addresses itself directly to Christ in the formula called the *Cheroubikón*, when it says:

> "No one is worthy . . . to draw near, approach or minister to You, King of glory. For it is a great and tremendous thing even for the heavenly Powers to minister to You. But, by Your inexpressible and immeasurable love for mankind, without any change or loss You have become man, You have become our High Priest and You have given us the sacred liturgical rite of this unbloody sacrifice. . . . I beg of You . . . give me the strength . . . to stand at this holy table and to consecrate Your sacred and spotless body and Your precious blood. . . . Condescend to have these gifts offered to You by me,

---

[18] See Dix, *op. cit.*, pp. 276-302.   [19] *Ibid.*, pp. 278ff.

Your sinful and unworthy servant. For You are the offerer and the offered, the sanctifier and the sanctified" [the most recent text reads: "the receiver and the one distributed"], "Christ, our God."

The same Dix, who is extremely cognizant of the difference between the two concepts, nevertheless admits that, even while insisting on the role of the Holy Spirit in the decisive moment of the Mass, the Eastern liturgies, even after the fourth century, maintained "with a happy illogicality," the ancient and universal concept that the earthly Eucharist is the action of Christ Himself, the High Priest of the heavenly altar, "who Himself offers, Himself prays, Himself consecrates, in the offering of the sacrifice." [20]

From the purely theoretical theological point of view, however, and aside from the question of the precise moment in which the consecration of the Eucharistic elements takes place, we fail to perceive all so much contradiction as Dom Dix sees between the idea that the stated consecration is done by the Holy Spirit and the idea that it is done by Christ. It is enough to recall the biblical thought that all that which Christ, now glorious at the right of the Father, does in the world, He does through the Holy Spirit, whom He Himself sends from the Father; thus, the action of Christ and the action of the Holy Spirit are not two diverse actions, but a single action of Christ in the Holy Spirit or through the Holy Spirit. Theoretically speaking, therefore, it is possible to emphasize quite well that which is, so to speak, the role of the Holy Spirit in the Mass without thereby abandoning the idea that Christ, our High Priest, now in heaven at the right of the Father, is the principal minister of the Eucharistic sacrifice.

At any rate the antiquity and the universality of the concept that it is truly Christ Himself who offers His sacrifice in the Mass is evident. The Council of Trent only reconfirmed this notion when it said that in the sacrifice of the Mass, "it is one and the same victim who by the ministry of the priests now offers Himself and who then offered Himself on the Cross." [21]

It is well known that the question of determining more precisely the manner in which Christ, now glorious at the right of the Father, really offers, as principal minister, each sacrifice that is carried out on earth has given rise among theologians to opinions sufficiently diverse; nor does it seem opportune for us to enter into the matter here.[22]

Nor is it necessary to dwell at length on the general notion that in the

[20] *Ibid.*, p. 292.
[21] Dz 1743 (940). It is known that this conviction gave rise to the iconographic theme of Christ celebrating the Mass Himself. See, for example, G. Millet, *Monumenta de l'Athos*, Vol. I, Paris 1927, plates 64,1 and 2; 118,2;

168; 218,2; 219,3; 256; 257; 261; and 262,1 and 2.
[22] See above, pp. 149ff. See also A. Coelho, *Corso di liturgia romana*, trans. by F. Maberini, Vol. I, Marietti 1935, pp. 175ff; Ch. Journet, *La messe présence du sacrifice de la Croix*, Paris 1957, pp. 80-128.

various sacraments it is Christ Himself who is the principal minister. We know that this doctrine was made explicit in its essentials by St. Augustine, in the course of the controversy over the validity of the baptism conferred by Donatists, when Augustine wrote those famous words:

> "Peter baptizes, but it is He (Christ) that baptizes; Paul baptizes, but it is He that baptizes; Jude baptizes, but it is He that baptizes." [23]

The doctrine of the *ex opere operato* efficacy of the sacraments is based entirely upon this presupposition.

And in general in this matter it will be well to remember the teaching of St. Thomas, already noted in a previous chapter, that every sanctification that God works in men is now made through the humanity of Christ as the physical instrument of His divinity.

Even in the sacramentals and in the liturgical rites instituted by the Church, just as in divine praise itself, it is always Christ who is the principal actor. As has been explained in a previous chapter, this takes place in a manner and in a degree somewhat different from that of the sacraments which work *ex opere operato*, but still in a manner ever superior to that which is operating in the private prayers of a Christian or in public but non-liturgical prayer. It is precisely here that we find the concept of the efficacy of the divine office and of the liturgical rites instituted by the Church being operative *ex opere operantis Ecclesiae*, intermediate between that of the *opus operatum* and the *opus operantis individui*. The special *ex opere operantis Ecclesiae* efficacy of the rites instituted by the Church and of the divine office proceeds directly from the fact that these rites and this prayer are in a special way actions of Christ, more so than in the case of prayer that is simply private or, though it be of one or more Christians, still unofficial.

If the basis for the efficacy of every Christian prayer, even private prayer, is always the union of the praying Christian with Christ, as member with Head, by reason of which in every prayer it is always in fact the Church and Christ who pray, it will be necessary to say that this takes place in a higher degree and with a superior quality when this prayer is liturgical prayer. With greater reason and in a wholly eminent way we must apply to liturgical prayer (and to all the liturgical rites instituted by the Church, since, as we know, these are operative essentially after the fashion of prayer) that which St. Augustine says in general about the prayer of a Christian:

> "God could not grant men a greater gift than to give them as their Head the Word through whom He made all things, and to unite them to Him as His members, in such a way that He would be Son of God and Son of man, God together with the Father and Man together with men; and that when we speak to God in prayer we would

[23] *In Io. tract.* 6, 7; see also CL, art. 7.

not separate the Son from God; and that when the body of the Son prays it would not separate the Head from itself; and that it would be the same Lord, Jesus Christ, Son of God, Savior of His body, who would pray for us and pray in us and be prayed to by us. He prays for us as our Priest; He prays in us as our Head; He is prayed to by us as our God. Let us recognize our voice in Him, therefore, and His voice in us. . . . He wanted to make the words of the psalm His own words also, when He hung on the Cross and said, 'My God, My God, why have You forsaken Me?' He is prayed to, then, in the form of God; He prays in the form of a servant; there the Creator, here the created. He took to Himself without change the creature which He was to change, and made us together with Himself a single man: Head and body. We therefore pray to Him, by Him and in Him; we say with Him and He says with us, we say in Him and He says in us the prayer of the psalm. . . . Let no one remark, therefore, when he hears these words, 'It is not Christ who says them' or 'It is not I who say them.' Rather, if he recognizes himself as part of the body of Christ, he must say both 'Christ says them' and 'I say them.' Do not say anything without Him, and He will not say anything without you." [24]

The great idea, then, is that the prayer of the Church is the prayer of Christ, and the prayer of Christ is the prayer of the Church. Christ and the Church, the same St. Augustine remarks somewhere else, because they are bridegroom and bride, are like two in one single flesh:

"From two, they become as one single person, head and body, bridegroom and bride. . . . If they are two in one flesh, why not two in one voice? Let Christ speak, therefore, because in Christ it is the Church who speaks, and in the Church it is Christ who speaks; the body in the Head and the Head in the body." [25]

It is not without reason, then, that the Second Vatican Council, following in the footsteps of St. Augustine and of the encyclical *Mediator Dei*,[26] affirms that the divine Office is in an eminent way the prayer of Christ Himself:

"Jesus Christ, High Priest of the New and Eternal Covenant, taking human nature, introduced into this earthly exile that hymn which is sung throughout all ages in the halls of heaven. He attaches to himself the entire community of mankind and has them join him in singing his divine song of praise.

[24] *Enar. in Ps.* 85:1.
[25] *Enar. in Ps.* 30:4.
[26] MD, no. 144 (Lat. 142): "By assuming human nature, the Divine Word introduced

into this earthly exile a hymn which is sung in heaven for all eternity. He unites to Himself the whole human race and with it sings this hymn to the praise of God."

"For he continues his priestly work through his Church. The Church, by celebrating the Eucharist and by other means, especially the celebration of the divine office, is ceaselessly engaged in praising the Lord and interceding for the salvation of the entire world." [27]

No matter, then, what part of the liturgy be considered: it is always and everywhere Christ who is on the primary level. It is Christ who offers the sacrifice of the Mass; Christ who sanctifies, who distributes His graces, in the sacraments; Christ who prays, who offers praise to the Father, in the sacramentals, in prayer, and in the divine Office. The Church, her ministers, her faithful, are the instruments of Christ in whatever the liturgical action. In the liturgy God does not look upon the men who are acting; He sees only Christ, who acts through men and associates men with Himself.

If we now join to this the express doctrine of the New Testament, in particular that of St. Paul and of the Epistle to the Hebrews, that Christ is Head also of the angels,[28] as well as the mind of the Roman liturgy, which affirms that it is through Christ that the angels themselves praise God,[29] it will easily be understood how Christ is the single "liturgist of the holy places and of the true tabernacle, which the Lord has erected and not a man" (Heb. 8:2) in the heavens; and how He is at the same time the single high liturgist of our terrestrial liturgy who, under the veil of the signs, under this sensible covering adapted to our nature, makes present and actualizes among us that same heavenly liturgy which He is celebrating before His Father.

Always and at every turn we come back to the great concept lived so intensely by the ancient Church and expressed so magnificently by Tertullian when he called Christ the *catholicus Patris sacerdos*,[30] the unique and universal priest, the "Catholic Priest of the Father."

6. Consequences for the Nature of the Liturgy

From what has been explained thus far in the present chapter it is apparent that the liturgy, under the veil of the sensible and efficacious signs of the sanctification and of the worship of the Church, is, in its own more intimate nature, an exercise of the priesthood of the dead and risen Christ, the *Kyrios*, Lord, who in it and through it transmits His own divine life to the world and leads the world back to God.

The liturgy, action of Christ, Lord and Priest. The sanctification of the Church in the liturgy is nothing else but the Christification or the paschali-

---

[27] CL, art. 83.
[28] See, for example, Col. 1:15-20 and Heb. 1:5—2:18. That Christ is the Head of the angels is certain, apart from the question of knowing whether it is also in this sense that

the grace of the angels is the grace of Christ.
[29] *Per quem maiestatem tuam laudant angeli.*
[30] *Adv. Marc.* 4, 9.

zation of the world, effected by Christ the Lord, Mediator and Priest, in the progressive assimilation of the world to Himself.

The worship which henceforth the Church in her liturgy renders to God can be only the act in which Christ the Lord, High Priest, unites the Church to Himself by associating her with Himself in the worship which He renders to God, and in which the Church, by allowing herself to be associated in this process, renders worship to her Head and Bridegroom and is united with Him in the worship which He renders to God.

Our earthly liturgy, viewed from the role which Christ plays in it, is therefore, under the veil of sensible signs, a continual epiphany of the priesthood of Christ now glorious beside the Father, an epiphany which He Himself realizes among us by associating the Church to His priesthood, which is always active. Viewed from the role of the Church, the liturgy is none other than a participation of men in the priestly activity of Christ, ever effective at the side of the Father, from whence Christ continues, in glory, the sacerdotal action which He had begun on earth from the first moment of His incarnation.

It is clear that these affirmations suppose in the liturgical reality an actual presence of Christ which transcends immensely the simple psychological sphere and is based on the hypostatic union, on the doctrine of the mystical body and the *gratia capitis*. In the liturgy Christ's presence is that of a physical reality: in His own person (Eucharist and sacrifice), or at least in His sanctifying power really and physically operative (in the other sacraments, sacramentals, divine Office).

In short, for an understanding of the liturgy it is indispensable to have discovered this truth: that Christ is present there *hic et nunc*, not as an abstract idea, but as a living person and as a living force emanating from a living person: "And therefore He is able to grant perfect salvation to those who approach God through Him, since He is always alive to intercede in their behalf" (Heb. 7:25), and to act in them, through them, and together with them.

Thus, in the liturgical reality, the present sacerdotal action of Christ, which began with the incarnation, is completed on Calvary and is prolonged in the presence of the Father, becomes a reality which enters into us really and presentially. Time is surpassed there, and suspended, so to speak. Christ, His sacrifice, His sanctifying power, His prayer, His action as Mediator with the Father, are present there, really and physically, under the veil of the sensible signs. All men throughout the ages are able to become individually, one by one, by participating in the liturgical reality, contemporaries of Christ; and this in a way of which Kierkegaard, Protestant that he was and totally submerged in the obscurities of psychologism, was unable to have even an inkling. It is not that men escape time and space and return to the time of Christ; but Christ, always living and present, draws men to Himself in the orbit of His priestly, sacrificial, and mediatorial action, which henceforth transcends every space and every time.

In this light we should see as the accurate expression of a reality beyond dispute a certain number of statements about the nature of the liturgy which are often taken in quite another way, as more or less poetical exaggerations of liturgists living far from the real world and from the needs of the modern apostolate. Thus, for example, when we say: the liturgy, under the veil of the sensible signs, is the actualization and the prolongation in space and time of the same priestly and mediating action of Christ, which He initiated on earth and continues now always at the side of the Father — an actualization which is made by Christ in the Church through her means and on her behalf.

In fact, far from being an exaggeration of the liturgists, this notion of the liturgy is simply a repetition in other words of the import of recent official documents of the ecclesiastical magisterium. The Second Vatican Council expresses it thus:

> "To accomplish so great a work Christ is always present in his Church, especially in her liturgical celebrations. He is present in the Sacrifice of the Mass not only in the person of his minister, 'the same now offering, through the ministry of priests, who formerly offered himself on the cross,' [31] but especially in the eucharistic species. By his power he is present in the sacraments so that when anybody baptizes it is really Christ himself who baptizes.[32] He is present in his word since it is he himself who speaks when the holy scriptures are read in the Church. Lastly, he is present when the Church prays and sings, for he has promised 'where two or three are gathered together in my name there am I in the midst of them' (Mt. 18:20).
>
> "Christ, indeed, always associates the Church with himself in this great work in which God is perfectly glorified and men are sanctified. The Church is his beloved Bride who calls to her Lord, and through him offers worship to the eternal Father.
>
> "The liturgy, then, is rightly seen as an exercise of the priestly office of Jesus Christ. It involves the presentation of man's sanctification under the guise of signs perceptible by the senses and its accomplishment in ways appropriate to each of these signs. In it full public worship is performed by the Mystical Body of Jesus Christ, that is, by the Head and his members.
>
> "From this it follows that every liturgical celebration, because it is an action of Christ the Priest and of his Body, which is the Church, is a sacred action surpassing all others. No other action of the Church can equal its efficacy by the same title and to the same degree." [33]

[31] Council of Trent, Session 22: Doctrine on the Holy Sacrifice of the Mass, ch. 2.   [32] Cf. St. Augustine, *Tractatus in Ioannem VI*, ch. 1, n. 7.   [33] CL, art. 7.

Père Roguet, commenting on a similar passage in *Mediator Dei*,[34] observes quite rightly:

> "The Church does not *succeed* Christ; she does not substitute for Him. Not only did Christ institute the worship she renders to God, the sacraments she administers, but He is always present in them, through His assistance to the Church, through His presence in the community, through His sanctifying power. From this truth comes the greatness of the liturgy, work of the Church and work of Christ at the same time. The liturgy is therefore something quite different from a ceremonial or a memorial." [35]

Again, under the veil of sensible signs, the liturgy is simply the continuation and the application to single individuals, in a succession of times and places, of the redemptive action of Christ. And again there is no oral sleight of hand in this, for the purpose of putting the liturgy in a more favorable light. This teaching has been reaffirmed recently and authoritatively by the Second Vatican Council:

> "For it is the liturgy through which, especially in the divine sacrifice of the Eucharist, 'the work of our redemption is accomplished.' " [36]

The encyclical *Mediator Dei* is even more explicit when it says:

> "It is an unquestionable fact that the work of our redemption is continued, and that its fruits are imparted to us, during the celebration of the liturgy, notably in the august sacrifice of the altar. Christ acts each day to save us, in the sacraments and in His holy sacrifice. By means of them He is constantly atoning for the sins of mankind, constantly consecrating it to God." [37]

In these phrases we easily recognize thoughts to which the liturgy itself not infrequently gives expression. Thus, the *Super oblata* prayer for the Second Sunday *per annum*, the same as was formerly designated the *Secreta* for the Ninth Sunday after Pentecost, and which is quoted both by the late council and by the same encyclical,[38] reads as follows:

> "Grant us, O Lord, we pray You, to take part worthily in these mysteries which we celebrate again and again; for every time that this commemorative sacrifice is celebrated, the work of our redemption is wrought." [39]

---

[34] MD, no. 20. See also no. 22: "The priesthood of Jesus Christ is a living and continuous reality through all the ages to the end of time, since the liturgy is nothing more nor less than the exercise of this priestly function."

[35] Roguet's edition of *Mediator Dei*, p. 10.

[36] CL, art. 2, quoting what was at that time a line from the *Secreta* for the Ninth Sunday after Pentecost. The same prayer is found in the present Pauline Roman Missal as the *Super oblata* prayer for the Second Sunday *per annum*.

[37] MD, no. 29.

[38] MD, no. 79 (Lat. 78).

[39] *Quoties huius hostiae commemoratio celebratur, opus nostrae redemptionis exercetur.*

The efficacious celebration of the paschal mystery, the universal objective of the liturgy. The paschal mystery is the whole and integral Christian mystery viewed in its central point which acts as organizer and catalyst for
the liturgy, to which central point all tends and from which all is derived:
Christ's passage, from death to life and His communication with the world.
This communication is made primarily in the efficacious celebration of the
sacred rites.

Thus the paschal mystery is at one and the same time something of the
present, of the past, and of the future, because it is something both historical
and metahistorical, now always in act, and which will be completed in the
future. It is at one and the same time an event, a rite, and a feast. It points
to a singular historical event of the past, its soteriological value transcending
space and time, and the embodiment of this value in an efficacious ritual
celebration, under the veil of sacred signs, for whoever participates therein
with the proper dispositions.

The liturgy has no other aim, no other object, than to celebrate the paschal
mystery in the aforesaid manner.[40] Therefore, every passage, every more
ardent passage from death to divine life by means of the sacred rites, is a
celebration of the paschal mystery.

For this reason in every sacrament and in every sacramental there is celebrated and made visible "the paschal mystery of the Passion, Death, and
Resurrection of Christ" (as well as personal soteriological participation for
all those who take part therein with the proper dispositions). "From this source
all sacraments and sacramentals draw their power."[41]

Baptism has a special claim to being the celebration of the paschal mystery,
because it is in baptism that a man makes his first and fundamental passage
from death to divine life, and his first fundamental assimilation to the dead
and risen Christ (Rom. 6:3-11). Penance is like a new baptism for the already baptized person who has afterwards fallen back into death; and the
anointing of the ill is an extension of penance.

The celebration of the Eucharistic mystery is by a very eminent title the
celebration of the paschal mystery; and all the other sacraments are directed
toward the Eucharist, without reference to which (at least by way of implicit
desire) none of the other sacraments confer grace.[42] Therefore the Eucharistic mystery is "the source of all graces"[43] and the source, then, of every death

[40] See the *Instruction* of September 26, 1964,
n. 7, and the works cited above in notes 3
and 4 of the present chapter.
[41] CL, art. 61.
[42] See St. Thomas, *Summa*, III, q. 79, a. 1,
ad 1; q. 80, a. 11, c. In 4, d. 8, q. 1, ad 1.
[43] *Catechism of the Council of Trent*, trans.
by McHugh and Callan, New York 1949
(11th printing), pp. 241-242: "As, however,
no language can convey an adequate idea of
its (*i.e.*, the Eucharist's) utility and fruits, pas-

tors must be content to treat of one or two
points, in order to show what an abundance
and profusion of all goods are contained in
those sacred mysteries. This they will in some
degree accomplish, if, having explained the
efficacy and nature of all the sacraments, they
compare the Eucharist to a fountain, the other
sacraments to rivulets. For the Holy Eucharist
is truly and necessarily to be called the fountain of all graces, containing, as it does, after
an admirable manner, the fountain itself of

to sin and every resurrection to divine life in us: it is the efficacious paschal celebration *par excellence*. Every Mass is a feast, actually the feast of Easter. Just as there is no Easter without the Mass, so too there is no feast without the Mass.

Therefore every celebration of the Eucharistic mystery is an *anamnesis*, that is to say, an efficacious memorial rite, for the benefit of anyone who participates in it with the proper dispositions; not only is it a memorial of the death but also of the resurrection of the Lord (and this is precisely the meaning of the *anamnesis* in every Mass). "When together we are nourished (with the Body and Blood of Christ) we truly celebrate His Pasch," says St. Athanasius.[44] "The paschal mystery," writes St. John Chrysostom, "has no greater intensity than that which is presently celebrated (in the Mass). It is one and the same. The grace of the Spirit is the same. It is always Easter." [45]

The weekly feast of Easter (i.e., Sunday) and the annual celebration thereof is simply the celebration with particular solemnity and psychological efficacy of the same Easter that is wholly alive in every Mass. Easter is *the* Christian feast.[46] Other feasts simply emphasize in a special way one of its particular aspects.

Thus we see the whole reality of what is implied by those four words of the liturgy, *per Christum Dominum nostrum*. The reality of the dead and risen *Kyrios*, one Priest, one Mediator, one Liturgist who continually celebrates the one liturgy, the paschal liturgy, existing in the world to tear the world away from death and to communicate to it the divine life with which He is filled: *Per ipsum, et cum ipso, et in ipso*.

This being the case, it is not at all extraordinary that the reality of the paschal mystery in Christ Himself and in us should have been strongly emphasized by the Second Vatican Council in its constitution on the sacred liturgy, *Sacrosanctum Concilium*.[47] It regards as urgent our reacquisition of the ancient Church's synthetic, sacral, mystic, and paschal understanding of the events of salvation and of their "celebration" in us, a goal which will be accomplished when we recognize that all these events of salvation are visible and alive in their concrete and universal focal point: Christ, dead and now risen.

celestial gifts and graces, and the Author of all the sacraments, Christ our Lord, from whom, as from its source, is derived whatever of goodness and perfection the other sacraments possess." See also the Encyclical of Leo XIII, *Mirae caritatis, A.S.S.*, Vol. 34 (1901-1902), p. 642: "It is from this same (Eucharist) that the Church draws and maintains all her power and glory, all her adornments of divine charisms, all her perfections." See also *Mediator Dei*, AAS, Vol. 39 (1947), p. 548. Quite rightly does the Roman Missal in the

Super oblata for the feast of St. Ignatius of Loyola, refer to the ". . . most holy mysteries in which You have established the source of all holiness. . . ."

[44] *Epistolae paschales* 4, 5.

[45] *In 1 Tim. hom.* 5, 3.

[46] See Cyprian Vagaggini, *"Pasqua la festa christiana,"* article in *L'Osservatore Romano*, April 22, 1962, p. 3.

[47] See P. Massi, *Il Kerygma pasquale nella costituzione del Vaticano II sulla liturgia*, Ascoli Piceno 1964.

9 THE LITURGY AND THE LAW

OF SALVATION IN COMMUNITY

"To accomplish so great a work [as that of the liturgy]," says the Second Vatican Council, "Christ is always present in his Church. . . . Christ, indeed, always associates the Church with himself in this great work in which God is perfectly glorified and men are sanctified. The Church is his beloved Bride who calls to her Lord, and through him offers worship to the eternal Father. . . . From this it follows that every liturgical celebration, because it is an action of Christ the Priest and of his Body, which is the Church, is a sacred action surpassing all others." [1]

Consequently, the same council is able to assume us: "Liturgical services are not private functions but are celebrations of the Church which is 'the sacrament of unity,' namely, 'the holy people united and arranged under their bishops. Therefore, liturgical services pertain to the whole Body of the Church. They manifest it, and have effects upon it. But they also touch individual members of the Church in different ways, depending on their orders, their role in the liturgical services, and their actual participation in them." [2]

The essentially communitarian nature of the liturgy could not find clearer or more concise affirmation. An understanding of this nature is of prime importance for one who would penetrate and live the liturgy, and make it come alive. And in this regard it is necessary to take into account a general

[1] CL, art. 7.   [2] Ibid., art. 26.

law in the plan of salvation effectively willed by God: the law of salvation in community.

With this law we come to grips with one of the more thorny questions that the liturgy poses to the modern mind: the relationship between the individual and society, between individualism and sociality, in the more jealously intimate area of our piety, our personal relations with God.

The modern spirit, as it has been developing since the late Middle Ages and the Renaissance, tends to emphasize strongly the narrowly individual and personal aspect of our relations with God. It fears every factor which lays claim to a functional intervention in defining the relations between the individual and God. Whether this factor be a person, tangible things, communities themselves, societies, or traditions, the modern mind tends to regard it as an intrusion. Only alone, it seems to modern man, is it possible to safeguard the spontaneity, the sincerity, the vitality, etc., of religious conduct, against the ritualist externalism, the naked mechanics of life, and empty conformism to social customs.

Now, however, to accept the liturgy means the acceptance not only of things that are in fact external and sensible, but even of official ceremonies, presided over by official authorities, who act in the name of the society as such, where the faithful are invited to conform their own religious sentiments to the thoughts and states of mind which are presumed to be those of the whole community, expressed in forms passed on to us from remote generations. All this is more than enough to raise in the modern mind the specter of collectivism, of legalism, of abstractionism, of conformism introduced into the very sanctuary of the religious conscience.

To resolve this problem it is necessary to show how the official and traditional communitarian aspect of the liturgical world not only does not injure the legitimate needs of the individual in the area of religion, but even that these legitimate needs cannot find true nourishment and development except in intimate connection with the liturgical world and even with its official and traditional communitarian character.

1. Protestant Communitarian Dimension and Catholic Communitarian Dimension

It is a common thing to make a strong appeal to the social nature of man as evidence that the individual cannot find his full development, not even his spiritual development, except in forms of religion which are social in character. And it is true enough that the social nature of man is taken into consideration as an explanatory element in respect to the social character of the Catholic religion. But, taken in itself alone, this consideration does not reach to the heart of the problem. The social nature of man does undoubtedly demand that religion in its practical aspects be somehow marked by certain communitarian characteristics; but it is not an adequate basis for determining the degree and the concrete intensity of these social characteristics, nor in particular does it determine in what sense that religion must be social.

To satisfy the social nature of man in the area of religion, that degree of sociality, for example, may be enough that is found in religious worship among the Lutherans, or even that of the Hindu Yogins. But the social character of Catholic worship is immensely more profound than that which could be logically admitted by a Lutheran or even imagined by a Yogin.

For a Protestant the sociality of religion and of worship wears itself out in functioning on the level of the psychology of the individual; for a Catholic, it has a function primarily and essentially of an order much more profound, which, along with theologians, we can term physical or even supernatural,[3] and is only incidentally of the psychological order.

Let me explain. When a Protestant speaks of man's sanctification, he is not talking about a really and physically transforming effect in man himself, nor does he have in mind physical participation in the divine nature, which elevates and physically transforms man to an order of divine being and action; rather, he is speaking only of an effect of the psychological order: a feeling of trust in the mercy of God.

For the Protestant the sacraments are not true and proper instruments of God's grace which, granting the proper dispositions including even the proper psychological dispositions, really produce in the recipient that which they signify; rather, they are but symbols destined to excite in the believer the aforesaid feeling of confidence in the mercy of God. For the Protestant, then, a sacrament functions no differently than a certain kind of preaching.

And what is of special importance, for many Protestants the Eucharist does not really and physically hold Christ; the Mass is not in itself really and physically a sacrifice, the unbloody continuation of the sacrifice of Golgotha, but only a memorial, a remembrance, with the purpose of exciting good feelings in the faithful. Consequently the priesthood, for the Protestant, is not a real and physical sharing in the priesthood of Christ so that the actions of the priest become really and physically instruments in the hands of Christ by means of which He actualizes in the sacrament His own sacrifice and really and physically sanctifies the faithful. The priesthood, for Protestants, is a deputation that a group of men gives to another man so that he may instruct them and excite in them sentiments of piety. The minister of worship in Protestantism is simply a delegate and representative of the community and not really of Christ. Finally, the Protestant community is not a priestly community because the priesthood is not established therein as an

---

[3] *Physical* here and in a theological context is opposed to the *purely moral*, and does not signify *material* or *sensible*.

essential and determinative element. The Protestant community is simply the sum total of the faithful who have fiducial faith. Beyond this sum total of individuals, there is no properly divine element needed to constitute the community.

In such a perspective, then, everything is limited to the narrowly psychological level. And this is why the Protestant cultic assembly does not transcend this level. Here worship is reduced essentially to a sermon, and the communitarian character of the Protestant religion found wholly in the social nature of preaching. It is not by chance that in a Protestant church the principal place is occupied by a pulpit. In the logic of Protestantism, acts of worship and the worshipping assembly are not physically necessary for the transmission of the divine life. In the relations between God and man, in the final analysis, such acts of worship have only a psychological utility which the believer can logically bypass if he finds ways more efficacious for himself. In a word, in Protestantism the community is not the intermediary of divine life itself for the individual, except in the sense that it is a useful means to excite in him right notions and good sentiments, especially the sentiment of fiducial faith.

It can easily be seen how, in the Catholic view of the world, the communitarian character of the religious life is immensely more profound. It belongs to the physical order before it comes into the psychological order, and here, therefore, the individual, in his relations with God, depends in a much more substantial way upon the community. Indeed, in the Catholic view, when it is said that God sanctifies a man, what is meant is that He works a real and physical transformation in his being, allowing him actually to participate in the mode of being and of acting proper to the Divinity. This transformation, however, does not take place without the sacraments, *in re*, or *in voto*.

The sacraments are genuine instruments and channels of grace, and they really effect what they signify. All the sacraments are ordered toward the Eucharistic Sacrifice. The Sacrifice itself does not take place without a sacramental and hierarchical priesthood. And this priesthood is a real and physical participation in the priesthood of Christ, which participation really and physically empowers the hierarchical priest to be His instrument through which Christ actualizes His sacrifice for us in a real but unbloody manner, and thereby really and physically sanctifies men. The hierarchical priesthood is a cause which formally constitutes a group of individuals into a community, i.e., the Church.

Indeed, according to Catholic doctrine, the Church cannot exist without a sacramental and hierarchical priesthood, including always Christ's vicar, the Pope. The Church, therefore, is not just the sum total of those who believe in Christ, but over and above this sum total there is a new element, divine and physical, the sacramental and hierarchical priesthood, conjoined to the

Bishop of Rome, the Sovereign Pontiff. The believers are not a community, they are not the Church, except insofar as they are united to this sacramental and hierarchical priesthood or insofar as they are included beneath it.

In Catholic doctrine the priest is not simply the delegate of the people, nor is he primarily their representative. First of all and essentially he is the delegate and representative of Christ, Head of His mystical body; the priest is empowered by Christ to act in His stead through a special quality belonging not just to the moral or purely juridic order, but to the physical and supernatural order: the priestly character and grace transmitted through the sacrament of orders. Only because the priest is, in the aforesaid manner, the delegate of Christ, Head of the mystical body, is he derivatively the representative also and the delegate of the faithful. This is the doctrine to which the encyclical *Mediator Dei* explicitly calls attention:

> "We deem it necessary to recall that the priest acts for the people only because he represents Jesus Christ, who is Head of all His members and offers Himself in their stead. Hence he goes to the altar as the minister of Christ, inferior to Christ but superior to the people." [4]

That is why, in Catholic faith, it is of necessity that the individual be really included (if not visibly at least invisibly) in the Catholic Church-community, concrete and visible, under the authentic hierarchy; that he be in real contact, at least invisible, with it. Nor does this necessity proceed from a simple utility of the psychological order, for the sake of attaining the more easily to a psychological end, but it is a necessity of the physical order; for without being so included, the individual is physically incapable of participating in the divine life.

Just as without an airplane a man is physically incapable of flying up into the air, so too, in Catholic faith, the religious life of the individual is radically and physically dependent on the Church-community as such, under the legitimate hierarchy. We are far indeed from the Protestant position. To justify so profound a dependence of the religious life of the individual upon the hierarchically structured community, it is not enough to take refuge in the generic social nature of man.

2. Salvation History and Salvation in Community according to Revelation

It is necessary, on the other hand, to consider this matter again under another doctrinal heading, and to remember that the relations between God and man are governed by the law of objectivity: the way by which God descends to man and man goes up to Him has been determined for man in most of its particulars by the free will of God. It but remains for man to conform himself to this free will of God, and to submit himself to it as to

[4] MD, no. 84 (Lat. 83); see also Robert Card. Bellarmine, *De Missa* 2, 4.

a given fact. It is through revelation that we know what God's will is in our regard. It is revelation and that alone which can allow us to know to what extent God has chosen to link the religious life of the individual to his membership and submissive inclusion in a determined society; and if God has also willed to allow us to know something of the reason for this determination, then this knowledge too pertains equally to that revelation to which we must address ourselves.

And in fact, revelation acquaints us with a most important aspect of the aims and plans designed by God in His dealings with men. The aspect of which we speak is this: in communicating His divine life to the world, He has not just willed to draw to Himself a certain number of individuals, each considered separately from the others as so many atoms; rather, it has been His design to found a city, a divine organic society, a people of God, a kingdom of God. Thus, single individuals cannot attain to the supernatural level nor can they reach the mode of existence which God has willed for them; they cannot have a supernatural existence at all, nor can they even develop themselves, except in close connection with and dependence, even physical, upon this community, this people, as God has effectively planned it. This is the law of salvation in community.

An immediate consequence of this law is that, in the supernatural area, conflict between the good of society and the good of the individual is simply impossible, because these two goods formally coincide and, by God's free will, they constitute but a single solitary supernatural good of the individual and of society — or better, of the individual in society.

To prove the reality of this law of salvation in community it would be necessary to explain the theological concept of the people of God, of the covenant, of the kingdom of God, in the Old Testament and in the New. This would be equivalent to explaining the whole theology of history in Christian revelation. It will be enough to recall briefly the main features, emphasizing here and there certain points that are of greater interest in view of our purpose.

The concept of the people of God and of the kingdom of God is present already on the first pages of the Book of Genesis, where it is made clear that in accord with God's design the whole of material creation has been ordered to the establishment and development of those friendly relations between God and men, evidenced in the grace and in the preternatural gifts which our first parents enjoyed prior to their sin.

For the sacred author, that initial state was the ideal point of departure from which mankind would have had to develop itself. For him, that ideal state would have had to be transmitted from Adam to his descendants; and if in fact this has not happened, the fault lies with our first parents themselves, in their having sinned.

Thus, from its very first pages, the Bible views the religious solidarity with Adam, in good or in evil, of all the individual members of the human race, as their factual status willed by God. For the Bible, religiously speaking, between God and every individual human being there is Adam; and there he stands, not only as the font of our physical origin, but also as the religious head of each individual, all of whom are freely constituted by God together with Adam in a solidarity and in a particular society under the royal power of God Himself. The Christian doctrine of original sin and therefore of redemption makes no sense at all without taking as presupposition that God has freely willed that all men be governed by the law of societal salvation in solidarity with a specific individual as head of this society.

This law appears to have been even more decisively applied in the conception of Israel, as it was concretely willed by God. The deeply societal, communitarian, and collective nature of the religion of Israel is a thing much emphasized by all scholars of the Old Testament.[5] In the Old Testament conception, the action of God toward Israel is directed essentially by this idea: God desires not only to concern Himself with the individual, but to shape for Himself a nation, a theocracy. To this people as such is confided the extraordinary mission of being the instrument of the inauguration of the kingdom of God in the world, in accord with the designs willed by God Himself: theirs is the mission of safeguarding the monotheistic faith, of preparing the environment into which the Messiah must be born, of furnishing the first recruits for the messianic kingdom; and of being, as it were, the point of departure from which this kingdom will go forth to conquer the world.

In Israel the individual is not able to participate in the messianic benefits, in part already present but for the greater part belonging still to the future, except as a member of the chosen people. Outside of this inclusion among the people by blood, by faith, by circumcision, by observance of the law, by worship, the individual is completely cut off from the current of life which God imparts. This is, in substance, the conception of the Old Testament, even if it is equally true that the prophets, especially beginning with Jeremias,[6] reacted against the vulgar exaggeration that many in Israel were attempting to make of this concept of communitarian religion and morals, by vindicating the proper rights and duties of the individual in his relations with God.

This prophetic vindication, in fact, was not intended to release the individual from the concept of salvation in community, but to remind him that this communitarian reality does not dispense the individual from the moral responsibilities of internal and heartfelt religion. Thus Israel's strong concept of salvation in community does not mean, as has sometimes been inti-

[5] See, for example, W. Eichrodt, *Theology of the Old Testament*, trans. by J. A. Baker, Vol. II, Philadelphia 1967, pp. 231ff.

[6] See, for example, F. Spadafora, *Collettivismo e individualismo nel Vecchio Testamento*, Rome 1953; A. Gelin, *The Key Concepts of the Old Testament*, New York 1955, pp. 64ff.

mated, that in Israel the religious individuality of each person was completely overwhelmed by the ties of collectivism. What it does mean is simply that, in Israel, the development of the individual religious personality was inconceivable outside the environment of a collectivist framework. In the Old Testament there is no trace of religious individualism understood in the sense of a religious life of the individual that springs up, develops, and achieves its end without some regard for a religious tie with the popular theocracy as such. From the religious viewpoint, society carries the individual, and the individual has value only in the people and in relation to the people.

In the Old Testament a characteristic designation of this theocratic people, besides the *people of God*, is *church of God: q^e hal Yahweh, ekklesía toû theoû*, or *ecclesia Dei* (Deut. 4:8-13; 23:1-9). It means the *assembly* of God, the *meeting* of God, and its import is that Israel is a religious people which, by the free and loving will of God, has been chosen, called, separated from all the others, assembled into a community devoted primarily to worship, and consecrated by God in view of a special mission.[7] Other characteristic expressions employed in the Old Testament to designate Israel as a religious community are: God's possession, His inheritance, holy nation, beloved of God, priestly people, object of God's promises.[8]

The Old Testament clearly announces also how this people of God, at the culmination of the ages when the Messiah will come, will achieve the end of its messianic mission. The prophets predict that when the Messiah will come the people will not grasp the solemnity of the moment, will be disobedient to God and will be unfaithful. Only a small group will remain faithful, the "remnant of Israel," "the seed" of Israel that will remain. They will rally to the Messiah and form around Him a new religious people, the continuation, the spiritual heir and fulfillment of the old unfaithful Israel, that messianic people itself for which it was Israel's mission to prepare.[9]

The Messiah comes and carries out God's plans. And in the New Testament the idea is abundantly clear that these plans, realized by Jesus Christ the Messiah, are none other than those which God had always had, since the creation of man: not just the salvation of individuals, but the creation of a people, of a strongly communitarian society which would be for those individuals the solitary and determinate means of salvation. The Messiah is the new Adam who, by new paths and on an immensely superior level, restores the religious condition of mankind which had been destroyed by the first Adam; and thus, in a way even more marvellous than that of the first

---

[7] See, for example, Karl L. Schmidt, "Ekklesía," in *Theol. Wörterbuch zum N. T.*, Vol. III (1938), pp. 502-539; A. Médebielle, "Église," in *Dict. de la Bible*, Suppl. Vol. II (1934), pp. 488-490; M. C. Matura, "Le Qahal et son contexte cultuel," in *L'Église et la Bible*, Desclée 1962, pp. 9-18.

[8] See, for example, R. Meyer and H. Strathmann, "Laós," in *Theol. Wörterbuch zum N. T.*, Vol. IV (1942), pp. 29-57.

[9] See, for example, S. Garofalo, *La nozione profetica del resto d'Israele*, Rome 1942.

Adam, He appears as the Head of the new mankind, a mankind that is redeemed.[10]

It is thus that in the redemption all men are consolidated with Christ. There is no man from now on who can live the divine life without being united, mysteriously but really, to Christ. This unity, indispensable for a sharing in the divine life, is immensely more profound and real than a purely moral union. Yet, it is not physical, if by physical union one means, for example, such a union as there is between my hand and my body, because the personal individuality of Christ and of the redeemed must remain always distinct. This union is generally termed *mystical*, not by way of denying that it is a union in the physical order, but by way of affirming that it is of the mysterious and supernatural physical order, which preserves intact the distinction of individuals. In the Christian economy it would be absurd to suppose that, religiously speaking, an individual could be born, developed, perfected without this physical-mystical union with Christ and without his complete submission to Christ, as to an objectively given fact willed by God.

But no one can attain to this same union if he does not include himself in the community which Christ founded as His body, His people, His Church. This Church of Christ is simply that people whose formation has always been, according to the Sacred Books, the purpose pursued by God throughout history: *My ekklesía*, Christ calls it; [11] *the ekklesía of God in Christ Jesus*, says St. Paul; [12] and *the new Israel, the Israel of God, the heirs of the promises, the true sons of Abraham*; [13] and *the holy people, the chosen people, the people beloved of God*.[14] All these designations, transferred to the Christian Church from the religious society of the Old Testament, are indicative of the close union between the two communities and the societal character found no less in the new economy than in the old.

Thus, addressing himself to the new Christians, St. Peter is able to say:

> "You are a chosen race, a royal priesthood, a holy nation, a pur-chased people, that you may proclaim the perfections of Him who has called you out of the darkness into His marvelous light; you who once were not a people, but are now the people of God; you who had not obtained mercy, but have now obtained mercy" (1 Peter 2:9-10).

St. Paul insists so strongly on the social, communitarian, organic aspect of the Church that he compares it to a living body, in which not only do the various members cooperate for the good of the whole, but they cannot even

[10] Consider St. Paul in Rom. 5:12-17.

[11] Matthew 16:18.

[12] See 1 Thess. 1:1; 2 Thess. 1:1.

[13] See, for example, Rom. 9-11: Gal. 3:29; 6:16; 1 Cor. 10:18.

[14] See, for example, Rom. 8:27, 33; 1 Cor. 6:1-2; Phil. 4:21; Col. 3:12. For the theology of the people of God in the New Testament see, for example, L. Cerfaux, *La théologie de l'Église suivant S. Paul*, 2nd ed., Paris 1948; Second Vatican Council, Constitution on the Church, *Lumen gentium*, cap. I-II.

exist at all without their being vitally included in the body. And it is this body, this total unity, and not just an aggregate of individuals, which, according to St. Paul, Christ has chosen to form:

> "Christ is Head of the Church, being Himself Savior of the body . . . (who) loved the Church and delivered Himself up for her, that He might sanctify her, cleansing her in the bath of water by means of the word of life; in order that He might present to Himself the Church in all her glory, not having spot or wrinkle or any such thing, but that she might be holy and without blemish" (Eph. 5:23-27).

In the primitive Christian community, as is evident from the Acts of the Apostles, this ecclesial and therefore sacramental and liturgical communitarian dimension of the new religion appears with marvelous strength and freshness. The primitive Christians knew the response of St. Peter on the day of Pentecost to the first converts, when they asked the Apostles, "Brothers, what must we do?" — and how the life of this first group of Christians was described by St. Luke: "And Peter said to them, 'Repent and be baptized every one of you in the name of Jesus Christ for the remission of your sins; and you will then receive the gift of the Holy Spirit.' . . . Now they who received his word were baptized, and on that day the number of the faithful was augmented by about three thousand. And they continued steadfastly in the teaching of the Apostles, in fraternal communion, in the breaking of bread and in prayers. . . . And they continued assiduously every day at the temple in one accord; and in their houses they broke the bread" (Acts 2:38-46). It was crystal clear, therefore, even from the first day, that in the new economy established by Christ, the link between the individual and God is the community and therefore the hierarchy, the sacraments, common prayer, the liturgy; and that for each individual these are the indispensable forms which he must make use of if he desires to find salvation.

Thus, in the transition from the Old Testament to the New, the plans of God in regard to mankind are not changed but fulfilled, even if in a manner much more marvelous than could possibly have been expected by the ancient Israelites. That which God intends is the formation of a people around the Messiah and not just the salvation as such of single individuals. The individuals are called to be included in this people whose Head is Christ. There will be for them no other path to salvation, development, and perfection, except inclusion in the bosom of this people, in harmonious accord with this community. In a word, they must find their own lives in the life of the Church. *Extra Ecclesia nulla salus.*

Nor does this purpose of God of forming for Himself a people reach its conclusion on this earth. It has its culmination in glory, as is described in the Apocalypse. Heaven is not so much a collection of the individual elect as the triumph of a people, the eternal triumphal liturgy of a city, the heavenly Jerusalem, made up of myriads of angels and of the faithful of the Lamb, who celebrate together the cosmic liturgy which will have no end; and they sing: "You have redeemed us, O Lord God, in Your blood out of every tribe and tongue and people and nation, and have made us a kingdom to our God" (an antiphon from Vespers for the Feast of All Saints; cf. Apoc. 7:9-12).

3. Church and Liturgy in the Law of Salvation

While single individuals are on this earth, if they are one day to be enumerated in the book of life when it is reviewed in the heavenly city of Jerusalem, they cannot now do otherwise than see to it that they are included in the Church, as the people of God and the society which God Himself has willed, and which is essentially determined as such by the hierarchical priesthood to which is entrusted the sacrifice and the ministry of the sacraments without which no one can attain to that life which is the only true life, and without which no one can be included in the mystical body of Christ.

By the general law of salvation in community is understood the ultimate dimension of the fact that only such a sacramental and hierarchical priesthood, acting in virtue of its mission, has the power, in the liturgical action, to transform an assembly of men into something immeasurably more profound than an aggregate of many individuals, believers though they be, into the sacral actualization (sacrificial, sacramental, prayerful) of the mystical body of Christ; into that people of God willed by God Himself and listened to by Him, in His whole plan for men; into an *ekklesía* which in the liturgical action is reunited as such to Christ, who is really present in person or in power, under the veil of the sensible signs of His ministers in the liturgical rites. In the liturgical action the single individual participants are actualized or become always more actualized as members of this reality, of the higher and divine order, which is the body of the Church united to its Head and vital principle, Christ.

This is why we say, as we explained in a previous chapter, that in the liturgical reality it is always the Church as such who acts, while her individual members act only insofar as they are her ministers and members, or members only; that is, insofar as they are included in the ecclesial reality, as Church, as family, as people of God. And that is why the divine efficacy of the liturgical action immeasurably surpasses the proper power personally inherent in the individuals who perform that action or who are in attendance thereat.

Once more it is seen that even if in the purely philosophical area there is a diversity of opinions on the question of knowing whether a society is really something more than the mere sum of its individuals or whether it is, on the other hand, simply a legal fiction as such, nevertheless, in the area of the supernatural life there can be no doubt that the Church as such can in no way be reduced to a mere legal fiction; rather, it is something real, which surpasses the sum of its individual members.

The Church is the mystical body of Christ, the characteristic of which is precisely that it immeasurably transcends any purely moral union effected by the sentiments of its numerous individual members and by their tending toward a common extrinsic end. Contrariwise, it is an actuality of the mysterious but nonetheless real order, which, in the framework of a hierarchical structure and through its special powers, really unites the faithful to Christ and the individual faithful among themselves, which leaving intact the distinction of personal individuality. These are mysterious realities, but undeniable ones from the Catholic point of view; and when they have been admitted, then the concept of *opus operantis Ecclesiae*, as has already been explained, becomes perfectly logical.

In conclusion: since the Church is the solitary means of salvation, with a well-defined character, from the Catholic point of view, it would be absurd to regard the proper and official and communitarian aspect of the liturgical world as an impediment to a strongly felt true piety and to the free development of the individual supernatural personality, *such as God wills it in every man*. In fact, that which God asks of each individual (and of this we have certainty through the revelation proposed to us by the Church) is not simply that he respond vibrantly to religion after such fashion as will appear best to the man himself, but that he make a vital and heartfelt personal response in tune with the determinate and absolutely objective realities imposed by God as a precise norm for each subject; and these realities are Christ, lived in the sacrifice, in the sacraments and sacramentals, in the Church: in other words the liturgical reality with its whole objective character, social and official.

Consequently the way to safeguard the spontaneity, the sincerity, the vitality of the religious conduct willed by God and to avoid its mortal enemy which is mechanical compliance, mere ritualism robbed of its vitality, cannot be found in flight from the liturgy or in reducing it to the bare minimum required for remaining within Catholic orthodoxy. The only way, in fact, is to penetrate and to live the liturgical reality in a manner so intense that all the thoughts, sentiments, and the whole life of the individual are impregnated and transformed by this reality.

It demands, in other words, that the Christian, in correspondence to his essentially communitarian supernatural existence, create for himself a communitarian religious psychology, by keeping himself precisely attuned to the objective reality of his nature, and, as regards his religious sensibility, that he not live in disharmony with his religious nature. Without this attunement of sympathies to the communitarian, ecclesial, and sacramental religious entity, the Catholic will not be able to feel fully at ease in the world of the liturgy. He will be tempted to avoid it as much as possible.

On the other hand, if a Catholic does succeed in shaping his religious sensibility in accord with the communitarian dimension of the liturgy, he will then live every day the dogma of the mystical body of Christ to the fullest; nor will he run the risk, not at all imaginary, of reducing this reality to a disembodied relationship on the level that is purely psychological and individual, even individualistic, between Christ and the believers, and between all believers among themselves, independent of and outside the ecclesial reality concretely willed by God.

And thus, in the final analysis, we are brought back again to the great law of objectivity: the way by which we are to go to God is imposed upon us by God Himself, and was freely determined by Him in its particulars. Now, this way is not only Christological-Trinitarian, but societal, ecclesial, hierarchical, and therefore liturgical. This is why in the order effectively willed by God, the individual, outside of the liturgical ecclesial community, is able neither to be born, to live, to develop himself, nor to achieve his end. To understand this reality and to attune one's own psychology and one's own sensibility to it is the only possible way of living the liturgy.

4. The Ritual Expression of the Communitarian Nature of the Liturgy; Its History and Its Present Status

Theologically speaking, every liturgical action is always of a profoundly communitarian nature. And this is the case even when, for instance, it is performed by a single individual with no others present, as in the private recitation of the breviary. This is a fact which tends naturally to manifest itself even in ritual expression; and in some way the nature of the liturgy demands this, just as the essence of a thing demands its own natural perfection.

The more perfect fruit of this tendency is the liturgical assembly,[15] as concrete expression of the ecclesial community [16] in the act itself which constitutes it and manifests it in the highest degree.[17]

[15] For an ample biblical-liturgical explanation of the assembly see P. Massi, L'assemblea del populo di Dio, Ascoli Piceno 1962; see also A. G. Martimort, "L'assemblée liturgique mystère du Christ," in La maison Dieu, n. 40 (1954), pp. 5-29; and also Martimort, The Church at Prayer, Desclée 1968, pp. 77-106.

[16] The sacraments and in a special way the Eucharist are certainly performed by the Church; but it is also true, under another aspect, that they make the Church. For the special function of the Eucharist under this aspect see, for example, N. Afanassief, "Le sacrement de l'assemblée," in Inter. Kirche Zeitschr., Vol. 46 (1957), pp. 382-396. Also of Afanassief, "L'Église qui préside dans l'amour," in La primauté de Pierre dans l'Église orthodoxe, Neuchâtel 1960, pp. 8-14; S. Strottmann, "Sur le sacrifice eucharistique fondement du rassemblement des croyants," in Irénikon, Vol. 33 (1961), pp. 41-55; L. Lécuyer, Le sacrifice de la nouvelle alliance, Le Puy 1962, pp. 199-226.

[17] The idea that the liturgical celebrations, in their natural communitarian and ritual perfections, and in a special way the celebrations

The term assembly here means the convocation, meeting, and efficacious celebration in Christ the Lord, dead and now risen, of the people of God as the living organism composed of its various hierarchically structured members, all of whom have their own roles to perform, as parts of the whole, but each in his own capacity, in his own time and in his own function,[18] without usurping that which pertains to the others, but also without being either physically or spiritually isolated from them.

The laws of the liturgical celebration [19] depend upon this conception of the liturgical assembly.[20] The history of the communitarian dimension in the ritual expression of the liturgy is the history of the observance or of the neglect of the laws of the assembly in its individual rites.

In point of fact, in the course of the centuries there is observable in this ritual expression, and especially though not solely in the Roman liturgy, an obscuring or even a diminution of that communitarian character of the liturgy. This has come about through the suppression of ancient rites which emphasized the communitarian character of the liturgy, through the reservation of some of these rites and prayers to the clergy alone, whereas originally they pertained to the whole community; and finally, through the infiltration of elements of private devotion which conform poorly to the original communitarian character of the liturgy.

In the Mass

In particular the communitarian nature of the essential liturgical structure of the Mass, as well as the history of its being obscured since the fourth and fifth centuries and especially in the West in the Middle Ages, has been treated quite substantially in two works, already classics in their field, of Dom Gregory Dix [21] and of Father Josef A. Jungmann.[22]

In these works one can discover how the Mass by its very nature and by its ritual structure is essentially an action of the whole ecclesial community, and most especially of that part which is present *hic et nunc*. What is treated of is, of course, the action of a community differentiated and hierarchically

of the Eucharistic mystery, are the principal manifestation of the Church, has been strongly emphasized by the Second Vatican Council: "Therefore all should hold in the greatest esteem the liturgical life of the diocese centered around the bishop, especially in his cathedral church. They must be convinced that the principal manifestation of the Church consists in the full, active participation of all God's holy people in the same liturgical celebrations, especially in the same Eucharist, in one prayer, at one altar, at which the bishop presides, surrounded by his college of priests and by his ministers" (CL, art. 41). Article 2 speaks in much the same sense when it describes the liturgy as the *epiphany par excellence* of the Church.

[18] See A. G. Martimort, *The Church at Prayer*, Desclée of 1968, pp. 90-107.

[19] See J. A. Jungmann, *The Liturgy of the Word*, Collegeville 1966.

[20] The norms themselves for liturgical reform so clearly delineated by the Second Vatican Council (CL, art. 26-40) are based on the concept that the liturgical celebration is an action of the assembly. See especially articles 27-28, 30-34, and 36.

[21] *The Shape of the Liturgy.*

[22] *The Mass of the Roman Rite.*

organized into its individual members and its individual ranks, each having its own specific part to play, without a confusion and without an equalization of roles. Nevertheless, it is always a unified action of a single community whose members are all active in working out a single drama which concerns all and in which all have an active role, each in his own way. In ancient times, therefore, there was no conception at all of some members or of some ranks of the community being present at the Mass only as spectators or simply as listeners. Still less was it conceivable that they should be occupied in meditation or private prayer with no connection or at best with but a loose connection with the action that was being dramatized as the action of all.

It is well known how, prior to the fourth century, this ritual structure of the Mass which expresses the latter's intrinsic nature as an action of the whole community, manifested itself in a number of different ways. And for the most part, as the reader will observe, these more ancient usages have now been restored, in the liturgical reforms subsequent to the Second Vatican Council, and dependent upon the legislatory actions thereof. In the early Church, for example, and prior to the fourth century, the prayers were said in a loud voice, audible to all present; and so they are again. There existed no "secret" prayer, neither for the priest nor for those present; nor does there any longer, to any extent that could be considered an abuse. There was no superimposition of prayers, of singing, and of other rites, as happened when the priest recited a prayer or a formula while the choir busily sang something else, or when the choir sang something which had no direct relationship to what the priest was doing; and again, the more ancient usage in this regard has for the most part been restored since Vatican II, so that what might be termed abuses of long standing exist no longer.

The parts sung or read for all were sung or listened to by all present, the priest included. The celebrant did not read privately for himself the parts being sung by all or read to all by the deacon or the lector; and this too is once more our present custom, the abuses of intervening years having been set aside in the reforms subsequent to Vatican II.

The prayers themselves were always prayers for all who were present, said in the name of all, either for all the brethren or for all men, or for all classes of men. There were no prayers in which the priest prayed in his own name or for himself alone, not even in respect to the sacrificial act which he was performing; and in general we can say that what changes may have crept into this structure over the years have been obliterated since Vatican II.

The language of the Mass was understood or was presumed to be understood by those present. When this supposition was no longer verified, there was no great delay in changing the language, as was in fact done at Rome, it seems, in the course of the fourth century. Since the Mass is not the prayer of the priest alone who celebrates it, but of the whole community which assists, it seemed obvious enough that it ought to be in the language which the community understood. Again, this was the reasoning of Vatican II in permitting certain restorations of vernacular usage. If in Christian antiquity, for a certain time and in certain places, the Mass continued to be celebrated in a language not understood by the people, the only reason for this was that in these instances the vernacular was not a literary language and there were not even as yet translations of the sacred books available in it.

The bishop, or whatever priest celebrates in his stead, before beginning a prayer said in the name of all, addresses the assembly with a phrase such as: "The Lord be with you"; "Let us give thanks to God"; "Let us pray"; "Peace be with you"; or some similar formula. At the end of the prayer recited in the name of all the people, all the people made it their own and explicitly ratified it with their "Amen." These customs too, insofar as they had fallen into disuse, have now been restored. And perhaps the congregation's ratification of the prayer is most apparent now, even as it was in early times, in the great Eucharistic Prayer of the Mass, the anaphora. Only the bishop or the priest who takes his place has the right to recite the Canon. Only he can consecrate the offerings by saying this great eucharist. In it he repeats that which Christ did, in His place and as His representative. Yet here too the whole people is associated in the prayer and ratifies it in its final "Amen."

Even in the communion rite those who received the body and blood of Christ from the bishop or the deacons responded to the proper formula, recited by the minister, with their "Amen"; and this usage too has now been restored.

The people were gathered about the altar; and the altar was not relegated to a remote part of the church, far from those assisting, so that they could see scarcely or not at all what was being done thereon. The altar was not hidden from the people. Again, the developmental changes which had taken place over the years and which militated against these ancient usages have largely been obliterated since Vatican II.

The Church of the earliest centuries could not imagine assisting at Mass without receiving Communion. All who assisted communicated because Communion is essentially and in the most profound sense the rite of participating in the sacrificial banquet. Indeed, it would be a strange way of "participating" in a common sacrificial meal to which one had been invited, or at a convivial sacrifice, which is precisely what the Mass is, if one were to come there only to watch the others eat. Communion was taken to those who were absent and unable to attend, precisely so that they might be able to participate in the fulfillment of the sacrifice.[23] In the modern Church con-

[23] See St. Justin the Martyr, *First Apology* 65 (Jurgens, no. 128).

siderable progress has been made in encouraging frequent reception of Communion ever since the time of St. Pius X.

In the third century the rite of the offering by the whole people made its appearance. The people offered to the priest the matter of the sacrifice which he then would consecrate. This placed a strong emphasis upon the communitarian character of the Eucharistic action: all offered, all communicated, even if only the celebrant might consecrate. This practice was maintained in the West until the eleventh century and even afterwards; [24] and now, after long centuries of disuse, it has been re-introduced as an optional rite in the Roman liturgy, under the form of the offertory procession in which the gifts are presented at the altar.

Another remarkable expression of the communitarian character of the Mass was found in the Roman custom (adopted at times by other bishops elsewhere) of the *fermentum*, according to which on festive days as a sign of union the Pope sent to the parish priests of Rome and to the bishops of the suburbicarian sees a fragment of the Bread he had just consecrated in his solemn Mass. The parish priests and the bishops then placed this fragment in the chalice of the sacrifice which they themselves were celebrating. This custom continued at Rome until the ninth century.[25] Fortunately the Second Vatican Council and its post-conciliar commissions showed in this instance that they were above any naked antiquarianism and refrained from restoring this rite.

Whoever was not part of the ecclesial community was not permitted to assist at the Mass. The Mass is the act *par excellence* of the ecclesial community; and it was the exclusive property thereof.

Essentially a communitarian action, the Mass remains always a differentiated action, in which each participant has his own specific role. It is the action of all, but in various ways. St. Clement of Rome was obliged to insist on this point in countering the disorders of the community in Corinth:

> "We ought to do in proper order all those things which the Master has commanded us to perform at stated times. He has commanded the offerings and the services (*prosphoràs kai leitourgías*) to be celebrated, and not carelessly nor in disorder, but at fixed times and hours. He has, moreover, by His supreme will, determined where and by whom He wants them to be carried out, so that all may be done in a holy manner, according to His good pleasure and acceptable to His will. Those, then, who make their offerings at the appointed times, are acceptable and blessed; for they follow the laws of the Master and do not sin. To the high priest, indeed, proper ministrations are allotted, to the priests a proper place is appointed, and upon the levites their proper services are imposed. The layman is bound by the

---

[24] See Righetti, Vol. III, pp. 248ff.   [25] *Ibid.*, pp. 404ff.

> ordinances for the laity. Let each of us, brethren, in his own rank, be well-pleasing to God and have a good conscience, not over-stepping the defined rules of his ministration (*leitourgías*) — in dignity." [26]

It will be observed how far this text is from the Protestant mentality which equalizes the powers of all in the liturgical action.

A more complete expression of the Mass as a unified action of the ecclesial community and showing the differentiation in rank willed by Christ is to be found in the ancient custom, which, however, could not be maintained for very long by reason of the practical necessities imposed by the increase in the numbers of the faithful, according to which in each local community, even on Sundays, there was permitted only one Mass, and that presided over by the bishop surrounded by his presbytery, by the deacons, by the other clerics and by all the people.

St. Ignatius of Antioch is a wonderful and most eloquent spokesman of this ideal:

> "You must all follow the bishop as Jesus Christ follows the Father, and the presbytery as you would the Apostles. Reverence the deacons as you would the command of God. Let no one do anything of concern to the Church without the bishop. Let that be considered a valid Eucharist which is celebrated by the bishop, or by one whom he appoints. Wherever the bishop appears, let the people be there; just as wherever Jesus Christ is, there is the Catholic Church. Nor is it permitted without the bishop either to baptize or to celebrate the agape; but whatever he approve, this too is pleasing to God, so that whatever is done will be secure and valid." [27]

> "Just as the Lord, being one with the Father, never did anything without Him either in His own person or through His Apostles, so you also must not do anything without the bishop and the priests. In vain will you try to make anything appear praiseworthy which you have done privately on your own account; only that which you do in common is praiseworthy. One prayer, one supplication, one mind, one hope animated by love, in the joy without blemish — such is Jesus Christ, whose excellence is beyond comparison. Hasten together, all of you, to one temple, to one altar, that is, to Jesus Christ, who is one and who, proceeding from the one Father, has remained one with Him and has returned to Him." [28]

> "Take care, then, to use one Eucharist, so that whatever you do, you do according to God: for there is one Flesh of our Lord Jesus Christ, and one cup in the union of His Blood; one altar, as there is one bishop with the presbytery and my fellow servants, the deacons.

---

[26] St. Clement of Rome, *Letter to the Corinthians* 40, 1–41, 1 (Jurgens, nos. 19–19a).

[27] St. Ignatius of Antioch, *Letter to the Smyrnaeans* 8 (Jurgens, no. 65).

[28] St. Ignatius of Antioch, *Letter to the Magnesians* 7.

In this way all that you do will be done in accord with the will of
God." [29]

Again we see how far the ancient Church was from the fundamental
presupposition of every logical Protestant: that of the essential self-sufficiency
of each individual in respect to all other individuals in their relations with
God. In the ancient Church there was a strong consciousness that the individual outside the hierarchically structured *ekklesía* was, from the supernatural point of view, absolutely nothing. Equally strong was the consciousness that the greatest expressive and efficacious ritual sign of this *ekklesía*
is none other than the participation of all the people in a single Eucharist,
a single prayer, a single supplication, in a single spirit, in a single hope and
charity, gathered around a single altar where the bishop presides in person,
as head of each local community, surrounded by the college of presbyters and
by the deacons. Here all the faithful assemble, united among themselves,
because they participate in a single Bread and in a single Cup which unites
them in the single Flesh and in the single Blood of the Lord Jesus.

In this perspective we can better appreciate what the celebration signifies,
with the whole ecclesial community gathered around its own bishop and,
by analogy, the liturgical celebration carried out by the lesser ecclesial community, the parish, gathered around its own pastor, the delegate and representative of the bishop, and the liturgical celebration or concelebration of the
universal ecclesial community, at least in its representatives, carried out
around the Pope, as can be seen on some occasions at St. Peter in Rome. It
also makes it more evident how the bishop is first and foremost the liturgist
par excellence of a local community, and why it must be regarded today as
a desirable thing that all, hierarchy and faithful, should reacquire something
of this ancient sense of the *ekklesía* in its communitarian liturgical expression
in order to re-vivify the communitarian and sacral dimension of the Church.
It is not without reason, therefore, that the Second Vatican Council has
forcefully confirmed these ideas.[30]

Unfortunately, it cannot be denied — Dix and Jungmann have already
documented its essential details — that everywhere, beginning with the
fourth century, and especially in the West in the Middle Ages, the sense of
the Mass as the action of the whole community, differentiated in its hierarchical structure, underwent in its liturgical expression and therefore also in the
psychology of the faithful, a notable diminution and was gradually obscured. Thus there were born those anomalies and contrasts between the
profoundly communitarian nature of the liturgical reality which is carried
out in the Mass, and its ritual and rubrical expression, such as are observable
to some extent even in the Mass in its present state. [This last remark was

[29] St. Ignatius of Antioch, *Letter to the Phil-
adelphians* 4 (Jurgens, no. 56).

[30] See CL, art. 41, cited above in note 17 of

the present chapter, in which the spirit of the
texts of St. Ignatius of Antioch, cited above,
is recaptured.

written prior to the promulgation of the Pauline Roman Missal; and while it may not be totally unjustifiable even at the present time, certainly today the anomalies of which Dom Vagaggini speaks are not nearly so notable as they may have been when he wrote.]

In the East, for example, as early as the fourth century and as found in the Sacramentary of Serapion, there appears a series of prayers to be said in the Mass by the priest alone; and this, of course, other than the great Eucharistic Prayer, which was always reserved to him. Thus the part reserved to the clergy alone was augmented. In the fourth century the offering made by the people was discontinued. In the East alone the placing of an iconostasis before the altar began to be the custom; and it continued to be enlarged until at last it ended up by hiding the altar more or less completely from the eyes of the people, and especially at the most solemn moment of the anaphora when the center doors were closed. Afterwards the custom was introduced by which the priest recited the prayers for all secretly and in a low voice (while the deacon and the people sang the litanies or other chants) only raising his voice at the final conclusion (*ekphónesis*) so that the people might answer with their "Amen." And above all, also in the East, the custom was introduced by which the priest recited secretly the whole of the anaphora, except for some *ekphonéseis*.

Nevertheless, all things considered, it seems to be undeniable that this lessening of the communitarian dimension of the Mass was even more notable in the West than in the East. The principal facts which would seem to demonstrate this point in regard to the West are:

a) the liturgical language was one which was no longer understood by the people;

b) the development of the low Mass and its extraordinary multiplication in some periods of the Middle Ages;

c) the fact that in these same low Masses there was present a server who was both able and obliged to respond to the celebrant even with those parts which of their very nature were intended for all the people — all of which was quite natural; but then it came about that he was regarded as the only one who had the right to make these responses, even when there were other participants in attendance, and even when the latter were present in considerable numbers; and thus the people were perforce prohibited from exercising their natural right of active participation at the sacrifice;

d) the introduction into the Mass itself not only of prayers said silently but even of prayers of an emphatically private character, in which the priest prays for himself and in his own name; [31]

---

[31] These prayers, of medieval Gallican origin, were nearly all concentrated at the entrance, at the offertory, and at the communion of the Mass. At the entrance there was the *Judica me, Deus*; *Introibo ad altare Dei*; *Adjutorium nostrum*; *Confiteor*; *Misereatur*; *In-*

e) the canon recited in a low voice;

f) in sung Masses, not merely the permission but the actual obligation on the part of the celebrant of reciting privately in a low voice those parts sung by all the people or read for all by the deacon or subdeacon or lector;

g) as in the East, the suppression of the offering made by the people; and also as in the East, a lessening in frequency and, in certain periods, the almost total absence of the Communion of the people;

h) Communion given outside of Mass even to those assisting at Mass;

i) execution by the *schola cantorum* even of those parts which ought to have been sung by the people; for when the music became more difficult, the people were no longer able to sing it. This was true even of Gregorian Chant when it became more florid around the eleventh and twelfth centuries, but was much more the case when polyphonic Masses began to be composed;

j) a growing custom on the part of the people of reciting, during Mass, other private prayers having either no connection at all or, at best, only a remote connection with the Mass at which they were assisting;

k) the prohibition, which lasted for a long time, of translating the Missal,

dulgentiam; *Deus, tu conversus*; *Ostende nobis*; *Domine, exaudi orationem meam*; *Aufer a nobis*; and *Oramus te, Domine*. At the Offertory: *Suscipe, sancte Pater*; *Deus, qui humanae substantiae*; *Offerimus tibi*; *In spiritu humilitatis*; *Veni, Sanctificator*; *Incensum istud*; *Lavabo inter innocentes*; *Suscipe, sancta Trinitas*; *Orate, fratres*; and the *Suscipiat*. At Communion: *Domine Iesu Christe, qui dixisti*; *Domine Iesu Christe, Fili Dei vivi*; *Perceptio Corporis tui*; *Panem coelestiam accipiam*; *Domine, non sum dignus*; *Corpus Domini nostri Iesu Christi*; *Quid retribuam Domino*; *Sanguis Domini nostri Iesu Christi*; *Quod ore sumpsimus*; *Corpus tuum, Domine*. Almost all of these prayers were in the singular; and even those said in the plural refer primarily to the priest himself. For the most part they are the *apologies*, so-called "because they are presented as a kind of confession or accusation which the priest makes to God, to excuse himself for his rashness in celebrating mysteries so august; and therefore they are, as it were, a protestation of unworthiness on account of his own sins, which are indicated generically or specifically. . . . The apologies, being the expression of personal sentiments, which, whatever their propriety, occupy the priest at certain moments of the Mass, are expressed in the singular, and are recited by him in a low voice, with a bow and with hands joined, quite apart from the assembly present there; they are addressed to Christ or to the Most Blessed Trinity, are rather purposeless in themselves, but in most instances tend to be of an expository nature, accompanying a formula, a gesture, or a liturgical ceremony, or are intended to occupy the priest piously during the schola's singing. All of these elements are in neat contrast with the liturgical customs of the ancient Church" (Righetti, Vol. III, pp. 144ff). In the reforms subsequent to Vatican II, nearly all of the prayers cited above have been expunged from the Mass; and of the few that remain in one way or another, nearly all have been reworded and are said in an audible voice, so that the former objections are no longer valid. If there remains in the Mass one or the other short "secret" prayers at the time of the celebrant's own reception of the sacrificial elements, these can scarcely be objected to by any reasonable persons. Not every change that comes about in the Mass in the course of time is to be termed an abuse; and there are such things as legitimate developments. Otherwise, we shall have to go back to saying Mass in Greek — or perhaps real purists would prefer Aramaic.

and more especially the ordinary of the Mass, into the vernacular. Thus the laity were reduced to "assisting" at Mass as mere silent spectators.[32] There is no need to insist further. True, many medieval abuses were eliminated or lessened by the reform of Pope St. Pius V in 1570 and by later reforms. Still, a certain number of abuses remained even to our own times, when the liturgy was still celebrated in a language not understood by the people and the canon was recited in such a way as not to be heard by those present. The problem of our times was one of bringing the people back to an active participation in the Mass as an action of the whole community.

Anyone who understood the incomparable theological, spiritual, and pastoral strength of the liturgy, could not but rejoice in the fact that the Second Vatican Council faced this problem squarely and with a wonderfully decisive and apostolic boldness that could only derive from a profoundly supernatural overview. The Council courageously established such basic principles as made it reasonably possible to predict that an effective solution to the problem would not be long in coming.[33] In fact, in the years since Vatican II, many of these reforms have already been carried out and others are even now in process. What might also have been predicted, however, can now be seen by all: that reforms in external matters and in rites, however important they may be, are not enough. External reforms have been carried out very well, one might almost say ruthlessly; but where is the reform of hearts that is even more necessary? In their eagerness to strain out all the gnats (abuses), have the liturgists spilt and lost the precious wine — the devotion, faith and fidelity of the people? As the external ritual becomes more refined and sophisticated, the percentage of Catholics in attendance dwindles, while the moral imperatives of pure and holy living have gone with the wind.

In the other sacraments

Something similar to what has just been said in regard to the Mass in respect to the ritual expression of its communitarian nature might also be said in regard to the sacraments. The intrinsic communitarian nature in each of the individual sacraments is no less evident than it is in the Mass. The sacraments, in fact, are something ecclesial, because they are the instruments of the grace by means of which, supernaturally speaking, the

[32] For more historical details on this evolution, see the excellent treatment by Jungmann in his *The Mass of the Roman Rite*, Vol. I, pp. 74-159 in particular. And again, we must note that while not every historical development in the liturgy is to be regarded as a departure from pristine integrity and an abuse, it is obvious enough that most of the developments noted above were in fact abuses, or easily lent themselves to abuse. While many of these developments persisted even up to the time of the Second Vatican Council, such of them as were clearly abuses have mostly been rectified in the conciliar and post-conciliar reforms.

[33] Of particular importance and interest in the Constitution on the Liturgy, *Sacrosanctum concilium*, are articles 26-42, 54, 57, and 118.

faithful are born, are nourished, are protected and perfected by the Church and in the Church, as organic members of the people of God, hierarchically structured and differentiated.

Thus baptism is not only the supernatural regeneration of an individual (Rom. 6:1-14) and his adoption as a son of God, but at the same time it is also and necessarily his visible initiation into the body of Christ which is the Church, thereby effecting his supernatural organic union with the other differentiated members of the same body. Nor does baptism constitute union with Christ, except in the Church and by means of the Church, hierarchically structured and differentiated.

Confirmation is not only the supernatural perfecting of an individual; it is also a perfecting of his being included in the people of God.

Penance is not only the reconciliation of an individual with God, but at the same time it is also and necessarily his reconciliation with the Church, with the community of the brethren whom the sinner offended and injured at the same time that he offended God.

That holy orders and matrimony have a deeply communitarian character is obvious and well-known, since they are destined immediately to provide for the material and spiritual multiplication of Christian society and for the formation of its hierarchical structure.

It would not be difficult for the historian to show how in the administration of these sacraments the ancient ritual expression brought their communitarian nature under strong emphasis, and how, contrariwise, in the practice of recent centuries, in consequence of various historical developments, this communitarian expression was frequently somewhat diminished or even obscured; as a result, in some cases the communitarian aspect has become clouded over in the psychology of the faithful.

For baptism and confirmation we have but to recall the ancient ritual of Christian initiation, performed solemnly only once or twice in the year, during the vigils of Easter and Pentecost, in the presence of the ecclesial community of the place presided over by the bishop who, as head of the ekklesía, introduced new members into the sacred community of the brethren. In such an atmosphere there was a very lively sense of the significance of the act of Christian initiation as an act of Holy Mother Church, who gives birth to new members; of the body of Christ, which aggregates to itself new cells; of the annual conscription of Christ's holy army.

If, on the other hand, we think of the usual manner in which baptism is administered, it will be obvious that there has been a diminution, in our psychological outlook, of its value as act of initiation and of entrance into an ecclesial community, an act which is of interest to the community as a whole. Today in a baptism, even in the best Christian families, everything seems to be limited to the concept of the regeneration of a soul or, if you will, to a family festival. The communitarian ecclesial aspect which the ceremony carries with it is barely perceived.[34]

Penance is the sacrament which for us has the most studiously private character. The whole is limited to a matter between ourselves and God, in which the priest, it is true, acts as intermediary and as minister, but in which we perceive only with difficulty anything of a communitarian ecclesial character. In the administration of the sacrament of penance, everything is private and secret: private confession, private absolution, private penance.

Contrariwise, in antiquity and up to the period of the sixth to the eighth centuries, when a change in discipline in regard to penance was effected, we find no sure evidence — the opinions of some to the contrary notwithstanding — of private sacramental penance for other than private sins, while there is ample evidence of public penance for public sins. This discipline of public penance involved confession, which, at least implicitly, was public for grave and notorious sins,[35] which were submitted for deliberation to the ecclesiastical assembly presided over by the bishop with his presbyters and deacons and in the presence of the people;[36] the excommunication of the sinner who "has sinned so grievously that he is cut off from communication in prayer and assembly and from every holy transaction";[37] public works of penitence or satisfaction, among which was the custom of prostrating oneself with tears not only before the bishop and the presbyters, but even before all the brethren of the community;[38] the public reconciliation accorded by the bishop in the presence of the whole community of the brethren, as a re-admission to peace not only with God, but also and necessarily with the Church and with the brethren.

Basic to this discipline, of course, is the concept that sin is not only an offense against God but also and at the same time an offense damaging to the whole *ekklesía*, which, therefore, is a thing of concern to the whole community. Thus, in regard to fornication, Origen was able to say:

---

[34] See the description of the present-day situation and some pastoral suggestions for remedying it in *"Le baptême entrée dans le peuple de Dieu,"* in *La maison Dieu*, n. 32 (1952), pp. 118-166. [Translator's note: Some progress in re-establishing the communitarian aspects of baptism has been made and gives every indication of continuing, in the few years since Dom Vagaggini wrote the above paragraph. The revised rite of baptism is well under way, only a few aspects of it yet remaining indefinite at this moment. It gives every indication of successfully overcoming the less laudatory aspects of what is outlined above.]

[35] Implicitly public, since the fact of submitting oneself to the assembly's deliberation and decision, with the bishop presiding, and of subjecting oneself to public satisfaction was equivalent to public confession. On the other hand, confession of secret sins was conducted in secret, before the bishop (and later, the priest) alone. Some helpful early references may be Origen, *Homilies on the Psalms*, Ps. 37[38]: Hom. 2, 6 (Jurgens, no. 485a); Socrates, *Hist. eccl.* 5, 19, with the parallel passage in Sozomen, *Hist. eccl.* 7, 16.

[36] See, for example, Righetti, Vol. III, p. 129.

[37] Tertullian, *Apology* 39, 4 (Jurgens, no. 281).

[38] See, for example, Righetti, Vol. III, pp. 131ff.

"It is not permitted me to take a member of Christ and make it a member of a prostitute. Say to it (your evil desire): I have become a temple of God; it is not permitted me to introduce anything unclean, nor is it right for me to violate the temple of God. And also: he who commits fornication sins against his own body; not only against this body which has become a temple of God, but also against that body of which it is said that the whole Church is Christ's body. He who soils his own body sins against the whole Church, since through one member the stain spreads throughout the body." [39]

In this light it is easily understood that the sin of any one member of the Church and the reconciliation of the sinner are matters of supreme interest to the whole community.

[Many of the author's desiderata are part of the new *Ordo Paenitentiae*; this reform of the sacrament of penance has now been promulgated in the United States.]

All the members of the community, therefore, each in his own way and in accord with the nature and the exigencies of the hierarchically differentiated structure of the *ekklesía*, the body of Christ, were able to intervene in the judgment and re-admission of the sinner. That is why Tertullian exhorted the penitents in this fashion:

"These are brethren and fellow servants, who share with you the same hopes, fears, joys, sorrows, sufferings, because they have in common with you the spirit of a common Lord and Father. Then why do you regard them as strangers? Why do you flee from the partners of your misfortunes as you would from those who would deride? The body is not able to take pleasure in the trouble of one of its members. It must necessarily grieve as a whole and join in laboring for a remedy. With one and two individuals, there is the Church; and the Church, indeed, is Christ. Therefore, when you cast yourselves at the knees of the brethren, you are dealing with Christ, you are entreating Christ. In the same way, when they shed tears over you, it is Christ who suffers, Christ who implores the Father. When it is a son who asks, the request is always more easily granted." [40]

---

[39] Origen, *Homilies on Josue*, Hom. 5, 6.

[40] Tertullian, *Repentance* 10, 4-7 (Jurgens, no. 316). Something of the communitarian aspect of penance existed in the Church in the United States until comparatively recent times. In many dioceses it was the custom that when a young couple attempted marriage outside the Church, before being re-admitted they were obliged, at the time of the homily during the High Mass on a Sunday morning, to stand before the communion rail in the front of the church, turn and face the congregation, and beg the pardon of all for the scandal they had given to the community. This horrible custom lasted well into the 1920's and 1930's. Certainly it was a marvelous expression of the communitarian character of the Church; but I [the translator is writing this note] doubt that any reasonable person would want it revived. In more recent years some efforts have been made in this country toward communal penance services, and in practice they take many forms. It is not improbable that the communal penance service, so long as the rather obvious abuses to which it might lead are precluded, can be found quite beneficial.

It is also known that in ancient times, at least in some places, the communitarian character of the sacrament of holy orders was rendered even more evident than it is today, through the effective intervention of the whole concerned community in the designation of candidates for the episcopate, priesthood, and diaconate of a specific church. Something of this is still in evidence today in the posting of the banns before diaconate and priesthood, and in the investigations that precede episcopal election.

In the rite of the sacrament of matrimony the expression of its communitarian nature has been maintained substantially intact; and in a certain respect it has even been strengthened — by the prescribing of an obligatory form and by the declaring of clandestine marriages invalid. Nevertheless, in certain regions and in certain classes of society, there is a strong tendency to avoid as much as possible the celebration of matrimony in the parish church and to search out chapels and smaller remote country churches, where every effort is made to obtain the intimate atmosphere of a restricted audience, rather than before the whole *plebs Dei* as represented by the ecclesial cell which the parish constitutes.

In the style of the liturgical prayers and in the breviary

Insofar as the nature and style of the liturgical prayers of the Roman liturgy are concerned, notwithstanding some infiltrations of a more private character and of medieval origin, they have, and particularly in the Mass, preserved their ancient communitarian imprint. There is the very obvious fact of the plural style of these liturgical prayers, by which, through the mouth of the celebrant, it is always the whole community that prays, as Church of God, people of God, family of God.[41] Already in the third century St. Cyprian of Carthage had observed:

> "Our prayer is public and common; and, when we pray, we do not pray for an individual but for all the people, because all the people are one."[42]

And St. Ambrose, only a little more than a century later:

> "The basis of justice, therefore, is faith. . . . And the Lord says in Isaias: 'Behold, I have set a stone in the foundations of Sion' (Is. 28:16), that is, Christ, the foundation of the Church. Christ, in fact, is the object of the faith of all, and the Church is a certain concretizing of justice. She is the common law of all; she prays in common, she works in common, and it is in common that she is put to the test."[43]

The communitarian character of the divine office was emphasized in the ancient Church even by the fact that it was conceived as a choral prayer to

---

[41] *Ecclesia tua, populus tuus,* and *familia tua* are expressions constantly recurring in the orations of the Roman liturgy.

[42] *The Lord's Prayer* 8.

[43] *De officiis* 1, 29, 142.

which, as to family prayer, the community as such, whether canonical or monastic, was obliged, although there was no obligation upon the individual members to recite it outside the choir. This latter obligation emphasizes, of course, in the modern Latin Church, the personal aspect of the divine office. In our present circumstances, this most clearly is not an evil. It is only to be desired that, in the psychological outlook of those concerned, it should not lose its primary character, that of communitarian prayer.

*   *   *

The Church, therefore, first and foremost in its liturgy, is seen on earth as the ultimate concretization of the divine law of salvation in a differentiated and structurally hierarchical community, outside of which, supernaturally speaking, there is, for the individual, no possibility either of life or of development, because "where the Church is, there is the Spirit of God; and where the Spirit of God, there the Church and every grace." [44]

The most effective general expression of this communitarian dimension of the liturgy among the faithful ought to be their liturgical parochial life. The parochial community, ordered around the altar and deriving all its strength therefrom, is, in a concrete sense, the place where the individual finds his inclusion in the universal ecclesial community. But the parochial dimension of the Christian life is fiercely opposed by many and various circumstances of modern life and especially, I think, by poorly formed habits of parochial attendance, resulting in a lack of interest in their respective parishes on the part of so many. Not without reason did the Second Vatican Council stress the necessity of revitalizing the parochial orientation of the faithful.[45] However, it seems certain that to achieve this revival, it will be necessary to re-habituate the faithful to an awareness of the great divine law of salvation in community.

And it is especially certain that only by considering matters against the background of this law will there be a true understanding of the fact of an ecclesiastical liturgical body of law, dependent upon competent ecclesiastical authority as the external and obligatory regulator of the liturgical life of the faithful.[46] In the happy renewal of liturgical understanding that is now in

---

[44] St. Irenaeus, *Adv. haer.* 3, 24, 1.

[45] CL, art. 42.

[46] That is why it may properly be regretted that in the definitive redaction of the Second Vatican Council's constitution on the liturgy, the matter in regard to the authority to which the regulating of liturgical reform and the life of the liturgy pertains, a matter which in the previous redactions had been explained, with a better theological sense, as consequence of the hierarchical and communitarian nature of the liturgy itself, was afterwards transferred to the beginning of the whole treatment of the liturgical reform (art. 22). So now liturgical reform is treated by taking as starting point the authority competent to regulate such reform. This is typically the juridic point of view. For the theologian, on the other hand, the legal authority in the liturgy (and the whole of liturgical law) is a consequence of the hierarchical and communitarian nature of the liturgy itself; the theologian does not take this legalist point of view. This is one of the examples (fortunately not very serious in the present instance) of the struggle in the Second Vatican Council between the prevail-

progress, this is a thing which some even among those who have a superior grasp of the meaning and strength of the liturgy seem to endure only with a certain impatience, forgetting that the restraints imposed by a solitary competent authority are part and parcel of the law of salvation in the differentiated and hierarchically structured community.[47]

In the history of the liturgy it cannot be denied, rapid as our survey has been, that there is perceptible a certain tension between the ritual expression of the communitarian aspect on the one hand, and of the personal character on the other, of every liturgical action and prayer. This tension, moreover, is in some way inherent to the very nature of the liturgy, inasmuch as the liturgy, in order to be the vital thing that it ought to be, demands that the reality proposed, the communitarian *éthos*, be interiorized and personalized by each of the believers who participates therein, and first of all by the priest himself. Otherwise, this necessary interiorization and personalization, weak as it will be, will easily tend to display itself in an almost autonomous manner apart from the communitarian framework which gave it its beginnings, and impose itself upon the ritual expression of the liturgy.

Hence there is a danger of reversing the roles: the subject's individual behavior, instead of modeling itself on the liturgical reality, seeks to draw the liturgy into its own service and make it express the subject's own tendencies, forgetting that the liturgy is an essentially communitarian reality.

A proper equilibrium in this area is difficult to maintain. At any rate, it is historically certain that the late Middle Ages and the baroque period, in the whole field of the liturgy and especially in the Mass, have left us an inheritance of usages and of ways of thinking in which we now quite rightly experience an urgent need of reaction, to bring into appreciation again the communitarian aspect of the liturgy. We could wish that personal participation in the liturgy were better understood as an attuning of the personality of the individual to the liturgical communitarian reality.

ing legalist mentality and the theological mentality.

[47] When we view the liturgy in this light we can easily see the theological aberration of the theories expressed in regard to authority and obedience in matters liturgical by *Paroisse et liturgie* in its January number for 1965. In regard to such theories, see also the observations of His Eminence G. Cardinal Lercaro, "*Nella Costituzione sulla sacra liturgia si esprime la dottrina autentica della Chiesa,*" in *L'avvenire d'Italia,* Tuesday, March 2, 1965, p. 3.

10 THE LITURGY

AND THE LAW OF INCARNATION

More than once in the course of our explanation of the nature of the liturgy it has been necessary to make some allusion to the law of incarnation. It is necessary now to dwell upon it explicitly, in order to gain a better understanding of the significance of the concrete and human character of the liturgy. Concrete and human, I say, because the liturgy is the place of encounter between God and man, beneath and through the veil of sensible signs and of men of flesh and blood; and this, of course, carries with it certain inescapable consequences.

1. The Law of Incarnation
in the Relations between Man and God

There are two aspects to this law of incarnation. First of all it signifies that God communicates divine life to man through and under the veil of sensible things, which means in turn that man is obliged to pass through these sensible things in order to receive that divine life. In the second place, it signifies that what results from that communication is an elevation of man to a divine mode of being and acting, and this not just in the purely moral order in a cognoscitive and affective line, but in the ontological or entitative order and, in this precise sense, in the physical order, so much so that even while the substantial distinction between God and man remains ever intact, man is raised up to a really divine state of being and of acting.

300

The law of incarnation, therefore, affirms a mysterious and very real theandrism, a marriage between the divine and the human manifested in the end result of the relations between God and man as well as in the life which leads to this result. The divine embodies itself, so to speak, in order to elevate the human to a divine mode of being and acting.

This law of incarnation largely determines and forcefully emphasizes the law of objectivity. In our relations with God the way to Him is objective and normative, viz., via His human-divine nature, sensible-spiritual —a way that is productive of a true participation in the divine nature, not merely in the cognoscitive and affective area, but in existence itself, which is at the root of the cognoscible, the volitional, and the sensible.

Christ, incarnate Word, God-Man, is the prototype in whom the aforesaid law is verified in the highest degree and under all the aspects. And it is natural that this be the case, since Christ is the concrete recapitulation of God's whole plan for man, the ring which weds man and God. In Him, human nature, from the first moment of its existence, is assumed by the divine Person. This is the mystery of that unprecedented union which theologians term *hypostatic*. In Christ a whole human nature, body and soul, is compenetrated by the divine Person and imbued, as it were, with the divinity, not only in the order of knowing and willing, but, what is much more basic, in the order of existence. The hypostatic union is the fullest and most real sanctification possible for a created being. It is the divine that descends into the human and the human which is drawn into the divine in the most perfect way conceivable. Here, then, is theandrism at its very source and summit, the prototype of which all other elevations to the divine order can be no more than imitations and participations.[1]

In Christ, you see, this communication is an incarnation. It is true that the divine Word took on not only a human body, but an integral human nature, soul and body. But in Christ, during His mortal life, the divinity was largely hidden beneath the veil of His body, the sensible and material element. That is why the incarnation constituted at one and the same time not only God's full revelation in the world, His epiphany,[2] but also His being hidden from the world. In the Man-God, Christ Jesus, God is hidden at the same time that He is revealed.[3]

[1] See, for example, this magnificent collect for the feast of Christmas in the Leonine Sacramentary: "*Omnipotens sempiterne Deus, qui in Domini nostri Iesu Christi Filii tui nativitate tribuisti totius religionis initium perfectionemque constare; da nobis, quaesumus, in eius portione censeri, in quo totius salutis humanae summa consisti*" (no. 1248; ed. Mohlberg, Vol. II, p. 159). Christ, who appears in the world on the day of His birth, is not only the source from whom all worship acceptable to God is derived (*totius religionis initium*), but also the highest perfection of this worship and of every sanctification that God works in men (*perfectio; summa*). For other men, it treats only of being united to Christ and of sharing in His fullness (*in eius portione censeri*).

[2] See Titus 2:11; 3:4.

[3] Quite rightly does Dionysius the Areopagite say: "In the humanity of Christ, the Superessential is manifested in the human es-

In order to see in Jesus of Nazareth the Man-God, it was not enough for His contemporaries to look at Him, perhaps even to live next door to Him. The divinity, even though it was manifested in Him, was manifested in a mysterious way; and it was able to be seen only with the eyes of faith. To the proud, to the self-satisfied, the humanity of Jesus, His visibility, His corporality, was a screen which hid His divinity. Only one who knew by means of faith how to penetrate this screen could reach the divinity which lay hidden behind Christ's humanity. This was the objective way, incapable of circumvention, which God imposed upon men, if they were to come to Him.

In order to connect all this with what was said above about the centrality of the paschal mystery, it is enough to note that the incarnation effectively willed by God in the same Lord Jesus was not, on earth, a merely static phenomenon, but one having also a dynamic aspect: it was something which had to evolve, to develop, to arrive at a goal.

In fact, the hypostatic union, which was perfect in its substance from the first instant of Jesus' existence, did not at first have all its connatural secondary effects on His human nature. The humanity in Christ was suffering humanity, subject in every respect, sin excepted, to our miseries, that humanity voluntarily accepting these consequences of original sin, even to death on the Cross; His divinity remained hidden beneath the form of the mortified servant of God. According as God willed it, the glorification of the humanity in Christ, to which He had a right, had to be subdued through humiliations, through His Passion and death. Only with the resurrection and His taking His seat at the right of the Father did Christ's incarnation achieve its full effect; because only then did the divinity so penetrate His human nature as to render His body glorious after overcoming in it every trace of the consequences of sin.

This, then, is the incarnation concretely willed by God, in which it was Christ's task to make us participants, by communicating to us in some way this existence and His status as incarnate Son of God, first humiliated and made to suffer even death, and only afterwards raised and made glorious.

This way in which God has willed to appear in the world and to communicate Himself to men, truly astonishing to human comprehension, is of inestimable importance in allowing us to gain some understanding of the ways of God's working among men and to show us the way which we must take in order to reach Him. In fact, for arriving at God the way of the incarnation was imposed not only upon the contemporaries of Jesus, but remains even today the only way that leads to the Father. It is a law.

In a certain way it can be said that what the humanity of Jesus was for His contemporaries, the sacraments are for us. Here the remark of St. Leo

sence, yet remains hidden after this manifes- remains hidden in the manifestation itself"
tation, or, to speak in a more divine way, (Ep. 3, PG 3, 1069 B).

the Great holds good: "That which was visible of our Redeemer was changed into a sacramental presence." [4] We are not able to go to God except by passing through these realities, sensible and spiritual at the same time, which are the sacraments, through which the divine sanctifying power is operative. The sacraments are not merely symbols to recall in us certain ideas and to stimulate our sentiments and volitions. No, they are truly instruments and channels of grace. And this grace is such that God communicates to us through the sacraments that grace which truly transforms us in the order of being and not only in the order of knowing and feeling. The transformation takes place in the order of existence and therefore in the order of acting.

The sacraments are sensible instruments by means of which God confers upon us a theandric being and life. This life is none other than a reflection, a derivation and participation, in the theandric life of Christ. Even the sacramental world, first of all the Eucharist, is therefore constructed entirely in accord with the law of incarnation. Even here the divine descends into the human, into the sensible itself, in order to elevate man to its mode of existence and action. Not without deliberation does St. Thomas declare that the sacraments are separate instruments of the Man-God, just as the humanity of Christ is the conjoint instrument of His divinity. And what he says of the sacraments holds good in its own way likewise for the sacramentals, the difference being that the sacraments work *ex opere operato* and the sacramentals *ex opere operantis Ecclesiae*. All this is based on the importance that the body has, primarily the physical body of Christ, in the plan of salvation. [5]

Similarly the entire Church is subject to the law of incarnation. God communicates Himself to us not only through sacrament-things, but through sacrament-people. In the Church, you see, there are men who have, by God's will, the authorized function of communicating divine life to others, so that it is indispensable to remain in contact with these men, in order not to be cut off from the current of life. These men are the authentic hierarchy of the Catholic Church: Pope, bishops, priests. We must go through these men in order to reach God.

They are instruments, intermediaries, quite visible and sensible, between ourselves and God. They are, among else, the possessors of the sacrifice, the administrators of the sacraments, and they preside over the public and official prayer of the Church. Theirs is the authentic mission, always by the will of God. Even here, therefore, the divine is communicated through what is human and sensible, and it is what is sensible that makes present and manifests the divine; and at the same time, in the very act which manifests the

---

[4] *Sermo* 74, 2.

[5] See C. Vagaggini, *"Caro salutis est cardo: corporeità, eucaristia e liturgia,"* in *Miscellanea liturgica in onore di S. E. il cardinale* G. *Lercaro*, Vol. I, Desclée 1965. On His sacraments as separate instruments of Christ, see St. Thomas, *Summa*, III, q. 62, a. 5 c.

divine, the divine is hidden. Here is the incarnation which comes to each of us individually.

Scripture becomes understandable only in the perspective of the incarnation. In Scripture God communicates to us what He knows, wills, and does through determinate written signs, determinate modes of speech and representation, in a determinate language, of a determinate era, of a determinate culture, even though it be far removed from ours, making use of determinate men, while respecting the individuality of each. And we, in order to communicate with God, are bound to these incarnate intermediaries which both manifest and hide His word.

Nor can we afford to forget that the divine is incarnate not only in men and in things, but even in time, because God, in communicating Himself to mankind, takes into account the element of time. In this regard revelation was objectively augmented until the death of the last of the Apostles; and afterwards there was and is yet a development of dogmas, a change of discipline, a history of the Church and of souls. There is always the law of incarnation; and with this law, it is impossible to reduce Christianity simply to a philosophy, to a system of ethics, or to a religious experience.

It would not be possible to insist too much upon that which we have already emphasized in the concept of sacred salvation history, namely, that Christianity, prior to its being a system of doctrine, of ethics, or a psychological experience, is first and foremost a historical event. Here, then, it is necessary to determine precisely what this historical event is to be called: it is the incarnation of the Son of God; God's manifesting of Himself on earth and His communicating of Himself to men in the Man, Christ Jesus. Whoever does not understand this will not be able to understand either St. Paul or St. John. To be a Christian means first of all to accept this historical event, this fact of the incarnation, with all the consequences which it implies for the relations between man and God.

These consequences we have now seen: the divine transforming us entitatively, in the very sphere of being, elevating us to itself, and making of us theandric beings in the image of Christ, communicating itself to us through and under the veil of things truly objective, both sensible and visible, namely, the sacrifice, the sacraments, the sacramentals, the human and visible hierarchy, the Scriptures: all of these are things which, each in its own way, are like a prolongation of the incarnation and, each in its own way, place each believer individually, in the course of the ages, in personal contact with this unique event of history. It is through these things, which are at one and the same time both divine and human, spiritual and sensible, that each individual who in the course of the ages is presented for a brief moment on the stage of history, is able and obligated to include himself in that extraordinary and ever permanent historical event, and thus to conquer space and time.

In communicating Himself to men God would have been able to choose another way. By freely choosing the way of the incarnation, what He has done is in substance, to take into account the nature of man and to treat man, spirit incarnate, in the style of man.

2. The Incarnation and the Liturgy

These remarks have not taken us away from the liturgy. It was necessary to speak of the incarnation in order to situate the liturgy in its proper framework. The liturgy is a prime example of the law of incarnation. The liturgical world, more than any other aspect of the life of the Church, is the world of the incarnation prolonged, made present, and participated in by men, in the sanctification which God works in the Church and in the worship which the Church renders to God. The liturgy is that reality in which men, through the veil of things both symbolic and sensible — sacrifice, sacraments, sacramentals, ceremonies and divine office — in the official and hierarchical worship of the Church, itself a thing both human and divine, are included within the historical event of the incarnation of the Son of God, participate in it and appropriate it to themselves in order to be transformed by it and to be elevated by it to theandric existence and theandric action, becoming images of Christ. And all this is to be understood in a sense that is strictly realist and objective.

There are two essential and evident characteristics of the liturgy that will not be understood except in the light of this law of incarnation: to wit, whether the liturgy be viewed as sanctification or as worship, it is *sensible and external,* and it is a *hierarchical action, officially regulated by authority* and presided over by official and responsible men. These are precisely the two characteristics which make the liturgy so offensive not only to every kind of disembodied idealism but also to every sort of individualism and anthropocentric psychologism.

That is why there remains in the liturgy always the threat of the scandal of the incarnation: *nonne hic est filius Ioseph?* Beneath all this humanity does there really lie hidden something divine? Is it really necessary to bind one's own interior freedom to this externalism, this materialism? And if so, what happens to adoration in spirit and in truth? Anyone who so reasons, had the choice been his, certainly would not have chosen the incarnation as the way to redeem the world, and, at any rate, not the way of incarnation in the *forma servi,* by which God did in fact appear on earth *in similitudinem hominum factus et habitu inventus ut homo* (Phil. 2:7).

Christ Himself, whose humanity was but a transparent veil through which, to the eyes of faith, the divinity shone forth, did not prevent that same humanity from being for many a stumbling block. How much more inevitable, then, that the externals and the human element in the liturgy, carried out by wicked men as conductors to the divine element, should also be a stumbling block and a scandal to many. Turning to those ministers of the sanctuary who, in the liturgical action, instead of facilitating as much as possible the efforts, in so difficult a matter, of the faithful to understand the liturgy, make it even more difficult by their negligence, clumsiness, and lack of appreciation of the role expected of them in the house of God — to such ministers as these might be repeated the words of Jesus: *"Necesse est enim ut veniant scandala; verumtamen vae homini illi, per quem scandalum venit."*

But the liturgy can also say, with Christ Himself: *"Beatus qui non fuerit scandalizatus in me."* Whoever, viewing the liturgy and living it, succeeds in overcoming the scandal of the incarnation, discovers life *et hauriet salutem a Domino.* Therefore the liturgy, like the Church itself and the sacraments which are actualized in the Church, is the continuous incarnate epiphany of Christ, just as Christ, when He was on earth, was, to the eyes of faith, the incarnate epiphany of God. In the liturgy more than in any of the other manifestations of the Church, the eyes of the believer, once they have overcome the obstacle of its externals and its materialness and the scandal of the incarnation, behold the epiphany of our great God and Savior Christ,[6] whom, in the liturgy, the believer, in his own way, sees, hears, and touches.

Each believer, going out from the liturgy, and especially from the Mass, is able in a very real way to make his own the words of St. John, who wrote of ". . . what we have seen with our eyes,[7] what we have looked upon and our hands have touched: of the Word of Life.[8] And the Life was made known and we have seen; and now we testify and announce to you the Life Eternal, which was with the Father, and has appeared among us — that One, I say, whom we have seen and heard, Him we announce to you, so that you too may have fellowship with us and that our fellowship may be with the Father and with His Son Jesus Christ. And this we write to you that you may rejoice and that your joy may be full."[9]

These notions have been authenticated with remarkable strength by the Second Vatican Council when, placing itself in the perspective of the incarnation, it allowed the liturgy to be seen as the place *par excellence* in which the faithful are able to experience in a living way the mystery of Christ and the genuine nature of the Church, not just an eminent epiphany, but the principal epiphany [10] of the nature of the Church. The mystery of Christ, therefore, is precisely, to recapitulate the matter, the mystery of the incarnate Son of God, dead and risen; and the genuine nature of the Church consists primarily in the characteristic that she is

[6] See Titus 2:11-13; 3-4.

[7] The Greek liturgy ordinarily chants after the communion of the faithful an antiphon which begins, "We have seen the true light, we have received the heavenly Spirit. . . ."

[8] At one time the faithful could say this literally, for it was in their hands that they received the consecrated Bread at communion (see Jungmann, *The Mass of the Roman Rite,*

Vol. II, pp. 378-380). In the post-conciliar reforms it has been left to the decision of the regional hierarchical authority what discipline in this matter shall prevail. The Bishops of the United States have thus far courageously refused to return to the antiquated discipline of reception in the hand.

[9] 1 John 1:1-4.

[10] Cf. CL, art. 41.

"essentially both human and divine, visible but endowed with invisible realities, zealous in action and dedicated to contemplation, present in the world, but as a pilgrim, so constituted that in her the human is directed toward and subordinated to the divine, the visible to the invisible, action to contemplation, and this present world to that city yet to come, the object of our quest." [11]

It is the theandrism of the incarnation more than any other quality in the Church that makes the liturgy come alive and is so apt to manifest it. Thereby — the text continues —

"The liturgy daily builds up those who are in the Church, making of them a holy temple of the Lord, a dwelling-place for God in the Spirit, to the mature measure of the fullness of Christ. At the same time it marvelously increases their power to preach Christ and thus show forth the Church, a sign lifted up among the nations, to those who are outside, a sign under which the scattered children of God may be gathered together until there is one fold and one shepherd."

This incarnationism in the Catholic conception of the world, so characteristically expressed in the liturgy, is perhaps the point that separates Catholicism and Protestantism most sharply. The fact is that every logical form of Protestantism, in the depths of its psychological outlook, entails a misapprehension of the total extension of the law of incarnation. This is because at the very root of Protestantism there is the appositional refusal to accept any sort of human intermediary upon which the soul depends in an essential way in its individual relations with God. As if to accept the Bible as the word of God and as objective norm of faith (except when interpreting its meaning in a purely subjective sense) did not already imply such an intermediary! And, similarly, for every believer the Apostles were and are such intermediaries.

And especially as if the human nature in Christ the Man-God were not precisely, for all men, in virtue of the incarnation itself, just such an essential intermediary as through God's will, no individual after the sin of Adam has been able, is able, or will be able to do without! And as if, by the same will of God and positive institution of Christ, the law which now governs the relations between individuals and God, were not that same law of incarnation upon which the relations of Christ's contemporaries with God depended! That is why every point in Protestantism, logically developed, is profoundly anti-liturgical and why in essence every revival of the liturgical spirit is a reconciliation to Catholic tradition; for every revival of the liturgical spirit is a revival of the spirit of the incarnation.

[11] *Ibid.*, art. 2.

11 THE LITURGY AND THE LAW OF

THE COSMIC UNIVERSALITY

OF THE KINGDOM OF GOD

I. LITURGY, MAN, AND THE

INFRAHUMAN WORLD

In speaking of a law of the cosmic universality of the kingdom of God, I mean simply to affirm the fact that in the order of the things which God has effectively willed, man, in the totality of his physical, psychic, spiritual, individual, and social structure, along with the subhuman creatures and the angelic world, are all ordered, each in his own way, in an organic unity — keeping intact, however, the possibilities and characteristics of each being — to a common end: the kingdom of God, which is to be joined together again in the heavenly Jerusalem. This being the case, this kingdom has the character and dimensions of a cosmic universality, extensively and intensively, which embraces the totality of all creatures ordered to an organically common end and which therefore have a certain reciprocal solidarity and interdependence, in a single universal symphony.[1]

In the light of this law it is not surprising, then, that the liturgy views the whole cosmos as an integral universe, united in worship. This will help us to understand a great many of the particular and characteristic traits of the liturgy, which can be regarded as particular manifestations of that general law which discovers in the liturgy an actualization that is already remarkably perfect, in such degree as our earthly condition permits perfection.

1. The Liturgy and the Full Actualization of the Whole Man

Revelation regards man as a substantial unit

According to revelation the whole man as a living unit in all the aspects of his substance and of his physical, psychic, and spiritual life, is totally ordered to the divine life, to be achieved in the heavenly Jerusalem. In this regard a special importance attaches to the doctrine of the substantial unity of man, teaching that he is a being at one and the same time both corporeal and spiritual, whose single parts, body and soul, are not in themselves independent and operative, but are only parts of a whole that is in itself independent and operative.[2]

Doctrinally it is this substantial compound, in the unity of its being, that is the concrete, stable, and total subject of God's interventions among us and of the development of divine life in us: creation, elevation, fall, redemption, slow and painful ascension to God in the striving for purification and ascent through coöperation with His grace, and, ultimately, in the state of final perfection to which we all aspire in hope. In this unfolding of our salvation history and in each of its individual moments, the body no less than the soul, in its own way, is interested, acts and cooperates in the substantial unity of the whole. Hence, not only the psychic faculties but also the physical faculties are concerned and they work together, each according to its own mode; and, among the psychic faculties, it is not only the spiritual faculties of intellect and will, but even the sentient faculties, the external and internal senses, the passions and feelings, that are concerned and which behave coöperatively.

It is really in the light of this doctrine that the dogmas of the incarnation, of the resurrection, and those which are concerned with Catholic ascetical practice must be considered. The Word, desiring the salvation of man, did not assume only a human soul, nor only a human body; rather, He "was

---

[1] The damned, whether angels or men, who, against the will of God, do not achieve the end to which they were destined, may circumvent God's plans of mercy, but they cannot escape His justice.

[2] A substantial union is one in which the individual component parts are not, in being and in act, such as are independent and operative in themselves, but one in which they are only parts of a whole that is in itself independent and operative.

made man"; He assumed, therefore, the whole human nature in the substantial unity of body and soul. Thus, He became perfect man in no lesser sense than that in which He is perfect God.

In man himself, beatitude and redemption will achieve their final perfection only when the divine life has transformed, and that without annihilating him, the whole man, body and soul, in the substantial unity of his being. Herein do we find some understanding of the perfect reasonableness and propriety of the doctrine of the resurrection of the body; and it was precisely in this perspective that the Fathers of the ancient Church defended this doctrine against the pagans who had such difficulty in admitting it.[3]

It is in this light, too, that we can understand the struggle which the Church has always carried on against every kind of asceticism that has for its basis the notion that matter, and the body in particular, is something in itself evil.[4] From this point of view there is nothing more foreign to the true Catholic mentality than the disembodied spiritualism of Orphic, Platonic, and Neo-Platonic tradition, with its strong tendency to reduce the whole of man to the human soul, and therefore to something purely internal; to consider the body, by reason of its very corporality, as the prison and tomb of the soul, and the senses as no more than chains which but impede the soul and prevent it from flying freely back to its original condition of pure spirituality.

In the history of the theory and practice of asceticism more than one private teacher has sometimes allowed himself to be so deceived by that excessive spiritualism as to fall in with a similar notion according to which a perfect Christian way of living can be achieved only by detaching oneself entirely from things here below and concentrating entirely on the celestial reality.

In the Catholic view of the world, however, in this striving toward the heights, the body must be regarded as subject and instrument, and not as a natural enemy. The body is subject and instrument, which must keep always to the role which pertains to it by its very nature, in serving the greater good of the whole. Every tendency in mortification and asceticism to disrupt the harmonious interplay between body and soul and to shift to the body the total responsibility for all human action will, therefore, have to be repressed. In the Catholic view of the world, the mortification of the body and of the senses and the very desire for death are simply a temporary means for maintaining the body's role of service to the whole, and which, in the final analysis, will redound to the benefit even of the body itself in the

---

[3] Thus, for example, with St. Justin the Martyr, *The Resurrection*, frag. 8 (Jurgens, no. 147); Athenagoras of Athens, *The Resurrection of the Dead* 15 (Jurgens, no. 150); St. Irenaeus, *Adversus haereses* 5, 6-7 (Jurgens, nos. 251-252); Tertullian, *The Resurrection*

of the Dead 53.

[4] See, for example, St. Clement of Alexandria, *Stromateis*, book 3 in its entirety (PG 8, 1097-1213; two particularly pregnant passages in Jurgens, nos. 420a-420b).

glorious resurrection. Christian mortification of the body and of the senses, therefore, has its basis in view of their true and perpetual vivification. It is not a question of abolishing the body and the senses, but of making use of them, of making them pliable and flexible instruments in service of the divine life in us.

Augustine himself, in the earliest days of his conversion and in the euphoria of Neo-Platonic spiritualism, did not perceive clearly enough how far distant the spiritualism of this philosophy, quite religious in appearance, was from the Christian spiritualism which teaches the incarnation and the resurrection of bodies. When, however, his Catholic sense had been somewhat sharpened, he finally discovered the man in Christ; in man, the body and the senses; and in the Church, the sacraments and the liturgy. Not infrequently in later times he expressly warns his readers against the imprecision of his initial thinking on this matter. Apropos of his book *De beata vita*, he says:

> "I regret having said that, in this life, happiness resides only in the mind of the wise man, and the condition of his body matters little. In reality, the perfect knowledge of God, that is, the maximum that man can have, is hoped for by the Apostle in the life to come, which alone should be called the happy life, for there the body too, incorruptible and immortal, will be subject to its spirit without trouble or resistance." [5]

Elsewhere he explained carefully the difference between the contempt of the body and of the senses practiced by the philosophers, and that practiced by Christians and especially by the martyrs:

> "The Christian martyrs acted prudently, therefore, and did not despise their bodies. Such a philosophy would have been perverse and worldly. It is the philosophy of those who do not believe in the resurrection of the bodies. They consider themselves great despisers of the body, because they regard bodies as prisons in which they think souls have been shut up for having sinned in a previous life.

> "But our God has made both body and soul. He is Creator of both, Redeemer of both, Author of both, Restorer of both. The martyrs, therefore, did not despise or persecute the flesh as an enemy. 'For no one has ever hated his own flesh' (Eph. 5:29). Rather, they took care of it precisely when they seemed to be neglecting it. When, still in the flesh, they endured temporal torments with faith, they were procuring eternal glory for that very flesh also." [6]

The case of Augustine is worth relating, I think, because the Neo-Platonic temptation is real enough even today.

Let us add that, according to revelation, the divine life concerns not only

---

[5] *Retractationes* 1, 2; see also 1, 4, 3.   [6] *Sermo* 277, 3.

the whole man, body and soul and the totality of his psychological makeup, but it sanctifies all his actions that are honest in themselves, and in particular his aesthetic creative activity, his efforts toward subjecting the world to himself technologically and organizing it toward the ends of human life. The words of Genesis (1:28), "Be fruitful and multiply and people the earth and subdue it," contain in germ the justification and even the possibility of the sanctification of all these activities, whether individually or socially undertaken, in which man cooperates with God in the work of creating and organizing the world.[7]

In short, in the Catholic view of the world, it is man, whole and integral, living and concrete, in the fullness and substantial unity of his being, corporeal, psychic and spiritual, individual and social, who must be vitalized by the divine life, and in that way be included in the kingdom of God.

The liturgy likewise views man as a substantial unit: soul and body

The liturgy too adopts this scriptural perspective. It is, in fact, precisely in this perspective of unified totality that the liturgy views man and vitalizes him, in its own way, in the concrete unity of his many-faceted existence: as an individual and social being; body and soul; with all his faculties and activities directed, in the organic unity of the whole, toward being sanctified by God and toward rendering worship to Him under the veil of sensible signs.

It is easy to show how in the liturgy it is not just the soul of the believer but the concrete totality of the believer in the substantial unity of his being, body and soul, that is sanctified by God, which is consecrated to God and which renders worship to God. Thus, in the liturgy it is as much the body as it is the soul that is actor and beneficiary, each according to its own natural exigencies and potentialities, in the substantial unity of the human being. That is why, in the liturgy, it is demanded of the faithful and of the hierarchy as well, not only an internal attuning of the soul to the action that is being performed — without a certain degree of this attuning, participation in the rites would be empty of any fruit of salvation — but even, in its own way, the attuning of the body itself.

This attuning of the body demands first of all a bodily presence at the liturgical action, at a specific time and place. It thus explains, among else, the law of bodily presence for satisfying the obligation of attendance at Mass.[8] It demands, in the second place and connaturally, the conforming of the various bodily attitudes to that which is suggested at every moment of the

---

[7] This is the basis of what today is called the theology of labor, of technology, and in general, of earthly realities. See, for example, G. Thils, *Théologie des réalités terrestres*, 2 volumes, Paris 1946-1949; M. D. Chenu, *Pour une théologie du travail*, Paris 1955.

[8] The anomaly of marriage by proxy seems to be justified by the fact that the nuptial blessing is not the sacrament of matrimony, but that this sacrament is a contract consisting only in the exchange of consent by the spouses.

liturgical action: either by the natural sense of what is expressed in the rites themselves, or by what is accepted custom in the Church and in society and is imposed by appropriate prescriptions of a rubrical or ceremonial nature.

It is, therefore, the law of the complete cosmic character of salvation which, in the last analysis, justifies the rubrical prescriptions of the ceremonies and imposes upon the ministers and the faithful specific bodily postures at the various moments of the liturgical action: genuflections, prostrations, bows, standing erect, striking one's breast, elevating the eyes, joining or elevating one's hands. It is the whole man who must attune himself to the liturgical action; the attunement of the body is a substantial part of the attunement of the man, in the same way that the body is, along with the soul, a substantial part of the man. Besides, in accord with the laws of psychology, the body and the soul exercise in turn a reciprocal action, so that the bodily attitude is the connatural expression of the internal attitude of the soul, when this has already been formed; and it is, in turn, an incitement to an internal attitude of soul, when such attitude has not yet been formed, or it will re-inforce that which is already present.

The fact that the external bodily attitude is able, in its own way, to generate corresponding sentiments in the soul explains why it is not a question of hypocrisy when the believer subjects himself to these external attitudes even when his soul is not yet in full accord, by reason of its internal sentiments, with these external attitudes. In this case the will, more or less reflexively, imposes upon the body a specific attitude for the sake of creating a corresponding sentiment in the whole soul. So long as there is always this prior will, at least virtual in character, there is absolutely nothing reprehensible in this manner of acting.

We can see why, therefore, in the liturgy and in particular in the Mass, the active role of the body in its various physical attitudes is relevant and the object of most careful attention.

But in the liturgy and in the Mass in particular the body is not just the essential co-agent but also the co-essential beneficiary. I want to point out that in these sacred rites there is a constant concern with the *welfare*, or supernatural salvation, not only of the soul but also of the body; and this is the case even if, as we would expect, the body is not considered separately from the soul or as if it were in disharmony with the ultimate end of the whole man.

If our body must play a part in the liturgy, the liturgy in turn is concerned with the body's welfare. It implores simultaneously the health of the soul and that of the body, always considering the body, of course, in its relation to the soul and to the last end of the whole man. If the Lenten liturgy emphasizes the mortification necessary for the equilibrium of the human composite, numerous postcommunion prayers, on the other hand, ask God to extend to our bodies the effects of the redemption, basing their petition on the general concept, biblical and traditional, of the Eucharist as a medicinal remedy bestowing bodily as well as spiritual incorruptibility and immortality.

This notion is epitomized in a masterful manner in the Roman Missal postcommunion prayer for the Monday after the first Sunday of Lent: "By partaking of Your sacrament, we pray You, Lord, may we experience help for soul and body, that both may be saved and we may glory in the perfection of the heavenly remedy." [9] And in many other instances the liturgy expressly begs that participation in the sacrifice be "a renewal of soul and of body"; [10] "welfare of soul and of body"; [11] "salvation of soul and of body"; [12] "sanctification of soul and of body"; [12a] "remedy and defense for soul and body." [13]

As is now well-known, the new rite for the sacrament of the anointing of the ill highlights the restoration to physical health, God willing, of the recipient. [14] In fact, there exist in all liturgies, historical as well as those of the present time, orations and Masses for the infirm, [15] as well as numerous anointings and blessings for the sick and even in view of specific ailments. [16]

The exsequial rites for the dead constitute a no less eloquent testimony to the concern which the liturgy has for the body. Finally, the liturgy makes it clear to all that the ultimate basis for this concern is the body's final resurrection into glory.

This respect and this concern which the liturgy exhibits for the body extends in a special way to the human senses. We will content ourselves here with showing as evidence of this concern the sanctification of the senses which takes place in the Roman liturgy in the present rite of baptism and in the administration of the anointing of the ill: the first and often the last interventions of the liturgy in a man's life.

---

[9] *Sentiamus, Domine, quaesumus, tui perceptione sacramenti, subsidium mentis et corporis, ut, in utroque salvati, de coelestis remedii plenitudine gloriemur.* See also the *super oblata* prayer for the 11th Sunday of the year.

[10] Postcommunion for the 26th Sunday of the year, ". . . *reparatio mentis et corporis*"; postcommunion for the Tuesday after the 4th Sunday of Lent, ". . . *auxilium*."

[11] *Super oblata* prayer for Wednesday in the octave of Easter, ". . . *salutem nobis mentis et corporis* . . ."; postcommunion for the Feast of the Most Holy Trinity, ". . . *salutem corporis et animae* . . . ."

[12] Postcommunion prayer for December 21, ". . . *salvationem mentis et corporis* . . . ." See also the postcommunion for the Friday after the 3rd Sunday of Lent.

[12a] *Super oblata* prayer for the 2nd Sunday of Lent, ". . . *corpora mentesque sanctificet.*"

[13] Alternative prayer of the celebrant before his own reception of communion, ". . . *prosit mihi ad tutamentum mentis et corporis, et ad medelam percipiendam.*"

[14] See Apostolic Constitution, *Sacram Unctionem Infirmorum* of Nov. 30, 1972, *in Acta Apostolicae Sedis*, Vol. 65 (Jan. 1973), no. 1, pp. 5-9.

[15] See, for example, the Gelasian Sacramentary, Mohlberg edition, no. 1535-43, on pp. 221-222; and in the latest (Pauline) Roman Missal, there is, among the Ritual Masses, a Mass *"ad ministrandum Viaticum"*; and in the votive Masses for various circumstances, there are Masses for the ill and for the dying.

[16] See, for example, in the modern Roman Ritual, title 9, ch. 4, no. 6-8; and the blessing of candles against maladies of the throat, on the feast of St. Blaise, title 9, ch. 3, no. 7.

The present order of baptism of adults, according to a most beautiful custom of the Oriental and Gallican type, expands the ancient rite in which the catechumen was signed on the forehead with the sign of the Cross, by having this *signatio crucis* traced on all his senses. The ritual expresses it thus:

> "With his thumb the priest traces the sign of the Cross on the forehead of each of the catechumens, saying, 'N., receive the Cross on your forehead: Christ Himself will guard you by reason of this sign of His love. Learn now to know and follow that Cross.'
>
> "While he signs them on the ears: 'Receive the sign of the Cross on your ears, so that you may heed the voice of the Lord.'
>
> "While he signs them on the eyes: 'Receive the sign of the Cross on your eyes, so that you may see the glory of God.'
>
> "While he signs them on the mouth: 'Receive the sign of the Cross on your mouth, so that you may respond to the word of God.'
>
> "While he signs them on the breast: 'Receive the sign of the Cross on your breast, that by your faith Christ may find a dwelling place in your hearts.'
>
> "While he signs them on the shoulders: 'Receive the sign of the Cross on your shoulders, so that you may take upon you the sweet yoke of Christ.'
>
> "Then, without touching them, the celebrant makes the sign of the Cross over all the catechumens together, saying: 'I sign you all in your whole being, in the name of the Father and of the Son, and of the Holy Spirit, that you may have life in eternity.' " [17]

It is evident that the rite has the significance of a sanctification of all the senses, each of which will have such an important role to play in the work of sanctifying the one being baptized, in his service of God in the Christian life which he is about to commence.

It was logical, therefore, that in the sacrament of the anointing of the ill, there was prescribed in the Pontifical of the Popes from the thirteenth century and in the Roman Ritual up to the present time, a sacramental anointing of the five senses of the same baptized Christian at the time of serious sickness: "Through this holy anointing and His most tender mercy, may the Lord pardon all the sins you have committed by the sense of sight . . . by the sense of hearing . . . by the sense of smell . . . by the sense of taste and the power of speech . . . by the sense of touch . . . by the power of walking. Amen." [18] By an Apostolic Constitution dated November 30, 1972,

---

[17] Newly revised Roman Ritual, baptism of adults, nos. 83-85, which differs only slightly from the older Roman Ritual, baptism of adults, no. 11.

[18] Roman Ritual, no. 8-9.

Pope Paul has provided now, however, for a simplification of the rite of the anointing of the ill, so that after December 31, 1973, only the forehead and hands are to be anointed. The sacramental formula is recited only once: *"Per istam sanctam unctionem et suam piisimam misericordiam adiuvet te Dominus gratia Spiritus Sancti, ut a peccatis liberatum te salvet atque propitius allevet."*

In this anointing of the body we see how effectively the liturgy expresses Catholic doctrine in its rejection of anything savoring of Neo-Platonism or of Gnosticism of whatever sort. Tertullian, in his usual lapidary style, had already pointed this out very forcefully:

> "Indeed, the flesh is the hinge of salvation. In that regard, when the soul is deputed to something by God, it is the flesh which makes it able to carry out the commission which God has given it. The flesh, then, is washed, so that the soul may be made clean. The flesh is anointed, so that the soul may be dedicated to holiness. The flesh is signed, so that the soul too may be fortified. The flesh is shaded by the imposition of hands, so that the soul too may be illuminated by the Spirit. The flesh feeds on the Body and Blood of Christ, so that the soul too may fatten on God. They cannot, then, be separated in their reward, when they are united in their works." [19]

Harmonious actualization of all the psychological faculties

Let us proceed. The liturgy and in particular the Mass — considering sung Mass and possibly even pontifical Mass as the natural prototype — in bringing into play all the various psychological faculties of man, has a balance all its own and not much different, it would seem, from that which is realized in other forms of piety or in other methods of prayer and meditation.

It is impossible not to recognize that the liturgy, and primarily the Mass, is concerned with the actualization and with the awakening, during the whole duration of the cultic action, of the whole psychological life of the community in attendance, whether in its cognoscitive part: external senses, especially the auditory and visual; imagination and intelligence; or in its affective part: emotions and will. The genius of the liturgy is such that it addresses itself directly to the whole assembly, and provides a basis which may serve to vitalize the religious life of all, and does not allow any of these various faculties to remain inactive for any length of time, but brings them all, individually and unobtrusively, into play, as a spiritual-physical unity. Thus the liturgy is presented first of all as a sacral action, spiritual and physical; in continuous development, and not primarily as a meditation.

[19] *The Resurrection of the Dead* 8 (Jurgens, no. 362). Irenaeus, writing against the gnostic claim that "salvation is something which concerns only souls, and that the body, being taken from the earth, cannot participate in salvation" (*Adv. haer.* 1, 27, 3), had already strongly defended the doctrine that "the flesh participates in life" (*Adv. haer.* 5, 3, 3).

This is true, at least, if by meditation we mean an individual internal exercise concentrated upon our relations with God and with sacred things, in a *wholly interior* way. And so much the more if by this exercise a person seeks in meditation to suspend all exterior activity of the faculties, and even all interior activity of the discursive type, to become absorbed in a simple contemplation of God, in a purely intuitive act. If that is approximately what we mean by meditation, then we must recognize that the liturgy is not primarily a meditation but a sacred action; not so much a *theoroúmenon* or *theoría* as a *drómenon*, is what the ancients would say. In the liturgy of the present day the moments directed to meditation, in the aforementioned sense, are rather few and quite short; but still, they are somewhat more extensive in the Pauline Roman Missal than they were in the so-called Tridentine.

In the ancient Roman liturgy, in the synaxis of the fore-Mass, there were moments when the deacon's invitation *flectamus genua* called people and hierarchy to meditational silence and private prayer for a brief interval of time, until interrupted by the deacon's *levate*, immediately after which the celebrant initiated the prescribed prayer again with the word *oremus*. But the intentions for the silent prayer were suggested beforehand to the whole assembly by the celebrant, with such phrases as: "Let us pray for the Church of God . . .; let us pray for our most blessed Pope . . .; for the priests . . .; for the deacons . . .; for the emperor . . ."; or similar phrases. In the Roman Missal in use until quite recently, some remnants of this usage were to be found on Good Friday, in the Easter Vigil, in the Ember Day Masses, and in a few other instances.

With the advent of the Pauline Roman Missal the *flectamus genua* has departed entirely, although on Good Friday the various prayers are still introduced with a phrase designating the persons and categories of persons being prayed for; but more important, this revised Roman Missal either prescribes or suggests among various times for silent prayer and meditation the following: during the penitential rite; after the *oremus*, before continuing with the official prayer; after the reading or after the homily; after the purification of the sacred vessels; and again for a moment, between the *oremus* and the recitation of the postcommunion prayer.

In ancient times the monastic recitation of the divine office sometimes had periods of private silent prayer, more or less prolonged, between the recitation of the psalms. But in the Canon of the Mass, the Mass of the faithful, there are no traces to be found at any time of any official pauses for private prayer or meditation.[20] The Mass is the sacred *action* above all others; it is something that is *done*; we need only recall some of the terms

---

[20] The interruption which now takes place at the *Memento's* for the living and for the dead merely substitutes for the ancient practice of the reading of names from written tablets called diptychs, which reading was done aloud by the deacon. The change came about with the advent of the Low Mass.

attaching to it: *eucharistian poieîn* or *eucharistiam facere*; *mysteria teleîn*; *sacrum facere; prosphoràn epiteleîn*, and *oblationem facere*.

In substance the Mass is the repetition of what Christ did at the Last Supper: *do this* in memory of Me. Christ, *making eucharist*, that is, *giving thanks*, took the bread and gave it to His disciples, saying: "Take this, it is My body"; and in like manner with the cup: *making eucharist*, He distributed it to His disciples, saying: "Take this, it is the cup of the new covenant in My blood." It was, in a transformed way, the sacred and convivial "eucharistic" *action* of the Jews. And sacred *action* is essentially what it always remains.

With these few remarks it was not my intention to imply that in the liturgy and in the Mass itself, and even in pontifical Mass, a certain individual concentration on the part of the priest and of the faithful, even very strong and of a psychological kind, is undesirable; nor did I mean to exclude that which belongs properly to the passive and mystical state; and much less did I mean to imply that such concentration and recollection is incompatible with the Mass, or impossible. I meant only to say that if this happens, and if it must happen (a question which must be examined more at length when we treat of the liturgy in relation to spirituality) the way which the liturgy itself opens for it is an abundant one, involving the varied, continuous, peaceful, simultaneous and communitarian actualization of the whole human psychological makeup: corporeal movements; the various senses, especially hearing and seeing; imagination; emotions; feelings; intelligence; will; and all this in the course of a sacred action which is uninterruptedly unfolded and in which hierarchy and faithful, each in his own role, must take an active part.

The liturgy does not invite the faithful, and much less the celebrant, in view of praying and uniting themselves to God, to isolate themselves from the common movements, songs, words, responses, or from the general circle of what is being said and what is being done.

All this, it is true, poses a certain problem, which we shall examine in due course: Is there not in fact a good case for accusing the liturgy of favoring too little the "recollection of the senses"; of being, on the other hand, too "distracting" and basically of being a superficial way to God, too external and popular — suitable, if you will, for ordinary and very imperfect minds? For the moment it will be enough only to state our awareness of the problem.

Intelligence, will, and sentiment in the liturgy

In respect, first of all, to the liturgy's nourishing of the intellect: to be sure, this nourishment is not of the academic sort. I would say that if you approach the liturgy with the expectation of finding there intellectual preoccupations in regard to revelation such as make up the principal content of scholastic theology, especially in its more ancient forms, but even in post-

Tridentine scholasticism, you will find very little. And this is for the very simple reason that the liturgy, generally speaking, was already fixed in its forms for a long time before scholasticism made its appearance.[21]

Nevertheless, this does not mean at all that the intellect does not find rich nourishment in the liturgy. Even without transforming them into disquisitions of a scholastic sort there are no prayers richer in doctrinal content than the prayers of the liturgy; and this is because in the liturgy there is constantly present the whole general plan of the sacred history of God's interventions in the world, the mystery of Christ, and the mystery of the Church; because everything in the liturgy is viewed in this framework in which all of man's sentiments towards God are poured out always as a response to this objective doctrinal reality present in the mind. With only a very few exceptions, occasioned by infiltrations of a later kind of religious sensibility in which the simple autopsychological sentiment of the subject prevails over the objective and therefore intellectual view of the doctrinal reality,[22] nothing is more foreign to the Roman liturgy than sentimental outpourings, the result of vague and superficial contact with an objective reality of which only the emotional aspect is noticed.

There are, on the other hand, objective doctrinal realities which remain on the primary level of the liturgical psychology. In this way vague sentimentality, however pious it may be, is always far overshadowed by clear intellectual vision: the vision of God, His wonderful deeds in the world in our behalf, and through His deeds, the vision of His perfections; of Christ in His earthly life and in His heavenly glory; of man in his misery; the history of redemption, prepared for in the Old Testament, realized by Christ in Palestine, still being realized for us in the ecclesial and sacramental reality; the heavenly Jerusalem and future glory together with the angels and the blessed with whom even now we enjoy a communion. Of great significance in this regard are the great anaphoral prayers of the Mass, whether in the Eastern or in the Western tradition.

And it is precisely because the intelligence which predominates in the psychology of the liturgy is not of the abstract metaphysical, discursive and deductive sort, but of a kind that is much more concrete, visible, intuitive, and historical, that the emotions and the will, in the total harmony of the

[21] Scholastic theology strove to examine the data of revelation from a point of view chiefly ontological, entitative or metaphysical. In the present Roman liturgy the Office of Corpus Christi — a very beautiful one, moreover, and composed with a remarkable liturgical sense — is probably the only one to bear some discreet traces of this scholastic way of thinking.

[22] In point of fact the rare exceptions which were able to be pointed out in previous editions of the present work — such things as the liturgical use of the hymns *Iesu dulcis memoria* and *Iesu decus angelicum*, taken from the *Iubilus rhythmicus de nomine Iesu* of an unknown author of the end of the twelfth or beginning of the thirteenth centuries, and objectionable features of certain feasts — have since been largely expunged from the liturgy through the ongoing work of liturgical reform.

human being, have an essential part to play in the liturgy. The liturgy never considers the objective world of dogma and of salvation history, which is ever present to the intellect, without responding immediately to it with a total adhesion of the affective and volitional faculties, under forms and gradations almost infinite: admiration, aspiration, desire, supplication, humble recognition of one's own misery, acts of faith, of hope, of charity, of humility, of compunction, etc. It is always at this level of affection and will that the liturgy completes the cycle of the total psychological actualization of the human being.

Various activities of life; esthetic sense; pedagogic efficacy

To be convinced that the liturgy sanctifies all human activities that are in themselves honest, whether individually or socially undertaken, it is enough to observe that the liturgy, by means of appropriate blessings in its ritual intervenes in all the circumstances of life from birth to the tomb and sanctifies every kind of human activity, in our day not even forgetting sport, and every sort of product of human labor and of technology. The theological theme of these sacramental blessings is almost always this: "Grant, O Lord, that those who are engaged in the activities connected with these things may be protected by You in body and in soul; that they may use these things in accord with right order and may conduct their activity in accord with Your will, so that they may come to love You, to serve You, and finally to enjoy You in heaven." Thus, along with a hundred others, there is a blessing for telegraphic apparatus, for the railroads, for electric machinery, for an archives, for a library, for a printing establishment, for a bridge, for a well, for a furnace, for an oven, for a ship, for an automobile, for an airplane, for a seismograph, and for mountain climbing gear.[23]

Here, for example, you may read and ponder the blessing of mountain climbers or Alpinists:

> "Through the intercession of St. Bernard, whom You have given as patron to Alpine dwellers and travelers, protect, O Lord, these Your servants; and grant that those who climb these peaks may come to the mountain which is Christ. Through the same Christ, our Lord." [24]

In this context of the sanctification which the liturgy provides for all human faculties and activities, it is only proper that a special emphasis be placed upon the exploitation, in the service of sanctification and worship, of man's esthetic sentiment, of his artistic activity and of the fruits which derive therefrom. That sentiment and esthetic activity are strongly utilized

---

[23] See the Roman Ritual, title 9, chapters 8-9. The liturgy has a tendency to introduce a new blessing with every new invention. See also CL, art. 79.

[24] Roman Ritual, title 9, ch. 8, no. 20.

in the liturgy is undeniable. Architecture, painting, sculpture, music, all are employed in abundance in the liturgy, as was explained above in chapter 2. Some historical restrictions in this area — the absence in remote Christian antiquity of figured representations, statuary and even of music, except for the simple popular hymns and songs which, there is reason to believe, were in use — can be explained by the historical circumstances of the times and especially by the fact that contemporary pagan worship employed these means in abundance. The Church was concerned with demonstrating to the faithful, even on the psychological level, the essential difference between pagan worship and that of Christianity. With the passing of that obvious danger, the liturgy began to make use, and does yet continue to make use, on a grand scale, of its natural artistic heritage.

But, of course, it cannot be denied that this esthetic display can present certain dangers. This is true of anything human if it is not used properly, not excluding even various psychic and physical aids employed in various methods of prayer and meditation. Here the danger will be of allowing oneself to be deluded by the liturgy's esthetic display, in an estheticism unaccompanied by a profound religious life. Still, it would be absurd to say that a wise exploitation of the esthetic sense cannot be of powerful service, as we explained in treating of art in chapter 2 above, to the holy ends of religious actualization in the liturgy, precisely by reason of man's deep substantial unity, which is corporeal, psychic, and spiritual at the same time.[25]

It is from this basic aptitude for accepting the whole concrete man and involving him completely in worship that the liturgy derives its extraordinary pedagogical efficacy, as is recognized by all. In the liturgy, so to speak, the religious object enters completely into the whole man and penetrates his depths through every pore of his psychology; and it does this quite unobtrusively, almost without his noticing it. Every age, every culture, every state of mind and every degree of perfection, each in its own way and in its own degree, finds nourishment in abundance in the liturgy.

In regard to the heritage of particular nations and the principle of adaptation

It is also, I think, this fundamental aptitude of accepting fully the concrete man as he is that explains in good measure the historical fact that, notwithstanding its strongly traditional character and its nature as a thing transmitted, not only every great epoch of history but also every notable ethnic group that has made use of the liturgy has left its imprint thereon as evidence of its own particular needs. And this constitutes in the liturgy a principle of development and of continuous adaptation which, along with

[25] Romano Guardini, in his various works on the liturgy, insisted very much on the concept of the liturgy as "disinterested activity" and on the concept of "liturgical playfulness."

the principle of permanence and conservation, especially active in the liturgy, makes of the liturgy a living experience rather than transforming it into a mere museum piece.

This power of adaptation to ethnic peculiarities, both spatial and temporal, has evidently been much more apparent and effective in periods of greater flowering of particular liturgies, whether Eastern or Western, while on the other hand, under a regimen of liturgical unification, such as prevailed more generally in the West, it has been somewhat less in evidence.

Actually the modern Roman liturgy, in appearances so far removed from the living and popular sensibilities of those who employ it, is not just the ancient Roman liturgy, but the fruit of the ancient Roman, modified and developed by notable medieval Gallican and Germanic influences. Whether, with a certain modern German author, we find this fact a source of great joy,[26] or whether, with other authors, we oppose this influence, being unable to forget the reverse side of the coin,[27] the fact is there, and it proves the great vitality of the liturgy.

After the post-Tridentine phase of static and rigid uniformity, the Roman liturgy at this very moment is giving a noteworthy and practical demonstration of this very vitality, with the impulse to reform and to new creation which characterizes it: a stimulus precisely to the principle that the liturgy is addressed to the concrete and living man in the totality of his being, and that therefore it must always be near to him.

The Second Vatican Council has reinforced, both for the liturgy in general [28] and for its individual parts,[29] the principle of mutability and therefore of the possibility of reform, with the proper cautions, of course,[30] of the ecclesiastical institution of the liturgy.

Much more, in the compass of this same regulatory principle, the same council has proclaimed, in particular, the rule of the necessity of adapting the liturgy to the temperament and traditions of various peoples, by expressly repudiating the idea of imposing even in this area a rigid uniformity, except, of course, in matters involving the faith or the common good of the whole Church. The words themselves of this proclamation are particularly solemn:

---

[26] Theodore Klauser, *Abendländische Liturgiegeschichte*, Bonn 1949, pp. 14-20, after showing how our knowledge of the part played by the Franco-Germanic Church has increased, concludes that "the meaning of all these historical discoveries with regard to our attitude toward the Roman liturgy is clear: It is Roman, but it is also ours (*Romana est, sed etiam nostra*)." See also A. Mayer-Pfannholz, "Die Liturgie und die deutsche Geistesgeschichte," in the *Zeitschrift für deutsche Geistesgeschichte*, Vol. I (1935), pp. 5-12; I.

van Acken, *Germanische Frömmigkeit in liturgischen Hymnen*, Freiburg 1937; H. Dausend, *Germanische Frömmigkeit in der kirchlichen Liturgie*, Wiesbaden 1938.

[27] For example, Ildephonse Herwegen, *Antike, Christentum und Germanentum*, Salzburg (Pustet), 1932; J. A. Jungmann, *The Mass of the Roman Rite*, Vol. I, pp. 74-141.

[28] CL, art. 21. See also MD, no. 49ff (Lat. 48ff).

[29] CL, art. 50; 62; 88; 107; 118; 123; 128.

[30] CL, art. 23.

"Even in the liturgy the Church does not wish to impose a rigid uniformity in matters which do not involve the faith or the good of the whole community. Rather does she respect and foster the qualities and talents of the various races and nations. Anything in these people's way of life which is not indissolubly bound up with superstition and error she studies with sympathy, and, if possible, preserves intact. She sometimes even admits such things into the liturgy itself, provided they harmonize with its true and authentic spirit." [31]

Among recent Popes who gave expression to the principle in the general area of the missions is Benedict XV; but this is the first time that this principle of adaptation has been expressed so strongly, and the first time that it has been expressly extended to the liturgy. Now it is made a principle for the whole Church, while taking special cognizance of mission lands.[32]

This principle is now admitted not only in the sense that it wishes to afford permission, within the very interior of the Roman rite and while safeguarding its substantial unity, for a very large measure of adaptability to local needs,[33] but even opens the door, in certain cases, especially in the mission lands, for even deeper changes.[34]

It considers the possibility, in certain places, of an evolution of the Roman rite that might arrive eventually, with the Roman rite as point of departure, at new rites corresponding more closely to the mentality of certain peoples. I am thinking especially of the African nations and those of the Far East, where in the first phase of their Christian life, the people received the Roman rite along with their faith. It is a wonderful opening for true Catholicity.

It is this same basic fact of the adhesion of the liturgy to the concrete and total psychology of man that explains the resemblance, sometimes quite striking, that the rites of the Christian liturgy are able to have with more or less parallel rites of non-Christian forms of worship, especially the more ancient ones, or even the fact that the ancient Christian liturgy adapted and Christianized various cultic usages in the Hellenistic and Roman environment. In all this, nothing could be more natural. Human nature is always the same; therefore it is logical that the psychological expressions in which that nature is embodied and in which it externalizes itself should also be fundamentally the same. The Christian liturgy takes this psychology into account; and that is why its rites are able to present noteworthy traces of a resemblance to rites which that same human nature has created elsewhere.

Consequently, given that the rites of worship in the Hellenistic and Roman environment, where the Christian religion first developed, were not infrequently natural expressions, or, at any rate, expressions honest enough in themselves of human psychology, it is in no way extraordinary, then, if the

[31] CL, art. 37.
[32] CL, art. 38-39; 65; 68; 119.

[33] CL, art. 38-39; 63b.
[34] CL, art. 40; 54; 119.

Christian religion, in certain instances, has thought it opportune to adapt these expressions by giving them a Christian spirit.

2. The Liturgy and the Involvement of the Infrahuman World in Worship, in Furthering the Ends of the Kingdom of God

The unity between man and infrahuman creation in revelation

According to revelation there is an intimate connection between man and infrahuman creation in the kingdom of God. Infrahuman creation is destined to serve the ends of this kingdom. This is achieved in man and through man, insofar as the infrahuman is of service to man in his achievement of the end assigned to him in the common kingdom. The infrahuman world is entirely at the service of the divine life in man.

Some essential characteristics of this insight into the intimate unity between man and infrahuman creation are to be found already in the first three chapters of Genesis.

In the narrative of creation in the first chapter of Genesis, there is a strong underlining, along with the transcendence of God, of the order and unity of the universe, by means of the schematic and progressive distribution of days and of the things created in them. The whole work of God has its culmination in the creation of man, to whose use and dominion, as representative and immediate vice-regent of God, all the rest is, by right, ordered and made subservient, while it will but remain to man himself, by means of his industry, to realize this dominion effectively (Gen. 1:28-30). Thus the infrahuman world is conceived as the theater where the history of man is unfolded and as a means to the ends to which man must attain.

These ends are specified in the second and third chapters of Genesis. Here, too, primarily, plants and animals are seen as ordered to man as their lord and master, under the supreme dominion of God.[35] Moreover, the author clearly intends to indicate that the highest purpose of man's life here below

[35] See Gen. 2:8-9, 17-21. The question is discussed whether to admit a genetic connection between the body of the first man and the body of animals. From the theological point of view, such evolutionism is admissible on certain conditions: first, that it be extended only to the body and not to the soul; then, that the theory suppose an extraordinary intervention of God at the decisive moment, transforming the animal body in such a way as to make it capable of receiving a human soul and thereby transforming it into a human body. On the metaphysical level, this transformation reaches into the very essence of the body, even if it be of small extent on the morphological level.

In such a perspective the connection between man and the infrahuman world, and hence the unity of the cosmos, and divine Providence itself, appear still more wonderful: all the lower creatures, mineral, vegetable and animal, tend and coöperate in a vast organized process to the formation of the human body, which is then endowed by God with a spiritual soul; and this human composite enters into participation in the divine life.

Man has his apex in Christ, in whom the lower world, the human world, the angelic, and the divine have their greatest unity.

was to be found in those gratuitous and amicable relations which the proto-parents enjoyed with God before their sin: the paradisial state. For the sacred author those familiar relations with God constituted the ideal of life, from which the history of mankind ought to have developed without disruption. Nevertheless, the course of man's history, unfortunately, because of the sin of our protoparents, did go astray from this ideal path. Such a deviation, for the sacred author, created not only a state of enmity between man and God, but a tension between man and inferior creation, which latter is no longer submissive to man but resists him.

By the express will of God, who in this way punishes man's rebellion against His dominion, the infrahuman world becomes for man a source of sorrows and tribulations (Gen. 3:16-19). Even after his sin man still has the right and the duty to make creation subservient to himself; but the history of primitive mankind makes it evident that from that moment on, the prog-ress of man's obtaining dominion was very slow and painful,[36] and that man-kind was obliged to begin, so to speak, at zero. In all this the fundamental idea is clear enough: the rupture of the unity between man and God, brought about by sin, results also in some way in the rupture of the unity between man and inferior creatures. The latter, in their relations with man, in some way follow the course of man's relations with God.

Such a basic concept is found throughout the Old Testament, emphasized and developed in various ways.

The concept of God, supreme Creator and absolute Master of infrahuman creation no less than of His other creatures, naturally enough, is found every-where in the Old Testament; and, in some passages, it is especially developed and lyrically celebrated, as in Job, chapters 38-41.

Infrahuman creatures are able and obliged to serve man in a special way for the legitimate sustenance of his physical life as previously decreed by God. In this regard the sense of the law of offering firstfruits is significant: it is precisely by this offering that man must acknowledge that all his nourish-ment is given him by God (Lev. 23:9-11, 15-17, 39-43; Deut. 26:1-11).

Furthermore the infrahuman world must be of service to man by raising him to a knowledge of God, of His existence, and of His attributes (e.g., Wis. 13:1-9).

The Old Testament develops in a special way the theme that the infra-human world is obliged to serve man by assisting him in the praise and adoration of God, by the very fact that this infrahuman world constitutes a revelation of God. Most numerous are the psalms and hymns which offer praise and adoration to God by taking their cue from a consideration of

---

[36] See, for example, the invention of the crafts and occupations according to Gen. 4: 17ff, which belongs, like Gen. 2 and 3, to the Yahwist tradition. That man, even after his fall, still has the right and the duty to sub-ject the earth to himself, is pointed out ex-pressly by the priestly tradition in Gen. 9:1-7.

the whole of creation, and in which also, in doing this, the psalmist invites in a certain way the same creation to praise and adore its Creator. Among these, worthy of special note because of their extraordinary beauty, are Psalms 8; 18A; 28; 103; 148 (all in the liturgical [Vulgate] enumeration); and the Hymn of the Three Young Men in the Fiery Furnace (Dan. 3:56-88): *Benedicite omnia opera Domini Domino.*[37] In these hymns the whole cosmos is truly viewed as a single unity which is referred to the glory of the Lord.

Also the Old Testament develops further the theme of Gen. 3:17-19, that if man, turning aside from the purpose assigned him by God, revolts against Him, and if, in particular, he makes wicked use of the things of the infra-human world, God will use those very creatures against man in order to chastise him and bring him back to repentance. Thus God uses the infra-human elements to punish an unfaithful Israel (Deut. 32:23-24); drought and famine, brought on by unseasonable weather and by illnesses among the cattle, are ordinary means employed by God as punishments (Joel 1:1-20; 3 Kings 8:35-40); with these same infrahuman elements He punishes sinners, His enemies, and the enemies of Israel (Deut. 32:31-33; Wis. ch. 11–12). At the same time, He places these same elements at the disposition of His friends and faithful servants, as happens in the miracles worked by the prophets, and when He gives a good and fertile earth to His friends, to His faithful people (Deut. 31:12-14; Wis. ch. 11–12), with abundance of flocks and harvests, etc. (Lev. 26:3-12; Amos 9:13-15; Joel 2:25).

So strong throughout the Old Testament is this idea of intimate association between infrahuman creatures and man, for the sake of man's relations with God, that in the second part of the book of Isaias (65:17-25) it is foretold that in the future God will perfect and give a perfect heart to His ideal, messianic, and eschatological people, and He will create a new heaven and a new earth as a place corresponding to what will then be their situation; and in this way the primitive harmony of paradise, a harmony between the inferior creatures and man under the supreme dominion of the Creator, will not just be regained, but will be made sublime.[38]

It is easy to verify how these ideas of the Old Testament on the unity of the infrahuman world and man, to the ends of divine life, are all taken up again and made more profound in the New Testament.

---

[37] See also Psalms (again in the liturgical [Vulgate] numbering) 96:11-13; 97:7-9; 146: 8-9; 147.

[38] See also Is. 11:6-8. A comparison between Is. 68:25 and Is. 11:6-8 suggests that even in chapter 11 of Isaias there is the idea of a return to a state of paradise, and that verses 6-8 are written not with man only in mind. The argument of Jean Steinmann that Is. 11:6-8

presents merely a symbolic tableau of the relations among men, and that the idea of vegetarianism appears in Scripture only later than the authorship of the first part of Isaias is not convincing (see Steinmann's *Le Prophéte Isaïe,* Paris 1950, pp. 169-170). In view of the texts, we would wish for other positive reasons for a contrary position. See also Is. 32:15-18; 35: 1-9; and 24:18-23.

This great and almost incredible profundity which the New Testament brings to bear upon these ideas is accomplished primarily through the message of the incarnation of the Son of God, the Word who "was made flesh" (John 1:14); and becoming in all things like unto men who "have blood and flesh in common, He in like manner has shared in these" (Heb. 2:14). Thus it is an integral and perfect human nature, not just a soul but a body as well, that was assumed by the Word, and became Christ the prototype and head of all creation in its totality: the point of physical encounter between God, man, and inferior creation. In the body of the man Christ, Word incarnate, the infrahuman world achieves the summit of union with God and of divine life.[39] And there, in the same divine Person of the Word, there takes place the most profound consecration possible of the human cosmos to the divinity; and this of the human cosmos as much in its static aspect as in its dynamic historical aspect; and secondarily, this consecration includes also the infrahuman world. This is precisely what is implied in the manner of expression employed by the *Roman Martyrology* for the 25th of December:

> "The eighth day before the Kalends of January: in the year 5199 from the creation of the world; in the year 2957 after the deluge; in the year 2015 from the birth of Abraham; in the year 1510 from Moses and the exodus of the people of Israel from Egypt; in the one hundred and ninety-fourth Olympiad; in the year of the foundation of Rome 752; in the forty-second year of the rule of Octavian Augustus: when the whole world was composed and at peace, Jesus Christ, eternal God and Son of the eternal Father, *desiring to consecrate the world by His most obedient coming*, having been conceived of the Holy Spirit, nine months after that conception, having been made man, was born in Bethlehem of Judah."

It is in no way extraordinary, then, if, in the life of Jesus, the whole infrahuman world seems to be perfectly submissive to Him and entirely at His service.[40] His behavior in respect to the things of the infrahuman world is such as must be imitated by every man: His perfect and tranquil command; His simple use thereof, with no hint of dualism, for the honest ends of human life (see Mark 7:14ff, and its parallels), thus establishing the basic

---

[39] St. John Damascene quite properly observes: "The Father's gracious will, in His only-begotten Son, has effected the salvation of the entire cosmos and restored the unity of all things. For since man is a microcosm, the knot that ties together all substances visible and invisible, because he himself is both, it was most fitting that the Lord and Ruler of all things should desire that in His only-begotten and consubstantial Son the unity of divinity with humanity be realized, and by means of this unity of divinity with all things, so that God would be all in all" (*Hom. de transfig. Dom.* [PG 96, 572ff]). In such a perspective as this, the modified evolutionism mentioned in note 35 above is seen as a preparation not only for the human body but even for the Incarnation.

[40] See, for example, Matthew 8:23ff and its parallels: the calming of the storm on the lake.

pattern for the future conduct of His Apostles.[41] Yet, how easily does man become a slave to inferior creation, by perverting its meaning and its right use.[42] Hence, the continual exhortations to remain interiorly free of them. For Jesus, lower creation is a mirror of clearest quality in which the Father is ever revealed. Shining through His parables is a marvelous sense of nature; but for Him, this is always just the point of departure from which He reascends to God and to the reality of the divine life, a way to illustrate the workings of providence and of the laws of the divine economy and of the divine life in the world.[43]

Finally, in the institution of the Eucharist and of baptism, material things and ordinary usages are intimately associated with the higher purposes of the transmission of the divine life to men.

Already in St. Paul we find explicitly the theory itself of the original unity of the whole cosmos, including infrahuman creation, in the plans of God; of the disrupting of this unity through sin; of its reëstablishment in Christ and through Christ and under His dominion, a reëstablishment already real and radical here below in the redeemed and in the means of redemption, and to be perfected in the future life in heaven, with the resurrection.

The principal texts are Col. 1:15-20 and Rom. 8:19-22,

> "The eager longing of the created world awaits the revelation of the sons of God. Indeed, creation was made subject to vanity, not willingly, but by reason of Him who made it subject, in hope, because creation itself will also be delivered from its slavery to corruption, and will attain to the glory of the sons of God. We know well that the whole of nature is as one in its groaning and in its labor pains from the beginning even until now."

Vanity and slavery to corruption, to which material creation is now subject, is the sin of the man whose use of that creation is contrary to God's ordinances and constitutes abuse; and the notion includes all the moral and physical consequences of this sin. It presupposes that prior to sin such slavery did not exist; man, at that time subject to God, made use of creation in accord with right reason. The future glory of the sons of God is the resurrection of the body and the final economy in the glory that is found with the "new heavens and a new earth" (1 Peter 3:13) which we await — where there will

---

[41] See, for example, Rom. 14:4. For Paul's reactions against dualist tendencies and the mentality thereof: 1 Cor. 8–10, especially 10: 25ff; Col. 2:22; 1 Tim. 4:3b-5; Titus 1:14ff; Heb. 13:9; 1 Cor. 7; 1 Tim. 2:15; 4:3a; 1 Cor. 11:9; 1 Tim. 4:4.

[42] See, for example, the parables of those invited to the wedding feast: . . . *alius in villam suam* . . . *alius vero ad negotiationem*

suam . . .; Matthew 22; Luke 14:16ff.

[43] See: the lilies of the field and the birds of the air; the young sparrows; the vine and the branches; the color of the sky, if reddening . . .; see the fig tree and all the trees: when they have fruit you know that summer is near; the parable of the sower; of the wheat, etc.

take place the perfectly sublime reëstablishment of the original order. This reëstablishment is, for the present, only initial and partial in us "who have the firstfruits of the Spirit"; and elaborating upon this mention of a firstfruits, "even we," the Epistle to the Romans continues at some length, "we groan within ourselves, awaiting the adoption of sons, that is, the redemption of our body; because it was in hope that we were saved" (8:23ff).[44]

In the Apocalypse, finally, this idea of the unity of the cosmos, including also infrahuman creation, directed toward the notion of a single city and people of God in the heavenly Jerusalem, is strongly emphasized: the use of material elements for the definitive punishment of the enemies of God; plagues; guardian angels of infrahuman elements, especially of material things, to see to their use in accord with God's established order; resurrection, glorious for the sons of God, opprobrious for evil-doers; hell with its torments for the enemies of God, punished by means of material elements; the new heavens and the new earth, corresponding perfectly to the condition of the man in whom the divine life has attained its full development; the eternal and cosmic liturgy of praise, in which even infrahuman creation is associated —

> "and every creature that is in heaven and on earth and under the earth and on the sea, and all the things that are contained in the sea, I heard them saying: 'To Him who sits upon the throne, and to the Lamb, blessing and honor and glory and power through the ages of ages'" (Apoc. 5:13).

There is, therefore, nothing more certain, nothing clearer in revelation, than the idea of the integration even of the infrahuman world into the universal cosmic unity to the ends of the divine life in man and through man, and most especially in the Man-God, through the Man-God and through His works.

The unity between man and infrahuman creation in the liturgy

This being the situation with the general view of the world according to revelation, it is in no way extraordinary that the whole of infrahuman creation, in its own proper way, is vitalized in worship in the liturgy.[45] The

---

[44] In regard to this theme in St. Paul see for example Lucien Cerfaux, *Christ in the Theology of St. Paul*, New York 1959, pp. 419ff. The theme of the reconstitution of the unity of the cosmos, including infrahuman creation, was afterwards taken up again and developed, most notably by St. Irenaeus, who includes it in his doctrine of the *anakephalaíosis*. See also E. Scharl, *Recapitulatio mundi*, Freiburg im Br. 1941.

[45] On this question see, for example, I. Herwegen, "*Das Verklärungsgedanke in der Litur-*

gie," in *Festschrift G. Hartling*, Kempten 1913, pp. 108-116 (reprinted in I. Herwegen, *Alte Quellen neuer Kraft*, Düsseldorf 1920, pp. 22-47); J. Pinsk, *Die sakramentale Welt*, Freiburg 1938 (French translation under the title *L'espérance de la gloire*, Paris 1952); J. Caspar, *Weltverklärung im liturgischen Geist der Ostkirche*, Freiburg 1939; A. Winklhofer, *Schöpfung und Liturgie*, Ettal 1951; H. Schulte, *Die Entsühnung und Heiligung der Welt nach dem römischen Pontifikale und Rituale*, Buenos Aires 1954.

liturgy is already the design of Christ in action, that design, I mean to say, which in a most real way has reëstablished the original unity of the cosmos disrupted by sin. The only thing is, this reëstablishment, for the present, has not attained the total extension to which it is destined. And even in those beings who have attained it, it is only in its initial stages, a first-fruits as it were; the rupture between infrahuman creation and man on the way to divine life has not yet been completely healed, because sin still reigns in the sinner, and its consequences, still sensible even for the just, will not be completely destroyed except in the general resurrection. And this is why, even in the liturgy, that reëstablishment of unity between man and infra-human creation directed towards the ends of divine life, even while it is most real, is still partial and initial.

Moreover, on this earth these same firstfruits, however real, are veiled, *in sacramento, in mysterio*. Only in heaven will everything be unveiled, in glory. Hence, even in the liturgy, the transfiguration of the infrahuman world to the service of the divine life remains *sub velo, in sacramento, in mysterio*. Only the eyes of faith will be able to perceive it.

Nevertheless, that reëstablishment and that transfiguration in the liturgy are real. They are manifested first of all in the liturgy of the sacrifice of the Mass and of the sacraments; next in the liturgy of the sacramentals, such as in exorcisms, consecrations and blessings; and finally, in the liturgy of praise, the divine office.

The greatest liturgical involvement of the infrahuman world in the cosmic unity, ordered to divine life, takes place in the Eucharist. The transubstantiation of the bread and wine, presented by the faithful, into the body and blood of Jesus Christ, truly immolated though gloriously reigning at the right of the Father and presenting Himself to Him as a victim of infinite worth, is, here below, the most extraordinary assumption, elevation, and transfiguration of the infrahuman world to the service of the divine life. With the exception of the assumption which took place at the first instant of the conception of the body of Jesus, in the hypostatic union of the Word, there is not, in the whole history of the world, a more marvelous example of the unitative significance which belongs to the cosmos itself in the plans of God.

The matter of bread and wine, of which, even while the accidents remain, the whole substance is changed into the substance of the body and blood of Christ, serves as a substratum and as a secret and transparent vehicle for the real and sacrificial presence of Christ; and thus, in its own way, it is profoundly associated with that whole flow of divine life which the Eucharistic sacrifice carries to men, living and dead, of joy to the angels and saints in heaven, and of glory to God. Thus, in the Mass, there is accomplished in the most perfect way possible before the creation of the new heaven and the new earth, after the fashion of firstfruits and *sub velo* and *in sacramento*, that redemption of material creation which is its liberation from slavery and corruption and sin, and which, according to St. Paul, all creation ardently desires in accord with the profound order established in created things by God Himself.

Among the other sacraments a similar, even if quite inferior, employment of infrahuman creation in the service of divine life is found especially in baptism and in the anointing of the sick. In these sacraments, in fact, in the so-called sacramental "matter" which, determined by the "form," constitutes the sacrament, material elements properly so-called are involved. It is of the faith, in fact, that in baptism the remote matter is water and the proximate matter is the washing in water of those being baptized. It is also of the faith that in the sacred anointing the remote matter is oil. Moreover, the opinion is deemed certain that this remote matter must be oil duly consecrated. The proximate matter of this sacrament is the anointing made with this same oil. Even in confirmation it is held that the remote matter is chrism consecrated by the bishop and the more common opinion maintains that the proximate matter is the imposition of the hands together with the signing and anointing with chrism. In these sacraments therefore, each in its own way, the material element, as instrument of God, is a concomitant grace, since the sacrament causes the grace which it signifies.

This rededication of the infrahuman creature to the service of the divine life is surely one of the more notable elements in the liturgical world of the sacramentals: exorcisms, consecrations, and blessings. Here, it is true, it takes place in a way which is inferior to that of the sacraments; [46] but it is nevertheless most noteworthy, particularly because of its broad extension, embracing, as it does, a very large number of elements. The seven sacraments look only to the principal circumstances of life. Three of these — baptism, confirmation, and holy orders — cannot be repeated. Two others, matrimony and the anointing of the ill, while they may be repeated in the same subject, are in fact repeated only with comparative rarity. Communion, even if daily, and confession, are but relatively rare moments when compared to the rest of the time and activities of man.

The world of the sacramentals, on the other hand, can be practically extended to almost all the objects with which a man comes into contact in his daily life and can pervade virtually every situation.[47]

In the exorcism performed over inanimate objects, their rededication to the service of the divine life takes place in this sense: through sin man gave to the demon the possibility of employing infrahuman creatures to exercise in various ways, direct and indirect, his malignant influence to the prejudice of the divine life, and to oppose the expansion and intensification of the kingdom of God. In extreme cases, not to be easily supposed, this demonia-

[46] Explained above, p. 87ff. [47] CL, art. 61.

cal influence can advance, with God's permission, to the point of obsession properly so-called. In an exorcism the prayer of the Church obtains from God [48] the expulsion of the demon from the object, in the case of obsession, or simply special divine protection for those who make use of the object with the proper dispositions. This special protection includes first of all a special providence of God to prevent any possible demoniacal influence on things, in such a way that a man in employing them according to their right ends as willed by God will not be hindered by the demon. Furthermore, it means also that actual graces will be accorded to those who make right use of such things with the proper dispositions.

Very instructive from this point of view is, for example, the prayer accompanying the exorcism of water as found in the Roman Ritual, in the rite for the blessing of holy water:

> "O God, who, for the salvation of the human race, founded Your greatest mysteries on this substance, water, graciously hear our prayers and pour out the power of Your blessing into this element, prepared for many kinds of purifications. In this way, let Your creature become an agent of divine grace in the service of Your mysteries, to drive away the demons and to dispel illnesses, so that everything in the homes and other places of the faithful that is sprinkled with this liquid may be preserved from every impurity and freed from every contagion. Let no pestilential spirit reside there, no breath of corruption. Drive out the lurking enemy with all his wiles. And if there be anything that might prove harmful to the welfare and tranquility of those who dwell therein, may it be put to flight by the sprinkling of this water; and thus may the health called forth by the invocation of Your holy name be made secure against every attack. Through Christ our Lord." [49]

In the consecration of inanimate things to the service of God by means of the sacramental rites, as in the consecration of a church or of a chalice, by virtue of the prayer of the Church God accepts the thing as reserved to His exclusive use and as removed from every profane use; and He accords special graces to those who make use of the thing with the right dispositions.

Even in the simple blessings of infrahuman things there is included the idea that God, always in consideration of the prayer of the Church, will grant, in accord with the designs of His providence, a special protection to the object itself and to the use which man makes of it, with a view to permitting him the more easily to work out his salvation. It is noteworthy that in the formulas of these blessings there is not infrequently a sense of the

---

[48] *Ex opere operantis Ecclesiae,* as was explained in its proper place.

[49] See also, for example, the exorcism over the oil to be blessed (*Roman Ritual,* title 9,

ch. 7, no. 8); and the exorcism of water as indicated for the former Vigil of Epiphany (*ibid.,* title 9, ch. 9, no. 28, 3).

cosmic unity of the kingdom of God and a consciousness that even infrahuman creation, in its own way, is called to a coöperation therein. Read, for example, the blessing of bees in the *Roman Ritual:*

> "O Lord God Almighty, who created heaven and earth and all the animals which exist therein and thereon, so that they might be useful to men, You have commanded that the ministers of Your most holy Church light tapers in Your temple, candles made from the product of the labors of the bees, during the performance of the sacred rite in which the most holy Body and Blood of Your Son, Jesus Christ, is confected and eaten. May Your holy blessing be upon these bees and upon their hives. Let them be fruitful and multiply, and keep from them every misfortune, so that their product may be of service in praising You, in praising Your Son and the Holy Spirit, and in praising the most Blessed Virgin Mary. Through the same Christ our Lord." [50]

Thus in the liturgical life exemplified in the sacramentals the following great realities of doctrine and of Christian life are given concrete expression and are placed in operation:

1) the unity of the cosmos;
2) the cosmic universality of the fall and of the reign of Satan;
3) the cosmic universality of the redemption accomplished in Christ as a liberation from the rule of Satan;
4) man as a microcosm and as focal point of the universe;
5) the sacred worth of sensible things as gift of God to man, and as instrument of man in going to God.

All of this is opposed in the highest degree to pantheism, polytheism, magic, naturalism, and to every kind of secularism.

It is not necessary to document at length how in the liturgy of the divine office the whole of inferior creation is given a place in the praising of God. This is evident first of all with the words themselves of the psalms and hymns of the Old Testament, especially with Psalm 148, *Laudate Dominum de coelis*, and with the hymn, *Benedicite omnia opera Domini Domino*. Another way in which the liturgy associates inferior creation to the praise of God and makes use of it in rediscovering Him and in elevating us to Him is through the symbolism of the infrahuman world, or better, by an exemplarism of the superhuman world impressed upon the infrahuman world. Most notable from this point of view is the cycle of light and of darkness in the hymns of the hours in the Roman liturgy.

Thus, in man and through man, in the liturgical action, the whole inferior world fulfills its higher destiny: to lead to the knowledge, to the glori-

---

[50] See also, for example, the prayers for the blessing of oil (*Roman Ritual*, title 9, ch. 7, no. 8); of wine for the ill (*ibid.*, title 9, ch. 7, no. 3); of animals (*ibid.*, title 9, ch. 5, no. 3).

fication, and to the adoration of God. The liturgy lends a consciousness and a voice — which is the Church's voice, or better, the voice of Christ — to all infrahuman things.

In short, in the liturgy there is realized a sublime concretization of the Catholic perspective of the relationship between nature and grace: grace which does not destroy nature, but purifies it of sin and elevates it.

See how a Protestant, otherwise indifferent to the liturgy and to the implications of this very teaching, has understood the grandeur of the logic in the Catholic belief that sin did not destroy nature:

> "The entry into the world of Catholic worship opens to our view a structure of beauty and triumphal grandeur. This structure is exalted in brilliant panoramic views of Greek antiquity. The panorama is characterized by the festive rejoicing of the gods, the celebration of the encounter with them in worship, and is crowned by the Christian cupola. In reality the temple has not been abolished. The idea which directed its construction and utilization is completed, elevated, and surpassed. And this is accomplished not with the toilsome justification characteristic of the recent Protestant attempts at a liturgical revival, but with the good conscience of a theology based on foundations broad enough to embrace, in its unsurpassable grandeur, all the values of sentiment and reason, and the intuitions of all religions and of all philosophies." [51]

[51] G. Harbsmeier, *Dass wir die Predigt und sein Wort nicht verachten*, Munich 1958, p. 146.

12 THE LITURGY AND THE LAW OF

THE COSMIC UNIVERSALITY

OF THE KINGDOM OF GOD:

II. LITURGY, SAINTS AND ANGELS

The liturgy is addressed to every living person in the totality of his being — being which has deep contacts even with the infrahuman world. But this totality of the living human being is not really fully explored if a person is considered as an individual separate from all other individuals. Man is a social being.

That revelation, and therefore the liturgy, does not consider man simply from the individual point of view but also from the social point of view in his relations with other men still living on this earth was sufficiently explained above, where we analyzed the law of salvation in community. It is necessary now to add that revelation, and, therefore, the liturgy, prolongs this consideration of the social aspect of every individual in relation to other men even beyond this present life, inasmuch as it establishes a deep union between the faithful who are still pilgrims on this earth and all the just who, since the beginning of the world, have been assembled in God's presence, the ultimate end of every life. Moreover, revelation, and, as always its constant follower, the liturgy, establish a deep union between men still on this earth and even the angelic world itself.

1. The Liturgy and the Just Who Have Arrived at Their Destination

A synthetic expression of this concept of the unity of the faithful on this earth with the justified in the beyond and with the angelic world itself in the heavenly Jerusalem is to be found in the Epistle to the Hebrews 12:21-23, a passage which we have already analyzed in another context. The general idea of this text is as follows: ancient Israel was constituted as a religious people, as the *q*ᵉ*hal* Yahweh, in a pact sealed in the blood of calves at the foot of Mount Sinai, preceded by a scene of majesty and terror, an action performed to instill in the people a most profound respect. Christians are constituted as the Church of God, the new people of God, the new Israel, by a new pact in the Blood of Jesus. Thus, whoever enters the Church does not draw near to a physical mountain in a scene of alarm and terror, but rather to a spiritual mountain, a celestial one, much more majestic and divinely awe-inspiring. It is the holy mountain, the superterrestrial Sion, the celestial Jerusalem.

Now, the celestial Jerusalem is the city of the living God, where the angels are, along with the just who have already arrived at the end of their pilgrimage. To all these, every Christian draws near, setting out as if to a city in which he has a role to play in the general unity of the kingdom of God: "You have drawn near to Mount Sion, to the city of the living God, to the heavenly Jerusalem, and to all the myriads of angels, gathered in a festive liturgy (*panégyris*) and assembly (*ekklesía*) of the first-born inscribed in the heavens, and to God, the Judge of all, and to the spirits of the just who have been made perfect (*teteleioménon*), who have arrived at their goal, and to Jesus, the Mediator of the new covenant, and to the sprinkled blood which speaks better than that of Abel."

Special note should be taken of such terms in this text as *to draw near,* the *panégyris,* and the *ekklesía;* terms which provide the heavenly Jerusalem and consequently the Church herself on earth with a certain perspective against the background of a liturgical concept: the Church here below is, as it were, *en route;* it *draws near* in the liturgical action, as in a procession, to the heavenly Jerusalem, and already has a role to play in the heavenly *festive liturgical assembly,* together with the just who have already been made perfect because they have already arrived at their life's goal, and, together with the myriads of angels, all are fellow-citizens of one and the same city.[1]

In the present paragraph and in the following, we will give only a nutshell explanation of the idea expressed in this text, illustrating the relations of our terrestrial and wandering liturgy with the world of the just who have already achieved their end, and with the same angelic world.

Communion with the souls in purgatory

The just who have already arrived at their goal must be considered as including not only the saints already in the glory of the beatific vision, of

---

[1] For the meaning of this liturgy and worship, see Ceslaus Spicq, *L'épître aux hébreux,*   Vol. I, pp. 227ff; 280ff; 311ff; Vol. II, pp. 214ff; 402ff.

whom the text of the Epistle to the Hebrews speaks directly, but also the souls in purgatory. Even if these latter, speaking most accurately, have not yet arrived at their ultimate end, they are, nevertheless, souls truly saved and perfectly secure of attaining to the beatific vision. Revelation teaches that even with these souls in purgatory we have a profound communion of supernatural life and of mutual concerns. This idea, of course, is reflected also in the liturgy.

The teaching of revelation that touches most closely, therefore, on this point of the relationships of the liturgy with all the just who have arrived at the end of their pilgrimage is basically the dogma of the communion of saints which unites the faithful still on their pilgrimage on this earth both with the saints of paradise and with the souls in purgatory. Derivations from this basic dogma are the dogmas of the liceity and utility of the worship of the saints, and first among them, the Blessed Virgin Mary; of the intercession of the saints for us; and of the sacrifice of the Mass, of the prayers of the Church and of pious works in behalf of the souls in purgatory. For our purpose in the present chapter, which is to see how there is ever present in the liturgy the law of the cosmic universality of salvation, it is not necessary to lay any special stress upon these dogmas. It is necessary, on the other hand, to show how they are profoundly and continually brought into focus in the liturgy itself.

Even for this it is not so necessary to retell the history of the worship of the saints and of the liturgy of the dead [2] as it is to bring into relief its meaning and its profound and resplendent penetration into the liturgy. The most authentic expression of that union which Christians were persuaded to preserve with all those who had died in communion with the Church was, from at least as early as about the middle of the second century, the celebration of Mass for them, whether at the time of their burial or on the anniversaries of their *deposition*, as it was called, or of their martyrdom. About the year 140A.D., the apologist Aristides of Athens wrote:

> "If one of the faithful dies, obtain salvation for him by celebrating the Eucharist and by praying next to his remains." [3]

In the apocryphal *Acts of John*, dating from about the middle of the second century, the Apostle John is represented as celebrating the *breaking of bread* over the tomb of Drusiana.[4] For Carthage the usage is testified to already by Tertullian and afterwards by Cyprian.[5]

[2] See for example Righetti, Vol. II, pp. 268ff; 330ff.

[3] See H. J. M. Milne, "A New Fragment of the Apology of Aristides," in the *Journal of Theological Studies*, Vol. 25 (1924), pp. 73-77; cited by Righetti, Vol. II, p. 330.

[4] See, for example, in Jesús Solano, *Textos*

eucaristicos primitivos, Vol. I, Madrid 1952, p. 721.

[5] Tertullian, *Monogamy* 10, 2 (Jurgens, no. 382); *An Exhortation to Chastity* 11. St. Cyprian, *Letter to His Clergy and to All His People* 39, 3 (Jurgens, no. 572); other references in Righetti, Vol. II, p. 330.

In the fourth and fifth centuries testimonies are abundant.[6] The Leonine and Gelasian Sacramentaries already have special formularies for Masses for the dead.[7] It was the custom in these Masses to announce publicly the name of the deceased for whom the Mass was being offered. This practice gave rise later to the diptychs of the dead, or whole lists of the names of the dead which were recited by the deacon during the Mass celebrated for them. Still later, there came to be a commemoration of the dead with a general formula, read in all Masses, whether for the deceased or not, as in the *Memento* for the dead in the first or Roman canon of the Roman liturgy. Such customs are common in one way or another to all the liturgies.

The basic meaning of these phenomena is clear enough. The Mass is a matter of deep concern even to the dead who have died in the Church; and from it they are able to derive great profit. And what profit can this be, if not that of being purified of the effects of sin, from which they still have need of being freed before they can finally be admitted to the enjoyment of the perfect peace and happiness of heaven, with the saints and with the angels, in which we ourselves hope one day to participate?

The names of the dead are recited publicly in the Masses celebrated for them, St. Epiphanius tells us,

> "in order that those present may be fully convinced that the dead still live, that, far from being annihilated, they do exist and live in God's presence; and also for the proclamation of that sublime dogma, according to which those who pray for the brethren have hope for them, as for those who have departed on a long voyage. . . . We make a memorial of the just and of the sinners: of the sinners to implore the Lord's mercy on them." [8]

And St. Cyril of Jerusalem writes,

> ". . . next, we make mention also of the holy fathers and bishops who have already fallen asleep, and, to put it simply, of all among us who have already fallen asleep; for we believe that it will be of very great benefit to the souls of those for whom the petition is carried up, while this holy and most solemn Sacrifice is laid out. . . . We . . . offer up Christ who has been sacrificed for our sins; and we thereby propitiate the benevolent God for them as well as for ourselves." [9]

It is hardly necessary to point out that in all this there is implicit the concept of a state after death which is not yet the definitive state of the beatific vision and of perfect peace, but in which souls have still a need to be purged

---

[6] See the *Apostolic Constitutions* 6, 30, 2-7; Funk edition, Vol. I, pp. 381-383.

[7] Leonine Sacramentary, Mohlberg edition, no. 1138ff; Gelasian, Mohlberg ed., no. 1628-

1695, pp. 238-247.

[8] *Adv. haer.*, 75, 3; 8; 9.

[9] *Catechetical Lectures* 23 [*Mystagogic* 5], 9-10 (Jurgens, nos. 852-853).

of certain effects of their sins, after which they will be admitted to the definitive state of beatitude. It is also implicit therein that, in order to secure this passage for those souls, the sacrifice of the Mass which we offer for them is, among other things, of great utility. It is the concept of purgatory and of our spiritual communion with the souls still detained there, a communion which is realized to the fullest in the liturgical sacrificial action.

This concept is to be found abundantly in the numerous other parts of the liturgy, both historical and present-day, which concern the dead, and which developed very quickly in all the rites.[10] Thus, for example, in the nocturnal vigil of the dead, already rather general in the practice of many churches as early as the fourth century; in the canonical Office of the Dead, in use at Rome at least as early as the end of the seventh century and in all probability even earlier; in the liturgical feast commemorating all the faithful departed, which feast exists today in all the rites and which in the West was definitively organized and diffused by St. Odo of Cluny towards the end of the eleventh century.[11]

In short, in the whole liturgy, whether considered from the historical point of view or in its present state today, that mysterious but real communion of divine life and of spiritual interests which unites us to every soul who has left this world in at least a basic peace with God and who will be our fellow-citizen in the heavenly Jerusalem, is profoundly operative. That sentiment, rooted so deeply in the human heart, that the legitimate ties which unite us to one another here below, in which there is something holy and sublime, will not be broken by death, but will continue beyond the grave, is not only held in the greatest respect by the liturgy — proving again that the liturgy addresses itself to man in his whole personality — but is made operative in an atmosphere of light and hope which is unknown to non-Christian religions. The liturgy always views this sentiment against the background of the heavenly Jerusalem, the common fatherland in which we all have the hope of one day being reunited.

Communion with the saints of heaven

Still more profound and present everywhere in the liturgies of our own time is the concept and the reality of the communion which unites us with the saints in heaven, and most particularly with the Blessed Virgin Mary. Our communion with the saints is, in fact, the fundamental concept implied not only in their memorials which were developed in the anaphoras beginning with the fifth century, but also in the liturgy of their feasts and, in general, in their invocations, which had a tremendous development in all

---

[10] See H. R. Philippeau, *"Origine et évolution des rites funéraires,"* in *Le mystère de la mort et sa célébration*, Paris 1951, pp. 360-399.

[11] For all these rites see, for example, Righetti, Vol. II, pp. 325ff.

the rites, beginning with the fourth and fifth centuries, and which occupy a position of prominence even today.

As is well-known,[12] the liturgical cult of the saints developed in the Church with the cult of martyrs as its starting point;[13] and in the beginning this latter was connected locally with their tombs and chronologically with the anniversary day of their martyrdom. Now, the specific way of liturgically honoring the memory of the martyr was to offer the sacrifice on his tomb. The *Martyrium Polycarpi* supposes as much.[14] The same custom prevailed at Carthage in the time of St. Cyprian. In fact, speaking of three Carthaginian martyrs, Celerina, Lawrence, and Ignatius, he tells his people:

> "We always offer sacrifice for them, as you will recall, as often as we celebrate the passions of the martyrs by commemorating their anniversary day."[15]

Texts from the fourth and fifth centuries speak also of the custom of celebrating nocturnal vigils at the tombs of the martyrs to commemorate their anniversary day. This usage is affirmed at least for the period *ca.* 420-450 A.D., the time at which the passion of St. Saturninus, Bishop of Toulouse, was written:

> "*Vigiliis, hymnis ac sacramentis etiam solemnibus celebramus.*"[16]

This manner of commemorating the saints liturgically was practiced even when, in the fourth and fifth centuries, the confessors and our Blessed Lady began to be venerated along with the martyrs.

Here too, therefore, the fundamental concept is of the reality and vitality of our communion in supernatural life and in spiritual concerns with the world of the saints who are already gathered to God, a communion which is realized to the fullest in liturgical action and primarily in the action of the sacrifice. The Mass, therefore, is seen always and in every instance as the place of encounter *par excellence* of the Church Militant with the Church Suffering and the Church Triumphant.

It is by reason of this basic concept that, beginning with the fifth century, the general commemoration of the dead in the formularies of the anaphoras is developed into an explicit commemoration of the saints, as the more noble part of those among the faithful who have already achieved the end of their pilgrimage and are gathered to God.[17] Hence, the *Communicantes* in our

[12] Righetti, Vol. II, pp. 325ff.

[13] The earliest notices of a liturgical veneration of the martyrs are to be found at the middle of the second century. See *The Martyrdom of Saint Polycarp* 18 (Jurgens, no. 81).

[14] *Ibid., loc. cit.* In the year 250 A.D., almost a hundred years after St. Polycarp's martyrdom, St. Pionius was arrested while celebrating the Eucharist for the anniversary of St.

Polycarp. See Eusebius, *Hist. eccl.* 4, 15, 46ff.

[15] St. Cyprian, *Letter to His Clergy and to All His People* 39, 3 (Jurgens, no. 572).

[16] 1. See also 6. And see the *Vies des saints et des bienheureux, par les bénédictins de Paris*, Vol. XI, Paris 1954, pp. 973-990.

[17] See, for example, Jungmann, *The Mass of the Roman Rite*, Vol. II, pp. 159-160; 170-179.

present-day Roman Canon. But here, different from what is seen in the other anaphoras, this memorial of the saints is notably separated from the *Memento* for the dead, and follows immediately after the *Memento* for the living. Its meaning in this context is quite indisputable; and the prayers can be paraphrased thus:

> "Remember, Lord, Your people . . . for whom we offer, and those too who are offering to You this sacrifice . . . so much the more since we are united in communion, first of all with the glorious ever-virgin Mary, Mother of God, and then too with Your holy Apostles Peter and Paul . . . whose memory we reverently celebrate . . . and by their merits and prayers grant that we may be assisted by Your help and protection in all that we do."

Here, as in most anaphoras,[18] the concept of communion is determined further in the intercession of the saints for us and in our veneration of them. St. Cyril of Jerusalem writes:

> "Then we make mention of those who have already fallen asleep: first, the patriarchs, prophets, Apostles, and martyrs, that through their prayers and supplications God would receive our petition. . . ."[19]

To this concept of the saints as our intercessors, which is presupposed in the invoking of them in the liturgy, there is joined also the idea that in the liturgy and especially in the Mass we are giving thanks to God for the marvels of divine life which were operative in the saints. Later, but always along with this idea, there developed the concept that we also honor the saints themselves for the excellence of the divine life which, by God's grace, they actually achieved, and that we take them as examples for our own imitation, inasmuch as we hope one day to be their fellow-citizens in the glory of the heavenly Jerusalem.[20] With this in mind we will better appreciate the breadth

---

[18] See F. E. Brightman, *Eastern Liturgies*, Oxford 1896, pp. 48, 12; 57, 8ff; 94, 32ff; 169, 21ff; 264, 25ff; 332ff; 388, 19-20; 406, 31-32.

[19] *Catechetical Lectures* 23 [*Mystagogic* 5], 9 (Jurgens, no. 852). Originally, it was said that the sacrifice was offered or that the prayers were said at Mass *for* (*hypér*, *pro*) the martyrs or the saints, just as it was said that the Mass was offered *for* the dead. The *hypér* or *pro* was taken in the broad sense of "on the subject of, in relation to" Jungmann, in *Die Stellung Christi im liturgischen Gebet*, p. 234, notes that in the Coptic Jacobite liturgy, at the time for the gospel the deacon invited the people to pray by saying to them in Greek, "Pray for (*hypèr*) the holy gospel," to which the people answered, "*Kyrie eleison*"

(cf. Brightman, *Eastern Liturgies*, pp. 155, 34-35). Later, the attempt was made to be more precise, and some ancient authors had difficulty explaining this *hypér*. Beginning with the fifth century, although traces of the ancient formula are still found, there is no longer any hesitation about the meaning given it: "At the altar we do not commemorate them (the martyrs) in the same sense as the others who have departed in peace, as if we prayed for them, but rather in order that they may pray for us and that we may follow in their footsteps" (St. Augustine, *In Io. tract.* 84, 1). See Jungmann, *Die Stellung Christi im liturgischen Gebet*, pp. 233ff.

[20] This last concept finds special expression in the *Nobis quoque peccatoribus* of the Roman Canon.

and depth of the reality of our communion with the saints in paradise which, under the veil of sensible signs, is really actualized in the liturgy; and we will better understand with what strength the law of the cosmic universality of salvation effectively pervades the liturgy.

All the liturgies, moreover, have given a particularly efficacious concretization to these ideas in a feast of all saints which developed out of a feast of all martyrs, attested to in various parts of the East since the fifth century.

In the Roman liturgy the Feast of All Saints on November 1, the origins of which, under somewhat varied forms and celebrated on different dates, reach back at least to the sixth century, brings into play in a most felicitous manner this reality of the union of our pilgrim Church, and particularly of our liturgy, with the festive throngs of the blessed in heaven. The *Vidi turbam magnam*, which constitutes, as it were, the central theme of the feast; the enumeration which the hymns, antiphons, and responsories make of the principal categories of the saints whom we invoke, whom we celebrate, whom we take as our models and to whom we attach ourselves; and especially the constant perspective of the great liturgy which, in heaven, the saints and angels fulfill without interruption before the throne of God and in the presence of the Lamb, as recounted in the Apocalypse 7:9-12, constitute, at the end of the liturgical year, a grandiose synthesis of the reality of the communion which unites us to the Church Triumphant.

The idea that our liturgy here below is none other than a beginning — such as were precisely suited to the pilgrim phase of a Church which lives in struggle and in faith — of the liturgy which is eternally carried out in the glory of the heavenly Jerusalem finds explicit expression in the liturgies, generally speaking, only in relation to the angelic hosts, to whose praises we beseech God, in the *Sanctus* of every Mass, to be allowed to unite our own voices.[21]

Nevertheless it cannot be denied that our liturgy is in fact but the beginning, the echo, and the shadow not only of the angelic liturgy, but also of the liturgy of the saints, and that it is in view of the saints also that our plea goes forth: "May our voices blend with theirs as we join in their unending hymn: Holy, holy, holy Lord. . . ."

The angelic liturgy and the liturgy of the saints in the heavenly Jerusalem is a single liturgy of a single *ekklesía* united in a single *panégyris*. To conceive of our liturgy, therefore, as a beginning, an echo, and a shadow of the liturgy of the angels is necessarily to conceive of it as a beginning, an echo, and a shadow of the heavenly liturgy of the saints.

> "I saw a great multitude which no man could number, made up of all nations and tribes and peoples and tongues, standing before the throne and in the sight of the Lamb, clothed in white robes and with

[21] In some Gallican texts, in the introduction to the *Sanctus* mention is made of the saints along with the angels. See the *Missale gallicanum vetus*, ed. Mohlberg, Rome 1958, p. 78, no. 283, 33ff.

palms in their hands. And they cried out in a loud voice, saying: 'Salvation belongs to our God who sits upon the throne, and to the Lamb.' And all the angels were standing round about the throne, and about the elders and the four living creatures; and they fell on their faces before the throne and adored God, saying: 'Amen. Blessing and glory and wisdom and thanksgiving and honor and power and strength to our God through all the ages. Amen'" (Apoc. 7:9-12).

And again the liturgy of the Feast of All Saints says:

"You have redeemed us, O Lord God, with Your blood, out of every tribe and tongue and people and nation, and have made us a kingdom for our God" (cf. Apoc. 5:10).

And the same liturgy adds in another antiphon:

"This hymn is in praise of all His saints, of all the children of Israel, the people that is near to Him; this is the glory of all His saints" (cf. Ps. 148:14; 149:9).

These children of Israel, the people that has the privilege of drawing near to God, that kingdom of those redeemed by the Lamb from out of every tribe and tongue and people and nation — this, in fact, is what we are ourselves together with the blessed of heaven. That hymn which is sung to the redeemed is, for the blessed, the great outcry of blessing, of glory and of thanksgiving which they send forth uninterruptedly to God who sits on the throne, and to the Lamb. For us it is first of all the great outcry of blessing, of glory and of thanksgiving which the pilgrim Church sends up, as St. Justin the Martyr describes it,[22] to the Father of all, through the name of the Son and of the Holy Spirit; and the president of the brethren likewise gives thanks to the best of his ability, in memory of the Last Supper, of the Passion, death, and resurrection of Christ, of His glorious ascension and of His future and tremendous coming, in thanksgiving to God for the work of creation and redemption and because He has made us worthy to stand in His presence as ministers of the altar. To this highest eucharist (thanksgiving) of the Church on earth, which is the Mass, there is joined in a secondary position the eucharist of all the rest of the liturgy in the sacraments, the sacramentals and in the praise offered in the divine office. And in all this the pilgrim Church does nought else but join its hymn to the hymn of the blessed in heaven.

2. The Liturgy and the Angelic World

In order to understand the relations between the liturgy and the angelic world it is of utmost necessity to have a clear conception of the unity which,

[22] See St. Justin, *First Apology* 65; 67 (Jurgens, nos. 128-129).

according to revelation, exists between the angelic world and the rest of the cosmos: man and infrahuman creation.

Unity with the angelic world according to revelation

Now, in this area, the teaching of revelation is most clearly and strongly inculcated both in the Old Testament and in the New. In substance the matter is simply this: in accord with God's plan the angelic world constitutes an inseparable unity together with the human world and the infrahuman. God does not deal with these three orders as separate and independent worlds, but as a single cosmos in view of a common general end, in the attaining of which each order assuredly has its specific part to play, but with a hierarchical interdependence, in such a way that the destinies and the history of each order is of the highest concern to the other orders, and all are in some way mutually involved in the destiny and history of each other.

The inclusion of the angelic world in a general cosmic universality is already apparent in the narrative of the second and third chapters of Genesis, even if only in a subtle way and on the secondary level of attention. The account of creation, of the paradisiac status, of man's fall and his expulsion from paradise, closes with the special detail that God "drove out the man; and He placed at the east [23] of the garden of Eden the Cherubim, and the flaming sword which revolves, to guard the access to the tree of life" (Gen. 3:24).

The Cherubim, in biblical tradition, are angelic beings in the service of God, dwelling in the place where God Himself dwells, and regarded as His corps of guards and the watchmen, as it were, of His dwelling. The author of the narrative supposes, quite naturally, that these angelic beings, the honor-guard and friends of God, were present when He created man and that, while man lived in a relationship of intimate familiarity and friendship with God, they were his friends also.[24]

Thus, in the intention of the author, the scene of creation, of man's original status and of his fall, is not related as a matter which is of concern only to God and to man and to infrahuman creation, but as one which concerns, at the same time, angelic creation. Before man's sin there was, under God's supreme dominion and in His friendship, a harmony between angelic creation and man: man was given to live in paradise, the dwelling-place of God and of the angels, in familiarity with God and the angels. This was the order willed by God, the original ideal. Sin disrupted the harmonious rela-

[23] It was there on the east that the solitary gate of paradise was to be found.

[24] Thus it seems probable that in Gen. 3:22 the words which God speaks immediately after the sin of man — "Behold! the man has become like one of Us, knowing good and evil!" — and before stationing the Cherubim as guards at the gate of paradise, are in fact addressed by Him to the angels. This is a not infrequent manner of representation in the Bible: see 3 Kings 22:19-22; in the Prologue to the Book of Job, 1:6-2:6; Is. 6:8.

tionships not only between man and God and between man and the infra-human creatures, but also between man and angels. Man's sin, his revolt against God, was at one and the same time an act of enmity toward the angels. The superior malevolent being, acting in the guise of the serpent, was already, it is presumed, in a state of antagonism toward God and His angels; and he seduced man, drawing him away from his role, turning him not only against God but against God's angels also.

Thus, in the drama which unfolds in the second and third chapters of Genesis, what is treated of is the whole cosmos conceived as a unity. What is narrated there in a straightforward way is the history of man; but this history is framed in the orbit of a general and unitative cosmic perspective of all things. The man in this history plays a role the total result of which is immeasurably more vast than mankind itself. The angelic world plays an essential part in this vast unity willed by God. It is concerned not less but much more indeed than the infrahuman world is with the status of man, with his history, and with his relationships with God. And man in turn is concerned with the condition of the angelic world, with the relationships which the angels of God have with mankind, as well as with the nature, history, and activities of that wicked being who hid himself under the guise of a serpent in order to drag man down to ruin.

This fundamental notion of the angelic world as playing an essential role, together with man and infrahuman creation, in the general cosmic unity willed by God, so apparent in the narrative of the second and third chapters of Genesis, is afterwards largely supposed, repeated, illustrated, and developed throughout the whole of the Old Testament. Its basic concept in regard to the angels is that they constitute the celestial court of Yahweh and, in respect to the world, are the army of ministers and executors of the will of Him who is the sole Creator, Master and Supreme King of all.

In this general framework, the Old Testament permits us to see the angels in their many and varied duties in carrying out the orders of God. In regard to Yahweh Himself and, so to speak, in His personal service, we find the cherubim of Ezechiel (ch. 1 and 10), who appear in the function of assistants at the throne and as the throne itself of God.[25] Those angels whom Isaias calls seraphim (6:1-3) also appear as assistants at the throne, while they sing the praises of Yahweh: *Sanctus*, almost as if in a liturgical function. In the psalms, and especially in those which sing the cosmic praises of God,[26] it is presumed that all the angels praise God and that this is in fact one of their essential functions. The precise concept of the fundamental unity of

---

[25] See also Ps. 17:11 (Vulgate). Dan. 3:55 supposes the same. And so also the representation of the cherubim surmounting the ark of the covenant in the temple of Solomon, 3 Kings 6:23-28; 2 Chron. 3:10-13.

[26] Principally Psalms (liturgical or Vulgate numbering) 28, 102, 148; and the canticle *Benedicite omnia opera Domini Domino*, in Dan. 3:51-90.

the angelic world with the rest of the cosmos for the purpose of the adoration and praise of God is quite notable in these psalms. The angels, as heavenly and superhuman beings in intimate familiarity with God are considered therein as the first circle of creatures, constituting all together a universal cosmic unity.

The role which the angels play in the service of Yahweh, in respect to the world and to men, as His intermediaries and ministers, is of grand and immense proportions in the telling of the Old Testament. They accompany the theophanies of God in the world.[27] They are always at His disposal to fulfill His orders: like the hundreds of thousands who stand ready to obey Him, according to Daniel (7:10); the "watchers" of whom the same Daniel speaks;[28] the seven who stand before the throne of God, according to Tobias (12:12-15); the angels of the nations: Michael for Israel (Dan. 10:13, 21; 12:1), other angels for other nations (Deut. 4:19; 32:8ff; Is. 24:21; Dan. 10:13, 20). Malachias (3:1) even alludes to the angel of the testament, most probably the angel to whom had been confided the special role of intermediary between God and Israel for the conclusion and the execution of the pact of Sinai.[29]

There are angels who act as intermediaries in the aid that God sends to men (e.g., Judges 5:20; Exod. 14:19; 23:20-23; Gen. 24:7); angels who are intercessors for single individuals, their protectors (Tobias; Job 5:1; 33:23-24; Ps. 33:8; Zach. 1:12; 3:1-8), who, among else, present men's prayers to God (Tob. 3:24-25; 12:12-15); and angels who console men (Gen. 24:7; 3 Kings 19:5; 4 Kings 1:15; Dan. 3:49; 6:22). Numerous texts[30] speak of the angels who are intermediaries of God, sent to punish men; and among these are the exterminating angels.[31]

In later Jewish theology, both the rabbinic and that of the apocrypha, this concept of the cosmic unity including the angelic world, was greatly developed. In this theology, angelology always takes a quite prominent position.[32] This accentuation is manifested, for example, in the concept of guardian angels, who intervene in the various circumstances of life (*The Testaments of the Twelve Patriarchs: Joseph* 6; *Targum Ps.-Ion.* on Gen. 33:10; 48:6); in the concept of the angel who accompanies each soul which appears before God after death (*Testaments: Aser* 6; *Levi* 5); in the very highly developed concept of the angels charged by God with the government of the material elements, such as the stars, the winds, the rains; in the deter-

---

[27] Gen. 18:2ff; Deut. 33:2-3; Job 38:7; Ps. 67:18 (liturgical or Vulgate); Dan. 7:10; Zach. 14:5.

[28] Dan. 4:10-14. See also Ezech. 9:1-10; Zach. 3:9; 4:10; Apoc. 1:4, 16, 20; 2:1, 8, 12, 18; 3:1, 7, 14.

[29] See also the apocryphal *Book of Jubilees* 6:19-22; 14:20; and in the New Testament,

Acts 7:38; Gal. 3:19; Heb. 2:2.

[30] For example, Exod. 12:23; 2 Sam. 24:16; 4 Kings 19:35; 1 Chron. 21:15-16.

[31] See Exod. 12:23; Ezech. 9-10; Job 23:2; Ps. 77:48 (liturgical or Vulgate numbering).

[32] See Joseph Bonsirven, *Le judaïsme palestinien au temps du Jésus-Christ*, Vol. I, Paris 1935, pp. 222-239.

mination of the various classes of the angels; in the development of recourse to their intercession and of their cult in general.

The New Testament regard for the concept of the unity between the angelic and the human worlds is simply a continuation of the Old Testament tradition. Nevertheless, these matters now take on a special color, by reason of the great new revelation of Christ, the incarnate Son of God. In Christ and through Christ, God has descended to earth in person; and by personally establishing His kingdom, the Church, He thus reestablishes, first of all in His own Son, in a manner more marvelous and in a degree immeasurably higher and more spiritual, the original unity of the whole cosmos, which had been broken by original sin. St. Paul gives direct expression to the synthesis of this concept in Col. 1:15-20.

The doctrinal points which, in the New Testament, appear to be of greater importance from the point of view which is our present concern, seem to be able to be reduced to two principal headings. First of all, there is the concept that the angels, since they are *par excellence* the court of God and His ministers, are present, even on the second level of the perspective, through the whole life of Christ and in His work: the annunciation of the birth of John the Baptist and the annunciation to Mary; admonitions to Joseph; the nativity of Christ, at which the angels who sang the *Gloria in excelsis* gave explicit expression to the concept of the reestablishment of the unity of the cosmos, whereby from now on men are once more the object of the divine approval (*eudokía, bona voluntas*), a happening which brings great joy to the angels themselves and for which they praise God, because, as is presumed, it is a happening in which they themselves are tremendously interested; the flight and return from Egypt; the beginning of the public ministry of Jesus (Mark 1:13; Matthew 4:11); afterwards, in the Passion (Matthew 26:53); in the resurrection; in the ascension; in the future parousia (Matthew 16:27 and parallels thereof; 13:39; John 1:51).

The second doctrinal heading is that the angels have an interest and take an active part in the life of the Church and of the faithful, so that they view in an interested way everything that is of concern to the divine life in men. There is an angel of the Lord, a special protector of the Church, the new Israel, just as there was for the old Israel (cf. especially Matthew 1:24; 2:13-19; 28:2; Acts 5:19; 12:7ff). There are angels who have the special care of little children (Matthew 18:10). The angels rejoice over the conversion of sinners (Luke 15:7). The angels in the Acts of the Apostles are presented as the protectors and advisers of the Apostles, particularly in view of the apostolic ministry of the latter (Acts 12:15; 8:26; 10:7, 22; 1 Cor. 4:9).

The same concept of the profound union between the human world and the angelic world is found operative throughout the whole of the Apocalypse. The general plan of this final book of the Scriptures is clear enough: the just both here below and in the heavenly Jerusalem comprise but a single city and a single kingdom, at the head of which is God and the Lamb. This single city, however, is in two distinct phases of development which are converging to a unification in a single reality. There is the heavenly phase where, together with God and the Lamb, the faithful angels and the just men who have already arrived at their goal are in peace and in glory. And there is the earthly phase, made up of the faithful who are still engaged in the struggle against the hostile city of Satan and the beast.

Between these two phases of the one city, however, there is a constant interchange and, as it were, an uninterrupted procession from one to the other. Those of heaven, the angels equally with the just, are concerned for the brethren still engaged in the struggle, and they assist them in every way. They present to God the prayers of the faithful; they beseech Him on behalf of the latter. The angels in particular serve as intermediaries between God and the faithful here below; they reveal to them the designs of God; they intervene in the battle as His ministers in order to punish the enemy, those who are attached to the beast, especially by means of the material elements, over which they have power. Under the leadership of their chief, Michael, they even engage directly in the struggle against Satan and his satellites. The city of God which still struggles on earth advances its citizens one by one to the heavenly city; and when at last the number of the predestined is filled, the two phases of the single city will be reunited in one only: the heavenly Jerusalem, with its eternal and cosmic liturgy.

The final phase is represented by the great doxology in chapter five of the Apocalypse:

> "And when He (the Lamb) had taken the book, the four living creatures and the twenty-four elders fell down before the Lamb, each one having a harp and golden bowls full of incense, which are the prayers of the saints. And they sang a new hymn, saying: 'Worthy are You, O Lord, to take the book and open its seals; for You were slain, and with Your blood You have redeemed unto God men from every tribe and tongue and people and nation; and for our God You have made them a royal and priestly people, and they shall reign upon the earth.' And I saw, and I heard a voice of many angels about the throne, and the living creatures and the elders, and the number of them was thousands of thousands and myriads of myriads, saying with a loud voice: 'Worthy is the Lamb who was slain, to receive power and wealth and wisdom and strength and honor and glory and blessing.' And every creature that is in heaven and on the earth and under the earth and on the sea and all those that are in them, I heard them all saying: 'To Him that sits upon His throne, and to the Lamb, be blessing and honor and glory and dominion through the ages of ages.' And the four living creatures said, 'Amen!' And the

twenty-four elders fell prostrate and worshipped Him who lives through the ages of ages" (Apoc. 5:8-14).

In this vision we stand at the summit and at the final conclusion of the idea, firmly fixed in all revelation even from the first pages of Genesis and in the most ancient inspired writings, of the intimate unity of the whole cosmos, human, infrahuman, and angelic, conceived as an extensive and intensive universe in accord with its common and ultimate end, the kingdom of God. The apocalyptic vision shows us that same cosmos which was visible in the drama unfolded on the first pages of Genesis, joined in the purpose of all such dramas, trials, and sorrows as are described and unfurled throughout the pages of Scripture, the end to which all of it tended. That end is the *panégyris* of the eternal, cosmic liturgy of all creatures in adoration and praise of the Lamb and of Him that lives in the ages of ages.

Unity with the angelic world in the liturgy: the angel of sacrifice

It is certain enough that more than one of the brushstrokes with which St. John in his Apocalypse paints the heavenly liturgy is the result of a kind of transposition to heaven of the Christian liturgy which we know on earth. Nevertheless, since the idea of the intimate compenetration between the human world and the angelic is so rooted in the whole of revelation, it is not surprising that this is largely taken for granted and then actively vitalized in the liturgy. Erik Peterson [33] and other authors after him [34] have documented this fact. For a sufficient understanding of the substance of their observations we can but refer those who desire fuller particulars to these authors themselves.

Insofar as the Mass is concerned, liturgical and patristic tradition emphasized the idea of the unity of the angelic world with men primarily in the concept of the angel of the sacrifice. When the Apocalypse speaks of the angel who, in paradise, on the symbolic golden altar which stands in the presence of God's throne, offers to the Most High the prayers of the saints (Apoc. 8:3-5), it must be inferred that this is, in a broad way, what happens with the greatest prayer of the faithful, the Mass. The implication, therefore, is that the sacrifice which the faithful offer here below is presented in heaven before the throne of God through angelic mediation. This concept is common to the various liturgies.[35] In Canon I of the Roman liturgy, the ancient

[33] *Das Buch von den Engeln*, Leipzig 1935.
[34] H. Dullmann, "*Engel und Mensch bei der Messfeier*," in *Divus Thomas*, Freiburg, Vol. 27 (1949), pp. 281ff; J. Daniélou, *Le mystère de l'Avent*, Paris 1948, pp. 94ff; *Les anges et leur mission*, Chevetogne 1952; and also of the Cardinal Daniélou, *The Bible and the Liturgy*, Notre Dame 1956, pp. 130ff.

[35] See B. Botte, "*L'ange du sacrifice*," in *Cours et conférences des semaines liturgiques*, Vol. 7, Louvain 1929, no. 209-222; also of Botte, "*L'ange du sacrifice et l'épiclèse au moyen âge*," in *Recherches de théologie ancienne et médiévale*, Vol. I, 1929, pp. 285ff; G. Fitzengard, *De sacrificio coelesti secundum S. Ambrosium*, Mundelein 1944.

Roman Canon, it finds particular expression in the prayer *Supplices te rogamus*, which, according to the more likely interpretation, can be translated:

> "Your suppliants pray You, O almighty God: command that this sacrifice be carried by the hand of Your angel to Your altar on high, into the presence of Your divine majesty. . . ."

The official translation in use in the liturgy as celebrated in the United States does not, of course, differ substantially from the above more precise translation: but it does have about it that cold, bare-bones emptiness that is so obvious throughout our poor emasculated "officially approved" vernacular:

> "Almighty God, we pray that your angel may take this sacrifice to your altar in heaven."

Be that as it may, whatever the variety of interpretations that have been proposed for this passage,[36] it is clear enough from a parallel text in the *De sacramentis* of St. Ambrose that the prayer beseeches God to have the sacrifice of the Church presented to Himself through the ministry of a holy angel, or rather, of the angels in general, so that in this way the sacrifice might be rendered acceptable to God. St. Ambrose, in the passage mentioned, refers to a prayer which corresponds to the *Supra quae propitio* and *Supplices te rogamus* of the present-day Roman Canon; and in the prayer known to Ambrose, the priest says:

> "Commemorating, therefore, His most glorious passion, His resurrection from among the dead and His ascension into heaven, we offer You this immaculate Victim, this spiritual Victim, this unbloody Victim, this sacred Bread and this Chalice of eternal life; and we beseech You and pray You to accept this oblation *on Your heavenly altar by the hands of Your holy angels.*"[37]

The same idea is expressed in the Greco-Egyptian liturgy of St. Mark, in this fashion:

> "The gifts of sacrifice, of offering, of thanksgiving, that have been offered to You, receive, O God, on Your holy, heavenly, spiritual altar in the heights of heaven, through the ministry of Your archangels."[38]

Angels and the Mass

No less common is the general concept of the presence of the angels at the sacrifice of the Mass. Some examples: in the Byzantine tradition the idea is brought into relief from the beginning of the sixth century in the hymn known as the *Cheroubikón*, which is sung at the time of the great entrance in the procession in which the oblations are carried solemnly to the altar:

[36] See Righetti, Vol. III, p. 336.   [38] Brightman, *Eastern Liturgies*, p. 129.
[37] St. Ambrose, *De sacramentis* 4, 6, 27.

> "We who mystically represent the cherubim and sing the thrice-holy hymn to the life-giving Trinity, lay aside all earthly cares, for we are to receive the King of the universe *who comes escorted by unseen armies of angels.* Alleluia."

In the Mass of the Presanctified in the same liturgy, in the corresponding procession of the now already consecrated oblations, the text sung is:

> "*Now the heavenly powers join invisibly with us in adoration.* Behold, it is indeed the King of glory who is coming in procession. Behold, that which is carried is the mystical sacrifice already completed. In faith and in awe do we approach to participate in life eternal."

In the same Byzantine Mass, in the prayer of the little entrance it is affirmed that the angels join with us in celebrating the liturgy of the Mass:

> "Master, Lord our God, who have established in heaven orders and armies of angels and of archangels for the liturgy of Your glory, bring it about that together with our entrance the entrance also of the holy angels be made, who *celebrate the liturgy together with us* and together with us sing glory to Your goodness."

In the Greek version of the Syrian liturgy of St. James the *Cheroubikón* is as follows:

> "Let all human flesh be silent! Let it stand with fear and trembling and have no earthly thought. For the King of kings, Christ our God, comes to be immolated and to give Himself as food to the faithful. *He is preceded by the choirs of angels with all the powers and dominations; the cherubim with many eyes and the seraphim with six wings, who cover their faces and cry out the hymn. Alleluia.*" [39]

In an Egyptian liturgy, probably of the sixth century,[40] at the moment of the kiss of peace the deacon announces:

> "Have your hearts in heaven. If anyone has had any dispute with his neighbor, let him be reconciled. . . . For the Father of men, His only Son and the Holy Spirit are present, watching our actions and examining our thoughts; *and the angels are moving among us and mingling with us.*"

Of course there is nothing arbitrary about the concept of the angels being present at the sacrifice of the Mass. It is based on the two propositions of revelation already pointed out above: that the angels constitute the court of God, their King and ours, and they are for that reason present wherever Christ, their King, is present; that the angels are our fellow-citizens, our

---

[39] *Ibid.*, pp. 41-42.

[40] Cf. Anton Baumstark, in *Oriens Christianus*, 1901, pp. 1ff.

guardians, and our intercessors with God. If these propositions are true in general, then the more particularly must it be true that they are present at that most sublime action that can be performed on earth, the Mass, wherein heaven and earth are united in a manner most real, however mysterious.

It is precisely in this sense that the Fathers explained the presence of the angels at the Mass. If we may but note three characteristic texts, St. Ambrose says:

> ". . . the angel assists when Christ is present, when Christ is immolated. . . . If the body of Christ is here present, here too are the angels present." [41]

St. John Chrysostom affirms that when the priest draws near to the altar to offer the unbloody sacrifice,

> "In that moment angels are in attendance upon the priest. The space around the altar is filled with the whole order of heavenly powers in honor of Him who lies thereon." [42]

And then there is the famous text from St. Gregory the Great:

> "Who among the faithful could doubt that at the very moment of the immolation, the heavens open at the priest's voice? In this mystery of Jesus Christ the choirs of angels are present; the lowest beings are associated with the highest, the earthly join the heavenly, and the visible and the invisible become a single reality." [43]

Again, from these two concepts of the angels of the sacrifice and of the presence of the angels at the Mass we are better able to understand the idea brought into the great anaphoral prayer of the Mass by means of the inclusion therein of the *Sanctus*. It is certain that the triple acclamation of *Holy* which, according to Isaias (6:3), the seraphim cried one to another in regard to the Lord was used by the Hebrews in the liturgy of the synagogue service and was called the *Kedushah*, that is, the *sanctification* — a sanctification, obviously, of the name of God.[44] That this Jewish usage should have its

[41] St. Ambrose, *In Lucam* 1, 12 (CSEL pp. 28, 12ff). *De sacramentis* 1, 6; see also 4, 7.

[42] W. A. Jurgens, *The Priesthood: A Translation of the Peri Hierosynes of St. John Chrysostom*, Macmillan, New York 1955, p. 95 (Bk. 6, ch. 4, no. 520).

[43] *Dialogues* 4, 58. From this same idea so masterfully expressed by St. Gregory there developed among the Fathers the theme that the Mass is an efficacious representation *in sacramento* or *in mysterio* of the heavenly sacrifice, in which the altar is the figure of Christ who offers Himself to the Father, and the deacons are a figure of the angels who surround it. See J. Card. Daniélou, *The Bible and the Liturgy*, Notre Dame 1956, pp. 130ff.

[44] For example, in the prayer called *Shemoneh Esreh*, the *Kedushah* was introduced after the third blessing in a text which in more ancient times may have been somewhat shorter: "You are holy, and holy is Your name, and holy ones praise You every day. Blessed are You, O Lord, holy God. *Reader:* We will sanctify Your name in the world even as they sanctify it in the highest heavens, as it is written by the hand of Your prophets: And they cried one to the other and said, *Congregation:* Holy, holy, holy is the Lord of hosts; the whole earth is full of Your glory (Is. 6:3). *Reader:* To those over against them they say, Blessed — *Congregation:* Blessed be the glory of the Lord from His holy place (Ezech.

counterpart from the very earliest times in a similar usage in the prayer of Christians will be in no way surprising, when it is remembered that in the prayer of our Lord Himself each day Christians call upon God, asking that His name may be hallowed or "made holy" on earth, just as it is among the angels in heaven.

It is probable that a passage in St. Clement of Rome alludes to a liturgical usage of the *Sanctus*.[45] But however that may be, from the fourth and fifth centuries, starting with the *Euchológion* of Serapion, its inclusion in the anaphora is well-attested as the usual thing in the East, from whence it passed into Spain and Italy. It seems to have been accepted in Rome in the first half of the fifth century.[46] After that period it is found in all the liturgies. By its very nature, the *Sanctus* in the anaphora is the song of the whole liturgical assembly: celebrant, assisting clergy, and people.[47]

The Mass is presented primarily in the framework of a great action of thanksgiving, praise, and blessing to God, as is expressed in the first place in the great anaphoral prayer. The inclusion of the *Sanctus*, therefore, is intended to emphasize that that supreme thanksgiving, that supreme praise and blessing which we render to God in the Mass is the best way by which we can associate ourselves here below with the eternal heavenly liturgy of the angelic world, and the moment in which the unity of the angelic world and of the human world finds its highest expression.

In fact, whatever the various changes introduced into the text of Isaias, all the Christian liturgies have strongly emphasized that that *Sanctus* of the angels with whom we associate ourselves in the Mass is not merely the acclamation of the seraphim in the temple of the earthly Jerusalem; rather it pertains to the solemn liturgy which all the angelic hosts carry out in the heavenly Jerusalem (cf. Apoc. 4:8). "Heaven and earth are full of Your glory" — so says the Roman liturgy. "More important is the addition in the song of the word 'heaven': *coeli et terra*. This is true of all the Christian liturgies, and only of them. . . . No longer is it the Temple of Jerusalem that resounds with the triple *Sanctus*, nor is it only the seraphim who cry out one to another; heaven has become the scene, and all the choirs of heavenly

3:12). *Reader:* And in Your holy words it is written, *Congregation:* The Lord shall reign forever, your God, O Zion, unto all generations. Alleluia (Ps. 145:10). *Reader:* Unto all generations we will declare Your greatness, and to eternity we will hallow Your holiness; and Your praise, O our God, shall never depart from our mouth, for a great and holy God and King are You" (cf. W. O. E. Oesterley, *The Jewish Background of the Christian Liturgy*, Oxford 1925, p. 143).

[45] St. Clement of Rome, *Letter to the Corinthians* 34, 5-7. Jungmann observes quite rea-

sonably in his *The Mass of the Roman Rite*, Vol. II, p. 132, that what makes it probable that we are dealing with a genuine allusion to a liturgical usage and not just a Scripture quotation is the fact that Clement's text joins Dan. 7:10 with Is. 6:3, just as most of the Eastern liturgies do, later on. Furthermore, verse 7 in the passage from Clement seems to refer to a liturgical assembly.

[46] See Righetti, Vol. III, p. 298.

[47] Quite properly pointed out and documented by Jungmann, *The Mass of the Roman Rite*, Vol. II, pp. 128ff.

spirits, the *militia coelestis exercitus*, are united in the singing. *Socia exultatione* they sing their song of praise, and their cry is *sine fine*." [48]

It is to this exultation of all heaven that worshipping Catholics, interrupting the great Eucharistic prayer with its triple acclamation of *Sanctus*, want to associate their own voices and to unite their own liturgy. Here it is that lesser things identify themselves with the higher, the earthly joins itself with the heavenly, the visible with the invisible, and together they become one.

And that is why in liturgical and patristic tradition the concept of the unity of the angelic world with the world of men attains its most vivid expression in the Mass.

Angels and baptism

Something similar can be seen in respect to the other sacraments also. In the liturgies and in patristic tradition there exists the concept too of an angel of baptism, who takes special care of the catechumen, intervenes in the sanctification of the baptismal water, is present at the solemn moment when the sacrament is conferred, and afterwards takes the baptized under his special protection for the rest of the lifetime of the baptized person.

Thus it is that in the present Roman Ritual, in the first part of the rite of baptism of adults, which is simply the ancient rite for establishing one in the catechumenate, there is clear allusion to the angel of baptism:

> "God of Abraham, God of Isaac, God of Jacob, God who appeared to Your servant Moses on Mount Sinai and led the children of Israel out of the land of Egypt, assigning to them the angel of Your mercy to protect them day and night; we pray You, O Lord, see fit to send Your holy angel from heaven to protect likewise this Your servant N. and lead him to the grace of baptism. Through Christ our Lord." [49]

The intervention of the angel in the preparation of the baptismal water — with its probable derivation from John 5:4, "the angel of the Lord descended from time to time into the pool and stirred the water" — is documented by Erik Peterson [50] with texts from Tertullian and from various liturgies. Tertullian says, for example, that "the intervention of the angel has given the waters a certain curative power," [51] and that we "are purified in the water under the direction of the angel, and thus we are prepared to receive the Holy Spirit"; [52] or even that "the angel of baptism, as mediator, prepares the way for the coming of the Holy Spirit by washing away sins." [53]

This same idea is found again in the Gelasian Sacramentary, in the rite for the blessing of baptismal water in an emergency situation, in preparation for the baptism of a catechumen who is gravely ill:

[48] Jungmann, *ibid.*, Vol. II, pp. 134-135.
[49] *Ordo baptismi adultorum*, no. 17.
[50] *Das Buch von den Engeln*, Leipzig 1935, p. 60.
[51] *De baptismo* 4, 5.
[52] *Ibid.*, 6, 1.
[53] *Ibid.*, loc. cit.

"O Lord, . . . we beseech You . . . send upon these waters, prepared for washing and giving life to men, the angel of holiness, that,
once the sins of the past life have been washed away and guilt has
been effaced, he may make a pure dwelling-place for the Holy Spirit
in those who are regenerated." [54]

In regard to the presence of the angel at the very moment of baptism,
Origen says:

"When the sacrament of the faith was given you, the heavenly virtues, the ministries of the angels, the assembly of the firstborn were
present." [55]

Didymus the Blind attests in turn:

"Visibly, the font generates our visible body by the ministry of the
priests. Invisibly, the Spirit of God, invisible to every intellect, im-
merses in Himself and regenerates at the same time our body and our
soul, *with the assistance of the angels.*" [56]

The great interest of the angels in the baptism of each individual finds
splendid expression in the patristic tradition embodied in the theme of the
admiration of the angels for the baptized as he emerges from the font. St.
Cyril of Jerusalem says to the newly baptized:

"The angels dance around you in chorus, saying, 'Who is this who
comes up in white garments and leaning on her beloved?' " [57]

St. Ambrose develops the same idea in explaining to the newly baptized
who are about to approach the altar:

"You have begun to approach. The angels have observed you and
have seen you approaching; they have observed that human condition
which formerly was soiled by the black stain of sin, and have seen
it suddenly resplendent. This has made them ask, 'Who is this that
goes up from the desert whitened?' The angels are in admiration,
therefore. Do you want to know why? Listen to the Apostle Peter
say that there has been given us that which the angels desire to see
(cf. 1 Peter 1:18). Listen again: 'What eye has not seen, nor ear
heard, this is what God has prepared for those who love Him' " (1
Cor. 2:9).[58]

Again: in this concept of the angel of baptism there is nothing arbitrary.
If, indeed, baptism is our birth into spiritual life and our reconciliation with
God, it constitutes, by that very fact, our reconciliation with the angels too,
and the moment at which we are effectively made their fellow-citizens, mem-

---

[54] Mohlberg edition, no. 606, p. 95.
[55] *In Ios. hom.* 9, 4. Other patristic texts are
cited by Peterson, *op. cit.*, pp. 62-69. See also
Per Lundberg, *La typologie baptismale dans*

l'ancienne église, Paris 1942, pp. 44-45.
[56] *De Trinitate* 2, 12 [PG 39, 672C].
[57] *Catechesis* 3: *De baptismo* 16.
[58] *De sacramentis* 4, 5.

bers of the Church and members predestined for the heavenly Jerusalem. It were incredible, indeed, that they would be absent or disinterested in an event of such great importance in our life and in theirs. If there is joy among the angels of God over one sinner who does penance, who can deny their joy at the birth of a sinner into divine life? [59]

Angels: penance, matrimony, and orders

"There is joy among the angels of God over one sinner who does penance" (Luke 15:10). It is precisely this same verse in Luke which forms the basis of the liturgical and patristic concept of the angel of penance, whether because he discovers the sins or because of a certain role which he has in their being forgiven the sinner.[60]

For the role played by the angels in Christian matrimony we may cite that text of Tertullian which speaks of "the happiness of that marriage which the Church arranges, which the sacrifice strengthens, on which the blessing sets a seal, which the angels proclaim, and which has the Father's approval." [61]

For the presence of the angels at the ordination of a bishop we can cite the *Apostolic Constitutions*, wherein it is recalled that when, in the ordination, the people attest that the newly elected bishop is truly worthy of the high office to which he has been called, it must be done "as if they were in the tribunal of God and Christ, in the presence of the Holy Spirit and of all the holy spirits charged with ministering" (see Heb. 1:14).[62]

Angels and the liturgy of the ill

It is not necessary to expound upon the details of the very important role which the angels have in the liturgy of the ill and of the deceased as it is found in patristic tradition and in the liturgies themselves.[63] Enough to remember from the *Commendatio animae* of the Roman Ritual such prayers as the *Proficiscere anima christiana* and the *Commendo te*; or from the

[59] Precisely and explicitly in this sense there is St. John Chrysostom, *Huit catéchèses baptismales*, (ed. Wenger, *Sources chrétiennes*, no. 50), Paris 1957, *cat.* 1, 2, p. 109; *cat.* 2, 20, p. 145.

[60] Texts in Peterson, *op. cit.*, pp. 72-73. In the Ash Wednesday prayer for the blessing of the ashes to be imposed on those who did public penance, there is a clear allusion to the intervention of an angel: ". . . deign to send Your holy angel from heaven to bless and sanctify these ashes."

It would not seem out of place at this point to recall from the *Divine Comedy* the angel who, at the entrance to purgatory, marks seven P's on Dante's forehead (*Purg.* IX, 103-

113), symbols of the seven capital sins, which would afterwards be cancelled out one at a time in the successive circles of the mountain of penance and purification through the ministry of other angels (see *Purg.* XII, 98; 115-135).

[61] *To My Wife* 2, 8, 6 (Jurgens, no. 320).

[62] *Const. apost.* 8, 4, 5.

[63] Noted in Peterson, *op. cit.*, pp. 74-75. An extensive inquiry into the role of the angels in death and in the passage from this life to the next, according to the Alexandrian and Cappadocian Fathers, has been made by A. Recheis, *Engel, Tod und Seelenreise*, in a thesis written at the Anselmianum, published at Rome in 1958.

funeral service, such antiphons as the *Subvenite sancti Dei* and the *In paradisum*.

> "Go forth, Christian soul, from this world, in the name of God the almighty Father who created you; in the name of Jesus Christ, the Son of the living God, who suffered for you; in the name of the Holy Spirit, who has been poured forth into you; in the name of the glorious and holy Mother of God, the Virgin Mary; in the name of the blessed Joseph, illustrious spouse of that same Virgin; in the name of the angels and of the archangels; in the name of the thrones and dominations; in the name of the principalities and powers; in the name of the virtues, of the cherubim, and of the seraphim; in the name of the patriarchs and prophets; . . . . May peace be your dwelling today, and may holy Sion be your habitation." [64]

The sense of the union of the human world with the world of the angels is very strong in the above *Proficiscere*; nor is it any less evident in the following prayers.

> "I commend you, dear brother [sister], to almighty God. . . . Then, when your soul goes forth from your body, may the radiant company of angels come to meet you. May the assembly of the apostles, our judges, welcome you. . . ." [65]

> "Come to his [her] aid, O saints of God; come forth to meet him [her], angels of the Lord, receiving his [her] soul, and presenting it to the Most High. May Christ, who has called you now receive you, and may the angels lead you forth to the bosom of Abraham."

> "May the angels lead you forth to paradise. At your coming may the martyrs welcome you and lead you on into the holy city of Jerusalem. May the choir of angels welcome you, and with Lazarus, who once was poor, may you have eternal rest." [66]

The Roman Ritual, in its burial rites, speaks even of an angel charged with guarding the place of burial:

> "O God, by whose mercy the souls of the faithful find rest, see fit to bless this tomb and assign Your holy angel to guard it. . . ."

[64] The *Proficiscere* is found already in the Gelasian sacramentaries of the eighth century. The mention of Mary and of Joseph, however, is modern. It is hardly possible to recognize this magnificent prayer in the transmogrified version given in the new, official American *Rite of Anointing*, nos. 146-147.

[65] See already in the Gelasian Sacramentary, Mohlberg ed., no. 1627, p. 238: "O God, in whom all mortals live, . . . your suppliants beseech You, command that the soul of Your servant N. be welcomed by Your angels and conducted into the bosom of Your friend, Abraham the patriarch. . . ."

[66] See also the burial prayers in the Gelasian Sacramentary (Mohlberg ed., nos. 1610-1611, pp. 234-235), "*Suscipe . . . ad te revertentem de Aegypti partibus*"; and "*Suscipe . . . revertentem ad te: Vestem . . .*"; and no. 1621, the prayer *Opus*. See also the offertory antiphon in Masses for the dead: "*. . . Sed signifer Sanctus Michaël repraesentet eas in lucem sanctam.*"

On the subject of the struggle against Satan in the liturgy of the dead we shall have something to say of the opinion in regard to the role of the good angels and that of the demons in the particular judgment, and on the theory of the *telónia*, in our next chapter.

Angels: canonical office, blessings

The presence of the angels at the liturgy of praise, the divine office, is a very common theme. So early an author as Origen (d.253/254 A.D.) had this to say about the prayers recited in common by Christians:

> "In regard to the angels, it is necessary for us to say this: If the angel of the Lord is with those who fear Him, then, of course, it is to be supposed, when they are officially gathered for the glory of Christ, that the angel of each one will be with each one of those who fear God, that is, with the one whom he is assigned to guard and direct; so that when the faithful are gathered, there are two assemblies, that of men and that of the angels." [67]

St. Benedict, in his rule, sums up in a few words the way in which his monks must recite the office:

> "We believe that the divine presence is everywhere. . . . But we should believe this especially without any doubt when we are assisting at the Work of God. To that end let us be mindful always of the prophet's words, 'Serve the Lord in fear' and again 'Sing praises wisely' and 'In the sight of the angels I will sing praise to You.' Let us therefore consider how we ought to conduct ourselves in the sight of the Godhead and of His angels, and let us take part in the psalmody in such a way that our mind may be in harmony with our voice." [68]

This conviction always remained vital in monastic tradition. Among the texts cited by Peterson [69] it is enough to note the gracious anecdote that Alcuin recalls in regard to Bede:

> "It is told that Bede said, 'I know that the angels are present at the canonical hours. . . . What would happen if they did not find me there with the other brethren? Would they not say, "Where is Bede?" ' " [70]

Mention of the angels recurs frequently in the consecrations and benedictions of the ritual. Two orations for the protection of houses are particularly classic examples:

> "Listen to us, Lord, holy Father, all-powerful, eternal God, and deign to send Your holy angel from heaven to guard, sustain, protect, visit and defend all who dwell in this house." [71]

[67] *De orat.* 31.
[68] Chapter 19.
[69] *Op. cit.*, pp. 76ff.
[70] *Epistola* 219 (no. 16 in some editions).
[71] Found already in the Gelasian Sacramentary; Mohlberg ed., no. 1558, p. 225.

The following prayer is said at the end of Compline:

"Visit this house, we pray You, Lord, and keep far from it every ambush of the enemy; may Your holy angels dwell here, to guard us in peace, and may Your blessing be always upon us."

In the next chapter we will see the important role that, according to the liturgy, belongs to the holy angels, in defending us against the attacks of Satan and the demons.

Angels and the liturgical year

The angels occupy a noteworthy position in the liturgy of the time from Advent to Epiphany. Thus during this liturgical period each year there comes to life again a remembrance of their importance in sacred salvation history and, in particular, of their ministry during the infancy of Jesus. On the Feast of Christmas the angels are present everywhere as personages essential to the whole scene.

The *Gloria in excelsis Deo et in terra pax hominibus bonae voluntatis*, which they sang at the birth of Jesus, was already used in the earliest days of Christianity, or so the evidence would indicate,[72] as the beginning of a great doxology, which was thus presented as a paraphrase and amplification of the angelic hymn; and at least as early as the beginning of the fourth century it passed into the liturgy, first at Matins and afterwards, in the West, in the Mass. Every time it is recited or sung, we recall the reëstablishment of peace between the angelic world and the human world, peace that was broken by the first sin and is reëstablished by the coming of Christ on earth.

This idea is set forth very well in the following *Collecta ad pacem* in the Mass of Christmas Day in the *Missale gothicum:*

"All-powerful, eternal God, who have made this day sacred by Your incarnation and by the Blessed Virgin Mary's giving birth; who, as the cornerstone, by Your incarnation have restored unity in place of the long-standing discord between angels and men caused by the transgression of the tree; grant to Your servants in the joy of this solemnity that, as they rejoice to see You share their early condition, they may be brought to union with the heavenly citizens, over whom You have raised the body You assumed."[73]

Finally, to have a panoramic view of the role of the angels in the liturgy, we must recall also the development of their direct veneration which, centering principally around the person of St. Michael the Archangel, appears in the East in the fourth century, and in the fifth century is found in full flower even in the West. It was from the first connected with the numerous sanctuaries dedicated to the Archangel throughout the Christian world. The Leonine Sacramentary already exhibited various formularies for Masses on

---

[72] See Righetti, Vol. I, p. 198.　　　　[73] Bannister edition, no. 16, p. 5.

September 30 for the anniversary of the dedication of a basilica on the Salarian Way, consecrated to the Archangel.[74]

The Gelasian Sacramentary, and afterwards the Gregorian, know a similar feast on September 29, a date which was retained in the Roman liturgy until our own times, in connection with the Feast of the Dedication of the Sanctuary to the Archangel Michael on Monte Gargano, famous from the end of the fifth or beginning of the sixth century. In this feast St. Michael was regarded as the leader of the heavenly armies; and thus, all the angels are venerated along with him. With the recent promulgation of the Pauline Roman Missal, the date September 29 is retained, but the formal object of the feast is changed from the *Dedication of the Basilica of St. Michael, Archangel* to *SS. Michael, Gabriel, and Raphael, Archangels.*

The feast of the guardian angels, on October 2, was celebrated in Spain and France already in the fifteenth century; but it was not extended to the universal Church until 1670.[75] It too is retained in the Pauline Roman Missal.

*   *   *

In concluding this study of the relationships of the liturgy with the just in the great beyond and with the angelic world itself, we can do no better than to quote the words of St. Augustine, who, perhaps better than anyone else, understood and found expression for the intimate union between the angelic world and the human world in the general framework of the City of God; an intimate union of which our liturgy here below is thoroughly interpenetrated as the anticipation, under the veil of mystery, of the cosmic liturgy of the heavenly Jerusalem:

> "All together we are the members and the body of Christ; not only we who are present in this place, but all Christians throughout the earth; and not only we who are alive at this time, but, actually, every just person who has passed through this life and will pass through this life, from Abel the just until the end of the world, as long as men beget and are begotten; every just person who exists now, not in this place but in this life, and every just person who is yet to be born — all together form the one body of Christ, and each one is a member of Christ. If all, then, are His body and each one is a member, He is surely the Head of this body. He is the Head of the body which is the Church, says the Scripture, the Firstborn, who holds the primacy in all things. And since it is also said of Him that He is always the Head of every principality and power, this Church which is now a pilgrim is united to that heavenly Church where the angels are our fellow-citizens. . . . Thus it is made a single Church, the city of the great King." [76]

[74] Mohlberg ed., no. 844ff.   [76] *Sermo* 341, IX, 11.
[75] See Righetti, Vol. II, pp. 329-334.

The pilgrim Church is united to that heavenly Church where the angels are our fellow-citizens, and where the just have gone before us; and thus we form but a single Church, the city of the great King. This will be fully perfected in the heavenly Jerusalem; but it is already real even now and here on earth. The time and the place where it is best manifested now is precisely at the liturgical celebration, where, in the highest degree possible while we are still here below, there is verified that "single city under the rule of a single King, or a single province, as it were, under the rule of a single Emperor." [77] Because in the whole of the liturgy, and, as St. Gregory says, in a special way in the Mass, weaker things are associated with the higher, terrestrial things are joined to the celestial and that which is visible with that which is invisible, it is but a single unity that is formed.

[77] St. Augustine, *Enarrationes in Ps. 36, Sermo* 3, 4.

13 THE TWO CITIES:

THE LITURGY AND THE STRUGGLE

AGAINST SATAN

It is incontestably evident and by now a commonplace that today among the faithful themselves the lively sense of this truth of the faith has been lost: that an essential aspect of the Christian life is its existential development as a continuing struggle against Satan and his satellites; as a dramatic and uninterrupted battle not only against abstract and impersonal evil, and not only against our own passions and evil inclinations, but precisely and in the final instance, against the Evil One and his followers.[1]

Today, when Christian people read in the gospels where the cures worked by Jesus are recounted, they become embarrassed; instinctively they are moved to attribute it to a popular manner of speech or conception (objectively erroneous) when many gospel personages whom we would regard

[1] See, for example, Henri-Irénée Marrou, "The Fallen Angel," in *Satan*, New York 1952, pp. 67-68: "Apart from professional theologians, professors whose habit it is to plod through the encyclopedia of dogma with steady and methodical steps, and apart from those privileged souls who are so far advanced in the way of perfection and the life of the spirit that they know every aspect of it, one might say by experiment, I am certain that among the Christians of our day there are very few who *believe* really and effectively in the devil; for whom this article of faith is an active element of their religious life. Even among those who say they are and think they are and want to be faithful to the Church's teaching, we should discover many who have no difficulty in acknowledging that they do not accept the existence of 'Satan.' "

simply as ill are spoken of as being possessed by a demon or by evil spirits. There is, for example, that shrunken woman who was quite unable to stand erect, and of whom Jesus said that "Satan" had held her bound for eighteen years (Luke 13:16). Then, I suppose, when these persons read the stories of the desert Fathers, they immediately attribute all demonic interventions to their ingenuousness and, if you will, to their carrying over into Christianity the popular pandemonistic mentality of the Roman and Hellenistic world; accordingly they were able to see Satan everywhere and they seem to be overly credulous of the struggle against the demons.

This modern mentality which began to take shape more firmly in the first half of the seventeenth century as a reaction to the psychotic preoccupation with Satanism and sorcery which was rampant at the end of the Middle Ages and especially from the fourteenth to the beginning of the seventeenth century [2] is not to be condemned in its entirety. It is evident, I suppose, that the demoniacs of the Gospel and the mentality of the ancients in respect to the devil and his real influence do pose a certain problem. But however that may be, it is beyond doubt that the modern mentality works its effect even among the most sincere of the faithful themselves, so as to minimize and obscure through a hidden tendency of psychologism and naturalistic individualism what is an important point of revelation.

According to revelation, in fact, the sacred history of God's communications with the world and of the response of the world is embraced essentially in a drama. Some of the angels fell away, and introduced physical and moral evil into the cosmos. From that moment on, the history of the world includes a struggle, not only between good and evil, between cultures, between inclinations, between decisions in regard to individual men, but it is a struggle of persons against persons: God and His followers on the one hand, the kingdom of Satan on the other. Two kingdoms, two cities in constant conflict! God's will permits it to be so. This struggle is of cosmic proportions and it involves everything that exists, persons and things.

It is man, on his earthly pilgrimage, still in an uncertain position or, at least, a variable one, who is at stake. His decisions, in one way or another, are of concern not just to him personally, and are not to be explained simply by the autonomous developing of his internal psychology; on the contrary, they are a part of the broad cosmic drama which is unfolding between the two cities. If all this is not thoroughly understood, it will result in making one of the essential aspects of the liturgy quite incomprehensible. On the other hand, as might be expected, there is nothing more suited to understanding and living this essential aspect of revelation than to understand and live this point of the liturgy.

[2] See, for example, a brief conspectus of events in Emile Brouette, "The Sixteenth Century and Satanism," in *Satan*, New York 1952, pp. 310-348.

1. The Struggle against Satan in the New Testament

It is not necessary for our purposes to treat the question of the gradual development of revelation in regard to demonology, as that revelation is found on various pages of Scripture. It will be enough to consider the finally developed notion of the Scriptures in regard to the struggle against Satan, as its practical aspects are reported in the New Testament.[3] We will, moreover, bring separately to the total picture which Scripture presents of this matter, the special shadings and accents which are to be found in its individual and principal authors.

The fact of Satan in the New Testament in general

In short, put it this way: the New Testament recounts the redeeming work of Christ as accomplished in its Author, Christ Himself, during His whole life; it recounts this redeeming work as manifested in the Church as such, or in its daily application and extension to each of the baptized; within this account the New Testament perceives, essentially and continuously, a very personal struggle against the devil and against his satellites, the demons. These make man a slave in body and in soul; and, in some way, they hold the whole infrahuman world in slavery. They are at the root of all the physical and moral evils which afflict mankind: sin, persecutions, temptations, passions, wicked inclinations, diseases, and death itself. Redemption, therefore, in Christ Himself and in us, necessarily includes a struggle against the devil and triumph over him, as well as over his satellite demons and the means which they employ in exercising their dominion, the result of which triumph is the liberation of man, body and soul, and through this the liberation also of the infrahuman world, from the power and slavery of Satan.

This drama which unfolds not just between good and evil but between kingdom and kingdom, city and city, between *person and person*, is not a concept of secondary importance in the New Testament, but a reality which is prominent in the first level of consciousness and in the descriptions of the inspired authors.

The first point in this picture is the conviction that evil, whether physical or moral, originated in a rebellion, which took place before the creation of the world, of angelic creatures against God. According to the authors of the New Testament, the fall of our first parents was brought about by the

[3] See, for example, J. Smit, *De daemoniacis in historia evangelica*, Rome 1913. E. Mangenot, *"Démon dans la bible et la théologie juive,"* in the *Dict. de théol. cath.*, Vol. 4 (1924), pp. 322-339. L. Bouyer, "The Two Economies of Divine Government: Satan and Christ," in *God and His Creation*, Chicago 1955, pp. 465-497; E. Staufer, *Die Theologie des neuen Testaments*, 4th ed., Gütersloh 1948, pp. 47ff; 110-111, 114, 2, 116, 3, 118, 3; S. Lyonnet, *"Le démon dans l'Écriture,"* in the *Dict. de spir.*, Vol. 3, col. 142-152. For a general treatment of demonology see, for example, E. von Petersdorf, *Demonologie*, 2 volumes, Munich 1956-1957.

wicked instigation of a perverted angelic being. It is the ancient serpent, the devil, Satan, who is the father of sin and of the sinner even from the beginning (Apoc. 12:9; 2 Cor. 11:3; John 8:44; 1 John 3:8; cf. Gen. 3:15).

Satan is not alone. He is surrounded by a multitude of perverse spirits (Eph. 6:12), the demons, who are his angels (Matthew 25:41; 1 Cor. 15:24-26; Col. 2:15) and, together with him, constitute a reign (Matthew 12:24ff) of ordered and organized activity (Matthew 12:43ff), under his leadership (Matthew 9:34 and with it 12:24).

With the fall of our first parents at the instigation of Satan, every moral and physical evil, and death foremost, made its entrance into the world and began its rule (Rom. 5:12ff). From that moment onwards every man here below is not only a sinner, enemy of God and object of His wrath (Eph. 2:3; Rom. 4:5; 1:18), but by that very fact a slave to the devil (John 8:34-47; Rom. 5:12-21; 6:16-20; 2 Peter 2:19).

Man is a slave not only in soul but even in body, made such primarily through the consequences of sin (Rom. 5:12ff), death and all that which makes death fearsome. It is the devil who controls the empire of death (Heb. 2:14).

Even illnesses of every kind are regarded always in their religious aspect as consequences of sin and hence as an exercise of the dominion of Satan (e.g., Matthew 12:22ff; Luke 13:16; John 5:14; 2 Cor. 12:7; Rom. 8:20; Mark 16:17; Matthew 10:1; Luke 9:1).

The influence of Satan on the body itself of man can go even as far as diabolic possession in our modern understanding of it. In some instances in which the New Testament speaks of men as being "possessed" and of the driving out of Satan (e.g., Luke 13:11-16), it is not certain that it is a question of diabolic possession in the proper sense; for perhaps they are truly only simple illnesses that are spoken of. These, however, are to be seen and judged, according to biblical tradition and as they really must be in any general religious view of the world, as a real exercise of the dominion of Satan over men, in consequence of sin. There are other cases that cannot in fact be reduced, even when viewed in a general religious context, to ordinary illness. Such, for example, is the case of the two obsessed Gerasenes, and the pigs which precipitated themselves into the lake (Matthew 8:28-34).

To resolve in principle the question of the demoniacs of the Gospels, it will be enough to distinguish two kinds of cases in which, in general, the Scriptures are really able to speak of diabolic possession. And though this possession is different both in kind and in degree, this is a matter which the Scriptures do not determine. There is the case of ordinary illnesses which today we would call "natural" phenomena, but which in a religious view of the world must be regarded as a real exercise of Satan's dominion over man in consequence of sin; and there is the case of that kind which even today is commonly agreed to be diabolic possession in the proper sense.

In Rom. 8:19ff, St. Paul speaks of infrahuman creation as subjected against its will to the slavery of "vanity" and of "corruption," because it is made subject to man, who abuses it by sin, the source and cause of vanity and moral corruption, with physical disintegration consequent thereupon. In the reasoning of St. Paul and of all the New Testament authors, this implies that the same infrahuman creation is made subject to Satan, at least in the sense that Satan stands at the beginning of the sinful abuse that man makes of it — the same Satan who is the origin of all "vanity" and of all "corruption." He can use it against man primarily by enticing him to concern himself with it and to use it in a spirit of sin and for sinful purposes.

According to the New Testament, paganism and idolatry are in a very special way the manifestation in the world of the dominion of Satan. Here it is a question not simply of erroneous understanding, but truly and properly of the worship of demons, who usurp to themselves the honors due to God (Rom. 1:18ff; 1 Cor. 10:10-11; Eph. 2:2; 2 Cor. 4:4).

When the authors of the New Testament say that man, and through man infrahuman creation itself, is found under the dominion of Satan and is enslaved to him, they do not exclude, of course, the responsibility of man himself. The formula in Second Peter makes explicit the speculative principle: "By whatever a man is overcome, of this also he is the slave" (2 Peter 2:19. See also John 8:34; Rom. 6:16).

The totality of all visible things external to ourselves is referred to in the New Testament, in an unfavorable way and insofar as it is subject to sin and to Satan, as *the world*; *this world* is used to indicate all the forces of evil which are organized in the world; *the age* and *this age* indicate the same insofar as they have free run in the length of time granted them.[4]

In St. Paul these concepts are connected with those of *the flesh* and *darkness*. Hence it is that Satan is called *prince of this world* or *prince of this age* (John 12:31; 14:30; 16:11; 1 Cor. 2:6-8; Eph. 2:2); and the devil and his wicked spirits are called *the rulers of this darkness* (Eph. 6:12). Satan is able to say to Christ, showing Him in an instant all the kingdoms of the earth: "To You will I give all this power and all the glory of these kingdoms, for they have been given to me and I give them to whom I will" (Luke 4:5). And St. John confesses that "the whole world is in the power of the evil one" (1 John 5:19). St. Paul is straightforward in calling him "the god of this age" (2 Cor. 4:4), i.e., having arrogated to himself the honors due to God, he assumes such a position in respect to those men who have followed him. He is in the "world" like a strongly armed man in his fortress (cf. Matthew 12:29).

---

[4] See, for example, M. Meinertz, *Theologie* pp. 37ff.
des neuen Testaments, Vol. II, Bonn 1950,

Christ's mission and work as struggle against Satan

From what has preceded it can be seen how the authors of the New Testament have viewed the entire mission and work of Christ as a struggle and a triumph against the power of Satan, and the kingdom of Christ as a kingdom engaged in a struggle against the kingdom of Satan. St. John puts it very concisely: "For this did the Son of God make Himself manifest, that He might destroy the works of the devil" (1 John 3:8). And the author of the Epistle to the Hebrews synthesizes the same idea in this fashion: "Since, therefore, children are participants in blood and flesh (i.e., men are made of blood and flesh), He (Christ) too, in like manner, has shared in these, in order that through death He might destroy him who had the empire of death, that is, the devil; and so that He might deliver them who throughout their life were kept in slavery by the fear of death" (Heb. 2:14-15).

Thus the expediency of the incarnation is considered in reference to the struggle and triumph over Satan, with a view to the liberation of men from his slavery. The instrument of this slavery to Satan is death and the fear of it that dominates the whole life of man. The means of overcoming Satan and freeing man was Jesus' own laying down of His life. When we consider that, according to the New Testament, sin, illness, and death are broadly correlative concepts indissolubly connected, it is easy to understand how it is possible for the authors to synthesize, as they do, the whole empire of Satan and the slavery of mankind in the single word *death*; and the redemption gained for us by Christ on the Cross, in order to free us from the slavery of Satan, which is also in fact the very aim of the incarnation, in the concept of *liberation from death*.

That which the author of the Epistle to the Hebrews thus synthesizes is repeatedly affirmed and explained in a more analytic fashion by the other New Testament authors. Characteristic of this point of view is the grouping of events at the inauguration of the public ministry of Jesus in the synoptics: baptism, temptation, beginning of the public ministry of Jesus in His preaching and in His working of cures. Immediately after His baptism "Jesus was led into the desert by the Spirit, there to be tempted by the devil" (Matthew 4:1 and parallels). The significance of the temptation, which is immediately precedent to the realization of the messianic work, is to demonstrate in this work the element of personal struggle between Jesus and Satan, a struggle which is of concern to all mankind. The protagonists of the two kingdoms are in immediate confrontation. Satan, in attempting to overcome Jesus, makes use of hints about a temporal messianism.

There is a remarkable parallelism between the situation of Jesus at the commencement of His messianic ministry and the situation of Adam at the first beginnings of mankind: the beginning and the re-commencement of the religious history of the human race; the first Adam and the second

Adam. Satan, the adversary, is in sudden confrontation with each of them. With the first Adam he is the victor; but with the second Adam, he is the vanquished. Probably this significance of the scene of the temptation was not lost on the evangelists.

And since, effectively, they have considered the temptation as an introduction to all the messianic work of Jesus and this same work as a struggle against Satan, their way of connecting the narrative of the beginning of the ministry of Jesus with the preceding temptation is obvious enough. The messianic work after the temptation is described by the evangelists as consisting in two things: in the preaching of the doctrine that the kingdom of God has come, and in the healings considered as one with the expulsion of demons. See, for example, the gist of the text of Mark immediately after his narration of the temptation:

> "Now, after John had been sent to prison, Jesus came into Galilee preaching the gospel of the kingdom of God. He said: 'The time has been fulfilled and the kingdom of God has come; do penance and believe in the gospel.' . . . He went to Capernaum; and immediately, on the Sabbath, Jesus entered the synagogue and began to teach. . . . Now, in their synagogue there was a man possessed by an impure spirit, who began to cry out, 'What have we to do with You, Jesus of Nazareth? Have You come to destroy us? I know who You are, the Holy One of God.' But Jesus rebuked him, saying: 'Be silent, and go out of the man.' And the impure spirit, after having convulsed him violently, went out of him, emitting a loud cry. All were amazed at this and began to ask each other: 'What sort of thing is this? What new doctrine is this? He commands with authority even the unclean spirits, and they obey Him.' . . . Now when it was evening and the sun had set, they brought to Him all who were ill and who were possessed by demons. . . . And He cured many who were afflicted by various diseases and cast out many devils. . . . He went about through all of Galilee preaching in their synagogues and casting out demons" (Mark 1:14-39).

The picture drawn by Matthew (4:17, 23ff), as well as that of Luke (4:31ff; 7:21), is substantially the same.

This is a picture that will be continued throughout the whole life of Jesus; so much so that in the catechesis of the primitive Church, His whole work from His baptism to His Passion was able to be summed up as follows:

> "He (God) sent His word to the children of Israel, announcing the good news of peace through Jesus Christ. He it is who is Lord of all. You know what took place throughout all of Judea: Jesus of Nazareth, how He began in Galilee after the baptism preached by John; how God anointed Him with the Holy Spirit and with power; and He went about doing good and healing all who were in the power of the devil, because God was with Him" (Acts 10:36-38).

The whole public ministry of Jesus is viewed as a preaching of the doctrine of the kingdom and as a liberation of those oppressed by Satan. In the New Testament the announcement of the arrival of the kingdom of God and the expulsion of demons is all one thing, because the expulsion of demons is the immediate effect and the irrefutable proof of the coming of the kingdom of God in the person of Jesus Christ (Matthew 12:22-32 and parallels).

For the evangelists this aspect of the struggle of Jesus against Satan, even when it is a question of the Passion of Jesus, remains always at the first level of their attention. Luke ended the detailed narration of the temptation with these words: "When he had finished every temptation the devil departed from Him until the opportune time" (Luke 4:13). For Luke, the opportunity awaited by Satan was, in a special way, the time of the Passion. In all the events of the Passion Satan is present, at a secondary level and as if hidden, but nonetheless really and efficaciously, so much so that Christ Himself says to the Jews, "But this is your hour, and the power of darkness" (Luke 22: 53).

How this power of darkness, which is certainly to be identified with Satan (see John 14:30; Col. 1:13, and especially Acts 26:18), is in action in the Passion of Christ is seen by the same Luke even in the fact that Satan, on that occasion, requests and is permitted to tempt violently all the Apostles and Peter most especially (Luke 22:31ff). If, thanks to the special protection which Christ, with His prayer for Peter, obtained for Peter himself and for all the other Apostles, Satan enjoyed no substantial victory over them, it is nevertheless true that he succeeded in entering into Judas and in persuading him to betray the Master to His enemies (Luke 22:27).

In Mark and in Matthew the Passion of Jesus appears as a struggle against Satan even by the fact that Peter, who had desired to circumvent this Passion, is reproved by Jesus as Satan the tempter (Mark 8:33; Matthew 16:23), as if to say that Peter is Satan's instrument.

John emphasizes this idea again. The moment of the Passion is presented as "the hour" of Jesus; that is, the time of the great test decreed by the Father and freely accepted by Him (John 12:27ff; cf. 7:30; 13:1). This test is the supreme struggle against Satan, the prince of this world, who at that moment draws near to engage Him in combat (John 14:30). But this hour will be the hour of the definitive victory over Satan, who will be expelled from his kingdom: "The prince of this world is coming; but in Me he has nothing" (John 14:30); "now is the judgment of the world; now will the prince of this world be cast out" (John 12:31); "the prince of this world has already been judged" (John 16:11). And John notes that "dipping the bread, He (Jesus) gave it to Judas. . . . And after that morsel Satan entered into him" (John 13:26-27).

That St. Paul would regard the Passion of Jesus as a struggle against Satan seems to me to be quite undeniable in view of 1 Cor. 2:6-8, ". . . a wisdom, indeed, not of this age nor of the princes of this age, who are passing away; but we speak of the mysterious wisdom of God, the hidden wisdom which God foreordained before all the ages, unto our glory, and which none of the princes of this age has known; for had they known it, they would never have crucified the Lord of glory." To me it does not seem possible to interpret the expression *the princes of this age* otherwise than of the hostile demoniacal powers who reign in this world. The expression is reminiscent of other similar ones in which it is quite evidently such powers that are referred to (Eph. 2:2; 6:12; 1 Cor. 15:24-28; Gal. 4:3-9; Col. 2:8). The crucifixion, therefore, for St. Paul just as for the evangelists, was due to the work of Satan and his angels.

If in the New Testament the Passion and the crucifixion of Jesus constitute the supreme moment in His struggle against Satan, it is natural that the triumph of Jesus, His exaltation manifesting itself in His descent into hell, in His resurrection from the dead and in His ascension, be considered as a triumph over Satan and the demoniacal powers. The general expression of this concept is to be found in the familiar text of the Epistle to the Philippians: "He humbled Himself, becoming obedient to death, even to the death of the Cross. Therefore God also has exalted Him and has bestowed upon Him the name that is above every name, so that at the name of Jesus every knee should bend of those in heaven, of those on earth, and of those under the earth" (Phil. 2:8-10). Heaven, earth, and the regions under the earth is a conventional expression to indicate the whole universe (cf. Apoc. 5:3, 13).

After His death, the glorious Christ, in an expression of victory, as if surveying all things by His descent into hell, His resurrection and His ascension, took possession of all of it as its victor and Lord: "This '*He ascended*', what does it mean, except that He had first descended into the inferior regions of the earth? He that descended is the same who ascended to the regions above the heavens, in order to fill up the whole universe" (Eph. 4:9-10). Thus did He harvest the fruits, in a special way, of His triumph over Satan and his satellites. He holds forevermore "the keys of death and hell" (Apoc. 1:18; cf. 9:1).

Even the text of Colossians 2:15, the interpretation of which in tradition and among modern exegetes is far from unanimous,[5] can be understood as reinforcing this idea. Possibly it expresses not only the superiority of Christ over the angelic powers, henceforth clearly subject to Him and to His service (cf. Col. 2:10), but, in particular, His triumph, obtained by means of His death on the Cross, over the perverted angelic beings who, by taking advantage of man's weakness, in accord with a very prominent Pauline theme, abused even the Mosaic Law itself by drawing him along more and more into transgressions and sin. Christ by abolishing the Mosaic Law with His

[5] See, for example, T. K. Abbot, "Epistles to the Ephesians and to the Colossians," in *The International Critical Commentary*, Edinburgh 1946 (reimpression), pp. 257ff.

death on the Cross, which Law, contrary to God' will, had become for mankind the occasion of greater sin, snatched away from Satan and from his
satellites, even this weapon of theirs, hanging it, like a trophy, on His Cross:
"and having disarmed the principalities and the powers, He made them a
spectacle before the whole world, dragging them away by His triumph on
the Cross." [6]

The whole life of Jesus, then, is conceived by the New Testament, as a
personal struggle against the devil and the demons; and the significance of
His work is that of a triumph over Satan and the hordes of hell — our liberation and the liberation of the material world itself from slavery to Satan. On
the very first level of the New Testament consciousness, therefore, there is
the image of Christ, given expression to by Himself, as the one who is
stronger and who enters by force the stronghold of the enemy, armed though
he be, overpowers him, snatches away his weapons, binds him and distributes
his goods as spoils (cf. Luke 11:20ff and parallels).

The mission of the Apostles as a struggle against Satan

This image is reinforced again if we recall how the New Testament conceives the mission of the Apostles, sent by Christ and charged with carrying
on His work. There is a perfect correspondence between the manner in
which the mission of Jesus is conceived and that of the Apostles: to preach
the kingdom of God and to expel Satan, even in narrow connection with the
working of cures. The three Synoptics coincide substantially even in the
way in which they refer to the charge received by the Apostles at the outset
of their mission. Luke expresses it thus: "Having called the twelve to Himself, He gave them power and authority over all the demons and the power
to cure diseases; and He sent them forth to preach the kingdom of God and
to heal the sick" (Luke 9:12 and parallels).

And then there is the note in Luke at the end of the mission of the seventy-
two disciples: "The seventy-two returned full of joy, saying, 'Lord, even the
demons are subject to us by the power of Your name.' And He answered
them: 'I was watching Satan fall from heaven like a bolt of lightning. Be-

---

[6] The text indicates a struggle of Christ
against these principalities and powers, their
violent spoliation against which they offer resistance, and their being punished. All of this
is quite incomprehensible if it is supposed that
the passage treats of the good angelic beings.
In fact, it suggests to us the general and
well-known theme of the struggle of Christ
against the demoniacal powers. That these adverse powers appear here as patron of the
Mosaic Law and that they serve it to our detriment is not in contradiction to the theme,
recurring elsewhere in St. Paul and throughout the New Testament, that the intermediaries and administrators of the Mosaic Law
are the good angels. In fact, there is in St.
Paul a third theme also, clearly indicated in
the present text (Col. 2:14), according to
which, because of the weakness of man, the
Mosaic Law, in spite of its divine origin and
the fact that the good angels are its administrators, was in actual fact the occasion for
man of even greater sinning and hence, in the
logic of Paul and of the whole of the New
Testament, an instrument of Satan.

hold, I have given you the power to tread upon serpents and scorpions, and over all the mighty of the Enemy; and nothing shall be able to harm you' " (Luke 10:17-19).

At the last mission of the Apostles, shortly before the ascension, the final verses of Mark (16:15ff) likewise convey a feeling strongly antagonistic to Satan, with the usual two themes of the preaching of the kingdom of God and of the expulsion of the devil in connection with the working of cures: "Afterwards He said to them: 'Go into the whole world and preach the gospel to every creature. He that believes and is baptized will be saved; but he that does not believe shall be condemned. The signs which shall attend those who believe are these: they shall cast out devils in my name; they shall speak new languages; they shall take up serpents in their hands; and if they drink any deadly thing it shall do them no harm; they shall lay hands on the ill and cure them.' "[7]

Most enlightening indeed are the terms in which St. Paul refers, before the Procurator Festus and King Agrippa, to the apostolic commission which he had received from the mouth of Jesus Himself, on the road to Damascus; when Jesus told him that He was sending him to Jews and Gentiles alike "to open their eyes that they may be converted from darkness to light and from the dominion of Satan to God, and that they may obtain, through their faith in Me, the remission of sins and their inheritance among the saints" (Acts 26:18; cf. 19:11-12; 16:18).

In all this there is nothing extraordinary. If the work of Jesus was conceived essentially as preaching the kingdom and expelling Satan, it was only natural that the mission of those who, by His name and by His power, would continue and realize His work in the world, should be conceived in the same way.

The general situation of the Christian and of the world confronted by Satan after Christ

In the New Testament it is not only the life and work of Jesus and of the Apostles commissioned immediately by Him that is conceived as struggle against Satan, but even the life and work of the individual Christian down through the ages and in every era of the Church until the end of time.

To convince oneself of this it is enough to read, for example, Rom. 6:1-16

---

[7] A manuscript of the fifth century (W, the Codex Freerianus in Washington), in referring to this same final commission, lays an even greater emphasis upon the feeling of antagonism against Satan, by interposing the following at the beginning of the text, between verses 14 and 15: "And to justify themselves (i.e., for their disbelief: cf. Mark 16:13) they said: 'This age of iniquity is subject to Satan, who prevents whoever is defiled by reason of subjection to the spirits, from receiving the truth and the power of God. Therefore reveal now Your justice.' Thus they spoke to Christ. And Christ answered them: 'The term of the power of Satan is completed. . . .' Afterwards He said to them: 'Go into the whole world and preach . . .'."

and Col. 3:1-4; and, for the particular role which the Eucharist plays in the life of the Christian, enough to subjoin to those texts John 6:32-59. The life of the Christian is a realistic *imitatio Christi*, not only in the moral order of sentiments and affections, but of the physical mystical order, and therefore of the moral also, because it is a participation in the manner of Christ's being and consequently in His way of feeling, of acting and reacting, in the presence of God or other realities. This participation is germinally established at baptism, which is the first radical assimilation to Christ, and which makes subsequent development physically possible; and it places upon every man a moral obligation, which continues to his last life's breath, of living ever afterwards in accord with all that baptism demands.

Certainly we are aware that the reality of Christ includes, essentially and realistically, struggle against Satan and triumph over him. It might well be said, therefore, that imitating that reality, which defines Christian life, will include, no less really and essentially, the aspect of struggle and triumph over Satan. This is a struggle and a triumph which has its radical beginning in baptism. The latter, inasmuch as it constitutes fundamental assimilation to Christ, is, for each individual, a radical triumph over Satan; yet, it is one which will thenceforth put a claim on all the rest of his life, sacramental and moral, until he draws his last breath. In fact, only with his final breath will the process of the *imitatio Christi* have its end, and only then will the reproduction of Him in the faithful appear definitively successful or definitively lacking.

If outside of this assimilation to Christ and participation in Him there is no salvation for man, it may well be said that, after Christ, whoever remains beyond His influence remains in slavery to Satan. There are but two kingdoms, the kingdom of God in Christ and the kingdom of Satan. Whoever belongs not to the one must belong to the other.

If Satan did not abandon the struggle against Christ until the last moment, for even the moment of His Passion and death indicated the paroxysm of his attacks, so much the more will he not abandon until their last breath the individual faithful of Christ, and the whole Church. Thus, the moment of death for each man and the final days of the Church itself will be indicated by the very strength of Satan's supreme endeavors. All of these things are clear enough *a priori*, by simple logical reasoning, when we consider what the New Testament has to say about the relations between Christ and Satan, and between the Christian and Christ.

It is not, however, a matter solely of *a priori* deductions made through the process of logic. Effectively, it is a matter of the situation of the Christian life, whether of single individuals or of the Church in general, described with an abundance of detail in the New Testament. According to the New Testament, the general situation of the world, after Christ, in its struggle against

Satan and his kingdom appears as follows. The world is divided into two kingdoms (cf. Matthew 12:30 as conclusion to the entire pericope; 13:36ff): the sons of God in Christ, and the adherents to Satan; Christ has conquered Satan and the world as well, insofar as the latter is Satan's dominion (John 16:33; Matthew 12:24ff). Whoever adheres to Christ, and in the degree that he does adhere to Christ, is freed from the slavery of Satan and is transported from the power of darkness to the light of the kingdom of Christ (Col. 1:13); whoever does not adhere to Christ sins thereby, and insofar as he does not adhere to Christ he is under the slavery of Satan, whose son he is (1 John 3:8-10). The Jews who resist Christ and faith in Him are under the slavery of Satan and they have Satan for their father (John 8:44; Acts 13:10). They are henceforth the synagogue of Satan (Apoc. 2:9). Once faithful Christians who abandon the faith fall back under his dominion (1 Tim. 5:15). In general all those who resist the faith and are in revolt against it are under Satan.

According to St. Paul (Eph. 2:2), Satan, in all the disbelieving spirits who are in revolt against God in spite of Christ's coming, still continues his work, just as he led Paul's Christians prior to their conversion from paganism: "You also have been made to live again (by God in Christ), you who were dead by reason of your sins, wherein once you walked according to the fashion of this world, according to the prince of the dominion of the air,[8] the prince of that spirit who now operates in the sons of disobedience" (Eph. 2:1ff). It is Satan who blinds those who do not wish to believe: "And if our gospel also is veiled, it is veiled only to those who are perishing, those whose unbelieving minds the god of this age has blinded, so that the splendor of the gospel of the glory of Christ, who is the image of God, might not shine for them" (2 Cor. 4:3-4). Whoever resists the truth is bound in chains by the devil (2 Tim. 2:25-26). Idolatry in particular, whether prior to Christ's coming or afterwards, because it is truly worship of the demons (1 Cor. 10:20-21; 2 Cor. 6:15-16; Apoc. 9:20), remains the privileged dominion of Satan. One of the major themes of the Apocalypse is that the worship of the emperor in particular, the worship of the beast of the Apocalypse, is worship of Satan.

In the situation of the world after Christ, therefore, the first concern and greatest endeavor of Satan is to prevent men from coming to the faith. It is the devil who carries away the word of life from the hearts of those who have heard the good news ("so that they might not believe and be saved" [Luke 8:12; cf. Acts 13:10; Luke 10:18]). He hampers the apostles in their missionary work (1 Thess. 2:18; 3:5).

[8] According to the notion of the ancients, the air is the natural dwelling place of the malicious spirits. In expressing it in this manner St. Paul merely supposes, without discussing it or, at any rate, without making it an object of faith, the common view of his own times.

Assuredly, Christians have been radically liberated from the slavery of Satan; but they are, for all of that, all their lives objects of his continual attacks. Satan is the roaring lion who goes about among Christians seeking someone to devour (1 Peter 5:8; cf. 2 Cor. 2:11; James 4:7). His temptations are of every sort: falsehood (Acts 5:3), pride (1 Tim. 3:6-7), incontinence (1 Cor. 7:5); and he is able to act under the appearances of zeal and piety so as to transform himself into an angel of light (2 Cor. 11:14).

Even physical means and maladies of every kind (cf. 2 Cor. 12:7) can become in the hands of Satan instruments for fighting against the kingdom of God.[9] In the logic of the New Testament, everything, even those things morally good or indifferent in themselves, and all the concerns of life, can be, in the broad view, the occasions of temptations and of sin for man in the actual condition in which he finds himself.[10] In some way the Evil One is behind every temptation and every sin; and therefore, in view of sin, everything can be regarded as an instrument in the hands of Satan, at least potentially such, in his war against mankind.

The life of the individual Christian as struggle against Satan

In point of fact the whole life of the Christian will be a continual struggle against Satan and his satellites, as St. Paul explained in his Epistle to the Ephesians (6:10-20), when he exhorted Christians to put on the armor of God in order to withstand the attacks of Satan:

> "Put on the armor of God so that you will be able to withstand the wiles of the devil. For our struggle is not with blood and with flesh,[11] but against the Principalities and the Powers, against the rulers of the world of darkness, against the wicked spirits in the air. Therefore, take up the armor of God, so that you may be able to resist in the evil day and, having done what you must, may remain on your feet. Be strong, therefore, girding your loins with truth and putting on the breastplate of justice, and having your feet shod with the preparation which the gospel of peace provides, in every case taking up the shield of faith, with which you may be able to quench all the fiery darts of the Evil One. And put on also the helmet of salvation and the sword

[9] It is the angel of Satan who buffets St. Paul (2 Cor. 12:7). It is almost certainly a question of a chronic illness that hampered the Apostle in his missionary work. In the context there is no suggestion whatever of carnal temptations.

[10] See, for example, in Matthew 13:3ff and its parallels, the parable of the sower; 6:25ff, in regard to excessive concern over food to eat and clothing to wear; 22:1ff, the parable of the guests invited to the wedding feast; 1

John 2:16, all that is in the world is concupiscence of the flesh, concupiscence of the eyes, and pride of life.

[11] In biblical language flesh and blood simply means *man*. Here we can see how much Paul's view differs from that of our modern naturalist psychologism, which tends to conceive the whole struggle of man against evil only as a struggle against human passions and evil tendencies, whether of our own or of others.

of the Spirit, which is the word of God. With all prayer and supplication pray at all times in the spirit" (Eph. 6:11-18).

Great vigilance, therefore, is demanded of the Christian, so as to give no entry to the devil (Eph. 4:27), to avoid his snares and to resist his attacks (2 Cor. 2:11; 1 Peter 5:8). It is not without reason that the Lord's own prayer ends with the petition (Matthew 6:13) ". . . and lead us not into temptation, but deliver us from the Evil One." [12] The most ardent desires of Christians are summed up in the prayer that the God of peace will speedily crush Satan beneath their feet (Rom. 16:20).

In the struggle against Satan the Christian has God's help, which will not permit him to be tempted beyond his strength; but along with the temptation he is given also the means whereby he will be able to bear it (1 Cor. 10:13). In the Apocalypse it is especially clear that the good angels, as messengers and instruments of God on behalf of man, engage actively in the struggle against Satan and his satellites, assisting the faithful thereby (e.g., Apoc. 12:7-10; 20:1ff *et passim*). In the Scriptures in general, on the secondary level of the struggle between the kingdom of God and the kingdom of Satan on earth, the good angels are always seen on the side of the kingdom of God (Gen. 3:24; Mark 1:13 and parallels; Apocalypse *passim*).

Among the means which enable the Christian to struggle efficaciously against Satan there is the whole bearing of a truly Christian spirit (Eph. 6: 11ff), and prayer especially (Eph. 6:18; Matthew 17:21; Mark 9:29). In the Scriptures, prayer and fasting are frequently conjoined (Tob. 12:8-9; Luke 2:37; Acts 14:23; 13:3). Thus, in Mark 9:29, in a variant reading less well attested in the manuscript tradition, fasting is mentioned along with prayer, for the driving out of demons. Moreover, by comparing 1 Peter 5:8, "Be sober and watchful, for your adversary, the devil, goes about seeking whom to devour," with Matthew 24:42-44, 49, where the sobriety demanded of those who watch is clearly to be understood as a sobriety in eating and in drinking, we are led to the conclusion that it is just such a sobriety as this that the author of First Peter recommends as a weapon in the struggle against the devil. Another means pointed out by St. Paul (Eph. 6:17) is "the helmet of salvation and the sword of the Spirit, which is the word of God" (see also Heb. 4:12), i.e., the Scriptures, no doubt, pondered upon and accepted as a rule of life, so that they are, as it were, the sword among the armaments of the Christian. Christ Himself, in the scene of the temptation, repelled Satan by opposing him with the words of Scripture (Luke 4:4ff).

Everywhere in the New Testament the invoking of the name of Jesus is

---

[12] *apò tou poneroũ* can be translated either *from evil* or *from the Evil One.* However, as we have already sufficiently demonstrated, in this whole matter the mind of the New Testament is concrete and personalist: the Chris- tian has need of being delivered not only from impersonal evil but from Satan himself, the source of every evil and of every temptation.

seen as the foremost weapon in the struggle against the devil (Mark 9:38; 16: 17; Matthew 7:22; Luke 9:49; 10:17; Acts 16:18; 19:13; Phil. 2:10. See also James 2:19). The ritual application, so to speak, of this principle, is found in the primitive catechesis announced by St. Peter:

> "Be it known to all of you and to all the people of Israel, that in the name of our Lord Jesus Christ of Nazareth, whom you crucified and whom God has raised up again, even in this name does this man stand here before you, healed. . . . Neither is there salvation in any other. For there is no other name under heaven given to men by which we hope to be saved" (Acts 4:10-12).

Nevertheless, invoking the name of Jesus is not conceived as a magic word with a mechanical effect (Mark 9:13-28 and parallels; Acts 19:13-16). It presupposes faith, prayer, mortification, and, in general, moral dispositions. Its invocation against the demons is equivalent, therefore, to a prayer to God through the agency of Jesus against them. The disciples, moreover, are obliged to keep in mind that the gift of expelling demons is a charism, and that it is more important to have God's favor than it is to have such a charism (Luke 10:18-20).

The life of the Church as struggle against Satan

What we have previously said of the life of the individual Christian, considered as a constant struggle against Satan, is likewise applicable, according to the New Testament, to the life of the Church itself as such. There are two groups of texts which are of great significance from this point of view. The first consists of the two classic texts on the primacy of Peter in the Synoptics: Luke 22:31ff, and Matthew 16:17-19; and the second, the whole book of the Apocalypse.

In the words of Jesus as reported by Luke and Matthew, there is a noteworthy and, after the manner of what we have been explaining up to now, a logical and natural intimate connection between the primacy of Peter and the concept of the struggle which the Church must carry on and will always have to carry on against Satan. According to Luke, at the last Supper Jesus said to Peter: "Simon, Simon, behold, Satan has desired to have you, that he may sift you like wheat. But I have prayed for you, that your faith may not fail. And you, when you have returned, strengthen your brethren" (Luke 22:31-32). In Matthew, after Peter's confession at Caesarea Philippi, Jesus said to him: "Blessed are you, Simon son of John, for flesh and blood has not revealed this to you, but my Father who is in heaven. And I say to you that you are Peter and on this rock I will build my Church, and the gates of hell will not prevail against it. I will give you the keys of the kingdom of heaven, and whatever you shall bind on earth shall be bound in heaven, and whatever you shall loose on earth shall be loosed in heaven" (Matthew 16:17-19).

In these two aforesaid texts, the fundamental concepts correspond. The most special function of preëminence in the Church, which Christ willed to give to Peter among all the other Apostles, has for its precise end the assuring thereby of the stability of that same Church and its final triumph over the attacks of Satan. While in Luke's text Satan is directly named, in Matthew it is "the gates of hell" that signifies Satan and his satellites, under the figure of a city assembled, at least as to its leaders, in deliberative, legislative, and executive [13] council, in order to attack the Church.

The conceptual background of the two texts, therefore, is the uninterrupted struggle between the kingdom of Satan and the kingdom of Christ. Satan spares no effort in his attempts to overthrow the work of Christ. In the text of Luke he is seen at work attempting to ruin it in its very nucleus, the Apostles. Christ saves it by the power of His special prayer in behalf of Peter, directed precisely to the purpose [14] of confiding to him the task — he now having recovered from his momentary straying — of seeing to it that the other Apostles and, by means of them, all the faithful, will persevere steadfastly against the same attacks of Satan.

In the text of Matthew the whole infernal kingdom is seen in rage against the Church of Christ, viewed under the image of a fortified antechamber to paradise. To see to it that it is able always to offer victorious resistance to these attacks, Christ will build it on the person of Peter as upon a rock unshakable. This means that, in that fortress, Peter, as vicar and first-minister of Christ, will have plenipoteniary powers recognized in heaven itself. So, thanks to Peter, the infernal forces will not prevail against the Church.

It can easily be seen, then, how profoundly the concept and the reality itself of the constant struggle against Satan gives evidence of itself in the thought and in the ecclesial work of Christ. The Church is viewed by Christ and organized by Him as a citadel, all the parts of which are subjected to the onslaughts of the infernal forces, which, nevertheless, by virtue of the special preëminence and special assistance given to Peter, will not be able to prevail against it.[15]

The whole of the Apocalypse has for its central theme, so to speak, the

---

[13] In biblical and oriental tradition, such councils were held in the public squares before the gates of the cities. *Hades* can signify death. But not even this would separate the concept from Satan, who, in biblical tradition, is the one who holds the empire of death (Heb. 2:14), just as Christ, triumphant over death, is the One who holds the keys of Hades (Apoc. 1:18). See H. M. Féret, "La mort dans la tradition biblique," in *Le mystère de la mort et sa célébration, (Lex orandi 12),* Paris 1951, pp. 1ff. Also O. Betz, *"Felsenmann*

und Felsegemeinde (Eine Parallele zu Mt. 16, 17-19 in den Qumranpsalmen)," in *Zeitschrift für die neutestamentliche Wissenschaft,* Vol. 28 (1957), fasc. 1-2, pp. 70ff.

[14] The concept of the relationship of finality between the prayer of Christ for Peter and the consolidation of the brethren is expressed in the text, by the particle *kai,* which, in biblical Greek, frequently has this sense. See M. Zerwick, *Graecitas biblica,* Rome 1949, no. 314.

[15] But woe betide anyone found outside that Church! See 1 Cor. 5:5.

struggle itself and the final triumph of the Church over Satan. It is acknowledged[16] that this historical background of the Apocalypse is the first and second persecution carried out by the Roman Empire against the Church, in the time of the Emperors Nero and Domitian. The author, in the language of the prophetic apocalypses of the Old Testament, has no other purpose than that of explaining to Christians, for their consolation and encouragement, the meaning of such persecutions. This being his purpose, he situates these persecutions within the general picture of a theology of history and of the ultimate end toward which that history is reaching. Now, this picture is of none other than the struggle between Satan and God; between the kingdom of Satan and the kingdom of God; between Satan, the demons, and men who follow them, on one side; and on the other, God, Christ, the good angels, the Church on earth, and the just already in heaven. The ultimate end of the development of this struggle is the final triumph of God and of His kingdom, and therefore of the Church, which triumph He will confirm on the day of judgment, over the instruments which Satan will have won for himself. Afterwards there will be but the passage of the present world to the future world of the heavenly Jerusalem.[17]

There is nothing more instructive, for our purposes, than to observe how in each of Boismard's division of the text, the Apocalypse's view of history is developed. Boismard[18] provides the following summary:

"Text II offers the more simple plan. Satan, spiteful because of his having been dispossessed of heaven, turns his anger against the inhabitants of the earth (12:7-12). The better to succeed, he takes into his service the beast with ten horns and seven heads (the Roman Empire), which unleashes a violent persecution against the Church (ch. 13). Fortunately, prospects of salvation appear: the vision of peace for those faithful to Christ (14:1-5), the prophetic announcement of the fall of Babylon (Rome) (14:6-13), the symbolic vision that announces the extermination of the pagan nations (14:14-20). After an interlude the purpose of which is to justify the apparent rigor of the divine decrees (15:1-4), a series of punishments is poured out over Babylon which, finally, is overthrown by an invasion of the people dwelling beyond the Euphrates (the Parthians) (15:5—16:21); fortunately, those faithful to Christ, warned in time, are able to flee (18:4-8). A lamentation over Babylon accompanied by a proclamation of triumph closes this first episode of the 'great day' of wrath (18:14, 22-23, 20; see 16:14). Afterwards, in their turn, the pagan nations which had allied themselves with the beast are exterminated (19:11-21). Then it is time for the judgment, which marks the tri-

[16] For all this see, for example, M. E. Boismard, *L'apocalypse* (*Bible de Jérusalem*), 2nd ed., Paris 1953, pp. 12ff. W. H. Heidt, *The Book of Apocalypse* in the New Testament Reading Guide series, Collegeville, Minn. 1964.

[17] Heidt, *op. cit.*, pp. 3-120.

[18] *Op. cit.*, pp. 13ff.

umph of Christ's faithful (20:11-12), the end of the present world
and the advent of the heavenly Jerusalem (21:1-8).

"Text I takes up again very nearly the same plan. . . . In an initial
vision God, who is enthroned in heaven, confides to the Lamb the
destinies of the world, or, more precisely, the sealed book which contains the decrees of extermination against the pagan and persecuting
nations (ch. 4—6; see Ezech. chs. 1 and 10). A series of visions announces the coming of the 'great day' of wrath (see 6:17; 9:15; 11:
18), in the form of an invasion by the Parthians, with their fantastic
cavalry (chs. 6—11, less the interpolations provided by text II). . . .
Finally, there are voices from heaven announcing: 1) the proximity
of judgment; 2) the extermination of the pagan nations; 3) the destruction of those who corrupt the earth (11:18). Babylon (Rome),
the prostitute, the corruptress of peoples, is the first to be exterminated
(chs. 17—18, less the text II interpolations of 18:1-3; see Ezech.
chs. 16 and 23); and her fall is accompanied by a lamentation (18:
9-13, 15-19, 21, 24; see Ezech. ch. 27), and by songs of triumph in
heaven (19:1-10). The fall of Babylon marks an era of peace for the
Church, the stabilizing of the Messianic kingdom (20:1-6; see Ezech.
chs. 34—37), preceded by the symbolic resurrection of the martyrs
(20:4; see Ezech. 37:1ff). At the end of these times the pagan nations
(Gog and Magog) attempt a final assault against Jerusalem (the
Church) and are annihilated (20:7-10; see Ezech. chs. 38—39); finally, it is time for the judgment (20:11-15; see Ezech. 29:21); and
then there is a description of the future Jerusalem (21:9—22:2; 22:6-
15; see Ezech. chs. 40—47)."

In this picture, it is easy to see how the Apocalypse can present the people
of God, since the sin of Adam, and more especially the Church herself in her
life on earth, as the great stake in the struggle between God and Satan. Satan,
therefore, appears therein, whether in the first or in the second series of texts,
as the great enemy and antagonist of God. The role that he has in human
history, and how he is the father of every sinner and of every persecution
against the Church is explained particularly in chapters 12 and 20.

Chapter 12 contains the famous vision of the woman and the dragon. The
woman described with such signs as are indicative of splendor (12:1; see Gen.
37:9; Cant. 6:9), who gave birth not without anguish, who was menaced
and persecuted by Satan, whether personally or in her progeny, is the people
of God which arrives at the Messianic times only in pain and agony.[19]

The raging red dragon is Satan. His tail which drags down the third part
of the stars of heaven is an allusion to the fall of those angels who followed
Satan. The male child born of the woman is the Messiah. When it says that

---

[19] See Micah 4:9ff and Is. 66:5. It is not
necessary to refer to the question of whether
or not in the woman of the Apocalypse the
author had in mind some reference to Mary.

the dragon stood ready to devour the newborn, it is an allusion to the struggle of Satan against Christ; and when it says that the male child born of the woman was caught up to God, it is an allusion to the triumph of Christ in His resurrection and ascension. The expulsion of Satan and of his angels from the aerial regions of the heavens to the lower regions of the earth is indicative of his being dispossessed through the work of Christ, in whose service the faithful angels remain. Then Satan enters into conflict with the woman, that is, the Church and her faithful, unleashing persecutions against her.[20] All this is to be found in the twelfth chapter.

Chapter 13 and the following indicate how, to accomplish this, Satan makes use of human instruments and primarily of the political religious force of the persecutory pagan powers and of false prophets, seducers in their service. Then follows the description of the persecutions and of the destruction of the persecutory powers. The greatest of all the antagonistic pagan powers, the Roman Empire, is destroyed. There follows a period of peace for the Church in which the reign of the Messiah is strengthened. During this lengthy period, vaguely described as a thousand years, Satan is bound and hurled into the abyss, "so that he might deceive the nations (i.e., the pagans) no more, until the thousand years should be finished" (20:3). In the mind of the author, certainly this does not imply for this same period the cessation on earth of every evil and of every sin, for there will still be pagan nations who, at the end of time, will unleash, in a final effort, the general persecution (20:7ff). It is the author's intention to indicate that in the Messianic millennium, Satan will be reduced only to a relative impotence. At the end of those times he will be loosed once more, and will be equipped with the great power of unleashing his final attack on the Church (20:7ff).

In short, the same thing which Matthew says about the Church under the figure of a citadel built on rock but still the object of attacks by Satan and his satellites, the last book of the scriptural canon, taking its cue from the first Roman persecutions, shows us in action in a powerful apocalyptic finale, providing a general view of history, at the same time realistic and concrete, as a struggle between the kingdom of God and the kingdom of Satan.

The struggle against Satan in the end times

Final period: according to the New Testament the paroxysm of the struggle of Satan against Christians and Church will take place in the end times of the world. Thus, with the passage of the ages, according to Scripture, it would seem that we ought not expect a diminution but an intensification of the attacks of the Evil One and of his apparent success against God's kingdom.

In the Second Epistle to the Thessalonians, St. Paul recalls his earlier in-

[20] For all of this, see the usual commentaries on chapter 12; e.g., Heidt, op. cit.

structions on the events of the last days and the signs which will precede the final coming of the Lord. First there must be a great secession or apostasy from Christ, and then the appearance of the Antichrist. Both of these events will be fruit of Satan's work. "The mystery," the secret "of iniquity, is already at work even at the present time" (2 Thess. 2:7), but for the moment its activity is carried on in secret. There is, in fact, for the present an obstacle which restrains or impedes its full manifestation.[21] But soon enough this obstacle will be lifted, the great secession from Christ will take place openly, and "the man of sin will be revealed, the son of perdition, the adversary who exalts himself above all that which is of God or which is the object of veneration, even to the point of seating himself in the temple of God, proclaiming himself as God" (2 Thess. 2:3-4). "His coming is marked, through the work of Satan, by every power and by signs and lying wonders, and by all the deceptions of injustice, for those who are perishing; for they have not received the love of truth which would save them. That is why God sends them a deceptive influence, so that they believe falsehood" (2 Thess. 2:9-11).

The substantial accord between Second Thessalonians and the Apocalypse is especially remarkable in the area of the concept of the supreme struggle that will take place in the end times between Satan and the Church. The chaining up of Satan in the bottom of the abyss during the Messianic millennium (Apoc. 20:1-3) corresponds to the idea of Second Thessalonians, that for the moment the mystery of iniquity works in secret, there being an obstacle which prevents its fully manifesting itself (2 Thess. 2:6-7). The releasing of Satan at the end of time, for a last general assault against the Church, of which the Apocalypse speaks (Apoc. 20:3), corresponds quite well to the manifestation of the Antichrist, spoken of in Second Thessalonians (2 Thess. 2:8). There is a parallelism also between the marvels of the Antichrist and his seductive force through the workings of Satan, things spoken of in Second Thessalonians (2 Thess. 2:10-12), and the seduction and general persecution which, according to the Apocalypse, Satan will unleash against the Church in the end times, by means of the pagan nations (Apoc. 20:8ff).

And finally, there is the last and definitive action in the struggle between the kingdom of God and the kingdom of Satan, the reduction to absolute impotence of every force opposed to God, which is to say, of Satan and his satellites: "Fire from heaven came down and devoured them. And the devil who deceived them was cast into the pool of fire and brimstone, where the beast and the false prophet already are; and they will be tormented day and

---

[21] 2 Thess. 2:6ff. The determination of what this obstacle is, according to the mind of St. Paul, is a question much discussed and probably insoluble. See, for example, J. Everret Frame, *Epistles of St. Paul to the Thessalonians* (*The International Critical Commentary*), Edinburgh, reprint of 1946, pp. 259ff.

night through the ages of ages" (Apoc. 20:9-10; see also 20:14-15; 2 Thess. 2:8). Following upon this will be the advent of the new world, the heavenly Jerusalem.

* * *

In conclusion, it is easy to see how profoundly rooted in the New Testament is the concept that the whole history of the world, especially the whole work of redemption, in Christ Himself and in each Christian individually — the life of the Church in all its aspects — contains, essentially and as an idea on the primary level of importance, an incessant and mortal struggle not only against impersonal evil, not only against human passions, but against the person of the Evil One and against the persons of those spirits who are his followers.

There is in this no trace whatever of genuine dualism, because God remains the supreme Creator and Master of all things. The concept expressed poetically in the prologue of the Book of Job (1:6ff) is always vivid and quite essential in the New Testament: that Satan not only is inferior to God and unable to do anything without His permission, but that, in some way, even against his own perverse will, he remains the servant of the inscrutable and infallible designs of God, whose directives he cannot escape.[22]

For this reason there is in the New Testament nothing that smacks of hopelessness, no nightmare or terror of Satan, no pessimism of any sort, but only optimism and confidence. Christ is the stronger (Luke 11:22); and it is He who has conquered the world (John 16:33). Final victory is assured. And for this it is enough to keep oneself united to Christ (see 1 John 2:13; 4:4; 5:4). Everyone who remains united to Him will infallibly conquer the accuser in the blood of the Lamb (Apoc. 12:10ff). At the same time, however, it is undeniable that Christian revelation is far removed from reducing the whole struggle between good and evil whether within man himself or outside of man, to a simple question of nature or of psychology, of tendencies and of passions. Scripture is far removed from modern naturalistic panpsychologism. As always, so in this too, Scripture is far and away more personalist and concrete.

2. The Principal Developments of Later Non-liturgical Tradition In Respect to the Struggle against Satan

If we keep very clearly in mind the position of the New Testament on the question of the life of the Christian and of the Church as an unceasing struggle against Satan and his satellites, it is not necessary, for the sake of explaining the liturgy, which is our precise purpose, to dwell at any length on

[22] See, for example, Luke 22:31, where Satan has "requested and obtained"; 2 Thess. 2:11, "therefore the Lord will send . . ."; Apoc. 22:3-7.

the ideas of tradition and of Christian theology outside the liturgical area, on this same matter.

Later Christian thought in regard to demonology, having developed from the New Testament with the general purpose of determining the facts more precisely, concerns itself with a series of questions the real importance of which is vested in dogmatic theology in general; and in particular, the question of the nature of demons and the question of the precise way in which their fall took place;[23] or with other questions which are directly concerned with the history of spirituality and asceticism, such as those of the psychology of temptations and of the discernment of spirits. These questions, however, are of no direct interest to our investigation, because there is no trace of them to be found in the liturgy. In respect to the point which does properly interest us, that of the concept of the Christian life and of the Church as a struggle against Satan in general, the position of tradition and of later theology can be synthesized in the following terms.

First of all: the substance and even, quantitatively speaking, the immense majority of the affirmations of later tradition on this point, is made up for the most part simply of repetitions of what is read in the New Testament. It would be easy enough, but of no particular importance, to report a multitude of extraliturgical testimonies, from which it would but be apparent that the view of the New Testament has always been preserved by patristic tradition and, ultimately, even by scholastic tradition.[24] On the other hand, it will be of interest to take note in the non-liturgical literature of certain points in regard to which later tradition does not merely repeat that which is already to be found in Scripture, but in some way renders it more explicit or determinate.

Demons: relationships to the human body, to paganism, and to the natural elements

The essential facts which are recorded in the New Testament in regard to the question of how, with what frequency, and in what sense the devil is able to be present in a man's body, in the elements, and in material things in general, can be reduced to these: behind every evil, moral or physical, there is always the influence of Satan; his influence even on the human body and on sensible things is real and can extend even to inhabitation or possession properly so-called; this influence which he has is particularly extensive in the area of those things which are connected with idolatrous worship.

---

[23] See the excellent treatment in E. Mangenot and T. Ortolan, in the *Dict. de théol. cath.*, Vol. 4 (1924), pp. 339-407.

[24] Anyone who needs to be convinced of this may read the overview of this whole question, traced from a point of view that is not much removed from our own, in the *Dict.* *de spir.*, Vol. 3 (1957), pp. 152-234: Jean Card. Daniélou, *"Démon dans la littérature ecclésiastique jusqu'à Origène"*; A. and C. Guillaumont, *"Dans la plus ancienne littérature monastique"*; F. Vandenbroucke, *"En occident"*.

Patristic tradition received these facts in their generality. What remained to be done was to come to know how to explain them further and to represent — if we may so phrase it — their application in a concrete fashion: and this, of course, is a matter not of faith but of explaining the faith.

In this matter there was in the Church during the patristic age a considerable variety of opinions — infinitely less, however, than was to be found in the heterodox sects — deriving in part from certain Jewish apocryphal works such as *The Testaments of the Twelve Patriarchs* and the *Book of Henoch*, and in part from Christian adaptation of certain characteristics of the demonology of the Hellenistic milieu. From these Judaic and Hellenistic influences there are derived, in the process of explaining the faith further, certain opinions which are widespread and of frequent occurrence in Christian antiquity.

Demons, it was thought, insinuate themselves into the human body and dwell therein; again, it is sometimes said that specific demons, the authors of specific vices, and specialists in such vices, as it were (for example, in the seven or eight capital sins), insinuate themselves into specific organs of the human body and dwell there, where they excite passions, incite to sin, and torment the soul.[25]

Another opinion is that the demons are everywhere present in localities where idolatry prevails. The demons are identified with the gods of the pagans. They hide themselves within the idolatrous statues in order to receive divine honors and to breathe in the odor of the sacrifices and of the incense which delights their physical passions. They preside at pagan worship, at divinations, they utter oracles, foster magic and astrology. They send dreams, anxieties, and obsessions of every kind. They practice their wiles of every sort in order to deceive men.[26]

The whole of pagan life — not just that area of it that is directly concerned with worship, but even those areas which might on the face of it seem to be purely civil, military, commercial, areas concerned with the theater, with honors military or civil, because these things are indissolubly connected with pagan worship — is completely permeated by demoniacal worship and is a

---

[25] This notion is found in *The Testaments of the Twelve Patriarchs: Reuben* 3, 3-6; and it recurs in the *Corpus hermeticum*, for example, XVI, 14-15. It is widely repeated by the heterodox sects, and can be found in the pseudo-Clementine literature, e.g., *Hom.* 9, 10, or in Valentinian Gnosticism (see Clement of Alexandria, *Stromateis* 2, 20, 14). Echoes of such notions can be found in Tatian, *Oratio* 18; Clement of Alexandria, *Paidagogos* 2, 1, 15; Origen, *In Ios. hom.* 15, 6; Minucius Felix, *Octavius* 27, 1-4.

[26] In all of this Christians accept first of all the general affirmation of the Scriptures that idolatrous worship is worship of demons. Later they accept the Hellenistic opinions in regard to the *daimónia*: intermediary spirits between the gods and men, relative to matters of worship, divination, dreams, etc. But while Hellenism kept more to the idea that these *daimónia* were beneficent beings, Christians came to regard them as pernicious beings, demons in our sense of the term, satellites of Satan. See, for example, St. Justin the Martyr, *First Apology* 5 (Jurgens, no. 112a); Athenagoras, *Supplication for the Christians* 23-26. Later this becomes a common theme.

formidable instrument of Satan for the enslaving of mankind. Tertullian, who is particularly firm in his insistence upon this theme, refers to the whole complexus of paganism, in view of its being Satan's tool, as *pompa diaboli*.[27]

Another opinion, based on positive data of the New Testament in conjunction with certain Hellenistic views along with those of the Jewish apocrypha,[28] consisted in regarding as quite frequent and, as it were, natural, especially in pagan surroundings, the influence of the demons on the elements, on plants and animals, for the sake of doing harm to men and impeding their salvation. Tertullian, for example, says:

> "The business [of the fallen angels, who are the demons], is to corrupt mankind. Thus, from the very first, spiritual wickedness augured man's destruction. Therefore do they inflict diseases and other grievous misfortunes upon our bodies; and upon the soul they do violence to achieve sudden and extraordinary excesses. Their marvelous subtlety and elusiveness gives them access to both parts of man's substance. To spiritual forces much is possible. Because they are invisible and imperceptible to the senses, they manifest themselves more in the results of their actions than in their actions themselves. So it is, for example, when, in the case of fruits or crops, something imperceptible in the air casts a blight upon the flower, kills the bud, and injures their development. It is as if the air itself, tainted in some unseen way, were spreading abroad its pestilential breath." [29]

In the three preceding cases — insinuation into and inhabitation of the human body by demons; entry of demoniacal worship into every aspect of pagan life, even in the civil areas thereof; harmful influence of demons on and through the elements of nature — it is easy to see that the influence of Jewish and Hellenistic views has not in fact created new points of doctrine, but has really only determined and concretized in a greater degree concepts which were already contained in the New Testament.

It can also be seen how a series of liturgical rites of an antidemoniacal import would be born in this climate: exorcisms of a man prior to his being

---

[27] See J. H. Waszink, "Pompa diaboli," in *Vigiliae christianae*, Vol. I (1947), pp. 13-41. A good resumé of Tertullian's thought in this matter is to be found in Cardinal Daniélou's "*Démon dans la littérature ecclésiastique jusqu'à Origène*," in the *Dict. de spir.*, Vol. 3 (1957), pp. 174-182. Be it noted that this position of Tertullian in regard to the demoniacal influence in a pagan society, apart from the question of whether it be direct or indirect, or, philosophically speaking, natural or not entirely natural, simply draws out the consequences of New Testament principles, from St. Paul in particular, in regard to idolatrous worship as worship of demons,

while drawing also on the Apocalypse in regard to the pagan powers as instruments of Satan.

[28] It involves the concept from the Jewish apocrypha that there are angels presiding over every material element (angels of the rains, of hail-stones, of the winds, etc.), along with the Hellenistic concept of the demons. Christianity is of a mind that initially it was a question of good angels charged with the administration of the universe; and that afterwards some of them fell away and became perverse.

[29] Tertullian, *Apology* 22, 4-5 (Jurgens, no. 278).

baptized, and blessings of an antidemoniacal import of various objects and of the elements of nature. In any case, these rites were not mothered in the womb of the false opinions of Judaism and Hellenism. They were nurtured at the breast of Scripture, the understanding of which, in this matter, can be said, however, to have been assisted in the patristic age by the convergence before the eyes of Christians of certain opinions derived from the Jewish Apocrypha or from a Hellenistic milieu.

Demons: relationship to baptism, to martyrdom, to monastic life, and to the particular judgment

In the general picture of the Christian life as a struggle against Satan, patristic tradition has made more explicit, even in areas outside the liturgical texts, the antidemoniacal dimension of a whole series of manifestations of the Christian life, the significance of which, in the struggle against the devil, was only implicit or, at any rate, very little emphasized in the New Testament. Sometimes these developments had great importance in the area of liturgical expression, as we will easily have occasion to see in what follows. It is a question first of all of the antidemoniacal dimension of baptism, a notion contained equivalently in the New Testament in the concept of baptism as death and resurrection with Christ, death to sin and the flesh, putting off the old man, the beginning of a new creature in Christ, etc. Afterwards there is the most notable development of the antidemoniacal dimension of martyrdom,[30] a notion which is explicitly mentioned in the Scriptures (Apoc. 12:11).

Baptism, martyrdom, the ascetical life of virginity and the monastic life are realities intimately connected with each other in ancient tradition, because martyrdom is regarded as the supreme witness and perfect development of baptism, while ascetical life and the monastic life are seen as surrogates of martyrdom.[31] Certainly there is nothing extraordinary about the fact that, given a clear perception of the profoundly antidemoniacal dimension of baptism and martyrdom, the ascetical life in general and, after the development of monasticism, the monastic life in particular, and especially in its eremitical form, came to be regarded as preëminent forms of that struggle against Satan which is the mark of the Christian.

Origen so develops this first notion that his whole spiritual doctrine, in its somewhat negative view of asceticism properly so-called, is practically de-

[30] Various testimonies to this from Hermas, St. Ignatius of Antioch, acts of martyrs, have been collected by Cardinal Daniélou, "*Démon dans la littérature ecclésiastique jusqu'à Origène*," in the *Dict. de spir.*, Vol. 3 (1957), pp. 179-182. The acts of the martyrdom of St. Perpetua have been studied from this point of view by F. J. Dölger, "*Der Kampf mit dem Aegypter in der Perpetua Vision. Das Mar-* tyrium als Kampf mit dem Teufel," in *Antike und Christentum*, Vol. 3 (1932), pp. 177-188. For Origen, see S. Bettencourt, *Doctrina Origensis ascetica, seu quid docuerit de ratione animae humanae cum daemonibus (Studia anselmiana 16)*, Vatican City 1945, no. 112ff.

[31] See Edward A. Malone, *The Monk and the Martyr. The Monk as the Successor of the Martyr*, Washington 1950.

veloped in all its details around the picture of the struggle against the devil.[32]
The second notion, that of the monastic life and especially its eremitical form
as a preeminent position in the struggle against Satan, constitutes one of the
fundamental concepts of Athanasius' *Life of Anthony*; and it recurs and is
strongly emphasized in all subsequent monastic hagiography. This is true of
St. Jerome's life of St. Paul the Hermit, his life of St. Hilarion, and his life
of Malchus; and it is true as well of the descriptions of the lives led by monks
as found in the *Historia monachorum*, the *Lausiac History*, and the various
Apophthegmata patrum, and Cassian's *Conferences*.

Evagrius Ponticus more than the other monastic writers theorized on this
aspect of the monastic life.[33] The principle is formulated in general that
the more conducive to perfection the life that the Christian leads, the more
severe and the more concentrated are the attacks of Satan's forces against
him in order to make him fall: attacks directed principally against those who
have arrived at a high degree of sanctity, practicing various forms of external
mortification, visible and sensible, of every sort.[34] It is not necessary for us,
in view of our purpose of investigating the liturgy, to delay much over this.

We must nevertheless make mention, because of the numerous instances in
which it has had an influence upon the liturgy, both historical and of the
present time, of the opinion which Origen borrowed from his Hellenistic en-
virons,[35] in regard to the role that belongs to the demons in the particular
judgment of each man after his death. Origen believes that the particular
judgment of each soul after death unfolds through a certain period of time,
as it would seem, among the spaces of the heavenly spheres which surround
this earth and which each soul must necessarily traverse in order to reach to
God. At the entrance to each sphere stand the demons, described sometimes
as lions ready to devour souls or at least to impede them on their way, and
now as toll-collectors (*telónai*) before whom the soul must pass an examination and to whom it must pay a tribute in accord with the vices and sins
with which it is still burdened.[36]

This imaginative way of representing and concretizing what the Christian
faith insists upon in regard to the particular judgment of each soul was very
widely accepted in the East in ancient times, and even in some parts of the

[32] See Bettencourt, cited above in note 30 of
the present chapter.

[33] See the details in A. and C. Guillaumont,
under "*Démon*," in the *Dict. de spir.*, Vol. 3
(1957), pp. 189-212.

[34] For Origen, see Bettencourt (cited in note
30 above, present chapter), pp. 67ff. For Evagrius Ponticus see "*Démon*" in the *Dict. de
spir.*, Vol 3 (1957), p. 203. The *Life of
Anthony* is especially typical of the approaches
of ancient literature.

[35] See P. Wendland, *Die hellenistische-

römische Kultur, Tübingen 1912, pp. 35, 170-
171.

[36] *In Lucam hom.* 23, Rauer edition, pp.
154ff. It should be noted, however, that Origen, in giving expression to this theory, is
conscious of the fact that his speculations go
beyond that which is "of the faith"; and he
gives his usual warning that his opinions are
of a private nature and tentative: "*periculo-
sum quidem, sed tamen strictim breviterque
tangendum.*"

West down to the thirteenth century.[37] The journey of the soul across the spheres, through various stages, before various toll-collectors, undergoing various examinations, accompanied by good angels who plead their cause, in particular, St. Michael, the great conductor of souls, or psychopomp,[38] and the snares set by the demons, the hateful examiners and collectors who desire to impede the soul's ascent to God — all this forms a theme which recurs broadly in the Fathers, in the apocrypha, and in the liturgy.

This too was a way of representing to the imagination, in accord with the cosmological and demonological conceptions of the Hellenistic milieu, the great theme in the Scriptures of the Christian life as a continuing and incessant struggle against Satan and the demonic hordes. From this it is possible to judge even now how much alive was this concept in the religious psychology of antiquity. It is in a similar climate that the various liturgies were born and shaped through the ages. It will easily be understood, therefore, how, in the liturgy, the reality of the struggle against Satan appears as an essential aspect of the Christian view of the world.

3. What Is De Fide and What Is Not De Fide in the Affirmations of the New Testament and of Later Tradition in the Matter of the Struggle against Satan

Having come thus far, there is now a question which cannot be avoided. Could anyone wish to say that the struggle against Satan, as it has been seen in the New Testament and even more so in its presentation by patristic tradition, does not present, objectively speaking, any question to the theologian, or that these affirmations as they stand, do not require explanation and determination? That would be to deny what is evident. It does not seem possible to avoid the spontaneous question of the modern reader: what, basically, must be believed in this matter? Perhaps someone will say to me: is it your intention, then, just to report to us the ingenuous opinions of the ancients in

[37] See J. Rivière, "Le rôle du démon au jugement particulier chez les Pères," in Rev. des sciences relig., Vol. 4 (1924), pp. 43-64. B. Serpilli, L'offertorio della messa dei defunti, Rome 1946, pp. 64-65. See also A. Recheis, Engel, Tod und Seelenreise, Rome 1958, pp. 152-158: Origen, Athanasius, monastic literature, Basil, Gregory of Nyssa. It is a question of an imaginative representation and not of a dogmatic exposition of the way in which the particular judgment takes place. Even today the preacher may sometimes appeal to the imagination in describing in a concrete way the torments of hell and the joys of paradise. St. Cyril of Alexandria is especially prominent among the Fathers for his detailed descriptions of the particular judgment (Hom. XIV,

De exitu animae [PG 77, 1072-1076]). He did not hesitate even to warn that "this Judge has no need of accusers and of witnesses, of proofs and of refutations. It is He that places before the eyes of the guilty all that we have done, said, and willed" (ibid., 1072). These descriptions of the journey and of the examinations of the soul at various stages thereof, taken as imaginative representations, presented no dogmatic difficulties, even if some of those who made use of such representations did not distinguish with sufficient clarity between the imaginative descriptions and the dogmatic reality.
[38] See, for example, B. Serpilli, op. cit., pp. 87ff.

the matter of demonology? What is at the roots of this embarrassing matter, and what will be the criteria which will permit us to make the necessary distinctions and clarifications? The following, then, is what I think must be said in this matter.

First of all: that the air is in a special way the dwelling-place of the demons was a Hellenistic opinion to which St. Paul alludes, but, as doctrine assures us, without making it the object of the affirmation of faith. There is nothing of dogmatic affirmation about the later opinions in regard to the specialization of certain demons in certain vices; nor in that of St. Michael as special psychopomp. We discount also the imaginative way in which, following Hellenistic cosmological and demonological opinions, Origen and so many others after him reported the relations between the individual soul and the demons immediately after death, in the particular judgment. The *telonia* constituted an opinion in reference to a way of concretely imagining a fact affirmed in substance by the faith: the particular judgment. The opinion in regard to the *telónai* is one which has no support in dogmatic tradition and, objectively speaking, was afterwards recognized as mythological.

A second point to be observed: it is not a question of accepting, without examination, the reality of all the supposed demoniacal visions of which, for example, so much is found in monastic literature and in ancient hagiography. Let us pose the question as to whether or not the beasts seen by St. Anthony, as recounted in St. Athanasius' *Vita Antonii*, or the little Ethiopians which Macarius believed he saw in the Church while the monks were in choir, and so many other similar cases, were truly diabolic apparitions. From the theoretical theological point of view it is perfectly possible. From the historical point of view there would seem to be no reason in many of these cases why we should deny them every probability *a priori*. There is nothing incredible about all this in the lives of the saints, for example, the Curé d'Ars. But that all such stories recounted are authentic is entirely another matter. It would be necessary to have a firm control over the many other possibilities, and a critique of the witnesses and of the facts in order to arrive at a well-founded opinion. In any case, from the theological point of view the matter has little importance.

A third point, and the most important: even after admitting the validity of the two preceding observations, there still remains, in the New Testament and in tradition, an immense body of demonological affirmations, still proving an embarrassment such as that of which we spoke above. In what does this embarrassment consist? With the exception perhaps of some rare instances in which no Catholic would dream of denying that the case may well be one of true and proper diabolic obsession or possession, in the vast majority of other cases, instances of physical, psychic, and moral imbalances in regard to which the New Testament and later tradition speak of diabolic influence, of demoniacal possession, a struggle against demons, etc., is it not really a question perhaps of physical, physiological, psychological and moral phenomena on a purely *natural* level? Why then must we have it that the devil is personally intervening? And if all those cases are natural, what still remains of the general affirmation of Scripture and tradition that the whole Christian life and the whole life of the Church is a continuous struggle against Satan and his demons? If it is basically a question of natural phenomena, would it not be more precise to turn the saying of St. Paul around and to declare that our struggle is not primarily against the principalities and powers and the rulers of this world of darkness, but simply against flesh and blood? Then we are dealing only with attempts to attribute the manner of expression employed in the Sacred Scriptures and followed afterwards by tradition to popular conceptions and traditions which are taken up and employed as vehicles of expression, without in any way making them the object of religious judgment or of faith.

Such, it appears to me, is really the crucial question in this matter. The embarrassment of which I spoke above proceeds simply from the fact that in Scripture itself and in tradition there does not seem to be readily apprehensible any neat response to the aforesaid problem.

The question hinges entirely on the concept of *natural* and, therefore, of *nature*. In these matters and in ourselves, what precisely is *natural*, and what is *not natural*, to be attributed to factors situated outside the range of *nature* in particular cases? Today it would appear that Scripture and ancient tradition attributed too many things, which we would regard as evidently *natural*, to factors outside the range of the *nature* of the beings in question. Without entering into the particulars of the complex question of what is natural and what is supernatural, I am nevertheless compelled to offer some account of the points which are indispensable to our purpose.

Anyone who has studied, in the course of general dogmatic theology, the question of the *natural* and the *supernatural* in its historical development and in its theoretical aspect, will not be in any way surprised that neither in Scripture nor in tradition is there to be found a completely exhaustive answer to the aforesaid question. And what is the reason for this?

The reason is simply that the concept of *nature* and of *natural* can be determined from two different points of view — not contradictory, but actually complementary — and can, therefore, have two different significations. Scripture and ancient tradition take one point of view; and we today instinctively take the other, without taking sufficient cognizance of its necessary complement, the first point of view. The coming to an understanding of this is, in the history of theology, a relatively recent accomplishment. Furthermore, I would not make bold to say that this is a matter perfectly clear in the minds of all theologians even yet.

In Greek and in Latin, the two languages in which the concept of nature is defined, whatever a man posits about the *nature* of anything, he is referring to that thing in the condition in which it was *natus*, that is, to all that constitutes this thing from its birth or coming to be; to the concrete historical nature of a thing with all the notes and qualities which it possesses from birth or origin by any title whatever. Here the concept of *nature* is determined from a concrete, historical point of view. In this sense, all that the thing has from its origins, all that which historically is primal and original in the thing, is *natural*. Whatever is afterwards subjoined to this thing and is other than pertinent to its primitive condition, whether for good or for evil, will be, in this perspective, an alteration of *nature*, and will be regarded as *not natural*. Factors which cause or bring to bear an alteration in this life will be considered first of all under their aspect of being factors which are *not natural*.

This perspective is not that of the philosopher, because in considering the thing in its concrete primitive condition, as it originated, it does not analyze entitatively that which is essence and that which is accident. It does not pose the question of knowing which among the various gifts the thing possesses are the ones which it might not have had from its very origins, and which are the ones without which it would have been absolutely impossible for it to have been originated or born in the first place, or to have been able to subsist afterwards in any condition whatever of its successive development.

This concrete historical perspective, you see, is the perspective of Scripture and of ancient tradition when looking to the *nature* of man and of things, to that which is natural to their being and to that which, contrariwise, is to be attributed to factors outside the range of their *nature*. For the New Testament and for ancient tradition, if something supervenes in respect to man or the world which is outside or contrary to the line of the original condition in which they find themselves, historically and concretely speaking, as they came from the hands of God, it is to be regarded, even if the word *natural* is not actually used, as an intrusion into man or into the world, and as a thing which is *not natural*. The New Testament and ancient tradition fix their attention solely upon this status of a person or thing; their attention is directed immediately and single-mindedly to the factor which has provided its historical existence, and to that which is extraneous to the *nature*, i.e., to the primordial condition, of man and of world.

This concrete historical mentality ruled almost uncontestedly in the history of Christian thought up to about the thirteenth century, when, little by little, in the consideration of things and therefore in the concept of *nature* as well, the other perspective began to show itself, the perspective of the entitative philosophical sort. Later, beginning with the sixteenth century, i.e., from the time of the anti-Protestant and anti-Baianist conflicts, this second perspective had perforce to be considerably emphasized as a weapon against the aforementioned heresies which not infrequently had difficulty in understanding the point of view of the Scriptures and of ancient tradition, and especially that which the more ancient point of view had intended to teach and properly defend.

The philosophical point of view, in considering these matters, wants to analyze them in their metaphysical structure, abstracting from their concretization in time, in space, and by individuation: to distinguish in anything first of all what there is in it that is necessary, and what is not necessary in it, whatever the state of its conditioning by time, space, and individuality, and to determine its each aspect according to the various degrees in the scale of necessary and universal being. In this perspective the *nature* of a thing is its very essence; necessary essence, universal, identical in all the individuals of the same species and concrete states in which they are to be found successively and simultaneously; and, more precisely, it is the essence of this thing inasmuch as it is the principle of its specific operations.

Seen thus, a thing is *natural* according to what appertains to it by *nature*, whether because of its constitution (as the body and the soul are *natural* to man), or because of what necessarily accrues to it (as in the case of man, to be corruptible, to be able to have sorrows and sicknesses, to be mortal, to have passions, to make perverse use of his liberty, and similar things), or because its activity is governed by *nature* as a necessary means to the achievement of a necessary end (as in the case of man, to be sustained by God in his every action, without which support he would not in fact be able to act).

The philosophical viewpoint of *nature* does not concern itself with the historical, concrete, *de facto* status of things, but only with their metaphysical structure. If a thing is in man and in the world in accord with the line of their metaphysical structure, in the aforementioned senses, the philosopher, therefore, in considering it, is not concerned with knowing if, historically speaking, such a thing is manifested effectively or less than effectively, or even if it is necessarily manifested in the primitive historical state of man and of the world: for him, it will simply be *natural*. This being the case, that man is in fact subject to corruption, to the noxious effects of the natural elements, that he has pains, sicknesses, emotions, passions, sometimes makes a perverse use of his freedom, are things which, for the philosopher and in the light of his solely philosophical perspective, are to be conceded; and they are all things that are simply *natural*, belonging to the original historical condition of mankind. To explain all this, for anyone who clings to the purely philosophical viewpoint, it is not necessary to have recourse to processes and agents outside the range of the *nature* of man himself.

It seems to me that these observations are the key to the resolution of the question with which we are concerned. If we wish to understand the mentality of the Scriptures and of ancient tradition — and hence, of the liturgy — in its conception of the redemption and of the whole life of the Christian and of the Church as a personal and concrete struggle against Satan, we must seek to understand how Scripture conceives the real and personal power of

Satan after sin. But to understand this same power we have to start not from the purely philosophical and abstract consideration of man and of the world, but from the consideration of their concrete historical status and condition prior to the sin in the earthly paradise.

Now, speaking concretely and historically, moral and physical evil holds sway over man not purely and simply as the result of man's willfulness, but as the effect of man's voluntary action under the influence and at the instigation of Satan, and as a manifestation not only of the struggle between good and evil, but between the kingdom of God and the kingdom of Satan. The state of being despoiled of the goods of grace and of the preternatural gifts, into which man has fallen through the influence of Satan, is a state of true sin, of aversion from God and of slavery to Satan. Every consequence of original sin to which we are so utterly subject, is always the exercise of Satan's power over the world and over us: not only personal sins, but even temptations of every sort, persecutions, tribulations, harmful influences of the infrahuman elements, misfortunes, maladies of every kind, and death. In the limitless scale of physical, psychic and moral evils to which we are subject and to which the world is subject, the influence of Satan, his power, and his incessant struggle against the kingdom of God is manifested. The perception of these things will present no difficulty to anyone who, in accord with revelation, takes the historical point of view in considering the paradisial state in which man, by virtue of grace and the preternatural gifts, enjoyed immunity from all these evils.

Today we pay too little heed to the preternatural gifts which man enjoyed prior to sin and which through the positive will of God, we should always have enjoyed. These gifts, though they went beyond the exigencies of nature philosophically considered, belonged to the state of nature in which man was originally constituted. By the will of God, they should have remained always part and parcel with that nature. To have lost them means that man is in a state contrary to the will of God and at variance with his primitive state. It means being in a state of sin. If the preternatural gifts are forgotten, it is not possible to grasp original sin, nor its consequences; and therefore, it will not be possible either to grasp the real influence of Satan over man and over the world after original sin, nor, ultimately, the effective extent of the struggle which we today are obliged to carry on against Satan. The Scriptures, when they introduce the personal struggle against Satan into the primary level of the concept of redemption, are perfectly logical in taking up this historical viewpoint.

In this perspective, the work of Christ and the gifts which He obtained for us are not just something which brings to perfection and crowns a world and a nature in themselves indifferent, as it were, or neutral in regard to God — as the naturalism so widespread today would more or less consciously prefer to believe — but they are a *redemption*, a *ransoming*, a *liberation* of man and of the whole cosmos. And this rescuing is not only from a state of hostility to God but also and even primarily from a person hostile to God, to that God who "has snatched us from the power of darkness and has transferred us into the kingdom of His beloved Son" (Col. 1:13).

This is the great catechesis which Scripture and ancient tradition, with the theme of the struggle against Satan, impart to our modern naturalism: after the first sin, man finds himself no longer in a normal state nor in a state of philosophic neutrality before God, but in a catastrophic state of aversion to Him; and in this state he not only stands before God, but has made a choice between God and the enemy and is thereby involved in the great dramatic and cosmic struggle which, ever since the fall of the angel, has divided the kingdom of God from the kingdom of Satan. Redemption in Christ, because it certainly restores grace to us — though not for the moment, of course, the preternatural gifts — reintegrates us anew and even now into the ranks of the kingdom of God; but it does not remove us from the struggle and from the possible and very effective and personal influence of Satan and his hordes, an influence which is exercised over us whenever any kind of physical or moral evil strikes us. This being the case, then, our struggle is really not against flesh and blood only, but primarily against Satan and his satellites who still operate through the vexations which flesh and blood inflict upon us.

Having admitted this, then a concern with determining in individual cases of physical or moral evil whether the personal influence of Satan and of his satellites, which operates through these evils, is direct or indirect, proximate or remote, is a justifiable concern and is in no way contrary to the aforesaid truth; whether that influence is exercised through forces and processes which, philosophically considered, are above *nature*, or, contrariwise, are simply *natural*; to what point and in what manner, in a determined case, the elements of demoniacal influence which, philosophically speaking, are *natural*, are intermingled with those which, in the same consideration, are not.

This concern is a legitimate one; and a more precise knowledge of the *nature* of man and of things, as well as of the processes and forces of this *nature*, in the light of philosophy and of the experimental sciences, helps us to satisfy it. And this has its usefulness in preventing us from exaggerating the influence of Satan over us and from conceiving of it as if it were exercised in ways which, philosophically and experimentally speaking, are all and always superior to merely natural forces, as happens in those cases in which today we speak of possession or of obsession properly so-called. This is something which revelation does not in fact impose upon our belief, not even when the New Testament speaks, in its own particular sense, of *possession* or of diabolic action.

Still, I do not see how it is possible to deny that, even after all these considerations, there remains still the fact of this secondary aspect: that behind every moral and physical evil that strikes us there stands effectively the personal influence of Satan. And, in fact, such a concern is not found in Scripture nor in ancient tradition, whose perspective in the manner in which it considers all things and so too in the manner in which it considers our relations with Satan is not, if I may repeat it again, primarily entitative, but rather historical; for it views all things primarily in the perspective of salvation history.

4. The Liturgy of Christian Initiation and the Struggle against Satan

With the aforegoing considerations, I believe that we are now sufficiently prepared to understand the liturgy in its theme of the struggle against Satan. If, indeed, the struggle against Satan seems to be so strongly emphasized in the sacred history, *viz.*, the mystery of Christ or the mystery of the Church which Christian revelation proposes to us as a general vision of the world, no wonder that the same struggle seems to be equally emphasized in the liturgy, which seeks only to concretize and actualize the mystery of Christ under the veil of sensible and efficacious signs.

As in revelation in general, so too in the liturgy, Satan is always and everywhere present, at least on a secondary level, as the great antagonist of the kingdom of God and consequently of the fulfillment of the mystery of Christ. The liturgical material of liturgies both past and present confirms this observation superabundantly. It is not my intention to make an integral collection of all these texts. We will achieve our purpose, however, by reporting them in what amounts to a formal integrity, i.e., by glancing through the whole area of the liturgy, divided into the liturgy of the seven sacraments, along with the rites immediately connected with their administration; the liturgy of those sacramentals which are not in themselves a part of the rites connected with the sacraments; and the liturgy of the liturgical cycles. We shall document these matters as much as is necessary in order to see that in fact, in the consideration of the liturgy, whether of the past or of the present, Satan is always present on a secondary level of perspective, as the great antagonist of the kingdom of God and of the mystery of Christ.

This struggle against Satan, liturgically speaking, is concretized first of all in the rites of Christian initiation, and especially in the baptismal rites. In the Bible (Rom. 6:1ff), baptism is presented as a single reality expressed sometimes in a negative way, sometimes in a positive way: death and resurrection; death to sin, new life of grace in Christ; death of the old man, birth of the new man in Christ. And we know that for the Scriptures sin and Satan, the old man and Satan, are indissolubly connected. It is perfectly natural, then, that the earliest generations of Christians should have formulated and ritually concretized the theme of baptism simply as a liberation from the slavery of Satan and birth of life in Christ in the liberty of the children of God.

Besides, according to the same New Testament, baptism signifies the decisive initial moment of the great passage from darkness to light and the beginning of the new life, which must afterwards grow and increase throughout the rest of our pilgrimage on this earth; the radical reïntegration of a man into the ranks of the sons of God. It was only natural, therefore, that the Christian would conceive of baptism precisely as the great initial moment of the struggle against Satan, the decisive moment of the first phase in which Christ and Satan do battle in individual souls: Satan, to keep that soul in his slavery; and Christ, to liberate it and to draw it to the light.

Finally, because according to Scripture the influence of Satan is more especially active and manifest in paganism and in the worship of idols, again it was but natural that the antidemoniacal value of baptism should be perceived and given prominence among the converts from paganism.

In fact, so early a writer as St. Justin the Martyr, speaking of the value of the name of Jesus as an exorcism, in connection, it would appear, with a profession of faith which might well be that of baptism, seems to allude to the antidemoniacal and exorcismal value of baptism.[39] Be that as it may, this antidemoniacal import is made perfectly explicit in Tertullian through the ceremony of the renunciation of Satan,[40] and is brought fully to light in the baptismal ceremonies of the fourth and fifth centuries and in the explanations given those same ceremonies by the Fathers of that era. The more characteristic rites exemplifying this dimension, common to all the liturgies, were the exorcisms and the renunciation of Satan. Even the blessing of the baptismal water, which is to be found in all the liturgies alike, contains as an essential aspect this antidemoniacal dimension. Moreover, there was annexed to practically all the concomitant rites, at least in the explanations of one or the other of the Fathers, a directly antidemoniacal dimension. For an understanding of this a cursory review of the principal baptismal rites which were in use from the fourth to the seventh centuries will suffice.[41] This will assist us also in gaining a grasp of the exact import of the antidemoniacal elements which have been preserved in the baptismal rites even to the present day.

The rites over the *audientes*

The ceremonies which accompanied the admission to the simple catechumenate in the ranks of the *audientes* or *auditores* [42] were all centered around

[39] *Dialogue with Trypho the Jew* 30; 85.
[40] *The Shows* 4; *The Crown* 13; *The Soul* 35.
[41] What these rites are can be seen, for example, in Righetti, Vol. IV, pp. 27-52. Some noteworthy material in regard to this point, extracted largely from the Greek Fathers of the fourth century, can be found in Jean Card. Daniélou, *The Bible and the Liturgy*, pp. 19-69, where the principal themes of the baptismal rites are reviewed, along with the explanations given them by the Fathers.
[42] Among the catechumens the *auditores* or *audientes* (hearers) formed a category distinct from those who, at the beginning of Lent, were scheduled to receive baptism at the approaching Easter, and who submitted themselves during this same period to a well-

the theme of liberation from Satan and the way now opened to Christ. This was true from the beginning with the ceremony of insufflation on the face, accompanied by a formula of exorcism. This insufflation was a gesture of contempt for Satan, the significance of which was made immediately clear by its being explicitly pointed out in the exorcism. The meaning of the ceremony was, in fact, so explained by John the Deacon in the ninth century:

> "After the insufflation he is exorcized, so that, the devil having been expelled from him, a way may be prepared in him for the entry of Christ, our God." [43]

This ceremony would have served the purpose of the ancient Church in keeping alive the notion of the historical and supernatural antagonism of Satan in respect to man and the world, a fact which can be seen from the argument which St. Augustine employs against Pelagian naturalism, in which he never tires of pointing out that this rite of exorcism is omitted for no one, not even for infants.[44] The rite was preserved in the Roman Ritual [45] almost

planned immediate preparation for the sacrament. These latter were known as the *competentes, electi,* or *photizómenoi* (those about to be enlightened, illumination or enlightenment being one of the names given to the sacrament of baptism).

[43] *Exsufflatus igitur exorcizatur, ut, fugato diabolo, Christo Deo nostro paretur introitus;* in his *Letter to Sennarius* 3.

[44] See, for example, St. Augustine's *De nupt. et concup.* 1, 22 [20]; *Contra Iul.* 6, 11, 5; *De gratia Christi et de peccato originali* 2, 45; *Opus imperf.* 3, 182. Consider the following passage: "The Christian faith does not doubt, though it is a thing which the heretics have begun to impugn, that those who are cleansed in the bath of regeneration are redeemed from the power of the devil, and that those who have not yet been redeemed by means of this regeneration, even if they be the infant children of those already redeemed, are slaves in the power of that same devil, unless they too be redeemed by the same grace of Christ. When the Apostle speaks of that blessing of God, that God 'who has delivered us from the power of darkness and has transferred us into the kingdom of His beloved Son,' we cannot doubt that the blessing of which he speaks applies to every stage of human life. Whoever denies that infants, when they are baptized, are delivered from that power of darkness, of which the devil is the prince, that is, from the power of the devil and his angels, is confuted by the truth of the very sacraments of the Church, which sacraments

no heretical novelty is permitted to destroy or change in the Church of Christ, because the Head of that Church rules and helps His entire body, members great and small alike. It is true, therefore, and in no way false, that the power of the devil is exorcized in infants; and infants renounce his power through the hearts and mouths of those who bring them to baptism, because they are unable to do it with their own hearts and mouths; and this, in order that they may be delivered from the power of darkness and be transferred into the kingdom of their Lord. What, then, is there within them, by which they are made subject to the power of the devil up to the very moment when they are delivered from it by Christ's sacrament of baptism? What is it, if not sin? The devil has found nothing else to enable him to put under his own control that nature of man which the good Creator made good. Nor have infants since they came to be alive committed any personal sins of their own. There remains but original sin, whereby they are made slaves under the power of the devil until they are redeemed by the bath of regeneration and by the blood of Christ so that they may pass into the kingdom of their Redeemer, after having frustrated the power of him who held them slaves, and having received the power by which they become no longer children of this world but children of God" (*De nupt. et concup.* 1, 22 [20]). It would be utterly erroneous to attribute this language to the exaggerations of Augustine. It is correct and indisputable. There but re-to the present moment. In the newly revised rites which, in the United States, are just now coming into use, the insufflation has disappeared, though a verbal exorcism, even in the baptism of infants, remains.

Following immediately upon the insufflation and exorcism, there was an imposition of hands to signify in a positive way the sanctification of the soul.

A later development in the West (elsewhere it was done at different points in the ceremony) is the imposition of the sign of the Cross on the forehead of the candidate: the *consignatio* or *sphragís*. The sign of the Cross is basically a sign of belonging to Christ and of consecration to Him; but derivatively, it is also a sign of recognition, of protection, of enrollment in the army of Christ, the ensign of the contest. It was easy, therefore, to perceive therein an antidemoniacal aspect; and so much the more easily might it be seen that the sign of the Cross in reference to Christ is not a conventional sign of any sort, but the instrument and the symbol of His Passion and hence of His greatest struggle and supreme victory over Satan. It is not without reason that this victory of Christ is more than once recalled in the New Testament in a context which speaks of His death and of the Cross.[46] The Fathers, therefore, and the various liturgies as well, do not fail to point out the antidemoniacal dimension of the *consignatio crucis*. St. Cyril of Jerusalem, for example, writes that in an upright conscience the Lord

> "gives the wondrous and salvific seal (*sphragís*), at which demons tremble and which angels recognize. Thus are the former put to flight, while the latter gather about it, as something pertaining to themselves." [47]

To understand fully the meaning of the *consignatio* it is necessary to situate this ceremony in the general picture of the significance that Christians attached to the sign of the Cross in the various aspects of their lives. Now, among else, the antidemoniacal significance of the Cross in the Christian life in general is strongly emphasized. In St. Hippolytus' *Apostolic Tradition* it is expressed in this way:

mains in it, as in the New Testament itself, a still undefined point, as we explained above. All that Augustine says must be retained as true: the power of Satan, even over infants not yet baptized, is real and personal; and calling it to the attention of our modern Pelagianism is no less necessary than was the defending of it against that ancient Pelagianism. Nevertheless, it is not necessary that, philosophically speaking, that power be exercised through means which are other than natural. It is not necessary, therefore, to hold that in those infants, for example, it is a question of what we today would call diabolic possession; — because for us today, diabolic pos-

session means the influence of Satan over the body of a man, exercised by means which, philosophically speaking, are *not* natural.

[45] *Ordo baptismi adultorum* no. 8; *Ordo baptismi parvulorum* no. 3.

[46] John 12:31-33, " 'Now judgment is passed on the world; now will the prince of this world be cast out. And I, when I am lifted up from the earth, will draw all things to Myself.' He said this to indicate by what kind of a death He would die"; Phil. 2:8-11; 1 Cor. 2:2-6.

[47] *Catechetical Lectures* 1, 3 (Jurgens, no. 808).

"When tempted, always reverently seal your forehead with the sign of the Cross. For this sign of the Passion is displayed and made manifest against the devil if you make it in faith, not in order that you may be seen by men, but knowingly (*per scientiam*) putting it forward as a shield. If indeed the adversary sees the power of the Spirit outwardly displayed from within . . . he takes to flight trembling." [48]

Tertullian gives us a glimpse of a common usage among Christians:

"At every forward step and movement, when coming in and going out, when putting on our clothes, when putting on our shoes, when bathing, when at table, when lighting the lamps, when reclining, when sitting, in all the ordinary occupations of our daily lives, we furrow our forehead with the sign." [49]

Lactantius says:

"Anyone who has seen how the devils adjured in Christ's name flee from the bodies they have been possessing, knows what terror the sign of the Cross inspires in the devils." [50]

Cyril of Jerusalem insists strongly on the antidemoniacal efficacy of the sign of the Cross and recommends that the Christian employ it on every occasion:

"Let us not be ashamed of the Cross of Christ, therefore. Even if others hide it, make its sign yourself openly on your forehead, that the demons, seeing the sign of the King, may flee trembling. Make this sign when you eat and drink, when you sit down, when you go to bed, when you rise, when you speak, when you are on your way — in a word, on every occasion." [51]

St. Augustine observes, in regard to the sign of the Cross, that

"unless it is made on the forehead of the believers, on the water itself by which they are regenerated, on the oil of chrism with which they are anointed, on the sacrifice by which they are nourished, nothing of all this is done as it should be." [52]

Tradition, therefore, has perceived in the sign of Christ, that is, in the sign of the Cross, that mark of God with which, according to the Apocalypse

---

[48] *The Apostolic Tradition* 37; ed. Dix, pp. 68-69. In the last sentence I leave out some words of difficult interpretation. In them, apparently, Hippolytus means that in tracing the sign of the Cross on his forehead, the Christian manifests outwardly the force of the Holy Spirit, whose temple he has become by his baptism; the spirit of evil must flee before this sign of the presence and the force of the Holy Spirit. See also Jean Cardinal Daniélou, "*Le signe de la croix*," in *La table ronde*, Dec. 1957, pp. 32-38.

[49] *The Crown* 3, 4 (Jurgens, no. 367).

[50] *The Divine Institutions* 4, 27.

[51] *Catechetical Lectures* 4, 14. See also 4, 13; 13, 3; 13, 22; 13, 40-41. The text quoted above (4, 14) is cited also by Jean Card. Daniélou, *The Bible and the Liturgy*, pp. 62-63. He calls attention also to Athanasius' *Life of Anthony* 13, and to St. Gregory of Nyssa's *Life of St. Gregory the Thaumaturge* (PG 46, 952A-C).

[52] *In Io. tract.* 118, 5.

·(7:2-3), the faithful of the end times will be signed as a mark of protection against the infernal powers and their satellites.[53]

In Rome and in Africa, from the third and fourth centuries, the *consignatio* was followed by the rite in which the candidate tastes of blessed and exorcized salt, a ceremony which is retained even today in all places where the Roman Ritual is in use.[54]

Beyond the symbolic meaning of preservation through divine wisdom, this rite is given also a protective dimension, for warding off the demons. This is particularly well-expressed in the prayer for the exorcism of the salt, as found in the Gelasian Sacramentary and still preserved in the Roman Ritual:

> "I exorcize you, salt, in the name of God the Father Almighty and in the love of our Lord Jesus Christ, and in the power of the Holy Spirit. I exorcize you by the living and true God who created you for the protection of mankind and who ordained that you be consecrated by His servants for the sake of new believers. We pray You, therefore, O Lord our God, that this salt be made a sacrament of salvation for putting to flight the enemy. Do You, O Lord, sanctify it, bless it, so that for all those who taste of it, it may be a perfect medicine to strengthen them, in the name of the Lord Jesus Christ, who will come to judge the living and the dead by fire." [55]

From the preceding remarks and observations it will easily be understood that even the admission to the simple catechumenate was and is yet considered essentially in the context of a liberation from Satan and an adhering to Christ.

The rites over the *competentes*

Such too was the sense of the ceremonies carried out all during Lent, as a proximate preparation for baptism, over those catechumens known as *competentes*, who, being inscribed in the official registers of the Church, were pledged to receive the sacrament of baptism at the approaching Easter. The preliminary examination, to which each candidate was obliged to submit before being admitted to the ranks of the *competentes* was clearly invested with a symbolism which concretized from the beginning the theme of the struggle against Satan and removal from his dominion to adherence to Christ.

Thus it is that in Syria, as is apparent from the *Catecheses* of Theodore of Mopsuestia and as has been pointed out by Cardinal Daniélou,[56] the candidate, during the examination in which his case was discussed, was obliged to remain standing on sack-cloth, barefoot, clad only in a tunic, with his

[53] See, for example, R. H. Charles, *The Revelation of John* (*The International Critical Commentary*), Vol. I, Edinburgh 1950, pp. 194ff.

[54] *Ordo baptismi parvulorum* 6-7; *Ordo baptismi adultorum* 13-15.

[55] Gelasian Sacramentary, Mohlberg edition, no. 288, p. 43.

[56] Jean Card. Daniélou, *The Bible and the Liturgy*, pp. 20-22.

hands extended in an attitude of prayer and with eyes lowered.[57] This behavior concretizes in a symbolic fashion the theme mentioned above. The
candidate shows thereby that he wishes "to manifest the servitude in which
the devil held him slave, and to excite the compassion of the judge." [58]

Standing thus before the ecclesiastical judges, he shows by his attitude that
he believes himself engaged in a struggle against the devil very like the
struggle of Christ Himself in the temptation in the desert. The mat of sack-
cloth, the original significance of which seems simply to have been that of
penitence, Theodore sees as signifying those "garments of skin" (Gen. 3:21)
with which God clothed Adam and Eve after their sin, and as a symbol of
the new condition into which they had fallen and in which the candidate for
baptism still finds himself: a condition from which, however, he is about
to be liberated.[59] Inscription on the registers of the Church among the candidates for baptism at the Easter following was, as it were, the positive
aspect of this new victory over Satan.

There is evidence also that afterwards, during Lent, there were two groups
of ceremonies which concerned the *competentes*. The first group, more properly catechetical in nature, was concentrated on the explanation of the Apostles' Creed (*traditio symboli*) and of the Our Father (*traditio orationis dominicae*), which, at a specified time, the candidates were obliged to be able
to recite from memory (*redditio symboli* and *redditio orationis*). At Rome,
by the sixth century, this rite was preceded by a brief introduction to the
four Gospels (*traditio evangelii*).

The second group of ceremonies, the *scrutinia*, was more directly purificatory by nature, and consisted primarily of exorcisms and prayers. The most
important *scrutinium* was the final one, and it took place on the very morning of Holy Saturday.

Although the first group of ceremonies was more directly catechetical in
nature, it was not entirely lacking of an antidemoniacal dimension. Thus, in
the *traditio symboli* of the Gelasian Sacramentary, the bishop, after having
recited the creed in the presence of the candidates, commented briefly on its
importance, saying among else:

> "You, therefore, should retain in your hearts this very brief formula
> which contains everything necessary for this profession of faith to
> serve you as protection at all times. For the power of these arms is
> always invincible, and serves the good soldiers of Christ against all
> the surprises of the enemy. Let the devil, who never stops tempting
> man, find you always armed with this creed; that, having conquered
> the adversary, whom you renounce, you may preserve incorrupt and

---

[57] Theodore of Mopsuestia, *Catechesis* XII,
prologue; Tonneau ed., p. 323.
[58] *Ibid.*, XII, 24; Tonneau ed., p. 361.

[59] Daniélou, *The Bible and the Liturgy*, pp.
21ff.

immaculate to the very end the grace of the Lord, with the help of Him whom you acknowledge." [60]

Neither is the *traditio orationis dominicae* entirely lacking in allusion to the devil, since the Our Father itself, directly or indirectly, contains as petition: "lead us not into temptation, but deliver us from evil"; or, as many of the Fathers understood it, "deliver us from the Evil One." [61]

It is, nevertheless, primarily in the *scrutinia*, which in the ancient Roman discipline were conducted on the third, fourth, and fifth Sundays of Lent, and particularly in the great *scrutinium* of Holy Saturday morning, that the antidemoniacal character of baptism has its principal emphasis. An overview of how these *scrutinia* developed, as is provided, for example, by the description offered by Righetti,[62] is sufficient basis for gaining an understanding of the fact that their significance was directly and entirely antidemoniacal, and this with a concreteness and vividness comprehensible only against the background of the New Testament and of ancient tradition such as we sketched above.

The scrutiny did not originally signify an examination of doctrine or of manner of living (even if something of this meaning did insinuate itself into the conception of the scrutinies towards the end of the fifth century); rather, it meant a scrutiny or examination of body and soul in order to free the catechumens from diabolic influences by means of exorcisms and prayers, to which were joined, on the morning of Holy Saturday, an anointing and the explicit renunciation of Satan. That is why the clerical exorcists were the principal ministers of the scrutinies.

Bishop Quodvultdeus of Carthage, a contemporary of St. Augustine, enumerates the *sacramenta* involved in the scrutinies as follows: exorcisms, prayers, religious chants, insufflations, sack-cloth, inclinations of the head, the humiliation of being barefoot.[63]

According to the *Ordo Romanus* XI of the sixth or seventh century, the *scrutinium* proper opens with the deacon's invitation to kneel in prayer; and probably it is concluded with an oration delivered aloud by the priest, to which all present responded *Amen*. This was followed by an invitation to the sponsors of the catechumens to make the sign of the Cross on the forehead of their respective godchildren. Next there was an initial exorcism, made by an exorcist, over the men and women separately. The same ceremonies were repeated a second and a third time with a second and third

---

[60] Mohlberg ed., no. 317, p. 51.

[61] In the text of the *Traditio* as given in the Gelasian Sacramentary the antidemoniacal dimension of the Our Father is emphasized in the introduction and in the petition, "lead us not into temptation."

[62] Vol. IV, pp. 43ff.

[63] Quodvultdeus, *Sermo ad compet.* 1, PL 40, 660-661. The Gelasian Sacramentary (Mohlberg ed., no. 283, p. 42) defines the scrutiny: "*Coeleste mysterium quo diabolus cum sua pompa destruitur et ianua caelestis aperitur.*"

exorcism made by different exorcists. The whole ceremony concluded with a prayer by the priest, with a second sign of the Cross made by the sponsors on the forehead of the catechumens, and with Mass. This ceremony of the scrutinies as found in the *Ordo Romanus XI* is substantially preserved in the Roman Ritual in its *Ordo baptismi adultorum*, while the *Ordo baptismi parvulorum* preserves only the final prayer of the priest.[64]

The character of the formularies of exorcisms are so well-known that it is scarcely necessary to dwell upon them. For the most part they consist in:

1) Addressing Satan with titles of contempt and opprobrium, such as unclean spirit, adversary, enemy of the faith, enemy of the human race, seducer, source of every evil and every vice, traitor, ancient serpent, etc.; and in reminding Satan of his sins, of the punishments meted out to him by God, of his defeats suffered at the hands of Christ, etc.

2) Words of command and threat made with authority and decision: flee, leave this place; give honor to Father, Son, and Holy Spirit; give honor to Jesus Christ.

3) Invocations of the name of God, of the Persons of the Most Holy Trinity, of the name of Jesus.

4) The sign of the Cross; and more recently, sprinkling with holy water.

The first exorcism in the *Ordo Romanus* XI, the text of which is found in the Gelasian Sacramentary, after calling upon God to send His angel to protect the catechumens, reads:

> "Therefore, accursed devil, recognize your condemnation and give honor to Jesus Christ, His Son, and to the Holy Spirit; withdraw from these servants of God, because our God and Lord Jesus Christ has seen fit to call them to His holy grace and blessing and to the gift of baptism. By this sign of the holy Cross which we place on their foreheads and which do you, accursed devil, never dare to violate." [65]

It is especially in the presence of these exorcisms that our modern naturalism experiences embarrassment. Righetti tries to shake it off by citing a passage from Duchesne:

> "In those ages there was a lively preoccupation with evil spirits, with their power, and with the necessity of obtaining the freedom therefrom not only of souls, but also of bodies, and of nature itself, whether animate or inorganic. It was believed that every object over which the name of Jesus Christ was not vigorously invoked, was subject to the activity of the demon and able to transmit it. That is why exorcisms were multiplied over the candidates at baptism. . . . Such an obsession may seem strange to us, but it had great importance in

---

[64] *Ordo bapt. adult.* 16-18; *Ordo bapt. parv.*   [65] Gelasian Sacramentary, Mohlberg ed., no.
9.   292.

its own time and, lest we forget, has left its very evident traces in the liturgy from ancient times even to our own days." [66]

This last sentence of Duchesne treats the whole matter as an antidemoniacal and antispiritual "obsession" of which those ages, through popular error, were the victim, and of which numerous traces are preserved in the liturgy of the present time only by the force of inertia.

I hope I have shown that such a way of explaining these matters, in accord with Duchesne's well-known modernist tendencies, is too simplistic and too hasty. It seems to me, on the contrary, that it was most proper indeed that those ages had a lively concern over evil spirits, over their power, and with the necessity of freeing from their influence not only souls but bodies also, and nature itself, both animate and inanimate or inorganic; and that they did well to believe that every object, over which the name of Jesus Christ was not vigorously (!) invoked was subject to the activity of the demon and capable of transmitting it. Otherwise all that revelation tells us about the paradisial state, about the fall of man, about original sin and its consequences, among them the slavery of mankind and of the world to Satan, about the redemption of Christ as struggle against Satan, and our liberation and that of the world from that same slavery — all this would be only a fable.

It will be valuable to repeat it: if in the position taken by the ancients, and therefore by the liturgy, there was or is something imperfect that could or can yet give place to exaggeration and to unjustified obsessions, this is not in the fact that they believed in the power of the malevolent spirits, and in the necessity of freeing from the power of those spirits not only souls but bodies also, along with nature itself, both animate and inorganic; nor is this imperfection in any way in the fact that they admitted that every object over which the name of Jesus was not invoked was subject to the activity of the devil and able to transmit it.

On the contrary, it is simply in the fact that in the ancient texts, many of which are still in use today, there is an area that remains undefined, because the question was in no way posed whether the influence of the demon is exercised in ways and in processes that, in the light of philosophy and of the experimental sciences, are to be termed natural, or whether in ways that are not simply natural; and hence what remains undetermined or undefined is at what point we are dealing with true and proper cases of possession in the modern sense; in other words, whether the diabolic influence being dealt with is direct or indirect.

Between the two possible attitudes toward this there is a great difference indeed. The first consists in admitting that the demoniacal influence exists

[66] Cited by Righetti, Vol. IV, p. 44, with reference to Duchesne's *Histoire de l'ancienne* *église*, Vol. III, p. 120 of the Italian translation: *Storia della chiesa antica*.

and is exercised, for the most part, through processes and ways which are, philosophically speaking, natural, and, after the sin of Adam, real, personal, and universal; that it is everywhere evident that man is the victim of physical and moral evil; that the life of the Christian and of the Church is a continual struggle against this influence; and that the whole liturgical complexus of the means of sanctification and of worship, and the exorcisms in particular, possesses among else, the aspect of being a protection for the Christian in this aforesaid struggle.

The second attitude consists in attributing the whole practice of the Church in regard to exorcisms — not to say the whole viewpoint of Scripture in this matter — to simply popular phantasy, excepting only those extremely rare cases, not otherwise interpretable, in which it is a question of true and proper possession in the modern sense of the term.[67]

In conclusion, therefore: when it is a question of the exorcisms of those about to be baptized, it is necessary to say that they are fully justified, even while admitting — and Scripture, tradition, and the liturgy itself in no way suggest otherwise — that in the immense majority of cases, it is not a question of possession properly so-called in the modern sense of the term. The exorcism, in the usual case, has the sense of a prayer of the Church to obtain from God, for the one about to be baptized, actual graces of various kinds. In the first place, in order to prevent any exercise of diabolical influence that might set up physical, moral, personal, or social obstacles, internal or external, as impediments to the effectiveness of the baptism. In the second place, to obtain for the one about to be baptized actual internal graces which dispose him to receive the sacrament in the most fruitful way possible.

The exorcism brings about this latter effect, among other ways, by symbolizing in an anticipatory and vivid way, and by presenting before the eyes of the one himself being baptized and of those who are praying for him, one of the aspects of the grace of future baptism, this aspect being none other than the liberation of the baptized from the slavery of Satan. Thus the exorcism is also a catechesis for the one about to be baptized and for those who are concerned with his welfare, a catechesis which disposes him to better understand, to appreciate and to desire — and therefore to receive — the baptismal graces. And from this catechetical point of view the exorcism is fully justified, even when it is a question of infant baptism.

It is undeniable, however, that the union of the rites of the catechumens with those which look to the immediate conferral of baptism, and even more, the general ignorance of the significance of these rites, are in a large measure detrimental to their being an effective catechesis. The first part of this difficulty has now been largely remedied by the revised rite of baptism, just now

[67] This mentality, sometimes unconsciously Pelagian, the fruit of our modern naturalism, would do well to read again and meditate upon the text of St. Augustine cited above in note 44 of the present chapter.

in process of publication, which permits the conferral of baptism in defined stages. The second part of the difficulty, the general ignorance of the significance of the rites, can, of course, be remedied only by effective instruction; and attendance at a course of instructions is now required, in many of the dioceses of the United States, of the parents and the sponsors of the child to be baptized.

Fully justified, too, are those exorcisms over infrahuman things, even if, as is for the most part verified, they are not in fact obsessed or possessed in the modern sense of the terms. This is because the diabolic influence on these things exercised with a view to harming man, can be real enough, even if it is exercised through ways and processes which, philosophically speaking, are natural. In this case the exorcism has the significance of a prayer to God, asking Him to prevent the diabolic influence from making use of such objects for the purpose of drawing man into sin or holding him there, and so that those who make use of these objects with the proper dispositions of mind may obtain every sort of actual grace needful to protect them from diabolic influence and to dispose them always in a better way to the divine influence of sanctifying grace.

Among the scrutinies, that of Holy Saturday morning had particular solemnity and importance as the most immediately preparatory to baptism. In this scrutiny, besides an exorcism of the usual sort and the *redditio symboli*, there were three special rites, all of an antidemoniacal character: the rite of the *Ephpheta* or of the *aperitio aurium*; the anointing; and the renunciation of Satan.

The *aperitio aurium* is connected with the initial exorcism and holds a position which in more ancient times was occupied by a simple sign of the Cross, which was frequently made at the conclusion of the exorcisms. The antidemoniacal dimension of the *Ephpheta* or *aperitio aurium* is clearly expressed in the formula which accompanied it, and which is preserved even to the present time in the Roman Ritual: [68]

> "*Ephpheta*, which means, 'Be opened', so that you may perceive the fragrance of God's sweetness. But you, O devil, depart; for the judgment of God has come." [69]

Even the anointing with oil on the breast and between the shoulders — in the East, the whole body was anointed — still preserved in the Roman Ritual,[70] though not without some changes in the revised rites not yet entirely completed, has a meaning which is preëminently antidemoniacal and antagonistic to Satan. The catechumen, who is about to join the supreme struggle against Satan by renouncing him definitively and who is about to

[68] *Ordo baptismi parvulorum*, no. 13; *Ordo baptismi adultorum*, no. 34.
[69] See the Gelasian Sacramentary, Mohlberg ed., no. 420, p. 68.
[70] *Ordo baptismi parvulorum*, no. 15; *Ordo baptismi adultorum*, no. 36.

escape his slavery through the baptismal immersion, was anointed beforehand in order to be healed and fortified with the strength of Christ, just as
an athlete makes his preparations, to fit his body not only for the hand to
hand combat of baptism, but to prepare himself for the struggle against the
enemy, a struggle in which he must be engaged for the rest of his life.[71]

St. Ambrose puts it quite succinctly: "We came to the font. You entered,
you were anointed. . . . You were anointed as an athlete of Christ, as if you
were a wrestler." [72]

The Eastern tradition is unanimous in this same interpretation.[73] In the
Sacramentary of Serapion, for example, the anointing is accompanied by this
prayer:

> "We do this anointing over those who approach for the divine re-
> generation, praying that our Lord Jesus Christ set healing and
> strengthening forces to work on their behalf, and thereby find out
> and heal every trace of sin and iniquity or of diabolical influence in
> their soul, their body, and their mind; that, by His grace, He grant
> them forgiveness, that, freed from sin, they may live in justice and,
> re-created by this anointing, purified by the bath and renewed in the
> Spirit, they may have the strength henceforth to overcome all the
> hostile powers and the illusions of this life." [74]

At Rome the renunciation of Satan came after the aforesaid anointing and
in more ancient times formed part of the baptismal rite proper. Among the
antidemoniacal elements of the baptismal rites, the rite of the renunciation
of Satan is one of the most ancient [75] and is still preserved today in the Roman Ritual.[76] In it is concentrated the whole symbolism of baptism as a
liberation from Satan and adhesion to Christ. The formula is remarkably
the same in the various liturgies. The object of the renunciation is regularly
expressed in three parts: Satan, his pomps, and his angels or his works. The
meaning of the expression "the pomps of Satan" seems to be sufficiently
clarified.[77] It is a matter, principally, of the manifestations of pagan worship,
especially its processions and the games which Christians were still tempted

[71] The texts of the liturgy and of the Fathers take into account the whole span of life
following baptism.

[72] De sacramentis 1, 2, 4.

[73] Pointed out by Jean Cardinal Daniélou,
The Bible and the Liturgy, pp. 40-42, where
texts are cited. See, for example, St. Cyril of
Jerusalem, Catechetical Lectures 20 [Mysta-
gogic 2], 3: "Just as the insufflations of the
faithful and the invocation of the name of
God, like flames of roaring fire, burn the
devils and put them to flight, so the oil ex-
orcised by the invocation of God and by
prayer receives such power that it not only
burns and destroys the vestiges of sin but also

puts to flight all the invisible powers of evil."
See also St. John Chrysostom, Huit catéchèses
baptismales (Wenger's ed., in Sources chrétiennes, no. 50), Paris 1957, Catechesis 2, 22-
23, pp. 145-146.

[74] Sacram. Serap. 22 (15); Funk ed., Vol.
II, p. 185.

[75] See even so early a writer as Tertullian,
The Crown 3, 2 (Jurgens, no. 367).

[76] Ordo baptismi parvulorum, no. 14; Ordo
baptismi adultorum, no. 35.

[77] See the discussion of J. H. Waszink,
"Pompa diaboli," in Vigiliae Christianae, Vol.
1 (1947), pp. 13-41.

to attend. In the angels of Satan it is difficult not to see an allusion, at least in the original signification of the term, to the demons, in accord with the expression found in the New Testament (Matthew 25:41; 2 Cor. 12:7; 2 Peter 2:4; Jude 6; Apoc. 9:11; 12:7-9); some of the Fathers, nevertheless, interpret the expression not of the demons but of the human instruments of Satan in the working of evil and in the tempting of Christians.[78] In this meaning, the expression approaches the variant "and all his works," preserved in the Roman tradition [79] and referring to various sins of every sort.

In the East the antidemoniacal dimension of the ceremony was especially emphasized by a series of symbolic gestures and postures, in particular, by turning toward the West and extending the hand when pronouncing the renunciation. Ancient Greek tradition located the gates of Hades in the West; and in the tradition of the Fathers the West was still regarded as the place of the kingdom of darkness. The significance of the gesture, therefore, was clear: "The devil, being darkness, has his empire in darkness. That is why you renounce this prince of darkness," St. Cyril explains, "while turned symbolically to the West." [80] In making this renunciation the candidate extended one or both of his hands, a gesture which accompanied every sworn pact or its renunciation; or he even breathed three times in the direction of Satan, as a sign of contempt for him; and then he turned to the East, elevated his hands and eyes toward heaven as a sign of prayer, and verbally professed his adherence to Christ.[81]

The blessing of the font and the postbaptismal anointing

Among the ceremonies which immediately surrounded the baptismal washing itself on Holy Saturday night, the one which had from antiquity most directly an antidemoniacal dimension was the blessing of the water for the baptismal font. It is attested already by Tertullian as a current practice,[82] and its meaning as sanctification of the water had, most probably from the beginning, a double aspect. There was the negative aspect, the expulsion of the demoniacal influence by means of an exorcism; and the positive aspect, the bringing down from above by means of calling upon God, of divine protection and power, with special reference to the Holy Spirit.[83] The consecra-

[78] See, for example, Theodore of Mopsuestia, *Catechesis* 13, 7-9; Tonneau ed., pp. 377-383.
[79] Found already in St. Hippolytus, *The Apostolic Tradition* 21 (Jurgens, no. 394i).
[80] St. Cyril of Jerusalem, *Catechetical Lectures* 19 [*Mystagogic* 1], 4. These rites are preserved even yet in the Byzantine liturgy. See the *Euchológion*, Rome 1873, p. 151.
[81] The renunciation is called *apótaxis*; the adherence, *sýntaxis*. See J. Card. Daniélou, *The Bible and the Liturgy*, pp. 30ff.
[82] Tertullian, *Baptism* 3. See Righetti, Vol.

IV, p. 58, and the bibliography cited there.
[83] St. Ambrose in his *De sacramentis* 1, 5, 18 says: "As soon as the priest enters he performs the exorcism over the creature which is water, and afterwards utters the invocation and offers the prayer that the font be sanctified and that there be in it the presence of the Holy Trinity"; and the same, 1, 5, 15: "You have seen water. But not every water heals. Only that water heals which has the grace of Christ. The element itself is one thing, and sanctification is quite another. The

tory prayer over the water in the Gelasian Sacramentary [84] — which is the
one still in use in the Roman liturgy — even if it is in composition a cento
of two distinct prayers, is clearly constructed on this plan of exorcism and
consecration.

How did such practices arise? Without a doubt, from the general concept,
based on the teachings of revelation in regard to the influence of Satan over
man and over the world after sin, of the usefulness of sanctifying, in order
to counteract the demoniacal influence, even the inorganic elements which
serve man, and in particular those which are employed for sacred purposes.
Moreover, in a secondary way, the Hellenistic idea which regarded certain
elements, air and water among them,[85] and certain places as the special
habitats of demons,[86] may very well have been a contributing factor.

By their very nature the rest of the baptismal rites, beginning with the
immersion in the piscina and the emergence therefrom, manifest the positive aspect of the whole ceremony: the new life in Christ, which the neophyte, having overcome the devil, had now achieved, was much more
strongly expressed here than in the prior part. Such is the case in the chrismal
anointing which, according to both Roman and African usage, the neophyte
received and does yet receive from a priest immediately after the baptism;
and similarly in the white garment, with which the neophyte was clothed,
and in the lighted taper which was placed in his hands.

This is not to say, however, at least in respect to the chrismation, that the
antidemoniacal dimension was entirely lacking in these rites. This dimension
is strongly emphasized not so much in the formularies of the chrismation
itself as in the blessing by which the chrism was prepared, the blessing
which was performed in the *missa chrismatis* of Holy Thursday. In the Gelasian Sacramentary, in the prayer which precedes the consecratory preface
of the chrism, it is expressed as follows:

> ". . . Lord, we pray You that by the anointing with this chrism
> You grant purification of soul and body to those who are coming to
> the bath of divine regeneration; so that, if any remnant of adverse

action itself is one thing, its efficacy quite another. The action is fulfilled with the water,
but its efficacy comes from the Holy Spirit.
The water does not heal if the Holy Spirit
has not descended thereupon and has not
consecrated it."
[84] Mohlberg ed., nos. 445-448, pp. 72-74.
[85] See, for example, Tertullian, *Baptism* 5.
[86] Even in other particular rites of the baptismal ceremony there is easily perceived the
antidemoniacal dimension which, moreover,
was certainly implied throughout. Thus in the
fact that the catechumen was obliged to strip
himself completely and enter naked into the
piscina there is sometimes seen a symbol of

the fact that in baptism, in which he participates in the death to which Christ submitted
Himself naked on the Cross, he conquers the
infernal powers just as Christ conquered them
from His Cross. In the immersion of the
catechumen in the piscina, from which afterwards he emerges, is seen an expression of
his victory over Satan, who dwells in the
depths of the waters. Sometimes the baptistries
were decorated with figures of stags panting
for the water while holding in their mouth
a serpent, to indicate that the catechumen
came to the saving waters of baptism only by
conquering the demon. See Jean Card. Daniélou, *The Bible and the Liturgy*, pp. 36-37.

spirits still adhere in them, it may go away on contact with this consecrated oil. Let no place be granted the evil spirits; let no opportunity be granted the deserting powers; let no possibility of hiding be given the perverse tempters; but, for Your servants who are coming to the faith and are to be cleansed by the operation of the Holy Spirit, may the preparation of this anointing be helpful toward the salvation they will receive in the sacrament of baptism by means of the birth of heavenly regeneration." [87]

It must be affirmed, therefore, that in the mind of the ancient Church the anointings which were made with the chrism consecrated on Holy Thursday, including even that of confirmation properly so-called, by the very fact that these anointings are made with the chrism, had a clearly antidemoniacal dimension.[88]

Confirmation

The antidemoniacal dimension of confirmation properly so-called, which sacrament the newly baptized received at the hands of the bishop, proceeds really from the general notion which regarded confirmation as the seal and fullness of baptism. It was only natural that there should be perceived in such a rite a meaning also of a perfecting and strengthening of the powers of the new Christian in view of the struggle against Satan which, even if in a situation radically different from that prior to his baptism, he must continue to carry on throughout his whole life.

The Euchologion of Serapion already gave expression to this notion, in its prayer for the blessing of the chrism with which the neophyte would be anointed:

"God of hosts, protector of everyone who turns to You and places himself in Your powerful hand and under Your only-begotten Son, we call upon You, that, through the divine and invisible power of our Lord and Savior Jesus Christ, You give this chrism a divine and heavenly power. May the baptized who will be anointed with it, with the salutary sign of the Cross of the only-begotten Son, by which Satan and all the hostile powers have been routed and discouraged, be regenerated and renewed by the bath of regeneration. May they become sharers more and more in the gift of the Spirit. Fortified by

[87] Mohlberg ed., no. 384, p. 61. See also the exorcism, *"Exorcizo te creatura olei . . . ,"* which comes immediately before the consecratory preface in the Roman Pontifical.

[88] In the modern Roman Pontifical the antidemoniacal dimension of the anointings made with the oil of catechumens and with chrism is explicitly affirmed not only in the pertinent exorcisms expressed in the consecrations of these oils, but also in the concluding stanza of the hymn *O Redemptor*:

Consecrare tu dignare,
Rex perennis patriae,
Hoc olivum, signum vivum,
Iura contra daemonum.

King of heaven everlasting,
Deign to consecrate these oils;
Make the juices of the olive
Strong against the devil's toils.
                    (W. A. Jurgens)

this seal, may they remain stable and immovable, unhurt and inviolable, protected from threats and surprises, living in the faith and knowledge of the truth to the very end, and awaiting the hope of life and of the eternal promises of our Lord and Savior Jesus Christ." [89]

And St. Cyril of Jerusalem, commenting on the confirmational anointing which, at Jerusalem, was made also on the breast of the neophyte, says:

"Afterwards you were anointed on the breast, so that having been clothed with the breastplate of justice, you might be able to stand against the deceits of the devil. Just as Christ, after His baptism and the coming upon Him of the Holy Spirit, went forth and defeated the adversary, so also with you: after holy baptism and the mystical chrism, having put on the panoply of the Holy Spirit, you are to withstand the power of the adversary, and defeat him, saying, 'I am able to do all things in Christ who strengthens me.'" [90]

With the above in mind I must confess that I see nothing at all aberrant[91] in that formula which gained entry into Western theology in the twelfth century, through the practical medium of the insertion into the *Decretum* of Gratian of a fifth century text, recovered from the Pseudo-Isidore, which stated that confirmation *augmentum praestat ad gratiam et robur ad pugnam* (confirmation gives an increase of grace and greater strength to fight).

The Eucharist

As if to its ultimate end, the whole rite of initiation tended to enable the new Christian, freed at last from the slavery of Satan and fully a member of the *ekklesía*, to participate in the Eucharistic sacrifice in communion with the other faithful. It is natural, therefore, that in such Eucharistic participation the emphasis would have been primarily on the positive aspect of the new life in Christ. Nevertheless, even in this action, preëminently specifying the new creature in Christ, an action in which this new creature achieves his maximum degree of expression and of realization, it was not possible to fail to observe a dimension of profound opposition to Satan and to his kingdom.

This was evident not only from abstract reasoning, but it had already been made sufficiently explicit in the New Testament. Not without reason did St.

---

[89] *Sacram. Serap.* 25 (16), Funk ed., Vol. II, pp. 186-187.

[90] *Catechetical Lectures* 21 [*Mystagogic* 3], 4 (Jurgens, no. 842a). Cyril insists on this concept; see also his *Catechetical Lectures* 3, 13; and 17, 35-37.

[91] As, following Dix, L. Bouyer apparently does in his "*Qu'est-ce que la confirmation*," in

Paroisse et liturgie, Vol. 34 (1952), pp. 65-67. For the recent problematics over the theology and pastoral liturgy of the sacrament of confirmation, see A. Adam, *Firmung und Seelsorge*, Düsseldorf 1959; and B. Luykx, "*Théologie et pastorale de la confirmation*," in *Paroisse et liturgie*, Vol. 39 (1957), pp. 180-201; 263-278.

Paul point out the absolute opposition between the table of the Lord and the table of demons (1 Cor. 10:20-21). Later tradition put an emphasis upon this idea. A secret or *super oblata* prayer of the Leonine Sacramentary, later repeated in various other sacramentaries, reads:

> "All-powerful, eternal God, who command those who participate in Your table to abstain from the diabolical banquet, grant to Your people, we pray You, that, rejecting a taste for profane and deadly food, they may approach with pure minds the banquet of eternal salvation." [92]

Participation in the Eucharist as an armament and protection against the demons easily became a traditional theme. After learning Psalm 22 during Lent, "The Lord is my shepherd, I shall not want," the catechumens chanted it solemnly, together with the whole sacred assembly, on Easter night, while they passed in procession from the baptistry into the church where the faithful were gathered; and they stood to assist for the first time at the Eucharist which the bishop would celebrate on the altar which they saw at the end of the church.[93] Having arrived at the words, "You have prepared a table before me in the face of those who persecute me," it was easy for these Christians, so profoundly moved by the liturgy, to think of the redemption as a liberation from the slavery of Satan and of the Christian life as a struggle against his kingdom; and they would see the Eucharist as protection and armament against Satan.

This in fact is made explicit by St. Cyril of Jerusalem when, after having insisted upon the reality of the Body and Blood of Christ in the Eucharist, he continued to address himself to the neophytes as follows:

> "The Blessed David explains all its power to you when he says, 'You have prepared a table before me in the face of those who persecute me.' The meaning of what he says is this: 'Before Your coming, the demons had prepared for men a table contaminated and polluted and full of diabolical influence. But after Your coming, Lord, You have prepared a table before me.' When man says to God, 'You have prepared a table before me,' what else does he mean but the mystical and spiritual table which God prepares for us in the face of the devils, that is, against them? And rightly: the former table was communion with the demons, but this one is communion with God." [94]

[92] Leonine Sacramentary, no. 76; Gelasian, Mohlberg ed., no. 53, p. 13. In the Ambrosian Missal the same prayer is the *oratio super populum* for the Feast of the Circumcision.

[93] See Jean Card. Daniélou, *The Bible and the Liturgy*, pp. 178-180.

[94] *Catechetical Lectures* 22 [*Mystagogic* 4], 7. It is the other St. Cyril, he of Alexandria, who remarks in his commentary on Psalm 22: "The mystical table, the Flesh of the Lord, makes us strong both against our passions and against the demons. For Satan fears those who take part with reverence in the mysteries" (PG 69, 841 C — cited by Daniélou, *op. cit.*, p. 183).

The theme of the Eucharist as armament and protection against the demons recurs frequently in the Fathers. St. John Chrysostom says:

> "God has given me also another weapon of protection. Of what kind? He has prepared a table for me, He has shown me a food with which He will fill me, and after I have been refreshed here I may overcome the enemy with more strength. When the enemy sees you go out from the Lord's banquet, he flees you as if you were a lion breathing fire from your mouth. Faster than the wind he leaves you and does not dare approach. When that cruel enemy sees your tongue red with blood, believe me, he does not resist. When he sees your mouth glowing red, he turns back, terrified." [95]

St. Cyril of Alexandria writes:

> "Consider again how useful it is to touch His holy flesh. It puts to flight many ailments and a throng of demons, it subverts the power of the devil and in a moment heals a great multitude. . . . May He (Jesus) touch us also, therefore, or better, may we touch Him in the mystical *eulogía*, that He may free us from infirmity of soul, from the devils' attacks and tyranny." [96]

How common among the faithful was this belief in the protective power of the Eucharist against evil spirits is demonstrated by the following narrative from St. Augustine:

> "Hesperius, a former tribune, lives in our region. He has a farm at Fussala, called Zubedi. Having observed that his house was being subjected to the harmful influence of evil spirits, who afflicted his animals and his servants, in my absence he asked our priests that one of them should come to the place to pray and cast out the devils. One of them went. There he offered the sacrifice of Christ's body, praying with all his heart that the vexation cease. By God's mercy, it ceased immediately." [97]

Even more characteristic, perhaps, is the discipline generally observed in antiquity, even if not without some contradictions, by which those who were believed to be possessed by the devil, if they behaved themselves properly and showed themselves ready to obey the injunctions of the clergy, were permitted to participate in the Eucharist; and this precisely because it was expected that the Eucharist would be their best medicine against the devil, and because it would be very dangerous to these sick people to deprive them of the Sacrament.

Canon 14 of the Council of Orange of the year 411 says:

---

[95] *Homily to the Baptized*, in the new critical edition of A. Wenger, *Jean Chrysostome, Huit catéchèses baptismales*, Paris 1957, *Catechesis* 3, no. 12, p. 158.

[96] *In Lucam* 4, 39-41; Jesús Solano, *Textos eucaristos primitivos*, Vol. II, no. 606. See also Cyril's *De adorat. in sp. et verit.* 3, *ibid.*, Vol. II, no. 533. And the citation from Cyril of A., in note 94 above.

[97] *De civ. Dei* 22, 8, 6.

"If possessed persons already baptized are taking measures for their own purification, delivering themselves to the care of the clergy and obeying their orders, by all means let them communicate, that they may be protected by the power of the sacrament from the attacks of the devil who infests them, or that their purgation may continue if they are already on the way to being cleansed." [98]

In the *Conferences* of Cassian, Apa Serenus does not approve the custom of certain churches, of excluding the possessed permanently from Communion:

"We do not recall that holy communion was ever forbidden them by our elders. Rather, they thought that, if possible, holy communion should be administered to them even daily. For you must not think that holy communion thus becomes the food of devils, according to that gospel saying, 'Do not give holy things to dogs,' which you have wrongly interpreted in this sense. Rather, it becomes protection for soul and body. When the possessed person receives holy communion, it burns the spirit who dwells in his members or who seeks to hide himself there, and puts him to rout as if it were a fire. Recently we have seen Apa Andronicus and many others cured by this means. On the other hand, the enemy will keep harassing the possessed person more and more if he sees him deprived of this heavenly medicine. The longer he finds him kept away from this spiritual remedy, the more intensely and frequently will he tempt him." [99]

The awareness of this aspect of the Eucharist as protection and armament against the devil brought about also in the ancient Church a better understanding of the seriousness of that excommunication which prevented one from participating in the Eucharist. The excommunicate remained dangerously exposed to the attacks of Satan. This is why excommunication, as St. Leo the Great warns, should not be inflicted except in most serious cases and after thorough examination:

"Communion must not be easily denied to any Christian. And this decision must not be made by a bishop in anger. . . . We have known some to be excluded from the grace of communion for deeds and words of little moment. Thus a soul for which Christ's blood was poured out, being punished with such cruel torture, has been abandoned wounded and, as it were, unarmed and stripped of all defense, an easy prey to the attacks of the devil, who then can easily make it his slave." [100]

[98] See Hefele-Leclercq, *Histoire des conciles*, Vol. II, part 1, pp. 442-443.

[99] *Conferences* 7, 30.

[100] *Ep.* 10, 8 (PL 54, 635). The context shows that the concern is indeed with Eucharistic communion (see the note *b* in the PL), which, from the fifth century on, could be designated by the term *communio* alone (see A. Blaise, *Dictionnaire latin-français des auteurs chrétiens*, under the word *communio*, 5). Thus the idea of St. Paul that one who is excommunicated is abandoned to Satan (1 Cor. 5:5; 1 Tim. 1:20) has its concrete application in the lot of one who is deprived of

The liturgies echo these ideas. For example, the anaphora in Book VIII of the *Apostolic Constitutions* makes explicit mention of the antidemoniacal theme in the epiclesis for the coming of the Holy Spirit upon the gifts:

> ". . . that He may make this bread the body of Your Christ and this chalice the blood of Your Christ, so that all those who partake of them will be strengthened in the true religion, will obtain the remission of their sins, will be defended from the devil and from his frauds." [101]

Some prayers might also be cited from the various sacramentaries, such as the following from the Leonine:

> "We pray You, Lord, that, having received Your mysteries with reverence, we may be armed against the weakness of our condition and against the deceits of the devil." [102]

And there is this, from the Gelasian Sacramentary:

> "May Your sacraments, O Lord, guard us and protect us always against the attacks of the devil." [103]

The same idea is found again in the following *post pridie* of the Mozarabic liturgy:

> "Sanctify the mystery, O Lord, give joy to the minister, illuminate the temple, decorate the altar, give order to the people, cure the sick, grant healing, listen to the prayers, that all, freed from the devil's deceits, may fear not him who lies in ambush for them but Him who cures them." [104]

From all the foregoing it ought to be clear that the concept of redemption and of Christian life as a struggle against Satan and a liberation from his slavery was quite essential to the whole of the ancient discipline of Christian initiation, especially the baptismal rite, and that it had penetrated the whole liturgical structure. It can also be understood how, in the psychology of those generations for whom the liturgy of initiation preserved its vital strength,

Eucharistic communion. This is normal, since communion in the sacrifice is the efficacious sign of ecclesiastical communion.

It might be asked whether the ancient custom of placing the consecrated host on the mouth or on the breast of the deceased did not also have an antidemoniacal significance. See Righetti, Vol. II, p. 391; and G. M Colombas, *S. Benito, su vida y su regla*, Madrid 1954, p. 210, note *a*.

[101] *Const. Apost.* 8, 12; 8, 39; Quasten's edition in his *Monumenta eucharistica et liturgica vetustissima*, Vol. IV, p. 44.

[102] Mohlberg ed., no. 1304. See also the postcommunion prayer in the Gregorian Sacramentary, formerly repeated in the Roman Missal: "Come to the aid of Your people, O Lord, we pray You; and as You have nourished them with the heavenly mysteries, so too defend them from the enemy."

[103] Mohlberg ed., no. 1220, p. 181. Like the postcommunion cited in the previous footnote, this prayer too was formerly repeated in the Roman Missal (secret prayer for the 15th Sunday after Pentecost); and again like the former, it has disappeared with the promulgation of the new Pauline Roman Missal.

[104] *Liber mozarabicus sacramentorum*, Férotin ed., no. 1395.

the dogmas of the fall from a paradisial state, of the catastrophic situation of hostility to God in which man and the whole world then found themselves, and of the reality of the struggle against Satan involving our whole life, were able to be a concrete reality and an invincible bulwark against the onslaughts of naturalism. One is well able to believe that if, for the modern generations of Christians, this same liturgy might reacquire something of that strength, it would be no small contribution toward lessening the dangerous menace of that naturalism whose tentacles are now stretching abroad.

5. The Struggle against Satan in the Liturgy of the Other Sacraments

The theme of the struggle against Satan has left its mark not only in the sacraments of Christian initiation, but in the other sacraments as well, just as we would be inclined to expect.

The liturgy of penance

In the liturgy of penance it seems natural enough that penance should have been conceived of as a new baptism. This concept is valid for the sacrament of penance as such, apart from the liturgical and disciplinary forms in which the sacrament is concretized. However, it is natural that it should have been psychologically more effective in the ancient Church, when the sacrament of penance remained concretized in the disciplinary and liturgical form of public penance, granted only once in a lifetime.[105] Under this discipline, not only by its effects but also by its non-iterability, penance seemed like a second baptism, and hence its parallelism with the first baptism was more sharply defined.[106]

[105] For the general history of penance, see Righetti, Vol. IV, pp. 119ff.

[106] On this concept in general, see the anonymous *Contra Novatianos*, published among the works of St. Athanasius (PG 26, 1316): "Just as the man baptized by a priest is enlightened by the grace of the Holy Spirit, so likewise he who makes his confession in penance obtains forgiveness through the priest by the grace of Christ." The same idea is found in St Leo, *Ep.* 108, 2 (PL 54, 1011): "God's manifold mercy comes to the aid of fallen mankind in such a way that the hope of eternal life is restored not only through the grace of baptism but also through the medicine of penance." *The Shepherd* of Hermas calls baptism the first penance and canonical penance the second penance, to which recourse can be had only once (*Mand.* IV, 3).

[The translator begs leave to add this note of his own: A fair acquaintance with the writings of the Fathers convinces me that they often exaggerated the non-iterability of penance for pedagogical reasons, so as to stress their genuine horror of repeated sinning, to convey the idea that repeated confession really should not be necessary for one who is truly a follower of Christ and who would not, therefore, repeat his sins, and to avoid any possibility of their seeming to give a handle to sinning by making forgiveness easy. Furthermore, and apart from the likelihood of different disciplines obtaining in different places at the same period, and in the same place at different periods, I believe it likely enough that it was specifically *public* penance that was done only once, while private reception of the sacrament remained iterable. Origen, among others, speaks explicitly of penance as a sacrament which is available only once: and yet he himself, in his *Homily on Psalm 37 (38)*, dating from between 240 and

Be that as it may, it was easy to pass from the concept of penance as new or second baptism to the concept of penance as a new or second overcoming of the slavery of Satan, into which the Christian, through certain specified sins committed after baptism, had fallen anew. See how Tertullian presents this matter:

> "Reluctantly I speak of a second, rather, a last hope, for fear that in mentioning penance as a remedy still available, I seem to allow room for sinning again. . . . Let no one decide to be more perverse because God is more clement, returning to sin every time he is pardoned. . . . We have escaped once; let us not expose ourselves further to danger with the hope of getting out unhurt. . . . But the implacable enemy never stops using his evil arts; rather, he becomes most furious when he sees a person fully liberated; he blazes up most, just when he is being extinguished. It is inevitable that he grieve and groan to see so many works of death destroyed in a person by the pardon of sins; to see wiped out so many entries which were going to stand in the record for that person's condemnation. He is maddened at the thought of that same sinner, now become a servant of Christ, one day judging himself and his angels. That is why he spies on the person, attacks him, besieges him, to see whether by some means he can either blind the eyes through fleshly concupiscence, or entrap the mind with worldly allurements, or shake the faith through the fear of the secular power, or make the person decline from the right road by means of perverse doctrines. He will keep tempting the person, trying to trip him up.

> "The devil's poisons, however, are foreseen by God; and although the gate of repentance has already been closed and barred by baptism, still, He permits it to stand open a little. In the vestibule He has stationed a second repentance, which He makes available to those who knock — but only once, because it is already the second time, and never more, because further were in vain. Is not even this once enough? You have that which you did not now deserve; for you have lost what you had received. If the Lord's indulgence grants you the means by which you might restore what you have lost, be thankful for a benefit which has been repeated, and which has in fact been amplified. For it is a greater thing to restore than it is to give, since it is worse to have lost than never to have received at all.

> "If anyone becomes a debtor to the second repentance, certainly his spirit should not be immediately downcast and undermined by despair. By all means, let it be irksome to sin again; but let it not be irksome to repent again. Let it be shameful to be endangered again; but let no one be ashamed to be freed again. Medicine must be repeated

242 A.D., says that he has *often* confessed his sins, and continues then to give advice on the selection of a regular confessor, adding fi- nally that if the confessor recommends public confession, one should humbly submit (Jurgens, no. 485a)].

for a repeated sickness. You will show your gratitude to the Lord if you do not refuse what He offers you again. You have offended, but you are still able to be reconciled. You have One to whom you may make satisfaction, and indeed He is willing!" [107]

Given these premises, it was only natural that in the development of the liturgical penitential disciplines and in the practices of those same rites and in their very formulas, a place should be found for expression among diverse other concepts, of the theme of the sinner fallen through the instigation of the devil, of diabolic deceits, of diabolic arts, etc.,[108] and the theme of his reintegration into divine pardon, into divine grace, into the Church, into the Eucharistic community in the company of the brethren, as his liberation from the power of the devil.

The juridic and public act by which one was placed officially among the penitents was excommunication. As official separation of the penitent from the body of Christ, from participation in the sacraments, the Eucharist in particular, and from the community of the faithful, it was considered, in accord with the very thought of St. Paul (1 Cor. 5:5; 1 Tim. 1:20) and as we emphasized above in regard to a text of St. Leo the Great, as an abandoning of the penitent into the hands of Satan "for the death of the flesh so that the spirit may be saved." [109]

The Middle Ages contributed a dramatic development to the scene,[110] and the *Ordo excommunicandi et absolvendi* of our modern Roman Pontifical, derived from medieval usages, emphasizes the aforesaid concept:

> ". . . we separate him from the reception of the precious body and blood of the Lord and from the society of all Christians and exclude him from the pale of Holy Mother Church in heaven and on earth. We declare him excommunicated and anathematized. We judge him damned to everlasting fire with the devil and his angels and all the reprobate, until he shall disentangle himself from the snares of the devil, return to correction and to penance and satisfy the Church of God which he has injured. We abandon him to Satan for the death of the flesh that his spirit may be saved in the day of judgment."

The idea that the penitent, as excommunicated, is under the power of Satan, recurs again in the prayers which are said during Mass for the public penitents.[111] So too in the liturgy of the eighth book of the *Apostolic Constitutions*, before the dismissal of the penitents and at the end of the first part

---

[107] *Repentance* 7, 2-4 (Jurgens, no. 314).

[108] Among the formularies which we have for the reconciliation of penitents, see those in the Gelasian Sacramentary, Mohlberg ed., nos. 354, 358, 364, pp. 56-58. Here it is recalled that man has been led into sin "*diabolo scindente . . . invidia diaboli . . . diabolica fraude . . . diabolica incursione.*"

[109] 1 Cor. 5:5. See St. Leo the Great, *Ep.* 10, 8; St. Jerome, *Adv. lucif.* 5.

[110] Righetti, Vol. IV, pp. 192-193.

[111] See, for example, St. John Chrysostom, *De incomprehensibili, hom.* 3, 7 (PG 48, 726); *In Matt. hom.* 71, 4 (PG 58, 666); and the *Apostolic Constitutions* 2, 57, 14; 8, 9.

of the Mass, there is prescribed for the penitents a litany recited by the deacon, to the petitions of which the people are requested to respond *Kyrie eleison*. The rite ended with an oration of the bishop over the penitents who were standing with heads bowed; and no doubt the oration was accompanied by an imposition of hands. Among else, the litany says:

> "Penitents, pray. All of us make ardent supplication for our brethren who are in penance, that the merciful God show them the way of repentance, receive their self-accusation and confession, 'speedily crush Satan under their feet' (Rom. 16:20), free them from 'the devil's snares' (2 Tim. 2:26) and from the violence of the demons, and keep them from every unlawful word, every shameful action and every evil thought." [112]

In this perspective the reconciliation of the penitent was naturally regarded as his liberation from Satan. St. Jerome sums up the essential actions and concepts of reconciliation in this way:

> "The bishop offers his oblation for the layman, lays his hands on him, invokes upon him the return of the Holy Spirit, and thus, making the people pray, reconciles to the altar the one who had been abandoned to Satan for the death of the flesh that the spirit might be saved. He does not restore a member to health until all the members have wept together. The father readily forgives the son if the mother in her commiseration prays him to do so." [113]

The formulas of reconciliation in the Gelasian Sacramentary insist repeatedly on the concept:

> "that the enemy not exult in the harm done to Your family . . . that the enemy no longer have power over his soul. . . . Renew in him, most kind Father, whatever has been corrupted by earthly frailty or violated by diabolical fraud . . . , whatever has been spoiled by action, by word, or even by thought, through diabolical deceit." [114]

These same ideas are repeated in the current Roman Pontifical,[115] and find noble expression in the Mozarabic liturgy. The two orations which we cite from the latter are filled with that profound theology which the authentic liturgical tradition always conveys:

> "Holy Lord, eternal Father, eternal God, we suppliants pray You, addressing Your merciful kindness, always full of indulgence, forgiving and gentle: You that are inclined to mercy and ready to pardon; You that are slow to punish and swift to forgive; You that not only

---

[112] *Apostolic Constitutions* 8, 9.
[113] *Adv. lucif.* 5.
[114] Mohlberg ed., no. 358, p. 57; no. 363, p. 58; no. 364, p. 58.
[115] See in the *Ordo reconciliationis poeniten-* *tium quae fit in feria V coenae Domini*, for example, the request of the archpriest, *Redintegra in eis . . .*; the preface of reconciliation; and the oration *Deus misericors, Deus clemens.*

do not desire that any should perish, but search out those who are hastening to perdition; You that, after having granted us the grace of baptism, have deigned to provide still a second chance for those who have fallen, so as to exclude forever the dominion of death.[116] Moreover, in order to remain ever propitious toward us, You have deigned to make Christ our propitiator at Your side in such a way that You are able always to hear Him gladly as He pleads against our offenses. Through Him, O Lord, we pray You to look upon the downcast spirit of Your servant N.; strengthen him, refresh him with Your indulgence. Give him rest after his labors, and restore to him that pristine robe which he has lost, so that he may receive from You his nuptial garment. Restore that which has fallen into ruin, reconstruct the foundations of Your temple so that it may once more be a proper tabernacle of the Holy Spirit and a dwelling-place where He may abide, even as it was before; and that the same Holy Spirit, dwelling there again, after having reconsecrated the·walls, may remain there and defend it, which indeed, will bring joy to all the Church. Grant him, O Lord our God, that he may begin from this holy day to reconcile himself to Your altar so that from now on he may be permitted to offer the sacrifices with an honest heart by means of Your priests, and to come forward to the Food of Your heavenly table. Do not permit him again to wander away from the truth and from the admonitions of Your commands, so that, having again acquired peace, he may receive the reward of immortality." [117]

"Beloved brethren, assist me in your prayers for the servant of God, N., whom our Lord Jesus Christ has this day deigned to restore to the bosom of His holy Church; that He may pardon him even the last farthing of his wicked ailment; that the Lord may restore him to His holy Catholic Church without any blemish, and that the devil will have no longer any power over him. May he be permitted to approach the holy altar of the Lord and to participate in the Body and in the Chalice as he did before." [118]

The liturgy of the ill

The liturgy of the ill comprised and does yet comprise penance, anointings with oil, Viaticum, and the *commendatio animae*. In all of this the antidemoniacal aspect is quite conspicuous. And again we note that this is in no way surprising, when we consider the intimate connection which, according to the New Testament, exists between sin, illness, death, and Satan; freedom from illness, from death, from sin and from Satan. The connection ought also be noted, which, according to Mark in his narrative of the first mission of the Apostles, exists between preaching penance, expelling demons, anointing the sick with oil and curing them: "Going out, therefore, they preached

---

[116] Synonymous with the dominion of Satan.   p. 98.
[117] *Liber ordinum mozarabicus*, Férotin ed.,   [118] *Ibid.*, p. 100.

that men should do penance; and they cast out many demons and anointed the ill with oil and cured them" (Mark 6:12-13).

In point of fact, in the ancient rites of the liturgy of the ill, the antidemoniacal idea was already expressed in the blessing of the oil with which they were anointed. The earliest known formula of such a blessing is to be found in *The Apostolic Tradition* of St. Hippolytus.[119] But certainly the usage was much more ancient. St. Irenaeus says that the gnostic Marcosians had a custom of anointing the dying with a mixture of oil and water, while reciting certain invocations,

> "to redeem the faithful who were about to leave this life . . . so that the dead might not be taken and detained by the principalities and by the higher powers, and so that their internal man, invisible, might ascend to a greater height." [120]

C. Ruch, citing the same text,[121] observes that Irenaeus himself affirms that the gnostics, in their worship, were indiscriminate in mixing gross and superstitious practices, pagan ceremonies, and certain Christian rites, more or less disfigured; for which reason "we may ask whether the Marcosian ceremony is not a transposition of a Catholic rite intended to save the soul from sin and from the devil, and to do away with the obstacles which prevented its ascent to paradise."

At any rate, it is certain that in the earliest incontestable evidence that we have of a Catholic usage of blessing oil for an anointing of the infirm, that which is treated of is oil mixed with water; [122] and that in the East the earliest formulas of its blessing already give to the future anointing an antidemoniacal character:

> "In the name of Your only-begotten Son Jesus Christ we bless these creatures; we pronounce over this water and this oil the name of Him who suffered, was crucified, arose and is seated at the right of the Unbegotten. Grant curative powers to these creatures, that whoever drinks of them or is anointed with them may be freed from every fever, from every demon, from every sickness; may they be a remedy of healing and of wholeness for those who receive them in the name of Your only-begotten Jesus Christ, through whom be glory and dominion to You in the Holy Spirit forever and ever. Amen." [123]

In much the same tenor there is the formula of the eighth book of the *Apostolic Constitutions*, where God is besought:

[119] Chapter 5, during the Mass, Dix ed., p. 10. See A. Chavasse, *"L'onction des infirmes dans l'Église latine. Les textes,"* in the *Revue sc relig.*, 1940, pp. 64-122 and 290-364.

[120] *Adv. haer.* 1, 21.

[121] *Dict. de théol. cath.*, in the article *"Extrême onction,"* Vol. 5/2 (1913), cols. 1931ff.

[122] St. Hippolytus, *The Apostolic Tradition* 5; *Euchológion* of Serapion 17 (5); *Apostolic Constitutions* 8, 29.

[123] *Euchológion* of Serapion 17 (5).

> "Sanctify, through Christ, this water and this oil . . . give them healing power, to banish ills, put the devils to flight, foil every ambush." [124]

In the tradition of the Roman sacramentaries, for the blessing of the oil of the infirm there was at first a prayer which contained only implicitly an antidemoniacal import; [125] but, from the beginning of the ninth century, it was preceded by an exorcism properly so-called, [126] which put a strong emphasis on the antidemoniacal dimension.

In the administration itself of the holy oil, according to the Roman Ritual in use until December 31, 1973, the antidemoniacal dimension of the whole rite was repeatedly emphasized. The first part of the rite contained nothing except the greeting of the priest as he enters the home of the person who is ill, and the sprinkling of the sick-room with holy water, while reciting a formula the import of which is clearly antidemoniacal:

> "Let no demons have access here; let the angels of peace be present."

The Lord was besought to dismiss from those who dwell in that house

> "every hostile power; free them from every fear and from every anxiety";

and petition was made also that the heavenly angel be present and

> "watch over, cherish, protect, visit, and defend all who dwell in this house." [127]

Afterwards came the administration of the sacrament of penance. In ancient times the *Pater* and the *Credo* were recited at this point: "The creed above all was regarded as a repellent to the devil and a safeguard against temptations." [128]

In the Roman Ritual referred to above, the anointings properly so-called were preceded by a prayer which is none other than the ancient formula of the sacrament, which, in the eleventh century, was said while anointing the head. It has a distinctly antidemoniacal character: "In the name of the Father and of the Son and of the Holy Spirit. May any power that the devil has over you be utterly destroyed through the imposition of my hands . . . ." [129]

---

[124] *Apostolic Constitutions* 8, 29.
[125] The collect *Emitte quaesumus* of the Gelasian Sacramentary (Mohlberg ed., no. 382, p. 61), preserved in the modern Roman Pontifical.
[126] At first this was the exorcism *Exorcizo te creatura olei*, which was in the ancient sacramentaries for the exorcism of the oil for the preparation of the chrism; the corresponding exorcism in the current Pontifical is the

Exorcizo te immundissime spiritus.
[127] *Ordo adm. extrem. unct.* no. 5.
[128] Righetti, Vol. IV, p. 242.
[129] *Ordo ministrandi Sacramentum Extremae Unctionis* no. 7. A new, revised *Order of the Anointing of the Sick* became obligatory on January 1, 1974. See the Apostolic Constitution *"Sacram Unctionem Infirmorum,"* of November 30, 1972.

The whole theological dimension which the liturgy attaches to the anointing of the ill with holy oil is perhaps best expressed in the Mozarabic liturgy, when, in an antiphon recited in the administration of this sacrament, reference is made to three Gospel texts containing sayings of the Lord:

> "The Lord said to His disciples, 'Receive the Holy Spirit'; 'In My name cast out demons'; and 'Impose hands upon the sick and they shall be healed.' " [130]

Sanctification of the soul, expulsion of demons, and healing of the body are precisely the three purposes of the anointing with holy oil, according to the liturgy and tradition.

After the administration of the holy oil the liturgy, in instances of severe illness, prescribes Viaticum. In view of the concept already explained above, of the antidemoniacal value of the Eucharist, it is easy to understand why tradition and the liturgies have emphasized in a special way the antidemoniacal dimension of the Viaticum. The formula of the pre-1974 Roman Ritual is quite explicit about this dimension:

> "Receive, my brother, this Viaticum (food for a journey), the Body of our Lord Jesus Christ, that He may guard you from the malice of the enemy and guide you to everlasting life." [131]

The *commendatio animae* is the final liturgical act with which the Church assists the living. In view of what we have seen up to this point, it should be in no way surprising that, in the care which the liturgy expends upon the final moments of a man's life on this earth, those moments which must decide, in the final accounting, what his eternal lot shall be, here too there is a noteworthy emphasis on the concept of the struggle against the devil.

In the pre-1974 Roman Ritual the antidemoniacal character shows forth strongly in the second part of the rite, which consists of a formula in part auguring hope and in part, followed by an oration to God with fourteen petitions to liberate that soul which is about to leave this world (*Libera Domine . . . sicut liberasti*).

The formula *commendo* appears after the eleventh century. It desires that the soul will no sooner have left this world than it will be met by the angels and the saints; and that it will not come to know hell. Then follows a directly antidemoniacal passage:

> "May that most foul Satan with his satellites fall back before you. May he tremble at your coming with your escort of angels and flee into the dread chaos of eternal night. May God rise up and His enemies be scattered; and may those who hate Him flee before His face.

[130] *Liber ordinum mozarabicus*, Férotin ed., p. 72. The formula for the anointing of the ill in the Milanese (Ambrosian) liturgy is: "*Ungo te oleo sanctificato ut more militis*

unctus et praeparatus ad luctam aëreas possis superare catervas."

[131] *De communione infirmorum*, no. 19.

As smoke vanishes, so may they vanish. As wax melts in the fire, so may sinners perish before the face of God. But let good men hold festival and rejoice in the sight of God. May all the legions of Tartarus be confounded and ashamed; and may the ministers of Satan not dare to bar your way. May Christ, who was crucified for you, free you from torment. May Christ, who condescended to die for you, free you from eternal death. May Christ, the Son of the living God, bring you into the ever green loveliness of His paradise, and may He, the true Shepherd, recognize you as among His sheep."

In the above expressions which request the defense of the soul and that it be accompanied by the angels against the snares of Satan and his satellites so that "they may not dare to bar its way" in its ascent to heaven, it seems to me to be undeniable that there is an allusion, however discreet, to the opinion about the *telónai*, the toll-collectors or examiners whom we mentioned previously. We do not mean, of course, that besides such an imaginative way of representing matters, these expressions are entirely devoid of any other sense. Ultimately and in any case, they constitute a prayer to God against the influences and the temptations which Satan would not fail to unleash against the faithful in those last moments of life. It seems probable to me that the figure of the *telonía* is presumed also by the fourteen petitions which begin with the *Libera Domine animam servi tui . . . sicut liberasti*.[132]

Finally, the reader will note an explicitly antidemoniacal dimension to the prayer to St. Joseph, inserted into the rite of the *commendatio animae* in 1913.

The liturgy of the ecclesiastical order of exorcist

In the liturgy of the ecclesiastical orders or ranks, the concept of the struggle against Satan, historically speaking, was concretized primarily in the creation in the West, beginning already in the third century, of the order of exorcist as a proper ecclesiastical rank with the specific function of casting out the devil by means of exorcisms. It is known that prior to the third century the power of expelling demons, exercised broadly by Christians,[133] was regarded as a charism and not as a permanent office deriving from hierarchical deputation or authorization as such within the framework of the organizational or administrative structure of the Church. The East held fast always to this earlier concept, expression of which is found in the *Apostolic Constitutions*:

[132] The same figure is easily recognizable in the theory of the gnostic Marcosians of whom St. Irenaeus speaks (*Adv. haer.* 1, 20), in regard to the anointing of the dying with a mixture of oil and water. Nor does it seem improbable that this same idea is presupposed

by the formula for Viaticum, cited above.

[133] For references and citations in regard to the exercise of this power in the earliest centuries, see J. Forget, "*Exorcisme*," in the *Dict. de théol. cath.*, Vol. 5 (1913), pp. 1770-1775.

> "The exorcist is not ordained by the laying-on of hands. This re-
> ward given to combatants depends on the free benevolence and grace
> of God through Christ in the outpouring of the Holy Spirit. The
> identity of one who receives the charism of healing is indicated by a
> divine manifestation, which makes known to all the grace that is in
> him." [134]

In Rome and in Africa, however, beginning with the middle of the third
century, there is clear testimony to the existence of a class of exorcists in the
ranks of the clergy, together with the priests, deacons, subdeacons, acolytes,
lectors, and porters.[135]

The ceremony and the form of the ordination of the exorcist are known
from the seventh canon of the so-called Fourth Council of Carthage, a text
which dates from sometime between the end of the fourth and the end of
the sixth centuries:

> "When the exorcist is ordained, the bishop gives him the book
> in which the exorcisms are written, saying, 'Receive it and commit
> it to memory, and have a power to lay your hands on the possessed
> person, whether he be baptized or catechumen." [136]

This remained the form for the conferral of the order of exorcist, as found in
the Roman Pontifical, until our own times, when, in the aftermath of Vatican II, the order has been suppressed.

In the admonition which the bishop gave to the exorcist and in the other
two prayers of the recent but now obsolete rite, there was a repeated insistence upon the concept that the exorcist received the *potestas* and the *imperium* to cast out demons; and the exorcists are called *spirituales impera-
tores* for casting out from the bodies of the obsessed the demons with all their
various perfidies.

Until about the fifth century, the exorcist continued to exercise his general
functions, "which, except in special cases, consisted for the most part in the
imposition of hands over the catechumens, repeated many times in the scrutinies, and perhaps even upon the sick." [137]

The creation of the order of exorcist and its establishment among the
ecclesiastical orders demonstrates the importance which the Church attached

---

[134] *Apostolic Constitutions* 8, 26. Note especially the equating of the terms *exorcist* and
one who receives the charism of healing.

[135] *Letter of Cornelius of Rome to Fabius of
Antioch* (A.D. 251), fragment preserved in
Eusebius, *Hist. eccl.*, 6, 43, 11 (Jurgens, no.
546a). Letter 23 in the Cyprianic corpus, *All
the Confessors to Pope Cyprian*, also makes
mention of an exorcist, in connection with
other ranks of clergy.

[136] Hefele-Leclercq, *Histoire des conciles,*

Vol. 2/1, p. 112. The acts of this self-styled
Fourth Synod of Carthage (A.D. 398), were
in reality composed probably about the year
500 A.D. in Provence or in Northern Italy.
See Andrieu, *Les ordines romani,* Vol. III,
pp. 615-619.

[137] Righetti, Vol. III, p. 275. That the exorcists might even have been entrusted with imposing hands upon the sick is suggested by a
consideration of the close connection between
illnesses and demoniacal influence.

to the concept and to the reality of the struggle against Satan. For centuries past none have been ordained to the order of exorcist, except as a step towards the priesthood; and, as noted above, even this is now suppressed in the reforms subsequent to Vatican II. The actual function of exorcist has long since devolved upon priest or bishop. Moreover, in many dioceses, the function of exorcising may not be performed over the possessed, properly so-called, without particular and special permission of the bishop. That the order continued to exist so long after its functions were reserved to others is in itself a testimony to the mind of the Church, which has insisted always upon the reality of the struggle against Satan; and explicit mention of this struggle is not entirely lacking in the various rites of ordinations still remaining, as for example in the ordination to diaconate.

The matrimonial liturgy

Even in the liturgy of marriage the concept of the struggle against Satan has left its traces. One of the reasons why it was felt to be a necessity that the Church interpose its blessing upon the marriage of Christians was precisely so that the new family which was being established might be free from the snares of the devil, against whose intrusions into matters matrimonial St. Paul had already put Christians on their guard (1 Cor. 7:2-5).

St. John Chrysostom says that it is necessary

> "to call in the priests and by prayers and blessings to reinforce the unity of sentiment which should prevail in marriage, that the husband's love and the wife's chastity may increase; that everything may tend to introduce virtue into the house; that all the devil's machinations may be removed; and that the partners themselves, united with the help of God, may lead a happy life." [138]

The protection of the newly married against the diabolical deceits is a theme which recurs in the matrimonial liturgies even in the most ancient formularies that have come down to us. Thus, in the solemn blessing of the bride as found in the Leonine Sacramentary, God is asked to strengthen her with all the necessary virtues, and there is joined to this in a phrase which was still preserved substantially in the previous Roman ritual in the blessing at the end of the nuptial Mass, the petition that "the excommunicated father of lies may usurp no power over her." [139] A parallel formula in the Gelasian Sacramentary reads: ". . . may You deign to strengthen the union of these spouses even as you strengthened that of their ancestors; may all the deceits of the enemy be kept far away from them, so that even in marriage they may imitate the holiness of the Fathers." [140]

---

[138] *In Gen. hom.* 48, 6.
[139] Leonine Sacramentary, Mohlberg ed., no. 1110, pp. 140 and 24-25.
[140] Gelasian Sacramentary, Mohlberg ed., no. 1454, p. 210.

At least as early as the sixth or seventh century there was introduced a liturgical rite for the blessing of the bridal chamber, still preserved in the Roman Ritual. Many of the formulas relative to this blessing of the bridal chamber have "an apotropeutic character, invoking the Lord to ward off from the nuptial chamber the deceits of the devil and the evil spells of wicked men." [141] With this meaning given to the rite it is more easily seen how the Middle Ages, with its too easy credence in the frequent influence of evil spirits against the happy outcome of marriage, propounded unhealthy evaluations. Nevertheless, the conviction that the influence of Satan was in some way responsible for sterile marriages was not a false one. Apart from the ingenuousness of medieval views, ultimately, the Church did not err when, by means of prayers and lustrations, she invoked the protection of God on the happy progress of the marriage and protected it against demoniacal influence.

Lastly, we ought note the blessing for a pregnant woman in the Roman Ritual. It is a prayer to God for the protection of the mother and the offspring, and their defense against the wiles of the enemy:

> "Accept the sacrifice of a contrite heart and the ardent desire of Your servant, who humbly supplicates You for the welfare of the child which you granted her to conceive. Guard that which is Yours and defend it from every deceit and injury of our bitter enemy; so that the hand of Your mercy may assist her delivery and her child may come happily to the light of day, be kept safe for the holy regeneration [*i.e.*, baptism], serve You always in all things and attain to everlasting life."

The blessing concludes with a lustration and an additional prayer that the holy angels will protect the house, the mother, and the child.

It was not a childish fear of the devil that dictated this and similar prayers to the faith of the Church, but a wonderful and supernatural vision of the whole plan of salvation, viewed integrally and without forgetting the real part which the devil, God's enduring antagonist, has in it.

6. The Struggle against Satan in the Principal Sacramentals not Immediately Connected with the Rites of the Seven Sacraments

Now that we have reviewed, from the viewpoint of the struggle against Satan, the liturgy of the seven sacraments with the whole complexus of the rites immediately connected with them, our examination of the liturgy of those sacramentals which are not directly connected with the ritual administration of the seven sacraments can be much more brief. A good many observations which would otherwise have to be made in a discussion of this

[141] Righetti, Vol. IV, p. 348, with reference there to A. Franz, *Die kirchlichen Benedik-* *tionen im Mittelalter*, Vol. II, pp. 176-185.

part of the liturgy have already been made in our analysis of the rites which accompany the seven sacraments, and need not be repeated now.

In general

In general one has only to glance through the Roman Ritual and Roman Pontifical and it will be impossible not to be impressed by the great number of rites, beyond those to which we have already made reference in the preceding exposition, which contain, expressed in a more or less emphatic way, evidences of the concept of the struggle against Satan and his kingdom. Anyone who cares to count them up will find that this theme enters into about fifty blessings, consecrations, rites of various kinds, frequently short but sometimes even quite lengthy, such as the dedication of a church or the liturgy of the dead.[142]

These rites are in reference to the most varied circumstances of ecclesiastical and Christian life in general. They concern ordinary and commonplace things of daily life: a blessing of a house, of a stable, a blessing against noxious insects; and they concern the rarer and more solemn moments of life: the consecration of a virgin, the dedication of a church, the liturgy of the dead.

This is itself a clear indication of how much this struggle against Satan and his kingdom is a reality still profoundly present in the whole liturgical complexus of even those sacramentals which have no immediate connection with the administration of the seven sacraments, and which impress themselves upon every facet of Christian life. To have a sufficient sampling of this part of the liturgy it will be enough to make some few observations in regard to holy water and lustrations, in regard to entreaties against storms, in regard to the blessing of virgins and of monks, and about the liturgy of the dead.

Holy water

The use of water blessed for purposes other than baptismal use seems not to have gained favor in the first centuries of the Church; the associations of such a practice, especially when of purificatory purposes, would have been too suggestive of similar usages in Judaism, paganism, or even in the hetero-

---

[142] See Egon von Petersdorff, "De daemonibus in liturgia memoratis," in Angelicum, Vol. 19 (1942), pp. 326-328. If perchance the matter be of interest to anyone, here is the list: From the Roman Ritual: blessings of candles, of bread, of ordinary oil; processions; litanies; blessing of gold, incense, and myrrh; blessing of crosses; of plants; of a school; of a fountain; of a pool; of a lime kiln; of fields; of a sick adult; of linen cloths for the sick; of salt and oats for animals; of a stable; of bells; against rats and other pestiferous animals; of St. Anthony's lilies; of children; of the stations of the cross; various blessings of scapulars and of water in honor of the saints. From the Pontifical: consecration of a virgin; blessing of a cornerstone; dedication of a church; blessing of a cemetery; of sacred vestments; of a new cross; of sacred sacramental vessels; of containers for relics; of bells; of crosses for those going to the crusades. The liturgy of the dead.

dox syncretist sects.[143] In the East, however, beginning about the fifth century, it would seem, there are traces of a blessing of water and of its ritual use outside of baptism.

The Sacramentary of Serapion presents us with the case of a prayer whose original purpose was evidently to serve only for the blessing of the oil of the sick, but which was afterwards adapted to serve also as the blessing for bread or for water.[144] It is interesting, nevertheless, for the antidiabolical dimension which it gives to the usage of these blessed things, and because its general tenor is much the same as that which will be found later in the typical formula for the blessing of holy water:

> "We call upon You, who have all power and strength, Savior of all men, Father of our Lord and Savior Jesus Christ, and we pray You to send from heaven the healing power of Your only-begotten Son upon this oil, that for those who will be anointed with it — or who will receive these creatures — it may serve to keep away all disease and infirmity, as an antidote against every devil, to put every impure spirit to flight, to expel every evil spirit, to extirpate every fever or chill or debility, to receive grace and the remission of sins, that it may be for them a remedy of life and of salvation, restoring health and wholeness to the soul, the body and the mind, and giving perfect salvation. O Lord, may every diabolical action, every demon, every assault of the adversary, every wound, every torment, every sorrow, every pain or thrust or jolt or evil shade, fear Your holy name which we are now invoking, and the name of Your only-begotten Son, and keep away from the interior and the exterior of Your servants, that glory may be given to the name of Him who for us was crucified, who rose from the dead, who bore our sorrows and our wounds, and who will come to judge the living and the dead."

In the West the blessing and use of holy water was introduced in the course of the sixth century. The Gelasian Sacramentary already contained the whole rite. Among else, it includes the blessing of the water, the exorcism over the same, the prayer while sprinkling the water, and the exorcism of the salt.[145] The substance of the rite and of later formulas for the blessing and aspersion of holy water is already contained therein; essentially it is a question of a rite purifying from the influence of the devil all those persons, places, or things over which the blessed water will be sprinkled. This is signified

---

[143] Tertullian, *Baptism* 5.

[144] *Sacram. Serap.* 19 (17), Funk ed., Vol. II, pp. 190-192. In view of the general tenor of the prayer, this theory seems certain enough to me. The adaptation was made in the title, where, after *"prayer for the oil of the sick"* there was subjoined *"or for bread or for water."* In the formula itself, it is oil only that

is spoken of at first; but afterwards bread and water are also included, and mention is made *"of these Your creatures."* The latter words are evidently interpolated, since they fit but poorly into the whole grammatical context of the phrase.

[145] Mohlberg ed., nos. 1556-1561, pp. 224-226.

clearly enough by certain characteristic expressions of the blessing, in which God is addressed, beseeching Him to pour out into this element:

> ". . . the power of Your blessing, that Your creature, serving Your mysteries, may have supernatural power for expelling demons and curing diseases. Whatever this water sprinkles in the homes of the faithful, let it be preserved from every impurity, delivered from all harm. Let no harmful spirit dwell there, no breath of corruption; may all the traps of the hidden enemy be removed, and may everything opposed to the safety and repose of those who live there be put to flight by the sprinkling of this water; and thus may the well-being implored with the invocation of Your holy name be safe against every attack." [146]

The prayer is found even yet in our *ordo ad faciendam aquam benedictam*. The other prayers of the Gelasian Sacramentary and of our own Roman Ritual, in respect to the matter which we are now discussing, are all of much the same import.

When we consider the frequency and importance which the use of holy water quickly assumed, and which in large measure that usage still retains, so that holy water has its part in the Church's blessings of every kind and in the daily life of the Christian, so much so that holy water together with the sign of the Cross is a sacramental of most frequent usage, it is easy to see how the reality of the struggle against Satan impresses its mark upon the whole life of the Church and has had to leave its mark on the life of every Catholic who understands what he is about.

Among these lustrations performed basically with holy water, one thinks first of all of those which, beginning with the Carolingian era, formed an essential part of the rite for the dedication of a church. After the preliminaries of the ceremony, the first part is, in substance, a taking possession of the edifice by means of lustrations with holy water, this taking possession being made while walking around the outside of the walls of the building (prior to the reform of the rite made in 1961, the trip around the outside was made three times), around the inside of the church, and around the altar, to purify them of every demoniacal influence. The antidemoniacal dimension in all these rites is quite explicit: the blessing of the water, with which this part of the ceremony commences; the prayer which the bishop recites upon completing the walk around the outside (*omnipotens sempiterne Deus, qui in omni loco . . .*); the proclamation which he makes upon entering the church after having traced a cross on the threshold: "Behold the sign of the Cross; let all spectres flee away"; the outline of the huge cross on the floor to indicate that Christ takes possession of the place.

---

[146] See, for example, the analysis of the rite made by Righetti, Vol. IV, pp. 381ff.; A. Franz, *Die kirchlichen Benediktionen im Mittelalter*, Vol. II, pp. 49-123.

Only after all this, when at last the demoniacal influence has been utterly restrained and put totally to flight, can the depositing of the relics (no longer a necessary part of the rite) and the pronouncing of the consecratory prayer take place, followed by a chrismal anointing of the altar.

The entreaties against storms

The modern Roman Ritual [147] contains a "procession against storms," in which, while the bells are rung, litanies are recited, followed by a psalm, by various versicles, and by five orations, among which is the prayer "*a domo tua* . . . ." This same prayer was found also in the Roman Missal, among the several orations against bad weather, until the promulgation of the present Pauline Roman Missal. The prayer has a clearly antidiabolical dimension. All of this is but a modest vestige of a liturgical rite which in the Middle Ages had taken on a grand proportion and frequency: the entreaties against storms.[148]

These rites were directly antidemoniacal, based on the belief that storms harmful to men are in some way the effect of diabolic influences. This belief was and is quite accurate, even if there remained, as we have so often pointed out, doubt as to whether such influence should be termed natural or supernatural. And since the distinction between the devil's use of natural and supernatural means was not well-drawn, it was easy for exaggerations and superstitions to arise. Nevertheless, in this oration which is still recited in the rite for protection against storms, "*a domo tua*," the Church maintains the idea of the connection between storms harmful to men, and the influence of Satan:

> "We pray You, O Lord, that the spirits of iniquity be driven away from Your family, and the scourge of stormy skies depart."

The consecration of virgins

We have already seen in its proper place how ancient tradition, making explicit the concepts of the New Testament, developed the themes of the ascetical life of virgins and of the monastic life as eminent forms of the struggle of the Christian against the devil. In the liturgy this idea has left its imprint on the rites of the consecration of virgins and of monastic profession.

The most ancient formula extant for the consecration of virgins is to be found in the Leonine Sacramentary.[149] Its consecratory preface is still central to the rite as used in our own times. Essentially the preface is an imploring of God to accept the proposed offering which the virgin makes of her life, and that He grant her the protection and the necessary graces so that she will be able to persevere and attain to the full significance of her resolve. In this

---

[147] Title 9, chapter 8.
[148] See Righetti, Vol. IV, pp. 399ff.

[149] Mohlberg ed., no. 1104.

framework there is sketched in broad strokes the theological meaning of virginity, by recalling first of all the original fall of man through the deceit practiced by the devil, and then the divine pedagogy of how God lifts man up again, inspiring in chosen souls the desire for greater perfection through total dedication to Him, and how He gives them the strength to overcome, through love and service of Him, even the deepest tendencies of nature.

These souls, however, have a special need of divine assistance, because the ancient enemy vents his rage against them in a special way. May God deign, therefore, to grant them His special protection

> "so that the ancient enemy, who surrounds the nobler resolutions with more subtle traps in his desire to spoil the palm of perfect continence, may not insinuate himself through some negligence of the mind and rob those who have made a vow of virginity of that which should be found even in the conduct of married women."

The theme of the virginal life, therefore, is portrayed as a preëminent form of the struggle of the Christian against Satan.

In the modern rite as found in the Roman Pontifical the same theme recurs in the prayer *Deus plasmator corporum:*

> "They desire to live in Your grace. May the champion of evil and enemy of good fail in his efforts to gain title of ownership over these vessels consecrated to Your name."

And the prayer *Exaudi*, for the blessing of their robes, asks that those garments
> "be a strong armor of defense against all the arrows of the enemy."

The monastic profession

In the liturgy of monastic profession the concept of the struggle against Satan has taken its concrete forms in connection with the idea of monastic profession as a second baptism.[150] To flee from the world and to embrace the state of perfection was regarded as being somehow parallel with the flight from the world and entry into a new life which was brought about in converts from paganism when they received baptism. This parallelism is expressed in the formulas of the rites. In this way it was quite obvious that monastic profession was viewed as a renunciation of the devil and his pomps and an adherence to Christ; and the whole of the monastic life is a state of preëminent struggle against the devil.

Some of these concepts, even in the concise but pregnant style of ancient Roman Latin, are found already in the prayer in the Gelasian Sacramentary: *"For those who are renouncing the world,"* [151] which seems simply to be the ancient Roman euchological formula for reception to monastic profession:

---

[150] See Ph. Oppenheim, *"Mönchsweihe und Taufritus,"* in *Miscellanea Mohlberg*, Vol. I, pp. 259ff.
[151] Mohlberg ed., no. 1574, p. 229.

"Be pleased, Lord, we pray You, to open the doors of Your grace to Your servants who are renouncing the pomps of the world and who, despising the devil, are taking refuge under the banner of Christ. Receive with a favorable countenance those who come to You, that the enemy may not be able to triumph over them. Grant them the aid of Your unwearying arm; surround their minds with the armor of the faith, that, happily protected on all sides as by a wall, they may feel the joy of having escaped the world."

Quite similar ideas are expressed in the Mozarabic liturgy:

"Receive, I pray You, Lord, this Your servant N., who is fleeing to You from the tempest of this world and the entrapments of the devil, that, in being received by You, he may feel the joy of being saved from the present world and rewarded by You in the world to come." [152]

In the later rites of monastic profession these concepts have always been preserved; but the idea of the struggle against the devil was somewhat softened. In fact, while the ideas of the above mentioned formulas in regard to flight from the world and renunciation of the world were preserved, it seems to me that in general there was no longer any direct mention of flight from Satan and renunciation of Satan and his pomps.

It will be noticed in these texts, however, that the concept of the struggle against the devil is expressed with an imagery that makes profession of monastic life a flight from the world and the devil, a withdrawal from their dangers. In the primitive monastic tradition it is appreciably the same concept that is expressed under an imagery that makes the profession of monastic life equivalent to engaging even more intimately in the struggle against the devil, and to a taking of the offensive, advancing to provoke that struggle.

This latter concept has been better preserved in Greek euchology, which, moreover, still gives explicit expression to the notion of monastic profession as a second baptism. To the monk who is about to receive the great habit and make his monastic profession, the priest says:

"Brother, today you receive the second baptism, in the superabundance of the gifts of the merciful God; and you are purified of your sins and become a son of light." [153]

It is strongly emphasized throughout the rite that the new monk is placed in a state in which the struggle against Satan will be continuous and intensified:

"And think no longer that in the life you have led hitherto you have struggled valiantly against the invisible powers of the enemy; but think that, from now on, you will have greater travails in the

[152] *Liber ordinum*, Férotin ed., pp. 86, 14ff.   [153] *Euchológion*, Rome 1873, p. 242.

struggle against him. But he will not be able to conquer you if he finds you protected by a strong faith and charity towards Him who leads you, and by promptness to every obedience and humiliation." [154]

Finally the priest beseeches God on behalf of the newly professed monk:

"Arm him with Your power and clothe him with the panoply of Your Holy Spirit; for his fight is not against flesh and blood, but against principalities, against powers, against the rulers of the darkness of this world, against the spirits of evil. Gird his loins with the power of truth, and clothe him with the breastplate of Your justice and Your exultation, and equip his feet with readiness to spread the gospel of peace. Make him wise enough to take up the shield of faith with which he may ward off all the fiery darts of the Evil One, and to receive the helmet of salvation and the sword of the Spirit, which is Your word." [155]

In various other allusions to these same concepts it is noteworthy that the various articles of the monastic garb with which the newly professed monk is clothed are interpreted as items in that panoply spoken of above, for the struggle against the devil.[156] And finally, another characteristic detail, the pericope read in the Mass at which the rite of profession takes place is none other than the passage in which St. Paul exhorts the Christian to invest himself in this panoply in his struggle against Satan (Eph. 6:10-17).

The liturgy for the dead

The concept of the struggle against Satan is found also in the liturgy for the dead. We have already referred twice to the way in which the ancients represented to the imagination the proceedings of the particular judgment of every man after death as an examination of the soul, in which the demons and the angels take part as opposing powers, and which examination is carried out in the presence of examining tribunals (*telónia*) during the voyage of the soul through the various spheres prior to its arrival at paradise.

It is in this imaginative representation that the concept of a certain continuation of the struggle against Satan, even immediately after the death of each man, is concretized in the liturgies for the dead. Allusions to this are found already in the Gelasian Sacramentary:

"Receive, O Lord, the soul of Your servant *N.*, returning to You from the land of Egypt. Send Your holy angels to meet him, and show him the way of justice. Open the gates of justice to him, and drive the princes of darkness away." [157]

---

[154] *Ibid.*, p. 243.
[155] *Ibid.*, pp. 244-245.
[156] *Ibid.*, p. 248.
[157] Mohlberg ed., no. 1610, p. 234. Whether

these elements pertain originally to the ancient Gelasian Sacramentary or were introduced with its Gallican revision is another question entirely.

And:

> "Be pleased, O Lord, to give him a place of light, refreshment and peace. May he be permitted to pass the gates of hell and the ways of darkness, and dwell in the habitations of the saints, and in the holy light which You promised long ago to Abraham and to his descendants." [158]

> "May Michael, the angel of Your covenant, assist him. Free his soul, Lord, from the princes of darkness and from the places of punishment." [159]

In the current exsequial rites there is the prayer *"Deus qui proprium est misereri . . . ,"* which formerly read:

> "O God, whose part it is ever to be merciful and sparing, we humbly pray You on behalf of Your servant *N.*, whom You have this day commanded to go forth from this world. Do not abandon him into the enemy's hands, or put him out of mind forever, but command that his soul be taken up by the holy angels and brought home to paradise; so that, having hoped and believed in You, he shall not endure the pains of hell, but possess everlasting joy."

It is interesting to note that while basically the prayer has been preserved in the Pauline Roman Missal, all references to Satan or hell have been expunged, so that the prayer in question now reads:

> "O God, whose part it is ever to be merciful and sparing, we humbly pray You on behalf of Your servant *N.*, whom You have this day commanded to go forth from this world, so that, having hoped and believed in You, You may grant him entrance to his true fatherland, and the boon of everlasting joy."

Even in the Pauline Roman Missal, however, there is an antidemoniacal dimension to the postcommunion prayer in the *Mass for the Dying:*

> "By the power of this Sacrament, O Lord, mercifully deign to sustain Your servant by Your grace, so that in the hour of death the enemy may not seem to prevail against him, but, accompanied by Your angels, he may be rewarded by passing over to life."

Certainly similar allusions, and even clearer ones, can easily be found in the historical liturgies,[160] nor are they entirely lacking even in the current revision of the liturgy. The offertory verse *Domine Iesu Christe*, formerly an integral part of all Requiem Masses, and now at least optional if an offertory verse is to be sung, is surely a most remarkable text, developed entirely in the framework of the imagery under discussion:

[158] *Ibid.*, no. 1617, p. 236.
[159] *Ibid.*, no. 1621, p. 236.
[160] See the suggestions of Boniface M. Ser-pilli, in his *L'offertorio della messa dei defunti*, Rome 1946, pp. 69-80.

"Lord Jesus Christ, King of glory, free the souls of all the faithful departed from the pains of hell and from the deep pit. Save them from the lion's jaws, that they may not be the prey of Tartarus and may not fall into the darkness; but may St. Michael, the standard-bearer, bring them into the holy light which You promised long ago to Abraham and to his posterity." [161]

From the point of view of dogma it should be noted that this and similar prayers are and indeed must today be understood, in the framework of the doctrinal development of eschatological theology, as prayers for release from the pains of purgatory, no matter the meaning which historically they had when they were composed nor the peculiarly material expressions which they contain.[162]

And certainly it is true that it is possible to speak in a fully orthodox sense of the struggle against Satan being carried on in some way after death, so long as the soul is detained in purgatory; for surely the fact that souls do not yet enjoy the beatific vision is a noteworthy remnant — or better, a consequence — of the power of Satan over souls after the sin of Adam. The power of Satan and its consequences will be fully and definitively destroyed only with the general resurrection, when *novissima . . . inimica destruetur mors* (1 Cor. 15:26).

7. The Struggle against Satan in the Temporal and Sanctoral Cycles

To give a substantially complete idea of the position which the concept of the reality of the struggle against Satan occupies in the liturgy it but remains for us to examine the liturgical cycles. This will be largely a matter of considering, from the particular viewpoint in question, the temporal and sanctoral cycles of the Missal and, in a considerably lesser degree, of the Breviary.

The Advent to Epiphany season

We know that the liturgical cycle embracing the period from Advent to Epiphany has as its general theme the mystery of Christ as the epiphanic coming of the Lord, prepared for, announced, and prefigured in the Old Testament; as historically realized in Palestine; as in process of realization *in mysterio*, mystically, in us; and as preparing for and prefiguring His eschatological epiphanic coming.[163] Likewise in all the liturgies, both histori-

---

[161] Serpilli, *ibid., loc. cit.,* is of the opinion that we are dealing with a text of Irish or perhaps Gallican origin. See also Marino Soressi, *"L'offertorio della messa dei defunti e l'escatologia orientale,"* in *Eph. lit.,* Vol. 61 (1947), pp. 245-252.

[162] The text of the offertory verse of the Requiem Mass, in view of its actual wording, requires somewhat more forcing than do other texts, in being fitted to this interpretation.

[163] See J. Lemarié, *La manifestation du Seigneur,* Paris 1957.

cal and current, an essential theme is bringing into prominence the redemptive value of this epiphanic coming, at all its various levels. But since in Scripture and tradition the redemption necessarily includes a struggle against the devil and our liberation from his slavery, it was only natural that this dimension should be present in the liturgy not only implicitly — for implicitly it is effectively present everywhere — but that it should also find explicit expression.

In the Roman Missal and Breviary of the present time the theme is scarcely hinted at except in the Advent hymn *Creator alme siderum*, in its second and fourth stanzas,[164] and more particularly on the very night of Christmas, in the lessons formerly pertaining to the second nocturn, taken from a homily of St. Leo the Great. In this homily the profoundly antidemoniacal meaning of the incarnation of the Son of God is strongly and explicitly related:

> "The Son of God, in the fullness of time fixed by the inscrutable divine counsel, assumed human nature to reconcile it with its Creator, that the author of death, the devil, might be conquered by that same nature which he himself had once conquered. In this conflict, which He joined for our sake, the Lord fought by rules of strict and perfect equity: the all-powerful God entered the lists with the cruel enemy not in His majesty but in our lowliness, opposing to him the same form and nature that we have, subject to mortality like ours, but free from all sin. . . . Be conscious, O Christian, of your dignity . . . remember that you have been snatched from the power of darkness and transported to the light and the kingdom of God." [165]

The same theme is found not infrequently in the ancient sacramentaries. The following two orations for the feast of the Nativity are given in the Leonine Sacramentary:

> "Grant, we pray You, Lord our God, that He who was born today to destroy the devil and pardon sins, may purify us from the infiltration of sin and defend us against the attacks of the enemy."

> "O God, who have not allowed the human nature You created to perish by the malice of the devil, apply the remedies of Your mercy, that man may not be overcome by the enemy's deceit but rather obtain redemption from Your goodness." [166]

In the Gelasian Sacramentary there is a recurrent idea that we have need of the protection of God against Satan in order to be able to celebrate Advent

---

[164] The original text of the hymn is preserved in monastic breviaries; but the antidemoniacal dimension is even clearer in the revised text made under the direction of Urban VIII, and which is the text found in the Roman Breviary. [Since this footnote was written, the original text has been restored in the *Liturgia Horarum*.]

[165] Office of Readings, formerly second nocturn, lessons 5 and 6.

[166] Mohlberg ed., nos. 1251 and 1275.

and Christmas worthily. Petition is made that these feasts will free us from the influence of Satan:

> "By virtue of these gifts, O Lord, we pray You, keep ever far from us the machinations of the devil, that we may celebrate with pure minds the Nativity of our Redeemer." [167]

> "Hasten, Lord our God, do not delay, and free us by Your power from the devil's fury." [168]

The Gothic Missal prays God that the Feast of the Nativity might signify for us our liberation from Satan; [169] and it points out that Christ, by subjecting Himself to the law of circumcision, has shaken off from our necks the yoke of the devil.[170]

The Ambrosian Missal, in its preface for the feast of the Madonna, the Sixth Sunday of Advent, in the framework of the Eve-Mary relationship, opposes the work of the serpent in and through Eve and the work of the Virgin, showing thereby that it is Mary's action that destroys the work of the serpent and of Eve.

In the *inlatio* for the Fourth Sunday of Advent, the whole mystery of Christ as epiphanic coming of the Lord, on its various levels — its annunciation in the Old Testament, its historic realization in Palestine, its mystic realization in us, and the parousia yet to be — is viewed by the Mozarabic Missal as having the precise aim of freeing mankind from the slavery of Satan.[171]

Lent as struggle of the faithful against Satan

It is in the cycle of the period from Quadragesima to Pentecost, however, and especially throughout the Lenten season, that the theme of the struggle against Satan occupies a position of greatest importance. This might easily be surmised from what we have already said of the importance of this theme in the liturgy of Christian initiation and in the penitential liturgy, the rites of which, in the ancient Church, were performed during this cycle and which pertained in a special way thereto. We need not repeat what has already been said about the conferring of the appropriate sacraments upon the catechumens and upon the public penitents.

---

[167] Mohlberg ed., no. 13, p. 8; Secret prayer for the Vigil of Christmas.

[168] *Ibid.*, no. 1150, p. 173. Sin, too, keeps us slaves through *obligation* or *ancient bondage*, from which it is besought that the Nativity of our Lord might free us. If this is not expressed quite as directly as it might be, still, it does touch very closely upon the theme of our slavery to Satan from which the Nativity of Christ frees us. In the Gelasian Sacramentary, Mohlberg ed., no. 1148, see the oration *Concede quaesumus omnipotens Deus ut qui*

sub peccati iugo . . .; in the Gregorian Sacramentary, Wilson ed., p. 115, the oration *Concede quaesumus . . .* , which is found also in the Roman Missal, formerly as the collect for the third Mass of Christmas Day, and now as collect for the Sixth Day within the Octave of Christmas.

[169] Bannister ed., no. 11, pp. 4, 2ff.

[170] *Ibid.*, no. 55, p. 18.

[171] *Liber sacramentorum*, Férotin ed., no. 32.

On the other hand, we do feel obliged to point out again how this whole period, and Lent in particular, was conceived as the period *par excellence* of the struggle against Satan not only for the catechumens and the public penitents, who were preparing themselves to receive at Easter the sacraments of initiation and of reconciliation, but also for all the faithful who, each year, celebrated and realized ever more profoundly in themselves the mystery of Christ as redemption.

Lent is conceived as the period of the great annual spiritual exercises of the whole Church, with its focal point on the mystery of Christ as redemption made necessary, prepared for, prefigured, and announced in the Old Testament; radically realized in the mortal life of the same Jesus Christ, principally in His Passion, death, resurrection, and ascension; and which is being realized *in mysterio* continuously, though in this period especially, not only in the catechumens and in the penitents, but also in the rest of the faithful, as the beginning and prefiguration of its perfect realization in the parousia.

For all the faithful the great means of this realization are, first of all, participation in the paschal sacraments in their whole liturgical context: the sacraments of initiation for the catechumens, of reconciliation and of the Eucharist for the penitents, of the Eucharist for all the other faithful. In the second place, there is prayer, fasting; good works toward others, especially the giving of alms to the needy; reading and meditating on the Scriptures; and, in general throughout this period, the more intense practice of the Christian virtues. The means of realization, therefore, is the general intensification of Christian life in all its aspects, focusing on the liturgical life in the paschal mysteries.

During Lent it is the intention of the Church that all the faithful should approach a little closer to that more perfect kind of Christian life which the ascetics, as a distinct group among Christians, hold up as an ideal, the realization of which they strive for throughout their whole life. The words of St. Leo the Great are well-known:

> "We ought to have for these great mysteries such an unending *devotio* and abiding reverence that we might remain always, in the sight of God, in that condition in which the Paschal Feast itself should find us. Such perfection, however, belongs but to the few. Since austerity is relaxed because of the frailty of the flesh, and our concern is with the various affairs of this life, it is inevitable that even sincerely religious souls be sullied by the dust of worldly things. Therefore has divine providence most salutarily decreed that, to restore our purity of soul, we should have the medicament of these forty days of exercises, in which pious works would be able to redeem the faults of other times, and holy fastings diminish them." [172]

---

[172] Homily from the former second nocturn of the First Sunday of Lent.

In such a perspective we might easily expect that Lent would be commonly regarded, in the liturgies of times past as well as in those of the present, as the time *par excellence* in which the Christian engages himself in the conflict with Satan. This, in particular, is the conception of Lent that is found in the Roman Missal and Breviary of the present time. This conception is expressed with perfect clarity in the oration, found already in the Gregorian Sacramentary, which formerly concluded the ceremony for the imposition of ashes on Ash Wednesday, and which now is recited, in the Pauline Roman Missal, as the collect of the Mass of Ash Wednesday:

> "Grant, O Lord, that we may begin with holy fasting the defensive operations of the Christian warfare, that in our fight against the spirits of evil we may be protected by the fortifications of self-denial."

It is an oration for the beginning of Lent, the whole of which season we see conceived as a time in which the faithful, gathered into ranks as soldiers of Christ in the struggle against the evil spirits, are concerned from the very first moments of the campaign with erecting, by means of fasting, strong ramparts of defense against the enemy.

The whole liturgical structure of the First Sunday of Lent, whether in the Roman Rite or in the Ambrosian, is colored by this same concept, with the Gospel pericope of the temptation in the desert. The Ambrosian usage recites, as did the Roman until recently, the account of Matthew. Now in the Roman liturgy, through the three-year cycle of readings, all three synoptic accounts of the same event are read: Matthew 4:1-11; Mark 1:12-15; and Luke 4:1-13. The consistent selection of the account of Christ's temptation in the desert for the Gospel reading on this First Sunday in Lent quite evidently is intended to show a parallel between the forty days upon which the faithful are about to enter and the forty days passed by Christ in the desert, these two periods being considered as times of battle at close quarters with the devil.

The parallel is reinforced by the use of Psalm 90 in the proper parts of the same Mass: the sacred text of that Psalm which Christ had invoked against Satan is now invoked by the Church as she wages the same battle. If the passages selected for the first reading (Gen. 2:7-9; 3:1-7; Gen. 9:8-15; and Deut. 26:4-10) and the second reading (Rom. 5:12-19; 1 Peter 3:18-22; Rom. 10:8-13) through the three-year cycle of our present-day liturgy are not as directly antidemoniacal as the Gospel pericope, still, the latter element is certainly there, and they are nonetheless pertinent.

This general sense of Lent as a period of special conflict against Satan is quite strongly and felicitously emphasized in the Mozarabic liturgy as well. Let us only indicate a few of the characteristic texts. After Moses and Elias, a third model whom the faithful ought to imitate during Lent is Christ Himself,

"who after a full forty days in the solitude of the desert brought to
nothing all the temptations of the devil." [173]

"By His fasting He won a glorious victory over the devil, and by
His example showed His own soldiers how to fight." [174]

During Lent, therefore,

"with all care, beloved brethren, we should observe the practice of
the fast and the struggle against the devil as against enemies of another breed, in daily attacks, day and night; for the devil subverts
with bad thoughts a person whom he has not been able to trick into
evil deeds, and solicits with false images in sleep the one whom he
has not been able to tempt while awake." [175]

Such being the general import of Lent we must undoubtedly think of
Satan as the prime antagonist envisioned in the numerous texts of this
season in which the Church asks God's protection against enemies.[176]

The conflict and the triumph of Christ over Satan in the liturgy from Palm Sunday to Ascensiontide

In the liturgy of this liturgical period, extending from Palm Sunday to
the Ascension, there is a strong reminder, just as in the New Testament itself,
that the Passion, death on the Cross, descent into hell, resurrection and ascension of Christ, are as so many acts in His conflict with Satan, and in his
triumph over him.

The theme of Christ's victory and the victory of the Christian over Satan
is brilliantly illustrated and proclaimed in the Palm Sunday procession.
This is expressed in the prayer for the blessing of the palms, as now found
in the Pauline Roman Missal:

"Almighty and eternal God, sanctify these palm branches with
Your blessing, so that we who follow jubilantly after Christ our King
may, by His merits, be made worthy to enter into the eternal Jerusalem";

but it was even more clearly expressed in the blessing formerly in use, preserved for a while in the revised Ordo for Holy Week, but now suppressed
with the promulgation of the Pauline Missal; [177] and perhaps best of all

[173] Liber mozarabicus sacramentorum, ed.
Férotin, no. 318.

[174] Ibid., no. 477. See the whole text.

[175] Ibid., no. 473. On the idea of fasting as
a way of carrying on the struggle against Satan, see the same, nos. 345-346, 514.

[176] See, for example, in the Pauline Roman
Missal the collect for Tuesday in the Second
Week of Lent; postcommunion for Friday in
the Fifth Week in Lent; and perhaps more
clearly in the so-called Tridentine Roman Mis-

sal, the postcommunion prayer for Wednesday
of the First Week in Lent, and the super
populum prayer for the Thursday of the First
Week in Lent, both of which are found already in the Gregorian Sacramentary.

[177] "Bless, O Lord, we pray You, these palm
branches; and grant that what Your people do
today to honor You in a material way may be
fulfilled spiritually and in deepest devotion,
by victory over the enemy and an all-pervad-
ing love of the work of Your mercy."

in the oration *Deus qui miro*, which had already been suppressed in the earlier revision:

> ". . . The palm branches in fact signify triumph over the prince of death; the sprigs of olive, on the other hand, announce in some way the coming of Christ, inasmuch as that coming is a spiritual anointing. For that blessed multitude of men already understood what these symbols prefigured: how our Redeemer, being compassionate on account of human miseries, was preparing to engage in combat with the prince of death for the life of the whole world; and how in death, He would be the Victor. Therefore did this people pay homage to the Lord with those branches which signified the glory of His victory and the sweetness of His mercy. And we who, in the fervor of our faith recall this action and this symbol, O Holy Lord, . . . we beseech You through Jesus Christ our Lord, that in Him and through Him, of whom You willed that we be the members, You might grant us victory over the kingdom of death, and allow us to merit to be sharers in His glorious resurrection."

Death on the Cross as victory of Christ over the devil, in accord with the very thought of the New Testament and of patristic tradition, and especially after the discovery of the Cross in the fourth century, is indeed a theme of great prominence in the various liturgies. In the Roman liturgy this theme is very highly developed in the ceremony of the adoration of the Cross on Good Friday. The general dimension of the rite is the adoration and glorification of the Cross as the ensign of Christ's triumph, a triumph won over the powers of hell. This triumphal significance of the Cross was given lyric expression by Venantius Fortunatus in the first three stanzas of his hymn *Pange lingua gloriosi lauream certaminis*:

> "Sing, my tongue, the glorious battle,
> Sing the last, the dread affray;
> O'er the Cross, the Victor's trophy,
> Sound the high triumphal lay,
> How, the pains of death enduring,
> Earth's Redeemer won the day.

> "He, our Maker, deeply grieving
> That the first-made Adam fell,
> When he ate the fruit forbidden
> Whose reward was death and hell,
> Marked e'en then this Tree the ruin
> Of the first tree to dispel.

> "Thus the work of our salvation
> Was of old in order laid,
> That the manifold deceiver's

Art, by art might be outweighed,
And the lure the foe put forward
Into means of healing made.
(J. M. Neale et al.)

The same concept is found also in the preface of the Cross, formerly said throughout Passiontide, but now heard only on the feast of the Exaltation of the Cross (Sept. 14):

> ". . . You founded the salvation of mankind in the tree of the Cross, that from the very source of death, life might spring up again, and that he who conquered by a tree might himself by a Tree be conquered, through Christ our Lord."

The Feast of the Exaltation of the Cross, and the now suppressed Feast of the Finding of the Holy Cross, are, as it were, but extensions of the Good Friday adoration of the Cross. Characteristic of the antiphons of these feasts are such expressions as:

> "Here is the Cross of the Lord! Away with you hostile powers! Victory belongs to the Lion of Juda, the Offspring of David."

> "By the sign of the Cross deliver us from our enemies, O our God!"

> "By the tree we were enslaved, and by the holy Cross emancipated."

Expressions of much the same tenor can be pointed out in the Mozarabic liturgy,[178] in the Gallican liturgies,[179] and in the Byzantine.[180]

Christ's descent into hell, along with His resurrection and His ascension, as triumph over Satan, is likewise a theme common to the various liturgies, and in accord with New Testament concepts.[181] In the Mozarabic rite, Christ

> "descended into hell, conquered death, made the devil powerless, abolished the laws of Tartarus . . . and made the whole human race rise up again, born to a new life";[182]

---

[178] *Liber mozar. sacr.*, Férotin ed., no. 739ff, especially no. 743.

[179] See, for example, the *Missale gothicum*, Bannister ed., no. 317ff; *Messale di Bobbio*, Lowe ed., no. 288ff, especially the *contestatio* at no. 292.

[180] See the feast of September 14 and that of the Third Sunday of Lent, *Triódion*, Rome 1879, e.g., p. 349, third stich; p. 351, stichs 2-4; p. 353, *cáthisma*; p. 356, ode 5, third stich; etc.

[181] For the best general expressions of these ideas in the Mozarabic liturgy, see the *Liber sacr.*, Férotin ed., nos. 615-616, 679, 704, 707, 752-753. For similar in the Gelasian Sacramentary, see Mohlberg ed., nos. 457, p. 75; 575, p. 89; 583, p. 90; 589, p. 90. In the

Gregorian Sacramentary, in the *codex ottobonianus 313*, the *praefatio in feria III post dominicam VI in palmis*, Wilson ed., p. 269; preface for the Ascension, *ibid.*, pp. 275–276. In the present-day Roman liturgy, see the two paschal hymns *Aurora lucis rutilat* and *Ad caenam Agni providi* (both from the monastic breviary); the hymn *Aeterne rex altissime*; and the hymn *Iesu nostra redemptio* (monastic breviary); and in the Roman breviary prior to the reforms of the 1960's, the second nocturns of Monday and Tuesday of Easter week; and the homily of St. Leo the Great in the second nocturn of the Ascension.

[182] *Liber mozarab. sacr.*, Férotin ed., no. 704.

and again:

> "You have liberated us from the dangers of hell . . . , You have reconciled us with God. . . . Having nullified any right that death had over us . . . You have given us hope of being freed unto heavenly beatitude. In the first-fruits of Your victory and of Your resurrection, You call us to the rewards of eternal blessedness. Desiring to prepare a place in heaven for the redeemed, You ascended, our precursor, to God the Father, whither You call us; and thus, our redeemer on earth and our propitiator in heaven, You free those who suffer here below and defend the slaves, calling them to Yourself." [183]

The struggle against Satan in the sanctoral cycle: martyrdom, especially of virgins, as victory over Satan

In the sanctoral cycle the principal theme, in respect to the matter that is of interest to us, is that of martyrdom, and especially the martyrdom of women, as victory over the devil. It is a theme connected with the theology of martyrdom, a subject of intimate and intense concern to the Christians of antiquity. Martyrdom, because it is a total giving of oneself to God in the fullest way conceivable, was regarded as the most perfect imitation of Christ and therefore the apex of the perfection of the Christian life.

Naturally, then, martyrdom would be regarded also as the highest victory of the Christian, or better, of Christ Himself in His members, over Satan. The routing of Satan in the martyrdom of the faithful was traditionally regarded as a victory of especially grand proportions and particularly shameful for him, when it was a martyrdom inflicted upon a woman. The idea has its basis in the concept of woman being the weaker (!) sex, and in the fact that, because Satan, in paradise was assured of his victory over the human race by a woman, his rout in the martyrdom of a woman is a more splendid revenge against him.

These ideas recur with great frequency in the Leonine Sacramentary and constantly in the proper prefaces of the martyrs. As we know, these texts were very much reduced in numbers in the successive Roman sacramentaries, which gradually omitted the larger part of the Leonine prefaces. The Pauline revision has again vastly increased the number of the prefaces in the Roman Missal, and there are now a few prefaces for various categories of saints, e.g., for saints generally, for holy martyrs, for holy pastors, for holy virgins and religious; but there has been no restoration of prefaces for individual martyrs.

A typical example from the Leonine Sacramentary is the Preface for the Feast of St. Cecilia:

> "It is truly fitting . . . in order that the triumph over the enemy of the human race might be great, that You not only destroyed the

[183] *Ibid.*, no. 707.

tyranny of the devil through Christ our Lord; and not only through the blessed martyrs of the male sex do You take a well-deserved revenge on the deceiver for the fall of the first man; but also through the weaker sex You justly take revenge against the enemy of our mother Eve; that he who laid low both sexes, taking advantage of their foolish trust of him in their paradisial happiness, now, by Your grace, may be ground underfoot by the one and the other." [184]

And another example, for the Feast of St. Stephen:

"It is truly fitting . . . because not only, through Jesus Christ our Lord, have You granted us, Your adopted sons, that cruel hell's deadly sting should be destroyed, together with him who had received the power to inflict it, the devil, and that death, contracted as punishment for sin, when it was undergone to satisfy justice, should lead to a reward; but such has been the generosity of Your superabundant grace that human nature receives all this not only in the person of our Redeemer but also in that of the faithful who have acknowledged Him. St. Stephen it was, levite of the New Testament and first martyr after the Lord's Passion, who first took this role and won this victory." [185]

As to similar prefaces, there is one in the Gregorian Sacramentary [186] and various others in particular recensions of the same.[187] Neither are these concepts rare in the Mozarabic *Liber sacramentorum*.[188]

The regrettable lacuna made by the lack of this concept of martyrdom as victory over Satan in our own modern Roman Rite has now been at least partially filled by the special preface for the feasts of martyrs.[189]

The angels and Mary and the struggle against Satan

Another biblical and traditional theme, afterwards common to all the liturgies, both historical and current, is the importance of the good angels in the struggle against Satan, the help which they lend us in this conflict, the prayers which we make to God or to the angels themselves for the continuance of this help. In the sanctoral cycle of the liturgy in the current Roman Missal this theme is found primarily in the Feast of the Archangels Gabriel, Michael and Raphael, celebrated on September 29, and in a feast of comparatively recent origin, that of the Guardian Angels, on October 2. In the Breviary the concept is found throughout, and particularly in the hymns.

---

[184] Mohlberg ed., no. 1180.

[185] *Ibid.*, no. 678. See also in the same Leonine Sacramentary, nos. 29, 159, 161, 164, 784, 826, 837, 839, 1183, 1185.

[186] Wilson ed., p. 10, for St. Anastasia.

[187] Codex R., *praefatio de pluribus virginibus*, Wilson ed., p. 242; *Codex ottobonianus* 313, for SS. Tiburtius, Valerianus, Maximus, *ibid.*, p. 273; for St. George, *ibid.*, p. 286; for one virgin, *ibid.*, p. 297; for several virgins, *ibid.*, p. 247.

[188] See, for example, Férotin ed., nos. 72, 81, 96.

[189] *Ordo Missae: Prex Eucharistica*, no. 66. See also nos. 64-65, 67-68.

It was found again in the prayers which Leo XIII ordered to be said at the foot of the altar at the end of Mass, and in the prayers which the same Pope ordered to be inserted into the Roman Ritual before the exorcism "against Satan and the apostate angels." [190]

On the other hand, the theme of Mary's role in the struggle against Satan appears relatively late in the liturgies, and only in compositions of recent origin does it assume some importance. This does not by any means signify that Mary's role in this domain is not objectively one of greatest importance. On the contrary, theological argumentation based on principles developed in this very exposition easily demonstrates that her role is a high one and immensely superior to that of the angels or of any other saint. It is simply a reflection of the fact that Marian theology developed relatively late, the broadest areas of its piety developing only in an era in which the liturgies had already become substantially set in their forms.

The earliest explicit liturgical mention of the opposition between Satan and Mary, as well as the earliest prayer which I can find in the West, invoking, through the intercession of Mary, God's help in defending us against the demon, is in a Mass of the *Missale gothicum* dated by its editor, Bannister, at the end of the seventh or beginning of the eighth century. In the *contestatio* of the Mass of the Assumption, Mary is called

> "splendid bridal chamber from which the worthy Bridegroom comes forth; light of the nations; hope of the faithful; plunderer of the demons." [191]

This title *plunderer of demons* is undoubtedly meant to indicate that she snatched away from the demons all their prey. In the same Mass the prayer after the *Pater noster* beseeches God:

> "Deliver us from every evil, from every sin, O God, author and creator of all good things; and through the intercession of the blessed Mary, Your Mother, defend us with daily protection against the daily plots of the enemy, O Savior of the world, who lives and reigns together with the Father and the Holy Spirit. . . ." [192]

Not even in the Middle Ages are liturgical texts of a similar tenor to be encountered with any frequency. A methodical examination of the documents now known has been made. Egon von Petersdorff, who did the research, says that the most ancient text he was able to find belongs probably to the thirteenth century, after which some are to be found in the *Sacerdotale romanum* of the sixteenth century, the prototype, as it were, of our Roman Ritual; and several in most recent liturgical compositions of the nineteenth and twentieth centuries.[193]

[190] Title 12, chapter 3.
[191] Bannister ed., no. 98.
[192] *Ibid.*, no. 102.

[193] Egon von Petersdorff, "*De daemonibus in liturgia memoratis*," in *Angelicum*, Vol. 19 (1942), p. 332. In the Greek liturgy there are

In point of fact, in Marian feasts of recent institution, the antidemoniacal element is of frequent occurrence and is expressed in these two themes: Mary has conquered the ancient serpent and, with obvious reference to the text of Genesis, she has crushed his head; Mary is our defense against the snares of the devil, and we ask her to defend us therefrom:

> "Tower impregnable to the dragon, star propitious to the ship-wrecked, protect us from deceits and guide us by your light." [194]

The struggle against Satan in the ferial office

To complete the picture of the importance which the reality of the struggle against Satan has in the liturgy, I shall only hint at a point which must be proven in a latter chapter: that all the psalms of the Old Testament which are in any way directed against the enemy — and, as you know, they are most numerous — when they are used in the liturgy, not only because of tradition, and that not merely of an arbitrary allegorism, but because of the intrinsic necessity of theological principles, can and must be understood as directed against Satan and his satellites. From this simple observation one can easily see how the reality of the struggle against Satan makes its entry as an important element in the concept of the ferial psalter.

The Roman liturgy of the ferial breviary reminds us of the struggle against Satan in a special way in the last canonical hour of the day, which is Compline. The *lectio brevis* at Compline is the admonition of St. Peter:

> "Brethren, be sober and watchful; for our adversary, the devil, goes about like a roaring lion, seeking whom he may devour. Resist him steadfast in the faith."

The hymn of Compline is a prayer to God for His protection against the snares of the devil, put in relation especially to possible dreams and impure phantasms and pollutions:

> "As dusk draws on to end the day,
> Creator of all things, we pray

some beautiful expressions in this same vein in the Acáthistos Hymn. See G. G. Meersemann, *Der Hymnos Akáthistos im Abendland*, Freiburg, Vol. I, 1958, pp. 27, 37, 45, 49, 53, 73, 77.

[194] Much this same sense is found in various texts for the Feast of the Immaculate Conception: the reading from Genesis in Matins, with the responsory after the first lesson; the Benedictus antiphon; and the third stanza of the hymn at Lauds. On the Feast of the Apparition of the Blessed Virgin Mary at Lourdes, on February 11, see the hymn *Te dicimus praeconio*, stanzas 3 and 5; the former ninth lesson, a reading from St. Bernard; and stanzas 4 and 5 of the hymn *Aurora soli*. In the now suppressed Feast of the Motherhood of Mary, October 11, see the third stanza of the Lauds hymn, *Te Mater alma Numinis*. Mention of the Blessed Virgin is made also in the exorcism "against Satan and the apostate angels" which Leo XIII inserted in the Roman Ritual, Title 12, ch. 3. This is in fact the first time a liturgical exorcism makes any mention of Mary: "*In nomine Iesu Christi . . . intercedente immaculata virgine Dei genitrice Maria . . . imperat tibi excelsa Dei genitrix Maria . . . .*"

> That in Your mercy You will keep
> Close watch to guard us in our sleep.

> "Let dreams and phantoms of the night
> Be far from us; and put to flight
> The enemy, lest we, beguiled,
> Awake to find ourselves defiled."
>   (*trans.* W. A. Jurgens)

The oration which concludes the hour is likewise a petition that God protect from diabolical deceits the house in which dwells the one who prays, along with all who dwell therein, that they may enjoy the special protection of the holy angels:

> "Visit, we beseech You, O Lord, this house, and keep far from it all the snares of the enemy. Let Your holy angels dwell therein, that they may guard us in peace; and may Your blessing be upon us always.

The proper and specific psalms of Compline, in the monastic tradition, the tradition in which this hour was born, are Psalms 4, 90, and 133 in the Vulgate (liturgical) numbering. The Roman breviary has reserved these to Sunday Compline, while on other days other Psalms are used.

It is evident that Psalm 90 was selected on account of its antidemoniacal dimension. It is the Psalm which had such great importance in the temptation of our Lord in the desert, and which figures largely in the proper parts of the Mass of the First Sunday in Lent, on which Sunday also one or the other of the Synoptic accounts of the temptation is read as the Gospel pericope. Psalm 90 does in fact speak of the protection which God affords His faithful, ordering even His angels into their service, so that they might escape unscathed from all the dangers and all the snares of the enemy:

> "You shall not fear the terror of the night *
>   nor the arrow that flies by day;
> Not the pestilence that roams in darkness *
>   nor" —

— so read the Septuagint and the Vulgate, and so too all the various liturgies —

>   — "the attack of the noon-day devil.
> Though a thousand fall at your side, and ten thousand at your right *
>   near you he shall not come.
>   . . .

> No evil shall befall you, *
>   no affliction come near your tent,
> For to His angels He has given command about you, *
>   that they guard you in all your ways.

> Upon their hands they shall bear you up, *
> lest you dash your foot against a stone.
> You shall tread upon the asp and the viper, *
> you shall trample down the lion and the dragon."

Even if the Hebrew text does not speak directly about demons, the Septuagint cannot be accused of arbitrarily mentioning them, if we but recall the connection which exists in the whole of biblical tradition, and in oriental tradition in general, between the dangers and illnesses which are mentioned there in the Psalm, and their cause, the demons. It is no exaggeration to say that the selection of this Psalm at Compline, especially in the monastic tradition which repeats it every day, is intended to impress upon the faithful at nightfall the remembrance of their essential condition as combatants against Satan, the temptations put to our Lord, the protection of the Most High, and the guardianship exercised by His angels.

*   *   *

In conclusion, it must be affirmed that the reality of the continual and cosmic struggle against Satan is an essential aspect of revelation and hence of the liturgy too; and that, if this viewpoint be lost, neither revelation nor liturgy is comprehensible. The sacred salvation history of the communications of God with the world and of the response of the world to these communications is in essence a drama of two kingdoms, two cities in conflict. The drama of every being is part of this more general and cosmic drama. The liturgy, for one who lives it, does not allow this drama to be forgotten; for revelation does not want it forgotten. In the liturgy the Church is seen

> "always in battle array, waging constant war against her enemies,
> of whom the Apostle says, 'Our fight is not against flesh and blood,
> but against principalities and powers, against the rulers of this world
> of darkness, against the evil spirits of the air.' " [195]

Only in this light can we understand why the liturgies never cease exhorting the faithful, even in generic formulas besides those of the more specific character which we have examined up to now, in their struggle against Satan; why they never cease asking God's protection for the faithful and for the Church, against Satan and his angels.

"Be strong in the war, and fight against the ancient serpent, and you will receive the eternal kingdom." So advises the Roman liturgy in the *Magnificat* antiphon at Second Vespers on feasts of the Apostles.

How well does the Mozarabic liturgy express it, when, at the end of the

---

[195] *Pontificale romanum*, ordination of deacons. For the importance which this biblical, patristic, and liturgical perspective holds in the evangelization of mission countries, see, for example, X. Seumois, "*La structure de la liturgie baptismale romaine et les problèmes du catéchumènat missionnaire*," in *La maison Dieu*, no. 58 (1959), pp. 83-110.

paschal feasts, viewing Lent and the whole Christian life as a struggle against Satan, it prays:

"Do not permit us, Lord, to forget the good things You have given us, raising us up to salvation when we were lost. Place between us and the irredeemable devil a perfect hatred, not that he may be enabled by Your leave to harm us, but that he may not be able to cause any further lapses in those whom You have enlightened with the knowledge of Your truth." [196]

And the reason why this divine protection is necessary is likewise explained quite well in the same Mozarabic liturgy:

"Grace has adopted man, but the devil is not yet confined to hell. Sin has lost its violence, but not its nature. We are able to fight, but we are in no position to stand safely at ease. The enemy has been despoiled but not annihilated, and of course he will rage against those who used to be under his dominion but whom he has now lost." [197]

[196] Liber mozarabicus sacramentorum, Férotin ed., no. 713. See, in the ancient liturgies, other generic prayers for obtaining protection against Satan; for example, in the Leonine Sacramentary, Mohlberg ed., nos. 78, 140, 182, 184, 266, 391, 418, 516, 518, 520, 533, 631, 1272.

[197] Liber mozarab. sacr., Férotin ed., no. 657.

PART 3 LITURGY AND BIBLE

14 HOW THE LITURGY

MAKES USE OF SCRIPTURE

The liturgy, as we saw in the first and second parts of the present work, is concerned with the mystery of sacred history, the mystery of Christ, the mystery of the Church. But the liturgy does not invent this mystery; it simply finds it in the Scriptures. It is for this reason that the liturgical expression of the mystery of Christ is wholly scriptural, especially in the Roman liturgy. It can in fact be said that in the Roman liturgy the non-scriptural compositions are not only relatively few in number; as a rule, they do no more than coördinate, underline, and interpret with great sobriety the thoughts of the scriptural passages, which always occupy the principal place.

Nevertheless, the liturgy reads Scripture in a well-determined sense, a sense all its own, and under a light of its own — which makes the liturgy a kind of law of interpretation. It is with clarifying this law that we are concerned. Without entering into details of a historical and descriptive kind,[1] I shall attempt to consider the matter from the more strictly theological-liturgical point of view.

[1] For the use of the Bible in the liturgy from the historical point of view, see, for example, S. Marsili, "La bibbia nell'ufficio divino," in Enciclopedia cattolica, Vol. II (1949), cols. 1578ff. This use, as a rule, derives from the apostolic practice, which in part has its roots in the practices of the temple and synagogues. The Jewish public prayer included also the reading of some passage of the Pentateuch (divided into 167 sections, read in three years)

1. The Foundation: The Concept of the Unity of the Two Testaments and of Sacred History

The law of the liturgical interpretation of the Scriptures can be formulated thus: The liturgy reads the Scriptures in the light of the supreme principle of the unity of the mystery of Christ, and therefore of the two testaments and of the whole of sacred history, an organic-progressive unity under the primacy of the New Testament over the Old, and of the eschatological realities over the reality of the present economy.

To understand the import of this law, we must refer again to the first chapter, and especially to that outline in which we traced the various phases of the mystery of Christ, and take account of the profound unity which binds these phases to one another. This intrinsic unity depends on the fact that history, centered in Christ, is wholly in the hands of a single, all-powerful director, God Himself, who grasps its threads firmly yet with complete respect for human freedom, and infallibly directs its course, whether in general or in its smallest details, to a single and precise end: the establishment of the heavenly Jerusalem of the redeemed in Christ together with the faithful angels.

In the historical unfolding of this plan, nothing escapes the supreme purpose of God. The phases which follow one another are all realizations and concretizations of one and the same supreme idea. They are ever more perfect approaches to a single ideal, because He who realizes them does not leave them to follow one another chaotically but in an orderly fashion, keeping

and a prophetic passage (Law and prophets). Other notable liturgical passages: the trisagion of Isaias; some psalms more especially in use, whether every day or according to a weekly distribution or on particular feasts. Everything leads to the conclusion that the Christians too, who in the beginning continued to frequent the temple and whose apostles willingly made their propaganda in the very meetings of the synagogues (Acts 13:15; 15:21), continued to read passages from the Old Testament and sing psalms even when they became separated from the synagogue in their worship.

St. Justin the Martyr, who is the first to give us an adequate description of the way in which the Eucharist was celebrated, mentions expressly (in the first part of the synaxis) the reading of the "Memoirs of the Apostles" and of the "writings of the prophets" (*First Apology* 67 [Jurgens, no. 129]). Tertullian adds mention of the singing of the psalms (*The Soul* 9). Later testimony is abundant.

The reading of the Scriptures and the chanting of the psalms took on a very great development in the liturgy, especially in the divine office, with the rise of monasticism in the fourth century. Then also the cycle of the scriptural readings of the Mass was fixed, often in agreement with the readings of the office, especially on the feasts and in paschal time. The cycle then established remained much the same until our own time and the liturgical revisions subsequent to Vatican II. But there also prevailed, especially under monastic influence, the system of the so-called *lectio continua*, that is, the concept of reading in the course of one year, especially in the office, the passages of Scripture in the order in which they follow in the collection of the sacred books. This too had its influence as historical antecedent upon the later status of the use of the Bible in the Roman liturgy; and at least the concept itself has clearly influenced the reforms of our own times.

For the use of the Bible in the liturgy from the more descriptive point of view, see the chapter by P. Jounel in *The Liturgy and the Word of God* (a fruit of the Strasbourg Conference, 1958), published by The Liturgical Press, Collegeville, Minnesota.

always in view the total picture and the ultimate goal. Thus there is an intrinsic connection between these phases: each one prepares and announces the one that follows and is like a first imperfect realization of it, a roughcast, while all are fullfilled in a most perfect way in the last, the general goal toward which they tend.

And since all the phases are nothing but an ever more perfect realization of the unique mystery of Christ, each one of the realities in which this mystery is successively concretized, besides being and signifying that which it is in itself, has also a functional meaning in respect to something else beyond itself which is like the future goal to which it tends. The mystery of Christ in the unfolding of salvation history is fulfilled, therefore, by successive roughcasts, as it were, in which the preceding ones prepare for, announce, and prefigure the subsequent ones.

It is through the texts of the Old and New Testaments that we know the realities of the phases in which the mystery of Christ is successively concretized. It follows that to understand in depth the meaning which the realities spoken of in the Scriptures have in the eyes of God (the only meaning that counts), it is necessary to consider them also in relation to the subsequent unfolding of the same sacred history, since only in this does each one find its connatural fulfillment, its full significance.

The whole of the Old Testament, then, and the realities of which it speaks, besides being what they are, prepare for, announce, and prefigure as if in an initial roughcast those realities which will be realized later in the historical life of Jesus and which are realized continually in the real, mystical life, liturgical and extraliturgical, of Christians in the Church, in the present economy between the ascension and the parousia. In their turn, the realities of the present economy prepare for, announce, and prefigure the realities which will be fulfilled in the final eschatological phase.

Practically speaking, this means that the complete significance of the realities of which the Old Testament speaks can be understood only by a person who places them in relation to the realities of which the New Testament speaks and to those which are now being fulfilled in the Church in the ascetical and mystical life, liturgical and extraliturgical, of Christians. It means also that to understand the full import of the realities which are now being fulfilled in the Church in the ascetical and mystical life of the faithful, a person must consider them first by looking backward in the light of the realities of which the New Testament speaks, and further backward to those of which the Old Testament tells; and then by looking ahead to the light of the future eschatological realities. For only thus will he understand how the realities which are fulfilled today in the Church in the supernatural life of the faithful were prepared for, announced, made possible, prefigured in the history of the world before Christ; how in their own way they were realized in the life of Christ Himself; and how, in their turn, they prepare for, announce, and prefigure the final consummation to which they lead.

Thus we find again, with reference to the Scriptures, the great concept of the four dimensions of the liturgical sign. Here is discovered *the essential principle which must guide the Christian in the reading and interpretation of the Scriptures and of the mysteries contained therein*, a principle repeated again and again by the Fathers of the Church and one which St. Augustine formulated much in this way: *The New Testament is hidden in the Old, and the Old is manifested in the New: In Veteri Testamento Novum latet et in Novo Vetus patet.*[2] It can also be formulated thus: The Christian economy, prepared for, made possible, and prefigured by the ancient economy, prepares for, makes possible, and prefigures the future eschatological economy.

This is the key to understanding in what spirit and according to what laws the liturgy makes use of the Scriptures.

2. The Fourfold Depth of the One Sense of the Scriptural Texts in General

This is the unshakable foundation of all those theories, so disconcerting to us, which held sway in antiquity and in the Middle Ages concerning the so-called various senses of the Scriptures. Their intention was simply to explain and systematize the observations made above. It cannot be denied, however, that in these explanations and systematizations, and especially in the trivial practice of the ancients, alongside the statement of principles which are quite correct there are found arbitrary applications. These proceed, not from scriptural foundations and traditions, but from extraneous

[2] See the *Quaest. in ev.* 73. We have already pointed out that there is today among historians a salutary reaction tending to understand more fairly and to re-evaluate in its proper elements, separated from the perishable elements, the patristic exegesis, which rests for the most part on the aforesaid principle.

Jean Cardinal Daniélou studied patristic exegesis from this point of view in direct connection with its so-called symbolic explanation of the liturgy in two of his works. In *Sacramentum futuri: Études sur les origines de la typologie biblique*, Paris 1950, he reviews the themes of Adam and paradise, Noah and the flood, the sacrifice of Isaac, Moses and the Exodus, the cycle of Josue. In *The Bible and the Liturgy*, Notre Dame 1956, he reviews the symbolico-theological explanations which the Greek Fathers of the fourth century, especially in their mystagogic and homiletic literature, have given of the sacramental rites and the liturgical feasts, and strives to show how this explanation rests, essentially, on the aforesaid

dogmatic-biblical principle and how only in a secondary way it is influenced by Hellenistic theories. On page vii ff. of *Sacramentum futuri* will be found also the list of the principal studies made up to now concerning these questions, studies of a general character or more specialized on the Old and New Testaments and the Fathers of the Church.

Also to be noted is J. Guillet's *Thèmes bibliques*, Paris 1951. He studies the development of revelation in regard to the following themes: 1) themes of Exodus: the march through the desert; 2) grace, justice and truth: the basic vocabulary; 3) the same: the evolution of the vocabulary; 4) themes of sin; 5) themes of damnation: the Satanic powers, the accursed places; 6) themes of hope: life; of possessing the land; the inheritance of Yahweh; the vine; 7) the breath of Yahweh. Almost all of these themes have also a noteworthy liturgical interest. See also M. Simon, *Verus Israel*, Paris 1948.

theories and tendencies, especially from the allegorical method which in the last stage of Hellenism was used widely in the moralizing and philosophical interpretation of the ancient poets and myths, a method which Philo of Alexandria had already applied to the interpretation of the Old Testament in the spirit of the medio-Plantonic Hellenistic philosophy.[3]

Therefore, in the theoretical determination of the problem of the so-called various senses of Scripture, leaving aside the question of patristic or medieval theory and terminology,[4] the following can be directly affirmed: to be thor-

---

[3] See J. Coppens, *Les harmonies des deux testaments*, Tournai 1949, with abundant bibliography. Célestin Charlier, *La lecture chrétienne de la bible*, 4th ed., Maredsous 1951, pp. 296ff. J. C. Joosen and J. H. Waszink, "*Allegorese*," in the *Realexikon für Antike und Christentum*, Vol. I (1950), pp. 283–293. Of basic importance in this question are the works of Henri de Lubac, *Histoire et ésprit. L'intelligence de l'écriture d'après Origène*, Paris 1950; *Exégèse médiévale: Les quatre sens de l'écriture*, 4 vols., Paris 1959–1963. See also Msgr. Garrone, *La porte des écritures*, Toulouse 1956; C. Burgard, *La bible dans la liturgie*, Paris 1958; X. Léon-Dufour, "*Renouveau biblique et vie spirituelle*," in "*Écriture sainte et vie spirituelle*," in *Dict. de spirit.*, Vol. 4 (1960), pp. 265–278.

The essential difference between Hellenistic allegory and the biblical concept which asserts that the ancient inspired texts and the things expressed in them have also a preparatory and prefigurative value proceeds in the last analysis from the fact that Hellenism knows nothing of the concept of rationality properly so called of history, and therefore of the intrinsic rational relation of preparation and prefiguration of the various phases in which history unfolds. In fact Hellenism — and the same is true of all the other ancient profane philosophies — knows nothing of a God who is personal and transcendent and at the same time directs, as Providence, the world, time, and history. Only on the presupposition of such a God is it possible to conceive of history as successive and rationally organized phases of a plan always in the process of being actualized, with a view to achieving an ultimate definitive end to which everything is ordered.

In Hellenism the cycles, infinitely repeating themselves and according to which history would unfold, a concept which is the summit to which philosophy could attain in this field, are not rational, but blind and mechanical. The *sympátheia* itself which, according to the Stoics, for example, penetrates things and

makes them akin to one another, thereby expressing the unity of the cosmos and permitting divination, is not a rational functionality ordering one thing to another, but something that is blind and purely natural.

Hence, in Hellenism, allegory is a simple arbitrary expression of the one who is speaking, by which a certain relation is arbitrarily established between two things or a thing and an idea, and in which one is expressed by means of the other. Allegory is not in things but only in the intention of the man. The choice of one thing rather than another to make the allegory of a third is arbitrary and is often decided by connections of likeness which are quite superficial and extrinsic. The reality or lack of reality of the "fact" which is used to make the allegory has no importance. Thus, for example, Hermes and a myth of his are used to express, in allegory, the importance and the vicissitudes of the developments of reason in man. The concern will be simply with a piece of philosophy expressed arbitrarily by men in relation to an invented story about Hermes. Even when the story is not invented but is actual history, the relations between the history and the idea which is meant to be allegorized are invented.

In the biblical concept, on the other hand, these relations are real in the things themselves because they are put there by one who was able to do this, God Himself, and who, thereupon, has also in some way manifested this intention of His to us.

For the influence of Hellenistic allegory on the Fathers, see Cardinal Daniélou's *Sacramentum futuri*; P. Guillet, "*L'exégèse d'Alexandrie et d'Antioche*," in *Rech. de sc. relig.*, Vol. 34 (1947), pp. 257–302; Henri de Lubac, " *'Typologie' et 'allégorie,'* " *ibid.*, pp. 180–226; also of Lubac, "*A propos de l'allégorie chrétienne*," *ibid.*, Vol. 47 (1952), pp. 5–43.

[4] This is a question whose theoretical solution proves quite perplexing to moderns (see Jean Gribomont, "*Les liens des deux testaments selon la théologie de S. Thomas*," in

oughly understood, the texts of the Scriptures, especially of the Old Testament, must be examined under four lights and, as it were, sounded to four depths.

First: in the light which these texts, and hence the things of which they speak, had or could have had in the minds of the persons living at the time when the respective texts were written and for whom such compositions were immediately intended. We call this the sense or meaning grasped by the contemporary mind, or better, the "contemporary depth" of a biblical text, viz., the *literal sense*, in technical biblical textbooks.

Second: in the light which these same texts and these same things have to the eyes of those who consider them at a later date in the context of events which happened sometimes generations or centuries after the composition of the texts under consideration. In fact, in God's intentions, these later events were destined precisely to concretize in a more perfect way that very idea concretized or expressed at first in a less perfect way, as in a roughcast, in the previous events and texts. It is clear, therefore, that the functional meaning of the prior texts and of the things expressed in them toward those later events will be evident only to the later witnesses of these events, who have at their disposal, for understanding the ancient things, a light which the people contemporary with the original setting could not make use of.

Thus, within the limits of the Old Testament itself, texts and events of an earlier age can have to the eyes of later sacred authors a significance, not arbitrary but true, which far transcends that which the more ancient contemporaries were able to perceive. Thus again, and with greater reason, the whole ensemble of events and texts of the Old Testament, for the sacred authors of the New—and for all the faithful who live after that decisive event which is the incarnation of the Son of God, His redemptive life and death and glorification—takes on a meaning which is not at all arbitrary because first it corresponds to the deep realities of the events, while immensely transcending anything the contemporaries of those events could possibly suspect. All this is the simple and inevitable consequence of the concept of the unity of the two testaments and of history. For the believer who lives in the economy inaugurated by Christ, texts and facts of the Old Testament are illuminated by a new light, because they are considered in view of the realities which have already taken place in Christ Himself, realities toward which the whole of the Old Testament tended functionally. This depth which is discovered by the light of the person of Christ we may call the "Christic depth" of the Old Testament.

Ephemerides theologicae lovanienses, Vol. 22 [1946], pp. 70-89, and especially 70-71). The reason for this, I think, is that in treating of the question they adhere too much to the terminology of the ancients, who spoke of the four "senses" of Scripture. Such a way of speaking, however, gives rise to many difficulties. It is necessary, I think, to pay heed to the things themselves without becoming entangled in the terminology in which the ancients expressed them.

Third: but Christ is never separated from Christians, nor are the Christic realities separated from those realities which take place after Christ in Christians and among Christians. Indeed, Christ is in some way extended and fulfilled in the Christian realities. Thus, in the light of the Christian realities, the texts of the Scriptures reveal a new depth. We call it the "Christian depth."

These Christian realities are either extrinsic to each individual and more directly social, such as the Church, the sacraments, the liturgy, or they may be intrinsic because they take place in the interior of each of the faithful, comprising in some way the vicissitudes of the ascetical and mystical ascent toward perfection. Indeed, the mystery of Christ in Christians includes precisely this. Truly, it must be said that these vicissitudes of the intimate and personal relations of each soul with God are in some way the ultimate seal in which the mystery of Christ is fulfilled in every soul. Although they must never be divorced from those realities which are also extrinsic and of which we have spoken, yet it is true that it is to this ultimate seal, intimate and personal, that all the rest is in some way ordained. It is certainly a mistake, therefore, to think that no account need be taken of these intimate and personal realities of ascetical and mystical life when the concern is with reading and understanding the Old Testament in the light of the Christic and Christian realities.

It is not my intention to justify here the arbitrariness of Origen and his school when, with their system of allegorical interpretation of the Scriptures, they claimed to read in every text of the sacred page even the smallest details of their systematic ascetical and mystical theories, however arbitrary those theories might be. Still, I do not see how anyone can reject the fundamental principle that in the Sacred Scriptures are prefigured and prepared the realities even of the highest ascensions of the perfect life in Christ, ascetical and mystical, and that, in fact, it is precisely these realities which, in the final accounting, will give us the strongest interpretive light for understanding the Bible in the sense intended by God. Nor do we wish to fully justify the manner in which the mystics are accustomed to read the Scriptures. We wish only to invite the reader to reflect whether, in this manner of reading, their fundamental principle is not correct, and whether the scientific reaction in the opposite direction has not been exaggerated. All this, as is easily understood, will be of great importance in the question of the relations between spiritual life and liturgy.

Fourth: a fourth light, finally, is necessary to exhaust, insofar as possible, the meaning of the Scriptures, whether of the Old or of the New Testament, namely, the light of the eschatological realities which have not yet occurred, but on which we are nevertheless informed in some way by the revelation of the New Testament. Indeed, with the arrival of the new economy which begins with Christ, the mystery of Christ, or sacred salvation history, has not

yet reached its fulfillment. It continues to unfold unto the ultimate goal of
cosmic eschatology. The complete significance of sacred history, whether of
the Old or of the New Testament, cannot be discovered, therefore, until the
second coming of Christ. The phase of the mystery of Christ in which we are
now living, and which serves as a light to the events and texts of the Old
Testament and the New, will itself be clarified in its ultimate meaning by
the events of final eschatology. Hence the meaning which the texts and the
events referred to in the Old and New Testaments take on in the light of
final eschatology — of which meaning we do even now through revelation
know something, however obscure that knowledge may be — can be called
the "eschatological depth."

Light which was available to the contemporaries; light which emanates
from the person of Christ; light which comes from the Christic realities extended and realized in Christians; light of the future eschatological realities
about which we are already in some way informed: here is the fourfold beacon, so to speak, which, projected on a text of the Scriptures, permits us to
discover successively, as it were, four levels and four depths of the one meaning which that text possesses. To be thoroughly understood, therefore, a text
of the Old Testament, the event, the person of which it speaks, must be considered in the light of the aforesaid four beacons; while to exhaust a text of
the New Testament, it is necessary to consider it also in the light of the reality
of the Old Testament, in the light of the realities which are now taking place
in Christians, and in the light of those which will take place in the eschatological future.

In any case, the meaning which a text or the event of which it speaks had
for the contemporaries for whom it was immediately written, not only may
never be denied, but rather, must always be explicitly affirmed or presupposed,
since the successive clarifications do not bear on the discovery of a sense
different from that of the contemporaries, but simply bear on its deepening,
always in the one line marked by it, though with a new depth at which the
contemporaries could never have arrived.

3. The "Contemporary Depth" in the Biblical Texts Used by the Liturgy

Actually, the meaning which a biblical text used by the liturgy had to the
eyes of the contemporaries for whom it was immediately written is always
explicitly affirmed or presupposed in the liturgical framework into which it
is transferred. Thus, when the liturgy, reading a text, sets it forth in a light
which far surpasses that meaning, this "surpassing" never means the annul-
ment or evaporation of the depth realized by contemporaries, because that
sense always remains as the basis of all the successive deepenings given it by
the liturgy.

This holds true for every type of text and of event referred to therein, both of the Old Testament and of the New:

1) whether it is a question of texts of the *historical* type, relating historical things and events, such as the history of the Exodus, the history of the judges, the histories of the books of kings, the histories of the Machabees, the history of Jesus, the history of the acts of the Apostles, etc.;

2) or whether it is a question of texts making *doctrinal* statements, such as those about the nature of God, His attributes (wisdom, goodness, love, justice, power, etc.), or about the general relations between God and men, about men's duties toward God, about the origin of the world, the value of life, the freedom of man, etc.;

3) or whether the concern is with texts of a *juridical* type, giving precepts and exhortations on morality (e.g., the ten commandments; exhortations to prayer, to patience, to mortification, to good works, etc.), or of a *liturgical* type (e.g., on the feasts and the manner of celebrating them);

4) or whether it is a question of *prophecies*: e.g., about the Messiah and the future messianic era.

Thus, for example, all the narrations related in the Bible, transferred in any way into the liturgy, keep the meaning which they had for the contemporaries to whom they were first addressed. Sometimes there may be a dispute about what precisely this meaning was, as, for example, in the stories of Job, of Esther, of Tobias, in the narrations of Genesis, etc. But this is a question of biblical exegesis, not of liturgy. Liturgically, we must simply assert that whatever is narrated in the Bible, when it is transferred to the liturgy, keeps the sense which it had for the contemporaries.

From this follows a most important rule for the interpretation of the liturgy: The accurate knowledge of the sense which the biblical texts used by the liturgy had for the contemporaries remains always the fundamental presupposition for understanding the use which the liturgy makes of them.

Thus, for example, the first presupposition for understanding in what precise sense the liturgy of the time from Advent to Epiphany interprets the messianic prophecies of Isaias about the future Messiah and about the kingdom of God which was to be established by Him must be above all the exact knowledge of what sense these prophecies had for the contemporaries for whom they were originally written. It is starting from this "sense" that one will have to understand the further "senses" of such prophecies as shown by the liturgy.

When the contemporary Jews (*c.* 550 B.C.) read, "Arise, be enlightened, O Jerusalem" etc. (Is. 60:1-6), they thought of the end of the exile and of a limitless glory of the people of God, whose capital, Jerusalem, under the reign of the Messiah, would become the center of the world. The essence of this interpretation of God's promise made through the mouth of the prophet was quite justified; God really did announce and promise that Israel would be forgiven spiritually, would be liberated from exile in Babylon, and Jerusalem would again become a center of life on earth that was divinely acceptable. The only trouble was that the Jews later concretized this revelation into a material and national ideology, while God intended a much more sublime, spiritual, and universal fulfillment of it, a fulfillment which was verified in the appearance of Jesus on earth (Epiphany) and is verified in mystery every day in the Church, in the Mass, and in souls.

When the liturgy of the Epiphany reads that prophecy in the Mass, it is the whole complexus that is under consideration. The further light which comes to this text with the advent of the Son of God on earth at Bethlehem and every day in the Church at Mass and in the souls of the faithful does not cause the message given Judaisim in exile to evaporate but presupposes it, so that the total theological-liturgical meaning of this text read on the day of Epiphany is this: What God promised and announced to the Jews in exile, namely, that in virtue of the Messiah the people of God would be liberated from their enemies and, resplendent with extraordinary glory, would become the center of the whole world, was indeed verified as if in a first very pale sketch in the end of the Babylonian exile, but in reality had its consummate fulfillment in a manner immensely more sublime than that which the Jews could suspect, with the appearance of the Son of God on earth in Palestine many centuries later and with the sacramental coming of the Son of God every day in the Church, in the Mass, and with His spiritual coming into souls. There is no interruption, therefore, but rather a sublimating continuity between the understanding which the contemporaries had of that oracle and the further insights stressed by the liturgy.

In the same way it must be said that the theological-ascetical interpretation of the psalms in liturgical use, to keep from being arbitrary, must start from the sense of the contemporaries, and the other "senses" must always, in some way, be connected with that original one and be a deepening of it, never foreign to it. Otherwise one would fall into full Hellenistic allegories, with no guarantee that we are still understanding the sacred text in the sense of the author, God. In a word: every interpretation of the Bible, including liturgical interpretation, which would want to abstract from the literal, historical sense, i.e., the meaning originally intended by the inspired author and understood by his contemporaries, would build on emptiness.

4. The Deepening of the "Contemporary or First Perspective" in the Texts of the Old Testament Used by the Liturgy

To understand the use which the liturgy makes of the Bible, we must resolutely affirm that the sense which contemporaries had or could have given to a biblical text at the time of its composition is always surpassed when such a text is used in the liturgy, surpassed precisely by means of that deepening which is obtained by putting the text into relation with the realities which have already taken place in the historical life of the Redeemer in Palestine; with the realities of the Christ-mystery which are verified in a real mystical way every day in souls and above all by way of the liturgy in the present period from the ascension to the parousia; and finally, with the future realities of eschatology about which we are already in some way informed.

Let us illustrate this rule with a series of examples showing the prolongation which the liturgy gives to the sense of the contemporaries. Let us consider first the liturgical use of Old Testament texts accordingly as the concern is with texts which express:

a) doctrinal affirmations about God, His nature and attributes; or about other things, especially about the relations between God and man;

b) moral, juridical, liturgical precepts and admonitions;

c) prophecies properly so called;

d) historical persons, things, and events.

Doctrinal affirmations

If the concern is with texts of the Old Testament which speak, whether under didactic form or under the form of prayer or some other form, of God's attributes, the fact that they have come to be inserted into the Christian liturgical picture and recited by the Church and by the believer in this framework interprets these attributes under a light much more profound than that under which they could possibly appear to the Jews. Actually, a philosophical analysis of such attributes is never made in the Scriptures, but the story of their manifestation through God's action in the world is told. Scripture does not analyze speculatively what wisdom or goodness or power or freedom is in God; rather, it shows God acting in the world with wisdom, goodness, power, and freedom.

Now the record of God's interventions in the world is that sacred salvation history which, as we know, is wholly centered in the mystery of Christ. It is clear, therefore, that with the manifestation of Christ and of the Christian realities, the attributes of God affirmed and sung in the Old Testament appear in the New with a depth unsuspected in the sole light of the Old, but obvious to that of the new reality. That is precisely what happens when the texts of the Old Testament affirming the attributes of God are recited in the liturgy in the further light of the realities of Christ, of the Christian economy, and of the future eschatology.

Thus, for example, in Psalm 135 [Vulgate or liturgical numbering], *Confitemini Domino quoniam bonus* (new translation: *Laudate Dominum quoniam bonus*), in which the refrain *quoniam in aeternum misericordia eius* is constantly interjected, the goodness and mercy of God is exalted as it is manifested in the creation and constitution of the world, in His providence toward His people, in the continual care which He takes of all men. It is clear, however, that when this psalm is sung in the Christian liturgy, this same attribute of the goodness and mercy of God takes on a much more profound meaning than it could have for a Jew.

Indeed, when the Christian says, "Praise the Lord, for He is good, for His mercy endures forever," his thought is not only of the creation and of God's providence toward the Israelite people, which already are notable manifestations of His goodness and mercy; but he recalls also that God has so loved the world as to give His only-begotten Son to save it; that God is charity, Father of the prodigal son and our Father; and that, sinners though we are, He has saved us out of pure mercy and has made us His adoptive sons in Christ and keeps giving us His Spirit. In fact, He has predestined us in Christ and gives us all the graces necessary to lead us to the beatific vision in a peace and happiness which eye has never seen nor ear ever heard, but which God prepares for those who love Him. In this light, which is precisely that of the liturgy, verses like these take on an unprecedented significance:

"Who remembered us in our abjection,*
for His mercy endures forever;
And freed us from our foes,*
for His mercy endures forever;
Who gives food to all flesh,*
for His mercy endures forever.
Praise the God of heaven,*
for His mercy endures forever."

In the same way when the same psalm (vv. 10-22) praises the Lord's eternal mercy in the liberation of the Hebrew people from Egypt and in the care He took of the people until the entrance into the promised land, the Christian recalls that this providential action of God toward the Hebrew people was all directed to the ultimate formation of the Christian people and of the Church, and that he himself forms part of this people, of this Church, which in its turn, is but a preparation and a foreshadowing of the heavenly Jerusalem. Hence here also the refrain "for His mercy endures forever" is illuminated by a much more profound light than could have been that granted to any Hebrew who sang it.

What will this light be, moreover, and what vital force will it take on if the Catholic who sings the psalm is not just a mediocre Catholic content to live in the state of grace while yielding to all sorts of imperfections, but one who has given himself earnestly and entirely to God, to the point of reaching the elevated states of perfection in the ascetical and mystical life, in the intimate experience of the mystery of Christ in himself! Actually this Catholic, in singing this psalm and its refrain, *quoniam in aeternum misericordia eius,* will have before his eyes not only the creative and redemptive economy of God in Christ toward men in general, and not even only toward Christians in general, but also toward himself, here and now, in a most particular manner.

God's attributes will appear to him not only in God's interventions in the world, but also in those interventions of God in himself personally, by which He has loved him, chosen him, purified him, and made him experience His indescribable intimacy, which in its turn is nothing but a pale shadow, a small anticipation, a distant preparation for that more sublime intimacy in the heavenly Jerusalem toward which God is setting him on the way. It is with all these realities, in the most scrupulous respect of the truth and of the one sense of the biblical text, that his chant of *quoniam in aeternum misericordia eius* will be colored. The case of St. Teresa with respect to the verse *misericordias Domini in aeternum cantabo* is well known. We shall have occasion to return again to this matter in treating of the relations between liturgical life and mystical life.

Another example: in Wisdom 10:20-21 one reads of the Hebrews after the crossing of the Red Sea: "Together they praised Your conquering hand, O Lord, because wisdom opened the mouth of the dumb and made eloquent the tongue of infants." And Psalm 97 begins thus: "Sing to the Lord a new song, for He has done wonderful things." Here the power of God shown in freeing His people from their enemies in a marvelous victory is exalted.

In the liturgy these texts for centuries were read alongside each other in the Introit of the Mass of Thursday after Easter and were evidently referred to the neophytes baptized on Holy Saturday. (Since the promulgation of the Pauline Roman Missal, this Introit consists only of the first passage, Wis. 10:20-21). In this context it is not hard to understand how the power of God, praised in these texts according to the sense which they had for the contemporaries, here takes on an immensely more profound sense. For that same power of God which was manifested in freeing His people, first from the Egyptians and then from their other enemies, is manifested in a manner still more surprising in the marvels of baptism, which is, in a more sublime way, for individual men and for the Church, what the liberation from Egypt and from other temporal enemies was for the Hebrews.

In Sirach 24:5-32 there is an encomium on the wisdom of God which is manifested in creation, how God has conceived it and carried it out (vv. 5-12), and especially in the law which He has given to the chosen people (vv. 13-32). The passage begins:

> "I came forth out of the mouth of the Most High, first-born before every creature";

and it ends:

"He who listens to me will not have to blush, and those who act by
using me will not sin; those who put me in the light will have life
eternal. All this is the book of life and the alliance of the Most High,
and the knowledge of truth."

Now, this passage frequently serves as one of the liturgical readings, with
evident reference to our Lady. In this context the sense with which the
encomium on the wisdom of God is colored is this: The wisdom of God,
which was manifested in a marvelous way in the creation of the world and
in the Mosaic law, manifests itself in a still more marvelous way in the Blessed
Virgin Mary. And in fact, one who thinks of the close relationship between
Mary and Christ, the concretized and incarnate Wisdom of God, one who
thinks of the marvels God has wrought in Mary, of the place she has in the
life of Christians, cannot help counting Mary among the most marvelous
works of the divine Wisdom: *beatam me dicent omnes generationes quia fecit
in me magna qui potens est*. There is nothing arbitrary, therefore, in her insertion into the message of scriptural passages which praise the wisdom of
God manifested in creation, in providence, and in the Torah!

Those texts also, so frequent in the Old Testament, in which God the
Creator is spoken of take on a wholly new light from the context in which
they have been inserted when they are read in Catholic liturgy. For the
liturgy, as the New Testament has already done (see Col. 1:15-20), reads the
work of creation in the light of Christ, of His work of redemption, and of
future eschatology, so that the vision of God the Creator which the Jew
could have is different from that which the Christian has.

Hence the oration after the ninth prophecy of Holy Saturday used to say:

"O God all-powerful and eternal, wonderful in the disposition of all
Your works, may those whom You have redeemed understand that the
creation of the world, which took place in the beginning, was not more
excellent than the immolation which Christ, our Passover, accomplished
at the end of the ages."

In the older rite the "first prophecy" was a reading from Genesis, the creation
narrative; now in the Pauline Roman Missal the same passage is the first
reading during the Paschal Vigil service. The oration which formerly was
read after the first prophecy may now be read after the first lesson. The text
of that prayer is: "O God, in a wonderful way You created man, and still
more wonderfully You have redeemed him . . ."; one may add: "still more
marvelously You will glorify him at the parousia."

The Old Testament often speaks of God present among His people, especially in the sanctuary. Very marked is the sign of God's presence in the
sanctuary in the passages of the Second Book of Paralipomenon, where the
erection and dedication of Solomon's temple is related. The deepening of the
sense of these texts is obvious when they are read in the Catholic liturgy for

the dedication of a church — material edifice of the spiritual Church, where God makes Himself present in the Eucharistic sacrifice and where the influx of sanctifying grace (derived from the Eucharist for every soul and which can go as far as the mystical experience of the presence in oneself of the persons of the Trinity) is immensely greater than in the temple of Solomon. In fact, in the Office of the dedication of a church, the continual allusions to the presence, still more extraordinary, of God among the people of the heavenly Jerusalem (see, for example, the responsory to the former eighth lesson, the chapter at Lauds, the hymns *Caelestis urbs Ierusalem* and *Alto ex Olympi vertice*, and the first reading of the Mass: Apoc. 21:1-5) prolong the sense of the texts of 2 Paralipomenon on the presence of God even to the triumphs of the Apocalypse.

The prophets of the Old Testament often sing the tenderness and the greatness of God's love for His people, comparing it to that of a husband for his wife (Osee 1:2; 2:3-15; 4:10-19; Jer. 12:7-9; 31:3; Is. 54:5-8; 62:4 ff; Ezech. 16; 23; Mal. 1:2). The whole Canticle of Canticles, after the fashion of a parable, is simply celebrating this conjugal love between God and Israel. The texts of the Canticle are sometimes read in the liturgy in the votive Mass for religious profession and on the feasts of various saints. Transported into these Catholic surroundings, those texts are read in the light of all those manifestations of the love of God for the Church and the individual souls within the Church, especially for Mary, in whose case the relations between God and Israel were but a pale foreshadowing. And in the background is always the heavenly Jerusalem where the nuptials of the Lamb with the Church and with individual souls will have their perfect fulfillment (Apoc. 19:7-9; 21:2 ff).

God the protector of the just and pious Israelite is very often sung in the psalms and in the sapiential books. These texts are often read by the liturgy in the light of the still more wonderful protections which God has granted the just of the New Testament (see, for example, the readings of the Common of Martyrs outside of Paschaltide).

In short, the Old Testament texts of a doctrinal type in which some attribute of God or something of the relations between the world and God is affirmed, when read in the liturgy, are, as it were, deepened and prolonged by it in the light of the realities present in Christ and in the Church and of the realities proper to the consummation of Christ's redeeming work in the eschatological future.

Precepts and admonitions

The moral, liturgical, juridical precepts and admonitions directed immediately to the Israelites in the Old Testament are often accepted into the New Testament and held valid in the new economy, and hence are repeated also in the liturgy. But it is clear that these precepts and admonitions as read in the liturgy, precisely because they are seen within the great reality of Christ, the Church, and the future consummation at the second coming, are illuminated by a new light.

For example, the commandment of the love of God and of neighbor, in which the whole decalogue is summed up, takes on in the New Testament a depth unsuspected in the Old. Indeed, it now appears that the precise sense of that supreme commandment is none other than that explained by St. John:

> "Consider with what love the Father has loved us, granting that we may be called and may be in fact sons of God. . . . Dearly beloved, we are now sons of God; but what we shall be is not yet manifested. We know that when it is manifested we shall be like Him, because we shall see Him as He is. And whoever has this hope in Him, sanctifies himself, as He too is holy. . . . Whoever is born of God does not commit sin, because he holds in himself a germ of Him. . . . Whoever does not practice justice and does not love his brother is not from God. This is the announcement that you have heard from the beginning, that you love one another. . . . Dearly beloved, let us love one another, because charity is from God. And he that loves is born of God and knows God. He that does not love has not known God, for God is charity. In this is God's love for us made known, that God sent His only-begotten Son into the world, that through Him we may have life. In this is charity, that without our having loved God, He has first loved us, and has sent His Son as propitiation for our sins. Dearly beloved, if God has so loved us, we also ought to love one another. No one has ever seen God. If we love one another, God dwells in us and His charity is perfected. From this do we know that we are in Him and He in us; because He has given us of His Spirit. And we have seen and we testify that the Father has sent His Son, the Savior of the world. Whoever confesses that Jesus is Son of God, God will abide in him and he in God. And we have known and believed in the charity which God has for us. God is charity, and he that abides in charity abides in God, and God in him. *Let us therefore love God, because God has first loved us*" (1 John 3:1–4:19).

Therefore: full continuity with the Old Testament and at the same time unprecedented deepening.

So also the precepts of the Old Testament against impurity are naturally preserved in the new economy, but motivated by an immeasurably more profound light, that explained by St. Paul:

> "Do you not know that our bodies are members of Christ? Shall I then make the members of Christ members of a prostitute? Never! . . . Or do you not know that your body is a temple of the Holy Spirit who is in you, whom you have from God, and that you are not your own? For you have been bought at a great price. Glorify God, therefore, in your body" (1 Cor. 6:15, 19-20).

In the same way the admonitions unto a holy life and good works which the Old Testament makes to the pious Israelite are read in the liturgy in the light of the Sermon on the Mount (Matthew 5:1–7:27) and of the theology of St. Paul and of St. John. In particular the themes of prayer, almsgiving, fasting, so frequent in the Old Testament, are preserved in the new economy, but deepened by the light of the doctrine and the examples of Jesus (Matthew 6:1–7:23): the forty days in the desert, His life of prayer; as well as in the light of the doctrine of grace, of the mystical body, of expiation, of assimilation to Christ.

The necessity of almsgiving is explained thus by St. John:

> "We know that we have been transported from death to life because we love the brethren. He who does not love remains in death. Whoever hates his own brother is a murderer; and you know that no murderer has eternal life abiding in him. From this we know the charity of God, because He has given His life for us; and so we ought to give our life for the brethren. Now if a man has some of the goods of this world and, seeing his brother in need, closes his heart to him, how does the charity of God abide in him? My little children, let us not love in words and with the tongue, but in deed and truth" (1 John 3:14-18).

And it is actually in this spirit that the Old Testament precepts and moral admonitions of a holy life are repeated in the liturgy. Thus it was, for example, when for centuries the decalogue was read in the Epistle of the Mass of Wednesday after the Third Sunday of Lent and of Wednesday after Passion Sunday — days of scrutiny for the catechumens who aspired to baptism on Holy Saturday. Especially in the Mass of Wednesday after the Third Sunday of Lent, the reading of the Gospel (Matthew 15:1-20), with its strong emphasis on the primarily interior basis of the observance of the decalogue, interprets the decalogue itself, read in the Epistle, in the light of the Sermon on the Mount. And many similar examples might be adduced from the liturgy, even in its post-Vatican II forms.

In the same way the continual appeals which the liturgy of Lent makes, with the very words of the Old Testament, to prayer, to fasting, to almsgiving, to penance, to good works in general, have, in the setting of the New Testament and of the liturgy, a much deeper sense than that which they could have had for the Hebrews, seen as they are against the background of the economy of Christ, of Christian existence as described especially by St. Paul and St. John, and of revealed eschatology.

The liturgical precepts of the Old Testament, too, are repeated in the liturgy, with reference to the Christic and ecclesial reality as it is verified in the liturgy itself. Thus, for example, when formerly on Good Friday, and in what was the ninth prophecy of Holy Saturday, there were read the precepts governing the liturgical celebration of the Jewish Passover from Exodus

12:1-11, it was clear that the sense of those liturgical precepts is to be seen against the background of the immolation on Golgotha and of its unbloody re-enactment in the Mass.

The liturgical precepts of Exodus (13:1-3, 11-13) and of Leviticus (12:1-8) concerning the presentation of the first-born in the temple, which are read in the breviary liturgy of February 2, are read with reference to the historical fact of the presentation of Jesus in the temple and to the real mystical fact of His sacramental coming in the Mass.

Very appropriately, therefore, did the former antiphon of the Candlemas procession, still recited in part in the first responsory after the first lesson of the breviary, proclaim: "Adorn your bridal chamber, O Sion" (understand Jerusalem and the Church), "and receive Christ the King. Welcome Mary with love; she is the gate of heaven. For she carries the King of glory, the new light. The Virgin stops, presenting in her arms the Son, begotten before the dawn. Simeon receives Him in his arms and to the nations heralds the Lord of life and death and Savior of the world."

Or the entrance antiphon: "We have received Your mercy, O God, in the midst of Your temple; as Your name, O God, so also Your praise goes even to the ends of the earth. Your right hand is full of justice."

It is proper also that the Catholic worshipper think of the full realization of these realities in the heavenly Jerusalem.

Prophecies properly so called

The continuance of the first or original message of the prophecies properly so called of the Old Testament when used in the liturgy is easy enough to understand; we have given an example of it above. Actually, any prophecy properly so called from the Old Testament in its essence touches upon the messianic work, the Messiah, or His reign in the last times, the eschatological era of history; or at least, among the prophecies properly so called of the Old Testament, it is this aspect that interests the New Testament and the Church.

Now, according to the New Testament, the Messiah of prophecy is Christ Jesus; and with Him begin the last eschatological times of which the prophets spoke. These eschatological times are not yet completed, but are still in progress; they will be completed perfectly in the second coming of Christ, in the parousia, and in the final, definitive establishment of the kingdom of God.

Thus, theologically speaking, the prophecies of the Old Testament about the Messiah and His kingdom, besides the message which they could convey to their first or original audience, can and should have, as it were, three further levels of deepened meaning, three further stages of integral realization, in the light of which the fundamental sense perceived by contemporary Israelites is prolonged and deepened: the level of Christ's historical life; the level of the real mystical realization of the mystery of Christ in souls and in the Church by means both liturgical (chiefly the sacrifice and the sacraments) and extraliturgical (as takes place every day in the present phase from the ascension to the parousia); and the level of final eschatology.

In the liturgy the prophecies of the Old Testament about the Messiah and His kingdom are important principally in the period from Advent to the Epiphany, the season during which the mystery of Christ, in its complete unfolding from the beginning of the world to the Apocalypse, is seen in the perspective of the Lord's epiphanic coming.

Secondarily, these oracles have a certain importance also in the Quadragesima-Pentecost period, the time during which the whole mystery of Christ is once more viewed in perspective, but from the viewpoint of redemption. Some particular feasts, such as those of the Immaculate Conception and of the Sacred Heart, may be added for consideration here.

In the Advent-Epiphany period, precisely because the primary objective is the unfolding of the mystery of Christ as that of the coming of the Lord, the scriptural background, particularly abundant in the breviary, is constituted of Isaian prophecies on the future Messiah, His coming, and His kingdom. Now, the sense which these prophecies had for Isaias and his contemporaries undergoes a continual transposition in the liturgy by way of deepening, because they are seen in the light of Christ's historical coming on earth in Palestine, of His continual real mystical coming in souls, in the Church, in the sacrifice of the Mass, in the sacraments, in the private life of every Christian soul, and finally in the light of His future second coming at the end of time.

Thus when the Roman liturgy on the Fourth Sunday of Advent recites the entrance antiphon, "Drop down your dew, O heavens, from on high, and let the clouds rain down the just one; let the earth open and bud forth the Savior" (Is. 45:8), this is indeed the cry of the Jews who, in the exile of Babylon, awaited the coming of the Messiah, liberation by the hand of Cyrus (see the former fourth lesson in the Office of Ember Saturday in Advent), and the establishment of the kingdom of God — all things which God was promising by the mouth of His prophet.

But in the vision of the liturgy, Is. 45:8 is also the cry of the whole Old Testament for the coming of Christ, an event realized by the incarnation of the Son of God and His birth of the Virgin Mary in Palestine. Is. 45:8 is also the cry of every Catholic who annually awaits the feast of Christmas, in fact, who each day awaits Christ's sacramental coming in the sacrifice of the Mass and His mystical advent into the soul. And it is, finally, the cry of this same individual as he awaits the second and triumphal coming of the Lord in the parousia and the beatific vision.

It is for this reason that in the collect of the vigil Mass of Christmas, the Roman liturgy can summarize the spirit of Advent and of the Isaian prophecies in the words: "You gladden us, O Lord, with the annual expectation of our redemption. Joyfully do we welcome Him also with a tranquil conscience when He comes as Judge."

In the same Mass of the Christmas Vigil there is read as communion antiphon the following passage from Isaias: "The glory of the Lord will be made manifest, and every living being will see the salvation by our God." This passage, in the sense here given it by the Roman liturgy, refers simultaneously:

1) to the Jews of the Old Testament who were awaiting the messianic liberation which God would grant to them and to the whole world with the incarnation of the Son of God and His birth of the Virgin Mary;

2) to the Catholics who daily await the sacramental coming of the same Son of God in the sacrifice of Mass and in Communion, and His mystical coming into the interior of their souls, and who annually await the feast of His nativity on Christmas Day;

3) to the same Catholics who hope for heaven and the parousia with the definitive, cosmic, and glorious establishment of the kingdom of God.

The same may be said of the text of Isaias 30:30, which begins the Roman formulary on the Second Sunday of Advent: "People of Sion! See, the Lord will come to save all the nations! The Lord will make the majesty of His voice heard, flooding your hearts with gladness." The reference of this text to the coming of Christ in the Mass and on the feast of Christmas is underlined by the Roman liturgy in the opening prayer of the Mass on the following Thursday: "Arouse our hearts, O Lord, and prepare the ways of Your Only-begotten, that through His coming we may serve You with purified souls."

The eschatological perspective of these prophetic texts from Isaias is emphasized by the liturgy at the very beginning of this liturgical season in that the Mass of the First Sunday of Advent throughout the three-year cycle features Gospel texts in which the Lord speaks of the end of the world and of His second coming at the end of time (Matthew 24:37-44; Mark 13:33-37; or Luke 21:25-28, 34-36).

In the Quadragesima-Pentecost liturgical period, Old Testament prophecy properly so called certainly has a lesser significance than it has in the Advent-Epiphany period. During this Quadragesima-Pentecost season the Old Testament, as will be seen later, is considered in its typological dimension as prefigurative of the mystery of redemption rather than in its dimension of prophecy properly so called of the same mystery. Nevertheless, even in this period three prophecies are stressed:

1) Psalm 21 (liturgical or Vulgate numbering), *Deus, Deus meus, respice*

in me, quare me dereliquisti?, read as the refrain in the responsorial psalm in the Mass of Passion [Palm] Sunday;

2) the Isaian prophecy on the "servant of Yahweh," read in the Masses of Passion [Palm] Sunday (Is. 50:4-7) and on Good Friday (Is. 52:13-53:12).

3) the prophecy of Joel (2:28-32), recalled in the discourse of St. Peter on Pentecost day and read in the Mass of the Vigil of Pentecost, as well as in various places in the Divine Office in the week following Pentecost.

The two prophecies of Psalm 21 and of the "servant of Yahweh" are concerned with the suffering and redeeming Messiah; and in each of them there is a brief hint at His triumph and at the marvelous fruits of His work. In the light of the historical presence of Christ, of the details of His Passion, death, and resurrection, of the revelation of His divinity, of the spiritual nature and of the universality of the redemption, the ultimate fruit of which is the heavenly Jerusalem, it is clear how much the liturgy, in the understanding of these prophecies, transcends the meaning originally germane to these passages.

In this light, then, we can see something of the new perspective given to verses such as the following: "You who fear the Lord, praise Him! Offspring of Jacob, glorify Him, all of you. A future offspring shall speak of the Lord, and the heavens shall declare His justice, for what He has done for the people to come" (Ps. 21:24, 32). The future offspring which the liturgy is thinking of here is the Church and the heavenly Jerusalem.

"The Lord God is my helper, and therefore I have not been confounded; therefore have I made my face as a very hard stone, and I know that I shall not be confounded. He who judges me is near at hand. Who will declare himself against me?" (Is. 50:7-8). This passage the liturgy reads in the light of clear faith in the divinity of Christ and of what He Himself said: "I lay down My life that I may take it up again. No one takes it from Me, but I lay it down of Myself. I have the power to lay it down and the power to take it up again. This is the command given Me by the Father. . . . I and the Father are one" (John 10:17-18, 30). It is evident that the liturgy reads the prophecy of Is. 53:1-12 in the framework of St. Paul's Letter to the Philippians (2:5-11) and of the First Letter of Peter (2:21-25).

In what sense the liturgy understands the prophecy of Joel on the gift of the Spirit of God to the faithful during messianic times (Joel 2:28-32) is made clear in the interpretation given it by St. Peter (Acts 2:15-21) and, in general, by the doctrine of St. Paul on the gift of the Spirit bestowed upon Christians, on the Spirit's role in the life which they are to lead, on the future glorification of the body in the resurrection as ultimate fruit of His presence in us (see, for example, Rom. 8 in its entirety).

Among the particular feasts on which the reading of the prophecies properly so called of the Old Testament has some importance should be noted: the Immaculate Conception and the reading of Genesis 3:15ff both in the breviary and as the first reading in the Mass: ". . . I will place enmity between you and the woman, and between your offspring and her offspring; he shall bruise your head, and you shall bruise his heel." The passage, even as understood by its Yahwist author and his contemporaries, presents a prophetic announcement of the Redeemer to be born of woman and of the victory which the human race through Him will win over the power of evil, the cause of man's first fall. Obvious to all is the resplendent light with which this oracle shines in the liturgy, which reads it in the context of the revelation on Mary as the Mother of God and on her Immaculate Conception. Hence the liturgy can comment, "Through a man sin has entered into this world, and by sin, death — in which all have sinned. Fear not, Mary! You have found grace before God" (responsory after the first lesson, and, in part, the Gospel reading of the Mass).

On the feast of the Sacred Heart, the readings of the Roman Breviary placed notable emphasis during the Office of Readings on the prophecies of Jeremias concerning the establishment of a new and eternal pact between God and the people at the time of the Messiah, a pact founded on God's love for the people and the sincere response of the same people to the love of God. These prophecies obviously assumed a new and profound meaning, read as they were by the liturgy, in the light of the revelation of God-love in Christ as it appears in St. Paul and in St. John, and of the Church as God's new people ever pilgrimaging their way to the heavenly Jerusalem. In the Liturgy of the Hours, supplanting the Roman Breviary, the feast is retained, but the reading is from St. Paul.

The meaning of persons, things, historical events, institutions. Typology

The deeper sense by means of which the New Testament and the liturgy surpass the simple sense which the contemporaries gave to certain texts of the Old Testament, when the concern is with the meaning attached to persons, things, historical events, institutions, has a special name, already used, though not exclusively, in respect to the New Testament, and which today is ever more universally accepted: it is called the *typological sense*. It is necessary to examine this special case more closely.

Typology in the Bible is a certain relation, as of roughcast and complement, which God has placed between two things in which He has intended to concretize successively one and the same aspect of the mystery of Christ, so that the antecedent object has the character of imperfect realization and, as it were, of sketch of that which will be more perfectly fulfilled in the subsequent thing.

The antecedent thing is the type: a first expression, a first roughcast, an initial prefigurative sketch. The subsequent thing is the antitype: the more perfect and more complete realization of the same objective. Between the type and the antitype, therefore, there is in the eyes of God an intrinsic relation of preparation and prefiguration: in realizing the antecedent thing God already had in view the subsequent thing. Thus it is clear that the full significance or whole *raison d'être* of the type in the historical development of the mystery of Christ cannot be understood except in reference to the antitype.

In typology, then, there is a thing which prepares, prefigures, and roughs out another thing, with a view to a successive and ever more perfect realization of the mystery of Christ. This "thing" may be a person, an inanimate thing, an event, a relationship or an institution. Typology presupposes the unity of the two testaments and of sacred history as it has been explained at the beginning of this chapter. It expresses this unity of sacred history in the mystery of Christ not only by means of an ever greater deepening of the total value of general abstract, doctrinal, moral, or prophetical statements, but by means of an intrinsic, preparative and prefigurative relation of one phenomenon to another.

The existence of typology in principle between the Old and the New Testaments is absolutely certain. The process appears already in the prophets, with whom there is seen the tendency to interpret the past events of Israel's history as a function of future events awaited. Past events are considered as preparing, announcing, and prefiguring future realities which be verified in the days of the Messiah. In fact, the thought of the prophets is that in the messianic era the more memorable events of Israel's ancient story will be renewed in some way, yet not in a mechanical and material repetition, but, as it were, in a more sublime and wonderful transposition.

It is above all else the story of the Exodus, the departure from Egypt and the entrance into the promised land, which is considered in this light (see, for example, Is. 11:11-12:6; 43:16-21; Jer. 23:7ff; 31:31-33). Thus the essential lines of the history of ancient Israel, besides preserving their function of delineating past historical reality, take on a further dimension of first imperfect realization of what God will do in messianic times. Then there will be, in a manner much more marvelous and sublime than that which took place at the first Exodus, a new passage through the sea, a new march of the people through the desert, new living waters gushing from the rock, a new luminous column of clouds, and especially a new and eternal covenant. This tendency is especially strong in later Judaism and finds its full development in the New Testament.

The great new announcement which the New Testament addresses to the Jews is simply this: Whatever had been prepared, announced, prefigured as in a first sketch in the Old Testament has now been fulfilled in the person of Christ and in Christians. The books of the New Testament are full of this idea.[5] St. Paul explicitly formulates the theory of it. It is his concept of the fullness of times (Gal. 4:4; Eph. 1:10); of the law as instructor which leads to Christ (Gal. 3:24; Rom. 10:4); of Christianity, goal toward which all previous history was tending (1 Cor. 10:11); of the true Israel which God had in mind already when He occupied Himself with the historical Israel (Gal. 6:16); of the true sons of Abraham in whom the promises made to him are fulfilled (Rom. 9:7ff). And, of course, we must not omit the concept of the law as first and prefigurative roughcast of the new economy (Heb. 10:1).

In these general themes, which express the continuative unity of the two testaments and of all history, typology properly so called has a most important place: the Old Testament not only prepares for and announces the New by means of a chronological succession or by means of theoretical doctrines and statements; but in the Old Testament, things, persons, and events have also the dimension of first imperfect and prefigurative realizations of things, persons, and events of the new economy.

This relation between realities of the Old Testament and realities of the New is explicitly referred to as *typos* and *antítypos* in four cases:

1) relation between Adam and Christ (Rom. 5:14);

2) relations between events of the Exodus and Christian life (1 Cor. 10:6);

3) relations between the priesthood and the liturgy of the tabernacle and the temple on the one hand, and the priesthood and the sacrifice of Christ on the other; the sanctuary of the temple and the sanctuary of heaven (Heb. 9:24; cf. 9–10:8);

4) relations between Noah's ark and baptism (1 Peter 3:21).

It would be arbitrary to say that these are the only passages of certain typological interpretation in the New Testament. Actually, in many other texts, without using the words *typos* or *antítypos*, the New Testament interprets the meaning of things, persons, and events of the Old Testament with an identical process, or one so similar as to make it exceedingly difficult to see what is the difference from the preceding cases. Thus, looking closely at things, it is impossible to escape the impression that in the New Testament the process of typological interpretation is really used on a broad scale.

Here are some examples which I have been able to discern:

1) the manna (and the water from the rock) — the Eucharist (John 6:48-58; see 1 Cor. 10:3);

2) the three days of Jonas in the belly of the whale — the resurrection of Christ after three days (Matthew 12:39); although here, perhaps, it is a question of a special case;

3) Elias — John the Baptist (Matthew 17:12);

[5] See L. Goppelt, *Typos: Die typologische Deutung des Alten Testaments im Neuen,* 1939; P. Lestringant, *Essai sur l'unité de la révélation biblique,* Paris 1943; P. van den Ploeg, "L'ancien testament dans l'épître aux hébreux," in *Revue biblique,* 1947, pp. 187ff.

4) Paschal lamb — Christ (Matthew 26:28 and parallel passages; 1 Cor. 5:7; see Exod. 24:8; Jer. 31:31; Zach. 9:11; Heb. 9:19ff);

5) the serpent in the desert — Christ on the Cross (John 3:14);

6) earthly Jerusalem — Church — heavenly Jerusalem (Gal. 4:25-27; Heb. 11:10; 12:22; 13:14; Apoc. 3:12; 11:2; 20:9);

7) the old covenant — the new testament (Matthew 26:28; 2 Cor. 3:6, 14; Gal. 4:24; Heb. 7:22; 8:8ff 9:15; 10:29; 13:20);

8) Moses — Christ (John 6:32; 1:17; Acts 7:37; 1 Cor. 10:2; Heb. 3:2ff; 11:26);

9) David — Christ (Acts 2:25ff);

10) Jacob and Esau — Christians and Jews (Rom. 9);

11) Jewish ascetical observances and feasts — Christ and Christian realities (Col. 2:16-23).

The existence and the legitimacy of the typological interpretation having been established in principle, the further question, which is of great interest today, is to know what are the precise laws which permit us, in a particular determinate case, to establish with surety and without becoming in any way arbitrary, how far the typological relation between a reality of the Old Testament and a reality of the New Testament extends in its details. For it is evident that, even while revalidating the principle of typological interpretation against the scientistic philological exaggerations which have predominated through the last century,[6] we dare not in any way relapse into the no less evidently arbitrary exaggerations into which many of the Fathers fell, and especially medieval authors, even when starting out from the right principle of typological interpretation.

The question has been the object of various studies.[7] The surest practical rule is simply to confine oneself to those cases of typology clearly attested by the Scriptures or at least hinted at in Scripture. And the principal reason is this: typology is a relationship of preparation and prefiguration between two things in different phases of sacred history, a relationship intrinsic to the things themselves because God Himself has placed it in them; hence it depends essentially on the divine creative intention and free will, and we cannot know it with certainty if God has not in some way manifested it to us.[8]

The authority of the Fathers in this field is decisive as to faith only if, according to all the general criteria of theology, it fulfills the conditions of moral unanimity so as to impose the things as being of the faith. In fact, according to general theological methodology, this moral unanimity is neces-

---

[6] C. Charlier, *La lecture chrétienne de la bible*, 4th ed., Maredsous 1951, pp. 6ff.

[7] This is precisely what the two works of Cardinal Daniélou, *Sacramentum futuri* and *The Bible and the Liturgy* are aiming at in large part.

[8] This is also what the encyclical *Divino afflante Spiritu* says; see the *Acta Apostolicae Sedis*, Vol. 35, (1943), p. 311.

sary if an apodictic argument is to be drawn from the Fathers alone, so as
to assert that a thing is to be believed and accepted as of the faith. These
conditions of moral unanimity will be difficult to verify for those cases which
are not already clearly proposed by the Scriptures themselves. With this in
mind, it is not at all sufficient to show that some typology has been affirmed
by one or even by various Fathers, or that it is affirmed in some text of a
historical or present-day liturgy, in order to be able to conclude at once
that this typology is to be considered a matter of faith.

On the other hand, to know the thinking of the Fathers about the typological interpretation of some passage of Scripture or of the liturgy will be
very useful in every case for understanding the symbolic meaning which
they attached to it, although it does not follow that this meaning must be
considered a matter of faith. In this regard the works of Cardinal Daniélou,
Sacramentum futuri and *The Bible and the Liturgy*, will be found very useful.

At any rate, the use of typology in the liturgy is quite abundant; but, by
observing things attentively, one will note that, as a rule, the Roman liturgy
confines itself to the cases already very clear, or relatively clear, in the New
Testament. Thus it is easy to find there the cases previously listed. Some few
examples will suffice:

On the passage through the Red Sea as a type of baptism, see the liturgy
of the Paschal Vigil, the oration after the third reading, and the blessing of
the baptismal water; the entrance antiphons of the Masses of Thursday,
Friday, and Saturday in the octave of Easter.

On the typology of the Eucharist, see the Mass and the Office of Corpus
Christi. On the flood as a type of baptism, see again the blessing of the
baptismal water in the liturgy of the Paschal Vigil. On the entrance into
the promised land as a type of baptism and entrance into the Church, see
the entrance antiphon of Easter Monday. On Elias as a type of John the
Baptist, see the feast of June 24, the Gospel passage read in the Vigil Mass
(Luke 1:5-17). On the typology Esau-Jacob, Ishmael-Isaac, and Jews-Chris-
tians, see the Masses of the Saturday after the Second Sunday of Lent and of
the Fourth Sunday of Lent in the pre-Pauline Roman Missal. On the typology earthly Jerusalem-Church-heavenly Jerusalem, see the Mass and the
whole Office of the dedication of a church. On the serpent in the desert as a
type of Christ on the Cross, see the feast of the Exaltation of the Cross on
September 14, *passim.*

Besides these cases of typology of biblical origin, the liturgy adds a certain
number of patristic origin, some of which, however, can easily be considered
as a simple development of elements already contained in the New Testament. Concerning our Lady, the liturgy develops a whole typology which is
not explicitly scriptural: Eve-Mary, a theme very much developed in the

patristic tradition [9] and connected in some way with Gen. 3:15, the promise of a Redeemer to be born of a woman; Judith-Mary; Esther-Mary. See on the feasts of our Lady the many texts taken from the books of Judith and Esther. The typology of the Eucharist is developed especially by means of the elements: sacrifice of Isaac-Eucharist,[10] sacrifice of Melchisedech-Eucharist.[11] That of baptism is developed, for example, by means of the theme: earthly paradise-baptism.[12] From the Fifth Sunday of Lent to Good Friday the characterization of Jeremias as a type of Christ is greatly developed in the liturgy.[13]

5. The Texts of the New Testament in the Liturgy: Their Deepening

The use of the texts of the Old Testament and the use of those of the New Testament in the liturgy present two rather different cases because their liturgical interpretation is made under two different perspectives. Actually the sense which the contemporaries for whom they were immediately written could see in the texts of the New Testament is already, under a certain aspect, their exhaustive sense. We who live today and read those texts are not, with respect to the immediate disciples of the Apostles, in such a substantially different situation as were the Apostles themselves with respect to the ancient Jews, as far as the understanding of the Old Testament was concerned.

From the time when the texts of the New Testament were written to the present day, nothing substantially new has happened in the mystery of Christ, sacred history, since, after the Apostles, there has not been nor will there be any new public revelation in the Church. The unfolding of salvation history to the very moment of the parousia does not therefore involve any event which may permit the contemporaries to see the texts of the New Testament in a substantially new light and depth comparable to that new light which the coming of Christ and of the Church brought to the comprehension of the Old Testament.

And yet, under another aspect, it is true enough that the texts of the New Testament read today in the liturgy are illuminated by a light wholly their

[9] See "*La nouvelle Eve*," parts 1 and 2, in *Études mariales. Bulletin de la soc. mariale franç.*, 1954 and 1955; and also Jean Card. Daniélou, "*La typologie de la femme dans l'Ancien Testament*," in *La vie spirituelle*, 1949, pp. 491-510.

[10] See Jean Card. Daniélou, *Sacramentum futuri*, pp. 97ff.

[11] See Jean Card. Daniélou's *The Bible and the Liturgy*, pp. 142ff. The sacrifice of Melchisedech as a type of the Eucharist is basically indicated already by the Scriptures in the Melchisedech-Christ typology.

[12] See Jean Card. Daniélou's *Sacramentum futuri*, pp. 13ff; as also his articles "*Terre et paradis chez les Pères de l'Église*," in *Eranos Jahrbuch*, Vol. 22 (1953), pp. 433-472, and "*Catechèse paschale et retour au paradis*," in *La maison Dieu*, no. 45 (1956), pp. 99-119. This typology also, "earthly paradise-baptism," has a scriptural basis in the Adam-Christ typology.

[13] This typology is already sufficiently hinted at by the Scriptures where Christ is presented as "the just one" and "the prophet" *par excellence*.

own. This light which is their own and is in some way new proceeds from three sources.

It proceeds first of all from the unfolding of ecclesiastical history and of the life of the Church as it has been fulfilled from the Apostles to the present day. This unfolding permits us to understand, under a certain aspect, more deeply than the contemporaries of the Apostles the precise import of some texts of the New Testament. Thus, for example, the growth of the Church lets us understand better the sense of the parable of the grain of mustard seed (Matthew 13:31ff and parallel passages), of the leaven (*ibid.*, 33ff), of the weeds (*ibid.*, 24ff), and in general the doctrine on the Church itself. Thus these passages, read in the liturgy (see the Gospel reading for the Sixteenth Sunday of the Year [Cycle A], and the Gospel readings for Saturday of the Sixteenth Week and for Monday and Tuesday of the Seventeenth Week of the Year), are illuminated by the experience of the history of the Church.

Another source of new light even more abundant is the evolution or successive explicitation of the dogmas and doctrines of the Church as it is admitted in the Catholic Church. For by the light of the doctrines clarified and the dogmas evolved and defined, many texts of the New Testament take on a depth of significance which the contemporaries of the Apostles certainly did not see with such precision.

Thus, for example, the doctrine of the Immaculate Conception, fully known in modern times, illuminates with a more profound light a phenomenon which the contemporaries of the Apostles certainly did not see with such clarity — the meaning of the angel's salutation to Mary: "Hail, full of grace! The Lord is with you!" (Luke 1:28). This text, by the simple fact of its being read in the liturgy of the feast of the Immaculate Conception (Gospel of the Mass), receives a very clarifying commentary.

The text of the Apocalypse on the woman crowned with twelve stars also receives a commentary all its own by the simple fact of its being recited as the first reading in the Mass of the feast of the Assumption of Mary, which is the feast of her triumph in heaven, body and soul.

And, in general, the development of the Marian dogmas is illuminated with the marvelous light of Mary's *Magnificat*: "My soul magnifies the Lord, and my spirit rejoices in God, my Savior, for He has regarded the lowliness of His handmaid. For behold, henceforth all generations shall call me blessed, because He that is mighty has done great things for me. . . . He has shown strength with His arm, . . . He has cast down the mighty from their thrones and has exalted the lowly" (Luke 1:46ff).

Similarly the development of the dogmas of the primacy and of the infallibility of the Roman Pontiff show forth in all their meaning the significance of the words of Jesus to Peter, "You are Peter, and upon this rock I will build My Church, and the gates of hell shall not prevail against it. . . . Whatever you bind on earth shall be bound in heaven, and whatever you loose on earth shall be loosed in heaven." These words, read as the Gospel pericope in Masses in honor of supreme pontiffs (*Lectionary*, no. 724, 1), are commented on by the very frame into which they are inserted by the liturgy.

A third and most abundant light which several texts of the New Testament receive from the liturgy is their reference to the liturgical action in which *hic et nunc* they are inserted, and hence to the personal situation of the believer who in this moment lives this same liturgical action. Thus, many texts of the New Testament, whether the concern be with historical texts on the life of our Lord or of the primitive Church, or whether it be with doctrinal texts or with admonitions of the Christian life, come out of the abstract sphere of simple past history or of doctrinal admonition in general and become personal realities present and operating in me at this moment.

This actualization of the sense of the texts of the New Testament is possible only in the liturgy because only the liturgy is wholly centered in the sacrifice, the sacraments, and the sacramentals; and in them, in a way which is mysterious and, while different in different situations, always nonetheless real, there is made present either Christ Himself in person (the Eucharist) or His redemptive power.

As we have seen, the liturgy in some way, *in sacramento*, makes present the whole mystery of Christ, sacred history, realizing it in individual souls. Now all the texts of the New Testament and the things of which they speak do nothing but express, under some aspect, this mystery of Christ, sacred history. It is for this reason that the liturgy actualizes the sense of the texts of the New Testament of which it makes use.

Thus, for example, the historical passages of the New Testament on the birth of our Lord, on the epiphany, on the resurrection, on the ascension, on Pentecost, read in the liturgy of the respective feasts, in the liturgical frame in which they are read, have not only the significance of a purely historical commemoration of the event, now past, to which they refer, but have also in the liturgical action the significance of a present application to each of the faithful of the value and redemptive fruit of that event. Thus the redemptive power of these events is in its own way newly actualized and prolonged because it is newly applied. Therefore it can be said that these events, in the liturgy, are really re-actualized, not as historical events (as if, for example, the Mass of Christmas renewed the nativity of our Lord in the same way that every Mass renews, in its own way unbloodily, the sacrifice of Golgotha), but in their redemptive power.

In this sense it is rightly said that the feast of Christmas involves in the soul of each individual believer who takes part in it with the correct dispositions an ever-renewed birth of Christ; the Epiphany, an ever-renewed manifestation of Christ; the Resurrection, an ever-renewed participation in His divine life; the Ascension, an ever-renewed participation in His glory at the Father's side; Pentecost, an ever new coming of the Spirit into the heart of the believer.

Thus when there is read in the liturgy on Christmas day, "In those days a decree went out from Caesar Augustus that all the world should be enrolled. . . . And [Mary] gave birth to her first-born Son and wrapped Him in swaddling clothes and laid Him in a manger," the sense of this reading is not only to recall the historical fact which happened in Palestine, but also to assert that that fact, in its redemptive power, is actualized today in every individual believer who takes part with the proper dispositions in the liturgical action which is going on. Thus Luke's narrative does not speak of a simple historical fact like other historical facts, which have no real contact with me and with what I am doing at this moment. That of which Luke speaks is a living reality which touches me personally. We participate for the first time and radically in the redemptive power of Christ's nativity in baptism; then, throughout our life we assimilate to ourselves that redemptive power more and more in participation in the sacrifice, the sacraments, the liturgical life of the Church and our extraliturgical Christian life.

The like may be said of all the other liturgical feasts which refer to historical events in which our redemption is realized. Every Holy Week is for us a further dying and a further rising in Christ. The narrative of the descent of the Holy Spirit on the Apostles, recounted in the first reading of the Mass on Pentecost, in the liturgical frame in which it is read, at the same time that it records the past historical event, proclaims its mystical sacramental realization in the souls of the faithful in the liturgical action.

The reference of the New Testament texts used by the liturgy and containing some moral admonition is clearly in view of the present liturgical action as well as of the personal situation of the believer who is participating in that liturgical action. For example: on Easter Sunday the second reading of the Mass is (optionally) from St. Paul's Epistle to the Colossians (3:1-4): "If you have risen with Christ, seek the things that are above, where Christ is seated at the right hand of God. Set your mind on the things that are above, not on the things that are of earth. For you have died, and your life is hidden with Christ in God. When Christ, your life, appears, then you also will appear with Him in glory."

The sense of this passage is not a simple repetition of what St. Paul was writing to the Colossians. But, by reason of the fact that this passage is read in the Easter Mass to the faithful who, whether the day before or a longer time before, have received baptism and confirmation and are now about to participate in the Eucharistic sacrifice, St. Paul's admonitions are considered as directed personally to the faithful here present. They refer to their baptism, either recent or in the more distant past, to their participation in the Eucharist, to the obligations which are derived from it, and to the certain hope which each of them personally has of reaching the goal of all life, which is glory together with Christ and in His likeness. It is not only the history of the Colossians which is here placed in perspective for me, but my personal situation while I participate in the liturgical action at this moment on Easter Sunday.

It is to me personally that another admonition of St. Paul is addressed, and which, like the one just considered, serves optionally as the second reading of the Mass on Easter Sunday: "Throw out the old leaven, that you may be a new dough, as you really are unleavened; for Christ, our Passover, has been sacrificed. Therefore let us celebrate the feast, not with the old leaven, the leaven of malice and wickedness, but with the unleavened bread of sincerity and truth" (1 Cor. 5:7-8).

It is just as clear that all the other passages of the New Testament read in the liturgy and referring to a moral teaching of Jesus or of the Apostles, or which describe the realities of the supernatural life which take place in every Christian, are read as addressed to each of the faithful present at the liturgical action. Thus, for example, the Sermon on the Mount (see in the *Lectionary* the numerous places where pericopes from Matthew 5–7 are read; and in particular, on the feast of All Saints, when the Beatitudes are read — with the further implication that these precepts and admonitions have been, as it were, the way which has led the saints to their glory). So also when on the Sixth Sunday of Easter (Cycle C) there is read the Gospel passage in which Jesus promises the coming of the Spirit and explains the conditions necessary for receiving Him and the effects of His coming (John 14:23-29): "If a man loves Me, he will keep My word, and My Father will love him, and We shall come to him and make our home with him . . ." — all this the liturgy interprets as addressed to each of the faithful present.

* * *

From the simple hints given in this chapter on the use of the Bible in the liturgy, it is seen how important it is to take account of the theological laws which apply.

From what we have said, the fact is made perfectly evident that the Church is living out a sacred history, just as revelation emerges primarily in sacred history. The Christocentrism of the liturgy becomes most vivid. Sacred history is the mystery of Christ, in Christ Himself and in His faithful. Christ appears as the pivot of the whole liturgy, of the whole Bible, of all history, of the whole life of the believer.

The perfect unity of the two testaments and of all history is found again precisely in the mystery of Christ, read in the Bible and realized in liturgical action.

The vitality and the presentness of the entire Bible is found not artificially but really, and in respect also to that which modern critical research has contributed to this study. The Scripture is no longer a simple history without connection with my personal situation *hic et nunc*. I am immersed in this immense dynamic current; the Bible is my history as I now live it in the liturgical action, as I live it outside the liturgy, as I shall live it eschatologically. I can understand myself only through the Bible in the liturgical action.

This liturgical reading of the Bible is the specifically Christian reading of the Scriptures. It is the only reading which brings into play all the meaning which Scripture has in the eyes of its principal Author. It is the theological reading of the Bible. The philological, critical reading, which by definition intends to confine itself to the sense of the contemporaries, is legitimate, useful, necessary, since every further reading must take its start from this; but such a reading is partial and incomplete.

The liturgical reading of the Bible is the biblical catechesis of the Church. The ignorance among the faithful of the mystery of Christ as it is taught in the Bible, the fact that they no longer live it, certainly proceeds in large part from the ignorance of the liturgy, from the fact that they no longer live the liturgy.

The aforesaid liturgical method of reading the Bible, which is the method in which it was read by Christ, by the Apostles, by the original Christian catechesis, by the Fathers of the Church, penetrated so deeply into the minds of the ancient and medieval faithful that ancient and medieval Christian iconography (and in part that too of the Renaissance) is incomprehensible without it.[14] There it is that the union of theology, Bible, liturgy, culture, and art is, as it were, made a tangible unity.

[14] A specialist, L. de Bruyne, has been able to write of ancient Christian art: "Aside from some representations borrowed directly from profane art (Orpheus, Amor and Psyche, etc.) and apart from symbolic signs, decorative motifs, and reminders of the earthly life, the repertory of this art is composed of symbolic figures and historical, allegorical, and representative scenes, *every one of them designed to evoke and illustrate Christ the Savior and the work of salvation prepared for in the Old Testament, done during Christ's earthly life, continued after His death by the Church and crowned in the life of beatitude.* . . . After peace came to the Church, Christian art developed freely in monumental compositions at the direct service of the liturgy and of the education of the faithful. The technique of the mosaic secured it a splendor which was often secular. Even while being fully aware of its new task, it does not deny its original basic character, and remains essentially symbolic. In the baptistries and the *martyria*, as well as in the basilicas, its cycles of biblical scenes, apparently only narrative, reveal better and better that the choice and the distribution of their scenes obey symbolic or typological laws. Thus they form a natural transition between the primitive symbolism of the catacombs and the true concordances of the Old and the New Testament as the Middle Ages will know them" (from the article *"Arte cristiana antica,"* in *Enciclopedia cattolica,* Vol. 2 (1949), cols. 48ff.

15 REMARKS ON THE CENTRAL THEMES OF THE INDIVIDUAL PSALMS AND THEIR REFERENCE TO THE MYSTERY OF CHRIST IN THE LITURGY

The manner in which the psalms are used in the liturgy deserves a detailed study, both by reason of the abundance of this use, especially in the breviary, and by reason of the special difficulties which are encountered in understanding their meaning as intended by the liturgy. I shall limit myself to a few reflections, intended more directly to clarify the general principles which, in the liturgy, govern the prolongation or deepening or transposition, if you wish, of the sense of the contemporaries in the psalms to the Christic, ecclesial, and eschatological realities, as well as the realities peculiarly personal to the individual who recites the psalms — in other words, to the mystery of Christ understood in its full extension.

1. The Consideration of the Psalms from the Point of View of the Great Theological Biblical Themes of Sacred Salvation History, or the Mystery of Christ

The study of the psalms in the liturgy has for its aim, in the last analysis, to help us make their recitation also our personal and deeply felt prayer. When we think of the part they occupy in worship, of the necessity of widely re-establishing their use among the people, of singing them in the liturgy, we can understand the capital importance of the question of how to make them also our personal prayer, especially for those of us who are obligated to the breviary and still more for those whose lives are such that besides the breviary obligation they have the additional obligation of choral recitation.

It would be naïve to think that in order really to pray the psalms, it is enough to "understand" them, in the sense of having a conceptual comprehension of them of the scientific or learned sort. It is certain, on the contrary, that holiness of life, even if not accompanied by such knowledge, is the one condition necessary and sufficient for achieving this result.

Actually, in one who has holiness of life there occurs infallibly, by the work of grace, an understanding of the psalms, not by a conceptual process of the scientific type, but an understanding gained connaturally and, as it were, by an attuning of two natures confronting each other, or by instinct and sympathy. For holiness means a way of being and of acting similar to the way of being and of acting which pertains to God and to divine things. But the psalms speak of nothing else but God and divine things. Hence, just as a mother's nature "understands" her son instinctively by an intuitive and not a conceptual process, or just as the chaste person reacts instinctively by sympathy or by repugnance before situations and objects which concern chastity, so the holy man vibrates with a connaturality before God and the divine things of which the psalms speak; and thus does he "understand" them.

And this understanding, which does not depend on intellectual acumen or abundance of erudite knowledge, but solely on grace and moral dispositions, is eminently a prayer which is so much the more intense as the holiness is greater, and reaches its apex in the mystical life, as will be better explained in a later chapter.

But this does not mean that the conceptual understanding of the psalms is useless for enabling us to make them more easily a true personal prayer. On the contrary, a conceptual understanding may help this aim considerably in two ways. First of all, it may help it as preparation, inasmuch as the conceptual understanding of the text disposes the discursive intelligence toward the things of which the text speaks; and, through the intellect, it disposes the will and the other powers which obey its command. Secondarily, it may help inasmuch as the conceptual understanding of the text may justify the way in which, even if more or less instinctively and without any formal deliberative study, we interpret it and apply it to our personal situation, seeing ourselves personally involved in what it says.

On the other hand, not all methods of proceeding in the study of the psalms are equally adapted to attaining this end. It is not enough to "understand" the psalms in the sense of knowing the original composer's message.

And we must realize also that the purely philological-historical study, while being the indispensable basis for a conceptual and exhaustive liturgical understanding of the psalms, is not by any means sufficient in itself to attain that understanding.

Under this aspect, for example, the otherwise important work of H. Gunkel [1] on the literary genres of the psalms is still far from satisfying the desires of anyone who wants to understand and live the liturgy. Let it suffice to say that his proposed grouping of the psalms into ten different titles [2] is made essentially from the literary-philological point of view of expression and not of religious thought or theological content.

On the contrary, to understand the psalms in their real depth, it is necessary to start out first of all from the viewpoint of their thought and seek to understand it against the general background of the mystery of salvation history, the mystery of Christ. In other words, while taking into account everything that exegesis and modern biblical theology have given us and are now giving us with ever greater perfection, we must ground the study of the psalms — as of all the Bible — decisively on the point of view which was essentially that of the Fathers. [3]

Accordingly, in this study it is indispensable to take into account everything that exegesis and modern biblical theology teach us; it is likewise clear that to imitate the Fathers in the general grounding of the study of the

[1] *Einleitung in die Psalmen*, Göttingen 1933.

[2] 1) Lamentations of private individuals; 2) hymns: 3) psalms of thanksgiving; 4) royal psalms; 5) lamentations of the people; 6) sapiential psalms; 7) alphabetic psalms; 8) psalms which speak of the lot of Israel; 9) psalms which contain stories; 10) psalms of eschatological content.

Père Tournay, *Les psaumes* (*Bible de Jérusalem*), 2nd ed., Paris 1955, pp. 59-61, groups the psalms according to literary genre under four headings: hymns, prayers, didactic psalms, prophetic and eschatological psalms.

In Italy we have the work of G. Castellino, *Libro dei Salmi* (*La sacra bibbia*), Marietti 1955. He groups the psalms under the following eleven titles: 1) individual lamentations; 2) psalms of trust; 3) public lamentations; 4) songs of thanksgiving; 5) hymns; 6) royal psalms; 7) psalms of Sion; 8) psalms of Yahweh King; 9) liturgy of Yahwistic fidelity; 10) sapiential psalms; 11) various prayers. In the work of Castellino will be found an excellent foundation for dedicating oneself to that first phase of the study of the psalms which is their consideration under the simple philological, critical, historical light according to the advances of modern science. See also

P. Dryvers, *Les psaumes, genres littéraires et thèmes doctrinaux* (trans.), Paris 1958.

[3] Foremost is St. Augustine in his *Enarrationes*. Even prior to him in time, and taking much the same point of view, there are Athanasius, Hilary, Ambrose, and many others. See the list of them in G. Castellino's *Libro dei Salmi*, pp. 34-37. See also B. Fischer, *Die Psalmenfrömmigkeit der Märtyrerkirche*, Freiburg 1949. P. Salmon, *"De l'interprétation des psaumes dans la liturgie. Aux origines de l'office divin,"* in *La maison Dieu*, no. 33 (1953), pp. 21-55; *"Le problème des psaumes,"* in *L'ami du clergé*, Vol. 64 (1954), pp. 161-173; and also of Salmon, *Les "tituli psalmorum" des manuscrits latins*, Rome 1959. L. Bouyer, *"Les psaumes dans la prière chrétienne traditionnelle,"* in *Bible et vie chrétienne*, Vol. 10 (1955), pp. 22-35. H. de Caudole, *The Christian Use of the Psalms*, London 1955. R. B. H. Scott, *The Psalms as Christian Praise*, London 1958. T. Worden, *The Psalms Are Christian Prayer*, London 1962. A. George, *Prier les psaumes*, Paris 1962. *I Salmi, preghiera e canto della Chiesa*, Turin, LDC 1964. S. Rinaudo, *I Salmi nel mistero di Christo e della Chiesa*, Turin, LDC 1965.

psalms against the theological synthesizing background of sacred history does not mean to imitate them in every detail of their interpretation; for example, when they see exclusively in a particular text and not in any other a particular point of the Christic, ecclesiological, ascetical and mystical, or eschatological dimensions of the psalms.

From the patristic commentaries on the psalms will be acquired first of all the sense of the theological synthesizing view of the cosmos as sacred history and, in the second place, the general mental habit of never considering as exhausted the sense of any thing, event, or text of the Bible before having caught a glimpse of the real relation which it has, in the eyes of God, with the various phases of sacred history or the mystery of Christ, up to its final eschatological phase. Granted this much, it is clear that in the particulars of the interpretation of any psalm, especially insofar as the philological and historical basis of this interpretation is concerned, we should have recourse to modern exegesis and biblical theology.

When this kind of study is developed and its fruit is popularized, a notable step forward will have been taken for the understanding of the psalms, of the liturgy, and of their mutual relations, as well as of the relations between Bible, liturgy, and spiritual life. I truly believe that such a step will be even more important and decisive than the reform itself of the breviary; it is a prerequisite toward the goal of making the breviary a book of prayer and of life for all who use it.

At any rate, to arrive at this result, it is indispensable to study the psalms, not just simply in the order in which they are presented in the Bible in their present collection, nor, at least the first time, in the order in which they are used in the breviary, for example in the ordinary Office of the several weeks; rather, it is necessary to regroup them from the point of view of their ideological, theological, and biblical content.

More precisely, this point of view must be that of sacred salvation history — the mystery of Christ — because, as has been explained, this is the primary aspect under which the Bible speaks of everything of which it does speak. The grouping of the psalms must be made, therefore, by following the great biblical theological themes of sacred salvation history according to the outline which was made in the first chapter, but taking into account those special nuances they take on in the Psalter.

Here a difficulty presents itself. Even starting out from the point of view of the biblical theological themes of sacred history, one and the same psalm may and often does contain a number of these themes, more or less juxtaposed or even mixed together.

The observation is correct. And from this is explained the fact that, even among those who have endeavored to follow this criterion in whole or in part, the lists of the psalms included under each theme — supposing that the theme itself is admitted by the different authors — often differ considerably.

Thus, for example, among the psalms which have as theme the kingship in Israel, von Rad[4] counts eight of them, in this order according to the numbering of the Vulgate (which I always follow): 2, 19, 20, 44, 71, 100, 131, 143. Lepin, on the other hand,[5] counts fifteen of them according to this order: 2, 17, 19, 20, 32, 44, 60, 68, 71, 88, 109, 117, 131, 137, 143. Among the penitential psalms, Lepin counts only five: 24, 31, 50, 102, 129; but Bernini[6] counts eleven of them, as individual penitential prayers: 18, 24, 31, 37, 38, 39, 40, 50, 68, 129, 142; three, as collective penitential prayers: 78, 89, 105; and, at the end, he also adds three hymns — of thanksgiving, 64; of prayer, 84; of praise, 102 — in connection with the remission of sins. The examples could be multiplied.

Yet the matter is not so grave as might seem at first glance. For, aside from the fact that for some psalms there may really be doubt whether one theme is treated rather than another (for example, in Psalm 100 is the concern with good resolutions of a sovereign or of a private pious Israelite?), in many there are different, sometimes even numerous, themes more or less juxtaposed or even mixed together, and hence, under one aspect they may be catalogued in one rubric and under another aspect in another.

This will mean that in the general grouping of the psalms according to the biblical theological themes of the mystery of Christ, attention must be paid first of all to the criterion of the principal theme of each one. Then if there are two themes, or sometimes even more, which seem equally dominant, the same psalm will have to be catalogued under different themes (for example, Psalm 18:1-7 treats the theme of creation, but 18:8-11 treats the theme of the law). Finally, it means that in order to study a theme integrally in the psalms, one must indeed study it first of all in those in which it occurs as the principal theme; after which it will be indispensable, practically, to go through the whole Psalter in order to discern the places where it is treated as a secondary theme or even by way of simple allusion.

It must not be forgotten, of course, that the study of the theme must be carried out over the whole of the Old Testament, since it is evident that the Psalter cannot be isolated. From this precise point of view it seems that the general method followed by Bernini in the study of the penitential psalms is quite good and to be recommended.

In fact, to find the whole background of sacred salvation history in connection with a theme of the Psalter, it is no less indispensable to pursue the

---

[4] See under the entry *Basileús* in the *Theological Dictionary of the New Testament*, Vol. 1 (1964), pp. 565-571.

[5] *Le psautier logique*, Vol. 2, Paris 1937, p. 413.

[6] G. Bernini, *Le preghiere penitenziali del salterio*, Rome 1953.

study of that theme even through the New Testament, without ignoring, moreover, those realities of the mystery of Christ which theology shows us, under various forms, in the Church, in souls, and even in eschatology itself.[7]

In short, according to what was said in the preceding chapter, what is important for the liturgy is that the study of the Bible and of the psalms in particular be made from the prevailing point of view of the great biblical theological themes of the mystery of Christ and that, in respect to each theme, there be kept in mind the intimate connection which the different phases of sacred history have among themselves in the eyes of God. Thus the text which for the original author spoke directly of one of these phases will be seen by us in intimate connection with the antecedent and subsequent phases.

It goes without saying that when we affirm that the psalms must be viewed against the background of salvation history or the mystery of Christ in its total extension, we are by that very fact recognizing at the same time that all the psalms, as indeed the whole of the Scriptures, speak of Christ, or, as St. Augustine puts it, of the *Christus/totus*: of Christ the Head, and of ourselves, His members. All the psalms, therefore, can, and in a certain sense, must be prayed as the prayer of the *Christus totus*. Christ offers them all as His prayer, and we pray them all as ours. It must be kept in mind, of course, that even though there exists between Christ and ourselves that ultimate union which is called the Mystical Body, there is not on that account a physical unity of person. And that being the case, certain of the psalms — those, for example, in which the sinner asks pardon for his sin — are prayed by Christ in one sense and by ourselves in another.

Nevertheless, even while admitting this, every psalm is the prayer of Christ and our prayer also.[8] In fact, there is no event nor aspect of the sacred salvation history of which the psalms speak which does not refer, as to its focal point extended into the eschatological reality, to Christ and to ourselves, His Christian followers.

2. General Grouping of the Psalms according to the Principal Theme of Each One in Relation to Sacred History and Their Extension to the Christic, Christian, and Eschatological Realities

For these reasons I think it will be useful to attempt to a general grouping of the psalms according to the principal theme of each one in reference to sacred history; and to indicate, for each theme, the type of reasoning, by way of transposition or deepening, by means of which the liturgy makes use of

---

[7] P. Guichou, *Les psaumes commentés par la Bible*, 3 vols., Paris 1958.

[8] See St. Augustine, *Enarr. in Ps. 85 proem.*

See also CL, art. 83. In this same regard, cf. F. Vandenbroucke, *Les psaumes et le Christ*, Louvain 1955, with bibliography.

it, beyond the sense of the original author, and sees in every psalm the Christic, ecclesial — also ascetical and mystical — and eschatological realities of the mystery of Christ in its whole extension. It is this transposition which *ipso facto* permits the individual who recites those psalms in following the liturgy to recite them as prayers which are personal and which are of immediate interest to himself.

Without giving an absolute interpretation to this attempt, it seems to me that the whole Psalter, from the point of view which interests us here, can be divided into ten categories:

1) Creation and general providence;
2) Election, separation, formation, and restoration of the people of God;
3) The king, head of the people of God;
4) Jerusalem, the capital city of the people of God;
5) The temple of God; the holy ark; and Sion, the holy mountain;
6) The law of the people of God;
7) The enemies of the people of God and the struggles of the people of God against them;
8) The penitent sinner among the people of God;
9) The just and pious man among the people of God;
10) Attributes of God and invitations to praise Him as the direct and the principal theme of some psalms.

The necessity of this last category, notwithstanding the fact that ultimately all the psalms have as their general objective the singing of the praises of God and of His attributes, will be clarified later in this presentation.

1. Creation and general providence. In this group the concern is with those psalms whose principal theme is to sing of God as universal Creator, Governor, and Provider of all things and for all men.[9] They are the following psalms, according to the numbering of the Vulgate: 8; 18:1-7; 28; 32; 89 (which under other aspects could also be put into the category covering the enemies of Israel or in the category of the penitential psalms); 91:1-7 (but the whole psalm, under another aspect, could be put into the category on the just man among the people of God; the different lot of the just man and of the sinner); 94 (under another aspect it could be included in the category on the attributes of God directly sung: the kingship of God); 103; 148.

The liturgy, making use of these psalms, does not stop at the consideration of the marvels of creation and of general providence — which, however, it contemplates no less than the Jews could — but deepens and prolongs this theme, conscious that in the intentions of God, and therefore in the truest way possible, creation and general providence were all directed to the redemption and to the special providence in Christ. "In a wonderful way You have created

[9] See A. B. Rhodes, *Creation and Salvation in the Psalter*, Chicago 1952.

man, and still more wonderfully You have redeemed him," says the alternative oration after the first reading in the Paschal Vigil, in which the Genesis account of creation is read (Gen 1:1–2:2). Or in the other alternative oration after the same reading: ". . . the creation of the world which took place in the beginning was not a more excellent act than the immolation which Christ, our Passover, offered at the end of the ages."

It is thus, for example, that the liturgy will think not only of the creation of man on the purely natural level but also of his elevation to the divine order and of his redemption, when it reads in the eighth psalm:

> "When at Your firmament I gaze — Your fingers' work,
> at moon and stars which You have poised in space —
> ah, what is man that You should think of him;
> ah, what is mortal man that You should care for him!
>
> A little less than angels You created him;
> with dignity and glory him You crowned!
>
> You gave him sway o'er all Your handiwork;
> all things You placed beneath his feet:
> yes, sheep and oxen, each and all,
> as well as all the roving beasts;
> the birds in the sky, the fish in the sea —
> whatever travels ocean's paths.
>
> O Lord, our Lord, how wondrous is Your name in all the earth!
>
> Above the firmament You have extolled Your majesty!" [10]

In fact, it is of Christ Himself that the liturgy will think, not just by arbitrary transpositions of meaning, but because, really, it is the holy humanity of Christ subsisting in the person of the Word which God in creating man had in view in the last accounting, and because in that holy humanity the whole creation of the world and of man takes its ultimate meaning. This is precisely what is supposed in Heb. 2:6-9 and 1 Cor. 15:24-28.

Again: on the day of the Immaculate Conception, the recitation of the same Psalm 8, "O Lord, our Lord, how wondrous is Your name in all the earth," has this antiphon prefixed to it by the (Benedictine) Office: "Admirable is Your name, O Lord, in all the earth, because in the Virgin Mary You have prepared for Yourself a worthy dwelling place." And to Psalm 18, "The heavens tell the glory of the Lord," the same liturgy prefixes the antiphon: "In the sun God pitched His tent." In all this there is presumed an understanding of the type of reasoning used by the liturgy to deepen the theme of the creation so as to see Mary in it, viz., if God is wonderful in the marvels of

[10] In the translation of James A. Kleist and Thomas J. Lynam, *The Psalms in Rhythmic Prose*, Milwaukee 1954.

creation, He is still more wonderful in the marvels of divine life which He has worked in Mary.

And in general: there is a creation and a providence — Christological in scope — which in its various phases on to its eschatological consummation is more wonderful still than material creation, and to which, as a supreme end, visible creation was ordained.

2. Election, separation, formation, and restoration of the people of God.

These themes recur as the primary objective in a certain number of psalms that are notably historical in content; in summary they recount the story of the people of Israel as the very special object of divine providence, of Yahweh who intended to form for Himself in Israel a people from among all peoples, dedicated and, as it were, reserved to Himself.

Our prolongation or extension of these themes is made with a reasoning of this type: the people of Israel and all that God did concretely for that people was but a first roughcast, still imperfect, of what God later did and concretized perfectly in the Church of Christ, the new people of God, the new Israel. All that God did in the election, separation, and formation of the people of Israel is not understood in its integral sense except by referring it to the election, separation, formation of the new and true spiritual Israel, the Church. This takes place principally in the sacraments and in the liturgical realities, especially in baptism and in the Eucharist.

Again: that same election, separation, and formation of the people of God in the Church will have its ultimate fulfillment in the eschatological realities of the heavenly Jerusalem.[11]

Nor may we forget the impact of these same spiritual realities upon the individual person, because it is in the election, separation, and formation of individual Catholics unto divine life that the Church is effectively realized; this may take place in the application to inviduals of the basic liturgical realities, especially baptism and Eucharist, but also in the more private ascetical and mystical experiences — or in the life beyond. It is thus, for example, that in ancient liturgical tradition one of the characteristic psalms recited on the occasion of the death of one of the faithful was Psalm 113, *In exitu Israel de Aegypto*, which sings of the divine prodigies on behalf of Israel in its liberation from Egypt.[12]

[11] On the theme of the election, separation, formation, etc., of the people of God in the Bible, see W. Eichrodt, *Gottes Ruf im Alten Testament. Die alttestamentliche Botschaft im Lichte des Evangeliums*, 1951; Th. C. Vriezen, *Die Erwählung Israels nach dem Alten Testament*, 1952; F. Asensio, *Jahveh y su pueblo, contenido teológico en la historia bíblica de la elección*, Rome 1953.

[12] See the *Apostolic Constitutions* 6, 27. The theme of the exodus from Egypt was well-known in the liturgy of the departed. See, for example, the Gelasian Sacramentary, Mohlberg edition, nos. 1610 and 1625, pp. 234 and 237 resp. In the Apocalypse the redeemed sing as hymn of thanksgiving "the Canticle of Moses, servant of God" (Apoc. 15:3).

The psalms in which these themes are especially developed are the following, in the numbering of the Vulgate: 76; 77; 80; 84; 94:5-11; 99; 104; 105; 106; 110; 113:1-8; 113:9-26; 120; 125; 134; 135:10-26; 146.

3. The king, head of the people of God. Here the concern is with the theme and the theology of the king as representative of Yahweh in the midst of His people and, as such, special object of God's love and care as well as His instrument for the realization of the kingdom which he always has in view. Special attention is accorded to David and to the Messiah-King, David's descendant.[13]

Christian prolongation or extension of this theme is done in the following way: just as Israel, as people of God, in the intentions of God had all her significance in relation to the future Church, so the king in Israel, inasmuch as he was representative of Yahweh in the midst of His people, special object of His love and of His protection, His instrument for realizing His kingdom, was but a first and imperfect roughcast of that which God later realized effectively in Christ. The royal psalms in which is expressed the theology of the king and of the kingship in Israel must all therefore be seen in their typological prolongation in Christ. So much the more must Christ Himself be seen in those psalms which already, according to the conscious intention of the human author, referred directly to the Messiah, and above all in Psalm 109.

These psalms are: 2; 17; 19; 20; 44; 71; 100; 109; 131; and perhaps also 143.

4. Jerusalem, the holy capital city of the people of God. It is the theme of Jerusalem, capital of the people of God, chosen by Him from among all, loved, protected, adorned in glory, spiritual center of unity of the chosen people, destined to become the glorious center of the whole world when the Messiah comes.

The extension or prolongation is done in this way: the earthly Jerusalem is a type of the Church and of the heavenly Jerusalem. Yahweh's concern for the earthly Jerusalem, the promises of glory made to her, all had in view the formation of the holy city, the Church, which in its turn prepares for and prefigures the heavenly Jerusalem of the Apocalypse.

The psalms which refer to this theme are principally: 45; 47; 86; 121; 147; and 124 may also refer to this theme. Under a certain aspect the group of so-called gradual psalms (119–127) may also be referred to it.[14]

---

[13] Concerning the religious and theological significance of the king in Israel, see, for example, J. de Fraine, *L'aspect religieux de la royauté israélite,* Rome 1954; and Eugene Maly, *The World of David and Solomon,* Englewood Cliffs (New Jersey) 1966.

[14] For this aspect and for the general study of the theme of Jerusalem, see Th. Maertens, *Jérusalem la cité de Dieu,* Abbaye de S. André 1954; J. Cales, "Le Ps. 87 (86): Sion le cité de Dieu mère des peuples," in *Recherches de science religieuse,* 1922, pp. 211ff. A. Gelin, "Jérusalem dans la dessin de Dieu," in *La vie spirit.,* Vol. 86 (1952), pp. 353-366. O. Rousseau, "Quelques textes patristiques sur la Jérusalem celeste," *ibid.* pp. 378-388. A. Colunga,

5. The temple of God; the holy ark; and Sion, the holy mountain.
The temple theme is very close to the preceding theme of Jerusalem, the holy city. The temple, the ark, is the place and the symbol of God's very special dwelling among His people, of His protective presence over the holy city, of the manifestation of his glory. It is therefore the place of special encounter between God and man, the heart of the nation, the place *par excellence* of prayer, of the most holy aspirations of every pious Israelite, of the abode of the priesthood, and of the worship of the people made in the name of all.

The deepening of these themes against the general background of sacred history is done by keeping in mind the following correspondences. On the one hand: holy ark, temple of Jerusalem, and Hebrew worship. On the other hand: Christ and the worship rendered by Him to God; universal Church; every soul as temple of God insofar as it lives in Christ; churches as material edifices and the Catholic worship rendered there to God; finally, the heavenly temple and the heavenly liturgy in the Jerusalem above.[15]

The presence of God in His people, concretized and symbolized in the ark and in the temple of Jerusalem, was only a pale shadow preparative and prefigurative of the presence and the manifestation of His much more extraordinary glory which He realized first of all in Christ and, by means of Him, in the universal Church, His new people and true new Sion, to which the ancient Hebrew people and the ancient Sion were ordained. Hence it was a preparation and prefiguration of God's presence in the individual souls who live in Christ and *in Spirit* and are thus, in an eminent way, God's temple and the place where His glory is manifested.

Moreover, it was a preparation and prefiguration of the presence of God in every single Catholic church building, which also, by virtue of the Eucharistic tabernacle, is, in a way far more true and sublime than the ark and the temple of Jerusalem, the place of God's presence among His people, of the encounter between God and man on this earth, where His glory — *shekinah* — continues to be manifested here below.

Finally, the universal Catholic Church and Catholic churches are only a pale shadow prefigurative and preparative of the temple of the heavenly Jerusalem in which the presence of God and the manifestation of His glory reach the apex and the ultimate end to which all the antecedent presences and manifestations of glory were ordained.

It is apparent that these perspectives, in the pre-Pauline Roman and Benedictine liturgy, are applied in a special way in the Mass and the Office of the dedication of a church. The psalms which refer especially to this theme are:

"*Jerusalén, la ciudad del Gran Rey*," in *Estudios biblicos*, Vol. 14 (1955), pp. 255-279. E. Testa, "*La 'Gerusalemme celeste': dall' antico Oriente alla bibbia e alla liturgia*," in *Biblia e Oriente*, Vol. 1 (1959), pp. 47-50.

[15] See Jean Card. Daniélou, *Le signe du temple*, Paris 1945. Yves Congar, *Le mystère du temple ou l'économie de la présence de Dieu à sa créature de la Genèse à l'Apocalypse*, Paris 1958.

14; 23; 49; 64; 67; 83; 86; 121 (it refers also to the theme of Jerusalem); 126 may also refer to this theme; 132; 133. It is regrettable that the current *Liturgy of the Hours* is insensitive to this rich liturgical heritage. Hopefully it will be remedied in the next "reform."

6. The law of the people of God. Here belong the psalms whose principal theme is the theology of the Mosaic law: its divine origin, its nature as manifestation of God's wisdom and love; its efficacy as sure guide of a life according to the will of God and therefore the only means toward true happiness, peace, security in travails, right estimation of the values of life. Hence the law is the constant object, in fact the only object, of the cares of the pious Israelite, who asks God to give him the intelligence and the strength to observe it.

The transposition is made in this way: the Mosaic law was only a pale shadow of the economy of grace inaugurated with Christ; it was destined in the intentions of God to serve men as a pedagogue to lead them to Christ, to the economy of grace in Christ. All the praises on the origin, nature, and efficacy of the old law are read in the light of the new economy of grace, whether in its public aspect or in its more intimate and personal aspect.[16]

The psalms which treat this theme are principally: 18:8ff and 118.

7. The enemies of the people of God. Of concern are those psalms in which the psalmist asks for help against the enemies of the people of God as such, especially at times of national anguish, as well as for the punishment and humiliation of these enemies; then, upon favorable response, he thanks God for the benefits and the protection granted.

The transposition is made thus: Israel was a people unique in the history of mankind by reason of its character and essentially religious function. And in this it depended entirely on the free divine choice which entrusted to it a unique religious mission. The enemies of Israel, inasmuch as they acted against the will of God, were therefore, for that very reason, enemies of God, at least insofar as they wanted to obstruct His religious plans for His particular chosen people. The enemies of religious Israel — and if in antiquity there was no distinction between the religious aspect and the political aspect of a people, so much the less was there such a distinction in Israel — were therefore, ultimately, the satellites of the city of Satan, at war against the city of God from the beginning of the world.

This struggle of Satan against the ancient people of God is the same that

---

[16] Very useful for the study of the theme of the law is the work of A. Deissler, *Psalm 119 (118) und seine Theologie (Münchner theologischen Studien),* Munich 1955. See also M. F. Lacan, *"Le mystère de prière dans le Ps. 119 (118),"* in *Lumiere et Vie,* Vol. 23 (1955), pp. 125-142. H. Duesberg, *"Le miroir du fidèle: Le Ps. 119 (118) et ses usages liturgiques,"* in *Bible et vie chrétienne,* Vol. 15 (1956), pp. 78-97. S. F. Logsdon, *The Victory Life in Ps. 119 (118),* Chicago 1960.

he, directly or by means of his satellites, carries on continually today against the new Israel, the Church and every one of her sons individually. The reactions of Israel against her enemies are therefore essentially the same as the reactions of the entire Church and of her individuual believers personally against Satan. It is for this reason that the Church and every single believer can legitimately, and in fact should, make his own, in the struggle which he has to carry on against Satan and the evil which Satan rouses up in the world, the prayers which the pious psalmists addressed to God to ask for protection against the enemies of their people, and the hymns of thanksgiving and jubilation for the protection He granted Israel on these occasions.

If we have difficulty making our own various expressions of these psalms in which imprecations are made against enemies of the people of Israel and in which the psalmists ask the most terrible exterminations, and sometimes even beg God never to admit those enemies to His pardon and His mercy, we find an answer by reflecting on the general relations between the Old and the New Testament.

One of the fundamental canons which determines these relations is, in fact, that the New Testament and its supernatural realities are not only in a relation of profound continuity and unity with the Old Testament, but also, and at the same time, in a relationship of transcendence. Thus the realities and the attitudes of the Old Testament not only prepare for and prefigure the realities and the attitudes of the new law and of the economy of grace in Christ, but also and by that very fact are more imperfect than the Christian realities. The Christian realities continue the realities of the Old Testament, not in that which was still imperfect and lacking in them, but only in that which was good and acceptable.

The fact is that the attitude of the Israelites in the Old Testament toward their enemies or the enemies of the nation was very imperfect; they did not yet know the perfection of universal charity and therefore did not distinguish sufficiently in the enemy between the sin and the sinner.

The reaction of the Old Testament toward enemies is good and unimpeachable as regards the attitude against sin, the work of Satan and of men insofar as they are his instrument, although free. But it is still imperfect as regards the manner of behaving toward the sinful enemy because it does not yet know the fullness of the charity taught by Christ, which totally rejects the sin but does not desire the death of the sinner; rather, it desires that he be converted and live.

Thus, in conclusion, in the new law of Christ, when use is made of the psalms in which the Israelite prays, or at any rate inveighs, against the enemies of the people or against his personal enemies, all this is accepted insofar as it refers to Satan and to sin. But as far as the sinful man is concerned, the desire of the Christian can only be that he be converted and live. Thus is resolved the question of the use in the liturgy of the imprecations against enemies and of the imprecatory psalms, whether against the enemies of Israel or against the individual enemies of the pious Israelite.

For example, when in Psalm 136, *Super flumina Babylonis*, the final two verses are read:

> "Men of the devastatrix Babylon —
> blessed is he who will repay to you
> the evils you have brought upon us!
>
> Blessed is he who snatches up your little ones
> and dashes them against a rock!" [17]

the Christian must think of Satan, also insofar as he works against the people by means of the sinful enemies of the Church. But he may not in hate wish any evil, either moral or material, upon the sinners themselves or upon the enemies of the Church. His thought stops at the desire for the destruction and the eradication of the evil — in other words, of the influence of Satan — in the world and of all those seeds of evil which Satan sows on earth. The "Blessed is he who snatches up your little ones and dashes them against a rock" necessarily means, in the mouth of the Christian: Blessed is he that can crush the sprouts of evil which Satan nurtures, by having recourse to the supreme and invincible opponent of all sin: Christ, God.

There is nothing at all arbitrary, therefore, in the traditional patristic interpretation of this verse as referred to Christic realities: "Who are the little ones of Babylon? Evil desires when they are being born . . .: when it is little, throw it . . . , throw it against the rock: and the Rock was Christ." [18] And in doing thus, whatever may be the way in which the Israelites and the contemporaries understood this verse, the Christian attains the deep sense which God had in view in it, because the *lex talionis* which He, by way of teaching, gave to the Hebrews, and according to which this verse is conceived, was not, in His intentions, anything but a condescension to the imperfection of that people and a first and distant roughcast of the law of charity which He would

---

[17] In the translation of Kleist and Lynam.

[18] St. Augustine, *Enarr. in Ps. 136:12*. Origen, St. Hilary, St. Ambrose, and St. Jerome had already commented in the same sense. Later there were John Cassian, and St. Benedict in his Rule, prologue 28; see the edition of Anselmo Lentini, Montecassino 1948, pp. 19ff.

[Another approach to this problem would be this: the psalmist is simply applying the Deuteronomic sanctions of divine punishment upon those who violate God's law — it is not a matter of personal revenge at all. The divine sanction of punishment upon violations of God's law are even more dreadful in the New Testament than in the Old, e.g., that of eternal punishment in hell surfaces nowhere in the psalms. Accordingly, just as the psalmist was simply repeating God's sanctions upon sinners according to revelation as he knew it, so the Christian in praying the psalms simply continues to give expression to our faith in God's punishment of sinners. It would pervert the Gospel to eliminate those passages in which Jesus speaks as God of wrath, pronouncing judgments of punishment upon the wicked; see Matthew 23:13-39; 25:41-46 and *passim* throughout the Book of the Apocalypse. Tr.]

later give to the Christians. In virtue of this law, the Christians would have to be irreconcilable enemies only of sin as well as of Satan and the damned because they are now definitely rooted in sin, while they would still and always pray and hope for the conversion of every living sinner.[19]

The psalms which refer to the theme of the enemies of the people of God are principally: 43; 46; 69; 65; 67; 73; 78; 79; 82; 88; 97; 107; 117; 122; 123; 124; 128; 136; 143; 149. Psalm 89 may also be counted as one of them.[20]

8. The penitent sinner among the people of God. This is the theme of the pious Israelite who feels that he is a sinner, confesses his sin, humbles himself, asks pardon of God, appealing to His boundless mercy, and thanks Him for the pardon received and the peace regained.

The transposition is made thus: the sentiments of the pious Israelite aware of his own sins and repentant for them should be with greater reason the sentiments of the Christian sinner, since the offense against God committed by the Christian is so much the more serious as he has been more the object of God's goodness and benefits, as the whole economy in Christ demonstrates.

The psalms which refer to this theme are principally: 6; 24; 31; 36; 37; 50; 129; 142.

9. The just and pious Israelite, the God-fearing man, the "poor man of Yahweh," among God's people. This theme is, in comparison to the others, the most abundant in the whole Psalter. Here we have those psalms in which the just and pious Israelite, who is referred to also as God-fearing and as the poor man of Yahweh, addresses God in the various contingencies of life.[21]

The deepening of these themes in the light of the Christian realities is done

---

[19] Since no instance of the application of the law of talion can be found in Jewish history, e.g., a person actually having his eyes gouged out in a legal process, it is erroneous to understand this principle in terms of revenge. Rather it is a principle cast in metaphorical language which simply demands just restitution for damages done. The precise kind or amount of restitution in a given case was determined either in the Law itself or through a legal process in court. The Catholic Church too regards this application of talion law as just and upright both in civil and in her own ecclesiastical practice.

[20] Various of these psalms refer to the wars of Israel against her enemies, e.g., 46; 59; etc. Some psalms which treat of the king of Israel or even of Jerusalem the holy city also refer to a similar theme. Concerning this theme of the wars of Israel and of their religious

character, see Fr. Schwally, *Semitische Altertümer: I. Der heilige Krieg in alten Israel,* Leipzig 1901; G. von Rad, "Deuteronomy and the Holy War," in *Studies in Deuteronomy,* London 1953, pp. 45-59.

[21] For this theme of the pious Israelite, the poor man of Yahweh, etc., see A. Causse, *Les "pauvres" d'Israel,* Strasbourg 1922; G. Castellino, *Le lamentazioni individuali e gli inni in Babilonia e in Israele,* Turin 1940. On the theme of the enemies of the pious Israelite, see Castellino's *Libro dei Salmi,* Marietti 1955, pp. 254-263. See also A. Gelin, *The Poor of Yahweh,* Collegeville, Minn. 1964. R. Sorg, *Hesed and Hasid in the Psalms,* St. Louis 1953. J. Coppens, "Les psaumes des Hasidim," in *Mélanges A. Robert,* Paris 1957, pp. 214-244. G. Pidoux, *La main qui guérit. Psaumes du malade,* Neuchâtel 1960.

in this way: whatever holds for the just man of the Old Testament holds for the just man of the New Testament, but in a more perfect way, hence more deeply, more spiritualized, since the idea of the just man of the Old Testament is but a first roughcast and a sort of pale reflection of the ideal of the just man in the New.

In a very special way the ideal of the just man drawn in the Old Testament and his way of behaving in the varied circumstances of life were fulfilled in a sublime way by Christ Himself, the just one *par excellence* and the model of all the just (see how these psalms, and in a special way those of the sub-themes a, b, and c [see below], are put by the liturgy on the lips of Christ, from the Fifth Sunday of Lent until Good Friday). Subordinately, this ideal is fulfilled in every saint of the new economy (see the use of these psalms on the feasts of the saints).

Some of these psalms enter into the literary category of the psalms called imprecatory. Their transposition into the Christian regimen is accomplished, as a rule, according to the principles explained above for the psalms of the same character in group seven.[22]

These psalms constitute more than half of the whole Psalter and may be distinguished into four sub-themes:

a) The just, god-fearing, poor man of God implores God's aid in various difficult circumstances of life, especially against the persecutions of enemies, sinners, unbelievers, calumniators, and oppressors: 5; 7; 9:22-39; 11; 16; 21; 25; 27; 30; 34; 35; 38; 41; 42; 53; 54; 58; 68; 69; 70; 85; 87; 93; 101; 108; 119; 139; 140; 141.

b) The same just man in the various circumstances of life, especially in the persecutions by his enemies, expresses to God the full trust which he retains in Him: 3; 4; 10; 12; 21; 26; 40; 55; 56; 61; 130.

c) The just man offers up to God his prayer of thanksgiving and praise after the benefits received from Him, especially in the various tribulations of life and in the persecutions suffered at the hands of enemies, sinners, oppressors, calumniators, and unbelievers: 9:1-21; 17; 22; 27; 29; 30; 33; 39; 60; 64; 66; 74; 114; 115; 137; 143; 145.

d); The psalmist sings of the different lot of the pious man and of the impious, of the just and the sinner. This theme is often touched upon also in the psalms of the three preceding categories, but it is found principally in the following psalms: 1; 7; 13; 15; 36; 48; 51; 52; 57; 62; 63; 72; 81; 90; 91:8-16; 111; 126.

10. Attributes of God and invitations to praise Him as the direct and principal theme of some psalms. The whole Psalter, and for that matter the whole Bible, has basically for its single theme God and His

---

[22] For Psalm 108 (109) in particular, see F. Baumgürtel, *"Der 109. Psalm in der Ver-* *kündigung,"* in *Monatschrift für Pastoral The-ologie,* Vol. 42 (1953), pp. 244-253.

attributes. The Psalter, and again the whole Bible, is not concerned with reflecting on God and His attributes or analyzing them with a philosophical procedure, but with describing them concretely and, so to speak, showing how they appear in fact in His interventions in the world, in His creative action, and in His providence toward men and toward Israel in particular.

It is equally true that the whole Psalter is an invitation to praise God and His attributes thus considered. From this point of view, there should not exist in the general ordering of the psalms one particular group which treats of God, of His attributes, of the invitation to praise Him, because this is found throughout the whole Psalter.

Nevertheless, examining some psalms closely, we notice that, under the same aspect of the theme of God, of His attributes, and of the invitation to praise Him, they have something special with respect to the rest. And what is special is that these themes constitute the direct, immediate, and, so to speak, exclusive object of the song. Also in them, almost always, the psalmist makes allusions to one of the themes which we have grouped in the preceding nine categories: creation, general providence, special providence for the people of Israel, etc. These allusions serve to bring out those attributes of God (majesty, and royal and judicial power; clemency, benignity, omniscience, goodness) and to motivate the invitation to praise Him. But in these psalms the concern is only with brief allusions, while the principal aim remains that of singing these attributes in their generality or of inviting in a general way to praise God.

The transposition of these psalms into the Christian regimen is intuitive: the Christian sings the attributes of God with so much greater reason inasmuch as he sees them manifested in a manner immensely more profound and magnificent, in Christ Himself, in the Church, in the ecclesial realities, in the realities of the inner life of perfection of the Christian, and in the future eschatology already announced. In the same way the general invitation to praise God is accepted and reinforced by the Christian because in him this invitation arises from the knowledge and the experience of the Christic, ecclesial — as well as personally individual — and future eschatological realities.

The psalms which refer to these themes are principally: the series of psalms which sing of God the universal King, powerful, saving, holy, just Judge of Israel and of the world: 85:8-10; 92; 93; 94; 95; 96; 97; 98. In these psalms it is the kingship of Yahweh that is sung in all the aforesaid aspects.[23] Psalm 102 sings of the clemency of God; Psalm 112, His loftiness and benignity; Psalm 138, His omnipotence, omniscience, and omnipresence; Psalm 144, His majesty and goodness. Psalms 116 and 150 are general invitations to praise God for His mercy and faithfulness, for His prodigies and His majesty.

[23] See H. J. Kraus, *Die Königsherrschaft Gottes im Alten Testament*, Tübingen 1951. J. Gray, "The Kingship of God in the Prophets and Psalms," in *Vetus Testamentum*, Vol. 11 (1961), pp. 1-29.

*   *   *

In concluding these two chapters on Bible and liturgy, it would not seem to be in any way an exaggeration to assert that to penetrate the world of the liturgy, it is of capital importance to understand its relationship with the Bible, to penetrate the profound spirit which actually determines the mutual relationships between Bible and liturgy.

I shall add, in fact — may it not be displeasing to the exegetes who neglect too much the question of the relations between Bible and liturgy — that it is of capital importance even for arriving at the total comprehension of the Bible, as it should be understood in a Christian and ecclesial context, and for bringing it about that the Bible is truly the nourishment of souls and of the whole life of the Christian. For it is principally in the liturgy that the Church uses and lives the Scriptures.

It is for this reason that liturgical renewal and biblical movement are profoundly connected and must keep step, so to speak, with each other. In practice it is illusory to suppose that one can bring Christians back to the sources of the Bible if they are not brought back to the sources of the liturgy; just as vice versa, it is illusory to think that one can bring back Christians to the sources of the liturgy if they are not brought back to the sources of the Bible. This is what has been happily understood by those promoters of the liturgical movement who are striving to link that movement to the renewed study of the Scriptures.[24]

But it is just as evident that the study of the Bible does not rise to this function of nourishing the life of the Church if it does not surpass the purely, or too prevalently, philological-historical or even apologetic phase, to raise itself clearly in every question to the level of integral biblical spirituality. And this takes place only by means of the study of the biblical theological themes in their development throughout the Bible against the background of salvation history in its various phases connected among themselves, even to the final eschatology.

Probably it is no exaggeration to say that when the sense of finding the Bible connaturally in the liturgy, and the liturgy in the Bible, once more becomes general among Christians, a great step forward will have been taken toward a more intense Christian life because the key to the unity of Bible, liturgy, and life will have been found. This was the essential aim to which the ancient monastic method of the *lectio divina* tended and does always tend — the *lectio divina* which is at the same time theological study, meditation, and prayer, centered essentially around the Bible as seen in the liturgy and the liturgy as understood by means of the Bible.

[24] To be noted in this sense are the reviews: *Bibel und Liturgie*, of Klosterneuburg near Vienna; *Paroisse et liturgie*, of the Abbaye de S. André, Bruges [Brugge], in the *Supple-* *ment: Lumière et vie* of June 1951. The publications of the *Centre de pastorale liturgique* of Paris also give notable importance to this aspect of the liturgical renewal.

It is true, as I said at the beginning of this chapter, that it is not enough to have a clear discursive intellectual vision of the great biblical themes and of their relations with the liturgical life in order that a Catholic may unfailingly live the liturgy with all the intensity desirable. For this something else again is needed — holiness of life. Still, habituating ourselves to finding naturally the relations between Bible and liturgy by means of the understanding of the great biblical theological themes against the background of salvation history considered in its unity, we are suitably disposing our conceptual intellect to cooperate as best it can in its own specific way in the work of our sanctification and of our worship in the liturgical life of the Church.

Keeping in mind what has been said in these two preceding chapters, it will be understood why the Second Vatican Council desires that "in sacred celebrations a more ample, more varied, and more suitable reading from sacred scripture should be restored"; why it inculcates the necessity of the homily as explanation of the Scriptures in their liturgical framework; why it actively encourages special celebrations of the word of God, such as Bible vigils.[25]

It will be understood, moreover, what the same Council meant when it stated: "In order to achieve the restoration, progress, and adaptation of the sacred liturgy it is essential to promote that sweet and living love for Sacred Scripture to which the venerable tradition of Eastern and Western rites gives testimony." [26]

Perhaps the expression "sweet and living love" is not a particularly felicitous one, since it might seem to imply that what is being treated of is a sentimental and more or less arbitrary way, even if well-intentioned, of reading the Bible. This is certainly not what the Council meant. On the contrary, it had in mind that total, theological reading of the Bible which is, as we have sought to demonstrate, the only scientifically integral manner of reading the sacred text.

[25] CL, art. 35. [26] CL, art. 24.

PART 4 LITURGY, FAITH, AND THEOLOGY

16 LITURGY AND FAITH

What are the precise relations between liturgy and faith, and between liturgy and theology? In particular, to what point does the liturgy oblige the faith of the believer, and what use can and should be made of the liturgy in theology? These questions have an importance much more concrete than might be thought at first glance, for the purpose not only of the right theoretical understanding of the liturgy but also for the efficacy of practical penetration of the liturgical movement in the Church. This efficacy depends in an essential way on the fact of whether or not the clergy themselves, first of all, will be persuaded of its true usefulness. But it cannot be seriously hoped that the world of the liturgy will become connatural in the theoretical religious thought and in the practical religious sensibility of the clergy as long as the clergy have not taken account of the precise place which that world holds in the general picture of revelation and of the life of the Church which they are accustomed to draw — or should be drawing — from the study of theology. And this depends in large part on the solution of the aforesaid questions.

First of all, what exactly are the relations between faith and liturgy? The answer is, in substance: *Lex orandi, lex credendi* — the manner in which prayer is said in the liturgy indicates what must be believed; and that which must be believed influences the manner of praying. The liturgy is, or involves, a certain way of proposing the faith to the adherence of the faithful, and is, or involves, a certain expression of this faith by the magisterium and by the people. The liturgy, it may be added, is a manifestation of the ordinary magisterium of the Church.

That all this, however, needs clarification and precise formulation is demonstrated by the simple observation that if the liturgy is taken as a whole, inasmuch as it includes both the historical liturgies and those now in force, and if a closer look is taken at what is contained therein, we find ourselves confronted with a whole, not only of great extension and variety, but also of notably different values as far as the faith itself is concerned.

Consider, for example, from this viewpoint, a collection of feasts like the following: the Assumption today, the Assumption immediately before its solemn definition, the Assumption again in the seventh-eighth century; the feast of the Presentation of our Lady in the temple; the feast of the Apparition of our Lady at Lourdes; the feast of Mary Mediatrix of All Graces, granted in 1921 by Benedict XV to several dioceses; the feast of the translation of the holy house of Loretto, likewise celebrated in several dioceses; the feast of the stigmata of St. Francis.

It is clear that the principle *lex orandi, lex credendi* in these different cases has a notably diverse meaning, and that the magisterium of the Church and the very adherence of the faithful are quite differently committed in each one of them.

Specialists are aware also that in some liturgies, otherwise orthodox and catholic, even doctrinal errors or at least formulas of an inexact and antiquated theology infiltrated, even if they were quickly eliminated for the most part. This is the case, for example, with certain formulas in the Mozarabic liturgy, to which the adoptionists Elipandus and Felix of Urgel later appealed.[1] Thus again, in liturgical documents of the Middle Ages there is the rubric which affirmed the consecration of the wine in the chalice by mere contact with the consecrated host, and a formulary of Mass "to alleviate the pains of hell."[2] In similar cases, too, it is obvious that the responsibility of the magisterium and the adherence of the faithful are things which, theologically, require distinctions and explanations.

It is for this reason that since the seventeenth-eighteenth century, in other words, from the time when modern historical liturgical science began to have some substance and when recourse to the liturgy began to be taken into consideration also in the controversies with Protestants, the need was felt to determine more precisely the relations between faith and liturgy, as well as the interpretative rules and the conditions by means of which this recourse would be effective in the exposition and defense of the faith.

[1] See D. de Bruyne, *"De l'origine de quelques textes liturgiques mozarabes,"* in *Revue Bénédictine*, Vol. 30 (1913), pp. 421-426. See also the Council of Frankfort of 794 A.D. in Mansi, Vol. 13, cols. 886 B ff.

[2] See M. Andrieu, *Immixtio et consecratio*, Paris 1924; F. A. Zaccaria, *Bibliotheca ritualis*, Rome 1776-1781, Vol. I, p. lvii.

After Father F. A. Zaccaria,[3] who at that period was the principal author to concern himself with this question, it kept attracting the attention, every now and then, of some theologian while he was explaining the method of theology in the tract called *De locis theologicis*. Nevertheless, it is true that all this always remained in the purely theoretical field, because no serious penetration of the liturgy ever really occurred in theology. What is, in our opinion, the reason, will be seen later.

Recently again some liturgist and theologians have tried to re-examine the same question of the relations between faith and liturgy. Karl Federer has done a good work of a historical nature by examining, on this point, the thought of the Latin Fathers up to the fifth century.[4] In a book by Ph. Oppenheim can be read a compilation of what modern authors generally say, from the theoretical point of view, about the same question.[5] M. Pinto, undertaking a similar compilation with the addition of the historical side, has attempted to order it in what he calls a sketch of a complete theological treatise on the theological value of the liturgy.[6]

Regarding the theory of the relations between faith and liturgy, it seems to me that several of the essential considerations have already been made by Zaccaria and may be regarded as points generally accepted. But I think that today they can be stated exactly and in a manner somewhat simplified, thanks to three points of doctrine on which present-day theology can say something more and better than the theology of the eighteenth century, namely:

a) there is today a more comprehensive and exact notion of the liturgy itself;

b) there is today a more precise awareness of the notion of the magisterium of the Church, of its relations with the Scriptures, tradition, history, as well as of the fact that what the magisterium proposes to the faithful it proposes with very different degrees of authority and of authenticity;

c) finally, there is today a more acute awareness of the fact of the evolution of dogmas and doctrines and of the various factors which contribute to that evolution.

It is under this light that we shall strive to re-examine the question.

[3] Especially: *Thesaurus theologicus*, 12 vols., Venice 1762; *Bibliotheca ritualis*, 3 vols., Rome 1776-1781.

[4] Karl Federer, *Liturgie und Glaube, Legem credendi, lex statuat supplicandi. Eine theologiegeschichtliche Untersuchung*, Freiburg in der Sch. 1950. Abbot Bernard Capelle has brought out more clearly the relations between authority of the liturgy and apostolic origin of the same (true or supposed) according to the same Fathers, in his article *"Autorité de la liturgie chez les Pères,"* in *Recherches de théologie ancienne et médiévale*, Vol. 31 (1954), pp. 5-22.

[5] *Principia theologiae liturgicae*, Turin 1947. Antecedent general bibliography on the same matter, *ibid.*, pp. xiii-xix.

[6] *O valor teológico da liturgia* (thesis of the Jesuit theological faculty of Granada), Braga 1952.

1. In What Sense the Liturgy is "Didascalia" of the Church

First of all, in what sense is the teaching authority of the Church involved in the liturgy? In a private audience[7] Pius XI said: "The liturgy . . . is the most important organ of the ordinary magisterium of the Church. . . . The liturgy is not the *didascalia* of this or that individual, but the *didascalia* of the Church." Thus there are summed up in a few words the relations which exist between the liturgy and the teaching authority of the Church — a few words which must, however, be explained. For if it is true that the liturgy is the teaching of the Church and is the most important organ of the ordinary magisterium, it is just as true that the liturgy is all this in a very special sense, which distinguishes it profoundly from the form of magisterium which the Church exercises outside of the liturgy, for example by means of catechisms, professions of faith, encyclical or pastoral letters. This special way depends wholly on the proper nature of the liturgy.

The liturgy as complex vital action of the whole Church, Christ's Mystical Body

This insight into the nature of the liturgy is what we have endeavored to explain in all the preceding chapters, especially in the first part, which treats precisely of the notion of the liturgy. Let us recall some essential points.

The liturgy is the complexus of the efficacious sensible signs of the Church's sanctification and worship. In it, through the instrument and the veil of sensible signs, God sanctifies the Church by means of Christ, her Head; and the Church, united to Christ as the members of the body are united to the head, through Him, renders her worship to God by associating herself to the very worship which Christ renders to the Father, making that worship hers, at the same time that she also makes Christ Himself the object of her worship. The liturgy, as the complexus of sensible efficacious signs of the Church's sanctification and worship, is the privileged place of encounter between man and God, in which man, by means of Christ the Mediator and Head, in the possession of the Holy Spirit, receives every good gift from the Father and returns to the Father, in the living and concrete actualization in himself of the mystery of Christ, of salvation history, of the Church, and of the unity of the whole cosmos. I hope that the kind reader who has had the patience to follow me thus far will not take these notions as an outburst of lyricism.

If this definition is true, every liturgical action — and the whole liturgy is essentially and primarily an action — is something more and better than the mere didascalic exercise of the magisterium of the Church. It is, in the super-

---

[7] See the text in Annibale Bugnini's *Documenta pontificia ad instaurationem spectantia*, Rome 1953, pp. 70-71. See also the encyclical *Quas primas* of Pius XI, dated December 11, 1925, in *AAS*, Vol. 17 (1925), p. 603, and in Bugnini, *op. cit.*, p. 57, no. 2.

natural order, a general and complex vital action of the whole Church as such, organizationally structured — hierarchy and faithful, each in its own place and in its own role — a vital action in which the whole Church (supposing the required condition) reaches here below its maximum actualization as body of Christ,[8] because in union with her Head, Christ, through the veil of the sensible and efficacious signs, she responds adequately to the sanctifying action of God in a plenary encounter of the human and the divine.

All this is something more than a mere exercise of the teaching power of the hierarchy with relation to the faithful. It is something in which there converge and are put to work the teaching power of the hierarchy, its power of governing and its power of sanctifying, as well as the response of the faithful to all this; and, above all, the action itself of Christ and of God. More than the exercise of the teaching power of the hierarchy, therefore, liturgical action — the proper conditions always being necessarily supposed — is the maximum vital encounter, under the veil of the sensible and efficacious signs, between man and God in Christ; the common and ultimate aim of the Church's teaching power, governing power, and sanctifying power is to stir up and to activate this encounter.

All this must be kept in mind if we want to specify precisely what are the exchanges between the exercise of the Church's teaching authority and the liturgy, to understand the special modalities which this exercise there takes on and the rules of interpretation according to which it must be understood.

Didactic end of the liturgy subordinated to the immediate end of worship

It is clear, indeed, that this exercise of the magisterium of the Church in the liturgy is utterly real, inasmuch as the liturgy involves, among other things, also a teaching of the magisterium, as well as an expression of the adherence which the faithful give to this teaching and by which, in its turn, it can be recognized.

But with what precise modality does the liturgy involve a teaching, a *didascalia*, of the magisterium? This can be inferred from the general doctrine of the relations between the liturgy as maximum exercise of the virtue of religion, and of the theological virtues. It can be inferred especially from the relationship between religion and faith, which the teaching of the magisterium has for its immediate aim to enkindle, and which the adherence of the believer to this teaching manifests.

When treating the question, "What relation is there between faith and religion?" St. Thomas arrived at this conclusion:

---

[8] This is a concept strongly emphasized by the Second Vatican Council: see CL, art. 26 especially, but also art. 2; 5-8; 41; 48; and 83.

"It is clear, therefore, that the act of faith belongs materially to religion, as also the acts of the other virtues; in fact, it belongs to it more,
since the act of faith is the first movement of the mind toward God. . . .
Moreover, faith has connections with religion inasmuch as faith is the
cause and the principle of religion. For no one would render worship
to God if he did not believe that God is Creator, Providence, and Re-
warder of human acts." [9]

The doctrine of St. Thomas on the relations between theological virtues
and the virtue of religion, apropos of faith in particular, is acknowledged.
What St. Thomas says here of religion in general holds still more of the
liturgy in particular, which, inasmuch as it includes worship, is the supreme
exercise of the virtue of religion. The relations between liturgy and faith
are therefore: in the first place, that the faith, its teaching and its acceptance,
is cause and principle of the liturgy, the faith being in man the first phase
of that movement toward God which in the liturgical action, under the veil
of the sensible and efficacious signs, is completed as encounter of the Creator
and the creature. But in the liturgy, in a more particular way, the faith is
also matter which is used by the virtue of religion active in worship, inasmuch as in the liturgical act the virtue of religion offers God the acts of
faith as homage due to Him as Creator and Providence.

This means that, while the teaching of the magisterium in general is
specifically directed to enkindling the faith, in the liturgy this teaching has
for its proper end that of arousing in the believer here and now the act of
faith, with a view to offering it *hic et nunc* in homage to God in the cultic
action. Thus the faith is not only a presupposition of the liturgy, but forms
part of the substance itself of the liturgical action: the liturgical action consists in part in offering to God *hic et nunc*, through sensible and efficacious
signs, acts of faith as homage due Him as Creator and universal Provider,
and it is to evoke these acts that in the liturgy itself the magisterium teaches
and exhorts, that is, exercises its didascalic function.

The homage rendered to God in the liturgy is not complete unless there
is added to the act of faith the act of hope and principally that of charity.
In charity, offered to God as homage due Him as Creator and Provider, the
cycle of worship is completed.

The teaching of the magisterium, its didascalic function, aims essentially,
therefore, in the liturgy, as activating in the faithful here and now faith,
hope, and especially charity, with a view to offering each to God in the
present act of worship, as homage due to Him.

It is for this reason that the liturgy is neither a catechism nor a sermon
nor a manual of dogmatic theology nor an encyclical nor a pastoral letter.

[9] *In Boethii De Trinitate*, lect. 1, q. 1, a. 2   *logica*, Vol. 2, p. 345.
(alias 11), Marietti edition, *Opuscula theo-*

In all these means of teaching used by the Church, the end is also to arouse in the believer faith, hope, and charity, this being the aim of every activity in the Church. But in these the concern is with an end which is distinct and remote. The proximate and proper end of a catechism, a pastoral letter, etc., is simply to instruct in the faith, but not with a view to offering the acts of faith *hic et nunc* in the expression of sensible and efficacious signs, in cultic homage due to God as Creator and universal Providence.

In other words, in the liturgy the concern is first of all to make the Christian people pray here and now in community, in an act of worship, and not simply to instruct them.

This, of course, does not prevent some parts or rites or usages in the liturgy from being more directly didactic. Such is the case, in particular, historically and theoretically speaking, of the first part of the Mass. Such is the character also of the creeds introduced into the liturgy, especially the so-called Nicene-Constantinopolitan and still more the so-called Athanasian. In fact, we must recognize the historical fact that in the course of the centuries, especially in times of dogmatic struggles and disturbances, there is no lack, either on the part of the orthodox or on that of the heterodox, of recourse to the liturgy to inculcate in a more notable didactic way and even, sometimes, in a polemic way, such and such a point of faith, for example, against Arianism or against semi-Pelagianism.

But all this does not change the fundamental fact that by the very nature of things the instruction imparted in the liturgy is a function proceeding directly and immediately from prayer. And this is true even in the parts of the liturgy which are more didactic than the rest, such as the homilies, the lessons, the direct exhortations, the professions of faith, especially in the first part of the Mass. Even these parts, because they are done precisely in the liturgical action, as part of it, tend in themselves and by themselves immediately to the cultic actualization of souls and, in this sense, take on a very different character from the extraliturgical teaching of the magisterium.

Then in the other parts of the liturgy — sacrifice, prayers, especially the prayer of the Divine Office, administration and reception of the sacraments and the sacramentals, all things which, from the liturgical and cultic point of view, have much greater and more essential importance than the homilies, lessons, exhortations, and professions of faith — in the other parts, I say, the didactic aspect is much less direct and explicit. In them, by contrast, the aspect of sanctification and the aspect of worship predominate over the aspect of teaching.

The direct didactic style does not predominate in the liturgy

This observation appears to be of no little importance. Thus it is understood first of all why the liturgy, as a whole, is not at all constructed in a didactic style. The very points of a more didactic nature are intermixed as a general rule with chants and prayers, as if to translate the teaching received into an act of worship at once.

If it were desired to examine the liturgy in the general picture of literary genres, it would have to be said that it constitutes a literary genre of its own. In the liturgy there is a notable predominance over the means of expression which are meant to communicate or simply to express clear and distinct concepts of a ratiocinative type with the immediate aim of enriching the intellect, of those which are in more immediate connection with the will and the feeling, in all its shadings, with a view to creating or expressing complex affective and intuitive states of mind more than simply conceptual states.

Thus in the Roman liturgy there are the various types of orations; the various types of hymns: hymns properly so called, psalms, canticles, tracts, sequences; the refrains or antiphons; the consecratory prefaces, above all the great Eucharistic prayers or Canons of the Mass; the exorcisms. These are all forms which, from the point of view of literary genre, are typical means for expressing volitions, desires, petitions, thanksgiving, admiration, praise, repentance, or simply faith, hope, love.

It is for this reason also that in every liturgy a lyrical and rhetorical tone predominates, with greater or lesser sobriety, over mere exposition. The extent of this phenomenon will be understood if one is aware of the profound rooting of symbolism and of typology in the liturgical expression, and if one recognizes the simultaneous actualization and, as it were, general orchestration which takes place in the liturgy of all the senses of man, as has been demonstrated in its place.

All this proves that the liturgy is not so much concerned with simply communicating clear and distinct concepts or with teaching as with attuning the whole concrete man and immersing him in a general environment of prayer and of surrender to God, in that environment of *devotio* which is the soul of worship.

Now, to create such an environment, teaching together with clear and distinct concepts can be used only in a certain measure and sparingly. This is the law of religious psychology known, if only obscurely, to all those who have some experience with mental prayer, and on which, under various forms, the mystics have not failed to insist.

They do so insist when they recommend that meditation should not exhaust itself completely in intellectual considerations and in reasonings, but must take care to put the will into motion and make the feelings cooperate. They insist on it again when they warn a person to be on guard against becoming preoccupied with making clear and distinct acts of intellect or even of will in prayer, and that, if the Spirit so moves them, they be content with a simple loving glance, because in prayer, in respect to the distinct acts of the faculties, this simple loving glance is the end not the means.[10]

When the liturgy places this didactic aspect on the second level, it is simply applying this law, mindful that its nature, insofar as it is worship, is to be first of all a prayer and not a form of teaching.

This is also, it seems to me, the kernel of truth in the arguments once used by the opponents of the vernacular in the liturgy when they said that it is essential for the liturgy to preserve a certain character of indistinct mysteriousness, a character which would be lost if it were performed in a language understood by all. This kernel of truth was insufficient to justify perpetuating the use in the liturgy of a language not understood by the people; however, it may now aid us to understand that the simple fact of bringing it about that the people have a liturgy in their own living language, while it may be a powerful means for achieving an external and conscious participation in worship, is not by any means the infallible panacea, sufficient in itself to reach its highest goal. There must be still other means precisely because the liturgy is not only, nor even principally, the teaching of a doctrine but an act of worship, a prayer.

Some of the clergy who "know Latin" still use the old Psalter; others, thankful for a clearer translation, and happy to recite the psalms in a Latin text they can "understand," along with those who have availed themselves of the privilege of vernacular recitation, imagine, rather naïvely, that they have finally resolved the question of how to "pray the breviary". They will easily be able to appreciate these observations when the first effect of the novelty has passed!

All this ought surely render more cautious some persons who seem to envision the ideal of making the liturgy a kind of rostrum of propaganda — a grand means of methodically teaching the Church's doctrine, or at least the doctrines of which the world today seems to have greater need. A rostrum of propaganda it is, if you will, provided it is not forgotten that, as worship, the liturgy has for its primary aim to make the people pray and that if it does not succeed in this, it is emptied of its true force.

The liturgy is very effective indeed in teaching

If the aspect of prayer is safeguarded on the first level, then it is true that the liturgy is an incomparable means of teaching, even if indirect, or rather, perhaps, so much the more effective and universal inasmuch as it is indirect and, as it were, amalgamated in a whole complex synthesis of acts and attitudes which, almost unconsciously, and, as it were, by all the possible en-

[10] See, for example, St. John of the Cross, *Living Flame of Love* 3, 30-62; St. Teresa, *Life*, 15, nos. 6ff: "But if doctrine is of great help before and after prayer, it seems to me that during prayer it should be of very little help, so as not to weaken the will."

trances of psychology, penetrate the mind of men of any class or culture.

It could be said that the total proper efficacy of the liturgy, even as teaching, derives from the fact that, rather than "teaching," it causes doctrine to be lived. Without pretending that every true participation in the liturgical action necessarily involves a knowledge and an experience of divine things which is properly mystical in the sense in which writers on the spiritual life speak of the mystical, still it is undeniable that the liturgy is directed to a communication and penetration of divine things which is more experiential than simply conceptual. Now it is known that the vital efficacy of experiential penetration is immensely superior to that of mere conceptual communication.

Thus considered, the liturgy appears as the principal means of the Church for causing her view of the world to penetrate vitally into the minds of the faithful, even if, in its complexus, it is a means of communication of doctrine less direct, less conceptually precise, and less intellectual than the other means which the magisterium habitually uses. It is the principal means in the sense that it is more vitally effective, more continual, more intuitive and penetrating, more popular and universal.[11]

2. Some General Rules for Determining the Extent to Which the Church Imposes Anything in the Liturgy as Being a Matter of Faith

Since the liturgy, as a means of teaching, is a means of teaching of the ordinary magisterium and, since, as a whole, it is less precise conceptually than the other means, in many cases it offers the theologian special difficulties when he considers it with the purpose of knowing to what extent, in a determinate case, recourse can be had to the liturgy to know conceptually the teaching of the magisterium.

This difficulty makes itself felt especially when it is desired to determine precisely, on a certain point, what is properly *de fide* in the liturgy and what is not, and what degree of adherence must be given to each element.

The question has real importance because one of the essential tasks of the theologian is precisely that of determining in any proposition what the magisterium proposes and with what degree of authority it proposes it. The

---

[11] Quite rightly, then, did Pope Pius XI observe: "To pervade the faithful and to elevate them thus to the happiness of the interior life, the annual celebrations of the sacred mysteries have an efficacy far greater than that of any other kind of document of the ecclesiastical magisterium, even those of the gravest import. These latter documents, in fact, for the most part reach only a few persons and those the more learned, while the former, the liturgical celebrations, strike home and instruct all the faithful. The latter speak only once, while the former, if you will, speak every year and perpetually. The latter address themselves primarily to the intellect, whereas the former influence in a salutary way the intellect and the soul, that is, the whole man" (*Quas primas, AAS*, Vol. 17 [1925], p. 603; in Bugnini, *Documenta*, p. 57, no. 2).

use which will be made of liturgy in theology will depend in large measure on the possibility of specifying these points in the liturgy.

It is for this reason that the post-Tridentine theologians, after Melchior Cano, who had attempted to determine the rules for resolving the same questions with regard to Scripture, tradition, and the other so-called theological loci, sought to do the same with regard to the liturgy, of which Cano had not spoken.

Starting with Zaccaria as a major source, theologians have proposed and do yet propose a rather complicated series of rules for determining in individual cases what they call the theological authority of the liturgy. It seems to me that the following observations may be made in this connection.

Philological and critical-historical research

First of all, the theologian who examines any element whatsoever of the liturgy — text, rite, or usage of the present or of the historical past, of the Roman liturgy or of another liturgy — must take into account what can be discovered concerning the meaning of this element by the simple and pure light of philology and of history.

For this phase of the inquiry it is necessary to try to see the philological significance of a word or of a text; what can be unearthed in any case from the proximate or remote context, from investigating the origin, development, vicissitudes of a text, a usage, an object. Here nothing more is required than to apply accurately and honestly the laws of philological and historical research. But this is demanded simply because the liturgy is composed of words, of phrases, of usages, of objects, etc., and because these elements in any case have a context and a history.

Up to this point we can, I think, agree perfectly with those modern liturgists who belong to the philologico-historical school, who keep insisting on the necessity of accurate technical, philological and historical research into the liturgy. They are right, I think, inasmuch as such research must necessarily constitute the indispensable basis for the study of the liturgy.

This phase, however, is far from constituting the whole of liturgical inquiry; in fact, it is nothing but the beginning. Its results are not at all the definitive results to which the theologian, or the believer as such, can attain. It is necessary to pursue another phase of research. This further phase begins at the precise moment when, from the elements obtained in the philological and historical phase, it is desired to give a higher judgment in the light of the doctrine of the faith, by which light whatever God has revealed and the Roman Catholic Church, through her responsible organs, proposes for our belief, is admitted as true. It is only at the end of this further phase that the full theological judgment takes place, the one which, for the believer, gives, insofar as possible, the definitive light on the value and the sense of any element of the liturgy.

It may be that this definitive theological judgment simply confirms, by another way and under another light, the historical and philological inquiry. But it is not necessary that this be so. In particular, at any rate, only this definitive theological judgment can give the believer the ultimate answer as to the extent to which the faith is involved in the single elements of the liturgy and the degree of adherence which the believer is bound to give to these individual elements.

Four principal rules for arriving at the theological judgment

This answer is obtained by following the rules taught by general theological methodology for finding out what is and what is not of faith. In particular, let the Catholic doctrine be recalled that revelation is contained in the Scriptures and in the oral Apostolic dogmatic tradition, and is proposed and explained to the faith of the believer by the magisterium of the Church.

This magisterium precisely because it is by Christ's will — which can be ascertained and proved also by historical-philological examination of the New Testament — the infallible and indispensable propositive means of revelation, is also, by the fact itself, the supreme proximate criterion by means of which the believer knows what he is to believe.

It is also known that a proximate infallible criterion of the faith is, speaking precisely, the present-day, living magisterium of the Church; it is never mere individual reason, either philosophical or historical or philological. The present-day and living magisterium is the supreme interpreter not only of the Scriptures and of the oral Apostolic dogmatic tradition, but also of its own thought and its own documents expressed even in more or less remote times.

It is known also that the authentic organs of the infallible teaching authority of the Church are the Catholic bishops, dispersed over the whole earth, united with the Roman Pontiff, when they propose with unanimity a matter as of the faith (called the ordinary and universal magisterium of the Church); the ecumenical councils together with the Roman Pontiff, who at least approves of them as such; the Roman Pontiff himself when he speaks *ex cathedra*. Also from the faith of the people united to their bishops and to the Roman Pontiff, can it be known what is of faith for a believer, inasmuch as from the faith universally embraced can it be known what the magisterium itself proposes as of faith.

Let it be observed also that in the liturgy, materially speaking, there are various elements: texts of the Scriptures; documents emanating from or approved as of faith by the ecumenical councils, such as the so-called Nicene-Constantinopolitan creed; many other elements of diverse origin and nature. In the liturgy the magisterium directly involved is the ordinary magisterium.

It is clear that this magisterium proposes as of faith the passages of the Scriptures and the decisions of faith of the ecumenical councils contained in the liturgy. For these documents, certainly matters of faith, there can be at most some doubt on their precise interpretation, but no doubt that in them the Church, also in the liturgy, proposes something as of faith.

On the other hand, the difficulty of knowing whether or not the magisterium, in a given element of the liturgy, really proposes something as of the faith, is met with also in all the other magisterial documents of diverse nature and origin. It is to resolve just this difficulty that the theologians strive to propose some directive methodological rules. It seems to me that, when all is said and done, the principal rules for this purpose can be reduced to four.

FIRST RULE: *The various elements of the liturgy involve that precise ordinary propositive doctrinal authority in which the individual members of the hierarchy share who have issued them or who have approved them.*

Let us recall that the liturgy, being by its nature an official act of the Church as such, hierarchically structured, depends essentially on the authentic hierarchy of the Church. The teaching authority of the authentic hierarchy which is engaged in it is not the extraordinary magisterium, but the ordinary. Authentic organs of the ordinary magisterium are the individual bishops in their own dioceses, and the Roman Pontiff throughout the whole Chuch. Any individual bishop, whoever he be, if he is not united with the Roman Pontiff, enjoys no doctrinal authority in the Church. A bishop, even if his life is such that he is habitually united to the Roman Pontiff, is not infallible, considered in himself alone. The individual bishops dispersed throughout the world in their own dioceses, and at the same time united with the Pope, enjoy infallible authority in proposing a doctrine only in the event that, together with the Roman Pontiff, they are all morally in agreement in proposing as of divine and Catholic faith a determinate doctrine concerning faith and morals. Let it be recalled that not just any morally unanimous agreement is enough, but that it is necessary that this morally unanimous agreement carry with it precisely the intention of proposing as of divine and Catholic faith a doctrine concerning faith and morals.

It is known that in ancient times the composition and the arrangement of the liturgy was up to the individual bishops for the particular portions of the Church entrusted to them. The liturgy at that time was of episcopal right. This means that in the ancient liturgies there is involved only that doctrinal authority which is within the competence of the individual bishops habitually in union with the Roman Pontiff and who issued or approved those liturgies at least by the use which they made of them.

Only in relatively recent times (sixteenth century), after various trials, was the right finally reserved to the Roman Pontiff of explicit supreme approval of the liturgical texts and rites in the whole Catholic Church. From that time on, the liturgy in the Catholic Church is of papal rite and the ordinary doctrinal authority (not necessarily *ex cathedra*) of the Roman Pontiff is more directly engaged. This is true even of the non-Roman liturgies in use today in the Catholic Church.

The preceding observations permit the establishment of some important norms when the concern is with determining what is proposed and must be believed as of divine and Catholic faith in the historical or present-day liturgies.

First consequence: there is no real difficulty if in some particular ancient liturgy, for a certain time, there infiltrated formulas or doctrines not correct, or downright errors. The individual bishops are not infallible. Thus is resolved, for example, the case of the Mass "to alleviate the pains of hell" in some ancient missals.

Second consequence: if there are elements common, or morally common, to all the liturgies, at least for a certain period of time, especially if this is verified from antiquity on, and if it is evident that, in the liturgies, these elements are proposed as of faith, this mere fact would already demonstrate by itself alone that the matter is really of the faith. However, it will be most difficult [12] to prove from the liturgy alone that the matter has really been proposed as of faith, and this with moral unanimity. In very many cases it will be possible, on the other hand, to demonstrate it easily by having recourse to other extraliturgical proofs, and without forgetting the evolution of dogmas in the individual periods. Thus, for example: the liceity of the cult of the saints, of relics, of images, the usefulness of the invocation of the saints, the baptism of infants for the remission of sins, the usefulness of prayer for the dead and of offering the sacrifice for them, and many other similar tenets.

Third consequence: from the time of the explicit approbation given by the Roman Pontiff, even by exercise of the ordinary magisterium, to the liturgies in use today in the Catholic Church, these liturgies can be considered in practice as immune from errors against faith and morals.

SECOND RULE: *What the magisterium proposes in the liturgy for the adherence of the faithful, and which the faithful accept, is proposed with diverse degrees of dogmatic authority, according to the matter in question; and the faithful, in the same way, provided that they are well informed of the intention of the magisterium, respond with an adherence that varies in degree and quality.*

This is simply a rule of general theological methodology: not everything that the magisterium proposes is proposed by it with the same degree of authoritative force or with the intention of engaging its responsibility or doctrinal authority and the faith of the believers in the same manner.

Some points are proposed by it to be believed with divine and Catholic faith under the pain of shipwreck of the faith; in them the magisterium engages all its infallible authority. Others, on the other hand, are proposed by

---

[12] See below, fourth rule.

the magisterium in lesser authoritative degree. This in its turn may vary from the degree which the theologians call proximate to faith, without being strictly of faith; to opinion simply admitted as such; to mere hypothesis, more or less generally admitted, which the magisterium does not intend for the moment to contradict, but concerning which, even while presupposing it, the magisterium does not intend to assume any special responsibility. Between these stances there can be an indefinite number of degrees and shadings.

In the same way, the faithful are not to give to whatever is proposed by the teaching authority the same degree and the same kind of adherence. The general rule is simply that the believer give to every single proposition of the magisterium that degree and that kind of adherence which the magisterium requires of him, neither more nor less. That which is proposed by the teaching authority as of divine and Catholic faith under pain of shipwreck of the faith itself, must be believed by the faithful with divine and Catholic faith and with closest adherence as required by the authority of God revealing, which is the formal motive of divine faith. To all the rest he must adhere with an adherence inferior in nature and in degree, according to the nature and degree of the proposition of the magisterium.

This general rule holds also for that proposal of doctrine of the magisterium which takes place, in its way, in the liturgy. In the various elements of the liturgy these degrees of proposal are very diverse. They are so much the more diverse and hard to distinguish because in the liturgy, as has been explained, the teaching aim is only indirect, while a didactic expression that is explicit and precise is very rare.

Let us take the example of the liturgical feasts. Many feasts propose a certain historical fact, which in some way is the object of the feast. But the degree or authority with which the magisterium proposes this fact and with which the faithful accept it as true varies greatly.

The fact of the resurrection of our Lord, which is the object of the feast of Easter, is proposed and believed as of divine and Catholic faith.

So also, today, after the definition of the Assumption, the fact of the Assumption of our Lady into heaven is so proposed in the feast of the same name, and so believed. But before the definition this fact was not proposed as of divine and Catholic faith, but certainly at least as extremely probable, proximate to faith. In more ancient times, the same fact was proposed by the liturgy as acceptable and praiseworthy.

The presentation of our Lady in the temple, which is in some way the object of the feast of November 21, is presented by the magisterium, on the other hand, only as a pious legend, even if in the feast there are ideas which are certainly proposed with a greater degree of authority, such as the idea that our Lady was consecrated in a very special way to God from her childhood.

The case of the translation of the holy house of Loretto, which was in some way involved in the feast of the same name, was also presented by the magisterium only as a pious legend. Points associated with the feast which have for object supposed apparitions, miracles not reported in the Scriptures, private revelations and the like, were admitted by the Church only as reports that could be lawfully and piously believed. Such is the case also with the apparition of our Lady at Lourdes and the stigmata of St. Francis.

In the same way, in the feasts which have for their object an idea or a doctrine, such an idea or doctrine are proposed by the magisterium, according to the particulars in questions, with very diverse degrees of authority. Thus, for example, the feast of Christ the King includes points which are of faith, while any liturgy on the mediation of our Lady in respect to all graces is, for now, only a theological opinion.

THIRD RULE: *The evolution of dogmas, doctrines, and opinions is reflected in the liturgy. Such development is admitted by Catholic faith and demonstrated by history.*

The Catholic faith, while rejecting the modernist transformistic concept of the evolution of dogmas, does admit their evolution in the sense of an ever greater explicitation of the same substantial truth, according to the times and the circumstances.

With greater reason a real evolution is admitted in mere doctrine and opinion. Thus a tenet which at a certain time in history could have the appearance of a mere opinion more or less founded and widespread, with the development and deepening of theological thought may become increasingly common doctrine and ultimately be proposed by the competent organs of the infallible teaching authority as dogma of divine and Catholic faith. On the other hand, an opinion more or less widespread at a certain time may come to appear less well-founded or even downright erroneous, and be abandoned.

That all this may be reflected in the liturgy in general, or in a particular liturgy, is obvious and does not present any special difficulties. The liturgy may reflect, more or less abundantly, the theological positions of an epoch and their evolution.

Thus the feast of the Immaculate Conception in the twelfth and thirteenth centuries reflected a theological position, and there were notable differences among the theologians about the object of the feast. But the same feast at the beginning of the nineteenth century, in the proposal of the magisterium and in the adherence of the faithful, reflected quite another state of the doctrine. And today it reflects still another.

Today the feast of Mary Mediatrix of All Graces, granted to several dioceses, still expresses only a theological opinion. But this does not mean at all that it will always remain in this phase.

It is understood also that, with the progress of this evolution, changes are made in the liturgy which are of interest to doctrine. Thus in the liturgical books, beginning with the twelfth century, there disappeared little by little the rubric which supposed that the wine in the chalice could be consecrated by mere contact with the host already consecrated.[13] Recently the rubrics concerning the matter and form of the sacrament of Holy orders have been modified by the Apostolic Constitution *Sacramentum ordinis*, in accordance with the decisions of Pius XII.[14] In the Mass of the Assumption, revised with the declaration of the dogma, there was no longer any mention made of the bodily death of our Lady, because the opinion that our Lady did not really die was beginning to gain ground. The Common of Supreme Pontiffs promulgated some thirty years ago reflected the contemporary development of theological thinking concerning the Roman Pontiff and the current *de facto* exercise of his authority. The great dogmatic disputes of the fourth to the eighth centuries over dogmas of the Trinity, of Christ, of Mary, of grace, of images, have left notable traces in the liturgies.[15]

The same evolution can bring it about that ancient formulas and rites which in the beginning had a very specific message for those who composed them or made use of them, later came to be interpreted in a different way. So, perhaps, the epiclesis in the Eastern liturgies; the object of the feast of the Immaculate Conception; the object of the feast of the Assumption.

An observation in this connection is opportune. Let us suppose that certain texts in our Roman liturgy for the dead, originally in centuries past really implied the opinion of delayed and not immediate retribution for the souls of the departed. At any rate, it is certain that such a text could subsist in the Roman liturgy to this day only because the Church understands it in such a way that in reciting it she does not intend by any means to deny the doctrine of immediate judgment and retribution. And it is in this sense that it must be understood today, because it is in this sense that the magisterium now proposes it. From this it can be seen how inadequate it is, in some cases, for establishing the meaning which a certain element in the liturgy has, to turn only to philology or to the meaning it may have had when it was first composed or inserted in the liturgy.

Likewise it must be said that today every Catholic must interpret the epicleses in use in the Eastern liturgies of the Catholic Church in such a way as to safeguard the doctrine that the form of the Eucharist is constituted only

---

[13] See M. Andrieu's *Immixtio et consecratio*, Paris 1924. The final disappearance of the last vestiges of this opinion took place, in the liturgical books, in the sixteenth century.

[14] *AAS*, Vol. 40 (1948), pp. 5-7.

[15] For the variations in the formularies of the Mass of the Sacred Heart, see A. Bugnini, *"Le messe del SS. Cuore di Gesù,"* in *Cor Iesu*, Vol. I, Rome 1959, pp. 59-94.

of the words of the institution, aside from the question of what possibly was the opinion of the original composers of these epicleses.

FOURTH RULE: *In practice, only by means of exhaustive theological study of each individual problem can the degree of authority of any point of the liturgy, historical or present-day, be determined.*

This fourth rule is by far the most important. In fact, if the preceding observations are admitted, the crucial point for the theologian or the believer who is concerned with knowing what doctrinal value such and such an element has which is found in the historical or current liturgies, is to know how to determine, in the individual cases, the degree of authority which the magisterium gave, at a given epoch, and gives today to this element.

Can the study of the liturgy alone lead to this result? Even from the liturgy alone it will sometimes be possible to have indications. The importance given to an element, whether it be found in one or several liturgies, or quite clearly in all, can suggest that in this the teaching authority is engaged more or less notably. The universality of the feast of the Assumption and its notable degree of solemnity may suggest a notable engagement of the ordinary and universal magisterium in the proposal of this point of doctrine.

But for the most part it will be exceedingly difficult, if not downright impossible, to determine with sufficient precision from the liturgy alone the degree of authority which the magisterium engages in proposing an element, even supposing — which is not always the case — that the very meaning of the element in question can be determined sufficiently from the liturgy alone.

The very antiquity and universality of the element is not an absolutely apodictic proof that it is proposed in the liturgy by the magisterium as a matter of divine and Catholic faith. It must not be forgotten that in order to be able to argue apodictically from the ordinary and universal magisterium alone that a doctrine is proposed by the Church as of divine and Catholic faith, it is not enough to show that in proposing this doctrine there is moral unanimity among the bishops united with the Roman Pontiff; it must also be proved that they propose it with moral unanimity precisely as a matter of faith.

A new proof of the difficulty encountered by anyone who wants to infer from the liturgy alone the precise degree of authority with which the magisterium there proposes a doctrine has been had in our own times in the brief discussions which preceded the definition of the Assumption. Many were asking what motive there could be for making this definition when, as they thought, the magisterium had already proposed that doctrine to the faith of believers for a long time in the very feast of the Assumption. In fact, to consider only the liturgical side of the question, and abstracting from the dogmatic bull of Pius IX, the reading of which, contrary to previous liturgical customs, had been introduced into the breviary for the feast of the Immaculate Conception, what difference could ever be established between the manner in which the Church proposed the Immaculate Conception to the faithful and the manner in which she proposed the Assumption? And yet this difference, from the dogmatic point of view, was very great.

Sometimes, it is true, by following attentively the historical development of the various liturgical elements, for example of a feast such as that of the Immaculate Conception in the West,[16] a progressive increase of emphasis and of authority on the part of the magisterium can be discovered. But, first of all, this is not always the case; and then it is ever a question of ascertaining an evidence of increase of general emphasis, the nature and degree of which cannot be specified by a consideration of the liturgical elements alone.

The successive liturgical changes brought about in the liturgy of the feast of the Immaculate Conception especially since the fifteenth century do not take on a precise significance with regard to the degree of obligation which the magisterium put into them until they are considered in the light of the contemporary developments of the theological controversy over the same matter, and in the light of other unambiguous manifestations of the feeling of those Roman Pontiffs who were concerned — in other words, in the light of the extraliturgical manifestations of the contemporary ordinary magisterium.

What is the reason for this state of affairs? The essential reason must be sought in the very nature of the liturgy. As has been said, the liturgy, inasmuch as it contains an action of the Church, is directly and essentially a worship, a prayer; and it does not involve an activity of teaching except in a very indirect way, for the very reason that the Church considers it useful and opportune to impel the faithful, while engaged in the liturgical action, to turn their whole mind to God in a response of worship and prayer.

And this explains, as has been observed, why the liturgy is neither a catechism nor a manual of dogmatic theology. The Church supposes in the liturgy that the congregation of the faithful who take part in it already know their catechism and that the clergy already know their manual of dogmatic theology. Supposing such knowledge — and, to be sure, recalling some point of it to mind on occasion — the Church in the liturgy is wholly concerned with making her children pray here and now.

This accounts for the observable fact that, without detriment to the truth, taking advantage of everything which she considers useful for leading the faithful to a worshipful and prayerful state of mind, in the liturgy the Church is occupied scarcely at all with advising the faithful, for every element used, with what precise degree of authority she intends to bind or not bind their faith in each one of the cases considered. Such preoccupations would be very far from the nature of the liturgy.

It follows, on the other hand, that for the one who is properly concerned

---

[16] See J. Löw in *Enciclopedia cattolica*, Vol. VI (1951), cols. 1659-1662.

with this aspect of things, the theologian, to satisfy his legitimate preoccupation, there must be recourse to the total theological study of the question with which he is concerned. Only this general theological study of the question, made according to the usual criteria of theology, will be able to give him, insofar as is possible, a sure answer as to the degree of authority and the sense in which the ordinary magisterium imposes a determinate element in the liturgy for the adherence of the faithful, and hence, to what degree and kind of adherence the faithful are held in their turn.

Thus, with what degree of authority the magisterium, immediately before the definition of the Assumption, imposed the same doctrine of the Assumption in the liturgy, could be determined with sufficient clarity only by the total theological study of the doctrine of the Assumption. Only thus could it be seen that up to that time, in the liturgy itself, the Church was not imposing the Assumption as a tenet of divine and Catholic faith, under pain of shipwreck of the faith, but with a lower degree of authenticity and of authority, although already very great at that time; let us say, with the theologians, as *proximate to the faith*, that is, as so probable that anyone who, by chance, had wanted to deny it would certainly find himself in grave and proximate danger of erring.

In what sense and with what degree of authority private revelations are proposed in the liturgy — as, for example, those made to St. Margaret Mary Alacoque, of which mention was formerly made in the lessons of the breviary during the octave of the feast of the Sacred Heart — can be determined only from the total theological study on the thinking of the Church concerning private revelations.

What meaning the exorcisms in the liturgy have and with what degree of authority the liturgy imposes what is said or implied about such exorcisms can be determined only by the general theological consensus on the topic.

Concerning many points relating to ecclesiastical or profane history which the liturgy seemingly supposes as historically true (for example, in the accounts of the lives of the saints in the former lessons of the second nocturn of the breviary), the Church asks for nothing more than mere human faith, a response which they merit according to the current state of historical knowledge. From this it is seen that when the Church makes mention of seemingly historical facts in the liturgy, she is doing nothing but accepting their truth hypothetically, according to the opinion — sometimes even the mere opinion of the crowd — of the time in which they were admitted into the texts; then, passing over this hypothetically supposed truth and not imposing its *de facto* acceptance, she concerns herself with disposing the faithful to the act of worship and of prayer which is the purpose of the liturgy.

We may conclude, for example, that statements concerning the presentation of our Lady in the temple or the translation of the holy house of Loretto, when made in the liturgy, are not made except as pious legends; and for this reason the Church does not intend in any way to support with her authority the historical veracity of these statements.

If these observations were kept in mind and if it were remembered that the purpose of the liturgy is to make people pray, many who, as a result of modern formation, have a very developed historical and critical sense, but not necessarily an equally vigorous sense of prayer, would perhaps be less scandalized to find that the Church is not in too much of a hurry to purify the liturgy from historical inaccuracies and errors or even from legends. Recalling, moreover, that the veneration given to the saints, in the last analysis, goes above all to God, one should not be too disturbed either by the fact of finding in the liturgy, if such is really the case, feasts of saints who never existed, or the veneration of relics that are not authentic.

3. Lex Orandi Lex Credendi:
Reciprocal Influences between Faith and Liturgy

The phrase from the *Indiculus* and its meaning

All things considered, therefore, what are the reciprocal influences between faith and liturgy? The formula *lex orandi lex credendi* is an abbreviation of a passage from the *Indiculus de gratia Dei*.[17] This latter is a document of the fifth century against the Pelagians and semi-Pelagians, in which are gathered a series of testimonies of the previous Roman Pontiffs about the questions of grace, concluding the whole (chapters 11 and 12) with an argument deduced from the liturgy. The document was compiled probably by St. Prosper of Aquitaine,[18] but certainly reflects the thinking of the Roman curia of that era, and has notable theological authority because the Roman See has since then always considered it as the exact expression of its point of view in the matter under discussion and, subsequently, has often appealed to it.

From the point of view which interests us, the essential passage is the following:

> ". . . Let us consider also the sacraments of the prayers which the bishops offer (*obsecrationem quoque sacerdotalium sacramenta respiciamus*), which, handed down by the Apostles, in the whole world and in every Catholic church are recited in the same way (*uniformiter celebrantur*), in order that the obligatory manner of praying may determine the obligatory manner of believing (*ut legem credendi lex statuat supplicandi*). For when the prelates of the holy people fulfill the man-

---

[17] See Dz nos. 238-249 (129-142). For the study of the proximate and remote context of the document, see Karl Federer, *loc. cit.* above in note 4 of the present chapter.

[18] Thesis of D. M. Cappuyns, articles in

Revue Bénédictine, Vol. 39 (1927), pp. 198-226; Vol. 41 (1929), pp. 156-170. The thesis is confirmed by the study of Federer referred to above in note 4, present chapter.

date entrusted to them, they support the cause of all mankind with the divine clemency; and, the whole assembly (*ecclesia*) groaning together with them, they ask and pray that the faith be given to infidels, that idolaters be freed from the errors of their false religion, that the veil be taken from the hearts of the Jews and the light shine on them, that heretics come to repentance and turn to the Catholic faith, that schismatics receive the spirit which will revive their charity, that the remedy of repentance be granted the lapsed, and finally, that the catechumens be conducted to the sacraments of regeneration and be welcomed into the bosom of God's mercy." [19]

The exact meaning of the phrase *ut legem credendi lex statuat supplicandi*, in the immediate context, has been sufficiently clarified by Federer [20] in relation to the text of St. Paul in 1 Tim. 2:1-4 and to the thought of St. Augustine, on which the author of the document certainly depends very closely. In the immediate sense of the author the formula means simply: in order that from the obligation which the Apostle lays on us (1 Tim. 2:1-4) and which the bishops satisfy in the liturgy, of praying for all that grace may be given to all (*lex orandi*), the obligation may appear clear also of believing against the Pelagians and the semi-Pelagians, that grace is necessary for all (*lex credendi*).

When the formula of the *Indiculus* is reduced to the more precise *lex orandi lex credendi*, and this is posited of the general relations which obtain between liturgy and faith, this does nothing but extend to the liturgy in general, understood as the law and norm of the official prayer of the Church, and to the faith in general in its relations with the liturgy, the somewhat more restricted reasoning of the author of the *Indiculus*.

It is well known that the modernists [21] supposed they could find in the formula *lex orandi lex credendi* their theories on the concept of the faith as blind feeling, completely extraneous to discursive reason, which is generated in the subconscious and is expressed in some way in the practical and religious life, especially in the liturgy. The liturgy in turn would be the generative rule of dogmatic formulas, and these would be nothing but an attempt to express intellectually the state reached at a certain moment of development by that same blind religious feeling. Thus the blind religious feeling, extraneous to reason and continually changeable, which somehow makes its states extrinsic in the liturgy, would also command the formulation and the meaning of the dogmas, as well as the necessity of their continual adaptation, even substantial, to its variation.

There is no need to waste time on such an interpretation of the formula *lex*

[19] Dz 246 (139).
[20] See page 123 of his work, for his conclusion.
[21] Especially George Tyrell, *Lex Orandi or*

Prayer and Creed, London 1903; and the same modernist author, *Through Scylla and Carybdis or the Old Theology into the New*, London 1907.

orandi lex credendi. It is completely foreign to the Catholic meaning and falls with the concept of faith and of dogma which it presupposes.

From the Catholic point of view, on the other hand, it must be said that the meaning of the principle *lex orandi lex credendi* is the following: the liturgy always presupposes and expresses a certain teaching and a certain belief in a very broad sense; but, in many cases it moreover presupposes and follows logically the divine and Catholic faith, in the strict sense, already made explicit; in other words, it supposes and follows the proposal and the acceptance of the dogmas; in these cases the liturgy expresses the divine and Catholic faith, already made explicit, makes it lived, and strengthens it in the believers. In still other cases the liturgy precedes the making explicit of the divine and Catholic faith, in other words the proposal and acceptance of dogmas, and is an occasional potent factor in this process of making it explicit.

The liturgy as expression and means of strengthening in the faithful the dogmas already made explicit

There is no need to insist on the affirmation that the liturgy, always and in every case, presupposes and logically follows a certain teaching of the Church and a certain belief in a very general sense. It could be said, in this sense, that the liturgy, always and in every case, presupposes and logically follows "the faith," if by "faith" is understood not specifically the divine and Catholic faith, which is properly of dogmas, but, in a very broad sense, belief in general, even that which refers to mere theological doctrines more or less widespread and common, to theological opinion, historical or other, even if singular and only accepted as hypothesis. But it is noticed at once that, in this case, it is very ambiguous to speak of "faith." It would be better to say simply that the liturgy supposes always and expresses at least an opinion and perhaps even a theological doctrine more or less widespread.

What is of interest, however, is to determine the relations of the liturgy with divine and Catholic faith. For this purpose we must recall first of all that in the liturgy some things are proposed and accepted as of divine and Catholic faith, as dogmas, while others are proposed and accepted with a lesser degree of authority. We must recall also the fact of the evolution of dogmas as admitted by Catholic teaching.

In those cases, therefore, where the doctrine implied in the liturgy is a doctrine which the teaching authority proposes as of divine and Catholic faith, the principle holds in a strict sense that the liturgy supposes and expresses the faith, that is, presupposes and expresses the divine and Catholic faith already proposed by the magisterium in other ways, makes it live again and strengthens it in the faithful. And why is this?

Every dogma of divine and Catholic faith involves, on the part of the

teaching authority, the determination of a doctrine as revealed and the imposition on all the faithful of the most grave moral obligation to adhere
totally and with the greatest firmness to such doctrine under pain of shipwreck of the faith itself.

It is necessary, therefore, that every formal dogma, that is, every doctrine
proposed or defined as of divine and Catholic faith, be so proposed and
defined in such a way that the precise point in question appears sufficiently
determined and that the intention of the magisterium to propose or define
such point as of divine and Catholic faith and to bind the faith of believers
with a corresponding obligation is sufficiently manifest.

Present canon law is simply clarifying and proposing explicitly a doctrine
which is demanded by the very nature of things when it says, "nothing
should be considered declared or defined as dogma if such is not manifestly
apparent." [22]

But the teaching authority implied in the liturgy is the ordinary magisterium. I should not want to say at all, as some theologians seem to affirm,
that the definition of a doctrine as dogma of divine and Catholic faith cannot
be made, at least today, except through the extraordinary magisterium of an
ecumenical council or of the Roman Pontiff speaking *ex cathedra*.

Yet it is undeniable that in coming to know (by means only of the ordinary
magisterium, even speaking outside of the liturgy with the direct means of
teaching which it usually employs) whether a doctrine is proposed by the
Church as of divine and Catholic faith, there are always special difficulties.
To know the morally unanimous thinking of all the bishops scattered
throughout the world and to know whether this thinking proposes a determinate point as of divine and Catholic faith is not at all a simple matter,
abstracting from the extraordinary magisterium. It is for this reason that, on
specific occasions, another form of magisterium, the solemn and extraordinary
one of the ecumenical council or of the Roman Pontiff speaking *ex cathedra*,
is necessary as a matter of fact.

At any rate, it must be said frankly that when the question of whether the
teaching authority proposes a determinate point as of divine and Catholic
faith turns upon a doctrine currently disputed among Catholics themselves,
there is no possibility, at least practically, of settling the dispute technically
by means of the ordinary magisterium alone, even considering its manifestations of direct teaching outside of the liturgy. If such a possibility existed,

---

[22] *Codex iuris canonici*, can. 1323 § 3. Let
it be noted that the expression "implicit definition" which is sometimes encountered in
authors is self-contradictory. A definition of the
magisterium is always explicit, since it means
by its very nature a determination of doctrine.
There are doctrines implicit in others already
defined; but, as long as they are only implicit,
they must still be deduced from the first, and
such deduction, until it is authorized by the
magisterium and therefore made explicit, can
never be regarded as a dogma of divine and
Catholic faith.

there would be no dispute on any particular doctrinal point among Catholics themselves.

This difficulty, inherent in the very nature of the ordinary magisterium in general, is notably aggravated when it is desired to settle a similar question by having recourse to the same ordinary magisterium as it is expressed in the liturgy alone. The very manner in which the teaching of the ordinary magisterium is involved in the liturgy, which is, as a whole, only indirect and implicit, has for its consequence the fact that from the liturgy alone it is not possible to know with sufficient clarity what the magisterium proposes as of faith and what it does not propose in that way, and that it is necessary to have recourse to other loci.

This means that the proposal of a dogma of divine and Catholic faith does not take place the first time by way of the liturgy alone, and that every time the liturgy involves such a dogma, this has been proposed by the magisterium through other ways, extraliturgical ways, before making its appeareance in the liturgy.

In these cases the liturgy is of its very nature an expression of the divine and Catholic faith already proposed by the magisterium and accepted by the faithful; the liturgy follows the faith, makes it live, and strengthens it in the believers.

The importance of the liturgy in the process of making dogmas explicit

But even in the case where the liturgy contains elements and doctrines proposed with a degree of authority less than that of dogma, its relation with the faith properly so called — divine faith in general, and also divine and Catholic faith — is very close and worthy of consideration. In these cases, it can be said in a very true sense that the liturgy precedes the divine and Catholic faith and in some way begets it.

It is a more precise knowledge of the evolution of dogmas that permits us today to have a better understanding of this important aspect of the relations between liturgy and faith. The liturgy is one of the principal contributors to the evolution of dogma, as that evolution is admitted by Catholic teaching. This is the kernel of truth which was contained in the modernist interpretation of the principle *lex orandi lex credendi*. But how and in what sense?

In order to understand this fact fully, it would be necessary to enter into the theological details which explain the evolutionary process by which simple doctrines, at first more or less widespread in the Church, come to be dogmas formally proposed as such. In particular, it would be necessary to clarify in detail the part which the so-called *sensus Catholicus* has or can have in this process. For it is primarily by means of the influence which the *sensus Catholicus* exerts, that the liturgy is a potent causative factor in the evolution of dogmas.

Without entering into the details of the discussions to which this matter gives rise among theologians, it seems to me that the following observations can be made on the subject.

Let us recall first of all that, according to Catholic doctrine, divine faith in general is an adherence of the intellect to a truth, an adherence formally given because of the authority of God who has revealed the truth. The formal or determining element in divine faith is that that adherence be intrinsically determined as by its cause: in the last analysis by nothing else but the authority of God who reveals.

Just as the act of the eye's seeing is intrinsically and formally carried out by the perception of light and by nothing else — wanting to see, opening the eyelids, having healthy organs are all prerequisite conditions, but they are not that which intrinsically and formally actuates the seeing of the eye — so the act of divine faith is an adherence of the intellect intrinsically and formally determined by the authority of God revealing and by nothing else.

That it be within our knowledge that God has revealed the truth to which we adhere in divine faith is an indispensable prerequisite for being able to give that adherence, but it is not the intrinsic determining element of the faith itself, because if it were otherwise, this would be transformed into adherence of knowledge, which is quite another type of intellectual assent. But it is really an indispensable prerequisite that it be within our knowledge that God has revealed; otherwise the assent of faith would be a blind and irrational assent, something which cannot exist in divine faith.

The means by which we come to know in some way that God has revealed a truth are also conditions prerequisite to the act of faith; but they are the means which lead to it and not the intrinsic determining element of this act itself. For the contemporaries of Christ, for example, this is the case with the miracles which He performed to convince them that He was truly the one sent by God and that the doctrine He was teaching was of divine origin. In theology they are called motives of credibility.[23]

We must remember further the distinction between divine faith in general, and divine and Catholic faith. When it is known to a person in a certain way, whether by means of a private revelation or by means of his own private reasoning, that God has actually revealed a truth, he is obliged to adhere to this truth because of the authority of God revealing; and his act of faith

---

[23] For this reason, in regard to the act of faith, theologians distinguish the motive of faith (authority of God revealing and nothing else) and motives of credibility, which are only prerequisite conditions for the act of faith. To have knowledge that God has revealed is a prerequisite condition as motive of credibility. Thus the theologians say that revelation itself, understood in a passive sense — the placing *ad extra* of the sign which manifests the will of God — is only a prerequisite condition by means of which we come to the knowledge of the intrinsic will of God which is manifested.

will always be by that very fact an act of divine faith. In the case of a private revelation, however, or of another private persuasion of his, this act of faith obliges him alone, personally. His faith is indeed divine, but private.

On the other hand, for the act of divine faith to be obligatory on all believers without distinction, it is a necessary prerequisite that the doctrine be proposed by the infallible teaching authority of the Church as revealed by God. If this proposal is verified, by this very fact all believers, under pain of shipwreck of the faith, must adhere formally to that truth by virtue of the authority of God revealing. This faith, therefore, is called divine and Catholic faith.[24] This is the faith properly due to dogmas formally proposed as such.

In this divine and Catholic faith the proposal by the infallible teaching authority is, for the believer, only an antecedent condition in order that he may be certain that God has revealed and may therefore give his assent determined intrinsically and formally by the sole authority of God revealing; just as the affirmation of the ambassador speaking in the name of the sovereign is only the means and the condition for knowing the will of the sovereign and not the intrinsic formal cause which makes us accept this will, this cause being solely the authority of the sovereign.

Third step: among the antecedent means or conditions, as motives of credibility which can lead man to an act of truly divine but private faith about a determinate truth, St. Thomas and the theologians admit what they call knowledge by connaturality, or by divine instinct, or by the Christian sense, to which we also have alluded in connection with the prayer of the psalms.

Thus, for example, St. Thomas says concerning the motives or antecedent conditions which may lead one to believe, "He that believes has sufficient motivation, which leads him to believe. For he is led to belief by the authority of divine teaching confirmed by miracles and, *what counts more (et quod plus est), by the interior instinct of God's inviting him to belief*. And therefore he does not believe lightly, since he has sufficient motive for believing." [25]

We are interested here in underlining this second kind of motive inducing to faith: the interior instinct of God's inviting belief. St. Thomas often speaks of this type of higher instinctive knowledge which applies broadly also to knowledge under the influence of the gifts of the Holy Spirit. He calls it by a terminology which is varied, but basically unified: for example, by connaturality, by contact, by affinity, by a certain union of the soul with God, without discourse, affective and experiential, simple and absolute knowledge, by natural disposition, as if by taste, by compassion, etc.[26]

What is it that is treated of in this knowledge by connaturality? It is a type

---

[24] I do not intend to speak here of what some theologians call ecclesiastical faith, because others — and, it seems to me, with more justification — deny the existence of such a type of faith.

[25] *Summa*, II-II, q. 2, a. 9, ad 3.

[26] See Victor White, "*Thomism and Affective Knowledge*," a series of articles in *Blackfriars*, Vols. 24 and 25, 1943 and 1944. B. Miller, *Knowledge through Affective Connaturality*, London 1961.

of knowledge in which the knower perceives the object precisely and formally under the aspect of its relations of conformity or difformity with his own concrete nature *hic et nunc*, inasmuch as the reactions of the object on his concrete nature in a determinate state are conformed to it or unconformed and hence generate sympathy or antipathy, attraction or repugnance.

This type of knowledge is found already in the sensitive knowledge, and then it is properly called instinct. Thus, for example, the bird perceives straw as useful for making its nest and bringing up its young; so also the lamb flees the wolf, which it perceives as harmful.

The same type of knowledge is found in the higher sphere of intellectual knowledge. As early a thinker as Aristotle gave the example in this connection of a chaste man, who, without discursive reasoning, judges of an action or of an object in the field of chastity with marvelous certainty, inasmuch as he simply pays attention to the reactions of repugnance or attraction of his nature confronted with such and such an act or object or decision.

The moralist too, who perhaps is not chaste, can judge of the morality or immorality of this action, but by referring to general concepts and to abstract universal principles and to deductive reasonings. He judges by referring to abstract concepts which everyone has or can have, discoursing and concluding; hence he can also communicate to others the motives of his judgment, which is a scientific judgment and can hold for all and not for him alone; he can persuade, and he can refute the objections to the contrary.

The chaste man, on the other hand, judges of the morality of the act simply by paying heed to the reactions of his chaste nature; hence he does not make a scientific judgment, he cannot communicate his "motives" to others, he cannot refute with his knowledge alone the objections raised against his attitude; he can only invite the others to put themselves in the same conditions in which he finds himself and to have the same experience which he has.

Of similar nature are the judgments commonly called "of taste." Hence comes the popular saying that there is no arguing about tastes. A similar distinction can be made between the mere critic of art who is not an artist, and the artist who is not a critic.

Now this type of knowledge exists also on the supernatural level of faith. Here recourse could be had to analyses of interior experience and to the numerous testimonies especially of those who have come to the faith as adults and have analyzed their conversion. They affirm that at a certain time they saw what they had not seen before; and that the decisive moment cannot be analyzed, still less explained to others; that intellectual inquiries, however, important they may have been, did not constitute this decisive moment, but were something previous and preparatory to it; and that there enters into it an experience quite unique. Without involving ourselves in research in this direction, let us only recall here the statement of St. Thomas that he who believes is led to "faith," among other things, by an instinct of God who invites him interiorly, while keeping in mind also the thesis of instinct and of the *sensus Catholicus* admitted by all.

How is this fact, this instinct, or sense if you will, explained in the supernatural field, especially in regard to faith? Let us recall that every act of supernatural faith is made always under the indispensable impulse of actual grace. Actual grace is a certain divine motion which is a passing participation, not permanent as in habitual grace, but given after the fashion of a transient motion, a participation in the divine nature itself and in its way of acting; for every grace is participation in the divine nature. It moves the will to command the intellect's assent to faith and, by means of the will, moves the intellect to assent.

But no grace enters the soul if the soul is not disposed and capable of receiving it. Theologians teach that the last disposition immediately previous — at least from the logical point of view — to the entrance of grace is given by the grace itself in the moment of its entrance into the soul.

At any rate, no act of divine faith can be made without the believer's being previously — at least from the logical point of view — modified and disposed by means of a passing participation, as of motion, in the divine nature under the influence of actual grace.

If we connect all this with what we have said about knowledge by instinct or by connaturality in general, we can understand why this is realized also in the act of divine faith. The soul of the believer, in the very act of believing, is previously — from the logical point of view — modified and elevated by a motion of grace which is participation in the divine nature, to a way of being and of acting which is formally divine, though participated. Hence, confronted with the object of faith, which is supernatural and divine, it finds itself, by means of the grace which is at work in it "tuned in," as it were, with the object and with the divine way of being.

Thus there is a harmonious consonance of nature or connaturality, as between the chaste man and the object or the act of chastity, as between mother and son, as between the artist and the object which excites artistic pleasure in him. The nature of the believer, under the influence of grace, placed before the object of faith, experiences reciprocal conformity with it; it perceives this conformity, not conceptually and in an abstract way or by reasoning, but by the mere reaction of conformity of its nature in the presence of the object; by instinct and connaturality.

This brings it about that the believer, under the efficacious grace of believing, behaves with instinctive impetuosity toward the object proposed to his faith as to that which is conformed to his inmost being.[27] The adherence to this object is infallible and most secure of itself, but is not conceptually

---

[27] This connaturality and impetuosity will be much more intense if the believer is already in a state of habitual grace, which is a permanent conformity of nature between God and man; it will be even more so if he finds himself, moreover, in a high degree of holiness of life.

analyzable or explainable, nor directly communicable to others by way of reasoning, as the teacher can directly communicate to the student a theorem of geometry.

Actually there enters essentially into that knowledge by connaturality and into that special type of judgment which follows upon it (it is true, it is credible; it is beautiful, it is good, etc.), an element not conceptual, but strictly personal and not communicable: in other words, such and such a reaction of one's own nature in the presence of such and such an object. Only one who finds himself in the same dispositions will be able to have the same experience and judge in the same way.

Precisely because that knowledge by connaturality constitutes for the believer a condition antecedent to the act of faith and a motive of credibility based on a strictly personal and not conceptually analyzable or directly communicable element, the believer himself is not capable of defending the reasonableness of that assent of his by way of reasoning against possible objections except by having recourse to arguments on another level and of another nature. For this purpose he will always and necessarily have to have recourse to considerations taken from a conceptual and not a purely personal level.

It is for this reason that the existence of motives of credibility based on knowledge by connaturality and their importance in the act of faith leave unprejudiced the necessity of the traditional apologetic, which has for its precise aim to defend on the level of conceptual, scientific, argumentative reasoning, and in the face of all, the reasonableness of the very act of faith which the knowledge by connaturality can base only on strictly personal and not conceptual grounds.

In this complex experience the believer not only perceives the reactions of his own nature in conformity with the object, but also that his act of assent is most reasonable; that he, and not only men in general, morally speaking, can and should believe, and can and should do it *hic et nunc* in the dispositions and at the moment in which he finds himself. Such is one of the effects of the efficacious grace of believing.

But this could not be unless the believer, under the efficacious grace of believing, saw in some way that God has really spoken and revealed the truth to which he assents at the time. This happens because in the knowledge by connaturality in which, under the efficacious grace of believing, he experiences his own nature in a reaction of conformity with the object presented to him, the believer perceives in some way the very voice of God who speaks to him personally in this moment and in these dispositions.[28]

[28] It seems that the believer arrives at this point by a kind of inference quite spontaneous, rapid and hardly conscious, summed up, for example, in the simple affirmation: the voice of conscience is the voice of God. Such a statement, in the aforesaid circumstances, seems to contain in summary fashion a syllogism more or less like the following: the impulse of nature which the conscience warns us must be followed is the voice of God; but such is the impulse of nature which I perceive *hic et nunc*; therefore the impulse of nature which I perceive *hic et nunc* is the voice of God.

The process described above can be verified not only when the concern is with giving the assent of divine and Catholic faith to a truth already proposed as dogma by the infallible teaching authority of the Church, but also in certain cases in which the truth to which the believer assents is not yet proposed as dogma of divine and Catholic faith. In these cases the believer to whom it is evident in a most certain way, though wholly a personal way and not conceptually explainable or demonstrable, that God has revealed this truth, issues an act of divine faith. He consents to the said truth formally by the authority of God revealing. But that divine faith is only private and obligates him alone personally; it is not yet the divine and Catholic faith due to a dogma proposed as such by the Church and obligating all believers.

Such knowledge by connaturality depends essentially on the action of grace on any believer and not on the acumen of his intellect or on his theoretical knowledge. God, moreover, is sovereignly free in the distribution of His grace and gives it only to those who are morally prepared for it. This means that the aforesaid knowledge by connaturality depends in its frequency and its intensity, insofar as it depends on man himself, on holiness of life: humility, mortification, faith, charity, prayer, etc.

It is here that one finally begins to understand the importance of the liturgy in relation to this same knowledge by connaturality. It is obvious that the liturgical life can be, and in fact very often is, the occasion of God's giving to individuals those superior knowledges by connaturality, not only about truths already proposed formally by the infallible teaching authority of the Church as dogmas of divine and Catholic faith, but also about other truths which the magisterium up to now has proposed only with a lesser degree of authority.

The fact that the faithful in the liturgy live those truths, even if not yet proposed as dogmas of divine and Catholic faith, is often the occasion for God to operate in such a way with His efficacious grace in individuals that they instinctively, by connaturality, keep penetrating and loving those truths more and more; in fact, that they acquire concerning these truths and concerning the fact that they are really revealed by God and contained in public revelation, a very strong certitude, even if of a strictly personal and undemonstrable nature; in other words, an intuitive certitude of divine faith, though only private.

Such certitude, under the direction of the Holy Spirit, who works efficaciously in the Church, occasioned in good part by the liturgical life, can gradually be diffused more and more among the faithful and among the members of the hierarchy itself. Thus there can come to be formed a state of persuasion and of private but rather general certainty, or even very general, about the fact that a truth, not yet proposed as dogma of the Church, is really contained in public revelation.[29]

---

[29] It is not necessary that it be able to be demonstrated in a strictly apodictic way, by

Such a state of certitude, more or less generalized, is then grounded in the knowledge by connaturality of the individual members of the Church under the influence of God's efficacious grace. It is the *sensus Catholicus* in action. This state of certitude, still private, may be accompanied in certain circumstances by the desire that such truth come to be defined also as dogma by the competent teaching authority with a view to the need or the advantage of the Church herself.

If at this point a new factor of a different order did not intervene, such persuasion concerning the truth in question would never be transformed into dogma to be believed with divine and Catholic faith. But if the definition of a competent organ of the infallible teaching authority intervenes — for example, of an ecumenical council or of the pope speaking *ex cathedra* — such a qualitative transformation is made, and a truth which was not yet formally dogma of divine and Catholic faith becomes such. This happens because the competent organ of the infallible teaching authority of the Church, in declaring a truth as revealed by God and therefore to be believed by all the faithful as dogma of divine and Catholic faith, enjoys the infallible assistance of the Holy Spirit.[30]

way of philological or historical reasoning alone, nor by way of logical deductive reasoning from another dogma already proposed, that such truth is contained in the Scriptures or in the oral dogmatic tradition immediately after the death of the Apostles. The idea of the truth in question may have been suggested in the Church by the Scriptures or by the oral Apostolic dogmatic tradition or by another dogma already defined, even if only by way of the argument from suitability. The fact that the idea has been suggested in this way is sufficient to prove that it has not become known by means of a new public revelation, a kind of revelation which was closed definitively with the death of the last of the Apostles. Afterwards, by means of the process of knowledge by connaturality, God has brought about concerning this idea, previously known by normal and natural ways from the sources which contain public revelation, a more or less widespread certitude of divine though private faith.

[30] She enjoys this assistance, of course, even in the case where it has not been previously demonstrated by way of a properly apodictic reasoning — made by starting from the Scriptures, from the oral Apostolic dogmatic tradition as it was immediately after the death of the Apostles, or from another dogma already defined — that the truth being defined is really, at least implicitly, contained in the Scripture or in the aforesaid tradition.

It is indeed a dogma of the faith that every truth proposed by the Church as of divine and Catholic faith is really contained in the Scriptures or in the aforesaid tradition, at least implicitly. But in order that the teaching authority be able to define a doctrine, it is not necessary that the fact that it is contained there be able also to be demonstrated with properly apodictic reasoning by way of reasoning alone. The infallibility of the magisterium does not depend on the fact, whether, before defining a truth, it sees and proves by way of apodictic reasoning that this truth is contained in the sources of revelation, but simply on the fact that in affirming or denying a thing as being of the faith, it enjoys the assistance of the Holy Spirit.

It is known that even the commission of theologians which Pius IX instituted with a view to the definition of the Immaculate Conception admitted as a principle that it was not at all necessary that, before the definition, it be able to produce the aforesaid apodictic proof by way of reasoning alone. (See V. Sardi, *La solenne definizione del dogma dell'Immacolato concepimento di Maria Santissima*, Rome 1904, Vol. I, pp. 791–796.) And in fact this properly apodictic proof by way of reasoning alone, (as opposed to many and good reasons of suitability) was never given either for the Immaculate Conception or for the Assumption of Mary.

Here it may be asked how, then, in such a

In this case, of course, the doctrinal authority which belongs to the dogma defined as such comes to it solely from the fact that, according to the Catholic faith, in defining a dogma the teaching authority enjoys the infallible assistance of the Holy Spirit. The process of knowledge by connaturality has served only as an occasion in the hands of God for inducing the competent organ of the infallible teaching authority to want to define and to define in fact, making use of that assistance which God has guaranteed to it.

In such a process of making a truth explicit we can see the importance of knowledge by connaturality as well as the specific role of the liturgy. In this case the liturgy has truly preceded the proposal of the divine and Catholic faith and, thanks to the process of knowledge by connaturality, has been one of the major occasions of the development of a doctrine into a dogma properly so called.

The reader who has followed this long reasoning has certainly been thinking continually of the case of the Immaculate Conception and of the Assumption. And rightly so. These two cases are the most recent and most conspicuous demonstration of the influence of the liturgy on the development of a dogma. They are not understandable without recourse to the *sensus Catholicus* or to knowledge by connaturality. I do not believe by any means that they are the only ones that can be cited in this connection, but only that they are the most recent and the most conspicuous. Nor could it be excluded *a priori* that such a process be repeated in the future. Who could be sure, for example, that the doctrine of Mary Mediatrix of All Graces is not on the same road toward definition?

case, the dogmas so defined can be effectively defended against the objections of non-Catholics.

The answer is essentially this: that such dogmas must and can be defended in an indirect way, that is, by recourse to general apologetics. In general apologetics the credibility of Christian revelation is demonstrated against the non-Christian; against the traditional Protestant it is demonstrated that, according to the New Testament, even interpreted solely with the help of philology and history, the proximate criterion of Christian truth is not the individual reason, but the infallible teaching authority of the Church, the organ of which is the hierarchy; against the Photian it is demonstrated that, admitting the Scriptures and tradition as criterion of the faith, and admitting that the organ of infallibility in the Church resides in the hierarchy, it follows that there cannot be in the same Church an effective criterion of truth which does not include the Roman Pontiff.

When these things have been proved, it follows from them that it is perfectly reasonable to admit, with Catholics, that a truth defined by the magisterium, for example by the Roman Pontiff, is a truth really revealed, since this magisterium is infallible by reason of the assistance of the Holy Spirit.

In other words, in the case of dogmas like the Immaculate Conception and the Assumption, the dispute with the non-Catholics must be waged not on the apodictic proof by way of reasoning alone to be supplied from the Scriptures or from the oral Apostolic dogmatic tradition as it appears immediately after the death of the last of the Apostles, but on the question of the proximate and infallible criterion of the Christian faith, that is, on the infallibility of the teaching authority of the Church, which always includes the Roman Pontiff.

17 POSITIVE-SCHOLASTIC THEOLOGY

AND LITURGY

I do not know whether I am deceiving myself in hoping to have helped a few readers in the preceding chapters to discover some of the theological riches which the world of the liturgy encloses. It may be that someone, having arrived at this point in our book, will ask himself how it is that little or no notice has been taken of the great biblical, dogmatic, spiritual visions which, with a little attention, can be discovered in the liturgy during the long years passed in the study of theology. It is quite probable that, concerning the theological perspectives delineated in the preceding chapters, many, from the general study of theology made in the seminary, have drawn only some notions on the question of liturgy and faith, treated in the chapter immediatly preceding.

In fact, in the general manuals of theology which are in the hands of all, aside from a hint given in the treatise on the theological loci, where it is noted that the liturgy can also be considered as a theological locus, as expression of the ordinary teaching authority, and aside from some brief allusions to a few texts, rites, or liturgical customs, scattered among the various treatises, for the most part among the arguments from tradition in relation to the proof of the individual "theses," the liturgy does not otherwise appear.

Then, if one reflects on the proper significance of the liturgy, as we have attempted to explain it, it is perhaps no exaggeration to say frankly that this is simply absent from theology as it is generally conceived. It is evident, in fact, that the question of the relations between theology and liturgy is much more profound and more vast than the question of the liturgy as *locus theologicus* or the sporadic recourse to the liturgy in the proof *ex traditione* of our manuals.

Nor does the course in liturgy, as it stands in the program of seminaries, change this state of affairs, because this course, as is well known, is conceived for the most part essentially as history of the liturgy and not as liturgical theology, when it is not still conceived actually as a course in rubrics now pretentiously labelled "the art of presidentially presiding."

1. The Question of the Relations between General Synthetic Theology and Liturgy

Taking up the question of the relations between theology and liturgy, I intend to treat of the insertion of liturgy into general synthetic theology, in other words, into what is now commonly called dogmatic theology and is precisely the object of the aforesaid manuals.

If the question of the relations between theology and liturgy were limited to the question of the utility, or even the necessity, of monograph studies and courses about the theological aspect of the liturgy, the discussion would soon be resolved on the theoretical level and in principle. It would merely be a matter of hoping that these monograph studies and courses, essays of which are beginning to appear, be effected on a large scale and thus come to deepen in some way our knowledge of the liturgy. At any rate, probably no theologian would have anything to object against such studies, barring afterwards the continued ignoring, more or less completely, of the liturgy in his dogmatic or general theology, as something extraneous and of another order.

Instead, the question to be examined is precisely whether, and to what extent, the liturgy is truly something extraneous to general theology and of another order, and whether that kind of attention and importance which theologians up to now have granted it in their general syntheses is enough.

I intend to speak primarily of the qualitative attention and importance they have granted to the liturgy and not at all of the number of pages they have devoted to it, of the number of liturgical quotations with which they have adorned their proofs of theses, this being a purely material and quantitative aspect, and therefore not resolutive, of the place which belongs to liturgy in theology. What must be sought is whether the very title or the ultimate methodological reason for which the theologians have admitted the liturgy up to now into general synthetic theology is sufficient. We intend, therefore, to bring forward the question of the primarily qualitative unity to be found, or to be recovered, between general synthetic theology and liturgy.

The question is similar to that which today, rightly, preoccupies so many theologians, of the unity to be found or recovered between general synthetic theology, dogmatic theology as it is called, and Scripture, or more exactly, biblical theology. That there exists a question of the unity to be found or recovered between Scripture and theology is today widely recognized by experts. Yet whoever has become somewhat accustomed to holding the Bible in hand and getting some taste of biblical theology according to the possibilities and the exigencies of present-day methods knows very well that the question of recovering the unity between Bible and theology is not resolved with a purely quantitative increase of biblical quotations in the scheme of the "theses" of our manuals. In question, rather, is a whole method of considering the qualitative relations between Bible and theology. The same holds true in its own way for the liturgy.

In fact, these two questions are much more closely connected than might appear at first glance. For what we have pointed out in its proper place must not be forgotten: that it is in the liturgy and through the liturgy that the orthodox reading and the deep sense of the Bible is connaturally recovered; also what we have often repeated and tried to demonstrate with practical examples must not be forgotten: that the world of the liturgy remains impenetrable for anyone who is not reshaped by the world of the Bible. If this is so, why should anyone wonder that the question of the relations between Bible and theology and that of the relations between liturgy and theology should be intimately united? This should seem obvious enough right from the beginning.

At any rate, it can be taken for certain that as long as the question of the qualitative relations between liturgy and general synthetic theology is not resolved theoretically and applied practically on a broad scale, the liturgical movement will not be founded on the rock which alone, in the final analysis, can guarantee its stability and strength. This is so because, as we have hinted, notwithstanding the more or less acknowledged discredit into which dogmatic theology has fallen with some people — because they are thinking of what they studied in the manuals in the seminary — it remains nonetheless undeniable that it is precisely in this theology that the general view of the world, as man can attain to it by revelation in conjunction with right reason, must be studied and proposed in a general synthesis.

To understand, in the last analysis, the meaning and the necessity of the liturgy, it is necessary to understand what is its specific place in every great question of which that synthesis treats; just as, to understand, in the last analysis, what is the meaning and the necessity of the study of the Bible, of the Fathers, of metaphysics in the Christian view of the world, it is necessary to understand what is the specific place of the biblical, patristic, metaphysical aspect in every great question of which general synthetic theology treats. In the preceding chapters we have merely given a series of essays of what may be the consideration of the liturgy seen against the background of the general theological synthesis and of what, in its turn, this synthesis may receive from the right consideration of the liturgy.[1]

Let it be observed, however, that in the question which we are posing here of the qualitative relations between liturgy and general synthetic theology and of the unity to be recovered between the one and the other, the primary and essential point of view which must guide us is not that of giving a greater impulse to the liturgical movement among the clergy and, through the clergy, among the Christian people. The determining point of view would then be that of the liturgical apostolate: a pragmatic point of view. The liturgist would be addressing the theologians because he perceived that, given the influence which they have or should have among the clergy, the chairs of theology would be excellent platforms for liturgical propaganda.

However true this may be, the theologian could and should reply that a chair of theology, by its intrinsic and specific end, *ex fine operis*, is meant only for the teaching of theology and for nothing else; and that to fulfill its specific and irreplaceable task in life, a science must be conducted and determined above all by the requirements intrinsic to the science itself and by nothing else; and that if the liturgy does not enter into dogmatic theology by intrinsic exigencies of dogmatic theology itself, substantially more than has been admitted up to now, the theologian has but one thing to do: to ask the liturgist to display his legitimate zeal in another field more suited.

All this is very true. And it is for this reason that the question of the relations between liturgy and theology must be considered essentially as a theological question and not as a liturgical question, so much less a question of the liturgical apostolate. I mean that what must be decisive on the relations between theology and liturgy is theology itself as the supreme science.

It is easy to see that the question, thus determined, depends on the nature of general synthetic theology and on the requirements of its method. But it is known that there have been and there are different ways of seeing and of acting among theologians themselves, in particulars of notable importance, about this question, in theory and especially in practice. It is obvious by the very nature of things that precisely in these divergencies must be sought the ultimate root of the different ways of considering and putting into practice the relations between liturgy and theology.

Historically the ways of conceiving the nature of theology and therefore its method have been three: the patristic method; the scholastic method, em-

---

[1] Let it be noted, however, that in the preceding chapters, with regard to many questions, we have neither made nor wished to make a complete synthesis such as should be made in general synthetic theology. There is no pretense at all, for example, that general synthetic theology would have nothing more to say on the Trinity, on Christ, on the angels, etc., than what we have said in the relative chapters!

bodied especially in the great representatives of scholasticism of the thirteenth and fourteenth centuries; and the method which we may call positive-scholastic, starting with the sixteenth century, which, with various adaptations and shadings, is more or less in command to this day, as is evidenced by the great majority of the manuals.

Before essaying a theoretical solution of the question, we shall analyze briefly these different methods, paying attention above all to the consequences which each of them has in the question of the relations with the liturgy. Let us begin with the positive-scholastic method because it is the closest to us.

2. The Actual Status of the Relations between Positive-Scholastic Theology and Liturgy

The origin of this type of theology: the desiderata of the fifteenth and sixteenth centuries

In the sixteenth century there arose a manner of conceiving the general theological synthesis which, while seeking to retain what had been in effect the major and most characteristic contribution of the scholasticism of the preceding centuries to the development of theology, namely, the deepened elaboration of the revealed data under the dialectical and ontological or entitative aspect, wanted at the same time to integrate it under another aspect.[2]

Actually, the spiritual and mystical authors as early as the end of the fourteenth century and those of the fifteenth century, and afterwards with greater insistence the humanists and, finally, with a clearly heretical spirit, the Protestants — aside from the inaccuracies, the real injustices, and the errors of their polemic against scholasticism — had brought out the necessity of elaborating some aspects of synthetic theology much more accurately than the scholastics of the preceding centuries had been concerned with doing.

The spiritual authors and, with another spirit and for other ends, the humanists, had insisted especially on the need of a more intimate and direct contact with the proper sources of theology which were contained in revelation, that is, with Scripture and tradition.

The Protestants, in their turn, were accusing the Catholic Church of having corrupted revelation itself by introducing into it, in the course of the centuries, a series of novelties, branding as such everything of which they did not approve in the Catholic Church of the sixteenth century. To demonstrate

---

[2] On the history of positive-scholastic theology see A. Humbert, *Les origines de la théologie moderne. Vol. I. La renaissance de l'antiquité chrétienne (1450–1521)*, Paris 1911. P. Polman, *L'élément historique dans la controverse religieuse du XVIᵉ siècle*, Gembloux 1932. M.-J. Congar, in article *"Théologie,"* in the *Dictionnaire de théol. cath.*, Vol. 15 (1943–

1946), pp. 411ff. E. Hocedez, *Histoire de la théologie au XIXᵉ siècle*, 3 vols., Paris 1947ff. E. Marcotte, *La natura de la théologie d'après Melchior Cano*, Ottawa 1949. R. Snoeks, *L'argument de tradition dans la controverse eucharistique entre catholiques et réformés français au XVIIᵉ siècle*, Louvain 1951.

their point they had recourse to the Scriptures and to the history of dogma and doctrine. It appeared necessary, therefore, for every question discussed, to demonstrate that the Protestant accusation of novelty was not founded.

Thus both the desire to give satisfaction to that which appeared justified in the requests of the spiritual authors and of the humanists and the necessity of the polemic against the Protestants drove the Catholic theologians of the period apropos of every question, to attach as premise to their treatment of the revealed datum, through the use of philosophy, an area in which the effort of the scholastics was concentrated, a prior and more accurate elaboration of the relation of Catholic dogma to Scripture and to ancient tradition.

This new task assigned to theology was called a *positive* task because in it, before passing on to the speculative elaboration of a question according to the scholastic custom, it was desired to *posit* firmly the very foundations and, as it were, the principles on which it was based.[3] It is for this reason that the designation "positive-scholastic" which is given here to this type of theology is fully justified.

This positive-scholastic theology, while being allied in the role of speculative elaboration to the prior scholastic tradition, still really constituted, taken all in all, a new way of conceiving the theological synthesis with a method of its own which did not coincide, absolutely speaking, with the former scholastic method as it appears, for example, in St. Thomas.

New tendencies

The new positive task, added to the speculative, and, abstractly speaking, characteristic of the new conception of theology, could have been developed and brought to its fulfillment in various ways. In point of fact, however, it was concretized in a well-determined ideal.

The whole Tridentine and post-Tridentine Catholic theology was undeniably dominated by the need of defense against the Protestant attack. The apologetic preoccupation, which is one of the tasks of every science, then passed easily to first place by reason of the practical necessity of contemporary circumstances. The predominant concern in the method of conceiving the theological synthesis and of treating the individual questions and, as it were, the ideal to which everything actually tended, was therefore the following: prior to seeing what philosophical reason can do about the various dogmas and the various doctrines proposed by the Church (argument from reason, *ex ratione*, into which the positive-scholastics transformed the former speculative task of the scholastics) to prove for every single question, against the new denials, and this in an apodictic way and with the aid only of philology and history, that those same dogmas proposed by the teaching authority are really contained in the Scriptures or in the tradition handed down to us by

---

[3] *Ponere principia.*

the Apostles and have always been taught as such by the Church. This was at least the ideal to which that whole theology tended, consciously or unconsciously, in its new positive task.

And let it be noted well that the ideal pursued tended to present from the sources, Scripture and tradition handed down by the Apostles, and precisely with the help of history and philology alone, and, moreover, directly for every single question discussed, an apodictic proof of the apostolicity of every doctrine taught by the Church, in such a way as to demonstrate, by the aforesaid method, that the Protestant accusation of novelty was unfounded.

Hence comes the ideal pursued by those authors of furnishing a chain of testimonies which prove with history alone that a given doctrine has been uninterruptedly taught in the Church since the time of the Apostles. The testimonies in a chain are characteristic of this type of theology. The ideal, direct and purely historical proof for every doctrine is the perpetuity of its tradition.[4]

Melchior Cano

This way of conceiving things went on gradually taking shape even before the Council of Trent in the first polemics with the Protestants. But to Melchior Cano[5] goes the honor of having explicitly worked out the methodology of this type of theology in his well-known work *De locis theologicis*.[6] Practically all of Cano's effort in this work tends to teach the theologian how, for each question, he must first of all *posit the principles* before passing on to the speculative elaboration of the doctrine by means of dialectic and philosophy. The "theological places" for Cano are precisely and above all those sources whose examination will permit the theologian to posit the principles solidly in the aforesaid sense. As is well known, he enumerates ten loci or places;[7] but he does not mention the liturgy.

[4] Of course, I am not denying at all that in some questions then disputed with the Protestants such an ideal could be attained, at least very nearly. I am doubtful only about two things: whether such an ideal was really attainable for every question disputed; and whether it would not have been more effective to carry on the dispute with the Protestants in the first place on the question of the proximate criterion of the faith in the Christian religion, and to show them, on the basis of the Scriptures, already in the light of mere philology, criticism, and history, that this criterion cannot be the individual reason, nor philosophical nor historical reason, but only the infallible teaching authority of the hierarchical Church. With this first point settled, the questions under dispute should have been distinguished: for those in which the apostolicity and the perpetuity of tradition could be demonstrated apodicti-

cally even by the historical way alone, recourse could have been had also to this way; for the others, on the other hand, in which such demonstration was not possible, recourse should have been had to the authority of the magisterium and to the legitimacy and the necessity of the development of dogmas.

[5] Died in 1560.

[6] First edition issued posthumously in 1563.

[7] But he makes no special point of a precise number. Among these loci, two contain revelation: Scripture and tradition; five interpret it: the Church (meaning the Christian people), the councils, the Roman Church, the Fathers, the scholastic theologians. The final three are loci which only help to elaborate and interpret further: human reason, philosophy, human history. As is known, later theologians reduce these loci to four: magisterium, Scripture, tradition, reason.

After Cano this general concept of theology enjoyed enormous development and bore those fruits which are admired in the magnificent post-Tridentine flowering.

At first it was the speculative scholastic roles which continued, as in the past, to be more developed by the great post-Tridentine commentators of St. Thomas.[8]

But afterwards more frequent and abundant recourse was had to the Scriptures, to the Fathers, to the previous theologians, and there was more often direct dispute with the Protestants in the *disputationes* which were added to the commentaries properly so called of the text of St. Thomas, or which actually developed separately as a form in itself without direct regard to the text of the *Summa*.[9]

In fact, with the work *Theologicorum dogmatum tomi IV* of Dionysius Petavius,[10] the positive aspect of the new theology is directly and separately elaborated. Petavius wanted to reconstruct the whole of theology simply by starting from the Fathers; or, better, it was on the patristic aspect of theological questions, elaborated with the greatest scrupulosity of critical and historical, objective and impartial method that was then possible, that he put his whole effort. In this sense he is rightly considered as the founder of simple positive theology, because he was the first to cultivate this aspect separately from the scholastic aspect and according to what at that time could be the strictest requirements of the critical and historical method.

He had, as is well known, many eminent continuators,[11] some of whom, such as the Maurists and Muratori, undertook to investigate with great fruit the historical aspect of the whole life of the ancient Church in general, raising up imperishable monuments of erudition.

Historical liturgy

In all this flowering of historical studies, occasioned in good part by the necessities of the Protestant polemic, liturgical inquiries did not remain behind. From the sixteenth century and the beginning of the seventeenth, against Protestant attacks directed more immediately against the ceremonies and liturgical customs of the Church and especially of the Mass, there arose a legion of Catholic defenders.

Among these some had recourse to a more theoretical kind of discussion, while others went forward already on the more directly historical terrain with

---

[8] Such as Bartholomew Medina († 1581), Dominic Bañez († 1604), Diego Alvarez († 1635), Thomas de Lemos († 1629), John of St. Thomas († 1644), the Salamancans (1631–1701), Francisco Toledo († 1596), Gregory of Valencia († 1603), Francisco Suarez († 1617), Gabriel Vasquez († 1604), Luis de Molina († 1600), Martinez di Ripalda († 1648), John de Lugo († 1660), and Leonard

Lessius († 1623).

[9] For example, already in several works of Suarez, and afterwards in the *Controversies* of Bellarmine.

[10] First editions of the four volumes from 1644 to 1650.

[11] For example, Louis Thomassin († 1695), Jean Morin († 1695), J. Habert († 1668).

the publication of ancient documents and with commentaries. To this second group belong, for example, Conrad Braun, some studies of Maldonatus and of Cardinal Bellarmine, and especially John Cochlaeus with his collection *Speculum antiquae devotionis circa Missam et omnem alium cultum Dei*, first published in 1549, and Melchior Hittorp with his corpus of medieval liturgies entitled *De catholicae ecclesiae divinis officiis ac ministeriis, varii vetustiorum aliquot ecclesiae Patrum ac scriptorum libri*.[12]

Thus there began to arise modern historical liturgical science which enjoyed a magnificent development during the seventeenth and eighteenth centuries with a series of scholars of the first rank: whether editors of Eastern and Western texts like Goar, Mabillon, Renaudot, Martène, the Assemani brothers, Joseph Simon and Joseph Aloysius, along with their nephew Evodius Assemani, to name only a few of the more noted; or commentators and authors of historical-liturgical monographs or studies of matters closely connected with the liturgy, such as Leon Allatius, Jean Morin, Cardinal Bona, Louis Thomassin, Martin Gerbert, Jean Grancolas, Benedict XIV, Joseph Catalani, to mention only some of the more noteworthy.[13]

Liturgy and theology in the positive-scholastics

It would be normal to expect that the theological field and the struggle which was being carried out in it against the Protestants should benefit from these new liturgical findings. But aside from the first general results in the polemic against the Protestants, as can be seen, for example, in Bellarmine, it was only toward the middle of the seventeenth century that the first somewhat consistent attempts to integrate the new liturgical material into the positive-scholastic theology began, or at least to construct a kind of liturgical theology, illustrating, in controversy against the Protestants, a whole series of theological questions from the liturgy, as Petavius had tried to illustrate the whole of theology from the Fathers.

This was the method employed in 1657 by François Carrière in his work *Fidei catholicae digestum singula eius dogmata et ritus iuxta SS. Patrum et Conciliorum doctrinam exacte declarans*. Leon Allatius and Antoine Arnaud, almost at the same time, gave noteworthy importance to the liturgy, Allatius intending to demonstrate the perpetual community of faith between the true Eastern and Western traditions, while writing against the Protestants; and Arnaud, more directly against the innovators, in his work on the perpetuity of the faith in regard to the Eucharist.[14] Bossuet also, in his controversy against the Protestants starting about 1677, and in his controversy with the Quietists, willingly appealed to arguments from the liturgy.

---

[12] Cologne 1568. For more particulars see Righetti, Vol. I, pp. 69ff.

[13] See Righetti, Vol. I, pp. 70ff.

[14] Leon Allatius, *De ecclesiae occidentalis et*

orientalis perpetua consensione, Cologne 1648; Antoine Arnaud, *La perpetuité de la foi sur l'eucharistie*, 3 vols., 1669–1674.

Around the middle of the eighteenth century the recourse to the liturgy to prove the dogmas of the Church according to the positive-scholastic concept, always with an anti-Protestant intention, began to enjoy notable vogue. In 1748 Muratori premised his work *Liturgia romana vetus* with a long dissertation in which he proved from the liturgy of the ancient Roman sacramentaries a series of dogmas especially concerning the Eucharist.[15] In 1767 J. B. Gener, in the six volumes of his *Theologia dogmatico-scholastica . . . sacrae antiquitatis monumentis illustrata,*[16] first set forth, for every question, the dogma according to the scholastic method, then illustrated it from inscriptions, from the liturgy, from numismatics, from seals, etc. In 1769 G. C. Trombelli began the publication of a *Tractatus de sacramentis per polemicas et liturgicas dissertationes distributi,* in which he treated of baptism, confirmation, extreme unction, and matrimony.[17]

Finally F. A. Zaccaria sought to systematize all that the liturgy could furnish to theology properly so called. In the second dissertation introductory to the first volume of his *Bibliotheca ritualis*[18] he treats, as we have already indicated in the preceding chapter, of the general theological value of the liturgy and of the rules to be observed by the theologian in making use of it. In eighteen corallaries to the fifth chapter, he reviews almost all the principal dogmatic theological questions and shows how Catholic doctrine in each of them can be confirmed or demonstrated by the liturgy. Thus there are proved from the liturgy: the revelation of the mystery of the Trinity; the divinity of the Word against the Arians and the Socinians; the divinity and the true humanity of Christ; the reality of His body; the virginity of Mary; the primacy of St. Peter and of the Pope; the infallibility of the Church; the superiority of bishops over priests; the necessity of grace against the Pelagians and semi-Pelagians; original sin. And there is proved also, in particular against the Protestants, that confirmation is a sacrament; that the Mass is a true unbloody Sacrifice; the real presence of Christ in the Eucharist; transubstantiation; purgatory; the cult and the invocation of the saints.

At this point we must ask what has been the result of this elaboration of the theological content of the liturgy by the systematic synthetic theologians properly so called, even if among those cited, only Gener could pass muster; the others, including Zaccaria, are rather authors of historical monographs who make some thrust into the theological field.

It is common opinion that the eighteenth century, from the viewpoint of speculative theology and general synthetic theology, was a century of notable

---

[15] Venice 1798, Vol. I, pp. 101–288. In 1759 Martin Gerbert published a work with the title *Principia theologiae liturgicae*; but it is rather a manual of liturgy. In another work, *Theologia generalis,* of which the *Principia theologiae liturgicae* formed a part, Gerbert often cited texts from the liturgy.

[16] Rome 1767.

[17] Other works of Trombelli also have interest from the liturgical point of view, such as two works on the cult of the saints and one on the cult of our Lady.

[18] Rome 1767, pp. xxv–liv; *De iure liturgico.*

decadence. The very names most quoted, such as Billuart, Gotti, Tournely, compared to the great post-Tridentine scholastics, have the appearance of lesser lights. But precisely in these lesser lights must be recognized the immediate forerunners of our modern manualists. It was they who began to write "courses" conceived after the manner of systematic manuals in which they attempted to sum up and to harmonize positivism, scholasticism, polemicism, and often also piety.

What is the place of the liturgy in these courses? Billuart, Gotti, Tournely wrote before the middle of the century, and more to the point, before Zaccaria. It would perhaps be too much to claim that they profited from the theological liturgical material scattered through the previous authors. And in fact we make the following observations:

In their treatment *de locis theologicis*, which these authors explain following Cano more or less, no mention is made of the liturgy. In their other treatises the liturgy has left the following principal traces: in the treatises on the sacraments they refer to the rites and ceremonies which the Church uses in the administration of the sacraments. Against the Protestants they defend the power of the Church in this matter, the lawfulness and the obligatory character of the observance of sacramental ceremonies; they also touch upon the question of the vernacular. In the treatise on the sacraments in general they treat various questions in general. Then at the end of the treatise on baptism, on confirmation, and on the Eucharist, they do the same in particular, with respect to each of these sacraments.

It is thus, for example, that at the end of the treatise on the Eucharist, they treat of the lawfulness of the low Mass, of the time of celebration, of the priestly vestments, of the principal ceremonies of the Mass, of which sometimes they also explain briefly the essential liturgical structure. In the same treatise on the Eucharist they also defend against the Protestants the practice of communion under one species, the custom of pouring a drop of water into the chalice, the cult of the Eucharist as it is observed in the Church, the prayers and the application of the Mass for the dead, and various other details.

Where does this material come from? Is it, at least in notable part, fruit of the previous liturgical studies to which reference has been made above? It is not at all necessary to suppose so. In all this these systematic theologians are doing nothing but following the tradition of St. Thomas himself, who in the same treatises touched on precisely the same questions.[19] They add a hint of anti-Protestant polemic, following in a very general way the explicit decisions of the Council of Trent on the same matters.[20]

Greater influence of the previous historical-liturgical studies, or at least of

---

[19] This matter will be better explained below. See the *Summa*, III, q. 66, a. 10; q. 70; q. 71; q. 72, a. 12; q. 83; *Supplementum*, q. 28.

[20] See Dz 1613 (856); 1643 (878); 1645–1661 (879–893); 1726–1759 (930–956).

POSITIVE-SCHOLASTIC THEOLOGY AND LITURGY

the historical studies connected also with the liturgy, is noted in these authors when they treat of the questions of the matter and form, the minister and subject of the individual sacraments, in which they also give some details on the development of the ecclesiastical practice in these matters, both in the East and in the West, doing it sometimes with explicit historical digressions.[21]

If to this are added various allusions to the liturgy, as brief and general as they are obvious, even inevitable, in some other treatises — such as allusions to the feast of the Immaculate Conception or of the Assumption, or to the ecclesiastical usage of the invocation and veneration of relics and images — an idea will be had of the quantitative place occupied by the liturgy in these general theological syntheses. And this may perhaps seem considerable in comparison to our present-day manuals, but taken in itself it is obviously not much.

Then if we consider the essential question of the formal aspect and, as it were, the precise visual angle under which these authors consider the liturgy insofar as they admit it into their syntheses, it is easy to see that the directly polemic point of view against the Protestants predominates immensely. Almost all the liturgical questions or questions in connection with the liturgy with which this theology is concerned are considered above all and almost solely in the preoccupation with refuting the Protestant assertions in these matters. The possible points of view which do not enter into the dispute with the Protestants are ignored. In this polemic against the Protestants, moreover, the ideal aimed at, besides some considerations of the theoretical order, is primarily to show the antiquity, even the apostolicity, of the point being defended.

It might have been thought that among the synthetic theologians who wrote after Zaccaria, the situation would be notably changed in favor of the liturgy. In reality this did not happen, except for the fact that some, not all, theologians in the treatise *de locis theologicis* made mention also of the liturgy in the sense of Zaccaria. But the mention which the liturgy has thus succeeded in winning with some theologians in the general treatise on theoretical methodology did not in practice make any great improvement in its situation in the rest of theology, even among the very theologians who had admitted it into that introductory treatise.

Typical from this point of view is the case of Perrone. The *Praelectiones theologicae* of this author (first edition in nine volumes, 1835-1842) has particular importance for us, first of all, because his way of projecting theological study and material is derived immediately from the positive-scholastic courses of the eighteenth century; these courses he abridges and reduces to a manual type quite similar to that of our own time; and second, because the *Praelectiones* of Perrone are, in turn, the source and the model from which the great majority of our present-day manuals are derived. It is readily seen how our

[21] For example, on the catechumenate; on public and private penance.

textbooks update these previous authors and, after Leo XIII, include references to St. Thomas; in treating theological questions his arrangement is followed and large works are abridged into a few volumes of convenient size. Perrone's *Praelectiones* has indeed been influential.[22]

What is the fate of the liturgy, then, in the treatises of Perrone?

In the tract *de locis theologicis* he makes express mention of the liturgy among the "general means which transmit the primitive dogmatic tradition to us and by which this can be surely known." After the magisterium of the Church, the councils, the acts of the martyrs, comes "the sacred liturgy," and after this again, "the practice of the Church in the administration of the sacraments and in religious worship."

In this last section also the liturgy is considered. Perrone has separated it from the first by an incorrect idea of the liturgy itself. It is evident that the author has taken a look at Zaccaria and at one or another of the monographs to which Zaccaria is himself indebted. He exalts the importance of the liturgy in theology as witness to the tradition and the faith of the Church: "The authority of the sacred liturgy is supreme and the liturgy must be considered as a witness, superior to any other, of the tradition and the faith of the Church. Only he could deny this who does not advert to the fact that in the liturgy the voice of the whole Church, its bishops and priests, speaks; and likewise the prayers, the laws, the rites, and the dogmas themselves bear witness."

Having indicated some rules for judging the authority of the liturgy in the individual cases (Perrone insists on the unanimity of the liturgies on any particular point), he adds that in the liturgy are found almost all the dogmas of the Church. And he makes a summary enumeration of them, following the heading of "corollaries" as used by Zaccaria.

He says also that from the liturgical practice of the Church in the administration of the sacraments can be inferred a public, perennial, universal, and constant testimony of the dogmatic tradition about the number, efficacy, particular effects of the sacraments, and the dispositions required in order to receive them.[23]

After these high-sounding declarations on the theological importance of the liturgy, it might be thought that in the course of the various treatises Perrone would make abundant use of it. In reality, even quantitatively, his use of the liturgy does not much surpass the use made of it by Billuart, Gotti, and Tournely.

In the treatise on the sacraments in general, Perrone speaks also of the liturgical ceremonies in general, in the administration of the sacraments, in order to refute the errors of the Protestants in this regard.

[22] In the original nine volume form, there were thirty-four editions up to 1888. In the reduction to a compendium (*Praelectiones . . . in compendium redactae*) of five volumes and afterwards of two volumes, there were forty- seven editions up to 1892.

[23] As a matter of fact, for Perrone, the force of the liturgical argument resides ultimately in the fact that it proves the apostolicity of a doctrine. See the following note.

The same can be pointed out specifically in regard to the ceremonies of the Mass at the end of the treatise on the Eucharist, in connection with which he has recourse again to the liturgy, in order to defend, always against the Protestants, the Catholic doctrine on the Real Presence, the cult of adoration given to the Eucharist, the propitiatory character of the sacrifice of the Mass for the living and the dead. He appeals also to the liturgy for the lawfulness and the usefulness of the cult of the saints and of relics. Perrone believes also that he can prove from the liturgy that there are seven sacraments. It may be that here and there in his treatises some other recourse to the liturgy can be found. But I do not think that even the most careful search could change the essence of what I said above, namely, that even quantitatively, Perrone presents little more than Billuart, Gotti, or Tournely.

Even from the qualitative point of view, that is, from the aspect under which mention is made of the liturgy in these cases, we are always at the same stance, essentially and directly in relation to the anti-Protestant polemic of the authors of the sixteenth and seventeenth centuries: to demonstrate from the liturgy that the Protestants err when they deny various points of doctrine. In all this the liturgy serves to demonstrate the apostolicity of the doctrine of the Church, denied by the innovators.[24]

And the synthetic, or, as they are usually called, dogmatic theologians after Perrone? Père Berthier, in his treatise *De locis theologicis*,[25] gives notable prominence to the liturgy as *locus theologicus*, but does nothing except recapitulate Zaccaria and Perrone; besides, he wrote no other treatises from which we could see how he would have put into practice what he says of the liturgy in his general methodology.

The most notable dogmatic theologian of the second half of the eighteenth century was Franzelin, continuator and perfecter of the concept of theology of Perrone and of the whole positive-scholastic tradition. But the fact is that Franzelin drops the use of the liturgy in theology almost completely. He wrote a very well-known treatise on theological methodology, *De divina traditione et Scriptura*;[26] but I do not find that he gives any importance in it to the liturgy. He names the liturgy among the "monuments of tradition," between the acts of the martyrs and penitentials,[27] but says nothing else about it, to my knowledge. He also wrote a *Treatise on the Sacraments in General*;[28] but I find no mention there of the liturgy either.

In his treatise on the Eucharist there is an allusion to the liturgical argu-

---

[24] A typical example is Perrone's way of reasoning on the number of the sacraments: *De sacramentis in genere* (edition of Vienna, 1843), Vol. 3, p. 240, no. 11. The same way of reasoning is found on the probative value of the epiclesis for the Real Presence, inasmuch as the epiclesis must be of apostolic origin: *De eucharistia, ibid.*, p. 150; on the cult of the saints, Vol. 6, pp. 279–280; on ceremonies in

general, Vol. 7, p. 291, no. 172. It is clear that at the basis of Perrone's argumentation there remains an insufficient understanding of the evolution of dogmas.
[25] Turin 1900, pp. 424–440.
[26] First edition, Rome 1870.
[27] Edition of 1875, p. 165.
[28] First edition, Rome 1868.

ment in the question of the Real Presence and of the propitiatory character of the Mass.[29] In the treatise on the Church [30] there is nothing about the liturgy. And yet Franzelin was Perrone's disciple and a scholar concerned with bringing up to date and perfecting the positive method. It would seem to indicate, then, that on this point of the liturgy, he decided that he should drop even that attention which Perrone, following the theologians of the eighteenth century, had still accorded the liturgy.

During the first quarter of the twentieth century the concept of positive-scholastic theology was more or less relegated to a second rung while the more purely scholastic concept of theology was re-evaluated and theology was simply presented in the framework of direct commentaries on the *Summa* of St. Thomas; [31] thereafter the manualists returned substantially to the positive-scholastic concept of Perrone and of Franzelin. They brought their compendia up to date, however, in two respects.

First of all, in the positive aspect, all strove with varying success to follow the progress of historical and critical studies, as well as to add to the refutation of the old Protestants the refutation of the liberals of the type of von Harnack and of the modernists.

Moreover, they developed more substantially than had Perrone and Franzelin the speculative or traditional scholastic aspect with a deeper and more continuous contact with the text itself of the *Summa*: happy fruit of the renascence of Thomistic philosophy under Leo XIII.

Such is the genealogy of almost all the present-day manuals of theology. The most noted, those which have served to form entire generations of the clergy in theological science are, for example: Tanquerey, Pesch, van Noort, Bartmann, Hervé, and Diekamp. The position of these manuals with regard to the liturgy is substantially this:

1) in general, its admission among the *loci theologici*, for the most part with simple mention and without any or at most a very brief explanation of its nature and of its use in theology;

2) allusion to the liturgical feasts of the Immaculate Conception and of the Assumption of our Lady in the relative questions on the Immaculate Conception and the Assumption;

3) an unexpected allusion to the liturgy when they speak of the sacramentals, with regard to which they say that the whole liturgy can be considered as a sacramental;

4) then, in the treatise on the sacraments in particular, in connection with each sacrament, occasional mention of the liturgy; allusions to liturgical data in connection with the question of the matter and the form of each sacrament;

[29] Rome, edition of 1899, pp. 83–84; 365–367.

[30] *Theses de Ecclesia Christi*, Rome 1887.

[31] As, for example, with L. Janssens and L. Billot.

5) somewhat more abundant recourse to the liturgy in the treatise on the Eucharist, with brief allusions, apropos of the question of the Real Presence, of the worship due the Eucharist, of the propitiatory value of sacrifice of the Mass for the living and for the dead;

6) new allusion to the liturgy in questions about the cult of the saints, of relics and of images, and in the question about the existence of purgatory.

The above is just about all that can be found.[32]

Then if we try to take into account what is the determining visual angle under which these manualists are interested in the liturgy, the conclusion is always the same: they are interested in it solely, or almost solely,[33] as an element which manifests tradition, and this with a view to proving, against the Protestants, against the rationalists like von Harnack, and against the modernists, the apostolicity, or at least the great antiquity, of the doctrine now proposed by the magisterium.

At any rate, the conclusion of this inquiry on the place which the liturgy actually has in the theory and the practice of positive-scholastic theology, especially in the manuals of dogmatic theology which are still in the hands of most priests, can be only one: in the reality of things as it appears to those who are theologians by profession, we are very, very far from the liturgy as *locus theologicus praestantissimus* or even only *locus theologicus praestans* acclaimed by the liturgists beginning with the seventeenth century,[34] and which some theologians too have occasionally re-echoed, parenthetically we might say.[35] Certainly the cleric who has studied theology in the positive-scholastic manuals will not, at the end of his studies, have acquired thereby any concrete idea of the pre-eminence of the liturgy in the construction of a general theological synthesis.

In fact, having arrived at this point, I cannot see how on reflection we can avoid this dilemma: either the positive-scholastic theologians, the manualists in particular, have been very deficient in assimilating into their general synthesis the theological-liturgical material which the liturgists had placed at

---

[32] Tanquerey, probably by reason of his eclectic-practical tendency, is, so far as I can see, more generous than the other manualists. He develops somewhat more the question of the liturgy as a *locus theologicus* and restores, from the scholastic and positive-scholastic tradition of the eighteenth century and of Perrone, the questions of the rites of baptism, confirmation, Mass, extreme unction, at the end of the respective treatises.

[33] I say "almost" only to be scrupulously accurate and to reserve the possible case where, in some point, allusion may be made to the liturgy as witness to the teaching of the present and living magisterium. If this case exists, it is certainly very rare. To demonstrate that the "thesis" formulated is truly the doctrine of

the Church, the theologians do not have recourse to the liturgy, but to the definitions of the extraordinary magisterium (to that of Trent, in the questions disputed with the Protestants) or to some definition *ex cathedra*, as in Mariology.

[34] The statements of the liturgists both of the seventeenth and eighteenth centuries and of recent times can be reduced to this formula. See some of these formulas reported by Ph. Oppenheim, *Principia theologiae liturgicae*, pp. 108 ff; of Zaccaria, Renaudot, Languet, Beaudoin. Of Oppenheim himself, on p. 72: *locus theologicus praestans.*

[35] Such as Bossuet and Perrone (*maximi faciendam esse*), quoted by the same Oppenheim, *op. cit.*, pp. 111–112.

their disposal and which they, the positive-scholastic theologians, following the laws of their own discipline, could have and should have incorporated into their construction to its own real advantage; or else, in the expression of the liturgy as "outstanding theological source" there is an equivocation. In this case, the synthetic theologians, they whose trade it is to have a finger constantly in the theological pie, knowing in one way much more exactly than the liturgists who are but occasional theologians, every single theological question and the real utility which may be obtained in it by recourse to the liturgy, and seeing, however, from the concrete facts, that this utility is reduced, in the final analysis, to something of very little moment, have allowed liturgists to proclaim their theory of the pre-eminence of the liturgy as *locus theologicus* and, in practice, as was their right, or rather, their duty, have taken no account of it. Now, dear reader, if you must be stuck, which horn would you prefer?

3. Whether the Positive-Scholastic Ideal of Theology Permits the Assimilation into General Synthetic Theology of the Theological Material Included in the Liturgy

The first question which must be examined is whether the positive-scholastic theologians, according to the requirements of the concept of theology which stands as the basis of their work, could and should incorporate the theological-liturgical material placed at their disposal by the liturgists much more abundantly than they have done or are doing, and with real advantage to their theology.

The positive-scholastic ideal of the apologetical proof from the sources

Let us recall first of all that in the part called "positive," the theological ideal of positive-scholasticism is to demonstrate apodictically and directly for every single question, and with a purely critical and historical method, in such a way that the conclusion must impose itself also against the Protestants, the rationalists, and the modernists, that the doctrine enunciated in the "thesis" is, at least substantially, of apostolic origin and not a novelty of the Church.

It is important for our purpose to be really sure that this is truly the ideal of positive-scholasticism in the positive part. This ideal, more or less clearly expressed since the sixteenth and seventeenth centuries, is expressed reflectively and with all desirable clarity in the authors of the nineteenth century and of our day, as can be seen, for example, in Franzelin, Scheeben, Pesch, van Noort, and Diekamp.[36]

---

[36] Franzelin, *De divina traditione et Scriptura*, Rome 1875, p. 3; Scheeben, *Handbuch der kath. Dog.*, Vol I (1927), p. 389; Pesch, *Institutiones propedeuticae ad theologiam*, 1903, pp. 9–10, no. 23; pp. 11–12, nos. 27–28; van Noort, *Tractatus de fontibus revelationis*, 1911, pp. 4 ff; Diekamp, *Manuale . . .* , Vol. I (1932), p. 3, nos. 3–4, 8.

The typical statement of Tanquerey holds good for all: "The *positive* is that which perceives from the sources of revelation the individual truths which must be believed, sets them forth and demonstrates them with arguments taken from the Scriptures and from tradition."[37] That Tanquerey means (in the sense explained above) the task of demonstration from the Scriptures and from tradition is proved, for example, by the following quotes: "Biblical theology and historical theology refer to positive theology. Biblical theology investigates the doctrines as they can be found in the Scriptures alone, by means of criticism and exegesis. . . . Historical theology derives and sets forth Catholic doctrine not only from the Scripture but also from the Fathers, from the councils and from the other documents of tradition,[38] with the intention of demonstrating that the dogmas which are now proposed by the Church for our belief are substantially the same that were preached by the Apostles and by Christ. Thus it differs from positive theology inasmuch as the latter pays less attention to the chronological order, and from the history of dogma inasmuch as this describes the progress of Christian doctrine without seeking to demonstrate, however, its unity and identity with the original revelation."[39]

Between positive and historical theology, for Tanquerey, therefore, there is only an accidental difference: positive theology pays less attention to chronological order; otherwise, both have for their purpose to demonstrate the identity, at least substantial, of the doctrine now preached by the Church with the original revelation contained in the Scriptures and in the apostolic tradition.

That this proof, moreover, in the mind of Tanquerey, should be made by the historical and critical way alone, is clear again, for example, from the following text: "Actually, the positive and historical method, for the themes of primary importance, is eminently suitable for refuting the errors of those who, with (von) Harnack, claim that Catholic dogmas have undergone a natural evolution; but if they were used for all questions, even for the accessory ones, in an elementary course they would be too long and tedious."[40]

Only if a person takes this ideal into account can he understand the typical scheme employed in the exposition of a theological question in positive-scholasticism. After the statement of the question, often even before, the thesis to be considered is briefly put; and the adversaries are kept in view. There follows a note enunciating the degree of authority proper to that thesis (of the faith; certain; common opinion; etc.) and, possibly, the declarations of the magisterium (for example, the text of a council) which prove such to be

---

[37] *De vera religione, De ecclesia, De fontibus revelationis,* 1922, p. 5.
[38] The liturgy, for Tanquerey, is one of these documents of tradition: *ibid.,* pp. 618, 640 ff.
[39] *Ibid.,* pp. 6–7.
[40] *Ibid.,* p. 8. Tanquerey would have it that

if proof by history alone is not used in fact in all the questions, this holds only for an elementary course, to avoid length and tedium. *Per se,* however, it should be used in every question.

actually the doctrine of the Church. Then come the "proofs" of the said doctrine. First of all the proof from the Scriptures; then the proof from tradition; finally, that from reason, at least theological reason or by reason of what is appropriate. The objections are examined either in the course of the individual arguments or at the end.

This procedure, typical of the positive-scholastic ideal, having made its appearance to some extent even from the beginning of positive-scholasticism, became solidly constituted toward the end of the seventeenth century; reduced to school form by Perrone, it was commonly adopted by subsequent manualists except for accidental modifications. In recent authors we find certain hesitations among those more sensitive to the requirements of the historical method.

The liturgy as proof from tradition of the apostolicity of a doctrine: the possibility of such a proof and its minimal actual usefulness for this purpose

The question now is whether the aforesaid picture of the positive-scholastic ideal requires, or at least permits, for the real advantage of theology a substantially more abundant and especially a qualitatively better utilization of the liturgy as a source than that formerly made of it by positive-scholastic theologians or the use made of it by the manualists even to our own times. To this question it seems to me that the answer must be unhesitatingly in the negative.

Here it could be asked whether possibly in the positive-scholastic scheme recourse should not be had to the liturgy immediately after the enunciation of the thesis, where usually texts are cited from the extraordinary magisterium, councils, or decisions *ex cathedra*, to show that the doctrine enunciated in the thesis is really the doctrine of the Church. Actually, the positive-scholastics do admit that the doctrine of the magisterium can be known from the liturgy. But these theologians do not have recourse to the liturgy at this point of the argumentation.

Reflecting on what we have set forth in the preceding chapter, we must admit that in neglecting the liturgy the positive-scholastics, granted their concept of theology, are led by a sure instinct. For we have seen that the liturgy is indeed important for knowing the thought of the Church on a determinate doctrine, but that this thought is not given in a direct and didactically precise way in the liturgy. To attain the needed precision a person must in practice have recourse to other means by which the magisterium expresses itself in a direct way, principally the decisions of the extraordinary magisterium.

When the positive-scholastics, therefore, in their effort to prove that the doctrine expressed in their thesis with the indicated degree of authority is truly Church doctrine, do not appeal to the liturgy but to the documents in which the magisterium expresses its thought directly and didactically, viz., the decisions of the councils and the teaching authority of the Pope *ex cathedra*, they know very well what they are doing. The liturgy, in such instances, would be of no use or of very little use, since in order to establish the meaning of a thesis and its precise didactic import in a determinate case, recourse must be had anyway to these other documents.[41]

And it is for this reason that in positive-scholasticism the liturgy, insofar as it enters in at all, enters normally as a mere element of the proof from tradition. Now we know that the ultimate purpose of this proof from tradition in positive-scholasticism is to supply an apodictic demonstration by the historical way alone of the apostolic origin — substantially apostolic, at least — of a doctrine presently taught as of faith by the Church. But what is to be thought of the use of the liturgy for this purpose?

It should be noted well that at the moment we are concerned with proving apodictically by the historical method alone and from the liturgy alone the apostolicity in some measure of a genuine tenet of faith. It is necessary, therefore, that this proof, to be valid, be made according to all the requirements of the historical method. I do not wish to deny at all that such proof can actually be made from the liturgy. But in how many cases will this be possible, given the actual state of the sources? It is certain that the positive-scholastics in the polemic of the sixteenth to the eighteenth centuries, and others together with them, whether before or after, have been led to exaggerate the number of such instances.

Recently an excellent scholar of ancient liturgy, patristics, and historical method, Abbot Capelle, summed up in this way his thinking in connection with a study on the same question in the Fathers: that the apostolic origin, as far as the liturgical elements are concerned, "has been too easily supposed and quite naively admitted, if not sometimes fraudulently affirmed,[42] is evident. But not everything is imaginary in this conviction. There is no doubt, for example, that the elementary ritual of baptism and of the Eucharist must necessarily have existed very early. Substantial agreements are noted between the ancient rituals of Rome, of Jerusalem, of Antioch, and of Alexandria. As far as the Mass in particular is concerned, the reading of the Gospel, the union between Eucharist and synaxis of prayer,[43] the solemn orations, the kiss of peace, the role of the deacons, the *Amen* of the people, the sending of

---

[41] It is for this reason that in the theses which express a doctrine of the faith, the positive-scholastics appeal to the decisions of the extraordinary magisterium, especially to the Council of Trent in the doctrines defined against the Protestants, to the First Vatican Council in those defined against the rationalists and the semi-rationalists, to the anti-modernist documents against the modernists, to

the decisions *ex cathedra* in the question of the Immaculate Conception, the Assumption, etc.

[42] Abbot Capelle alludes to the case of the author of the so-called *Constitutiones apostolicae*.

[43] The two parts of the Mass, referred to for centuries as the Mass of the catechumens and the Mass of the faithful.

the Eucharist to the absent, are equally common traits, extraneous both to Scripture and to Jewish custom. It can be held *probable* that they derive from the primitive organization of worship at Jerusalem. *The belief in an apostolic tradition, if it has sometimes been too generally accepted, is founded nevertheless on a primeval reality, the importance of which cannot be measured.*" [44]

I have emphasized certain passages by the use of italics. The word *probable* must be noted, and the last clause, in which it is stated that the apostolic primeval reality of the liturgy in its precise elements *cannot be measured*, i.e., its extent cannot as yet be estimated. As is seen, in the judgment of an expert, if we address the liturgy with the precise aim of furnishing by means of it alone the purely historical apodictic proof of the apostolicity of the doctrines now taught by the Church, we cannot escape being almost always deluded.

Of course, if instead of apodictic arguments we are content with probable arguments, we shall be able to gather a greater share of them in the liturgy; and more yet, if instead of claiming to go back all the way to the Apostles, we are content with reaching a more or less remote antiquity.

But, to tell the truth, even so the recourse to the liturgy, in the totality of the theological argumentation of the positive-scholastic type, will have a rather limited usefulness. For, if I am not mistaken, in all or almost all the cases in which the antiquity of a doctrine proposed today by the Church can be demonstrated by means of the liturgy, the same can be done and rather better with other and more effective arguments, as with texts of the Fathers or of the councils, etc.

For example, even by the historical way alone the conviction held in the Roman Church of the fifth-sixth century concerning the primacy and infallibility of the Roman Church can be demonstrated from the liturgy alone of the Leonine Sacramentary; but the same can be demonstrated with just as much or with even more effectiveness from the very texts of St. Leo, from the Council of Chalcedon, from the statements of the legate Philip in the Council of Ephesus, from the texts of Boniface I, Zosimus, Innocent I, etc.

From the texts of the liturgy the faith of the Church in transubstantiation and in the Real Presence can certainly be demonstrated, beginning with the fourth-fifth century; but it can be done just as well by recourse to the texts of the Fathers of the same epoch or even of a previous age.

And so for other cases. Thus the liturgical argument has no more value than that of a confirmation.

And in general it can be said that all the theses of positive-scholasticism could easily be adorned, decked out as it were, with citations of liturgical texts and customs. But the usefulness of such a procedure would be almost nothing. These, it seems to me, are the reasons which explain why, despite the effort of the liturgists, such as Zaccaria and others, to prepare liturgical

---

[44] "*Autorité de la liturgie chez les Pères,*" in   Vol. 21 (1954), p. 20.
Recherches de théol. ancienne et médiévale,

material of theological value at the disposal of the dogmatic theologians, the liturgy in reality has never seriously penetrated into dogmatic theology. The present-day positive-scholastic manualists have followed the intrinsic logic of things when they have in good part practically expelled from their theology that bit of liturgy which Perrone, for example, still tried to preserve.

With all this, shall we perhaps say that the theory of the liturgy as "outstanding theological source" is a fiction? Pardon my naïveté, but I cannot quite refrain from posing another question: How can it be doubted, after the mere reading of these modest essays on the theological meaning of the liturgy, that the liturgy is really loaded and overloaded with theological material of highest value? And theological material, be it noted, from which something about the meaning and the force of revelation can be perceived which is not given by the other ways of theological knowledge.

The knowledge and the deepening of the revealed truths, for example, of which I have treated in the first three parts of these essays, which can be gathered from the liturgy, is not a mere repetition or confirmation of what can be gathered about them from the Bible alone or from the Fathers or from the directly didactic documents of the magisterium alone; so much the less from theological speculations. The liturgy contributes something of its own, a *quid proprium*, to the better knowledge of revelation itself which we know by the other theological means. What this aspect of its own is, will appear better in what follows. If this is so, the liturgy cannot remain outside of dogmatic theology, supposing the task of dogmatics is to use all the lights that can contribute to deepening the scientific knowledge of its object.

This means that if in positive-scholastic theology the theological material of the liturgy, notwithstanding the good intentions and the attempts of the positive-scholastic theologians, remains essentially and must remain essentially outside of the theological synthesis, the true reason cannot be because this material is not assimilable into this synthesis or does not belong to it or has no value for it, but because there is some imperfection in the manner in which this theological synthesis is conceived. It is an inflexible methodological and historical law: When any reality, duly ascertained, is not organically incorporable into a previous scientific construction, even though it does belong to the object of that construction, this is a sign that there is some deficiency in the manner in which the aforesaid synthesis has been conceived and carried out. The reality brought to light obliges the scholar to rethink and control his construction and his method.

Insufficient assimilation of the liturgical material in positive-scholasticism by reason of the exaggerated preoccupation with apologetics

It is not my intention here to evaluate all the reasons underlying the labor that bore fruit in positive-scholasticism. In judging the final product, however, there is not an expert today in the fields of exegesis and biblical theology who is satisfied with the manner in which, very often, the biblical theological material is used and incorporated in this type of theology, especially in our usual manuals. And as we said at the beginning of this chapter, every expert understands that the concern is not simply with the quantities of biblical quotations nor with accuracy alone and with texts as being truly appropriate, but with the qualitative manner of conceiving the relation between biblical theological material and dogmatic synthesis.

The same ·may be said in its own way of patristic theology. There is not today an expert in patristics and in the history of dogmas and doctrines who remains satisfied with the manner in which, very often, this historical-theological material is assimilated into the theology of the manuals. I say this to make it clear that I hope I will not look like a knight errant when I set forth some remarks on the way in which, in many cases, positive-scholasticism conceives the theological ideal.

The essential remark is that in the positive-scholastic ideal of theology there is a certain exaggeration of the apologetical concern and of the task of defense against adversaries, real or only methodological, a task which, for that matter, is incumbent upon every science. This exaggeration is manifested in two fields.

First of all it is manifest in the very manner in which the material is presented. The choice of the questions treated, the relative importance which is given to each one, the precise aspect under which it is primarily considered, the place granted to it in the general synthesis, are in many cases too much determined by the polemic against the Protestants, to which is later joined that against the enlightenment, against the liberal rationalists like von Harnack, and against the modernists. Thus the old scholastic problems are developed in a sense dependent more upon the ideas of the adversaries whom it was necessary to refute than on the intrinsic necessities of the matter considered in itself.

It is certain that positive-scholasticism has had the merit of broadening and deepening the theological propositions of the old scholasticism. This is demonstrated, for example, by the creation and the insertion into the general theological synthesis of three new treatises whose matter was discussed by the old scholastics in a few questions, often scattered somewhat throughout theology: the treatise called *de locis theologicis*, or the sources of revelation; the treatise on the Church; the treatise on general apologetics. Also the problematics of other treatises was notably enlarged.

It is no less certain, however, that this broadening has been conceived with a too exclusively polemical preoccupation. This is demonstrated in the first place by the fact that it is hardly manifested at all in the treatises which touch on matters not placed directly in question or but little disputed by the Protestants, by the enlightenment, by the liberal rationalists, or by the modernists, e.g., *De Deo uno*, the Trinity, the angels, Christology. A profound contact with the Scriptures, tradition and, of course, the liturgy, made with the predominant concern of knowing better the message of revelation in itself, would easily lead to a notable broadening and deepening of the problematics germane to these subjects.

The polemic approach is also evident from the fact that any new questions introduced by positive-scholasticism into the general theological synthesis are precisely those aspects denied by the Protestants, then by the enlightenment, and lastly by the liberal rationalists and by the modernists — and almost nothing other. It is thus that the treatise on the Church concerns itself wholly with the defense of its visibility, and in particular with the primacy and infallibility of the Roman Pontiff; the spiritual nature of the Church as mystical body is almost entirely forgotten. It is thus again that general apologetics, conceived primarily against the enlightenment, is understood as a sort of bridge to lead the atheist to theology, and that the whole orientation is anti-illuminist and anti-Protestant. The question of our relations with the Eastern Churches is treated in a clearly inadequate way.

The treatise on grace is almost wholly centered on the question of actual grace and of free choice; and the aspect of divine sonship and of deification, which is the predominating aspect of the Scriptures and of tradition in these matters, is relegated to a very secondary level; what is said of it is again in regard to a question disputed with the Protestants, that of our justification: whether it is intrinsic or merely imputed.

The problematics of the treatises on the sacraments in general and in particular (and the treatise on the Four Last Things), compared to that of the old scholastics, exhibits as new only the topics disputed with the Protestants and with the more recent rationalists, above all the question of the institution of the sacraments by Christ.

The treatise on the Eucharist, too, is all by way of defense against the Protestant denials, above all concerning the Real Presence and the reality of the sacrifice.[45]

The second field in which the exaggerated preoccupation with apologetics is manifested in positive-scholasticism is its way of using, in the individual questions, the proper sources which contain revelation, that is, the Scriptures and tradition, in the so-called positive part of the theological task. As has been seen, when positive-scholasticism appeals to the Scriptures and to tradition, it does so with the direct and highly predominant concern of proving by a purely historical way against real or methodological denials that the doctrine taught today by the Church and expressed in the thesis is truly of apostolic origin.

I am not denying at all that this proof by the historical way alone can

---

[45] The inevitable influence of the polemic in the very problematics of a science is not, of course, denied. But there are ways and there are ways. The old scholasticism, for example, is not predominantly polemic but irenic, expositive, contemplative.

truly be made in several very important cases, above all in the question of the proximate criterion of faith, in which the primary error of Protestantism occurs.

It is undeniably a notable merit of positive-scholasticism to have realized and to have developed this proof for the cases in which it was possible. Moreover, when one thinks of the airiness with which the first Protestants were assigning to much later dates the "birth" of the Catholic dogmas which they did not want to admit, and how much more cautious the Protestants themselves and the rationalists have now become in accusing the Catholic Church of novelty (it is well known that von Harnack himself at the end of his life recognized that the essential elements of Catholicism were already present in the Church at the end of the first century and the beginning of the second), one cannot but recognize that the activity of the positive-scholastics has been beneficial and providential, even when they did not succeed absolutely in giving the proof of apostolicity.

Still it is certain that the aforesaid mentality of appealing to the sources, seeing in them too exclusively what can be extracted from them against the Protestants, etc., has its inconveniences. It is not up to me in my capacity to analyze all of them. Nor do I intend to insist on the fact that certainly there are cases — and they are more numerous than the positive-scholastics have been ready to admit — in which that proof by the historical way alone cannot be made,[46] and in which, to defend their faith against the Protestants, the Catholics must have recourse to other ways, above all to the fundamental question of the proximate criterion of faith. This proximate criterion, when examined according to Scripture and tradition, is not human reason taken individually or philosophically or historically, but the infallible teaching authority of the hierarchical Church.

It is certain that more than once the exaggerated anxiety to provide direct historical proof against the Protestants, etc., has led positive-scholastics not to recognize these cases and to diminish their number unduly, as if at that time there did not exist any other way of defending the Church. This led to the danger, not imaginary, of requiring in those cases more of history than it can give, and of bringing forth proofs historically and critically inadequate. Thus they fell into the same peril into which their own adversaries themselves often fell: they asked too much of history alone; they ran the risk of arousing doubts in the faithful themselves, who saw that the proof was insufficient, and of exposing our faith to ridicule by unbelievers, who, as St. Thomas says apropos of inadequate proofs of a philosophical order, imagine that we believe for similar unsound reasons.

But let us consider rather the cases in which apodictic proof can really be

---

[46] For example, the Assumption; see Diekamp, *Manuale* . . . , Vol. 2, p. 427: "the proposition cannot be proved from history"; the sacramental characters, see the same, Vol. 4, p. 28; the number of the sacraments, *ibid*, p .68.

made by the historical way alone. Even in these instances, the rather restricted viewpoint from which the positive-scholastic ideal leads to using Scripture and tradition with a view to furnish the aforesaid proof brings it about that the positive-scholastic too often does not give due attention to the aspect of the evolution of dogmas and doctrines, whether it be the objective evolution in the very orbit of Scripture before the death of the last Apostle, or the subjective, explicitative evolution after the death of the Apostles.

This evolution is real, and it is up to the theologians to make it known and to explain it to us in relevant passages. Instead, the positive-scholastic readily puts all the texts of the Scriptures of the Old Testament or of the New which refer to a question on the same level and uses them indiscriminately, paying little or no attention to their respective epoch, their different authors, the different tendencies which they manifest, etc.

Then for tradition, excessive preoccupation with a chain of testimonies easily risks causing the perspective of explicitative evolution to disappear; no explanation is given why in some cases recourse is had to the testimony of a writer, for example Tertullian or Origen, while in others it is declared that he cannot be admitted as witness to the faith of the Church; in other instances texts are wrenched from their context and are therefore not convincing.

But the unsuitability of the exaggerated prevalence of the apologetic viewpoint in positive-scholasticism which is of greater interest to us from the liturgical viewpoint is the following. Even in the cases where the apodictic proof of the apostolicity of a doctrine can be made by the historical way alone, if recourse is had to Scripture, to tradition, to the magisterium, with too great a dependence on the aforesaid mentality, the contact with the sources of revelation will be determined in its extension and in its quality more by the problematics of the adversaries than by the intrinsic theological riches of the sources themselves.

Not all the data actually contained in the Scriptures, in tradition, in the exposition of the magisterium even in our day will be assimilated, but only some, namely, the data affecting the dispute with real or fictitious adversaries; the sources are tapped but only under a determinate and restricted aspect, that in which the adversaries have erred. Immense riches contained in the sources remain unexplored and will not be assimilated into the theological synthesis because the adversaries are not involved, or because the dispute with the adversaries does not touch such values.

Now it is easy to see that the sources of revelation, for the theologian, are not there merely to permit him to prove that the adversaries of the Catholic faith have erred; rather, these sources offer very many and very important other things of primary value in the construction of any general theological synthesis.

Theology is above all and in the first place the scientific effort of the believer himself to penetrate and contemplate the riches of the revelation to which he assents in all its breadth and depth. This irenic function — let us call it such — this penerative, contemplative, expositive function of theology must necessarily be primary and determinant, and take precedence over any apologetic or defensive function.

The defensive or apologetic function does belong necessarily to every science because it cannot be said that one has penetrated and possesses a matter scientifically as long as he does not know also how to answer the doubts or the objections of the opponents. But the defensive function, which is rather negative in the general synthesizing view of every science,[47] must be subordinated to the penetrative or expositive function. It is not the defensive function which can determine in the last analysis, either quantitatively or qualitatively, either the problematics, or the use of the sources, or the general skeleton of the synthetic construction.

The ultimate reason for this evaluation is that apologetic functions are regulated in an essential way by the opinions of adversaries, which are variable and purely accidental with respect to the truth itself, while the penetrative or contemplative function is regulated solely by the content and essence of the science itself. It is the essence or content which is always the object of scientific inquiry, and which, in the final analysis, determines procedure; to be a science, a science must be concerned primarily about its own proper subject matter.

It is therefore the exaggerated predominance of the apologetic aspect of positive-scholastic theology in its so-called positive part that is the root of the dissatisfaction which it arouses (especially as it is often handed down in our usual manuals) among all experts in biblical theology, historical theology, and liturgical theology.

The reading and the study of the sources of theology which, thanks be to God, is now being done more and more generally, with the primary intention of simply penetrating as far as possible into all the riches of these sources considered in themselves and by themselves, renders acute the perception that positive-scholastic theology, especially that of the manuals, does not assimilate as it should all the material at its disposal in the sources and does not take sufficient account of that material in its general synthesis.

Concluding judgment

It is in this general perspective that we can finally give a judgment on the question of the use of the liturgy in the general synthetic theology of positive-scholasticism.

[47] I am not speaking, of course, of monographic treatises, which by definition consider only one aspect or one part of a question, but only of synthetic treatises. In a monographic treatise it is legitimate to limit oneself even to the simply defensive and apologetic aspect. But dogmatic theology is synthetic theology, not monographic.

Looking closely at matters, we see that positive-scholastic theology has considered only two questions pertinent to liturgy.

In the general theological methodology of Melchior Cano it is asked whether the liturgy is a kind of *locus theologicus*. The reply in substance: the liturgy is a theological source which is included in the more general theological source of the ordinary magisterium. By means of the liturgy, therefore, certain rules being observed, it can be determined what the ordinary magisterium teaches about a certain question and what the Christian people who accept that magisterium profess.

Then, in the rest of its theological treatises, positive-scholastic theology has been interested in the liturgy only as an element of tradition by means of which it may be possible to prove, in a purely historical way and in particular against the Protestants, the apostolicity of some specific doctrine or custom in the Church.

Now it is evident from what we have explained that to see in the liturgy only these two possibilities means ignoring the enormous theological riches which the liturgy possesses and interesting oneself in two aspects which are real but secondary and, all in all, of only slight usefulness anyway in any theological synthesis. For we know that the liturgy, as a source from which can be determined what the magisterium proposes didactically, has only slight importance because it is by its nature a rather indirect manifestation of the magisterium and because, in order to specify its meaning and its degree of authority it is practically necessary, in every case, to have recourse to all the other sources of theology, in particular to the direct manifestation of the same magisterium, especially in its extraordinary and solemn interventions.

We know also that the liturgy as an element for proving by the historical way alone the apostolicity of a doctrine or of a usage in the Church is of secondary importance and utility in a general theological synthesis; there are two principal reasons for this: either such proof cannot be made by the liturgy alone, or if it can be made, it can generally be made also and better by recourse to the other ways, especially to the texts of the Fathers and to the Scriptures.

If, therefore, in the practice of positive-scholastic theology the liturgy does not appear in fact as the "outstanding theological source," the reason for this is the too restricted way in which positive-scholasticism considers the liturgy; and this attitude is a result of its general mentality in conceiving its theological task, being too dominated by the viewpoint of forming directly for every doctrine the apologetic-historical proof from the sources.

The deficiency of the use of the liturgy in positive-scholastic theology is therefore a simple consequence of a certain narrowness in the viewpoint from which that theology considers its proper sources, in particular the magisterium, the Scriptures, and patristic tradition. As to the theological use of the liturgy, however, there is this further drawback. The magisterium, the Scriptures, and patristic tradition, even when considered with the too restricted preoccupation of reading in them primarily what can be useful for the anti-Protestant, anti-rationalist, and anti-modernist polemic, still always have an importance which is not only considerable but capital for the systematic theologian, although in doing so he is still far from exhausting all the theological riches which these sources contain. The liturgy, on the other hand, considered in the same perspective, loses almost entirely any real importance for the purposes of the theological synthesis.

The liturgy presents itself to the systematic theologian neither solely nor even primarily to show him what the ordinary magisterium proposes didactically, and neither solely nor primarily as an element of tradition from which he can gather, against the Protestants or others, a historical proof of the apostolicity of the doctrine of the Church.

The liturgy presents itself to the theologian primarily to teach him how the Church — hierarchy and faithful — under the veil of sensible and efficacious signs, lives its faith every day and has lived it in the past, in the actual encounter of sanctification and worship with God and the supernatural world.

This is the liturgy's own specialty and wealth, which the theologian cannot know in any other theological source, in any other *locus theologicus*.

Now to know how the Church lives its faith in the actual encounter with God under the veil of sensible and efficacious signs of sanctification and of worship has, in connection with every great question of which synthetic theology must treat, an importance which the systematic theologian cannot ignore, because it manifests greater and more proper horizons and depths about that same faith, horizons and depths which cannot be perceived, or cannot be well perceived, except in the liturgy.

What are these horizons and these depths of revelation which the theologian cannot discover except in the liturgy? In the preceding chapters I have attempted to elucidate some of them. I think it can be concluded that by neglecting the liturgy, the systematic theologian either will not see or will not understand and will not set forth in all their real force and import, according to revelation itself, the following concepts among many others: revelation primarily as sacred history, and sacred history as mystery of history, mystery of the Church, mystery of Christ always in the making; the Christological-Trinitarian route of the derivation of every good from God and of its return to God, and therefore the force of the Trinitarian life in the Church and, in particular, the import of that statement that every sanctification is made *in Spiritu*; the real force of the actual presence of Christ in the Church and the real import of His priesthood and ceaseless priestly activity; the reality and the precise meaning of the universal priesthood of the faithful; the whole import of the law of incarnation; the profound force of the reality of people of God, of salvation in community, of solidarity, of communion of saints, of mystical body; the real unity of the infrahuman, human, angelic cosmos, and hence the cosmic import of the redemption; the implications of the bodily-spiritual nature of man in the substantial unity of his being; the eschatological tension in the Christian life; the redemption as struggle always going on against Satan; the importance of the Scriptures in the Christian life and the Christian way of reading the Old and New Testament, and therefore the ever-living actuality for every single one of the faithful of the whole of Scripture, even of the Old Testament and of the psalms in particular; the Mass as center of the whole sacred economy *hic et nunc*; the nature of the Church and especially the worship of God as its primary end to which are ordained all other means and powers and from which are derived all its energies. And I do not at all pretend to have exhausted the list; I have recalled only the outstanding points which can be gathered from the preceding chapters.

But why cannot the theologian understand these things, or understand them well, except in the liturgy? Because Catholicism is indeed a doctrine and a system, but a doctrine and a system which is at the same time a life always being lived: Christ living in the Church, the Church living in Christ. But Christ living in the Church and the Church living in Christ is above all and primarily the liturgy in act. It is for this reason that the very doctrines of Catholicism cannot be penetrated to their depths if the liturgy is neglected.

But, of course, to attain this end it is necessary to approach the liturgy simply with the intention of finding in it, apropros of every great question, how the Church, under the veil of sensible and efficacious signs, has lived and does live her faith every day in the actual encounter, in sanctification and worship, with God and the supernatural world. The liturgy must be approached, therefore, with a broader view, less directly polemic and more simply positive, penetrative, and contemplative than that view which positive-scholastic theology has been able to bring to it, by reason of the historical contingencies of the birth and the development of positive-scholasticism. It is beside the point to add that the polemical method is nevertheless one which has and which continues to benefit us greatly.

18 THEOLOGY AND LITURGY

IN ST. THOMAS

In order to obtain an adequate appreciation of the relations between theology and liturgy in scholasticism, it seems sufficient to limit ourselves in a special way to St. Thomas, because it is in him that the concept itself and the theological practice which were proper to scholasticism have their purest exemplar, one most significant for its influence upon later theologians.

Now if one studies rather closely the place of the liturgy in the theological synthesis of St. Thomas, after having studied it in positive-scholasticism, one is pleasantly surprised to find a quite different situation; even if it has notable need of being deepened and perfected, still it is richer and more fertile than that of the later positive-scholastics.

Throughout the *Summa*, in particular, there are, for whoever knows how to note them, very considerable elements of liturgical theology and hints which reveal a rather more profound understanding of the place of the liturgy in systematic synthetic theology, even if, objectively speaking, they cannot yet be called adequately developed.[1]

[1] The following have treated of the liturgy in St. Thomas: H. Hering, "*De loco theologico liturgiae apud S. Thomam*," in *Pastor bonus*, Vol. 5 (1951), pp. 456–464; C. M. Travers, *Valeur sociale de la liturgie d'après* *S. Thomas*, Paris 1946. There are worthwhile observations in the notes to the French translation of the *Summa*, ed. Revue des Jeunes, *Les sacrements*, Paris 1945, of A. M. Roguet.

This material involving liturgical theology in the *Summa* is found principally in the treatise on the Old Law as far as its ceremonial precedents are concerned (I-II, qq. 101-103); in the treatise on religion and on worship in general (II-II, qq. 81-100) especially where religion is considered in itself and in its acts (qq. 81-87); and in the whole treatise on the sacraments in general and in particular (III, qq. 60-90; *Supplementum*, qq. 1-68). Moreover, throughout the theology of St. Thomas the liturgy figures in various questions as one of the "authorities" in the framework of the *quaestio* and of the dialectical process of the *sic et non*.

It seems that the study of all this material from the point of view which interests us here can be conveniently divided into three subheads: the general fundamental notions of St. Thomas in the *Summa*, which can spark an elaboration of the concept of liturgy and therefore serve as basis for the construction of a general liturgical theology; the direct and methodical insertion of liturgical considerations into the Thomistic theological synthesis; and the use of the liturgy as "authority" throughout the whole theology of St. Thomas.

1. Fundamental Notions of the *Summa* Which Can Serve as Basis for a General Liturgical Theology

As for the presence in St. Thomas of fundamental notions which can serve as a basis for the construction of a general liturgical theology, let it suffice to recall some of the elemental concepts in his theology of religion and of worship in general, in his treatment of the sacraments, and in his comments on worship in the Old Testament; from these sources we ourselves have often culled in the first part of this work concerning the concept of liturgy.

Theology of religion and worship

From St. Thomas we have an accurate analysis of the two concepts of religion and worship (II-II, qq. 81-87), as well as of the concept of *devotio* (q. 82), of prayer in its various kinds (q. 83), and of sacrifice (q. 85), all things of highest importance for framing ideologically the concept of the liturgy. Aside from certain particular points about which there may be some dispute, such as placing the virtue of religion among the simple potential parts of the cardinal virtue of justice, these analyses constitute the solid foundation of any theology of the liturgy.

Particularly important is the emphasis which St. Thomas gives everywhere in the treatise on religion and worship to the following distinction: religion considered in its interior aspect and religion considered in its outward expressions justified by the bodily-spiritual as well as social nature of man, but always relative to the interior attitude of soul which constitutes the dynamic life-giving force of every act of religion.

Theology of the sacraments in general

Concerning the sacraments in general (III, qq. 60–65), there is to be pointed out above all the great concept of sign; it is precisely that concept of sign which has served as basis for the elaboration of the concept of liturgy in the first part of the present work. Not only is there in the works of St. Thomas a whole philosophy and theology of sign,[2] but it is no exaggeration to say that this concept represents the keystone of his mature theology throughout the whole treatise on the sacraments in general and in particular.

This fact has rightly been given a strong emphasis by those recent commentators (notably Père Roguet[3]) who have tried and are trying to construct in some way a liturgical theology starting from St. Thomas. In all this St. Thomas is the heir and, in some way, the perfecter of the theological thought of St. Augustine and, through him, of the whole symbolical, theological, liturgical tradition of ancient patristic literature as well as of the thought of the early Middle Ages. In the *Summa*, the mature expression of his thought on this point, not only does St. Thomas say that sacrament must be placed in the genus of sign (III, q. 60, a. 1), but he actually defines the New Testament sacrament as "the sign of a sacred thing inasmuch as it is sanctifying for men" (a. 2).

He presents, moreover, the doctrine of the threefold dimension of signification proper to the sacramental sign; here he echoes again the grand symbolistic, realistic vision of the Fathers: "A thing is called a sacrament, properly speaking, which is ordained to signifying our sanctification. Now in this there are three aspects which can be considered, namely: the cause itself of our sanctification, which is the Passion of Christ; the form of our sanctification, which consists in grace and the virtues; the ultimate end of our sanctification, which is life eternal. All this is signified in the sacraments. Therefore the sacrament is a sign commemorative of that which has preceded, that is, of the Passion of Christ; demonstrative of that which is operative in us by the Passion of Christ, namely, grace; and prophetic, that is, foretelling future glory" (a. 3).

To this same fundamental doctrine of the sacrament as sign St. Thomas links his explanation of the composition of every sacrament: a sacrament consists of (a) a sensible thing with the potential of further determination (*res*); (b) an element that specifically determines its special meaning (*verba*) — the so-called hylomorphism applied to the sacraments (aa. 4–7); (c) a causality by which every sacrament is an efficacious sign, i.e., one which effi-

[2] See A. M. Roguet, the work cited in the preceding note, pp. 257–346. Also the study of Travers depends wholly on the notion of sign, for the work is divided into two parts: social value of sign; social value of Christian signs.

[3] *Op. cit.* So too with Travers, *op. cit.* See also H. Schillebeeckx, *De sacramentele heilseconomie. Theologische bezinning op St. Thomas' sacramentenleer in het licht van de traditie en van hedendaagse sacramentenproblematik*, Antwerp 1952.

caciously causes precisely that which it signifies (III, q. 62), or, as later theologians have said, *efficit quod figurat* or *significando causat*. The explanation of the individual sacraments hinges wholly upon the sign proper to each as the expression of the particular grace which it confers.

Another basic concept of the treatise on the sacraments in general in St. Thomas (and this too is of considerable importance for liturgical theology) is that of the twofold indivisible end of the sacraments, sanctification and worship, with worship having a primacy over sanctification inasmuch as sanctification is consequent upon worship (III, q. 60, a. 5 c.; q. 63, a. 6 c.).

A third important concept is that the worship of God, to which the sacraments are directed, is specifically Christian worship, namely that begun by Christ, especially on Golgotha, always continued by Him, and to which He associates the faithful, uniting them to Himself and making them sharers in His worship of God; it is therefore the worship of God in Christ. For St. Thomas, it is precisely in view of this worship of God in Christ that the sacramental characters have their specific function — the sacramental characters "are nothing else but a certain participation in the priesthood of Christ, derived from Christ Himself" (III, q. 63, a. 3) The result is that the whole of Christian worship is nothing but Christ's worship continuously actualized by means of the Church, with the Church, and through the Church. This last concept receives further precise application in St. Thomas in the doctrine of the sacraments as separate instruments of the divinity of Christ, just as His humanity is its conjoint instrument.

Finally, there is in St. Thomas the concept that all the sacramentals and the various liturgical rites are ordained to the sacraments as their principal (see, e.g., III, q. 65, a. 1 ad 6), while among the sacraments all are ordained to the Eucharist, sacrifice and sacrament, which thus appears as the center and sun of the whole complexus of the Church's worship and sanctification (III, q. 56, a. 3).

It is true that in all this St. Thomas speaks directly of the seven sacraments, that is, of those major rites of the liturgy which are of divine institution and work *ex opere operato*, and not of the whole liturgy. The treatise of St. Thomas on the sacraments in general is directly and exactly a treatise on the seven sacraments in general and not a treatise on the *sacramenta*, that is, practically, the whole liturgy in the patristic sense.

This precise perspective involved a certain possible danger: one could end up by constructing a theology of the seven sacraments separated from its connatural frame of liturgical theology in general and even that the liturgy would be expelled from the theological synthesis. In St. Thomas himself such an eventuality is in part avoided, as will be seen below; later theologians, on the other hand, did not know how to escape this danger.

But it is also true that to have emphasized strongly the seven major liturgi-

cal rites, over against the rest of the liturgical complexus which surrounds
them in the practical life of worship in the Church, has permitted the scholastics, and St. Thomas in particular, to make the very notable and necessary
progress of determining exactly what, among all the liturgical rites in general, distinguishes specifically the seven major rites and is proper to them,
especially with respect to their institution, their efficacy, and their necessity.

Theology thus achieved the reflective and analytical consciousness of our
distinction, within the liturgical complexus, between sacraments on the one
hand and sacramentals, liturgical rites, and liturgical prayer on the other, a
distinction which is of capital importance in the theological study of the
liturgy, as the reader has been able to see in the first part of this book; previous to St. Thomas theology had been too indeterminate on this important
matter.

In the first part of this present work we showed that the great concepts
mentioned above and put by St. Thomas at the basis of his theology of the
seven sacraments can and should be applied to the whole liturgy by means
of an opportune and necessary broadening and perfecting, with exception
being made for the special manner in which these concepts are verified in the
seven sacraments.

Theology of the worship proper to the Old Testament

We can show that in the mind of St. Thomas himself these concepts, exceptions being made for the differences required by the matter in the individual cases, admit of an extension beyond the restricted sphere of the seven
sacraments. A typical example is had in his treatise on the theological significance of the worship of the Old Law (I-II, qq. 101–103), especially in connection with the significance of its ritual signs (q. 102). Here St. Thomas not
only applies to all the ritual signs of the Old Law the principle expressed
by him in connection with the meaning of the sacramental signs of the New
Law — that these signs have a value demonstrative of a present spiritual reality,
a value commemorative of a past reality, and a value prophetic of a future
reality (I-II, q. 60, a. 3) — but, with a terminology somewhat different and
derived more directly from the ancient patristic tradition, he specifies the
details of individual parts:

> "The end of the ceremonial precepts is twofold. For they were or-
> dained to the worship of God for that time and also to prefigure
> Christ. . . . Therefore the reasons of the ceremonial precepts of the
> Old Law are deduced from a twofold consideration: first, from the
> motive of the divine worship which was to be observed at that time.
> This kind of reason is indicated by the very letter of the Scriptures:
> the object was either to avoid idolatrous worship, or to recall some
> benefits from God, or to inculcate the divine excellence, or even to

express the disposition of mind which was then required in the worshipers of God. The second consideration apt to indicate the reasons of the ceremonial laws is in view of the fact that they are ordained to prefiguring Christ. Thus these reasons are figurative and mystical, whether with respect to Christ Himself and to the Church, which belongs to allegory; or with respect to the customs of the Christian people, which belongs to moral signification; or with respect to the state of future glory, inasmuch as we are introduced to it by Christ, which belongs to the anagogic signification" (I-II, q. 102, a. 2).

Thus the ceremonial precepts of the Old Law had (a) a significance with respect to contemporary reality, viz., the interior dispositions with which the worship of God was offered, including removal from idolatrous worship and faith in the divine excellence; (b) a significance with respect to a past reality, viz., the benefits of God then recalled; (c) a significance with respect to a future reality, subdivided in its turn into a threefold object: Christ Himself and the Church, the moral customs of the Christian people, and final glory to come.

Although all this is here expressed by St. Thomas in a somewhat involved way, by reason of the influence of the patristic terminology on the various senses of the Scriptures (for which reason the question of the article is "whether the ceremonial precepts have a literal cause or only a figurative one"), still it is quite easy to recognize in his observations the foundation of what we have called in the first part of this present book the fourfold dimension of signification of every liturgical sign.

Actually St. Thomas, in the articles of questions 102 and 103, explains the meaning of the whole Old Testament liturgy according to this plan, which is of undeniable theological value, even if, naturally, in assigning in detail the figurative meanings of the individual rites, he often falls into the allegoristic fancies of Philonian and medieval Jewish origin (Moses Maimonides is often cited in these articles), and into some of patristic or medieval Christian origin.

These fancies, as we know, are derived from the contamination of the biblical concept of typology and figuration with the Hellenistic concept of allegory, and from the fact that, already to some extent the Fathers, but more especially the writers of the Middle Ages, had forgotten the rule, which we have explained in its proper place, that the precise figurative meaning of the liturgical rite (and this holds good also for the liturgical rite of the Old Law) is determined by the competent authority which has instituted it and which explains it through its competent organs of expression (in the case of the Old Testament, by the Scriptures themselves and by the Church) and not by the whimsical choice of any private person whomsover.

At any rate, may what we have said suffice to prove the existence of fundamental principles in the synthetic theology of St. Thomas, principles which can serve as a basis for the construction of a fundamental liturgical theology, especially of the basic concept of the liturgical rite as sign of the fourfold dimension of sanctification and of worship.

That St. Thomas, besides the theoretical view of the fundamental theological principles concerning the nature of the liturgy, had a healthy and very fine traditional liturgical sense and, as it were, instinct, is demonstrated clearly by the Mass and the Office of the feast of Corpus Christi which, as is well known, are his work, and in which is notable, among else, the symbolico-realist sense, or the sense of the various dimensions of the liturgical sign.

2. The Direct and Methodical Insertion of Liturgical Considerations into the Thomistic Synthesis

From what we have propounded thus far in our work, it should be evident that almost all the questions which constitute the principal subject matter in the usual propositions of synthetic theology have, among other things, also a liturgical aspect, and, so to say, a liturgical dimension.[4] It follows that the individual theological propositions cannot be fully elaborated — as theological propositions, note well — if, among other things, the treatment of the theological-liturgical aspect which they involve is not integrated in them.

Synthetic theology is obligated, in fact, to assimilate into the synthesis of every proposition all related material of theological value — which is found abundantly, as has been seen, in the liturgy — by means of which some aspect can become known which cannot be known, or at least cannot be known adequately or similarly, in any other way.

We ask ourselves now how St. Thomas conducted himself, from this point of view, in his general theological synthesis, that is, whether and to what extent he inserted into his synthesis the theological-liturgical aspects pertinent to individual questions.

Let us consider first the type of insertion known as direct and methodical. (That which takes place sporadically or by an indirect way will be apparent to us from the use of the liturgy in St. Thomas as "authority" as developed in the next section of this volume.)

The methodical and direct insertion of liturgical aspects into questions treated in the *Summa* occurs in only three instances: first of all, and in a relatively perfect way, in the treatise on the sacraments in particular; then,

---

[4] From the themes treated in the preceding chapters, it can be seen that among the treatises which constitute the whole of our dogmatic theology, there exists a liturgical question for the following: methodology, the triune God, angels, infrahuman creation, man, Christ, Church, sacraments. It would not be hard to make the same demonstration for other treatises.

in the theology of human actions where St. Thomas treats of the virtue of religion in connection with the cardinal virtue of justice; and thirdly, in the treatise on the Old Law.

In the treatise on the sacraments in particular

In covering the theology of the sacraments in particular, St. Thomas certainly had the preoccupation of inserting systematically material of theological value taken from the liturgy. Practically speaking, he intended to explain the individual sacraments in their context of liturgical ritual. It is thus that, in the treatment of each sacrament, he pays attention not only to all those details of a liturgical nature which concern the substance of the sacrament, such as its matter and form, but, moreover, inserts an explanation of the liturgical context proper to the administration of the respective sacrament.

In the treatises on baptism there is a special article "whether the rite which the Church uses in baptism is appropriate,"[5] in which the principal liturgical rites used in the administration of baptism are explained. In the same treatise is also inserted an explanation of the essential points of the liturgy "ad faciendum catechumenum,"[6] and of the rite of circumcision as prefigurative and preparative of baptism.[7] At the end of the treatise on the sacrament of confirmation there is an article in the same vein, "whether the rite of this sacrament is appropriate."[8]

In the treatise on the Eucharist liturgical aspects are taken into consideration by St. Thomas more fully than in the other sacraments. He treats of the custom of mixing water in the wine at the offertory;[9] the custom which is met with in antiquity of increasing the consecrated wine with unconsecrated wine order to have it suffice for the communion of the faithful;[10] the Eucharistic fast; the communion of those who do not have the use of reason; frequent and daily communion; communion under one species;[11] concelebration;[12] distribution of communion by priest and by deacon;[13] the obligation of the consecrating priest in the Mass, and the obligation of the priest to celebrate;[14] finally and in a special way he treats "of the rites of this sacrament."[15] Here he speaks of the time of celebration, of the place of celebration, of the sacred vessels, of the whole *ordo Missae* as far as the principal formulas and the principal rites are concerned, of the method of correcting the various defects which may be incurred in the celebration of the Mass.

With regard to penance, the propriety of the liturgical rite of solemn penance is explained.[16] In the sacrament of anointing the sick there is an explana-

[5] III, q. 66, a. 10.
[6] III, q. 71, a. 2 and a. 3.
[7] III, q. 70, a. 3.
[8] III, q. 72, a. 12.
[9] III, q. 74, a. 6-8.
[10] III, q. 77, a. 8.

[11] III, q. 80, a. 8-12.
[12] III, q. 82, a. 2.
[13] III, q. 82, a. 3.
[14] III, q. 82, a. 4 and a. 10.
[15] III, q. 83.
[16] *Supplementum*, q. 28, a. 3.

tion of the propriety of anointing the parts of the body indicated by the liturgical rite.[17] At the end of the sacrament of orders the meaning of the priestly vestments and of the pontifical insignia is explained.[18]

As can be seen, St. Thomas inserted into the synthetic theology of the sacraments a considerable amount of material of a liturgical nature. By contrast, this material is excluded unanimously, it seems to me, from the theological syntheses of our present-day manuals, no doubt because it is not considered to be of theological interest. St. Thomas, on the other hand, considered that this liturgical material rightly is of theological interest, an interest which he found, for the most part, through a consideration of the appropriateness of the liturgical rite in view of its purpose. Likewise he was wont to observe whether the rites were suited to the ends of the several major sacraments in the administration of which such rites occur. He would also devote space to the figurative reasons for the rites, that is, their symbolism.

I do not wish to assert that today, in order to find again a more profound unity between the theology of the sacraments and sacramental liturgy in general, it will suffice simply to repeat what St. Thomas has said concerning liturgical aspects associated with each sacrament. It cannot be denied, however, that the observations of St. Thomas in explaining the liturgical rites of the sacraments (apart from the comments on propriety and on figurative relationships which he makes) very often touch authentic and profound theological values — theological values, moreover, which are likewise traditional. For in the articles of St. Thomas listed above, there often converge a goodly number of theological-liturgical themes of patristic origin, which the Fathers were accustomed to develop in their explanations on the rites of Christian initiation to the catechumens and to the neophytes. The *De sacramentis* of St. Ambrose and various works of St. Augustine are cited more than once by St. Thomas in this context. The medieval tradition on these matters also, often collected in the works of a canonical nature such as the *Decretum* of Gratian, constitute an important source for further study.

In the treatise on the virtue of religion

The systematic insertion of liturgical aspects into the theological synthesis of a treatise is also found in St. Thomas' treatment of the virtue of religion. He provides us with a series of articles covering the liturgical aspect of this virtue. Such articles investigate whether the virtue of religion has some exterior act;[19] whether prayer should be vocal;[20] whether it can properly be said that the parts of prayer are supplications, orations, petitions, and thanksgiving;[21] whether adoration involves bodily acts;[22] whether it requires a

---

[17] *Supplementum*, q. 32, a. 6.
[18] *Supplementum*, q. 40, a. 7.
[19] II-II, q. 81, a. 7.

[20] II-II, q. 83, a. 12.
[21] II-II, q. 83, a. 17.
[22] II-II, q. 84, a. 2.

determinate place.[23] The whole of question 85 of the *secunda secundae* treats of sacrifice as the highest act of the virtue of religion. Question 86 on oblations and on first fruits also touches often on the liturgy. The two articles of question 91 are directly of a liturgical nature, treating of the vocal praise of God and of liturgical chant. In question 94, apropos of idolatry, images in worship are considered.

In the treatise on the Old Law

Finally, in the treatise on the Old Law, St. Thomas inserts systematically a treatment of the theological significance of the liturgy of the Old Testament, considering that liturgy in itself, in its reasons or significations according to the purpose of each liturgical rite and prescription, and in its duration and efficacy.

Thus in a first question he explains the nature of the liturgy of the Old Law inasmuch as it was meant for the worship of God directly, or indirectly as a preparation of heart and mind. Then he explains the propriety of this liturgy's being figurative of Christ and of the future glory,[24] the reason in general for the multiplicity and diversity of its rites,[25] and the distinction of its individual parts into sacrifices, sacraments, and sacred observances.[26]

In the second question the meaning of these parts according to the nature and the purpose of each one is explained. A first article establishes the general fact that such meaning must have existed for everything in the liturgy even of the Old Testament.[27] Then, specifying what we have called the significative dimensions of the liturgical signs, it is shown in general that for the liturgy of the Old Testament, these must be sought in the literal or figurative sense of the texts.[28] Then the question passes on to the explanation of the meaning of the individual parts of the liturgy according to the foregoing principles: explanation of the meaning of the sacrifices,[29] of the *sacra*, in other words, of the sacred temple, the sacred places, the sacred vessels, the sacred ministers;[30] of the sacraments: circumcision, paschal lamb, consecration of priests (and here the meaning of the priestly vestments is also discussed), oblations, purifications;[31] explanation of the meaning of the sacred liturgical observances, such as the prohibition against eating certain foods, certain animals, blood, etc.

In the third question the duration of the ceremonial liturgical precepts of the Old Testament is discussed inasmuch as they did not exist by precept prior to the Law[32] and were abolished by Christ,[33] as well as the efficacy

[23] II-II, q. 84, a. 3.
[24] I-II, q. 101, a. 1 and a. 2.
[25] I-II, q. 101, a. 3.
[26] I-II, q. 101, a. 4.
[27] I-II, q. 102, a. 1.
[28] I-II, q. 102, a. 2.
[29] I-II, q. 102, a. 3.
[30] I-II, q. 102, a. 4.
[31] I-II, q. 102, a. 5.
[32] I-II, q. 103, a. 1.
[33] I-II, q. 103, a. 3 and a. 4.

proper to them in the era of the Old Law.[34] As can be seen, the complexus of questions is quite exhaustive.

So far as I know, outside of these three treatises on the sacraments, on the virtue of religion, and on the Old Law, nothing similar is found in the *Summa* involving the systematic insertion of liturgy into the theological synthesis of individual treatises.[35]

3. The Use of the Liturgy as *Auctoritas* in the Framework of the *Quaestio* and of the Method *Sic et Non* Throughout the Theology of St. Thomas

This does not mean that in the other treatises which make up the synthesis of the *Summa* the liturgy does not enter in at all. On the contrary, in going through these treatises it is possible to glean a certain number of appeals to the liturgy. In order to understand, however, the precise stance from which these appeals are made and hence the limits of their value, it is necessary to keep in mind the general scholastic picture of the *quaestio* and of the method *sic et non*.[36]

The *auctoritas* and the *quaestio* in the scholastic method

It is well known that scholastic effort, whether philosophical or theological, from the viewpoint of method, begins from positive data, namely, the statements or opinions, for the most part put down in writing, of previous authors who, in the matter taken under examination, are supposed to constitute "authority" in some way. The sayings of these authors, which sum up in a determinate question their respective position, and also the authors themselves who have pronounced them, are called *auctoritates*.

[34] I-II, q. 103, a. 2.

[35] Some questions and articles of other treatises, however, without directly explaining the liturgical aspect, touch on questions and propose concepts which are often very important. Thus in the treatise on Christ and on our Lady, in a series of questions, ideas of great liturgical value are touched upon. In *pars tertia* questions 22 (on the priesthood of Christ) and 26 (on Christ as Mediator) are important for the concept of the liturgy in general and for clarifying the place which belongs to Christ in the liturgy. Question 25, especially articles 3 to 6, is important for the worship of Christ (e.g., Sacred Heart, wounds of Christ), for the veneration of images and relics. The following questions also are important for various reasons: 27, on the sanctification of our Lady; 29, on her espousal; 30, on the annunciation. The following questions on the life of Christ are important for the theology of the corresponding liturgical feasts: 35, on the birth of the Savior; 36, on the manifestation of Christ after His birth; 37, on the observance of the legal precepts in the case of the infant Jesus; 39, on the baptism of Christ; 45, on the transfiguration of Christ; 46, on the Passion of Christ; 50, on the death of Christ; 51, on the burial of Christ; 52, on His descent into hell; 53, on the resurrection of Christ; 57, on the ascension of Christ; 58, on His sitting at the right of the Father. In the *Supplementum*, q. 71, where prayers for the departed are discussed, there are several observations of liturgical theology, as also in question 72, where the invocation of the saints is discussed.

[36] See J. de Ghellinck, *Le mouvement théologique de XIIᵉ siècle*, 2nd ed., Bruges-Brussels-Paris 1948, pp. 472 ff; M. D. Chenu, *Introduction à l'étude de S. Thomas d'Aquin*, Paris 1950, pp. 106 ff.

In philosophy it is Aristotle, the philosopher *par excellence*, who, after the rediscovery of his works, is naturally the great *auctoritas*. In theology the *auctoritates* are quite varied: the Scriptures; the Fathers; "the saints"; the more recent theologians; the *doctores*; the councils; the Church in general, especially the Roman Church. The liturgy, whether in its texts or in its rites or in its feasts, is one of the *auctoritates* in theology. Although St. Thomas does not say much on the subject, it seems certain that for him the *auctoritas* of the liturgy is reduced to the *auctoritas* of the Church, whose *consuetudo* it manifests, especially in the rites and the feasts, and hence, in some way, whose faith it manifests, whether in the rites or in the feasts and in the formularies.[37]

In the scholastic method the *auctoritates* constitute the point of departure of the inquiry; and at the same time these *auctoritates* give rise to the *quaestio*, inasmuch as opposing *auctoritates* (those for and against a certain solution [*sic et non*] in a certain matter) raise, for the theologian, a question, a doubt, and impose an alternative in his solution according to whether he follows one faction or the other among the *auctoritates*.

Thus there arises naturally the well-known system of scholastic exposition in every discussion. It consists, in every article, of first propounding a question (*Quaeritur utrum . . .*). Then follows the expression of the doubt in one of its alternatives (*Et videtur quod . . .*), supported immediately by a series of *auctoritates* who seem to militate in its favor (. . . *enim* . . . and the series of *obiectiones* which support the first alternative). In the fourth place follows one or more *auctoritates* in favor of the opposite solution (*Sed contra est*). In the fifth place the resolution of the doubt (*Respondeo*, or *Dicendum*). Finally, the explanation of the *auctoritates* contrary to the solution chosen, which are generally those set forth in the first series, that is, in the *obiectiones* (*Ad primum ergo. Dicendum*).

It is known also that in the solution of the doubt, the procedure which is by far the most prevalent in scholasticism, principally in St. Thomas, and the primary preoccuption from which the solution of the doubt is sought, is not the philological-historical treatment of the opposing *auctoritates* with the intention of simply gathering the historical thought of each one, the point of view which was or is his, or even the historical development of a doctrine in time (although these aspects are not completely absent). Rather, the preferred procedure is the consideration of the reality in itself and as it appears

---

[37] In connection with the recourse to the *auctoritas* of the liturgical feast of the Conception of Mary, St. Thomas speaks of the *consuetudo* of the churches which celebrate this feast: *Summa*, III, q. 27, a. 2 ad 3. Of the authority in theology of the custom of the Church in general, St. Thomas says that it is greatest and must prevail over the very authority of the Fathers and the doctors: II-II, q. 10, a. 12 c. See also III, q. 78, a. 3 *sed contra; Supplementum*, q. 29, a. 8 *sed contra* 1 and in the body of the article; *Supplementum*, q. 72, a. 2 *sed contra* 3.

from analysis by means of philosophy and dialectic. From such analysis the initial doubt is resolved in one direction or another.

In scholastic theology the *auctoritates* which are scattered throughout the individual articles, whether in the initial objections or in the *sed contra* or in the body of the articles or in the responses to the objections, have above all a dialectical ontological function, not directly historical or apologetical.

For example, in citing as authority a passage of St. Augustine or of St. Jerome or of any other saint or doctor, the concern is not primarily, as it is with us today, with knowing the historical thought on the subject, and still less the whole historical thinking of these Fathers, or the general evolution of their thought. Nor is the concern primarily, as it is with the positive-scholastic theologians, with building a chain of evidence to demonstrate that the present doctrine of the Church is really contained in tradition or in Scripture.

The primary concern of the scholastics in citing the *auctoritates* is simply to raise a doubt, a question, of an ontological-dialectical order, philosophical or theological; to incline the inquirer from without to a determinate solution of the same order; to support or confirm, at least apparently, that solution by authority.

When, therefore, the *auctoritates* contradict one another or the proposed solution, care is taken, primarily by means of the dialectical distinction of different points of view, which it is said each of these *auctoritates* has taken in his statements, to demonstrate if possible that the contradiction is only apparent. Only in extreme necessity will it be admitted that the contradiction is real and hence that one of the *auctoritates* must be sacrificed. But this will be done with great repugnance and with a highly respectful manner of speaking, preferring for the most part, with some apt turn of words or some expression of hesitation (*expositio reverentialis*), to cover up, as it were, the *auctoritas* found to be in error.[38]

Examples of the recourse to the liturgy as an *auctoritas* in the framework of the *quaestio* in the *Summa*

All this holds also for the liturgy. It is in this framework of the *auctoritates* in the *quaestio* and in the *sic et non* that St. Thomas, throughout the whole of theology, even outside of the treatises which have been considered more directly above, has a certain recourse to the liturgy. Father Hering, in his article on the liturgy as *locus theologicus* in St. Thomas (referred to in footnote 1 of the present chapter), points out fifty-seven appeals of this kind in the whole of the *Summa*, sixteen of which are in the treatises on the sacraments and forty-one for the rest of theology, including moral theology. It is clear enough, then, that it cannot be said that this kind of recourse is very abundant.

---

[38] See Chenu, the work cited in note 36 above, pp. 126 ff. therein.

At any rate, here are some examples. In the treatise on the unity of God, in arguing against the divine omnipotence there is cited as authority a collect of the Dominican Missal in which it is asserted that God shows His omnipotence mostly by pardoning and having compassion, which would seem to insinuate that He can do nothing but pardon. On the uncertainty of the number of the predestined, there is cited the prayer, "God, to whom alone is known the number of the elect who are to attain supreme happiness."[39]

In the treatise on the Trinity, to support the thesis that in God the relations and the essence are really identified, there are cited in a *sed contra* the words of the preface: *"Ut in personis proprietas"* and *"in maiestate adoretur aequalitas."*[40]

In favor of the positive answer to the question of whether an exclusive way of speaking can be correctly affixed to a term which in God expresses a person, the words of the *Gloria* are cited, "You alone are most high, Jesus Christ." In the reply St. Thomas brings out the fact that the text of the *Gloria* adds "with the Holy Spirit in the glory of God the Father."[41]

In the treatise on the angels, in favor of the thesis that the angels can be in a place, there is cited in a *sed contra* a text of the Dominican liturgy in which God is asked that the angels dwelling in this house may protect us.[42]

In the treatise on sadness, in favor of the thesis that the contemplation of the truth alleviates sadness and pain, St. Thomas cites from the lessons of a current breviary the words of St. Tiburtius, who, walking on burning coals, said, "I think I am walking on roses."[43]

In the treatise on martyrdom, discussing the questions whether martyrdom is an act of fortitude, whether it is an act of virtue, whether it requires death essentially, recourse is had every time to the authority of the liturgy.[44]

In his Christology the authority of the *"O felix culpa . . ."* of the paschal exultation is invoked to confirm the thesis that after sin, human nature has been raised to a greater dignity than that which it enjoyed before sin.[45] The liturgy is invoked again on behalf of the thesis that in Christ there was union of soul and body;[46] on behalf of the thesis that the Cross is to be adored;[47] and St. Thomas interprets the precise sense of the liturgical text in which it is said that the Word took flesh from Mary.[48]

In the treatise on Mariology, St. Thomas discusses the authority and the meaning of the liturgical feast of the Conception of Mary.[49]

In the treatise on the Four Last Things allusion is made to the liturgical

[39] I, q. 25, a. 3, obj. 3 and ad 3; I, q. 23, a. 7 c.

[40] I, q. 28, a. 2.

[41] I, q. 31, a. 4, obj. 4 and ad 4.

[42] I, q. 52, a. 1.

[43] I-II, q. 38, a. 4 c. See also II-II, q. 123, a. 6.

[44] II-II, q. 124, a. 2 c.; a. 3, ad 1 and ad 2;

a. 4 in the objections and in the replies.

[45] III, q. 1, a. 3.

[46] III, q. 2, a. 5.

[47] III, q. 25, a. 4 c.

[48] III, q. 31, a. 5, obj. 1 and ad 1.

[49] III, q. 27, a. 1, *sed contra*; a. 2, obj. 3 and ad 3.

prayers for the dead [50] and to the Church's custom of invoking the aid of the saints in the litany.[51]

Of course, St. Thomas from time to time has recourse to the authority of the liturgy in other works besides the *Summa*; [52] nor should it be forgotten that this recourse is often had also in those treatises analyzed above on the sacraments in general and in particular, on the Old Law and on religion in general, in which the liturgical aspect is more directly and systematically inserted into the general synthesis.

Concluding judgment

What, in conclusion, is the judgment that may be formed of the relations between theological synthesis and liturgy in St. Thomas? The place which the liturgy occupies in the theological synthesis of St. Thomas is certainly worthy of the greatest consideration on the part of theologians.

But, first: it is not the use of the liturgy as *auctoritas* throughout the framework of the scholastic *quaestio* and of the method *sic et non* that leads to its notable insertion into the synthesis of St. Thomas. If in this synthesis there are, as in fact there are, points in which the force of the theological value of the liturgy has penetrated, this takes place substantially by reason of the two facts analyzed above, namely, that St. Thomas has systematically inserted the liturgical aspect into the three treatises on religion in general, on the Old Law, and on the sacraments in general and in particular; and still much more because, in these same three treatises, he analyzes and strongly emphasizes a series of basic concepts, first among them the concept of *sign*, which can serve as foundation for the construction of a fundamental theology of the liturgy.

It is, substantially, in virtue of these two facts that in St. Thomas the relation between synthetic theology and liturgy appears notably richer and deeper than in the later positive-scholastic theology. In fact, here we can take account better of the ultimate reasons for the inferiority of this positive-scholastic theology, especially of that of our present-day manuals, in comparison to that of St. Thomas, in the question which concerns us.

This theology, starting from the sixteenth century, in the treatise on the sacraments in general and in particular, has so relegated to the second level the concept of sign, in order to insist instead almost exclusively on that of efficacy, that it has practically forgotten the idea of sign, or at least has left it

---

[50] *Supplementum*, q. 69, a. 4 ad 2; q. 71, a. 2 ad 4.

[51] *Supplementum*, q. 72, a. 2 ad 3.

[52] For example, *Opusc. de rationibus fidei* 9, the existence of purgatory; *Opusc. de forma absolutionis* 1, citation of a hymn; *Quodlibet.* 12, q. 9, a. 2, devotion to the saints; *Quodlibet.* 6, 7, and *In Ioann. lect.* 5, the symbolic meaning of the space of the edifice of a church; *Quodlibet.* 3, q. 13, a. 29 and *Quodlibet.* 5, q. 13, a. 28 (see also *Summa*, III, q. 66, ad 1; I-II, q. 103, a. 3 ad 4), on the symbolic meaning of time and of feasts in the liturgy; *In Ioann. lect.* 5, on the sanctoral and on the dedication of a church.

inoperative. A sacrament has indeed continued to be defined as the efficacious sign of grace, but, wholly preoccupied by the polemic against the Protestant denials, the theologians concentrated on the concept of efficacy *ex opere operato* and on the divine institution of the seven sacraments, paying little attention to the aspect of sign.

The practical result was the obscuring, in the psychology of the theologians and of the faithful, of the symbolic-realistic value of the sacraments and of the whole liturgy; the separation of the study of the seven sacraments from their connatural liturgical whole of *sacramenta*; the consideration of the liturgical rites of the seven sacraments in a purely apologetic manner against the Protestants at first, and later the simple exclusion of this matter from the theological synthesis altogether.

Another reduction effected by positive-scholasticism was to exclude from its theological synthesis the treatise of St. Thomas on the Old Law and especially on the liturgy of the Old Law. If the matter was given any attention at all, it was regarded as exegetical and as the object, at most, of pious reflections.

The treatise on religion and worship was also expelled from the dogmatic synthesis and transferred to moral theology. This, in its turn, was conceived more and more in a casuistic and juridic sense, for which reason religion and worship were treated much more in order to indicate what are the sins against them so that such might be avoided, rather than to show what is the positive import of religion and worship in the Christian life.

Another exclusion was that of the Christology contained in the section *De vita Christi* in which St. Thomas had scattered several considerations of real value to liturgical theology.

With respect to the position which the liturgy occupies in the theological synthesis of St. Thomas, what are the *desiderata* which theology today can express? Aside from many other minor details, it is easy to see that, among the theological treatises in the *Summa*, there are still many in which there is not a trace of any attempt to assimilate liturgical aspects organically. As has been pointed out repeatedly, this attempt exists only in the treatises on religion, on the Old Law, on the sacraments; and in some way, if you will, but a very imperfect way, in Christology. What is the reason for this state of affairs?

Perhaps the answer is that St. Thomas concerned himself, quite systematically, with explaining in his general theological synthesis only the liturgical rites and, in some way, liturgical facts in general. He did not concern himself with the theological thought included not merely in the rites but in the whole liturgical complexus, especially in the liturgical prayers or formularies and in the festive liturgical cycles. Therefore in the treatises on the Old Law, on the seven sacraments of the New Law, and on religion in general, the liturgical aspect is quite developed, while it is not so developed in other numerous treatises.

In the first part of this present work, however, I have attempted to show, with a series of examples, even if they were not exhaustive, that for the other treatises too there is rich liturgical material of theological value which can and should be assimilated into the general theological synthesis, such as for the treatises on God, on the good and bad angels, on material creation, on man, on Christ, on the Church; and it would not be hard to continue with matter for the treatises on Mariology, on grace, on the virtues, and on the Four Last Things. In St. Thomas, for these treatises, the liturgical aspect finds a certain echo only through some insufficient recourse to the liturgy as *auctoritas* in the framework of the *quaestio*.

Moreover, it is known that in the concerns of the synthetic theology of St. Thomas there is a strong preoccupation with the ontological and, as it were, metaphysical analysis of the realities in which he is interested. But the perspective of sacred salvation history, as it has been explained in the first chapter of this work, while well enough preserved by St. Thomas in the treatises on the Old Law and on the sacraments, precisely in virtue of the value given there to the concept of sign, to symbolism, and to liturgical aspects in general, is much less safeguarded in the other treatises, precisely those in which the liturgical aspect is not systematically assimilated.

It is not by chance that a parallel deficiency is observed in these other treatises in bringing out the aspect of sacred history and in assimilating the liturgical theological aspect. As long as the perspective of sacred salvation history is not proposed as the natural and necessary background in the explanation of every great theological question, the liturgy cannot display all of its potentialities in the theological synthesis itself.

We may perhaps go further and ask why there is this objective deficiency in St. Thomas in the assimilation of the aspect of sacred salvation history, or of theology of history, in the aforesaid treatises. The reason must be sought in his manner of conceiving the ideal of theology. Not only did he follow, rightly, the Aristotelian principles of the concept of science, and hence, legitimately and rightly, pursue the ideal of theology as a science; but further, preserving from the same Aristotle some conceptions and indeterminations, not at all necessarily connected with the same principles, he held, more or less consciously, that properly and strictly speaking, only philosophy is science (aside from mathematics and, if anything else, philosophical physics) and that the properly scientific method is the deductive method. Induction for him is prescientific and has its importance only inasmuch as it is preparatory to philosophical (and mathematical) deduction; and, logically enough, it is not to be used except in that strict measure which is useful to such a purpose.

In particular, neither Aristotle nor St. Thomas arrived at the concept of history as science properly so called. Applying this to theology, it follows not only that this is conceived as science, but exclusively, properly speaking, as science of the ontological or entitative aspect of revealed things which is worked out essentially by the use of philosophy and of the deductive method. Because history in this concept is not properly science, nor its method a properly scientific method having value by itself, the more properly temporal aspect of revelation, that which is scientifically gathered only by means of the application in theology of the critical-historical method, and hence revelation as sacred history and its reflection in every great concept of our faith, remains, properly and logically speaking, outside of theological science. Thus the whole ontological method is too exclusively assimilated to the philosophical method, and theology itself is too exclusively restricted to the consideration of the directly timeless aspect of the revealed data.[53]

We easily see, then, why the Second Vatican Council, for the sake of rediscovering the unity between theology and liturgy, desired that every branch of theological science should develop in considerable detail, according to the exigencies of its proper object, the aspect of salvation history.[54]

[53] Then it becomes impossible to assimilate in an adequate way into the synthetic theological construction the temporal aspect of revelation inasmuch as it is primarily a sacred history. Father M. D. Chenu, in his work *La théologie au XIIᵉ siècle* (Paris 1957), redraws the general picture of the symbolist-allegorical mentality, and hence of the sense of revelation as sacred history which the twelfth century still preserved from the previous tradition (pp. 159–220 and 62–89). He indicates its origin, its development and its decadence through excess, something which rightly provoked the reaction which became acute at the beginning of the thirteenth century. The thirteenth century practically expelled "symbolical theology" from the picture of sacred *doctrina* conceived as systematic synthetic theology on the basis of the Aristotelian concept of science. Yet Father Chenu, approving of the reactions against the excesses, rightly points out: 1) that a "symbolical theology" on the bibli-cal background of sacred history is not only legitimate but necessary even in synthetic theology, and that today it is rightly sought to find it again; 2) that the very scholastics of the thirteenth century, even in their reaction, preserved, as it were, blocks of that traditional theology, such as the questions of which we have spoken above in the *Summa* of St. Thomas (as well as in works like the *Breviloquium* of St. Bonaventure and in the commentaries on the Scriptures). [Nine of Chenu's essays appear in *Nature, Man, and Society in the Twelfth Century*, edited and translated by Jerome Taylor and Lester K. Little, Chicago 1957.]

"The Spirit is in history—it is the lesson given by Origen, patron of all allegorism, and which always holds true—and all the biblical revivals have made this concept the law of their mystique as well as of their method" (Chenu, *op. cit.*, p. 209).

[54] CL, art. 16.

19 THEOLOGY AND LITURGY

IN THE FATHERS

It might be thought that in order to resolve the question of the organic insertion of the liturgy into general synthetic theology there would be no point in turning to the Fathers. Certainly the Fathers did not construct general theological syntheses even if some initial efforts, of a somewhat different character, however, toward compendious expositions of Christian doctrine can be pointed out among patristic authors, such as the *Perì archôn* of Origen, the *Enchiridion* of St. Augustine, and the *Pegè gnóseos* of St. John Damascene.

Still it is certain not only that they produced nothing comparable to the medieval *Summas* and still less to the modern theological textbooks or manuals, but also that in their quite varied theological concerns and in the very abundant corresponding literary production, the concern with such general syntheses was not at all on the first level of their psychology, as it was, by contrast, in that of the theologians beginning toward the end of the twelfth century.

Yet, even if the Fathers did not write *Summas*, this does not mean that they had not arrived at a general theological conception more or less synthetic of all things, a conception which can be discovered from their works and in which the liturgy has its more or less clearly marked place. It is under this aspect that an inquiry into the relations between theology and liturgy in the Fathers can be of real use to us.

It is certain, in fact, that in the Fathers there is a liturgical theology considerably developed under the twofold aspect in which every theology is developed: the irenic aspect, simply expositive of the faith to believers; and the polemic aspect of the defense and proof of the same faith against the real or hypothetical unbelievers. In the first, the theological riches of the liturgy are simply set forth for the believer. In the second, recourse is had to the liturgy to prove the foundation and the obligation to believe a point of the faith against the denials or the objections, real or hypothetical, which are brought against it.

1. Patristic and Post-patristic Literature
of Theological-liturgical Interest until the Twelfth Century
in the West and the Sixteenth Century in the East

The patristic literature of theological-liturgical interest can be catalogued, from the rather extrinsic viewpoint of literary genre, in five principal groups.[1]

In the first can be put the catecheses to the catechumens and to the neophytes concerning the meaning of the rites of Christian initiation: the mystagogic literature or the literature of initiation properly so called. The principal rites whose theological meaning is explained in these works are those of the *traditio* or *redditio symboli*; of the *traditio orationis*, that is, of the Our Father; the pre-baptismal rites such as exsufflations, exorcisms, anointing; the rites of baptism; of confirmation; of the Eucharist, including the Mass.

The two little works of Tertullian, *De baptismo* and *De oratione* (between 200 and 206 A.D.), can already be counted in this category. In the fourth century, with the full development of the organization of the catechumenate, there is a group of very important works in this class: the eighteen *Catecheses* of St. Cyril of Jerusalem (384 A.D.), besides the five *Mystagogic Catecheses* of the same Cyril, or, as some hold, of his successor in the see of Jerusalem, John of Jerusalem; the *De mysteriis* of St. Ambrose (*ca.* 387–391 A.D.) and the *De sacramentis*, now with ever greater unanimity recognized as of the same author; the catechetical homilies of Theodore of Mopsuestia of about 392;[2] the two catecheses *Ad illuminandos* and the eight baptismal homilies recently rediscovered of St. John Chrysostom[3] and what remains to us of the mystagogic teaching of St. Augustine to the catechumens and neophytes.[4]

This type of liturgical theological work explaining the rites of the Christian initiation to the catechumens and the neophytes broadened itself beginning with the fifth century and subsequently developed, in spite of the discontinu-

---

[1] Several of these works are pointed out by Jean Card. Daniélou in *The Bible and the Liturgy*, pp. 8–17.

[2] Recent edition of R. Tonneau and R. Devreesse, *Les homilies catéchetiques de Théodore de Mopsueste*, in the series *Studi e testi*, Vol. 93, Vatican City 1949.

[3] PG 49, cols. 223 ff, perhaps of the year 383 A.D.; *Jean Chrysostome, Huit homilies baptismales*, ed. A. Wenger, Paris 1958.

[4] See Sermons 211–216, 224–229, 272. The *De catechizandis rudibus* and the *De symbolo ad catechumenos* are works of the same kind.

ance of the catechumenate, to the point where it created what may well be called a new literary genre: treatises explanatory of the liturgy in general, whether the concern was with works of the synthetic type or with monographs on particular points.

In this literary genre there takes place a twofold broadening with respect to the previous mystagogic genre: it is no longer addressed only to the catechumens and to the neophytes but to all the faithful, sometimes to some more advanced group of the faithful, often even the clergy or the monks; not only are the rites of the initiation explained but also, more or less fully, the other parts of the liturgy. In the East, for example, they dwell at length on the explanation of the consecration of the oils and of the myron; everywhere the ordinations of bishops, priests, and deacons are explained; then the explanation of other rites such as public penance is introduced; of marriage; the consecration of virgins, of monks; the rites of burial; the rites of the consecration of a church. In fact, the field always widening, they passed on to the explanation of the meaning of the arrangement and the furniture of the church; of the priestly vestments and also, of certain parts at least, of the canonical Office and of the liturgical seasons and liturgical feasts. This type of explanation of the liturgy continued throughout the Middle Ages both in the East and in the West.

In the Greek-speaking East, among the productions of this type it seems that the first to be taken into account is the *De ecclesiastica hierarchia* of Pseudo-Dionysius,[5] a work which had very great influence on works of the same kind which followed it. Among these must be noted in particular the *Mystagogy* of Maximus the Confessor,[6] the liturgical *Commentary* bearing the name of St. Sophronius of Jerusalem,[7] and the *Rerum ecclesiasticarum contemplatio* attributed to St. Germanus of Constantinople.[8] In the later Byzantine period, this kind of literature is represented principally by the excellent explanation of the divine liturgy (the Mass) by Nicolas Cabasilas[9] and by the theological-liturgical works of Simeon of Thessalonica.[10]

[5] PG 3, cols. 369–584. See R. Roques, *L'univers dionysien*, Paris 1954, especially at pages 245–302.

[6] PG 91, cols. 657–718.

[7] PG 87, cols. 3981–4002. The essential part of this work seems to be of the eighth century.

[8] PG 98, cols. 383–453; *Protheoria*: PG 140, cols. 413–468. On these and other Byzantine mystagogies, see F. E. Brightman, "The *Historia Mystogogica* and other Greek Commentaries on the Byzantine Liturgy," in the *Journal of Theological Studies*, Vol. 9 (1907–1908), pp. 248 ff; 347 ff.

[9] Nicolas Cabasilas († after 1363), *Explanation of the Divine Liturgy* (= Mass), PG 150, cols. 367 ff. See the recent French translation

with introduction and notes by S. Salaville, N.C. *Explication de la liturgie* (*Sources chrétiennes 4*), Paris 1943. His work *On the Life of Christ* also contains many things of theological-liturgical and ascetical value about the sacraments (PG 150, cols. 443–726). See also M. Lot-Borodine, *Un maître de la spiritualité byzantine du XIVᵉ siècle: Nicolas Cabasilas*, Paris 1958.

[10] Simeon of Thessalonica († 1429), especially his *Tractatus de sacramentis nec non de officiis et ritibus ecclesiasticis* (PG 55, cols. 176 ff) and his opuscula *On the Divine Temple, on the Deacons, on the Priests, on the Bishops, on the Sacred Ornaments which they Wear, on the Divine Sacrifice and on What-*

In the Syriac literature we have in this field the liturgical Homilies of Narsai of Edessa; [11] the commentaries on the liturgy by George, bishop of the Arabs, and by Moses bar Kepha.[12] In the eighth-ninth century the commentary of John of Dara on the *Ecclesiastical Hierarchy* of Pseudo-Dionysius; in the twelfth and thirteenth centuries we have the treatises of Dionysius bar Salibi, of Jacob Severus bar Shakko or of Edessa [13] and especially the great commentary of Gregory bar Hebraeus.[14]

In the West, explanations of the liturgy of the same type were developed starting in the seventh century with St. Isidore of Seville,[15] opening the way

ever Is Done There Divinely (PG 55, cols. 697 ff). The work of R. Bornet, *Introduction aux commentaires mystagogiques à la "divine liturgie" dans l'Église byzantine du VIIᵉ au XVᵉ siècle*, on the press when Dom Vagaggini was preparing the fourth Italian edition of this present work, will shed considerable light on these liturgical-theological works, both under their critical-historical aspect (an area in which there are many problems, especially in regard to works attributed to Sophronius, Germanus, and to Theodore of Andida), and under the aspect of their real value, theological and spiritual.

[11] Died after 503. *Explanation of the Divine Eucharist, of Baptism and of the Priesthood*; edition of R. H. Connolly and E. Bishop, *The Liturgical Homilies of Narsai*, Cambridge 1909.

[12] Of George, bishop of the Arabs († 724), we have an *Explanation of the Mysteries of the Church*; see R. H. Connolly and H. W. Codrington, *Two Commentaries on the Jacobite Liturgy by George Bishop of the Arabs and Moses bar Kepha*, London 1913. Of Moses bar Kepha († 903) we have the commentary on the Mass, in the work just referred to. W. de Vries, *Sakramententheologie bei den syrischen Monophysiten*, Rome 1940, pp. 21 and 9–10, indicates, moreover, other treatises still unpublished: *On the Myron; On the Unwritten Mysteries Which are Observed in the Church according to the Tradition of the Holy Fathers; On the Mysteries of the Consecration; On Baptism.*

[13] For the commentary on the *Ecclesiastical Hierarchy* of Pseudo-Dionysius by John of Dara, see Assemani, *Bibliotheca orientalis*, Vol. 2, p. 211. Of Dionysius bar Salibi († 1171) we have an *Explanation of the Liturgy* (see H. Labourt, *D. bar S., Exposition liturgiae*, in *Corpus scriptorum christianorum orientalium, Scriptores syri*, series 2, Vol. 93, Paris 1903). De Vries, *op. cit.*, p. 22, indicates as still unpublished a commentary on the consecration of the myron and one on the rites of ordina-

tion. Jacob bar Shakko († 1241) treats of the liturgy in the second part of his *Book of the Treasure* (see Assemani, *Bibliotheca orientalis*, Vol. 2, p. 239).

[14] It is the sixth part of a great work of general dogmatic theology: *Book of the Lamp of the Sanctuary*. This sixth part is entitled *On the Earthly Priesthood*. In it are treated the degrees of the earthly priesthood and the consecrations. These consecrations are the ordinations of the bishop, of the priest, and of the deacon; the lower ordinations which take place with the mere extension of the hand over the ordinand; the consecration of the myron; the anointings of baptism; the Mass and burial services are also treated. The scheme of the general dogmatic treatise is as follows: On knowledge in general; The nature of the whole of dogma; The nature of God; The incarnation; The angels; The earthly priesthood; The devils; The rational soul; Freedom; Foreknowledge and predestination; The last things; The resurrection and paradise. As can be seen, the treatment of the liturgy is organically included in the essay of general synthesis of the whole of dogma. See Radbert Kohlhaas, *Jakobitische Sakramententheologie im 13. Jahrhundert. Der Liturgiekommentar des Gregorius Barhebraeus*, Munster i. W. 1960. Other parts of the work have appeared in the series *Patrologia orientalis*. R. H. Connolly has edited an *Expositio officiorum ecclesiae Giorgio Arbelensi vulgo adscripta* in the *Corpus scriptorum christianorum orientalium, Scriptores syri*, series 2, Vol. 92, Paris 1913 (reprinted at Louvain 1953).

[15] Isidore of Seville († 636), *De ecclesiasticis officiis* (PL 83, cols. 737 ff.). The first book treats, among else, of: The elements of liturgical prayer: songs, formulas, psalms, etc.; The order and prayers of the Mass (Mozarabic); The canonical hours; The liturgical seasons and feasts; The liturgical fasts. The second book treats of: The various orders of the faithful; clerics, monks, penitents, virgins, widows, etc.; Baptism; The anointing with chrism; Con-

for the abundant literature of the medieval allegorists,[16] whose father can be said to be Amalarius of Metz.[17]

In this medieval literature prior to scholasticism can be noted, for our purpose, the essay of Rhaban Maur *De clericorum institutione*,[18] in which he attempts to make a sort of *Summa* of all that a cleric was supposed to know at that time. The work consists of three books. While the third book contains a kind of theory on clerical study in general and on preaching, in the first two everything that the clergy should know is practically set forth in the framework of the liturgy in the following order, inspired by the *De ecclesiasticis officiis* of Isidore:

I. The Church and her various orders (ch. 1–13); the priestly vestments (ch. 14–23); the Christian initiation: catechumenate, baptism, confirmation, Eucharist (ch. 24–33);

II. The canonical hours (ch. 1–9); non-canonical or private prayers (ch. 10–16); fasts, continence, works of mercy (ch. 17–28); public penance, satisfaction, reconciliation of sinners (ch. 29–30); liturgical seasons and feasts, in which is included also the treatment of the sacrifices for the dead, of the dedication of churches, etc. (ch. 31–46); the elements of liturgical prayer: canticles, psalms, hymns, etc. (ch. 47–55); rule of faith, creeds, catalog of heresies (ch. 56–58).

The Scriptures are spoken of in connection with the readings of the Office (II, 53–54) and of the preparation for preaching (III, 1–15), to the service of which is also directed the whole *trivium* and *quadrivium* (III, 16 ff).

Another literary genre which is of interest for the theology of the liturgy is the homilies on the liturgical feasts. The most ancient, of course, are those on the paschal feast; we still have one of the second century, of Melito of

firmation. Among the expositions of the Gallican Mass must be noted the one falsely attributed to St. Germanus of Paris (PL 72, cols. 88 ff), of the end of the seventh century.

[16] For more details on this liturgical-theological literature of the Middle Ages to the twelfth century, see Righetti, Vol. I, pp. 62–67, where there is a list of the principal names and works. The theological-liturgical value of these works needs to be studied more carefully than it has been thus far. For this purpose an indispensable work is that of M. D. Chenu, *La théologie au XIIe siècle*, Paris 1957, in which is given an excellent general cultural theological picture of the twelfth century. In a special way see chapters 3 (Awareness of history and theology), 7 (The symbolic mentality), 8 (Symbolical theology), 9 (The Old Testament in medieval theology). Chenu rightly notes that "it would be a grave historical and theological error to relegate to the margin of the development of theology in the twelfth cen-

tury — as if they belonged only to the oratorical or poetic art — the works which, in greater number than in the following century, elaborated thus [i.e., by means of the symbolic method] the revealed data and the traditional content of the faith" (p 185). [*Translator's note*: Nine of Chenu's essays appear in *Nature, Man, and Society in the Twelfth Century*, edited and translated by Jerome Taylor and Lester K. Little, Chicago 1957.]

[17] The liturgical works of Amalarius († 853) are edited by J. M. Hanssens, *Amalarii episcopi opera liturgica omnia*, 3 vols. (138–140 in the series *Studi e testi*), Rome 1948 ff. His principal works of theological-liturgical interest are: *De ecclesiasticis officiis libri quattuor* (also in PL 105, cols. 985 ff), which treats of the liturgical year, ordinations, the Mass, the Divine Office; and the *De ordine antiphonarii*, which contains an exposition of the structure of the canonical Office.

[18] PL 107, cols. 293 ff.

Sardes,[19] and one, perhaps of the third century, which is inspired by the treatise of St. Hippolytus of Rome on Easter.[20] Starting with the fourth century, in the patristic literature still preserved to us, the homilies on the feasts of the whole liturgical year abound, as little by little the genre was broadened and determined until it took on its substantially definitive form during the sixth-seventh century. Cardinal Daniélou points out the special importance among the Greeks of the homilies of the Cappadocian group, primarily some sermons of Gregory of Nazianz and of Gregory of Nyssa;[21] but there are others too.[22] Among the Latins can be pointed out the ninety-three sermons of Zeno of Verona;[23] the paschal sermons of Gaudentius of Brescia and of St. Maximus of Turin, at least such as are attributed to him;[24] especially the numerous sermons of St. Augustine on the liturgical feasts of the temporal and sanctoral cycles;[25] all the homilies of St. Leo the Great[26] and many of St. Gregory the Great, without counting the medieval authors who, until the scholasticism of the thirteenth century, continued on a broad scale the theological-liturgical genre of the Fathers in their homiletics of the Christian feasts.

The paschal letters which the patriarchs of Alexandria used to address to their faithful at the beginning of Lent constitute a theological-liturgical genre of their own. Some by St. Athanasius[27] and by St. Cyril[28] are preserved.

Finally, various theological patristic works of different kinds are of occasional and sometimes even considerable theological-liturgical interest. Thus, for example, in St. Augustine, Letters 54 and 55, and the *De cura pro mortuis*

---

[19] Published by Campbell Bonner, *The Homily on the Passion by Melito, Bishop af Sardes,* (in the series *Studies and Documents,* 1940). A more recent edition is that of M. Testuz, *Papyrus Bodmer XIII. Méliton de Sardes, Homilie sur la Pâque. Manuscrit du III* siècle, Geneva 1960. See also S. Czerwik, *Homilia paschalis apud Patres usque ad saeculum quintum,* Rome 1961, pp. 27–28.

[20] See P. Nautin, *Une homilie paschale inspirée du traité sur la Pâque d'Hippolyte* in the series *Sources chrétiennes,* Vol. 27, Paris 1950. See also the material published in volumes 36 and 48 of the same series.

[21] Jean Card. Daniélou, *The Bible and the Liturgy,* pp. 16–17.

[22] See Eusebius of Caesarea, fragment of a homily on the solemnity of the Pasch (PG 24, cols. 693 ff); homily *In Epiphaniam* under the name of Titus of Bostra (see J. Sickenberger in *Texte und Untersuchungen,* Vol. 21/1, 1901); Amphilochius, *Homilies* (PG 40, cols. 163 ff); Eulogius of Alexandria, *Homilies on the Psalms* (PG 86, cols. 2913 ff); Sophronius of Jerusalem, *Sermons* (PG 87, cols. 3201 ff).

[23] Principally on the paschal mysteries (PL 11, cols. 476 ff).

[24] Gaudentius: PL 20, cols. 827 ff. Maximus: PL 57, cols. 221 ff. For the critical question, see P. Bongiovanni, *S. Massimo di Torino e il suo pensiero teologico,* Turin 1952; and M. Pellegrino, "Sull'autenticità di un gruppo di omilie e sermoni attribuiti a S. Massimo di Torino," extract from the *Atti della Accademia delle scienze di Torino,* Vol. 99 (1955-1956), Turin 1955.

[25] See also the material among the *Sermones dubii* or *supposititii* in PL 39.

[26] PL 54–56. See also *S. Léon le grand, Sermons,* Vol. 1, translated by R. Dolle, introduction by J. Leclercq (*Sources chrétiennes,* Vol. 22), Paris 1947; Vol. 2, *ibid.,* Vol. 49, 1957.

[27] In Greek, PG 26, 1360 ff. In Coptic, ed. of L. Th. Lefort, *S. Athanase, lettres festales et pastorales en copte.* Text and French translation in *Corpus scriptorum christianorum orientalium,* Vols. 19/20 of the Coptic series, Louvain 1955.

[28] PG 77, cols. 402 ff.

gerenda. Cardinal Daniélou calls attention also to the *De Trinitate* of Didymus the Blind [29] and to St. Basil's treatise on the Holy Spirit.[30]

Of special interest sometimes are certain polemic dogmatic works, for the recourse which the Fathers have in them to the liturgy with the intention of demonstrating a specific point of the Catholic faith against those who doubt or deny. We shall examine below, separately, this aspect of the use of the liturgy in the Fathers. The most important patristic works from this point of view are St. Augustine, his *De peccatorum meritis,*[31] his *De baptismo,*[32] his *Opus imperfectum,*[33] his *De dono perseverantiae,*[34] and his *De Genesi ad litteram*;[35] St. Jerome, his *Dialogus adversus Luciferanos*[36] and his *Contra Vigilantium.* The *Indiculus de gratia Dei* and the *De vocatione omnium gentium*[37] are probably by Prosper of Aquitaine.

In order to have a rather complete picture of the patristic literature of theological-liturgical interest,[38] it must not be forgotten, either, that this is the golden and creative age of the liturgy itself and that therefore it is possible to perceive from the liturgical texts themselves in what degree their composers possessed the theological sense of the liturgy.

2. The Approach to the Liturgy Taken by the Fathers of the Church was Primarily Irenic and Theological

Is it possible, by drawing upon all this material and putting together the elements scattered over the individual authors, rather than attending to the exact position occupied in the total picture by the individual authors themselves, to trace a general picture of the place which the liturgy occupies in the general theological vision of the Fathers? With the proper precautions this seems possible and legitimate.

It must be observed initially, however, that the Fathers are not interested in the liturgy either from a developmental historical point of view or from the rubricist point of view, as the moderns are, but from the point of view of its spiritual or theological value. This, moreover, with them, not only is not separated from, but is rather intimately connected, much more than with the scholastics or the positive-scholastics, with catechetical, ascetical, hortatory-moral, or even mystical purposes. In this we have a characteristic trait of the relations between liturgy and theology in the Fathers. The moderns, on the other hand, are interested up to now in the liturgy from the almost exclusively rubricist or historical point of view. The scholastics and the positive-scholastics

---

[29] 2, 12–14; PG 39, cols. 668 ff.
[30] Ch. 25–27; PG 32, cols. 173 ff.
[31] 1, 23; 1, 63.
[32] For example, 2, 12.
[33] For example, 2, 181 and *passim.*
[34] For example, 15; 63.
[35] For example, 10, 63.

[36] 8.
[37] PL 51, cols. 209 ff; 664 ff.
[38] For other patristic testimonies of lesser interest, in addition to St. Basil's treatise on the Holy Spirit, a work already mentioned, see K. Federer, *Liturgie und Glaube,* Freiburg in der Schweiz 1950.

were indeed interested in it from the theological point of view, but it is easy to see that their concerns were much less immediately associated with catechetical, hortatory, ascetical, and mystical objectives.

A second observation: the method of presentation pursued by the Fathers in treating the liturgy is predominantly expositive, irenic, and even contemplative; they sought above all to address the faithful and explain to them the theological significance which the liturgy has for the believer who practices it, as well as its ascetical-moral value. All of the liturgical-theological works listed above move almost exclusively in this perspective, a perspective in which the great richness of the theological-liturgical subject matter of these works is made clear.

Apologetic treatment of the liturgy, with a view primarily to proving against doubters and unbelievers, or at least against hypothetical doubt and disbelief, the obligatory character of such and such a point of doctrine taught by the Church, is indeed present, but nonetheless secondary and occasional in patristic literature. When the Fathers are interested in the liturgy, their interest is to show and explain the riches of the Church's doctrine to those for whom the foundation of this doctrine is a fact already accepted and not disputed. It is to this end that the directly mystagogic tracts look, also those explanatory of the liturgy in general, the homilies on the liturgical feasts, the allusions to the liturgy in the Lenten pastoral letters of the bishops of Alexandria, and a good part of the occasional allusions to the liturgy in various works and dogmatic treatises.

Hence one cannot help being astonished at finding authors who want to investigate "the theological value of the liturgy" [39] but who limit their study of the Fathers to the question of "the liturgical argument in the Fathers," in other words to the one question how and in what sense the Fathers had recourse to the liturgy to prove against anyone who denies or casts doubt on, at least from a methodological viewpoint, the truth of a doctrine taught by the Church. Such authors say not one word about all the other theological-liturgical perspectives encountered in patristic literature, as if the apologetic value were the sole aspect which interested the Fathers in discussing the liturgy.

It is clear that such an orientation of research is completely inadequate to make us understand what was the theological value of the liturgy for the Fathers.[40] The fact remains that all the recent authors who have concerned

---

[39] For example, M. Pinto, *O valor teologico da liturgia*, Braga 1952.

[40] Since, therefore, Father Pinto's whole work is limited to the question of the value which the liturgy has to prove, from the sources of revelation, a certain point of the Church's doctrine to anyone who really or methodologically denies it or casts doubt on it, it is clear that from the whole work it is impossible to get an adequate idea of the theological value of the liturgy. No mention is made even of the aspects of the liturgy more important and richer in theological value. The same question of the value of the liturgy for proving from the sources of tradition the binding force of a specific point of doctrine is the only one which

themselves with the relations between theology and liturgy in the Fathers, except, to my knowledge, Cardinal Daniélou, who, in his various works, sets out more or less consciously from a different stance, in doing so have presupposed the positive-scholastic concept of theology, as we have explained it above. In this concept, it will be remembered, by reason of a strong prevalence and exaggeration of apologetics, the essence and the primary preoccupation of theological effort lies (methodologically, at least) in proving against anyone who denies a specific point of the Church's doctrine its reasonableness with respect to the sources. But it is completely gratuitous to suppose that such was precisely the concept of theology with the Fathers.

The attention which is given to the liturgy in patristic literature is therefore above all theological, irenically and expositively theological, with strong hortatory, ascetical, and mystical connections, directed above all to believers, not in an effort to prove that the doctrine of the Church is truly to be found in the sources, but primarily in an effort to penetrate this doctrine by contemplation, so to speak, to penetrate its practical import also, its comprehensivity, and its beauty.

3. Mysterion, Mysterium, Sacramentum in the Theological-Liturgical Explanations of the Fathers

But can anything more be said about the intrinsic nature of this theology? There is a great concept which is its general basis and determines all of it: the concept of *mystérion, mysterium, sacramentum*. The liturgy is seen by the Fathers in the framework of the *mysteria* or *sacramenta* which for them dominate the whole of revelation.

The form under which the modern reader is struck by this fact from his first contact with the patristic liturgical literature is the rather unwelcome impression that everything in it is submerged in "allegorical" explanation. Saying this, the modern reader expresses a completely negative judgment. For him, allegorical explanation means arbitrary explanation, and hence one with no real usefulness, not even under the merely edifying aspect, at least for us today.

But, after what we have said in the first part of this work about the concept of liturgy and in the third part about liturgy and Bible, it becomes clear that the modern reader must take another look at his instinctive aversion to the theological-liturgical allegories of the Fathers; he must make more distinctions and separate the portion of indisputable theological value — much

interests Bernard Capelle in his article "*Autorité de la liturgie chez les Pères*," in *Recherches de théologie ancienne et médiévale*, Vol. 21 (1954), pp. 5–22. No adequate idea of the relations between theology and liturgy in the Fathers is to be sought here either, therefore.

The same may be said of the work of K. Federer already cited, which, moreover, intends explicitly to limit itself to the explanation of the principle *legem credendi lex statuat supplicandi*.

greater, no doubt, than the modern reader has been led to admit — from possible or real exaggerations. And, together with other reasons, the following considerations oblige him to do this: the examination of the concept of liturgy centered on the concept of sensible sign; the doctrine of the various dimensions of meaning proper to this sign; the doctrine that the existence and the precise import of this sign in individual cases is determined and therefore knowable in a certain way, viz., by the free will of God manifested to us through revelation, or by the will of the Church, knowable according to the ordinary ways of theology; finally, the doctrine of the intimate relations between liturgy and Bible in the general framework of sacred history and of the profound unity which pervades its individual phases.

Without doubt during the third-fourth century, the concept of *mystérion, mysterium, sacramentum* appears clearly as the key to the whole irenic, expositive theological vision of the liturgy in patristic literature. In the first part of this work we have hinted more than once at the content of this concept in the Fathers.

Origin and development of the *mystérion* concept

Recent research [41] permits us to form a rather exact idea on the roots of this concept, on the general line of its development starting with its substantially definitive formation as it is manifested, for example, in Origen, and on its fundamental common meaning in all subsequent patristic literature.

The ultimate root from which the concept proceeds is the nucleus of scriptural doctrine (which we have explained in its place) with the name of sacred or salvation history, inasmuch as it includes a vision of the universe centered in: the economy of God in the world, that is, His interventions in the world and the effects which they cause in history — the communication of divine life and salvation; the various phases of this economy: time before Christ; Christ; Christian ecclesial history and realities; eschatological and heavenly realities; the relationships which bind these phases to one another as preparation, figure, image, *typos*, symbol, and complement; the advent of Christ in the flesh and the events of His mortal life as center on which everything first

[41] From the time when Odo Casel launched his theory (around 1923) up to the present time, this question has been the object of numerous inquiries. Besides the works cited in the first part of this book, p. 30, notes 20-21; and p. 105, note 13, see the abundant bibliography in H. Schillebeeckx's *De sacramentele heilseconomie*, Antwerp 1952, pp. xxv–xxvii. The same author, pp. 35-106, gives a good summary of the recent conclusions of the inquiries made about the concept of *mystérion, mysterium, sacramentum* in the Bible and in the Fathers. After Schillebeeckx see C. Mohr-mann, "*Sacramentum dans les plus anciens textes chrétiens*," in the *Harvard Theological Review*, Vol. 47 (1954), pp. 141–152. M. Verheyen, "*Mystérion, Sacramentum et la Synagogue*," in *Rech. sc. rel.*, Vol. 45 (1957), pp. 321–337. P. Visentin, "*Mystérionsacramentum dai Padri alla scolastica*," in *Stud. patavina*, Vol. 4 (1957), pp. 394–414. J. Gaillard, "*La théologie des mystères*," in *Rev. thom.*, Vol 57 (1957), pp. 510–551. P. Th. Camelot, "'*Sacramentum.*' Notes de théologie sacramentaire augustinienne," *ibid.*, pp. 429–449.

converges as preparation and prefiguration and from which everything after Him derives as participation — in particular, the present phase, the ecclesial one, as realization participated in by men until the end of time; the divine realities in Christ, prepared and prefigured before Christ, realized in root and in a plenary way in Christ Himself in His earthly life: current foreshadowing and preparation for future eschatological and heavenly realities.

The various sacred authors of the New Testament accent now one, now another aspect of this vast panorama. The synoptics bring out especially the preparative and prefigurative relationship of the Old Testament to Christ. St. Paul, better than others, embraces all together and uses in this context the words "shadow," "figure," "*typos*," and even the word "*mystérion*." But *mystérion* for St. Paul is simply the eternal free and loving plan or counsel of God, known by Him alone and only recently revealed to believers, of saving all men — Jew *and* Gentile — precisely in Christ and in the Christian realities according to the aforesaid scheme. The crucial point in which and from which St. Paul contemplates this whole *mystérion* of the free and loving will of God (Eph. 1:9) is the calling of the Gentiles together with the Jews to this same salvation, in one body, the body of Christ which is the Church (Eph. 1–3). And since St. Paul does not tire of repeating that Christ in His concrete person is the center and fulcrum of this whole *mystérion* or counsel of God, he, at least at the end of his life, had a tendency to refer to Christ Himself in His person and in His concrete work as "the mystery," "the mystery of piety," as he says in 1 Tim. 3:16. See also Col. 2:2 according to the variant reading "the mystery of God, that is, Christ," which seems preferable.

In the apostolic Fathers the same concepts are repeated, with substantially Pauline expressions and ways of seeing things; and the individual points in which it is believed that the Old Testament is preparation and figure of the realities of the New are determined and extended. Justin, moreover, already applies on a considerable scale and in a determinate way the concept of *mystérion* to this symbolic, allegorical, and typical dimension of the texts, facts, and persons of the Old Testament. He conceives the traditional and scriptural doctrine that the whole Old Testament is preparation and figure of Christ and of the Christian realities in the form that the whole Old Testament is full of "mysteries." Beginning with Justin, it becomes certain that the historical events of Christ's life also are called *mystéria*, such as the incarnation, the nativity, the Passion, the death on the Cross, the resurrection, and the ascension.

After Justin, very gradually, the tendency was to express the whole panorama of the divine economy in the world, as it has been recalled above, whether in its entirety or in its details, with the concept of *mystérion*.

It seems undeniable that the general mentality of Platonic tradition contributed no little to the semantic evolution of *mystérion*. The mentality of the

Platonic tradition was accustomed to considering the heavenly world distinct from the earthly world while the whole world of sensible realities was regarded as symbol, image, shadow, and secret participation in the invisible heavenly realities; the sensible world's whole reason for existence lies in its function of being shadow and image designed to lead us to the participative contemplation of the invisible heavenly realities. The author of the Letter to the Hebrews already expressed somewhat in this perspective the common view of the relation between realities of the Old Testament and Christian realities, as well as the relations of Christian realities to the eschatological and heavenly ones.[42]

The fundamental meaning of *mystérion* as it appears, for example, in Origen

In Origen, who was wholly imbued with this Platonic mentality,[43] there is found in an already quite ripe state the aforesaid tendency to conceive the scriptural and traditional doctrine of sacred history, in its entirety and in its bond of unitary correspondence which unites its multiple phases as well as objects, persons, and events proper to each, under a series of expressions which seem centered in that of *mystérion*; to this *mystérion* concepts of image, symbol, shadow and truth, sign, type, letter or body and spirit, etc., seem to converge more and more.[44] This in Origen is the central vantage point around which he organizes his whole outlook. For him the study of dogmatic theology, of the Scriptures, of ascetical and mystical theology, in fact the very object of higher knowledge or gnosis which he considers the supreme end of theological effort and of life, is, practically speaking, the study of the *mystérion*, that is, of those relations of image, symbol, shadow and truth, sign, type, letter or body and spirit, etc., which bind together the individual parts of sacred history and all things contained therein.

Then if it is sought to determine in Origen the fundamental and very general meaning of *mystérion* and of related concepts, the conclusion is arrived at that for him *mystérion* (symbol, image, etc.) is (a) something perceptible or sensible but embodying a hidden divine reality which it (b) manifests to whoever has the sense to perceive it, and communicates in some way to whoever is sympathetically disposed to it — a divine reality in relation to the economy of God in the world. This is the fundamental meaning which is afterwards common to all subsequent patristic literature.

[42] See Ceslaus Spicq, *L'épître aux hébreux*, Vol. 1, pp. 73 ff.

[43] See, for example, *In Cant. com.* 2, ed. Baehrens 8, 160; *In Io. com.* 1, 24, ed. Preuschen 4, 31; *In Gen. hom.* 9, 1, ed. Baehrens 6, 88 f; *In Rom. com.* 3, 7 (PG 14, col. 943); *Contra Celsum* 7, 31, ed. Koetschau 5, 283; *In Cant. com. 3*, ed. Baehrens 8, 208 ff; *Peri archôn* 2, 11, 4, ed. Koetschau 5, 187.

[44] See the basic study by Hans Urs von Balthasar, "Le *mystérion* d'Origène," in *Recherches de sciences religieuses*, Vol. 26 (1936), pp. 513 ff; Vol. 27 (1937), pp. 38 ff. Also, H. Crouzel, *Origène et "la connaissance mystique,"* Bruges [Brugge] 1960, pp. 21-209.

In this concept their are two terms: that which is perceptible and the divine reality. The two terms are really distinct: the perceptible thing is not the divine reality purely and simply; the two terms, however, are intimately united by a unity of participation. And in this sense that which is perceptible is already in some way the divine reality; it is such under another form, in a different and participated manner of being. Therefore the relations of union between the two entities are relations of image (ontologically understood) to reality, to truth; of manifestation, signification, communication, and effective participation; of type and antitype; of sign and thing signified; symbol and thing symbolized; preparation, figure, and fulfillment. The mystery (and related concepts) is always the epiphanic manifestation, for whoever has the sense to perceive it, of a divine reality of the order of salvation in the form of a sensible thing, which in one sense hides it from anyone whose organs are not adapted to perceiving it, but in another sense manifests it to whoever has those senses, and communicates it because, in some way, it really contains it.

With the aforesaid general meaning in mind, we can understand the extremely varied use which Origen makes of that concept, whether with the term *mystérion* or with equivalent or related terms. Hans Urs von Balthasar [45] sums it up in this way: the primordial *mystérion* is Christ Himself in His concrete person, man and God. In Him *par excellence* is verified the example of a tangible reality which, in some way, really contains hidden in itself while manifesting to the believer and communicating to whoever is disposed, a sacred, divine reality necessary for salvation. This sacred reality in Christ is God, the Word Himself, the divine'life. Christ, says Origen, was a sign of contradiction because "one thing was seen in Him and another understood. Flesh was perceived and God was believed." [46]

Flowing from the *mystérion* of Christ is the *mystérion* of the words of holy Scripture, incarnation *sui generis* of the Word, which at the same time hide themselves from whoever has not the sense to understand them, manifest themselves to whoever understands them spiritually, and communicate themselves to whoever is prepared for them. [47] In the Old Testament, says Origen, "everything that is done, is done *in sacramentis.*" [48] For him this is a maxim which holds good for all of Scripture. If to this is added his persuasion that all man can desire to know — anything useful for reaching his end — is contained in the Scriptures and that it is a question only of discovering it, and that this knowledge is something which constitutes precisely the essen-

[45] *Op. cit.*

[46] *In Rom. com.* 4, 2 (PG 14, col. 968). The flesh of Christ was the garment covering spiritual things (*Peri archôn* 4, 2, 8); the human actions of Christ were symbols of His divine actions (*In Matt. com.* 16, 20). See also Schillebeeckx, *op. cit.*, pp. 66 ff. M. Harl, *Origène*

et la fonction révélatrice du verbe incarné, 2 vols. (*Coll. patristica sorbonensia*), Paris 1958.

[47] See, for example, *In Matt. Com. ser.* 27, ed. Klostermann, p. 45.

[48] *In Gen. hom.* 9, 1, ed Baehrens, pp. 87, 18. See also *In Gen. hom.* 10, *ibid.*, p. 95; "Everything that is in Scripture is a mystery."

tial object of gnosis or higher and salutary knowledge, it will be readily understood why, for Origen, the whole labor of explaining Christian doctrine is substantially a labor of explaining the meaning of the "mysteries" contained in the Scriptures.

Second only to the primordial *mystérion* of Christ is "the *mystérion* of the Church" from which we must be carefully on our guard not to separate ourselves,[49] because "outside this house, that is, outside the Church, no one is saved." [50] This is true because in the Church is realized the entire coming and presence of Christ: *Ecclesia . . . in qua tota totus est adventus Filii hominis.*[51] In the Church too, all things, besides being really what they are, have the value of *mystérion*, of symbol, of image, etc. So too, then, with the ecclesiastical hierarchy: "The bishop, the priest, the deacon, are symbols also of the truths which correspond to these names." [52]

This is the case also with the rites of worship which constitute precisely the third sphere of the *mystérion* of Origen, derived from the two preceding ones. Origen speaks in this sense not only of baptism and the Eucharist,[53] but also of the "ecclesiastical observances" in general, including also, as the context clearly indicates, the liturgical rites in general.[54]

Thus, from the apostolic Fathers to Origen, the great scriptural vision of the world as sacred salvation history always in the making and of the relation of roughcast, image, figure, preparation, realization, fulfillment, which unites the various phases among themselves — pre-Christian, Christic, ecclesial, eschatological — is enlarged and determined. This determination and broadening may be highlighted as follows: (a) details of the Old Testament are increasingly considered as image, figure, type, etc., of the realities of the new economy and even of the future heavenly economy and are more frequently related to single factors of the Christic and Christian economy; hence the prefigurative and preparatory background of the Old Testament is accentuated; (b) in the details of the sense-perceptible events of the life of Christ on earth and in tangible aspects of the constitution and life of the Church, the Fathers, and Origen in particular, pay heed with ever greater insistence to their symbolic-real value, expressive of a present spiritual reality; (c) this whole tendency of a symbolic-realistic vision of things and of sacred history

---

[49] *In Iob selecta* 20, 15 (PG 12, col. 1035).

[50] *In Ies. Nav. hom.* 3, 4-5, ed Baehrens, pp. 304 ff (Jurgens, no. 537).

[51] *In Matt. com. ser.* 47, ed. Klostermann, pp. 98, 3 ff. *Adventus* can translate *parousía* or *epidemía*, which imply coming and presence.

[52] *In Matt. com.* 14, 22, ed. Klostermann, pp. 338, 10 ff. For what these truths are, see *In Matt. Com. ser.* 10, ed Klostermann, pp. 17 ff: individual and social interior sacrifices; the eternal heavenly hierarchy: the Lord, the patriarchs, and the archangels.

[53] For baptism see, for example, *In Io. com.* 6, 17, ed. Preuschen, pp. 142 ff. Clement of Alexandria already termed baptism *mystérion*, opposing it to the false pagan 'mysteries (see the *Protreptikos*, 12, 118-120). For the Eucharist and the Mass, see *In Ex. hom.* 13, 3, ed. Baehrens, 6, 274; *In Lev. hom.* 13, 3, ed. Baehrens, 6, 471 ff; *In Num. hom.* 7, 2, ed. Baehrens, 7, 39 ff; *In Num. hom.* 16, 6, *ibid.*, 151 ff; *In Ps.* 37 hom. 2, 6 (PG 12, col. 1386 D).

[54] *In Num. hom.* 5, 1, ed Baehrens, pp. 25 ff.

is expressed more and more in the general concept of *mystérion*, of which the other concepts such as image, symbol, figure, sign, etc., tend to become particular aspects or else synonyms.

The application of *mystérion* to the whole liturgy beginning with the fourth century

Beginning with the fourth century, all this flowering out becomes a clearly characterized phenomenon grounded on the general concept of *mystérion* as explained above and presupposed by all.[55] At the same time, the application of *mystérion* is extended ever more and more to individual liturgical details, so that by this term there is understood explicitly not only the essential rites of the Christian initiation — baptism, confirmation, and Eucharist, including the whole Mass — but also the rites of the catechumenate, such as the Lord's Prayer, the creed, the exorcisms, etc. Then, as has already been pointed out,[56] starting from the fifth century, the term is progressively applied to the myron, to ordinations, to the consecration of the church, of monks, of virgins, to funerals, liturgical feasts, the canonical hours. At the end of this process, the liturgy in its entirety and in its details is explicitly envisaged under the concept of *mystérion*.

The situation is substantially the same in the Syrian Church — to such an extent that Father de Vries, when he seeks to treat of the theology of the sacraments among the Syrian Monophysites, is constrained to set down in advance that the object of the Syrians' treatises from which he will take his material is simply the liturgy. These treatises are entitled typically "*On the Mysteries of the Church.*" Under this concept Moses bar Kepha, for example, includes: "The renunciation of Satan, the acknowledgement of Christ, the anointing with the sign of the Cross, baptism, confirmation with the holy myron; the prayers which are said in priestly functions; why we do not kneel on Sunday and on the day of Pentecost; why when we pray we look to the East; why we venerate the Cross, etc. All these are mysteries of the Church."[57]

Other authors, besides all the rites of initiation, include in these explanations of the "mysteries" the consecration of a church, of the myron, of priestly vestments; processions; the profession or consecration of monks; individual objects found in the church, such as the altar, the candelabra, the chalice, the paten, *etc.*; the rite of funerals, in short, the whole liturgy. "'Mystery' for the Syrian theologians is any tangible thing or any action which, in a mysterious,

---

[55] See the texts cited in the first part, pp. 29 ff, e.g., the concept of St. John Chrysostom: "it is a mystery when we consider in sacred things that which goes beyond what we see" (*In ep. 1 ad Cor. hom.* 1, 7); and that of Theodore of Mopsuestia: "Every mystery is the indication in signs and symbols of invisible and ineffable things" (*Catech.* XII, 2).

[56] Above, p. 30, notes 20 and 21.

[57] W. de Vries, *Sakramententheologie bei den syrischen Monophysiten*, Rome 1940, pp. 30 ff. In regard to the matter of kneeling or not kneeling on Sunday and Pentecost, see Canon 20 of the First Council of Nicaea (Jurgens, no. 651z, with its note).

secret way, refers to a suprasensible reality." [58] "What is characteristic in all these treatises and demonstrates the fundamental concept of the Syrians with regard to the rites of the Church," says the same author, "is that, in connection with all the rites and objects of worship, they ask first of all and always: What do they mean? Why are they a 'mystery'? All these treatises are commentaries on the liturgy, they are full of explanations, often complicated and far-fetched, of what the individual ceremonies and the individual objects of worship signify. To explain secret meanings is the principal aim of these writings." [59]

Mystérium and Sacramentum among the Latins

The same way of considering the thesis in questions prevailed in the Latin churches. Here the underlying concepts find expression in the words *mysterium* and *sacramentum*. While *mysterium* is simply the Latinization of the Greek word *mystérion* and is found already in the oldest Latin versions of the Bible, *sacramentum* is of Latin origin. It comes from *sacrare* and might signify the thing which consecrates, the thing consecrated, or the very act of making a thing sacred.[60] For the ancient Romans *sacramentum* was primarily a military term: the *sacramentum militiae* which every new recruit had to undergo upon his entrance into the Roman army. It involved a religious rite of initiation, a consecration to the protecting divinities of the army and included an oath of loyalty on the part of the recruit.

This word, together with the word *mysterium*, were already used in the oldest Latin versions of the Bible for the Greek *mystérion*, a term which St. Paul, for example, used; the word *mystérion* also appears in late Greek ecclesiastical literature, preserving the same sense in all cases. Note, however, that, at least in Tertullian, *sacramentum* brings out forcefully the aspect of moral obligation and that of an oath of loyalty included already in the Greek *mystérion* (although rather secondarily). Thus *sacramentum* as synonym of *mysterium* was used to indicate the same ideas that the Greek indicated with *mystérion* and was connected with the same concepts with which *mysterium* was connected, such as *signum, figura, symbolum, imago*.

Thus it is explained how the fundamental concept of *mysterium* and *sacramentum* in the Latin Fathers is the same as that of *mystérion* among the Greeks.

Speaking of the Eucharistic bread and chalice, St. Augustine can say to the neophytes: "These, brethren, are called *sacramenta* because in them one thing is seen and another understood." [61] And he can also speak "of the signs which, when they refer to divine things, are called sacraments." [62]

---

[58] W. de Vries, *op. cit.*, p. 32. We would have to add, as de Vries himself points out on p. 33, "and, in some way, causes it."

[59] *Ibid.*, p. 32.

[60] On *mysterium* and *sacramentum* among the Latins, see Schillebeeckx, *op. cit.*, pp. 89 ff.

[61] *Sermo* 272.

[62] *Epist.* 138, 7.

Also the objects to which the expressions *mysterium* and *sacramentum* are applied are the same ones which the Greeks and the Syrians called "mysteries," "mysteries of the Church," that is, not only Christ Himself, the Scriptures in their typical, allegorical or spiritual sense, and the Church as such, but also all the rites of worship and practically the whole liturgy: rites, prayers, feasts, liturgical practices, liturgical objects.[63]

Reflections of this "mystery" terminology in the liturgies

Naturally this terminology of *mystérion*, *mysterium*, and *sacramentum*, with the related terms of image, sign, type, shadow, figure, etc., passed on a large scale into the vocabulary of the liturgical formularies of the historical and present-day liturgies, which, as is known, are substantially the fruit of the liturgical creativity of the patristic age.[64]

But something which is more important still is that the great majority of the liturgical compositions, even if they do not explicitly have the words *mystérion*, *mysterium*, *sacramentum*, image, etc., are basically structured in the perspective of the ideology which these expressions suppose. In other words, the aforesaid idea of *mystérion*, *mysterium*, *sacramentum*, etc., or, if you will, the idea which we have called in its proper place sacred history and efficacious sign with its various dimensions, constitutes the natural background — may we call it the "woof"? — of the liturgical compositions themselves: a woof which is idealized, which is repeatedly recalled in a more or less explicit way, which shapes prayer in all its forms — praise, adoration, petition, repentance — as well as colors all teachings, advice, aspirations. The same woof serves as criterion for the choice of the biblical readings in the liturgy, or, at any rate, as criterion for their interpretation.

---

[63] For St. Augustine see above, p. 30, notes 20 and 21. The *De mysteriis* of St. Hilary of Poitiers is a treatise on the typological, allegorical, spiritual meaning of the Old Testament. The two works of St. Ambrose, *De mysteriis* and *De sacramentis*, are in explanation of the rites of Christian initiation. This way of understanding the *sacramenta* and the *mysteria* by identifying them with the whole liturgy when they are said of the rites, remained practically unchanged in the West until the twelfth century (see A. Michel, "*Sacramentaux*," in the *Dict. de théol. cath.*, Vol. XIV/1 [1939], pp. 467 ff; D. van den Eynde, *Les définitions des sacrements pendant la première période de la théologie scolastique*, Rome 1950, pp. 1050–1240), when with the introduction of the distinction between *sacramenta* and *sacramentalia*, due, it would seem, to Peter Lombard, attention began to be directed to the question of what distinguishes our present

seven sacraments from the rest of the liturgical rites.

[64] It is easy now to account for the abundant use of this terminology, for example in the Leonine Sacramentary, consulting the glossary of the Mohlberg edition at the words *mysterium*, *sacramentum*, *figura*, and *imago*. Some examples taken from the Leonine and Gelasian Sacramentaries in the Mohlberg editions: Church as *sacramentum*, Gelasian, no. 432; *sacramentum* and *mysterium* are said of the Eucharist and the Mass, constituting in the Leonine the great majority of the passages where these terms occur; said of baptism, Leonine, 67, 23; Gelasian, nos. 485; 500; 508; 513; said of liturgical feasts and celebrations, Leonine, 21, 12; 48, 22; Gelasian, nos. 456; 637; of matrimony, Leonine, 138, 33; of the Apostles' Creed, Gelasian, no. 310; of incense, Gelasian, no. 429; of holy water, Gelasian, nos. 444; 445.

Thus, I think, it can be safely asserted that the background of the liturgical compositions of the patristic age is always and everywhere the *mystérion*, *mysterium, sacramentum* in the broad sense and according to all its dimensions, dimensions that are always supposed if not more or less fully in evidence. These dimensions of the *mystérion* are the same ones which in the first part of our book we called the dimensions of the liturgical sign, viz., relationships to the past realities of the Old Testament; to the historical events of the life of Christ; to the divine realities of grace which the liturgical rites communicate at present; to the dispositions of worship in the mind of the faithful, with the moral obligations which they involve; to the future eschatological and heavenly realities. The whole is bound together by the relationships of efficacious sign, of image, of figure, of first roughcast and the like.

The theological explanation of the liturgy in the Fathers as explanation of its mysteries

Such being the state of affairs, it is easy to understand how, in the patristic literature, the theological explanation of the liturgy is nothing other than the explanation of the "mysteries," of the "sacraments," or better still, of the "mystery," of the "sacrament," which contains the liturgy in its entirety and in its individual parts; of its "mystical" (*mysticus*) significance, as it was called,[65] and this in reference to the various dimensions of the *mysterium* indicated above.

What Father de Vries noted in connection with the Syrians — that a characteristic of their treatises on the "mysteries of the Church" is their essential concern with seeking, for every liturgical rite, gesture, or object, what it "signifies," why and in what sense it is a "mystery" — must simply be said of the whole patristic literature in reference to its irenic explanation of the liturgy.

Naturally in this task which the Fathers set for themselves, there are shadings and diverse tendencies, according to the greater or lesser insistence now on one, now on another of the various facets of the mystery. In this regard, a comparative study of the whole of the theological-liturgical literature of the Fathers is still necessary to discover better and characterize better its various tendencies and traditions. It seems, however, that the Latin line of the Fathers, at least before the seventh century, such as Tertullian, Ambrose, Augustine, Leo the Great, Zeno, and Gaudentius, follows a rather simple, single course; in treating the liturgy as *mysterium* and *sacramentum* they seem to pay heed above all to relationships between the realities of the Old Testament[66] and Christ, not neglecting the aspect of moral obligations. Among

---

[65] Let it be noted that the adjective *mystikòs* derives from the same root as the noun *mystérion*.

[66] The explanation in the Fathers, whether Greek or Latin, of the mystery of the sacraments and of the liturgical feasts in their re-

the Latins, St. Augustine, as might be expected, is the one whose view surveys most completely the various facets of the entire *mysterium*. Among other things he points out with great force and insistence the doctrine of the Mystical Body. But, in general, the Latins seem to keep close to the great schemes of sacred history itself and themes that are dogmatically certain.

Among the Greeks, too, there exists the tradition by which the *mystérion* of the liturgy pays attention above all to the relations of the liturgical realities with the Old Testament and with Christ Himself. Origen adds to it some further interest by his figurative evaluation of the different steps of the soul's ascent toward the heights of gnostic perfection. Nevertheless, among the Greeks another tendency represented by the Pseudo-Dionysius had much greater influence.

It can be said that this tendency relegates to a second level the liturgy's *mystérion* relationships with the Old Testament and, in general, with the temporal and historical aspect of revelation; this tendency stresses the *mystérion's* value as image bridging the human and the divine; it relishes the transcendent and abstract, or metaphysical in the neo-Platonic sense. It is the transcendent and, as it were, metaphysical God, more than the God of sacred history, who is considered as operating and whom the worshiper seeks to attain through the signs of the liturgy. Not by chance is this tendency called "theurgic." It peeps out in Theodore of Mopsuestia, through opposition to historical-biblical allegory; and it is developed to the highest degree in the Pseudo-Dionysius,[67] passing afterwards to all the Syrians, who depend heavily upon the Pseudo-Dionysius, to Maximus the Confessor, and thence, more or less, to the whole subsequent Byzantine tradition, including, even if in a very sober way and devoid of the Dionysian metaphysical tendency, Nicolas Cabasilas and Simeon of Thessalonica.

Discretion to be observed in these explanations: advantages and disadvantages

Among the Fathers of the Church the fundamental concept of *mystérion*, as it has been explained above, is undeniably based on the solid rock of Scriptures and of dogma. We ourselves in the first and third parts of this book have done nothing but take it up again and try to revalidate it. It is just as certain, however, that in the single details of the figural references which they established among the various phases of this mystery, and especially

lations to the Old Testament is precisely the object of the study of Jean Card. Daniélou in his *The Bible and The Liturgy*.

[67] For the liturgical theology of the Pseudo-Dionysius and its general setting, see R. Roques, "*L'univers dionysien*," in *Théologie*, Vol. 29, Paris 1954, pp. 92 ff, 245-302. In the Pseudo-Dionysian *mystérion* the divine realities of

which it is the sensible sign and symbol are essentially the action of purification, of illumination, and of perfecting, which God, the supreme Thearchy, exercises through the various ranks of the hierarchy, celestial and terrestrial. The whole vision of the world is strongly timeless; and the aspect of sacred history almost disappears.

with the phase of the Old Testament, all the Fathers, some more and some less, went beyond bounds, becoming at times quite arbitrary.

It still remains, however, to carry to fulfillment the labor of judicious discretionary selection in this liturgical-figurative theology of the patristic literature begun by Cardinal Daniélou.[68] Besides a historical inquiry into the origin of the individual figural references and into the extension which the individual opinions have in this field, the fundamental theoretical criterion of this discretionary selection must be the principle established by us in the first part of this book: that the liturgical signs, inasmuch as they signify a supernatural reality, are not simply natural signs, but free signs; and that in the liturgy, therefore, an object, a gesture, a word, an entire rite should be "mystery" or sign of a spiritual reality referring to the action of God through Christ in the world or to the worship which man renders to God in Christ; of what precise reality it should be the sign; to what degree and under what specific aspect it should be a sign; for all this depends solely on the free will of the competent authority who has established it and of the competent authority who makes use of it, not on private opinions.

So it remains for private persons to discover the intentions of the competent authority responsible in each instance through the ordinary way of historical, critical, philological, psychological, philosophical, theological research. The fact that something lends itself naturally to being the figure and image of something else does not mean at all that it is actually the figure or image or mystery of that other. It is still necessary to see whether the competent authority which established and makes use of the point under discussion actually meant to put that nexus of sign or of mystery between the two liturgical data, and in what precise way and to what extent.

We know that as far as the substance of the Mass sacrifice and of the sacraments is concerned, the competent authority who instituted them is Christ alone. What the spiritual realities are, therefore, to which the sacraments in their substance refer as mysteries in the sense explained above, depends solely upon the will of Christ, which we can know through the ordinary ways which make revelation known to us. The same holds true of the Old Testament types in their bearing upon the realities of the New.

For other parts of the liturgy the competent authority is the Church, whose intention with regard to the precise meaning of the "mystery" which liturgical details have, we can know through the origin and the history of given details, through the texts which accompany them, etc. It is necessary, therefore, to pass through the sieve of this criterion all the figurative liturgical theology of the patristic literature, and to reject forthwith those details in it

[68] Principally in his two works *Sacramentum futuri* and *The Bible and the Liturgy*. For the same discretion to be observed in the theologi-cal-liturgical literature of the Middle Ages in the West until the twelfth century, see above, note 16 in the present chapter.

which do not stand up under this scrutiny, even if they were of ancient usage and more or less common among the Fathers themselves.

The fruit of this discretion should be the revalidation of a sane figurative liturgical theology and, in general, of the concept of sign, figure, etc., and therefore of symbolism and of the *mysterium* in theology. In fact, the concept of sign and the possibility of its application in the whole of theology is the great patristic contribution in this field. The first great advantage of having considered the liturgy primarily in this way and, in its explanation, of having always posed as the first question that of the meaning of the individual signs — in other words, of the sense of the "mysteries" contained therein — is that by this very fact it will have been considered primarily against the background of sacred history. The second great advantage is that the liturgy will have been considered in its entirety, through the working out of a theology of the "sacraments" or "mysteries" of the Church in general, and through the analyzing of the theology of the seven greater sacraments in this general picture. This means that in the Fathers the theology of the seven sacraments will be found in the connatural framework of liturgical theology in general. In fact, to consider in the liturgical rites primarily the aspect of sign or "mystery" or "sacrament" in the sense of the Fathers is to consider primarily that which is common to the whole liturgy.

We know also that these advantages were paid for with one disadvantage: that of not arriving at a sufficient distinction of our seven greater rites, or sacraments, from the rest of the liturgy, a distinction which looks essentially to their special origin, efficacy, and necessity, as compared to all the others. It is undeniable that in the patristic concept of *mystérion*, *mysterium*, or *sacramentum* the aspect of sign is given such predominance that the aspect of efficacy, while really contained therein and noted by the Fathers, still remains hardly analyzed by them in its proper aspects.[69]

It was the great merit of Western scholasticism, especially that of St. Thomas, precisely to have elaborated in the concept of *sacramentum* or *mysterium* the aspect of efficacy which had been left too indeterminate in the patristic tradition; and this elaboration of the aspect of efficacy permitted the reflective and full recognition of the very special place which belongs to our seven sacraments in the whole complexus of the liturgy.

But we know now that while in St. Thomas himself the balance between the two aspects, sign and efficacy, of the *sacramenta* was quite notable and hence his insertion of the liturgy into the theological synthesis was quite satisfactory, at least in the treatise on the sacraments, in the later scholastics this balance was lost; so much attention was paid to the aspect of efficacy that the aspect of sign was too much forgotten, and hence the liturgy was practically

---

[69] A significant fact: Schillebeeckx, who in his work analyzes at some length the aspect of sign in the aforesaid concept in the Fathers, can indicate relatively few and general patristic expressions (pp. 80–81) which regard to the aspect of efficacy.

expelled from the theological synthesis. A more just revalidation of the aspect of sign, learned in the school of the Fathers, but with respect for all the later advances of theology, of exegesis, and of history, should lead to the rediscovery of a closer unity between liturgy and the theological synthesis in general.

4. The Question of the Authority of the Liturgy and Its Polemical Use in the Fathers

If the concept of *mystérion, mysterium, sacramentum* is the center on which the greatest interest of the Fathers in their theological view of the liturgy converges, it is still true that they have also had recourse to the liturgy as source of theological argumentation against the doubts or denials about a determinate point of the Church's doctrine. They have considered the liturgy as an "authority" [70] for resolving these possible doubts of believers and for refuting the denials of those who were in error. To what extent and in what sense they did this has been substantially clarified by recent studies, above all by those of Federer and Capelle.[71] It will suffice here to report the results briefly.

The authority of the liturgy for the Fathers is such as to impose the obligation of the observance of the rites, words, and customs of which it is composed, and the obligation of assent to the beliefs implied in them. The Fathers, therefore, have recourse to the liturgy when they consider it opportune to inculcate such obligations. This recourse, as is natural, is especially notable in doctrinal controversies. It will suffice to indicate the principal ones.

Controversies in which recourse to the liturgy was notable

Already in the anti-gnostic controversy of the second century St. Ignatius of Antioch [72] and, in a still more developed manner, St. Irenaeus [73] appeal

---

[70] St. Augustine in particular clearly connected the question of the probative value of the liturgy with the question of the *auctoritas*, a concept which is, as is well known, of basic importance in the whole procedure of Augustine. See, for example, M. Löhrer, *Der Glaubensbegriff des heiligen Augustinus in seinen ersten Schriften bis zu den Confessiones*, Einsiedeln 1955, pp. 81 ff. See also A. H. Wagenwoort and B. Tellenbach, "*Auctoritas*," in the *Realenziklopedie für Antike und Christentum*, edited by Theodor Klauser, Vol. I (1950), pp. 904–909.

[71] Karl Federer, *Liturgie und Glaube. Legem credendi lex statuat supplicandi. Eine theologiegeschichtliche Untersuchung*, Freiburg 1950. To clarify the meaning of the principle of the pseudo-Celestinian chapters, *legem credendi lex statuat supplicandi*, he inquires into the use of the liturgy as proof of the faith in the questions disputed with non-Catholics, in

Prosper of Aquitaine, Augustine, Ambrose, Optatus of Milevis, Cyprian, Tertullian, and the Fathers before Tertullian. Bernard Capelle, in his article "*Autorité de la liturgie chez les Pères*," in *Recherches de théol. ancienne et médiévale*, Vol. 21 (1954), pp. 5–22, reviews once more the texts of the Fathers about the authority of the liturgy as proof of the faith, to bring out more strongly that, in their eyes, the liturgy has such authority in virtue of the universality with which it is practiced in the Church, which universality, in its turn, indicates its apostolic origin, apostolicity being the ultimate foundation of the authority of the liturgy, according to the Fathers.

[72] *Letter to the Ephesians* 20, 2 (Jurgens, no. 43); *Letter to the Smyrnaeans* 7, 1 (Jurgens, no. 64).

[73] *Adversus haereses* 1, 3, 1; 4, 18, 5 (Jurgens, no. 234); 5, 2, 2-3 (Jurgens, no. 249).

to Eucharistic practice and to the sense of the Real Presence of Christ which the Church attaches to it to refute the gnostic dualist doctrine of the appearance of the body of Christ and of the essential perversity of matter, with the consequent impossibility that the body share in the divine life, especially in the resurrection of the flesh.[74] Tertullian, against this second point of the gnostic doctrine, draws the argument not only from the Eucharist but from the entire rite of Christian initiation.[75]

In the controversy on the validity of baptism conferred by heretics, which put St. Cyprian of Carthage and Pope St. Stephen at odds, one of the essential points, in fact *the* essential point, was precisely that of the authority of the relative liturgical custom in the respective churches.

In the Trinitarian controversies, recourse to the authority of the liturgy had an important role. Origen, for example, appealed to the anaphoral prayer in his disputes with the modalists.[76] The recourse to the Trinitarian liturgical texts was the order of the day in the controversy between Arians and anti-Arians. The most famous case is the controversy over the meaning of the liturgical doxology, as we know of it through St. Basil's work *De Spiritu Sancto*.[77] No less typical is the case of the anonymous Arian who recalled ironically to the Catholics the texts of their liturgy, implying, in his view, the Arian doctrine.[78] We have already hinted in chapter seven [79] at the impact which the same Arian struggle had upon liturgical compositions up to the early Middle Ages.

In the Donatist controversy, too, there is found some recourse to the liturgy in Optatus of Milevis [80] and in St. Augustine.[81] St. Jerome, in his turn, did

[74] The argument consists in pointing out what is implied, with respect to the essential goodness of matter, by the Eucharistic practice of the Church, in which our body itself receives the body and blood of Christ, and in showing the contradiction which there is in following that practice and denying the doctrine which it implies.

[75] The text of Tertullian's *The Resurrection of the Dead* 8, 2-3, is famous: "No soul whatever is able to obtain salvation unless it has believed while it was in the flesh. Indeed, the flesh is the hinge of salvation. In that regard, when the soul is deputed to something by God, it is the flesh which makes it able to carry out the commission which God has given it. The flesh, then, is washed so that the soul may be made clean. The flesh is anointed so that the soul may be dedicated to holiness. The flesh is signed so that the soul too may be fortified. The flesh is shaded by the imposition of hands so that the soul too may be illuminated by the Spirit. The flesh feeds on the Body and Blood of Christ so that the soul too may fatten on God. They cannot, then, be separated in their reward when they are united in their works" (Jurgens, no. 362). See also *Against Marcion* 1, 14.

[76] Origen's *Disputation with Heraclides* was rediscovered as part of the papyrus find at Tura, only in 1941. See the edition of J. Scherer, *Entretien d'Origène avec Héraclide et les évêques ses collègues sur le Père, le Fils, et l'âme*, Cairo 1949, pp. 128–129.

[77] We have spoken of the controversy above, pp. 218, 221.

[78] See the fragments published for the first time by Angelo Cardinal Mai; new edition in Mohlberg, *Sacramentarium veronense*, Rome 1956, pp. 201 ff.

[79] Pp. 218 ff.

[80] *Contra Parmenianum Donatistam*, 2, 20; 3, 12.

[81] *Contra epistulam Parmeniani*, 2, 10, 20; *De baptismo contra Donatistas* 4, 23, 30; *Epist.* 185, 9, 39.

not fail to appeal to the liturgy to defend against Vigilantius the cult of saints and of relics.[82]

But it was especially the Pelagian and semi-Pelagian controversy that gave occasion on a broad scale to the appeals to the authority of the liturgy. St. Augustine makes such appeal in practically all the essential points disputed with Pelagius and the semi-Pelagians: original sin and its consequences, relations between grace and free choice, predestination, perseverence, and especially in the necessity of grace for any supernatural good work whatsoever, even in its beginning.[83] Two points in particular of the liturgy serve Augustine as basis for his argumentations. In the question of original sin: the baptism of infants with the rites which precede it and make its meaning incontrovertible, especially the rites of the exorcisms and of the *exsufflatio*; [84] for the question of the necessity of grace for every salutary work even in its beginning, as well as for the question of predestination and of perseverance: the prayers of the liturgy, whether of petition or of thanksgiving.[85] The argument against the semi-Pelagians drawn from the orations of the liturgy is particularly developed in Letter 217. It is precisely this argument which was later taken up again by Prosper of Aquitaine for the very purpose of the polemic against the semi-Pelagians on the necessity of grace even for the beginning of the salutary good work, and which thus passed into the *Indiculus*, where it was summed up in the well-known formula *legem credendi lex statuat supplicandi*.[86] It is known also that the anti-Pelagian and anti-semi-Pelagian controversy had very considerable influence on the Roman liturgical compositions of the fifth and sixth centuries.[87]

In the Christological controversies also, the liturgy and liturgical arguments had a certain importance.[88]

In the last period of what is sometimes termed the late patristic age, before the thirteenth century in the West and the sixteenth in the East, there was

---

[82] *Contra Vigilantium.*

[83] See the detailed documentation in Karl Federer, *op. cit.*, pp. 23 ff.

[84] See *De peccat. meritis* 1, 63, 34; *Opus imperf.* 2, 181; *Epist.* 194, 10, 43-46. The bare bones of the same argument are found already in Origen, *Homilies on Leviticus* 8, 3 (Jurgens, no. 496), and it is at least implied in the *Letter of Cyprian . . . to Fidus* 64, 5 (Jurgens, no. 586).

[85] In various texts Augustine has directly in view not only private prayers but also liturgical prayers, e.g., *De dono persever.* 15, 7; 33, 13; 63-65, 23.

[86] See above, pp. 529 ff.

[87] For the semi-Pelagian controversy in the Leonine Sacramentary, see Cyprian Vagaggini, *"La posizione di S. Benedetto nella questione semipelagiana,"* in *Studia benedictina in memo-*riam gloriosi transitus S. P. Benedicti, (*Studia anselmiana*, 18-19), Rome 1947, pp. 46–53; C. Mohlberg, *Sacramentarium veronense*, p. lxxiv.

[88] Especially by reason of the alterations and novelties which the Monophysites introduced into the liturgy in favor of their opinions, and the protests of the orthodox against the changes introduced into the Mass by Nestorius and Theodore of Mopsuestia; by reason of the alteration of the rite of the *commixtio* with the Eutychians; by reason of the abandonment of the rite of the addition of a few drops of water in the chalice with the Armenians; and by reason of the introduction into the *Trisagion* of the clause "who was crucified for us" by Peter the Fuller, patriarch of Antioch in the time when Timothy the Cat was patriarch in Alexandria.

still a series of dogmatic controversies in which the recourse to the liturgy was more or less frequent: the controversy over images; [89] that aroused by Spanish adoptionism; [90] the long Photian and Caerularian controversy, continued later in that between Catholics and the Greek dissident Church. [91]

Finally, a point of doctrine which the Fathers, from ancient times, had to defend many times and for which they had recourse to the authority of the liturgy, was the liceity and the utility of prayers for the dead and of the offering of the sacrifice of the Mass for them. [92]

The thinking of the Fathers on the connection between the authority of the liturgy and its apostolicity and universality

Of more interest than a list of the controversies in which recourse was had to the authority of the liturgy is the mentality in which this recourse was had. The authority of the liturgy was admitted in the sense that, by reason of the fact that it contains certain usages and rites and implies certain doctrines, the observance of these usages and of these rites and belief in these doctrines are obligatory. But, for the Fathers, on what is this binding power based in the final analysis? Of what nature is it? Is it of the same degree for all the rites, usages and beliefs implied in any way in the liturgy, or are there distinctions and degrees to be reckoned with? And among the liturgies themselves, are there such distinctions and degrees? And if so, what will be the criterion for determining such distinctions and degrees?

To pose these and similar questions in connection with the Fathers is equivalent to asking whether and to what extent and with what success general methodological rules were made for determining the theological au-

---

[89] For the recourse to the liturgy in St. John Damascene, see B. Studer, *Die theologische Arbeitsweise des Johannes von Damaskus*, Ettal 1956, pp. 55-75, especially pp. 62 and 70.

[90] Elipandus and Felix of Urgel, to support their adoptionist theory, appealed to some texts of the Mozarabic liturgy. The Council of Frankfurt of 794 refuted this opinion. See above, p. 510.

[91] The principal liturgical points brought up by this polemic are: the insertion of the *filioque* in the so-called Nicene-Constantinopolitan Creed, which, in the West, began to be sung in the Mass in the sixth century; the liceity of the long series of liturgical usages which Caerularius and the Greek controversialists of the era reproved in the Western Church, especially the use of unleavened bread. (See M. Jugie, *Theologia dogmatica christianorum orientalium*, Vol I, Paris 1926, pp. 268 ff, 311 ff; M. Gordillo, *Compendium theologiae orientalis*, 2nd edition, Rome 1950, p. 168). The question of the epiclesis also had an important part

in this controversy. (See M. Gordillo, *op. cit.*, pp. 174 ff). And in general, for all the questions disputed between Catholics and Photians (including the primacy of the Roman Pontiff, the Immaculate Conception, and the various questions touching on the sacraments and the Last Things), the recourse to the authority of the liturgy has always been quite frequent by both parties even up to recent times.

[92] See, for example, Cyril of Jerusalem, *Catechetical Lectures* 23 (*Mystogogic* 5), 9-10 (Jurgens, nos. 852-853); Epiphanius, *Haer.* 75, 8-9 (PG 42, cols. 513 B; 516 A-B); Chrysostom, *In ep. 1 Cor. hom.* 41, 5 (PG 61, col. 361); *In ep. ad Philem. hom.* 3, 4 (PG 62, cols. 203 ff); *In Act. hom.* 21, 4 (PG 60, col. 170); Eustathius of Constantinople (sixth cent.), *Sermo in eos qui dicunt animos humanos . . .* (PG 80, cols. 319-380); St. Augustine, *De haer.* 53; *Sermo* 172, 2, 2; *Enchiridion* 110, 29; *De cura pro mortuis gerenda* 3; 6.

thority of the liturgy. Such an inquiry would be similar to seeking in the Fathers those general methodological rules governing the relations between faith and liturgy which we have tried to determine theoretically in chapter sixteen.

It is clear, however, that the precise determination of such rules presupposes a detailed elaboration of the great concepts which constitute the basis of theological criteriology, as, for example, if we may enumerate some: the relations between magisterium and revelation, between magisterium and Scripture, between magisterium and tradition; the distinction between the different degrees of authority in which the magisterium proposes anything; the distinction between matters of faith and morals and matters not of faith and morals; the determination of the authentic organs of the magisterium; the position of the individual bishops and the special position of the Roman Church and of the Bishop of Rome in this magisterium; the fact and the implications of the evolution of dogmas and of doctrines. It means, in a word, that to seek out with what mentality the Fathers had recourse to the authority of the liturgy implies necessarily to touch upon the whole question of theological criteriology.

An immediate observation is that we must not expect to find in the patristic period a clear and complete solution of the question, but rather successive approaches and various shadings, sometimes of considerable difference. The second is that the question of the nature of the authority of the liturgy in the patristic period will be intimately associated with the concept of tradition because, as is known, it is in the framework of this concept that the Fathers, in practice, unfold what they elaborate by means of theological methodology and criteriology.

Now "tradition" for the Fathers can have a very general meaning to indicate, objectively speaking, everything salutary that the living Church of every age proposes to the faithful: teachings, precepts, customs; and whatever they regard as tradition is so regarded precisely because the Church has received it from Christ by means of the Apostles and in virtue of the apostolic succession which connects it with them; further, in virtue of the infallible assistance of the Spirit, the Church has preserved it, and transmits it faithfully.[93] It is from this stance that the patristic age worked out what it proposed about the question of the authority of the liturgy. The liturgy has authority because it forms part of tradition objectively considered. Now tradition, in the patristic concept, involves these elements: Church, Apostles, apostolic succession, Holy Spirit. But I do not say that when the authority of the liturgy was based on tradition, the Fathers were thinking in an equally clear way about each of these elements; nor that they made a profound analysis of them and determined to what extent the individual details of the liturgy

[93] See A. Deneffe, *Der Traditionsbegriffe*, Münster i, W. 1931.

which obligate the Church are derived from the Apostles or are the fruit of the assistance of the Holy Spirit.

The method of justifying the authority of the liturgy in the general framework of the concept of tradition which, in the documents that have come down to us, makes its first historical appearance already in the patristic age and remains a fundamental idea throughout that era, is that method which bases the authority of the liturgy on the fact that it is a "good" of the Church received from the Apostles — in other words, on its apostolicity.

This frame of mind which tended to trace back to the Apostles, in a general way and not otherwise determined, the liturgical and disciplinary practice of the Church undocumented by the Scriptures is very ancient. We find it demonstrated already by the pseudo-apostolic titles and actual antiquity of the first literature of liturgical interest, such as the *Didache* or *Teaching of the Twelve Apostles*, the *Apostolic Tradition* of Hippolytus, the *Didascalia of the Apostles*, the *Apostolic Constitutions*.[94]

At any rate, when, in the documents which we have, the author begins to justify explicitly the authority of a specific liturgical practice not indicated in the Scriptures, he has recourse to its apostolicity, demonstrated, in its turn, by the universality of its observance in the Church. If a liturgical practice is commonly observed in the churches, the conclusion is drawn, without further distinctions, that it is of apostolic origin and hence has the very authority of the Apostles. This is done by Tertullian,[95] Origen,[96] Basil,[97] Augustine,[98] and the author of the *Indiculus*.[99]

In some circumstances observations were made which, if deepened, could have introduced important distinctions and shadings into the aforesaid concept. But this deepening, with respect to the liturgy, did not take place. Thus, St. Irenaeus, when he has to oppose the gnostic pretense of a secret apostolic tradition, appeals to the unanimity and universality of the faith in the various Christian Churches as proof of the true apostolic tradition that they really possess. The lack of unanimity and of universality among the heretics demonstrates, in his view, the non-apostolicity of their doctrines; but when it is a

---

[94] If the reality of the evolution of ecclesiastical discipline and practice is admitted, and hence if it is supposed that there is no desire to trace back *directly* to the Apostles all the particular disciplinary and liturgical practices in use in the Church, this mentality is perfectly justified, inasmuch as it wants to assert that the whole structure of the life of the Church goes back to the Apostles, directly or indirectly, immediately or mediately. Cappelle, *op. cit.*, pp. 10 ff., rightly notes that in the first three works cited above the pseudo-apostolic title does not seem to imply anything, in the mind of their authors, except the general persuasion of the apostolic origin of the life of the Church in general and that the gimmick of those titles seems to have been only a literary genre. For the *Apostolic Constitutions*, on the other hand, Capelle thinks that it is a question of a real fraud properly so called.

[95] *De corona* 3 and 4.

[96] *In Num. hom.* 5, 1, ed. Baehrens, p. 26.

[97] *De Spiritu Sancto*, ch. 25-27.

[98] For example, *De baptismo* 2, 12, 7; 4, 31, 24.

[99] Dz 246 (139); "Let us look to the *sacramenta* of the priestly supplications, which, handed down from the Apostles, are uniformly celebrated in the whole world and in every Catholic church." See also Dz 247 (140).

matter of determining a sure criterion in the questions or practices involving the faith and for which unanimity does not exist among the Christian Churches themselves, he appeals to the special authority of the Church of Rome, based on a special title of apostolicity of its own; and he knows very well that for practices which are also liturgical and in which the faith is not involved, as in that of the date of the celebration of Easter, the lack of unanimity among the Christian Churches is of no consequence; and that, in fact, different practices can sometimes appeal equally to different apostolic traditions.[100]

Also in the discussion between St. Cyprian and Pope St. Stephen on the validity of the baptism of heretics and on the necessity or not of rebaptizing them if they turn to the true Church, lacking unanimity of liturgical practice among the Christian Churches, it was necessary to have recourse to another criterion to determine what was the true apostolic tradition in this connection. It is known that Pope Stephen once more sees this criterion in the special authority and apostolicity of the Church of Rome,[101] while St. Cyprian ends up by taking refuge in the charismatic criterion of the inspiration which every bishop receives directly from the Holy Spirit.[102]

On the question of the ultimate criteria of the Catholic faith, the importance of the living presence of the Holy Spirit in the Church was also observed,[103] but it does not seem that this observation was explicitly related to the question of the authority of the liturgy.

Cyprian[104] and Augustine,[105] on the other hand, in relation to the same question, hinted at the argument of the holiness of the Church, which holiness guarantees that what she does and says in the liturgy are not empty games or vain things.

There was also insistence sometimes on the possibility that different Churches might legitimately follow different practices in questions which do

[100] See, for example, *Adv. haer.* 3, 3, 1 (Jurgens, no. 209); 3, 3, 2 (Jurgens, no. 210); 3, 4, 1 (Jurgens, no. 213); 4, 26, 2 (Jurgens, no. 237); 5, 20, 1 (Jurgens, no. 257). The texts of Irenaeus on the special authority of the Church of Rome are well known. For the position of Irenaeus in the question of the date of Easter, see Eusebius, *Hist. eccl.* 5, 24, 11-18 (Jurgens, no. 265).

[101] See Cyprian, *Letter to Pompey of Sabrat* 74, 1 (Jurgens, no. 601a); and Firmilian of Caesarea, *Letter to Cyprian (apud Cypr.)* 75, 16-17 (Jurgens, nos. 602-602a).

[102] For Cyprian the divine tradition from the Apostles remains always the ultimate criterion; but in case of disagreement, in order to recognize what is the true tradition of the Apostles, he appeals to the Holy Spirit, who guides every bishop. This holds, be it noted well,

only for the cases in which unanimity does not exist among the Churches; for if unanimity exists, this for Cyprian is a sign of the presence of the Spirit and therefore of the true tradition. See Cyprian, *Letter of Cyprian in Council with Thirty-Six Other Bishops, to Certain Clergy and Laity of Spain* 67 (68), 5 (Jurgens, no. 588).

[103] Especially Irenaeus, *Adv. haer.* 3, 24, 1 (Jurgens, no. 226). Also Tertullian, *The Demurrer against the Heretics* 28, 1 (Jurgens, no. 295).

[104] See in this connection the conclusion of Federer, *op. cit.*, p. 74.

[105] Augustine is very insistent on the fact that what the Church does cannot be a vain or false jest. See, for example, *De pecc. meritis* 1, 63; *Epist.* 217, 1-7.

not affect the unity of the faith,[106] an observation which could have led to the clear distinction, among liturgical practices common to all the Churches, of practices which involve a doctrine of faith from those which do not. Moreover, the common practice, followed broadly in all the Churches until the fifth and sixth centuries, of introducing into the liturgy new compositions and new rites, even in matters which were very important and which at first sight could have seemed untouchable — as in the very anaphora of the Mass and, to a certain extent, in the rites of Christian initiation — might, upon theological reflection, have made apparent, in a manner more clearly and insistently than actually happened, the fact of the historical evolution of the liturgy and the principle of the liceity of such evolution and adaptation according to circumstances and without detriment to the faith. In fact, however, this evolutionary process, theoretically speaking, was only glimpsed exceptionally and in a hazy way, for example, by St. Basil,[107] rather than being clearly observed by the majority of theologians.

Likewise, in patristic antiquity, there are found only a few hints at a concept, which has great importance for the question of the authority of the individual parts of the liturgy, viz., the concept of a true evolution of dogmas themselves after the death of the Apostles, an evolution which, without being transformist, is still something more than a mere variant in that it presents an equivalent formulation explicitly and clearly proposed since the apostolic age.[108]

All in all, then, we must acknowledge that in the patristic age the authority of the liturgy was recognized commonly and from the very beginning for deciding questions in doubt or disputed; and that, actually, in the doctrinal polemics, a not unimportant recourse was had to it. But as far as the reflective elaboration of rules was concerned which would permit the determining of this authority in particular cases, and which would provide the means to a theological explanation of its nature, it seems that we must admit that the situation still remained one of general observations associating this authority with the authority of the Church, which, in its turn, was based on the Apostles; there was little concern about continuing the analysis of the concept or about its application to the liturgy in general and to its individual parts, historical or contemporary.

The preceding conclusion leads us to affirm once more that, in the theological reflection of the patristic age about the liturgy, the question of its authority for deciding disputed questions does not at all occupy the first place, and it

---

[106] Irenaeus on the question of Easter (see Eusebius, *Hist. eccl.* 5, 24, 11-18 [Jurgens, no. 265]). Also Firmilian of Caesarea, *Letter to Cyprian (apud Cypr.)* 75, 6.

[107] In the question of the new doxology introduced by him: *De Spiritu Sancto* 25-27.

[108] As affirmations of the fact of the evolu-

tion of dogma we may cite Origen, *The Fundamental Doctrines* 1, Preface, 3 (Jurgens, no. 444); St. Gregory of Nazianz, *Oratio* 32, 24; St. Augustine, *Sermo* 294, 4; *De civitate Dei* 16, 2; *De baptismo* 2, 4, 5; *Contra Iul.* 1, 6, 22; *Enar. in Ps.* 52, 22; *De praedest. sanct.* 14.

is not principally in this point that the wealth of the liturgical theology of the Fathers consists. This wealth consists rather in the irenic exposition which they make to the faithful of the intrinsic theological content which the liturgy has for the believer, who, having overcome, or never having experienced, doubts or disputes, accepts peacefully as included in the sources of revelation that which the Church proposes, and desires only to contemplate its content and to conform his life better to it. This wealth, as we have demonstrated, is wholly centered about the idea of *mystérion, mysterium, sacramentum*. For a knowledge of it, we must have recourse not as much to the polemic treatises of the Fathers as to their mystagogic literature properly so called, to their explanations of the liturgy in a more ample sense, and to their homilies on the liturgical year; furthermore, we must have the courage to come face to face with an understanding of what seems to many today to be their allegorical lucubrations on worship.

5. Theology as Gnosis in Patristic Thinking — Positive Aspects and Negative Aspects

Having arrived at this point, we may ask *why* the state of the facts involving theological liturgy is precisely such as it is in the Fathers. When the concern was with finding the ultimate reason which explained the actual position of the liturgy in the positive-scholastic syntheses and in that of St. Thomas, it was necessary to have recourse to that which was their way of conceiving theology, in other words, the purpose for which they pursued it. In like manner, to understand the ultimate reason why in the theology of the Fathers the liturgy figures in the aforesaid way and perspective, we must go back to that which was their theological ideal.

The theological ideal of St. Thomas was determined by his interest in the *entitative* order of things, in other words, by the Aristotelian ideal of *essences*, with the presupposition that the empirical sciences and, in particular, history, are not true and proper sciences. The positive-scholastic ideal added to the process and heavily accented historical-apologetical demonstration from the sources. The patristic ideal in the expositive and not directly polemical efforts was, on the other hand, *gnôsis*, or, in Latin, *sapientia*: higher knowledge, or deeper wisdom.

Origin and nature of the theological ideal of gnosis

Without entering into details on the *gnosis* concept, may it suffice to hint at its principal characteristics. Its origin is the biblical ideal expressed in the phrase "*knowledge of God*," *da'ath Yahweh, gnôsis toû theoû*, or simply *knowledge, da'ath, gnôsis*. The concern is not at all with mere conceptual knowledge of God, of the world, and of life, but with a religious knowledge, implying a general attitude of one's whole being and above all of the will and the affections, and hence of all one's moral activity. In *da'ath Yahweh* or *gnôsis toû theoû*, the love of God, the knowledge of God, the fear and reverence of God, the observance of His commandments, wisdom, are inseparable. It is therefore an all-embracing spirit of knowledge and of effective love, in which, according to the Hebrew mentality, we are not concerned with distinguishing and analyzing in a quasi-philosophical frame of mind the various faculties and their various acts.

Man cannot attain *gnôsis* or *knowledge of God* without revelation, which is the supreme manifestation of the gratuitous benevolence and love of God for men. As St. Paul will say later, continuing exactly the mind-set of the Old Testament, man could not know God if God had not first known man.[109] It is for this reason that the Scriptures constitute the book of the knowledge of God, because in them man, through the intervention of God in the history of the world, can see and experience how and how much God has known and does know man, and hence know the religious value of all things and how man can and should know God. The result is that *da'ath Yahweh, gnôsis toû theoû, meditation* and *penetration* of the sacred history in the Scriptures are intimately united. The assiduous meditation and penetration of sacred salvation history in the Scriptures is for man the eminent source of *gnôsis*.

It now seems more and more probable that the Hellenistic *gnôsis*, apart from the conception of a personal and transcendent God which, together with all the consequences that this implies, marks the profound divergence between the Hellenistic and the Hebrew world, demonstrates not only a notable coincidence of ideals with the Jewish *gnôsis*, but also, for an essential part, a historical derivation from it or from a common source.[110]

At any rate, when, in the subapostolic age, the first notable movement of greater deepening of the simple faith began among Christians, their ideal was naturally formulated in terms of *gnôsis* which indicated, whether in the Jewish biblical tradition or in the Hellenistic environment of the age, higher religious knowledge, not of a purely conceptual order, but a complex psychological state or an order volitional and affective at the same time, implying moral preparation and purification in the subject who tended to such heights as to the supreme purpose of life. Besides the general common points, this ideal of *gnôsis* had its own characteristics among Christians, which distinguished it from the parallel non-Christian movements with which we generally associate the term *gnôsis* or gnosticism today, and also its own various nuances, tendencies, and successive developments.

---

[109] See Gal. 4:9. St. Paul, in Eph. 1:1-9 and 2:41-10, and St. John, in 1 John 4:10-19, say, with similar mentality, that the love of man for God presupposes the love of God for man. See J. Dupont, *Gnosis. La connaissance religieuse dans les épîtres de S. Paul,* Louvain 1949, pp. 51 ff.

[110] See E. Peterson, "*Gnosi,*" in *Enciclopedia cattolica,* Vol. 6 (1951), col. 879 ff. Or better still, J. Dupont, *op. cit.,* cols. 347-367. The Dead Sea scrolls are confirmatory.

Properties of the *gnôsis* were the centering of the theoretical and practical vision of the world in Christ and in the Christian realities; and the rule of faith or of the points clearly and explicitly proposed by the ecclesiastical preaching, as indispensable basis and inescapable norm of every deepening of true *gnôsis*. Common between Christian *gnôsis* and *gnôsis* of Jewish tradition was its intimate connection with the deeper knowledge of the sacred salvation history of God's interventions in the world as it is taught in the Scriptures.

There were nuances, diverse tendencies, and successive developments in conceiving the ideal of *gnôsis* among the Christians themselves by reason of the fact that some, such as Clement of Rome, the Pseudo-Barnabas, and the author of the *Epistle to Diognetus*, under the more properly Jewish influence of the ideal of the *gnôsis*, conceived this above all as interpretation of the Scriptures, in a Christic and Christian sense, be it well understood, especially by means of a broad typological and allegorical interpretation of the Old Testament.

Starting with the Apologetes of the second century, there began to be included in the Christian gnostic ideal a certain recourse to Hellenistic philosophy, thus accentuating the conceptual aspect of the deepening of the faith toward which they were attempting to reach out. Against this tendency there was the lively reaction of St. Irenaeus, who, concerned with the excesses to which the actually heretical and syncretistic *gnôsis* had led, recalled forcefully the rule of faith and of ecclesiastical preaching as the unavoidable norm of any *true gnôsis*, and was not far from fearing any use of the speculations of the Hellenistic philosophical type in the true Christian *gnôsis*.

But this over-severe position, which tended to deprive the true *gnôsis* of the aid which it could derive from a right use of philosophy, was overcome by St. Clement of Alexandria and especially by Origen. They were wholly intent on the construction of a great Christian gnostic system in which the cenceptual philosophical elaboration on the basis of the rule of faith and of ecclesiastical preaching was put to the service of that ultimate end of an order not only conceptual but also volitional and affective, and, we would say today, also mystical, at least in the broad sense, as act and state of adherence of man to God, an adherence which includes love and enjoyment.

Starting with the fourth century, the expositive irenic theological ideal in the East remains substantially that of Origen, but corrected, especially of those imperfections which, in Origen's construction, are derived from the use of a series of philosophical concepts taken from the Hellenistic environment and fundamentally ill-adapted to that end to which Origen himself wanted to make them serve. Moreover, the great dogmatic struggles from the fourth to the eighth centuries gave the theological production of that era a strongly polemical preponderance, while the aspect of the expositive irenic and therefore gnostic ideal was kept alive principally in the homiletic, ascetic, and liturgical literature.

In the West the gnostic ideal of theology shone principally in St. Augustine, and through him it continued predominant in later authors until the birth of scholasticism. It is the Augustinian *sapientia* as the goal to which tends, in the believer, every inquiry into and deepening of the faith as enjoyable understanding of God, an understanding which is mystical in tendency, even as the term mystical is understood today.

In this ideal of theology as *gnôsis*, two things must be carefully pointed out in view of the aim of our present study.

The mystic and therefore experiential aspect belongs, in the mind of the ancients, to the ideal of the *gnôsis* as its supreme crowning, *intrinsically*, by reason of its own nature inasmuch as it is higher religious "knowledge" *sui generis* of God and of other things in their hierarchy of religious values. The ancients did not know the Aristotelian-scholastic distinction of the *finis operis* — "end of the work" — and the *finis operantis* — "end of the agent"; but once this distinction is admitted, it must be said that, for them, the mystical-fruitive aspect belongs to the gnosis *ex fine operis* and not only *ex fine operantis*, and that the purely conceptual knowledge in the complexus of the gnosis is not, to say it once more with a later scholastic expression, *sui gratia* (i.e., for its own sake), but *alterius gratia* (i.e., for the sake of another), that is, in view of that higher "knowledge" which is the sapiential intellect of St. Augustine.

Second observation: as in the Jewish tradition, so also commonly in the Christian tradition of *gnôsis*, not only is *gnôsis* intimately connected with meditation upon Scripture and the interpretation thereof, and hence essentially scripturistic; but moreover, in the Scriptures themselves it considers above all the aspect of the sacred history of God's interventions in the world and of man's response to God, which is concretized principally in the journey or return of the soul to God, the whole considered in its profound unity. The *gnôsis* of the Pseudo-Dionysius and the tradition dependent upon him is probably the one which tends more to dissociate itself from this point of view by its more distinctly metaphysical character, although it is not of the Aristotelian tradition but of the neo-Platonic.

How the liturgy enters into the picture of theology as gnosis: merits and defects

This brief glance at the ideal of theology as *gnôsis* in the patristic age helps us, I think, to understand the place which the liturgy occupies in theology, and the merits and defects of the position of the Fathers in this field. To begin with, in theology as *gnôsis*, the expositive irenic value of the truth considered is always on the first level of concern, since *gnôsis* tends essentially and intrinsically to actuate in the believer himself a certain practical psychological state which is a complexus embracing both cognitive and affective elements at the same time. The things considered there will be so, therefore, primarily in relation to the value they have for the believer himself toward the aforesaid end, which is an end more contemplative than defensive, more intuitive than simply conceptual. It is for this reason that theology as *gnôsis* will be interested in the liturgy above all and primarily for its positive irenic value. In this point the position of the Fathers coincides with that of St. Thomas and differs from that of the positive-scholastics.

In the second place, the consideration of reality as *mystérion* is connaturally an essential point of every *gnôsis* and hence of theology as *gnôsis*. In fact, in the *gnôsis* of more distinctly Jewish tradition, an essential object of consideration is the sacred history of God's interventions in the world and of man's response to these interventions, all things which, from the properly Christian point of view, are centered in Christ. But this constitutes precisely the essential nucleus of the concept of *mystérion* in St. Paul and then in the greater part of the whole later theological tradition, in which the principal object of the *mystérion* remains always sacred history in its unity and the reciprocal correspondence of its various phases.

It is true that in the concept of the *mystérion* as represented in the thought of the Pseudo-Dionysius and of the authors dependent upon him, sacred history passes somewhat to the second level and a more metaphysical view of things comes to the fore. But, as we have said, in the Pseudo-Dionysian tradition it is not a question of a metaphysical view of the Aristotelian type, but rather of the neo-Platonic type; of a type, therefore, in which there is strongly on the first level a vision of the world centered on the concepts of symbol, image, participation, etc. Now, as we know, this aspect too is one of the essential characteristics of the concept of *mystérion*. The result will be that in theology conceived as *gnôsis*, the interest which will bear on the liturgy will be connaturally centered in its value as *mystérion*, as actually happens in patristic theology.

But the concept of theology as *gnôsis*, as it is applied in the patristic age, has also, objectively speaking, its undeniable defects. The principal defect seems to consist in the fact that there remains undetermined and actually missing the role which belongs, in the total gnostic theological complexus, to the properly scientific process, as it was particularly deepened, even if not carried to perfection, by St. Thomas on the Aristotelian bases of the concept of science. I mean that, comparing the ideal of theology as *gnôsis* as it was practiced in the patristic age to the ideal of theology as science as it was developed by St. Thomas, we see that in the former this scientific process, considered in itself, remains notably lacking.

Aside from the legitimacy, the utility, and under a certain aspect, even the necessity of a theology conceived as pure and simple science, I still would not want to accuse the patristic ideal of theology of not having been an ideal solely and purely scientific, in the sense, for example, of St. Thomas, or of having ordered the purely scientific ideal to something extra-scientific or supra-scientific. I would accuse it only of having been, objectively speaking, still rather imperfect in that scientific process which it did use and which it did order to a further end.

In fact, I do not see how anyone can question the legitimacy of the patristic ideal of the deepening of the faith culminating in the actuation, not purely conceptual, but intuitive and volitional-affective, and, to this same purpose, having recourse also to the conceptual inquiry not as an end in itself, but by ordering it precisely as a part in the whole to that higher end. Otherwise, from the moment that recourse is had to conceptual inquiry of the scientific type, it becomes indispensable that this, before being used and ordered to an end which differs from itself and surpasses it, be actuated in the most perfect way possible and according to the rules imposed by its nature.

But it is precisely in this that the patristic theology, objectively speaking, remains still imperfect, compared, for example, to that which was later realized in this field by St. Thomas. The Aristotelian distinction of the *finis operis* and the *finis operantis* is, objectively, indispensable because, making it understood that the scientific process can be ordered to something different from itself not by the end of the work but by the end of the agent, it recalls what are the requirements of the scientific process considered in itself and what is required for being perfect in itself before being used for another purpose.

This imperfection in the patristic theology is manifested principally in two respects.

The scientific entitative analysis of the deposit of faith, in other words, the philosophical aspect and the philosophical bases implied in it, still remains generally rather imperfect. The deepening of this aspect of the faith cannot be realized without the instrument of an elaborated Christian philosophy which, by its intrinsic truth, is unitary and coincides with the profound exigencies, whether explicit or implicit, of the faith itself. Now, in the patristic *gnôsis*, the philosophical instrument, despite the notable advances realized even in this field by the Fathers, is, after all, deficient. In philosophy the Fathers are eclectic and proceed more by occasional soundings than with a systematic method.

Moreover, concepts of the neo-Platonic type predominate in their philosophical eclecticism. For the most part, they adhered to these concepts not only because the whole tendency of the age was in that direction, but also by reason of the religious afflatus which pervades them and which, at first sight, might seem quite conformed to the Christian spirit, but whose roots, logically considered, are instead deeply contrary thereto. The Fathers avoided the difficulty sometimes by interpreting neo-Platonsim in a Christian sense, against the logic of its inmost nature, and sometimes by not following it to its logical consequences.[111] At any rate, they never arrived at the systematic working out of a Christian philosophy which, by responding to the intrinsic truth of things, would be a valid instrument in the probing of the questions of an ontological order which the faith posits.

A further consequence was that the systematic working out and ordering of theological knowledge remained always imperfect in the patristic age. It remained substantially in the status of monographs and essays occasioned and limited more by the contingent circumstances of the pastoral art and of the defense of the faith than by the desire to work out in an integral and ordered manner theological knowledge in itself, according to its intrinsic requirements and under all its aspects.

These two defects are reflected also in the use of the liturgy in the theology of the Fathers, above all in the fact that this use is not systematically extended to the treatment of all the theological questions in which it could and should have its role. The effort of theological synthesis being deficient, the place which the liturgy can and should occupy in such a synthesis does not appear sufficient. In the patristic age the theology of the liturgy is exhausted in monographs.

The defects are reflected, in the second place, by the fact that the foundations of a rather philosophical order which are at the basis of the liturgy itself are not much worked out. Exception must be made of St. Augustine, however, in whom, more than in all the other Fathers, are found precious observations in this field which will later be widely used by St. Thomas, as, for instance, on the concept of sign, of image, of participation, of worship, and of sacrifice.

[111] For this point see, for example, R. Arnou, *cath.*, Vol. 12/2 (1935), pp. 2258 ff. *"Platonisme des Pères,"* in the *Dict. de théol.*

20 SUGGESTIONS FOR THE SYSTEMATIC INCLUSION OF THE LITURGICAL-THEOLOGICAL ASPECT IN THE INDIVIDUAL QUESTIONS OF GENERAL SYNTHETIC THEOLOGY

The preceding review of the position which the liturgy occupies in the various historical types of theology should naturally be crowned with at least a roughcast positive solution of the question of how to assimilate organically into the general theological synthesis the material of theological value included in the liturgy.

Since theoretically, by the very nature of things, and historically, as we have tried to show in the preceding chapters, the solution is influenced in an essential way by one's concept of theology, it is necessary to start out from the concept of theology in order to see how the liturgical aspect of the deepening of the faith can be profitably employed in the individual treatises of general synthetic theology. At the end we shall make some observations on the question of the liturgy in the program of teaching.

1. Theoretical Notes on the Concept of Theology

In the preceding chapters I have endeavored to characterize the three major ways in which the ideal of theology was concretized throughout the history of Christian thought: theology as gnosis or wisdom in the patristic period; theology as science of the entitative aspect of revelation with the scholastics and especially in St. Thomas; theology primarily as apologetic-historical demonstration of the sources and secondarily as illustration of the entitative aspect of the faith with the positive-scholastics.

The question of the attitude to be adopted toward these three types of theology and of the corrections and improvements to be brought to them is, at bottom, at the center of the whole turmoil which troubles theology today. It can be said that theology is in search of a theological ideal of its own, at least in the sense that the need is felt of making certain corrections and bringing certain improvements to that which the previous theological traditions have handed down to us in this field. There is taking place today in the history of theology something like what happened in the second and third centuries, when the ideal of theology as gnosis-wisdom was worked out; in the eleventh to thirteenth centuries, when the ideal of theology was fixed as entitative science of the revealed; and in the fifteenth to seventeenth centuries, when the positive-scholastic ideal of theology was formed. Keeping to the indispensable and skeletal essentials and without entering into too technical details, reserved for another work, it seems to me that the following observations in this connection will suffice for our purpose.

The concept of theology as science must be taken as basis

First of all, it is indispensable to take as basis the ideal of theology as science. Here we stand with St. Thomas and the positive-scholastics and depart, in a certain sense, from the patristic concept of theology as gnosis. In a certain sense, I say, for, as we have indicated above, there can be no doubt about the legitimacy and, under certain aspects and in certain circumstances, even the utility and the necessity of conceiving the deepening of the faith in such a way as to make the whole process converge on the precise aim of an actuation of the subject which is not purely conceptual but intuitive and practical-affective, and to direct the conceptual effort itself to this actuation.

But the legitimacy of such a process, which is gnosis itself, takes nothing away from the legitimacy, the utility and, under a certain aspect, the necessity of a deepening of the faith of an essentially conceptual type, which will be a conceptual, higher, mediate, certain, and evident knowledge of this faith; and this is precisely what is understood by scientific knowledge. In fact, the distinction of the end of the work and the end of the agent is indisputable: the end of the work being the intrinsic and essential end of the work itself, as the intrinsic and essential end of the work of painting is to make pictures and nothing else but this; while the end of the agent is an end extrinsic and accidental to the work itself, which the agent can decide in conformity with his talent, as the painter can exercise his painting ability with the end of acquiring fame or simply for gain. Such being the state of affairs, it is a matter of necessity to conclude that the end of the work of the scientific process is nothing more nor less than to gain conceptual knowledge in a way that is mediate, certain, and evident.

This means that if anyone directs conceptual scientific knowledge to a different end, such as that of an intuitive and practical-affective actuation of the subject, as happens precisely in the gnosis, this end will accord with the scientific process in view of the end of the agent and not simply by reason of the end of the work itself. The result is that the process of gnosis, as the Fathers understood it, is, in its totality, from the point of view of philosophical analysis, a process of a mixed nature, composed of a scientific aspect and an extrascientific aspect. But the mixed genus supposes the pure genus, as plurality supposes unity. Hence the process of gnosis itself, in order to be attained to in the most perfect way possible, supposes a development as perfect as possible of the scientific process in itself. Thus theology as gnosis not only is not prejudicial in any way to the legitimacy, the utility, and the necessity of theology conceived as pure science, but rather demands it and supposes it.

Aside, then, from the legitimacy, the utility, or even the necessity of a theology as gnosis, the scholastics, and St. Thomas above all, starting out from the Aristotelian bases of the concept of science, were guided by a sure instinct when, to improve the inheritance of patristic theology, they set about developing and technically perfecting a theology as science. This alone can give, among other things, a systematic consistency to the deepening of the faith. It is for this reason that after the scholastics, and above all St. Thomas, had vindicated this aspect of things, notwithstanding the criticisms which had been and still are directed at their theology, no theologian who proposes as his end the general systematic synthesis of theological knowledge has ever been able to renounce the point of view of theology as science. Whoever, therefore, wants to determine the place of the liturgy in the general theological synthesis, must be clearly aware that his concern is with determining the relations between liturgy and theology conceived as science.

Not only the inquiry from the entitative aspect but also the inquiry from the empirical-historical aspect, having scientific value by itself, must be included as an integral part in theology as science

But this does not mean at all that the ideal of theology must be purely and simply that of St. Thomas or of the positive-scholastics, by reason of the fact that both set out from the concept of theology as science. We know that for Aristotle and for the scholastics, science properly so called is only philosophy, especially metaphysics; mathematics, especially geometry; and, if anything more, physical philosophy; in other words, science, strictly speaking, is only deductive science. Induction was indeed admitted, but, theoretically speaking, only as a prescientific moment and simply preparatory for deductive science, considered the only true science.

For them the empirical inductive process cannot have its own scientific value. History in particular, and hence philology and criticism, are not sciences properly speaking. I am not saying that such a position is necessarily connected with the basic principles of the concept of science posited by Aristotle and rightly accepted by St. Thomas. Indeed, I hold that those principles do not at all imply such a consequence. But Aristotle and the scholastics did not think in this latter way, or at least they did not see the thing clearly.

A consequence of this was above all the despotic predominance of the deductive ideal, and in fact of the philosophical, this is, ontological, entitative ideal in the whole field of scientific research. This was already verified to some extent in Aristotle himself, notwithstanding the experimental and empirical tendency to which, in practice, his inmost nature prompted him, but especially and with great clamor, in a good part of his medieval disciples, for whom it will suffice only to look at their deductive physics and astronomy. The result was a notable deficiency in their grasping, in actual reality, of the more individual, concrete, empirical, and temporal aspect.

In fact, history and the empirical sciences, with their essentially inductive method, have precisely the specific mission of grasping this aspect more profoundly than philosophy can, which is limited to the ontological and hence universal and timeless aspect of being; and yet, without philosophy, the empirical and historical sciences themselves cannot grasp the individual as such, this being the direct object of the senses and not of intellectual knowledge.

This state of affairs with regard to the ideal of science had its repercussions in the concrete way in which the scholastics and St. Thomas himself actuated their ideal of theology. Thus there was not only an ideal of theology as science, but an ideal of theology as ontological or entitative science, with a method not only essentially but almost exclusively deductive, at least in the sense that, in the theological field also, induction — and hence the study of the Scriptures, of tradition, of the magisterium, of the liturgy — is not considered as having scientific value in itself, but only prescientific and therefore pretheological value, preparatory to deduction of an entitative order.

From this there follows another consequence. If it is to fulfill solely a prescientific function preparatory to deduction, the inductive process for the most part need not be very profound and accurate. The necessary basis for theological deductions of an entitative order is for the most part easily and quickly obtained with even a rather superficial consideration of the Scriptures, of tradition, or of the teaching of the magisterium. Hence in theology considered as an entitative science, the elaboration of the individual, empirical, and temporal aspect of the things of faith remains notably deficient, whereas it could have been obtained much more accurately and profoundly by means of the properly scientific application of the empirical and historical method. Theology and its method are thus assimilated in an exaggerated way to philosophy, especially to metaphysics and its method, and so the ontological and timeless aspect of the faith is taken too exclusively into consideration, to the detriment of its more concrete, empirical, individual, and temporal aspect.

This fact has great importance for the organic and systematic assimilation of the liturgy into the general theological synthesis. For the liturgy, like Scripture, tradition, and the magisterium, depends in great part on the concrete, empirical, and temporal aspect of the faith. Consequently, and by the same token, the liturgy is scientifically knowable only through the empirical, philological, critical, historical method, considered not as a simply prescientific phase, preparatory to the deductive method, but as a scientific method in itself, applied to the liturgical rites, formulas, and objects.

Let us consider the sallies made in the second part of this book into a series of themes like the Trinity in the liturgy; Christ in the liturgy; the liturgy and the infrahuman world; the liturgy, the angels, and the devils; the liturgy and man; the liturgy and the Church. It is easy, I think, to understand that the conclusions reached there are, first of all, of properly theological value, inasmuch as they manifest in their own way a certain aspect of the faith, because they make it easier to understand certain aspects of it about the Trinity, Christ, the angels, etc. In the second place, these same results are not obtainable by a simply ontological-deductive way nor by simple induction considered only as a prescientific phase, preparatory to deduction of an ontological type, but only by an inductive historical method having properly scientific value already by itself. Whoever, therefore, denies the properly scientific value of the inductive method and of history, and asserts that only philosophy is science properly so called (and mathematics and philosophical physics, which have no special interest in theology), and that the scientific method properly so called is only the deductive method, if he is logically consistent, will not be able to assimilate organically into his general synthesis many theological values which the liturgy does in fact contain in abundance.

This, therefore, is the conclusion which must be drawn in the question which concerns us: the concept of theology as science must indeed be taken as basis, but science must not be limited to entitative science alone and its proper method limited to the deductive method alone; rather, science must be understood as embracing empirical-historical science as much as entitative science; the empirical-historical inductive method must be considered a scientific method just as much as the entitative method, and the inductive method must not be considered as simply a prescientific phase, preparatory to the deductive method.

The scientific process must be conceived as consisting of a double phase, not simply reducible one to the other, but complementing each other and contributing, both one and the other, to establishing together the integral scientific knowledge of any object: the empirical-inductive phase, proper to the empirical-historical sciences, and the ontological deductive phase, proper to philosophy. The theological science, therefore, must be conceived as a whole consisting of two integral moments: the empirical-historical inductive moment and the ontological properly deductive moment.[1]

The working out of the theological value of the liturgy in general synthetic theology enters in great part into the working out of the empirical-historical aspect of the datum of faith and hence into the first phase or moment of the integral method of theology as science. This first phase includes, among other things, the scientific working out of biblical thought under all the aspects which are of interest to theology concerning a determinate question; the scientific working out of the way in which, after the Apostles, the faith was and is: a) defended; b) made explicit; c) studied and explained by the Fathers and by theologians; d) proposed in a directly didactic way by the magisterium; e) lived by the whole Church in the encounter between God and man under the veil of the sacred sensible and efficacious signs of sanctification and worship. This last task is precisely the task of the scientific working out of the theological value of the liturgy by means of the empirical-historical method.

In all this I hold that we should not be doing anything more than carrying to conclusion the Aristotelian-Thomistic principles themselves of the concept of science and of its application to theology, broadening the too narrow way in which Aristotle himself and the scholastics had limited science to entitative (and mathematical) science and to the deductive method.

2. General Place of the Elaboration of the Liturgical Aspect in Theological Inquiry Thus Conceived

Differences of the positive-scholastic, scholastic, and patristic positions

A final review to distinguish our position from that of the positive-scholastics. Positive-scholasticism also starts from the point of view of theology as science and concerns itself with including in it the historical-critical aspect. But in this historical-critical aspect, positive-scholasticism gives an exaggerated predominance to the concern for the apologetic proof of the faith from the sources of Scripture and tradition. In Chapter 17 we explained at length how this takes place and why, objectively, it constitutes a defect which has significant consequences in the way in which positive-scholasticism has recourse to the sources of theology, including the liturgy.

---

[1] These two phases, which in the field of profane science constitute two specifically different kinds of sciences and of methods, in theology are only two moments or integral parts of a single science and a single method because both phases are made formally theological by the formal light, specifically unique, which formally unifies in itself that which in the profane field falls under specifically different sciences. See St. Thomas, *Summa*, I, q. 1, a. 3 ad 2.

In short, science, being simply a knowledge of the being of things — conceptual, mediate, certain, evident — controls its problematics, its systematization and, in general, all its requirements, primarily and essentially in view of the very being of things and not on the dispositions of the subject, which, with respect to being, are accidental and may vary infinitely according to the circumstances of time and place. It is for this reason that the irenic, contemplative function, simply expositive of the being of things as it is in itself in its wholeness, is necessarily primary in every science with respect to the defensive function, which, on the other hand, depends essentially also on the dispositions of the subject against which the defense is made. So it is in every science, and so too in theology as science.

In theological science, therefore, the simply contemplative function of the being of revealed things as it is in itself in its wholeness must be put in a primary position, as determining the whole process; and the defensive function against the objections of pure reason of the real or hypothetical adversary must be put only in a secondary position, subordinate to the first.

In this way of conceiving the ideal of theology, the liturgy is considered and investigated:

First: primarily in its theological value rather than in its historical, still less in its rubricist, value. In this the Fathers, the scholastics, the positive-scholastics, themselves are followed; while the position of the modern solely historical liturgists, not to say the historicist, and still more the position of the rubricist liturgists, is surpassed.

Second: the liturgy is investigated primarily in its simply irenic, expositive theological value, inasmuch as in the liturgy it is seen how the Church, under the veil of the sensible and efficacious signs of sanctification and worship, lived and lives every day every point of its faith as sacred history always in the making and as encounter in Christ between God and men. Therefore the liturgy is considered above all in its value of *mystérion, mysterium, sacramentum*. Here we find again the position of the Fathers, and somewhat of St. Thomas himself, and we distinguish it from the position of the positive-scholastic. In fact, the consideration of the liturgy as authority to prove against real or hypothetical objections that a specific doctrine is contained in the sources of revelation, in the aforesaid way of conceiving theology, is real but secondary.

Third: the liturgy is investigated not only in its entitative foundations by means of analyses of the philosophical type and by the deductive method, as St. Thomas in particular does very well, but also in its actual more concrete and temporal state, by means of the scientific use of history and related sciences and of the inductive method. This permits the discovery in the liturgy itself, under the veil of the sensible and efficacious signs of sanctification and of worship, of the supreme constants and, as it were, the supreme laws of the free economy of God in the world and of the return of man to God — in other words, of salvation history, in connection with every great question with which general synthetic theology is concerned. We have given examples of it in the second part of this book. In this point the position of St. Thomas is perfected and integrated, assimilating into theology as science the great vision of salvation history which constitutes the richness of liturgical theology in the patristic tradition.

Exposition

When the ideal of theology which has been suggested here is put into practice in the individual treatises of theology, the expositive scheme itself, and therefore that which strikes one at first glance in every type of theology, will differ not rarely, and even notably, from the patristic monography, from the scholastic scheme of the *quaestio* and *articulus*, and from that of the positive-scholastic *thesis*. The expositive scheme in every type of science and the outer garment, as it were, in which it presents itself at first sight tends naturally to become the precise instrument of the intrinsic ideal which is proper to it.

The irenic, expositive theological monography of the Fathers, with its strongly concrete, hortatory, and rhetorical flavor, serves well enough the ideal of theology as gnosis. The scholastic *quaestio* is a technically elaborated instrument of the ideal of theology as science with almost exclusive elaboration of the ontological and timeless aspect of the faith. The positive-scholastic "theses," in which the doctrine to be held is enunciated and which is followed by the *probatur* "from Scripture, from tradition, from theological reasoning," suits very well, on the other hand, the predominantly apologetical-historical ideal from the sources of the positive-scholastics.

What will be the tendencies which will be manifested in the expositive garment of the ideal of theology suggested above? Pursuing a strictly scientific ideal, the expositive garment will be systematic and not monographic nor hortatory nor rhetorical, as it is in the Fathers.

But the expositive scheme of the treatises will reflect a contact much more integral than in scholasticism with the empirical-historical aspect of revelation in its proper sources, Scripture, tradition, directly didactic magisterium, liturgy. The exposition will tend to bring out the fact that the elaboration of this more directly empirical-historical aspect of the revealed datum is held to have properly scientific value already by itself and not simply as prescientific moment preparatory to the ontological elaboration. For this reason, not only will a broad analysis be made of the empirical-historical aspect of revelation without being limited to the utility it may have for the further ontological analysis and deduction; but also in the exposition itself within the individual treatises, for the most part, this empirical-historical analysis will be separated more clearly from the ontological analysis.

In fact, there will be a tendency to give priority to the empirical-historical analysis of revelation, developed and distinct in itself, as has been said, over the entitative analysis. This is because revelation presents itself above all as a sacred history, and the entitative aspect, however important and basic it may be, is presented there as the remote basis and as its background on the second level of attention; and because, in the whole cycle of scientific knowledge, the natural movement is from the concrete and temporal to the abstract and timeless universal.

All this renders unsuitable the scholastic scheme of exposition in the *quaestio* and the *articulus* conceived essentially through an ideal of science in which empirical-historical knowledge enters only as a prescientific moment preparatory to ontological deduction and is of no interest, as a rule, except insofar as it is useful to that end.

The scheme of the positive-scholastic "thesis" also, as habitual scheme of exposition, will appear unsuitable because it is a scheme of an ideal directly and predominantly apologetic. The postive-scholastic scheme of the thesis which is "proved" from the sources will be substantially preserved only when the apologetic defense comes into play and in the cases in which the direct and apodictic historical proof from the sources can be effectively made.

In short, instead of the patristic monography of a strong hortatory and rhetorical character, there will be systematic and scientific treatises. In them, instead of the positive-scholastic "theses," there will be for the most part chapters of simply irenic orientation expositive of the revealed datum, of a mixed character, ordered in accord with the necessities of methodic or real polemic, with points, sometimes even with whole chapters, of a more directly apologetic character. And these chapters, instead of being each a scholastic *quaestio* with a series of *articuli* of the same kind, inquiry essentially ontological in which the empirical-historical aspect is of interest only as prescientific and preparatory moment, will be:

1) sometimes, and for the most part primarily, a broadly conducted inquiry into the empirical-historic aspect of the revealed data, for the scientific value which it has in itself as it is manifested in Scripture, in the Fathers, in the directly didactic magisterium, in the liturgy;

2) sometimes a directly ontological investigation of the same datum.

The internal structure of the individual chapter will follow no rigid scheme, but will be determined each time by the concrete matter which must be organized and explained in the chapter. In the same way St. Thomas does not follow rigid schemes *in the body* of the individual articles. By contrast, the tendency to rigid schematicism in the "theses" of positive-scholasticism is not lacking in serious drawbacks.

As far as the exposition of the theological-liturgical matter in particular is concerned, it will follow that this will figure for the most part in the individual treatises, in special chapters of a primarily empirical-historical and irenic-positive type, alongside similar chapters on the biblical thought and possibly on the traditional thought about the matter which constitutes the object of each individual treatise.

3. The Liturgical Aspect of the Individual Treatises of General Theology

At this point we may try to specify what will be the liturgical aspect of the individual theological treatises of general synthetic theology, conceived in the perspective explained above. Once the general order of the treatises is determined,[2] it can be seen with relative ease, I think, in a certain number of cases, how the liturgy enters into each of these by referring to the essays we have developed in this book. For other treatises, on the other hand, we are not in a position to give more than general suggestions. Their determination requires, as is obvious, execution of the whole program of which we wish to indicate only the principles here.

General theological methodology, which has for its task to explain the nature of theology, its proper method, its sources and its criteria, must necessarily treat of the liturgy among these sources. Having indicated its specific nature, it must explain in what sense it is a source of theological knowledge, under what exact perspective theological knowledge is reflected in the liturgy, and in what way the theologian should make use of it.

In short, general theological methodology must explain the general principles of the use of the liturgy in general synthetic scientific theology, which involves in practice a brief allusion to the material treated by us in the first part of this book on the proper nature of the liturgy, and a résumé of the chapters of the present fourth part on liturgy, faith, and theology.

In the treatise on the triune God [3] the theologian must show in one chapter by itself how and under what precise view the Church in the liturgy always lived and lives her faith in the triune God. The concern in practice is with that material which we have explained in Chapter 7 in the second part of this present book, in the essay on the liturgy and the Christological-Trinitarian law of the economy of God in the world.

In the treatises on the good and bad angels must be inserted practically the

[2] Order means arrangement of "before and after" with respect to a principle. Since revelation presents itself above all as a sacred history, and since theology is the scientific study of revelation, in general synthetic theology as science the principle of the distribution of the knowable must be taken from the object itself of theology considered according to the respective succession in sacred history. Thus, substantially, the following arrangement is obtained: theological methodology; triune God; creation in general; angels; infrahuman creation; man in his origin, nature, and history before Christ; Christ and His Mother; the grace of Christ and the infused virtues; the Church of Christ; the sacraments of the Church of Christ; the actions of the Christian; the Last Things.

[3] Conceived as a single treatise in two parts.

substance of our essays on the liturgy and angels, and on the liturgy and the struggle against Satan; and in the treatise on infrahuman creation, the matter of our essay on liturgy and infrahuman creation.

In the treatise on man, his origin, his nature, and his history before Christ, must be inserted practically the matter of our essay on the liturgy and the plenary actuation of the whole man. Moreover, in the part of this treatise where there is explained theologically the history of mankind after Adam's sin up to Christ, and therefore also the general theological significance of the Old Testament, there must be an explanation also of the theological significance of the liturgy of the Old Law. Thus there enters anew and with modern criteria into the general theological synthesis that matter about the general theological meaning of the Old Testament which St. Thomas, by theological instinct and by preceding tradition, had still rightly preserved and which the later theologians, on the other hand, expelled from their syntheses.

In the treatise on Christ must be inserted the matter of our essay on the *Kyrios* and the one liturgy and the one liturgist; and, in general, all that matter, developed to some extent throughout our present work, which brings out the role of Christ in the liturgy and how in the liturgy the Church lives her faith in Christ. In Mariology too a special chapter should be devoted to Mary in the liturgy. And where the concern is with the significance and legitimacy of the cult of the saints, the liturgical theology of the saints must be explained.

Also in the treatise on the grace of Christ and the infused virtues it must be explained, in a chapter by itself, in what way and under what perspective of its own this aspect of the Christian reality is actuated in the liturgy.

In the treatise on the Church, conceived as a single treatise and, like all the others, precisely of a dogmatic nature, but including, also like all the other dogmatic treatises, a series of questions of an apologetical order, a chapter should be reserved to the treatment of the Church in the liturgy. In this chapter, among other things, the liturgy should be explained as ecclesial communitarian act, the supreme actuation of the Church itself; and reference should be made to the liturgy in its relations with the law of incarnation and of salvation in community, as we have explained in the appropriate chapters of the second part.

The proper place in the general theological syntheses in which the nature of the liturgy — therefore all the matter of the first part of this book — should be explained directly *ex professo*, is the treatise now called "on the sacraments in general." But the treatment which this tract has received in the scholastic tradition and which the positive-scholastics, as has been seen, have further restricted, must be notably broadened.

A treatise must be constructed which will not be only a treatise on the seven greater sacraments in general, but a treatise on the *sacramenta* or *my-*

steria in general in the patristic sense. In it, that which belongs properly to the seven major rites, especially with regard to their institution by Christ, to their efficacy *ex opere operato,* and to their special necessity for salvation, must have its own proper place, safeguarding those clear distinctions between them and the other *sacramenta* which constitute the progress realized by the scholastics over the previous theology in this matter. Still, it is necessary to reposition the theology of the seven greater rites in general much more closely into its general framework of the *sacramenta* or *mysteria* in general, or, more to the point, in the framework of the liturgy in general. This ought to safeguard even more perfectly than did St. Thomas himself, and certainly more perfectly than did the later theologians, the great patristic and radically biblical concept of *mysterium* or *sacramentum* as the connatural soil in which the whole complexus of the sensible sacred signs of sanctification and of worship grows and bears fruit.[4] The treatise on the sacraments in general must therefore be a theological treatise on the liturgy in general.

In the treatise on the sacraments in particular, for every individual sacrament there must be taken up again and perfected, with modern criteria, the explanation of the theological value of the liturgical aspect of the celebration and administration of each of them, a subject matter which St. Thomas still retained but which was eliminated by the later theology.

In the treatise on the actions of the Christian, in other words in that which today is commonly called moral theology, at least in that part which treats of the Christian perfection to be attained and which today is commonly called theology of Christian or ascetical or mystical perfection, the questions "liturgy and spirituality" must be inserted. This is a subject of which we will treat in the next chapter of our present work.

In the treatise on the Last Things there must be a treatment of the eschatological faith as revealed in the liturgy in a special way, by an analysis of the theological value of the liturgy of the dead.

4. Observations on the Curricula and on the Teaching of the Liturgy in Seminaries and in Theological Faculties

At the end of this chapter it seems opportune to make some observations, suggested immediately by what has been said thus far, on the teaching of the liturgy in the curricula of seminaries and of theological faculties.

The present status

The curricula of seminaries and of theological faculties generally assign one or two hours a week for an entire year to the teaching of the liturgy. To those

---

[4] The work of H. Schillebeeckx, *De sacramentele heilseconomie,* Antwerp 1952, certainly marks an effort in this direction which must be pursued and perfected.

students who might be particularly interested in the liturgy there is given, at the most, in theological faculties, the possibility of following special elective courses in this matter. These courses of liturgy were conceived at one time as courses in rubrics; today they are conceived essentially as courses in the history of the liturgy. If there are exceptions in this connection, they cannot yet be very numerous.

It might be said that the whole of this present book has for its purpose the demonstration that this way of studying liturgy is legitimate and necessary, but that at the same time, if limited to this alone, it is utterly insufficient for the uncovering of the full riches of the liturgy. The true worth of the liturgy is its theological value, as has been demonstrated up to now, and hence its ascetical and pastoral value, as will be demonstrated in the following chapters.

It must be said, therefore, that, as long as the teacher has not led his students into the theological, ascetical, and pastoral sanctuary of the liturgy, he must not delude himself into thinking that he has introduced them at all into the true world of the liturgy. A mere historical introduction, if there is not added to it in some way a theological, ascetical, and pastoral introduction, is far from obtaining this effect. It is for this reason that theological students, in the great majority of cases, come out of the seminaries and theological faculties without having been truly introduced to the liturgy. This failure does not proceed essentially from the insufficiency of the number of courses they have heard in this matter, but from the qualitative way of conceiving these courses. The question of the teaching of the liturgy in seminaries and in theological faculties, therefore, seems to be the question of the introduction of the students to theological liturgy and, consequently, ascetical and pastoral liturgy, the foundations of which we are striving precisely to explain in this present book.

Consequences deriving from the union of theological knowledge and especially from the union of theology of the liturgy with general synthetic theology and the Scriptures

An initial observation must here be made. We have often had occasion to observe the profound unity of the world of the liturgy as it is conceived in this book with the world of the Scriptures and with the world of what is generally called dogmatic theology. In fact, under a certain aspect, the aim of this book is precisely to find this unity again. There follows at once a consequence of great importance for the teaching of the liturgy in seminaries and in theological faculties: for initiating the students to this world of the liturgy, the professors of dogmatics and of Sacred Scripture ought have the mentality, the status and the importance of the professor of liturgy.

Add to this consideration something which will now become more apparent: the profound unity between Christian perfection and liturgy and between pastoral and liturgy; hence to the general aim itself of introducing the students to the liturgy, the importance of the professors of these subjects; and it must be said that the very nature of things demands that, in practice, the whole teaching of theology be, as it were, naturally immersed in a liturgical atmosphere. This is true because the principal matters of this teaching have a certain liturgical dimension, which, developed according to the intrinsic requirements of these matters, constitutes a continuous link with the liturgy in theological teaching. In some way it prepares for the liturgy and makes it appear to be that which, under a certain aspect, it really is, a point of convergence of the whole faith and of the science which has for its precise object the study of this faith and of this life.

From what has been explained up to now, it must be evident that there is an importance to the way of conceiving the teaching of dogmatic theology and of Scripture, for the sake of the liturgical formation of students in theology.

For dogmatic theology the matter has already been explained sufficiently in our critique of the various types of theology in relation to their capacity for assimilating organically the material of liturgical theology.

For the teaching of Scripture the foundations have been laid in the third part of our present book, where the relations between Bible and liturgy were treated of, as also in the second part where the relations between liturgy and the great laws of the economy of God in the world were explained. There it was possible to make the observation that the great liturgical-theological themes are no other than the great biblical-theological themes; or that the great themes concerning the way in which the economy of God in the world and the relations between God and man appear in the liturgy do not differ substantially from the great themes between God and man, as these themes appear in the Bible.

It is enough to recall a few: the whole vision of the world as the sacred history of God's interventions and of man's response or non-response (sin and virtue); the unity of all the phases of this sacred history and therefore the great concept which dominates it of preparation, shadow, participation, complement, image, type, and antitype, etc.; the law of objectivity; the law of the Christological-Trinitarian movement; the centering of the whole economy in Christ; the law of cosmic universality or unitotality; the law of incarnation; the law of salvation in community; the struggle between the two cities.

These perspectives which constitute the foundations of the liturgy are typically biblical views. Thus the liturgy appears really as a certain way in which the biblical view of the world is made concrete and is lived under the veil of the sensible efficacious signs of sanctification and of worship. Hence the importance, for the liturgical formation of the students, that in the course of Scripture these and similar perspectives be not only studied but given that basic prominence which they have in scriptural thought.

Thus we arrive, considering the matter from the point of view of the unity between Bible and liturgy, at the same conclusion to which so many other considerations lead: it is of necessity that the study and the teaching of Scripture, first of all, transcend the phase of the too exclusive preoccupation with apologetics and launch out into the positive and quasi-contemplative consideration of all the riches of the Bible considered in themselves; and second, that this same study and teaching of Scripture, while being based on an indispensable critical, philological, and historical foundation, rise to the properly biblical-theological view of things.

In the study of dogmatics, of liturgy, and of the Bible, there will be observed a movement which impels them all to a more simply irenic, contemplative, and integral consideration of their object, in the due prominence given in each of these disciplines to the great themes of salvation history. The same might be said of moral, ascetical-mystical, and pastoral theology.

On this basis of their common task of scientifically illustrating the sacred history of salvation, the various branches of theological learning, each in its own way and in accord with the necessities of its proper object, will rediscover their connatural relation with the liturgy and their connatural and reciprocal unity, with utmost benefit for the teaching of theology and for the unity itself of ecclesiastical formation.

This idea has been very much promoted by the Second Vatican Council. What we have said above can be regarded as commentary on the words of article 16 of the Constitution on the Sacred Liturgy:

> "The study of sacred liturgy is to be ranked among the compulsory and major courses in seminaries and religious houses of studies. In theological faculties it is to rank among the principal courses. It is to be taught under its theological, historical, spiritual, pastoral, and juridical aspects. In addition, those who teach other subjects, especially dogmatic theology, sacred scripture, spiritual and pastoral theology, should — each of them submitting to the exigencies of his own discipline — expound the mystery of Christ and the history of salvation in a manner that will clearly set forth the connection between their subjects and the liturgy, and the unity which underlies all priestly training."

There are some, perhaps, who will fear in this way of viewing things a confusion of object among the theological disciplines. The answer is that between dogmatic theology commonly so-called — which would better be called simply general synthetic theology and which would include all the so-called dogmatic treatises plus moral theology and the theology of Christian perfection — and the other branches of theological knowledge, in seminary curricula and in theological faculties, including the Bible and the liturgy, the relation is not as between one and another part of a whole, but as between the whole synthetically considered and expounded, and a monography intended to set forth in a more analytical and detailed way one aspect or one part of this whole. The courses on the Bible and on liturgy are therefore monographic courses as compared to the course of general synthetic theology; and they treat monographically and analytically of an aspect which general synthetic theology has by its very nature an obligation to treat, though synthetically. Thus the unity of theological knowledge must be saved along with a due distinction of tasks in its teaching.

Reciprocal relation and respective proportions of the historical aspect, the juridical, the theological, the ascetico-mystical, and the pastoral aspects in an integrated general initiation to the liturgy

The present work does not intend to be an integral fundamental course in liturgy or an integral introduction to the liturgy. It has for its aim to bring to light the theological aspect of a fundamental course in liturgy or of a general introduction to the liturgy. Hence it does not enter into our task to draw up and discuss a precise program for the teaching of the liturgy.

Nevertheless, since, according to the opinion which the whole book is attempting to prove, this theological aspect constitutes the essential and by far the predominant part of the liturgy, it may be useful to indicate what are the practical consequences of this way of seeing things on the program of its teaching conceived as a complete initiation to the whole matter.

Aside from the question of the total hours available for the teaching of the liturgy and therefore apart from the reductions of curriculum to which one will be obliged in practice; aside also from the secondary displacements of materials and their practical distribution which it will sometimes be possible to effect in rather diverse ways, there remains the fundamental fact that a teaching of the liturgy which will have the value of a complete general initiation will comprise these four headings: general introduction, or fundamental liturgy as it is called; the liturgical cycles; the Mass; the other sacraments and the sacramentals. Another firm point is that, in any hypothesis, an integral initiation to the liturgy must necessarily treat the four aforesaid points under the historical, theological, ascetical, pastoral and juridical aspects.[5] The question turns solely on the reciprocal relationships of these aspects and on their respective proportions in the whole.

From our whole study follows the thesis of the necessary predominance of the theological point of view as determining and synthesizing, and even as coordinative for the teaching of the liturgy, which teaching ought to be an integral initiation to this subject in its diverse aspects according to the relative objective importance of each one in the whole. In this perspective the his-

---

[5] This point too has been confirmed by the Second Vatican Council: CL, art. 16, quoted in full above.

torical point of view cannot be anything but basis and presupposition in view of the elaboration of liturgical thought which is achieved in the theological treatment of the liturgy. In a general initiation to the liturgy, one must dwell on the historical aspect only in the exact measure that is necessary or useful for the induction of liturgical theological thought from the texts and from the facts in which it is embodied.

The ascetical and pastoral aspect, in its turn, will have to enter into the general introduction to the liturgy as consequence of the theological aspect. Concretely, the ascetical-mystical aspect, or simply the liturgy's value for one's spiritual life, aside from an ample treatment of the question in general theological liturgy, must proceed, in every specific question, from the liturgical-theological treatment itself. It will be sufficient, when occasion presents itself, to underline it opportunely. If from the theological treatment of a point of liturgy, as of the Mass, of the liturgical year in its whole or in its individual parts, of the sacraments or of the sacramentals, its value to spiritual life does not appear at once or obviously, but, at the end of such treatment the need is felt, in order to reach this end, of adding a sort of ascetical *ferverino*, similar to those *scholia pietatis* with which some theologians think it fitting to crown their "theses," we may be sure that the supposed theological explanation of the liturgy is radically lacking at least through some congenital defect. The theological-liturgical point of view of a question, inseparably connected with the biblical point of view of the same — the liturgy, as has often been repeated, being but a concretization *sui generis*, under the veil of the sensible and efficacious signs of the Church's sanctification and worship, of the biblical concept of history and of life — is always and necessarily vital by itself.

Nor can the pastoral aspect in liturgy be but the consequence of the theological aspect discovered with the aid of historical inquiry. When the communitarian character of the Mass is discovered, there flows from it spontaneously a series of questions on how to lead the great body of the faithful back to living the Mass again as a communitarian act. And in general, when the true nature and the richness of the liturgy is discovered and the separation between people and liturgy is noticed, the question is necessarily posed of how to lead the people back to the liturgy and the liturgy to the people.

Thus it is inevitable that, whether in general liturgy or in the treatment of the liturgical cycles or of the Mass or of the other sacraments and of the sacramentals, after the exposition of the historical basis and of the theological nucleus, the pastoral consequence also be described. This is in fact the case because liturgical science has for its object an action. The liturgy is, after all, an action. And the science of an action involves necessarily the study, at least theoretical, of the way in which to make the action practical. We shall have to return to this point again.

In its turn, the study of the positive legislation in this perspective cannot be understood as anything but subsidiary to the study of theological liturgical thought and hence of the pastoral problems which the liturgy raises. In other words, it will be necessary to devote oneself to the laws of worship only insofar as there is involved in them in a particular case some theological or pastoral value. As to the rest of the positive legislation, matters of rubrical interest, that which it is necessary for the young clergy to know must be taught them in another place, and largely by practical means.

Such being the state of affairs, if anyone were to ask me whether the matter explained in the present book can be considered as constituting a real integral course in fundamental liturgy or a general introduction to the liturgy, I would answer in the affirmative, reserving only the addition, perhaps, of some brief notions on liturgical law and the rubrics,[6] and certainly of a lengthy historical chapter. In this chapter a schematic panorama should be set out, according to the most recent research, of the genetic historical development of the Christian liturgy in its totality, pointing out the essential documents and the characteristic traits of the contribution that each epoch has made to its formation. This chapter can be prefixed to the whole treatment.[7]

[6] See, for example, Ph. Oppenheim, *Tractatus de iure liturgico*, 2 vols., Turin 1939. Similar brief but essential notions can easily be inserted, e.g., at the end of our Chaper 9 on the liturgy and the law of salvation in community.

[7] It should comprise the following points: the *terminus a quo* of the liturgy, i.e., what Jesus did; the liturgy from the Apostles to Constantine the Great in 314; from the peace of Constantine to Gregory the Great; the Middle Ages in the West from Gregory the Great to the Council of Trent; the formation of the present-day Eastern rites; the liturgy in the West from the Council of Trent to the beginning of the nineteenth century; the present liturgical movement. [And, several years having now elapsed since Dom Vagaggini wrote the above note, the translator would take leave to modify the last point to something along this line: the modern liturgical movement prior to Vatican II, while adding an additional concluding point: the post-conciliar and continuing liturgical reform.]

PART 5 LITURGY AND LIFE

21 LITURGY AND SPIRITUALITY

Just as the ascending cycle of life is fulfilled in the most perfect possible union with God here below, which union, since the good tends naturally to communicate itself, is followed by the return toward men to help them also rise to the high goal, so too, the cycle of science is fulfilled in a spirituality, as doctrine of life for attaining that maximum union, and this spirituality is followed by a pastoral science, as theory of the return toward men to help them attain the same goal.

In a theory of spirituality and of pastoral, science achieves the maximum contact with life that is permitted it while it remains science. Beyond that, life itself is lived in concrete and individual act, in the domain of prudence and of art of every kind which direct the individual act in the concreteness of individual circumstances, something which it is not permitted to any science to do.

Such is the case with science in general, and so too with liturgical science in particular. It is for this reason that a general theological liturgy, as general part of an integral liturgical science, must be completed in the exposition of a liturgical spirituality, to be followed by the exposition of a liturgical pastoral. In the theory of the relations between liturgy and spirituality and between liturgy and pastoral, liturgical science achieves the maximum contact with life, the maximum of which it is capable.

647

1. Spirituality and Spiritualities

We have said that a spirituality as doctrine is the doctrine of the way of achieving the most perfect union with God that is possible here below. Let us make this notion more precise by recalling some general concepts necessary for determining the concept of liturgical spirituality.

The notion of spirituality

Spirituality does not simply coincide with doctrine of the Christian life. The doctrine of the Christian life includes also the doctrine of the way of obtaining sanctifying grace for the first time and of preserving it to such an extent as is indispensable for salvation. Spirituality, as it is understood here, supposes the Christian life in act, and is concerned only with the tendency to perfection in the Christian life.

Perfection means the state of a thing in which it is not lacking anything of what it should have. The perfection of man can be considered in the natural order and in the supernatural order; and in both cases it can be considered either as perfection in being or as perfection in doing. Doing follows the order of being and presupposes it. But, especially when the concern is with free actions, doing does not always follow the requirements or the higher possibilities of being. When it does not follow the requirements, it is a sinful action. When it does not follow the higher possibilities, it is an imperfect action. The spirituality of which we are now speaking considers the perfection to be attained by man in the supernatural order — presupposing nature, however — and this whether in being or in doing.

Christian being is grace as participation in the divine nature. Specifically Christian doing, which corresponds to the aforesaid Christian being, is the actions of the infused Christian virtues, moral and theological: faith, hope, and charity, especially the actions of charity, the highest of the virtues.[1] Union with God in being is achieved through sanctifying grace. Union with God in doing is achieved, here below, principally through the act of charity.

Both sanctifying grace and act of charity can be possessed or done in a greater or lesser degree; and here below they are always subject to perfection and to diminution. Their increase depends on God, who infuses them, and on the merit which, after first grace, everyone can and should acquire in accord with grace.

The maximum degree with respect to which each person derives the greater or lesser perfection of his sanctifying grace and of his actual charity depends on the free positive will of God, who has established for each person the final degree of grace which he is to attain, as well as the degree of the

---

[1] It is not necessary to touch here upon the question of the gifts of the Holy Spirit because not all theologians admit that they involve a question of habits specifically different from those of the infused virtues.

same grace and charity which everyone should have at every moment of his life.

Christian perfection here below is, therefore, for each one, to have at every moment of life that degree of sanctifying grace and that degree of actual charity which God has established for him at that moment. But among mere creatures here below, only the Virgin Mary was perfect in this sense. For others there cannot be question of anything but tendency and approach to perfection.

To tend to perfection is to tend to have at every moment that degree of sanctifying grace which God requires for each one (the perfection of his Christian *being*) and to act in every instance with the degree of actual charity corresponding to the degree of being (the perfection of his Christian *doing*). Union with God and the imitation of Christ or the assimilation to Christ, which are merely other concepts for expressing, with some proper nuances, the same thing, consist both in the former and in the latter tendencies.

In this tendency to the Christian perfection of being and of doing, man, supported by God, by Christ, by the Virgin, by the angels, and by the saints, and hindered by the devil and by all his activities in us and outside of us, has at his disposal a series of means, given in part by the nature itself of things and in part imposed by the free positive will of God, means which he must duly use in order to attain his end.

These means are ordered to the aforesaid twofold aim: to the perfection of Christian being, by means of the increase of sanctifying grace which God has connected in some way with their use; and to the corresponding perfection of Christian doing, in the exercise of the moral and theological virtues, especially of charity, in connection with a deeper vital knowledge of God and of other things, above all of ourselves, in relation to Him, and in the purification from vices and from imperfect tendencies.

The tendency to perfection, the approach to the goal, as a living experience, is subject to development, with successive progress and the possibility ever of regressions, temporary or definitive. God on His part respects this law of nature, though without being bound absolutely to it. There is therefore a *terminus a quo* and a *terminus ad quem*. The *terminus a quo* is sin and imperfection, the *terminus ad quem* an ever greater sanctifying grace or actual charity.

The movement toward perfection includes, therefore at every point of its trajectory, an ever greater separation, an ever more intense purification from sin and from imperfection, and a continual increase, at least in its total result, of sanctifying grace and of actual charity, as well as of the other virtues. The subject of this purification and of this improvement is the whole man in his being and in his various faculties.

In every movement from a *terminus a quo* toward a *terminus ad quem* there are differences in being and in doing between the general status of one who still finds himself close to the point of departure, the general status of one who is obviously approaching the point of arrival, and the status of one who finds himself in an intermediate position. Hence, in the way of Christian perfection also, the authors rightly distinguish the beginners, the progressing, and the perfect. This distribution is not meant to be a clear-cut indication of the passage from one state to another, but a distinction of general status, clear enough on the whole at any given time.

The three phases are also called, with terminology derived from the Pseudo-Dionysius, the purgative, the illuminative, and the unitive way. For it is certain that in the beginners still relatively close to the point of departure, the labor of purification and of separation from sin and imperfection is still habitually predominant, while in those relatively close to the goal the unitive attraction to God is habitually much stronger.

Moreover, in the progressive journey toward perfection, in every action and at every point on the way, man is always active and passive at the same time under different aspects, while God is always active. In fact, every supernatural action is always and at the same time, though under different aspects, entirely of man and entirely of God. Through grace, God always acts in man and for man; otherwise the action would not be supernatural; and under this aspect man is always passive inasmuch as he is always receiving. But at the same time it is man who acts truly and completely in that action; otherwise it would not be the action of man, and man would be receiving it as if he were dead. Hence in every action man is, under a certain aspect, always active. Here it is the whole problem of grace and freedom that confronts us.

It is not our intention to explain how, in some way, this twofold assertion can be reconciled. We are interested rather in noting that at different moments of the total progress toward perfection the grace of God may act with greater or lesser intensity, and man may also have a greater or lesser awareness of this more intense action of grace in himself.[2]

At certain times and on certain occasions this action of grace may be of such quality and so intense, and man may be so aware of it that he has the clear impression that the action which follows from it is done by God in him in a way superior to the ordinary, rather than done by himself with the ordinary concurrence of God. Then man, psychologically speaking, has a feeling that he is, as it were, more passive than active.

But in reality it is never a question of an absolute passivity, as if man received the action of God in himself like a dead person or an inert thing, in which case the action which he puts forth would not be his own action in any way. Indeed, that so-called passivity is an intense life, but one which works

---

[2] Concerning this awareness, see, for example, J. de Guibert, *Theologia spiritualis ascetica et* *mystica*, 2nd edition, Rome 1939, pp. 356 ff, nos. 399–403.

on a level of powers immensely superior to the ordinary surface activity, which always involves a certain labor and a certain troublesome effort.[3]

There can be periods of the spiritual life in which the action of grace is of such quality and is so notably intense that the activity of that more passive than active way is habitually dominant. In other periods, on the other hand, man is left to his ordinary way of acting with the ordinary concurrence of God's grace, and with greater experience and psychological awareness of the more or less serious difficulties he must overcome.

A similar reasoning can be made with regard to the two ways of acting of the intellect: the discursive or, by way of simple experiential and direct apprehension, the intuitive. In every supernatural act of faith there is alongside the discursive aspect a certain aspect of direct and non-discursive experience. Or it even happens that in certain acts the intuitive aspect of a simple glance, under the influence of grace, which, as participation in the divine nature, confers of itself a certain connaturality and harmony with divine things, may increase and prevail over the discursive aspect. When such is the case, the man, psychologically speaking, hardly adverts or almost does not advert at all to the reasoning process, while knowledge of the sort called intuitive-experiential and direct predominates in his psychological awareness. And in certain periods of life this condition can become relatively habitual.

Let us unite the three preceding observations: predominance of the unitive attraction to God in charity over the labor of purifying from sin and from imperfection; psychological predominance of the sensation of passivity over that of laborious and painful activity; predominance of intuitive knowledge over the discursive. This is the basis of the common distinction between ascetical act and mystical act, habitually ascetical life and habitually mystical life. Thus it appears that this traditional distinction rests on an indisputable reality.

Diverse spiritualities within Catholicism

Our aim now is to determine the concept of liturgical spirituality. To use the phrase "liturgical spirituality" may seem to restrict the concept of Catholic spirituality in general to a well-defined type of Catholic spirituality in particular.

Are there, then, different kinds of Catholic spiritualities? In fact, the authors do speak of different "schools of spirituality." Thus, in particular, they speak of Benedictine spirituality, Franciscan, Dominican, Ignatian, Carmelite, Salesian, Berullian spirituality. And today, from a somewhat different point of view, there is much talk of spirituality for the diocesan clergy and of spirituality for the laity. These are not arbitrary designations.

[3] See, for example, St. John of the Cross, *The Ascent of Mount Carmel*, (in the critical edition of Fr. Crisogono de Jésus, *Vida y obras de S. Juan de la Cruz*, Madrid 1955): II, 15, 2; II, 12, 8; II, 14, 6. Throughout the rest of our work, whenever referring to St. John of the Cross, our references will be to this Spanish critical edition of Fr. Crisogono de Jésus.

In what sense, then, is it possible to speak of different spiritualities within the bosom of the single Catholic spirituality? And indeed, is the liturgy a spirituality at all, or does it include a spirituality which can be called liturgical spirituality? And if the existence of a liturgical spirituality is admitted, is it perhaps a question of one among the many schools of spirituality? A school of spirituality accidentally forgotten by the ascetical and mystical authors? Or else is liturgical spirituality only another name for what the authors call Benedictine spirituality? Ah, so many questions which must be clarified!

In the first place, at any rate, it is certain that it will not be possible to speak of different Catholic spiritualities or of different schools of Catholic spirituality except within well-defined limits, since there are certain elements necessarily common to every Catholic spirituality. In the question, therefore, of the concept of different spiritualities, as well as in the question of the proper nature of each one with respect to the others, it appears to be of capital importance to specify first of all what are the elements necessarily common to every Catholic spirituality. These elements concern the end and the means of spirituality.

The end common to all Catholic spirituality. While the end absolutely ultimate and common to all created things is the glory of God, the specific ultimate end of all spirituality is, as we have said above, the approach to the perfection of Christian *being* in sanctifying grace and of the corresponding Christian *doing* in the Christian virtues, principally in charity. This means that if there are to be differences among the Catholic spiritualities, these differences can reside only in that which is in the nature of a means, as related to the aforesaid end.

We must therefore specify the nature and the relative necessity of the individual means with respect to the aforesaid end if we are to be able to distinguish where, in all Catholic spiritualities, there must be agreement, and where, on the other hand, within the bounds of the general agreement, there exists a margin of possible diversities.

The common means, if considered generically. Actually, the means for tending to Christian perfection must be distinguished as common means, necessary for all, and special means, the use of which for attaining the same purpose is not necessary for all but may be for some, at least in certain circumstances. However, if the matter is looked into closely, it can be said that the means for tending to Christian perfection are the same and necessary for all if they are formulated generically; and they become special means necessary for some but not for all if that generic formulation is specified and concretized. Moreover, if the means are considered in their quality of being generic, they are indeed necessary for all and invariable; but the proportion of the relative use and of the relative psychological importance given to each of them in the totality of the whole complexus is not invariable. These distinctions, of great importance for our purpose, are clarified by the enumeration of the two categories of means.

The basis and point of departure for the tendency toward perfection is to be in the state of grace. Hence all the means necessary for preserving this state of grace are, *a fortiori*, necessary means for tending to the perfection of the Christian life. First among all is the observance of the commandments of God and of the Church. Among the commandments of the Church now there is also that of assistance at the sacrifice of the Mass on Sundays and holydays of obligation, as well as that of annual confession and reception of Communion in the Eastertime. Here it may be asked whether a greater frequency of participation in the sacrifice of the Mass and in the sacraments in general is to be reckoned forthwith among the means necessary for all, that there may be a true tendency to Christian perfection.

It will perhaps be objected that there are instances of saints in antiquity for whom it seems to be difficult to demonstrate — even without positing circumstances beyond their control — that they made use of frequent reception of the Eucharist and possibly of the sacrament of penance, especially in certain periods of their lives; and nevertheless, they retained their fervor.

Without calling into doubt the subjective right conscience of these saints and their good will in the aforesaid circumstances, it is, at any rate, a question of abnormal cases. Possibly they can be explained not only by the development of sacramental practice in the Church, but even by there being in certain individuals, or some locales and in specific eras, a less sharply developed explicit awareness of the importance in the Christian life of participation in the Eucharistic Sacrifice and, incidentally, in the sacrament of penance.

The anomaly of the situation becomes apparent upon recalling that to have grace it is necessary to have also at least the implicit desire for the Eucharist, as was explained above.[4] This means that for such an end, participation in the Eucharistic Sacrifice, at least by implicit desire, is necessary — and in the event of mortal sin, in the sacrament of penance also — because participation in the Eucharist is always participation in the Sacrifice. Thus it can easily be seen how very unusual would be the case of a person's enjoying the full flowering of an intense life of grace with reference only to an implicit desire for the Eucharistic Sacrifice (and incidentally for the sacrament of penance), and without such a desire's being frequently translated into an actual participation.

On the other hand, if there is to be a tendency or striving toward Christian perfection, certainly the following are means indispensable for all: a noteworthy spirit of prayer and of praying in general, exercised not only in the liturgical action but also outside of it, in the whole of life; a noteworthy spirit

[4] Pp. 171-173.

and exercise of meditation as discursive consideration of God and of other things, oneself in particular, in relation to God, above all about Christ and the work of salvation, with a view to acts of will and of affection. Meditation and prayer imply, in particular, that one's vital attention and emotions will range over the whole field of revelation, although this may happen with different nuances.

Other indispensable means are the frequent examination of one's own life and of one's own ways of acting: the fulfillment as exactly as possible of the duties of one's own state as well as of the duties of justice and charity toward one's neighbor according to each one's obligations; the desire for perfection with a substantially fervent spirit of will in tending to it; docility to the inspiration of grace; and a certain spirit of mortification.

The use of these means, even formulated generically as above, demands in practice, although in different degrees and with different shadings for each person, the engagement of all the human faculties: intellect, will, emotion, memory, etc. It is necessarily at the same time an exercise of the theological and moral virtues and purification from evil or imperfect tendencies, something which always implies a more or less difficult struggle.

Possible diversities with regard to further specification and concretization of the same means. Examples. If the aforesaid common means in their general formulation are certainly necessary to all, it is not so with their further specification and concretization. Here, then, in the sphere of the same Catholic spirituality, there will be a broad margin for differences, even notable differences. And it is here that the possibility arises of different schools or tendencies of spirituality. They arise essentially from the employment, for attaining the aim common to all, of diverse means, inasmuch as these diverse means are but specifications and concretizations of the common means necessary for all. A series of examples will clarify what we are talking about.

A certain use and frequenting of the sacraments, especially of the Eucharist, is a common and necessary means for any tendency whatsoever to Christian perfection. But the intensity of this frequenting and of this use, as well as the psychological importance which will be given to it, may vary immensely from one person to another in a determinate total way of striving concretely to perfection.

A certain participation in the liturgy of the Church, at least in that of the Sacrifice of the Mass, is also a common and necessary means for all. But here too, the frequency of this participation and the psychological importance which will be given to it among the other means for tending toward perfection may vary, even greatly.

The exact fulfillment of the duties of one's own state in life is an indispensable means. But the state of life for each one, within a very broad margin, is an object of free choice. Although in every state of life which is honest in itself one must serve God and strive to Christian perfection, still every state of life tends to its own particular end, which, with respect to the common end of Christian perfection, functions as a particular means. The end proper to the conjugal state is one thing, that of the diocesan priest another, that of the religious another, and among the religious themselves there are as many proper ends as there are orders, congregations, associations, etc.

The common and necessary means of the fulfillment of the duties of one's own state may therefore be specified and concretized in a great variety of ways. And since the fulfillment of the duties of one's own state is certainly an element of great importance in spirituality in general, the variety of the different states of life will have no little influence as an element of great importance in spirituality in general; likewise the variety of the different states of life will have no little influence as an element diversifying spirituality within the general common limits of Catholic spirituality.

With the particular duties of each state there is also connected a particular framework of life which determines in an essential way a series of points in the particular life of each person, such as the relations with others as far as their quantity or frequency is concerned; as far as the spirit with which they will be had is concerned; and as far as the persons who will be visited are concerned; the horarium of the day and of the night; the amount of time assigned to each duty and, in particular, to the duties of piety; the predominant concerns of each one; the kind of work in which one engages.

In all these points it is necessarily a very different kind of framework of life in which, let us suppose, a parish priest, a businessman, a hermit, a missionary in a pagan country, an assistant in Catholic action, a cloistered nun, a hospital sister, or a journalist has to live and sanctify himself or herself. The importance of the different frameworks of life which will be had especially in view of determining the particular spiritualities is obvious. When today, for example, there is talk of the necessity of a spirituality for the laity and a spirituality for the diocesan clergy, the idea is simply to draw attention to the necessity of taking due account of the particular duties of each state and of the framework of life proper to the laity and to the diocesan clergy in the specific way of conceiving and of presenting to them their duty and their way of tending to Christian perfection.

Meditation and prayer, and in fact a noteworthy spirit of meditation and of prayer in the whole of life, are means common and necessary to all in advancing toward Christian perfection. Now, meditation and prayer involve a certain centering of vital attention and of affectivity on the totality of the truths presented by Catholic dogma. Although the Catholic must accept the whole of dogma in its totality and, in some way, must also live by all the truths proposed by it, still, in a given individual or group of individuals, the psychological attention and the affectivity can be concentrated rather on one point than on another, in such a way that in its vital attention the first point will be directly on the first level and will constitute the great dynamism of life, while the other points will be considered and lived by starting from the first. This is so much the more legitimate as Catholic dogma is a vital whole whose single parts are intimately connected, for which reason whoever lives to the fullest any point whatsoever is brought necessarily to living them all, even if, so to speak, in a certain order and as if in a certain synthesis of its own, starting from the first point.

Thus it is quite possible to give the greatest vital attention to the dogma of the indwelling of the Persons of the Trinity in the souls of the just and, starting from this dogma, to consider the others vitally and to live them really, in such a way as to make of the first dogma the great dynamism toward perfection. This was the way, for example, of Sister Elizabeth of the Trinity. But it can be done just as well by starting from the dogma of the adoption as sons of God, as did Dom Marmion; or starting from the dogma of the states of soul of the incarnate Word, as does the so-called French school of spirituality. A more intense vital attention given to a dogma or to a group of dogmas, as compared to that given to the others, can therefore be a source of notable nuances and, as it were, of different tonalities in the bosom of the same Catholic spirituality.

Much the same thing can be said in considering the different aspects of a single dogma. In the Trinity, no doubt, one can devote himself to a deeper concentration on the intra-Trinitarian life, whereas someone else will concentrate more on the Christological-Trinitarian movement of the interventions of God in the world, as was explained above in Chapter 7. In Christ, we can look either more to His divinity or more to His humanity; and if to His humanity, sometimes starting from the Jesus who was born, lived, suffered, and died in Palestine, and sometimes from the *Kyrios* of the paschal mystery, as was stated in Chapter 8.

In the Eucharist it is possible to place the emphasis now on the sacrifice, and especially on the sacrifice of the Church; and again, on the Real Presence.

Connected with the preceding phenomena is that of particular devotions and devotional practices. It seems to me that we may call devotions, in the medieval and modern sense, preferential personal habitual psychological attentions of individuals or of private groups, given to a certain aspect of revelation or to its specific concretization, stronger than those which the presentation of this aspect induces by itself when it takes place in the general and relative proposal of the individual dogmas made officially by the magisterium, especially in the general panorama of the liturgy. From devotions in this sense are derived extraliturgical devotional practices and exercises of piety, in which the aforesaid special attention and affectivity is expressed and nourished.

Thus, for example, the devotion to the Eucharist as Real Presence will be, in an individual, his habitual concentration of vital attention and of affection on the dogma of the Real Presence of Christ in the Eucharist, concentration which in this individual is of particular intensity as compared to the habitual vital attention and the affection which he gives to the other dogmas, while the relative emphasis given to this dogma as compared to the emphasis given the others in the official presentation of them which the magisterium makes, for example, in the liturgy, does not of itself lead to such particular and preferential concentration.

The devotion to the Sacred Heart, on the other hand, is not only a preferential concentration of vital attention and of affection on the dogma of the love of Christ and of the whole familiar life of His person, but also of the concentration of this dogma in the symbol of that part of His body which is His heart of flesh.

Private visits to the Blessed Sacrament and the custom of the nine First Fridays are, for example, devotional practices in which the aforesaid devotions are expressed and nourished.

It is clear that the devotions and devotional practices in their proper object, in the intensity and in the importance which they assume in the total complexus of the spiritual life, are also elements which notably differentiate various types of spirituality.

Other differentiating elements may be the psychological "methods" of meditation, of prayer, of examination of conscience, etc., as specific concretizations of the general common means of prayer, of meditation, and of personal spiritual examination. Spiritual readings and conferences are also particular concretizations of the general means of meditation, of prayer, of examination of conscience, and are also elements which differentiate among the various types of spirituality, by reason of the authors recommended, by reason of the themes preferred, by reason of the methods followed.

Another very important differentiating element is the specific equilibrium which in any particular given type of spirituality is given in the whole complexus of the spiritual life to the use of the various human psychological faculties, especially intellect, will, and affection. Although in every Catholic spirituality all these faculties will have to be exercised in some way, still the relative importance which is given now to one and now to another in the total picture may be quite different.

Thus there will be spiritualities of a predominantly intellectual type, as in the Pseudo-Dionysius or in Tauler; others of a predominantly voluntarist type, as in St. Ignatius of Loyola; others of a predominantly affective or emotional type, as in St. Bernard or in St. Francis of Assisi. And in each one of these types there can be further and notable gradations.

Every Catholic spirituality must necessarily base itself on the fact that in the supernatural act both God and man must intervene, both grace and human effort. But here also the psychological nuances in concentrating with a certain insistence now more on the one and now more on the other of the two factors may have no small consequences in the shaping of the character of a particular spirituality. In one there may predominate the awareness and the preoccupation with the human effort to be made, though with grace; and in the other, the awareness of the divine grace with which the human effort must cooperate.

Similarly, viewing this matter under the aspect of the *subject-object* pair, there is no Catholic spirituality which can be exempted from considering and from taking into due account both the one and the other. But even here there can be various gradations. We have already explained this in Chapter 6: some can put the emphasis on the object, while others will emphasize the subject, or at least they will give the subject a direct and much fuller attention than do the former.

The same can be said of the binomial pair *individual-community*. Every Catholic spirituality must be fundamentally and at one and the same time both individual and communitarian. But some will concentrate primarily on the community in which and through which the individual must find his salvation, while others concentrate on the individual who must find his salvation in the community and through the community.

In every Catholic spirituality there must be an intense exercise of the moral and theological virtues, as well as a firm conviction of the superiority of the theological virtues over the moral. But even here, within the limits of orthodoxy, there can be a diversity of emphases, which are able to constitute elements of considerable differentiation among the various types of spirituality. There can be a psychology which is concerned primarily with the exercise of the moral virtues, which have for their immediate object not God Himself, the ultimate end of all the virtues, but a certain human material to be used concretely and in a proper manner as a means to arrive at the end, God, who can be attained to immediately only through the theological virtues.

Anyone who is dominated by this psychology makes it his first concern to order himself aright through human affairs, by attending first of all, so to speak, to putting his own appetites for the use of created things on the solid foundation of right order, so that in this way he can conduct himself better before God in the prompt exercise of the theological virtues, charity most especially.

Others, contrariwise, are able to put a psychological emphasis on the exercise of the theological virtues, which have God for their immediate object. They are concerned primarily with attaining to this highest object in the better way, keeping it constantly in view even when exercising the preparatory moral virtues, and trusting not a little, indirectly and reflexively as it were, in the rectifying and purifying power of the same theological virtues in respect to the human appetites for created things.

Moreover, among the moral virtues themselves it is possible to concentrate now more on one and now more on another, as for example, on obedience, on penitence, on poverty, or on humility, and to make them, in a certain way, the pivotal point of that whole dynamic reaching out for perfection.

It is true that when one such virtue tends strongly to be for anyone a notably unifying and coordinating pivotal point for his whole spiritual psychology, it tends, by that very fact, to broaden itself to the point that it joins its own thrust, almost as if mixing itself, with the thrust of the other virtues, particularly the theological virtues, or even with the whole of the spiritual life. This is about what happens, for example, to the thrust of *pénthos* or *compunctio* in the ancient monastic tradition, to that of humility in St. Benedict and to poverty in St. Francis of Assisi.

This is natural and inevitable precisely because of the profound unity of the spiritual life, so that if anyone reaches vitally to the depths of one, he necessarily comes upon all the others. Nevertheless, it remains true that such a discovery of the other virtues and such a synthesizing of them is made in this case by starting from one well-defined moral virtue; and the final result thereof, in its totality, has a very distinct character of its own, different from all other vital syntheses made up of the same materials but proceeding from a different starting point.

Even among those who put an emphasis on the theological virtues there can be differences, even rather marked differences, either because faith, hope (characterized by trust or by a fiducial sentiment), and charity are diverse virtues, or because theological charity itself has for its primary material object God Himself, and for its secondary object every rational creature capable of eternal beatitude. Fixing the psychological emphasis now directly on God, and again on the creature beloved of God as the secondary material object of theological charity, makes for a notable diversity in the syntheses of the spiritual life, such a diversity as is found, for example, in the Carthusian spirituality as distinct from the apostolic spirituality of someone like St. Vincent de Paul or from that spirituality heralded for the parish clergy by Thils or Michonneau.

Finally, we have seen that the ascetical aspect and the mystical aspect of the spiritual life, with their corresponding states, are distinctions not only legitimate but necessary. No Catholic spirituality of whatever sort can ignore their distinction and their intimate union, even apart from the position which is adopted in regard to the controversial question of the relations between Christian perfection and the mystical life, and of the universal call to the mystical life. Nevertheless, it is still evident that every spirituality, as a doctrine of the tendency to Christian perfection, will have a notably different appearance according to the general attitude that it takes in the aforesaid questions. It will be either a spirituality notably centered upon the ascetical aspect, like that, for example, of St. Ignatius of Loyola or of St. Vincent de Paul; or it will be a spirituality in which the whole complexus is frankly directed toward mystical experience, as, for example, in St. Teresa of Avila, in St. John of the Cross and, in general, in the Carmelite tradition derived from them.

Conclusion

These seem to be the diversifying elements of greater importance which, in the bosom of the same Catholic spirituality, are able to give rise to diverse spiritualities. It is clear, therefore, that the factor distinguishing one spirituality from another within the dimension of Catholic spirituality is not the presence of certain elements that are absent in another, if such elements are considered and formulated in a generic way. That which distinguishes one spirituality from another is simply the diverse concentration of the same common generic elements, dogmatic, moral, ascetic, mystic, liturgical, biblical, devotional in character, and especially the entire diverse but harmonious balance obtained by the diverse but synthetic and vital ordering of these same elements, through the psychologico-vital predominance given now to one and now to another. To borrow the apt comparison of Fr. J. de Guibert,[5] it is somewhat like the fact that with the same flowers, especially if they are numerous and varied — and the elements composing a spirituality are numerous and varied indeed — it is possible to arrange many bouquets of varied appearance; or again, with the same construction materials, while respecting the basic necessities of a house, it is possible to build houses of different styles and variously oriented in their surroundings, according to necessities and particular tastes.

According to necessities and particular tastes, we say. And this touches upon the question of the reason why, in single individuals or groups of individuals, one specific spirituality rather than another will find its place. And the reason is precisely this: the whole complexus is differently constructed because of differences of nature, of character, of education, of special circumstances of life, of vocation, of gifts of grace, of the states and frames of life that have their own special goal, of the necessities of the Church. It is clear that in this matter the various end products arise from vital experiences and not from artificial or cerebral structures. Hence the importance, in this area, of great religious personalities, like the founders of orders, or of religious movements in their creative period and period of fervor.

[5] "En quoi diffèrent réellement les diverses écoles catholiques de spiritualité?" in Gregorianum, Vol. 19 (1938), pp. 263–276. Also of de Guibert, La spiritualité de la compagnie de Jésus, Rome 1953, pp. xvii ff.

It is not our task to enter further into the determination of the various schools or tendencies, historical or present-day, of spirituality, that have been born and, in part, flourish even yet in the Church. Most certainly it is not our task to distinguish them one from another and to characterize them sufficiently. It would be a difficult task, not only because up to the present time the attempts made in this direction have been few and have frequently been carried out with criteria far from satisfactory,[6] but also because, as in all vital matters, even though between certain extremes the differences may be sufficiently clear, in many other cases we find ourselves confronted by boundaries as indistinct as the boundaries between the colors of a rainbow.

2. Concept and General Characteristics of Liturgical Spirituality

The preceding observations in regard to the concept of spirituality in general and to that of diverse spiritualities even within the one Catholic spirituality were made for the purpose of allowing us to clarify the concept of liturgical spirituality.

Concept

Well, then, what is liturgical spirituality? Now we are able to respond in brief: Liturgical spirituality is that spirituality in which the specific concretization and the proper synthetic relative ordering of the diverse elements common to every Catholic spirituality as a means toward Christian perfection are determined by the liturgy itself. It should not really be necessary, but still, in order to calm the timorous, we can subjoin the following: . . . are determined by the liturgy itself lived by each one according to the suitabilities of his own proper state in life. Some few observations will aid in understanding the import of this definition.

First of all, it should not be necessary to observe anew that when it is said that liturgical spirituality is spirituality defined by the liturgy, the term "liturgy" is intended in the plenary sense, the explaining of which is the purpose of the whole present work, and not, for example, in the sense of rubrics or

[6] The best work in this area is Fr. J. de Guibert, *La spiritualité de la compagnie de Jésus*, Rome 1953. Less satisfactory, however, are the attempts at collaborative works, in which the commission to make a profile of the individual spiritualities is confided to one of their presumed representatives. The frequent result is that the individual authors describe the spirituality of their proper group through elements that are generic and therefore common to all. Not infrequently we find ourselves in possession of a panegyric to the collabora-

tor's own professed spirituality rather than a serious definition. See, for example, *Le scuole cattoliche di spiritualità: Settimana di spiritualità promossa dall'università del S. Cuore*, Rome, April 1943; 3rd edition, Milan 1949. On a particular argument, *Il sacerdote e la spiritualità: Ciclo di lezioni all'università Gregoriana* (given in 1945), Rome 1946; J. Gautier, in collaboration with others, *La spiritualité catholique*, Paris 1953; *Seid vollkommen: Formen und Führung christlicher Askese*, edited by K. Rudolf, Vienna 1955.

of the external apparatus of the rites. To retain the rubricist or ritualistic concept of the liturgy, and then to speak of liturgical spirituality is little less than absurd.

Moreover, after what we have clarified above, it should appear as a crystal-clear truth that a liturgical spirituality not only has a different end than that which is common to every spirituality and that it tends to Christian perfection of being in grace, and of acting in charity; but also, it necessarily contains, when formulated in terms of what is general to all, all the common elements of every Catholic spirituality, as common means of tending to the same perfection. This is truth crystal-clear; but by that very fact, it is all the more important in the practical area to preclude, for example, anyone's supposing — whether he be friend or enemy of the liturgical movement — that liturgical spirituality is the spirituality of him who regards as sufficient for tending to Christan perfection the use of the means offered us by the liturgical action itself; to preclude anyone's supposing that in such a spirituality it is no longer necessary, for example, to cultivate outside the liturgical action a general desire for perfection, the spirit of prayer and of meditation with the vital attention owed to the individual dogmas of the faith, control of himself and of his own tendencies, the spirit of mortification, a spirit of substantial fervor of the will, docility to the inspirations of grace, to say nothing of the fulfillment of the duties of one's own proper state, and of the exercise, painful and purificatory, of the moral virtues.[7]

In practice, "barking up the wrong tree," and that more or less consciously, is always a possibility. Nevertheless, it will not be a useless effort to warn in advance against such errors now that we are on the very threshold of a discourse on liturgical spirituality; and sufficient to demonstrate such errors would be some of the tendencies which manifested themselves prior to the encyclical *Mediator Dei*, and against which that encyclical itself was obliged to intervene.[8] It should be quite clear that liturgical spirituality is a spirituality that extends not only to those moments in which the believer participates in the liturgical action but to the whole of his life, even outside the liturgical action, devoting it entirely to the endeavor toward Christian perfection and extending to his whole life the use of those common means which, for that end, are indispensable in every Catholic spirituality.

Liturgical spirituality takes its own proper character from the simple fact that in it the specific concretization and the relative synthetic ordering of those common means, whether in the liturgical action itself or outside of it, are determined by the liturgy itself. This means that the manner in which the common elements of every Catholic spirituality are presented, realized,

---

[7] This is what liturgical spirituality means to F. Vincent, "*La spiritualite salesienne,*" in J. Gautier, *La spiritualite catholique,* Paris 1953, pp. 211–212. After which, naturally, it is child's play for this ponderous author to ridicule such a "spirituality."

[8] MD, nos. 123–137 (Lat. 121–135); 173–185 (Lat. 171–183).

and lived in practice in the liturgy, whether individually in themselves or in the relative importance which is given them, is accepted not only as the concrete manner of viewing and living the Christian reality and of straining toward perfection during the moments of the liturgical action, but also in all the rest of life outside the liturgical action. In this way the *forma mentis*, so to speak, of the liturgy is reflected in all the rest of life and determines it in its entirety as a straining toward perfection.

We do not mean the above to be understood in the sense that would exclude elements not found at all in the liturgy. To do that would imply, for example, that liturgical spirituality excludes the practice of the rosary or of the way of the cross or of corporal penances because they are not found in the liturgy! We meant it rather in the sense that all that which is taken up and gathered into the liturgical spirituality is attuned to the spirit of the liturgy, is brought into relation with it, and is regulated by it both quantitatively and qualitatively. When we say regulated by it, we mean ordered and subordinated to the liturgy, the values of which are deemed the source and illumination of one's whole life in its efforts toward perfection.

In liturgical spirituality, the disposing and subordinating of everything else to the liturgy means that everything outside the liturgy is regarded and lived either as preparation for the liturgical action or as its derivation and amplification. So it is with private prayer and meditation, private devotions and other pious exercises outside the liturgy; and so too with private mortifications, readings and study, the fulfillment of the duties of one's state in life, the apostolic ministry, etc.

It was stated that in liturgical spirituality the ordering and the quality of the elements which compose the spiritual life are determined by the liturgy lived by each one in accord with the opportunities of his own state in life. This makes it clear from the beginning that liturgical spirituality does not at all demand one particular state of life rather than another, but is adapted to all states; and in consequence thereof, it cannot be a leveling factor in regard to the varieties of states of life nor of the diverse characteristics which these different states carry with them.

This being the case, the ascendancy which the liturgical action exercises in the liturgical spirituality over the rest of human activity in the straining toward perfection is a *qualitative ascendancy*, but not necessarily also a quantitative one. A quantitative ascendancy of the liturgical action in life is had when in the very schedule of the day's works, or in life in general, the amount of time assigned to participation in the liturgical action is so notable that it predominates even extensively over other concerns, at least over the spiritual ones. On the other hand, a qualitative ascendancy is had when even if, speaking in regard to extension, non-liturgical occupations constitute the greater part of a man's habitual occupations, but are nevertheless in some way so attuned to the mind of the liturgy that they are lived in a spirit of preparation for the liturgical action, the Mass especially, or as derivation from it.

Quantitative ascendancy or predominance of the liturgy in one's life, as for example with persons who have the choral obligation of the Divine Office, inasmuch as this may be a matter strange and abnormal, does not of necessity carry with it also a qualitative ascendancy. Alas, it is really not extraordinary to find people who have spent a good part of their lives in the fulfillment of liturgical offices, and who, even after so many years, have not yet discovered the liturgy.

What we have said up to this point does no more than call attention again to the ideas either clearly affirmed or at least implied in articles 9-12 of Vatican II's Constitution on the Sacred Liturgy. The two following propositions are determining factors:

First, the general principle that "the sacred liturgy does not exhaust the entire activity of the Church."[9] This principle is applied first in the same article 9 to activities of ministry and apostolate. Afterwards, in article 12, it is extended to the spiritual life in general:

> "The spiritual life, however, it not limited solely to participation in the liturgy. The Christian is indeed called to pray with others, but he must also enter into his bedroom to pray to his Father in secret; furthermore, according to the teaching of the apostle, he must pray without ceasing. We also learn from the same apostle that we must always carry around in our bodies the dying of Jesus, so that the life also of Jesus may be made manifest in our mortal flesh. That is why we beg the Lord in the Sacrifice of the Mass that 'receiving the offering of the Spiritual Victim' he may fashion us for himself 'as an eternal gift.' "

In the second place, the proclamation in article 10 of the equally general principle: "Nevertheless the liturgy is the summit toward which the activity of the Church is directed; it is also the fount from which all her power flows."[10] This principle too is first applied in the same article 10 to the activities of ministry and apostolate, and afterwards in article 13 to activities of piety and of asceticism properly so called which have their place outside the liturgy and are termed "pious exercises" or "devotions." These exercises are highly recommended, on the condition, however, that they harmonize with the liturgy in such a way that they are "in some way derived from it, and lead the people to it, since in fact the liturgy by its very nature is far superior to any of them."

Even in the area of the spiritual life properly so called, the liturgy, therefore, is proposed by the Council, not as an absorptive element, but as the factor which orders and shapes all the rest — in a word, as the summit to which

[9] CL, art. 9.   [10] CL, art. 10.

all else tends and at the same time as the source from which all else gains its strength. This is precisely the concept of liturgical spirituality delineated above.

Some general characteristics of liturgical spirituality considered in the liturgical action itself

Such being the generic nature of liturgical spirituality, let us view the matter a little closer and see what its principal characteristics are. These characteristics ought to be determined first of all in the liturgical action itself; and they should show themselves afterwards as reflections, so to speak, in the extraliturgical forms of piety, of pious exercises, and of activities in general.

The characteristic of liturgical spirituality which stands out most noticeably at first sight is, no doubt, the strong accent which it places on the ecclesial communitarian aspect of salvation. Every Catholic spirituality, as we have said, is necessarily and at one and the same time both individual and communitarian. But, since in liturgical spirituality it is really the liturgical action which determines qualitatively the special balance in which elements common to every spirituality are viewed and lived, and since such liturgical action is presented primarily as communitarian action not only in its recondite essence — if we may use the term — but connaturally, even in its extrinsic expression and in its more intimate psychology, the communitarian aspect in liturgical spirituality is necessarily on the first level. Its being communitarian does not make of it a shapeless mass nor does it imply any confused equalitarianism; it is hierarchically communitarian, in accord with the very structure of the Church.

It follows that a liturgical spirituality without a communitarian religious psychology and sensibility is not possible, even if the believer were, in a particular instance, a real zealot for the Church and for the liturgical formulations. To shape a liturgical spirituality it is necessary, then, to exercise the greatest care in creating and shaping this religious sensibility and this communitarian spiritual psychology. Here the danger of excess which must be avoided will be of neglecting the personal attunement of the individual to the objective and communitarian reality.

As was explained above, one of the points of differentiation among the spiritualities is the relative balance in which the various dogmas of the faith are presented and lived. We already know, especially from the second part of our present work, what the proper balance of the liturgy is in this area. Let us recall for ourselves a panoramic view of the whole: from the *sacramenta*, especially from the Mass, and from the assembly of the people of God, lived in act, it goes on to a general picture of the relations between God and man and to history as sacred salvation history, profoundly unified in all its phases, from creation and from the Old Testament to the heavenly Jerusalem; history always in act which, thoroughly involving the individual, is fulfilled *hic et nunc* under the veil of sacred signs, sensible and efficacious, of the sanctification and of the worship of the Church, primarily in the Mass, and hence in the corresponding moral attunement, ascetic and mystical, of each individual. And afterwards, the Christological-Trinitarian movement which descends from God to man and rises up from man to God in the formula from the Father, through the Son, in the Holy Spirit, to the Father, Blessed Trinity, one only God in three Persons.

The efficacious and ever-present mediation of Christ, God and man, our Head and High Priest, who lived on earth and suffered and died, completing on Golgotha the sacrifice of Himself, but having risen and now glorious at the right of the Father, not only intercedes continuously for us but effects our assimilation to Himself in the paschal mystery. And all this in such a way that for us there is no grace from God nor return to God nor glory to God except through Him and with Him and in Him, the *Kyrios*, dead and risen, in participation with what He is and does. We are concerned with the communitarian dimension, ecclesial, socially structured, incarnate, of our relations with God in Christ; with the dimension of the intensive and extensive unity of the whole cosmos in our relations with God: in the totality of the human being; in the connection with the infrahuman world; in union with the members of the mystical body on earth, with the saints — first of all with Mary — and with the souls in purgatory, fellow-citizens with the angels, on the march toward the heavenly Jerusalem, our common fatherland, where the heavenly and cosmic liturgy is already in act, of which ours here below is but a shadow and a distant anticipation.

There is an awareness that while we are taking part in the cosmic drama of the two cities in conflict *ab initio mundi*, our struggle is not merely against flesh and blood, but above all against Satan and his satellites.

This is the proper framework in which the liturgy, in its own way, proposes all dogma and makes it a thing to be lived. It is a framework, nevertheless, so rich that it allows broad possibilities to each one who approaches it to ponder in turn, with greater or lesser insistence now on one and now on another of its wonderful facets.

There is another distinctive element of liturgical spirituality, which looks to the way in which the object-subject binomial is viewed and lived. We have already touched on this question in Chapter 6, where we insisted on the fact that among the various possible orthodox attitudes in this area, the proper position of the liturgy is to place the object on the primary level, concentrating the attention of the subject on it in order to rouse the subject to action and, if necessary, to bring about a strengthening of the subject primarily through his concentration on the object. Therefore, as we have several times pointed out, liturgical spirituality, even while being concerned with stimulating the subject to attune himself morally with the object, is quite moderate as compared, for example, to some of the spiritualities born, or at least definitively constituted as types in themselves, in the sixteenth century, in respect to the matter of directly leading the subject to an introspective turning in upon himself and to a psychological analysis of his own condition.

This does not mean that in liturgical spirituality there is no importance attached to the examination of conscience and to the general inspection of oneself. This is an element that no Catholic spirituality can dispense with, under one form or another. But there are various ways of examining oneself, and various psychologies in doing it. In liturgical spirituality one is moderate in his psychological self-analysis of his own states and in taking an account of his own thoughts and actions. It does not follow that introspective analyses, even quite sharp, simply have no place in a climate of liturgical spirituality, but only that in this climate they will always be tempered by the majesty of the object which lays a strong claim to being the psychological focal point.

Moreover, in liturgical spirituality, the characteristic traits and, as it were, the light under which this same object (be it God, Christ, the Eucharist, our Lady, etc.) is presented to the consideration of the subject are imposed from without, that is, by the liturgy itself, and, under the light of the liturgy, by the Bible and by dogma in general.

Also, in this more than in other spiritualities, there is a greater demand made upon the subject that he first see and hear, and then accept and conform himself thereto.

From this follows, in liturgical spirituality, the importance of understanding the liturgy, its rites, its texts, and its feasts. And it is easy to perceive that almost all the literature of liturgical spirituality consists first of all in these explanations of the object itself of the liturgy much more than in descriptions of subjective states or in exhortations or in resolutions.

We might say that liturgical spirituality is more ex-troverted than introverted, taking these terms in their narrower etymological sense of "turned outward" and "turned inward."

The question of the way, proper to the liturgy, in which the liturgy achieves, psychologically speaking, the balance between the binomial pairs God-man, grace-human effort, since it is closely connected with that of the balance between the pair object-subject, is resolved in the same direction: the liturgy gives a certain predominance to consideration and to awareness. of God and of grace. But this does not in any way imply the complete renunciation of any concern for calling forth and stimulating the moral cooperation of the subject, a matter which will be seen more clearly when we treat explicity of the exercise of the moral virtues in a climate of liturgical spirituality.

In any case, it is clear enough even here that the way proper to the liturgy to stimulate the moral cooperation of the subject is to have him concentrate his attention more on God and on grace than on himself and on his own capabilities, even as assisted by grace. This is precisely the reason why the liturgy is in the habit of fixing men's attention, will, and emotional processes in all their gradations more on God who knows and loves man than on man who knows and loves God. This consideration will be completed by what we shall have to say later about the distinct prevalence in the liturgy of the theological virtues over the moral, a prevalence not only theoretical and entitative, which no Catholic spirituality would dream of denying, but even psychological and practical.

Another note characteristic of liturgical spirituality is in respect to the relative balance with which it brings into operation the various psychological faculties of man: intellect, will, and emotion or affection. This aspect of the liturgy too, which touches upon a criterion of no small importance in the determining of a spirituality, has previously been clarified in Chapter 11. The constant care of the liturgy in considering and treating man as a totality and as a unity, somatic, psychic, and spiritual, was seen; its broad utilization even of the external senses, not excepting the esthetic sense, for the purpose of the spiritual actuation of the whole man; its way of addressing itself to the intellect more intuitively and admirationally than discursively and analytically, as can happen, on the other hand, when, for example, we fix our attention on the metaphysically constitutive aspect of entities, or the formal philosophical motives of individual virtues and actions, or on the prudential pondering of actions from the viewpoint of their pros and cons; nor does this prevent the liturgy from keeping always present before the intellect the dogmatic panorama of that picture of sacred salvation history referred to above. We saw too, in its proper place, the care which the liturgy takes, softly and almost intuitively, but nonetheless constantly and, as it were, immediately, to make every actualization of the faculties flow together so as to produce a general attitude of the volitive-affective type, in accord with all the gradations of prayer, of *compunctio*, and of lyricism.

Every Catholic spirituality is necessarily in some way theocentric and, under another aspect, Christocentric; and it is dogmatic, ecclesial, and biblical as well. I say, *in some way* and *under a certain aspect*. What I wish to convey by these terms is that similar notes, generically formulated, do not distinguish one Catholic spirituality from another. That is why it is a useless labor, when attempting to characterize one spirituality in the face of another, to have recourse, as is frequently done, to similar notes in their generic quality, and to say, for example, that a particular spirituality is distinguished by its love of God, service of God, love of Christ, service of Christ, imitation of Christ, or even that it is a spirituality that follows the teaching of the Church in all things, that it has no other code than the gospel, etc., etc.

The special way that liturgical spirituality has of being a dogmatic spirituality is not only in its constantly setting before the eyes of the faithful the revelation proposed by the Church, but what is more, in its proposing it in that proper synthetic proportion and in that proper concrete coloration, with the *sacramenta* as starting place, in the general framework of sacred salvation history, in the Christological-Trinitarian movement, etc., as pointed out above.

The theocentrism of the liturgy is that which results concretely from its stance in the manner in which the binomial pair is lived: object-subject, God-creature; from the psychology deriving from the universal formula-reality: from the Father, through the Son, in the Holy Spirit, to the Father, Blessed Trinity of one only God; from the noteworthy predominance, both psychological and practical, given to the exercise of all the theological virtues; from the spirit of adoration, thanksgiving, and praise which pervades it through and through.

The proper way of the liturgy's being Christocentric is likewise tied in to the universal formula-reality: *Per Christum Dominum nostrum; Per ipsum, et cum ipso, et in ipso est tibi Deo Patri omnipotenti . . .* ; to the fact that the features of Christ are viewed by starting from the *Kyrios* of the paschal mystery. Spirituality based on the liturgy is ecclesial in the precise sense that in it the Christian life and the straining toward perfection are lived concretely in the real and psychological framework of the people of God as mystery of the Church always in act under the veil of sensible and efficacious signs, and that this way of living the Christian life and the tendency to perfection is none other, as will become clearer below, than the very way of living them proposed by the Church as pertaining to such a spirituality by a title that pertains to none other.

Liturgical spirituality is a biblical spirituality in the concrete sense that the whole Christian life and the striving for perfection are lived as mystery of Christ, of the Church, of history, through continually putting the Bible into act, be it Old Testament or New, as expression, always present and efficacious, of the same realities always in act, as has already been explained to some extent in the second part of the present work and more particularly in the third part.

It is not necessary to explain further in what concrete sense liturgical spirituality can and must be considered by a most special title a sacrificial and sacramental spirituality, after the notion of the liturgy which we have set forth in the first part of this book, and that which we have given, in particular in Chapter 5, in regard to the Mass as synthetic realization and expression of the whole liturgical complexus and hence the center and sun of the same.

It is against this background that we are to understand also the proper manner in which liturgical spirituality is Eucharistic spirituality. The Eucharist is always viewed therein in its connatural organic context, which is to say,

in its sacrificial context. Communion is, in the first place, sacramental participation in the sacrifice of the Cross through the eating of the Sacred Victim
who is immolated therein for us. A primary consideration here is that we receive the Real Presence at Mass, so that sacramental communion and the sacrifice itself are accomplished together. The Sacrament is reserved in view of
the possible reception of Communion by one who is unable to be present at
the sacrifice. Naturally, liturgical spirituality must take into account what is a
concern of every Catholic, that which today is referred to as Eucharist worship and devotion, that is, the worship and devotion dedicated to our Lord
present in the reserved Sacrament. Only it insists on the fact that the primary
duty of every Christian is to participate actively and fully in the Sacrifice and
to receive Communion therein.[11]

Liturgical spirituality and extraliturgical forms of piety

The preceding passages expository of liturgical spirituality are directly
relevant to the liturgical action itself. But we have also stated that we are not
thereby limiting liturgical spirituality to a spirituality centered solely on the
liturgy. How, then, is such a spirituality to be expressed and realized in
extraliturgical forms of piety or in "pious exercises"?

The answer is enunciated by the Second Vatican Council in its Constitution on the Sacred Liturgy, which summarizes in a few words what had
already been explained about this matter in greater depth in the encyclical
Mediator Dei.[12] The Council document states:

> "Popular devotions [i.e., pious exercises] of the Christian people,
> provided they conform to the laws and norms of the Church, are to be
> highly recommended, especially where they are ordered by the Apos-
> tolic See . . . But such devotions should be so drawn up that they
> harmonize with the liturgical seasons, accord with the sacred liturgy,
> are in some way derived from it, and lead the people to it, since in fact
> the liturgy by its very nature is far superior to any of them." [13]

Among the pious exercises or popular devotions we can reckon meditation,
examination of conscience, retreats, and the spiritual exercises. Of these we

[11] A manifestation of this spirit is to be found
in Vatican II's constitution *De sacra liturgia*,
art. 55, where "the more perfect form of participation in the Mass whereby the faithful,
after the priest's communion, receive the Lord's
Body from the same sacrifice, is warmly recommended" (i.e., with hosts consecrated at
the same sacrifice in which they are participating); and Communion under both species even
for the faithful is introduced anew in various
instances. For the history of the rites and customs in this area, see A. G. Martimort, *La
Chiesa in preghiera*, pp. 454–503; H. Fischer,
Eucharistie-Katechese und liturgische Erneuer-

ung, Düsseldorf 1959.

[12] MD, especially nos. 172–185 (Lat. 170–
183). The encyclical insisted on the point, and
was even somewhat polemical about it, because
of certain abuses in this area, which had manifested themselves especially in Germany. See
M. Kassiepe, *Irrwege und Umwege im Fröm-
migkeitsleben der Gegenwart*, 2nd edition,
Würzburg 1940. However, Kassiepe is to be
read with due caution because in not a few
instances he oversteps the bounds and finds
fault even with the more authentic liturgical
movement.

[13] CL, art. 13.

shall have more to say further on, since they are most immediately connected with the ascetical effort in the striving toward perfection.

Among the devotions which are of more direct interest to us in the present context we would mention the recitation of the rosary, the month of the Sacred Heart, the month of the Blessed Mother, triduums, novenas, the stations of the Cross, and the like.

First of all it is necessary to affirm not only their legitimacy and the fact that they are to be recommended, within the proper conditions set down for them, for Christian people in general, but also, with due regard for fitness and suitability, which a pastoral centered on the liturgy has the task of determining, the possibility, when particular circumstances demand it, of utilizing them fruitfully even in a climate of clearly liturgical spirituality.

For this to happen it is requisite that such pious exercises "be so drawn up," especially in reference to the liturgical seasons, and in regard to their quantity and quality, "that they harmonize . . . with the sacred liturgy."

This harmony, however, is not to be understood in the sense of a simple juxtaposition, as if it were a question of two independent ways of equal value for reaching to God, left to the free choice of each person with the sole restriction that no artificial antagonisms be interposed between the one way and the other. The harmony which is spoken of here is a harmony of subordination under the primacy of the liturgy, "since the liturgy by its very nature far surpasses" any kind of popular devotions; and this harmony must show itself in the fact that popular devotions "are in some fashion derived from the liturgy, and lead the people to it." It could not have been stated more clearly. It is the inevitable consequence of the principle that the liturgy, even though it does not exhaust in itself all the action of the Church, is nevertheless the summit to which all else tends and the font from which all else derives.

In a climate of liturgical spirituality such are in substance the relations between the liturgy and extraliturgical pious practices: there is no way an ostracism of extraliturgical popular devotions on the part of the liturgy, but simply their being shaped and ordered in their relative quantity and quality by the spirit of the liturgy as a preparation for living the liturgy more intensely and as amplification and extraliturgical outflowing from the liturgical life itself.

Two things in this area, therefore, are certain: first, that a strong life of piety, even outside those moments of actually assisting at the liturgy, and internal piety expressed even externally in a certain way, is necessary in anyone who wants to strive seriously for Christian perfection; second, that in a climate of liturgical spirituality the specific way in which that life of extraliturgical piety is concretized in its quantity and in its quality is by its being subordinated to the liturgy and its being defined by the spirit of the liturgy, as preparation for the liturgical life and as enhancement thereof.

Insofar as further particular delimitations of the terms of their use is concerned, so that in individual instances that correct ordering of these exercises is verified, a correct ordering quantitatively and qualitatively, through their subordination to the liturgy, it is a question of prudential tact in matters supernatural, the solution to which depends upon the concrete necessities of individuals or of groups of individuals, with reference to their degree of spiritual development, their culture, their temperament, the times and places. This much was already called to our attention quite rightly in the encyclical *Mediator Dei.*[14]

A truly good judge in particular instances can only be one who has all three of the following qualities: he will have really penetrated the world of the liturgy; he will himself be habitually and thoroughly imbued with a spirit of prayer; he will have pastoral experience in the care of souls. There is nothing more deplorable in this area than those pretended apostles of the liturgy who think they have entered into the spirit of the liturgy but are nevertheless notably lacking in the habitual spirit of prayer and, for the most part, even of true pastoral experience in the care of souls, and who believe that they are themselves authorized, under the pretext of liturgical spirit, not only to minimize every kind of extraliturgical pious practice, but even to disparage these practices, or, what is worse, actually take the field against them.

However that may be, it is certain that extraliturgical practices must be set in order through their being subordinated to the spirit of the liturgy. It is evident, therefore, that the fact that a certain extraliturgical practice of piety can be shown generically to benefit the religious spirit of a particular individual or group of individuals so that given their particular conditions, it helps them in some way to pray, cannot be, for those who have the responsibility of it, anything but a specious pretext that it dispenses them from the obligation of entering into and living the world of the liturgy, a pretext for neglecting to lead to the liturgy with a suitable catechesis and instruction those in their charge.

Liturgical spirituality and extraliturgical activities

The question of the relations between the liturgy and extraliturgical activities is resolved in an entirely similar fashion in the climate of liturgical spirituality.

And in this matter too, we are not abandoned to our own arbitrary judgment. The Second Vatican Council has explained it all quite thoroughly. Let us read again the pertinent texts, with a special eye to the aspect that is of interest to us in the present context.

> "The sacred liturgy does not exhaust the entire activity of the Church. Before men can come to the liturgy they must be called to faith and to conversion. . . . Therefore the Church announces the

[14] MD, nos. 108 (Lat. 107); 179 (Lat. 177).

good tidings of salvation to those who do not believe. . . . To believers also the Church must ever preach faith and penance; she must prepare them for the sacraments, teach them to observe all that Christ has commanded, and encourage them to engage in all the works of charity, piety and the apostolate." [15]

"Nevertheless the liturgy is the summit toward which the activity of the Church is directed; it is also the fount from which all her power flows. For the goal of apostolic endeavor is that all who are made sons of God by faith and baptism should come together to praise God in the midst of his Church, to take part in the Sacrifice and to eat the Lord's Supper.

"The liturgy, in its turn, moves the faithful filled with 'the paschal sacraments' to be 'one in holiness'; it prays that 'they hold fast in their lives to what they have grasped by their faith.' The renewal in the Eucharist of the covenant between the Lord and man draws the faithful and sets them aflame with Christ's insistent love. From the liturgy, therefore, and especially from the Eucharist, grace is poured forth upon us as from a fountain, and the sanctification of men in Christ and the glorification of God to which all other activities of the Church are directed, as toward their end, are achieved with maximum effectiveness." [16]

These two articles of the Council are the *magna charta* of liturgical spirituality in the question of the relations between the liturgy and extraliturgical activities of every kind.

It is evident that the activity, whether of the individual Christian or of the Church, is not wholly exhausted in the liturgical action. Nor, all things considered, can the liturgical action properly so called have, in the totality of the life of the clergy in general, in respect to their other occupations, even a quantitative prevalence in reference to time. Liturgical spirituality, therefore, cannot mean, even for the clergy, a material absorption of other ecclesiastical activities by the liturgical action. For the vast majority of the clergy, there cannot even be a habitual material predominance of liturgical activity properly so called over other pastoral ecclesiastical activities such as instruction, administration, penetration and safeguarding of the interests of religion, and the winning over of those who are strangers to the faith.

And nevertheless liturgical spirituality, precisely because it is a complete spirituality which runs over into every facet of life, determines in its own way even these activities, gathering them together in a single spirit, directing them to Christian perfection in the edification of the Church and in the perfecting of individuals. Liturgical spirituality, therefore, regards these activities and lives them as means preparing one for the liturgical life and as effects deriving therefrom.

[15] CL, art. 9.   [16] CL, art. 10.

Thus in a climate of liturgical spirituality the missionary carries on his missionary activity with a view to leading him who is a stranger to the faith to live the Christian life and to live it fully, as is done in the liturgical action, and especially in the active and even psychologically complete participation in the communitarian sacrifice of the Mass. In doing this the missionary builds up the Church by contributing on his part to its being led to the fullness of the age of Christ in the liturgical action.

Considering this matter under the aspect of the missionary's own striving toward perfection, we can say that he is devoting himself to his missionary activity as to a fulfilling of the duties of his state that devolve upon him in the vineyard of the Lord, with a view to being able to live fully his encounter with God in the liturgical action, primarily in the Mass. Under another aspect we can say that the missionary, in consequence of having lived his encounter with the Lord in the liturgical action, especially in the Mass, gives himself to his missionary activity in order to accomplish the demands which the liturgical life imposes: to fulfill with generosity the duties of his own state and to share with others, in accord with his proper calling, the treasures which God has shown us and has caused us to live in the liturgical action.

In this way and in every way the liturgical action, and the Mass most especially, not only does not diminish at all the multiplex extraliturgical activity of the missionary, but even strengthens it immensely; for it gives his activities an incomparable clarity and unity of total purpose in a powerful supernatural dynamism of realization, while of itself it shapes and qualitatively dominates his whole life, unifying and enlivening its multifaceted workings. In this sense the whole of life is a liturgical life — we mean qualitatively liturgical.

What has been said of the missionary's extraliturgical activity is likewise true of all the other extraliturgical activities in the Church, whether of the hierarchy as such or of the individual faithful.

There is nothing extraordinary in all this. The total activity of the Church is directed without exception to the sanctification of souls in their contact, at least in desire, with the sacraments. And even if sanctification and worship be inseparable, sanctification itself is ordered to the worship of God and not vice versa. The highest worship of God, whether of the Church as such or of single individuals, takes place in the liturgy, most especially in the Mass, supposing always the complete moral attunement of the subject. Everything in the Church, therefore, is ordered to the liturgy, primarily to the Mass.

Moreover, there is no activity whatever that can have any supernatural value without grace. But as we explained in its proper place and in keeping with the Catechism of the Council of Trent, in respect to the Mass as focal point of the liturgy, every grace derives from the Eucharist, sacrifice and sacrament, like individual little streams pouring out from their common source. All the supernatural activity of the whole world derives, then, from the liturgy, most especially from the Mass, and is directed back to the liturgy, most especially to the Mass. Liturgical spirituality, focusing the whole of Christian life and the striving toward perfection on the liturgy, simply takes cognizance of this fact and tries to live accordingly.

That this manner of viewing matters will have great practical consequences on the spirit and method according to which all one's various activities are carried out would seem to be a thing quite obvious; and it has direct bearing upon the question of liturgical pastoral. It is enough to reflect for the moment on the fact that if the liturgy is the fount from which every activity in the Church derives and the end to which every activity tends, then no method for the practical execution of this activity can be recommended if it is one that, in practice, allows us to forget that this activity derives from active participation in the liturgy and must lead us back to active participation in the liturgy, primarily in the Mass.

Is liturgical spirituality but one among the several schools of spirituality?

In order to gain an understanding of the nature and general characteristics of liturgical spirituality, we began this chapter with an explanation of what spirituality in general is, and in what sense, within the bosom of the single Catholic spirituality, it is possible to speak of diverse spiritualities. With this approach to the question it would be easy to come to the conclusion that whatever be the value of liturgical spirituality, it is but one spirituality among the many others existing in the Catholic Church: one school of spirituality alongside so many other schools, and basically the Benedictine school of spirituality.

It is time now to dispel this illusion. Liturgical spirituality is not one among many other schools of spirituality admitted or even recommended by the Church; much less is it to be identified with Benedictine spirituality. No, liturgical spirituality is the spirituality of the Church by a title which is suitable to none other.

Certainly the reader will not have failed to notice that when we were speaking of the idea and general characteristics of liturgical spirituality, we did scarcely more than comment on articles 9 to 13 of Vatican II's Constitution on the Sacred Liturgy. And this to such an extent that we can say that liturgical spirituality is simply the spirituality described in the aforesaid articles.

The proof is quite weighty; for it is evident that the Council would not have concerned itself with proposing to the Church a new school of spirituality among the many already existing. Its purpose was simply to set down the principles of life and of action that are valid for the whole Church. What it means, then, is that even if these principles do amount to a spirituality, this is not in any way to be regarded as one spirituality among the many. How can this be?

Let us call to mind first of all that which we said above about the concept *opus operantis Ecclesiae*, in regard to the various degrees in which the Church as such is, so to speak, involved in whatever is done in her bosom, for example, in prayer. Every prayer uttered by any individual whomsoever in the bosom of the Church, that is, so long as such individuals be united in faith, in sacraments, and in obedience to the legitimate hierarchy, is in a most real way the prayer of the Church. It is the Church, the body of Christ, it is Christ Himself who prays in the prayer of the individual. That prayer, then, can never be regarded by God, much less heard by Him, as offered separately from the body of the Church, and separate from Christ Himself, in whom it is offered.

The various prayers offered in the bosom of the Church and which, therefore, are all in a certain sense prayers of the Church, these the Church herself as such makes her own and regards them as her own by various titles. Thus all the prayers offered in the bosom of the Church are most assuredly prayers of the Church, but all are not such in the same degree nor by the same title because even though the Church and Christ Himself accept them all as their own, there attaches to them various degrees of obligation and of authenticity before God.

In the case, for example, which we referred to elsewhere, in which, in a parish, the parochial community, under the presidency and guidance of the pastor and upon the recommendation or even the explicit command of the competent ecclesiastical authority, solemnly recites the rosary or makes a solemn way of the Cross, this is the prayer of the Church by a different title and in a much superior degree, with a corresponding degree of efficacy *ex opere operantis Ecclesiae* much superior to that which is to be found in the case of one of the faithful who recites privately a prayer even highly praised and recommended by ecclesiastical authority, for example the rosary or the *Anima Christi*.

The recitation of the rosary, therefore, even under the official guidance of the pastor and upon the recommendation or command of the competent authorities, not being regarded, at least at the present time, as a properly liturgical act, must be considered as a prayer of the Church in a degree and by a title different and inferior, with a corresponding efficacy *ex opere operantis Ecclesiae* inferior to that of all liturgical prayers properly so called. Liturgical prayer is prayer of the Church, the body of Christ and bride of Christ; and hence it is the prayer of Christ Himself in His Church, by means of the Church, and at the pleasure of His Church, to a degree and by a preëminent title which does not pertain to other prayers offered in the

Church, even though they be prayers legitimately recognized or warmly recommended by the Church.

Liturgical prayer is not simply one of the many modes of prayer legitimately recognized and used by the Church; rather, it is a prayer which, in respect to the others, is far and away beyond comparison in dignity and in efficacy. This is simply the doctrine of the greater dignity of liturgical prayer in respect to private prayer. This much is explicitly affirmed by the Second Vatican Council:

> "Every liturgical celebration, because it is an action of Christ the Priest and of his Body, which is the Church, is a sacred action surpassing all others. No other action of the Church can equal its efficacy by the same title and to the same degree." [17]

Pius XII had already stated:

> "Unquestionably liturgical prayer, being the public supplication of the illustrious Spouse of Jesus Christ, is superior in excellence to private prayers." [18]

The same Pope also said:

> "This form (private) of worship the Church does not merely tolerate; rather, she fully recognizes and recommends it, without in any way implying anything prejudicial to the preeminence of liturgical worship." [19]

Having arrived at this point, the rest of the reasoning process is easy. Since liturgical prayer is not simply one of the many kinds of prayer legitimately recognized, used, or even recommended by the Church, but is the prayer of the Church herself by a title which pertains to none other, a title which without antagonism or contradiction places liturgical prayer in a category different than any other kind of prayer, by reason of its dignity and efficacy, so too the spirituality which focuses on liturgical prayer, therefore, is not simply one among the many spiritualities recognized or even recommended by the Church, but on the contrary, it is the spirituality belonging peculiarly to the Church by a title which belongs to none other, and this with no antagonism or contradiction in regard to the other spiritualities existing in the Church and which she recognizes or even recommends.

The Church, therefore, just as she has her official prayer which is her prayer by a special title, even while admitting and recommending other forms of prayer, has also her official spirituality, which is her spirituality by a special title, precisely determined by that official prayer, even while admitting and recommending other forms of spirituality. The Church not only lays down

[17] CL, art. 7.
[18] MD, no. 37.

[19] Discourse of September 22, 1956; in *AAS*, Vol. 48 (1956), p. 714.

the main lines and the limits common to every Catholic spirituality, while allowing the liberty of further specification and concretization within these same limits, but beyond this she herself proposes a specification and concretization which she regards as hers by a special title. In the same way it is proper that she determines not only what are the essential characteristics which every Catholic prayer must have, but beyond this she specifies and concretizes those characteristics in an official prayer which is hers by a preëminent title, even while admitting and recognizing other ways of specifying and concretizing the general characteristics of Catholic prayer.

It was seen above that while the Church admits or warmly recommends certain extraliturgical forms of piety, it is intended by all means that these harmonize with the spirit of the liturgy and that this harmony, in the mind of the Church, be a harmony of subordination and not simply of juxtaposition. It is logical to suppose that such be also the thought of the Church in regard to spiritualities in some way different from the official spirituality, which is liturgical spirituality; that the Church, I mean to say, while recognizing the legitimacy and the utility of these other spiritualities, or even recommending them, means always to do this with the presupposition of their being harmonized with the spirit of the liturgy.

An objection might be raised at this point. If it is said that the Church, while admitting forms of spirituality other than the official liturgical form, intends, nevertheless, that they harmonize with the spirit of the liturgy, does this not in itself tend to confirm that the Church intends to take away from these spiritualities the characteristic notes by which they differ from liturgical spirituality and to reduce them thereby to a solitary official spirituality?

Certainly such a reduction cannot be in accord with the mind of the Church, which, while recognizing on the one hand the possibility of diverse forms of spirituality in the bosom of the selfsame Catholic spirituality, could not on the other hand demand the suppression of those very notes which are the precise characteristics which distinguish those spiritualities from liturgical spirituality. Such a conclusion does not follow from the requirement that all spiritualities be colored by the spirit of the liturgy; for this harmonization can have various forms and degrees, and the Church certainly does not demand that it be pushed to the point of simply adopting all those characteristics which were indicated above as belonging properly to liturgical spirituality.

It seems that that harmonization with the spirit of the liturgy, of spiritualities not properly liturgical, which is demanded by the Church is sufficient if through these other spiritualities a real care is taken, in the words of Pius XII, in making "the divine cult loved and spread daily ever more widely, and in making the faithful approach the sacraments with more longing desire," [20] especially the Eucharistic Sacrifice; and if through these other spiritualities,

[20] MD, no. 181 (Lat. 179).

the participation of the faithful in the Eucharistic Sacrifice tends to be such a participation as that spoken of by the Second Vatican Council as "full, conscious, and active participation," [21] and communitarian as well.[22]

Naturally, such care, if taken seriously, cannot but make its effects sensibly present through every facet of a spirituality. But even while admitting this, there can still remain broad margins to differentiate it from the official liturgical spirituality strictly and properly so called, sufficient, it would seem, even with the harmonizing of all spiritualities with the spirit of the liturgy, to safeguard in each of them those characteristic traits which give them their own distinct individuality. When the necessary harmonization with the spirit of the liturgy of the most diverse forms of private piety and of the exercises in which these forms are expressed is properly carried out, the liturgical form of piety properly so called does not deprive these other forms of their legitimate notes of distinction. In no case is this harmonization, be it even by subordination, simply equivalent to absorption.

So much the less, then, need there be any fear that the thorough spirituality by the spirit of the liturgy, a thing to be desired, is an attempt to establish an inadmissible monopoly of one school in the field of spirituality or to bring into danger, in this matter, the principle of broad liberty mentioned by Pius XII in respect to the concrete manner of making retreats and the spiritual exercises:

> "As regards the different methods employed in these exercises, it is perfectly clear to all that in the Church on earth, no less than in the Church in heaven, there are many mansions; and that asceticism cannot be the monopoly of anyone. It is the same Spirit who breatheth where He will; and Who with differing gifts and in different ways enlightens and guides souls to sanctity. Let their freedom and the supernatural action of the Holy Spirit be so sacrosanct that no one presume to disturb or stifle them for any reason whatsoever." [23]

Are liturgical spirituality and Benedictine spirituality one and the same?

It must be observed, finally, that liturgical spirituality strictly so called admits even within itself a considerable variation and diversification, greater even, so far as I can see, than is admitted by the various individual schools of spirituality. This is due to the fact that liturgical spirituality is much tied in to the experience of a single individual or a specific group of people or a particular segment of life.

Father de Guibert, who more and better than others has studied the question of that which in general determines the distinctions between different spiritualities, believes it necessary to place on the first level of these distinctive factors the personal experience of some great personality or saint. A founder of an Order, for example, through circumstances of temperament, of sur-

---

[21] CL, art. 14.
[22] CL, art. 26.

[23] MD, no. 179 (Lat. 177).

roundings, of vocation and special gifts, realizing in his own life a specific balance of the factors common to every spirituality, shows by his own experience the validity of such a formula and thus gives rise to a distinct school of spirituality within the bosom of the general Catholic spirituality.[24] This, however, is not the case with liturgical spirituality properly so called, which owes its origin, not to the experience of a saint nor in any way to a group of saints nor to a particular movement temporally and locally specified in the Church, but simply to the supernatural instinct and the continued experience of the Church as such, in that which she holds as most authentic.

Moreover, it seems to me, that Father de Guibert does not grant sufficient importance, among the factors which concern the origins of various schools of spirituality, to the special area of life in which they were conceived, or, if you will, to the specific duties of a particular state in life which the various schools really have, most frequently, as their purpose and through the most perfect possible fulfillment of which they expect to lead their adherent in the direction of Christian perfection.

Thus, the same Father de Guibert rightly emphasizes the fundamental importance which the concept of "service" of God or of Church has in Ignatian spirituality. But it does not seem to me that he ever emphasizes in a sufficiently explicit way, even if it is a matter implicitly evident everywhere, that this service of Christ, in Ignatian spirituality — especially outside the *Exercises*, which, everyone knows, are intended to bear directly upon the choice of a state in life — does not remain simply a generic concept. The concept of total service is found generically in all the spiritualities, for example, in that too of St. Benedict.

Insofar as it is a distinctive characteristic of Ignatian spirituality, service has a quite concrete meaning; for it signifies the service of Christ in the varying forms of apostolate to which the Jesuits dedicate themselves in their frame of life, in the disposition of time and of surroundings experienced by them. The service of Christ, concretely speaking, means the service of Christ within the framework of the duties of the Jesuitical state. Thus, the concept becomes truly determinate through a particular spirituality, as Father de Guibert does quite rightly point out. As much would have to be said, I think, for all the great schools of spirituality, at least for the greater ones, in which their purposeful possession of a specific framework of life and of duties of a particular state seem to be a constitutive element of primary importance.

And this is probably the reason why it always poses a most delicate problem which, in the long run, is likely to carry with it some real difficulties when a specified spirituality is adopted by one who lives a notably different style of life. The same thing happens when, as is much more frequently the case, an individual or a community takes up a type of activity, or even a style

---

[24] See the two studies by Father de Guibert cited above in note 5 of the present chapter.

of life, which carries with it duties of a state in life notably different from those which were contemplated in the type of spirituality in which the individual or community continues to live.

Nevertheless, while all this is certainly true of the various schools of spirituality, it is not so with liturgical spirituality. The latter is not the product of the experience of a specific personality, nor has it been conceived by the Church as appropriate to a specific group of people in specific circumstances; rather, it is to be realized in quite disparate styles of life and in persons who are bound to very different duties of their state: by the hermit as well as by the missionary; by the cloistered nun as well as by the mother of a family or by the businessman; by the monk as well as by the parish priest; by the farmer and the laborer as well as by the university professor; by the teacher as well as by the student.

The Church, proposing the Mass and the sacraments as the center, even the psychological focal point, of Christian life and dynamism, as the organizer even in a subjective way of the striving toward perfection, addresses herself to all states of life, embracing within herself the purpose of all. She invites each to draw out even psychologically and subjectively all the connatural consequences of the fact that the Mass, at which he must in any case assist, and the sacraments, which he must in any case receive, are objectively, in a Catholic and ecclesial regimen, the pivotal point and the center of his relations with God. The Church says to all: Live intensely and to the very depths of your subjective psychology the Mass and the sacraments in the framework and in the spirit that I propose to you, and in which, in any hypothesis, you must participate; and not only will your Christian life be assured, but even your striving toward perfection.

This means that liturgical spirituality, even in the strictest meaning of the term, will have to be able to admit notable gradations of varied concrete realization and of practical application to different styles of life, even while it is always and everywhere marked by a qualitative predominance of the liturgy as the element which determines the general balance of the various common means of perfection and their specific concretization.

It signals especially that particular kind of concrete realization of liturgical spirituality properly so called which is achieved when not only a qualitative but even a quantitative prevalence in one's life is given to the liturgy, as happens with those who give to the choir obligation of the Divine Office a prevalence, even quantitatively, or at least devote to it a noteworthy amount of time in comparison to that given to other occupations. This kind of liturgical spirituality properly so called is not possible except in a well-defined style of life, and it cannot in fact, in its particular specification, be proposed for all.

It is a custom among authors, when they speak of various schools of spirituality, to enumerate among these that which they call the Benedictine school.

It is not my intention to discuss here to what point the Rule of St. Benedict and the history of spirituality among the monks who for some fourteen centuries have in some way followed that Rule may authorize us to speak of a Benedictine school of spirituality. It is extremely probable that exhaustive research would demonstrate that when we speak of *Benedictines* as a unit, instinctively meaning thereby the Benedictine *Order*, in this field, as in many others, it is possible to so speak only by reason of many and great oversimplifications and by reason of more or less arbitrary assimilation of the *ordo monachorum* to a modern Order.

However, taking matters as they are today among the confederated Benedictines, it can really be said that among them, beginning with the last decades of the nineteenth century, under the impetus given by Dom Guéranger, there reigns a strong tendency to a common spirituality of the strictly liturgical type, defined not only by the qualitative prevalence given to the liturgy but even by its quantitative prevalence, or at least by a very notable amount of time given to the liturgy in comparison to the amount of time given to other occupations. The fact that some of these Benedictine monasteries, from the time of Don Guéranger, were the instigators of the liturgical movement in various countries, and, up to the end of the Second World War, its greatest and most effective promoters, gave rise to the notion that simply equates liturgical spirituality with Benedictine spirituality.

Such an identification, however, is ambiguous and dangerous from the point of view of the liturgy. Benedictine spirituality is *one* specific kind of *liturgical* spirituality, but it is not to be identified as *the* liturgical spirituality; it does not entirely exhaust the whole content. Whoever does not see this clearly will instinctively come to believe that the liturgy and liturgical spirituality are the property of the Benedictines, almost in the same way that it is popularly believed that a certain devotion is the property of a certain Order, a certain pious practice the property of another. For the instinctively suspicious it would follow that the efforts to make the liturgy known and lived must be regarded as no more than the efforts which are made by every religious Order when it preaches in behalf of its own chapel. And thus the liturgy would be debased, in the opinion of many, to the means of carrying on a monkish rivalry between chapel and chapel, between refectory and refectory!

Finally, in the majority of cases, by identifying liturgical spirituality with Benedictine spirituality, the implication is made that the liturgical spirit and liturgical spirituality are really not for ordinary mortals; rather, that they demand restrictive surroundings, culturally and spiritually chosen, responsive to the esthetic refinements of Gregorian Chant, where the possibility exists of numerous ministers about the altar so that the sacred rites can be performed in all their fullness and with all decorum, etc. Especially will it be believed that the bishop in the practical difficulties of a diocese, the missionary in spreading Christianity anew, the pastor of a country parish among country-folk, or a city pastor at the head of a large parochial operation have nothing to gain by addressing themselves and their subjects to the school of the liturgy.

How contrary to the truth all this is will be seen still better in the chapters on liturgy and pastoral. Fortunately the liturgical movement, from the Second World War until the present time, has gone forth definitively from the Benedictine monasteries, and it is in large measure in the hands of dedicated pastors of souls involved in a struggle that is most real, and eminently ecclesial and universal, for the Christianization or re-Christianization of the world. The fruit of this pastoralization and universalization of the liturgical movement can be seen in the accomplishments of the Second Vatican Council. The spirit of the liturgy has worked its effects therein; and there could be nothing more gratifying to those Benedictines who have truly penetrated this spirit.

3. Liturgical Spirituality and the Ascetical Effort of Striving to Perfection

When speaking of the general notion of spirituality, we also recalled the precise meaning and the necessity of the distinction between the ascetical aspect and the mystical aspect of the striving toward Christian perfection. We know that this distinction, presupposing the common role that belongs as much to God and to grace as it does to man and human effort, in every supernatural action, is based in the first place on the different intensity, perhaps even with a psychological awareness, now of the human effort and the pains that it may cost, even though it is always assisted by grace, and now on the action of God with the consequent greater passivity of man and ease of action; and in the second place, on the presence or absence of a prevalence of the intuitive aspect over the discursive. Each of the two aspects is of value simultaneously for purifying from sin and imperfection, and for uniting to God.

After having examined the notion and general characteristics of liturgical spirituality, we must consider it more in particular under this double aspect, ascetical and mystical, in the striving toward perfection.

Liturgical spirituality and the ascetical effort in general

It should not be necessary to call attention explicitly to the fact that in liturgical spirituality ascetical effort on the road toward perfection is really and consciously deemed indispensable no less than it is in any other kind of Catholic spirituality. It cannot be other than a question of vulgar deception if some, under the pretext of liturgical spirit and of liturgical spirituality, have come to a theoretical contempt or to a practical neglect of the undeniable necessity of the ascetical effort, under all its forms, in the work of sanctification. To such as these, it is necessary simply to recall the catechism lesson which teaches that the very *opus operatum* of the sacraments demands of every adult, if their fruits of sanctification are to be obtained, good moral dispositions and hence his cooperation.[25]

And when persons such as these join us in the liturgy and in the liturgical spirit, they can see for themselves how foreign is the omission of ascetical effort or the actual contempt for it in anyone who takes a pride in the liturgy, while the liturgy itself does not cease recalling it in every way, for example, during all of Lent and on so many other occasions, as we will explain in due course. On the contrary, it is time now to remind ourselves of what we have already explained in its proper place about the moral and obligatory dimension of every liturgical sign; from that teaching it is easy to see how closely morals and liturgy are connected by way of intrinsic constitution and not only by way of exhortations and vague admonitions.

To suppose, therefore, that ascetical life and liturgical piety can be, I will not say contrasted, but simply separated, is such an aberration that from the theoretical point of view it is not worthwhile for anyone to expend his efforts in refuting the notion, since it is so very evident that it is an aberration deriving from an ignorance of the nature of the liturgy and of the most elementary principles of the spiritual life in general.[26]

We can only ask how it could be possible for there to exist even a vague theoretical tendency to regard these realities, asceticism and the liturgical spirit, as actually separate, or even how they could be regarded as being only tenuously connected. Whatever is said, this attitude is as good as manifested by some who aspire to be liturgists while accepting this pretended fact and peacefully accommodating themselves to it. The same attitude often shows up among those who, though diffident to the liturgical movement, wish to reassure more and more those who are suspicious of them, and to persuade them that, in any case, enthusiasm for the liturgy in the majority of cases does not provide a firm and solid basis for the spiritual life of the clergy and

---

[25] Vatican II's Constitution on the Sacred Liturgy explicitly inculcates the principle that for the sacred liturgy to produce its full effect, "it is necessary that the faithful come to it with proper dispositions, that their minds be attuned to their voices, and that they cooperate with heavenly grace lest they receive it in vain" (art. 11). See also the admonition of MD, nos. 28–37.

[26] In reference to this matter see the conclusion reached in the encyclical *Mediator Dei*: "In the spiritual life, consequently, there can be no opposition between the action of God, who pours forth His grace into men's hearts so that the work of the redemption may al-

ways abide, and the tireless collaboration of man, who must not render vain the gift of God. No more can the efficacy of the external administration of the sacraments, which comes from the rite itself (*ex opere operato*), be opposed to the meritorious action of their ministers or recipients, which we call the agent's action (*opus operantis*). Similarly, no conflict exists between public prayer and prayers in private, between morality and contemplation, between the ascetical life and devotion to the liturgy. Finally there is no opposition between the jurisdiction and teaching office of the ecclesiastical heirarchy, and the specifically priestly power exercised in the sacred ministry."

faithful, the basis, precisely, that is to be found in a strong and realistic ascetical effort.[27]

Personally I think that in both cases the rationale is really the same — to
wit, arbitrarily considering liturgical spirituality from a very incomplete and
false viewpoint, as if liturgical spirituality were a spirituality that is satisfied
with the liturgical action alone, strictly so called, that which is done in those
moments when one is present in the church, without concerning oneself at
all with what comes before or after. Even if in the liturgical action itself the
aspect of ascetical effort be anything but absent, as we shall soon see, still,
if liturgical spirituality is understood as limiting itself entirely to the liturgical
action with no concern for the before and the after, it is evident that in such
a "liturgical spirituality" the ascetical effort will be completely inadequate;
but the fact is, to call such an attitude "liturgical spirituality" is really self-
contradictory. As if it were possible to be serious about living the liturgical
action spiritually without being concerned for the before and the after! As
if there could be a spirituality which does not extend its influence to the
whole of a man's life, and did not gather up all his energies and all his actions
and direct them to his striving for Christian perfection! It should be enough,
then, simply to recall the notion of liturgical spirituality as we explained it
above in order to disabuse some and to reassure others.

The ascetical effort on the way toward perfection is manifested principally
in discursive meditative activity, to which are annexed examinations of conscience and spiritual retreats, and in the laborious practice of the theological
and moral virtues. Let us review these aspects from the point of view of their
realization in a climate of liturgical spirituality, whether in the liturgical action properly so called or in the ordinary life of the Christian outside the
liturgical action.

The value of discursive meditation included in the liturgical action

The role of discursive meditative effort in the striving toward perfection is
well known. It must occupy the external senses and the imagination, it must
persuade the intelligence, it must shape the affective or emotional sensibility,
and principally it must stir up the will, in respect to God and to things divine.
The will, in its turn, thus strengthened, can afterwards direct the intelligence
more easily, dominate the affective sensibility more profoundly, and command the imagination, the external senses, the whole body in order to submit
the whole man ever more intensely to God.

The pivotal point of discursive meditation is the exercise of imagination
and of ratiocination as phases of addressing oneself to prayer and to the
arousing of volitional sentiment in respect to God. This volitional affection
includes practical resolutions of the will on specific points — as when some-

---

[27] See the account told by Abbot Capelle,   giques, Vol. 1, Louvain 1955, p. 78.
"Liturgie et progrès moral," in Travaux litur-

one decides to abandon such and such a sin or to perform such and such an act of virtue at the next opportunity — and simple volitional sentiments of pleasure in God. The simple volitional sentiment of satisfaction or pleasure has in view the end of turning specific resolutions of the will toward practical action.

That stirring up of the simple volitional sentiment having been achieved more or less rapidly, sometimes quite rapidly, through discourse and possibly through specific resolutions of the will, it continues on in the character of the goal that was being sought. What remains in it is no longer meditative discourse properly so called, but its end, which is simple non-discursive union. And it remains thus so long as the simple volitional sentiment lasts, which may be for only the briefest of moments or for an extended length of time. As soon as it dies down, the simple volitional sentiment gives back to prayer and to the discursive effort as much time as is necessary for its being rekindled. And thus time is spent in discursive meditation, in prayer, in making acts of the will and practical resolutions, and in the simple glance of love.

The difference between beginners and those who are no longer mere novices is that in the former, habitually and not just on particular occasions, what predominates is their discursive effort, their making of resolutions, and only relatively infrequently and for short periods do they arrive at the repose of simple affection, while with the latter the contrary is the case. In certain phases of the spiritual life, it is frequent that these latter, as soon as they begin some discursive consideration through imagination or ratiocination about God and about other things relative to God, or as soon as they commence some volitional resolution, pass immediately to simple volition and remain there even for a quite extended period of time. In all the phases of the development of the spiritual life, therefore, the discursive meditative effort is present in its own way, and it is necessary that it be called upon with greater or lesser frequency.

The themes which the meditative effort can bring to imagination, to reasoning, to the formulation of prayer, to resolutions of the will are as vast as the whole field of dogma, the life of Christ, the example of the saints, the virtues to be practiced and the vices and imperfections to be avoided.

All this must be verified and is verified in its own way in liturgical spirituality, whether in the liturgical action itself or outside of it. That the liturgical action itself embraces an abundant exercise of discursive meditative activity is easily understood. For this it is enough to refer back to what we have already said in Chapter 11 in regard to the plenary actualization of the whole man in the liturgy, in a special way in regard to the actuation of the external senses, of imagination, of the esthetic sense, of discursive intelligence, of the will, and of the affections or emotions.

The value of discursive meditation included in every liturgical prayer is shown even by the fact that the typical schema which was later "rediscovered" by the systems of methodical prayer (preparation-body-conclusion) has always been in substance that of the liturgy. Thus in the first part of the Mass there is: a) an introduction: singing of the entrance, collect, which have the purpose of first creating a general atmosphere and of placing oneself in the presence of God with a view to that which is to follow afterwards; b) a body: biblical readings and their explanation, intercalated with reasonings, sentiments, colloquies, petitions, singing of psalms, alleluias, and the homily; c) closing: the creed, followed by the common petitions or prayer of the faithful, with its presidential conclusion.

It has been observed [28] that the typical format of methodical prayer presents a remarkable parallelism with that of the traditional Office of Matins: recognition of the place and preparatory prayer=invitatory and hymn; three points of meditation=three nocturns with their pertinent lessons; affections and colloquies after each point=responsories; thanksgiving=$Te\ Deum$. Nor is the preparation of the points lacking, for in this we can see a correspondence to the First Vespers of feasts.

But it is not so necessary to demonstrate the fact that discursive meditative activity is exercised in the liturgical action as it is to see what special shadings are given to this activity therein.

In the first place, it is to be observed that the liturgical action itself does assuredly have discursive meditative value; but it remains primarily action and communitarian action of the whole Church in the sense explained in Chapter 16. The concept of action does include, but at the same time really goes beyond, that of discursive meditative activity. Let us say, then, that what we mean is that the liturgical action itself has also a discursive meditative value, but of meditative-action. The liturgical action, therefore, can be conceived neither entirely nor even predominantly as a simple framework more or less convenient for substantially private meditation. The discursive meditation which must in some way be realized in each liturgical action must remain substantially, as befits the spirit of the liturgy, in the framework of a communitarian action, in which it takes an active role in the attuning of itself therewith as completely as possible.

The temporal frame of the discursive meditative activity in the liturgical action is, of course, marked by the temporal frame of the liturgical action itself. Hence it will have its center in the Mass, in the canonical hours, in the feasts, and in the annual liturgical cycles. But there will be a remarkable difference according to the different styles of life in which the liturgical spirituality is actuated. For those who admit even a quantitative predominance of the liturgy in their lives, as with those who live within the framework of the choir obligation, the whole day is centered around liturgical actions and is marked by the discursive meditative activity in accord with the succession of the canonical hours. We are presuming that the canonical hours are not said all at once, which might exaggerate their quantitative and qualitative predominance over the whole day.

In every exercise of meditative activity there must be provision for a certain recollection of the external senses. Even the liturgical action does this in its own way. Normally the very surroundings of a holy place, of a sacral community, and the separation, even physical, from the profane will already tend toward this recollection. Therefore in the very surroundings of the liturgical action a further disposition of the external senses does not take place for the most part, as would be done through the most complete suppression possible of their acts, as when care is exercised not to notice nor to hear that which is going on around us. Indeed, the liturgical action invites us to see and to hear all that is expressed and verified in it; it invites us to recite, to sing, to follow the movements of the whole community. It must be said, therefore, that in the liturgical action that disposition of the external senses necessary in every action that is to have meditative value, in order to lead the whole man to a total attunement with the divine, takes place more in their being connaturally turned toward the sacred objects than in their utter suppression.

In any case, to one who finds himself actually or habitually in a state of profound interior recollection — a situation that begins to be verified in the prayer of the simple glance — it is connatural and certainly in no way impossible, even while participating normally in the common movements, recitations, chants, to close the eyes more or less uninterruptedly, or if you will, even while keeping them open but not fixing them upon precise objects of attention, and in this way to follow more easily the rhythm of internal recollection. This is why it was quite the usual thing with the monks of antiquity that each one as soon as possible should learn the Psalter from memory, so that while the process of reading would occupy his eyes as little as possible, the monk, by his internal recollection, would be able to recite or chant the psalms as if he had composed them.

However, here we see how important it is that in the liturgical action everything be done with simple calm and recollection and that everyone avoid anything that might in any way disrupt this sacred climate of God's presence and prove a distraction to the senses and the attention. Here we can recognize the importance even of the rubrics, the ceremonies, the movements of the choir and of the people, and primarily the common recitations and the singing, that they be so well known and so connaturally executed by all that for the celebrants their execution proves not to be a point of conscious concern and a cause of continual psychological tension, nor for the faithful the occasion for continual distractions.

The themes that the liturgical action regularly proposes to the discursive intelligence and its own proper way of presenting them in a total synthesis are already known to us from the second and third parts of this present work and from part two of the present chapter: starting from the sensible and efficacious sign and the communitarian reality, it proceeds to the Christological-Trinitarian movement, to Christ the single liturgist, our Head and Mediator, etc. Nor do we dare forget the great themes that are more directly moral and anthropological, of which there is an abundance in this panorama: creation, the last things, the aim of life, elevation, fall, corruption of nature through original sin, sin in general, struggle against sin and the devil, good works, penance, and mortification.

It is worthy of note that the way in which these themes are proposed by the liturgy, inasmuch as they are presented always in the framework of salvation history, as the history of God's interventions and of man's response or lack of response — in a concrete and intuitive way, therefore, because they are centered always on the person of Jesus, the incarnate Word, His life, what He did and suffered in the flesh — the very way in which these themes are presented in the liturgy serves, so to speak, to concretize and condense them, whether they are directly dogmatic or directly moral. Hence in the liturgy meditation can always find a point of departure in the life, passion, death, resurrection, and present glorified state of Christ. In subordination to Christ, our Lady and the saints have the same function. We know also the prevalence which the liturgy, in the way in which it presents the totality of dogma, accords to the consideration of God as object over man who is subject. Among other motifs, these themes, considered as material for meditation, are characterized by their breadth, variety and synthetic vision.

The aspect of practical resolutions in the exercise of the will is present everywhere in the liturgical action, but usually in a way that is more indirect than direct. It is not the habitual style of the liturgy to conclude its considerations with a resolution of the will in such form as I will, we will, I promise, we promise, etc., but with a prayer: Lord, grant that we may live rightly, give us the grace to avoid sin, to engage fruitfully in fasting, to practice charity, etc. And this is natural in a *forma mentis* in which God is always the focal point of our consciousness.

On some solemn occasions, nevertheless, those which involve the pledging of one's whole life, the liturgy does know and give solemn expression to such forms as I will, we will, we promise: in baptism, in the renunciation of Satan and in the adherence to Christ; in the renewal of the baptismal promises, now happily included in the ceremonies of the Paschal Vigil; in religious profession; in the blessing of an abbot; in the consecration of virgins; in the rite of holy orders.

In the liturgy the activation of the will in a simple affection of admiration, gratitude, satisfaction in God is everywhere and continually intermingled in the whole complexus, first of all in the prayers of thanksgiving and of praise and in the general sense of compunction present in all the liturgy; and it is preferred because of its style which is, for the most part, smoothly rhetorical and lyrical. All this gives the liturgical action, considered as discursive meditative exercise, a note of being more volitionally affective than voluntarist.

Objections and responses

But this is the precise point at which there arises a series of objections against the real efficacy of the discursive meditative action in the liturgy. The whole system, considered from this precise point of view, can seem too impersonal to be really efficacious. The liturgy, at first sight and directly, by the very fact that it is proposed to all and speaks in the name of a community and not, for the most part, of a single person, does not seem to involve sufficiently the single individual person, because it seems to bespeak rather a common level for all, in a sphere that seems impersonal.

Moreover, as a method of discursive meditation, the liturgy seems to present too much material all at one time for consideration, while the individual who is following the liturgical action has no leisure in which to fix his will upon any specific point. Being wholly turned toward homage, praise, thanksgiving, eyes fixed always directly on God, is an attitude that seems to favor very little a consciousness of oneself; nor does it seem to be a propitious climate for exciting the will to practical resolutions toward amending one's life and the actual acquisition of such rectitude. Finally, the obligation to consider specific themes on specific occasions does not seem to allow the individual sufficient freedom of choice, since on these same occasions there may be demands placed on his attention by other themes; for example, his inclination might be to consider the Passion of our Lord, but the liturgy is of the Christmas season; or he might be inclined to meditate on the *Gesù bambino*, but it is Pentecost week.

These objections, however, are not at all precise. Their imprecision stems from the fact that they minimize too much the real possibility of personalization that is intrinsic to the liturgy. This possibility is connected with that dimension, even personal, of every liturgical sign, to which we called attention more than once in the first and third parts of the present work.

Even if the perspective of salvation history, the mystery of Christ, as it is presented in the liturgy, has direct universal value transcending the individual, the individual is certainly not absorbed by it nor in any way neglected by it, but is regarded as included in it, having some role throughout. The general laws of the relations between man and God, as they are reflected in salvation history, as they are concretized and are lived in the liturgical action, have value even for single individuals because the relations which God has with single individuals are substantially, by His own free will which follows certain consistent patterns, the same as those which He has with the totality of men, which relations are given expression in the Bible and especially in the psalms. Thus in the general history of these relations and in the laws thereof, each individual can and must see his own personal history and the factors which determine it.

For example, as has been stated in its proper place, each individual who lives the liturgy can and must apply the themes of the psalms to himself. The psalms which sing of the mercy of God toward Israel, these the believer must understand by applying them to himself and deepening their meaning in his own regard until he sees therein not only the most sublime and wonderful mercy of God toward the Church as such but even toward himself personally, calling to mind his vocation in Christ, his Christian life in the Church, and the graces with which he personally has been filled to overflowing by God. And it is the same with all the other themes which the liturgy proposes for our discursive meditation: the Christological-Trinitarian movement in the *a, per, in, ad* schema, the universal *per Christum Dominum nostrum*; the theme of election, separation, obedient behavior; the problem of sin; the events of the Old Testament as prefigurative and preparative of the Christian realities; the moral obligation present in our every contact with God; the eschatological tension of expectation, etc. Each individual who lives the liturgical action must see himself in all this, always and everywhere. And this not by some arbitrary supposition, but because each individual is truly included therein in his own way. Since it is a question of things which involve him personally and in which he himself has a role, from the spiritual point of view his life is but a certain reflection and a particular concretization of these realities.

In the second chapter, where we treated of the quadruplex dimension of the liturgical sign, the conclusion was drawn that the liturgy, in its internal structure, is like a very extraordinary mirror in which are reflected and epitomized, as real and present, all the relations between God and men. This is understood not only of the common and general relations between God and men, but even of the personal relations of each individual with God. In the liturgy, in respect to the consciousness of ourselves to which we must in one way or another be led when we concentrate our attention on God, what St. Gregory the Great said about Scripture can and must be verified, for after all, the Scriptures constitute a considerable part of the liturgical texts:

> "Sacred Scripture comes before our eyes like a mirror in which we can contemplate our inner countenance. There we can perceive what is beautiful and what is ugly in ourselves: there we can learn how far we have progressed toward perfection, and what a distance still separates us therefrom." [29]

[29] *Moralia* 2, 1, 1.

For the same reason each individual must remember to apply to himself the moral admonitions in the liturgy and its exhortations to good works. Hence, he must make practical decisions in regard to his own life; he can and must pray as his own personal prayers the hymns of thanksgiving, of admiration, of praise, of repentance, of petition for assistance in avoiding sin, in practicing virtue, and all the other prayers which the liturgy in any way raises to God.

The more intensely an individual lives the spiritual life in general, so much the more vivid and profound will be the significance for him of this phenomenon of personalization of the whole liturgy. What St. Gregory the Great says of Scripture must be said also of the liturgy: *crescit cum legente.*[30] And this explains why this personalization of the liturgy achieves its highest degree of perfection in the mystical life properly so called of one who participates therein, a thing which we will see more clearly as we go along.

Since the material for discursive meditation presented to the individual in the liturgical action is in fact most abundant, it must be observed that for the achievement of meditative harmony of the subject with the things proposed it is not actually necessary nor is it even practically possible for anyone to pursue with equal diligence each of the individual points proposed to him. A general but profound concentration of the mind on God, or that which takes its cue from a more particular concept without following with equal diligence all the others constitutes the best attunement of the mind to the liturgical action.

Finally it can be observed that the subjection of the individual, up to a certain point, to meditation on obligatory themes on certain feastdays and seasons of the year does not seem after all to carry with it such great inconveniences, since we can see that the same thing is done even in those methods of meditation in which, under this aspect, the dominant factor is an extreme diligence that can be called — and we do not mean it in a pejorative sense — personalist and individualist. In the *Exercises* of St. Ignatius, for example, the one making the exercises is required to follow in a very rigid way the themes assigned for the individual weeks and individual days; he is not permitted to change them about at will. Indeed, from this point of view, it would have to be said that the liturgy is remarkable for its variety and flexibility.

It is true, in any case, that the special way of leading the individual subject to a consideration of himself is, I say it again, to teach him to view himself against the background of the general laws, objective and communitarian, of salvation history, as part of an immense totality. And this explains why, in the liturgical action, at least as it is now, there is not left to each single individual the liberty of choosing for himself the particular time that he will pause for silent reflection or how much time he will then devote to reflection on a particu-

---

[30] *Ibid.*, 20, 1, 1.

lar point which is more personally pleasing to him. The liturgical action must concern itself with the community as such in its totality and with the necessities of public action.

The observations against the efficacy of the liturgical action in respect to its discursive meditational value, therefore, were imprecise and exaggerated, Nevertheless, it is undeniable that those objections do contain a kernel of truth. The specific individual is not aimed at directly; he is not completely free in his choice of a theme for meditation which may be more satisfying to him at this precise moment; he is not permitted to pause quietly and devote such time as he wants in fixing his imagination, his thought, his affections on a specific point without paying attention to what is being done or said around him. Can it be said that these possibilities would not have some considerable advantages, and that they are not, at least at certain times, inescapable necessities? I think not.

The very history of the liturgy shows that these necessities have been recognized and that in ancient times they were taken into account in the liturgical action itself much more than today. We are referring to the phenomenon of interspersing moments of prayer, more or less protracted, and of moments of personal meditation and of silence within the liturgical action itself. An attempt was made in this way to satisfy, within the public and communitarian action itself, the more personal needs of single individuals. These interspersions in the Mass took place particularly at the moment of the great intercession. The celebrant, exhorting all to prayer, also expressed each time the specific intention for which all should pray; the deacon, on days of special penitence, invited all to kneel with the expression *Flectamus genua*, and after a moment signaled them to rise again with the command *Levate*. The celebrant then continued with a brief common oration, as an official summing up of the private prayers just offered. The ancient euchological formula was: reading-homily-psalm-private prayer in silence-concluding oration by the one presiding.

For centuries the last vestiges of this usage was to be found in the *Flectamus genua* and *Levate* of Good Friday and the Ember Days. In the reforms subsequent to Vatican II, and in the recently promulgated Pauline Roman Missal, the disposition of the Ember Days and the decision of retaining or not retaining the *Flectamus genua* and *Levate* on Good Friday is left to local conferences of bishops. But in any case, the revised Roman Rite does provide numerous short periods for silent reflection, personal prayer, and momentary meditation throughout the Mass every day.

In the monastic tradition, joined to the choral Office was the interspersion of moments, more or less protracted, of private prayer-meditation after each psalm or group of psalms. Such private prayer closed with an oration delivered in an elevated voice in the name of all by the president of the assembly: the *oratio psalmica*.[31]

If this system of intercalations fell very quickly into disuse, it is most probably because it had very little real practicality in reference to the necessities of communitarian action, and not because it was not in fact an attempt to respond to a need. In any case, the system has fallen into disuse, and this need can be responded to only by private prayer and meditation outside the liturgical action. Nor does the restoration through most recent revisions of the liturgy of some few short moments for silent prayer and meditation within the liturgy obviate the necessity of lengthier periods of meditative prayer outside the liturgy.

Discursive meditation outside the liturgical action in a climate of liturgical spirituality

We must, then, simply say once more what we have already said so many times before, that liturgical spirituality cannot in fact make the claim that in the life of striving toward Christian perfection it is possible to fulfill sufficiently the need of discursive meditation by being satisfied with that discursive meditative action actually contained in the liturgical action itself as it is presently structured if, at the same time, no attempt is made to prepare for and to prolong this exercise outside the very moments of participation in the liturgy.[32]

This meditation outside the very moments of the liturgy is so much the more necessary, even for one who centers his whole spirituality in the liturgy, the more one's life is led in distracting surroundings, or the more intimately one is engaged in a kind of work that is less closely connected with the things of God, and the less habitual one's recollection is.

Insofar as the precise form and the specific methods of devoting oneself to this meditation are concerned, it seems to me that all the forms and all the methods suggested by the spiritual authors of proven reputation can be worthwhile, in accord with the circumstances and personal needs and differing moods of the individuals. For one who lives a habitually recollected life, the exercise of discursive meditation outside of the liturgy can also, if need be and in the degree necessary, take the simple and much more flexible form of reading-meditation, in accord with the ancient monastic method of the *lectio divina*.

For others it will be necessary or useful, according to their moods and dispositions, to have a more schematically rigid and analytic form, such as

---

[31] See Cassian, *Inst.* 2, 3. See also in the *Dictionnaire de spiritualité* the article "Contemplation," in Vol. 2/2 (1953), pp. 1931–1932, 1941. L. Brou, *The Psalter Collects*, London 1949. M. Coune, "*Les oraisons psalmiques*" in *Paroisse et liturgie*, Vol. 39 (1957), pp. 306–

324. An attempt at restoring the psalmic prayers in the modern setting was made in the *Salterio corale* of the LDC, Turin 1965.

[32] The encyclical *Mediator Dei* emphasizes the usefulness and the necessity of this meditation: nos. 32, 37, and 174 (Lat. 172).

those suggested, for example, by St. Ignatius. This may be especially the case at certain times of life, in order to control more easily the imagination and the sensibilities, if it is recognized by experience that they are difficult to control, in view of achieving the recollection indispensable to spiritual exercise.

For the themes of these meditations it is clear that in liturgical spirituality nothing presented in Catholic dogma and moral is excluded, be it even the almost entirely philosophical reflection on the duties of the creature toward the Creator or meditation on the last things. Even here it is the needs of the individual that constitute the determining factor. But it is also obvious that the themes chosen will be viewed especially in the light of the vision of the world that the liturgy provides.

First of all, therefore, it will naturally be a question of themes connected in some way with the Mass, with the sacraments, the sacramentals, and in a special way with the feasts and liturgical seasons, whether as seen in the Missal, in the Breviary, in the Pontifical, in the Ritual, or even in the Scriptures.

The liturgical books themselves and the Scriptures in association with the liturgy, possibly even some extracts of patristic writings, always in association with the liturgy, are, even outside the liturgical action, the connatural books for meditation in a climate of liturgical spirituality. Here, moreover, for those who do not understand Latin — and not infrequently, because of the intrinsic difficulty of the texts, even for those who do know Latin — a good translation of the texts will be of the utmost utility; and for many, in view of a progressive introduction to the world of the liturgy, it will be necessary also to have brief commentaries on the liturgy, first of all on the liturgy of the Missal.

For the Missal there are already numerous commentaries of some merit; yet, new ones will have to be written in accord with the Pauline Roman Missal. For the Ritual and the Breviary, similar commentaries exist, if I do not err, only for selected parts. And here again, revisions will have to be made and new ones written for the revised liturgy of the Breviary and Ritual. It is hardly necessary to point out how valuable it would be for making the liturgy the efficacious font of life, first of all for the clergy and then even for the faithful, to have complete editions of the Breviary and of the Ritual with brief commentaries similar to those that are available for the Missal, and in which, if necessary, very short references might be made to the historical aspect, while the primary point of concern would be with the theological, biblical, and ascetical aspects of the rites and of the texts.

It would be quite useful also for meditation in the climate of liturgical spirituality to have books of meditations drawn directly from the liturgy. There already exist, as you know, various works of this kind, such as the *Année liturgique* of Dom Guéranger, which has its usefulness even yet, especially in its five-volume condensation;[33] the *Liber sacramentorum* of Cardi-

---

[33] Italian translation from the press of the Edizioni Paoline. An English edition, unabridged and in 15 volumes, was published at Dublin and elsewhere between 1870 and 1903, under the title *The Liturgical Year*.

nal Schuster, and works of a similar kind.[34] The best works of meditation and spiritual reading in the spirit of the liturgy, already classics in their field, are those of Dom Marmion.

Naturally, outside the liturgical action, meditation even in the climate of liturgical spirituality can and must follow along lines more free and personal than within the liturgical action. This is especially evident in respect to the ability to linger peacefully and with due leisure over specific considerations which answer better to the necessities or inspirations of the moment, as well as to their applications and the consequent personal resolutions.

Spiritual exercises in the climate of liturgical spirituality

Closely connected with exercises of discursive meditation outside the liturgical action are the examinations of conscience and the periodic recollective retreats. It is not necessary to insist on the usefulness and the actual necessity of the one or of the other. From our point of view it is enough to note that the practice of periodic times of recollection or even of the exercises properly so called, in the climate of liturgical spirituality, is naturally made to coincide as much as possible with the preparation for the greater liturgical feasts.

In the official spirituality of the Church, Lent has been conceived in just this way, and most especially as the consecrated annual spiritual exercises of the Christian people in preparation for the Paschal triduum. It could be that for some just and proportionate case — not to be presumed too easily, as happens all too frequently — the week or the three days of annual exercises in the modern sense of the term, now of quite general custom, might not be able to be made during Lent. In such a case we must be much on our guard, in the climate of liturgical spirituality, lest this time be allowed to pass by without spiritual observance, in harsh contrast with the Masses which the priest then says each day and the breviary which he must recite each day. Another period of somewhat similar character is the joyful season of Advent in preparation for Christmas.

Thus, in liturgical spirituality, the Paschal triduum and Christmas, the mystery of Christ as incarnation or epiphanic arrival of the Lord and as redemption, being repeated each day and each year under the veil of sensible and efficacious signs, constitute the two great affairs of the soul even outside the liturgical action properly so called. The other great feasts, e.g., Ascension, Pentecost, Assumption, All Saints, constitute just so many other points of reference which may be naturally connected with the periods chosen for a time of greater recollection .

Naturally, in the climate of liturgical spirituality, the days devoted to the exercises have their focal point on active and communitarian participation in the liturgy, primarily in the Mass.

---

[34] For example, Pius Parsch, *The Church's Year of Grace*, English translation by William　G. Heidt, O.S.B., Collegeville, Minn. 1953–1959 (five volumes).

Liturgical spirituality and the active exercise of the theological and moral virtues

Ascetical effort on the road toward perfection, beyond that expended in discursive meditative activity, in the examination of conscience, and in the practice of spiritual retreats, manifests itself primarily in the active practice of the theological and moral virtues. How does this happen in liturgical spirituality, whether in the liturgical action itself or outside of it? To clarify this question we have to start with the notion of the liturgy explained in the first part, that it is a complexus of the sensible and efficacious signs of the sanctification and of the worship of the Church. Under the double aspect of the sanctification that God works in His Church and the worship that the Church renders to God, the liturgy is so intimately connected with the active exercise of the theological and moral virtues that the spirituality which is centered on it and takes its particular flavoring from it is necessarily a spirituality in which the active exercise of these virtues occupies a prominent position.

The first thing to be observed in this matter is that the liturgical action itself, insofar as it is sanctification which God works in His Church, is the privileged place where man, in the sacraments, obtains from God sanctifying grace *ex opere operato* and, in the rites of ecclesiastical institution, actual grace *ex opere operantis Ecclesiae.* Now, actual and sanctifying grace constitute the indispensable divine existence and dynamism which man must possess and in some way bring into action in the practice of any of the theological or moral virtues.

It is evident, therefore, that spirituality centered on the liturgy, by the very fact that it is concerned most seriously with tapping as continuously, as constantly, and as immediately as possible the greatest and most efficacious sources of grace, is also profoundly and constantly concerned with establishing a solid foundation, not only in reality but also in the consciousness of the faithful, for the practice of the virtues and for the moral effort toward perfection, on the primary and indispensable basis of the assistance of God completely compenetrating even our free and meritorious actions.

The liturgical action and the exercise of faith, hope, and charity in the framework of the virtue of religion. That in this spirituality there is an abundant active exercise of the theological and moral virtues can be seen by considering in the first place the liturgical action itself inasmuch as it is worship. To put it briefly: in the liturgical action as worship there is present eminent and continuous exercise of faith, hope, and charity first of all in respect to the primary object, which is God. This takes place in the area of the real exercise of the virtue of religion, compenetrated by sentiments of humility, reverence, submission, compunction, flowing in their turn into the sentiments of adoration, with prayer of praise, of petition, and of thanksgiving. Moreover, in the liturgical action itself insofar as it is worship, there is continuous consideration, exhortation, promise, and prayer to God in respect to the extra-liturgical exercise of all the other virtues, and especially of works of charity of every kind toward one's neighbor and of the other moral virtues.

The key to the understanding of this assertion is simply what we have already said in Chapter 4 about the singular nature of the virtue of religion — the maximum actualization of which takes place precisely in the liturgical action as worship — and its relations with the theological and moral virtues. Let us call to mind the three fundamental points on which theologians are in agreement: the general meaning of the virtue of religion in the Christian life as response of man to the profound debt which he owes God as the source, ultimate ruler, and end of all created beings; the transcendence of the virtue of religion over all the other moral virtues because of its more intimate closeness to God Himself; the intimate relationships between the virtue of religion and the theological virtues, not only because the theological virtues are the more immediate and efficacious source of the virtue of religion and the virtue of religion is a favorable matrix in which the theological virtues are exercised, prosper, and develop, but even beyond this, because the same acts of the theological virtues are like the more noble and more sought-after material of which the virtue of religion makes use in order to put itself into act. This explains to us how the intrinsic nature of the liturgical action, insofar as it is cultic activation of the virtue of religion, always carries with it of necessity a continuous putting into action of the virtues of faith, hope, and charity, considered first of all in their primary material object, which is God.

In fact, religion is the virtue which renders to God the homage due Him as creator, supreme ruler, and ultimate end of creatures. As the natural virtue of religion presupposes belief in the existence of God, in His being creator, ruler, and supreme end, the hope that He will accept our homage, the will to be in conformity with His will, the natural love of God, so too the exercise of religion presupposes the supernatural virtues of faith, hope, and charity. Faith, hope, and charity command the act of homage due to God; by their rule they cause the virtue of religion, as St. Thomas expresses it: *suo imperio causant.* With this phrase it can already be seen how faith, hope, and love of God are always and everywhere in operation in the liturgical action as cultic activation of the virtue of religion. They are the inexhaustible interior well from which the liturgical action everlastingly gushes forth, and without which that living font of living worship would suddenly dry up.

Again, the homage which the virtue of religion renders to God as supreme creator, ruler, and end of all things has for its essential and primary matter the internal dispositions and acts of man's mind in which dispositions and actions the various virtues consist. For every disposition and act of virtue, beyond being that which it is in itself, has also a value as homage to God, which man can and must render to the creator, supreme ruler, and end of all things.

The act of temperance in the use of food and drink, for example, is an act of a certain moderation in eating and drinking. But a man can and must perform the act of temperance not only for the sake of the beauty which is present in the preserving of a proper moderation, but also in order to render thereby due homage to God, recognizing in Him the creator, the supreme ruler, and the final end of all things, to whom all the actions of a man must be freely ordered and subordinated.

In acting in this way a man activates not only the virtue of temperance but also that of religion; or better, the virtue of religion makes use, as it were, of the matter of the act of temperance in order to activate itself by offering the act of temperance as due homage to the creator.

Since worship is first of all an internal disposition of mind, the matter which it offers in homage to God is first of all those internal dispositions and acts of the mind in which the virtues consist. But among them, excelling in the highest degree, are the dispositions of the mind and the internal acts in which the three theological virtues of faith, hope, and charity, consist. These, more than any other virtue or disposition of mind, have religious value precisely because, more than any other virtue or disposition of mind, beyond being what they are by reason of their own formal object, they have the value of homage to the creator, supreme ruler, and end of all things.

In fact, and charity foremost among them, they imply more than any other virtue the reverential recognition, the humility and submission, the complete dedication of self with sentiments of adoration and praise, which constitute, as it were, the general psychological atmosphere of the virtue of religion. It is, therefore, in the offering to God of acts of faith, of hope, and especially of charity, as supreme homage due to Him as creator, supreme governor, and end of all things, that the act of the virtue of religion and therefore supreme worship finds its primary realization.

It is necessary, nevertheless, to say also that if in the offering of faith, of hope, and particularly of charity, the supreme worship of God is realized, then the highest faith, the highest hope, and the highest charity which are offered in worship to God on this earth are precisely the faith, the hope, and the charity by which homage is done Him in the Christian cultic action, primarily the Mass; for the Christian cultic action, primarily the Mass, is, in fact, the supreme worship rendered to God on this earth.

This is because the faith, hope, and charity which are offered in homage to God in the liturgical action are, by a superior title belonging to no other act of faith, hope, or charity made by any individual or group of individuals whatsoever, even be it in the Church, the faith, hope, and charity of the Church herself. In the same way that the official liturgical prayer, because it is, by a special title belonging to no other prayer, the prayer of the Church as the integral mystical body of Christ, head and members, and is therefore of a dignity and efficacy which transcends every other prayer here below, so too the act of faith, of hope, and of charity, of which that same liturgical prayer is but the expression, transcends in dignity every other act of faith, of hope, and of charity on this earth because it is an act of faith, hope and charity granted a special and preëminent title of esteem by the Church as such, by her very head, Jesus Christ, and presented by this special title in worshipful homage to God.

This is but the general teaching of the transcendence of liturgical prayer and worship over non-liturgical prayer and worship, explained in reference to the concept of *opus operantis Ecclesiae*. Let us call to mind that no prayer and no worship of any sort on this earth is accepted by the Father if it is not presented by Christ Himself and considered in some way by Him as His own act. In the eyes of the Father, nothing whatever done by men has supernatural value, nothing whatever done by men is accepted by Him unless it is done through Christ and with Christ and in union with Christ: *per ipsum, et cum ipso, et in ipso*. So it is with prayer of every sort and with acts of virtue of whatever kind.

In the Church, however, there are various gradations in which this can take place, as is shown by the concept itself of *opus operantis Ecclesiae*. The highest degree in which this can come about after the *opus operatum* is precisely that which is fulfilled in the liturgy. It is in the liturgy that there is achieved the highest possible degree of identification of the individual, who is interiorly attuned to the liturgy, and of his acts of prayer, of faith, of hope, and of charity, with Christ Himself and with His acts of worship of the Father; the individual is united to Christ and to His acts by a most special title; or still better, it is Christ Himself who draws to Himself by a most special title, in the worship which He renders to the Father, that individual and his acts of faith, of hope, and of charity as acts rendered in worshipful homage to the Father.

From this it can be seen not only how closely the exercise of the theological virtues is connected with liturgical worship in the very nature of the things involved, but also how the exercise of these virtues here below attains the highest degree of worth before God precisely in the liturgical action. In this perspective the doctrine of St. Augustine takes all its value, he having held that the profound meaning of worship and indeed, of the whole Church, is precisely the building up on this earth of faith, of hope, and of charity: *aedificatio fidei, spei, et caritatis*,[35] and especially of charity which, once built up, will not any more be destroyed.

In view of the foregoing considerations it should be in no way surprising

[35] See D. Grabner, *St. Augustine's Doctrine Concerning the Edification of Faith, Hope and Charity and Its Place in the Theology of the Liturgical Year*, manuscript thesis defended at the Anselmianum in Rome, 1956. The perspective of the *opus operantis Ecclesiae* was lacking to St. Augustine himself, and without it he could not perceive the proper value of the exercise of faith, hope, and charity within the framework of the liturgical action.

if faith, hope, and charity show themselves present everywhere in the liturgy even in a cursory examination. It is enough only to recall that the natural background of the liturgy, always presupposed and in some way made explicit, is the sacred history of God's interventions in the world as mystery of Christ always in progress in accord with its various levels: the historical level of preparation and past actuation; the mystic level of present actuation through the grace of participation in the mystery of Christ in the liturgy and in moral life outside the liturgy; and the level of the eschatological future as the ultimate goal to which the whole complexus is directed.

It is easy to see how the historical level of preparation and of past accomplishment, as well as the mystic level of present participation, are entirely and necessarily the object of faith. Except by faith we cannot perceive the meaning of history prior to Christ as preparation for Christ; the really divine significance of the life of Christ from incarnation to Golgotha, to the resurrection, to His being seated at the right of the Father, and to His sending of the Holy Spirit; the significance of the present life as participation by grace in the mysteries of Christ under the veil of sensible signs and in the intimacy of the individual life.

It is just as easy to see how the realization of the future eschatological level up to the glorious resurrection of bodies and the definitive restoration of the reign of God in the heavenly Jerusalem, the level which is always insistently present in the liturgical perspective, as has been explained in its proper place, can only be the object of faith and hope at the same time. Just so, the help of grace which the liturgy continually awaits and implores of God is the object of hope, so that the blessed end which is ever before the eyes of hope might be happily achieved. Whoever knows a striving toward a future good, difficult to attain but still attainable at least with the help of another, knows hope. This is precisely the case with the liturgy, which is addressed constantly to future supernatural goods.

It is no less clear that the constant presentation of these levels, from which the readings, prayers of petition, thanksgivings, adorations, exhortations, professions of faith, etc., take their cue — in short, all that which constitutes the complexus of the liturgical texts — is directed always, in the final analysis, to its ultimate end, the actuation of the love of God as the ultimate response, however inadequate, of man to the prevenient and paternal love of God, which, in its turn, is the final word which alone explains God's interventions, loving, gratuitous, and always in action in history, to draw men to Himself.

This is in substance the content of the observation made in the encyclical *Mediator Dei*, following a path already laid out by St. Augustine:

> "The worship which she [the Church] offers to God, all Good and Great, is a continuous profession of Catholic faith and a continuous

exercise of hope and charity, as Augustine puts it tersely: 'God is to be worshipped,' he says, 'by faith, hope and charity.' " [36]

In the sacred liturgy we make explicit profession of faith, not just with the celebration of the divine mysteries, with the fulfilling of the sacrifice, and the administration of the sacraments, but even in the reciting and singing of the creed, which is like the distinctive mark or membership pass of Christians, with the reading of other documents and of the sacred letters written under the inspiration of the Holy Spirit. The whole liturgy, therefore, has a content of Catholic faith, to which the faith of the Church attests publicly. The same must be said also when it is a question of the other theological virtues: "In faith . . . in hope, and in charity we pray always with constant yearning." [37]

In conclusion, it is to be noted that in the liturgical action the exercise of faith, hope, and charity toward God is so prominent and continuous that it would be impossible for this characteristic not to impress itself deeply upon the whole spirituality that focuses itself on the liturgical action.

No less characteristic, however, is the fact that in the liturgical action faith, hope, and charity are made so deeply operative because they are activated by the virtue of religion and in the framework of the virtue of religion which is directly expressed in the liturgy as worship. Generally reckoned among the moral virtues, which have for their object the establishing of a certain moderation in human actions, religion is, in any case, rightly regarded by all not only as supreme among the moral virtues, but also the most selfless, the most theological or theocentric of all.

And this is the case precisely because the human actions which religion regulates are those in which our debt to God as supreme creator, ruler, and end of all things is expressed. Even from the point of view of the exercise of the moral virtues, it seems clear that the liturgy, involving both God and man, is centered more directly on God than on man. In fact, among the same moral virtues, there is an enormous emphasis on that which, among them all, is most directly concentrated on God. Its characteristics are its sentiments of admiration, of reverence, of submission, of praise, of adoration, of *devotion* as total dedication of oneself — all sentiments which look directly to God.

The liturgical action and the exercise of *compunctio.* But if we may repeat, it is not that the liturgical action (in the exercise of the moral virtues which find immediate acticity therein) is concentrated so much on God that man is forgotten. Even here man is bound to be present, but as a reflection of the attention that is devoted directly to God. Now, the specific sentiment which man has as reflection in his own regard while he concentrates his attention directly on the excellence of God as creator, supreme ruler, and end of all things is that which the ancients called *pénthos, compunctio, compunction*: a

---

[36] St. Augustine, *Enchiridion* 3; MD, no. 47 (Lat. 46).

[37] St. Augustine, *Epist.* 130 *Ad Probam* 18; MD, no. 48 (Lat. 47).

general sentiment produced by humility, by regret and sorrow for one's own offenses and deficiencies, by contempt for oneself, tempered by a fiducial consideration of God's mercy.[38]

The liturgy is an optimum medium for the natural growth of compunction. Of some bearing on this proposition is the following anecdote of an ancient Palestinian ascetic:

> "A brother met one of the elders in the laura of Soucas near Jericho, and asked him, 'How's it going, Father?' The elder answered, 'Rotten!' So the brother said to him 'How come, Abba?' The elder answered, 'Well, on account of the thirty years handrunning in which I stand every day in prayer before God. Because of the countless times I curse myself when I say to God, "*Be not compassionate to those whose deeds are evil*"; or even "*Cursed be all those who hold themselves aloof from Your commands*," while I myself am aloof from them and my deeds are evil. Sometimes I even say to God: "*You will destroy all those who speak lies*"; and I myself continue every day to lie. Even while in my own heart I harbor wicked thoughts, I say to God, "*The thoughts of my heart are ever before You*." Though I really do not fast, I say, "*My knees are made weak by my fasting*." And again, even while I bear angry thoughts against my brother, I say to God, "*Forgive us as we forgive others*." While I think of nothing else but eating my bread, I say, "*I have forgotten to eat my bread*." Though I sleep until morning, I say in the Psalm, "*In the middle of the night I arise to confess Your name*." Though really I have no compunction, I say, "*I am aggrieved and I groan and my tears have become night and day my bread*." Full of pride and of physical comforts, I make myself a laughingstock when I sing, "*Look upon my humility and my sorrow and forgive all my sins*." And I am not really prompt, but I say, "*My heart is prompt, O Lord*." In a word, my whole liturgy and my whole prayer have been changed into my reproach and my shame.' The brother said, 'I think, Father, that David said all this about himself.' But the elder sighed and said, 'Brother, brother, what are you saying? Surely if we do not do what we sing about, we are on the road to perdition!' "

Father I. Hausherr, who transcribes the above anecdote,[39] observes that the ascetic who took the liturgy seriously did not find therein occasions for ecstasy only, and that, nevertheless, the good old man, at least on one point, exaggerated his condition when he said, to wit, that he did not have compunction; the whole passage, in fact, proves quite clearly that the contrary is true. It shows how this precious state of mind can be marvelously nourished by the liturgy. This presumes, of course, that the liturgy is taken seriously. Just as, besides, the exercise of so-called mental prayer or that of meditation must be

---

[38] See I. Hausherr, *Penthos. La doctrine de la componction dans l'Orient chrétien*, Rome

1944.
[39] *Ibid*., pp. 46–47.

taken seriously in order to make it a true dynamism of moral force unto real practice of virtue.

The moralization force of the liturgical action in respect to the exercise of works of charity toward one's neighbor and of the moral virtues in the practical life. It remains undeniable, however, that the liturgical action considered in itself, from the stance of the operative exercise of the theological and moral virtues, has its limits. The very exercise therein of theological charity is in some way limited because the charity so strongly and preëminently exercised in the liturgical action is in direct reference first of all to God Himself, the primary object of this theological virtue. The creatures loved by God are the secondary object of the same virtue, and they are also quite notably, even if secondarily, the object of love in the liturgical action, but under the form of prayer, of good will, of good wishes.

At the same time, however, the exercise of the external works of charity and of mercy toward one's neighbor is necessarily but nonetheless notably lacking. This is more especially the case with the faithful, whereas the priest himself, leading the action, fulfills this exercise in a prominent way in administering the sacraments, in instructing, and in leading the prayers. But even in the case of the priest, numerous works of charity toward his neighbor, which he has the duty of performing, are not exercised in the liturgical action itself. Essentially, the exercise of most of the moral virtues, such as repentance, chastity, temperance, obedience, humility, fortitude in such forms as courage, perseverance, etc., are not exercised in any prominent way within the liturgical action itself.

Is recognizing these limits equivalent perhaps to saying that the liturgical action has no noteworthy moralizational efficacy in respect to the practice of works of charity and to the exercise of the numerous other moral virtues, religion excepted, and that, for this reason, the liturgical action has no notable moralizational force in the ordinary affairs of life? By no means. On the contrary, it is a fact that the liturgical action, the aforesaid limitations notwithstanding, has nevertheless a prominent moralizational force even in respect to extraliturgical life and hence in respect to the exercise of the works of charity toward neighbor and of the other moral virtues in the practical order.

And this for various reasons. In the first place the more generic, because the liturgy holds constantly before our eyes that which can be called the complete general framework of man's religious situation in the proper balance of the respective roles that pertain to man and to God: creation, elevation, earthly paradise, fall, nature corrupted, sin, last things, devil, weakness of man, necessity of grace, restoration in Christ alone, aim of the Christian life to be reclothed in Christ, imitating Christ, *per ipsum, et cum ipso, et in ipso,* communion of saints, communitarian sense and acute awareness of the Mystical Body reality. And in all this the necessity of cooperation and of ascetical effort.

Thus, in that ascetical effort the believer is ever cautioned that it would all be for nothing if he were not to trust in Christ; and he is not, after all, simply an atom, even if conscious and free, carried away in the vast current of divine life which descends to the world from Christ and rises again to God from the world through Christ. This vision is the bearer of a dynamic force in the ascetical life and effort because it is the bearer of certitude and optimism: the certitude of hope and the optimism of our communitarian participation in Christ's victory.

In the second place, the liturgy, even psychologically, is full of moralizational force even for the extraliturgical life, since it provides incessant reminder of the necessity of the ascetical effort in the practice of the virtues in all of life, every moment praying God to give us the strength to actually make that ascetical effort. And the liturgy accomplishes this by considering the practice of virtue in all of life either as necessary preparation for a worthy participation in the liturgy or as a necessary consequence of having participated therein.

What we can call the psychological-moralizational catechesis of the liturgy is not a thing of small import in the liturgy, as is proved by the basic fact, already explained, of the moral and binding dimension of every liturgical sign. In particular, the pre-festive periods, primarily Lent, Advent, and the vigils, have the eminent aim of the moral preparation of the life of the Christian with a view to the worthy celebration of the approaching feast.

The theme of good works to be performed, therefore, is always in strong relief in the liturgy. One of the great postcommunion themes is the prayer to God that the participation in the Sacrament which just now took place may bear fruit for the faithful, enabling them to lead lives of virtue and to meet all the necessities of Christian existence, so as to be able one day to arrive happily at the goal of life in the enjoyment of the beatific vision. Another great theme, especially in the liturgy of the saints, is that of the imitation of their virtues and of their labors for the cause of God.[40]

Another typical example of the moralizational force of the liturgy is found in the exhortations which accompany the conferring of holy orders the consecration of virgins, the blessing of abbots, and monastic profession. Without counting up the extremely numerous Scripture passages read in the liturgy

---

[40] For these themes see, for example, the Collect for Wednesday in the First Week of Advent: *Praepara, quaesumus, Domine Deus noster, corda nostra*; Postcommunion for the Midnight Mass of Christmas; Collect for the Second Mass of Christmas Day; Collect for Monday in Holy Week; *Super oblata* prayer for Tuesday of Easter week; Collect for Thursday in Easter week; Collect for Friday in Easter week; Collect for the Second Sunday of Easter; Collect for the Memorial of St. Francis Xavier (Dec. 3); Collect for the Memorial of St. Francis de Sales (Jan. 24); Collect for the Memorial of St. John Bosco (Jan. 31). Further examples could be easily but needlessly multiplied. (For the full impact of the argument the Latin text as given in the official *Missale Romanum* published by the Vatican Press must be consulted; as in most other similar cases, the English version tends to be too imprecise and vague. Tr.).

which contain and frequently are substantially moral admonitions put into a direct relationship with the liturgical action that is taking place, it is obvious enough that they are quite numerous.[41]

A further reason why the liturgical action possesses a very pronounced psychological moralizational force is that in the liturgy, and in liturgical spirituality in general, the necessity of moral action in the whole of life is proposed from the viewpoint of the specific motivation of rendering honor and homage to God, which is precisely the proper motivation of religion. Now, this is the most noble, most disinterested motivation, at the same time quite efficacious psychologically, in view of the action. It is easily seen how important are psychological motives in the moral life, animating and sustaining our efforts: for example, magnanimity drives us on and encourages our effort, making us enthusiastic for a high ideal.[42]

> "The highest and most immediately adapted motive to the supernatural exigencies of our moral progress is that of the virtue of religion: our obligations to God and the honor which is due Him. *Qui gloriatur in Domino glorietur*! It is a motive that gives great support to our moral effort, considering the perfection which we must win not only as human grandeur worthy of praise, but as an actualization in which the honor of God is involved. . . .
>
> "It would be especially interesting to analyze the psychological conditions of magnanimity and to demonstrate the powerful dynamism which it finds in the virtue of religion. The stability and the firmness of our moral life will truly be as much more secure as our ideal is higher and more unifying and our confidence more serene.
>
> "Religion which forces us to consider the honor of God provides the highest ideal for the concentration of all our moral efforts. Such an ideal is not only the highest but also the most selfless. It is this which gives to the religious soul its fiducial stability. We can be certain that we are not deceived if we work not for our own glory but for that of God.
>
> "We notice that St. Thomas himself has pointed out (in regard to magnificence, but the same holds good for magnanimity) this psychological connection.
>
> " 'The end of magnificence is to do great works. The works done by man are ordered toward some end. But no end whatever of human works is so great as the honor of God. And hence magnificence performs its great work first of all in relation to the honor of God. For this reason the philosopher says in his fourth book of *Ethics* that "especially honorable are first of all those things which pertain to the divine sacrifices. The magnificent man is especially concerned with these matters."

---

[41] Typical examples are to be found not infrequently in the first readings from the Old Testament, and even more frequently in the second readings, especially when the latter are from St. Paul.

[42] See St. Thomas, *Summa*, II-II, q. 129.

And therefore magnificence is joined to holiness, because its effects are directed primarily to religion, that is, to holiness.' "[43]

It must be added that the specifically religious motive of the honor and homage of God is used, and in fact not infrequently, in a more or less intense way, as a dynamism and a psychological lever to galvanize man in the practice of virtue and in charitable action, even by methods and schools which place no special emphasis on the liturgy. But it is also true that a spirituality clearly centered on the liturgy is not wanting in this potent psychological lever of moralizational function and in this incitement to the exercise of the virtues in the practical life; and by the very fact of its being centered on the liturgy, which, inasmuch as it is worship, is directly the supreme exercise of the virtue of religion, it possesses that very lever in a direct and transcendent way.

The preceding consideration is connected with another piece of evidence also tending toward a better understanding of the moralization force of the liturgy. And it is that in the liturgy, as in Scripture itself and in accord with the very style of the Scriptures, the immediate motives of individual moral actions are habitually taken not so much from the philosophical-ontological consideration of the nature of things as from the sacred salvation history of God's free and concrete intervention in the world. This is a matter which was sufficiently explained in our first chapter. Now, the specifically Christian motive and a constant supernatural vision of things is evidently a most powerful lever for the exercise of the virtues in the practical life.

Finally, the moralizational efficacy of the liturgical action is the result of the connection between worship and *devotio*. As was made clear in Chapter 4, *devotio* is a general and basic attitude of the will, always prompt to serve God and all that concerns His honor. This basic attitude is like the immediate humus in which worship sprouts and grows. Now, it is properly from this same attitude of *devotio* that the force and efficacy of every prayer and meditation proceeds, and of every resolution in view of the effective expression of charity through the exercise of the virtues in the practical life.

Thus the liturgical action, since it is, as worship, *devotio* in act, indeed, in its supreme act, behaves at the same time like a general dynamic charge, if you will, but nonetheless real, which efficaciously induces one to dispose his whole practical life to the service of God in the homage due Him. Even if this attitude of *devotio* did not lead to some particular point of the exercise of a specific virtue, nevertheless, when necessary, "it will make fruitful all the particular resolutions which the exercise itself of our moral life can,

[43] I. Mennesier, *St. Thomas d'Aq., Somme theol.* (ed. *Revue des jeunes*), *La religion*, Vol. I, Paris 1932, pp. 333–335. The final paragraph is from St. Thomas, *Summa*, II-II, q. 134, a. 2 ad 3.

on reflection, suggest to us; and it will elevate them all in reference to the ability to improve." [44]

The analysis of the psychological moralizational force of the liturgical action, even in respect to the exercise of works of charity and of the moral virtues which do not find their immediate practical application in any notable degree in the liturgy, carries us far indeed from the opinion of some people, not very well-reasoned anyway, to the effect that outside the strictly cultic function of adoration and praise, the liturgy cannot make any serious penetration into a man's interior moral ascetical labors nor in his apostolic and charitable activities in respect to others.

Liturgical spirituality and the real exercise of virtue in extraliturgical practical life. To complete this picture of the ascetical exercise of the theological and moral virtues in a climate of liturgical spirituality, it is enough to add that liturgical spirituality takes into account, of course, the necessity, in view of an efficacious straining toward Christian perfection, of a broad exercise of the theological and moral virtues in the extraliturgical area. It is not necessary to insist once more on the fact that liturgical spirituality is not really a spirituality that expects to confine itself absolutely to the liturgical action; rather, it is a spirituality in which the spirit of the liturgy, without suppressing the necessity of an extraliturgical life, for example, precisely by the exercise of works of charity and of the moral virtues, which have no occasion to be exercised within the liturgical action, still imbues the whole effort toward Christian perfection, and that which one must necessarily do outside the liturgy.

Does this mean, then, that in the climate of liturgical spirituality even the active exercise of the theological and moral virtues outside the liturgical action is imbued by the spirit of the liturgy? Let me say it again: it means that this extraliturgical exercise is regarded psychologically as necessary preparation for the proximate future active participation in the liturgy, and is the extension and necessary consequence of active participation in the liturgy already having taken place. Outside of the liturgy and in the area of the duties of one's proper state, the Christian virtues are practiced, especially those, to be sure, which normally find their only opportunity for exercise outside the liturgy, in order to be able to participate as fruitfully as possible in the liturgy, and because participation in the liturgy already having taken place demands, as necessary consequence, that such virtues be practiced in the Christian life.

Thus without falling into a deleterious narrowness of viewpoint and without limiting Christian life to liturgical action, liturgical spirituality has the enormous advantage of preserving the necessary and extremely beneficial

[44] I. Mennesier, *op. cit.*, p. 331.

unity of the activity and of the whole effort expended in striving for perfection, centering it, even psychologically, in that which theology calls the center of the Church's life, actually proposing it to us as such, that is, the liturgical action, principally the Mass.

An outstanding example of the profound mutual influence between liturgical action and practice of the virtues, especially the moral virtues, in the ordinary life outside the liturgy is given us by the Church herself in the official way in which she conceives and proposes to live Lent as a period of annual exercises and of more intense spiritual life. This more intense spiritual life, even while having its strong central point of radiation and attraction fixed in the liturgical action itself during this period, is nevertheless integrated, in the mind of the Church, with a broad extraliturgical practice of every kind of virtue, especially of works of charity toward neighbor (almsgiving is held in great respect) and works of penitence, temperance, perseverance, concentrated especially on fasting. The ember days and the vigils are, in this respect and in the spirit of the Church, assimilated to Lent.

Conclusion

At the conclusion of this article on the ascetical effort in the climate of liturgical spirituality, it can be asserted without fear of contradiction that the liturgy itself and the spirituality which is centered on it, by their intrinsic nature, bespeak a very great exercise of the theological and moral virtues, and they imply therefore a very strongly binding and moralizationally efficacious ascetical effort in the whole business of life. Liturgy and liturgical spirituality, even while constantly demonstrating, as we have had occasion to point out now and then, that they are themselves strongly theological and theocentric, are not quietistic, nor semi-quietistic, nor are they aesthete, nor do they draw one away from the healthy realism of every day life. Even while having their eyes fixed always on God, they do not forget man and his inherent weaknesses. Indeed, they aspire to heal him and to reveal him the better to himself, precisely by enticing him to a strong concentration on God.

If some who are diffident about the liturgical movement have their doubts about all this, it is simply because they have insufficient knowledge of the liturgy. And if some who claim to be liturgists seem by the practice of their own lives or by certain of their affirmations or fuzzy tendencies to lend weight to the aforesaid doubt, it is because they too have little knowledge of what the liturgy essentially is, and perhaps they have not even a clear notion of what spirituality is. It is ever so urgent to dispel these uncertainties so that all may be able to draw near without hesitating and to approach freely "the primary source of the true Christian spirit."

Perhaps someone will say: But is it not at least possible that in liturgical spirituality there are certain dangers present, such as a false estheticism or excessive ritualism or insufficient moral engagement? The answer to this is simply that the human element comes into everything; there is nothing that man cannot abuse, and so, of course, these dangers are possibilities; indeed, in anything in which something of the human has a part, there are specific areas of danger open to man's abuse and must be most carefully guarded against. Being of divine institution does not exclude the Mass itself nor the sacraments from such dangers. So much the more, then, will it have to be said that in every spirituality, understood as a particular concretization of the common means for striving toward Christian perfection, there can be and certainly are specific dangers against which a man must be on his guard. On the historical level it inevitably happens that some person will "come a cropper" therein.

Every spirituality has had those who, if not properly its critics, were insistent at least on pointing out its inherent dangers. Thus, in regard to a certain spirituality which insists directly and rather heavily on the aspect of voluntary or even voluntaristic self-determination in view of the moral practice of the good, of the correction of defects, of apostolic service, there is no lack of those who would speak of moralism, psychologism, activism, and similar things. Others, in reference to such another spirituality as tends clearly to direct its whole effort to mystical experience, have talked of introspection, experientialism, and so forth.

In reference to one or the other types of spirituality there is frequent talk of individualism and of the lack of an ecclesial communitarian sense of piety. Justifiable accusations? It is easily shown that they are not. An indication of certain dangers inherent in the aforesaid spiritualities, for anyone who does not have the wisdom to use them well, even if such dangers are in no way really necessary? I do not think that recognizing this necessarily implies any lack of respect for the aforesaid spiritualities nor in any way diminishes their real value. I repeat: anything that is in any way touched by mankind, so that there is the possibility of man's abusing it, carries with it its own specific dangers. This is true of the spirituality, official and otherwise, of the Church herself.

Why is there this possibility of abuses in the liturgy itself in the sense of externalism and an esthetism contrary to the necessary and healthy personal ascetical effort in the spiritual life? Because the liturgy, by its very nature, necessarily carries with it at one and the same time both internal worship and its externalization. Now, internal worship, considered in itself, is not subject to measure, nor is there in it the possibility of excess; for its measure is its being without measure, for man is never able to honor God as much as God is worthy of being honored.

But the externalization of internal worship — like the externalization of charity — is subject to right measure, in accord with what is fitting to the nature of man, the regulations of the Church, the circumstances of person, of place, and of time. In this area there can be abuse, either by excess or by defect. In concrete cases, therefore, prudence has to enter in to regulate the externalization of worship and, in accord with the aforesaid criteria, to prevent abuses. External worship is, as it were, the expression of internal worship and an encouragement thereto. Anyone who in the concrete situation of his own circumstances does not make use of external worship in such a way as to make of it a means for the greater expression and excitation of internal worship is abusing external worship.

The admonitions, therefore, which some are pleased to address to those who are devoted to the liturgy are not without foundation. Neither are those warnings devoid of foundation which others issue to those who are devoted to other kinds of spirituality, lest they fall into moralism, psychologism, introspectionism, and individualism. We recognize, therefore, that the danger of externalism, of the lack of serious moral involvement, sometimes of esthetism, can threaten anyone who, not understanding the liturgy and the spirituality based on it, abuses it rather than uses it rightly; and that to avoid such a danger it is enough to understand the liturgy and, having understood it, to live it in earnest.

4. Mystical Life and Liturgical Spirituality

As a complete doctrine of the way of striving toward Christian perfection, there is no spirituality which does not have to concern itself with the mystical aspect with which this striving is or can be clothed. It is not our task to expound *ex professo* on the concept of the mystical and on its specific role in the development of Christian life. That role we shall ignore, or, if need be, we may merely point out the way to the questions discussed by the various Catholic theologians in this field; for us it will be enough to start from points accepted by all and to clarify the questions which these points pose in liturgical spirituality.

Some points of doctrine in regard to the mystical life

These points are chiefly the following. The essence of the mystical act as the supernatural act of loving awareness of God (contemplation), transcends the faculties even to such a degree that man's ordinary manner of acting, with the assistance of grace, is of a kind that is more instinctive, more simply intuitive than discursive; and in this way of acting man is — and, in a certain way, he is aware of it — psychologically more passive than active, in the sense that in the very activity itself he is spared the labor of the act. It could even be said that the mystical act is an infused act of awareness of God and of love of God, of a kind that is more intuitive than discursive, more passive than active, and, in a certain way, psychologically perceived as such (infused contemplation).

The second point which we must recall is the diversity of the degrees of infused contemplation or of mystical acts. To describe them in detail, it is usual today to take as basis the descriptions which were offered by St. Teresa of Avila, from a psychological point of view, of her own personal experiences, completed for the most part by certain observations made by St. John of the Cross. But while, according to the descriptions of the mystics, the characteristics of the beginning of infused contemplation are quite clear, and the general fact of the existence in infused contemplation of diverse degrees of intensity and perfection is certain, the question of the individual degrees in particular, of the distinctive notes, of their respective perfection, and of their order of succession is much less certain.

In this area St. Teresa does not pretend to do anything but describe her own personal experience; but we are tempted, of course, to take her experience as a point of universal reference because of the marvelous and not easily improvable psychological descriptions which the saint has left us and by means of which she has, as it were, set them on display before us. But it is frequently most difficult, well nigh impossible, to go beyond generalities and get to the particulars, to reconcile these outlines of St. Teresa with what the other mystics have told us about their experiences; and it does not seem that the only reason for this is that these other mystics have not been able to give us as precise a psychological description of their experience, but also because it does not seem to be necessary to understand the plans of St. Teresa as having absolute and universal validity.

The third point which must never be lost sight of is the clear distinction gained by this time between the essence of the mystical phenomenon and the accidental epiphenomena which may but need not necessarily accompany it. Among these are reckoned not only visions, revelations, internal vocalizations, external somatic phenomena of ecstasies, levitations and the like, but also some other physico-psychic feats, such as specific reactions of the affective sensibility, the suspension of somatic movements, the suspension of speech, of the exterior activities of the external senses, of the imagination. The essence of the mystical phenomena does not consist of these things.

Nevertheless, if these epiphenomena accompany the mystical phenomenon, it is either because the subject, by reason of his temperament, reacts thus to that which is essential to the phenomenon, without these reactions being produced by the direct intervention of God, or because God Himself does indeed produce them directly but as secondary phenomena accompanying the essential mystical phenomenon, and taking into account always the temperament of the subject and the particular circumstances.

As you know, theologians like to discuss the question of the precise relations between mystical graces and Christian perfection, whether or not the latter is attainable without the former. Connected with this is the other question of the universal call to the mystical life, as well as that of the graces which characterize the mystical life, whether or not they are to be desired. In any case, we are able to be in some way disposed to those graces, and when God is pleased to bestow them on someone, there is a grave obligation not to impede the divine operation. In liturgical spirituality, then, just as in any other kind of spirituality, the question of the relations between the liturgy and mysticism cannot be evaded.[45]

The question

Now, the nature and the style of the liturgy can raise the question of compatibility or, at least, of the possibility of a harmonious relationship between liturgical spirituality and the mystical experience. At first glance it might seem that liturgical spirituality excludes or at least hinders to a considerable extent the birth and the development of mystical acts and mystical states.

Liturgical spirituality, especially in the liturgy itself, is actively communitarian. It involves an abundant use of sensible signs, of prayers, even vocal prayers, as well as a noteworthy exercise of the external senses and of the imagination. All this seems but little reconcilable with the mystical act, or, at least, to be but poorly equipped to create an atmosphere favorable to the mystical.

Someone will surely inform us that actually the greatest mystics spoke but little about the liturgy; for example, St. Teresa, and even more notably, St. John of the Cross.[46]

Indeed, it would seem that what they say about the mystical acts and mystical states, and especially of the way in which man must conduct himself so as to be prepared for them, at least to the point of not hindering them in any way when God grants them, were notably contrary to the style of the liturgy. Specifically, it is a matter of the warnings which St. Teresa and St. John give to those who are just beginning to receive the grace of mystical contemplation, when they begin to try that which St. Teresa calls the prayer of quiet, which is the first step in the mystical state properly so called. It is the moment in which discursive meditation begins to become laborious, because the soul is called to an ever more simple way of conversing with God,

[45] See R. Hoornaert, "*Liturgie ou contemplation*," in *Études carmelitaines*, Vol. 17 (1932), pp. 177–215.

[46] Hoornaert, *op. cit.*, pp. 181–182 and 187–190, has pointed out how much attestation there is in the lives and in the works of St. John and St. Teresa to their adherence to the liturgy. See also J. Villet, "*Bible et mystique chez St. Jean de la Croix*," in *Études carmelitaines*, Rome 1949, pp. 12–18, on the influence of the liturgy on the biblical citations in St. John. Fr. Lucien Marie de St. Joseph, "*Oraison et prière liturgique chez Ste. Thérèse d'Avila*," in *Carmel*, 1960, pp. 92–114. It may be observed, in any case, that it is not enough to lead the choral life, or to have a great respect and general esteem for the sacred rites, or even to be imbued in a generic way with a great spirit of the praise of God in order for one to be said, without qualification, to have "a liturgical mind," at least in the sense which we intend when we speak of liturgical spirituality.

like a simple loving glance and repose in Him, without distinct notice of particular objects, but with a simple general loving attention, without effort of the senses, of the imagination, nor of discursive reasoning.

In this condition, in fact, it is recommended first of all that the soul not disturb itself with ratiocinations, vocal prayers, specific imaginations, acts of the will in respect to precise objects, and so much the less, then, with specific activities of the senses. On the contrary, having recognized the true signs of having been called, it is recommended that one abandon the way of discursive meditation and maintain tranquillity in that vague general awareness of God which is a vital act much superior to all other acts. We recall, for example, the following passage from St. John of the Cross:

> "Consequently, many times the soul will be found in this loving and tranquil awareness without laboring in any way with the faculties regarding specific acts, not working actively but only receiving; and many other times it will be necessary to assist oneself by means of discourse, but with moderation and without effort, in order to maintain oneself in that awareness. When this has happened, therefore, the soul does not labor at all with her faculties. Indeed, to tell the truth, in this situation, the heavenly and delightful intelligence becomes operative of itself in the soul, while the soul has nothing else to do but to fix its loving attention on God *without desiring to know or to see anything.*

> "Hence God communicates Himself to the soul passively, just as one who has his eyes open receives the light passively, and has nothing to do for his part except to keep them open. The reception of supernatural light is passive understanding; and therefore it can be said that the soul does not labor, not because it does not understand, but because that which it does understand is not the fruit of its own industry and consists only in the accepting of that which is given it, whatever comes its way through divine illuminations and inspirations.

> "Although the will receives freely the general and vague awareness of God, it is nevertheless necessary, in order to receive this light more simply and abundantly, to exclude other more tangible and sensible lights of extraneous awareness or forms of discourse; for there is nothing of this latter that can compare to that serene and limpid light. And therefore if *in this process someone were to wish to conceive and consider particular objects, however spiritual, it would impede the clear, simple, and general light of the spirit,* by interposing there these clouds. The light and the vision of these objects would only be an impediment for anyone who would place such a screen or other obstacle before his eyes.

> "It is evident, therefore, that not until the soul is successful *in purifying itself and in emptying itself of all these intelligible forms and images* will it dwell in that pure and simple light, being transformed in it into a state of perfection. That light does not remain abidingly in the

soul, for the forms and veils of creatures, which envelop and embarrass the soul, impede it by diffusing it. But if the soul decide to reject every veil or impediment, keeping itself in its pure nakedness and poverty of spirit, now suddenly simple and pure, it will be transformed by the simple and pure Wisdom, who is the Son of God. Now that there is in the enamored soul a lack of that which was naturally there, suddenly the divine is supernaturally infused into it; for nature abhors a vacuum.

"The spiritual man, therefore, may achieve a certain stability in his loving awareness of God, and an intellectual repose, when he is unable to meditate, though he will appear to be doing nothing. Little by little, and most rapidly, a heavenly peace will be infused into his soul, with marvelous and sublime knowledge of God and of divine love. *Let him not upset himself with imaginations or meditations or discourses of any kind*, so as not to disturb his soul and draw it away from its tranquillity and contentment, only to carry it off to where it will find only revulsion and pain." [47]

Joined to this passage and to so many others of a similar flavor is the firm and well-known insistence of St. John of the Cross in recommending to the spiritual man who desires to strive toward perfection that he "divest his soul of its natural perceptions of external objects" and that he "make vacant" his imagination or phantasy "of all the forms and imaginary perceptions that can gain natural entry there," [48] and to apply the same procedure of

[47] From *The Ascent of Mount Carmel*, the *Subida* 2, 15, 2-5, pp. 595-596 in the critical Spanish edition of Fr. Chrisogono de Jésus, *Vita y obras de S. Juan de la Cruz*, 3rd ed., Madrid 1955.

[48] *Ibid., Subida* 2, 12, pp. 582-583. Book I of the *Subida* treats of the divesting of the soul of the perceptions of external stimuli; Book II, chapter 12, treats of the emptying out of the imagination. Book III, chapters 35-44 (pp. 734 ff), speaks at considerable length of images, oratories, churches, places, and ceremonies, in admonishing the spiritual man on how he is to comport himself in respect to all this.

Saint John has in mind the tendency to externalism, to display, and sometimes, even to superstition, which he saw all about him in the Spain of the sixteenth century. And he is, therefore, singularly intent upon guarding against the dangers which, in these matters, so far from nourishing a profound devotion, do not more than tickle the palate with external and visible things, which, in the majority of cases, only hinder one's arriving at a true union with God in nakedness of spirit.

In reference to prayer in churches and in oratories, while recognizing repeatedly that "the suitable and appointed place for prayer is the church and the oratory, and images serve a purpose" (*Subida* 3, 40, 1; p. 744), he never tires of advising the spiritual man to select for a matter of such great importance "that place which will be of less concern and less attraction to the senses. The place must not be luxurious (such as some like to have); otherwise, rather than serving for recollection of spirit it will only provide diversion. On the contrary, solitary and even wild places are quite suitable, where the spirit can ascend earnestly and directly to God, unimpeded and undetained by visible things, which sometimes do indeed help to elevate the spirit, but only if we immediately forget them, to make our abode again entirely in God" (*Subida* 3, 39, 2; p. 743). "Choose the most solitary and deserted place possible" (*Subida* 3, 40, 2; p. 745).

"For the spirit to approach God by this manner of means it is proper to observe that beginners are permitted, and it may even be necessary for them, to find some sensible joy in images, oratories, and other visible things nullification or evacuation to the memory and to the discursive understanding, as he explains in Books II and III of the *Ascent.*

With all this certainly I do not wish to insinuate that St. John of the Cross, and still less St. Teresa, positively regard the frank acceptance of the liturgy as a way ill-suited to the development of the mystical life, for the reason that the liturgy, so clearly bound to the senses, to external rites, to communitarian manifestations of piety, would be regarded by them as poorly suited to nourish that nakedness of spirit which is quite essential to that life. I wish only to call attention to the fact that in the great mystical teachers of the sixteenth century, who, with their concentration on the psychological and descriptive aspect of union with God, did make such great progress in mystical doctrine, the place which the liturgy may have or is able to have in the contemplative experience is not explained.

A text from Cassian

To resolve this question, the experience and the exact testimony of these same mystics is of capital importance, as with everything else that concerns the mystical. The first thing to be seen, therefore, is whether or not in the history of mysticism there be any testimonials in which the mystical and the liturgical seem to be in some way normally united. These cases do exist and they show, in fact, that liturgy, spirituality, and mysticism can go together very well, and together they can even prosper gloriously. These cases and these testimonials, by broadening and filling out our information about the mystical experience, keep us from making unjustified judgments and from drawing invalid conclusions from certain affirmations, such as those cited above from St. John of the Cross.

The most complete case history of the perfect marriage between liturgy, liturgical spirituality, and mysticism seems to be that of St. Gertrude. But because it is an example of liturgical spirituality that can be profitably studied under various aspects, I propose to treat it more fully by itself in the next chapter. Here in the present chapter I shall have recourse to other testimonials.

---

of piety, because they have not yet weaned their palates away from the things of the world; and hence, by means of a taste for holy things they may the more easily abandon all their other cravings; as we do with a baby, when we want to take one thing away from him, we give him another, so that his hands will not be empty and he will not cry. If, then, he desires to make progress, the spiritual man is obliged to divest himself even of the aforementioned tastes and appetites in which the will can delight. The pure spirit is but very little attached to any of these things; rather, it relies entirely on interior recollection and on mental converse with God; and whatever use it makes of images and of oratories is only a temporary means. It is elevated suddenly to God and forgets all that pertains to the senses. Consequently, while it is better to pray in the most suitable places, nevertheless, that place must be chosen where the mind and the spirit will find less hindrance in ascending to the Lord" (*Subida* 3, 39, 1; p. 743).

The fact remains that St. John is not speaking of liturgical prayer, nor of the sacraments and ceremonies, etc., except in relation to the danger that they might nourish the sensible appetites for external and visible things, and thus hinder that nakedness of spirit necessary for true contemplation. See also, for example, St. Teresa, *The Way of Perfection* 26–29, 31.

Now, among these there are some, ancient and modern, consisting in psychological descriptions of acts and states characterized as mystical experiences, which exclude even the slightest doubt about the basic fact of the perfect possibility of the act of mystical contemplation properly so called, in the communitarian liturgical action itself, while the mystic takes an active role therein with perfectly normal external behavior.

First of all I will transcribe and analyze a text of Cassian from *Conferences* 10, 11, wherein he recounts the second conference of Abba Isaac, on prayer. The text treats directly of that which Cassian calls the perfect prayer, and which for him means nothing else but the very apex of mystical contemplation. The general context should be kept in mind.

Conferences 9 and 10 speak of prayer as the goal of the monastic life. The ninth speaks of prayer in general, of its various kinds and of its presuppositions, that is, of the ascetical purification of one's whole life as the indispensable foundation of prayer. It speaks also of the various gradations of prayer; and in particular allusions are made to the most sublime of these gradations: the "pure" prayer, *pura et sincera oratio*, the ardent prayer, perfect prayer, *ignita oratio, perfecta oratio* (9, 25-27).

The tenth conference, after having refuted the error of the anthropomorphites, who maintained that God has a certain human form which some of them deemed important to be able to represent in prayer, treats the question of the way or method by which to rise to the perfection of prayer. An easy and much recommended way is that of ejaculatory prayers, in which it is possible to achieve a very high gradation of prayer: *pura et brevis oratio*. In this regard the versicle is recommended, *Deus in adiutorium meum intende*, which can serve to realize in some way perpetual prayer, the *iugis oratio*, that is, a state in which the mind renews in itself with the greatest frequency the awareness of God's presence (*perpetua Dei memoria*) and elevates itself to Him constantly in pure and brief prayer. All of this presupposes, of course, the moral purification of life by means of ascetical effort.

At this point (chapter 11) the conference begins again to speak of perfect prayer, now as the interior sanctuary to which all the preceding purifications and prayers but serve as the introduction:

> "Whoever shall have arrived at this state and will advance onwards from it (i.e., from the state of purification and of the constant remembrance of God) possesses in it not only the simplicity of innocence, but what is more, endowed with the virtue of discretion, he has become the exterminator of the venomous serpents by keeping Satan under his feet. He has achieved, by the alacrity of his mind, the state of the spiritual stag, and he will find his pasture on the mountains of the prophets and apostles, that is, in their highest and most sublime mysteries.
>
> "Thriving ever more on their nourishment, he will make his own all the sentiments of the psalms, and he will begin to sing them in such a

way, with deep compunction of heart, that he will utter them not as compositions of the prophet, but as coming forth from himself, as his very own prayer. Or at least he will believe that they have been made his own, composed, as it were, with him in mind, recognizing that that which is stated in them did not take place only at an earlier time, for the prophet or in the prophet, but that it take place and is fulfilled every day and in himself. In fact, only then do the Scriptures open themselves to us, only then are they clearly manifest to us, with, so to speak, their veins and marrow exposed, when our own experience not only perceives the meaning of Scripture but anticipates it, and the significance of the words is made clear to us, not by means of learned explanations thereof, but through the verification supplied by experience itself.

"Then, while we renew in ourselves the same interior affection in which each psalm was sung or written, we will ourselves become like their authors and will anticipate the meaning of the psalms rather than follow after it. That is to say, knowing that to which the words vitally correspond before they are conceptually formed, when we come to meditate on them we will be reminded, so to speak, of what has happened to us, or is happening in us every day. While we sing we recall the effects of our negligence and the battles we have won; the benefits that Divine Providence has granted us and the losses that we have suffered at the instigation of the enemy; the injuries because of fickle and too easy forgetfulness, the consequences of human fragility, and the deceptions of our blind ignorance. All these things we shall indeed find expressed in the psalms, so much so that by viewing therein, as in a mirror of finest quality, all that has befallen us, we shall recognize it all the more perfectly. And this will take place in such a way that, having been taught by experience, we will recognize these things not as having heard them, but by touching them as something actually present; and we will utter them from the interior affection of the heart not as if from memory but as if implanted in us by their very nature, understanding their meaning not by the reading of the text but under the guidance of antecedent experience.

"To such degree that our mind arrives in this very act at that pure prayer of which we spoke in the preceding conference, that is the degree to which the Lord has granted us to attain. This prayer not only does not pause to consider any sort of images, but what is more, it is not formulated in any kind of expression using words or utterances. Rather, with inexhaustible joy of spirit, it is expressed in the ardent yearning of the mind, with inexpressible rapture (*excessus*) of the heart; and the mind, passing over all things sensible and visible, pours out this prayer before God with groans and sighs unutterable."

Let us note first of all that the passage certainly wants to indicate how the monk can rise to the supreme degree of that perfect prayer which is treated of directly in the final paragraph of the text: the pure prayer that was spoken of in conference 9, 25-27; ardent prayer in the rapture of the soul: *excessus mentis*, beyond images and words.

That it is a matter of contemplative and mystical prayer, properly so called, of a very high order is evident from the description that Cassian gives of it in conference 9, 25, where he attributes to it the following notes: actually known only to a few;[49] knowable only by experience;[50] this experience is intuitive rather than discursive, in a general awareness but without specific objects;[51] not distinguished or characterized by vocal sounds, movements of the tongue, nor by the utterance of words;[52] it is infused by illumination with divine light;[53] the sudden and unexpected character of this illumination is notable, for it strikes the mind with a *stupor subitae illuminationis*;[54] it is of short duration;[55] the soul, when it receives this illumination, is, as it were, drawn out of itself; and when the illumination ceases, the soul returns into itself (*in semetipsam reversam*) and to its ordinary discursive way; but even then it cannot analyze its experience rationally, nor can it speak of its experience, because that experience remains unutterable.

Elsewhere Cassian indicates some of the effects brought about by ardent (*ignita*) prayer. Sometimes the joy which pours into the soul is so great and of such a nature that the soul emits exclamations, sighs, and shouts that it cannot contain. At other times, on the contrary, the soul, because of the great amazement that it feels, is thrown into a profound silence which hinders or takes away its every word and leaves room only for an unutterable and ardent conversation with God. At other times again only tears can suffice in some way to give some relief to the joy that is felt.[56]

Basically, for Cassian, ardent or inflamed prayer means those brief moments in which the soul, under the influence of a special divine grace, is elevated above its own habitual state, even if of constant recollection of God and, in some way, of constant prayer, and reaches the apex of actual union with Him.

In chapter 26 of the ninth conference Cassian speaks of the various occasions that can give rise to this ardent prayer. The natural terrain in which it germinates is *compunctio* in the broadest sense of its use among the ancients. Therefore the various causes which give rise to various compunctions are as many as the occasions by which "the soul is inflamed and set on fire and incited to pure and most fervent prayers."[57]

Among these occasions we may note: spiritual exhortations and confer-

---

[49] *Perpaucis cognitam.* See also *Conferences* 10, 10.

[50] See also *Conferences* 10, 9.

[51] *Omnem transcendens humanum sensum . . . conglobatis sensibus . . . .*

[52] *Nullo non dicam sono vocis, vel linguae motu, vel ulla verborum pronuntiatione distinguitur . . . mens . . . non humanis atque angustis designat eloquiis.*

[53] *. . . quam mens infusione coelestis illius luminis illustrata, non humanis designat eloquiis.*

[54] *Conferences* 9, 27.

[55] *. . . in illo brevissimo temporis puncto . . . .*

[56] *Conferences* 9, 27.

[57] *Conferences* 9, 26.

ences; the death of a loved one; the singing of some verse of a psalm: "Sometimes, indeed, while we were singing, a verse of some psalm has given rise in us to the ardent prayer."[58] The connection between ardent prayer and active normal participation in the singing of the psalms deserves close attention: "Sometimes, on the contrary, it has been the modulation of the sonorous voice of a brother's singing that has excited the minds of the amazed singers to intense supplication."[59] Here the ardent prayer is triggered simply by hearing the beautiful singing of another. "We know too that the gravity and distinct enunciation of those singing the psalms has instilled great fervor in those present." These particulars complete quite well the picture provided by the text cited above, where ardent prayer is spoken of only in association with the recitation and singing of psalms by those themselves who are favored by it.

Progress towards this apex of perfect prayer, which is the subject matter of the text of chapter 11 of conference 10, is characterized there as follows: it supposes that moral purification has already been acquired; this being the case, reading and constant meditation on the Scriptures with true profit for the soul and with understanding of their mysteries becomes possible; at this point the very singing and recitation of the psalms acquires an entirely special power of spiritual prayer; and thus one arrives at the supreme degree of prayer, ardent prayer.

Even the special prayer which occurs in the third phase, during the recitation of the psalms, is certainly a prayer of properly mystical nature. This is proved by its personal character — experiential, intuitive, transcending and preceding ordinary discursive knowledge, in which the soul, under the actual influence of mystical grace, sings the psalms as if it had composed them itself on the spur of the moment — because the source from which the profound understanding of the words of the psalms is derived is the internal harmonious disposition itself which precedes the actual formation of the words in the mouth and their discursive conceptual understanding in the intellect.

The words of the psalms then arouse in the soul echoes of life well beyond the simple concepts of reasoning in search of explanations and of understanding. It is here that the highest personalization of the Scriptures in the liturgical action takes place. The singing itself is like an extraordinary mirror and becomes for the one praying a vital review of his state, in which the soul not only hears but sees and touches its own most intimate relations with God.

We may well ask whether, according to Cassian, praying the psalms as just now described is simply to be identified with the most perfect prayer, or with the ardent prayer of which he speaks at the end of the text cited; or whether ardent prayer is for him a higher form of prayer. I think that for

[58] *Nonnumquam etenim psalmi cuiuscumque versiculus occasionem orationis ignitae decan-* tantibut nobis praebuit (*ibid.*, 9, 26).
[59] *Conferences* 9, 26.

Cassian what is called the most perfect prayer or ardent prayer is a form superior to that just now described in regard to the psalms, because when he speaks of most perfect prayer he always insists on the fact that it transcends images and words, while that described immediately above seems in some way to be expressed in the words themselves of the psalms.

Nevertheless, it is certain that for Cassian the singing and the recitation of the psalms can be the occasion by which perfect prayer, ardent prayer, is released, so much so that this can take place in the very one who is singing, and even while he is singing: *interdum etenim psalmi cuiuscumque versiculus occasionem orationis ignitae decantantibus nobis praebuit.*[60]

I think, therefore, that for Cassian ardent prayer is the supreme degree of mystical prayer known by him, transcending in itself, in its simplicity, every image and word, but which can also take place and continue for some time in someone even while he is singing or reciting the psalms; and it is of such great intensity that sometimes (Cassian has in mind the monk in his cell) it provokes even the suspension of words and of other activities of the spirit.[61]

Whatever view one takes, two things are certain in regard to the experience recounted by Cassian: first, that mystical contemplation properly so called can take place while participating, even actively and normally, in the liturgical action; second, that the liturgical action itself is a very favorable terrain in which, proceeding from compunction, the aforesaid contemplation can develop and progress even to the point that it may become the occasion of achieving the highest order of prayer.

Thus, for Cassian, the communitarian singing and recitation of the psalms, far from being a hindrance to mystical experience, is a natural seed bed — presupposing the moral purification of life and the vital habit of reading and meditating on the Scriptures as well as on the constant presence of God, nourished in some way by the habit of ejaculatory prayers — in which we grow up to the higher order of contemplation, the effects of which are, among else, sometimes unrestrainable joy, sometimes an entirely internal amazement, and sometimes an abundance of tears, even external.

In summary, it is a panoramic view of the ascetical-mystical life so familiar to the whole monastic tradition of antiquity. In this tradition, far from forgetting the liturgy in the ascent toward perfection, there is always assigned to the liturgy its own connatural place in the whole process. The Venerable Guigo I, the great Carthusian prior general and legislator († 1136), epitomized the principal aspects of this spirituality, without enumerating them in their logical order, as follows: *suavitates psalmodiarum, studia lectionum, fer-*

---

[60] *Conferences* 9, 26.

[61] *Conferences* 9, 27: *Nonnumquam vero tanto silentio mens intra secretum profundae taciturnitatis absconditur, ut omnem poenitus sonum vocis stupor subitae illuminationis includat omnesque sensus attonitus spiritus vel contineat intrinsecus vel amittat.* The context shows that Cassian is talking about a monk in his cell, when he speaks of the fact that sometimes, under the influence of this same grace, there is a bursting forth of groans and of shouts of joy heard by those nearby the cell.

vores orationum, subtilitates meditationum, excessus contemplationum, baptismata lacrymarum.[62] The logical order would be: *studia lectionum, subtilitates meditationum, fervores orationum, suavitates psalmodiarum, excessus contemplationum, baptismata lacrymarum.*[63]

The testimony of the Venerable Marie of the Incarnation, Ursuline

In regard to this same question of the relations between the liturgical life and the mystical life, the testimony of Marie of the Incarnation,[64] a French Ursuline of the seventeenth century, is highly informative. This mystic, who lived after St. Teresa of Avila, whose works, moreover, she read very quickly and was certainly influenced by them, had in a degree no less than St. Teresa herself an extraordinary gift for describing, frequently in quite minute detail, the proper psychological states in the graces of union and contemplation.

But she gives us in addition something which neither St. Teresa nor St. John of the Cross were able to give: the example of a most intense mystical life, quite unbroken and in its highest orders, lived first of all for eleven years in the world in the full hubbub of daily affairs and, after the parenthesis of eight years of peaceful cloistered life with the Ursulines of Tours, for some thirty-three years in the full missionary activity in Canada in its first uncertain days of colonization, always in exterior circumstances so far distant from those which, too easily, are supposed to be indispensable for the full flowering of the mystical life — circumstances, indeed, which are much closer to the actual life of nearly all the faithful. From this point of view, Marie of the Incarnation, in the very area of experience and of mystical teaching, is an indispensable complement to St. Teresa and to St. John of the Cross.

She complements them also in the area of the relations between liturgy and the mystical life. The passages in the writings of Marie of the Incarnation which do indeed speak of this are relatively rare but ever so significant. She herself notes that from her childhood and afterwards even in the very circum-

---

[62] *Consuetudines* 80, 11 (PL 153, col. 757).

[63] Tears, of course, are the quite accidental effect of contemplation. The ancients, we know, held this gift in very high esteem because of its close connection with compunction.

[64] Marie Guyart, born at Tours in 1599, died at Quebec in 1672. Even from childhood she received remarkable graces, with a strong tendency to contemplation. In 1617 she married Claude Joseph Martin, a silk manufacturer. She had a son, Claude Martin, who later became a well-known Maurist. Widowed in 1619, she gave herself more intensely to prayer and to works of charity. In 1620 she entered upon the mystical life properly so called. From 1621 she lived in her sister's house; and in 1631 she joined the Ursulines at Tours.

In 1639 she went to Canada as head of a group of sisters, and in the midst of the dangers and difficulties of those early days of the colonization of the country, she became, both for the French settlers and for the Indians who frequented the missions, the soul and, as it were, the spiritual mother of the colony. Over and above the numerous letters of a spiritual nature and others of great historical and civil interest for the early days of Canada, she wrote by order of her confessors two general relations, of special interest from the mystical point of view, about her own life and the graces which God had given her: the first relation in 1633, and the second in 1654. The critical edition is by A. Jamet, *Marie de l'Incarnation, ursuline de Tours, Écrits spirituels et historiques*, 4 vols., Paris Quebec 1929–1939.

stances of the cares of a married woman, the liturgy was for her the source
of a profound religious life:

> "One of the things that has greatly assisted my spirit of devotion is
> the ceremonies of the Church, which, from my childhood, powerfully
> attracted my spirit. I found them so beautiful and so holy that I saw
> nothing comparable to them. After I had grown up and had become
> capable of understanding their meaning, my love was augmented by
> the wonderment that I felt in seeing the sanctity and the majesty of the
> Church. This augmented also my faith and bound me to our Lord in a
> manner really quite extraordinary. I gave vent to thanksgivings for His
> having vouchsafed to let me be born of Christian parents and for hav-
> ing called me to the vocation of a daughter of the Church. The more
> I progressed in knowledge, the more I felt emotion and love for these
> holy ceremonies of the Church. . . .
>
> "I had a faith so alive to all that the Church does that it seemed to
> me that this was my very life and nourishment. Once I thought I would
> be suffocated in the general procession of a jubilee. Then I found my-
> self among the first to enter the church to see the ceremonies and the
> solemn office performed there on this occasion. My whole preoccupation
> was internal, in respect to what I saw and heard.
>
> "On the occasion of a procession of the Blessed Sacrament my heart
> and my spirit were so ravished in God that in looking upon this Sacra-
> ment of love, it seemed that it was all directed to me. I had so narrow a
> view that I walked about at random like a person who has had too
> much to drink. I did not know if people noticed it or what would be
> thought of it.
>
> "In this state I thought I was in the midst of true devotion because I
> did not know that there was anything else beyond praying to God and
> serving Him by frequenting the sacraments and not committing volun-
> tary sins. Thus when I made my confession I found myself quite just,
> and my spirit felt satisfaction from one confession to another.
>
> "But the Spirit of God urged me on to make a confession of all my
> transgressions since infancy. As I have said, He wanted from me a
> great purity that I did not understand, nor did I know the reason why
> He wanted it." [65]

Thus Marie, looking back much later to that first phase of her spiritual life
as preparatory to the future and much more sublime communications of
God, gave an excellent account of the important role which the liturgy and
active participation in the ceremonies had in her developing spiritual life.

In 1619, scarcely two years after a marriage entered into at the will of her
parents, the death of her husband left her with an infant of six months and
the care of a silk business. Henceforth Marie followed entirely the course of
interior life to which the Spirit drew her. She remained in the world, in the

[65] *Relation of 1654*, Jamet edition, Vol. 2, pp. 170 ff.

midst of economic difficulties, humiliations, apprehensions about her son, concerns ever so humanly absorbing and distracting. She lost practically all her possessions, liquidated the silk business, and retired to a solitary life of prayer and penitence.

In 1620, in a vision in which she saw herself immersed in the blood of Christ, she was called decisively to enter into the mystical life properly so called; and from the very beginning she received the highest graces. But driven again by the Spirit, for the purpose of a deeper self-mortification and practice of charity, in 1621 she began to act as helper and virtually as a servant in the domestic and commercial affairs of her sister and her sister's husband, who had a thriving drayage business; nor did she fail to concern herself with the numerous workmen in the business, wagoners and porters. She was completely occupied with cooking, with clients, with goods to be loaded or unloaded at the river, often into the middle of the night, with the sleeping quarters of travelers, with the ill, with the storerooms, with the stables, and even with fifty or sixty horses with which, she says, "I had to busy myself."

In the midst of this incredible hubbub, when Marie was day and night at work, the graces of the interior life pursued her ever more profoundly and constantly. Interiorly she never lost sight of God, who was always present to her. At first it happened very quietly. But afterwards the calls made to her were more intense and violent, with moments in which she was so forcibly drawn along that she would scarcely begin to pray when she would have to retire to a hidden place and find somewhere to sit lest she fall down in the presence of others. One day when she was in this condition, she was given the promise of spiritual espousals: "I will espouse you to Me forever, I will espouse you to Me in the faith" (Osee 2:19-20). Of such occasions she writes:

> "I felt myself powerfully attracted in a moment without having time to do anything by way of internal or external act. It seemed to me that I was submerged in God, which deprived me of every power of action. . . . It was impossible for me to linger voluntarily over anything whatever because of that internal preoccupation which drew me irresistibly along. It deprived me of the power of praying vocally. If I wished to say the rosary, it transported my spirit and deprived me of speech and it was seldom that I could say it. It was the same with the Office.[66] Sometimes, even so, the meaning of the psalms was made clear to me with a gentleness that I would not know how to express; and in these instances I was at liberty to recite the Office."[67]

Here, in short, Marie is found in that habitual state which the mystics called spiritual betrothal. She experiences moments of sudden and violent attraction to God. This at times deprives her of the power of vocalizing

[66] The Little Office of the Blessed Mother, which Marie frequently recited.

[67] *Relation of 1633*, Jamet edition, Vol. 1, p. 159. See also the *Relation of 1654*, same edition, Vol. 2, pp. 227 ff.

prayers, of saying the rosary, of reciting the psalms; but at other times she is not only left free to recite them, but what is more, she is given an unutterable experiential understanding of their meaning. Bear in mind that this was always a matter of private recitation. The experience to which Marie of the Incarnation briefly alludes coincides quite closely with what Cassian had to say about ardent prayer.

Before arriving at the state of perfect union with God, permanent and in the very depths of the soul always peaceful even in the midst of sufferings of every kind, it is necessary to pass, the mystics tell us, through the passive purifications of the senses and of the mind so that the faculties may be reduced to perfect simplicity and malleability in the hands of God in their way of acting in the fact of things most divine. And in regard to these things most divine, we mean even the things that are the objects of these faculties as they come into play in the liturgy.

When in 1654 Marie of the Incarnation wrote the second relation about her life, she made some interesting observations on this very matter. The passive purifications, Marie notes, come about through the fact that God gradually "suspends" the operation of the senses, of the imagination, of the memory, of the discursive intellect, and of the will itself.

> "On account of this operation, a veritable crucifixion of the more noble faculties, what happens? Can one believe that these faculties are able to remain fixed and suspended, as in death? It is incredible how very painful this amputation proves to be for them, especially in the solemnities which are carried out in the Church, where the mysteries of our redemption are presented, which mysteries had previously been a delicious nourishment for them and in which they found their greatest satisfaction. . . . through the lights which the Holy Spirit communicated to them about each of the holy mysteries. And now it is not possible for these faculties to pause to dwell upon the mysteries.
>
> "Sometimes one who is led on this way enters in fear, not being able to understand how he can be on the true path while not being able to dwell upon those things which are the most holy and the most solemn in all the Church. Then he reacts violently, trying to snatch away the intellect from the laziness into which he thinks it has fallen. But in vain; all this is but ignorance and imperfection. After repeated violence on various occasions, he realizes by experience that there is nothing to be gained by such efforts, however great, since the faculties of the soul have lost their natural use in a supernatural way." [68]

One can only wait for God Himself to apply the remedy. Let it be noted that in similar cases, ever more profound "suspension" of the senses, of discourse and of will, in regard to the objects of the liturgy just as in regard to other objects, that which constitutes a hindrance and has need of purification

---

[68] *Relation of 1654*, Jamet edition, Vol. 2, pp. 458–459.

is not the fact that the faculties are concerned with the objects which the liturgy presents to them, but the manner in which the faculties are concerned with them. That passivity is never absolute, as we have pointed out in its proper place. The faculties, when they are purified in their activities in regard to the object of the liturgy, are not faculties inactive and as if dead; rather they are the same faculties now acting in a more sublime way in respect to these objects.

Meanwhile, when Marie was still living in her sister's house, not long after that transitory state of spiritual betrothal, even in the midst of concerns and an almost incredible hubbub, she received the most sublime graces of experiential knowledge of the incarnate Word and of the Trinity. Moreover, beginning in 1628, she received the grace of a profound and constant union with God — mystical marriage — in whom her soul, at least in its deepest part, consequently remained ever immersed, even when, in its inferior part, she had still to undergo great trials and temptations, or, in any case, to endure terrible sufferings.[69]

Already in a very perfect state of habitual union, Marie entered the Ursuline convent at Tours in 1631. Two months after her entrance, and for the third time in her life, she had a vision of the Blessed Trinity during which the three divine Persons took complete possession of her soul and she possessed the three Persons "in the fullness of participation in the treasures of the divine splendor."[70] It was the highest of the graces which Marie received, the strongest presentiment of the beatific vision, as she says.[71]

But the inferior part of her soul had still to pass through three years of the most intense moral suffering, so much so that one evening, through God's workings, all her gifts were dispersed as if she had never had them; but still, from this experience she derived tremendous spiritual advantage by way of an ever more perfect purification. Thus she entered into a more and more habitual and profound state of union with God.

Henceforth her most varied occupations and her greatest sufferings only touched, so to speak, the surface of her soul and could not distract it from her fundamental and permanent union with God. She received an experiential understanding by which to comprehend the meaning of the Scriptures.[72] Marie has described with great delicacy even the more subtle movements of her own psychology in this habitual state of highest mystical contemplation.

[69] In these sufferings psalmody not infrequently constituted her only comfort: "The only thing which would give me rest was psalmody, which seemed to dispel all my pains, and which filled me with such an excess of interior joy that the meaning of the words and of the phrases was made clear to me and sometimes I leaped up within myself because of it, and I believe my joy may have been visible even externally" (*Relation of 1633*, Jamet edition, Vol. 1, p. 313).

[70] *Relation of 1654*, Jamet edition, Vol. 2, p. 286.

[71] *Relation of 1633*, Jamet edition, Vol. 1, p. 299; *Relation of 1654*, same edition, Vol. 2, p. 286.

[72] *Relation of 1633*, Jamet edition, Vol. 1, pp. 301–303; *Relation of 1654*, Jamet edition, Vol. 2, p. 288.

And in particular she has given us two highly effective descriptions, written one after the other, of the movements of her psychology in this order of union with God during the moments of the recitation of the choral Office. These texts are important to our present study. I do not think there exists a psychologically more convincing testimony to the possibility and to the fact of the perfect marriage between normal active participation in the liturgical action and habitual mystical union of the highest order. In her *Relation of 1633*, Marie writes:

> "In regard to my union with God, in the midst of all my crosses, when, at the apex of all my sufferings, I go out of obedience through the house or on the pathway through the garden, I feel my heart crushed by the constant onslaught of living and ardent love; and sometimes it seems that this heart must tear itself loose and, as it were, come forth from its place to be lost in Him who is its life. Even if the inferior part suffers much, the superior part feels more vigorous and capable of acting with the very greatest purity and delicacy, since it is not encumbered by anything whatever to impede it, nor does it transmit anything to the senses, but it keeps everything in itself.
>
> "When I am in the refectory the reading arrests the senses, and this makes it so that I am in constant attention to God. I do not remember ever having lost this attention, be it even for only a moment. . . .
>
> "At recreation, even if I am recreating with sisters, my heart, nevertheless, is none the less attentive. When I am working, the thing most capable of being a distraction that I have had to do until now, I do not feel this internal occupation as such strong and ardent onslaughts as when I go walking through the house, but I feel my heart quietly attentive and aspiring to God, and sometimes I notice that this is more frequent when I am doing my needlework; for, as I said before, I find that this attention is ever present even when I am in the midst of my crosses. These do not in any way work against my attention to the Divine Majesty, but, on the contrary, they excite me the more and urge me on all the more to speak to Him, the greater are the necessities in which I find myself.
>
> "When I assist in choir in the singing of the psalms, while the other side recites a verse, I am in possession of a familiarity with our Lord in respect to the meaning of what is being said, or my thoughts follow wherever He leads me; and when our side recites its part, I pass from interior to exterior act; and thus, one corresponding to the other, I do not lose that intimacy with His Divine Majesty. Nevertheless, I do not at this point feel the familiarity with our Lord, because of my using my voice, as when the other choir is reciting. But my spirit does not fail me thereby. In the one instance I have a freedom to speak interiorly, and in the other it is necessary that the voice be brought into play; and this brings it about most certainly that I feel the less that which is happening interiorly.

"When the meaning of the psalms or of the other things that we sing in choir is unveiled to me, a contentment comes over me which I cannot properly describe, because I feel in every way transported, that is, internally and externally, by a spirit of gaiety, like that which overtook David when he danced before the ark of the covenant. This happens to me especially at Lauds, where all creatures one after another are invited to praise God, and I desire that my spirit be inspired all internally to these divine praises.

"When I am heavily weighed down by my crosses, I do not feel these moments of joy, but only a simple attendance upon God, whom I tell of my sufferings, according to that which we are reciting, which sometimes is very much in accord with what I suffer. The more demanding the needful conformity to His holy will, the greater the strength that is to be drawn from a consideration of His holy promises. In a word, I find therein nourishment for every straitened circumstance.

"Frequently there are mental distractions, especially when I am undergoing a trial, since at such a time all is withdrawn into the depths of my soul, while I speak with God in the way that I have stated, with great simplicity and without any feeling; while my imagination is unable to feed itself on spiritual things, I have to hasten from one part to the other, recalling objects with which to occupy myself. This annoys me very much, even though such activity has not the strength to detach me from the union with God which has come upon me." [73]

Marie of the Incarnation wrote this passage in 1633, at the very time she found herself in the dispositions which she analyzes here. The passage has, therefore, the value of a document of primary importance. In the *Relation of 1654*, written more than twenty years later, she speaks again of the same thing and clarifies, with interesting particulars, some points only touched upon in the former relation:

"I understood in French everything that I sang and recited in Latin in choir. And this so transported my spirit that if I had not done violence to what was external, it should have been apparent to those about me. By singing I was raised up, and it aired my spirit and touched my senses. These participated to a considerable extent, so much so that I had strong inclinations to dance, to clap my hands, and to excite the whole world to the singing of the praises of a God so great, so deserving that all things should be consumed by His love and service, and by being made His spouse; that all the world should *rejoice and dance for contentment in the remembrance of the belly of the bridegroom* (see Cant. 5:14), just as I rejoiced and was made glad by the power of these divine words. With an indescribable exuberance I was moved by inclinations to excite the whole world to sing an *Eructavit* in proclaim-

[73] *Relation of 1633*, Jamet edition, Vol. 1, pp. 336 ff.

ing the grandeur and the prerogatives of my Spouse, whose words were to me spirit and life.

"In singing the psalms I beheld His justice, His judgments, His grandeur, His love, His impartiality, His beauty, His magnificence, His liberality, and finally, that in the eyes of the Church, His spouse, He had *hands as turned on a lathe and full of hyacinths* (Cant. 5:14) and other things apt to the transfusing of their fullness of purity into the souls of those who love Him. I saw that the goodness of this divine Spouse had placed me in an abundant and fertile pasture, that it kept my soul in good condition, providing for it superabundantly, so that I was not able to remain silent. . . .

"My spirit was so full and fruitful in regard to all that was sung in choir that day and night it shaped my conversation with my heavenly Spouse. And it took me outside myself, so much so that when I went about the convent I was in constant rapture. And it was the same when I was at work. Sometimes it was over the purity of the laws of God, and how all things proclaim His glory. The psalm *Coeli enarrant gloriam Dei*, etc., had charms that struck me to the heart and stirred my spirit: 'Yes, yes, my love, your testimonies are true; of themselves they justify, the proud they make wise; send me through all the world to teach them to those who know them not.' I would have desired that all should know and enjoy the delights which my soul was sampling.

"From this point my spirit was carried to another. It was an endless chain. Once, in the midst of such feelings, I spoke in French instead of Latin; it was while I was praising within myself the sacred Person of the Word, through whom all these things were being done. It was a *Laudate*, in the impulses that the psalmody brought about in me." [74]

Liturgy and the prayer of quiet

The foregoing examples show how a good harmony is possible between the liturgical life and the highest degrees of mystical experience. The case of Marie of the Incarnation certainly refers to mystical marriage. The experiences of which Cassian and St. Gertrude speak seem to be closer to what St. Teresa calls "spiritual betrothal" or "intense union" and what St. John of the Cross calls "divine touches." [75]

It might still be possible to entertain a doubt as to whether or not such a harmonization is possible with respect to initiation into the mystical life, which involves what St. Teresa calls the prayer of quiet and the sleep of the faculties.[76]

In these situations one begins to experience what in the mystical life is called "binding" or "suspension" of the faculties, and this seems difficult to

---

[74] *Relation of 1654*, Jamet edition, Vol. 2, pp. 288 ff.

[75] See, for example, in the Spanish critical edition of the works of St. John of the Cross,

the *Subida* 2, 27, 4–6, pp. 653 ff; and the same, 2, 32, pp. 664 ff; *Cant.* 25, 5–8, p. 1035 ff; the same, 26, 2, pp. 1040–1041.

[76] See her *Vita* 14–17.

reconcile with active participation in the liturgy. The advice which spiritual authors give to those who enter upon the mystical life, not to impede themselves with discursive reasonings, with vocal prayers, etc., refers primarily and properly to these initial degrees.

Nevertheless, the example of the mystics shows that even the prayer of quiet and that of the sleep of the faculties, in spite of the "binding" which accompanies them, constitute no exception to the general rule of being able to be left sufficiently free so as to be able to participate actively and in a normally external manner in the liturgical action.

The same St. Teresa notes explicitly that in the prayer of quiet and of the mystical sleep, the suspension of the faculties notwithstanding, it happens frequently that the soul does not entirely lose the power of giving itself over in a normal way to extenal actions, even if somewhat arduous, especially if such actions are in reference to holy things or to the exercise of charity. She alludes directly, moreover, to the recitation of the Psalter while in this state.[77]

In any case, let us see two quite characteristic examples. They are taken from the life of Maria Cecilia Baij, abbess of San Pietro di Montefiascone, a mystic who died in 1766. While firmly engaged in these states of prayer, she once recited Terce with the other nuns, and on another occasion she accompanied the singing of the community on the organ in a normal manner.

> "I went into the choir to say the hour of Terce. Jesus remained close by me. I said Terce with my mouth, but I did not know where I was. I never opened my eyes except once, and then it seemed to me that I was in some other place. In truth, I was entirely outside of myself. I had lost all use of my senses. Jesus told me that I should lean on Him, and I did, resting my head on Him, nor did I draw away. I saw my Spouse, so noble, so beautiful, so gracious, with His mane of hair in ringlets and like threads of gold; and I was caught up in wonderment. I was very much refreshed. He said, I know not to whom: *Innixa super dilectum suum.* Meanwhile I slept in great tranquillity. A troublesome thought occurred to me because of this in regard to my observance and of not satisfying the Divine Office; but I decided that it was all right. . . . While I finished Terce I was asleep. Asleep, not really; but I was enjoying a great tranquillity. . . . But to tell you the truth, Father, I do not know where I may have been or what my condition was. I did not know where I was, *but I was not asleep, because I said Terce with the other nuns, even though my eyes were closed and I was like a bag of straw.*" [78]

Again she writes:

> "In an instant I found myself perfectly united with Jesus. He stayed with me, occupying me completely; and indeed, He was entirely in me and like another me, so much so that I saw Him most clearly in myself:

---

[77] *Vita,* 15, 8. See also 15, 1 and 17, 4.
[78] See P. Bergamaschi, *Vita della serva di*   *Dio Maria Cecilia Baij,* Vol. 2, Viterbo 1925, pp. 282–283.

He rested Himself in me, filling me up completely. . . . I was satiated and full of all that I could desire, taking my repose in a fullness of enjoyment; and this enjoyment brought me no exuberance of merriment, but only the greatest tranquillity. All the faculties of the soul were engaged in this same enjoyment, incapable of receiving any other object. I was incapable then of knowing what human misery and weariness is, while my humanity remained entirely abandoned in the same tranquillity and enjoyment. I was subject neither to pain nor to distraction. I was totally deprived of everything that carries our humanity with it. In short, I did not know how to do anything but take supreme enjoyment in a most perfect tranquillity, incapable of any further desires. I saw only Jesus in me, who filled me up entirely. In this vision, in this tranquillity, I have remained for a long time without being able to speak even a single word to my Spouse, because I was not able to do anything but remain in this state of enjoyment. *I was not deprived of this even during the time that I spent in sleep; only the bodily senses were involved, afterwards returning again to their same tranquillity.*" [79]

In the face of these examples, perhaps someone will say that these are exceptional cases and, as it were, miraculous. Actually, the contrary is true. It must in fact be said that such is the normal case, at least when it is a question of participation in the liturgical life.

The inquiry made on this point by Father Poulain leads, at any rate, to such a conclusion. In chapter fifteen of his classic work *Des grâces d'oraison*, he treats of the phenomenon of the "binding" and of the "suspension" of the faculties in the mystical life. He defines such a phenomenon as an impediment to the voluntary production of acts "additional" to the mystical union, that is, acts which are not the union itself nor its cause nor its consequence — in particular, discursive intellection, imaginations, external actions. This binding is evident in ecstasy and, analogously, to a greater or lesser degree even in the prayer of quiet, which is like a minor partial ecstasy.

But Poulain notes that the experience of the mystics obliges us to distinguish three types of this "tranquillity of quiet." He calls them: a) *praying quiet*, when the mystic engaged in it is at the same time impelled to pray even in formulas; b) *jubilant quiet*, when he feels the need of expanding himself in ardent colloquies or even in singing; c) *working quiet*, when the mystic is able at the same time to perform external works

From this we see once again that the mystical grace of quiet or tranquillity, in what is essential to it, is not entirely opposed to participation, even active participation, in the sacred rites. The same author observes that in tranquillity there can be a facility in reciting prayers aloud. "Generally the priests do not experience serious difficulties in reciting the prayers of the Mass." [80]

---

[79] *Ibid.*, pp. 280–281.
[80] A. Poulain, *Des grâces d'oraison*, chapter 14, no. 18.

The same is evidenced for the recitation or the singing of the Office in choir. "Desiring to gain an understanding of the facts, and rather than abandoning myself to *a priori* notions, I made enquiries into this matter in several contemplative convents. The most usual response was that there is a slight hindrance, but easy to overcome. At the very least, they add, it is possible to arrive at a material recitation of the words, with the main attention remaining fixed on the internal divine action. Only most exceptionally have others declared that the hindrance can be most strong, while others, quite the opposite, say they have never experienced this difficulty." [81]

The reason why mystical experience and active participation in the liturgy go together so very well

The fact remains, therefore, that normal, externally active participation in the liturgical action can accord very well with the mystical experience in all its gradations. But what is the reason for this? The key to the answer to this problem is the distinction between the essence of the mystical activity and the accidental phenomena which, in certain circumstances and with certain persons, may sometimes accompany it.

The so called "suspension" of the faculties, and especially of the senses, both internal and external, in the measure in which it results in the inhibiting of the normal external involvement demanded by active participation in the liturgy is not, when it comes about, the essence of the mystical activity in any of the gradations thereof, but merely an accidental epiphenomenon which sometimes accompanies it in certain subjects because of their particular condition.

The fact that a particular subject does or does not experience this epiphenomenon depends, for the most part, more upon the education of his religious sensibility than upon his innate temperament.[82] Normally it happens that when this sensibility has been shaped to the liturgical and communitarian sense, active and normal participation in the liturgical action is either not disturbed at all or else very little by the mystical intrusion.

It is to be noted that the exterior paralyzing phenomena of ecstasy are simply accidental epiphenomena and not necessary to the mystical grace that the subject receives on these occasions; that these physical aspects lessen and afterwards even gradually disappear completely in those who are habituated to them.

[81] *Ibid.* chapter 14, nos. 19–20.
[82] The cases of some saints, such as St. Joseph of Cupertino, St. Philip Neri, and St. Ignatius of Loyola, are explained in this way. See Poulain, *op. cit.*, chapter 14, no. 16. The historians of spirituality have not, on the other hand, failed to notice the almost total lack of the inhibitory phenomena in regard to the normal external use of the senses by the mystics of Helfta, Mechtild and Gertrude, whose religious sensibility was quite notably shaped according to the style of active participation in the liturgical action. See, for example, the article "Contemplation" in the *Dictionnaire de spiritualité*, Vol. 2 (1953), p. 1989.

It is to be noted also that in the higher orders of the mystical union, and especially in spiritual marriage, the union, even habitual, with God does not entirely prevent one's giving himself at the same time to external affairs, even profane and quite absorbing. The affirmations of St. Teresa on this point are well known.[83]

The descriptions which Marie of the Incarnation offers of this same state in her own regard are still more relevant for their psychological refinement and by the fact that they refer as much to the permanent union of spiritual marriage [84] as to a prior state.[85]

Besides, we saw above the very explicit affirmation of St. Teresa about the possibility of giving oneself normally to external affairs in spite of the suspension of the faculties in the prayer of quiet and in the mystical sleep. If such a possibility exists in regard to external and even profane affairs, how much more easily, then, can we affirm that it is possible when it is a question of active participation in the liturgical action! [86]

[83] *Interior Castle*, 7, 4.

[84] *Letters on Conscience Matters*, A. Jamet edition, Vol. 1, p. 360.

[85] She describes her own state while she was in the midst of the uproar of porters, of wagoners, and of the tasks of superintending a river transportation firm. In the midst of all this "I experienced a realization that our Lord desired that I should be so engaged, and He soothed my sorrow with the remembrance of His words: 'My yoke is sweet and My burden is light' (Matthew 13:11). Afterwards He infused into my soul the reality and the efficacy of these divine words, so that He calmed my sorrow and sent His ways running through my soul, amid the more coarse and material things in which I was physically involved, while my spirit was bound to the superadorable incarnate Word. If the clock strikes, the soul is forced to calculate the hour; and this interval necessarily interrupts the soul's loving colloquy with its Beloved. If it is necessary to speak to someone nearby, the glance of the soul does not go out to Him whom it loves; after the neighbor responds, the soul's colloquy begins again, and attention to whatever is necessary does not keep it from its own. The same happens in writing, in which the attention is twofold: to its divine object and to the matter at hand. When it is necessary to dip the pen into the ink, this time is precious, because the spirit and the heart engage in their colloquy. Even if others are present, it can in no way prove a distraction" (*Relation of 1654*, Jamet edition, Vol. 2, pp. 230 ff).

[86] It may be well to note with H. Brémond (*Histoire littéraire du sentiment religieux en France*, Vol. 6, pp. 146 ff), directly in reference to Marie of the Incarnation, that the attentive reading of the mystics shows how false is the opinion that would have it that behind the expression "suspension" of the intellect and of the will there is no more than a kind of vacuum, a kind of sleep or insensibility through a lack of life. Properly, it is the contrary that is true: it is a question of a life so hidden and superior, but ever so real and intense, of those same faculties that it is beyond discursive intellection and specific acts of the will in reference to individual and precise objects.

The same must be said of the expression "passivity" of the superior faculties, which in mystical contemplation are most highly active, but with an activity which does not involve the agitation and the forceful effort of their ordinary manner of action, because in mystical contemplation they receive their actions, even if it is a question of a reception that is immensely active.

When the intellect and the will are thus "suspended," it is not entirely necessary that they be thereby incapable of rendering their service to the senses through the exteriorly normal disengagement with external actions. On the contrary, "the senses are free to such an extent that the soul, having arrived at this state, is able to act without distraction in the affairs in which its condition involves it" (*ibid.*, p. 166). Then one's external occupation, even if it is profane, rather than impeding the soul in that union which binds it in its very depths to God, "relieves it, because when the senses

Contemplation in the liturgy and contemplation outside the liturgy

In regard to the liturgy and contemplation, Jacques Maritain, in a disputatious attitude toward the liturgical movement and with the intention of defending the extraliturgical contemplative ideal regarded by him as being threatened, supported the following thesis: contemplation is an end superior to worship and therefore to the liturgy; and the liturgy is itself ordered to contemplation.[87]

It is necessary to reply that the thesis formulated in this way is simply ambiguous. It is false if, with such an affirmation, one means to say that contemplation, in a purely private act and outside the liturgy, is superior to liturgical worship, and that it is therefore the end of this liturgical worship to lead one to such private contemplation. It is true, on the other hand, in the sense that the liturgical worship is ordered to contemplation in the liturgy itself as to the interior perfection of active participation, normally interior and exterior, in the liturgical action.

In other words, when the interior union, which must be realized in every

are occupied and engaged, the soul is but that much more free" (*ibid.*, p. 167). Or, as the same author observes, "during this union, the center of the soul has no longer the trouble of dominating, of taking hold of the surface faculties of sensible intelligence, these being occupied with other objects." How much more, then, we may add once again, will the soul, while the senses are externally occupied, remain free to give itself to its higher union with God, if the objects with which the senses are occupied are those of the liturgy!

[87] Jacques and Raissa Maritain, *Liturgy and Contemplation*, trans. by Joseph W. Evans, New York 1960. See especially pp. 19–23. What follows summarizes what I wrote in *Rivista ascetica e mistica*, Vol. 7 (1962), pp. 8–34, in the article "*Contemplazione nella liturgia e contemplazione fuori della liturgia.*"

[*Translator's note*: The "thesis" given above, as one which the Maritains defend, suffers both from being an oversimplification of the Maritains' thought, as well as from being wrested from its context. Presumably it is Dom Vagaggini's summation of what the Maritains say on pp. 19–21 of the work cited. The passage actually reads:

"The liturgical cycle manifests in sacred signs the states of Christ and the participation of the Mystical Body in the mysteries of His humiliation, of His redemption and triumph. . . . It is clear, however, that the states of Christ such as they were lived in the intimacy of His soul are something greater than the signs . . . which manifest them. Likewise, as concerns the Church or the Mystical Body,

something is greater—not certainly than the Holy Sacrifice . . .—but greater than the very sublimity of the lessons, of the prayers and the singing, of the sacred rites and symbols . . . which manifest the participation of the Church in the states of the Lord; this something greater is this participation itself . . . , it is the suffering and the love through which the Church applies all along the course of time the merits and the blood of Christ; and it is the contemplation of the Church, that contemplation which enables it to experience in some way the mysteries of God the Savior, and which takes place . . . in human persons joined together as one in its communion. This contemplation of the Church . . . is clearly superior to the great liturgical voice which manifests it; . . . the liturgical service never succeeds in manifesting this contemplation of the Mystical Body in an entirely adequate manner, for in itself it is ineffable. It is to it that the liturgy wishes to lead souls, and it is from it that the liturgy superabounds."

On page 61 of the same work, the Maritains make it clear that the object of their polemic is in fact those "who, presenting themselves as the barristers of the Sacred Liturgy itself, reprove, in the name of the public prayer of the Church, mental prayer, solitude with God, and silent contemplation." Certainly Dom Vagaggini can in no way be reckoned among these latter. But neither can anyone pretend that such as these latter do not exist; and it is they who must answer for having for so many years given a bad name to the whole of the liturgical movement.]

true and active participation in the liturgy, arrives at its perfection, it becomes at the same time contemplation or contemplative participation. The liturgy is certainly ordered to such contemplation as to its proper interior perfection, not in that it would then cease to be liturgy, but inasmuch as it becomes contemplative liturgy. Contrariwise, the contemplation done outside the liturgy in a purely private act is ordered to liturgical worship and, under another aspect, must be derived from it.

To understand this, without entering into such particulars as are discussed by theologians themselves, let us take as our point of departure a hypothesis most prejudicial to the liturgy. Let us suppose, then, that while contemplation is an infused act of charity, worship, according to the opinion of Thomists and of St. Thomas himself, is formally an act of the virtue of religion, itself a moral virtue, a potential part of justice.

Even in this hypothesis the exercise of the virtue of religion cannot be realized except by offering in homage to God, as Creator and Supreme Providence, the act of such another virtue as serves it in the role of the matter by which it may be actualized.[88]

It is true that actual worship can exist, even if most imperfectly, even in the absence of charity, for example as in the case of one who assists at Mass in a state of mortal sin and who offers to God his dead faith and hope. He would not offer anything to God if he did not believe in Him and if he did not hope that God accepts our acts of homage.[89] But it is also true that charity is the most noble matter that the act of religion can offer to God and in which it can itself be actualized. And it is true that charity is always included in the concrete act of worship of one who is in the state of grace, and the more perfect this act of worship is, the more necessary it is that the charity offered in it be perfect.

In regard to the chanting of the psalms, St. Augustine has stated: "Whoever sings in praise not only sings but also loves him in whose praise he sings. In praise there is the speaking out of one who is confessing; in singing, there is the affection of one who loves."[90] This holds good for every liturgical action performed by one who is in the state of grace.

[88] See St. Thomas, *Summa* II-II, q. 82, a. 2, ad 2; and *In Boetii de Trin. lect.* I, q. 1, a. 2.

[89] See St. Thomas, *In Boetii de Trin. lect.* I, q. 1, a. 2.

[90] *Enarr. in Ps.* 72, 1. Answer can also be made here to the sophism that is frequently proposed in this matter. The usual sophism runs: contemplation is formally an act of charity, the queen of all the virtues. Liturgy is formally an act of religion, a moral virtue. Therefore contemplation (and what is meant is contemplation outside the liturgy) is superior to the liturgy.

The answer is that the liturgical action in its concrete state is never exhausted in the exercise of the solitary and bare virtue of religion, since the virtue of religion cannot be actualized without having as it were for its matter, the act of some other virtue. Whenever the liturgical action is done in the state of grace, concretely it always includes charity; and if it is a question of a perfect participation in the liturgy, it necessarily includes perfect charity. Such a liturgical action, then, *in its concrete state*, is not inferior to non-liturgical contemplation, but superior to it. In fact, it includes charity, and something more; that is to say, the cultic offering

The fact, then, that in worship the virtue of religion offers charity to God, does not deprive the latter entirely of its own nature; it does not reclassify charity, demoting it to the rank of the moral virtues. In this perspective of the analysis of the ontological aspects of things, the offering is certainly formally an act of religion and not of charity, but the thing offered is an act of charity and not of a moral virtue.

If, therefore, it is supposed that contemplation is an infused act of charity, it must be said that it is not possible to give full and perfect participation in the liturgy unless it is at the same time contemplative participation. Here, then, is the sense in which the liturgy is ordered to the mystical life: as to an essential aspect of itself.

Let us recall now the doctrine of the superiority of liturgical prayer over prayer that is purely private, in virtue, at least, of the former's being the *opus operantis Ecclesiae*, and we will understand why the contemplation in a purely private act is inferior in dignity and ordered to that contemplation which is the interior aspect of the active participation in the liturgy.

Let us recall also the three principles that the Second Vatican Council posits as the foundation of the relations between the liturgical and the non-liturgical in the life of the Church:

1) "Every liturgical celebration, because it is an action of Christ the Priest and of his Body, which is the Church, is a sacred action surpassing all others. No other action of the Church can equal its efficacy by the same title and to the same degree." [91]

2) "The sacred liturgy does not exhaust the entire activity of the Church. . . . Nevertheless the liturgy is the summit toward which the activity of the Church is directed; it is also the fount from which all her power flows." [92]

3) "Popular devotions of the Christian people . . . are to be highly recommended. . . . But such devotions should be so drawn up that they harmonize with the liturgical seasons, accord with the sacred liturgy, are in some way derived from it, and lead the people to it, since in fact the liturgy by its very nature is far superior to any of them." [93]

Private contemplation outside the liturgy constitutes no exception to these rules.

of that very special worship, superior to every private cult, which is the liturgy.

Even if, therefore, abstractly speaking, in the order of importance (formally speaking, is what the scholastics would say), charity is superior to worship, concretely speaking (*per accidens* the scholastics would say, which means that something is in fact verified, though its being true is not the unavoidable consequence of its very nature), when the liturgy is enacted with charity, it is not inferior but superior to contemplation outside the liturgy. It is incredible what jokes are played by that pseudo-metaphysical mentality which, by dint of its abstractionism, loses the sense of the concrete and of the totally real.

[91] CL, art. 7.
[92] CL, art. 9–10.
[93] CL, art. 13.

Conclusion on liturgy and the mystical life

In conclusion, it is not a paradox to affirm that the liturgy and the mystical life can easily go together hand in hand, even while both prosper vigorously. At the end of the preceding article a conclusion was properly drawn that there can and must be an excellent marriage between liturgy, liturgical spirituality, and ascetical effort, striving toward perfection. But just as at the end of that article specific dangers were frankly recognized, which, in the liturgy and in liturgical spirituality just as in any other kind of spirituality, can be a threat to serious ascetical activity in the striving toward perfection, so too it must be recognized that liturgical spirituality carries with it some dangers; and again just as in any kind of spirituality in the area of the mystical life, these are dangers against which one who is devoted to the liturgy must always be solicitously alert.

St. John of the Cross certainly is not complete in his way of considering the role of the liturgy in the mystical life. In any case, for one who is devoted to the liturgy and to liturgical spirituality, the strong warning issued in his writings, that it is necessary that the spiritual man, anxious to dispose himself for the graces of mystical union with God, not dally with the externals of the rites nor with sensible inclinations to the external trappings of worship, but, with the serious preparation of an already mortified life, that he make use of them as a means to grasp promptly the interior quality to which they must lead and which they, by their very presence and continued activity in the liturgical action, must nourish and sustain — for one who is devoted to the liturgy and to the liturgical action, his strong warning about this is, I say, all but useless.

Apart from the proper gradations in which it is realized in liturgical spirituality, bareness of spirit remains in it an axiom, as in any kind of spirituality, for disposing oneself or for being disposed to mystical union. That is to say, in regard to the use of external things and one's involvement with them, even in a question of worship, in liturgical spirituality just as in any other spirituality, the mystic must achieve a certain paradoxical state: he must be very much present and involved while remaining very much absent and free. Present not only to the spirit or content of the rites, which is God, Christ, the Church, the mystical body of the brethren, acts of faith, hope and charity; but present physically, and with the normal external use of his senses, to the external community and to the external communitarian action in which he actively participates.

And yet he is absent, because although he makes use of and is immersed in these externals, at the same time that he makes use of them and is immersed in them, he transcends them. To see that the paradox is only apparent and that its achievement is possible — or better, that God can set us down in the midst of such an achievement — consider the case of Marie of the Incarnation and what was said of her above.

St. John of the Cross, therefore, reminds him who is devoted to the liturgy and who desires to dispose himself for mystical union and for transcendence, of the external character of worship. And he does so not without reason, because the devotee of the liturgy can find himself threatened from that quarter. Nor is it without reason that the same St. John of the Cross and St. Teresa, proposing a kind of spirituality which gives no special prominence to the liturgy but lays the greatest stress upon the interiorization of the individual, never tire of warning their disciples against a possible yearning for experientialism or spiritual appetites and against the possible desire for visions and the like. Why such insistence? Because they know instinctively that these are the risks run by an inexperienced disciple regarding strong interiorization by an individual when that interiorization is not especially concentrated on the liturgy.[94]

Conclusion of the chapter: liturgical spirituality and present-day aspirations

Thus it seems to us that the liturgy is capable of being the center of a complete spiritual doctrine, and hence the pivotal point of a style of Christian life well adapted to the purpose of leading one to the highest state of perfection. It is liturgical spirituality, the official spirituality, which the Church as such proposes to all her children. The practical counsels, given concretely in individual cases for the purpose of leading souls on this way, look to the application and, as it were, to the art of liturgical spirituality. It is possible for some of them to constitute a species of theoretical-practical directory that will include the foundation common to all spiritual direction in every kind of Catholic spirituality, but viewed always in relation to the centering of one's whole life on the liturgy.

It is certain also that in its totality liturgical spirituality is clearly distinguished from other spiritualities. And it is no less certain that today many are discovering liturgical spirituality anew and find it in conformity with their deepest aspirations: aspirations to an essential quality, which is at the same time a reflection of individual values in their unitarian and hierarchically relative objectivity and a certain going direct to the heart of things; an aspiration to the communitarian quality and to the framing of the indi-

---

[94] I cannot believe that this particular insistence of St. Teresa and of St. John of the Cross against the possible hankering after experientialism, after visions, etc., is entirely explained by the necessity of guarding oneself against the atmosphere of false mysticism then pervading Spain through the influence of the *alumbrados*. St. Ignatius of Loyola lived in the same era and in the same area, but he did not in quite the same way feel the necessity of forearming his disciples against the seeking out of mystical experiences or against the desire for visions and such like. In fact, the danger of false mysticism in spirituality does not seem really to have been a threat to the disciple of Ignatius.

vidual in the organic structure of the whole, on which he depends and which he in turn enlivens; an aspiration to immediate contact with the prime sources of Christian life, in particular with the ecclesial life in action and with the world of the Bible with the flavor and the gradations of its own that are had in the Bible itself; an aspiration to the unity of spiritual, biblical, theological, and apostolic life, a unity which, as will be even more apparent in the chapters about liturgy and pastoral, finds its connatural bond precisely in the liturgy.[95]

At the Congress of Lugano in 1953, a German author, treating precisely of the various types of spirituality through the ages and desiring to characterize our own time, gave his report the forthright title: "The Liturgical Era in the Life of the Church."[96] It is true, of course, that this is a matter of a convinced liturgist. But on the other hand, the author said no more than has since been affirmed by the Second Vatican Council:

> "Zeal for the promotion and restoration of the sacred liturgy is rightly held to be a sign of the providential dispositions of God in our time, and as a movement of the Holy Spirit in his Church. It is today a distinguishing mark of the life of the Church, and, indeed, of the whole tenor of contemporary religious thought and action."[97]

[95] See also Cardinal Lercaro, *Attualità della liturgia, Atti della prima settimana liturgica nazionale*, Parma 1949, pp. 81–89.

[96] E. Fischer, "*L'era liturgica della vita della chiesa*," in *Partecipazione attiva alla liturgia,* *Atti del III congresso* . . . , Lugano 1953, pp. 55–71.

[97] CL, art. 43. These are almost verbatim the words of Pius XII in his *Discourse* of September 22, 1956.

22 THE EXAMPLE OF A MYSTIC:

ST. GERTRUDE AND LITURGICAL SPIRITUALITY

When it is a question of spirituality, examples have their particular importance in view of integrating theory. When it is a question of liturgical spirituality in particular, it seems that among the writings of spiritual authors, the most complete example that permits a concrete examination in one single person of a lively realization of liturgical spirituality, at least under its most important aspects, is still that of St. Gertrude, called the Great, the mystic of Helfta, born in 1256 and died in 1302 or 1303.[1]

Naturally we are treating of an outstanding example, in which, as in all

[1] Whether she was a Cistercian or simply a Benedictine is a point of discussion. But even if the monastery of Helfta, near Eisleben, Germany, was not juridically joined to the Cistercian Order, it is nonetheless certain that the spirit and the influence of St. Bernard were felt most strongly in the spiritual tone of that house. In the same convent, besides St. Gertrude, there flourished at the same time three other noteworthy mystics: Gertrude of Hackeborn, abbess; her sister, St. Matilda or Mechtild of Hackeborn; and Gertrude of Magdeburg.

The two works of St. Gertrude the Great that are preserved for us are the *Legatus divinae pietatis*, or *Revelations*, of which she wrote in her own hand Book 2, while she dictated to a confidante Books 3, 4, and 5; and this confidante in turn joined to them, after the death of Gertrude, Book 1, which, in relation to the rest of the work, has the function of an introduction. Her other work still extant is the *Exercitia spiritualia*. The critical edition of the monks of Solesmes is: *Revelationes gertrudianae et mechtildianae I. Sanctae Gertrudis Magne . . . Legatus divinae pietatis. Accedunt eiusdem: Exercitia spiritualia*, Poitiers-Paris 1875. Our citations refer to this critical edition.

such ardent examples in the matter of spirituality, especially when it is desired to take them as a practical guide, it is necessary to have sense enough to read with prudence and discretion. What I mean to say is that even in St. Gertrude, studied from the viewpoint of liturgical spirituality, it is necessary to know how to distinguish therein what is characteristic of every liturgical spirituality and what pertains especially to the person who embodies that spirituality, what is due to her sex, to her personal temperament, to the special frame of life that was hers, to the era in which she lived and which, in her own way, she reflected, not forgetting either the particular grace and proper mission that God gave her. It is not that this second series of facts is without importance in the question that concerns us. It is a matter of things that do not enter *per se* into liturgical spirituality and which, therefore, need not necessarily be desired and much less so imitated by anyone among us who wishes to attune his spiritual life to the liturgy.

Nevertheless, the factual presence of these things in St. Gertrude helps us to understand better how an authentically liturgical spirituality, without necessarily requiring them, is not entirely opposed to them — indeed, how a liturgical spirituality is capable of admitting and assimilating secondary realities.

It is necessary also to keep in mind from the start that while we are using St. Gertrude as an example of liturgical spirituality, she is certainly not such a totally perfect or complete example as we should like to have today. Varied and complete as is the experience of the totality of Gertrude's own life, there are still lacking in her liturgical spirituality two things in particular which for us today are rightly regarded as being of great importance: its experiential application in a pattern of life which the Catholic who lives in the world today knows; and the great pastoral experience in the bosom of a parish, or of great movements and clusters, for example, as in Catholic action, such as we today are accustomed to know. But this simply means that no example from the past, much less an example from the Middle Ages, however instructive it may be, will be able to dispense our contemporaries from realizing themselves, by their own inquiry and at their own risks, not only a liturgical spirituality in general, but that liturgical spirituality which is acclimatized to our special needs as men of the twentieth century.

1. Premises

Liturgy and spirituality in the works of St. Gertrude in general

As an example of liturgical spirituality, Gertrude makes known first of all the general fact, which from the very first strikes even the superficial reader of her writings, that the liturgical vision of the world really constitutes in her the primary and unifying form of her way of living in depth the life of the spirit. The liturgy, as the liturgical action of Mass and Communion,

of the canonical hours, of the feasts, of the liturgical times, constitutes the
psychological frame, not only external but internal as well, of attention, of
desire, of love, in the coordination of which her life unfolds as a search for
God, as a fruitful union with Him, and as a return to men in order to lead
them to God. In this life everything is either action lived in the reality of
the Mass and of Communion, of the canonical hours, of the feasts and liturgical times; or preparation for life to be lived in the action of these realities
in the liturgy; or the extension and consequence of the same.

The *Legatus divini amoris* treats only of that which happens to Gertrude
in the Mass, at Communion, at Matins, at the canonical hours, and on feasts;
or of that which happens in preparing for these events; or again, of that
which happens in consequence of them or at least in connection with them.
With the exception of the seventeen chapters of the first book, which is of
a general biographical character and was written by her confidante, among
the one hundred and ninety-nine chapters of the remaining four books of
the *Legatus* there are very few in which there is no reference either to the
Mass or to Communion or to the canonical hours or to the feasts or to some
such liturgical action; and not much more numerous are those which speak
of something which happens other than during these liturgical actions or in
preparation for them or in consequence of them.

In the other work of Gertrude, the *Exercises*, the essential objects of concern are Christian initiation, comprising baptism, confirmation, and Communion; the anniversary of the taking of the religious habit; the anniversary of virginal consecration; the anniversary of monastic profession; its
renewal — and all this in strict reference to the liturgical actions. Afterwards
there is an exercise rather in the form of the canonical hours for preparing
oneself for death, and two others for exciting oneself to divine love and for
giving thanks to God.

Moreover, the *Legatus* and the *Exercises* are, even in their composition
and literary expression, entirely imbued with the liturgy by reason of their
being strewn throughout with passages liturgical in their reminiscences.
This is so much the case that especially in some parts of the *Exercises*, the
work takes on the appearance of a cento made up from the liturgy and from
Scripture, and the latter itself often enough coming to it by way of the
liturgy.

Meaning and value that Gertrude gave to her imaginal visions

We cannot, however, remain silent about two problems which make quite
difficult the interpretation and correct assessment of the real value of the
Gertrudian writings, so much so that even from first contact with them, they
can alienate the reader or at least hide from him the real treasures which
they contain. The first difficulty is that the *Legatus* speaks constantly of visions and of the reception of divine discourses. The whole work seems to do

nothing else but endlessly relate visions seen and words supposedly heard in these visions. Moreover, some of these visions are related in a way that seems foreign to us, in an imaginal complexity of description that is difficult or even irritating — like that in which the members of Christ flourish in so many branches which grow and expand; or that of the Heart of Jesus like a palace with so many rooms; or that of His body clothed on the right half in splendid garments, while the left half is naked and covered with ulcers.

All this tends to turn away many readers who at first contact have the impression that they are in an atmosphere of naïve visionaryism, which, when pondered upon, even if it relates things which really happened, leaves the disagreeable impression that it seems actually to make sanctity and the ideal of life that it proposes consist in these experiences.

The second difficulty is that these visions and discoursings, as well as the sentiments which accompany their telling, are clothed in large measure in images derived from the amorous relationships of betrothals and marriages between man and woman or, at any rate, in expressions and imageries indicative of such a feminine sensitivity that the modern reader, not being able to put psychoanalysis completely out of his mind, is easily tempted to level a charge of sensuality or eroticism more or less hidden and sublimated.[2]

Both of these difficulties are facts to be reckoned with, and in the modern reader they easily produce a disagreeable impression that can hinder him from arriving at the true marrow of the Gertrudian writings.

But just as it is true that the first impression is not purely subjective, it is equally true that to stop there and form a definitive judgment of the Gertrudian writings would be to commit an egregious error. Certainly the reader who makes a careful examination for himself and who has experienced charity will not fall into this trap, for he will know well enough what it is in which Christian perfection consists, and the truth of the Pauline maxim: *omnia munda mundis*. He will resolve the problem *ab intrinseco* without difficulty.

Indeed, no reader of ordinary intelligence ought to fall into such a gross error if he but take the trouble to inform himself first of all what was, for Gertrude herself and for the confidante to whom she told or recounted her experiences, the real value that they attached to these visions.

In the Gertrudian writings there is a series of informal observations on this very question of the import and value of the visions. First of all, let us take note of what Gertrude says when addressing herself to the Lord, even if only in a chance saying, about a mystical grace of union and of a vision of such special grandeur that she was afterwards amazed that she could continue to live: "I am not unaware that Your unfathomable omnipotence,

[2] See for example 3, 18, pp. 151–157; 3, 21,   3, 42; 3, 45; 3, 50; 3, 63, p. 236; 3, 71, p. 253.
pp. 165–166; 3, 29, p. 175; 3, 38, p. 201;

through the abundance of Your mercy, is accustomed to temper the vision, the *amplexus*, and the *osculum*, as well as the other signs of love, in strict accord with the place, the time, and the person."[3] It is a precious observation of broad application which enables us to understand how in Gertrude's reflection the law of divine condescension has not been ignored, the law which adapts the way of communicating these same mystical graces to place, to time, and to person.

Still more precisely, in regard to the mystical graces which were bestowed upon Gertrude, she herself and her confidante as well repeatedly make a clear distinction between that which, in these graces, is most sublime and inexpressible, and the imaginal aspect applied in their description. The imaginal aspect is, as it were, the inferior part of those graces; and though it cannot be doubted that even this aspect, in Gertrude, came truly from God who shaped such images in her,[4] nevertheless she and her confidante consider that these had solely a symbolic value for the didactic purpose of instructing others, so that by means of images and symbols the reader might be drawn gradually to the most intimate experience of union with God.

One day, on the feast of the Annunciation, while the community, beset at that time by various difficulties, recited the psalm *Miserere* in honor of our Lady, Gertrude saw the Madonna herself holding in her bosom a certain number of chests of perfumes, and she then adorned them with precious gems which the Lord handed to her. Gertrude was instructed by our Lord that these chests of perfumes signified the difficulties which the community had endured with patience, and the precious stones signified the prayers which the same community had offered to the Madonna.

> "When Gertrude asked the reason why the Lord should provide her then with such a material vision and should so frequently do the like, the Lord propounded to her that responsory which is sung on that same feast, about the closed gate which the prophet Ezechiel saw in the spirit, and said to her: 'As once the manner and the ordering of My incarnation was shown to the prophets by means of mystical symbols, images, and in figures, so even now spiritual and invisible things cannot be expressed to the capacity of the human intellect except by means of figures and comparisons to things known. No one, therefore, ought to disparage that which is shown through images of corporeal things, but everyone should strive, by means of images of material things, to deserve to taste the sweet understanding of spiritual joys.'"[5]

---

[3] See 2, 21, pp. 101–102; and also 3, 48.

[4] Gertrude's confidante, speaking of this imaginal aspect, cites (4, 25, p. 382) a text of St. Bernard (*In Cant.* 42) which, distinguishing in the act of mystical contemplation between the contemplation properly so called and the imageries which accompany it, says that the former comes from God, while he deems

that the latter are formed in us by the ministry of the angels. In any case, it is clear that Gertrude's confidante was persuaded that in Gertrude's case those images were not at all the product of her own making, but that they came to her by divine inspiration (1, 1, p. 10).

[5] 4, 12, p. 334.

Besides the simple reason of giving praise to God, it was for this precise purpose of leading others, by means of these imaginal descriptions, as by means of painted portraits, to taste one day of those higher intimacies of divine union that Gertrude, in obedience to the express command of God and against her own natural inclination,[6] consented to write and to dictate.

> "You Yourself are witness that I truly desire that You be praised and given thanks for the fact that Your superabundant mercy has not fled away from my unworthiness. And I desire also that You be praised in this: that some who read this writing may take delight in the sweetness of Your mercy, and then, attracted in this way, they may have even greater experiences of Your intimacy. Students learn the alphabet first, but finally arrive even at the study of logic; and in this same sort of progress, may they, through the portrayal of these images, be led to taste in themselves that hidden manna which cannot be accurately expressed through any combination of corporeal images and which becomes the sole desire of him who has once tasted it." [7]

The same ideas are repeated with insistence by Gertrude's confidante.[8]

Hence, for Gertrude, the explanation of the meaning of the individual visions is important. As far as she is concerned, it is in this explanation that they have their whole substance and all their usefulness. She never fails to explain them, at least briefly.

But did Gertrude believe that these explanations were inspired by God? Her sister in religion who wrote the first book of the *Legatus* was convinced of it; she did not admit the possibility of seeing therein no more than the work of Gertrude herself.[9] But the saint herself seems to have been more cautious. In the fourth book, in two separate instances she explicitly poses the question of whether or not the explanations which she proposes of her imaginal visions might not be regarded afterall as a fruit of her own industry. And the response, which she relates as if it came from Christ Himself, is, in both instances, most circumspect.

Once on the vigil of the Nativity, during the singing of Vespers and at the doxology of the hymn, *Gloria tibi, Domine*, Gertrude saw a multitude of angels who flew about through the whole chapel, in and out among the sisters, and sang with them. Then she asked the Lord the meaning of this sight.

> "But my question received no response from the Lord. Nevertheless, it was a cause of great concern to me, and I pressed my query. Finally, through divine inspiration, I understood that when the angels are present at our liturgical offices here below, they beseech the Lord to deign to make like unto them in the purity of their hearts and bodies those who attempt to imitate them in their devotion."

[6] See 2, 5, pp. 70 ff.
[7] 2, 24, p. 113.
[8] For example, *Prologue*, p. 4; I, I, p. 10;

4, 25, pp. 381–382; 4, 48, p. 435; 5, 36, p. 613; *et alibi*.
[9] I, I, p. 10.

Thus Gertrude had finally found the meaning of the vision, but, she well knew, not without having sought for it herself with a certain anxiety. And for that reason she had a doubt:

> "Hence I began to fear, as is natural, that I had found this meaning not through divine inspiration, but through my own intellection. And in this regard a consoling response was given me by God: 'Do not fear. Your will is fully united to Mine, and it cannot want anything except what I want, for which reason it desires My praise in everything. Thus all the angelic spirits are subservient in such a degree to your pious will, that even if they had not prayed for you, as you have mentally understood that they did, by the very fact that you desire that they do it, without doubt they should have taken care immediately to do it with great zeal. Indeed, because you have been made Empress by Me, the Emperor, all My heavenly leaders are so much disposed to obey you that if you were to tell them to do something which they had not yet done, immediately, in order that your words might be fulfilled, with great promptness they would undertake to comply zealously with your good pleasure.' " [10]

But still we must admit that all this notwithstanding, the aforesaid explanations which Gertrude, supposedly by divine inspiration, gave to the visions might in reality have been the fruit of her own human endeavor and not a special divine inspiration properly so called. But Gertrude was not really afraid of this conclusion, or at any rate the Lord admonished her not to be afraid of it. For on another occasion when she was tormented by that same doubt as to the divine origin of her explanations, Christ answered her:

> "Why, then, would it have to lessen the value of My gift if in fact I have given it in a more subtle way, by means of your natural abilities which were created by Me in order to serve Me? What I said in a deliberative way in creating man, 'Let us make man in Our image and likeness' (Gen. 1:26), is more wonderful and more pleasant than what I said in creating the other things, 'Let light be made, let the firmament be made' " (Gen. 1).

Gertrude did not feel fully satisfied, since she noted: "Anyone, by using his own perception, would be able to propose various explanations discovered by himself, and defend them, too, by the authority of the Scriptures, even without having arrived at a knowledge of them through the influence of Your grace." But, provided that certain specific prior conditions be verified, the Lord found nothing troublesome in this event:

> "The Lord answered: 'But add this also, that if anyone, having considered all things, is aware that his will is so much united to Mine that in nothing, not even in the slightest matter, be it pleasant or disagree-

[10] 4, 2, p. 297.

able, can he desire what is not in harmony with My good pleasure; and moreover, if in all that he does or suffers, he desires only My praise and glory, so that in everything he renounces what is useful to himself and his own advantage, such a one can affirm with certitude whatever good he has found by the exercise of his own faculties accompanied by an internal savor, so long as it do not lack the supporting witness of the Sacred Scriptures and it be able to be of advantage to his neighbor . . .' " [11] [such a good is My gift].

As you see, the precautions are many. However, these conditions being verified, the question of knowing whether the proposed explanations have been truly inspired by a special grace or whether they are the fruit of the natural endeavor of the one who proposes them simply loses all its importance. It is incumbent upon us to point out that Gertrude knew this very well and that she was, therefore, far from attributing any decisive importance to the origin, whether properly supernatural or only natural, of the lessons which she drew from her visions.

And it is certain that she held most firmly to these teachings in imparting them to others. To such a degree, in fact, that on one occasion when the Lord left to her the choice of being illuminated either in a completely superior and most profound way, but incommunicable to others, or in a lesser but communicable way, she preferred the latter because it would be more useful to others.

> "She had in fact two ways in which to enjoy God. In the one way, her mind so overflowed that she was transported so completely in Him that afterwards she was able to tell very little of it for the advantage of her neighbor. The other way consisted in this, that sharpening the senses in meditation the Scriptures, with the cooperation of the Lord, she acquired a spiritual understanding of them with wonderful zest and delight as if she frolicked face to face with the Lord, as sometimes one jokes at table alone with an intimate friend. In this second way it was possible for it to be useful to others. It was this that the Lord asked her, inquiring whether she would prefer that He attend on her in the first way, or whether she herself would serve Him in the second way. But she, not seeking her own advantage but the advantage of Jesus Christ, preferred to be of use in this work unto His praise; and rather than satisfy her own inclination, she let the rest go and tasted how sweet is the Lord." [12]

All this seems to refer directly to those doctrinal explanations which Gertrude imparted to others in regard to her imaginal visions. It does not seem to me that she had any doubts about the properly supernatural origin of those same visions even in their imaginal apparatus. But she does not at all exaggerate its importance. As her confidante says, we can better understand

[11] 4, 14, pp. 343 ff.   [12] 4, 2, p. 290.

her sincerity when she chooses to apply the term "imaginational portrayals" to everything in the didactic service of others in order to draw them the more securely to that most hidden manna *"quasi per ascensorios gradus imaginationum."* [13] There is, then, nothing in Gertrude that can be termed visionary in a pejorative sense.

We may ask ourselves, then, why this exuberance of imaginal visions. The answer is provided us by Gertrude's own principle which we quoted a few pages above: God proportions His way of communicating Himself in view of place, time, and person. Gertrude is a medieval woman. The thirst for symbolism in the piety of the Middle Ages, and not in the piety alone, is a phenomenon too well known and too general in that era to require any particular demonstration of it here. [14]

Expressions and images from married life

The same principle that God adjusts His way of communicating His gifts in view of place, time, and person helps us to understand, and to reduce to its proper proportions, the other phenomenon, irritating when first we meet it, in the Gertrudian writings: her use of erotically evocative expressions and images. Gertrude indisputably places herself within the mystic tradition called "nuptial"; for she lives and explains the mystical relations of the union of her soul with God in the imaginal framework and in a vocabulary derived from the relationships of espousals and marriage, following the example of the Canticle of Canticles and applying its systematization not only to the relations between the Church and God, but even to the relations of individual souls with God. All the mystics of Helfta, as well as some of the other German mystics of the thirteenth century, [15] lived in this atmosphere.

They were influenced primarily by St. Bernard. St. Gertrude, for her part, aggravated the matter. But certainly it is true here if anywhere: *omnia munda mundis.* It is right, nevertheless, to subjoin this observation: we do not wish in any way to misunderstand the legitimacy, in St. Gertrude nor in so many other saints, men and women, made secure by their own eminent sanctity, of representing and expressing the highest secrets of mystical union with God, transcending every imagery and sensibility, with nuptial images and vocabulary.

Nevertheless, it is certain that this procedure is not necessarily connected with mysticism. There are authentic mystics who ignore it completely. Such, for example, is St. Ignatius of Loyola. Moreover, it cannot be doubted that the use by a mystic, man or woman, of this manner of representation, and

[13] 5, 36, p. 613. In substance it is the well-known doctrine of which St. John of the Cross gave a classic expression in the *Subida* 2, 17, pp. 602 ff.

[14] See, for example, M. D. Chenu, *Nature, Man, and Society in the Twelfth Century*, edited and translated by Jerome Taylor and Lester K. Little, Chicago 1968, chapter 3, pp. 99 ff.

[15] See, for example, the article *"Contemplation,"* in *Dictionnaire de spiritualité*, Vol. 2 (1953), cols. 1972 ff.

especially in an intense and insistent degree, depends, in the final analysis, upon such natural factors as sex, sensitivity, temperament, education — factors which, if you will, God adapts, making use of them as any other elements of nature, good in themselves.

From this it is easily inferred that in reading such writings which employ these representational and expressive elements with some consistency, each one, in accord with his own temperament, can either take it in stride or, if need be, simply pass over it. What is essential is that the reader not allow himself to be hindered by those *ascensorii gradus imaginationum*, which in the Gertrudian writings are somewhat disagreeable to our legitimately different sensibilities, from arriving, as Gertrude's confidante says, at those most secret intimacies and at the most pure and excellent fonts of wisdom, which gush out abundantly from these writings and which cannot at all be communicated by way of imagery to anyone who has not had the experience of it.[16]

A view of the external life of St. Gertrude

Finally, a glimpse of the external framework of the life that St. Gertrude lived. Presenting her, as we are, as a good example of liturgical spirituality, we must not forget, if only to have a better understanding from the outset of the limits of this example, the particular background of the life that was hers. This background was that of a monastery of Benedictine nuns. The characteristic of the ordering of a life of this kind is, as you know, that its precise focal point is on the carrying out of the liturgy: Mass and Divine Office.

The hours of the *Opus Dei* gave a rhythm to the whole day, and the liturgical feasts to the entire year. Thus the liturgical calendar is the actual calendar not only externally but even internally in a life of this kind. The precise characteristic is seen in Gertrude too, who, in fixing the time of the mystical graces of which she speaks, does not consider the year except in reference to its feasts and liturgical cycles, nor the day except in reference to the hours of the *Opus Dei*. It is a matter, therefore, of a picture of life in which the liturgy dominates not only qualitatively but even quantitatively.

The rest of the occupations in the monastery of Helfta were made up of the ordinary obligations of the offices necessary for the ongoing business of a community and of study. Humanistic studies were held in honor, but rather as a preparatory phase and for the instruction of the young children who received their education in the monastery.

The specifically monastic study was the *lectio divina*, ie., planned study of the Scriptures, of the Fathers and of more recent authors, in relation to the great themes of the spiritual and liturgical life. So understood, the *lectio divina* was a direct preparation for living the liturgical life in depth. The pas-

[16] See 5, 36, p. 613.

sage from the *lectio* to contemplation was regarded as a natural and continuous experience.

The ladder of this ascension, well known in monastic tradition, was *lectio, meditatio, contemplatio*; or more fully, *lectio, meditatio, oratio* (ejaculatory), *contemplatio*.[17] The Gertrudian writings make frequent allusions to these steps. Thus, at the end of the whole work, after having indicated its aim and purpose as the first step "through the range of physical imagination" toward mystical experience, Gertrude's confidante concludes:

> "Meanwhile, the more simple readers of this book, who are not capable of swimming by themselves in the ocean of divine mercy, place themselves at least on course by using this means, and launched by the delight of the good offices which have been done toward neighbor, they can give themselves to *reading*, to *meditation*, to *contemplation*, and thus commence finally to taste for themselves how sweet is the Lord, and how really fortunate is one who hopes in Him and who devotes to Him his every thought." [18]

In this picture of life in her monastery, Gertrude does not seem ever to have occupied administrative offices of any importance; at least there are never any allusions to such in her writings. Perhaps she helped St. Mechtild in the direction of the choir.[19] In the observance of all the regular exercises and ordinary works she was meticulous:

> "She observed the statutes of the Order with such great delight of mind, like attendance in choir, the fasts, the common works, that she never omitted them, except for grave illness." [20]

Even from childhood she was of alert mind, better than average:

> "Lovable, clever, and talkative, tractable to such a degree that anyone who heard her stood in amazement of it. In school she sparkled with such great liveliness of intellect and ingenuity of mind that she surpassed all those of her own age and her other equals in every kind of knowledge." [21]

When an interest in study awakened in her, she gave herself to it with avidity and a passion. After her conversion to a more perfect life, she always believed with remorse that she had, in the years of her adolescence, allowed herself to take too human a delight in her studies. Even after she had entered into the mystical life, her studies, or more accurately the *lectio* of the Scriptures and of the Fathers, remained always an object of her most lively concern.[22]

In Gertrude's monastery, contact with the outside world was quite rare. In the case of Gertrude herself, it was reduced to a minimum. As a child of only

---

[17] See, for example, in *Dictionnaire de spiritualité*, Vol. 2 (1953), under the article "*Contemplation*," cols. 1946, 1960.

[18] 5, 36, p. 613.

[19] See 5, 1, p. 510.

[20] 1, 11, p. 32.

[21] 1, 1, p. 7.

[22] See 1, 1, pp. 8 ff; 1, 4, p. 18.

five years she entered into apprenticeship in the monastery. It may be that she lost her parents at so young an age, or perhaps she was sent to the monastery "exiled by her parents." Certainly she did not have, at least in the neighborhood of the monastery, parents or friends whose natural affection she might enjoy. At about the age of thirty-four and perhaps earlier, she did not remember ever having seen a mother caressing her child.[23] All this did not prevent her from having an ecclesial sense shaped to a most excellent understanding of the various kinds of life and of the various necessities of the Church.[24]

These hints will suffice as a preparation to understand the Gertrudian writings in general. To study them more closely in the framework of a liturgical spirituality, we will examine them from the point of view of ascetical purification and of the exercise of the virtues, of the vital relative attention given to the various dogmas of the faith, of the mystical life properly so called, and finally, of extraliturgical prayer and devotions.

2. Purification, Exercise of Virtues, and Liturgical Life of Gertrude

In general

The aspect of purification in the spiritual life continues in its own way throughout the whole of life, even when the soul has reached the very summits of mystical experience. In Gertrude it is not a question of dramatic struggles against vice and evil inclinations. Having entered the convent in her infancy and never having left it, there she led always a life of extraordinary purity and chastity even in the earlier period when she was simply an honest and praiseworthy religious, with a passion for study but without any special spiritual fervor.

Her conversion to an ardent spiritual life took place when she was twenty-six years of age, in consequence of an agitation of her conscience that lasted for a month, and especially because of a vision which she had in the dormitory one evening after Compline; in that vision Christ made her understand that He wanted her all to Himself. This conversion is simply the moment in which Christ, by drawing her to Himself, frees her definitively from the all too natural affection which she had until then nourished for her studies and leads her to a true knowledge of herself, infusing into her at the same time a lively feeling of her imperfections and disorders in respect to the supreme purity of life which God demands.[25] Then she begins to reflect ever more and more on how she ought to correspond to the graces of God and live a life of union with Him:

[23] See 1, 16, p. 52; 3, 30, p. 130.
[24] See, for example, 3, 69; 3, 89; 3, 90.

[25] See 2, 1–2.

"You inspired me to know that if I, in the gratitude due You, would pour back continually to You, like a stream of flowing water, the graces which You infuse into me; and that if, to this end, giving myself ever more and more to the practice of virtue, I would grow straight as a tree in good works; and that if, more than this, I would renounce earthly things and fly free as a dove, desiring only heavenly things and thereby separate my bodily senses from the tumult of things external, occupying myself interiorly with You alone, my heart would become for You a most pleasant dwelling place." [26]

Then Christ gave her the grace of a higher and constant feeling of His presence in her, a feeling which, as she attests after nine years, never left her afterwards except once for a period of eleven days, because, as she believed, she had allowed herself to enter into too mundane a conversation.[27] From that moment on, Gertrude clung to Christ with total detachment, with a wonderful state of liberation from everything else, by reason of which

"at every moment she is ready to receive My gifts, Christ said, because she never allows her heart to cling to anything that would keep it from Me." [28]

Defects and imperfections still remained in her, of course, God permitting them for the sake of her humility.[29] But they were cauterized ever more deeply in their very roots, primarily by a profound sense of her own unworthiness and of the goodness, mercy, and lovableness of God, a feeling which always accompanied every new grace that she received.

Compunction

Thus it is that a profound and sincere sentiment of compunction, along with an ardent sentiment of gratitude to God, pervades the writings of Gertrude, a sure indication of her constant state of mind.

The second book of the *Legatus*, written by Gertrude herself, opens with this exclamation:

"O abyss of uncreated Wisdom, may You call upon the abyss of wonderful Omnipotence, in order to extol a benevolence so stupendous that by the superabundance of its mercy it flowed even to the deep valleys of my distress!" [30]

Having completed the same Book 2, in a chapter summing up and listing the major benefits which she had received, she does not forget to add a list of her ingratitudes; [31] and she concludes the whole of it with the following prayer:

"Grant to all those who read this writing with humility that they may have compassion on my unworthiness and compunction for the

[26] 2, 3, p. 63.
[27] *Ibid.*, p. 64.
[28] 1, 11, p. 35.

[29] See 1, 3, p. 17.
[30] 2, 1, p. 59.
[31] 2, 24, pp. 109–112.

sake of their own progress, so that from the golden thuribles of their charitable hearts a perfume may arise to You so sweet that it may amply supply for my every defect of ingratitude and negligence." [32]

Gertrude's confidante and the witness of her life, who exalts for emulation her sense of justice, her burning zeal for the salvation of souls and for the glory of God, her carefulness in the regular exercises, her compassionate and considerate charity, her sense of delicate purity and her extraordinary trust and confidence in God, nevertheless extols as the most notable among all her moral virtues — her humility:

> "Among the most resplendent virtues with which God so wonderfully adorned her like a shining star in order to dwell in her, it was humility that shone most brightly in her — humility, which is the receptacle of all the graces and the safeguard of all the virtues. Her humility was such that she accounted herself so unworthy of God's gifts that she was in no way able to admit receiving a gift for her own sake, but she considered herself a channel by means of which, by some mysterious divine arrangement, grace sought to overtake the elect of God.
>
> "But she regarded herself as most unworthy and believed that her reception of graces was totally unfruitful. She endeavored only, either by writing or by speaking, to spread them abroad for the advantage of others. . . . She did not think there was anyone so vile that had God's gift been given to him it would have been received more fruitfully than by herself. Nevertheless, she did not flee at all from these gifts; rather, she kept herself in readiness at every moment to receive whatever gift God might bestow on her and afterwards to spread it abroad for the advantage of her neighbor, as if it were something she had received not so much for herself as for others, by the narration that she would make of it for them. . . .
>
> "Her humility was such that when she was walking, in order to abase herself the more, she said to the Lord, 'I believe, Lord, that the greatest of Your miracles is really this, that the earth supports me, unworthy sinner that I am.' " [33]

It is certain that Gertrude's feeling of her own unworthiness and of the mercy and goodness of God was the great instrument of her ever more profound purification. For long years illness consumed her and caused her very often to keep to her bed. This too, of course, in the hands of God was an instrument for achieving His very purpose, her purification. But from what we can see of it in her writings, even in this matter the end was achieved not really so much by means of her pain as such as by means of an ever more intense appreciation of God's goodness and lovableness and of her own unworthiness, a feeling which God infused into her in the graces of union which He accorded her along with her illness.

---

[32] 2, 25, pp. 113 ff.   [33] 1, 11, pp. 31–33.

Now, all this takes place in Gertrude in strict relation to the liturgical life, so much so that in her the graces of intense union with God, the profound feeling of her own unworthiness, the recognition and correction of her faults, and her liturgical life are things quite inseparable one from another. She was visited by God on the vigil of the Annunciation while the community was holding chapter after Lauds:

> "How You have visited me from on high, O Oriens, with the inmost feelings of Your mercy and sweetness, no writing can tell. Grant me then, You giver of every gift, to immolate for You a sacrifice of jubilee on the altar of my heart so that I might attain, as much for myself as for all Your elect, to the frequent experiencing of that sweet union and that unitive sweetness which was a stranger to me until this very hour.
>
> "Thinking again of my life, whether earlier or later, I confess in all truth that it is a matter of a grace as gratuitous as it was unmerited. From that moment You have gratified me with a knowledge of You clearer than any light; and in that knowledge the sweet love of Your friendship has drawn me most powerfully, a more potent force for my correction, than the severity of the pains which I have merited. But I do not recall having had the fruit of such graces except on those days on which You have called me to the delights of Your royal table." [34]

The final words are worthy of special note: the knowledge of God and the love of His friendship experienced in the graces of union were a more potent factor in attracting Gertrude than the other means of correction; and all this is connected with the liturgical action, especially on days when she received Communion. It is indicative of her general manner of progress in purification.

Purification from tendencies to the less good

But in the writings of Gertrude in this area, we have more than mere general affirmations. More than once within the framework of the liturgical life does she allude to the purification of specific tendencies to the less perfect. Several times there is mentioned a certain tendency to impatience.[35] To recite only one such instance:

> "Around the feast of St. Bartholomew, through an inordinate sorrow and impatience coming together at the same time, she fell into such darkness that she believed she had lost in great measure the joy of the divine presence. This lasted until the moment when, on a Saturday, it was mitigated and she cheered up, feeling the darkness lifted through the intervention of the Virgin Mother of God while the antiphon *Stella maris Maria* was being sung in Mary's honor.
>
> "The next day was a Sunday, and she was gladdened when, through the divine condenscension, her accustomed tranquillity returned; and when she remembered her former impatience and her other faults, she

---

[34] 2, 2. See also 2, 24, p. 107.
[35] For example: 2, 15; 2, 16, p. 144; 3, 4. See also 1, 11, p. 35; 1, 12, p. 39; 1, 16, p. 51; 3, 30, p. 191; 3, 55, p. 229; 3, 63, p. 237; 4, 2, p. 288.

> was quite displeased with herself and began to supplicate the Lord for
> her correction with such great abasement of spirit, because of the mul-
> tiplicity and severity of the faults which she thought to find in herself,
> that she said to the Lord almost in desperation: 'Alas, most merciful
> Lord, put an end to my evils, which I commit without end or measure:
> *Libera me et pone me iuxta te et cuiusvis manus pugnet contra me.'* "

Then the Lord made her understand that she must not lose hope; that
these difficulties and faults did not mean that she did not have charity; and
that charity covers up a multitude of sins, while He was accustomed to distress His elect by remorse of conscience simply to disengage them from the
things of this earth.[36]

Gertrude, intelligent and quite impassioned for reading and study, also
possessed a natural gift of being a good speaker. She was one of those persons
who when they talk on a subject in which they are interested, can treat of
it with such hidden ardor of mind and with such great discretion that they
naturally enchant their audience.[37] After her conversion to the perfect life,
she used this gift in doing good to others.[38] But this in itself could present
some danger of vanity or of complacency. One day she noticed that she no
longer succeeded in attracting others by her speaking as she once did. So she
said to the Lord:

> " 'How will You be able to draw some of them to Yourself by means
> of me, unworthy as I am, if I have lost in great part that gift of speak-
> ing and of instructing others which formerly I had?' And the Lord
> answered her: 'If you had the gift of speaking effectively, you might
> perhaps think that it is by your own eloquence that you succeed in
> drawing men to me. You have lost it, then, so that you may know that
> it is not by your power but by My special grace that you succeed so
> well.' "[39]

By nature Gertrude had a delicate mind, sensitive to the beauties of nature.[40] Her writings, and especially the images in which, like a mysterious
reflection of her more sublime graces, there is in some way translated the experience of her mystical union, show at bottom a temperament naturally delicate and ardent, such that had it not been safeguarded by its surroundings and
specially protected, fortified, purified, and sublimated by grace, it might well
have been able to go astray into sensuality.[41] This straying, certainly, did not

---

[36] 3, 4, pp. 121 ff.
[37] 1, 1, p. 9.
[38] See, for example, 1, 1, pp. 8 ff.
[39] 4, 30.
[40] See, for example, 2, 3; 1, 8, p. 26.
[41] There is the fact, to which we alluded
above, of the use of a vocabulary in Gertrude
that evokes the erotic. Be it noted that the
phenomenon is not sufficiently explained by
the influence of the style of the Canticle of

Canticles. This latter book, as has been observed
by Father Doyère (*Le mémorial spirituel de S.
Gertrude*, Paris 1953, p. 31), is not at all an
essential source for the inspiration of the *Legatus*, especially not for Book 2, written by Gertrude herself. Even what little place the Canticle occupies in the writings of Gertrude probably obtains through liturgical channels rather
than in a direct way.

take place at all. But it is to be understood that such a nature, habituated from infancy to the beauties of the choral Office, may have been able, even after complete dedication to God in the life of perfection, to taste in the liturgy something apart from the manna of the spiritual life with which God continually provided her, something of its appeal in being artistically beautiful. This holds true in particular for the Gregorian Chant, the esthetic power of which is a thing recognized by those who are expert in it.

It is certain that Gertrude deeply loved assisting at Divine Office, especially on feast days; and it was the greatest mortification for her to be deprived of it by her not infrequent illness.[43] Indeed, it seems that in this matter she may have had properly to submit to those passive purifications through which souls called to the highest peaks must pass. Nevertheless, the Lord gave her to understand that being deprived of the Divine Office because of illness contributed greatly to her sanctification and to her being purified of every purely natural affection.[44]

It is certain also that she deeply loved Gregorian Chant.[45] But even here God took care to purify her from taking too human a sensory satisfaction in it.

> "On a certain feast when she was prevented from singing because of a headache, she asked of the Lord why He allowed this, a thing which had actually happened to her more frequently on feasts; and an answer was given her: 'To prevent it from happening that, raised up by the melodiousness of the chant, you might be less suited to My grace.' She replied, 'Your grace, O Lord, would be able to protect me in advance against this defect.' But the Lord said, 'It is more advantageous to a man that the occasion of his fall be taken away by the increased burden of such an illness. In this way he acquires the double merit of patience and of humility.' "[46]

On another occasion:

> "When she had finished the whole of Lauds with devout attention, she began to wonder whether it was because of some carelessness on her part that she had deserved not to receive such great enlightenments as she was accustomed to receive from prayers said with such devotion as she had expended on these Lauds. God instructed her with these words: 'Rightly have you been deprived of the internal sweetness of spiritual illumination so that by allowing you to pursue your own will, you found human satisfaction in the melodiousness of the chant. Know, however, that your merit of future recompense has been augmented for you in the degree that you have preferred My service to your own convenience.' "[47]

---

[42] See 1, 9.

[43] See 3, 30, p. 189; 4, 9, p. 324, and numerous other places in Book 4.

[44] See, for example, 3, 30, p. 189.

[45] See, for example, 2, 16, p. 87; 3, 30, no.

17, pp. 85 ff; 3, 59; 4, 14; 4, 41, p. 417; 4, 46, p. 426.

[46] 3, 30, pp. 185 ff.

[47] 4, 41, p. 418.

In Gertrude there are even clear traces to be seen of a basic character that might have been able to develop into fierceness even with bursts of resentment and anger.[48] One evening she lapsed into a display of temper. The following morning, during prayer, Christ showed Himself to her in a compassionate manner, which excited in her a strong remorse of conscience and the resolution that she would prefer that Christ did not appear to her at all rather than show Himself to her at a moment "when I have neglected to combat the enemy who drives me to things which are so displeasing to You." [49]

Another time she strongly resented the observation made to her by one of her sisters in religion that in order truly to discover Jesus she ought to keep watch over her own senses and feelings like a shepherd over his flock:

> "I received the observation with but little gratitude, judging that it scarcely applied to me, knowing that You had shaped my mind otherwise than to serve You as a mercenary serves his master. I pondered the matter in my bosom with abasement of spirit from dawn until dusk."

That evening, however, at the end of Compline, while she was recollected in prayer, Christ made her to understand that in that comparison there was nothing unbecoming, but that on the contrary it was quite fitting.

> "And You added that every time anything would want to draw my feelings either to the right, like joy and hope, or to the left, like fear or sorrow or anger, I should immediately make use of the rod of the fear of You, and controlling my senses, offer those feelings, like a tender newborn lamb cooked in the heat of my heart, as food for You." [50]

In a similar way God instructed her on the necessity of disinterested unselfishness even in prayer,[51] and on the necessity of the desire for suffering.[52]

Purifying force of the liturgy

In St. Gertrude, then, as it appears in the *Legatus* and in the *Exercitia*, we find nothing of that painful and dramatic struggle of active and passive purifications which can be seen in the lives of so many saints and so many mystics especially. From the first moment that we are able to follow her, she seems to us to be like a body of water, pure and crystalline, with only a ripple showing here and there.[53] The progress of purification, which certainly must have needed to take place even in her, from the moment of her entry into the mystical life, insofar as we can observe it in such documents as we have, does not stand out with any great emphasis. We have pointed out whatever clear traces of it that we have come upon in her writings.

[48] See, for example, 2, 12; 2, 13; 2, 1, toward the end: *cervicem meam indomitam* . . . .
[49] 2, 12.
[50] 2, 13.
[51] 2, 16, p. 87.
[52] 3, 5.
[53] See what Christ said of her: "Even from her infancy I have carried her as it were and protected her in My arms, keeping her spotless until the moment when she voluntarily united herself to Me with all the power of her will. And then, in turn, I gave Myself to her with all My divine strength" (1, 3).

But what interests us here is the fact that this aspect of purification fits itself naturally and without complications, just like the other elements of her sanctity, into the framework of her liturgical life, which is her life of the spirit. The graces of union and of illumination, received in close connection with her liturgical life, naturally exercise their purificatory power over the imperfections which still mark her in some degree, imperfections which are apparent to her precisely because of the light shed upon them by these graces. Thus the moral effort which she makes is in no way complicated, but is quite simple and at the same time efficacious.

We do not see extraordinary penances of any sort nor complicated methods for the examination of one's own conscience and for the practice of the moral virtues. What we do see in her is simply a great love for the *lectio divina*: the meditative study of the spiritual Fathers and particularly of the Scriptures, so much so that "having changed from grammarian to theologian, she never tired of pondering . . . finding therein honey for her mouth, music for her ears, and spiritual exultation for her heart." [54] We see in her a great zeal for the observances of her monastery,[55] for prayer, for Matins, and the regular exercises and practices, from which, as we have seen, she dispensed herself only for reasons of grave illness.[56]

Especially do we see Gertrude utterly overflowing with yearning and desire for loving encounter with God in the liturgical action. These encounters are the great dynamic force of her spiritual life as well as for internal ascetical and purificatory effort, because it is from these encounters that she obtains the light and strength to see ever better and better her own imperfections, to detest them, desiring to be free of them and resolving to labor to that end.

In a special way the preparation for the liturgical feasts and for participation in Communion at the sacrifice of the Mass have for her the very greatest moral and ascetical importance. She wants to come prepared to her encounter with God. Hence this desire to be enlightened by God Himself in order to prepare herself in the way that is most pleasing to Him.[57] Hence the exercises which she performed in order to prepare herself for the liturgy and the prayers addressed to God so that He Himself might prepare her for it with every kind of virtue.[58] Hence the graces of enlightenment about her own imperfections on these very occasions.[59]

Ascetical effort and consciousness of grace. The *suppletio*

Thus there was a fear even of arriving at the time of Communion or of a feast insufficiently prepared. But who, trusting in his own efforts, is able to consider himself sufficiently prepared for the encounter with God? Gertrude knew it well enough. What recourse then did she have? To the constant practice of the *suppletio*, that is, to pondering on the merits of Jesus Christ,

[54] 1, 1, p. 8.
[55] 1, 8, p. 24.
[56] 1, 11, p. 34.
[57] See, for example, 4, 20; 4, 21; 4, 23.
[58] For example, 4, 37–38.
[59] For example, 4, 2, p. 288; 4, 7, p. 319.

on His sorrows, desires, prayers, on the love of His most holy humanity; to uniting herself to them and to offering them to the Father so that they might *supply* for her unworthiness, her negligences, her faults, her sins.[60] Gertrude frequently had recourse in the same way to the merits of the Madonna and of the saints.

Having done this, notwithstanding the strong awareness of her own unworthiness and the little value of her ascetical efforts in preparing herself for her encounter with God in the liturgical action, she was perfectly at peace. There is in her not only not the slightest trace of a Jansenistic or Pelagian or semi-Pelagian mentality, but not even of a subconscious overestimation of voluntarist effort of man in his relations with God. Without blemish of lassitudinal or quietistic tendency, her psychology is peacefully ruled by the consciousness of the sovereignty of grace and of the *suppletio* that Christ affords to the poor human efforts of all those who are united to Him with sincere good will and purity of heart.

> "By reason of her aforementioned trust in God, she had such a gift in regard to Communion that she was never able to read anything in the Scriptures or hear any discoursing of men about the danger of communicating unworthily that would hinder her from willingly communicating, basing her position on a firm trust in the mercy of the Lord. She deemed her own efforts of so little account and of such negligible value that she never omitted receiving Communion because of any negligence in prayer or in the like exercises by which one prepares himself habitually for Communion. She considered that in view of that most excellent and gratuitous gift, every human effort is but a drop of water in a vast ocean.
>
> "And even if she did not seem to see any possible way sufficiently worthy to prepare herself to receive Communion, nevertheless, trusting in the incomparable munificence of God more than settling herself on any kind of preparation, she but strove to receive that same Sacrament with a pure heart and devoted love. All the spiritual gifts that she received she attributed to trust alone, deeming them so much the more gratuitous the more she came to understand that she had received from the giver of every grace, without merit on her part and truly gratuitously, that noble gift of trust." [61]

It is easy to see from the above how eminently positive, Christocentric, and Theocentric would be the asceticism of Gertrude. It is one of the fruits of her formation in the school of the liturgy. In the inseparable combination of God and man, grace and human effort, the liturgy centers one's attention more on God and more on grace than on man and human effort; and its proper way of healing man and stimulating his effort is precisely by fixing his attention and his love primarily on grace, on Christ, and on God.

[60] See, for example, 4, 17; 4, 28; 4, 35, p. 402; 4, 39–40. See also the *Exercitia* 7, pp. 699 ff.   [61] 1, 10, pp. 29 ff.

Love as unceasing homage of praise and thanksgiving

Hence it is that in the life of Gertrude as seen in her writings, insofar as the exercise of virtue is concerned, she seems to be immersed primarily in the practice of the theological virtues, first of all in the love of God exercised constantly as unceasing homage of praise and thanksgiving, prompted by remembrance of His grandeur and of His goodness, experienced ever more profoundly in graces received. Love ever in act as unceasing homage of praise and thanksgiving — this seems to be the formula which truly expresses the dominant note of this life so like a lyric sung to God. Dominant, yes, but of course many other harmonic notes accompany and enhance it, among which there is the profound feeling of compunction for her own destitution.

The second book of the *Legatus* and the *Exercitia*, the works written in Gertrude's own hand, are characteristic of this aspect of her practice of virtue. And much the same picture is bound to be reflected also in Books 3, 4, and 5 of the *Legatus*, which were dictated by her. The picture we have of her is typical of the spirit of the liturgy, viz., the spirit of love, of worshiping, and of thanksgiving — a thanksgiving centered *par excellence* on the Eucharist, which determined her purification of blemishes and her acquisition of virtues.

3. The Liturgical Life in St. Gertrude and the Vital Relative Attention Given to the Various Dogmas of the Faith

In order to gain an understanding of the liturgical character of a spirituality, no less important than the consideration of how purification and the exercise of virtue are conceived in it is the ascertaining of which among the truths of faith actually dominate the vital explicit attention or even the subconscious psychology of a specific individual, and what relative importance is accorded each. We know sufficiently well what the special balance is that the liturgy proposes in this area to the psychology of the believer.

Now, it is noteworthy how, in Gertrude, the great skeletal framework of the liturgico-dogmatic view of the world, explained in the first three parts of the present work, is reproduced in a quite faithful manner, except, by way of defect, that some features are emphasized insufficiently or not at all — primarily the total lack, I believe, of the viewpoint of salvation history in its Old Testament preparation, along with an insufficient emphasis on the struggle against Satan [62] — and except, by way of excess, that there is in Gertrude a notable proliferation of a series of "devotions" already in the modern sense of the term. How these latter are to be related to the liturgical context is a matter which will be taken up later.

However, let us make it clear right now that these devotional considerations, such as the Sacred Heart of Jesus, the Passion of Christ, the members of Christ, His wounds, although they may at first glance impress a modern

---

[62] See, for example, 4, 29, pp. 481 ff; 5, 32, p. 606; *Exercitia* 1, pp. 619 ff, 625; 5, p. 671.

reader of the *Revelations* and of the *Exercises*, and although the historians of spirituality, in researching the birth and development of modern piety, may in fact be pleased to emphasize them, in the psychology of Gertrude they do not upset the respective balance of the dogmas of the faith according to the view proposed by the liturgy. They are subordinated, they are integrated, or, if you will, they are amalgamated with it, but they do not stifle it. So much the less is that stifled, as we have seen in its proper place, which a modern reader of the *Revelations* might be tempted to call, a bit hastily, the exaggerated importance given to visions and revelations in the concept of the spiritual life which derives from these works.

On the contrary, considering the matter in depth, we notice that that which really dominates the psychology of our mystic is none other, in its essence, than the great dogmatic stance of the liturgy.The liturgy, then, is not only the external framework of Gertrude's life but the internal form as well, which determines her view of the dogmas of faith and the relative position which she accords to each in their totality.

The Trinity

In the *Legatus* and in the *Exercitia*, the first thing which one encounters is Christ, always and everywhere. Moreover, it is perfectly apparent that Christ is first of all the Mediator. From Christ there is a progress regularly to the Father, to the Trinity, and even if less frequently, to God. The center and apex of Gertrude's attention is not simply Christ, nor simply the Trinity; her mind follows a Christological-Trinitarian movement.[63] Gertrude's mental process goes ceaselessly from Christ to the Trinity, in respect to which she makes frequent use of the formula *fulgida semperque tranquilla Trinitas*,[64] and to which she likes to make reference in terms of the liturgical formulas of the feast of the Trinity.

This feast, with its way of considering the mystery primarily from the intratrinitarian point of view and its strongly admirational and contemplative formulas, seems to have been most dear to Gertrude.[65] Her visions very frequently have their precise object in what takes place in heaven in the presence of the Trinity. Frequently she sees herself in the presence of the Father to whom Christ presents her.[66] Sometimes it is the Madonna or her own guardian angel who performs the same office for her.[67] Most frequently she contemplates Christ who supplicates the Father for herself or for men and who offers for them His merits in substitution for their sins and imperfections.[68]

On the feast of the Assumption:

[63] See, for example, 2, 5, pp. 70 ff; 2, 7, p. 73; 3, 12, p. 136; 4, 2, pp. 290 ff; 4, 12, p. 336; 4, 35, p. 399; and especially 4, 41.

[64] For example, 2, 7, p. 73; 2, 11, p. 80.

[65] See, for example, 4, 41.

[66] For example, 3, 17, p. 147; 3, 19, the whole chapter and especially on p. 159; 3, 30, pp. 177 ff; 4, 19, p. 360.

[67] For example, 3, 23.

[68] For example, 3, 18, pp. 151–153; 3, 30, pp. 184 ff; 3, 31; 3, 40, p. 204; 3, 41; 4, 6, p. 316; 4, 9, p. 324; 4, 25; 4, 39, p. 412.

"While at Vespers, in the antiphon *Haec est dies* the words *hodie Deus homo factus* were being sung, and the community, out of reverence for the most noble incarnation of the Lord, prostrated itself to the ground, the Son of God and Supreme King, as if moved by those words, and remembering how, urged on by love, He was made man for our sakes, raised Himself excitedly from His royal throne; and, standing reverently before God the Father, He said: 'My brethren have come to me' (Gen. 46:31)." [69]

And again there is the following passage:

"On *Invocavi* Sunday, when Gertrude felt that she was less prepared to receive the Body of the Lord, she begged Him with a devout heart that, to supply for a fault of hers, which was that because of physical illness she had been constrained not to keep the Lenten fast, He might deign to grant her His own most holy fast in which, while on earth and for our salvation, He had mortified Himself for forty days and forty nights.

"At this petition the Son of God, raising Himself suddenly with a joyous countenance and genuflecting with reverence before God the Father, said: 'I, Your only-begotten Son, coeternal and consubstantial with You, by My unsearchable wisdom, know the defects of human frailty better than she or any other human can possibly know them. Having great compassion on her manifold frailty, I offer You, O Holy Father, the priceless abstinence of My holy mouth to make amends and to supply for all the faults of which she is culpable in act or omission, in frivolous conversation. I offer to You, O Holy Father, the abstinence of My ears for all the sins which she has committed with her ears. I offer You also the abstinence of My eyes for all the stains she has upon her because of some illicit glance. I offer You also the abstinence of my hands and my feet for all the sins committed by her in working or in walking. Most lovable Father, I offer You finally My deified Heart for all the sins which she has committed in her thoughts, in her desires, in her will.'

"Then her soul, standing before God the Father, seemed to be clothed in garments of white and red, like a daughter wonderfully adorned in various ornaments." [70]

And later on:

"Hence, the Holy Spirit Paraclete, making Himself present and standing before her soul, illuminated with His wonderful divine splendor that part of her soul in which she herself, as was stated above, saw the magnitude of her own vileness. And thus, by the power of the divine light, that soul was stripped of all its vileness and was happily immersed in the very font of light eternal." [71]

[69] 4, 12, p. 337.
[70] 4, 17, pp. 354 ff.

[71] 4, 17, p. 357.

Later on the same occasion, at the reading of the Epistle during Mass the Lord instructed her that the words recurring there, *in Spiritu Sancto,* mean that the good intention of practicing virtue comes to us as gift of the Holy Spirit.

Other times again it is Gertrude herself who offers everything to the Father by means of the Son, or by means of the Son and the Holy Spirit, as in the formula: "Lord, I offer this work to You by means of Your only Son, in the power of the Holy Spirit, in praise eternal." [72] She even offers to the Father the Son Himself and His merits, or the Sacred Host.[73]

Still other times it is the Father who speaks to Gertrude or, at any rate, blesses her or adorns her with virtue.[74] Or again it is the Holy Spirit who appears to her, operating in her or in others.[75] In regard to the Holy Spirit, there is in Gertrude a noteworthy formula which she frequently uses: *in Spiritu Sancto,* or *in virtute Spiritus Sancti.*

Finally, more than once Gertrude contemplates the Trinity in heaven, who infuse joy and delight into the saints:

> "On the feast of All Saints she knew in spirit the mysteries in regard to the glory of the ever venerable Trinity, and how the blessed and glorious Trinity, in Itself without beginning and without end, overflowing with every sweetness, joy, and happiness, imparts to all the saints joy, glory, and eternal happiness. But, prevented by human frailty, that which she saw so clearly in the mirror of divine light she was utterly unable to explain to the range of human understanding, except for the few following things which she was able, only poorly and in disconnected fashion, to express by means of comparisons." [76]

With these last expressions there is clearly an allusion, as we will better understand when we study the question directly, to an inexpressible vision of the Trinity, considered by mystical authors to be the highest grace that can be received here below.

Christ the Mediator

Be that as it may, it remains a fact that Gertrude rose to the Trinity through Christ, man and God, with particular emphasis on His humanity, united in Him to His divinity, and as Mediator between God and men.[77] A characteristic text:

> "On the solemn feast of the refulgent and ever tranquil Trinity, out of reverence for the Trinity, Gertrude read this versicle: 'Glory be to You, imperial, most excellent, most sweet, most kind, resplendent and ever tranquil and indescribable Trinity, equal and single Godhead,

[72] 3, 30, p. 184.

[73] For example, 3, 18, p. 153; 4, 25; 4, 39, p. 412.

[74] For example, 4, 2, pp. 288–289, 292.

[75] For example, 3, 48; 4, 17, p. 357.

[76] 4, 55, p. 471. See also 4, 12, pp. 334 ff.

[77] See, for example, 3, 20, p. 162; 4, 35, p. 406; 4, 41.

existing before all ages and forever.' While she was offering this prayer to the Lord, the Son of God appeared to her in His humanity, in which, Scripture says, He is less than the Father. He stood before the venerable Trinity, in the sweet springtime and bloom of youth. And He had over His every member a flower of such beauty and splendor that its equal could never be found among things visible and material. By this it was signified that since our human insignificance can in no way accomplish the unattainable praise of the most excellent Trinity, Christ Jesus, in His humanity, in which, it is said, He is inferior to the Father, has taken upon Himself our small effort and, ennobling it in Himself, has made of it a worthy holocaust to the supreme and indivisible Trinity.

"While Vespers was afterwards being sung, the Son of God, holding in both His hands His most worthy Heart in the form of a lyre, presented it to the most glorious Trinity. By means of that Heart in the form of a lyre, all the words which were being sung on that feast resounded most sweetly in the presence of God. The song of those who sang without any special devotion and just because it was the custom, or who sang for human pleasure, those heavier strings, they sent forth a low grumbling of bass notes. But those who wanted to sing with devotion the praise of the venerable Trinity sent forth, as if with higher notes, a clear melody of sweetest music.

"Afterwards, while the antiphon *Osculetur me* was being sung, a voice from the throne said: 'Draw near, My beloved Son, in Whom I am in every respect highly pleased, and give me, to my delight, a most sweet kiss.' Then the Son of God, in human form drawing near, gave a most sweet kiss to the incomprehensible Divinity, to which only the most holy humanity happily attained to being united in a bond of inseparable union. . . .

"Gertrude understood then that on that feast every time the Son was named, God the Father caressed His most beloved Son in a way incomprehensible and inexpressible. By that caress the humanity of Jesus Christ was wonderfully clarified; and by that clarification of the humanity of Jesus all the elect conceived a new knowledge of the incomprehensible Trinity.

"During the morning Office, while the antiphon *Te jure laudant* was being sung at Lauds, Gertrude praised the venerable Trinity with the same antiphon and with all her strength, with the intention that if it were possible at the moment of her death to sing the same antiphon with such devotion as to lose her life by consuming all her strength in praising God, most gladly would she do it. Then it seemed to her that the whole resplendent and ever tranquil Trinity, with great kindness deigned to incline Itself toward the most worthy Heart of Jesus, which, like a lyre, began to vibrate wonderfully and to resound sweetly in the presence of the Trinity. And the Trinity set three strings in that lyre-like Heart which would be able without interruption to supply for

Gertrude's every defect, with the invincible omnipotence of God the Father, the wisdom of the Son of God, and the benevolence of the Holy Spirit, according to the good pleasure of the Most Blessed Trinity." [78]

When we recall that texts of a similar bearing are scattered throughout the whole of Gertrude's writings; that linked to the same concept expressed in these texts is the theme of the *suppletio* by means of Christ, so central to the spirituality of the mystics of Helfta and so important, in particular, to our Gertrude; that the same themes of the Sacred Heart, of the Passion of Christ, of His wounds, of the Eucharist as Real Presence, so much emphasized in her that they are intimately connected to that theme of the *suppletio* by means of Christ and as so many ladders by which Gertrude ascends through Christ to the Father; that finally, as will be clearer in what follows, the mediation of Christ is constantly in evidence in Gertrude in the mystical graces themselves of her highest contemplations, then can we understand how profoundly did this saint live the *per Dominum nostrum Iesum Christum Filium tuum* of the liturgy.

Heavenly liturgy

Another central idea in the spirituality of Gertrude is the habit of viewing the celestial realities in the light of the liturgical actions to which they correspond; of passing from the earthly liturgy to the heavenly liturgy, from the liturgy of men to that of Christ, of the angels, and of the blessed. Many of her visions have for their object precisely that which is taking place in heaven while the liturgy is being performed on earth. The texts cited up to now in regard to the Trinity and Christ represent examples of these. But some of them have other characteristics, like the vision of Matins of the feast of the Assumption, sung in heaven by Christ, by the angels, and by the blessed while the community was singing it on earth.[79]

Also worthy of note is the vision of the Mass celebrated by Christ in heaven, with the angels and the blessed, at which Gertrude assisted in spirit, while on earth her community sang the Mass *Gaudete in Domino*, at which, prevented by illness, she was unable to be present. All the parts of a Mass were sung on this occasion by Christ, by the angels, and by the saints. After the *Sanctus*, for example, when the saints had finished singing *Dominus Deus sabaoth*,

> ". . . the Lord Jesus, true Priest and High Pontiff, getting up from His imperial throne and elevating His most holy Heart, which appeared in the likeness of an altar of gold, seemed to present it with His own hands to God the Father and to immolate Himself in a manner so incomprehensible and inexpressible that no creature, however worthy, could aspire to understand it in any way at all. At the same moment that the Son of God offered His divine Heart to God the

[78] 4, 41, pp. 415–416.   [79] 4, 48, pp. 434 ff.

Father, the bell sounded in the monastery chapel for the elevation of the Host. And thus it happened that simultaneously the Lord fulfilled in heaven what was being done on earth through the ministry of the priest, while Gertrude was entirely unaware of what hour it was or of what was being sung in church." [80]

The reader will marvel at the profound theological and traditional concept, explained in its place, which attaches to these imaginal representations. The same concept is present in other visions where Christ appears while He presides at Mass or at the liturgical offices which are being fulfilled in the church or in the chapters of the nuns.[81] Among these visions, most noteworthy is that of Christ, ever surrounded by the angels and saints, who presides in person over the rites which take place on the vigil of the Nativity in the community chapter.[82]

The total unity of the cosmos

In Gertrude there is an acute sense, derived specifically from the liturgy, of the unity of the whole cosmos: angels, saints, souls in purgatory, men or Church on earth — a unity or unitotality which finds its maximum concretization and realization precisely in the liturgical action.

Mary. Undoubtedly Mary occupies a prominent position in the spirituality of Gertrude, as would be expected especially in the case of a soul living in the primitive Cistercian tradition. From Christ Himself Gertrude received Mary as her special protectress and guide.[83] That is why she says at the end of the second book of the *Legatus*, in the chapter summing up the graces she had received up to that time:

> "To fill up Your benefits to overflowing You added to them even this, that You gave me Your most sweet Mother, the Blessed Virgin Mary, as my protectress, and You commended me often and lovingly to her affection with as great an earnestness as ever any faithful husband could commend his spouse to his own mother." [84]

Christmas, the feasts of Mary in the cycle of the liturgical year, especially the Purification, the Annunciation, and the Assumption, were always times of intense spiritual preparation and of great graces for Gertrude. And in general, all the liturgical texts which refer to Mary were occasions for Gertrude to raise her thoughts and affections to her. Mary always occupies a position of honor in the picture in which Gertrude, on these occasions, receives her special graces. Take, for example, a text characteristic of the concept which she formed of the position occupied by Mary in heaven and on earth, on the feast of the Annunciation:

---

[80] 4, 59, pp. 490–491. Similarly in St. Mechtild, *The Book of Special Grace* 2, 5.
[81] For example, 4, 59; 3, 17.
[82] 4, 2, pp. 293 ff. The same is found in St.

Mechtild, *The Book of Special Grace* 1, 7.
[83] 3, 1, p. 118.
[84] 2, 23, p. 108.

"During Matins, while the invitatorium *Ave Maria* was being sung, Gertrude saw three most efficacious beams of light coming from the Father, the Son, and the Holy Spirit. She saw them penetrate with a most sweet impulse the heart of the Virgin Mary and rise again from her heart with efficacious impetuosity to return to their place of origin. By this inflowing of the Most Blessed Trinity it was given to the Blessed Virgin to be the most powerful after the Father, the most wise after the Son, and the most kind after the Holy Spirit.

"Gertrude understood also that every time the angelic salutation, that is, the *Ave Maria*, is recited with devotion by the faithful on earth, the aforesaid beams of light overflow and run over into the Most Blessed Virgin with greater force, and flow back again from her most holy heart and so, with wonderful delight, return to their source. From that superabundance some rivulets of joy, of delight, and of eternal salvation are splashed over, as it were, on all the saints and on all the angels and even on those here below who recite the *Hail Mary*. Thus in each one there is renewed all the good that anyone has ever obtained from the salvific incarnation of the Son of God." [85]

Angels. No less strong is Gertrude's sense of the unity with the angelic world. We have seen that in the visions of what takes place in heaven around the Most Blessed Trinity, or in those of Christ, who presides invisibily at the liturgical offices on earth, the angels are always present like a court around the king. This is only one point in which Gertrude manifests her sense of unity with the angels. There are others which show that this unity was for her a reality which she lived profoundly. In the summational chapter at the end of the second book of the *Legatus*, she thanks God not only because He has given her the Madonna for her special protectress, but also because He has accorded her the constant protection of the angels:

"Moreover, You have frequently deputed to my special service the more noble princes of Your palace, not only from among the choirs of the angels and the archangels, but even from the highest choirs, according as Your mercy, O most kind God, judged that it would be most beneficial to me, with the intention besides that they might incite me to be more submissive to them in the spiritual exercises." [86]

Her guardian angel has a special position in Gertrude's attention. On one occasion:

"When Gertrude was assisting at Mass as devoutly as she could, having arrived at the *Kyrie eleison*, it seemed to her that the angel assigned to her by God as her guardian angel took her as a baby in his arms and presented her to God the Father, saying: 'Lord God, Father, bless this Your little daughter.' . . . After that the same angel pre-

[85] 4, 12, pp. 334-335.   622-623; 2, pp. 627-628; 4, pp. 686, 688.
[86] 2, 23, p. 108. See also the *Exercitia* 1, pp.

sented her in a similar way to God the Son, saying: 'O Son of the King, bless this sister.' . . . Finally he presented her to the Holy Spirit, saying: 'O Lover of men, bless this Your spouse.' " [87]

Another time it seemed to Gertrude that she saw her guardian angel in heaven standing between her soul and God, behind them; and she saw him "embrace the Lord with one arm, with the greatest reverence and delicacy, and with the other arm, her soul," excusing himself for this familiar gesture by reason of his office, in which he had frequently to bring God to this soul.[88]

It was on the same occasion that:

> "One day, when the feast of the Archangel Michael was drawing near, Gertrude stood up to advance to Communion. She remembered that though she was unworthy, she had obtained from the divine liberality the most benevolent ministry of the other blessed spirits. Desiring to recompense them in turn, she offered the vivifying Sacrament itself of the Body and Blood of the Lord, saying: 'In honor of Your so great princes, beloved Lord, I offer You this wonderful Sacrament in eternal praise and for an increase of their joy, of their glory, and of their blessedness.' Then the Lord, engaging the Sacrament in His divinity in a wonderful way and uniting to Himself the Sacrament offered Him, administered from It such inexpressible delights to the blessed angelic spirits that even if formerly they had had no share of blessedness, they seemed now to be made abundantly joyful in it and overflowing with all its delights. Then the holy angels in order of their proper rank genuflected with greatest reverance before Gertrude. . . ." [89]

Thus they gave thanks to her. The traditional conviction that the angels are present at the liturgical offices is found also in Gertrude. For the presence of the angels at Mass, one need but examine again what we have reported already above in regard to the visions of Christ celebrating the Mass. The following example shows the presence of the angels during the psalmody of the vigil of Christmas:

> "At Vespers, while in the hymn the words *Gloria tibi, Domine* were being sung, she saw a great multitude of angels flying about over the community; and together with the community, the angels made the same verse resound with their melodious and jubilant voices. Then she asked the Lord how men were to profit by the fact that the holy angels, uniting themselves to their praise, sang the psalms along with them. And since she received no answer at all from the Lord to this question, she grew anxious and more and more diligent in her inquiry until finally, inspired by God, she understood that when the holy angels are present at our solemnities here on earth, they supplicate the Lord so that He might deign to make like the angels in true purity of heart and body those who strive to imitate them in their devotion." [90]

[87] 3, 24, pp. 167–168.
[88] 4, 53, p. 466.

[89] 4, 53, pp. 465–466.
[90] 4, 2, p. 297.

Saints. That Gertrude kept constantly present the thought of the saints is shown by the fact that in her visions of heaven she always beholds the saints who, along with the angels, are around Christ and the Trinity, and who, along with the angels, assist Christ when He says Mass there or presides invisibly at the liturgy here below. It is shown also by the considerable series of revelations, referred to especially in the fourth book of the *Legatus*, of particular saints and in respect to them, through the course of the liturgical year. Gertrude shows a special affection for St. John the Evangelist, whom the Lord gave her as her special protector,[91] for St. Benedict, St. Bernard, St. Augustine, and St. Gregory.

Souls in purgatory. Historians of spirituality have pointed out the tender solicitude of Gertrude for the souls in purgatory. Every day she tried to come to their assistance with her prayers, in the offering of which she found great profit even for herself. Once on Christmas Day, during the Mass *Dominus dixit*, she tried to revitalize her fervor but was not successful until the moment she began to pray for sinners, for the souls in purgatory, or for those in any way afflicted. With this prayer, Gertrude suddenly felt its effectiveness. And this was rather a habitual thing. She remembered especially in this regard a certain evening when she resolved that in every memento that she would make of the souls of the departed she would include the souls of all the faithful departed by reciting the collect *Omnipotens sempiterne Deus, cui numquam sine spe misericordiae* . . . ; and for the memorial that she was accustomed to make for her parents, she would recite the prayer *Deus, qui nos patrem et matrem. . . .* At this Christ showed Himself immensely pleased.[92]

But it was principally during the liturgy and especially at Mass that Gertrude prayed for the dead. Thus, one day close to the feast of the Ascension:

> "At the elevation of the Host, she prayed to the Lord for the souls of all the faithful departed, that He might deign to loose them all from their miseries in view of the celebration of His joyous ascension. Then she saw the Lord reach down into purgatory something like a long rod of gold with as many grapples on it as were the sighs of affection which had been directed to Him for those souls. On each of the grapples some souls were drawn up out of their place of pain into the peaceful meadows of repose. She understood from this that every time common prayer was offered in a spirit of charity for the souls in purgatory, liberation was granted to the greater part of those who, while they lived in the flesh, had devoted themselves to the works of charity." [93]

The Church Militant as Mystical Body and Communion of Saints. All this tells us with sufficient clarity that in the psychology of St. Gertrude the concept of the mystical body of Christ as a union, under Christ Himself, of

[91] 4, 4.
[92] 2, 16, p. 87.
[93] 4, 35, p. 404.

the Church Militant with the angels, the saints, and the souls in purgatory was a living reality. But no less acute in Gertrude is her sense of the Church Militant considered in itself, as mystical body of Christ and communion of saints, with various members, various functions, various needs, in which, from the supernatural point of view and by God's free acceptance, those who plead are in some way united to all the others, from the moment when God accepts their interventions and merits for the benefit of those others; while each individual has precise duties for the benefit of the whole body.

The concept of a Christ who in some way is identified with the faithful themselves, His members, even though they be less perfect or outright sinners, finds strong expression, for example, in that vision in which Gertrude seemed to see the Lord:

> ". . . who, by the form of His own body, was permitting His mystical body, the Church, to be seen; that mystical body of which He has deigned to call Himself and actually be the Spouse and the Head. It appeared, in fact, that on the right half of His body He was clothed with solemn royal garments, whereas on the left He was naked and almost entirely covered by ulcers. Gertrude understood that by the right half was signified all those elect of the Lord in the Church who had been armed in advance by Him with the sweet blessings of special grace, while the left signified all the imperfect who are still in their faults." [94]

The whole vision seeks to inculcate the necessity of every Christian's dealing with great prudence and charity with every other member of Christ, not only the good but sinners as well. Toward the end of the same chapter cited immediately above, there is the observation:

> "If, therefore, the Lord Jesus Christ shows by this revelation that He is identified with the Church in such a way that the good are the right part of His body and the imperfect are the left part, then every Christian ought to attend with the greatest care to how he serves the members of Christ, whether they be the healthy or the infirm." [95]

The reality of the sharing in merits and prayers among the members of the Church Militant was felt very strongly by Gertrude, as the following text demonstrates:

> "Because a certain other person had very devoutly entrusted herself to Gertrude, she, as usual, took up her cause, and as soon as she began to pray she sought to obtain from the Lord that He might allow that same person to share in all that He would deign to do by means of herself, all unworthy, in watchings, in fastings, in prayers, and in other works of piety.
> "The Lord replied to her: 'Certainly I will communicate to her all

the benefits that the condescension of My divinity constantly and gratuitously works in you and will work even till the end.'

"And Gertrude answered: 'The whole of Your holy Church shares in what You deign to work whether in me and by means of me, all unworthy, or by means of Your other elect. Ought that person not, therefore, receive something special from this Your mercy, by the fact that I desire, with special affection, to have her participate in all the benefits which You accord to me?'

"The Lord replied: '. . . even if the whole Church participates in the individual benefits accorded to any one of the faithful, nevertheless he that receives them has the greatest profit from them, and therefore he to whom one desires to communicate them with special affection also receives from them a greater fruit and progress.' " [96]

Hence Gertrude knew the necessity of praying for the whole Church Militant and of satisfying for all the negligences and all the offenses that are done against the Lord. The Lord Himself more than once instructed her in how to achieve this aim, as when He told her to divide the day into three parts:

"From Matins until None render praise and thanksgiving on the part of the whole Church from the depths of your heart for all the benefits which, from the beginning of the world until today, were ever given to men, and especially for that venerable benefit by which each day from the rising of the sun until None, without interruption, I am immolated on the altar as a sacrifice to God the Father for the salvation of men. But men, not appreciating this benefit, give themselves to gluttony and drunkenness, showing themselves utterly ungrateful for My favors. For their deficiencies do you endeavor with affection to offer your gratitude on their behalf. . . . Afterwards, from None until evening, do you every day endeavor to practice good works in union with My most holy intention, in which I did all the works of My humanity, to supply for that universal negligence with which the whole world failed to respond with due appreciation for the benefits which I granted it. . . .

"Afterwards during the evening recall in heartfelt grief the impiousness of men by which not only do they fail to repay Me, as in terms of due service, for the infinite benefits they have received from Me, but worse than that, every day they endeavor to provoke Me to anger with their various kinds of sins. For the sake of their betterment, do you offer Me the pains and the bitterness of My most innocent death." [97]

With this in mind, Gertrude frequently endeavored by her prayers, her good works, and especially by her love to supply for the sins and negligences which are done in the Church.[98]

[96] 3, 76, pp. 268–269.
[97] 4, 14, p. 343.
[98] See, for example, 4, 21, pp. 362–364.

In this context there was in Gertrude a very strong awareness of the fact that the Divine Office recited officially in the Church has a special value as impetration before God, so that, because it is done at the command of the Church as such, whoever recites it officially does so *in persona Ecclesiae*; and God, by reason of this title, accepts those supplications to the benefit of the whole Church.

One day while she was praying for a person who had recommended herself to her prayers so that she might be able worthily to fulfill her obligations in the office of hebdomadarian in the recitation of the psalms before the whole community,

". . . she saw in spirit the Son of God conducting that person before the throne of God, where He Himself prayed to His heavenly Father that He might grant her, for her assistance and for the attaining of all her desires, that intention of fidelity and of love with which He Himself, the Son of God, desired the praise of God the Father and the salvation of the human race.

"Scarcely had the Son so prayed to the Sovereign Father than the person for whom Gertrude prayed suddenly appeared to her adorned with the very garments of Christ Himself. In the same way that the Son of God stands in the presence of the Father placating Him for the Church, so too this person, like Queen Esther, stood in the presence of the Lord God and Father with His Son to pray for the people, that is, for the community. And while thus she fulfilled the obligation of her Psalter, the heavenly Father accepted the individual words of it under a double aspect: as a master who accepts from a bailsman the debts that such a one pays on behalf of the debtors, and again as a master who accepts gratefully from one who is His procurator the monies offered to Him for distribution to His dearest friends. The Lord seemed also to grant to the aforesaid person all that she had desired to obtain by her prayers for her community." [99]

The whole of creation. The concept of the unity even of inferior creation in the great panorama of the kingdom of God, although it has but very little emphasis in the Gertrudian writings, is nonetheless expressed there with sufficient clarity. In the following passage, concerning the events which took place at a celebration of the feast of the Epiphany, we can see something of Gertrude's anxiety to lead all creation back to obedience to its Creator:

"While the Gospel was being read, *Et procidentes adoraverunt eum*, etc., Gertrude, urged on by the example of the most blessed Magi and inflamed in the spirit, prostrated herself in great devotion at the feet of the Lord Jesus, adoring Him on the part of all beings, heavenly, earthly, and infernal. And since she could find nothing that she might offer Him worthily, with anxious desire she began to pass in review the whole world, seeking among all creatures to see if she could not find something worthy to be offered for His unique pleasure.

[99] 3, 82, p. 275.

> "And while she was thus excited and breathless, hastening about in her search in the thirst of burning desire, she came upon some objects which every creature ought rightly despise because they did nothing for the praise and glory of the Savior. But Gertrude seized upon them avidly and endeavored to lead them to render that same glory and praise which it is the duty of every creature to give. Thus she drew into her heart by her burning desire all the pains, fears, sorrows, and anxieties that ever any creature has suffered not for the praise of the Creator, but through the depravities of their own weakness. And she offered them to the Lord as myrrh of finest quality.
>
> "Then she drew into herself all the simulated sanctity and devotion of all the hypocrites, pharisees, heretics, and the like. And this too she likewise offered to the Lord in place of the sacrifice of the most fragrant incense.
>
> "In the third place she endeavored to draw into her heart all the human affections and false and impure love of all creatures. And this she offered to the Lord as precious gold. And all these things together, completely purified of every blemish and wonderfully ennobled in her heart by the ardor of her loving desire like gold purified in the crucible, she seemed to present to the Lord." [100]

That this restlessness of Gertrude to lead all creatures back to the praise and glory of the Lord extended even to inferior creation can be seen also in the sixth of her *Exercises*, the one in which the soul is aroused to praise the Lord and to render thanks to Him. In this, among other things, Gertrude admonishes the reader:

> "As if enraptured beyond yourself before the immensity of the riches and of the blessedness of your Lord, by the inestimable beauty of His praise, by the glory of His saints, and by the sweet splendor of His glorious countenance, invite all creatures to praise God with the hymn *Benedicite omnia opera Domini Domino*." [101]

Gertrude's confidante, pointing out with insistence her deep sense of compassionate charity for all the suffering, adds that she extended this sentiment even to all the inferior creatures:

> "She had a great sense of pity not only for mankind but for all creatures — to such a degree that if she saw any sort of creature, bird or sheep or whatever, suffering any pangs of hunger or thirst or cold, suddenly, from her inmost heart she was filled with compassion for the handiwork of her Lord and, with devotion, she endeavored to offer to the eternal praise of the Lord that trouble of the irrational creature, in union with that dignity by which every creature is supremely perfected and ennobled in Him, desiring at the same time that the Lord, taking pity on His creature, might deign to alleviate its needs." [102]

[100] 4, 6, pp. 316–317.
[101] *Exercitia* 6, p. 684.
[102] 1, 8, p. 26.

How easily the prayer of Gertrude took on that general cosmic sense embracing heaven and earth is shown, for example, by such a text as the following, concerning her conduct at Mass:

> "In the way that was her custom, at the first *Agnus Dei* she prayed for the whole Church, that the Lord might guide it in all things. At the second *Agnus Dei* she begged that the Lord might mercifully loose the souls of all the faithful departed from their pains. At the third *Agnus Dei* she desired that the Lord might augment the merits of all the saints and all the elect who already reign with Him in heaven." [103]

The Mass

Authors of the history of spirituality unanimously point out the importance of the Eucharist in the spirituality of St. Gertrude, and they rightly explain this fact by referring to the great current of Eucharistic piety which developed in the thirteenth century and culminated in the institution of the liturgical feast of *Corpus Domini*, or *Corpus Christi*. Indeed, it is impossible not to be struck by the eminent position which the Eucharist occupies in the spiritual life of Gertrude. It should be enough only to remember her very explicit statement in which, after nine years since her having entered upon the mystical life, she declared that she did not recall that her great and frequent graces of union had ever been accorded her except on days on which she received Communion.[104] This matter is confirmed by her biographer when she speaks of the extraordinary desire that Gertrude always had of receiving Communion and of that confidence that induced her to receive it.[105] We know also the importance that the question of preparation for Communion held for her.[106] No less noteworthy is the psychological importance that the moment of the elevation of the Host at Mass had for Gertrude.[107]

We are concerned with pointing out first of all that this Eucharistic piety of Gertrude remains strongly centered on the Mass; and in the second place, that the Mass itself, which for our saint is the sun which illumines her spiritual life, is known and lived by her as the moment in which the real presence of Christ, under the Eucharistic species, is brought about. Gertrude's explicit affirmation that her greatest preparation for Communion is her habitual assistance at Mass is characteristic. One day when she was prevented from assisting at Mass, she complained to the Lord:

> "Behold, my most Beloved, I cannot attribute to Your foreordination the fact that today I am not able to assist at Mass. And how can I now

---

[103] 4, 39, p. 414. See also 4, 13, p. 399; 4, 55, pp. 471–472.

[104] 2, 2, p. 62.

[105] 1, 10, pp. 29–30.

[106] See, for example, 3, 18.

[107] See, for example, 3, 15, p. 141; 3, 18, p. 153; 3, 30, p. 190.

prepare myself to receive Your most sacred Body and Blood when, as it seems to me, my best preparation is always habitual assistance at Mass?" [108]

With this in mind, the intimate union in Gertrude's psychology between Communion and Mass is evident. The Mass itself, then, is for her, first of all, the sacrifice in which Christ is inexpressibly immolated on the altar to the Father by the ministry of the priest for His Church. She considers in the Mass its value as thanksgiving, as expiation, as propitiation, and as vicarious substitution. Once, on the feast of the Assumption, at the elevation of the Host, Gertrude heard the Lord say: "I come to offer Myself in sacrifice to God the Father for My members." [109]

On another occasion, but again at the moment of the elevation,

". . . while she was offering to the Father the same sacrosanct Host in worthy expiation for all sins and supply for all negligences, she understood that her soul was presented before the divine Majesty as an object of that divine good pleasure, of which the object was Christ Jesus, splendor and image of the eternal glory, Lamb of God without blemish, who at the very same moment had offered Himself on the altar for the universal salvation of mankind. Therefore God the Father, through the most innocent humanity of Jesus Christ, regarded Gertrude as pure and unspotted by any sin, and by Christ's divinity He saw her enriched and adorned with every virtue that the same glorious divinity produced in Jesus in His most holy humanity. . . .

"Then God gave her to understand that every time one assists at Mass with devotion, pondering on God who offers Himself there in the Sacrament for the common salvation of the universe, he is truly considered by God the Father according to the good pleasure that He has in the sacred Host that is offered to Him." [110]

In the same spirit, in the seventh exercise, Gertrude praises the goodness, mercy, and liberality of God for His great gift of the Eucharistic sacrifice:

"O goodness, O mercy, O sweet liberality of God, You keep hidden in Your treasury a marvelous gift which makes the heavens stand in amazement and excites the admiration of all the earth, nor is there anything its equal to be found through the ages. Every day on the altar You offer for me to God the Father such a sacrifice, such a perfumed holocaust as surpasses every merit and can truly satisfy for all my debts. To the Father You present the Son in whom He takes all His pleasure, to offer reparation to Him and to reconcile me to Him, O, by this mystery that is able to make up in the most complete way possible for all my imperfections and to make amends for all my deficiencies, do You renew my life!" [111]

---

[108] 3, 8, p. 126.
[109] 3, 16, p. 146.

[110] 3, 18, p. 153.
[111] *Exercitia* 7, p. 714.

4. Mystical Life and Liturgical Life in Gertrude

Mystical life: its principal aspect in the spirituality of St. Gertrude

St. Gertrude is first and foremost a mystic. When she began the drafting of her writings, nine years had already passed since she had begun to receive her more remarkable mystical graces. In the years that followed her writing of the second book of the *Legatus*, she received those graces uninterruptedly until her death. The reader who is somewhat versed in mystical literature has no difficulty in recognizing in the Gertrudian writings many graces of the kind that we today would refer to as contemplation properly so called.

He would recognize them at least in the sense that he will catch a glimpse of them. For Gertrude almost never makes more than an elementary psychological description of these states. Still less is she concerned with distinguishing degrees and gradations or with explaining them from a theological point of view, even in a summary way. Here there is nothing comparable to the psychological introspections and to the analyses so acute in St. Teresa of Avila.

In accord with the whole earlier tradition, particularly of the West,[112] Gertrude hardly even hints at the subjective importance of the properly contemplative and mystical action and state in regard to her experiences. On the contrary, she is concerned entirely with praising God for them and with reporting about those inexpressible graces what has been able in some way to be reflected in her imagination and in her discursive intellect, describing the persons, the objects, the scenes, the images which have been presented to her in her "visions" and to draw from them admonitions and directives for living that will be of profit to others.

But let us now recall what we said at the beginning of this chapter in regard to the value which Gertrude attached to her imaginal visions and to the interpretations which she proposed for them. She knew very well that that which she relates of the "visions" that she describes, as well as the notions that she draws from them, was not but the least and most inferior part of the graces which she received, that part which she could in some way communicate to others. She says of the things that she can communicate that they can serve only as the first rudiments and allurements to attract her readers in some way and lead them to take the first steps in view of arriving one day at the experiencing of the inexpressible tastes of the true manna which transcends every human representation. Remember that Gertrude wrote these things

> ". . . so that those who will read them may take delight in the sweetness of Your mercy and, thus attracted, they may have greater experiences of Your intimacy. Students learn the alphabet first, but finally

[112] See, for example, *Dictionnaire de spiritualité*, Vol. 2 (1953), under the article "Contemplation," cols. 1929 ff.

arrive even at the study of logic; and in this same way, may they, through the portrayal of these images, be led to taste in themselves that hidden manna which cannot be accurately described through any combination of corporeal images and which becomes the sole desire of him who has once tasted of it." [113]

The hidden manna, therefore, is something far beyond Gertrude's imaginal descriptions and discursive concepts.

From the short but quite frequent allusions made in the Gertrudian writings, we understand clearly enough that it is a question of mystical graces properly so called and, in particular, of contemplation properly so called, with the characteristics common to them which all tradition has recognized and with the nuances proper to the Cistercian tradition to which Gertrude belongs. They are those moments which Gertrude describes with the usual remarks about an extraordinary awareness of the presence of God; of union with Him experientially perceived, characterized by its sudden bursting through upon her soul and by its inexpressibility — for it is beyond images and discursive concepts — and hence by its incomprehensibility except to one who has likewise had experience of it.

Mystical graces without psychological tensions or conflicts with the liturgical life

We are especially interested in knowing what was the relationship in Gertrude between this mystical life and her liturgical life. Now, we are verifying in the case of our saint not only the actuality of so many and such great mystical graces in a person whose spirituality was at the same time centered in the liturgy, but we see, moreover, that these higher mystical graces and the most sublime contemplation properly so called are actualized in large measure right in the midst of the communitarian liturgical action or in strict connection with it. And this takes place without the mystical invasion being in any way harmful to her public communitarian participation in the liturgical action and without her public and communitarian participation in the liturgy being an impediment to the mystical invasion. On the contrary, in fact, they mutually sustain and nourish each other.

The mystical invasion takes place in Gertrude during processions, during the Mass, during the choral recitation of the canonical hours, during a sermon in chapel, during the liturgical offices that the community performs in the chapter hall; nor does it make any difference whether someone is singing or reciting, or whether she herself is singing or reciting, or whether it it is one of the intervals of silence which are found interspersed among these actions. Or it may even take place before or after the liturgical action, possibly continuing what had already begun during the liturgical action, or beginning before the liturgical action and continuing during it. And the

[113] 2, 24, p. 113.

texts betray no kind of psychological tension or conflict in Gertrude between the mystical invasion and her active participation in the liturgy.

To be perfectly precise about it, such a tension is evidenced in the Gertrudian writings only one time, insofar as I can discover, when one day in choir all of a sudden the mystical presence of God seized upon her to such an extent that she could no longer follow with any exactitude the ritual movements of the community. But the fact is pointed out with the express statement that it was a unique occurrence, having happened only once. It happened on Quinquagesima Sunday, on which the Mass began with the words *Esto mihi*; and the occurrence is recounted in the *Legatus* 4, 15, as follows:

> "In the Mass, when Gertrude, by means of the Introit, called upon the Lord, the Lord applied those words of the Introit to Himself, as if those words might seem to pertain specifically to Him because of the offenses which He was receiving in those days.[114] And He said to Gertrude: 'You, O my beloved, would be My protectress, proposing that if you were able to do it, you would protect Me from the offenses which are committed against me especially in these days. Hunted down by the others and seeking a place to rest, I find refuge in you.'

> "Then Gertrude, constraining Him with all her powers, endeavored to draw Him into her intimate confidence. And behold, suddenly she found herself so strongly withdrawn from her bodily senses and interiorly united to God that she could no longer conform herself to the movements of the community when it sat or when it stood. Observed by one of the sisters, she realized that she had not been doing what the others did. And she prayed to the Lord to be able, by His help, to control her body so that no singularity would be noticed. The Lord replied to her: 'Leave your affection with Me, that love of yours, so that it may take your place at my side, and then you may take care to have control of your body.' "

And Gertrude responded:

> " 'O most beloved God, even if a power of mine can take my place, I desire rather that the control of my body be entrusted to my reason and that I, with full liberty, be able to occupy myself totally with You.' From that moment she obtained the gift that even while united internally to God in the highest degree, she was never prevented from carrying out with exactness the things that she had to do externally." [115]

---

[114] As is clear elsewhere in the same chapter 15, the offenses alluded to were those occasioned by the *Mardi gras* or *Carnevale*. The text of the Introit antiphon of the Quinquagesima Mass was: *Esto mihi in Deum protectorem, et in locum refugii, ut salvum me facias: quoniam firmamentum meum, et refugium meum es tu: et propter nomen tuum*

dux mihi eris, et enutries me.

[115] 4, 15, pp. 349–350. The final phrase in Latin is: *Quod ex tunc dono accepit quod nunquam sic fuit Deo unita interius, quin recto moderamine exterius facienda sequeretur.* Certainly our translation captures the thought that is intended to be conveyed by this somewhat ambiguous phraseology. Certainly it was not

Insofar as I can discover, there is no other allusion in the Gertrudian writings to such impediments during the liturgical action, neither prior to the Sunday in question nor afterwards.

Principal mystical graces received by Gertrude in the liturgical action itself or in connection with it

In Gertrude, nonetheless, similar graces of union and contemplation given her during the communitarian liturgical action were frequent and even of the highest kind ever since the beginning of her entry into the mystical life. As we know, in Gertrude, in accord with the very distinctly Cistercian tradition inaugurated by St. Bernard, these graces are expressed most frequently in the form of the mystical betrothal derived from the Canticle of Canticles, and with such themes as the amorous glance, the *amplexus*, the *osculum*, and the like.[116] How frequently similar graces came to Gertrude, with greater or lesser intensity and properly during the liturgical action, can be seen from the following, her own general declaration:

> " 'I know,' she said, addressing herself to the Lord, 'that Your unsearchable omnipotence, according to Your abundant mercy, is accustomed to moderate the glance, the *amplexus*, the *osculum*, and the other demonstrations of love quite opportunely in accord with the place, the time, and the persons. And I have frequently experienced — for which I give thanks to You in the union of the mutual love of the ever venerable Trinity — the gratuitous gift of Your most sweet *osculum*; to such an extent that sometimes while I sat and inwardly attended You by reciting the canonical hours or the vigils for the dead, frequently in the course of a single psalm ten times or even more You impressed Your *praedulce osculum* upon my lips, that *osculum* which surpasses all perfumes and honey; and how frequently have I observed Your loving glance toward me, and I have felt Your most intimate *amplexus* in my soul.' "[117]

Nor can we believe that the most profound species of that union in the form of the glance, etc., would not be realized in Gertrude during the liturgical action itself and while she actively participated therein along with the

---

intended to say that from that moment on Gertrude did not have such great favors as before, like internal union with God, but only lesser gifts which left her the free control of her external actions. Indeed, the occurrence here narrated is the same as that narrated in 2, 8 and 2, 14. But, after the occurrences alluded to in 2, 8 or in 2, 14 Gertrude certainly received graces just as great. See, for example, 2, 16 (cf. 2, 23, p. 108); 2, 21; 2, 22; 4, 25; 5, 25. The confidante of Gertrude simply means to say, therefore, that the graces of

union which Gertrude received after that *Esto mihi* Sunday, even though they were not lesser, they nevertheless did not any longer prevent her from correctly performing the necessary external movements, as she had been prevented from doing on that particular Sunday.

[116] See, for example, allusions in J. Déchanet, "*La contemplation au XII*e *siècle*," in *Dictionnaire de spiritualité*, Vol. 2 (1953), under the article "*Contemplation*," col. 1954.

[117] 2, 21, p. 101–102.

other nuns. The same chapter 21 of the second book gives, among else, a most clear example of it. Once during Lent:

"On the Second Sunday, before Mass while the procession was beginning and the responsory *Vidi Dominum facie ad faciem, etc.*, was being sung, my soul was illuminated by an incomprehensible splendor of divine light that manifested itself. And there appeared to me, as it were, a face which pressed itself to my face: 'not shaped, but shaping,' as Bernard says, 'not dazzling the eyes of the body, but making joyful the countenance of the heart; pleasing, not by appearance, but by the gift of love.' [118] In this vision sweet as honey, while Your eyes, like rays of the sun, seemed to press directly upon my eyes, in what way Your gentle sweetness penetrated not only my soul but my heart as well and all my members, is known to You alone; and as long as I shall live, I will serve You with dedication, in gratitude for it. . . .

"I felt that from Your divine eyes a light incomprehensible and sweet entered into my eyes and, penetrating my whole being, brought about in all my members a strength wonderful beyond compare. At first it emptied out, so to speak, all the marrow of my bones; then it annihilated those same bones together with their flesh, to such a degree that my whole substance had no feeling of existence other than that divine splendor, which, frolicking in itself, gave my soul an incomprehensible joy and serenity.

"But what more shall I say of this most sweet vision? To tell the truth, it seems to me that the eloquence of all tongues speaking to me for a whole lifetime would never have persuaded me of the possibility of such a remarkable way of seeing You, not even in the heavenly glory, if Your condescension, my God, the only salvation of my soul, had not persuaded me of it by experience. I am glad, however, to add that if in divine matters it were to happen as in human — but the strength of Your eye immensely surpasses that which I myself see in this vision — truly, that soul to which such a vision is conceded, be it only for a moment, would not be able to remain in its body if the divine strength did not hold it there.' " [119]

Gertrude adds that never again up to the time of her writing this was it granted her to experience the divine strength as she had experienced it in that most wonderful glance of love which God cast upon her.

But prior to this, Gertrude had already received a very similar grace once on the eve of Christmas.

"O unapproachable heights of wonderful power! O utmost depths of unsearchable wisdom! O immeasurable bounty of coveted charity! . . . Even to me in the exile of my pilgrimage is granted the permission and the joy of reporting, in the measure of my small capacity, on the firstfruits of those most joyful delights and sweetest gentleness in which my

[118] St. Bernard, *In Cant.* 31, especially no.6.   [119] 2, 21, pp. 100 ff.

soul, united to God, becomes one only spirit with Him. The overflow-ing of this happiness does in fact so diffuse itself externally that it has granted even to me, miserable dust that I am, the boldness of skimming off some little drop of it in the following manner.

"On that most sacred night, when, by the sweet dew of the divinity, for the sake of the whole world the heavens dropped down as it were honey, my soul, like a fleece bedewed on the threshing-floor of charity, endeavored by its meditation to make itself present in that supercelestial region where the Virgin gave birth, like a ray of light, to her Son, true God and true man, and to make itself useful there by its exercise of de-votion. As if by an instantaneous miracle I understood that He was held out to my soul, and it received, as if in its own heart, a tender new-born babe, in which, certainly, was hidden the highest and surely the best of gifts.

"While my soul held Him within itself, it suddenly appeared to be changed entirely into the same color as He was — if, indeed, one can call that a color which cannot be compared to anything visible. Then my soul had an inexpressible knowledge of those most sweet words: 'God will be all in all' (1 Cor. 15:28), even while knowing that it must contain its delight in the depths of its heart, and it was gladdened be-cause it did not lack the agreeable presence of its Spouse with His most joyful caresses.

"In this state my soul drank with insatiable avidity the following words, as if they were a goblet of honey offered me by the Lord: 'As I in My divinity am the image of the substance of My Father, so you will be in your human nature the image of My substance, because you will receive in your deified soul the emanations of my divinity as the air re-ceives the rays of the sun; and thus penetrated right to the marrow by this unitive force, you will be made capable of an even more familiar union with Me.'"[120]

At the end of the second book of *Legatus*,[121] Gertrude explicitly counts this grace among the greater ones which she had until that time received, together with that of the *Esto mihi* Sunday, and another received on one of the Sundays after Pentecost. Speaking of all these together, she says:

"You invited me to such a union with Yourself that I marveled more than at a miracle, in the fact that, after those moments, I was able once more to live as man among men."

In the two preceding descriptions of graces of mystical union during the liturgical action, let the following characteristics, among others, be noted in regard to these occurrences: the suddenness with which the grace of the

[120] 2, 6, pp. 71–72. See St. Teresa, *The Castle* 6, 10, 2 and 5.

[121] 2, 23, pp. 108–109. Another general for-mula of a mystical immersion in God by the light of the Holy Spirit which occurred during the Mass of the First Sunday of Lent while Gertrude was listening to the reading of the Epistle is to be found in 4, 17, p. 357. See also 4, 37, p. 414.

mystical union properly so called bursts in upon Gertrude; the fact that the sudden passage to contemplation properly so called is immediately preceded by meditation; the passage from Christ to God, from the humanity of Christ to the divinity; Christ always appears there as Mediator; the characteristic of the union's penetrating the foundation of the substance of the soul so much so that it is referred to in expressions of immersion and transformation of Gertrude's substance in the divine light; the characteristic of extreme sweetness; that of the foretaste of the vision and union of heaven; the affirmation that without special divine protection, anyone who receives such graces would die.[122]

In Gertrude, moreover, on at least two occasions, the grace of mystical union during the liturgical action itself takes the form and the degree of a stabbing and transverberating pang of love. The first occasion was in 1287 or 1288 A.D. on Gaudete Sunday in Advent, during Mass, when, before Communion she felt herself induced to ask the Lord that He might transfix her heart with a dart of love. Having received Communion, she saw, as it were, a ray of the sun leave the heart of Christ, like an arrow, from an image of the crucifixion depicted in her missal, and come toward her. Several times it approached and then drew back, only to approach again; and finally it wounded Gertrude: "And this continuing for some time, it tenderly excited my love."

She felt the full effect of it on the following Wednesday, an Ember Day in Advent, when, during a ceremony after the Mass, in connection with the Gospel reading *Missus est* of that day, the faithful venerated the Annunciation and the Incarnation.

> "And then You made Yourself present like the sudden impressing of a wound upon my heart with these words: 'Now let the welling up of all affections unite as one; that is, let all your pleasure, hope, joy, sorrow, fear, and all your other feelings settle in my heart.'"[123]

But much more characteristic, efficacious, and important in the life of Gertrude was the second transverberation of love. It is worth the trouble of quoting the passage in its entirety:

> "A certain friar, preaching in the chapel, said among else: 'Love is like a golden dart, and whoever strikes something with it acquires

---

[122] It is always difficult and frequently futile to try to discover in the mystical graces experienced by various other saints the individual degrees through which God caused St. Teresa to pass and which she describes according to her own experiences. First of all, it remains to be demonstrated that the stages through which God caused St. Teresa to pass represent the only scheme possible. Then there is the difficulty that the other saints mostly do not describe their own states with psychological precision. Nevertheless, in regard to these graces of St. Gertrude, it is possible to discern what St. Teresa describes in the sixth mansion of the *Castle* in regard to the union called "intense" and that which she calls "spiritual espousals." See the résumé of St. Teresa's treatment of the graces of union in F. Cayré, *Manual of Patrology*, Vol. 2, pp. 819 ff.

[123] 2, 5, pp. 68–69.

as it were a proprietary right over what is struck. He is foolish indeed, therefore, who makes earthly things the object of his love while neglecting the things of heaven.'

"Being much inflamed by these words, Gertrude said to the Lord: 'Would that I might have this dart. Without delay I would want to transfix You with it, O delight of my soul, so as to be able to keep You always.' While she was saying this, she saw the Lord turn to her holding a golden dart; and He said to her: 'You would be willing to wound Me if you had the golden dart; and since I have it here, I wish to transfix you in such a way that you will never again be as you were before.'

"Now that dart seemed to be bent into three points, at the front, in the middle, and at the end. This was intended to signify the triple force which love impresses on the soul it wounds. When the first point pierces the soul it wounds it in such a way that, like an illness, it renders completely tasteless all transitory things, so much so that from then on one can no longer take delight or consolation in any of them. The second point, piercing the soul, wracks it as with a fever. And just as a person with a fever, because of the grievousness of his affliction, looks with great impatience for a medicinal remedy, so too the soul, with a yearning that goes beyond mere impatience, clings to God with a burning desire, because it seems to the soul that it will be utterly impossible without Him even to draw a breath. The third point, finally, in piercing the soul leads it to joys so inestimable that they cannot be described by any sort of comparison, except that with these joys it is almost as if they separate the soul from the body and happily engulf that soul in the torrents of the divinity, which streams are sweet as nectar." [124]

This occurrence took place not very long before the death of Gertrude. She had already had a very strong desire for death, and by this occurrence that desire was greatly augmented in her. [125] In the life of St. Teresa of Avila, her transverberation as well as the description and explanation which she herself gives, in this regard, of the mystical phenomenon of the piercing of love, [126] is too well known to require our laying any great stress upon it.

[124] 5, 25, pp. 581–582.
[125] See, for example, 5, 23 ff; 1, 10, pp. 30–31.
[126] The essentials of the relationship as Teresa describes it in her *Life* are as follows: "I felt that I was dying from my desire to see God. He was my life, and I knew not how to find Him in any other way except through death. The transports of this love . . . were such, however, that I no longer knew what to do. There was nothing any more that could satisfy me; I was beside myself and truly it seemed to me that my soul had been wrenched from my body. . . . The transports of which I am speaking . . . are totally different from those which proceed from sensible devo-

tion. . . . The soul aches because of the absence of God; but it is not that absence which brings about another pain, which is caused by a certain dart which from time to time penetrates the very heart and the vital organs, so that though one still lives, he is rendered incapable of doing or of willing anything.

"While in such a state, the soul knows well that it desires nothing else but God, and it seems to the soul that the arrow by which it is wounded is coated with the juice of an herb that prompts it to hate itself and to love the Lord with such a love as would be willing even to sacrifice its life. The way by which God makes such wounds in the soul is inexpressible and cannot be explained. Those

St. Teresa, in the gradation which she makes, drawing upon her own personal experiences, among the various degrees of mystical union and contemplation, places that of the piercing of love immediately before the highest degree, which is spiritual marriage. But it is not necessary that this be properly the precise degree that is indicated.

In Gertrude there is also realized the mystical phenomenon called exchange of hearts,[127] which consists essentially in a profound transformation of the will and of the affections brought about in a supernatural manner by God, by which, from time to time, this will and these affections are united to the will of God to such an extent that the person so favored, in a degree of superior perfection, does not will and does not love anything else except that which God loves and wills. It is called exchange of hearts because sometimes this grace is accompanied by an intellectual or imaginal vision in which it is symbolized by an exchange of hearts between Christ and the mystic. Gertrude, writing the second book the *Legatus* in 1289, attested that she had at various times received this grace:

> "Moreover, among so many graces, You have granted me the inestimable familiarity of Your friendship, giving me in various ways and in a superabundance of joy the most noble ark of divinity, Your deified Heart. Sometimes You gave it to me generously, and sometimes, as a most precious sign of our mutual familiarity, You exchanged it with mine. Thus, in Your Heart, You manifested to me so many intimate aspects of Your secret judgments and of Your joys, and have

wounds produce such a torment that though one still lives, it is as if the soul were drawn outside oneself; but at the same time it is all so sweet that there is no pleasure on earth that can compare with it. And for this reason, as I have said, the soul would like to die from the force of such a pain. . . .

"How many times, when I find myself in this state, does there come to mind the passage in David: *Quemadmodum desiderat cervus ad fontes aquarum!* Then it seems to me that this short verse is realized literally in me. The soul, not knowing what else to do, goes in search of some remedy, and when that favor is not accompanied by great violence, it seems that the torment can be somewhat alleviated by means of some penances. . . . But that first torment is too great. . . . It has no remedy here. The medicines of this earth are too base, and they are not able to heal a wound that is so sublime. To be able to alleviate it a little and to make it a little more bearable, there is nothing to do but to seek the remedy in God Himself. But the soul sees no remedy at all except death; and it is by death alone that it expects the full enjoyment of its only

Good. . . .

"While I was in this state, it pleased God to favor me from time to time with the following visions. I saw an angel near to me, at my left side, an angel in bodily form. . . . That cherub, then, held in his hand a long golden arrow, the point of which was iron; and it seemed to be tipped with fire. It seemed to me that he stabbed me with it several times in the heart, driving it right into my vital organs, which were then torn out of me when he withdrew the arrow, leaving me enveloped in a furnace of love. The agony of that wound was so vivid that it caused me to emit those groans of which I have spoken more above; but it was at the same time of so great a sweetness as to keep me from wanting it to end and to seek for some other satisfaction outside of God. . . . Between the soul and God there passes then a sweetness that is idyllic" (*Vita* 29, 8 ff. For a résumé of the same, see the *Castle* 6, 2, 2).

[127] See, for example, *Dictionnaire de spiritualité*, Vol. 2 (1953), under the article "*Coeurs (échange de)*," cols. 1046 ff.

so frequently liquefied my soul with Your most friendly caressees that if I had not known the depths of the superabundance of Your goodness, I would not have been able to believe at all that You had ever shown such benevolent tenderness even, among all creatures, to Your most Blessed Mother who reigns with You in heaven." [128]

From the Gertrudian writings, or so it seems to me, further particulars in regard to the extraordinary graces to which Gertrude alludes in the passage above are not to be extracted.

In the mystical graces referred to above — exchange of hearts, piercing of love, God all in all, *vidi Dominum facie ad faciem* — is that also included which the spiritual authors call transforming union, the same which St. Teresa calls spiritual marriage? Even if such data as we have are not perfectly clear, still, it seems undeniable. Even from the beginning of her mystical life, the expressions in Gertrude in which her relations with Christ are given in a matrimonial terminology are most numerous. But is it always properly a question of what St. Teresa later called spiritual marriage?

In the Gertrudian writings, it is true, the mystical graces conceded to St. Gertrude have numerous features which St. Teresa, for her part, regards as characteristics of that superior state. Thus, in the first place, the general idea of the soul's having become but a single unit with God, one only spirit with Him, in the sense of a most perfect conformity to His will.[129] It is primarily and precisely in reference to this feature that the above-mentioned graces are related by Gertrude. The same feature is strongly emphasized by her biographer in the first book of the *Legatus*. Once therein she speaks of this matter as of a future grace which God would certainly accord to Gertrude, as was revealed, so she says, to a certain person:

"She will arrive, moreover, at such a union with God that her eyes will see only that which the Lord will deign to see by means of them, and her mouth will utter only that which the Lord will deign to speak by means of it, and likewise with all the rest. When or in what way the Lord will bring it about, He alone knows, and those to whom it is happily granted to experience it. They do not know it, not even those who have recognized most profoundly in Gertrude the gift of God." [130]

The features mentioned, to wit, that Gertrude will not see, will not speak, etc., anything except that which God will want to see, to speak, etc., are characteristics of the state of supreme union.

Another time, in regard to an inquiry of St. Mechtild about St. Gertrude herself and the answer given by the Lord, the perfect conformity of will between Gertrude and Christ is mentioned as already having been accomplished:

[128] 2, 23, p. 107.
[129] See St. Teresa, *Castle* 7, 2, nos. 3–5.
[130] 1, 16, p. 51.

"And when Mechtild asked . . . the reason why at every moment Gertrude was in a hurry to finish whatever it came into her mind to do, so much so that, to her own knowledge, she was constantly either praying, writing, reading, instructing her neighbor, or counseling and consoling her, the Lord answered: 'I have united My Heart with such bounty and so inseparably to her soul that she has become but a single spirit with Me; in everything and about everything she is in harmony with My will, just as her own members are in harmony with her body, or just as when she thinks to do something, her hand, in consequence thereof, suddenly moves to do it, and when she thinks to look at anything, her eyes suddenly obey and open to it.

"So too Gertrude is prompted, by My grace, to do at every moment what at that moment is My will. I have chosen to dwell in her in such a way that her will, and hence the actions of her good will, have become, as it were, the right hand of My Heart, by means of which I do that which I will. For Me, her intelligence is like an eye because it devotes itself to understanding what is pleasing to Me. The driving force of her spirit is for Me like a tongue because under the impulse of that spirit, it speaks what I desire to speak. Her discretion is for Me like a sense of smell, so that I incline the ears of My mercy to that to which she is inclined by her compassionate pity. And her intention is for Me like feet, because she intends what it suits Me to follow. Thus, by the driving force of My spirit, it is necessary that she be always in a hurry, so that having finished one thing she will be ready to do another according to My intentions.' "[131]

What Christ had to say about Gertrude is repeated in much the same way by other persons:

"Never will you be able to find Me on earth with greater delight than in the Sacrament of the altar; and after that, in the heart and in the soul of this one who loves Me, in whom, miraculously, I have made all the love of My divine Heart converge. . . . I am all hers; with all delight do I give Myself to her embrace. Divine love has united Me inseparably to her, just as fire fuses gold and silver together and makes electrum."[132]

Another sign of the supreme degree of union is, according to St. Teresa, the ardent searching for the glory of God alone in all that one desires or does, with tranquil indifference not only to the fact of having or of not having divine pleasure and consolations, but even to that of continuing to live or to die, while before the desire for death, as a means of going immediately to the joy of the Lord, was most ardent.[133] This feature too is pointed out as being present in a high degree in Gertrude by her biographer:

---

[131] 1, 16, pp. 50–51.

[132] 1, 4, pp. 15–16. See, for example, in St. Teresa the comparison of the two candles which unite their flame: *Castle* 7, 2, no. 4. In the *Legatus* 4, 32, it says that Gertrude was received by the Lord "as a soul perfected in the spiritual state."

[133] See St. Teresa, *Castle* 7, nos. 2–3, 6, and 8.

> "If sometimes the Lord withdrew from her the graces to which she was accustomed, not even this could distress her. Indeed, it was almost a matter of indifference to her whether she had them or not, except that in her trials hope made her strong, because she knew with certitude that everything worked to her benefit, whether matters external or matters internal. . . . Because of her forementioned trust, she frequently desired to die, but even this in union with the divine will, because at any given moment it was a matter of indifference to her whether she lived or died. By death she hoped to gain beatitude, and by life an increase of praising God." [134]

Another distinctive feature of the supreme degree of union and one which again is found in Gertrude is the most burning zeal for souls, the perfect union of Martha and Mary in a single person [135] insofar as one's proper state permits it.

Let us see again the graces of contemplation of the Most Blessed Trinity conceded to Gertrude, considering them as part and parcel of the highest degrees of the mystical life.

In the Gertrudian writings there are various allusions to the highest graces of mystical contemplation of the Most Blessed Trinity which were given to Gertrude on various occasions during the liturgical action. But her confidante who relates these experiences, doing her best to assure us that Gertrude really had these graces, even notes with insistence that such graces, more than all the others, are highly indescribable and that Gertrude herself was unable to express more than the smallest part of those realities which it had been given her to contemplate. Thus in one passage, which we have already related above in a different context:

> "On the feast of All Saints she knew in spirit the mysteries in regard to the glory of the ever-venerable Trinity, and how the blessed and glorious Trinity, in Itself without beginning and without end, overflowing with every sweetness, joy, and beatitude, imparts to all the saints joy, glory, and eternal happiness. But, prevented by human frailty, that which she saw so clearly in the mirror of divine light she was utterly unable to explain to the range of human understanding, except for the few following things, which she was able to explain, only poorly and in disconnected fashion, by means of comparisons." [136]

The same confidante of Gertrude, at the end of a chapter on the graces received by the saint on various occasions on the feast of the "resplendent and ever-placid Trinity," adds:

[134] I, 10, pp. 29–30.

[135] St. Teresa, *Castle* 7, 4, no. 12ff. For St. Gertrude see for example 1, 11, pp. 31–33: she wants to receive the gifts of God in order to communicate them to others, herself being but the channel of communication; she is free of vainglory; 1, 5, pp. 18–19: anxiety to communicate to others the gifts received from God; otherwise she considers them as having been cast into a dung-heap; she cannot believe that the gifts received from God are really for herself, and regards them as received for the sake of others. See also 1, 1, pp. 8–9; 1, 7, p. 3; 2, 5, pp. 70–71; 2, 24, p. 113.

[136] 5, 55, p. 471.

"As for the graces and consolations which Gertrude, on this eminent feast so dear to her in a special way, received from the divine munificence after those related above or even earlier, lacking the words which could express such things to the range of human intelligence, even for these as for others known only to God, may there be praise and thanksgiving unto Him, as is especially sung in the liturgy of this very day." [137]

Another most notable mystical grace of union together with contemplation of the Trinity was given to Gertrude one time while the liturgical action was taking place in the church, but at which she, being ill in bed, was unable to assist in body, even though she was united there in heart. On this occasion, as she herself recounts, by means of a special grace of conformity to Christ, she received a most profound conformity to the Trinity by way of a seal and a fire in her soul which, having cauterized it of its human defects, reestablished in it, according to the teaching of St. Bernard, its ancient likeness unto God which had been lost through the sin of Adam.[138]

Even if the documents do not allow us to determine with precision the phases of the development of the various degrees of the mystical life of Gertrude up to that supreme degree of spiritual marriage, it seems, nevertheless, impossible to doubt that this supreme degree had been broadly achieved by the saint.

Gertrude offers us also noteworthy instances of mystical graces that not only were not brief but which actually lasted for days or even for years with an intensity more or less great. Already at the beginning of her entry into the

---

[137] 4, 41, p. 418.

[138] "When the time for the procession was drawing near, after having received the vivifying nutriment, I pondered on the Lord within me. I knew that my soul really became as soft as wax before the fire, and it remained pressed to the bosom of the Lord as if to receive a seal. And suddenly it seemed to expand itself all around Him and even to penetrate to the interior of that Sanctuary where the fullness of the divinity dwells corporeally, and thus to be stamped with the character of the resplendent and ever-placid Trinity" (2, 7, p. 73). Gertrude concludes this narration by exalting the omnipotence of the divine love, which is like a devouring fire, which operates first in secret but afterwards erupts externally, dries up human imperfections, makes the hardness of the will yield, and destroys every wickedness in the soul until it makes it pour out a grand hymn of thanksgiving. This fire alone reestablishes in us the supernatural likeness unto God which man had prior to sin and which sin itself destroyed. It is a matter, then,

of a special grace of conformity to the Most Blessed Trinity. It will be noticed again how it is always through Christ, through the humanity of Christ, that Gertrude is led to the Trinity and conformed thereto.

Another noteworthy mystical grace, received in immediate connection with liturgical prayer, was that which came to Gertrude when, one day, wearied by her illness, she assisted at Matins seated apart in a place reserved for the ill, without being able to take part in the choir with the other nuns. It was Matins of the feast of the Assumption of Mary. Beginning at the sixth responsory, Gertrude was enraptured in spirit to assist at the same Matins which was being sung at that very moment in heaven, and she had a wonderful understanding and delight in all the corresponding texts, of which she afterwards recounted something "sicut ad exteriorem intellectum possunt exponi." This lasted until the end of the Te Deum, when she returned into herself, feeling that her body itself had been wonderfully fortified by this grace (4, 48, pp. 434–435).

mystical life, she enjoyed a most special and continual presence of Christ in herself. When she wrote of it that grace had already continued for nine years.

> "One evening when I was about to go to bed, while I was on my knees in prayer, there suddenly came into my mind that passage of the Gospel: 'If anyone loves Me he will keep My words, and My Father will love him and We will come into him and make in Him Our abode' (John 14:23). And inside, in my heart of mud, I felt You making Yourself present. . . . From that moment, my God, You have made Your presence known, sometimes more serenely, sometimes more severely, accordingly as my life is either more reformed or more careless. . . .
>
> "In spite of the vagaries of my mind and the unsuitable pleasures in which I took delight, when, after some hours, or, alas, some days or even, I fear, some weeks, I returned to my heart, I always found You there; and I could never take refuge in the pretext that You had withdrawn Yourself from me even for an instant from that time until today, nine years now, except one time for eleven days, before the feast of St. John the Baptist. That happened to me because of my having had a mundane conversation, or so it seems to me, on a Thursday, and it lasted until the Monday that was the vigil of St. John the Baptist, during the Mass *Ne timeas Zacharia*." [139]

Another time, for the greater part of Good Friday and all of Holy Saturday, she was in a continuous ecstasy. Her confidante relates the matter thus:

> "I do not think I should pass over in silence how firmly Gertrude adhered to the remembrance of the most sweet Passion of Christ, with such great devotion, and so ardently and continuously that she seemed almost to ruminate on it, as if it were honey in her mouth, a song in her ears, and a celebration in her heart.
>
> "On the most holy day of Good Friday, one time, hearing the sound of the call to the liturgical rites, she was moved to the marrow of all the powers of her heart, as if it were a forboding that they were ready to announce to her the agony of her only Friend, most faithful and most dear, and as if she were going in haste to assist breathlessly at His death; and she gathered up all her powers within her to recall the Passion of the Lord and to recompense with most faithful love her Beloved who had suffered for her.
>
> "And thus for the whole of that day and even through the Holy Saturday following, her soul was, as it were, glued to the soul of her Beloved to such a degree that it seemed most difficult for her to apply herself to anything with her external senses, except only those things to which the obligations of charity called her; and to these she adapted herself without any hesitation, as on all occasions. . . .
>
> "Spending the greater part of that most holy day and the Saturday

---

[139] 2, 3, pp. 63–64.

following almost outside her senses, mostly she remained so enraptured and above what is sensible that afterwards she was unable to bring within the range of human understanding by any kind of imagery anything of what had been allowed to penetrate her understanding by that mutual familiarity with her Beloved, so sweetly close to her in so strong a union, and inseparably united to her by the power of their mutual love, like two liquids poured together.

"This is not a sign of imperfection but of the highest perfection, as Bernard attests in his commentary on the Canticle, when, in regard to the words *murenulas aureas faciemus tibi* (Cant. 1, 10), he says: 'When by divine power, something sparkles in the mind, shedding its light over the spirit suddenly and as if with the rapidity of a lamp, then, in order to moderate such a splendor and in order to make use of its lesson, suddenly it is accompanied by images of lesser things, infused by God and proportioned to the senses, by means of which that most pure and most resplendent ray of truth is in some way tempered and made more tolerable to the soul itself, which then is the more easily able to communicate it to whom it will. . . .' So says Bernard.

"Therefore that is not to be deemed a lesser grace which God of His own accord deigns to pour into a soul and keep it intact there, without phantasms of corporeal images, between that soul and Himself alone, as under the seal of a most intimate friendship." [140]

Already in the first or second year after her grace of entry into the mystical life, Gertrude received from Christ the invisible stigmata, while she was standing in the refectory pondering, in a more fervent way than usual, upon a prayer in which she asked Christ directly to impress upon her soul the marks of His passion:

> "In that moment, while my mind was occupied most devoutly in these thoughts, I felt that God was giving to me, most unworthy though I am, the grace that I had long since asked for in that prayer, namely that I might know in spirit that in the interior of my heart the marks of Your most holy, venerable, and adorable wounds were impressed as if corporeally. By these wounds You healed my soul and You gave me a love potion sweet as nectar." [141]

A practical lesson from St. Gertrude in regard to the relations between mystical life and liturgical life

In conclusion, our examination into the relations between the mystical life and the liturgical life in Gertrude gives us, by way of example, a great practical lesson. This lesson is that the whole mystical life, comprising its highest degrees, as they are known to us from the experience of the saints, in what is essential to it — and, let us add, what is desirable in it — is perfectly able and

---

[140] 4, 25. See pp. 381–382.
[141] 2, 4, p. 67. In chapter 23 of Book 2, Gertrude reckons this grace as among the most significant which she had until then received.

entirely at ease in being born, in developing, and in maturing within the framework of a liturgical spirituality, namely, in that spirituality in which the elements common to every Catholic spirituality are viewed and lived in that relative proportion and balance which is imposed by the predominance, at least qualitative, of the values of the liturgical action as the element which determines and orders all the others to itself.

Indeed, the practical lesson which Gertrude gives us is that the mystical life is perfectly able and entirely at ease in being born, in developing, and in maturing in a framework of life where the liturgical action is the element not only qualitatively determinative but also quantitatively predominant.

Finally, the practical lesson that Gertrude gives us is that the mystical graces, even the greatest, and contemplation, even the highest, in what is essential to them, are perfectly capable of being realized in the communitarian and public liturgical action without harm to normal active participation in it, to say nothing of their verification in the extraliturgical part of a life dominated by liturgical spirituality.

In a word, the example of Gertrude frees us once and for all, if there is need of it, from the suspicion and from the fear which a reader not sufficiently adept might be tempted to base on his reading of the modern mystics, especially those of the sixteenth century and principally St. Teresa of Avila and St. John of the Cross: that is, the suspicion and fear that a liturgical spirituality, accepted fully and integrally, especially if it is centered not only qualitatively but quantitatively too on the liturgical action, might be a framework but little adapted, not to say directly counterproductive, to the preparation and development of the mystical life because of its being a framework too "distracting."

The overcoming of this foolish fear has a most remarkable result, practical as well. It is enough to call to mind something of the question debated in mystical theology about the relations between Christian perfection and the mystical life and about the general call to the mystical life.

The example of Gertrude, probably better than any other, also shows us in a concrete way that whoever admits, with the necessary gradations and explanations, the inseparability of Christian perfection and the mystical life, and the general call to the mystical life, is able in a placid way to order his life with all his heart, fully and integrally, around the liturgy just as the Church presents it, giving it even a quantitative predominance, if he so desire it or if his personal or communitarian vocation lead him to it in such a degree, without vain fears and reticence, while keeping always for his goal the higher purpose to which God calls men here below.

Thus do we prove, by way of example, after the proof by way of theoretical reasoning, that liturgical spirituality, for all that it is a spirituality within the reach of all, is not a spirituality of second rank, good only for the unlettered and for novices in the way of perfection; on the contrary, it furnishes the Christian life with a complete framework which assimilates to itself and orders within itself all the elements needed to lead one who follows it to the highest perfection. How, then, is it possible for anyone to entertain doubts about it when it is a question of the spirituality of the Church as such, which she still today proposes to her children?

5. Extraliturgical Prayer, Meditation, Devotions, and the Spirit of the Liturgy in St. Gertrude

A life of purification and the exercise of the virtues, vital relative attention to the individual dogmas of the faith, the mystical life even in its highest manifestations—we have seen that in St. Gertrude all of this is centered in the liturgy and determined by it.

It still remains, however, to examine one whole area of Gertrude's spiritual life in which the determining influence of the liturgy is seen as no less evident—that of her prayer outside the liturgical action itself and of her "devotions," in the modern sense of the term.

For the prayer and meditations of Gertrude outside the liturgical action, clearly we are not obliged to show that Gertrude, even outside the liturgical action, always prayed and meditated much and intensely; this is a truth crystal clear in the case of any saint. It is a question rather of seeing how even this meditation and prayer outside the liturgical action is in her case substantially determined by the values of the liturgical action.

"That her devotion might be in harmony with the liturgy"

In fact, examining Gertrude's case, we see that her abundant meditation and her constant prayer outside the liturgical action, in their intrinsic structure and in the psychology of our saint, not only do not stifle the values of the liturgical action, they are not contrary to them, but they are not even superimposed on them or merely juxtaposed to them. Extraliturgical prayer and meditation in Gertrude are ordered and subordinated to the liturgical values as their preparation and amplification.

In the Gertrudian writings there are, in reference to the present matter, two explicit observations which are of the utmost value and which give us the key to the understanding of the spirit of the extraliturgical prayers, meditations, and exercises of Gertrude in relation to the spirit of the liturgy. Her confidante says:

> "So that Gertrude's devotion might be in harmony with the liturgy (*et ut devotio ipsius concordaret cum officiis ecclesiae*), on *Oculi* Sunday, in her usual way, she desired to be taught by the Lord those special exercises which she would be obliged to make during that week. The Lord answered her: 'Since at this time there is read in the liturgy

the history of Joseph, who was sold for thirty piasters, take an example therefrom, and by reciting thirty-three *Pater Noster's*, purchase from Me My most holy life, in which for thirty-three years I worked for the salvation of the world. Then communicate the fruit of it to all the Church for her true salvation and for My eternal praise.' When she had done it, she saw that the whole Church was like a bride adorned and wonderfully embellished by the fruit of the most holy life of Christ." [142]

The same confidante also says:

"Another time, keeping her mind occupied with the Passion of the Lord, she understood that the act of ruminating the orations or the lessons of the Passion of the Lord has a value infinitely greater than any other kind of exercise." [143]

In these two texts, note the affirmation that Gertrude was accustomed to be solicitous that her devotions should be in harmony with the liturgy of the time in which she then found herself, and that she deemed the best exercise of the spiritual life to be that of pondering upon or ruminating the orations and the liturgical lessons, at least about the Passion. That these two affirmations, even if they refer in their context to two specific cases, had for Gertrude the value of a universal maxim, we can see from the way in which, outside the liturgical action, she did her prayers, exercises and devotions.

Exercises of St. Gertrude and the liturgy

In this area, in fact, we know very well what the "method" of Gertrude was, not only from the *Legatus* — already a persuasive witness — but also from her *Exercitia*. In composing these *Exercises*, Gertrude was perfectly a woman of her times. Beginning already in the seventh and eighth centuries, there appears in the West a whole literature of booklets of prayers, composed by private persons and intended to be privately recited, in which the personal piety of the authors and of their particular eras, outside the liturgy, took a free course.[144]

This literary genre expanded itself broadly in the Carolingian era, but especially from the eleventh century and afterwards. Great names contributed to its enrichment, like Peter Damian, John Gualbert, John of Fécamp, and Anselm of Aosta. Toward the end of the thirteenth century, still as expression and nutriment of private piety outside the liturgical action, the "Books of Hours" were born, detached from the Psalter properly so called; and they enjoyed great success, especially in the fifteenth century and up to about the sixteenth.

[142] 4, 20, pp. 360–361.
[143] 3, 41, pp. 205–206.
[144] See, for example, a quick panoramic view of this matter, with further bibliography, in

J. Leclercq, "*Dévotion privée, piété populaire et liturgie au moyen âge,*" in *Études de pastorale liturgique,* (*Lex orandi,* Vol. 1), Paris 1944, pp. 149–173.

Well then, all those who are versed in this literature have pointed out the intimate connection which exists between these productions of private extra-liturgical piety and the liturgy, in view of these Books of Hours having their origins in the liturgy, although gradually they became more and more detached from it.

It is a literature of extraliturgical piety which finds expression in a liturgical perspective, in terms borrowed from the liturgy, with liturgical extracts and reminiscences, whether biblical-liturgical or patristic-liturgical, intermixed with some private composition, these also of the same tenor, with a view to preparation for the liturgical action or to its extension.[145]

Gertrude fits perfectly into that current. Her biographer tells us that after Gertrude's conversion, when the grammarian became a "theologian":

> "She composed also a number of *orationes*, sweeter than honey, and many other edifying compositions of spiritual exercises, in a style so dignified that even those who were masters of the art not only did not find anything to be corrected in them, but were themselves very much delighted by their grace and by the charm of the scriptural quotations with which they were strewn, a thing certainly apt to make them well received by theologians and by pious persons alike." [146]

Her *orationes* have perished, but we still have a collection of her exercises. In view of these *Exercitia*, Gertrude remains one of the more significant

[145] Father Leclercq, an expert in this literature, characterizes it in the following way, in an extract which we will here cite in full, since it applies so aptly to the *Exercises* of St. Gertrude: "This devotion is born of the liturgy and, far from being separated from it, it draws on the liturgy for its inspiration and extends it. It borrows entire formulas or reminiscences from the liturgy. The booklets of prayers constantly cite a great variety of parts from the Office and from the Mass: responsories, antiphons, lessons, collects, sequences, prefaces, etc. . . . These collections are usually composed, moreover, only of select passages; they retain and gather together either psalms of the working of grace, and of supplication, and biblical canticles of much the same type, or, they may extract from the psalms only those verses which express supplication, and intercalate them with texts borrowed from the liturgy.

"With the passage of time the freely inspired part becomes greater and greater, and a fault emerges, in that the liturgy begins to occupy a gradually diminishing place in these Books of Hours. At the same time, however, throughout the Middle Ages private devotion demands from the liturgy the interior framework upon which it is constructed: a distribution of texts according to the temporal and sanctoral cycles, and according to the canonical hours; a division into psalms, lessons, versicles, and prayers; compositions in the form of hymns or litanies, such are the elements by which, very frequently, the booklets of prayers and Book of Hours imitate the liturgy.

"Private prayer fits itself quite naturally to the communitarian worship of the Church and adopts the latter's "style": to the sobriety and classic purity of the ancient prayer it joins the freshness and charm of the medieval spirit. The liturgy forms the spiritual climate where devotion flourishes; the liturgy keeps the latter in contact with the doctrinal sources by which it is itself nourished, the Scriptures and the Fathers; the liturgy summons private devotion ceaselessly to the contemplation of the profound truths which the cycles of the mysteries of salvation recall each year; and finally, the liturgy assures private devotion of a firm theological basis, and, at the same time, of a share in the dignity, simplicity, delicacy, and general flavor which characterize the liturgy" (*op. cit.*, pp. 154–155).
[146] I, 1, p. 9.

representatives of the medieval literature of prayer. Taking the liturgical point of view, which is what interests us, let us note their content.

The first exercise is a meditation which calls to mind again Christian initiation: baptism, confirmation, the Eucharist, following the principal headings of the ritual with the intercalation of prayers and aspiration for the revivification of the soul with faith and charity, the graces then received. Gertrude introduces this exercise thus:

> "At specified times, especially at Easter and at Pentecost, take care to call to mind the remembrance of your baptism, so as to be able to present to the Lord at the end of your life your garment of baptismal innocence without blemish, and the seal of your Christian faith unbroken. Desire to be reborn in God in the sanctity of a new life and to receive a new infancy from the Spirit." [147]

The second exercise, using the same method, recalls the liturgical ceremony of monastic investiture. The third makes present, always in the same way, the essential part of the liturgical rite of the *consecratio virginum*; the fourth, that of monastic profession as distinct from the consecration of virgins. The fifth exercises in its present state is composed, or so it would seem, of what were originally two exercises, distinct from each other but each having for its purpose the "revitalization of love." It does not follow, as do the preceding, the general format of a liturgical action, but with a most elevated lyricism which is naturally expressed in languages interwoven of biblical and liturgical reminiscences, it gives free vent to sentiments of love. The first part of this fifth exercise divides the day into three periods; morning, midday, and evening; the second part of it is divided into seven periods according to the seven canonical hours. The sixth exercise, entitled "of praise and thanksgiving," does not follow the plan of a liturgical rite. And again its manner of expression is lyric and personal; but nonetheless it is couched in the language of liturgical and scriptural reminiscences and with the intercalation of whole psalms and canticles, in a language bespeaking the most profound attitude in which the soul that lives the liturgy in earnest is unconsciously and irresistibly shaped, the attitude of adoration in praise and thanksgiving. The seventh exercise is that of a day dedicated to reparation for sin in preparation for death. It is divided into seven periods according to the seven liturgical hours, in which are intertwined seven principal episodes of Christ's passion according to their historical succession, in their respective hours.

In regard to preparation for death, Gertrude composed another exercise entirely on the plan of the last sacraments as received by one who is ill. Let us see Gertrude herself, shortly before her death, following this exercise. Her confidante writes:

[147] *Exercitia* 1, p. 618.

"Gertrude had written a quite useful instruction on the way in which every man, at least once a year, ought devoutly call to mind his death. . . . The first day should be consecrated to meditation on his future last illness; the second to meditation on confession; the third, on extreme unction; the fourth on Communion; the fifth on death. Once, when she herself had decided to observe that which she had written for the instruction of others, ..." [148]

This will suffice to convince us of the continuity in Gertrude between liturgical prayer and extraliturgical prayer. An attentive reader of the second book of the *Legatus*, that written in Gertrude's own hand, might easily have perceived this already, since the chapters of this book, in large measure, are but ardent prayers, primarily of praise and thanksgiving in strict harmony with the graces she received in the liturgical action, and interwoven throughout with liturgical reminiscences.

Devotions and the liturgy in Gertrude

No less than with her composition of booklets of prayers and of exercises, Gertrude was the product of her own era by the strong place that was given in her piety to a series of "devotions" in the modern — or, if you will, medieval — sense of the term. But in Gertrude even these are ordered by the liturgy and subordinated to it, as amplifications not necessarily demanded by the liturgy, but certainly in no respect contrary to it, and actually, with due observance of proper precautions, eminently capable of being harmonized with the liturgy. The piety of Gertrude can in fact be taken as an excellent example of the possibility of a strong marriage between the medieval-modern devotional spirit and the liturgical spirit.

It is well known that in the Middle Ages, beginning especially with the Carolingian era and then with a renewal after the eleventh century, devotions and devotional practices underwent a tremendous development. [149] No less certain is the fact that in the same era there was a strong ebb and flow between liturgy and devotions, not only in the sense that many devotions had their origins in the liturgy, but even in the sense that the liturgy itself received, differing in abundance and rapidity in different geographical areas, not a few elements which in the beginning had a purely devotional origin. [150]

Beginning with the ninth century, with the reform movement headed by St. Benedict of Aniane, many Benedictine monasteries, for example, introduced into the common prayer of the communities not a few of these devotions of once private origin. A more notable instance of this was the frequent

[148] 5, 27, p. 584. See also 5, 4.
[149] See, for example, allusions to this in L. Gougaud, *Dévotions et pratiques ascétiques du moyan âge*, Maredsous 1935.
[150] Abundantly and very swiftly in the areas north of the Alps; much more parsimoniously and more slowly, not infrequently with reluctance, in the liturgy of Rome. See, for example, J. Leclercq (article cited above in note 144), pp. 155-156, note 104.

or even daily recitation in common of the Office of the Dead, as a supererogatory Office. Later the Little Office of the Blessed Mother was also added to it. Cluny developed this tendency abundantly. The Cistercian movement, on the other hand, signaled a certain reaction in this area, but preserved a number of usages that were already sufficiently established, like the supererogatory Offices of the Dead and of the Madonna.

It is in this Cistercian movement that the monastery of Helfta participates. In the Gertrudian writings we find frequent allusions to the practice of these two Offices, with the consequent strong general emphasis given to devotion to the Madonna and to solicitude for the release of the souls in purgatory.

Devotion to the humanity of our Lord in general

In the area of devotions, however, the most notable expression in Gertrude, as in the other mystics of Helfta, is devotion to the humanity of Christ which shows itself in various ways. After having received its initial decisive impulse from St. Bernard himself, this devotion had been growing more and more since the beginning of the eleventh century, and was given further increase still later by the Franciscan movement.

The liturgy, of course, presents Christ always and everywhere as our great and single Mediator with the Father. The Christ brought to the attention of the faithful by the liturgy, even in antiquity, is not only Christ as God, but as God and man at one and the same time, as our Head and our Priest even in His humanity. The mysteries of Christ which recur in the liturgy as particular aspects of His single mystery are the mysteries of His humanity united to the divinity, primarily the mysteries of His infancy and of His Passion, death, resurrection, and ascension.

It is true, nevertheless, that in the liturgy, which took shape substantially before the Middle Ages, the humanity of Christ is presented primarily as humanity already glorified. It delays very little over the consideration of His humanity as it was before His resurrection, in the sense that, as a general rule, the attention of the liturgy passes quickly over that phase and leaps suddenly to the remembrance that that humanity is by this time in its state of glory. In a word, the liturgy considers not so much the Christ in His condition as an infant, as an adolescent, as an adult, and as a man subject to sufferings, the man of sorrows; nor does it consider very often or search for examples of the human sentiments of the man-God infant, adolescent, adult, victim; rather, it considers much more frequently the Christ who was born, lived, and suffered but is now glorious — not so much the *Christus patiens* as the *Christis passus et gloriosus*.

Be that as it may, especially from the beginning of the twelfth and thirteenth centuries, medieval piety in regard to the humanity of Christ preferred to center its attention and its proper sentiment on the *Christus patiens*,

on Christ the adult, on Christ the infant, on the humanity of Christ as such
in the various phases of His life prior to His resurrection, endeavoring to
re-present to itself and to re-live His feelings of that time, although, of
course, it did not really forget that Christ is now glorious. It is a question
of accentuation, but in this sense, that in the way in which medieval piety
regarded the humanity of Christ, one is able rightly to speak of a certain
misplacement of accent as compared with the way in which the liturgy presented that humanity. Within these limits, it may be said that devotion to
the humanity of Christ was born in the Middle Ages.

Typical iconographic expressions of this devotion were, for example, the
Christmas cribs and the new way of representing the Crucified in the agonies
of His torment. Devotional expressions of this movement were, for example,
the devotions to the Gesù Bambino, to the crib, to the various members of
the body of Christ, to the Passion of Jesus, to the wounds of Jesus, and the
way of the Cross. Mystical expression of this same tendency is seen, for example, in visions of the infant Jesus and in reception of the stigmata.

Devotions to the Sacred Heart in particular

The mystics of Helfta, and St. Gertrude in particular, were a part of this
current. Within this current, indeed, St. Mechtild and St. Gertrude, if they
were not actually the initiators, seem at any rate to be of considerable significance among the prime movers in the devotion to the Sacred Heart
properly so called, which essentially involves the consideration, united to a
most special and habitual affection, of the Heart of Christ's flesh as the
symbol of His love. This is a matter of spirituality and is so evident in the
Gertrudian writings that there is no necessity of our dwelling upon it.[151]
The Sacred Heart of Jesus is seen everywhere in strong relief in the relations
between Gertrude and God.

For us it is of interest to note how this devotion, in Gertrude, is carefully
wedded to her liturgical spirit. On close examination, it is seen that the role
which the Heart of Jesus has in the relations of Gertrude with God and in
her way of viewing all things is simply that which, according to the liturgy,
is the role of Christ, Head and Mediator at the side of God the Father,
whereby we have our solitary access to God and through whose means all
the graces of God come to us. It is simply the universal *Per Christum Dominum nostrum* concretized in the symbol of the Heart of Jesus, along with a
strong attention to the immense and gratuitous love of Christ for men as
the ultimate dynamism and ultimate explanation of His sacerdotal and mediational redemptive work.

At the end of the second book of the *Legatus*, after having summarized

---

[151] See Cyprian Vagaggini, "*La dévotion au
Sacré Coeur chez Sainte Mechtilde et Sainte*
Gertrude," in *Cor Jesu*, Rome 1959, Vol. 2,
pp. 31–48.

the essentials of the extraordinary graces received by her in the nine years that had passed from the moment of her total gift of herself to God, and after having thanked the supreme Giver of all gifts, Gertrude concludes:

> "With these thoughts and with all those that now crowd into my mind, I render to You that which belongs to You. With the sweetly melodious organ of Your divine Heart, under the action of the Holy Spirit Paraclete, I sing to You, O Lord God, Father adorable the praise and thanksgiving of all Your creatures in heaven, on earth, and in the lower regions, who are, who were, or who will be." [152]

Gertrude expresses the same thought when she speaks of the Heart of Jesus as a lyre which sings divine melodies in the presence of the Father or of the whole Trinity,[153] or where she calls that Heart the "organ of the Most Blessed Trinity," [154] the divine organ which plays to the supreme delight of the whole Trinity and all the heavenly court; [155] and she represents it as a golden altar on which Christ offers Himself to the Father;[156] as a smoking thurible in the presence of the Trinity, the smoke of which carries with it the prayers which the Church is raising up to God, and which gives to those prayers their wonderful splendor and perfume; [157] as a fountain pouring out from the open side of the Lamb into a golden chalice of propitiation, even for the souls in purgatory.[158] These images and many others of like kind are nothing else but a concretization of the *Per Christum Dominum nostrum* of the liturgy.

Hence, the theme of the *suppletio* as major determination of the *Per Christum Dominum nostrum*, itself united to the theme of the Sacred Heart; that which is done here below has no value before God except in union with the merits and prayers of Christ in heaven, in union with the Sacred Heart:

> "Another time Gertrude endeavored to sing and to recite with attention each individual note and each individual word. But she was too frequently, by human frailty, prevented from doing so. With great sadness then, she said to herself, 'Can such an exercise be of any use to one who is so unstable?'
>
> "Unable to abide such sadness, the Lord presented to her, as if with His own hands, His deified Heart in the appearance of a burning lamp, and said: 'Behold My Heart, organ ever most sweet to the venerable Trinity. I set it before the eyes of your mind. Be assured that you may trust it to supply for all that you are unable to succeed in doing. Thus anything that you do will appear most perfect in My eyes. As a servant stands always close by his master ready to do all that he desires of him,

---

[152] 2, 23, p. 109.
[153] For example, 4, 48, pp. 434 ff; 4, 41, p. 416.
[154] 3, 49, p. 219.
[155] 5, 1, p. 500.
[156] 4, 59, pp. 490–491.
[157] 4, 26, p. 384.
[158] 4, 17, p. 366.

so too from now on My heart will stand ever near to you so that at every moment it may supply for all your negligences.' " [159]

Basically, Gertrude has ever before her eyes the Christ now glorious, seated at the right of the Father *ad interpellandum pro nobis*, a reality which is, as you know, the foundation of the liturgy. And, focusing her attention and sentiment on the humanity of the same Christ and on His love, she introduces into that viewpoint the concept of the Sacred Heart as symbol of this redemptive, mediational, priestly love, the single gate to the Father, the only channel of graces, which alone gives value in the presence of the Trinity to the poor efforts that are made on earth in order to achieve heaven.

Devotions to the members, to the wounds, to the passion of our Lord

It is in this same climate that there develops in Gertrude the devotions to the Passion of the Lord, to His members, to His wounds, devotions which also have a noteworthy prominence in the piety of our saint. In a characteristic passage, Christ Himself tells Gertrude what she must make clear to men for their greater utility:

> "It is very useful to men to let them know that it will be extremely advantageous for them to remember this: that I, the Son of the Virgin, for the salvation of men, stand in the presence of the Father. Every time they, through human frailty, sin in their hearts, I offer My own immaculate Heart to the Father in reparation for them. When they sin with their mouths, I offer My most innocent mouth. When they sin with their hands, I present My pierced hands. And so also with all the rest; for every way in which they sin, My innocence immediately placates God the Father, so much so that every repentant sinner easily obtains pardon. I would wish, therefore, that My elect, every time they obtain for their sins the pardon which they request, might give thanks to Me, because it is I who have entreated for them that which they have so easily obtained." [160]

In this text we see very clearly the general sense of the devotion to the members of the body of the Lord, including His Sacred Heart; to His Passion, and to His wounds. To repeat: it is a matter of the general dogma of Christ the Redeemer, Mediator, Head and Priest, chiefly in His Passion, who now continues His work beside the Father; the general dogma that is concretized in these devotions in a more explicit way than is done in the liturgy, by the consideration, accompanied by strong sentimentality, of the individual members of Christ's humanity which were, on earth and in their own proper way, the substantial instrument of redemption.

Hence the attention and the affection of Gertrude for the members of the

[159] 3, 25, p. 169.   [160] 3, 40, pp. 203–204.

body of the Lord. On Christmas Day she recites a prayer, *laudo, adorno, etc.*, 225 times in honor of the 225 members of which, according to medieval physiology, that body was composed. And in so doing, Gertrude obtains the purification and sanctification of her own 225 parts.[161] But it is especially in her meditating of the passion that Gertrude is most attentive to the members of the Lord, as on that Passion Sunday when,

> ". . . inspired by God, she began to salute from the depths of her heart each member of the Lord which, for our salvation, was tormented with various agonies in the Passion. And while she was saluting each member of the Lord, suddenly from each one by divine power a wonderful splendor shone forth which irradiated the soul of Gertrude."[162]

In the same way Gertrude had a very great devotion to the holy wounds. According to a medieval opinion, these wounds numbered 5466. In preparation for the feast of the Ascension, we find Gertrude reciting 5466 times, in honor of the 5466 wounds of the Lord, the following prayer:

> "Glory be to You, most sweet, most gentle, resplendent and ever placid, most mirthful and most glorious Trinity, for the rosy wounds of my only Beloved."[163]

It was in general in the consideration of the Passion of the Lord that Gertrude found her greatest contentment. The testimonies to this in her own writings are insistent and characteristic. Her confidante tells us explicitly that Gertrude

> ". . . meditated with great devotion, ardently and almost unceasingly, on the most sweet Passion of Christ. She seemed almost to ruminate, as if it were honey in her mouth, music in her ears, and a celebration in her heart."[164]

The Passion presents itself to Gertrude very realistically, as in the scene of the flagellation which she once saw on the First Sunday of Lent, when:

> "About the hour of Terce, the Lord appeared to her in the position of the flagellation at the column, bound and standing between two soldiers, one of whom seemed to beat Him with thorns and the other with a knotted whip. And both of them beat Him on the face until His face seemed so pitiable as to break the heart and move to deepest compassion anyone who would look upon it.
>
> "So much was this the case, that through the whole day, whenever Gertrude recalled that scene, she was unable to hold back her tears. She thought that no man on earth had ever been in such miserable cir-

---

[161] 4, 2, p. 293.
[162] 4, 22, p. 364.
[163] 4, 35, p. 399. See also 3, 9; 3, 13–14; 3,

49; 3, 73; 4, 2, p. 291; 4, 21, p. 363.
[164] 4, 25, p. 381.

cumstances as those in which the Lord then appeared to her. That part
of His face which was beaten by the thorns seemed to her to be so lacer-
ated that even the inside of His eye was wounded, and was bruised as
well by the knots of the whip. So bitter was the Passion that the Lord
seemed to turn away His face; but when He turned it away from the
one soldier, the other became more ferocious and more enraged against
Him." [165]

Here too the love of Gertrude is renewed by means of the image of the
Crucified,[166] and, finally, by the mystical phenomenon of the stigmata referred to above. In accord with the general liturgical spirit in Gertrude, this
devotion is expressed in her especially in connection with the liturgical days
of Holy Week, or at any rate, in the period from Lent to the Ascension, as
well as on the ordinary Fridays of the week.

Conclusion

Let us repeat that in order to be able today to propose Gertrude as an example of liturgical spirituality, it is necessary to keep in mind the limitations of this example — as, of course, we should have to do with any example. In Gertrude's case the limitations are imposed in view of the fact that
she constitutes a medieval example, far removed from us, and because she
is a nun, and a Benedictine nun.

Nevertheless, it can be said, to begin with, that even today and outside the
Benedictine communities, there are more than a few of us who find ourselves
living within a framework of life not so very much different from that in
which Gertrude lived. Enough to remember those communities which keep
the choir obligation. Now, even among these, they are not rare of whom it
may be said that, although a notable part of their time is spent in choir and
in liturgical functions, they have not yet discovered the liturgy. The example
of Gertrude can be a very salutary one in making them aware of such an
anomaly.

For so many others today, however, the frame of life in which they must
live is really quite different from that in which Gertrude lived. But even for
them, careful consideration of the case of Gertrude has great value. This
value, first of all, is in the example of the marvelous interiorization of the
liturgy in the sense of the perfect attunement of the individual with the
objective reality of the liturgical world. In Gertrude everyone can see how
well the liturgy can accord with an intense spiritual life.

Or more precisely, everyone can see, in particular, in Gertrude, how the
most intense and integral liturgical life is able to enter into a perfect marriage with a mystical life of the highest sort. They can see how liturgical

---

[165] 4, 15, p. 348. See also, for example, 3,   [166] For example, 3, 41; 3, 43.
39-45; 4, 4; 4, 15-16; 4, 22.

prayer and private prayer and meditation can and must go together. Indeed, they can see how liturgical spirituality and private devotions can and, to a certain point, must go together because it is not possible that one who lives the divine life intensely, even be it within the framework of the liturgy, will not have also some devotions, in the sense explained above; and they can see that it is only normal that these devotions be taken up, escorted, and vivified by the spirit of the liturgy which dominates them and shapes them.

23 LITURGY AND PASTORAL:

THE PRINCIPLES

Anyone who were to end his considerations in regard to the liturgy on the theme of liturgy and spirituality as a striving toward Christian perfection, especially on the particular point of the relations between liturgy and mysticism, would be in danger of remaining with the impression that liturgy and the spirituality which is centered in the liturgy are perhaps something with a solid theological basis and, if you will, very beautiful, but, at the same time, very aristocratic; something which is achieved by a class of elect souls and hence not only cannot lay claim to the serious attention of the masses of the people, especially today when they are dechristianized or in proximate danger of becoming so, but also cannot, on the account of its being for the few, lay claim to the interest even of all those who, among the great masses, are in earnest before God about their spiritual duties and responsibilities.

The study of the relations between liturgy and pastoral will complete our panoramic view of the general theology of the liturgy and must dispel the aforementioned impression, by letting us see how deeply the liturgical question penetrates into the concrete situations which today are stirring up the work of the Church and directing it to all Catholic people, principally and properly to the masses of the faithful.

It is not our task to enter into minute particulars of the work of liturgical pastoral; nor yet to enter into the particulars of the theoretical questions which are posed by the relations between pastoral and the liturgy of the Mass, of the sacraments, and of the liturgical year — these matters being reserved to special theological liturgy. We can hope only to shed some light on the general theological principles which govern these areas and to provide a glimpse of the general perspectives which will show their application to these matters in their totality.

1. On the Notion of Pastoral in General

Definition of pastoral

By pastoral in the broader sense we mean here the art of leading and conducting the people to Christ. Equivalent notions are, for example, the art of leading and conducting the people to Christ and Christ to the people; the people to God in Christ and God in Christ to the people; the art of realizing and maintaining the encounter between the people and Christ. By making explicit some points, actually contained already in the aforesaid concept, we can define pastoral as the art of leading and conducting the people to Christ and Christ to the people, within the structure of the Church, through the means indicated by Christ Himself together with those determined by the Church, and with those which may perchance be imposed or which may seem advisable by the very nature or by the concrete *de facto* condition of the people.

The encounter takes place when the people receive the sanctification of God in Christ and respond as they must to this action of God in Christ. Since, however, this sanctification and this response are able to take place in varying degrees, pastoral tries to achieve the most perfect degree possible. It seeks, therefore, not only to snatch away the people from mortal sin so that they will live in the state of grace, but likewise to lead them to the fullest possible development of this grace.

Pastoral presupposes, among so many other things, that God deals with men in accord with the law of salvation in community; that this community is the hierarchically structured ecclesial community in which God deals with men through other men, His agents, on whom it is incumbent, by this title, to perform their tasks as instruments of Christ; to be, as it were, shepherds under the supreme Shepherd. Pastoral presupposes, moreover, that God himself has determined, up to a certain point, the modality of His encounter with men and has left further determinations of it to the Church; that in the work of the pastors in the Church it is God Himself in Christ who is working externally, while internally He is operative with His grace.

Pastoral is an art

Pastoral theology is the theological science of the art of leading and conducting the people to Christ. It is very important to understand that pastoral (i.e., pastoral practice) is an art and that pastoral theology is the theology of this art. Every art, and every science that has for its object an art, stands in intimate relationship to the actual execution of the work toward which it tends and in which it is completed. It is thus that the military art, and therefore the military science which has the military art for its object, tends intrinsically to military practice and is fulfilled therein.

Every art and every science of an art draws the principles which direct its operation from the material with which it is concerned namely, (a) from the end to be achieved; (b) from the immutable nature of the things involved; and (c), from their actual though contingent status, either as it is more or less habitually verified, or, (and this is more usually the case) as it actually is at the moment when being considered.

At the moment of acting, in order for the end to be achieved, the action must conform itself to the current status of the things involved. It is thus that, to return to the example, already noted, the maxims and the principles which are the ultimate fruit of military science, having a connection with military practice, have been elaborated for the purpose to which this practice specifically tends, i.e., for the army's obtaining a victory; from the nature of the things involved therein, i.e., of man, of space, of time, of the means used, like the type of armaments employed; in the third place, from the contingent status, habitual or of the particular moment, of the things involved. As this status changes, the concrete action and the principles which formulate the directives of the operation must also change so as to conform to it.

The contingent habitual status of the things involved cannot be ascertained except by induction from many experiences, direct or indirect; the actual status at the moment of operation can be known only by immediate experience and immediate intuition, which implies facility and rapidity in grasping that status and adapting the action to it. In regard to this facility in comprehension, either it is possessed by nature, or it is achieved, at least in part, by long experience; and, in either case, it is subject to development.

From this we can see that experience is sovereign in the practice of every art and in every science of an art. For in every art, it being a question of a concrete operation in view of achieving a specific end, the action must conform itself not only to the generic and immutable nature of the things involved, but to their particular condition at the moment of action. Under penalty of failure to achieve the pre-established end, the theoretical principles of the science are constantly mulled over or re-thought as necessitated by the concrete changes in the situation. That is why, in this area, even when it is a question of the science of an art and not only of its practice, there is a perfectly justifiable instinctive distrust which shows itself in regard to those whom we may call armchair experts. And that, too, is why in the practice of an art sovereign importance is to be accorded to intuition, to the facility and rapidity of grasping the concrete status of the things involved and of conforming the action thereto in view of achieving the end, a facility or ease which, as we have said, is had from nature or is in part acquired, but is always developed and improved through long exercise.

But long exercise and practical intuition in acting are not enough to acquire the science of an art. For this there is the necessity also of expending one's efforts in reflection and in theoretical synthesizing about one's own actions and the actions of others. In the practice of an art, broad experience and practical intuition are of extreme importance; but in the science of that art and therefore in the guidance and direction of others in that art, there is a necessity also for reflection and the faculty of synthesizing.

All this holds true in its own way in regard to pastoral and pastoral theology. The art of leading and conducting the people to Christ and Christ to the people, precisely because it is an art, must be carried off under an unchangeable aspect and under an aspect changeable and contingent.

The unchangeable aspect is determined by the following factors: first of all, by the end itself, i.e., leading and conducting the people to Christ and Christ to the people, and that within the bosom of the Church; and then, by a series of means determined as indispensable to the end by the positive will of Christ Himself, e.g., orthodox morality and faith; the sacraments; the hierarchical structure of the Church; and moreover, there is the nature of man who must be led and conducted to Christ, with all that which necessarily derives from that nature.

The more or less changeable aspect, on the other hand, is represented by the contingent and changeable, habitual or temporary dispositions of the people to be led and guided to Christ and by the positive means of ecclesiastical institution, freely determined by the Church as specific concretizations of the means imposed by nature, by revelation, or by the positive free will of Christ. In these ecclesiastically instituted means there is included a great part of the liturgy and all the positive disciplinary canonical legislation.

Pastoral must take all this into account. In it the end and the unchangeable means, as well as the means which are *per se* changeable, being of positive ecclesiastical institution, can be known through abstract teaching, by which one can learn the nature of a thing, the positive will of another, and the legislation of a society. The habitual or temporary dispositions of the people, in regard to their conductibility and the guidability to Christ, can be known only through experience and intuition.

In pastoral activity the conforming of the concrete action to the actual but temporary dispositions of the subject in view of leading and guiding him to Christ, having taken into account his nature, the positive will of Christ, and the discipline of the Church, is the object of the pastoral art as pastoral prudence in an individual act. On the other hand, pastoral theology, as pastoral science, directs the pastoral action only in the universal and in the abstract, indicating and scientifically motivating the general principles which regulate it and which afterwards cannot be applied to individual cases in the concrete except under the guidance of pastoral prudence.

The people as object of pastoral

The object to which pastoral is directed is the people. Here we will make this concept more precise, for the sake of the singular importance which it has in the question of the relations between pastoral and liturgy. The Church has the duty of leading and conducting every single human being to Christ. Indisputably, salvation contains a profoundly individual aspect. But, with full respect to this "individual" reality, there is also the law of salvation in community, as we have already explained in its proper place. Because of this latter, the individual reality of salvation cannot reside wholly outside the community, much less run counter to the community; it is accomplished within the structure of the community and through the community.

As always when a reality, especially if it is a norm of action, is composed of two terms — and so much the more if these terms appear to be antithetical, like God-man, grace-freedom, object-subject, individual-community — the method and the practical results are notably different if, in respect to the two terms, even without actually eliminating one of them in favor of the other, nevertheless, a stronger accent is placed on one of them at the expense of the other. So too when it is a question of the pastoral art.

No pastoral can ignore, and no Catholic pastoral does ignore either the individual aspect of the salvation nor the communitarian aspect. But nevertheless, there can be, and there actually are, notable variations of method and of results if, in the theory or in the practice of pastoral, the accent is placed on the individual rather than on the community, or conversely, on the community rather than on the individual. In the first case, the formula which expresses the object of the pastoral will be: to save the individuals by leading them and by preserving them to Christ within the bosom of the community. In the converse case, the formula will be that the object of pastoral is: to guide and preserve to Christ the community in which and through which the individuals are able to be saved.

The two formulas have very practical diverse consequences, both for the missionary pastoral in non-Catholic countries and for the pastoral that is exercised in so-called Catholic countries. For several years now there has been considerable discussion about the specific aim of the missionary activity in the foreign missions. The solution accepted by all was that in those countries the specific aim of the missions was the establishment of the Church in which the individuals might be saved.[1] In this formula the communitarian aspect of the missionary activity in general is clearly placed on the primary level.

Abbé Michonneau has rightly drawn attention to the fact that an analogous problem exists even for the pastoral that is practiced in traditionally Christian countries, especially in our own times, when Christianity is for the most part more nominal than real. Abbé Michonneau notes that for the most part there are two great tendencies in the apostolate: on the one hand there are the "saviors of souls," and on the other, the "builders of Christianity."[2] The "saviors of souls" are stirred up directly by the greatest possible number of souls to be saved by any reasonable means among the men who are alive today; the "builders of Christianity," on the other hand, find their motivation in the problem of Christianizing society as such. These latter want to build what will mature in the future, even if in so doing they must spend a longer time and be temporarily prevented from reaching a certain number of individuals whom, were they to adopt the other system, they might be able to influence more or less efficaciously. They cling to this point of view so that tomorrow a more Christianized society may be able more surely to guarantee salvation, in the bosom of the community, to a greater sum total of individuals.

The difference in the two points of view resides essentially in the greater or lesser importance given to the communitarian atmosphere in the salvation of the individual. Those whom Michonneau calls "builders of Christianity" look more to long term results and proceed in a more communitarian way.

Theologically speaking, there is no doubt from the theoretic and abstract viewpoint that the communitarian concept ought to have precedence, precisely because it thinks and acts more organically, with plans which, although they must take longer to mature, are ultimately more efficacious for the end which is desired. The motto which Pius XI gave to the foreign missions, "build the Church," upon mature reflection and slightly modified in its expression, must necessarily be the motto of every pastoral: to guide and preserve the community to Christ so that in the community it may be possible, ultimately and more effectively, for a greater number of individuals to find salvation. The direct object of pastoral, therefore, must be the people, not in the sense of disconnected individuals, but as community, the vital matrix and atmosphere of the individuals.

To consider pastoral in a communitarian way means to accord a great importance in pastoral to the populace as a whole and to make it the object of greatest care, precisely because it is the mass of the populace which constitutes the mass of the community and which the Church has for her mission of guiding and preserving souls to Christ in as large a number as possible.

[1] See the encyclical *Evangelii praecones* of Pius XII, June 21, 1951. See also I. Paulon, *Plantatio ecclesiae. Il fine specifico delle missioni*, Parma 1953.

[2] See Georges Michonneau, *Revolution in a City Parish*, Westminster, Maryland, 1949, p. 52. (This is the English edition of the work which appeared in its original French under the title *Paroisse, Communauté Missionnaire*.)

The Church must extend her pastoral care to all groups, excluding or neglecting none. Pastoral, like the Church herself, is not and cannot be classist or racist in any of the meanings that the political scene attaches to these terms today. But where the community constituted or to be constituted is composed primarily of the common masses, it is obvious that the pastoral ought to be first of all a pastoral of the common masses. Since, then, this is the general rule and so broadly valid that cases to the contrary, in comparison to the rule, are relatively rare exceptions, logic and the end itself of pastoral demand for the most part that pastoral be popular, i.e., that it be adapted to the status of the masses of the people whom it must lead and preserve to Christ. Exceptions are admitted, be they legitimate and necessary, in restricted groups and in milieus that are not of the masses of the populace.

When, therefore, we say that pastoral is addressed to the people, it is necessarily intended to mean not only the people as community, but more than that, in view of the general rule, the people as community of the common populace. That this necessity is more urgent today and more widely recognized is obvious from the simple consideration that it is properly the mass of the people that is greatly dechristianized or in immediate danger of becoming so — the great scandal of our times, as Pius XI said; and it is nonetheless obvious when we consider that the conditions of this mass are greatly changed and continue to change every day, and that every day this mass achieves a position of greater consequence in the life of society, so much so that the importance which formerly attached to other social classes, allowing them to determine the general ways of society, is today ever more and more transferred immediately to the common masses.

For the Christianization of great masses of people in the very countries that are traditionally Christian, pastoral, more than being predominantly a pastoral to a sympathetic community, must, more than in times past, be a missionary pastoral, that is, a pastoral that conquers the masses foreign to the Church or alienated from her, and not only a pastoral that preserves those who have remained faithful. The fact that pastoral must be of the missionary sort not only in pagan lands but, in not a few cases, even in lands traditionally Christian in name, is well known by this time, after the warning given by Abbé Godin and his friends.

Every pastoral involves a raising up of the people because the goal to be achieved, God in Christ, is a transcendent goal. But it is a raising up of an essentially spiritual kind, but not necessarily and *per se* of a cultural kind. In pastoral, elevations of another sort cannot be taken into account except as means to an essential end. Pastoral must summon the people to elevate themselves to God in Christ, and hence to all those means toward this end which were indicated by Christ as necessary always and for all.

This essential elevation necessarily carries with it difficulties and sacrifices which the pastor cannot spare his people, because these difficulties and sacrifices are inherent to the transcendent end to be achieved. But beyond these necessary sacrifices, he cannot and must not demand of the people others that are not necessary for the end in view. The pastor must adapt to the people all the changeable and adaptable means for the achievement of the final goal; he must not impose unnecessary sacrifices, since such are not demanded by Christ for the achievement of that end.

In this sense, every pastoral affords not only an elevation of the people but requires also an adaptation to the people; and we can speak not only of carrying the people to Christ but also of carrying Christ to the people. Among these adaptations, one of the more important is the factor of progress, because pastoral involves an education and in every education the factor of time is essential.

The communitarian cell, conquering or maintaining the people for Christ, is the parish. In this cell pastoral action is concretized in a practical way in four kinds of activity: a) preaching and catechesis; b) administration of the sacraments, of the sacramentals, and in general, the carrying out of the liturgy; c) those which are referred to nowadays as parochial works, such as Catholic action, recreational groups, general works of instruction, those of beneficence and the like; d) individual contacts not covered in the three preceding categories.

2. The Union between Pastoral and Liturgy

What we have said until now about the notion of pastoral in general is in the nature of a simple review of those points which are of greater interest to us in determining the relationships between pastoral and liturgy. Now, in this area the first point to be considered is that these relationships are already quite intimate because pastoral, in order to achieve its end, cannot do without the liturgy.

The liturgy, by its nature, focus, and goal, is the font of pastoral

The Second Vatican Council had a decisive word to say about the union between liturgy and pastoral. In fact, its assertion that the liturgy, even while it does not exhaust the whole activity of the Church (art. 9), is nevertheless the summit toward which this activity is directed and the font from which all her power flows (art. 10), is understood by the Council not only in relation to the spiritual life of the faithful in general (art. 11–13), as we have explained above,[3] but also and directly in relation to the ministry of pastors. Such is the import of articles 9 and 10. Let us read these articles again in the present context:

> "The sacred liturgy does not exhaust the entire activity of the Church. Before men can come to the liturgy they must be called to faith and to conversions. 'How then are they to call upon Him in whom

[3] Chapter 21 above, pp. 664 ff.

they have not believed? And how are they to believe in Him of whom they have not heard? And how are they to hear without a preacher? And how are men to preach unless they be sent?' (Rom. 10:14-15).

"Therefore the Church announces the good tidings of salvation to those who do not believe, so that all men may know the one true God and Jesus Christ whom He has sent and may be converted from their ways, doing penance (cf. John 17:3; Luke 24:27; Acts 2:38). To believers also the Church must ever preach faith and penance; she must prepare them for the sacraments, teach them to observe all that Christ has commanded (cf. Matthew 28:20), and encourage them to engage in all the works of charity, piety and the apostolate, thus making it clear that Christ's faithful, though not of this world, are to be the lights of the world and are to glorify the Father before men.

"Nevertheless the liturgy is the summit toward which the activity of the Church is directed; it is also the fount from which all her power flows. For the goal of apostolic endeavor is that all who are made sons of God by faith and baptism should come together to praise God in the midst of His Church, to take part in the Sacrifice and to eat the Lord's Supper.

"The liturgy, in its turn, moves the faithful filled with 'the paschal sacraments' to be 'one in holiness'; it prays that 'they hold fast in their lives to what they have grasped by their faith.' The renewal in the Eucharist of the covenant between the Lord and man draws the faithful and sets them aflame with Christ's insistent love. From the liturgy, therefore, and especially from the Eucharist, grace is poured forth upon us as from a fountain, and the sanctification of men in Christ and the glorification of God to which all other activities of the Church are directed, as toward their end, are achieved with maximum effectiveness" (*art. 10-11*).

These statements are so much the more important because, in the intention of the Council, they constitute the very heart of the Constitution on the Sacred Liturgy, the predominantly pastoral orientation of which is well known.[4] And there is a reaffirmation of this in the *Instruction* of 26 September 1964, in which we read:[5]

"First of all it is necessary that all be convinced that the aim of the Constitution of the Second Vatican Council on the Sacred Liturgy is not only to change the liturgical forms and texts, but much more to promote that formation of the faithful and that pastoral activity which have the liturgy for their summit and source. The changes introduced into the sacred liturgy are directed to this end" (no. 5).

"It is understood that the purpose of ordering this pastoral activity around the liturgy consists in making the paschal mystery come alive;

---

[4] See Cyprian Vagaggini, "*Lo spirito della Costituzione sulla liturgia*," in *Riv. lit.*, Vol.   51 (1964), pp. 5-7.   [5] *AAS*, Vol. 56 (1964), pp. 878-879.

it consists in manifesting that paschal mystery in which the incarnate Son of God, made obedient even to death on the Cross, is exalted in the resurrection and in the ascension, so much so that He is constituted the one who communicates to the world the divine life by which men, dead to sin and formed to Christ 'live no longer for themselves, but for Him who died for them and rose again' " (2 Cor. 5:15).

"This takes place through faith and through the sacraments of the faith, principally through baptism and the sacrosanct mystery of the Eucharist, around which the other sacraments and sacramentals are ordered, as well as the cycle of feasts in which the paschal mystery is unfolded annually in the Church" (no. 6).

"Therefore, even if the liturgy does not exhaust the whole activity of the Church, it is still necessary to see to it with care that pastoral works be connected with the liturgy as they ought, and at the same time, that pastoral liturgical activity is not performed separately and, as it were, detached from the other pastoral works, but in such a way that it is intimately united to them.

"It is especially necessary that there be an intimate union between liturgy, catechesis, religious instruction, and preaching" (no. 7).

"Let the bishops, therefore, and their helpers in the priesthood, grow each day in the knowledge that their whole pastoral duty is ordered around the liturgy" (no. 8).

The basic thesis of these authoritative texts, therefore, is clear: the liturgy, already by its very nature, without in the least nullifying nor absorbing into itself the connatural variety of extraliturgical pastoral works, always necessary, must nevertheless be the focus, the goal, and the font of the whole pastoral ministry.

The proof of this thesis? Basically, it is because the end of every pastoral has its maximum fulfillment in the liturgy, and principally in the celebration of the Eucharistic mystery. The other numerous works to which the Church must dedicate herself are understood as preparatory means to the plenary celebration, externally and spiritually as perfect as possible, of the liturgical actions, especially of the Eucharist; and as prolongation and consequence of those very actions in the whole of life.

We know what the end of pastoral is: to lead, in the way established by God Himself, the people to Christ and Christ to the people; or again, to say the same thing in equivalent terms: the sanctification of men and the glorification of God in Christ, as it is stated in article 10 of the Constitution; or still again, as it is expressed in number 6 of the Instruction: to make it possible for men to enter vitally into the paschal mystery.

But is it really true that the maximum achieving of the end of every pastoral takes place in the liturgy and in the first place in the Eucharistic mystery? First of all, let us recall the law of objectivity, of which we wrote in

Chapter 6: the way by which man must go to God, the terrain and the place where the encounter comes about, are matters freely established by God Himself in their essential specifications; and this free will of God is known to us only through revelation.

Now, in accord with this will, to be saved it is necessary to enter into the process of the paschal mystery; and no one enters into such a process without faith and the sacraments of faith. What saves is not faith alone (including hope and charity) nor the sacraments alone, but faith (hope and charity) together with the sacraments of the faith. For, by the free will of God there is no faith as He wills it for us, that is, authentic salvific faith, without reference, at least in implicit desire, to the sacraments; and the sacraments do not produce their salvific effect without faith.[6] When it is said that grace is not bound to the sacraments, this means that it is not bound to the actual use of the sacraments for those who cannot draw near to receive them; but in the present order, for the conferring of grace, God demands at least the implicit desire to receive the sacraments.

Among the sacraments primacy belongs to the Eucharist. All the other sacraments are ordered to the Eucharist "as to their end."[7] By very strong argumentation this is verified also of the sacramentals and of all the other extraliturgical activities of the Church.

The Eucharist is "the fountain of all graces."[8] From the Eucharist "the Church draws and maintains all her power and glory, all the charisms with which she is endowed, all her goods."[9] "This sacrament has by itself the power of conferring grace. No one has grace prior to receiving this sacrament, except by a certain desire to receive it, a desire made on his own in the case of adults, or by the desire of the Church, as happens with infants." In a word: "In this sacrament the whole mystery of our salvation is contained."[10]

Let no one say, this is true enough of the Eucharist, but not of the liturgy, because the liturgy does not exhaust itself entirely in the Eucharist.

For if anyone says that, we would have to answer him that man, in his concrete reality, is the king of creation, even if he is not such equally through each of his parts, but formally, through his intellect. This is true because the

[6] See J. Gaillard, "Les sacrements de la foi," in Rev. thom., Vol. 67 (1959), pp. 5–31; and of the same author, "Saint Augustin et les sacrements de la foi: verbum fidei in Ecclesia Dei," ibid., pp. 664–703. L. Villette, Foi et sacrement, du Nouveau Testament à saint Augustin, Paris 1959. E. H. Schillebeeckx, "Parole et sacrement," in Lumière et vie, no. 46 (1960), pp. 24–25. C. Floristan Samanes, La palabra y el sacramento en la acción pastoral, Victoria 1961. O. Semmelroth, Wirkendes Wort, Frankfort 1962. M. D. Chenu "Foi et sacrement," in La

maison Dieu, no. 71 (1962), pp. 69–77. Ph. Schuermans, Parole de Dieu et rite sacramentel, Brussels 1963.
[7] St. Thomas, Summa, III, q. 65, a. 3, c.
[8] Catechism of the Council of Trent, trans. by John A. McHugh and Charles J. Callan, New York 1934 (11th printing, 1949), p. 242.
[9] Leo XIII, encyclical letter Mira caritatis, in ASS, Vol. 34 (1901–1902), p. 642.
[10] St. Thomas, Summa, III, q. 79, a. 1, ad 1; III, q. 83, a. 4 c.

intellect pertains to man not only in a substantial and essential way but forth-rightly as the substantial determining part in respect, we submit, to the body or to the other faculties.

In a similar way, it is proper to say that the liturgy, in its concrete reality, is the apex and font of the life of the Church, and in a special way of her pastoral activity, even if it is not such in an equal way in all its parts, but formally, because of the Eucharist; for the Eucharist pertains to the liturgy not only in a substantial and not in an accidental way, but straightforwardly in such a way that it is the heart and focal point thereof, or the determining part in respect to the other components of the liturgy.

Moreover, the other parts of the liturgy are first of all the other sacraments. But even by means of these the liturgy is the summit and font of the whole supernatural life of the Church, since these sacraments achieve their effects of the sanctification of man and the glorification of God primarily *ex opere operato.*

The sacramentals themselves, although they have not the same end nor efficacy nor importance as the sacraments, and so much the less when it is a question of the Eucharist, nevertheless achieve those effects *ex opere operantis Ecclesiae.*

That is why *Mediator Dei* [11] says that in the liturgy "the worship rendered to God by the Church in union with her divine Head is the most efficacious means of achieving sanctity." The Second Vatican Council simply reinforces the same doctrine when, in its Constitution on the Sacred Liturgy, it con-cludes article 10 with the words: "From the liturgy, therefore, and especially from the Eucharist, grace is poured forth upon us as from a fountain, and the sanctification of men in Christ and the glorification of God to which all other activities of the Church are directed, as toward their end, are achieved with maximum effectiveness."

It is because of this that the liturgy, by its very nature, is the center, apex, and font of every pastoral activity; and it ought to be said that the end of pastoral activity is achieved not precisely *by means of* the liturgy, but, more exactly, *in* the liturgy.

This implies that, considering the various activities which pastoral has for its expression and distinguishing directly liturgical activity from all the others, the liturgy ought not be conceived as a means ordered to extraliturgi-cal activities, but, on the contrary, extraliturgical activities are to be regarded as means ordered to the liturgy, that is, to the encounter between the people and God in Christ in the liturgy, and as effects deriving from the liturgy. The liturgical movement, certainly because of the great danger of our being able to invert the proper order in the very act of underlining the intimate connec-tion between general pastoral and the liturgy, has never ceased reminding

[11] MD, no. 26.

us of this truth, especially in view of the importance of its clearly pastoral bearing.[12] Let us see, for example, one of the many formulas in this regard:

> "The Christian community has its principle of life on the altar. All the work of the community leads to the altar, to Christ, and from the altar it draws its strength. But community about the altar leads anew to community in life. The end and goal of every Christian community is to give, on the one hand, expression to the new supernatural unity established by baptism and the Eucharist; and on the other, to lead men to this supernatural life, to the Church, to the liturgy, to the Mass, and to the Eucharist." [13]

Even in the practical order the consequences of these principles in the whole area of pastoral are enormous and quite obvious. An ideal is proposed to pastors, an ideal of a pastoral totally centered on the liturgy — a program, that is, in which the most varied pastoral activities — especially catechesis, teaching, religion, preaching, Catholic action movement, biblical movement, etc., are performed with a vision of the whole intimate union in reference to the ideal of the plenary participation of the people in the liturgy, especially in the Eucharistic Sacrifice, as the goal to which all else is ordered and the source which leaves the mark of its spirit on everything.

If we ponder, then, on the fact that one of the most legitimate and perceptible modern needs is that the whole formation of the clergy be imbued already in the seminary with a pastoral character, that this character mark the whole of their study of theology, we shall catch a glimpse of the logical consequences of the principles set forth above.

Objections

Why do some seem to have difficulty in admitting these theses? For three reasons, I think. And the first is the strongest: because of the vague psychological fear that there may derive from them a discrediting and a neglecting of the other pastoral and missionary works and of the so-called apostolate in general, and that use might be made of the aforementioned theses in order to propose to all priests and to all active religious an ideal which, for lack of a better term, may be called "Benedictine."

The second reason stems from a false or at least imprecise theoretical reasoning about the preeminence of the charity which is called upon for support in repelling the aforesaid supposititious danger.

The third reason is that they forget the doctrine of the *ever-present* (and

---

[12] See L. Bouyer, *"Quelques mises au point sur le sens et le rôle de la liturgie,"* in *Études de pastorale liturgique*, (*Lex orandi I*), Paris 1944, p. 384, nos. III–IV. See also, *"A propos de liturgie missionnaire,"* in *Paroisse et liturgie*, Vol. 32 (1950), pp. 11–24, articles by Chevrot, de Meester, de Féligonde. On the same theme: the whole of no. 40 (1954) of *La maison Dieu*, with the conclusions of the congress of S. Geneviève de Versailles, 1954, pp. 165–168.

[13] B. Hernegger, *Solidarietà cattolica*, 1948, p. 144.

this is the nub of the matter) and capital function, in the historical order of salvation, of the humanity of Christ, and more particularly, of His most sacred and now glorious body and His most precious blood.

Exercise of charity in the works of the apostolate and in the liturgy

This is very nearly how some reason in regard to charity: they ask themselves, what is more noble, more perfect, more useful and necessary for the Church, to be active in the liturgy or in the apostolate? And of course they answer: charity has a primary place over all else; the apostolate is an act of charity; the liturgy is an act of worship, a certain external way of expressing religion, a moral virtue. It cannot, therefore, be superior to the apostolate.

In truth, such reasoning is all too common. First of all, there is a suspicion that one who so reasons has yielded to the frequent and very strong inclination shared by many to regard the liturgy as merely the external part of worship, the apparatus of ceremonies. And then, of course, it is no longer difficult to make a respectful and obsequious bow to the "liturgy" by declaring it beautiful and useful and holy, though of marginal interest in the Christian life. If I have had the good fortune to find a reader who has followed this work to the present point, certainly it is not necessary for me to refute at any great length such a concept of "liturgy."

Moreover, if one wishes to compare the nobility, the utility, etc., of the liturgy with the works of the apostolate, one should not compare the act of the virtue of religion, formally considered and in the abstract (since it is the solitary act elicited by the virtue of religion, formally considered and in the abstract) with the works of the apostolate formally elicited by charity; rather, compare the liturgical exercise that is, as within the structure of the liturgy, of the act formally elicited by charity, with its exercise in the works of the apostolate.

This is because the liturgy does not wholly exhaust itself in the exercise of the virtue of religion, even if it is dictated by charity, in the same way that the act of paying a debt is wholly exhausted, formally, under the aspect of the exercise of virtues, in the exercise of justice; on the contrary, the liturgy always allows acts elicited *hic et nunc* by faith, and (presuming the state of grace) by hope and especially by charity; and what is more, it offers these acts to God *in persona Ecclesiae*, in public worship, by the virtue of religion, as homage due Him in His capacity of Creator and Ruler of all things.

The ultimate reason is the singular relationship, explained in its proper place, that exists between the virtue of religion and the other virtues, especially the theological virtues, and first among them, charity. Charity not only commands or dictates the act of religion, but it is itself, moreover, the most noble material by which the act of religion is assisted in actualizing itself in its highest degree. Honor is rendered unto God first of all by faith, hope, and especially charity;[14] for the supreme act of religion is to offer God the act formally elicited *hic et nunc* by charity, by which He is loved more than all things else, in the homage due to Him as Creator and Ruler of all things. This is precisely what happens in the liturgy.

If, therefore, someone wishes to compare the liturgy with the works of the apostolate, what he must ask himself is, *ceteris paribus*, which is more noble, useful, etc., the act of charity exercised in the liturgy or the act of charity exercised in the works of the external apostolate?

Now, in order to give a technical response to a question of this kind, it is absolutely necessary to distinguish the consideration of the thing taken only in itself by its proper and intimate nature (*per se*, the scholastics would say) from the consideration of the thing by certain accidental circumstances, not necessary but which do in fact prevail in it (*per accidens*, in scholastic terminology). The answer, therefore, is that *per se* the charity exercised in the liturgical act is in every way more noble, more necessary, and more useful to the Church, but that by certain accidental circumstances it may frequently happen that the charity exercised in the work of the apostolate is more necessary and in accord with duty.

Really, in the external and internal worship that is Catholic liturgy, performed with love for God, first of all charity is exercised in its primary object, which is God Himself; whereas, in the activities of the apostolate, performed with charity, charity is exercised in its secondary object, which is neighbor. And already for this reason the act of charity exercised in worship is *per se* superior to the acts of charity exercised in the apostolate.

Moreover, this act of charity within the liturgical action is offered to God *in persona Ecclesiae*, in communitarian action as action of the Church and of Christ Himself by a title which belongs to no other action, — not even to charity, even when it is done in the Church, but not as an act pertaining to the liturgy properly so called.

Therefore that act of charity toward God has a value and an efficacy *per se* superior to any other non-liturgical act of charity because of the *opus operantis Ecclesiae*, as was explained in Chapter 3 in regard to liturgical prayer in general. As in liturgical prayer in general, in which God looks upon and regards the prayer of the Church, the mystical body of Christ, Head and members, as having a special superior title, because of which title He listens to and accepts that prayer, so too in the act of charity sent forth by the faithful in worship, He looks upon and regards the act of charity of Christ Himself and of His Church as having a special and superior title which does not belong to the other acts of charity sent forth by the faithful outside the liturgy. All this goes to show that in every way, considering things as they are in their very nature and independently of contingent circumstances, how-

---

[14] See St. Augustine, *Enchiridion* 3.

ever long-lasting, in which they may be found, the liturgical action remains the most noble, most necessary, and most useful action in the Church; and in relation to other acts, it lays claim to these titles by reason of its end and its source, not its means.

This does not mean that it could not, by reason of contingent circumstances in regard to some persons or the whole Church, so much the more so if the circumstances be of long duration, be more useful or necessary for a specific person or persons, perhaps for the majority outright, not to devote themselves beyond a certain limited time, to the liturgy, in order instead to devote themselves the more to other works, especially of the apostolate. Circumstances of this kind might be, first of all, one's personal vocation, determined by one's own temperament, by physical and psychological possibilities, by divine inspiration, etc. Then there are the necessities of fact in which the ecclesial society in a specific era, in a specific geographic area, etc., may find itself. Furthermore, there are the contingent necessities of souls and other like eventualities.

Thus it can happen, and in fact does frequently happen, that even if it is *per se* more perfect and more useful to perform the liturgy, nevertheless, because of human weakness, it is not needful for such individuals to be engaged too long or too frequently in the liturgy, since to do so would actually militate against the desired end. Moreover, even if it is *per se* more perfect to take part in the liturgy as often as possible, still, for a John Doe who has a personal vocation to other works, the contrary may be the case; or even in a situation in which the Church finds herself in great danger and urgent need, it may be necessary that many dedicate themselves to the works of the apostolate.

There is nothing surprising in all this. The classic example in the profane area, brought forward already by Aristotle, is well known and indisputable: by its nature, independently of contingent circumstances, it is more noble to philosophize than to extinguish a fire; but when in the particular circumstances the fire is burning down the house, for all those present and for society at large it is more perfect and more useful to extinguish the fire than it is to philosophize. It is more perfect to philosophize than to eat; but when one is hungry, for him it is more useful to eat than to philosophize. It is *per se* more perfect and useful to philosophize than it is to pave a street, to erect a bridge, or to build a machine; but when society has need of a street, of a bridge, and of machines, for the duration of that necessity it is more useful to construct them. For man in general, it is more perfect to philosophize than to work the land; but for John Doe, who has neither the temperament nor the capacity to philosophize, it is more perfect and useful to till the soil. And so on *ad infinitum*.

Practically, then, it does not follow from the fact that we can say that the liturgical action, performed with charity, is *per se* more noble and useful to the Church than the other works of apostolate, that in the Church those who dedicate even the quantitatively greater portion of their time to the liturgical action ought to be more numerous, nor even that they must necessarily be numerous at all; much less does it follow that in the ecclesial society there can be any excuse for neglecting the works of the apostolate of every kind, in accord with the concrete needs in which the Church finds herself.

As for the indisputable fact that philosophizing is *per se* more noble than any other human action in the natural order, it does not follow therefrom that in society, as it actually exists, there ought to be more philosophers than farmers or bricklayers or engineers or physicians or soldiers. Nevertheless, by the fact that, because of the concrete circumstances in which human society finds itself, it is inevitable and necessary that if this society is to be well ordered, the farmers, engineers and physicians must be much more numerous than the philosophers, it does no injustice to those who are manual laborers or professional men to insist strongly that, in any case, philosophizing is more noble than cultivating the fields or building houses.

Perhaps someone will say that if the needs of the Church are in fact such, in society as it actually is, that the number of those who dedicate a greater part of their time to the works of the apostolate must be as great or even greater than the number who devote the major part of their time to the liturgy, then there is no validity to our painful insistence on the *per se* superiority of the liturgical action. Nor indeed will there be a lack of someone, infected by that old nominalism which so frequently today, disguised as existentialism, is given an air of great novelty, to say that our *per se's* are abstractions which never come into hard contact with the reality of things.

It is an error. First of all, the fact that the liturgical action is *per se* the more noble and useful thing assigns to the other activities of the Church their point of reference and of concentration, the end to which they must lead, thereby giving them their necessary unity, their right ordering, and their respective qualitative value. And this is of immense value, even practically, in combating the useless waste, the exaggerations, the lack of coordination, the disorganized and fruitless labor of so many who think they are doing a great deal because they are always in motion.

Then too, the same fact indicates to every priest in his own personal life of sanctification that even if the time which he spends in the liturgical action, expecially in the Mass, is relatively short in respect to his other activities, it is, nevertheless, properly in that liturgical action, and first of all in the Mass, that he must find the dynamic center and the vital nucleus of his day.

Finally, the above-stated doctrine must make known a thing which many, even though they be well intentioned, do not sufficiently understand, and that is: admitting that, because of concrete circumstances, not all, nor necessarily even the greater number of the faithful or of priests or of religious, have to lead a type of life in which the liturgy has even a quantitative predominance, nevertheless, it remains not only legitimate but even useful and holy and necessary that there be in the Church, in accord with the personal vocation that God gives to everyone, some individuals and even groups and whole societies who make their own this kind of life, and that the Church might suffer no small loss in the absence of these.

To understand all the needs of the mystical body of Christ is much more difficult than one might suppose. Here too there is a distinguishing of tasks and a hierarchy of values. See St. Paul, 1 Corinthians 12.

So, when it is asserted that the liturgical action must be goal and font of every pastoral activity, it is not intended to mean that pastoral activity is wholly exhausted in the liturgy; nor that extraliturgical activities are not important, or rather, even essential to the end of pastoral and of the liturgy itself; nor that the ideal which is being proposed is that every parish should be changed into a monastery, and every parish priest a monk. What it does signify is that in virtue of the very end that it pursues, among the various activities in which pastoral engages there can be neither opposition nor disconnection nor even mere independence; rather, there is a qualitative hierarchy by which, qualitatively, all these activities are subordinated to the liturgy and ordered thereto. I insist upon saying *qualitatively* because certainly no one would contend that for a parish priest, engaged in pastoral activities, the greater part of his time ought necessarily and always be consecrated to the liturgy.

In summary we need but repeat, and basically for the same reasons, that which we said of the relations between liturgy and extraliturgical activities when we spoke of the relations between spirituality and liturgy. There is no absorption or disparagement of extraliturgical activities by the liturgy; but nevertheless it is necessary that they be directed in a unified way to the liturgy and that they be qualitatively subordinated to the liturgy as to the reality in which the aim of all pastoral is fully realized.

The physical body of Christ and salvation

Anyone who forgets the function *ever-present*, in the historical order of salvation, of the most sacred and now glorified body of Christ, will not be able to understand, in the natural order willed by God, the irreplaceable function of the sacraments and especially of the Eucharist and hence of the liturgy; nor will he be able to see why in theology it is rightly said that no one today can have grace without some real relation, at least in implicit desire, (and this desire, to be sincere, must be carried into act as soon as possible and permissible), to the sacraments and especially to the Eucharist; nor will he be able to perceive the real force of the theological maxim that says that that which saves is not faith alone nor hope alone nor even charity alone nor any kind of psychological act alone, but faith (with hope and charity) *and the sacraments.*

Really, the reason for all this is that even today there is no grace that does not come from God through the glorious humanity of Christ the Lord, His body included, as the instrument of His divinity. The Church was not constituted, nor does it continue to exist, except in relation to the whole human nature of Christ, His physical body included. Therefore, in order to receive salvation, we must have contact even with this body. And such contact must be, by the will of God — which marvelously takes into account the human nature which, in Christ and in us, is spirit and body — at least in implicit desire, not only spiritual, by faith and charity, but even physical, although of a totally special order, that is, sacramental.

In the Christian economy actually willed by God, this is precisely the irreplaceable function of the Eucharist. The mystical body of Christ, in its birth, subsistence, and growth, is inseparably united to His physical body by means of the sacrament of the Eucharist. God has ordered all the other sacraments toward the Eucharist, and by means of the Church He has ordered the whole liturgy to the Eucharist as well, in a totality which, precisely because of this ordering, constitutes the heart of the new religion.

This is substantially the doctrine of St. Thomas, who but repeats the doctrine of St. John Damascene and of the Greek tradition, while the latter, in turn, has its roots in the Evangelist, (John 6:48-65), and in St. Paul.[15] The Angelic Doctor writes:

> "The sacraments cause grace instrumentally. This is explained as follows: Damascene (*De fide orthodoxa* 3, 13) says that the human nature of Christ was an instrument of His divinity. . . . Thus, indeed, the very touch of Christ was the instrumental cause of the healed condition of the leper. Just as the human nature of Christ was an instrument for the realization of the effects of His divine power in corporeal things, *so too in matters spiritual.* Hence the blood of Christ shed for us has the power to wash away our sins . . . and in this way the humanity of Christ is the instrumental cause of our justification. *This cause is applied to us spiritually by means of faith, and corporally by means of the sacraments: for the humanity of Christ is spirit and flesh. . . .*[16] Hence the most perfect of the sacraments is that in which the body of Christ is really present; that is, the Eucharist, which, as Dionysius says (*Eccl. hier.* 3): 'carries to perfection the work of all the other sacraments.' The other sacraments share something of that power by which the humanity of Christ acts as the instrumental cause of our salvation."[17]

---

[15] See L. Cerfaux, *The Church in the Theology of St. Paul*, trans. by Geoffrey Webb and Adrian Walker, Herder and Herder 1959, pp. 262–286, 320–356.

[16] Quite rightly, then does St. Leo the Great say in his *Sermo* 74, 2: "*Quod itaque Redemptoris nostri conspicuum fuit, in sacrosancta transivit*—What was visible in Christ was changed into a sacramental presence."

[17] St. Thomas, *De veritate*, q. 27, a. 4 c.

Psychological efficacy of the liturgy under the pastoral aspect

Thus the nature of pastoral and of the liturgy lets us see not only the intrinsically pastoral value of the liturgy but also its central position as source in the complexus of pastoral activities. In respect to these considerations, those inferred from the didactic psychological efficacy of the liturgy are secondary. Nevertheless, they too help us to understand its total pastoral strength.

The singular didactic psychological efficacy of the liturgy proceeds essentially from the fact that the liturgy, in its totality, is not an abstract catechesis, but is by right and by nature, even if not perfectly verified in fact in the conditions of any specific time, a catechesis-action in which, to wit, knowledge is conveyed not only by means of the abstract communication of concepts but by actually doing something. This is always the more efficacious way even in dealing with intellectuals, and so much the more so with non-intellectuals, when the end is not the simple transmission of a series of impersonal concepts, but the communication of a total vital posture; and this is precisely the case with pastoral, which seeks to provoke and maintain the vital encounter of the people with Christ.

Moreover, in the liturgy this communicating by doing is, by right and by nature, a communicating by doing in community. And this again corresponds eminently to the specific end of pastoral, which, as we saw above, is aimed directly to the people, the community of the common masses. This has been pointed out insistently by Abbé Godin and his friends, and it is a point that anyone can easily establish for himself:

> ". . . the majority of our people think only collectively. Only a small percentage is capable of individual thought, and it is these who discuss and reflect on social and religious questions. The others, the great majority, are not aware of any personal capabilities along such lines; they are submerged in the vague 'personality' of the group to which they belong. They think as a unit and subscribe only to those ideas which the group holds, whether that group is their union, their fellow-workers, their political party, or their friends." [18]

> "The mass of men think as a group, and they will be converted only as a group." [19]

> "Our people have everything to learn. We think . . . that our people can be influenced only by community action, by which they can *live* their praise of God and *live* the life of Christ. After all, what is the liturgy but the collective life of the whole Christian community 'through Christ, with Christ and in Christ,' directed towards the Father? If we can realize this, we are fulfilling our task, provided we really reach this end." [20]

[18] G. Michonneau, *op. cit.*, p. 7.   [20] *Ibid.*, pp. 39–40.
[19] *Ibid.*, p. 53.

Another reason for the psychological pastoral efficacy of the liturgy is, for example, that, as communitarian catechesis-action, the liturgy continues in the practice of the faithful all their lives, at least on all Sundays and holydays of obligation. A large part of the faithful stop the practice of attending any other kind of religious instruction quite early; but they continue to assist at Mass. Now, the Mass has within it the possibility of abundant spiritual nourishment for the most diverse needs and the most varied levels of spirituality and states of mind and soul, so that each one can draw upon it according to his own capacities and his own needs; and this nourishment, by its very nature, is preeminently suited to build one's Christian life on a rock.

Finally, one can notice always in the theme of the pastoral psychological value of the liturgy that, employing advantageously the concept and the vital experience of the ecclesial community, not a haphazard community but a hierarchically structured one, great value is placed at the same time on the vital assimilation of the realities represented by parish, parish priest, bishop.

Missionary value of the liturgy

Pastoral necessarily has at one and the same time two different aspects, one of conquest, which is its missionary aspect, and one of preservation or of perfecting. Its aspect of conquering is seen in relation to non-Catholics and to those who are Catholic in name only or who, for whatever reason, are alienated from the practice of Christian life; and it is conservational and perfective in regard to the faithful who are already participating in the Christian life.

That the liturgy has pastoral value for the preserving and perfecting of the Christian life of the faithful who are already participating in the life of the Church is obvious and needs no belaboring. But if we may address ourselves only to those — and there are more than a few among us today — who, by looking at everything (and under some aspects they are perfectly justified in so doing) from an anti-Communist stance, estimate the utility of every pastoral work in direct ratio to its value as a defense against Communism. Since they are almost always far from suspecting that, in their anti-Communist concern, the labor required to develop an intense liturgical life in the people might be of very great utility, we are happy to advise them of information about experience to the contrary, extremely probing and moving, reported by the bishops and the clergy of the Soviet zone of East Germany.[21] They will discover what it can mean for a people, unfortunately

[21] W. Weskamm, Bishop of Berlin, "Formation and Life of the Parish Community," *Worship* 28, February 1954, pp. 138–152. A. Spülbeck, Apostolic Administrator of Meissen (East Germany), "The Celebration of the Restored Holy Week in East Germany," *The Assisi Papers*, Collegeville 1957, pp. 176–185.

fallen under a Communist regime and in a grave religious persecution against the faith, to have had the good fortune of having been educated in time to an intense liturgical life with a living communitarian participation in the sacred mysteries. It is a demonstration ever so convincing of the pastoral force of the liturgy in keeping the body of believers faithful to Christ in any emergency.

But beyond this preservative function, does the liturgy have also a pastoral function of conquest, i.e., of conquering for Christ? This is the question of the missionary value of the liturgy, whether in non-Catholic locales or among those Catholics who are such in name only.[22]

It cannot be denied that the liturgy, by its inner nature, all the requisite conditions being verified, precisely because it does represent the highest actualization of the Catholic community and of individual souls who take part in it as the supreme encounter in sanctification and worship with God in Christ, is concerned directly and in the first place with its initiates, those Catholics who are already participating in the life of the Church. Indeed, in the ancient Church not even the catechumens were permitted to participate in the more central and essential part of the liturgy, so lively was the conviction that participation in the sacred mysteries is a grace that belongs to the faithful alone.

Among the pastoral works, therefore, the liturgy cannot be regarded essentially and directly as an instrument of conquest; rather, it is the end and the gate of arrival toward which the individuals "conquered" are to be directed. Missionary pastoral has its primary instruments in preaching and in extra-liturgical catechesis, oral or written, in the general works of instruction, of beneficence, of Catholic action, etc., and in personal contacts of every kind.

Certainly a misunderstanding in this area might easily lead to a perversion of the liturgy itself, leading to its being made a direct and necessarily

---

[22] See, for example, Y. Daniel, "La vie liturgique et l'apostolat missionnaire en milieu ouvrier," in Études de pastoral liturgique, (Lex Orandi I), Paris 1944, pp. 212–224; P. Doncoeur, "Conditions fondamentales d'un mouvement pastoral de liturgie," with discussion, ibid., pp. 53–80. L. Bouyer, "Quelques mises au point sur le sens et le rôle de la liturgie," ibid., pp. 379–389; a happy coordination and conclusion. Kl. Tillman, Die Liturgie missionarisch gesehen, Freiburg, 1947. J. Hofinger, "Necessità e speranze per la diffusione della fede nella terre di missione," in Partecipazione attiva alla liturgia, Atti del III congresso internazionale di studi liturgici, Lugano 1953, pp. 111–126. No. 40 (1954) of La maison Dieu is devoted entirely to the problem of Évangélisation et liturgie, liturgy and other apostolic activities: Congress of S. Geneviève de Ver-

sailles, 1954; conclusions of the congress on pp. 165–168. Bishop W. van Bekkum, "The Liturgical Revival in the Service of the Missions," The Assisi Papers, Collegeville 1957, pp. 95–112. J. Hofinger, "The Evangelizing Power of the Liturgy," Worship 28 (July 1954), pp. 338–357. The two basic works on the question of missions and liturgy are J. Hofinger et al., Pastorale liturgique en chrétienté missionnaire, Brussels 1959, (see especially Hofinger's own chapter 2, "Valori permanenti del culto nei paesi di missione"); and Liturgy and the Missions. The Nijmegen Papers, Collegeville 1960. On the concrete problems of the adaptation of the liturgy in the missions, beyond the two preceding works, see also X. Seumois, L'adaptation dans le culte, CIPA 1957, nos. 2–4, pp. 49–450.

very changeable instrument of propagandizing, of apologetics, of polemics or, at any rate, to its being made primarily an instrument of instruction directly adapted to the locale to be conquered. But all this is contrary to the genuine nature of the liturgy, which is primarily prayer and sacred actuation, by the community of the initiates, of the mystery of Christ under the veil of sensible and efficacious signs of sanctification and worship. Such a misunderstanding might even lead to frivolous criticism of the present structure of the liturgy as well as of the type of life led by those who concentrate their contemplative life in the liturgy. Sometimes, among well-intentioned promoters themselves of a more pastoral consideration of the liturgy, carried away, besides, by a burning missionary zeal, we can notice the obvious imprecisions and ambiguities of their statements in this area.[23]

Nevertheless, admitting that by its very nature the liturgy looks primarily to the faithful who already follow the life of the Church is not the same as conceding that it is entirely destitute of any missionary value properly so called. Indeed, on the contrary it is full of such. The essential reasons are: a) the force of attraction which, by the mysterious working of grace and the no less mysterious awakening of the more profound aspirations of nature, the liturgy, if it responds fully to its aim and is carried out as it always should be, can connaturally exercise and not infrequently does actually exercise, even in a casual contact, over those who are strangers to it; b) the even stronger force of attraction which is exercised over the selfsame strangers by the simple spectacle and the simple contact outside the liturgy with individuals and with a community reflecting the divine life which they habitually draw from the liturgy; c) the force of missionary expansion which is developed and which must be developed connaturally, in the bosom of a community living the Christian life to its fullest in its connatural center, the liturgy.

I say it develops and must be developed. Let us recall the doctrine of the binding dimension of every liturgical sign. This dimension of obligation looks not only to the private moral life of the individual whom it must lead to a conformity with the exigencies of the liturgical action in which he has participated, but it looks also to his grave missionary obligation of bearing witness to Christ and of proclaiming His mystery in the world in which he lives. Therefore, although he is a wanderer and stranger in the world, he must nevertheless be the leaven of the world.[24]

---

[23] Examples can be found in the various interventions of P. Doncoeur, article cited in the preceding note; in some statements of G. Michonneau which have quite rightly aroused opposition; see *Paroisse et liturgie*, Vol. 32 (1950), pp. 11–24.

[24] Not without reason did the Constitution on the Sacred Liturgy of the Second Vatican Council (art. 2 and 9) point out this connec-tion between authentic participation of the faithful in the liturgical life and the obligation of bearing witness and of the mission to the alienated and to the strangers. In France the liturgical congress of 1954 at S. Geneviève de Versailles rightly insisted on this same association. See *La maison Dieu*, no. 40 (1954), and the conclusions of that congress given therein on pp. 165–168. For example: "Before

In a word, the pastoral missionary force of the liturgy proceeds primarily from the fact that the liturgy is not only preëminently suitable to create a vital Catholic atmosphere, but from the fact also that it is itself necessarily the center and the focal point of that vital Catholic atmosphere, with the whole dynamism of attraction and expansion which this implies.

This has been so well understood by those who, stirred up by the missionary problem, whether in the nominally Christian locales or in those of the foreign missions, have believed that in order to achieve a purpose so close to their hearts, one of their primary duties and, under a certain aspect, the foremost, is precisely to bring the people to the liturgy and the liturgy to the people. It is no accident that, in France at least, the liturgical pastoral movement has gained a new and powerful impetus precisely in the company of Abbé Godin and his admirers, the missionaries of labor and the promoters of the concept of the missionary parish community. In 1944, in the congress that called into being the organization of the *Centre de Pastorale Liturgique* at Paris, Father A. M. Roguet gave expression to the missionary inspiration of the new action center as follows:

> "Even the idea that guides us is a missionary idea. We have not come together for a scholarly work of restoration. We are not a congress of archeologists, nor of esthetes, nor of fragile eccentrics of the past, amateur dabblers in things of rare beauty. What moves us, what inflames us is a missionary anguish. Certainly, we have placed in our title the beautiful epithet of *pastoral*. But the good pastor, the good shepherd, is not he alone who in tranquillity pastures selected and well-nourished flocks in a well-locked sheepfold; it is he who forces his way through the briers for the recovery of his lost sheep. It is he who is consumed by an intense pity for the famished throng, worn out, dejected, like sheep without a shepherd (Matthew 9:36; 14:14; 15:32).
>
> "We are obsessed by the thought of those vast crowds who live without ideals or who are captivated by liturgies purely human, indeed, often less than human, of the classes, of the masses, in the games of the sports arena, in the dark shadows of the cinema, and who, in any case, disown the inexhaustible source of joy, of power, of salvation which well forth from our Christian mysteries. We suffer when we see our churches so frequently empty, or even full of a people resigned, who come there out of habit, oppressed by the tedium of a worship that they bear like an inevitable servitude or which they reduce to an individualist and sentimental practice." [25]

the assembly which sings the praises of God there is the evangelization which puts men on the road to faith and baptism. After the assembly there is the whole of life which is exercise of charity. Between the former and the latter stands the assembly itself, a privileged moment in the life of the Church. . . ."

[25] *Études de pastorale liturgique,* (*Lex O-* *randi I*), Paris 1944, pp. 8–9. [The translator begs leave to add: This passage from Father Roguet was a very eloquent piece of oratory in 1944; and of course in 1965, when Dom Vagaggini last quoted it, it may still have been impressive. Eight years later it leaves a taste in one's mouth, rather like the wrong end of yesterday's cheroot, at least here in America,

Let us see, too, how the liturgy is fitted into the program of parochial missionary renewal by Abbé G. Michonneau, whose work *Paroisse, communauté missionnaire*, well known in English under the title *Revolution in a City Parish*, has been called an eye-opener about the modern parish:

> Q. *"Anyone who assists at services in your church can see that you go to considerable effort to get the people to share in the liturgy. Do you think that the prayers of the people have any great importance, from a missionary viewpoint?*
>
> A. "They are tremendously important. The Christian life to which we are trying to attract souls is not, we realize, merely a way to pray; but since it is the life of Christ, and since Christ lived to give praise to the Father, we can say that the Christian way of life is principally a worship of God. Our goal is 'to make our brothers Christian,' but it is obvious that they will not suddenly start coming to Mass or to devotions; they will come only by degrees, impelled by the growing conviction that Christianity is a complete way of life. It is only at the last stage that we

where we can see the results of liturgical reforms, or, if you prefer, the abuses of reforms that were in themselves at least partially legitimate but poorly introduced and more or less unsupervised: once our churches were filled with men and women worshipping God—some devoutly, some lukewarm; now the lukewarm have been vomited out, they no longer attend at all; and those who once were devout now come out of duty, angry on their arrival, angry through the mysteries and angry when they return to their homes.

And I am angry as I write these words. I am angry because I am old enough to have been around when Father Roguet was speaking in 1944, and I remember the events of those years. I am angry that anyone who calls himself a priest can call the Mass, celebrated under any decent circumstances, a thing of tedium, when Christ is made present on the altar. I preferred to conduct the liturgy in Latin, perhaps, among else, for esthetic reasons or because I am an archeologist; but I celebrate most often in English or German or Lithuanian for the sake of the people and so as not to have to fight with those who are now managing to manipulate the liturgy in the Church which is in pilgrimage in the United States so as to make its conduct suit their own peculiar notions of what is proper; but in any case, I never find it boring or tedious to meet my God in any language.

But speaking again of 1944 and the events of those years, I still cannot recall without tears the millions, almost certainly more than fifty million, who died senselessly because of

an ideology that found its perverted expression in the words of a once-grand civil hymn that had originally celebrated the patriotic sentiments of a people united not so much by bonds of nation and government as by language, "Deutschland über alles." Fitted with new words (usually *Glorious things of thee are spoken* or *Praise the Lord! ye heavens adore Him*) and borrowed from various hymnals, some already quite old, Catholics here in America are now singing Hayden's *Deutschland über alles* at Sunday Mass and offering it to God as a hymn of praise. True, many are ignorant of what they are singing; and in all fairness to Haydn, let it be recalled that he thought he was writing it as an anthem for Austria and the Holy Roman Empire of the German Nation. The problem is largely with what it became afterwards.

But if many are ignorant of what they are singing, many others are not; and it is they, the knowledgeable ones, who leave church in anger and perhaps do not return. I do not know if they can be excused; but neither would I dare to say that they have not been given cause. And the scandal has come from their own shepherds. That is why I am angry. And if I seem to make a great deal of only one rather bizarre instance, be assured that it is but one example where a multitude might be cited; and it is itself only the symptom of a real illness that lies much deeper, and which can be generalized as a nearly total lack of understanding of what the liturgy is while utilizing it for arbitrary, personal, subjective purposes.]

shall have to worry about assimilating them into the praying, sacrificing Church.

"But in the meantime, it is essential that we give these prospective converts the kind of Christian worship that will continue to attract them, that will keep them coming, once the first breach is made in their paganism. Also we must use it to teach them, and draw them gradually along to a full realization of the Christian mysteries.

"As a matter of fact, almost the same could be said for the Christians themselves, especially the young ones. If we want to keep them in the Church, we must let them share her life and not be mere spectators. If we want them to become dynamic apostles, our ceremonies must help them to become conscious of the meaning of Christianity." [26]

The same conviction of the immense missionary value of the liturgy has been becoming more and more widespread in the locales of the foreign missions, where the problem of bringing the liturgy to the people and the people to the liturgy has, for obvious reasons, an even more vital importance than in countries traditionally of the Christian faith. In 1953, at the liturgical congress in Lugano, eloquent witness was borne to it by the missionary Father Johannes Hofinger, S.J. Among else, he noted:

"When we speak of the apostolic, missionary, pastoral, and catechetical importance of the liturgy, certainly it is not without a fear of what I would want to call a betrayal of the liturgy itself, the fear that in the missions, at least, the liturgy could and would come to be regarded as ancillary to preaching. This must not be. If ever one of the two must be ancillary, it must not be the liturgy in relation to preaching, but preaching in relation to the liturgy. . . .

"But in the final analysis, then, in our apostolic work we ought to have for our manifest purpose the glory of God; the whole conception of religion is theocentric. If we examine our missionary labor in this light, and not only that work which is missionary in the strict sense, it will be made clear that the liturgy, the worship offered by the new people of God, is plainly at the very core of all missionary labor. . . . In shaping the people of God to a true Christianity, an ample and intelligent participation in the liturgy is more efficacious than any kind of catechizing. . . .

"Today in China, practically speaking, we have lost all our schools . . . and this is so much the more disastrous because our missionary method in China was based almost entirely on the schools. . . . It is a time of persecution and the people no longer have anything. Had it been forseen in time, the people might now have the liturgy of the word, the possibility of functions, if not liturgical, then paraliturgical, but shaped on the model of the liturgy, and all this in the Chinese language, with good readings, hearing which the Christian might still

[26] Michonneau, *Revolution in a City Parish*, p. 25.

have been able to be formed. But we lack these things, and we lack them because we have not at least a part of the liturgy in the vernacular. . . .[27]

"We must look to this point also, that after the catechetical value of the liturgy, it has a social value as well. . . . It is of great importance that the people of God gathered in the same church to celebrate the same mysteries have at their foundation a true and intimate familial community if they are not to be submerged and absorbed into the pagan majority. . . . Even in the famous Chinese mission, which is among the best, it is not now possible to speak of more than one percent of the population. Think of the wicked influence of the pagan majority, against which the weak minority must stand on the defensive and purely on the defensive, when we would wish that we might be conquering others to Christianity. For this to happen, however, what vitality our Christianity must needs have! We would have to reckon ourselves a lively people of God and would have to be a powerful ferment. But whence shall we draw this power if not from the liturgy?" [28]

Liturgy and ecumenism

By this time it is clear that the liturgy is one of the critical areas in which the rapprochement of separated Christians takes place.[29]

The first fact to be noted is the existence of a movement, both private and official, which is of most notable proportions, interested in the reestablishment of liturgical life and liturgical thought, in the bosom of the community born of the sixteenth-century Reformation. And this is found not only among the Anglicans,[30] who in this area always preserved a much more traditional

[27] It is well known that the Holy See had at various times, especially in regard to China, started out in this direction with broad concessions, including that of having the prior part of the Mass in Chinese. If the attempts never quite got off the ground, certainly it was not the fault of the Holy See. Cf. F. Bontink, *La lutte autour de la liturgie chinoise aux XVIIe et XVIIIe siècles,* Louvain 1962. See also N. Kowalski, *"Römische Entscheidungen über den Gebrauch der Landessprache bei der heiligen Messe in der Missionen,"* in the *Neue Zeitschrift für Missionswissenschaft,* Vol. 9 (1953), pp. 241–251.

[28] J. Hofinger, *"Necessità e speranze . . .,"* article cited above in note 22 of the present chapter. Another article entirely in the same vein is that of Bishop van Bekkum, cited in the same note 22. Bishop van Bekkum says: "I am firmly convinced that this liturgico-pastoral work of our Holy Father and the

liturgical reforms that it carries with it are of the greatest importance and urgency, even for the missions and especially for the missions. In the missions themselves this is still not understood everywhere with sufficient clarity" (p. 121). And he concludes his relation thus: "One point at least must clearly emerge: if the appeal of the Pope will be well understood in the missions and if it will be responded to with action, future generations will recognize and praise the liturgical pastoral work of Pius XII even and especially as a great missionary endeavor" (p. 137).

[29] There is a general bibliography on this question in H. Schmidt, *Introductio in liturgiam occidentalem,* Herder 1960, pp. 231–234.

[30] See *Liturgy and Worship: A Companion to the Prayer Books of the Anglican Communion,* edited by L. Clarke and Ch. Harris, London 1947 (first edition, 1932); also, the review *Parish and People,* issues of 1948–1949.

stance and a position close to that of the Catholic Church, but even among the Lutherans [31] and the Calvinists.[32]

This movement first started in Germany shortly after the First World War as the result of a spiritual and pastoral need much like that which, about the same time, gave rise to the Catholic liturgical movement, which, moreover, exercised afterwards no small influence on it. Due especially to the so-called Berneuchen Group, under the leadership of Wilhelm Stählin, the movement quickly began to concern itself more and more broadly even with the area of liturgical theology.[33] And it counts by this time among the leading movements of the separated Churches, even if it is not without misunderstandings and sources of opposition.[34]

A second important fact: the liturgical question has become explicitly one of the basic problems of the world ecumenical movement.[35]

How is all this to be explained? Basically, by the fact that the resurgence

[31] See *Theologie und Liturgie. Eine Gesamtschau der gegenwärtigen Forschung in Einzeldarstellungen*, edited by L. Hennig, Kassel 1952. Note in particular the article of F. K. Müller, "*Die Neuordnung des Gottesdienstes in Theologie und Kirche*," in the same, pp. 198–339, a panoramic view and analysis of the Protestant liturgical movement in Germany against the background of contemporary theological tendencies. *Leiturgia: Handbuch des evangelischen Gottesdienstes*, edited by F. K. Müller and W. Blankenburg, 4 vols., 1954–1961, a powerful work with ample bibliography and many reports useful even for Catholics. See also E. Lengeling, "*Der gegenwärtige Stand der liturgischen Erneuerung im deutschen Protestantismus*," in *Münchner theologische Zeitschrift*, Vol. 10 (1959), pp. 83–101 and 200–225. C. Mahrenholz, "*Zwanzig Jahre lutherische liturgische Konferenz Deutschlands*," in *Lutherische Monatschrift*, Vol. 1 (1962), pp. 154–162. W. Blankenburg, "*Offizielle und inoffizielle liturgische Bestrebungen in der Evangelischen Kirche Deutschlands*," in *Liturgisches Jahrbuch*, Vol 13 (1963), pp. 70–83.

[32] For French-speaking Calvanism, see R. Will, *Le culte*, 3 vols., Paris 1925–1935; R. Paquier, *Traité de liturgie*, Neuchâtel 1954 (the movement started by him was called *Église et liturgie*); the works of the Protestant monks of Taizé, with the review which gives expression to some of their ideas, *Verbum Caro*; and especially the works of M. Thurian, such as *Joie du ciel sur la terre, Introduction à la vie liturgique*, Neuchâtel 1946; *La confession*, Neuchâtel 1953; *La confirmation, consécration des laïcs*, Neuchâtel 1957; *L'Eucha-*

ristie, mémorial du Seigneur, sacrifice d'actions de grâces et d'intercession, Neuchâtel 1959.

For the Dutch Calvinists, see J. F. Lescrauwaet, *De liturgische beweging de nederlandse Hervormen in oecumenisch perspectief*, Bussum 1957. See also J. M. Droin and A. Senaud, "*Renouveau liturgique catholique et renouveau liturgique reformé*," in *Paroisse et liturgie*, Vol. 38 (1956), pp. 11–17.

[33] This can be seen, for example, in the work of P. Brunner; see especially his "*Zur Lehre vom Gottesdienst der im Namen Jesu versammelten Gemeinde*," in *Leiturgia*, cited above in note 31: Vol. 1 (1954), pp. 83–364); and *Grundlegung des Abendmahlsgesprächs*, Kassel 1954.

[34] See, for example, G. Harbsmeier, *Dass wir die Predigt und sein Wort nicht verachten*, Munich 1958; W. Hoechstaeder, *Liturgische Erneuerung?*, Munich 1961. But there is nothing surprising in this opposition when we consider the obstacles with which the liturgical movement was confronted in Catholic circles.

[35] In 1951 this matter was made the subject of a special session and special report of the World Council of Churches: *Ways of Worship. The Report of a Theological Commission of Faith and Order*, edited by P. Edwall, SCM Press, London 1951. In the Netherlands since 1962 there has been a specialized review on the relations between liturgy and the ecumenical movement: *Studia Liturgica: An International Ecumenical Quarterly for Liturgical Research and Renewal*, Rotterdam. The reviews which are concerned with ecumenism always give considerable attention to the liturgical question.

of the liturgical spirit and of liturgical practice carries with it, among ourselves and among separated Christians, a growing awareness and a deepening of elements theological and spiritual, biblical and traditional, which, in the protection of Catholic dogma, lead spontaneously to a noteworthy reconciliation of positions even on the basic points which have until now kept us divided.

For example, one of the major obstacles to a fair judgment of Catholicism that has until now been encountered among separated Christians is their making insufficient distinction between Catholic faith and Catholic theology; or more precisely, the failure to distinguish between the Catholic faith and Western scholastic medieval theology, between the Catholic faith and post-Tridentine positive-scholastic theology. They have had a tendency to ascribe directly to the Catholic *faith* the lack of completeness and the deficiencies, real or supposed, which they see in scholastic theology or in positive-scholastic theology. Among the usual accusations nurtured in such a psychological background, there is always the one of estrangement from the Bible and from certain aspects of ancient tradition in favor of a conceptualization excessively philosophical (meaning scholastic) in tone or plainly distorted.

Usual, too, is the accusation of an excessive prevalence given, in the Catholic Church's way of thinking, to juridical categories to the detriment of her mystical aspect, and to the functions of the clergy to the detriment of the concept of the people of God and of the universal priesthood of the faithful.

How certain aspects of scholastic and positive-scholastic theology are able to give some support to judgments of a like kind is easily seen by recalling what was said in chapters 17 and 18 in regard to these two kinds of theology and their limitations.

Another source of objection against the Catholic Church has been the tendency of separated Christians to attribute to the Catholic faith the limitations and deficiencies, real or supposed, which they think must be pointed out in the area of the piety and the devotions of the Catholic people.

One may ponder, for example, on the age-old accusations addressed to us by Protestants in general for the way, at least in practice, in which, it seems to them, the Catholic people conduct themselves in the area of Marian devotions, of the veneration of saints, and of some modern devotions and devotional practices. The most frequent objections in this regard are that these devotions are detrimental to biblical Christocentrism, that they constitute in practice a semi-Pelagianism in their anxiety for acquiring merits, that they displace the psychological attention of the faithful from the central Christian dogmas to marginal aspects, with a tendency to slip away into superstition.

The Orthodox, on the other hand, for at least a century past, have insistently reproached Catholic piety for the lack of a vivid perception of the paschal mystery, which perception, they assert, is one of the characteristics of their Churches in virtue of the union which, contrary to what could be found among Catholics, exists with them between liturgy and piety and spirituality in general.

In short, for separated Christians, the Catholic Church, in the area of ideas and piety, has lost or at least obscured much of the biblical and traditional riches which, they would have it, are better preserved in Protestantism or in Orthodoxy. This is not the place to investigate the extent to which such accusations may be justified. One thing, however, is certain, and every attentive reader of this work can easily verify it: the liturgy and the liturgical movement strongly urge the Catholic theologian to complete and to balance the scholastic and positive-scholastic points of view with a series of overviews which will focus on the matter with the dominant and directly apparent perspectives in which revelation is set forth in the Scriptures and in many facets of patristic tradition.

In such an exposition the first level of consideration will always be concerned with the subject matter of revelation, not so much under its analytical ontological aspect (characteristic of scholastic theology), nor yet the juridical and apologetical (dear to the hearts of positive-scholastic theologians); rather, it will deal with such topics more concretely in the way in which they actually appear in the sacred history in which our salvation is ever in act. Sacred history; *mysterium* and *sacramentum*; an acute awareness of the preeminence of God; Christ *Kyrios*, the Mediator who rules all, ever present and ever operative; the Church as "sacrament of unity, namely, the holy people united and arranged under their bishops"; [36] mystical body; universal priesthood; paschal mystery as summing up the whole of salvation; eschatological straining; inseparable unity and balance between faith and sacrament of the faith, between Word and sacrament — these ideas, among various others, constitute the quintessence of the liturgical panorama. The liturgical movement urges that a strong emphasis be placed on these ideas in theology in general, in the theory and in the practice of spirituality,[37] as well as in pastoral organization and in concrete pastoral action.

Here, then, is the capital fact of ecumenism: a movement typically intra-ecclesiastical, just as the liturgical movement is, it impels Catholic life and

---

[36] CL, art. 26. [The reader will have noted the total absence of any mention of the moral requirements inherent in sacred salvation history. Would ecumenism founder if the grave sinfulness of artificial contraception or abortion were inserted into the dialogue? Since sin and redemption from sin constitutes the sole underlying reason for the existence of salvation history — and contemporary liturgy — the tendency of professional liturgists to eliminate "sin" from their thinking and writing eliminates its pastoral value practically speaking; the methodology and content of the Bible is essentially different—see *The Major Old Testament Theme*, No. 30 in OTRG series by William G. Heidt, O.S.B.—Tr.]

[37] I have had occasion to document these two facts in detail in "*Liturgia e pensiero teologico recente*," an article in the booklet of the same title, Rome 1961, pp. 21–76; and in "*Orientamenti e problemi di spiritualità liturgica nella letteratura degli ultimi quarant'anni*," in *Problemi e orientamenti di spiritualità monastica, biblica e liturgica*, edited by C. Vagaggini, (Edizioni Paoline), Rome 1961, pp. 489–584.

thought toward such a deep and improved awareness of their own riches to be exposed in a completing of scholastic and post-Tridentine theology, as well as of the theory and practice of modern spiritual and pastoral life, with a noteworthy progress toward the achieving of an integration and more perfect theoretical and practical balance in respect to the total riches of revelation and its potentialities. At the same time the traits with which the thought and life of the Church will in this way be enriching themselves will emphasize the presence of precisely those elements which separated Christians have been inclined to believe were absent or too much neglected in the Catholic faith.

This convergence of the liturgical and ecumenical movements is of incalculable importance in the modern problem of ecumenism. And it is a natural thing besides because the better way for Catholics to engage in a sane ecumenism is always that of perfecting their own theology and their own spiritual and practical life in accord with the intrinsic needs thereof, so as to realize for themselves and to testify to others, in the most unified and balanced way possible, the intrinsic potentialities of the faith itself.

What is to be expected of the liturgy under this ecumenical aspect is already understood.[38] In this perspective one understands also the exceptional favor with which the Constitution on the Sacred Liturgy of the Second Vatican Council was received even in those non-Catholic groups which have at heart the reunion of all Christians.

No less surprising, to the purposes of a rapprochement with the Catholic Church, are the fruits of the liturgical movement in the Protestant communities. In the Lutheran and Calvinist Churches it is directly and substantially a matter of a much more positive appreciation of the incarnational, sacramental, priestly, and communitarian aspect of salvation, and at the same time, a much more biblical and traditional balance between faith and sacrament, Word and sacrament, and the subjective and objective aspect of salvation.

In particular, the liturgical movement has brought into not a few of the Protestant communities a new investigation of the more traditional meaning of the various sacraments, especially of the Eucharist (Real Presence, sacrifice, relationships with Golgotha, with Communion, eschatological value); of baptism, in the discussion about infant baptism; and of confirmation, in the question of its nature and of its relation to baptism.

Indeed, the liturgical discussions, through the intrinsic connection which ties together all the theological problems when they are examined in some depth, have contributed to a deepening appreciation of the more traditional

[38] See E. Beauduin, "Dialogue oecuménique et équilibre de la théologie," in Irénikon, Vol. 27 (1954), pp. 275–291. See also Ch. Moeller, "Liturgie et oecuménisme," in Quest. lit. et par., Vol. 32 (1951), pp. 166–170. Th. Filthaut, "Liturgische Erneuerung und oekumenische Aufgabe," in Liturgisches Jahrbuch, Vol. 11 (1961), pp. 9–29.

meaning of Christological problems (it is not possible to understand the liturgy except in reference to the very structure of the person of Christ), of problems about the nature of the Church, as well as the problems, in some respects even more fundamental, of general theological methodology, such as the question of the *sola Scriptura* and of tradition, and of the philosophy presupposed and made ancillary in theology.[39]

As to our relations with the dissident Orientals, the importance of the liturgical movement can be seen even in the particular fact that the liturgical tradition, always lively both in the West and in the East, was formed essentially in the centuries before the schism and that it therefore constitutes the natural common ground for a rapprochement.

It is well known that the Orthodox of a deeply religious culture, who are in contact with the realities of the Catholic liturgical movement, have been considerably and favorably impressed by it, not only because a whole series of prejudices and accusations made against the Church in this area are put to flight thereby, but also because, pondering upon the situation, they have thereby been forced to an awareness that the dimension of the mystery of Christ, in which in the past they frequently gloried as if it were a traditional characteristic of the Eastern Church in contraposition to Catholics, is in reality much more developed and more profoundly viewed by Catholics than in their own Churches. For that reason there is today among the Greeks (well-known political circumstances make it impossible among other reasons) some tentative interest in developing a liturgical movement after the model of our own.[40]

It can be taken as certain, in any case, that if Catholics of Latin or Oriental rite who live among the dissidents were to develop a powerful liturgical movement after the fashion of that in Western countries, it would have very interesting consequences in many lands, such as Palestine, Lebanon, Syria, Mesopotamia, Turkey, and in Greece itself, to say nothing of other countries when they will be able to be liberated from the Communist yoke. It is certain, in fact, that the dissidents who, in the places mentioned, come into contact

---

[39] Some of these results can be seen in *Ways of Worship*, (cited above in note 35), pp. 15–39; in the article of J. Meister, "*Zur Fragestellung und Begrifflichkeit der Arnoldshainer Abendmahlsthesen*," in *Die Eucharistie im Verständnis der Konfessionen*, edited by Th. Sartory, Recklinghausen 1961, pp. 262–282; and that of G. Reidick, "*Zur Diskussion über die Arnoldshainer Abendmahlsthesen*," *ibid.*, pp. 285–329 (these two articles are on the discussions which took place in Germany between Lutherans and Calvinists, in regard to the Eucharist); in the works of W. Stählin, especially *Berneuchen: unser Kampf und Dienst*

für Kirche, Kassel 1937; *Vom göttlichen Geheimnis*, Kassel 1936; *Um was geht es bei der liturgischen Erneuerung*, Kassel 1950. Also in the works *Theologie und Liturgie* and *Leiturgia* (cited above in note 31), in those of P. Brunner (see above, note 33), and in those of M. Thurian (see above, note 32).

[40] P. Trambelas, *The Liturgical Movements*, (in Greek), Athens 1948. E. Timiadis, "*Les tendances actuelles de la pensée dans l'église de Grèce*," in *Paroisse et liturgie*, Vol. 37 (1955), pp. 29 ff. See also in the same, pp. 287 ff.

with our worship, especially in the Latin rite, cannot but marvel at what the full Catholic life does for those who are engaged in it.

From this sketch about the eminent even if indirect pastoral, missionary, and ecumenical value of the liturgy, we can see how far the reality of the liturgy actually is from the notion that makes it consist only of monastic trappings, or even worse, that it is restricted entirely to elect circles of Christians and, as it were, to the aristocrats of spirituality, while the parish priests, the missionaries, the militant laity, caught in the narrow confines of apostolic necessities and with the duty of defending and conquering in the Christianization of the world, cannot and must not waste their time with it. Such a notion, indeed, unfortunately expresses well enough what is not infrequently the mentality found in certain circles which, however laudable their purpose, speak and dream only of the apostolate.

The reality, however, is actually that the liturgy, even without absorbing into itself the other pastoral and apostolic works indispensable for conquering and maintaining the people for Christ, is not only an eminent means of pastoral and of the apostolate, but is forthrightly the center and the goal to which the whole of pastoral and the whole of the apostolate must lead, and the source from which they proceed even in their most varied forms. In the final analysis, in fact, they tend to create that community which is alive in Christ and which finds its maximum expression precisely in the community liturgy.

Liturgical pastoral a characteristic of the present phase of the liturgical movement

Since the end of the Second World War, the consideration of the pastoral aspect has properly become the great dynamic force which has caused the liturgical movement to progress in such rapid and gigantic strides that it has by this time become a movement of so great a universal interest that according to the solemn witness of the Second Vatican Council: "It is today a distinguishing mark of the life of the Church, and, indeed, of the whole tenor of contemporary religious thought and action." [41]

The seeds of the clearly pastoral stance of the liturgical movement, contained in the directive given by Pope St. Pius X to Dom Lambert Beauduin and treasured by him, the first to revivify the liturgical ideal,[42] were very much enfeebled in the period between the two great wars. But they took hold again and began to germinate like weeds around 1944-1946.

[41] CL, art. 43. See Pius XII, discourse of 22 September 1956 to those attending the Congress of Assisi, in the *Atti* of the congress, p. 15.

[42] His work as promoter was given expression in a pastoral dimension as early as 1909 in the periodical *La vie liturgique*, flanked afterwards by the Liturgical Weeks, the relations of which were regularly published in the *Semaines liturgiques*, and in the review *Les questions liturgiques et paroissiales*, beginning in 1910. See O. Rousseau, "*Dom Lambert Beauduin, apôtre de la liturgie et de l'unité chrétienne*," in *La maison Dieu*, no. 40B (1954), pp. 128-132.

In German-speaking countries, Father Pius Parsch intensified his propaganda for a "popular" liturgy — which placed a strong emphasis even on the vernacular question — supported, besides, by an intense biblical catechesis.[43]

In France in 1944 there grew up in Paris the *Centre de Pastorale Liturgique*, through the initiative of men directly involved in the apostolate and with the quite explicit purpose of guiding the liturgical movement into a clearly pastoral dimension, as can be seen from the programs of the Center itself [44] and in the review *La maison Dieu*, the much-quoted exponent of the same goal.

Other liturgical circles now set out with the same purposes in mind, and periodicals already long existing began to work in the area of the liturgy. Among these the Belgian review *Paroisse et liturgie* [45] was very widely disseminated among the French-speaking parochial clergy because of the liturgical pastoral material of immediate usefulness which it placed at the disposal of its readers.

Beginning about 1946, the intensity of the liturgical movement, now channeled in a pastoral dimension, was taking hold in the various countries, and certain reforms were being so urgently demanded — some persons, always with their aim of a liturgical pastoral before them, did not even hesitate to begin to introduce "reforms" without waiting for proper authorization — that the episcopate virtually everywhere began to concern itself directly with the liturgical question. Liturgical commissions were started among the bishops, and national liturgical centers under episcopal surveillance, always with a predominantly pastoral tone, sprang up.

With the intervention of the encyclical *Mediator Dei* in 1947, intended to mark out the proper path and to reprove certain deviations, the movement for a liturgical pastoral again dashed ahead on the course that, already under the pontificate of Pius XII, brought about the first clamorous reforms, marked always by a directly pastoral concern.

The movement has achieved its highest theoretical expression in the Constitution on the Sacred Liturgy of the Second Vatican Council, the predominantly pastoral stance of which is well known. Nor is it any less obvious that there is a preeminently pastoral concern in the directing of the general work of the reform of the liturgy, in execution of the general directives of the Council.

It can be said that the ultimate fruit of this continual laboring and of those experiences which confronted the concept and the reality of pastoral in general with the concept and the reality of the liturgy has been the formation,

---

[43] See, for example, the biographical notice "*In memoriam Pii Parsch*," in *Liturgisches Jahrbuch*, Vol. 4 (1954), pp. 230–236; Ch. Rauch, "*In memoriam: Un promoteur du mouvement liturgique, Pius Parsch*," in *La maison Dieu*, No. 40B (1954), pp. 150–156.

[44] *Études de pastorale liturgique*, (*Lex Orandi* I), Paris 1944.

[45] Edited at the Abbaye de St. André, in Brugge (Bruges), Belgium.

by this time already acquired, of the concept of pastoral liturgy or, better, of liturgical pastoral.

The expression *liturgical pastoral* can mean: 1) the stratagems of the pastoral art for efficaciously inducing the people to live the liturgy intensely; 2) the value of the liturgy for achieving the general aim of pastoral, which is to lead and guide the people to Christ and Christ to the people; 3) the general way of conceiving and putting pastoral into practice by consciously centering it in the liturgy. All three of these meanings are justified, but the third is the fullest; and it is the one which we mean when we speak next of liturgical pastoral.

3. Active and Plenary Participation: The Goal of Liturgical Pastoral

Since the end of every pastoral is to guide and conduct the people to Christ and Christ to the people, and to realize and maintain the encounter between the people and Christ, when this pastoral is consciously centered on the liturgy, that is, when this pastoral is a liturgical pastoral, its end will be to guide and conduct the people to Christ and Christ to the people in the liturgy, and to realize and maintain the encounter between the people and Christ in the liturgy. To this end, the pastoral effort will consist in conducting the people to the liturgy and the liturgy to the people in order to be able to realize and maintain the encounter between the people and Christ.

But we know that the sun and center of the liturgy is the sacrifice of the Mass, the place of maximum encounter between man and God in Christ Jesus, where, presuming the necessary moral attunement, God in Christ sanctifies man in the highest degree and man in Christ renders his worship to God in the highest degree. Sun and center of the liturgy, the Mass is therefore necessarily sun and center of the liturgical pastoral, the primary purpose of which is to conduct the people to the Mass and the Mass to the people.

Plenary participation, external and internal

So that the aforesaid encounter may be realized, just any sort of presence or any sort of participation in the liturgical action will not suffice. It is not a question of a purely material, purely external encounter, but of an internal encounter, an encounter of the soul. Liturgical pastoral, therefore, must have for its aim not only a material conducting of the individual into a church so that he may in one way or another participate in the liturgy, but a creating in him of an internal moral attunement with the liturgical reality as sanctification in Christ and worship of God in Christ.

This attunement, as much in its external aspect as in its internal, admits of different degrees of perfection. A liturgically orientated pastoral, if it is to realize the full encounter of the people with Christ, must strive under both these aspects to achieve the maximum possible perfection, in accord with the connatural demands of the liturgy itself and of the development of the divine life in the faithful. The goal, therefore, is *plenary* participation, that is, that participation in which the Catholic, responding with perfect attunement to the given objective of the celebration, displays in full the possibilities of the supernatural activities included in his supernatural existence as a man deputed to the worship of God in Christ.

Quite properly, then, does the Constitution of the Second Vatican Council insist repeatedly on the concept of *full* participation as the goal of liturgical pastoral [46] just as much as it is the goal of the reform itself of the liturgy.[47]

Active

The full encounter with Christ in the liturgy demands an internal and external participation of the one present there, not only in a passive way like a silent spectator who but watches an action done by others, but an active participation as suits one who fulfills his own role in the activity when the action in which he takes part is, by an intrinsic exigency, also his own action. The liturgy is, in fact, by its very nature, an action not only of the priest but of each of the faithful present, although in a way that is not properly that of the priest and hence without an equation of roles and without a confusion thereof.

To clarify this point, let us recall first of all the concept of the priesthood of all the faithful, as has already been explained in its proper place. The intrinsic nature of the liturgy as action and the intrinsic nature of the Catholic as having been clothed, by means of his very baptism, with the "royal priesthood" by which he is deputed to make that liturgical action his own are such that the Catholic does not participate perfectly in the liturgy if he does not participate not only internally as well as externally, but also actively, vitally, and consciously.

If instead of the internal structure of the liturgy in relation to the depths of the participant's very being, one considers the liturgy's psychological efficacy over the individual, the same conclusion is reached. Without active participation the liturgy does not endow the one who so assists with its full psychological moral effect. Indeed, in the absence of active participation, there

[46] CL, art. 14: "Mother Church earnestly desires that all the faithful should be led to that full, conscious, and active participation in liturgical celebrations which is demanded by the very nature of the liturgy, and to which the Christian people, 'a chosen race, a royal priesthood, a holy nation, a redeemed people' (1 Peter 2:9; see 2:4-5) have a right and obligation by reason of their baptism."

[47] CL, art. 14: "In the restoration and promotion of the sacred liturgy the full and active participation by all the people is the aim to be considered before all else, for it is the primary and indispensable source from which the faithful are to derive the true Christian spirit. Therefore, in all their apostolic activity pastors of souls should energetically set about achieving it through the requisite pedagogy."

CL, art. 21: "In this restoration both texts and rites should be drawn up so as to express more clearly the holy things which they signify. The Christian people, as far as it is possible, should be able to understand them with ease and to take part in them fully, actively, and as a community." See also CL, art. 41.

is a cessation or at least a considerable diminution of what is, from the didactic educative point of view, the liturgy's principal characteristic — its being a concrete vital instruction by means of the action itself, in which the vital posture is transmitted not so much by concepts and reasonings as by living and actualizing a sacred situation with one's whole person at the very moment of its enactment.

Communitarian

There is still something else that is necessary: that external and internal, active and conscious participation must be at the same time a communitarian participation. Liturgical pastoral strives for this. And the intrinsic nature of the liturgy demands this perfection no less than its psychological efficacy demands it. As to its intrinsic nature, since the liturgy as worship is the vital action of the whole mystical body, Head and members, as a sacred community:

> "Liturgical services are not private functions but are celebrations of the Church which is the 'sacrament of unity,' namely, 'the holy people united and arranged under their bishops.' Therefore, liturgical services pertain to the whole Body of the Church. They manifest it, and have effects upon it. But they also touch individual members of the Church in different ways, depending on their orders, their role in the liturgical services, and their actual participation in them." [48]

To participate perfectly and actively in the liturgical action necessarily means, therefore, to participate actively in the action which is by right the action of the whole community in the act of worshipping; of the whole assembly of the sons of God as *ekklesía* in Christ Jesus, in the presence of the Holy Spirit, who gathers in one all who were otherwise dispersed. Ac-. tive participation, even externally communitarian, is but the expression, also extrinsic, of this communitarian need, ontologically intrinsic to the liturgy.

Consideration of the liturgy under the aspect of its psychological efficacy leads to the same conclusion. Indeed, this psychological efficacy consists in large measure in the fact that in the liturgy the vital religious posture is transmitted to the believer not merely inasmuch as he lives the sacred action actively and with his whole person, but also and in greatest measure because he lives actively in the community of which he forms a part. It is here that the psychological force of the influence of the atmosphere of the community and of the masses comes into play in the creation and in the strengthening of the ordered behavior vital to man. The existence of this influence has been ably demonstrated by social and mass psychology," [49] and the psycho-

[48] CL, art. 26. The term "sacrament of unity" was loaned to the Council by Cyprian of Carthage, *The Unity of the Catholic Church* 7 (Jurgens, no. 557, p. 222).

[49] See, for example, J. Froebes, *Lehrbuch der experimentellen Psychologie*, Vol. 2, Freiburg im Br. 1929, pp. 508 ff.

logico-phenomenological analysis of worship, in its social and communitarian aspect, has been especially illuminating in the case of the liturgy itself.[50]

Naturally the social and communitarian character of the liturgy, inasmuch as it pertains to the theological essence thereof, is secure in every liturgical action from the moment that the action is performed with all the conditions requisite to validity, even if it is carried out by one priest alone, without any of the faithful in attendance there.

Thus the Mass offered in these circumstances is still by its theological nature an action of social and communitarian nature; thus too with the solitary recitation of the breviary carried out by one who is canonically obligated to the Office. In the same way, one or several of the faithful who assist at Mass in a purely passive way or while occupied in private devotions which have only the most general connection with the Mass which they are hearing are performing an action which, by its essential theological nature, is a social and communitarian act. In this sense every liturgical act validly performed and every valid assistance at a liturgical act has social value and is not deprived of its social fruits.[51]

From this it follows that further social and communitarian characteristics, of an internal nature as also external, which are subjoined to the conditions strictly required for the validity of the liturgical act give to this act a greater fullness of sociality and communitariety in respect to that sociality and communitariety already contained in the simply valid act by reason of its theological substance. This greater fullness means, first of all, a greater internal and external subjective attunement of the believer to the objectively social and communitarian character of every valid liturgical action.

When, therefore, it is said that liturgical pastoral is concerned essentially with giving a social and communitarian expression to the celebration, it simply means that liturgical pastoral is concerned with persuading the faithful to respond in the most perfect way possible even in their internal and external subjectivity to the necessarily social and communitarian character of the liturgical actions. It means, moreover, that this response, as social and communitarian as possible, is within the normal exigencies instrinsic to the liturgy itself, in the same way that the perfection of a thing, even if accidental in respect to its essence, is nevertheless within the normal exigencies intrinsic to it.

And in all this there is nothing abnormal, because pastoral does not strive merely to a goal of leading the people to an encounter of just any sort with Christ; rather, it aims and must aim at the perfection of this encounter. Hence liturgical pastoral has not a goal of arriving at a merely valid celebration of the liturgy on the part of the priest celebrant and of persuading the

[50] See, for example, R. Will, *Le culte*, Vol. 2, *Les formes du culte*, Paris 1929.

[51] See CL, art. 27; and MD, nos. 96–97, 107 (Lat. 95–96, 106).

faithful to a merely minimal participation therein in order to obtain some sort of spiritual fruit from it or to satisfy the possible juridic obligations which they have of attending; rather, it necessarily proposes to persuade both the priest and the people in the liturgical act to that ideal of full life which is achieved only when all the possibilities of being nourished by the divine life which the liturgy offers are exploited to the fullest, in a way that is connatural to the spirit itself which shapes the liturgy — all this in view of fostering as much as possible the union of those participating in the liturgy with Christ, and among themselves in Christ.

Thus, in treating of active and communitarian participation, internal and external, as the ideal essential to liturgical pastoral, it is necessary to avoid every opinion that might seem to imply that without such ideal participation the sacred action is not able to achieve its essential purpose and, at the same time, to be persuaded that such participation represents precisely the ideal to which, observing the prudence necessary to every action of this kind, liturgical pastoral must strive with every legitimate means.

Hierarchically structured

Nevertheless, the active participation of the faithful in the liturgical action as their own action, to which liturgical pastoral aims, does not involve any confusion between the specific role of priest celebrant and the role of the faithful in the liturgical action. Each has an active role in the liturgical action, but each in his own way. For the Mass, in a special way, we refer the reader again to what was said in its proper place about the difference between the hierarchical priesthood and the priesthood that is common to all the faithful. It may be recalled particularly that in the Mass:

> "The unbloody immolation at the words of consecration, when Christ is made present upon the altar in the state of a victim, is performed by the priest and by him alone, as the representative of Christ and not as the representative of the faithful. It is because the priest places the divine Victim upon the altar that he offers it to God the Father as an oblation for the glory of the Blessed Trinity and for the good of the whole Church. Now the faithful participate in the oblation, understood in this limited sense, after their own fashion and in a two-fold manner, namely, because they not only offer the Sacrifice by the hands of the priest, but also, to a certain extent, in union with him. It is by reason of this participation that the offering made by the people is also included in liturgical worship.
>
> "Now it is clear that the faithful offer the Sacrifice by the hands of the priest from the fact that the minister at the altar in offering a Sacrifice in the name of all His members represents Christ, the Head of the Mystical Body. Hence the whole Church can rightly be said to offer up the Victim through Christ. But the conclusion that the people offer

the Sacrifice with the priest himself is not based on the fact that, being members of the Church no less than the priest himself, they perform a visible liturgical rite; for this is the privilege only of the minister who has been divinely appointed to this office; rather, it is based on the fact that the people unite their hearts in praise, impetration, expiation, and thanksgiving with the prayers or intention of the priest, even of the High Priest Himself, so that in the one and same offering of the Victim and according to a visible sacerdotal rites, they may be presented to God the Father. . . .

"In order that the oblation by which the faithful offer the divine Victim in this Sacrifice to the heavenly Father may have its full effect, it is necessary that the people add something else, namely the offering of themselves as a victim." [52]

Of all the people

And now another step. The ideal toward which liturgical pastoral aims, considered in its totality, cannot be solely nor even principally the active and communitarian participation in the liturgy by special groups in the community of the faithful, as would be the case with religious communities and, in general, groups selected on account of social degree, culture, spiritual elevation and the like. Every situation in which the practical result in the majority of cases is the confining of active and communitarian participation to such groups is necessarily regarded by those who are entrusted with the charge of general liturgical pastoral as tending away from the ideal and therefore to be avoided.

It is understood, of course, that when we say that such situations are to be avoided, we mean that they are to be avoided by the use of such means only as are pastorally legitimate, from which are excluded all such means as would be contrary to obedience to the hierarchical authority of the Church, because pastoral in general and liturgy in particular are functions not of private individuals, even be they priests, but of the Church as such, which is essentially hierarchical.

Moreover, the general principle of every regulation must, of course, be kept in mind: that in the introduction of any change the general concrete situation and the actual repercussions which this change can have in the life of society must be taken into account. This is a matter which looks not so much to the theory as to the prudence of management, which can be had only by one who knows the prevailing general situation and who considers the question in the totality of all its ramifications. All this holds good in the face of those who, reasoning in the abstract on the ideal of liturgical pastoral, arrogate to themselves a right which they do not have of manipulating changes on their own authority.

[52] MD, nos. 92–93, 98 (Lat. 91–92, 97). See also CL, art. 48.

Nevertheless, safeguarding always the aforementioned principles, it remains true that a situation the practical result of which is that, in the majority of cases, active and communitarian participation in the liturgy will be confined to a select group of the faithful is necessarily viewed by liturgical pastoral as a situation to be avoided. And this is simply because the pastoral which is centered on the liturgy depends upon the laws of general pastoral, one of which, as we saw above, is that it must tend first of all to the common masses of the people. The litu₁gy, viewed in its pastoral aspect, an aspect, which is necessary and intrinsic to it, tends, therefore, to be primarily and by its inmost nature popular. That which liturgical pastoral means to realize, therefore, embraces a participation in the liturgy, in the Mass, which participation is not only internal but also external, vital and active, a participation of the people as popular community.[53]

Convergent in the diocese or in the parish

Finally, in the pastoral centered on the liturgy, everything converges, on the local level, on the diocese as focal point and, in a more restricted range, the only one, concretely speaking, within the habitual reach of each of the faithful, on the parish.

The Constitution of the Second Vatican Council gives formal expression to the first point:

> "The bishop is to be considered as the High Priest of his flock from whom the life in Christ of his faithful is in some way derived and upon whom it in some way depends.
>
> "Therefore all should hold in the greatest esteem the liturgical life of the diocese centered around the bishop, especially in his cathedral church. They must be convinced that the principal manifestation of the Church consists in the full, active participation of all God's holy people in the same liturgical celebrations, especially in the same Eucharist, in one prayer, at one altar, at which the bishop presides, surrounded by his college of priests and by his ministers." [54]

If, therefore, active, full, and communitarian participation of the whole people of God in liturgical celebrations and particularly in the Eucharistic celebration is the goal of liturgical pastoral, then liturgical pastoral must address itself to the achievement of this goal primarily in the celebration of the Eucharist centered around the bishop of the diocese. The reason: this is,

---

[53] In German-speaking areas it was Pius Parsch who insisted especially upon this popular dimension; in France, Father Doncoeur, and to some extent the whole movement which he headed at the Centre de Pastorale Liturgique, never tired of flinging darts at the propagators or supposed propagators of a certain liturgical esthetism. See Doncoeur's "Conditions fondamentales . . . ," cited above in note 22; and his "Comment se pose le problème de la liturgie populaire," in Les questions liturgiques et paroissiales, Vol. 27 (1946), pp. 173–183.

[54] CL, art. 41.

in fact, on the local level, the principal action in which the Church collectively realizes and manifests herself.

Why? Because the Church, as it says elsewhere in the Constitution,[55] "is the 'sacrament of unity,' namely, a holy people united and arranged under their bishops." This means, in the terminology of St. Cyprian of Carthage, from whom these expressions are taken, that the Church is a society, the cause and symbol of the unity which, by means of the communication of divine life and the overcoming of the fragmentation brought about by sin, unites men with God and with each other in the participation in the life and in the unity which unites the Father, the Son, and the Holy Spirit. Therefore the Church can be defined as "a people reconciled in one by the unity of the Father and of the Son and of the Holy Spirit."[56]

In this reconciliation and creation of unity through communication of divine life, the bishop is the external, human, and immediate principle of transmission and of cohesion. Primarily "it is from him that the faithful who are under his care derive and maintain their life in Christ." With that in mind, the Church can be defined not only as "a people reconciled in one by the unity of the Father and of the Son and of the Holy Spirit," but also as "the people joined to the priest [i.e., to the bishop] and the flock clinging to their shepherd."[57]

The universal Church is formed of the union of the local churches by virtue of the communion of bishops among themselves under the primacy of the Pope, the supreme visible principle and guardian of unity.

If, therefore, the Church is that "sacrament of unity" in which men, by their right as being sons of God, but now estranged from Him and from each other because of sin, are reconciled anew and ordered around the bishop by being made into a holy people in the participation in the life of the Trinity, it is only natural that, concretely and speaking on a local level, the principal realization and expression of the Church is to be found in that action in which a group of the faithful, around their bishop, receives externally and internally in the most perfect way possible that unity of life and expresses that reconciliation which overcomes the dispersion brought about by sin.

This action of which we speak is the liturgical celebration, principally of the Eucharist, surrounding the bishop. Therefore "all should hold in the greatest esteem the liturgical life of the diocese centered around the bishop, especially in his cathedral church."

So too, "the bishop is to be considered as the High Priest of his flock." This means that he, *first of all*, is to be considered such; for in the acts in which he exercises his function of high priest, there is found on the local

---

[55] CL, art. 26.

[56] St. Cyprian of Carthage, *The Lord's Prayer* 23.

[57] St. Cyprian of Carthage, *Letter to Florentius Pupianus* 66, 8 (Jurgens, no. 587).

level the principal realization and manifestation of the Church: that is, he achieves in the first place the very end of the episcopal function.

In the first place, true, but not *exclusively*; for we know that the liturgy does not exhaust the whole activity of the Church but is only its apex and source, the central and organizational but non-exclusive element which, far from dispensing with the other numerous works of ministry and apostolate, demands them peremptorily as presuppositional conditions and as logical consequences.

Just as the Church, therefore, without exhausting herself entirely in this nor any other action, is herself more in the celebration of the Eucharist around the bishop with the full participation of all the people, so too the bishop, without exhausting his function in that of high priest of his people, nor in any other activity, is nevertheless himself and fulfills the function by which he is what he is more on this very occasion than in any other. Consequently the diocese, which is precisely the concrete structuring of the Church in a specific place around the bishop, is in the first place, even if not exclusively, a sacral and markedly Eucharistic structure.

All these are ideas which clearly demand that we draw for ourselves a new picture both of the bishop and of the diocese, presently conceived only too often as entities almost exclusively juridic and administrative. A new picture must be drawn, more pastoral and sacral in its dimensions, and in a general ecclesiological perspective in which the supernatural ontological reality of grace and of the participation therein by men, primarily in the sacral sacramental (*sacraments* in the broad sense) way, are conceived as clearly primary and determining in relation to the juridic structures.

A new picture again, in the sense of a greater appreciation of the reality of the local Churches within the bosom of the universal Church. By the local Church we mean *the* Church *in* or even *at* such and such a place: the Church at Bologna, at Paris, at Sydney, at Cleveland, at Erie, at Youngstown, at Dorset, etc. Or even, as it says in *The Martyrdom of Saint Polycarp*, "the Church of God which sojourns in Smyrna," i.e., which is in pilgrimage at Smyrna.[58]

This is an ecclesiology that is certainly implied in the whole liturgical reality; and hence it is that which is presupposed and briefly hinted at in the Constitution on the Sacred Liturgy and so happily developed in the Constitution on the Church of the Second Vatican Council.[59]

---

[58] *The Martyrdom of Saint Polycarp*, Address (Jurgens, no. 77). See also the note in Jurgens on the term *sojourning, paroikoûsa* in the Greek, from which comes the term *parish*, used very early and occasionally in the sense of *diocese*.

[59] I have illustrated these ideas in *"La Chiesa si ritrova nella liturgia,"* in *Riv. lit.*, Vol 51 (1964), p. 343; and in "The Bishop and the Liturgy," in *Concilium*, English ed., Vol. 2 (1964), pp. 7–24. The liturgical movement has made a great contribution to the recent deepening, even theologically, of the notion of the bishop and of the diocese. This can be seen in the literature on this question that prepared the way for the decisions of the Second

What has been said of the bishop and of the diocese as focal point of the liturgical pastoral must, *mutatis mutandis*, be said also of the parish priest, helper and vicar of the bishop in a more restricted portion of the flock, and of the parish, especially the territorial parish. Indeed, in a certain sense, what was said above about the diocese ought here be accentuated. In fact, practically speaking, the parish is the concrete nucleus proportioned to the individual, through which the believer enters into the diocese, lives his life in it in supernatural community and, through the diocese, enters into the universal Church.

Plenary active participation of the faithful in the liturgical celebrations, especially in the Eucharist, focuses practically, therefore, on an organized but restricted community, principally on the locally organized parish. So too, in turn, the life of the parish, though not exhausting the totality of its activity in the liturgy, would have communitarian liturgical celebrations, principally the Mass, as the apex toward which all else tends and the source from which the whole strength of the parish emanates. This is an explicit conclusion of the Constitution on the Sacred Liturgy:

> "As it is impossible for the bishop always and everywhere to preside over the whole flock in his church, he must of necessity establish groupings of the faithful; and, among these, parishes, set up locally under a pastor who takes the place of the bishop, are the most important, for in some way they represent the visible Church constituted throughout the world.
>
> "Therefore the liturgical life of the parish and its relation to the bishop must be fostered in the spirit and practice of the laity and clergy. Efforts must also be made to encourage a sense of community within the parish, above all in the common celebration of the Sunday Mass." [60]

When one considers, however, how strong and how numerous and from how many directions today are the forces which tend to disrupt and fragment the parish, it is easy to see why the liturgical movement, which strives with all its might to give new vigor to the sacral and dynamic focal point of the parish, is of interest to every parish priest.[61]

Vatican Council. See the panoramic view of the theological tendencies on the episcopate and the bishop prior to the Council in the *Herder-Korrespondenz*, Jan. 1958, pp. 188–194: *"Was ist ein Bischof?"*; Oct. 1961, pp. 31–39: *"Die Nachfolger der Apostel."* Notable among the works of this recent literature are A. G. Martimort, *De l'évêque*, Paris 1946. *Episcopus, Studien über das Bischofsamt*, Regensburg 1949. E. Guerry, *L'évêque*, Paris 1954. A. M. Charrue, *"L'évêque, dans l'église,"* in the *Rev. dioc. de Namur*, 1957, pp. 1–13. J. Lécuyer, *"Épiscopat,"* in *Dict. de spiritualité*,

Vol. 4 (1960), pp. 879–907. K. Rahner, *Episkopat und Primat*, Freiburg im Br. 1961. In regard to the diocese, see J. Colson, *Qu'est-ce qu'un diocèse?*, Paris 1958; F. Poggiaspalla, *La diocesi e la parrocchia*, Brescia 1950.

[60] CL, art. 42.

[61] On the parish see D. Grasso, *"Osservazioni sulla teologia della parrocchia,"* in *Gregorianum*, Vol. 40 (1959), pp. 297–314 (prefaced by a broad bibliography). See especially F. X. Arnold, *Comunità di fede*, Rome 1959; Congress of the *Union des oeuvres* at Besançon in 1946 (*Paroisse, chrétienté communataire et*

4. Three Presuppositions and Two General Directions for the Work of Liturgical Pastoral

From a consideration of the nature of liturgical pastoral and of the goal of active participation which it proposes, one can sketch out in general strokes the way which must be taken in order to achieve that goal. First of all, there are three very general presuppositions to be kept in mind.

Formation of the clergy

The first fact, clear as crystal, is that pastoral presupposes a pastor; and liturgical pastoral presupposes a pastor who has understood what the liturgy is and what its pastoral strength can be. Indeed, since the practice of liturgical pastoral is an art, and an art which must communicate a vital attitude, liturgical pastoral presupposes that the pastor is vitally permeated by his own experience of this reality which is the liturgy, by his own experience of its pastoral strength, of its meaning, and of the necessity of that active participation to which he must lead the people.

That the liturgical movement in its first stage must by all accounts have for its goal primarily the clergy, and in the first place the parochial clergy and, more precisely, the young cleric destined for the parochial priesthood has always been evident enough, and it is even more so today, now that the movement has entered decisively into its pastoral phase.

It is as much as made explicit in the Constitution of the Second Vatican Council: "Yet it would be futile to entertain any hope of realizing this [of leading all the faithful to full, conscious, and active participation in liturgical celebrations], unless pastors of souls, in the first place, themselves become fully imbued with the spirit and power of the liturgy and capable of giving instruction about it. Thus it is absolutely essential, first of all, that steps be taken to ensure the liturgical training of the clergy." [62]

The situation in regard to the liturgical formation of the clergy varies considerably, of course, from one place to another. It is evident, nevertheless, that even if, on the level of principles and of general legislation, the Council has solemnly codified the more profound questions of the liturgical movement even in this area, so much so that they can no longer be ignored by any bishop or priest, nevertheless, on the practical level, a great many priests have done little or nothing about it.

Why? The answer can be given in a few words by quoting what was said in this regard by Bishop Willem van Bekkum, Vicar Apostolic of Ruteng in Indonesia, when, speaking specifically of the missionaries, he testified to their general deficiency in the liturgical question and inquired:

missionaire); Congress of Lille in 1948 (*Structures sociales et pastorale paroissiale*); Congress of the Pastoral Institute of Vienna in 1953 (*Die Pfarrei: Gestalt und Sendung*). On the theme of parish as liturgical community, see *La*

maison Dieu, no. 36 (1953), with bibliography, pp. 141–149. See also F. Toniolo, *Parrocchia e liturgia*, 1949; H. Chery, *Comunità parrocchiale e liturgia*, Brescia 1948.

[62] CL, art. 14.

"Where did this strange concept have its origin? Certainly formation played a decisive part. We missionaries simply had no liturgical upbringing in our childhood. Our seminary training, too, unfortunately offered no opportunity of making good this deficiency, for 'liturgical instruction' was interpreted as being an introduction to the rubrics; and at the most, there was a rapid survey of the history of the liturgy by way of supplement. Thus it came about that, for most of us, the real outward and inward participation in and experience of the liturgy never really became flesh of our flesh. As long as that does not occur, the value, the essence, and the riches of the liturgy are not fully grasped, and judgments concerning the missionary importance of properly celebrated liturgy will remain faulty." [63]

These affirmations are valid, evidently, not only for missionaries but for many members of the clergy, and especially for those who completed their formation decades ago.

The Council, therefore, after having affirmed the principle of the liturgical formation of the clergy, proposed the general norms which from now on must regulate the instruction of clerics in the liturgy (art. 15 and 16) and their spiritual and pastoral formation in the same field (art. 17). Nor did it forget to give an exhortation to help priests already engaged in the ministry to a better understanding of the liturgy so that they may live it themselves and share it with the faithful (art. 18).

In reference to the matter of instruction in the liturgy, beyond affirming the necessity that this duty be entrusted only to teachers who are technically prepared for it, and that the liturgy be presented integrally as much under the theological and historical aspects as under the spiritual, pastoral, and juridic aspects, it is worthwhile to note also what is said about the unity that must be maintained in the teaching of theology in all its branches, with the liturgical vision of things revealed (art. 16). We have explained above [64] the capital importance of the perspective opened by this article of the Constitution for regaining the unity of ecclesiastical learning and of clerical formation.

Clear diagnosis of the people

After seeing to his own formation, the first rule for the pastor who will have to lead his people to their liturgical goal will be to have an exact idea, indeed, a perception as acute as possible, of the actual state of the people with whom he must deal in the concrete, in regard to the present condition and the actual possibilities of their external and internal, active, communitarian, parochial participation in the liturgy.[65] This much is certain: it is

[63] Bishop van Bekkum, "The Liturgical Revival in the Service of the Missions," *The Assisi Papers*, Collegeville 1957, p. 96.

[64] Chapter 20, especially pp. 638–641.

[65] In this matter it will be necessary to apply to the liturgy the technique of observation now employed in recognizing the social situation within a specific milieu. See G. Le Bras, *"Litur-*

necessary to take the people as they are and where they are in order to elevate them afterwards to the goal proposed.

Even here the situations are as diverse as the individual countries, the individual regions, the individual parishes. Certainly the work that remains yet to be done is immense in its complexity. It is not my task to enter into details, but it is more than evident that, on a broad scale, there exists between the people and the liturgy an abyss of dissociation and lack of understanding. This is the case first of all, as one would expect, between the liturgy and those people who until now have been only nominally Christian, viz., that body who, after their First Communion, learn nothing more or almost nothing more of the Church and of religion; and next there are those whose religion consists in making their Easter duty and assisting sporadically at Sunday Mass. Beyond descriptions of the more general sort,[66] recent soundings taken by systematic inquiry, with the aid of modern methods of statistical control, reveal every day more and more the breadth and depth of this phenomenon of dechristianization, no less than its intimate connection with the lack of solid education in the liturgy and the consequent lack of liturgical life.[67]

But, with the occasional exception of an oasis here or there, even that remnant of people who have remained faithful know but little indeed of the liturgy and of active participation therein.[68] That individualism has had and does even yet have many adverse repercussions even among the faithful

gie et sociologie," in Mélanges en l'honneur de Mgr. M. Andrieu, Strasbourg 1956, pp. 291–304; "Inchiesta circa la frequenza alla Messa domenicale nel comune di Bologna," in Piccolo sinodo diocesano, Bologna 1961, pp. 223–276.

[66] For Italy, see, for example, C. Richelmy, I preti in Italia, Rome 1956. For France, see Godin, France pays de mission?, Paris 1943. F. Boulard, Problèmes missionnaires de la France rurale, Paris 1945; G. Michonneau, Revolution in a City Parish, Westminster, Maryland 1949. A general panorama of the whole world, in B. Hernegger, Solidarietà cattolica, trans. in the Edizioni Paoline at Rome, 1948.

[67] Examine the picture drawn by Bishop Ilario Roatta in 1955, a picture which, unfortunately, had no need of precise controls because it did no more than portray the situation that anyone could have observed on almost any Sunday: "The statistics of attendance at Sunday Mass indicate a dreadful desertion. Many of the baptized have given up habitual attendance of Mass. Others have diminished the frequency of their attendance. Others keep on going to Mass, but only out of force of habit or because of Church discipline. Many are present only physically. Around the priest

celebrant, silence and boredom; among the more eager in attendance there is a form of assisting dictated by the whim of the individual, in which they go their own way, follow their own thoughts, read their own books, say their own prayers. . . .

"But in spite of all, the Mass has remained the trench where religious practice makes its stand, where testimony of fidelity to Jesus is borne, where the bond with Christ's redemption is preserved. In this trench, which is the essential line of battle, it is necessary to remain, to gather strength, to prepare to advance. In this trench there is abundance of supply: in it is the source of Life itself" (from "Catechesi della Messa," in the Rivista liturgica, Vol. 42 [1955], p. 271). The Council has made this its program; but how much remains yet to be done!

[68] See G. Card. Lercaro, Ritorniamo alla liturgia solenne, a discourse delivered at the Congress of Sacred Music in 1954, French text appearing in the Revue Gregorienne, Vol. 35 (1956), p. 44. P. Doncoeur, Conditions fondamentales . . . (see above, note 22 of present chapter), pp. 53–56. G. Michonneau, Revolution in a City Parish, pp. 26–28.

themselves who remain attached to the Church is generally easy enough to recognize.[69] It must be understood that in any hypothesis the first step in resolving the problem of rechristianization is to have the courage — much rarer than one might be inclined to believe — to make a very realistic diagnosis of the true situation in which our people presently find themselves.

Progressiveness

A further rule for liturgical pastoral, as for every kind of pastoral, will be to remember always that to guide the people back to the liturgy is a question of education and of the shaping of religious psychology and of communitarian religious psychology, and that it is necessary, therefore, to prepare oneself to create or to restore this psychology, taking into account the pedagogical principle of progressiveness and the indispensable time required for achieving the goal. Certainly anyone who would think that the work of the liturgical education of the people is a thing that can be easily achieved by frivolous and amateurish means without serious effort and a spirit of methodic perseverance is bound to meet inevitable and grave disappointments.

In any case, it is necessary to recognize and to have the courage to denounce in certain circles even the necessary concern over prudence and over progressiveness when it has become, as it does all too often, an abusive pretext for not moving at all or for going ahead only with an intolerable slowness. It is quite clear that in the business of the liturgical elevation of the people, pastors cannot take comfort in the thought of their prudence if they refuse to concern themselves with entering joyfully and wholeheartedly into the spirit of the directives imparted by the Church in the Second Vatican Council.

Elevating the people to the liturgy

Turning now from these very general presuppositions, we find that the whole pastoral labor centered on the liturgy unfolds substantially in two directions: bringing the people to the liturgy as it is today and bringing the liturgy to the people. This means making a wise selection among the various forms of liturgical celebration permitted by current legislation, choosing those which are better suited to the active participation of the people in their specific circumstances, as well as trying to obtain and studiously requesting, through proper channels, with proper respect and proper obedience, from the competent authorities, the reforms of the liturgy itself deemed useful for the achievement of its goal.

[69] In addition to the text referred to in the preceding note, Cardinal Lercaro had this also to say: "Both breathing in the same atmosphere, naturalistic humanism has been at odds with egotistical individualism and has even knowingly broken the pledge of brotherhood inherent in the liturgy"—*Rivista liturgica*, Vol. 41 (1955), p. 257. B. Hernegger, *op. cit.*, pp. 87 ff. G. Michonneau, *Revolution in a City Parish*, pp. 29 ff.

To elevate the people to active participation in the liturgy as it is today is by far the most important and most urgent task of liturgical pastoral, a task of which it will never be absolved. This task belongs by right and by duty to all the clergy under the direction of the hierarchy, and, along with them, under that same direction, there is a role to be played also by Catholic teachers and educators, starting with priests themselves. If the clergy do not fulfill this duty of theirs, the liturgical reforms, even the most beautiful of them, can very quickly be brought to bitter disappointment. This is true first of all because, in any hypothesis, the encounter between the people and Christ, which is the end of every pastoral, always includes the elevation of the faithful to a superior state, a state contrary to that into which a corrupt nature strives to ease them; an elevation which always portends stress and difficulty of every sort, in the overcoming of which the help of the pastor is required.

To this general consideration the liturgy itself adds another more specific. And it is that the liturgy, even in the actuality of a celebration entirely in the vernacular, and of a revolutionary and unheard-of adaptation, as complete as possible, of its variable part to the style of expression in use among the people today, will always carry with it a very great and substantial part which will not be accessible to the people except by means of a basic elevation of themselves to what is above. The realization of this elevation will remain always the essential and most urgent task of liturgical pastoral.

The reasons for this fact, it seems to me, are four. The first and general reason is that the liturgy remains always and necessarily a complexus of signs which are not natural, but freely chosen by God and by the Church to express spiritual and supernatural things, known by faith, in reference to the sanctification which God in Christ works in His Church and the worship which the Church, in Christ, returns to God. Now, for a knowledge — and especially for a vital knowledge — of these realities hidden under the veil of sensible signs, the faithful, and principally the people in their totality, will always and continually have need of being elevated with the help precisely of liturgical pastoral. What I mean to say is that the people will always have need of being instructed and catechized in regard to the vital theological meaning of the liturgical assembly and of its individual rites.

The second reason, specifying more closely the preceding general one, is that the Scriptures remain always and necessarily one of the more essential points of the whole liturgical structure, whether as direct catechetical reading, as in the first and second readings and in the Gospel readings in the Mass; or as a formula of prayer, as in the psalms and canticles; or as the general expression from which the other liturgical compositions take their cue and with the spirit of which they are imbued. Now the Scriptures, even if recited in the vernacular, remain always a world apart to which the people have need of being elevated, whether because of what is said therein or because of the way in which these things are conceived and expressed, which, apart from the question of language, remains always foreign to the people. It is the law of the incarnation coming into play.[70]

The third reason is that the liturgy, even in that part of it which is, absolutely speaking, variable, must remain deeply anchored in tradition. The traditional character of every religion demands as much; and the especially traditional character of the Catholic religion as factual data received and transmitted and slow to evolve even in its parts *per se* changeable cannot demand less. Indeed, the very laws of sound religious psychology demand it. Consequently, the Catholic liturgy will be strongly anchored to the past, precisely in order to give the present generations a way of living in connecttion with their forebears. Thus every generation must necessarily be guided and introduced to those traditional forms which they simply do not find spontaneous to them. And there again, the constant necessity of liturgical pastoral.

Finally, the fourth reason is that habituated use itself brings it about that once the novelty of a form of religious expression has worn off, its significance naturally tends to be effaced in the awareness of the faithful, thus making a necessity of continual laboring for revivification and rekindling of attention; and this brings with it anew the necessity of a continual elevating of the people to the liturgical form.

Bringing the liturgy to the people

The second task of liturgical pastoral is to bring the liturgy to the people. Furthermore, this embraces two aspects. The first proceeds from the fact that the ecclesiastical laws themselves in force today leave to the priest, always under the surveillance of the bishops — who, in their own dioceses, are able to restrict this liberty — a certain margin of free choice among diverse forms of liturgical celebrations of various rites, and primarily of the Mass, a margin considerably greater than is generally appreciated. Liturgical pastoral makes it the duty of every priest to use this margin wisely, choosing the forms better suited in a specific set of circumstances to bring the liturgy as close as possible to the people; and it indicates at the same time the right way to achieve this result.

The second aspect of the general direction of the labor of bringing the liturgy near to the people proceeds from the fact that the status of the liturgy itself in its changeable parts, because of historical contingencies free in them-

---

[70] It is the grave problem of how to make the Bible the vital book of today's Christian. Happily, the problem is brought into sharper focus by the fact of the liturgy in the vernacular. See P. Grelot, "*La parole de Dieu s'adresse-* *t-elle a l'homme d'aujour'hui?*" in *La maison Dieu*, no. 80 (1965), pp. 151–200. There can be no solution to the problem except through a suitable catechesis, which presupposes an adequate formation of the clergy.

selves, is, in various points even of some importance, still today too far re-moved from any real possibility that the people have of active participation.

Here, then, is where the question stands of possible reforms. Even though the realization of these reforms belongs in the final instance to the supreme authority of the Church, nevertheless, the ordinary pastor who has the liturgy at heart is able and, in some way, must cooperate in his proper role in this labor, possibly by his study and always with the suggestions which his own pastoral experience will afford.

24 HINTS ON THE MEANS OF LITURGICAL PASTORAL: IN PARTICULAR, PREACHING AND LITURGY, CATECHISM AND LITURGY

Having explained the general principles of liturgical pastoral, it remains still to explain the means. This we will do in the spirit of the present work, which is that of clarifying the theological dimensions underlying the liturgy.

It is not necessary, therefore, for us to draw up a list of all the means by which one can achieve the goal of guiding and conducting the people to the liturgy and the liturgy to the people. Much less, then, is it necessary for us to enter into the practical field of their detailed application. Our intention will be only to point out the general principles of the theological liturgical order which are very closely involved with some of these means.[1]

1. Premise: Initiation to the Liturgy

The liturgy, as we have already explained so many times, is *sacramentum, mysterium*, mystery of Christ, paschal mystery, because it is the complexus

---

[1] After the Council had happily completed its work on the level of general legislation and of directives for reform, many additional questions of a practical pastoral order were bound to arise, and these the Consilium for the Implementation of the Constitution on the Sacred Liturgy is still dealing with, and many of the rites are still in process of revision. It would not be practicable at present and in the present work to enter into detailed patriculars of the means of liturgical pastoral except insofar as the underlying theological principles are concerned. In any case, much of the available textual material will continue to remain in the process of its practical evolution.

of the sensible and efficacious signs of the sanctification and worship of the Church.

To introduce someone to the liturgy, therefore, is necessarily to introduce him to the "mystery." But an integral introduction of man to such a "mystery" cannot really be completed in an instruction by way of the transmission of concepts about the same; rather, it must be an "initiation." That is, it must be an introduction to a concrete fact-action, and therefore an introduction that is of interest to the whole man, body and soul — not only his conceptual and discursive function, but also his will, his sentiment in general, his imagination and sensibility; an introduction, moreover, that leads to experiencing the thing, that is, coming to know the liturgy by participating therein.

And this is because the liturgical mystery is not only an aggregate of concepts but a concrete fact of the existential order, a complex sacred and communitarian action, in a community hierarchically structured, in which the one being initiated is a real actor and not merely a spectator. And he is an actor who, to do what pertains to him, must really get himself involved therein with his whole concrete being, in view of realizing in himself a vital all-embracing attitude in response to the reality with which he is brought into contact.

Thus, to bring the faithful to the liturgy and the liturgy to the faithful necessarily includes two aspects, one practical and the other theoretical.

The practical aspect consists first of all in getting the faithful to take an active role in the liturgical celebrations properly so called, hopefully choosing among the various forms and degrees of participation permitted by authoritative legislation for a specific rite, that which is best suited to the liturgical formation and to the concrete situation of the faithful with whom one is then dealing.[2]

In the second place and in a subordinate way, even the celebrations of "pious exercises" or popular devotions can be of use to the aforesaid practical initiation, provided that, in regard to their frequency, the time of celebration, and their structure, they be in total conformity and subordination to the spirit of the liturgy, as the Council itself requires.[3] And this requires, of course, that many of the popular devotions in common use today be rethought in a sense more conformable to the liturgy.[4] If this is done, they

---

[2] Insights and directives of this type are given in the "Introductions" found usually at the beginning of the rite, e.g., of the various sacraments, the Sacramentary, the Lectionary, the Liturgy of the Hours, in the books containing the officially approved vernacular text of the respective rite.

[3] CL, art. 13.

[4] For the rosary, see Anthony N. Fuerst, *This Rosary*, revised and enlarged ed., Mil-

waukee 1943; A. M. Roguet, "*Lectures pour le rosaire*," in *La maison Dieu*, no. 30 (1952), pp. 149 ff; F. Weisgerber, *Votre rosaire, comment le prier?*, Clervaux, Luxembourg 1954; *La couronne des mystères. Pour méditer le rosaire avec l'année liturgique*, a booklet edited by the CPL, Paris 1958. J. Godefroid, *Catéchèse biblique du rosaire* (*Coll. Par. et Lit.* 34), 1958. For the devotions in regard to the Passion of our Lord: J. Godefroid, *Catéchèse bibli-*

will be able to be of use in preparing the faithful to understand and live the liturgy.

Among these popular devotions a special position can be accorded — because it is possible to give them a structure identical to the authentic celebration of the prior part of the Mass, in which case they will be an excellent help to understanding the same — to the so-called "celebrations of the word of God," i.e., Bible services or Bible vigils, so highly recommended by the Council. It would even seem, in the light of the Council documents, that such celebrations may be able to be admitted by the competent authority as a true liturgical form.[5]

In the third place, observing due prudence and caution, the same purpose of practical initiation to the liturgy can be served in certain circumstances even by the so-called "paraliturgies," or paraliturgical services in which the exteriorly expressive aspect of a liturgical celebration is developed in almost a panoramic way.[6]

The theoretical aspect of this initiation embraces the various branches of liturgical catechesis. The principal branches are: direct liturgical catechesis, which has for its immediate object the explanation of the liturgy; and preaching, teaching catechism to children, and instruction in religion, insofar as these maintain their necessary connection with the liturgy.

que des dévotions de la passion, ibid., 1960. For Eucharistic devotions, see the collaborated work *Pastorale liturgique des dévotions eucharistiques, ibid.*, 1959.

[5] CL, art. 35 § 4. See the more detailed norms indicated in the *Instructio* of 1964, nos. 37–39. Numerous plans for such celebrations can be found in *Lumiere et vie* (supplement to *Paroisse et liturgie*) from no. 7, largely under the signature of Th. Maertens, who also writes on the theory of these celebrations in *"Bible et liturgie. Les lois et l'organisation d'une celebration de la parole,"* in *Paroisse et liturgie,* Vol. 33 (1951), pp. 9–18. Numerous examples and plans for such services have been published since the early 1950s.

[6] When paraliturgical services first began to be discussed around 1940, included in this category was the form that much later came to be called "celebrations of the word of God," Bible services, or Bible vigils. Distinction is opportune, however, because they are two very different things. What is now termed paraliturgical are services somewhat akin to scenic representations or scenic portrayals of a religious nature and having a certain general character that puts them in relation and approach to the liturgy properly so called. These have definite limitations, and dangers which must be avoided: those who assist at them may

begin to mistake them for the real article, the true liturgy, and come to prefer them to the liturgy, as being more understandable and more "efficacious." That is why these paraliturgical services have given rise to considerable polemical writing (see, for example, J. Boutet, *"Où vont les paraliturgies?"* in *Paroisse et liturgie,* Vol. 29 (1947), pp. 111–119. See also the admonition of the French episcopate in *La maison Dieu,* no. 42 [1955], p. 31).

To respond to the requisite conditions, the paraliturgical service must be arranged by truly competent persons. Numerous schemata are given in *Paroisse et liturgie* and in its supplements: see the indices thereto for 1955, pp. 439ff. See the collections published by CPL of Paris: *Le Seigneur vient; Triduum paschal (recueil noté); Triduum paschal pour les fidèles.* C. M. Travers, *"Liturgie et paraliturgies de la quinzaine pascale,"* in *La maison Dieu,* no. 19 (1949), pp. 87–113. *"Quelques paraliturgies proposées par le CPL pour la Mission de Brey,"* ibid., no. 17 (1949), pp. 162–174. *Paraliturgies de Noël,* edited by the ACJB, 127 rue Marie Térèse, Louvain. *Veilées de Noël,* edited by the *"Semeur,"* Lyon. Ph. Verhaegen, *"Paraliturgies de Noël,"* in *Paroisse et liturgie,* Vol. 33 (1951), pp. 349–352. *Veilées de Noël,* a collaborated work in the *Collection Paroisse et liturgie,* no. 36.

In some way the theological principles which we have sought to explain in this present work are involved in all the aforementioned means of liturgical pastoral, both practical and theoretical. The reform of the liturgy must itself be guided by a clear vision of such principles. To have brought this into prominent relief is one of the greater services of the Constitution on the Sacred Liturgy issued by the Second Vatican Council. It seems necessary, nevertheless, to insist in particular upon the theological liturgical bases that are demanded by the strict relationships between preaching and liturgy, and between liturgy and catechism.

2. Preaching and Liturgy

The ideal of a pastoral totally ordered around the liturgy as the apex toward which the action of the Church tends and the source from which all its power emanates cannot but have profound repercussions on the whole problem of preaching in general.[7]

In fact, the liturgical Constitution of Vatican II speaks as follows: ". . . the ministry of preaching is to be fulfilled most faithfully and carefully. The sermon, moreover, should draw its content mainly from scriptural and liturgical sources, for it is the proclamation of God's wonderful works in the history of salvation, which is the mystery of Christ ever made present and active in us, especially in the celebration of the liturgy."[8]

The weight of these words is perceived in the affirmation of a near identity of content in preaching, Scripture, and liturgy. These three realities, it says, are concerned almost totally with the same thing: the wonderful deeds of God, always, even today, present and operative in us, in salvation history, that is, the mystery of Christ ever present. The task of preaching is to announce these deeds or this mystery that the Scriptures narrate and which the liturgy, more than anything else, makes present and operative in the faithful

---

[7] Father D. Grasso, *L'annuncio della salvezza. Teologia della predicazione*, Naples 1960 pp. 341–360 (see also *Gregorianum*, Vol. 42 [1960], pp. 35–42), draws attention to the ambiguity of terminology in this matter and proposes that the general concept of *preaching*, as transmission of the divine message, be subdivided into *evangelization* or *kerygma*, as either the first global announcement of Christianity in view of conversion or as the imparting of a new synthetic awareness to the faithful of what the faith implies; *catechesis*, as the preaching made to those who have already accepted the first global exposition of the faith, in order to lead them more deeply into the elements that their acceptance implies; *homily*, as catechesis in the framework of a liturgical action, especially Eucharistic, and in direct connection with it.

This terminology can be defended on the basis of the scriptural and traditional data— even if this data is not always perfectly clear and consistent—of the ancient Church; and it is in any case useful for specifying more precisely the different genre of preaching in view of the purpose and particular exigencies of each. Among these genres we might point out the preaching of novenas, triduums, etc., and that of meditations or instructions for retreats, exercises, etc. Here we will take preaching in its generic sense, but having in mind that preaching which is addressed to the faithful and which, according to circumstances, is either catechesis or homily.

[8] CL, art. 35 § 2.

every day. The result of all this is an inseparable union of preaching, Scripture, and liturgy.[9] For a proper understanding of all this it is necessary to analyze carefully the nature and characteristics of preaching.[10]

Notion of preaching

Preaching can be defined as the oral announcement of the message of God to the community of the faithful, made by the Church, to induce them to respond to the vital exigencies which are the subject of the message. By expressing in a more precise way some of the elements already contained in the definition, we can say that preaching is the oral announcement of the message of God centered on the mystery of Christ, sacred history, or paschal mystery, made by the Church through her authentic ministers, to the community of the faithful who follow one another through the ages, to induce them to respond to the vital exigencies which are the subject of the message. It is of sufficient interest to our purpose to illustrate this notion somewhat.

It should be noted first of all that the aforesaid definition is not arbitrary or aprioristic. The notes included therein derive from the end itself that preaching pursues. Before passing to a more in-depth examination of some of these notes, let us see in brief how the aforestated definition is found by proceeding from the specific end of preaching.

This end does not coincide simply with instruction, even be it religious instruction, theoretical or practical, in the truths of Christianity. Instruction, in fact, is the specific act of the teacher or professor. The preacher is not simply an instructor or professor of religion. Theoretical instruction in a science is addressed directly to the intelligence alone and, of itself, aims simply at the transmission of concepts by way of reasoning. Practical instruction in an art aims *per se* solely at technical training in the performance of the external acts related to the work of this art. Preaching, even while it embraces an instruction in doctrine, goes beyond the purpose of instruction, whether in a doctrine or in an art. It aims directly at moving the affection and the will of the hearer to induce him immediately to take a certain vital attitude in the face of the truth announced, a certain personal decision binding one's own being in view of that truth.

[9] The *Instructio* of September 1964 says: "Careful attention must be expended, nevertheless, that all the works of pastoral be in a proper relation to the sacred liturgy, and, at the same time, that liturgical pastoral not be carried on in a separate and independent way, but in intimate union with the other pastoral activities. Especially necessary is a strict bond between liturgy and catechesis, religious instruction and preaching" (no. 7).

[10] For general information see the excellent work of D. Grasso, *L'annuncio della salvezza*, with its ample bibliography, cited above in note 7 of the present chapter. See also M. Flick and Z. Alszeghy, "*Il problema teologico della predicazione*," in *Gregorianum,* Vol. 40 (1959), pp. 671–744; D. Grasso, "*Nuovi apporti alla teologia della predicazione*," *ibid.*, Vol. 44 (1963), pp. 88–118. S. Maggiolini, *La predicazione nella vita della chiesa*, Brescia 1961. E. Robben, *Il problema teologico della predicazione*, Rome 1962. P. Massi, "*Catechesi e predicazione liturgica*," in the *Riv. lit.*, Vol. 51 (1963), pp. 131–147.

Preaching has a common aim along with the rhetorical art of oratory — in the sense of the art of persuading by means of speech in view of inducing the hearer at that very moment to a specific affective volitional attitude to a thing. What is proper to preaching is that the truth which it announces is a religious truth, and the engagement of affection and will which it seeks to stir up is a religious engagement in respect to God, to be pleasing to God.

But if that is what the end of preaching is, then its content, i.e., the truths which it proclaims, cannot be other than the truths and other matters concerning God. Indeed, in the supernatural order, these truths can be only those which God has revealed, through which men know His will in their regard and in respect to other matters, as well as the way to go to Him and to please Him, that is to say, the vital attitudes which must be adopted in His presence. But the truths revealed by God are the message, the word of God; and this, in turn, is in fact centered entirely in Christ and coincides, in its basic structure, with the sacred history of salvation, the mystery of Christ, the paschal mystery, mystery of the Church, as we have already shown in Chapters 1 and 8.

At the same time, because of the law of incarnation and the law of salvation in community, the revealed word of God, which preaching must induce men to make a concern of their own, has for its necessary and solitary designedly authentic organ the Church, acting through her authentic agents. The individual must receive the word of God from the Church through her authentic ministers. Moreover, and always because of the same law of salvation in community, the individual receives the word which concerns him in the bosom of the community. By means of the Church, God proposes His revealed word to the community, and in and through the community to single individuals.

Let us see why, in brief, given the proper aim of Christian preaching, to move the affection and the will of man in God's presence to a supernatural order, oral preaching to the faithful cannot be other than the announcement of the message of God, centered on the mystery of Christ, the paschal mystery, sacred salvation history, made by the Church through her authentic ministers to the community of the faithful who succeed each other through the ages, to induce them to respond to the vital exigencies that that word carries with it.

Preaching as mystery. Does preaching belong somewhere between the sacraments and the sacramentals?

This general concept of preaching gives rise to several matters worthy of note, constituting as it were a theology of preaching, which reflection on the same has recently discovered or rediscovered, and rightly endeavors to bring into prominence. Among these let us take note of some that are of major interest to our present purpose.

The first is the concept that preaching is a *mysterium*, a *sacramentum*; *mysterium* and *sacramentum*, of course, in the general sense of ancient tradition, which we already know, involves a sensible sign, efficacious in its own way, significant of supersensible realities in relation to God's economy of salvation in Christ.

The sensible sign in this case is the word of the minister of the Church spoken in the midst of the community assembled to hear him. The supersensible reality in relation to salvation, to which the sign is referred, is the fact that the assembly is an assembly, or *ekklesía*, of God in Christ Jesus; that the word of the priest to the assembly is the word of God which He, by means of the Church and through her ministers, addresses at this very moment to such an assembly gathered together by Him, and by means of that assembly and in that assembly, to single individuals; the fact again that God is served by those sensible words of the priest, which fall upon ears of flesh, to transmit to the hearer His supersensible word, that which speaks internally to the heart and to the soul of each man; that that word of God, announced sensibly by the priests, is in this way, in the hands of God Himself, an efficacious instrument which, in some way, through the Spirit and the power of God who is served by it, realizes in the hearer that which it announces. By "in some way" we mean insofar as God unites to the external word of His minister that internal word of His Spirit with which He internally strikes the intelligence and the heart of the hearer and, granting the moral dispositions of the one receiving, renders efficacious in him the external word of the preaching; indeed, He causes echoes of life to reverberate in him, which are a conversion ever new, an obligation before God ever new, an adherence to Him ever new, and ever more profound in faith, in hope, and in charity.

But precisely how does God, in the sermon "unite" the internal power of His Spirit to the external word of the minister? This is the problem of the proper efficacy of the announcement of the word of God. Even in Catholic circles a better solution to this problem is now being sought, after the happy demise of the era of the almost exclusive apologetic defense against the Protestant exaggerations which tend to exalt the word at the expense of the sacraments.[11]

It cannot be said at this time that theology has achieved a perfect clarification of the question. The following points, nevertheless, seem certain enough.

1) It is not enough to say that the sermon is the *occasion* for God's giving of His grace. For that purpose, God can make use of anything as occasion.

[11] See the bibliography in D. Grasso, "*Nuovi apporti . . .*," (cited above in note 10), pp. 91, 99–103; 117–118; also his "*L'annuncio . . .*," (cited above in note 7), pp. 277–292. Schillebeeckx and Semmelroth, cited above in Chapter 23, note 6. A. Günthör, *Die Predigt*, Herder 1963, pp. 42–63.

It might be necessary to say at least, however, that the sermon is for God the special occasion of His giving of grace. But in what does this special character consist? That is the problem. Moreover, the concept of occasion is not sufficiently explanatory of the biblical texts, which, in respect to the prophetic or apostolic preaching, have a language much more direct and more forceful.[12]

2) *Per se*, every sermon, in the intentional area of knowledge and affection, has for him who receives it — and saving always his free will — a causal efficiency dispositive to the first reception or to the successive augmentation of sanctifying grace; indeed, it brings always to his knowledge the action and the will of God in regard to men in general and in regard to himself in particular, and at the same time it presents to him an invitation and an exhortation to conform himself to that will. This being the case, it is already apparent that preaching has the value of actual grace, and therefore every sermon belongs, in the broad sense, among the sacramentals.

3) When the sermon is made part of a liturgical act, as an element prescribed or even only permitted by the Church, it is also a sacramental in the proper sense, at least by the same title that makes such of every liturgical act of ecclesiastical institution. Insofar as it is a sacramental, the sermon has the efficacy of an instrumental cause properly so called of the grace which is principally *ex opere operantis Ecclesiae*, but also, by a subordinate title, *ex opere operantis* of the individual who hears it and of the minister who preaches it. Let us recall that according to common teaching the efficacy of the sacramentals in respect to grace is referred to the actual grace which they cause after the manner of prayer, and taking into account the general laws which regulate the granting of prayer.

When, therefore, it is said that the sermon, inasmuch as it is a sacramental, operates as a cause principally *ex opere operantis Ecclesiae*, this means, as we have already explained,[13] that God makes use of the sermon to grant, to those who are well disposed, actual graces, such as sentiments of faith, hope, and charity, repentance, etc., while the persons themselves are open to sanctifying grace or to its increase and sympathetic to the dignity and the prayer of the Church which is in some way actualized in the very act itself of preaching. This, of course, gives even greater prominence to the character of *sacramentum*, which the sermon possesses in the broad sense.

4) Some go further in this direction and speak, in regard to the announcement or proclamation of the word of God, of something intermediate between the sacramentals and the sacraments properly so called.

It is certain that the sermon is of divine institution: "Go and preach"

---

[12] See Acts 14:3; 20:32; 1 Cor. 1:18; 4:15;   4:12; James 1:21.
2 Cor. 5:19; 1 Thess. 2:13; Phil. 2:16; Heb.   [13] Chapter 3, pp. 111 ff.

(Mark 16:15; cf. Matthew 28:19-20; Luke 24:47-49). In this respect it resembles the sacraments in the strict sense and not the sacramentals.

The privileged character, moreover, of the announcement of the word of God in respect to the other sacramentals is undeniable whenever this announcement is none other than the reading or proclamation of the Scriptures as word of God purely and simply, even though it is pronounced through the instrument of a minister. The actual presence, *sui generis*, and the operative force of God and of Christ in this word [14] is certainly of a nature and degree superior to that which is verified in the other sacramentals. It is logical to conclude that its efficacy too is superior.

Is all this still valid when it is a question of the sermon as explanation of the Scripture announcement of the word of God in the broader sense? Even understood in this way, the sermon has not only the privilege of divine institution, but also, insofar as it concerns the Church in its totality, the guarantee of infallible divine assistance for the safeguarding of its purity in the spirit of Christ.[15] Therefore, considered even under this aspect, it remains by an eminent title the word of God and of Christ enunciated by the Church in which, by an eminent title, the divine power is present.[16]

It is certain, nevertheless, that only with the seven sacraments properly so called, and not with the sacramentals nor with the proclamation of the word of God nor with its explanation, has God granted the concession of sanctifying grace *ex opere operato*.

It seems, therefore, that in the sacramental economy, understood in a broad sense, it is possible to speak of the proclamation of the word of God as something intermediate between the seven sacraments proper and the sacramentals of simple ecclesiastical institution.

It is evident that all this is of no small importance for gaining a better understanding of the dignity and of the necessity of the proclamation of the word of God in the Church and for a more balanced view of the relations between word and sacrament.

Thus, even through that exterior proclamation of the word of God made by the minister of the Church to the assembly of the faithful, there is fulfilled, in the succession of the ages, in the single individuals who appear on the earth, the mystery of Christ as mystery of the salvation which the Father works for

---

[14] See CL, art. 7: "He [Christ] is present in his word since it is he himself who speaks when the holy scriptures are read in the Church."

[15] It is noteworthy that in the four Gospels there is substantial agreement on the point that Jesus, in commissioning the proclamation of His doctrine to all the world, connected His infallible assistance to that commission. See Matthew 28:18-20; Mark 16:15-20; Luke 24:45-49 (cf. also Acts 1:7-8); John 14:25-26; 15:26-27.

[16] See also the *Didache*, 4, 1: "My son, remember him night and day who spoke to you the word of God. Honor him as the Lord, for where the majesty of the Lord is told, there the Lord is." And the *Apostolic Constitutions* 7, 9: "Indeed, where instruction about the Lord is imparted, there the Lord is."

men through Christ in the Spirit. All this impresses upon Christian preaching a profound mysterious character, making it a sacred thing, a sacral action, making it appear as part of the great mystery of Christ ever in action, the history ever in action of the Church ever being actualized.

Anyone who reflects on how, especially in our own times, the preacher is constantly threatened by lack of faith in his duty, by lack of confidence in the usefulness of his toils — all things which, by deadening his enthusiasm and his strength of mind, are hindrances for him in his work, because they take away the confidence, the boldness, the *parresía* indispensable to the minister of the word [17] —will understand how important it is to regain the awareness of the character of mystery which pertains to Christian preaching, to regard it as that which it really is: sacred mystery, part and aspect of the great mystery of Christ, the mystery of sacred salvation history.

Prophetic character of preaching

Having rediscovered, without the shadow of pseudomysticism, the mystical character of Christian preaching, we rediscover also, without any illuminist aberrations nor with so much as a hint of revivalism or pentecostalism, its prophetic character. In the definition, this character is implied in the term *announcement* or *proclamation*. That, primarily, is what distinguishes preaching from the concept of teaching. For, as we said above, teaching or instruction is directed of itself alone either to simple communication of concepts to the intelligence of another by way of reasoning or to the technical skill in the execution of external acts in a specific area; whereas preaching aims, if necessary, to persuade the intelligence, but only as a means of getting to the affections and the will. Moreover, the distinction is evident by the fact that *announcement* is the concept suited to indicate the communication of individual historical events: an event, especially if it is in act, is announced or proclaimed, not instructed or taught. Finally, the difference in concepts can be seen by the fact that *announcement* has also the value of message, as transmission of words and of will to others, especially if it is in the form of a proclamation or an appeal.

Now, under all these aspects, the preacher is eminently an announcer, a herald. To urge along the affections and the will of men toward God, he transmits to them essentially the knowledge of an event, ancient but ever in act and belonging even to the future: the intervention of God in history, in Christ, which includes and, under a certain aspect, is essentially the word or

---

[17] See, for example, H. Schlier, article *"Parresía"* in the *Theological Dictionary of the New Testament*, Vol. 5 (1967), pp. 871–886, esp. 879 ff. The temptation for the preacher to a lack of confidence in the utility of his own work is not simply a modern phenomenon, even if today it is acutely manifested. See the admission of the deacon Deogratias of Carthage and the exhortations given him by St. Augustine in his *De catechizandis rudibus* 3 (2) ff; 14 (10) ff.

message of God to the world in the form of a proclamation and of an appeal
to men.

But these are precisely the essential traits of the prophet, especially in the
Old Testament: the messenger of God to the people, who announces God's
bursting in, past, present, and future, into the history of the people and of
individuals, the intervention of God centered on the Messiah then to come,
and who transmits the word and the will of God as proclamation and appeal
to the chosen people and through them to all mankind. Christian preaching,
therefore, is an announcement of a prophetic nature. It is certain that we can
learn much from this intrinsically prophetic nature of preaching. Among
else, this preaching logically demands of the preacher a strong awareness of
the necessity of his full dedication and continued dependence upon God,
upon His word, upon His Spirit, of whom he can be no more than the announcer and the instrument.

Content of preaching: salvation history, mystery of Christ, the central object of preaching

From the mysterious nature, sacral and prophetic, of Christian preaching
is derived what must be its content. We can say it is the word of God, the
truths of the faith, revelation. It is all one. I mean that all revelation, all the
truths of the faith, the whole word of God is the object of Christian preaching. However, the truths of faith are many and their aspects are multiplex,
and all are the revealed word of God, at least implicitly; for there is nothing
in the Catholic faith that is not in some way revealed by God, even the dogmas made explicit in the course of the centuries.

But God has revealed all this in a certain order, in a certain perspective, in
which each individual point and each individual aspect occupies its own
relative position in the totality. We know that this order and this perspective
are constituted by the sacred history of salvation, mystery of Christ, paschal
mystery, ever in act, as general framework or general background against
which is described all that is proposed in revelation. It is not without reason
that we have deemed it necessary even from our first chapter to bring this fact
into the light, so decisive, it seems to us, is its importance in the Christian
view of the world, whether in the general area of theology or in the biblical,
liturgical, spiritual, or pastoral field.

We have explained sufficiently that sacred history, the mystery of Christ,
is always in act because it is not only something that took place in the past
and is to be fulfilled in the future, but it takes place and is being fulfilled in
the world, in every Christian, constantly, every day, primarily by way of the
liturgy, to which there must be a response of moral adherence in the depths
of the soul of every man. In this daily fulfillment of sacred history, mystery
of Christ, the announcement of the word of God has its specific role, which
it is now our task to determine precisely.

We have also explained sufficiently that when it is stated that revelation is presented primarily as a sacred history, mystery of Christ and of the Church, it is not intended to mean that revelation does not also contain a speculative aspect, either metaphysical or, as we have termed it, entitative; this aspect is everywhere quite real, but commands a secondary level of attention, like the remote basis of a thing. The magisterium of the Church has, through the course of history, frequently made individual points explicit, especially because of the necessity of defending doctrine against errors, as when it defined the consubstantiality of the three Persons of the Trinity; or the unicity of person and duality of natures in Christ; or the possibility of knowing with certitude the existence of God by reasoning from the causality of created things, and the like.

In these cases and in many other similar instances, the background of the entitative nature of individual points of sacred history, mystery of Christ, which are actually found in the Bible, but only on a secondary level of attention, have been made explicit and have been defended by the magisterium and, in this sense, they are brought up to the primary level of attention of believers. They too are word of God no less than the others.

In the same way, let us keep in mind that in the general framework of sacred salvation history, the moral aspect, although of great importance and quite clearly made explicit everywhere in that same Bible, is nevertheless so presented therein that the moral obligations and duties in the Bible seem to be derived immediately from the interventions of God in Christ in the sacred history of salvation and only remotely, for the most part, from reasons of the natural intrinsic constitution of beings or from the philosophical analysis of the virtues and vices.

Even the opposition and defense against errors contrary to the faith is everywhere present in revelation and already in the Bible; one thinks, for example, of the anti-pagan controversy in the Old Testament and of the anti-Judaizing controversy in the New. This too, evidently, is word of God. But it is no less evident that the disputation against the adversaries, in the general synthetic framework of revelation as salvation history, is a derived and secondary aspect, however important it may be, in respect to the positive and expositive irenic exposition of the facts and of the doctrines for the use of the believer. These considerations are of no small importance to that question which we are endeavoring to clarify.

It follows, in fact, that to preach sacred history, mystery of Christ, paschal mystery, does not imply that one does not take into consideration in his preaching other important aspects of revelation, nor that he must limit himself to one only aspect as "sacred history." In particular, it does not at all mean that in preaching one may leave out, without giving it due prominence when necessary, the more entitative and, as it were, speculative aspect of Christian doctrine, even as expressed in precise definitions, nor even its apologetic aspect; so much the less, then, will preaching sacred history be intended to mean giving only minor prominence to the moral aspect of the Christian life.

Centering one's preaching on God's interventions in the history of the world, in Christ, does not mean either that the general outline of the sacred history that we sketched in the first chapter of our book must be the object of every sermon. That framework is the prospective synthesis of those realities. We do not pretend that every sermon must have for its object the explaining of sacred salvation history in that prospective synthesis.

Most assuredly it is necessary that the preacher never lose sight of the salvation history perspective, and that every now and then, be it only with a brief word or a passing allusion, he recall it again to his habitual hearers. But, for the rest, he will have to explain in unending variety, now one particular point, now another, of the word of God, either in its dogmatic or moral or even apologetic aspect. What is essential is that the preacher recall to mind and every now and then explain to his audience that every single point that he makes is a certain portion of the mystery of Christ ever in act, a facet of salvation history, and that as such it can best be understood in the totality of the perspective in which God has revealed it to us.

Sacred history, mystery of Christ, the central object of preaching by an intrinsic necessity of the nature of preaching itself

But why must preaching be centered on sacred history or the mystery of Christ in the sense explained above? The fundamental reason is the nature itself of preaching as the announcement of the word of God.

The word of God in its sources, the holy Bible, the ordinary teachings of the magisterium of the Church, and tradition, must be presented primarily as a complexus of revealed truths centering on the concept of sacred history ever in act; for this constitutes the general framework in which and against the background of which the individual particular points are viewed in perspective.

That the word of God in its sources is truly centered on the concept of sacred history, after what we have already said in the first chapter, requires no further demonstration insofar as the Bible is concerned. It is enough to add here that in the New Testament the preaching of salvation viewed in this perspective is frequently called *kérygma*,[18] and that when today, for the

[18] See, for example G. Friedrich, article "*Kéryx, kerýsso, kérygma*," in the *Theological Dictionary of the New Testament*, Vol. 3 (1965), pp. 683–718. A. Retif, "*Qu'est-ce-que le kerygme?*" in *Nouvelle revue théologique*, Vol. 71 (1949), pp. 901–922. In regard to the concept of *kérygma* see the bibliography compiled by A. Liégé in *Parole et mission*, Vol. 13 (1961), pp. 619–622. Additionally: C. H. Thompson, *Theology of the Kerygma. A Study in Primitive Teaching*, London 1962. A. Turck, *Évangélisation et catéchèse aux deux premiers siècles*, Paris 1962. F. Petit, *Proclamer la parole. Ce qu'enseigne la bible sur la prédication*, Paris 1963. The terminology of the New Testament in regard to the various types of preaching is variable. It can be taken, however, that in principle, *kérygma* indicated in a

revival of preaching, it is demanded that in substance preaching be or become again kerygmatic,[19] what is meant is basically that it must focus once more in its connatural general framework on its dynamic and vivifying center, which is the sacred history of salvation, the mystery of Christ, the paschal mystery ever in act. The same holds true in regard to theology, inasmuch as some are demanding a kerygmatic theology.[20]

It should not be necessary to insist further on the fact that in the proposals of the ordinary magisterium all revelation is centered in the sacred history of salvation.[21] In fact, the ordinary magisterium is expressed chiefly in the creed or symbol of faith, the summary and cue card of the whole of the general ecclesiastical teaching. But the creed, as we pointed out in Chapter 1, is totally constructed on the schema of salvation history. Moreover, the ordinary magisterium has, in its own way, a strong voice of its own in the liturgy, in which, as we have never grown tired of pointing out, the whole of revelation is presented and viewed as sacred salvation history ever in act and under the veil of sensible and efficacious signs of the sanctification and worship of the Church.

In regard to the most ancient tradition of the Church,[22] here too we can appeal to the same symbol of faith. Indeed, as is well known and as we have pointed out sufficiently in Chapter 6 à propos of the Trinitarian thought expressed in the most ancient baptismal liturgy, the symbol of the faith is intimately connected, in its ancient historical formation, with the baptismal profession and the rule of faith, both documents created as summaries of the faith and both drawn up in accord with the schema of the sacred history of salvation.

special way the aforesaid preaching in view of leading to the faith, and the *didachè* and *didascalia* indicated especially a further introduction and deepening in the faith itself. However, all the degrees of the announcement of the word were centered essentially on sacred history as mystery of Christ. It is well known also that the fact of the resurrection was regarded as the pivotal point of this sacred history and that the whole plan of salvation was thus presented as the knowledge of the paschal mystery and as participation therein. See H. Schürmann, *Aufbau und Struktur der neutestamentlichen Verkündigung*, Paderborn 1949.

[19] There seems to be a special predilection for this terminology in German-speaking circles, and in particular among the group of Innsbruck theologians, since the launching of the idea by J. A. Jungmann in his *Die Frohbotschaft und unsere Glaubensverkündigung*, first edition, Regensburg 1936. On the necessity and the possibility of the paschal mystery's being again today the focal point of preaching,

see F. X. Arnold, *"La catéchèse en partant du mystère central de l'histoire du salut,"* in *Evangéliser*, Vol. 15 (1960), pp. 211–223.

[20] The well-known controversy over this was aroused by the aforesaid Innsbruck theologians. See E. Kappler, *Die Verkündigungstheologie*, Freiburg in der Schweiz 1949, and the bibliographical and doctrinal résumé in *La scuola cattolica*, Vol. 78 (1950), pp. 350 ff.

[21] The same must not be expected of the proposals of revelation in the interventions of the extraordinary magisterium of the councils or of the definitions *ex cathedra*, precisely because the extraordinary magisterium is sporadic and intervenes primarily (prior to the definition of the Immaculate Conception there were no exceptions to this at all) for the defense of a specific point of doctrine against possible errors and not with the intention of proposing the whole of revelation to the faith of believers.

[22] See A. Turck, cited above in note 18 of the present chapter.

For later tradition up to the twelfth and thirteenth centuries, the fact that the whole of revelation was viewed and synthesized in the West primarily in the framework of the sacred history is abundantly demonstrated by the history of theology in antiquity, which was first of all simply expositive to the faithful and not polemic, as well as from preaching, especially catechetical preaching to the catechumens.

For the non-polemic theology, as we have said already in Chapter 19 in respect to the relations between liturgy and theology as found in the Fathers, the centrality of salvation history is implied in the very concept of the gnosis, which was the ideal of patristic theology, as found in St. Irenaeus of Lyons. It will be worth the trouble to see, for example, how Irenaeus expresses what the object was of the true orthodox gnosis: Its task

> ". . . is to labor over all that which has been said in parables and to incorporate it in the body of the faith; to explain the way in which God acts and His plan in reference to humanity; to explain how God was magnanimous whether in the matter of the apostasy of the rebellious angels or in the disobedience of men; to show why one and the same God has made some things temporal beings and others eternal or celestial; to understand why this God, who is invisible, has appeared to the prophets, and this not just under one form only but under various forms; to explain why various covenants were offered to mankind, and to teach what the character proper to each of them was; to search out the reason why God included all men in the disobedience in order to show mercy to all, to tell with gratitude why the Word of God was made flesh and suffered; to explain why it is in these last times that the Son of God has appeared, and why, therefore, the Beginning has appeared at the end; to uncover all that which is in the Scripture about the faith and about things to come; and not to be silent about how it has happened that God, against every hope, has made the Gentiles coheirs with the saints, one only body with them and sharers with them; to explain how this poor mortal flesh will be reclothed with immortality and this corruptible flesh with incorruptibility; to proclaim how that which was 'not My people' has become 'My people,' and how they who were 'not beloved' have become 'beloved,' and how the woman abandoned has had more children than she who had a husband." [23]

If one recalls that Irenaeus, certainly exaggerating somewhat his point of view, intended to exclude as it were from his investigation of the true gnosis all those questions which are not directly and clearly determined by the Scriptures, and especially those which we would today refer to as belonging to the speculative order,[24] and that he insists forcefully on the rule of faith, of which

---

[23] St. Irenaeus, *Adversus haereses* 1, 10, 3. See also 4, 33, 1; 4, 33, 7; and 4, 31–33 *in toto*.

[24] See, for example, *Adv. haer.* 2, 18, 7; 2, 27, 1; 2, 28, 3; 2, 28, 6 (Jurgens, no. 204); 2, 28, 7.

he intends that no further investigation shall add anything,[25] it will easily be understood how it is that in the ideal of theology which he cherishes, the biblical character and that of the sacred history of salvation is preeminent.

In the theology of Origen, under a certain aspect, the properly temporal and historical point of view of revelation suffers from being somewhat obscured. Under another aspect, however, the concept of salvation history dominates his whole synthesis inasmuch as, being strongly preoccupied with the degrees of the ascetical mystical ascent of the soul to God, he keeps ever present the concept of the three gradations in this ascent here on earth, completed by a fourth degree which is perfected in the eschatology, in the beyond. Origen constantly rediscovers these degrees foretold and prefigured in the various episodes of salvation history, so that in some way this history finds a place everywhere in his perspective. It is the basis of all his allegorical interpretation of Scripture, assiduous contact with which remains always the fundamental canon of his method, not only in all his exegetical and dogmatic works but even in his numerous sermons or homilies to the people.[26]

In St. Augustine the concept of this sacred salvation history or, as he calls it, *dispensatio, dispensatio temporalis, historia, historia dispensationis, administratio, narratio*, etc., so dominates his whole way of viewing revelation that when writing his *De vera religione* about the year 390 A.D., he could say: "The essence of this religion which we must follow consists in the history and in the prophecy of the temporal dispensation of Divine Providence for the salvation of the human race, to reform it and to refit it for life eternal."[27] His great synthetic vision of revelation as salvation history continuously in act remains present everywhere in Augustine's theological works, so much so that it has rightly been said: "The aspect of sacred history constitutes not just some sort of secondary viewpoint but an essential characteristic of the theology of Augustine. His clarity is at its best when he explains the creed. One thinks, for example, of his *De fide et symbolo*, his *Enchiridion*, his *De agone christiano*, etc. But this theme bursts in everywhere, practically from the time of his writing the *De moribus* and the *De genesi contra manichaeos* (387-389 A.D.), where Augustine treats of the Christian mysteries of salvation."[28]

The central position of the concept of sacred history in patristic theology is in full bloom in the West until the twelfth and thirteenth centuries, in ser-

[25] See, for example, *Adv. haer.* 1, 10, 1-2 (Jurgens, nos. 191–192).

[26] See, for example, Cyprian Vagaggini, "La natura della sintesi origeniana e l'ortodossia e l'eterodossia della dogmatica di Origene," in *La scuola cattolica*, Vol. 82 (1954), pp. 192–195. Henri de Lubac, *Histoire et esprit: l'intelligence des Écritures d'après Origène*, Paris 1950.

[27] *De vera religione* 7, 13.

[28] M. Löhrer, *Der Glaubensbegriff des hl. Augustinus in seinen ersten Schriften bis zu Confessiones*, Einsiedeln 1954, p. 186; the theology of St. Augustine in regard to faith against the background of the sacred history is treated in particular on pp. 186–202.

mons and in catecheses to the faithful and to the catechumens.[29] The whole mystagogic literature, of which we spoke in Chapter 19, is centered essentially on the concept of sacred history, mystery of Christ ever in act, viewed from the starting point of the liturgy of Christian initiation. It should be noted that the *Demonstratio apostolicae traditionis* of St. Irenaeus can be included in this same literary genre, it being a compendium of the teachings of the faith, very like a simple amplification of a catechesis, constructed on the plan of the creed and hence on that of sacred history: unity and trinity of God, God the creator, creation, fall, Abraham, Moses, judges, kings, prophets, fulfillment of prophecy in Christ and in His kingdom, which is the Church.

Even here, however, as in so many other things, Augustine is the supreme representative of the patristic tradition. This is a matter often enough pointed out by scholars [30] and should not be surprising after what we noted above in regard to sacred history as the central concept of his theology: that in his sermons to the people in general and in a special way in his catechesis to the catechumens he considers sacred history, *temporalis dispensatio salvationis*, as the principal object and the focal point of preaching, or better still, as the general framework which contains and within which are ordered the individual points to be made in preaching.

In his *De catechizandis rudibus* Augustine makes explicit the theory of what must be the object and the manner of the catechesis of catechumens, and at the end of the work he gives two examples, one of some length, the other short. The whole is conceived according to the rules of rhetoric, in the framework of the *narratio* and of the *exhortatio*. Here the *narratio* is simply the *temporalis dispensatio salvationis*. He begins with creation and briefly narrates the whole sacred history up to Christ and the Church, and then passes to the resurrection of the flesh and to the future life.[31] Everything is centered

---

[29] On the general history of preaching in respect to its content, see Y. Brilioth, *Landmarks in the History of Preaching. Donellan Lectures*, Dublin, 1949 and London (SPCK) 1950. The author, a Protestant, gives a rapid panorama of the question. He wrote a work on the same theme but in more depth in Swedish: *Predikaus historia*, Lund 1946. See also A. Niebergall, "*Die Geschichte der christlichen Predigt*," in *Leiturgia*, Vol. 2, Kassel 1955, pp. 181–352, with ample bibliography in regard to the general history of preaching. Among the earlier authors deserving of special note is H. Hering, *Die Lehre von der Predigt*, Berlin 1905, pp. 1–247. Some allusions will be found also in E. Weisemann, "*Der Predigtgottesdienst und die verwandeten Formen*," in *Leiturgia*, Vol. 3, Kassel 1956, pp. 8–22. B. Dreher, *Die Osterpredigt von der Reformation bis zur Gegenwart*, Freiburg im Br. 1951. In his treatment of the theme, Dreher restricts himself to Easter sermons; but in so doing he reflects admirably on the whole development of the history of preaching in general from the point of view of the general character of its content. He also gives a quick introduction to paschal preaching prior to the sixteenth century.

[30] See, for example, B. Capelle, "*Prédication et catéchèse selon S. Augustine*," in *Les questions liturgique et paroissiales*, Vol. 33 (1952), pp. 55–64. Jean Card. Daniélou, "*L'histoire du salut dans la catéchèse*," in *La maison Dieu*, Vol. 30 (1952), pp. 19–35. F. van der Meer, *Augustinus als Seelsorger*, Cologne 1953, pp. 404 ff. M. Pontet, *L'exégèse de S. Augustin prédicateur*, Paris 1954, pp. 35–110.

[31] *De catechizandis rudibus* 5; 10–11.

on Christ. Before His coming, everything tended toward Him; afterwards, everything derives from Him, particularly His Church, which is His kingdom and His body.[32]

The whole *dispensatio* has its ultimate explanation and end in love. God wants to show His love and wants to arouse the response of our love. In unfolding the *narratio*, the catechist must have no other purpose than to arouse in his audience faith, hope, and especially love.[33]

The *exhortatio*, which contains admonitions against temptations — among which, as is well known, there is also a warning of an apologetic type to be on guard against pagans, heretics, and schismatics — and the precepts of an honest Christian life, comes at the end as a logical consequence of the *narratio*; and in the *exhortatio* everything is viewed in the direct light of the facts stated in the *narratio* itself.[34]

The explicit explanation (always in the framework of sacred history, mystery of Christ ever in act) of the *sacramenta* of Christian initiation is left by Augustine until after baptism, and is given by him to the neophytes, as is apparent from his sermons addressed to them. This is connected with the law of the *arcanum* which still existed in his time. When custom abolished that law, this explanation of the *sacramenta* found its natural place in the general format of the sacred history catechesis where the Church is treated.

The *narratio* is evidently not conceived by Augustine as pure "narration" but also as explanation. Hence in some way and in accord with the capacity, the need, and the utility for the hearers themselves, those questions are touched upon which the *narratio* itself raises: ". . . so that the causes and the reasons behind the individual things and individual events that are narrated may be explained." [35] In the catechesis, however, all this must tend to exhibit and to excite love: in the explanations we must refer the things and the events narrated "to that end of love, from which the eye must never be distracted, neither of him who speaks nor of him who listens." The explanation must never lose itself in difficult questions in such a way that it would result in a forgetfulness or in an obscuring of the grand structure of the sacred history; for indeed, it must tend to shed light upon it: "At any rate, we must not expound upon these reasons in such a way that, having abandoned the subject matter of the *narratio*, our mind and our tongue become lost in knotty and difficult questions. Indeed, the truth of the reason adopted for explanatory purposes must be like the golden thread which is fastened about a gem for a purpose, but which does not by any excess disturb the simple beauty of the ornament: "*sed ipsa veritas adhibitae rationis quasi aurum sit gemmarum ordinem ligans, non tamen ornamenti seriem ulla immoderatione perturbans.*" [36]

Words of gold. The reasoned explanations to which recourse will be had

---

[32] *Ibid.* 8.
[33] *Ibid.* 6–8.
[34] *Ibid.,* 11.

[35] *Ibid.* 10.
[36] *Ibid., loc. cit.*

must serve as it were to bind the gems in their settings of sacred history and to bring into prominence something of its general union and design, not indeed to make one's listeners forgetful of it and so much the less to confuse them. Therefore, the function of the reasoned explanations is clearly subordinate to the *narratio* itself of sacred history, with the purpose of making the latter better understood.

Augustine contemplates even the possible circumstance, and what to do in such an event, of having for a catechumen one who is a rhetorician — we might say an intellectual, which would be about the equivalent in our times, or straightway, a scholar.[37]

Naturally, it will be necessary to treat each person according to his own state and his own dispositions, and to take into account that which he already knows, in order not to bore him. But, admitting this, the essential matter that will be announced to the scholar does not differ from that which is announced to the ignorant. If perchance it will be heeded, Augustine admonishes, in a discreet way but with substantial firmness, the intellectuals should be put on their guard against presumption, so as to strengthen in them the humility of which they have already given some evidence by asking for baptism; otherwise, the same way will be followed for both.[38]

From all this it is easily understood that for St. Augustine, as for the whole mentality of ancient tradition, the central content and the unifying concept, everywhere present and most prominently, of the catechesis of adult catechumens, is not different from that of ordinary preaching to the faithful; and it is the same as the central content and unifying framework of theology, no less than of the ordinary teaching of the magisterium, of the Bible itself, and of the liturgy as well. Now it is possible to catch a glimpse of the marvelous unity which, in this conception, unites Bible, magisterial teaching, liturgy, tradition, theology, ordinary preaching to the faithful and catechesis of the catechumens — a unity for which our own times are rightly sighing! The bond which unifies all these members is the primacy of emphasis given to the reality of salvation history that each is called upon to explain.

Thus do we understand anew why article 16 of the conciliar Constitution on the Sacred Liturgy specifies precisely salvation history as the basis on which the unity of all sacred learning must be reconstructed.

This unity remained alive until the twelfth and thirteenth centuries, and after that it began to diminish insofar as the relationships among theology, Bible, preaching, and catechesis were concerned, though it remained intact, of course, in respect to the relations between Bible and ordinary teaching of the magisterium, as well as among Bible, magisterial teaching, and liturgy.

---

[37] *Ibid.* 12–13.

[38] Ibid., 12: ". . . *Ut caveat praesumptionis errores, quantum eius humilitas quae illum adduxit, iam sentitur admittere. Caetera vero secundum regulas doctrinae salutaris, sive de fine, quaecumque narranda vel disserenda sunt, sive de moribus, sive de tentationibus, suo modo percurrendo quo dixi, ad illam supereminentem viam* (= charity) *omnia referenda sunt.*" See also *ibid.,* 13.

We do not mean that theology and preaching then ignored salvation history. To ignore it is impossible in a Catholic regimen, and so much the more is it impossible to deny it. But that concept had less prominence in the way in which individual questions were treated in the theological synthesis, and hence in preaching, which is always in some way dependent upon the state of theology.

In saying this I am far indeed from wanting to suggest that from the twelfth and thirteenth centuries and aferwards theology did not in its own way make an enormous contribution that can and must be used to gain a better understanding of the same mystery of Christ ever in act. This contribution in regard to the questions of the entitative order — or, if you will, of the speculative order — which are posed by the same sacred salvation history, and, beginning with the sixteenth century, even by the properly historical and biblical exegetical order, has been and is enormous; and it would be absurd to pretend that it can be taken lightly.

It is not a matter, therefore, of heralding an indiscriminate and naïve "return to the Fathers." We wanted only to show that while preserving the indispensable contribution of the speculative order and, more recently, even of the historical biblical exegetical order, which the scholastic and later ages made to the more profound understanding of revelation, it is urgent to reestablish in the awareness of theologians, whether in the general organization of all their respective material or in their manner of viewing individual questions, the full value of the great concept of sacred history, mystery of Christ ever in act, as the general framework of all revelation, of theology, and of preaching.[39]

Beginning with the twelfth and thirteenth centuries, theologians began to take strong cognizance of the necessity that in the explanation of revelation *causae rationesque reddantur*, as St. Augustine said; [40] and they focused their attention on the causes and reasons of the entitative speculative order and, thanks to this analytic concentration, they made an admirable contribution in this very area, which can and must serve to provide a deeper understanding

[39] It must be recognized, unfortunately, that among those who, north of the Alps, are rightly predicting a new appreciation of the concept of salvation history, especially in theology and preaching, in regard to the point that, in any case, this new appreciation must take place without sacrificing the later contributions, especially of the scholastics, in regard to a more profound elaboration of the speculative aspect of revelation, clarity of expression in the statement of their ideas is not one of their points of particular reknown. There is among them, in fact, a nebulosity of idea which, often enough, has practical consequences. It touches, as you see, upon the question of the nature and method of theology, on which rests, in the final analysis, that unity among Bible, theology, liturgy, and preaching. To explain in full depth how it is possible and necessary in the investigation of revelation to give to the aspect of sacred history the primary emphasis that belongs to it without sacrificing the speculative scholastic contribution nor the critical, historical, and apologetic contribution of more recent theology, pertains to the general methodology of theology.

[40] *De catechizandis rudibus* 10.

of revelation. The later centuries, especially from the sixteenth and after-wards, did something similar in regard to the causes and reasons in the his-torical, critical, and apologetic order, also making a notable contribution in this area.

Otherwise, this analytic concentration was accompanied, unfortunately, by an excessive neglect, in the general way of organizing the whole theological synthesis and especially in regard to the treatment in individual questions of the sacred history aspect, the mystery of Christ ever in act, as the general and primary framework of the whole complexus, a background which must never be lost from view. The result of this is that with the passage of time the later theologians, descendants of the great scholastics of the thirteenth century and of the Tridentine theologians, have not kept sufficiently in mind, or simply forgot entirely, the admonition of St. Augustine referred to above, and which is valid not only for preaching and catechesis but also for theology itself: to wit, "We must not expound upon the reasons in such a way that, having abandoned the subject matter of the *narratio*, our mind and our tongue be-come lost in knotty and difficult questions. Indeed, the truth of reason adopted for explanatory purposes must be like the golden thread which is fastened about a gem for a purpose, but which does not by any excess disturb the simple beauty of the ornament."

We have seen that insofar as catechesis is concerned, Augustine certainly intended that explanatory reasons as well as specific commandments and moral exhortations, and even apologetic hints to put one on guard against non-believers, be joined to the *narratio*; but all this surely demands that we never lose sight, smothering it, as it were, in the minds of our listeners, of the background and the general line of sacred history, mystery of Christ. We do not pretend, therefore, that in preaching, and so much the less in theology itself, there can be any neglect of the explanatory causal, moral and apolo-getic viewpoints, but simply that everything be allotted its proper proportion in the totality and that no unjustifiable hypertrophication be allowed "to dis-turb the simple beauty of the ornament"; in other words, that the whole com-plexus and the individual parts appear always and clearly as explanations of the mystery of Christ ever in act, from which the eyes and the heart of the preacher, no less than those of the theologian, the exegete, and the liturgist, must never be distracted.

In conclusion, the very nature intrinsic to preaching as announcement of the word of God, contained in the Bible, presented in the teaching of the magisterium and in the liturgy, demands that its object or content be in the first place none other than the sacred history of salvation ever in act, as was actually the case in ecclesiastical tradition up to the twelfth and thirteenth centuries.

Sacred history, mystery of Christ, and modern goals of a revival of preaching

At this point it is easy to perceive how a more conscious centering of preaching on salvation history ever in act, demanded by the very nature of the proclamation of the word of God, corresponds exactly to the great propriety of those deep aspirations which today are manifested virtually everywhere in regard to a renewal of preaching. What, then, are these just aspirations? Running through the recent literature which treats of this question,[41] it would seem that we can summarize them in the following points.

It is desirable that preaching have a closer connection with Holy Scripture. Not that preaching in the age immediately prior to our own did not depend upon the Bible. But there are ways and there are ways. Today when it is demanded that there be a more biblical preaching, it is meant that the Bible should serve not just as an arsenal of examples and of narratives for the illustration of themes in themselves of a rather philosophical moral nature, even if such themes be found in the Bible; rather, what is meant is that the message itself of the Bible should be preached in its integrity and in the perspective in which the Bible presents it.

It means that in modern preaching there must reappear in full prominence the great themes of the preaching of St. Paul as they are found in his Epistles; the great themes of the Gospel and of the Epistles of St. John, of the Apocalypse, of the Acts of the Apostles; and that through these themes, exactly as is done in these same documents, the figure of Jesus, His preaching as it appears in the Synoptics, the concept of the reality of God, the meaning of history and of human life, the meaning that the Old Testament has for mankind is to be surveyed and reanimated.

In the second place, it is desirable that preaching be more theological in the sense that it be theocentric, that its prospect be primarily that of what God has done for us, and that it present our moral obligations as the necessary response to the love of God for us, shown in His deeds.

It may be thought that preaching in the period immediately prior to our

---

[41] Already for some years the excellent review *Les questions liturgiques et paroissiales*, in its "*Bulletin de littérature liturgique*," has provided an annual bibliographical report prepared by B. Botte, for which we recommend consulting the index at the end of each volume. Some pertinent items of information can be garnered from numerous articles which *La maison Dieu* has devoted to this question on the relations between liturgy and preaching. Up to 1954, see the list in no. 39 on p. 6. Among these articles see especially "*La crise de la prédication*," in *La maison Dieu* no. 13 (1948), pp. 104–107. F. Louvel, "*La proclamation de la parole de Dieu*," *ibid.*, no. 20 (1949). A. Liégé, "*Contenu et pédagogie de la prédication chrétienne*," *ibid.* no. 39 (1954), pp. 23–27. L. Bouyer, "*Conditions d'une prédication vraiment pastorale*," *ibid.*, pp. 38–58. A. M. Roguet, "*Les sources bibliques et liturgiques de la prédication*," *ibid.*, pp. 108–118. *Le prêtre ministre de la parole*, acts of the Congress of Montpelier of 1954, UOCF 1955. See especially therein Jean Card. Daniélou, "*Parole de Dieu et mission de l'église*," pp. 41–56. G. Barra, *Tempo testimonianze*, Milan 1956. J. Ries, *Krisis und Erneuerung der Predigt. Studien zur Situation der Verkündigung*, Frankfurt am M. 1961. N. Fournier, *Esigenze attuali della catechesi*, (Italian trans.), Brescia 1963.

own times was too moralistic, because, some say, at that time preachers frequently satisfied themselves with a superficial moralism that might suffice for an honest philosopher, even if not a Christian. If by this it is meant to imply that preaching must not touch upon, or even that it must relegate always to a secondary place, the moral themes of the commandments, our obligations as creatures, the dangers which threaten our soul, the judgment, etc., such an accusation of moralism hurled against our current preaching would certainly be unfounded, nor would it be possible to give ear to the implied demands. St. Paul, not to speak of Christ Himself, certainly never neglected the moral aspect.

No, what we mean to say is basically that very often moral preaching has been too detached from the general context in which the commandments and the moral obligations are presented in the Scriptures, that is, in the perspective of the sacred history of salvation, the mystery of Christ. What is desired, and rightly so, is that there be a greater insistence on those motives of our moral actions which derive immediately from the action of God in the world in Christ Jesus, and that if it is necessary or useful to have recourse also to motives which do not *per se* transcend the philosophical order, this must not be allowed to obscure the more properly supernatural and specifically Christian motives and aspects of our actions.

No less ardent is the desire that preaching be in some way more Christo-centric, that it may speak everywhere and always of Christ and in a special way be centered on the paschal mystery in Christ, in ourselves, in all the world. And again, not that other points of revelation are not to be touched upon; rather, in the sense primarily that Christ Himself should be most frequently the direct object of our preaching; but especially, that in all the points presented to view we do not neglect to show in the order of divine revelation the indissoluble connection, on the level of God's salvation, that everything has with Christ dead and raised up again as the solitary way by which every good thing comes to us from God and by which every being returns to God.

A most frequent complaint is in regard to the abstractionism of current preaching; it has a bookish flavor not only because it knows too much of the school of dogma and moral but especially because the very way in which it views the objects of which it speaks is too impersonal and abstract. It is especially lamentable that in this preaching God seems more like a distant and transcendent idea than a living Person with whom our relationships are such as are had between person and person. It wants, therefore, to be made more concrete.

To this same problem of concreteness belongs the desire that preaching must be in contact with the true situation, personal, familial, social, economic, etc., in which our faithful do in fact find themselves today, the problems which are of vital interest to them in their daily lives. On this point, however, it is necessary to observe that there exists two kinds of concreteness and of correspondence to the real needs and problems of the faithful: one which is only superficial, and the other of some depth. The concreteness in matters superficial is that of the journalist or chronicler of events, as when one would speak of politics, elections, parties, etc., of business and social questions, of fashions, of some current happening that has made an impression on all, and the like kind of thing. Apart from political matters, in which the greatest prudential judgment is demanded, we do not say that these other questions cannot be touched upon, and even frequently, according to the needs of one's audience, serving perhaps to capture their attention in order to draw them along afterwards to higher things.

What we do say, however, is that in any case, this is not the kind of concreteness that gives substance and lasting fruit to preaching; rather, the concreteness wanted is the kind which knows how to plumb the depths of the universal concerns that are smoldering, perhaps not yet clearly adverted to, in the heart of every man and which the preacher must be able to bring before the eyes of those who hear him. Of such a kind are, for example: the recognition of the bounds of one's own abject misery, and of having need of God; of God's paternal love, and His mercy; a sense of responsibility in life and before God; the recognizing of self as a sinner; the awareness of the obligation of conversion; a sense of the equality of all men in the face of God, in the face of death, in the face of the moral law; a sense of the shortness and of the fragility of life; the need for Christ; that there is joy only in being at peace with God; and the like. The other circumstances of the more superficial concreteness can serve as an introduction to this concreteness of a more substantial kind.

Today one is frequently conscious even of the demand that Christian preaching must be eschatological; there should be no fear of announcing the meaning that history has in the eyes of God and the ultimate goal to which it leads, that is, the heavenly Jerusalem. Modern man has a sense of the general development of history. He is pleased to know himself and to perceive himself as part of a great totality, the beneficiary of all the preceding pains and the artisan, in his own way, of the final result that will most assuredly come after him. To labor for a future goal, arduous but possible, gives a man great dynamic impetus. It is like the mainspring of a watch; and among Catholics it is called hope.

Finally, everyone feels strongly the need of a preaching more clearly centered on the basic truths of the faith, presented in a systemmatic way, and panoramically complete; precisely as must be done with adults who are to be initiated to the Christian faith. Basically it is a question of a treatment characteristic of that which was realized in the ancient Church in the catechesis of the catechumens. The faithful in modern times have need of an initiation in the sense of a catechesis that

". . . must unify the diverse aspects of the Christian mystery and safeguard the organic balance of revelation. This is apparent from the kerygmatic origin of the Christian *Credo*. The living faith is nourished first of all by synthesis. A catechesis that did not constantly present the unity of Christianity as an organic whole deriving from a primitive nucleus and epitomizing itself therein would not cause the unitary reality of the Christian mystery to spring up in hearts.

"The commission to memory of a body of articles of faith would remain. Care will be taken, therefore, to attribute to every aspect of the Christian mystery the importance which belongs to it according to its proximity to the center of revelation. This means first of all that there will be no place for points of pseudospeculative curiosity, empty of the vital religious juices, or for the subtle developments of points on which the word of God is more discreet. It means also that care will be taken not to yield to the imbalances that subjective spiritualities, peripheral devotions, and theological disputes introduce fatally into the presentation of the faith.

"While the solemn magisterium is watchful to protect the faith against deviations from orthodoxy, catechesis, which expresses the ordinary magisterium, must take care not to present unduly the latest among the specifically defined dogmas as the most important dogma. Catechesis is not to be principally anti-heretical, although it must respond to the appeals and to the difficulties of the modern mind." [42]

It may be added that today, even among simple people, there are more and more who desire a solid religious nourishment and who remain, not invited, but subjected to those sermons based entirely on a superficial sentimentalism, even if their themes are of a religious nature; and they understand, in any case, that sentimentalism can perhaps sometimes produce really spectacular bonfires of straw, but certainly puts no lasting coals on the hearth of spiritual life.

Abstracting for the moment from the liturgy, what we have given above is, I think, a panorama, rather complete, of the better-founded desires that frequently, and virtually everywhere, are expressed today in regard to the improvement of preaching.

Now, it is a very remarkable thing and easily understandable on a moment's reflection how all these demands find their point of convergence in the fundamental necessity of the intrinsic nature itself of the announcing of the word of God, that it be centered on sacred salvation history, mystery of Christ ever in act. It is not necessary to explain further how this focus gives preaching that character of dogmatic stability which, without loosing itself in dry intellectualism, never indulges in a facile and superficial sentimentalism; it is equivalent precisely to that synthetic and organically unified per-

---

[42] A. Liégé, "*Contenu et pédagogie de la prédication*," in *La maison Dieu*, no. 39 (1954), pp. 35 ff.

spective in the presentation of revelation, a need for which is felt, without falling into an abstract systematization.

It is obvious, too, that to view revelation in the perspective of sacred history, mystery of Christ ever in act, is equivalent to presenting it under an aspect of a strongly eschatological dynamic tension, and that this viewpoint is eminently suited to avoiding the danger of abstractionism, quite rightly to be feared in our times; for sacred history, mystery of Christ, announces in the first place an event and not just an abstract system. And it is no less evident that such a presentation centered entirely in Christ and on the paschal mystery is theological and biblical.

Intimate union between preaching and liturgy

In the preceding explanations about the notion of preaching in general, there is scarcely any allusion to the question of its relations with the liturgy; but, after all that we have said, there should be no difficulty in clarifying these relations. Meanwhile, it is noticeable that among the desires expressed today in regard to the hoped-for renewal of preaching, the rediscovery of the intimate connection between preaching and the liturgy occupies a position of particular prominence. This is one of the great themes of the liturgical movement in general,[43] no less than of the modern yearning for a pastoral renewal of preaching.[44]

It is worth the trouble to note that this yearning for a rediscovery of a closer union between preaching and liturgy is making no little progress — though not without some resistance, it is true — even among various Protestant groups; and this too is connected, of course, with that same liturgical renewal which is visible among them almost everywhere. In 1950, W. Stählin, the Lutheran bishop of Oldenburg, Germany, denying the opposition that some Protestants were willing to see between preaching and liturgy, wrote:

> "The liturgy of the Church is the mother of Christian preaching, and liturgical life is the best preparation for preaching; no other work, theological, exegetical, or dogmatic, can be fruitfully substituted for it. . . . The separation of preaching from the liturgy and from the sacraments of the Church is properly the cause of the weakness of our preaching and the root of its decadence, if we may be permitted to so speak." [45]

[43] All the liturgical pastoral reviews are presently treating of this theme. As we said before, Les questions liturgiques et paroissiales has an annual bibliography of this material. La maison Dieu has devoted three special numbers in their entirety to it: no. 16 (1948), Prédication biblique et liturgique; no. 30 (1952), L'économie du salut et le cycle liturgique; no. 39 (1954), Aux sources de la prédication. See also

P. Massi, "Catechesi e predicazione liturgica," in Riv. lit., Vol. 50 (1963), pp. 131–147.

[44] See, for example, the acts of the Congress of Montpelier on preaching: Le prêtre ministre de la parole, UOCF 1955. N. Fournier, Esigenze attuali della catechesi, Italian edition, Brescia 1963.

[45] See Les questions liturgiques et paroissiales, Vol. 32 (1951), p. 281.

Really, considering the nature of preaching, as explained above, and the nature of the liturgy, as we already know it, we can see that in general their union is necessarily quite close; that in fact the highest actualization of preaching takes place connaturally when it takes place in immediate connection with a liturgical act, or better still, as a part of that act; that the content of preaching and the content of the liturgy coincide to such a degree that the liturgy has a strong need for preaching, whereas it is itself the end of preaching, which, in turn, if it is what it should be, cannot but have for its content, direct or indirect, the very world of the liturgy.

The intimate union between preaching and liturgy in general is perceived, in the final analysis, as dependent upon those laws which govern the relations between man and God, specifically in a Catholic context, it being the aim of preaching just as much as it is the aim of liturgy, each in its own way, to actualize those relations.

The first of these laws is the free cooperation that man must lend to the work of God; God descends to the encounter with man, but man must freely dispose himself to this encounter, placing himself in the dispositions demanded in order to be pleasing to God. Afterwards the law of objectivity comes into play: the modalities of this encounter and of the dispositions in which man must place himself so as to be pleasing to God in the supernatural order are determined by the free will of God Himself. Man not only cannot realize them of himself, but he cannot even know them of himself.

First he must hear the revelation which God Himself makes to him in the word which He addresses to him. It is in this revelation that he first comes to know that his encounter with God is accomplished only in Christ, which implies that to unite himself to God he must be united to Christ, to the death and resurrection of Christ, because only in this way, through Christ, will he receive the sanctifying influence of God; and, uniting himself to the worship which Christ, as Head of mankind, renders to God, he will be able to render to God the worship which is due Him and which He wants. Thus, it is through the word of God that man comes to know, along with the basic import and meaning of the liturgy, that his encounter with God in Christ takes place fundamentally by way of the liturgy.

And again, it is by hearing the word of God that man will know what are the moral dispositions which God demands and in which he must place himself in order to be pleasing to God, and hence to unite himself to Christ in order to receive for himself the sanctifying influence and to make his own the worship which Christ renders to God. He will know, in short, that essentially these dispositions are faith, hope, and principally charity — faith in the word of God, in His interventions in the world in Christ, in sacred history as mystery of Christ dead and raised up again ever in act; hope in the achievement of the goal, the ultimate end of the unfolding of that same salvation history; charity, as response of man to the love of God recognized as the final motivation that has given and does yet give meaning to the interventions of God in the world, to the mystery of Christ ever in act.

There are other laws which come into consideration: that of the incarnation and of salvation in the ecclesial community: Christ acts in the Church; the liturgy is *ecclesial* action. By *ecclesial* we mean to designate what is done by Christ through the agency of ministers authentically delegated, and which action pertains to the whole community of believers, in such a way that single individuals must participate therein by actually including themselves in the community. But even the word which God addresses to individual men passes through the Church, that is, through her ministers authentically delegated and in the bosom of the community. Man must receive God's revelation, must hear his word, through the teaching, the announcements, the proclamation, the explanation which the Church makes of that word in the community.

Thus the Church is the authentic depository of the liturgical rites wherein the encounter between man and God takes place, no less than she is of the word of God through which man knows the place and the meaning of this encounter and the dispositions which he must bring with him in order to participate fruitfully therein. The ministers of the Church are at the same time the authentic ministers of the rites wherein, in Christ, the encounter between man and God is realized, and the authentic ministers of the word of God which makes known the meaning of the rites and the dispositions which must accompany them in order that the encounter may take place in them.

Now, it is necessary for a man to have constant reference to this word of God because, as a defense against the *fascinatio nugacitatis* and the passions and the dangers of every kind that endeavor to draw him away in the opposite direction, he has always the need of calling to mind the goal of encounter with God in Christ and the dispositions in which he must keep himself in order to achieve that goal. In other words, he needs constantly to be concerned with the word of God in order to excite in himself faith, hope, and charity, by means of which, in the liturgy, he will be able to keep himself attuned to Christ dead and raised up again, as he receives from that word its sanctifying influence and unites himself to the worship which Christ, as Head of mankind, renders to God. And that is why the Church must constantly proclaim, announce, and explain the work of God to men, no less than she must celebrate the liturgy. The ministry of the sacrament and the ministry of the word — the word too, in its own way, is *sacramentum* or *mysterium* — must never cease in the Church, because each, in its own way, is always necessary so that the encounter between men and God may take place.

The ministry of the liturgical rite and the ministry of the word are complementary. Without the ministry of the word the rite runs the risk of remaining unfruitful for the faithful who do not understand the meaning of it and do not approach it with the necessary moral dispositions. The ministry of the word is logically precedent because it is in it that God gives the first blow to the soul and disposes it; *fides ex auditu*. But without the ministry of the rite, the ministry of the rite, the ministry of the word is of no avail, because, by the positive will of God, the encounter of man with God takes place in the rite and because there is no giving of grace without at least a desire for the Sacrament.[46]

All this can be seen already in the mission of the Apostles:

> "Go, therefore, and teach all nations, baptizing them in the name of the Father and of the Son and of the Holy Spirit, instructing them to observe all that I have commanded you" (Matthew 28:19-20).
>
> "Go into the whole world and preach the gospel to every creature. Whoever will believe and will be baptized will be saved; but whoever will not believe will be condemned" (Mark 16:15-16).
>
> "Peter, standing up with the eleven, raised his voice and spoke out to them. . . . Now, on hearing these things they were pierced to the heart and said to Peter and to the rest of the Apostles, 'Brothers, what shall we do?' And Peter said to them: 'Repent, and be baptized every one of you in the name of Jesus Christ unto the remission of your sins. . . .' And they were persevering in the teaching of the Apostles and in the Communion, in the breaking of bread and in the prayers" (Acts 2:14-42).

And that is why, from its very first day, the Church has built herself on the ministry of the word, followed immediately by the ministry of the liturgical rite.

The word of God, after the Apostles, is basically the Scriptures, proclaimed and explained by the Church, ancient and modern. That is why the announcing of the word of God consists basically in the reading, the proclamation of the Scriptures, which is followed by their explanation and application, that is, the sermon, which the Church makes through the agency of her authentic minister.

The highest actualization of preaching occurs when it is an integral part of the liturgical action, i. e., the homily

From what has been said above, we can pass without difficulty to the fact that the supreme and most connatural actualization of the sermon is verified when it is in immediate connection with the liturgical act, that is, when it

---

[46] See the great insistence of the liturgical Constitution of Vatican II on the reading, the proclamation, the preaching, indeed, on the celebration of the word of God, together with its insistence on the celebration of the Sacrifice and of the sacraments (CL, art. 6, 9, 24, 48, 51–52, 56, and most clearly in art. 35) and, parallel with this insistence, the emphasis placed on the paired concept, faith and sacraments (see art. 59 and the *Instructio* of 1964, no. 6, in *AAS*, Vol. 56 [1964], p. 878).

is the homily of the Mass.[47] Actually, the end of preaching is to proclaim the word of God in order to lead the hearers to the necessary moral dispositions so that the encounter with God may be able to be verified in them as fully as possible. But we know that this encounter, supposing the necessary conditions, is verified in the first place precisely in the liturgical action and principally in the Mass. So we see why the sermon is itself actualized in the most connatural way in the first place when it disposes the faithful more closely and immediately to the encounter with God in the liturgical action, principally in the Mass.

The most perfect and connatural expression of the sermon, therefore, is the homily properly so called, as explanation of the word of God — previously proclaimed in the liturgical Scripture reading in the prior part of the Mass — delivered by the president of the assembly, ideally the bishop but normally his substitute, the parish priest, to his faithful. There the sermon realizes its proper nature in the highest degree: in the assembly of the faithful as *ekklesía* or meeting of God in Christ Jesus with a portion of the great Church, the portion in pilgrimage in a specific territory; a meeting in which the local *ekklesía* actualizes itself in the highest degree in Christ Jesus and expresses its own mystery under the veil of the sensible and efficacious signs of sanctification and worship; an authentic and ideally communitarian and ecclesial proclamation of the word of God made by an authentic minister of the Church in the reading of the sacred books; an ideally communitarian and ecclesial explanation of the word itself, as amplification of the preceding reading, made by the authentic head of the local *ekklesía*; and the whole as proximate preparation to the supreme reception of sanctification and to the supreme worship rendered to God in the Eucharistic Sacrifice itself, which immediately follows.

Now the connatural and traditional plan of the euchological liturgy or, if you prefer, the liturgy of the word, begins to unfold: the reading of an extract from the Scriptures; an explanatory homily; the singing by the congregation of a hymn, or of a psalm and antiphon, with a refrain repeated by the people; the invitation to prayer; brief silent prayer; conclusion of the prayer recited aloud in the name of all by the president of the assembly. In this totality, the sermon appears clearly as an integral part of the whole liturgical action.[48] And this is even more apparent when the sacrificial liturgy

---

[47] See Élie Fournier, "When the Council Speaks of the Sermon," in *Lumen Vitae* [English edition], Vol. 19 (1964), pp. 115–130.

[48] The Constitution on the Sacred Liturgy regards the matter in this same perspective: "By means of the homily the mysteries of the faith and the guiding principles of the Christian life are expounded from the sacred text during the course of the liturgical year. The homily, therefore, is to be highly esteemed as part of the liturgy itself; in fact, at those Masses which are celebrated with the assistance of the people on Sundays and feasts of obligation, it should not be omitted except for a serious reason" (CL, art. 52). The *Instructio* of 1964 explains in no. 54: "With the terminology of 'homily to be expounded from the sacred text' is understood the explanation of some

follows immediately upon the euchological liturgy of the word. This arrangement, as is well known, either took place from the beginning among Christians, or at least it very quickly became the normal arrangement, because already in the notices of St. Justin the Martyr the two parts of the Mass are naturally united, and in the prior part there is explicit mention of the plan involving reading, homily, and prayer.[49]

It is a matter so much the more significant that, as the late Cardinal Bea so properly noted,[50] this direct union between the proclamation of the word, or the reading and explanation of the Scriptures, and the sacrifice is a phenomenon proper to Catholicism and is not found among the Jews nor among the pagans; and it may perhaps go back even to the very example of Christ, who, at the institution itself of the Eucharist at the Last Supper, prefaced that institution with various admonitions, consolations, and instructions.

The content of the liturgy as content of preaching

Finally, that which must be the essential content of preaching, namely, the sacred history of salvation — mystery of Christ ever in act — is none other than the essential content of the liturgy, inasmuch as the liturgy, as has already been explained in the first part, is none other than a certain present realization, in various places and in the succession of the ages intervening between Pentecost and parousia, of the mystery of Christ — salvation history ever in act — under the veil of the sensible and efficacious signs of the sanctification and of the worship of the Church. It follows that preaching, in virtue of its content, if it is truly that which it ought to be, is always and necessarily, at least in an indirect and general way, even if it has not for its direct object the liturgical rites or texts, an explanation which will be intimately connected with the liturgical reality, because it will be an explanation of that very reality. A preaching centered on the sacred history that is the mystery of Christ ever in act will, therefore, necessarily be a preaching profound in its liturgical spirit, just as also it will be a biblical, theological, Christocentric, and concretely practical preaching.

A purely moralizing preaching, without reference to the Bible and to the

---

aspect of the lessons of Sacred Scripture or of some other text from the Ordinary or from the Proper of the Mass of the day, taking into account either the mystery that is being celebrated or the particular needs of the audience."

[49] St. Justin the Martyr, *First Apology* 67 (Jurgens, no. 129). In regard to this plan of the euchological liturgy or the liturgy of the word, see J. A. Jungmann, *Der Gottesdienst der Kirche*, Innsbruck 1955, Vol. 4, pp. 40 ff. [Translator's note: In regard to St. Justin's *First Apology*, here referred to, the work was written between the years 148 and 155 A.D.;

and the same passage (ch. 67) also mentions that a money collection is taken up at the Mass and is deposited—not with the trustees or other competent laity!—but with the "president," i.e., the presiding bishop or priest, to be distributed to the needy at his discretion—a remarkably practical point indeed].

[50] A. Cardinal Bea, "The Pastoral Value of the Word of God in the Sacred Liturgy," *The Assisi Papers*, Collegeville 1957, pp. 76–77. See also St. Thomas, *Summa*, I–II, q. 102, a. 4, ad 3.

liturgy, is not a Christian preaching because it does not find the nutriment of its growth in a specifically Christian terrain. A biblical preaching without reference to the liturgy is incomplete because it does not let us see how the biblical realities are fulfilled in us each day, or at least it forgets the principal point in reference to which they are fulfilled. A liturgy without reference to the Bible is incomprehensible because it no longer appears as that which it is intended to be, that is, as the fulfillment in us, under the veil of the sacred signs, of the biblical realities.

This is why those who are concerned today with a renewal of preaching in the biblical, theological, Christocentric, and concretized sense are instinctively drawn to rediscover the vital union between preaching and the liturgy; while those who, starting from a more directly liturgical concern, are unwilling to have preaching remain estranged from the liturgical spirit, but want it to be a preparation to living the liturgical life to its fullest, instinctively demand that it be, more than it was in the past, directly biblical, theological, Christocentric and concrete. Once more, sacred history — mystery of Christ ever in act appears as the vital nucleus, and hence the unifying bond, of all these realities.

Such being the intimate bond between preaching and liturgy, a bond by reason of general content, by reason of connatural union in place and time and by reason of their being reciprocally complementary and indispensable ways of leading man to full encounter with God, it is natural that preaching, even when it has not the liturgy for its direct object, take care nevertheless to extend its observations, be it only with a simple allusion, so as to show how each point of the mystery of Christ that it explains has its counterpart in the liturgical realization.

Indeed, it is quite natural and necessary that preaching, since it is directly liturgical catechesis, should frequently have for its direct object the liturgy itself, or better, the very mystery of Christ ever in act as it is concretized in the liturgy: in its rites, in its formulas, in its readings, in its feasts, in its cycles; and that by properly starting from the liturgy, preaching may bring its audience to rediscover that same mystery of Christ which it must always explain under forms that, so to speak, are infinite.

Always, and especially in more recent times, the liturgical movement has concerned itself not only with directing preachers to this dimension in a general way, but even with furnishing them with abundant plans and examples of such a preaching. The result of it has been not at all inconsiderable. By this time there exists a whole library of liturgical preaching.[51]

---

[51] For the general French bibliography up to 1947, see R. Pierret, "*La bibliotèque du prédicateur liturgique*," in *La maison Dieu*, no. 12 (1947), pp. 73–85. This bibliography is divided under three headings: 1) The Teachers and the Models; 2) Preaching the Mystery of Christ in the Temporal and Festal Cycles; 3) Preaching on the Sacred Functions: a) Canonical Hours and Psalms; b) The Mass; c) Sacramental Liturgy.

After 1947, the following are especially good: A. M. Roguet, "*Qu'est-ce que la prédication*

From the preceding exposition a no less evident corallary follows: an intense spiritual life centered on the liturgy is not only not a detriment to the formation and preparation, remote and proximate, of the preacher, but it is in fact the generally connatural atmosphere in which this preparation will mature. With much greater reason in a Catholic regimen will the profound truth of the statement of the Lutheran Bishop W. Stählin be apparent: ". . . the liturgy of the Church is the mother earth of Christian preaching, and liturgical life is the best preparation for preaching; no other work, theological, exegtical, or dogmatic, can be fruitfully substituted for it"; for in a Catholic regimen it is immensely more true than any Protestant could suspect that the liturgy of the Church is the uninterruptedly present realization through all times and places of the very object and end of preaching: the mystery of Christ ever in act; and that it is, therefore, really first of all in that liturgy that the preacher is permitted to penetrate vitally to the highest degree of that reality which constitutes the object which he will afterwards be obliged to announce to mankind.

3. Catechism and Liturgy

Upon reflection it is seen that catechism and liturgy are two realities no less intimately connected than are preaching and liturgy, so that the liturgy is no less important for the solution of the problem of the catechetical instruction of children in their religion than it is for the problem of the renewal of preaching in the case of adults.

liturgique," in Évangeliser, Vol. 9 (1954), pp. 99–104. H. Jenny, "Prédication selon la liturgie. La sainte quarantaine," in L'union, Vol. 78 (1951), February, pp. 15–22; "Prédication selon la liturgie. Le coeur de l'année liturgique: quatrième dimanche du carême jusqu'à Quasimodo," ibid., March, pp. 49–57; "Prédication selon la liturgie: temps paschal," ibid., April, pp. 21–26. All three of these above articles of Jenny provide optimum plans for liturgical preaching. H. Oster, Le grand dessin de Dieu dans la pastorale et la prédication (Ésprit liturgique 10), Paris 1955. L. Bopp, Liturgie und Kerygma, 4 vols., Regensburg 1952–1960. J. A. Jungmann, "Liturgie et histoire du salut," in Lumen Vitae, Vol. 10 (1955), pp. 281–288. P. Parsch, Die liturgische Predigt, 10 volumes for the whole liturgical year, with various sermon plans, Klosterneuburg-Vienna. P. W. Esser, Der Einfluss der liturgischen Erneuerung auf der Messpredigt von der Erscheinung der Enzyklika Mediator Dei, Munich 1956. S. Rinaudo, Il mistero della salvezza, LDC, Turin 1964.

On the problem of how to include instruction in Christian doctrine in a harmonious way in the liturgical year, see Élie Fournier, "Doctrinal Sermons for Sundays and Feastdays according to a Liturgical Plan," in Lumen Vitae (English edition), Vol. 14 (1959), pp. 113–126; 347–364; 532–548; 708–738; Vol. 15 (1960), pp. 121–148; 321–350; 517–555. Many outlines for liturgical sermons have been published in the Bulletin paroissial et liturgique and in its successor, Paroisse et liturgie; and by this time all the pastoral liturgical reviews publish sermon sketches. The best series of short homilies or homily sketches that we have seen in English are still the two volumes written by Msgr. Thomas J. Kelly and published (without his name appearing therein) by the Diocese of Cleveland: Preach the Word: Sermon Topics on the Gospels, Cleveland 1954; and Preach the Word, Part II, Sermon Topics on the Epistles, Cleveland 1957. Monsignor Kelly makes available therein, among else, his especially fine insights into the thought of St. Paul.

The modern question of the catechism

There is, in fact, a problem about the catechism, and it is not a small one. There is the problem of how to conceive and draw up the book which is called a catechism or Christian doctrine, even prior to the question of how to teach it to children. The question, then, is identical to the problem of how to announce the word of God to the people, but transferred to the level of children.

Since the end of the Second World War this problem has been once again one of the great subjects of daily discussion in Catholic circles of all countries, because, as is obvious, on its solution depends in large measure the success or failure of the effort toward re-Christianization in which the Church virtually everywhere finds herself presently engaged. In directing their attention to this matter, no small contribution is made by the deepening of child psychology and the theoretical and practical development of pedagogy in general. The great efforts toward a revival of theological studies, the biblical movement, the catechetical movement, and, last but not least, the liturgical movement itself are fruitful in this same area. As a matter of fact, this subject has been and is always, sometimes more, sometimes less, the object of numerous studies.[52]

As always when an atmosphere of renewal is manifested in some area, it begins with a diagnosis of the present situation, with the evidences of deficiency and the formulations of goals. In the area of catechisms, the re-

[52] Consider the fact of the catechetical centers which have been formed in so many countries. The first was the *Centre international d'études de la formation religieuse*, founded at Louvain in 1934, now situated in Brussels, along with the *Centre documentaire catéchétique*. In 1937 the former published *Où en est l'enseignement religieux? Livres et méthodes de divers pays*, Paris and Tournai. Since 1947 the same *Centre international* has been publishing the review *Lumen vitae*, which concerns itself with the problems and publications in this area. In Italy there is the *Centro catechistico salesiano*, founded in 1939, with its review *Catechesi*, SEI Turin. See also the review *Sussidi*, Como, since 1937; *Rivista de catechismo*, Brescia; *Via, Verità e Vita*, edited and published by the Edizioni Paoline, Rome. For the general situation in Germany see J. A. Jungmann, *Katechetik*, Freiburg im Br. 1953. In the United States and other English-speaking countries the classic work is still that of Msgr. Anthony N. Fuerst, *The Systematic Teaching of Religion*, 2 vols., New York 1939, a work based on Fr. Michael Gatterer's *Katechetik*.

Especially since the last war and to the present time, the reviews of a pastoral liturgical nature have concerned themselves with the relationships between catechism and liturgy. *Les questions liturgiques et paroissiales* in the *Bulletin de littérature liturgique* is active in the problems of catechism (see in the indices under *catéchisme*, and *enseignement religieux au enfants*). Numerous articles and recensions on the same matter are to be found in *Paroisse et liturgie*, which, moreover, published a very useful supplement *Nôtre catéchèse*, from 1951 to 1960.

For a general bibliography on the subject, see the most excellent *Il contenuto della catechesi. Saggio di bibliografia sistematica a ragionata*, edited in 1962 by the *Centro catechistico salesiano*, Via Maria Ausiliatrice 32, Turin. This bibliography is divided into five sections: 1) introduction to the problem; 2) general principles on the content (of the catechism); 3) the Bible, permanent dimension of the catechism; 4) the liturgy, permanent dimension of the catechism; 5) personal and communitarian witness: the Church.

proaches have been of the kind that we are accustomed to — accustomed to in general, at least, since the time of the Council of Trent and especially since the influence of the so-called Enlightenment of the eighteenth century — in the first place that they are too abstract and are therefore directed too exclusively to the intellectual capacity alone of the child, aiming primarily at systematic and analytic exposition of doctrine, with formulations intellectually precise from the abstract dogmatic and moral point of view.

The same approach, having become more and more common since the second half of the nineteenth century — with the inclusion in the catechism of the salient episodes from the religious history of the Old and New Testaments — has frequently produced an amalgam rather than a reworking, because the episodes narrated have simply been intermixed or juxtaposed to the questions of the old catechism. This being the case, the catechism puts a very strong emphasis on the notional aspect of the Christian religion and hence on the apologetic aspect also, as well as on the moral aspect of obligation or commandment; and in practice, relying almost entirely on the memory of the child, the catechism almost always presents its matter in question and answer form.

It can be seen that the catechism conceived in this manner is, for the most part, no more than a brief summation of the manuals of positive-scholastic theology, of which we spoke in Chapter 17, a summation thought suitable for children because it is as bare and concentrated as possible. It is noteworthy also that this way of conceiving the catechism presented the least inconvenience when society and families were still deeply Christian and the education of the sentiments and will of the child, as well as of his communitarian sense, liturgical and ecclesial, was largely supplied by the family and by the environment in which the child lived, by frequenting the church along with his parents, etc. Today, however, these conditions are no longer prevalent; and the pedagogical deficiencies of a catechism conceived in the aforesaid manner are much more apparent and dangerous; so much the more since, in all the other branches of teaching, the science and practice of pedagogy has made such great progress.

Counterpoised against the basic complaint is the desire that first of all catechisms and the teachings therein be conceived in an educative dimension that is more global, integral, and hence more concrete; that they be strongly centered on the concrete world in which the child lives, and that they bring into play his whole person, imagination, affection, will; hence, that they be more intuitive and synthetic, less abstract and analytic. It means especially that they be placed much more in contact with the Bible and the liturgical life of the Church; that moral be presented in a more positive way, that Christ be the center of this instruction, etc., etc.

Solution to the question of the catechism by centering it on sacred history—mystery of Christ, thus achieving an intimate union between catechism and the liturgy

In view of what we have already said about preaching, it will not now be so difficult to see in what direction the search must go for a solution to this problem of the catechism, except, of course, that the difficulty of the practical implementation of a program will be great enough.

Really, what is catechetical instruction of the children and what is its purpose? It is simply the methodical initiation of the child to Catholic faith and morality. What we mean to say, then, is that the catechesis of the child, *insofar as content is concerned*, that to which he must be initiated, does not differ from the preaching and catechesis of the adult. Only the form of presentation, the depth of inquiry, and the didactics differ.

The content of the catechesis for a child, therefore, is none other than the same sacred salvation history—mystery of Christ ever in act, as general framework of all revelation. The catechesis of a child, no less than that of the adult, has no other purpose than to lead him to the encounter with God, in a special way, as we know, in the liturgy, and this in the fullest way possible in view of his age. By the intrinsic exigences of the operation, the catechesis of the child, no less than the preaching to an adult, must therefore be theological, biblical, Christocentric, liturgical, vital, and concretely practical.

It follows from this that catechism, both the printed book and the teaching thereof, no less than the preaching and catechesis addressed to adults, must be focused on sacred history—mystery of Christ ever in act, so that in catechism too the whole of revelation is viewed against this background, as much in the general distribution of the material content as in the special way of treating the individual questions. The catechism, no less than the preaching to adults, must never neglect anything of that which Christian revelation contains but must view each matter in its relative importance, starting from the picture of the salvation history—mystery of Christ, as we have already said in regard to preaching.

In particular, the nature of catechism demands, insofar as the intellectual capacity of the child will permit, that it not omit an initiation even to the abstract and, as it were, speculative formulation of certain truths of revelation, like God, His attributes, grace, moral obligations. But the nature of catechism, and even just a good pedagogical sense, demands no less imperatively that the child be introduced even to these truths in some way through sacred history, starting, as it were, from this same concept which must remain always on the primary level of attention.

This is precisely what the Bible and the liturgy do, wherein, for example, the omnipotence of God is not taught by means of an abstract definition, but God is shown acting in the world with great power, from which fact one can pass more easily to the affirmation even of a more abstract character, that God is omnipotent; and wherein sanctifying grace is not taught by starting out with a definition that might inform the child that it is a created accident, a quality inhering in the soul, etc., but the effects of sanctifying grace in us are enumerated and described: that it frees us from sin and from the anger of God, that it makes us His adopted sons and brothers of Jesus Christ and permits us to be able one day to arrive at the contemplation of Him in heaven.

Likewise the nature of catechesis demands that our moral obligations be placed in strong relief, precisely as is done in the Bible. But also as is done in the Bible, they will be shown first of all as naturally deriving from the interventions of God in the world on our behalf; and therefore they will always be viewed, so to speak, in the strong shadow of sacred salvation history. So too the necessary allusions to the defensive apologetic aspect, especially against errors common in the atmosphere wherein the child is living, will be made in such a way that this consideration will not take a precedence over the simply irenic expositive aspect of doctrine.

As we said above in regard to preaching, by focusing its whole complexus and its individual considerations on the reality of sacred history as the mystery of Christ, the catechism will automatically rediscover its most profound union with the Bible, it will become more theological and Christocentric, it will lose its quality of abstractness to be reclothed in a more concrete and vital aspect and, by that very fact, it will respond even to those deep pedagogical needs which child psychology has by this time revealed. In a special way, the catechism will thereby rediscover its profound union with the liturgy. Really, if everything in the catechism is focused on the mystery of Christ ever in act, then the liturgy will logically be present in some way everywhere therein as the point in which sacred history finds its most complete fulfillment in us today.

So conceived, the catechism will necessarily be an indispensable preparation to the liturgical life; and the liturgical life will appear as the sacral concretization, under the veil of the sensible and efficacious signs of the sanctification and of the worship of the Church, of the world of the catechism; the world of the catechism will be lived sacrally in its most important act. Then not only will the explanation of the liturgy, especially of the Mass and its significance, find its natural and important place in the totality of the catechism, but what is more, the general atmosphere of the catechetical education of the child will be profoundly liturgical, and in virtually all of its individual points and details it will be brought to an emphasizing of their extensions and concretizations in the liturgy. It will be brought to a rediscovery, so to speak, of the catechism in the liturgy. What a great advantage all this will provide for the unity of the religious formation of the child is easily foreseen.

The new German catechism as example

For some decades now, in various places, many persons have been toiling with this dimension of the intimate connection between catechism and liturgy, and their labors have borne good fruit.[53] Some liturgical commentaries on catechism have been prepared.[54] Plans and examples of catechetical lessons for children and youth are being prepared, all bearing the stamp of the spirit and even of the texts, rites, feasts, and festive cycles of the liturgy.[55] Others unite, in a way more or less ample and perfect, catechism and liturgy in the redactions themselves of the ordinary catechisms, carrying them on, for that very reason, to a certain enlargement and to a certain rectification.[56]

Among the productions of this last kind, deserving of special attention is the German catechism [57] prepared for all the dioceses of Germany in 1955. It is the fruit of the long and patient labor of specialists, commissioned by the conference of German bishops, with a desire to approach as closely as possible to the ideal of the catechism demanded at this time by the development which has been occasioned in many areas of ecclesiastical life by the catechetical movement, the biblical movement, the liturgical movement, the pastoral movement, and the theological movement. The new German catechism has rightly been hailed by those who are competent as an advance of

[53] For this section see the general bibliography given in Il contenuto della catechesi. Saggio di bibliografia . . . . (cited in the notes immediately preceding), pp. 22–35.

[54] See, for example, J. Colomb, Aux sources du catéchisme, 3 vols., Desclee, Paris 1947; also of Colomb, and with the same publisher, La doctrine de vie chrétienne au catéchisme, 3 vols., 1952. A. Groegaert, Commentaire liturgique des leçons du catéchisme, 3 vols., Dessain, Malines 1953 ff.

[55] Noteworthy in this is the review Nôtre catéchisme, which, beginning with no. 13 of March 1953, changed its title to Nôtre catéchèse, and is published as a supplement to the review Paroisse et liturgie, at the Abbaye de St. André in Bruges [Brugge] Belgium. See also S. Riva, La didattica sacramentale nella catechesi del ragazzo, Milan 1954.

[56] The catechisms and religion texts published since about 1945 have endeavored more or less successfully to take into account the relations between catechism and liturgy. Thus the French catechism of Quinet and Boyer of 1947 at the end of each lesson points out some few things about the liturgy in relation to the matter treated. The Dottrina christiana of the Edizioni Paoline in Rome, for the fourth and fifth classes (1954–1955) juxtaposes to each catechism lesson a lesson on liturgy and one

on Church history. The religion text of U. Rossi, Nella luce di Dio. Studio della religione, Rome 1957, devotes Part 4 of the work to the liturgy. See also U. Pasquale, Catechismo e anno liturgico nella scuola elementare. Guida di lezioni catechistiche, LDC, Turin 1957. In the United States the series Our Quest for Happiness, a broadly collaborated work of which the more notable authors are Msgr. Anthony N. Fuerst and the late Bishop Clarence Elwell, did noble service in our high schools from the 1940s well into the 1960s, but has now largely fallen into disuse. Perhaps it would have been better to revise it again than to discard it; at any rate, nothing of its quality and substance has since been published to take its place.

[57] Katholischer Katechismus, Herder, Freiburg im Br. 1955. An English version incorporating some slight adaptations to make it more suitable for the English-speaking world was first published in 1957 by Herder and Herder under the title A Catholic Catechism; and numerous impressions and editions under the same title and others have been published since. It has also been made available in Spanish, Italian, French, Dutch, Portuguese, Polish, Japanese, and, I have no doubt, other languages as well.

considerable importance in the history of the catechism and of the liturgical movement itself.[58]

However that may be, here we have the opportunity to gain an understanding, through a concrete example, of the matter that ought to go into the writing of a catechism to be centered directly upon sacred history — mystery of Christ ever in act, and how it results spontaneously in a profound biblical, theological, Christocentric, liturgical, concrete and vital atmosphere, eminently pedagogical according to the most certain principles, scientifically ascertained, of the psychology of the child and of adolescents.

The general criterion was to conceive the whole catechism not only as a book of instruction in religion, addressed only or at least principally, to the intelligence, but also as a book of religious education, a book, that is, which, in the face of the matter treated, engages not only the intelligence but also the imagination, the affection, and the will of the pupil and which therefore considers in every individual question the vital and personal implications as well. Moreover, without failing to leave a good portion to memorization with the traditional method of question and answer, it was found desirable to engage as broadly as possible the active cooperation of the pupil. The whole work was given a stance along strongly concrete lines, achieved quite simply by the general atmosphere of sacred history — mystery of Christ ever in act, which remains throughout the general viewpoint on the first level of the points considered.

The matter of the German catechism is divided as follows. In three introductory questions a panoramic view is provided of: 1) our vocation as Catholics, 2) in the bosom of the Catholic Church as guardian and teacher of our faith, 3) in order to enter into the kingdom of God and to take part one day in the heavenly banquet to which God has invited us. Then follow the four major parts: 1) God and our redemption; 2) the Church and the sacraments; 3) life in accord with the commandments; 4) the last things. At the end of the book there is an appendix of selected prayers. Basically the plan follows the construction of the creed, with the natural inclusion of the moral part on the commandments, between Part 2 on the sacraments and Part 4 on the last things, as the means the observance of which, in the bosom of the Church and together with the use of the sacraments, leads us to eternal life. Clearly it is a salvation history stance.

But, however important in itself, the general distribution of the matter alone is not sufficient to give to the reality that is sacred history the position of general framework and primary element determining the whole spirit

[58] From the more directly liturgical point of view, it has been studied by F. Schreibmayr, "Glaubensgrundlagen des Gottesdienstes im neuen Katechismus," in Liturgisches Jahrbuch, Vol. 5 (1955), pp. 219 ff. Kl. Tilmann, "Der Gottesdienst im neuen Katechismus," ibid., pp. 226 ff. J. Goldbrunner, "Die gottesdienstliche Feier als Verwicklichung des Katechismus," ibid., pp. 235 ff.

of the treatment. It will be the way of considering and expounding upon the individual questions that will decide the matter. In the catechism that we are examining, in each individual question, generally constituting the object of a single lesson, the plan followed is much like this: the proposal of the matter or of the question, starting almost invariably from a text of Scripture, narrative or parabolic if possible, or sometimes starting from the liturgy; then explanation of the text, from the viewpoint of the question which is the object of the lesson, with a strong emphasis given to two or three theoretical points contained therein; then follows a series of questions without answers, to stimulate the labor and thought of the pupil; afterwards there are two or three questions with answers, again containing the two or three aforesaid theoretical points according to the traditional catechism method of question and answer to be committed to memory; then follows the formulation of an affective resolution of the will derived from the doctrine explained: "for my own life, therefore, I ought . . ."; afterwards there are short scriptural passages which summarize the same matter; and then, under the title "from the life of the Church" (sometimes "from religious customs"), the pointing out of the connection of the aforesaid doctrine with the liturgy, wherein, by means of some characteristic examples, it is called to mind how it is found in the liturgical usages, rites, feasts or texts; the lessons almost always end with a task to do and frequently with a short poem suitable for memorization.

What is the position of the liturgy in the total plan? It is present everywhere, and not merely juxtaposed but intimately blended with the question treated. In general the liturgy is treated when the Church is spoken of, and more precisely, where her functions are treated: her doctrinal function, her function in regard to sanctification and worship, her governing function. Afterwards the liturgy is treated à propos of the individual sacraments, and especially, of course, with the Eucharist. With this latter great prominence is given to the Mass as action of the Church and as Sacrifice; and, after having spoken of the reservation and adoration of the Eucharist, there are added, always in reference to the Mass, the essential notions that are more directly liturgical.

But the presence of the liturgy in the catechism is derived still more from the fact that the general atmosphere in the way that individual questions are conceived and viewed is profoundly liturgical. And this first of all, because maximum prominence is given not just in one point, but virtually throughout, to those doctrines which are the foundations of the liturgy, such as the Church as people of God; the communion of saints; Christ, now at the right of the Father, universal Mediator ever present among us; presence of the Holy Spirit, Sanctifier; God, our Father who directs all things to the goal of the heavenly Jerusalem; and the ecclesial life of each Catholic. Afterwards, and even more, the liturgy is present in the catechism because the world which proceeds from the catechism in its entirety is none other than the world of the liturgy, precisely because of the focusing of its whole general perspective on the reality of sacred history — mystery of Christ ever in act, constantly illustrated by the Scriptures. And finally, the liturgy is made present therein because throughout the individual questions, especially in the part of the plan which has the general title "from the life of the Church," care is taken to refer every important point explained to its verification embodied in the liturgy.

Thus the liturgy is present in the catechism not just because a part of the catechism or a part juxtaposed to the catechism treats of worship, a thing that by this time all catechisms do and which in itself constitutes a noteworthy progress, but because the very atmosphere of this catechism is liturgical. What might be called the liturgical dimension of the individual questions — no less than their biblical dimension, their moral dimension indicative of certain obligations in life, and, to some extent, even their speculative dimension — is connaturally considered as a constituent part of the whole exposition. In this way, proceeding from the general framework and, as it were, the common terrain in which each question is viewed concretely in sacred history — mystery of Christ, for example, in the Bible, there is a natural transition, insofar as the pedagogical limitations of the child permit and require it, to the general conclusions and, as if by a more abstract principle of order, to the considerations of the moral order of vital obligation, and thence to the considerations of the order of liturgical life.

One or two examples, taken from questions which might seem to lend themselves but poorly to explanation in this liturgical dimension, will make the whole thing easier to understand. The first introductory question treats: "Of the richness of our calling and of our duty on earth." It is constructed as follows. The whole question is developed by taking the rite of baptism as starting point. For the most part, in the other questions, this point of departure is taken from the Bible.

> "Before baptism the priest asks the person to be baptized: 'What is it you ask of the Church of God?' The one being baptized answers, 'The Faith.' Then the priest asks, 'What is it that the faith will offer you?' The candidate answers, 'Life eternal.' The priest then admonishes the one being baptized: 'If you wish to enter life eternal, observe the commandments: "You shall love the Lord your God with your whole heart, with your whole soul, with your whole mind, and your neighbor as yourself."' "

Then there is a brief commentary on that rite and those words from the viewpoint of the lesson's object:

> "When we were brought to baptism, the priest received us in the name of God's Church. By the words of the priest we were welcomed by the whole community of the faithful, the countless numbers of the saints, and by Jesus Christ Himself, our Savior and Redeemer, who

wants to lead us by means of the Holy Spirit into the house of the Father.

"By means of baptism, the rich treasures of God's Church were opened to us: faith, which Christ gave us; the sacraments, with which He gives us divine life; the commandments and His own holy example by means of which He shows us the way to heaven.

"In baptism, through our sponsors, we professed the faith, renounced the devil and sin, and promised to live as children of God. Therefore we must carry out our task on earth as children of God: we must acknowledge God and endeavor to know Him better, to love Him with all our heart, to adore Him and to serve Him with all our strength.

"If we behave on earth as children of God and do His will, we shall live with Him afterwards forever."

Then follows a series of reflections in the form of questions with no answers provided:

"Consider: 1. Who received us when we were brought to be baptized? 2. What treasures have been opened to us by baptism? 3. What did our sponsors do for us at baptism?"

And then a question with its answer given:

"1. Why are we on earth? We are on earth to know God, to love Him, to serve Him, and, at the end, to live with Him forever."

Then follows a resolution:

"*For my life*: I want to be thankful to God always that I am a Catholic. I want to ask God frequently what it is that He wants from me."

Then some phrases from the Scriptures relative to the aforesaid theme:

"*The word of God*: "You have come to the city of the living God, to the heavenly Jerusalem, to the myriads of angels, to the festive assembly, to the Church of the first-born whose names are enrolled in heaven, to God, the Judge of all, to the souls of the just who have been made perfect; and to Jesus, the Mediator of the new covenant' (Heb. 12:22-24). — 'Fight the good fight of the faith, win the eternal life to which you have been called' (1 Tim. 1:12). — 'It is written: "You shall love the Lord your God, and Him only shall you serve"' (Matthew 4:10)."

This is followed by a lesson from the saints, an exercise to perform, and a short poem or the like for possible memorization:

"*The teaching of the saints*: 'Man was created to praise God, his Lord, to honor Him and to serve Him, and in this way to save his own soul'" (St. Ignatius of Loyola).

"*Exercises*: 1. On what occasions are the promises of baptism renewed? 2. What words can you use to thank God for the gift of faith?

> *"'No treasure is more splendid,*
> *No honor nor good of this world is greater*
> *Than the Catholic faith.'"*
>
> — St. Augustine of Hippo

That is how the German catechism presents the matter which in our traditional catechisms was focused in the question: "Why did God make you?," with its answer: "God made me to know Him, to love Him, to serve Him in this life, and to be happy with Him in the next." It is easy to see in the texts cited in what sense and with what fruit such a concept can and must be made, as it were, to gush forth from the context of salvation history — mystery of Christ ever in act; it can and must be presented in its biblical and liturgical dimension; viewed, therefore, in a way ever so concrete without thereby renouncing its precise and abstract formulation; and engaging in reference to it not only the intelligence of the child but also his imagination, his affection, his will, and not only his passive receptivity but also his active cooperation in inquiry.

Another example is Lesson 9, in reference to the explanation of the holiness of God. It takes its cue from the text of Is. 6:1-5, the vision of Isaias in the temple, with the seraphim who were calling out: "Holy, holy, holy is the Lord." Then it explains the text, pointing out that God is infinitely exalted above every creature and that since He is holy, it is right and necessary on that account that angels and men adore Him. He always loves what is good and detests what is evil, and wants us to be holy too. Then there is a series of reflections, in the form of questions without the answers being provided, in regard to this same content.

Then the question, "Why do we say that God is holy?," with the answer given: "We say that God is holy 1) because He is infinitely exalted above every creature; 2) because He always loves what is good and detests what is evil." Following this there is a resolution, "For my own life: Because God is holy and has made me holy too, I will love what He loves and detest what He detests."

Then the Scripture passages, "Be holy, because I, the Lord your God, am holy" (Lev. 19:2). — "This is the will of God: your sanctification" (1 Thess. 4:3). And finally from the life of the Church: "In every holy Mass we can join in the song of the angels, 'Holy, holy, holy Lord, God of power and might. Heaven and earth are filled with Your glory. Hosanna in the highest!'"

If questions which at first glance seem so little suited to be made to pour out sacred salvation history or to be viewed in a liturgical context as the above two questions about the goal of life and the holiness of God can be so easily and fruitfully embodied in the context of salvation history, a biblical and profoundly liturgical context, we but leave it to the reader's imagination what results may be derived by the same procedure when it is a question of matters in which the biblical and liturgical involvement of salvation history is clearly evident to all, such as that of the life of Christ and of the redemption, of the operations of the Holy Spirit, of the Church and the sacraments, of the last things. Here, once again, one can reach out and touch, as it were, how much the liturgy is truly the point of convergence in which Bible, dogma, teaching, and pastoral action of the Church are concretized, and how the liturgy can and must be the center to which everything converges in the religious education of the child.

And this will be even more forcefully apparent if one will but recall that the liturgy, for catechetical education, does not represent just a great treasury of texts and of rites to which one can refer in order to draw forth the concepts which one must inculcate in the child — as, on the contrary, in spite of all, the Bible necessarily remains — but it is also action and drama lived in act, in which the child, outside of the catechism lessons, can and must take an active part in accord with his own capacity, and normally, throughout his whole life.

Thus, what the child has learned through theoretical instruction is afterwards lived by him, verified in a practical concretization vital to that which he participates in, and which will constitute ever afterwards the central act of his Catholic existence. It can easily be sensed how great is the organic unity that the liturgy, as doctrine and as life, when understood and lived as it ought to be, is capable of giving to the whole religious education of the child.

Consider too the well-known and grave problem of catechetics: that of the formation of qualified catechists, without which, of course, the best theories and the best textbooks will not resolve the problem of an efficacious teaching of catechism to children. Think what a real understanding and a deep liturgical life can mean for the catechist, and it will be seen, even from this standpoint, why the liturgy seems to be such a really crucial point in the religious education.[59]

We have seen, then, that no matter the way of considering the question of the relations between catechism and liturgy, one arrives at the same conclusion. It is a conclusion that takes us far away, very far indeed, from the concept of the liturgy as a reality of marginal interest in the life of the Church, to which all those who are engaged in the great struggle for the spiritual transformation of the world cannot and need not devote more than their rapid and superficial attention, abandoning it in a haphazard way to those who, having withdrawn from the world and from the fray, have the leisure and the desire to dedicate to the liturgy that precious time which others would do better to consecrate to more serious and important tasks.

[59] See, for example, B. Capelle, "*La messe dans la vie du catéchiste*," in *Travaux liturgiques*, Vol. 1, Louvain 1955, pp. 152 ff. J. A. Jungmann, *Catechetica*, Rome, Edizioni Paoline, 1956, pp. 55 ff.

EPILOGUE

The purpose of this work was to shed some light upon the theological structure of the liturgy, to consider it in its totality, showing how only this way of viewing it makes its whole meaning clear in a unified synthetic vision, putting its living structure and, as it were, its most intimate vital nucleus under the glass, starting from which all the immense potentialities of life are developed and around which they converge in an orderly fashion.

What, then, is this most recondite vital nucleus of the liturgy which hides it in itself but manifests the riches of it? It is its very nature as complexus of sensible and efficacious signs of the sanctification and of the worship of the Church. If at the end of this work such an affirmation can seem too banal and bare, enough then to remember that it treats of the sanctification which God in Christ works in the Church and in her worship, first of all, by faith, by hope, and especially by charity, which the Church in Christ, united to Christ and by means of Him, offers to God with a dignity and efficacy which, in virtue of the *opus operatum* and of the *opus operantis Ecclesiae*, transcends every other dignity and efficacy. Therefore the liturgy in the ecclesial period from Pentecost to parousia appears simply as sacred history — mystery of Christ, continuously actualized under the veil of the sensible and efficacious signs of sanctification and worship, the supreme encounter between God and mankind in Christ, the point of convergence of the whole antecedent sacred history and the point of departure of all subsequent sacred history *donec veniat.*

It is this reality that explains the whole concept of the liturgy and orders the elements which compose it, as has been explained in the first part. Again, it is this reality which makes understandable why and how the great laws of the economy of God, His plan for the world, are reflected and fore-shortened in the liturgy, as was shown in the second part. Since that economy or plan is none other than sacred history itself, the mystery of Christ, it is no wonder that in the liturgy, which is that sacred history or mystery of Christ ever in act, concretized under the veils of sensible, efficacious signs of the sanctification and of the worship of the Church, the supreme laws of that history are reflected everywhere in the highest degree.

It is in view of that vital nucleus that the relationships between liturgy and Bible are understood. The Bible is the world of sacred history — mystery of Christ, on all the various levels of its development. The world of the liturgy cannot, therefore, be other than the world of the Bible concretized and em-bodied and, as it were, concentrated in all its dimensions, under the sensible signs of the sanctification and worship of the Church.

It is by taking this same point of departure that the relationship between liturgy and faith is understood. The faith, in fact, is entirely centered in sacred history-mystery of Christ ever in act. Thus the liturgy is none other than this same faith translated, lived, and in some way — more indirect than direct — even taught, under the veil of the sensible and efficacious signs of the sanctification and of the worship of the Church.

And it is by starting again from this same place that we come to under-stand the relationship of the liturgy with theology, whether with theological theory in general or with the various historical kinds of theology. Theology in general being the scientific study of revelation which originally is presented primarily as sacred history-mystery of Christ ever in act, any theology that takes due account of this perspective cannot help uncovering and pointing out at each step the liturgical dimension of its object. It will, therefore, be more or less intimately connected with the liturgy, as it employs, more or less, that identical perspective under which revelation has its primary presentation.

In the final analysis, the same point of view determines the relationship of the liturgy with spirituality as a striving to Christian perfection of being, of sanctifying grace and of the action of charity. Supposing the necessary condi-tions of moral attunement, in the liturgy, precisely because it is sacred history as the mystery of Christ ever in act under the veils of the sensible and effi-cacious signs of the sanctification and worship of the Church, there is veri-fied in the highest degree encounter of God who, in Christ, sanctifies man, and of man who, in Christ, evokes his love of God, offering it in Him and through Him, in the supreme homage due to God as Creator and Provider. Because of this, the liturgy is connaturally the center and the soul of the whole striving toward perfection in the way in which Mother Church officially pro-poses it to her children.

Finally, always for the very reason that the liturgy is sacred history-mystery of Christ continually actualized, in this period from Pentecost to parousia, under the veil of the sensible and efficacious signs of the sanctification and of the worship of the Church, it is, no less connaturally, the center of convergence and the goal to which the whole pastoral and missionary activity of the Church tends, as well as, under another aspect, the source from which that activity derives. Really, this activity but strives to realize and maintain the encounter between the people and Christ, which encounter, because the liturgy is just that which we have said it is, is achieved in its highest degree precisely in the liturgy and through the liturgy.

Thus the liturgy appears as the greatest concretization, the center of the relations between God and man in the period of time intervening between Pentecost and parousia; the privileged place of the encounter in Christ between God and mankind, where all the creatures of the infrahuman as well as the angelic world, all history, past, present and future, come together; where all faith, Scripture, theology, spiritual life, pastoral and missionary life of the Church converge.

Certainly such statements cannot but seem extremely exaggerated, not to say dithyrambic, to one who has never seriously reflected on the fact that the whole world of creatures, the whole history of humanity, the whole of the faith, the Scriptures, theology, spiritual life, the pastoral and missionary life of the Church have no other focal point than the sacred story of God's interventions in the world and of the response of creatures thereto; the sacred history centered in Christ, as mystery of Christ ever in act *ab origine mundi* even to the consummation in the heavenly Jerusalem. The preceding statements about the liturgy must inevitably appear exaggerated, I say, to anyone who has never seriously reflected on this fact and has never perceived that the liturgy is none other than sacred history-mystery of Christ ever in act, concentrated in the time intermediate between Pentecost and parousia, under the veils of the sensible and efficacious signs of the sanctification and of the worship of the Church.

To the patient reader who has followed me from the beginning, all this will not seem to be an unrefined panliturgism and an attempt to swallow up the whole life of the Church in order to reduce it to a universal ritualism, or, in the majority of cases, to a universal monachism; no, it is simply a synthetic vision of the reality wherein the single elements, without undue absorptions and simplistic reductions, are considered and ordered in the light of the supreme reality, the ministry of Christ.

The Second Vatican Council affirmed this doctrine in a solemn manner when it proclaimed that the liturgy is not only "the summit toward which the activity of the Church is directed; it is also the fount from which all her power flows." [1]

[1] CL, art. 10.

Anyone who has discovered that the mystery of Christ is verified in the highest degree in the liturgy is certain that he has found a great dynamic force of life. It is a fact that the effort toward a deepening of theology, the strong interest in the spiritual and mystical life and the studies pertaining thereto, the biblical movement, the pastoral movement, the Catholic action movement, the ecumenical movement, and the missionary movement, all phenomena so characteristic of our own time, are even now orientated in large measure toward the liturgy; just as also the liturgical movement, in turn, is uniting itself ever more intimately to these manifestations of vigorous and perennial life in Christ. This convergence is impressive in itself.

INDEX OF NAMES

ANALYTICAL INDEX

In the following index the term *feast* is used broadly as including memorials, optional and obligatory, feasts properly speaking, and solemnities.

ABEL: the first just, 360; his sacrifice a typological figure and preparation for the sacrifice of Christ, 170; his blood a figure of the blood of Christ, 336.

ABRAHAM: his history as sign, 63; his sacrifice a figure of the sacrifice of Christ, 170; father of the New Israel, 280, 478; in the *Martyrology* at the 25th of December, 327; A., and the rite of baptism, 354; A., and the Mass for the Dead, 436; A., and the liturgy of the dead, 357; A., and the history of special salvation, 871.

ABSTRACTNESS: in liturgy and catechesis, 670f; A. and preaching, 876–877, 879–880.

ACÁTHISTOS HYMN: and its theme of the triumph of the Cross, in the struggle against Satan, 448.

ACTIONS OF THE CHRISTIAN: theological treatment of the A. of the C., and relationship to the liturgy, 637.

ACTIVITY: every human A., honest in itself, is sanctified by the liturgy, 320f; extra-liturgical A., considered and viewed in the climate of liturgical spirituality as means ordered to the liturgy and as effects deriving therefrom, 670f, 708f, 811–816; meditative-discursive A. in the liturgy, 696.

ADAM: figure of Christ, 458, 478; Christ is the New Adam, 279, 280; our solidarity with Adam, 277–278; A. and the primordial situation of mankind in a parallelism with Christ, 367–368; A. and his sin, importance thereof for the history of the salvation centered in Christ, 14–15, 24, 72–74, 83f, 89–90, 104, 160, 277–278, 307, 344, 380, 406; A. and Eve, and their garb after their expulsion from the terrestrial paradise in relation to the prebaptismal garb, 402; A. and his sin, in St. Bernard, 788.

ADAPTABILITY: of the liturgy to the various needs which present themselves, 321–322.

ADAPTATION, LITURGICAL: 322f.

AD COENAM AGNI PROVIDI: hymn, 444.

ADIUTORIUM NOSTRUM: 291.

ADMINISTRATION: as history of salvation, in St. Augustine, 870.

A DOMO TUA: prayer, 432.

ADOPTION: as sons of God, and spirituality, 656.

ADOPTIONISM: and the liturgy, 614; Spanish A., and the liturgy, 510, 614.

ANTHROPOLOGY, THEOLOGICAL: anthropological themes in the liturgy, 688–689; the treatment of theological anthropology and the liturgy, 635–636.

ANTHROPOMORPHITES: a Christian sect, 717.

ANTICOMMUNISM: pastoral works and liturgy today, 824–825.

ANTITYPE: 476f, 602.

APERITIO AURIUM: or rite of the *Ephpheta*, 407.

APOCALYPSE: 329, 469, 473, 482.

APOLOGETICS: the apologetic function of theology is secondary to its irenic contemplative function, 567–568; necessity of traditional A., notwithstanding knowledge through connaturality, 538; the positive-scholastic ideal of A. from the sources in theology, 558f; positive-scholasticism's exaggerated preoccupation with A., because of its having given insufficient place to the liturgy in its theological synthesis, 563–568; the apologetic function and the irenic function in every science and the question of the liturgy in theology, 631–635; A. in the scholastic method, 582f; apologetic point of view, real but secondary in the patristic interest in the liturgy, 559f; A., revelation, and preaching, 865f. *See*: ARIANISM; MODERNISM; PELAGIANISM; SEMI-PELAGIANISM; PROTESTANTISM.

APOLOGIES: so-called, in the Mass, 291–292.

APOSTLES: their remembrance in the Mass, 341; and the struggle against Satan, 374; their mission as a struggle against Satan, 371f, 421–422.

APOSTOLATE, EXTERIOR: and liturgy, 811–821.

APOSTOLICITY: of the liturgy, in the opinion of the Fathers, 511, 560–563, 611–619; A. of a doctrine proved from the liturgy in positive-scholastic theology, 560–563, 565–566.

APÓTAXIS: or renunciation, and its antidemoniacal significance, 409. *See*: *SYNTAXIS*.

APPROPRIATIONS, TRINITARIAN: and the *a-per-in-ad* formula, 200–201.

ARCHITECTURE: and liturgy. *See*: Art.

ARIANISM: use of the liturgy in the Arian controversy in general, 208f, 515; influence of the Arian polemics on the patristic way of considering the Trinity, 204f; and on the conclusion of prayers, 213–217; on the anaphoras, 226–230; on the doxologies of the Eastern liturgies, 217–223; on the final doxology of the Roman Canon, 221; on the medieval Western doxologies, 222f; anti-Arian character of the feast of the Most Blessed Trinity, 243–246; the Arians interpret in accord with their views the ancient rule by which every liturgical oration must be directed to the Father through the mediation of Christ, 210, 612; from the 4th century and especially in the East, as a reaction to A., there is an accentuation of the direct consideration of Jesus Christ as God in the unity of the Divine Nature with the Father and with the Holy Spirit, 249.

ARK OF NOAH: figure of baptism, 478.

ARK OF THE COVENANT: in the O. T., a figure of Christ, of the Church, of the Christian Churches, of the Christian faithful, 497; A. of the C. is the throne of God in the temple, 345.

ARMENIANS: their abandoning of the rite of the drop of water in the chalice, 613.

ART: as sign in the liturgy, 50–59; concept of A., 51f; concept of A. and esthetic pleasure, 51f; A. and morality, 53–57; religious A.: notion, possibility, conditions, 57f; liturgical interpretation of the Bible, and ancient art, 485–486.

ASCENSION: as event of sacred history, and liturgy, 15, 91, 372, 440, 457, 465; the O. T. reaches out even to the A. as event of the sacred history centered in Christ, 160; as *mysterium*, event of sacred history, 600; as mystery of the humanity of Christ, in the liturgy, 797; A. and liturgical proclamation of the pertinent biblical passages, 484; is directly connected to the mystery of the Cross, 111; is not in itself a meritorious action of Christ, 111; the mystery of Christ after the A. is completed mystically in the faithful, 472–473; the remembrance the Church makes of the A. in the Eucharist, 343; its remembrance in the Mass in general, 163; its remembrance in the anaphora of St. Basil, 167; its remembrance in the Roman Canon, 170, 227, 350; as a liturgical feast, 176, 582, 696; A. in the context of the temporal liturgical cycle, 240f; liturgical feast of the A. as triumph over Satan, 442f; A. as an event triumphal over Satan, 370–371, 381, 444–445.

ASCENSION, ASCETICAL-MYSTICAL: in Origen, includes fourfold gradation, 870.

ASCENSORII GRADUS IMAGINATIONUM: in mystical experience, 748.

ASCETICAL AND MYSTICAL: and teaching of liturgy, 640f.

ASCETICAL PRACTICE: investigation of the ascetical aspect of the liturgy, xx; A. P. in the abstract, 310; A. P. more severe in Lent, 439f; the ascetical and mystical as illuminative principle for the Christian liturgical reading of the Bible, 460f; ascetical aspect of the striving for Christian perfection, 649f; A. P. and liturgical spirituality, 672f; ascetical point of view in the patristic interest in the liturgy, 596f; ascetical purification and liturgical spirituality in the life of St. Gertrude: compunction, 752f; purification from tendencies to impatience, 754–757f; from tendencies to vanity, 755; from tendencies to short-temperedness, 757f; from tendencies to sensuality and esthetism, 755–756; purificative force of the liturgy in the life of St. Gertrude, 757; ascetical striving, consciousness of grace, and the liturgy, 758f; love as unceasing homage of praise and of thanksgiving, 760; A. P. and demonology, 383f; *See*: MYSTICS.

ASCETICISM: the Church rejects an A. that despises matter and the physical body, 310.

ASHES: their imposition on Ash Wednesday is a symbolic sign of penitence, 45; Ash Wednesday, 45, 356.

ASH WEDNESDAY: and the struggle against Satan, 441.

ASPERSION: or sprinkling, in the rites over the *competentes*, 404.

ASSEMBLY: the liturgy by its nature involves the whole assembly, 316–317; the liturgical A. as ritual expression of the communitarian nature of the liturgy, 284f; Christian A. as personal sign, 59; liturgical A., its theological significance, 91–92; the A. in the Eucharistic celebration is hierarchically structured, 285f; A. of the People of God: in the sacraments viewed integrally, it ascends to relationships with God, in so far as they are sacred history, 665–666; one of the greatest problems of the A. today is that of active participation, 292f; *See*: EKKLESÍA.

ASSIMILATION TO CHRIST: in light of which the precepts and admonitions of the O. T. are understood, 471; A. to C. as tending or striving to be a Christian and to act like one in a perfect way, 649.

ASSISTANCE OF THE FAITHFUL: not a condition for a valid liturgy, 841.

ASSUMPTION OF MARY: infallible definition thereof, 540–541; A. of M. and its historical proof, 576; declaration of the dogma makes the meanings of the *Magnificat* more profound, 482; various degrees of expression of faith in respect to the feast of the A. of M. in different eras, 510, 523; A. of M. in the positive-scholastic manuals, 556, 561; development of the dogma of the A. of M., 541; no apodictic proof of the dogma of the A. of M. from reason alone, 540–541; proof by other than historical method, 566; definition of the A. of M., and the liturgy, 523, 528, 541; liturgical feast of the A. of M., 482, 510, 523, 525, 553, 556, 696.

ASTROLOGY: and demons, 385.

ATTRIBUTES OF GOD: liturgical use of O. T. texts which speak of the A. of G., 464f, 468–469; A. of G. in the Psalms as a principal theme, with the invitation to praise God, 492–493, 502f; A. of G. which appear in a Psalm as divine personal manifestations to the believer, 466–467.

tological-Trinitarian movement, 233; apostolicity of the baptismal rite in its essential nucleus demonstrated and defended, 561f; B. of heretics valid, and the dispute between St. Cyprian and Pope St. Stephen, 617; controversy over validity of B. administered by heretics, and the liturgy, 612; treatment of B., and liturgy, in the *Summa* of St. Thomas, 579; B. instrumental cause of grace according to the Council of Trent, 99; B. in the theological treatises of the positive-scholastic theologians of the 18th century, 551; monastic profession as a second B., 433f; B. and Christian initiation in St. Gertrude, 742; B. in the theological reconsideration involved in the liturgical movement in progress among Protestants, 834–835.

BAPTISMATA LACRYMARUM: and mystical experience in its different degrees, according to the Ven. Guigo I, Carthusian, 721–722.

BAPTISM OF CHRIST: the feast, 582.

BAPTISM OF JOHN: 44.

BAPTISTRIES: their decoration in antiquity, 410.

BEATITUDES: proclaimed on the feast of All Saints, they recount what have been the ways of the saints in achieving their heavenly homeland, 485.

BEES: blessing of B., 333.

BENEDIC: prayer reaffirming the antidemoniacal significance of the Palm Sunday procession, 442 n. 177.

BENEDICITE OMNIA OPERA DOMINI DOMINO: 326, 773.

BENEDICTINES: Benedictine spirituality and liturgical spirituality, 651, 679–683; liturgical movement and the B., 682; external view of Benedictine spirituality in the case of St. Gertrude, 749f.

BERNEUCHEN GROUP: its importance for the Protestant liturgical movement, 831.

BETROTHAL, SPIRITUAL *or* MYSTICAL: the same or much the same phenomenon that is referred to also as mystical or spiritual espousals, nuptials, or marriage: 729, 782 n. 122; as a transitory mystical experience of the Ven. Marie of the Incarnation, 724f; in St. Gertrude, 779, 782 n. 122.

BIBLE: and liturgy, 453–505; as *sacramentum* in St. Augustine, 29. *See*: SCRIPTURE.

BIBLICAL QUESTION: modern B. Q. and the liturgical question, 544.

BINDING OF THE FACULTIES: as mystical experience in apparent contrast to active participation in the liturgy, 729f; an obstacle to performance of any acts "additional" to mystical union, such as discursive intellections, imaginations and external acts, 731f; *See*: ECSTASY.

BISHOP: as sign in the liturgy, 60; the B. as celebrant liturgist representing and incarnating the local community, according to St. Ignatius of Antioch, 288f; high priest of the flock, 845; immediate human external principle of the transmission and cohesion of divine life, 845; Christological-Trinitarian dimension of the consecration of a B., 237f; liturgical movement and revalidation of the theology of the B., 844f.

BLESSED, THE: in heavenly glory, they already form, with the angels, a communion with us, 319; the B. and the angels engage unceasingly in the heavenly liturgy, 342–343.

BLESSINGS: in general, 88–89, 331; B. and angels, 358f; B. constitutive of things, sacramentals, 86–88; B. invocative, as sacramental actions, 86–88; B. of persons: of an abbot, 175, 690, 695; of infants, 86; of a pregnant woman, 428; of the sick, 86, 88; of the people, with the Blessed Sacrament, i.e., the ceremony of Benediction, 86; of spouses, 86; B. of natural products: B. of things and the reconsecration of infrahuman creation to the service of divine life in the world, 88, 332–333, 386–387; of water, 88, 175, 429–430; of baptismal water, 239, 354, 397, 409; of the paschal lamb, 175; of animals, 332; of bees, 333; of fields, 86, 88; of candles, 88;

CATECHESIS: in primitive Church, 486; biblical C. of the Church is essentially the liturgical reading and explaining of the Bible, 486; biblical C. and the liturgical movement in the work of Pius Parsch, 837; catechetical efficacy of the liturgy, C. as communitarian action, 677f, 827f; liturgical C. is the most important task of liturgical pastoral, 847–854; direct liturgical C., 855–858; general preaching and the spirit of the liturgy, 858–867; principal mystagogic works of the C. of the Fathers to the catechumens, 591–596; liturgical C. in the festal homilies of the patristic age, 594f; catechetical interest of the Fathers in the liturgy, 596f; C. and *kerygma*, in the N. T. and in patristic tradition, 867f; sacred history as principal object of C.: by the very nature of what is involved, 867–875; according to patristic tradition, especially according to St. Augustine, and up to the 12th–13th century, 871–875; C. and preaching, 858f; C. as program of pastoral, 816; direct liturgical C. in respect to preaching, catechism, instruction in religion, 857; C. distinguished as *kerygma* and as homily, 858; C. ought to be centered on the essential truths, as was the case in catechizing the catechumens in antiquity, 878; C. for children ought to be theological, Christocentric, biblical, liturgical, vital, and concrete, 890; C. of children ought to have for content the sacred history, mystery of Christ, 890; for an effective C. the formation of capable catechists is likewise indispensable, 890.

CATECHISM: and liturgy, 887; C. has direct relationship to preaching, 858; C. is indispensable preparation for the liturgical life, 891; its union with the liturgy, 890; the solution to the problem of the C. is to center it squarely on the sacred history, mystery of Christ, 890f; modern problem of the C. and movements critical of the traditional C., 888; C. for children, and the liturgy, 887–892; major criticism of the C.: it is too abstract, 889; requires too much memorization, 889; notional apologetic and moral aspects too prevalent, 889; the C. ought to be: more totally educative, more concrete, more intuitive and synthetic, 889; the C. ought to inculcate the moral obligations in the light of the sacred history, mystery of Christ, 890–891; the new German Catechism as an example of a solution to the problem of the C., 892; the new German C. calls not only the child's intellect into active coöperation, but also his imagination, sentiment or emotion, and will, 897; the German C. and the sacred history, mystery of Christ, 894–895; the German C. and the relevant position which the liturgy occupies therein, 895; the German C. is operative in a liturgical atmosphere, 895; it draws basic doctrines from the liturgy, 895; the German C., in a biblical atmosphere, is theological, Christocentric, liturgical, concrete, vital, eminently pedagogic, in accord with scientific psychology, 893; division of matter of the new German C., 893; essentially it follows the structure of the Creed, 893; and has, therefore, the posture of sacred history, 893; catechistic centers and journals, 888 n. 52; literature in respect to a C. of a liturgical spirit, 888 n. 52.

CATECHUMENATE: as *mystérion* of the liturgy, from the 4th century, 604; C. and liturgy in the positive-scholastic theologians of the 18th century, 553.

CATECHUMENS: Lent was the primary period of their struggle against Satan, 439; in the *scrutinia* the precepts and admonitions of the O. T. were repeated, 471; rites of the C. united with those of baptism, 406; the C. according to the *Indiculus de gratia Dei*, 530.

CATHISMA, THE: and the theme of the triumph of the Cross as triumph over Satan, 444.

CATHOLIC ACTION: and the universal priesthood of the faithful, 143f.

CECILIA, ST.: example of a female martyr as one of the most complete forms of victory in the struggle against Satan, 445–446.

CENTRE DE PASTORALE LITURGIQUE: at Paris, xxii–xxiii.

CEREMONIES: and object of liturgical science, xx; C. as sensible signs, 22f; fourfold dimension of the sensible signs in the C., 82f; C. justified by the fully cosmic character of salvation, 312–316; C. in the usages of the sacraments, and the theology thereof, according to the positive-scholastics of the 18th century, 552f; apostolicity of the ceremonies, in Perrone, 554–555 n. 23–24; significance of the C. of the O. T., according to St. Thomas, 576f; C. and controversy with Protestants, 549f.

CHARACTER, BAPTISMAL: enablement to worship, 152.

CHARACTER, SACRAMENTAL: of baptism and confirmation, an enabling for worship, according to St. Thomas, 139; S. C. and Christian worship, 139–143.

CHARITY: and liturgy, 515; faith, hope, and C. exercised in the liturgical action in view of the virtue of religion, 697–702; is it more perfect to devote oneself to works of C. or to the liturgy? 816–821; C. as constant actualization of the virtue of religion, 698–699; C. is not the same as faith and hope and is, therefore, differently stressed, 659; C. as action of a Christian realizing his being, which is grace insofar as it is participation in the divine life, 648; C., with faith and hope, has, according to St. Thomas, God for its object, 129; C., with faith and hope, is superior to the virtue of religion, 130–131; C. is the total worship offered to God by Christ, 899; C. as supreme homage to God in worship, 699–700; C. is the essential disposition for worship and sanctification, 881; C. is a constant demand of the liturgy, 817; exercise of C. in the liturgy and in the external apostolate, 816; C. in regard to a total presence in worship, 737; C. in regard to edification in worship, according to St. Augustine, 700. See: LOVE; VIRTUES, THEOLOGICAL.

CHEROUBIKÓN: song of the Byzantine liturgy, 350–351 [Translator's note: the very familiar and most excellent setting of this hymn is that of Dmitri Stepanovich Bortnyanski]; C. in the Syrian Liturgy of St. James, 351 [Translator's note: the text of this C. is paraphrased in the popular hymn, "Let all mortal flesh keep silence," commonly sung to a 17th-century French melody].

CHERUBIM: in the terrestrial paradise, 344; C. in Ezechiel, 345; C. in the liturgy of the ill, 357. See: ANGELS.

CHINA: significant example of the lack of liturgical adaptation in the missions, 830.

CHRISM: as mystérion according to the Pseudo-Dionysius, 30; blessing of the C., 411–412.

CHRIST: Image of God, 38; New Adam, 279; High Priest of the Father, 151, 220, 222f, 245, 250f, 259, 262f, 265f, 272; the one Liturgist, whose principal action is the liturgy, 99–112, 103, 250–266, 258–259, 272–299; sole Mediator, 336; Head of the angels, 266; His present state of glory, 267, 689, 797; Priest of the liturgy, in antiquity, 797; King, 176; name of Jesus sign of victory, and its antidemoniacal dimension, 397, 404; focal point of sacred history, which, therefore, is the mystery of Xt., 14f; Xt., primordial mystérion in Origen, 601f; Xt. in the anaphoras and in the Roman Canon, 224–230; the Christological theme in the Greek anaphora of St. Basil, 163–169; Christian worship of the Father as Christ's worship, as Head of His Church, in which Christians participate, and the Christian's worship of Christ, 20 n. 2, 134f, 139–143, 264f, 512f; the priesthood of Christians as participation in the priesthood of Xt. by virtue of the sacramental character, 139–143, 146–156; the heavenly priesthood of Xt., 254–259; the presence of the glorified Xt. in the liturgy, 259–266; the question of the re-presentation of the historical salvific actions of Xt. in the liturgy and the theory of Odo Casel, xxii, 104–112; these actions, insofar as they are theandric, exercise an influence of efficient, meritorious and exemplary causality in the distribution of graces to men, 109–112; Xt. in His humanity is the instrumental efficient cause, the meritorious and exemplary cause, and hence the source of the perfecting and sanctifying which take place in liturgical worship, 23f, 69f, 74, 102–112, 264f, 301 n. 1; Xt. is the principal minister of our liturgy under all its forms, 261–266; the whole of the liturgy, in its orations, in its doxologies, in the Mass, in the sacraments, in the sacramentals, and in the liturgical cycles, is constructed according to the Christological-Trinitarian movement in which Xt. always appears as the great Mediator through whom all graces come to us from the Father and all things return to the Father, 191–246, 666, 669, 689, 691f; Xt., the prototype of the law of the incarnation, and hence of the Church, of the Bible, and of the liturgy, 301–304; Xt., the prototype and Head of creation in its unified totality, and the point of physical and moral encounter between God, man, and infrahuman creation, 327f; the temple of Jerusalem a figure of Xt., 497f; the king of Israel a figure of Xt. in the Psalms and in the liturgy, 496; the just man in the Psalms a figure of Xt., 501f; Xt. and creation in the Psalms and in the liturgy, 492f; Xt. the illuminative principle in the interpretation of the O. T., 456–481; liturgy probative of the divinity of the Word, of Xt., of His true Humanity and of the reality of His physical body, according to F. A. Zaccaria, 551; the work of Xt. (baptism, temptations, public ministry) as struggle against Satan in the N. T., 366–371, 441–442; the more ancient tradition always considers in Xt. the Man who was born, who suffered and died, but is now glorious at the right of the Father, the Xt. who is the *Kyrios,* hence our High Priest and Mediator, 195–206, 219f, 226f, 230f, 254–259, 661f, 797f; the anti-Arian controversies produced in the liturgy a more frequent insistence on the divinity of Xt. directly considered, and hence on the Word and Son as equal to the Father in the inter-Trinitarian life, 204f, 207f, 215f, 218f, 223, 226f, 234; in the piety of the Middle Ages there was a disposition to accentuate a concentration of attention and sentiment on the historical humanity of Xt., especially in respect to His resurrection; but it left but little mark on the liturgy, 797f; unity of the mystery of Xt. from the incarnation to the parousia, 112; Xt. as an object of meditation in the spirit of the liturgy, 688f; mediation of Xt. and explanation of His life in the liturgical feasts, according to St. Thomas, 582 n. 35; Xt. the Mediator, and liturgical life in St. Gertrude, 763f, 780f, 788 n. 138; Xt., Priest and Pontiff in St. Gertrude, 765; devotion to the Humanity of Xt. in St. Gertrude, and the spirit of the liturgy, 797f. *See:* CHURCH; MYSTERY; SACRED (SALVATION) HISTORY.

CHRISTIAN, THE: and the struggle against Satan, 386.

CHRISTIANIZATION: and liturgy, 824–830.

CHRISTMAS: proper object and fourfold dimension of the significance of the C. cycle, 90; feast of C. and the angels, 359; redemptive power of the feast of C., 483–484; C. and the struggle against Satan, 437f; and the prophecies of Isaias, 473f; with the other phases of the mystery of Christ, C. is centered sacramentally and liturgically in the Mass, 175–176; the time preparatory to C. is similar in some respects to Lent, 696; we share in the redemptive power of C. for the first time in baptism, 484; the hymn *Gloria in excelsis Deo* already in remote antiquity was taken as the beginning of the greater doxology, 359; in the West from the 11th century emphasis was placed on Jesus, historical Man, prior to His resurrection, and therefore especially on His birth and on His Passion, 249; C. as *mystérion* since the time of Justin, 600; theological question in St. Thomas, 582 n. 35; apparently the liturgy does not leave the theme of C. to the free consideration of the faithful outside its specific time of year, 690.

CHRISTOCENTRISM: of the liturgy, 102, 485f, 668f; liturgical preaching and desire for a more Christocentric preaching, 877, 879f. *See:* CHRIST.

CHRISTOLOGY: and liturgy, 636; Christological controversies and liturgy, 632; treatment of C. and the liturgy, in St. Thomas, 582 n. 35, 585f.

CHRISTOLOGY, THEOLOGICAL: and rules for the use of the liturgy in the controversies of the patristic age, 614f.

CHRIST THE KING: the feast of Xt. the K. includes an idea that is of the faith and not simply a theological opinion, 524.

CHRISTUS PASSUS ET GLORIOSUS: of primary consideration up to the Middle Ages, 797.

CHRISTUS PATIENS: consideration since the Middle Ages, 797–798.

CHRISTUS TOTUS: Head and members, according to St. Augustine, 492.

CHURCH: the mystery of the C. is sacred history, mystery of Christ, 16–18; the C. is the Messianic community, a holy people, the new people of God, new Jerusalem, sole receptacle of the Holy Spirit, the Body of Christ, outside of which there is no salvation, 16f, 114f, 278f, 281; the C. is the new Eve, 17; the C. is the mother of the living, 17; the C. is the bride of Christ, 17; the C. is the only bride of Christ, 17; the C. is the object of sanctification in the liturgy, 69f, 74f; the C. is a society *sui generis* and not simply the sum total of the individuals of whom she is composed; an indissoluble totality, which results from the union of Christ, the Head, of the hierarchy mandated by Christ as mediator between God and man, and of the people who, through the hierarchy, are united to Christ, her Head, 120–123; the C. is the Body of Christ, 16f, 116f, 120–123, 279f, 282f; the C. is the "sacrament of unity" in the renewal of ecclesiological theology of the Second Vatican Council, 272; the C. is formed not from bottom up but from top down, 120f; the growth of the C. comes about in a sacramental way, 12f; the liturgy as action of the C., as action of Christ in the C. and through the C., as the integral worship of the mystical Body of Christ, Head and members, 112–123, 258–266, 279–299; the C. and the law of salvation in community, 279–299; the C. and the law of incarnation, 303f; the C. as such is actualized to the highest degree in the liturgical action, principally in the Mass, 91–95, 161, 282f; the C. is the trustee of the ministry of the words and of the liturgical rites, 881f; the C. determines the existence and the meaning of the liturgical signs which are not of divine institution, 43–47; the C. prays in the prayers of all the faithful; but there are differing degrees of intervention in her intercession before God, 114–117, 120–123; (*See: OPUS OPERANTIS ECCLESIAE*); the C. and the struggle against Satan, 377–381; the C. and the temple of Jerusalem, 497–498; the history and life of the C. provides a light by which certain N. T. texts can be understood more profoundly, 481–482; the C. as *mystérion* derived from the *mystérion* of Christ, according to Origen, 601f; the C. in Eph. 3:21: doxology, 217; in the final doxology of the anaphora of Hippolytus of Rome and in the doxologies of the same author's *Traditio apostolica*, 221–222 n. 50; infallibility of the C. proved from the liturgy, according to F. A. Zaccaria, 551; theological treatise on the C., and liturgy, 636; C. and positive-scholastic theology, 563–568. *See: EKKLESÍA*; MYSTERY OF CHRIST; SACRED (SALVATION) HISTORY.

CHURCH BUILDING: consecration of a C. and Christological-Trinitarian dimension, 239; rites of the consecration of a C. explained by the Fathers, 592–596; Christian C. and temple of Jerusalem, 497f.

CIRCUMCISION: Christ, in submitting Himself to C., lifted from our neck the yoke of the devil, 439; C., according to St. Thomas, prefigures baptism, 579; significance of C., according to St. Thomas, 581.

CITY: the two cities indicate the struggle between the City of God and the City of Satan: this struggle in the liturgy, 362–451, 498.

CITY, FUTURE: or Celestial City. *See*: JERUSALEM, HEAVENLY.

CLERGY: and the liturgical movement, 542–543, 848f.

CLUNY: its significance in the development of the liturgy, 797.

COELESTIS URBS IERUSALEM: hymn for the office of the dedication of a Church, 469.

COELI ENARRANT GLORIAM DEI: 729.

COLLATIONS *or* CONFERENCES: of John Cassian, which work develops the theme of the struggle against Satan, 388, 415, 716f.

COLLECTIVISM AND LITURGY: *See*: COMMUNITY; INDIVIDUAL.

COMMANDMENT OF LOVE: of God and of neighbor, summarized in the decalogue, assumes a greater depth in the N. T. than in the O. T., 470.

COMMANDMENTS OF GOD: necessary means for maintaining oneself in the state of grace, and the basis for progressing toward perfection, 653.

COMMANDMENTS OF THE CHURCH: means for maintaining oneself in the state of grace, and the basis for progressing toward perfection, 653.

COMMEMORATIONS OF THE DEAD: 338f; as a liturgical feast, it is spread abroad in the West from the 10th century through the work of St. Odo of Cluny, 339; with the commemorations of the saints, indicative of the strong sense of the communion of saints in antiquity, 340–341.

COMMEMORATIONS OF THE SAINTS: developed in a specific form in the anaphoras, alongside those of the dead, at least from the 5th century, 340; an indication of the strong sense of our communion with the saints, in antiquity, 340–341.

COMMENDATIO ANIMAE: its Christological-Trinitarian significance, 239; its antidemoniacal dimension, 338–339, 421f; *C. A.* and the role of the angels in the liturgy of the ill, 356.

COMMENDO TE: as a volitional and exorcistic formula in the *commendatio animae* in the Roman Ritual, it is expressive of an antidemoniacal dimension, 424f; *C. T.* and the role of the angels in the liturgy of the ill, 356.

COMMIXTIO: rite of the *C.* changed by the heretical Eutychians, 613.

COMMUNICANTES: of the Roman Canon, its significance, 340–341.

COMMUNIO: as a term, already in the 5th century it indicates Eucharistic Communion, 415.

COMMUNION, EUCHARISTIC: in Christian initiation, E. C. formed a homogeneous rite with baptism and confirmation, 174; in ancient times the liturgical action of the Mass was inconceivable without the E. C. of the people present, 287; in the Middle Ages the E. C. of the people is somewhat lessened in frequency, 292; E. C. has also something of the aspect of the reconsecration of the infrahuman world, 330; E. C. under both species for the faithful in certain instances reintroduced by the Second Vatican Council, 670; E. C. under the sole species of bread in the treatment of the Eucharist in St. Thomas, 579; E. C. under both species, 552, 579; E. C. outside Mass, 292; importance of the first Communion of children in respect to matrimony, 171–172; daily Communion, C. under one species, C. of the priest during Mass, and distribution of C. by the priest or deacon, according to St. Thomas, 579; E. C. is the central object of attention in the works of St. Gertrude, 742.

COMMUNION OF THE SAINTS: in the liturgy the C. of the S. is real and concrete, but practically limitless, 341–342; it is found, with other realities, above all in the liturgy, 571; the C. of the S. is presented constantly by the liturgy, 704; dogma that unites the faithful on earth with the blessed in heaven and with the souls in purgatory, 337; C. of the S. especially vital with Mary, 339; C. of the S. and the liturgy, 335–343; C. of the S. is realized to the fullest in the sacrifice of the Mass, 340.

COMMUNISM: importance of the liturgy as an anticommunist function, in actual experience, 824–825.

COVENANT, ETERNAL: perfect realization of the Old Covenant, 477–478.

CREATION: not considered metaphysically in the Bible, but in relation to concrete history, 7; in the Bible, C. concerns not only God and man, but angels too, 344–345; C. reveals the unity between man and the whole cosmos, 324f; effect of the attributes of almighty God in the Psalms, with the consequent invitation to praise Him, 502–503; liturgy takes C. as a thematic point of departure, 493–494; is a theme which the liturgy constantly brings to consideration, 704; recalled in the old oration after the first reading of Holy Saturday, 468; recalled in the old oration after the ninth reading of Holy Saturday, 468; manner in which the liturgy understands the texts of the Bible which speak of C., 494–495; and those which speak of God the Creator, 468; C., elevation, and Christ and Mary, 494–495; C. as a theme of sacred history in catechesis, 871.

CREATION, INFRAHUMAN: I. C., man, and angels in the laws of the cosmic unified totality of the kingdom of God, 308–309, 324–329; I. C. and unity with man in his service for the ends of the communication of divine life in the world is itself all the more marvelous if mitigated evolution is extended to the body of man, 324, 327; I. C. in the service of man for the praise of God, etc., 326; I. C. opposed to man after the latter's sin, 326; I. C. serves God in the assisting of His friends and in the punishment of His enemies, 326; working of I. C. in the liturgy to the ends of the kingdom of God, 324–334; maximum reconsecration of I. C. to the divine life, in the incarnation of the Word, 327; I. C. and attitude of Jesus, 327f; I. C., Eucharist and baptism, 328; I. C. and the theory of the unity of the cosmos in St. Paul, 328; I. C. and the unity of the cosmos in the Apocalypse, 329; I. C. is made present in worship in the liturgy, 329–334; I. C. is associated to the praise of God in the Divine Office, where it is granted a certain consciousness and voice, 333–334; use of I. C. in the liturgy through symbolism and example, 333–334; I. C. and the dominion of Satan after man's fall, according to the N. T., 364f; and according to later tradition, 383–389; I. C. and the spirit of the liturgy in St. Gertrude, 772f.

CREATOR ALME SIDERUM: Advent hymn, and the struggle against Satan, 438.

CREDIBILITY: See: MOTIVES OF CREDIBILITY.

CREDO: as antidemoniacal formula and formula strengthening the faith, 423. See: CREED.

CREED: and baptism, 231; Christological-Trinitarian structure of the C., 231–234; in the liturgy, 515; antidemoniacal dimension of the C., 423; its construction in accord with the schema of sacred salvation history, 9, 868; Apostles' C., 9, 30, 233; so-called Athanasian C., 9 n. 5, 209, 233, 515; Nicene C., 9 n. 5, 233; so-called Nicene-Constantinopolitan C. (the present Mass C.), 209, 233, 515, 520, 614 n. 91; Roman C., 233.

CRIB, CHRISTMAS: devotion to the C. C. in the piety of the Middle Ages, 798.

CROSS: in the life of Christ everything tends to the C., in which the fullness of our redemption is accomplished and in which Christian worship has its beginning, 111–112; adoration of the C. as a sign of the triumph of Christ over Satan, 443; antidemoniacal significance of the sign of the C., 399f; the C. and the struggle against Satan, 442f; the feasts of the C. and their antidemoniacal significance, 444.

CRUCIFIX: represented since the Middle Ages in the torment of its human pain and agony, 797–798; devotion to the image of the C. in St. Gertrude, 801–802.

DA'ATH: Hebrew term, absolute state da'ah, cognizance, knowledge; refers particularly to a knowledge of God, in the O. T., 619; da'ath Yahweh, cognizance of Yahweh, in the O. T., 619–620.

DEVOTION: notion of, 132f; D. and moralizational power of the liturgy, 707f; D. and relations with religion, 127f; D. has its culmination in the Sacrifice, 148; D. and liturgy, 516f; D. as total dedication to God is developed in the liturgy, 702; for St. Cyprian, devotion and faith are the armaments of the Christian, a reminder of his *sacramentum*, 77; according to St. Leo, D. must emerge above all during Lent, 440; philosophical and theological analysis that St. Thomas makes of it, 573.

DEVOTIONS: notion, 132–133; particular D., 655f; varying importance given to D. by different Catholic schools of spirituality, 657f; extraliturgical D. and liturgy, 820f; medieval prayerbooks and private D., and liturgy, 793f; the D. of St. Gertrude, 760–775, 796–802; Eucharistic D.: reservation of Eucharist and liturgical spirituality, 670; Vatican II and Eucharistic D., 856 n. 3; Marian D. and accusations of Protestants, 832; private D.: according to the mind of the Church, private D. are subordinate to the liturgy, 663; modern D. and accusations of Protestants, 832.

DEVOVERE: meaning of the term, 132.

DIATHÉKE: the notion of covenant in the O. T. and in the N. carries with it a strong call to the binding of the contractual parties, 79.

DIDACHÉ: or instruction, as means of further introduction to the faith after *kerygma*, 868 n. 18. *See: DIDASCALÍA.*

DIDACTICS: didactic end and cultic end of the liturgy, 512–515; in the liturgy the direct didactic style does not predominate, but nevertheless the liturgy has great didactic efficacy, 515–518.

DIDASCALÍA: or instruction, as means of further introduction to the faith after *kerygma*, 868 n. 18; in what sense the liturgy can be called the Church's *D.*, 512–518.

DIOCESE: is the natural point of convergence of the liturgy, 844f; the liturgical life of the D. ought to be centered about the bishop, 845; the D. ought to become the sacral and Eucharistic entity *par excellence* and not merely a juridic administrative entity, 846.

DIPTYCHS: of the living and of the dead, 317 n. 20.

DISCIPLES: the mission of Christ to the 72 disciples and its antidemoniacal dimension, 371f. *See:* APOSTLES.

DISCRETION: a virtue of the spiritual man, according to John Cassian, 717.

DISPENSATIO: or *dispensatio temporalis*, Latin term, literally (temporal) dispensation, a concept of the sacred history of divine salvation (salvation history), according to St. Augustine, 870.

DIVINATION: in tradition after the N. T. it was a common opinion that in pagan life and, therefore, in the practice of D., the demons are everywhere present, 385; Christians in antiquity accepted the general affirmation of the Bible that idolatry is worship of demons, along with the Hellenistic opinion about the *daimonia*, spirit intermediaries between the gods and men in worship, in D., and in dreams, 385–386.

DIVINE COMEDY: in *Purgatory IX*, Dante introduces the angels who, after penance and purification, sign the forehead of the penitent with the sign of restoration, 356 n. 60.

DOCILITY: to the inspirations of grace, 654, 662.

DOCTRINAL CONTROVERSIES: those of the patristic age, in which notable polemic recourse is had to the liturgy, 611–614; Adoptionism, 614; Arian, *See:* ARIANISM; Christological, 613; Donatism, 612; Gnostic dualism, 612; Modalism, 612; Pelagian, 613; Semi-Pelagian, 613.

DOCTRINE, CHRISTIAN: 887f. *See:* CATECHISM.

conclusion of the Ambrosian Canon, 230; the doxology distinguishes the Divine Persons but at the same time reaffirms their unity of nature, 244; doxology according to the *De Spiritu Sancto* of St. Basil, and the controversy thereon, 218, 221, 612, 618 n. 107.

DRÓMENON: i.e., that which is being carried out: the liturgy is presented first of all as a sacred action, 317.

DUALISM: no traces of real dualism exist in the N. T., insofar as it is a sacred history, 383; reactions of St. Paul to dualist tendencies, 328 n. 41; dualism and liturgy, *See*: FLESH; BODY.

DULIA: worship, 134, 136.

DUTIES: of justice and charity, and the liturgy, 654; of one's own state, and the striving toward perfection in general, 654f, 680; liturgical spirituality does not presuppose a specific state of life, but is proposed by the Church as being capable of realization in the carrying out of the D. of whatever state of life, 673f, 679–683; D. of one's particular state of life, along with the moral virtues, the desire for perfection, prayer, mortification, and coöperation with grace, as indispensable to liturgical spirituality, 662; D. of one's own state of life, and how they are subordinate to the liturgy, viewed as preparation or consequence of the liturgical action, 663; D. of one's own state of life and their general relationship to the practice of virtue, 708.

EAST: symbol of Christ, 409.

EASTER: and the faith of Christians, 523; and the triumph over Satan, 444f; homilies on E. in the patristic age, 594f; Paschal letters of the Bishops of Alexandria, 595; the Paschal Mystery attested by the Apostles concretizes the whole mystery of sacred history, mystery of Christ, mystery of His priesthood, mystery of the Church, and, therefore, mystery of the liturgy, 250–251; efficacious celebration of the Paschal mystery, 270f; history of Paschal preaching in respect to its content, 871 n. 29; Jewish Passover, 471f. *See*: CHRIST; EUCHARIST; *KYRIOS*; LITURGY; RESURRECTION; SACRED (SALVATION) HISTORY.

EASTER MONDAY: and the typology of entry into the promised land, baptism, and entry into the Church, 480.

EASTERN CHRISTIANS: not united to Rome, and importance of the liturgical movement, 835; their own modern liturgical movement, 835.

ECCLESIA DEI: *See: EKKLESIA*.

ECCLESIASTICAL OBSERVANCES: according to Origen, they comprise the liturgical rites and are included in the concept of *mystérion*, 603.

ECCLESIOLOGY: theological treatise on the Church, and liturgy, 636; E. in positive-scholastic theology, 564. *See*: CHURCH.

ECONOMY, DIVINE: or E. of salvation: as an aggregate view of the world in which God intervenes in respect to salvation, 599; is governed by certain supreme laws, 183f; already according to the ancients, the D. E. is centered in the Paschal mystery, 868 n. 18; of basic and indispensable importance thereto is the Humanity of Christ, 303; is necessarily reflected in the liturgy, 900; its laws are illustrated by Jesus in parables bearing on created nature, 328; is object of the true *gnôsis*, saving wisdom according to Irenaeus, 869; after Justin, the view of the D. E., is conceived as *mystérion*; its relationship to *mystérion*, the divine reality, according to Origen, 601; the proper object of preaching is the divine realities in relation to the D. E., 861; D. E. of grace: prefigured, prepared, and initiated by the O. T., 499; D. E. of Christ in act is the liturgy, 329; new D. E.: Christ is the ideal of the saints in the new D. E., 501f; D. E. of Christ; as basis of Lent, gives a different dimension to the words of the O. T., repeated and proclaimed in that liturgical cycle, 471; new D. E. has its roughcast in the biblical and liturgical theme of the Old Law, 477–478, 498; D. E. in Christ: gives the repentant sinner a deeper sense of the divine realities, 501.

ECSTASY: as mystical experience, produces an impediment to the additional acts of mystical union, 731.

ECUMENISM: the basic importance that the liturgy has today for ecumenism, 830–836.

EDEN: 344. *See*: ADAM; ANGELS; FALL OF ADAM.

EFFICACY *EX OPERE OPERATO: See: OPUS OPERATUM.*

EFFICACY OF THE LITURGY: the liturgy as efficacious sign, 23, 96–123; pedagogic E. of the L., 320f, 515f, 729–739.

EGYPT: liberation from E. in the Psalm *In exitu Israël de Aegypto* and liberation from this world, in the liturgy for the dead, 495.

EGYPTIAN LITURGY: 351.

EIKON: image; real natural sign which is related to the thing signified, 35; its meaning as sign, image, symbol, 36, 38.

EJACULATIONS: the habit of ejaculatory prayers nourishes the awareness of the constant presence of God, according to Cassian, 721.

EKKLESÍA: E. toû Theoû is the *Qᵉhal Yahweh* of the O. T., the People of God, the sacred assembly of God, the Israel of God, the religious people chosen and set apart by God in the O. T. in view of a special mission, 279; *E.* or Church as the assembly of men, the assembly made by God in Christ Jesus, which has its maximum realization in the liturgical assembly, and first of all, therefore, in the Mass, 43, 59, 91, 279, 280, 282, 290, 294, 336, 412, 840, 861, 884; the concept of *E.* demands of the community a full active participation, internal and external, 840; *E.* is the assembly of the first-born inscribed in heaven, 258; *E.*, community of the blessed of the heavenly Jerusalem, in a single liturgy, cosmic and eternal, 342; the sin of but a single member damages the whole *E.*, 295; the homily is made by the head of the *E.*, the sacred assembly, as an immediate amplification of the word of God proclaimed in the liturgy, 884. *See*: CHURCH; CHRIST.

EKPHÓNESIS: plural, *ekphonéseis*; final part, said in a loud voice, of a prayer the preceding part of which is recited by the priest in a low voice, 291.

ELECT, THE: catechumens more specially obligated to the next baptism, 397–398 n. 42. *See: COMPETENTES.*

ELECTION: and formation of the People of God and of the Church, one of the great themes of the Psalms, and its use in the liturgy, 495f; biblical theme which the liturgy proposes for discursive meditation, 691f.

ELEMENTS: materials and objects used as signs in the liturgy, 50. *See*: BLESSINGS; CONSECRATION.

ELEVATION: of man on the part of God is one of the biblical themes always proposed by the liturgy in a balanced way with the other biblical themes of salvation history, 689, 704.

ELIAS: typological figure of John the Baptist, 478, 480; in Lent the faithful ought to imitate E. and Moses, 441.

EMBER DAYS: 693, 709.

EMITTE: prayer for the blessing of the oil, 423.

ENEMIES: the Psalms against the enemies of the People of God and how they are to be understood in the liturgy as speaking about the struggle against Satan, 498–501; in the thematics of the Psalms, the enemies of God are Israel's enemies, 498.

ENERGOUMENOI: i.e., possessed persons; Eucharistic Communion of the baptized E. and the related controversy, 414–415. *See*: DEMONIACS.

ENLIGHTENMENT: i.e., the age of E.: the E. determined the choice of questions treated in theology, 564–565; influence of the E. on catechism of the 18th century, 889.

ENTRANCE INTO THE CHURCH: typology as entrance into the promised land, and baptism, 480.

EPHPHETA: or rite of the *aperitio aurium*, its antidemoniacal dimension, 407.

EPICLESIS: consecratory by the coming of the Holy Spirit in the Mass: its explicit formulation in the anaphora does not take place before the end of the third century, 226; in the anaphora of Hippolytus, 225; in the Eastern liturgies, 525; in the Roman Canon, 228f; in the Mozarabic and Gallican liturgies, displaced, minimized or suppressed by the 6th century, 229–230; in the Ambrosian liturgy, 230; the invocation to the Holy Spirit does not exclude the part of Christ in the Mass, 262; in the Eastern liturgies the E. was interpreted as preserving the teaching that the form of the Eucharist is solely the words of institution, 525–526; its antidemoniacal dimension in the Mass, 416; epicletic oration in confirmation in the Roman Rite, 235; E. for the coming of the Holy Spirit on the sinner in the rite of reconciliation of penitents, 236–237; in the sacramentals, 239f; question of the E. raised in the Caerularian controversy, 614; Apostolic origin of the E., according to Perrone, 555 n. 24.

EPIPHANIC COMING: of the Lord: as object of the Advent-Epiphany cycle, 90f, 176f; second coming of the Lord: *See*: PAROUSIA.

EPIPHANY: the Messianic prophecies of Isaias read in the liturgy of E. are interpreted primarily according to the contemporary depth, 464; the related biblical passages read in the liturgy of E. signify the prolongation of that salvific event even to our times, 483–484; the incarnation of Christ is the highest epiphanic expression of God's presence in the world, 301–302; E. as event of salvation history, an integral part of the ecclesial liturgical cycle, 176; the liturgy is the continuous incarnate E. of Christ, 305f; in the Mass a real E. of the Word takes place, 161; position of the angels in the liturgy of E., 359; the feast of E. is mentioned by St. Thomas in connection with liturgy, 582 n. 35; E. of the Church: primarily the liturgy, 31; the Second Vatican Council has reaffirmed that the principal E. of the Church is the liturgy, 306–307.

EPISCOPATE: superiority of the E. over the presbyterate studied by F. A. Zaccaria, 551. *See*: BISHOP.

EPISTLE TO THE HEBREWS: on the heavenly priesthood of Christ, 254f; and relations between the heavenly and earthly liturgies, 259f.

EPISYNAGOGÉ: in the Epistle to the Hebrews, is the liturgical assembly, 259.

ERRORS: even doctrinal, are possible in the historical liturgies, 510, 522.

ERUCTAVIT: 728.

ESAU: with his brother Jacob, expresses the typology of Jew and Christian, 479.

ESCHATA, TA: the final times, the last days: all time is proceeding thereto, 13; in the E. Christ carries out fully the whole of history, 15. *See*: ESCHATOLOGY.

ESCHATOLOGY: the fulfillment of the final times is a sign of the profound dynamism of salvation history, 12–13; E. and sacred salvation history, 15–16; eschatological dimension of the Mass, 161, 170; eschatological dimension of the Advent-Epiphany cycle, 176–177; eschatological dimension of the Lent-Pentecost cycle, 176–177; E. and the feast of All Saints, 178, 342; final times and the struggle against Satan, 381f; eschatological figurative dimension of the temple of Jerusalem, 497; eschatological dimension of the people of God in the Bible, 496; eschatological viewpoint and exercise of hope in the liturgy, 701; E. as liturgical interpretative principle in the biblical texts, 456–485, 490, 492–503; desire for a preaching that is more reflective of the theme of E., and liturgical preaching, 878. *See*: JERUSALEM, HEAVENLY.

ESPOUSALS, SPIRITUAL *or* MYSTICAL: *See*: BETROTHAL, SPIRITUAL *or* MYSTICAL.

ESTHER: like Job, Tobias, and certain persons of Genesis, her history is to be understood first of all according to the contemporary depth, 463; E., as a figure of Mary, is a typological figure of liturgical and not strictly biblical origin, 480–481.

ESTHETICS: esthetic pleasure in art, 50f; E. in the service of a religious end: possibility and conditions, 53f; in the service of the liturgy, 57f, 320f.

ESTHETISM: danger of E. in the liturgy, 32; 684f, 844 n. 53.

ESTO MIHI: Mass, 778, 781.

EUAGGÉLION: or mystery of the life and death of Christ, is the primary object of the catechesis of the Apostolic Church, 251.

EUCHARIST: how, by its means, the Holy Spirit is received, 24 (*See*: EPICLESIS); E. and sensible signs, 63f; Eucharistic realism of the ancients under the expressions of image, symbol, etc., 37f; the fourfold theological dimension of the E. and of baptism is already proposed by the Bible, 76–80; principal viewpoints by which the texts of the N. T. receive light and fulfillment from the liturgy, 483; its typology in the liturgy, 478f; E. and manna in the desert, 79; the Epistle to the Hebrews in 6:4 and 13:10 alludes to the E., 259; the supreme E. on earth, i.e., action of giving thanks to God, is the Mass, 343; E. connected essentially to the resurrection, 80; the E. is a medicament for immortality, even corporeal, 313f; E. and future glory, 79–80; the E. is conceived by the pre-Nicene Church primarily as action of Christ Himself, 261f; in salvation, the glorious Humanity of Christ has a basic and ever-present function, 821f; the E. carries out the mystery of Christ and in virtue of the *opus operatum* is something given and received objectively, 100; by means of the E. Christ is personally present in the liturgy, 267; according to Odo Casel, there is present not only the Christ of Golgotha, but the historical Passion of Golgotha, 105; the E. involves the personal presentness of Christ, 110; the E. together with baptism is the principal means of formation of the People of God, 495; the E. is made by the Church, and it nevertheless makes the Church, 284 n. 16; the E. is structured according to the law of the incarnation, 304; inasmuch as it transforms man, the E. is an essential part of the liturgy, 27–28; the E. is the end to which the other sacraments are ordered, 171–174; according to the Catechism of the Council of Trent, the E. is "the fountain of all graces," 172f, 814; the other sacraments confer grace only through a certain desire for the E. in those who receive them, 171f; as sacrifice and sacrament, the E. unites in the highest degree the aspect of worship and the aspect of sanctification, and is therefore the focal point of the liturgy, 126; the E. makes better known the essential goodness of matter, 612f; E. and the restoration of infrahuman creation to the service of divine life in the world, 329–334; the E. associates ordinary material things with the sanctification of man, 328; the E. is the highest liturgical intervention in the infrahuman world, 330; without the E., no other sacrament confers grace, according to St. Thomas, 270; E. has even an antidemoniacal dimension, 412–417; for the Christian, the E. already in the N. T. has a supreme role in the triumph over Satan, 372f; participation in the E. is the supreme armament of the Christian against Satan, 413; during Lent the E. is the primary means for living the mystery of Christ in its antidemoniacal dimension, 440; the elementary ritual of the E. is of proved Apostolicity, 561–562; the E. in the anaphora of St. Basil, 167f; the E. in patristic literature of interest to liturgical theology, 591f; the E. as *mystérion* in Origen, 603; E. as *mysterium*, 604f; the E. as *sacramentum* in St. Augustine, 29–30; the *res* of the E. in St. Augustine is the unity of the Body of Christ, 30–31; belief in transubstantiation proved from the liturgy and from other documents of the 5th–6th century, 562; E. as sacrifice and sacrament is the center of worship and of sanctification, in St. Thomas, 575; real presence and transubstantiation proved against the Protestants by Zaccaria by means of the liturgy, 551; treatise on E. and the liturgy in the positive-scholastic theologians, 565; treatise on the E. according to Franzelin, 555–556; treatise on the E. in Perrone, against the Protestants, 555; treatise on the E. in the theological manuals of the 19th century, 556; in consequence of the liturgical movement among them, today the Protestants are reconsidering the traditional theological aspects of the E., 834; E. in the spiritual life of St. Gertrude, 774f; in the spirituality of the Church, either the sacrificial or the sacramental aspect of the E. can be emphasized, 656; in the E. sacrifice and sacrament, the liturgy places the accent on the sacrifice (*See*: MASS; SACRIFICE), and modern piety more on the sacrament of the real presence, 670; extraliturgical devotion to the E., under the aspect of the real presence, and liturgy, 656, 670.

EUCHARISTÍAN POIEIN: *eucharistiam facere*: among the ancients, indicates the sacred action *par excellence*, 318.

EUDOKÍA: divine pleasure, is the salvific manifestation of God to men in the unity of the cosmos, 347.

EUTYCHIANS: heretics who, in consequence of their doctrine, changed the rite of the *commixtio*, 613 n. 88.

EVE: mother of the human race, figure of Mary, 480f; E., Mary, and the struggle against Satan, 439; typology on the figure of E. in the rites over the *competentes*, 402; E. named in the prayer of a martyr who has obtained victory over Satan, 446.

EVIL: origin of E. from the fallen angels, 364f.

EVOLUTION: historical E. and authority of the liturgy, 618; E. of dogmas: *See*: DOGMA.

EVOLUTIONISM: mitigated and non-materialistic E. does not exclude but actually confirms the unified designs of God in the cosmos, 324.

EXALTATION OF THE CROSS: expresses the typology of the bronze serpent in the desert and Christ crucified, 480; the feast of the E. of the C. and its antidemoniacal dimension, 444.

EXAMINATION OF CONSCIENCE: is one of the "pious exercises" recommended by the Second Vatican Council in harmony with the liturgy, and subordinate thereto, 670; as a means toward perfection, 654, 667–668; useful and necessary in climate of liturgical spirituality, 696.

EXAUDI: prayer for the blessing of the garments in the consecration of virgins, and its antidemoniacal significance, 433.

EXCESSUS CONTEMPLATIONUM: is the fifth degree of spirituality, according to the Ven. Guigo I, 722.

EXCESSUS MENTIS: ravishing of the mind in pure prayer, according to John Cassian, 719.

EXCOMMUNICATION: its real significance, 415, 419.

EXEGESIS, PATRISTIC: its basis and its being appreciated anew, 458 n. 2.

EXEMPLARISM: in the Epistle to the Hebrews, 258f; biblical, traditional, and philosophical bases of Christian E., and its use in the liturgy, 36–43; E. and the association of infrahuman creation to the praising of God in the liturgy, 333–334.

EXEQUIES: of the dead and their natural connection with the Mass, 175; are one of the proofs of the care which the liturgy has for the physical body of the faithful,

722–729; according to the research of Poulain, 731–732; in St. Gertrude, 776–792; why M. E. and active participation in the liturgical action are most compatible, 732–738; esthetic experience in the service of the liturgy: possibility, conditions, dangers, 50–59, 319f, 683f, 844 n. 53. *See*: KNOWLEDGE BY CONNATURALITY; INTUITION; MYSTICS; PEDAGOGY.

EXPERIENTIALISM: and its danger in the mystical life, 738.

EXPIATION: Christian: one of the themes which sheds light on the precepts and admonitions of the O. T., 471.

EXPOSITION: of theological science and the question of the liturgy in theology, 633f.

EXSUFFLATIO: St. Augustine uses the E. and the exorcisms as arguments in the question of original sin, 613. *See*: INSUFFLATIO.

EXTERIORISM: indicated by St. John of the Cross as a possible ambient danger in the spiritual life, 715.

EXTERNALNESS: interior worship and exterior worship in the liturgy, 136–139; E. and internalness in the liturgy ought to be viewed in the light of the law of incarnation, 305; E. of the law of salvation in community and of the law of the unified totality of salvation, 136–139, 252f; E. and possibility of "scandal in the liturgy," 305–306; danger of exteriorist formalism in the liturgy, 136–139, 737f. *See*: SIGN.

EXTREME UNCTION: *See*: ANOINTING OF THE ILL; ILL.

FACULTIES, HUMAN PSYCHOLOGICAL: and their actualization in the liturgy, 316–324, 515f.

FAITH: divine F., divine and Catholic F., ecclesiastical F., 535; proximate criterion of F. is the infallible magisterium of the Church, and not individual reason, whether philosophical or historical, 566; motives of F. and motives of credibility: the question of the point to which dogmatic F. is implied in the liturgy, 509–541; rules for determining to what point the liturgy implies something as being of the F., 518–529; relation between F. and liturgy according to the modernists, 529–533; F. among the moral dispositions prerequisite in the liturgy, 71; F. makes one present to the spirit of the liturgical action, 737; F., hope, and charity will not save without reference to the sacraments, 811–816; the exercise of F., hope, and charity in the liturgical action and in liturgical spirituality, in view of the virtue of religion, 697–702; liturgy does not exhaust itself in the virtue of religion, but includes acts elicited *hic et nunc* by F., hope, and charity, 817f; acting like a Christian in reference to the action of the infused Christian virtues, moral and theological, corresponds to being a Christian, which is a grace of participation in the divine nature, 648; in spirituality some place a different stress on F. than they do on hope and charity, 659; liturgy as *protestatio fidei*, 71, 701–702; only F. can perceive the restoration of cosmic unity in the liturgy, 329f; F. and the significance of the liturgical assembly, 84f; profession of F. at baptism and its Christological-Trinitarian structure, 230f; the timeless, entitative, metaphysical aspect, and the temporal, concrete aspect of the F. and the question of the assimilation of the theological values of the liturgy, 629f; the primary and natural object of F. is God as God, 698f; implicit F.: necessary to salvation for those who live according to their conscience, 115 n. 19; according to St. Thomas, F. is a theological virtue because it has for its immediate natural object God Himself, 130; in St. Thomas, F. as a theological virtue is superior to the virtue of religion, of which it is in fact the root, 130f; F., hope, and charity *suo imperio causant* religion, according to St. Thomas, 698; F. along with hope and love, is aroused by the catechist in the narration that he makes of salvation history, 871f; by heeding the word of God, man knows that F. is among the moral dispositions that God demands for the acceptance of worship and bestowal of sanctification, 881; worship by F., hope, and charity, that Christ, in the Church, renders to God, 899; F. in relation to liturgy is wholly centered on the sacred history, mystery of Christ, 900.

FALL OF ADAM: as theme proposed to the intelligence by the liturgy, 689, 704; fall of man, and angels, 344–345.

FAMILY: fathers and mothers of families, and the universal priesthood of the faithful, 144.

FASCINATIO NUGACITATIS: attraction of fatuous things a real danger for a man drawn to the supernatural, 882.

FASTING: and the struggle against Satan, 376, 442; F. and Lent, 667f; how the liturgy understands the precepts of fasting in texts of the O. T., 471; Eucharistic fast, according to St. Thomas, 579; F., with prayer, good works, reading and meditating on the Bible, is a means of realizing *in mysterio* the mystery of Christ, 440; F. as *sacramentum* in St. Augustine, 29–30; the *res* of F. is spiritual mortification according to St. Augustine, 30; by Divine Providence, F. and pious works during Lent cancel out guilt, according to St. Leo the Great, 440; F. as one of the sacramentals after the 13th century, 86.

FATHER: First Person of the Trinity: and Christological-Trinitarian movement in revelation and in liturgy, 191–246; F. as the *a quo* and *ad quem* of the sanctification and worship of the Church, 24; according to the ancient rule, liturgical prayer is addressed to the F. through the agency of Jesus Christ, 210; this aforementioned rule based on the Bible and on tradition, 210; the F. invoked in the introduction, in the body, and in the conclusion of liturgical prayers, 209–217; biblical tendency to reserve to the F. the name of God, the appellative Our Father, and to regard whatever the O. T. says of God as said of the F., 210–212; the F. in the older texts of the N. T. and in ancient Christian literature, 212f; doxologies of the N. T. addressed to the F. alone, or to the F. through Christ, 217f; the F. in the anaphoras and in the Roman Canon, 222–230; in the sacraments, 230–240; in the Lent-Pentecost cycle, 240f; why there is no feast of the F., 243; the F. in the Epistle to the Hebrews, 255 n. 12.

FATHERS: of the Church: theology and liturgy in the F., 590–625; principal patristic literature of theological liturgical interest, 590–596; principal patristic literature in which the liturgy was polemically employed, 596; various tendencies in the theological liturgical writings of the F., 607f; liturgy viewed by the F. primarily in a theological irenic way, 595f; theology and preaching of the F. centered on the concept of sacred salvation history, 867–876; the F. too readily supposed the apostolicity of the liturgy, 511 n. 4, 561f; and their realist manner of viewing the concepts of image, figure, symbol, etc., 37f; private opinion of the F. not enough to determine the existence and meaning of the liturgical signs, 46f, 479f; F. and universal priesthood of the faithful, 144f; F. and manner of conceiving the Trinity, 194f, 203–206; how the F. understood the relationship between the heavenly and the earthly liturgies, 260f; the opinions of the F. on the struggle against Satan, 383–389; biblical foundations and Hellenistic influences on the typology, and biblical and liturgical allegorism in the F., 458 n. 2, 459 n. 3, 466, 598–611; example of the F. in the manner of understanding the Psalms, 490; patristic theology in the positive-scholastic theologians, 564; the F. as *auctoritates* in the scholastic method, 582f; "return to the F.," and its significance for the modern age, 874.

FEASTS: Jewish F. as figure of the Christian F. and realities, 479; liturgical F. and liturgical cycles as signs, 90; general meaning of liturgical F., 175–179; their fourfold dimension of significance in reference to the liturgical signs, 90f; the liturgical F. do not have for their direct object the individual Persons of the Trinity considered in their intra-Trinitarian life, but in their relations with salvation history, 240f; history and significance of the feast of the Most Blessed Trinity, 243–246; every feast is of interest also to the concrete personal situation of its individual participants, 483f; special grace and redemptive power of the individual F., 483f; the object of the liturgical F. is proposed by the magisterium to the faith of believers in varying degrees of authority, 522f; liturgical F. explained by the Fathers especially in their homilies, 592–596; liturgical F. as connatural centers of reference for meditations, spiritual exercises, and periods of recollection in a climate of liturgical spirituality, 686, 695, 696; F. and liturgical spirituality in St. Gertrude, 741f.

FERMENTUM: hierarchical and communitarian character of the sacrifice expressed by the custom of the *F.*, 288.

FERVORES ORATIONUM: are for the Ven. Guigo I one of the principal aspects of the monastic spirituality of the Middle Ages, 721–722.

FIDES EX AUDITU: is the first jolt that God gives a man through the ministry of preaching, 883.

FIGURE: as *sacramentum, mysterium*, image, symbol, 605; necessity of reëstablishing a sound figurative liturgical theology, 610f; as a terminology connected with the concept of *mystérion*, it enters broadly into liturgical formulations, 606f; in the Fathers up to Origen the sacred history involves various phases, from the F. or preparation, roughcast, or initiation, to the fulfillment of the reality, 603f; in salvation history the F. is a preparation for higher realities, 599f; correctness of the observations of Adolf von Harnack on the concept and relation of figure, symbol, and thing itself, 37–38; ancient and modern mentality on the concept of F., 36–42.

FILIOQUE: and liturgy, 614 n. 91.

FINDING OF THE CROSS: liturgical biblical theme, 444.

FLECTAMUS GENUA and *LEVATE*: and silent prayer during the liturgical action, 317, 693.

FLESH: its basic importance in the spiritual life, 316, 612. *See*: SOUL AND BODY; BODY.

FLIGHT FROM THE WORLD: later formularies soften somewhat the concept of the primitive idea of the flight from Satan and of the repudiation of his pomps, 434.

FONT, BAPTISMAL: antidemoniacal dimension and Christological-Trinitarian dimension of the blessing of the B. F., 239, 409.

FORM CRITICISM: in the investigation of the authority of liturgy, 519f.

FOR THOSE WHO ARE RENOUNCING THE WORLD: prayer in the Gelasian Sacramentary, for use at monastic profession: its antidemoniacal dimension, 433f.

GALLICANISMS: in liturgy: the Gallican origin of many prayers and doxologies of the Middle Ages addressed directly to the Trinity or directly to Christ, 223, 243. *See*: LITURGY, GALLICAN.

GARMENT, BAPTISMAL: and its antidemoniacal significance, 410.

GARMENTS, PRIESTLY: their significance explained by the Fathers, 591–596; in the explanation of St. Thomas, 580; P. G. of the O. T., according to St. Thomas, 581.

GAUDETE IN DOMINO: Mass of the Third Sunday in Advent, 765, 782.

GENESIS: some narratives of G., like those of Job, Esther, and Tobias, are to be understood primarily in their contemporary depth, 463.

GLORY, HEAVENLY: in the fourfold dimension of every liturgical sign the H. G. is signified in the eschatological dimension, 69–95; fore-announced in the Jewish worship of the Old Law, 135, 577; as invisible spiritual reality signified in its liturgical sign, 103f; in the sacraments as prognostic signs, according to St. Thomas, 75; in the sacramental sign, baptism, 76–78; in the sacramental sign, confirmation, 80; the Eucharist is connected with the resurrection, and hence with the H. G., 79; in the sacramental sign, penance, 80–81; in the sacramental sign, anointing of the ill, 81; in the sacramental sign, holy orders, 81f; in the sacramental sign, matrimony, 82; in the sacramentals, 90; in the sign, liturgical assembly, 91; in the feasts and in the liturgical cycles, 90–95; one of the liturgical themes as objective dogmatic reality proposed to the liturgical psychology of the faithful, 319; the ill are prepared for the H. G. by the rite with which the Church assists them, 174. See: ESCHATOLOGY; JERUSALEM, HEAVENLY.

GLORY OF THE LORD: in view of the texts from Isaias read in the Vigil Mass of Christmas, 473.

GNÔSIS: Jewish G., is connected essentially with the meditation and interpretation of the Bible, 622; Jewish G., the source of a notable part of Hellenistic G., 620; Hellenistic G., according to recent studies, takes its origin from Jewish G., 620; heretical and syncretistic G., dangerous to Christian faith and therefore combatted by Irenaeus, 621; origin and nature of the concept of G., 619–622; Christian G. focuses all the theoretical and practical realities on Christ, in connection with the knowledge of the Bible as salvation history, 621; therefore the true G. is salvific biblical knowledge, 619–620; but the G. toû Theoû is not merely intellectual knowledge about God, but involves will, sentiments, and practical behavior, 619f; G. has its source in the Bible, meditated upon and penetrated, 620–621; in the Fathers of the 2nd and 3rd centuries the ideal of theology as G.-Wisdom predominates, even if it derives of differing tendencies, 621, 628; G. represents the ideal of the Fathers in their irenic, expositive labors, 619, 869; the true G. is, for Irenaeus, normative as rule of faith and for ecclesial preaching, 621; G. as superior knowledge through which one ascends by degrees, according to Origen, and the study of the mystérion, 601, 608; G. or salvific knowledge is, according to Origen, the work of discovering and explaining all the salvific mysteries contained in the Bible, 602–603; the G. has become less biblical and more metaphysical since the time of the Pseudo-Dionysius, 622; patristic G. has the defect of an insufficient philosophical instrumentality, 624; patristic G. for the later theologians is a mixed process, scientific and extrascientific, 628; ideal of the G. the ultimate root of the position of the liturgy in the theology of the Fathers: advantages and defects, 622f.

GNOSTICISM: the liturgy is clearly opposed to the spirit of G., which is inimical to matter and wants to save only the soul, 316; anti-gnostic and liturgical controversy: Ignatius of Antioch and Irenaeus of Lyons appealed against dualistic G. to Eucharistic practice and to the real presence, 611f; Irenaeus combats the supposed secret Apostolic tradition of G., appealing to the unanimity and universality of the faith in the various Churches, 616–617.

GNOSTICS: the Marcosian G. usurped the Christian rites, 422, 425.

GOD: as spouse of His people in the thematics of the Psalms, 469; protector of the just and pious Israelite in the thematics of the Psalms, 469; the portrait of God against Satan does not involve a genuine dualism, 383; City of God, 360; See: CITY; biblical tendency to reserve the name of God to the Father alone, 210f; the "God" to whom the ancient liturgical orations are directed is the Father, even if the conclusion of the prayer is simply Per Christum Dominum nostrum, 210f; in the Gregorian Sacramentary some orations are addressed directly to the Son, and hence the *Deus* (*Domine*) is understood of the Son, 217; various manners of considering the mystery of God in the unity of His nature and in the Trinity of Persons, 192–196; the God of the liturgy is, nevertheless, the Trinitarian God, 207f; the unity of the divine nature in the liturgy, 207f; God and man, grace and human strength in liturgical spirituality, 101, 665–666; how the liturgy, in the light of the Christic, Christian, eschatological realities, understands the texts of the O. T. that speak of the attributes of God and of His actions in the world, 465–469, 502f; God the King in the Psalms and in the liturgy, 503; holiness of God in the new German catechism, 897; treatise on triune God, and the liturgy, 635; treatise *De Deo Uno* in St. Thomas, 585.

GOD-FEARING, THE: in the Psalms and in the liturgy, 501f.

GOLGOTHA: the sacrifice of Christ was already prefigured in Jewish worship, 135; the immolation on G. and its prolongation in the Mass shed light upon the liturgical precepts of the O. T., recalled in the liturgy, 471; the liturgy of Christ the Priest in His earthly life culminates in the sacrifice of G., and continues in the heavenly worship, 259; the Mass is the unbloody prolongation of the sacrifice of G., 140, 159; for Odo Casel, in the Eucharist not just the glorified Christ who suffered on Golgotha is made present, but also the historical action on Golgotha, 105f; but if the Mass represented the Passion of G. in its numerical individuality it would be a bloody sacrifice and hence in it Christ would be meriting anew, 109; the meaning of Christ's life up to G. is perceived only by faith, 701; the Protestant liturgical movement is reconsidering the Eucharist and its relationship to G. in a more traditional sense, 834f.

GOOD FRIDAY: the great prayers of G. F., 317.

GRACE: sanctifying grace is signified in every liturgical sign, 26f, 69f, 72–76; the grace necessary for an act of faith is at the same time cause of a knowledge by connaturality, 536–541; Pelagian and semi-Pelagian controversies on G., and the liturgy, 525, 530, 613; G. and human strength in spirituality in general, 669; manner of living the binomial pair *G.-human strength* in liturgical spirituality, with consciousness of grace predominating, 667; necessity of grace recalled by the thematics of liturgical spirituality, 705; since the liturgical action is the privileged place where the grace necessary for the performance of all supernatural works is obtained from God, the spirituality concentrated in the liturgical action places G. at the center of consciousness, 697f; ascetic strength and awareness of G. in the liturgical spirituality of St. Gertrude, 758f; G. is caused by the Eucharist in itself, and by the other sacraments through a certain desire for the Eucharist, 172f; treatise on G., and liturgy, 636; treatise on G., and liturgy, in positive-scholastic theology, 551, 565.

GRATIA CAPITIS: and liturgy, 267.

GREAT DAY: in the Apocalypse, the G. D. is the day of the triumph of Christ and of His judgment, 379f.

GREEK LITURGY: position of Mary in the struggle against Satan according to the G. L., 447–448 n. 193. *See*: BYZANTINE LITURGY.

HADES: as the locale of demons, the Greeks placed it in the West, 409.

HAEC EST DIES: Vesper antiphon for the feast of the Assumption, 762.

HARMONY, UNIVERSAL: ancient stoic and gnostic theme in the theology of sign, 41.

HEARTS: exchange of H., as a mystical experience, in St. Gertrude, 784f.

HEAVENLY COURT: 345, 347. *See*: ANGELS; SAINTS.

HELFTA: monastery of St. Gertrude, 732 n. 82, 740, 748, 749, 765, 797, 798.

HELL: formulas of Mass "to alleviate the pains of H.," 510, 522; H. described in terms perhaps too concrete, 389.

HELLENISM: and influence on the opinions in respect to the demons, 385f, 388–389; H. and *gnôsis* in Origen, 621; difference between Hellenistic allegorism and biblical typology, 459 n. 3, 577.

HIERARCHY: without H. the Church does not exist, 121f; but the H. alone is not the Church, 122; the Church is the indissoluble totality which results from Christ the Head, from the H. as a human-divine intermediary structure, agent of Christ, and from the people which, through the H., is united to Christ the Head, 122; the individual elements of the liturgy have their doctrinal authority imparted to them by the individual members of the H. from whom they proceed or by whom they are approved, 520f; the H., depository of the word of God and of the liturgical rites, 882; the H. determines the fact and the meaning of the individual liturgical signs which are not of divine institution, 44–47; the liturgical movement esteems anew the episcopal and parochial H., 844, 847; earthly and heavenly hierarchies, according to Origen, 602f.

HISTORIA: expresses the concept of sacred (salvation) history in St. Augustine, 870.

HISTORIA DISPENSATIONIS: expresses the concept of sacred (salvation) history in St. Augustine, 870.

HISTORY: for Aristotle and the scholastics, H. is not a science in the proper sense, 588, 628f; among the sciences, H. gets a better grasp of the temporal aspect than do the others, and hence a better grasp of the concrete and individual aspects of being, 629; historical aspect and philosophical aspect of entities, 3–10, 390–396; H. and theology, 566f; the predominatingly historical ideal of liturgical science, xx f; H., philology, and criticism, in research into liturgy, 519f; historical research on liturgy in the 16th to the 18th centuries, 549f; what faith the liturgy demanded in the supposedly historical details of the lives of the saints in the Second Nocturnes of the Breviary, 528f; H. in the scholastic method, 583f; what consequences St. Thomas' opinion in regard to history's not being a science has for him in the question of the relationship between theology and liturgy, 588–589.

HISTORY OF RELIGIONS: how the similarities between Christian liturgical rites and the religious rites of other religions are to be explained, 323f.

HISTORY, SALVATION: *See*: SACRED (SALVATION) HISTORY.

HOLINESS: of the Church and authority of the liturgy, according to St. Cyprian and St. Augustine, 617; H. of God, and a catechism according to the spirit of the liturgy, 897.

HOLY SPIRIT: worship, liturgy, baptism, sacraments, prayer *in Spiritu*, 24; the H. S. and the Christological-Trinitarian movement of revelation and of liturgy, 191–246; the H. S. in the conclusion of the liturgical prayers and the meaning of *in unitate Spiritus Sancti*, 215–216; H. S. and Church, 16f; H. S. and sacrifice, 223f; the H. S. in the anaphoras and in the Roman Canon, 223–230; in the sacraments, 230–239; in the Lent-Pentecost cycle, 240f; in the Epistle to the Hebrews, 255 n. 12; H. S. and baptism, 354; and blessing of baptismal water, 354–355, 409f; the H. S. in the defining of dogmas, 539; how the liturgy of Pentecost interprets the prophecy of Joel on the gift of the H. S., 475; gifts of the H. S., 648 n. 1.

HOLY THURSDAY: every Mass contains its memorial, because every Mass contains all the phases of the mystery of Christ, from Advent to All Saints, etc., 176; in the *Missa chrismatis* a strong antidemoniacal dimension is made explicit, 410–411.

HOMILY: explanation of the word of God proclaimed in the liturgical biblical reading, 883f; the H., when it is an integral part of the liturgical action, is the highest

I., as proof of the care that the liturgy has even for the body, 313f; liturgy of the I., and the struggle against Satan, 421–425.

ILLNESSES: and Satan, 364f, 367f, 371f, 375.

ILLUMINISM: *See*: ENLIGHTENMENT.

IMAGES: concept, 35f; ancient realistic mentality and modern mentality in regard to the concept of I., and to its related concepts, and the importance of this for the history of theology and for the liturgy, 36–42; I. and *mystérion*, 601f; dogmatic controversy in regard to images, and the liturgy, 38, 525, 614; images of worship and worship of images, according to St. Thomas, 582 n. 35; in connection with the dimensions of *mystérion* as sacred history, 607; the concept has a considerable role in the neo-Platonic view, especially in the Pseudo-Dionysius, 40f, 623; concept broadly explained by St. Augustine, 625; the connected terminology passed into the liturgical formulas, 606.

IMAGO: realism of this notion, and of the related notions of species, figure, symbol, *mysterium, sacramentum*, in the ancients, 35f, 36, 37–38; concept connected by the Latins with the concepts of sign, figure, symbol, i.e., *mystérion*, 605; in the Leonine Sacramentary, 606.

IMITATION OF CHRIST: is not only moral, in regard to sentiments and emotions, but also physico-mystical, 373; the more perfect I. of Xt. is martyrdom as total dedication to God, 445f; or assimilation to Christ as union with God, as focal point of Christian spirituality, 649; is common to all the Christian spiritualities, 668.

IMITATION OF THE SAINTS: great theme of the liturgy of the saints, 705.

IMMACULATE CONCEPTION: the I. C. of Mary was proposed by the magisterium of the Church to the adherence of believers, in the feast of that title, with differing degrees of authority in different ages, 524f; I. C., an example, along with the Assumption, of the importance of the liturgy in the process of making dogmas explicit, 540 n. 30; feast of I. C. as triumph of Mary over Satan, 448; feast of the apparition of Lourdes as triumph over Satan, 448; in the feast of the I. C. the O. T. prophecy of the Messias is explained, 473; O. T. prophecies have importance for such a feast, 476; how the liturgy interprets Gen. 3:15f on such a feast, 476; on the feast of the I. C. the liturgy evolves the typology of Judith and Esther, 481; the liturgy reads the N. T. Marian texts in the light of the doctrine of the I. C., 451f; the doctrine as known today sheds light on the Angelic Salutation, 483; in the feast of the I. C., Psalm 8 acquires a particular interpretation, 494; the I. C. in the 12th and 13th centuries was a theological opinion looked upon in various ways by theologians, 524; the feast of the I. C. reflects varying states of the doctrine through the centuries, and at the beginning of the 19th century reflected a different state of the doctrine than it does at present, 524f; on the liturgical side alone in the 19th century there was a great diversity in the proposition of the I. C. and of the Assumption on the part of the Church, 526–527; Pius IX accepted the principle that for a dogmatic definition it was not necessary to produce an apodictic proof by way of reason alone, 540 n. 30; example of the influence of liturgy on dogma, 541; I. C. and liturgy in the positive-scholastics of the 18th century, 556; on the question of the I. C. the positive-scholastics have recourse to the *ex cathedra* definitions, 560; references to the feast of the I. C. in the theological syntheses of the 19th century that do not ignore the liturgy, 553; references in the modern theological manuals, which accord no great position to the liturgy, to the liturgical feast of the I. C. in the dogmatic question of the I. C., 557; in St. Thomas, 582; St. Thomas discusses the authority and the meaning of the feast of the I. C., 585; in the Photian question on the I. C. there was notable recourse to the liturgy, 614 n. 91; the magisterium intervenes primarily against errors and not to propose doctrine integrally: the definition of the I. C. is the first exception to this general rule, 868 n. 21.

IMPERIUM: of casting out demons received by the exorcist, 426.

IMPOSITION OF HANDS: important gestural sign, 49; a sign known already in Judaism, 44; as a *sacramentum*, in St. Augustine, 30 n. 20; positive rite of sanctification over the *audientes*, 399; I. of H. and the Holy Spirit in the reconciliation of penitents, 236, 420; in the sacrament of orders, 237; proximate matter of confirmation, along with the consignation and the chrism, 331; and the antidemoniacal dimension of the anointing of the ill, 423.

INCARNATION: the law of incarnation in the relations between man and God, 61–62, 136f; 300–305; meaning of this law, 300f; I. of the Word, full manifestation and hiddenness of God, 301; the liturgy as a prime example of the law of I., 305f; I., and possibility of scandal in the liturgy, 305–306; liturgy a constant, incarnate epiphany, and the hiddenness of Christ, 305f; I. and sin of Adam, 14 n. 9; Scripture is, in its own peculiar way, an incarnation of the Word, 602; I. and the struggle against Satan, 367, 438; I. of the Word and unity of the cosmos, 327; law of I. and liturgical pastoral, 852–853; I., beginning with Justin, as event in the life of Christ and *mystérion*, 600; I., beginning of the exercise of Christ's priesthood, culminating on Golgotha, 256, 267; considered in the light of the dogma of the substantial unity of man, 309f; the preparatory historical phase of the O. T., reaching out to its realization, 160; in the liturgical view, the whole O. T. cries out for the I., as do the faithful, 473f; brings unheard of depth to the ideas of the O. T. on the unity of the infrahuman world with man, to the ends of divine life, 326–327; is one of the biblical and traditional themes of Christian exemplarism, 42; the actual divine dimension is perceived only by faith, 701; with the redemption, the I. is the great beacon-light of the soul, even outside the liturgical action, 696; decisive event viewed by the faithful, which transcends greatly the significance of the O. T., 460; living I. as an abstract spiritualism is insufficient for its proper understanding, 253; in the early days of his conversion, St. Augustine's neo-Platonism was remote from Christian incarnational spiritualism, 311.

INCENSUM ISTUD: prayer introduced into the Mass in the Middle Ages, drawn from Gallican usage, 292 n. 31.

INDICULUS DE GRATIA DEI: and the principle of *lex credendi*, 30 n. 20, 529f, 613, 616.

INDIVIDUAL, THE: and liturgy: in the liturgy the fact and the meaning of the liturgical signs is not determined by private individuals; those signs not of divine institution are determined by the Church, 44–47; I. and community in spirituality in general, and the possibility of diverse emphases, 658–659; the moral dispositions and moral obligation of the individual who joins in the liturgy are involved in every liturgical dimension, 69–76; the liturgical action and the texts which are read therein have reference even to the concrete moral situation of the individuals who participate therein, 483f; reference of the Psalms in particular to the individual realities of those who recite them, 487f, 495, 497; the liturgy is preoccupied to the highest degree with the obligation of the individual subject, but conceives it as his response to the objective realities imposed by God according to the law of objectivity, 184–190; the I. in revelation and in the liturgy is not able to be born, to subsist, and to develop except in the context of the community, according to the law of the communitarian character of salvation, 272–299; liturgical spirituality is essentially communitarian, 665f; the individual personalization of the liturgy, possible and necessary, is realized to the highest degree in mystical experience in the liturgy, 689f, 692f; 720; the I., and personal experience of the faith, 535–540;

the I., and collectivity in the religion of the O. T., 278f; the I., and community in pastoral, 808–811; the I., and the liturgy, in the example of St. Gertrude, 802–803.

INDIVIDUALISM: in spirituality, 711; I. and estrangement of the people, even the faithful, from the liturgy, 840f. *See*: INDIVIDUAL, THE.

INDWELLING: of the Divine Persons, 126–127; Divine Persons and spirituality, 656.

INDUCTION: and deduction in science, according to Aristotle and the scholastics, 628.

INDULGENTIAM: apology in the Mass, 291–292 n. 31.

IN EXITU ISRAËL DE AEGYPTO: 495.

INFALLIBILITY: of the Roman Church: as a persuasion existing in Rome in the 5th and 6th centuries, demonstrated by the historical method alone, by examples from the Leonine Sacramentary, 562; I. of the Pope: the development of this dogma makes fully comprehensible the passage, "You are Peter . . .," 482–483.

INFANCY: historic I. of Christ presented in the liturgy, 797–798.

INFANTS: blessing of, 88; I. and desire for Eucharist, 171–173; baptism of I., original sin, and liturgy, 522, 613; exorcism over I., 398; catechism for children, and the liturgy, 887–899.

INFLUENCE, DEMONIACAL: after Adam the D. I. is real, personal and universal, 406.

INITIATION, CHRISTIAN: Lent is its specific time of preparation, 439; again today there is an introduction to the liturgy as "mystery," 856; a catechesis that unifies the aspects of the Christian mystery while safeguarding the balance of revelation, 878; liturgy of C. I. the point of departure for considering the sacred history, mystery of Christ, 871; has its apex in Communion in the Eucharistic Sacrifice, 402f; C. I. and the Lent-Pentecost cycle, 177; Christological-Trinitarian dimension of C. I., 230–234; C. I. and the struggle against Satan, 396–417; principal rites of C. I. and the exercises of St. Gertrude, 795; rites modified by the various Churches in the unity of the faith, 617–618; as *mystérion* in the theology of the Fathers from the 4th century onwards, 604; the patristic themes of C. I. are taken up again by St. Thomas, 580; *sacramenta* of C. I. as explanation of sacred history in St. Augustine, 872; as theme for consideration in the works of St. Gertrude, 742.

INITIATION, PAGAN: rite of initiation in the pagan mysteries, 77.

INLATIO: of the Mozarabic Missal, 439.

INNIXA SUPER DILECTUM SUUM: 730.

INNOCENCE: baptismal, and penance, 418.

IN NOMINE PATRIS ET FILII ET SPIRITUS SANCTI: and the Christological-Trinitarian dimension, 239.

IN PARADISUM: in the liturgy of the dead, and position of the angels, 357.

INSIGNIA, PONTIFICAL: in the teachings of St. Thomas, 580.

IN SPIRITU HUMILITATIS: its Gallican introduction into the Mass, 292 n. 31.

INSTINCT, CHRISTIAN: in the faith, 535; and the liturgy, in the evolution of dogmas, 539f.

INSTRUCTION: didactic end of the liturgy real but secondary, and realized more indirectly than directly, 513f; observations on programs of instruction in the liturgy, 637–643; I. in dogmatic theology, in exegesis, in ascetical theology, in mystical theology, and the liturgy, 638f.

INSTRUCTION, RELIGIOUS: does not coincide absolutely with the specific end of preaching, 859.

INSUFFLATION: and the struggle against Satan, 398; insufflations burn and put the demons to flight, according to St. Cyril of Jerusalem, 408; as *sacramentum* of the scrutinies, according to Quodvultdeus of Carthage, 403; as a theme in patristic literature, of liturgical theological interest, 591. *See*: EXSUFFLATION.

INTELLECTUALS: the catechesis of I., according to St. Augustine, 873f.

INTELLIGENCE: among the various psychological faculties exercised in the liturgy, the I. that is exercised is of a type more concrete, historical, and intuitive than scholastic and speculative, 318f, 516, 657f.

INTERCESSION: of saints, and liturgy, 341.

INTERIORNESS: and liturgy. *See*: INDIVIDUAL, THE; EXTERNALNESS.

INTROIBO AD ALTARE DEI: its introduction of Gallican origin, 291 n. 31.

INTROVERSION: and liturgy, 102.

INTUITION: and discourse in mystical experience, 650f; knowledge by I., sanctity of life and personal prayer of the Psalms, 488f; the liturgy involves less ratiocination than it does intuition, 516. *See*: KNOWLEDGE BY CONNATURALITY.

INVASION, MYSTICAL: in St. Gertrude, as an experience during the liturgy, 777.

ISAAC: in connection with the angel of baptism, the baptismal rite of adults names the God of the Patriarchs, to which Patriarchs an angel was assigned, 354; as a patristic typological theme in the modern theological revalidation thereof, 458 n. 2; and Israel in biblical typology as figure of Christian and Jew, 481.

ISHMAEL: and Isaac in biblical typology as figure of Jew and Christian, 480.

ISIS: in the pagan mystery religions that celebrate a death and resurrection, 105.

ISRAEL: as the $Q^e hal\ Yahweh$, religious people, 336; honored God as Founder of the Covenant, 135; the historical events of I. retain their reality, but in the N. T. they assume a reality even more profound, 477–478; the events undergone by I. in the typology of the prophets, 477; immediate subject of the precepts and admonitions of the O. T. that are repeated in the N., 469–470; between I. and God, Malachias places as intermediary the angel of the covenant, 346; receives an angel from God in the Exodus: a theme in connection with the angel of baptism, 354; theme of the conjugal love of I. and God in Canticle of Canticles, 469; I., subject of special Providence, as theme in the Psalms, 503; enemies of I. as theme of the Psalms, 493, 498f; the wars of I. against her enemies, as theme of Psalms, 501; the sons of I. receive from God the word of the peace of Christ, 368; the new I. is the Church, 16–18, 336, 495f; as new I., the Church has an angel of the Lord, 347; the redeemed sons of I. have the privilege of approaching near to God, 343; the prayers of thanksgiving made by I. for the protection of God are properly made by the Christian in the struggle against Satan, 498f; the Psalms which sing of God's mercy to I. are understood by the Christians as being extended to the Christian realities, 691.

IUDICA ME DEUS: its Gallican introduction into the Mass, 291 n. 31.

JACOB: in the ritual of baptism of adults the God of Abraham, of Isaac, and of J. is so designated as the One who assigned an angel to these; and all this in relation to the angel of baptism, 354; J. and Esau, according to the typological interpretation of Romans 9, are a figure of Christian and Jew, 479; J. and Esau as figure of Christians and Jews in the liturgical typology, 480.

JANSENISM: every indication of a Jansenistic mind is absent from the *suppletio* of St. Gertrude, 759.

JEREMIAS: patristic typology of Jeremias as figure of Christ, 481.

JERUSALEM, EARTHLY: according to Isaias, in its temple the Seraphim sing the *Sanctus*, 353; capital of the People of God and center of the world in the times of the Messias, according to the contemporary depth of Isaias, 463–464; its typology as figure of the Church and of the heavenly Jerusalem, 479f, 496; as the Holy City of the Psalms, 496.

JERUSALEM, HEAVENLY: signified by the eschatological dimension of every liturgical sign, 71–95; final terminus of sacred history, 9–18; object of Christian hope, 701; and goal intended by God in the election, separation, and formation of a sacred people, 495f; central vision of the feast of All Saints, 341f; and Church according to Ch. 12 of the Epistle to the Hebrews, 258, 336; in the H. J. perfection of cosmic unity is achieved according to the viewpoint of the Apocalypse, 347f; according to the viewpoint of Heb. 12:21f, Apoc. 5:8-14, 21–22:5, where the cosmic liturgy is celebrated, 12; and the final convocation of the Church, 16f; the Church is preparation for the H. J., 17f; in the unity of sacred history, all its phases tend toward the H. J., 42; its cosmic and eternal liturgy is the perfection of the present liturgy of the Church, 59; its worship is the final cause of earthly worship, 71–72; its eternal worship is the exemplary cause of earthly worship, 72; its worship is signified by the signs of earthly worship, 73f; its worship has as prophetic sign the liturgical sign, 74; genuflection, for example, is a prophetic sign of our worship in the H. J., 84; the prayer of the Church is a prophetic sign of the eternal liturgy in the H. J., 85; the sacramentals are the initial reintegration of things to the service of the divine life in the world, as will come to perfection in the H. J., 89; in their fourfold dimension, the sacramentals as prophetic sign of the eternal cosmic prayer of praise in the H. J., 89–90; the sacraments as prophetic sign contain the spiritual realities of the glory and worship of the H. J., 103; Jewish worship as first roughcast of worship in the H. J., 135; our union with the H. J. gains expression in the Sacrifice from the *Nobis quoque peccatoribus*, 170; the final triumph of the mystery of Christ in the H. J. brought out by the liturgy of the feast of All Saints, 178; according to the view of Heb. 12:22f, it is Christ Himself who introduces the faithful into the H. J., 258–259; Christians, with the liturgical action in Christ, are already near to the H. J., 258–259; in its teaching the Second Vatican Council recalls that the H. J. is our future city according to the perspective of the law of incarnation, 306–307; the unified totality of the cosmos is ordered by divine law to the H. J., 308; man is ordered in his completeness and in his totality to the H. J., 308–309; in the liturgy, intelligence, will, and sentiment are ordered to God and to the divine realities, among which is the H. J., 319f; in the Apocalypse the unity of the cosmos through the H. J. is emphasized, 317; the angels and the just of the H. J. form a unity with men on earth, 335f; final terminus of the pilgrimage of the People of God on earth, 335–336; the liturgy emphasizes our unity with the dead, our fellow-citizens in the H. J., 339; the liturgy emphasizes also our unity with the just, our fellow-citizens in the H. J., 341; the liturgy of the angels and of the blessed in the H. J. is a single liturgy, 342; the just on earth already form a single city with the H. J., 347f; in the liturgy the *Sanctus* of the Seraphim according to the text of Isaias is the very angelic liturgy of the H. J., 353; the angel of baptism indicates that in this rite the Christian is a fore-enrolled member of the H. J., 355f; H. J. and liturgy of the ill, 357f; unity of the angelic world and human world in the perspective of the H. J. in St. Augustine, 360–361; arrival in the H. J. after the final phase of sacred history, which is the judgment, is the decisive factor in the struggle against Satan, 329, 382; as to the unity of the two Testaments in Christ, the H. J. is its end, 456; the prophetic figure of the liberation from Egypt and the entry into the promised land, and the H. J., 466; in the liturgy of the dedication of a church, God is sung as supremely present to His people in the H. J., 469; the precepts and admonitions of the O. T. are realized to the fullest in the H. J., 472; the H. J. is fruit of the universality of redemption, 475; the H. J. sheds light on the prophecies, 476; typology of Earthly Jerusalem-H. J., 479; the same, in the Psalms, 496; in the H. J. the election, separation, formation, and restoration of the People of God is completed, 495; H. J. in the typology of the temple, of the Ark, and of Sion, the Holy Mountain of God, 495; H. J. as biblical theme proposed to our consideration in a balanced liturgical spirituality, 665, 701; the H. J. is a suitable and needed theme for preaching, 878; the H. J. is a suitable and needed theme also in catechism instruction, 894; the H. J. is the consummation in Christ of the sacred history, 901.

JEWS: and Christians, and their biblical typology under the figure of Esau and Jacob, 480.

JOB: the story of Job, like that of Esther, Tobias, and some passages of Genesis, is to be considered primarily in its contemporary depth, 463.

JOHN THE BAPTIST: his typological figure is Elias, 478; the feast of J. the B. manifests the biblical typology of Elias-J. the B., 480.

JONAS: in the belly of the whale is a figure of the resurrection of Christ, 478.

JOSEPH, ST.: and his position in the liturgy of the ill, 357; the prayer to St. Joseph inserted in the Roman Ritual in 1913 has an antidemoniacal dimension, 425.

JOSEPH OF CUPERTINO, ST.: as example of a saint subject to frequent ecstatic experiences, 732 n. 82.

JOSUE: the cycle of Josue is an example of the modern revalidation of the patristic exegesis based on the principle *Novum Testamentum in Veteri latet, Vetus Testamentum in Novo patet*, 458.

JUDGES: with the reading of the Book of J., the liturgy proposes the events recounted therein first of all in the depth of its contemporaries, in such a way as not to empty it of its historicity, 463.

JUDGMENT: the great day of J. will signify the triumph over Satan and the passage to the heavenly Jerusalem, 379; the particular J., and the role of demons, according to Origen, 387f; particular J. and the opinion of Origen, which follows Hellenistic ideas, of the demons as *telónai*, 388f; final act of the Apocalypse in the view of the heavenly Jerusalem, 379f. *See*: TELÓNAI; TELONÍA; TELÓNIA.

JUDITH: in a non-biblical but liturgical typology, J. is a figure of Mary, inasmuch as the Redeemer had to be born of a woman, 481.

JUST, THE: who, with the angels, form the heavenly Jerusalem, 336.

JUST MAN, THE: the just and pious Israelite of the O. T., in the Psalms and in the liturgy, 501f; the just man of the N. T., 502.

JUSTICE: as a cardinal virtue, 129.

KEDUSHAH: sanctification, a synagogue prayer containing the *Sanctus* of Isaias, 352.

KERYGMA: is the first announcement of the Gospel, followed by a deepening catechesis and by the homily on the liturgical action, 858 n. 7; in the N. T. and in patristic tradition, as a manner of conceiving the catechesis centered on Christ and sacred history, 867–875.

KING: as head of the People of God in the Psalms and in the liturgy, 496.

KINGDOM OF GOD: in the O. T., 277; messianic kingdom, 278.

KISS OF PEACE: 31, 351, 561.

KNOWABILITY OF GOD: by means of things, 42.

KNOWLEDGE BY CONNATURALITY: and esthetic pleasure and the liturgy, 52–55; and explicitation of dogmas, 535; and art and taste, 536; and liturgy in the evolution of dogmas, 539–540; and personal prayer in the Psalms, followed by a higher degree of penetration of divine things, 488; and mystical experience, 651. *See*: INTUITION.

KNOWLEDGE OF GOD: *i.e.*, man's knowledge about God: involves not only intellectual knowledge, but also religious knowledge, which involves will and sentiments and the practical life, 619–620; experimental knowledge of the Word and of the Trinity in the Ven. Marie of the Incarnation, 726.

KOINONOS: theme of the communitarian banquet connected with covenant in the O. T., 79.

KYRIE ELEISON: response of the people to the deacon's litany before the dismissal of the penitents, 420.

KYRIOS: *Dominus*, Lord, a title in reference to the risen Man now in His state of eternal glorification, toward which His whole historical life tends, 247f; a strong awareness is needed of the fact that there exists one only Jesus, He that is in glory, our High Priest with the Father, 248f, 252; only against the background of the *K.* and of the Paschal mystery is it possible to have an integral concept of the present priesthood of Christ, 254; universal Mediator, in the Epistle to the Hebrews, 257; in His eternal mediation with the Father, the *Kyrios*, by means of His Humanity, communicates to us His divine life, 250, 266; the consequences thereof for the nature of the liturgy, 266f; Sole Priest, Sole Mediator, Sole Liturgist, who carries out continuously the one liturgy, Paschal in character, which communicates divine life to the world, 271; in considering the Man Christ the emphasis can be placed either on the historical Jesus who lived and died in Palestine, or on the *K.* of the Paschal mystery, 656; every grace from God and every return to God is made always and only through the *K.*, 666; liturgical spirituality is Christocentric because it begins in the deeds of the *K.* of the Paschal mystery, 669.

LABOR: theology of L. and the unified totality of salvation, 312 n. 7.

LAITY: in the Church, and in the question of the universal priesthood of the faithful, 143f; active role of the laity in the liturgy, differentiated, however, from that of the high priest and the levites, according to St. Clement of Rome, 288–289; since the Middle Ages the L. were reduced more and more to mute and inert spectators of the Mass, 291f; the liturgical movement and the revalidation of the theology of the lay state, 838–842.

LAMB: by whose blood the faithful are able to overcome the Enemy, 383; who with God is Head of the heavenly Jerusalem, and redeems men of every tribe, language, people, and nation, 342–343; and the liturgy around the throne of the L. in heaven, 342, 348–349; marriage of the L. in the Apocalypse, 82, 469.

LAMB, PASCHAL: in the O. T., a figure of Christ, 479; sacrament of the P. L. in the O. T. according to St. Thomas, 581.

LANGUAGE, LITURGICAL: historical question of L. L. in antiquity, in the Tridentine era, and today, 286–287, 291; vernacular language and liturgy in the missions, 829–830; kernel of truth in the arguments of the opponents of the vernacular in the liturgy, that the preservation of a certain character of mystery is essential to the liturgy itself, 517; even in a liturgical celebration entirely in the vernacular, liturgical catechesis will always remain the principal and indispensable means of elevating the people to the liturgy, 852; vernacular in the liturgy, in the work of Pius Parsch, 837; the question of the L. L. touched upon by the positive-scholastic theologians of the 17th and 18th centuries, against the Protestants, 552.

LAST SUPPER: and Golgotha, 149f.

LAST THINGS: theological tract on the last things, and the liturgy, 637; in St. Thomas, 586; in the positive-scholastics, 565; as moral and anthropological theme habitually brought to our attention by the liturgical action, 689, 695; as theme proposed by liturgical spirituality, in balance with the other great themes of revelation, 704.

LATREIA, LATRIA: bondage, supreme worship of adoration given by man to the Divine Nature, 134, 136.

LAUDATE DOMINUM QUONIAM BONUS: 465.

LAVABO INTER INNOCENTES: of Gallican origin, its introduction into the Mass in the Middle Ages, 292 n. 31.

LAW, LITURGICAL: the error of conceiving the liturgy and liturgical science essentially as L. L., the rubricist view, xx, 638f; the juridic viewpoint in the liturgy, and in its teaching, 640f; L. L. theologically understandable only on the basis of the law of salvation in community, 298f; in ancient times L. L. was dependent upon the bishop, and from the 16th century, essentially on the Pope, 520f; the treatise De iure liturgico of F. A. Zaccaria, 551 n. 18; the Tractatus de iure liturgico of Ph. Oppenheim, 643 n. 6.

LAW, MOSAIC: as theme of the Psalms, is transposed into the economy of grace, according to the law of the pedagogue, 498; M. L., Christian economy, and liturgy, 498; the M. L., according to St. Paul, is the means abused by the wicked angels to make men sin, 370; even the M. L. was built on many rites, sacramenta, 63; significance of the liturgical precepts of the M. L., according to St. Thomas, 581.

LAW, OLD: treatise on the O. L. and liturgy in St. Thomas, 581f; theology of worship of the O. L., according to St. Thomas, 576f.

LAW OF INCARNATION: is one of the laws which God establishes in His relations with man and which regulate the liturgy, 66, 184; God has willed that in His relations with men, He save them by means of other men, not, however, in a merely abstract way, 66; Christ, the Word of God, is God's supreme communication to men, the living epiphany of God and hence an Incarnation according to the L. of I., 301f; the L. of I. presides over every encounter between God and man in the internal worship which must also be made external, 138; L. of I. and liturgy, 300–307; the L. of I. requires that the people be elevated to understand and assimilate the Bible in the liturgy, 852; the sacramental world and, therefore, the Eucharist which is its center, is constructed according to the L. of I., 303–304; the L. of I. takes into account the encounter between God and man in a regime of sacramenta, that is, of signs, 62; its depth is discovered by theologians primarily in the liturgy, 571; its close connection with ecclesial preaching, 882; L. of I. repudiated by Protestantism, 307.

LAW OF OBJECTIVITY: formulation: our way of going to God is not left to our free choice nor to our whim, but is imposed on us by God, 62; takes into account the encounter of God with man in sacramento, in a regime of signs, 62; one of the laws the observance of which God has willed in His relations with men, 66; in its liturgical fulfillment, God carries out the mystery of Christ and communicates it to men, 102f; is the primary basis of the liturgy, 184, 191; its norms and structure, 183–190; Church and liturgy in the law of salvation in community refer us always to the L. of O., 284; is the distinctive element in liturgical spirituality, 666–667; in order to be saved it is necessary to enter into the Paschal mystery, and hence to participate in the Eucharist, according to the L. of O., 814; close connection of the L. of O. with ecclesial preaching, 882.

LAW OF SALVATION IN COMMUNITY: is one of the laws established by God in His relations with man, which laws are of great interest to the liturgy, 184; Church and liturgy in the fulfillment of the L. of S. in C. always refer us to the law of objectivity, 284; L. of S. in C. takes into account the encounter of God with man *in sacramento*, in a regime of signs, 62; in salvation history, God saves man by means of other men, according to the law of incarnation, 66; its formulation, meaning, and structure, 272–299; the L. of S. in C., according to revelation, 276–282; it is explained with the concept of the people of God in the O. T. and in the N., 279; L. of S. in C. and relations with the individual conscience in the O. T., 278f; the Church is, on earth, the maximum concretization of the L. of S. in C., 297; such a law in the ecclesial and liturgical life, 282; and relations with the angelic world, 335; as one of the profundities of revelation, the theologian truly discovers it only in the liturgy, 570–571; is always presupposed by pastoral, 805f; in pastoral it is realized, nevertheless, in respect to the individual, 807; and its close connection with ecclesial preaching, 882; the restraints established by authority in the field of ecclesiastical liturgical law are part and parcel of the L. of S. in C., 298–299.

LAW OF THE COSMIC UNIVERSALITY OF SALVATION: is one of the laws established by God in His relations with man, which is of major interest in liturgy, 184; its formulation, meaning, and structure, 335–361; and dogma of the communion of saints, 337; pervades the reality of our communion with the saints, always carried out in the liturgy, 342.

LAW OF THE FREE COÖPERATION OF MAN: and its close connection with ecclesial preaching, 881.

LAW OF THE PEDAGOGUE: in the perspective of St. Paul, the L. of the P. or Instructor proclaims the fulfillment in Christ of all that which was prefigured, fore-announced, and prepared for in the O. T., 478; application to the Mosaic Law of the L. of the P. as guide to the economy of grace in Christ, 498.

LAW OF THE RESPECT OF NATURES: in dealing with man, God acts according to the style of man, because He takes into account the concrete nature of man, incarnate spirit, 304–305; man, spirit and body, in order to be saved, must have contact, even physical albeit sacramental, with the Humanity of the Risen Christ, that is, with the Eucharist, 821–822. *See:* STYLE OF MAN.

LAWS OF THE DIVINE ECONOMY IN THE WORLD: and liturgy, 183–451. *See the chapter heading in Part II of the present work for the individual laws.*

LAZARUS: and the liturgy of the dead, 357.

LECTIO: as vital study of the Bible and of the Fathers in St. Gertrude, 750, 758.

LECTIO CONTINUA: of the Bible, in the cycle of one year and in the natural sequence of the sacred books, during the Middle Ages and under monastic influence, 455 n. 1.

LECTIO DIVINA: the monastic method of the L. D. as study, meditation and prayer of the Bible and of tradition in intimate connection with the liturgy, 504, 694, 720f, 749–750, 758.

LEGEM CREDENDI LEX STATUAT SUPPLICANDI: i.e., *lex credendi lex orandi*: history and validity of the principle, 509, 529f; in recent views on the Fathers, 597 n. 40, 611 n. 71; against the semi-Pelagians, the argument on the necessity of prayer, found afterwards in the *Indiculus de gratia Dei*, 613; according to this principle the liturgy is one of the chief occasions for the evolution of dogma: modernist interpretation, 533f.

LEGENDS: in the Breviary and in the liturgy in general, and the manner of interpreting them, 528f.

LEGISLATION, LITURGICAL: *See:* LAW, LITURGICAL.

LEITOURGIA: from *leiton ergon*, "a work that is in regard to the people," in religious and cultual sense, term already used in the Septuagint, 19; in the thought of St. Clement of Rome, 288–289.

LENT: and the struggle against Satan, 439f; the Church's annual period of greater spiritual exercises, 440, 696; L. and liturgical spirituality, 709; L. and mortification of the body, 313–314.

LENT-PENTECOST: general significance of this liturgical cycle, 176f; its Christological-Trinitarian structure, 240–246; how the liturgy of this period understands the prophecies of the Servant of Yahweh and of Joel on the Holy Spirit, 475; and the Mass, 176.

LETTER AND SPIRIT: concept akin to that of *mystérion*, 601.

LEX CREDENDI LEX ORANDI: See: LEGEM CREDENDI LEX STATUAT SUP-PLICANDI.

LIBERA DOMINE . . . SICUT LIBERASTI: prayer of the liturgy of the ill, 424.

LIBERATION FROM EGYPT: of the People of God as sign of God's eternal mercy, and the transposition of it that the Christian must make, 466f; Psalm "*In exitu Israël de Aegypto*," and the liturgy of the dead, 495.

LIBERATION FROM SATAN: and the way opened by Christ, central theme of the rites over the *audientes*, 397–398.

LIFE: relationship between liturgy and L.: liturgy and spirituality, liturgy and pastoral, 647–902; liturgical manner of presenting the question of the aim and goal of L. in the new German catechism, 894; liturgical spirituality and exercise of the virtues in the extraliturgical practical L., 708f; active L. and contemplative L. in liturgical spirituality, 816–821; Christian L. and the struggle against Satan, 372–377; L. of the Church as struggle against Satan, 377–381. *See*: ASCETICAL PRACTICE; CATECHESIS; CATECHISM; MYSTICS; PASTORAL; PREACHING.

LITANIES: in the entreaties against storms, and the antidemoniacal dimension, 432.

LITTLE OFFICE: of the Blessed Mother, in the Middle Ages, 797.

LITURGICAL ACTION: the litany as sacred action, 284–293, 316f; L. A. is sacred action in relation to the concrete and personal situation of the individuals who participate therein, 483f; and grace, 696, 705; and *compunctio*, 702; and contemplation, 734; its efficacy and psychological moral force, 704, 706f; and the exercise of the theological and moral virtues, 704; and mystical experience, 732; preparation and consequence of the practical life of virtue, 704–705, 708; and concentration of the external senses, 688.

LITURGICAL CYCLES: their general significance, 175–177; proper object and fourfold theological dimension of the general significance of the Advent-Epiphany cycle and the Lent-Pentecost cycle, 90f, 176–177; general significance of the sanctoral cycles (Marian, of the angels, of the saints), 178; L. C. explained by the Fathers, 592–596; Christological-Trinitarian significance of the L. C., 240–246; L. C. and angels, 359f; L. C. and struggle against Satan, 435–451.

LITURGICAL YEAR: its fourfold theological dimension, 90f; homilies on the L. Y. in the patristic period, 594f. *See*: LITURGICAL CYCLES.

LITURGY: conceived as liturgical law, as part of canon law, as liturgical history, as pastoral L. and as theological L., xx–xxiv, 582–643, 637f; manuals on L. have been conceived as if the L. were a part of canon law, xx; various ways of conceiving liturgical science, xx–xxiv; theological interest in L. awakened shortly before the Second Vatican Council, xxiii; general theological L. and special theological L., xxiv; historical research into the L. indispensable, xxi; notion and necessity of theological L., xxiii–xxiv, 98, 572, 697; notions of the *Summa* of St. Thomas that can serve as basis for a general theological L., 573–577; necessity of an integral concept of L., xxi; concept of L., 3–179, 511f; technical definition of L., 19–32; essence of the L. expressed by its definition in terms of genus and species, as point of reference and of deduction for all that which is said of it in liturgical science, 34, 899f; L. as sensible sign, 22; L. as sensible, efficacious signs, 23; L. as complexus of sensible and efficacious signs, 39; definition of L. and doctrine of the *opus operatum*, 23, 27; definition of liturgy and doctrine of the *opus operantis Ecclesiae*, 23, 27; definitions of the L. in *Mediator Dei*, 20 n. 2; L. and terminology, 19–20; L. and its own literary genres, 516; how the L. uses the biblical texts, 455–486; how the Christian L. understands the liturgical precepts of the O. T. in its use of those texts, 471; the L. as summit and fount of the action of the Church, according to the happy expression of the Second Vatican Council, xix, 664, 736, 846; the L. in no respect exhausts the whole life of the Church, 664; L. as phase and manner in which the meaning of revelation is fulfilled in us, 3; L., focal point in which a concrete view is taken of the Bible, dogma, tradition, magisterial teaching, and theology, is the vital center of the pastoral life of the Church, 638f, 873f, 898; the L. makes present and realizes *in sacramento* in individual souls the sacred history, mystery of Christ, 483; the liturgical feast of Easter as *sacramentum* in St. Augustine, 29–30; L. and spirituality in general, 647–739; L. and the theological virtues which the teaching or instruction of the ecclesial magisterium must raise in the faithful, 513f; qualitative predominance of the L. in liturgical spirituality, 681; discursive meditation must take place in the L. and remain in the area of a communitarian action, 686–687; L., spirituality, and mystical theology can go together excellently and prosper, 716f; the L. is the supreme cultic fulfillment of the virtue of religion, 698; L. and the exercise of faith, hope, and charity in the area of the virtue of religion, 697f; L. and "pious exercises": distinction, relationship of subordination and derivation of one from the other, 117–120; earthly L. and heavenly L., 259–266, 344f; L. and the struggle against Satan as one of the laws of salvation, 362–451; the L., and especially the Eucharist, is the fulfillment and reconsecration of infrahuman creation to the service of the divine life in the world, 324–334; the L. is popular by the exigency of its intrinsic nature, 843f; L. as action, and communitarian action, of the whole mystical body of Christ, Head and members, 284, 316, 512f, 687, 838; L. is plenary fulfillment of man according to the law of the cosmic universality of the kingdom of God, 308–324, 686; physical presence at Mass for the fulfillment of one's obligation is demanded by the harmony which must reign in the L. among the sensible and supersensible realities, interior and exterior, 312; in what sense "the L. is the *didascalia* of the Church," 512–518; the L. as *didascalia* tends by its very nature to promote in the faithful the theological virtues, by offering homage to God in a cultic act, 514; the L. always involves a *didascalia* of the magisterium and an adherence thereto of the faithful, 513; L. and missions: in the climate of liturgical spirituality the missionary builds up the Church through the fullness of the age of Christ in the liturgical action, 674; missionary value of the L., 824–830; L. and pastoral: the principles, 804–854; in a theory of spirituality and pastoral, liturgical science achieves its greatest possible contact with concrete life, 647; pastoral psychological efficacy of the L., 823f; the L. has great didactic efficacy, 517f; L. and modern aspirations: essentiality, objectivity, communitariety, organicity, immediate contact with the prime sources of the Christian life, 738f; in the L. a unity of spiritual life, biblical and theological life, and apostolate is formed, 738–739; L. and modern technology, 320; L. and human labor, 320; L. and sports, 320; L. as *mystérion* according to Origen, 601f; L. in the view of theology as *gnôsis,* according to the Fathers, 622f; theological explanation of the L. in the Fathers as explanation of its "mysteries," 607–611; authority of the L. and its polemic use in the Fathers, 611–614; the Fathers unite the concept of authority of the L. with that of its apostolicity and universality, 614–619; use of the L. in the theology of the Fathers, 625; L. and theology in the Fathers from primarily irenic perspective, 596f; doctrinal errors possible in the historical liturgies,

and saints in heaven, 342f; the heavenly liturgy of the blessed is a single *panégyris* with that of the angels, 342f; in the heavenly liturgy of the angelic world there is a better way of associating oneself therein, than there is in the Mass, 353f; heavenly liturgy as transpositional theme of the Psalms, 497f; heavenly liturgy and earthly liturgy in St. Gertrude, 765f, 788 n. 138.

LITURGY, EGYPTIAN: and position of the angels in the Mass, 351.

LITURGY, EUCHOLOGICAL: the connatural plan of the E. L. is: readings, homily, song, silent prayer, final oration of the one presiding, 692f.

LITURGY, GALLICAN: and question of the epiclesis of the Holy Spirit in the Mass, 229; and triumph of the Cross as triumph over Satan, 444; its influence on the Roman Missal, 291–292 n. 31.

LITURGY, GRECO-EGYPTIAN: of St. Mark, and unity of the angelic world in the liturgy, 350.

LITURGY, MOZARABIC: and the question of the epiclesis of the Holy Spirit in the Mass, 229; and Lent as special period of the struggle against Satan, 441f; and the triumph of the Cross as triumph over Satan, 444.

LITURGY, SYRIAN: of St. James, and position of angels in the Mass, 351; *Cheroubi-kón*, 351.

LITURGY OF THE HOURS: *See*: BREVIARY, ROMAN; HOURS, CANONICAL; OFFICE, DIVINE.

LOCI THEOLOGICI: after Melchior Cano the post-Tridentine theologians attempt to determine the use of the *L. T.* in the theology, and hence too the use of the liturgy, though not designated such by Cano, as *locus theologicus*, 519; tract on *L. T.* and relationship between faith and liturgy after F. A. Zaccaria, 519f; in the tract on the *L. T.* even the liturgy is treated as a *locus theologicus* insofar as it is an expression of the ordinary magisterium, 542f. *See*: SOURCES.

LOURDES: apparition at L. and its liturgical feast, 524.

LOVE: how the liturgy understands the Old Testament texts which teach the love of God for man and the love which man ought to have for God and for his neighbor, 701; God's love of us and our love of God and of neighbor, and the history of salvation according to St. Augustine, 870; our love of God and its actualization in the liturgy is actualization of the prevenient love of God, 701; as increasing homage of praise and thanksgiving to God in the life that is wholly centered on the liturgy, 759f; *See*: CHARITY; VIRTUES (theological); love of God as a lively sentiment which the preacher must know how to arouse, 871–872.

LOVE OF GOD: with faith and hope, is always in action in the liturgy, 698; the natural love of God includes the will to be in conformity with His will, 698. *See*: CHARITY.

LYRICISM: and liturgy, 516.

MACHABEES: the meaning that such a historical book had for its contemporaries is always explicitly affirmed or presupposed in the liturgical frame of reference into which it is transferred, 463.

MAGIC: difference of the concept of *opus operatum* from that of M., 70, 101; in the liturgical life of the sacramentals great realities are put into operation, which are totally opposed to M., 333; in tradition after the N. T. it was a common opinion that in pagan life and therefore in M. the demons are everywhere present, 385.

MAGISTERIUM: proximate criterion of the faith, 520, 566; difficulty of knowing what is *de fide* from ordinary M. alone, 531; in the liturgy the M. imposes its authority

in differing degrees in different instances, 509f; therefore, even though it be indirect, the M. is involved in the liturgy, and hence the liturgy is *didascalia* of the
Church, 512–517, 560f.

MAGNANIMITY: as psychological motive to animate and sustain the human faculties,
706–707. *See*: MAGNIFICENCE.

MAGNIFICAT: is illuminated by the development of Marian dogmas, 482; antiphon
at the M. in II Vespers of the Apostles, and the struggle against Satan, 450.

MAGNIFICENCE: has for its end the doing of great works, of which there can be none
greater than those directed to the honor and glory of God, 706–707. *See*: MAG-
NANIMITY.

MAN: in the law of the cosmic unified totality of the kingdom of God, together with
the infrahuman creatures, with the angels and the blessed of heaven, with the souls
in purgatory, 300–361; M. is regarded as a substantial unity of body and soul in
revelation and in the liturgy, 309–316; human activity, honest in itself, sanctified
by the liturgy, 312; actualization of the human psychological faculties in the
liturgy, 316–324; theological treatment of man and liturgy, 636.

MANNA: figure of the Eucharist, 478; the Eucharist in the fourfold dimension of its
liturgical sign is commemorative even of the M., 79.

MANUALS OF THEOLOGY: of positive-scholasticism of the 20th century, and the
liturgy, 556.

MARAN ATHA: "The Lord is coming." *See: MARANA THA*.

MARANA THA: "Come, O Lord!" Final invocation of the Eucharistic prayer in the
Didache, and manifestation of the eschatological dimension of the Eucharist, 161.

MARIA LAACH: its importance for the theological liturgical movement, xxiii.

MARIOLOGY: theological treatment of M., and liturgy, 582 n. 35, 583 n. 37, 585, 636.

MARRIAGE, SPIRITUAL *or* MYSTICAL: *See*: BETROTHAL, SPIRITUAL *or*
MYSTICAL.

MARRIAGE CEREMONIES: explained in the liturgical tracts of the Fathers, 591–596.

MARTYRDOM: as participation in the priesthood of Christ, 146; and universal priesthood of the faithful, 143; as priesthood and sacrifice exercised outside the Eucharistic priesthood and sacrifice but still as preparation therefor and derivation therefrom, 146, 151, 155; is the highest expression of personal sacrifice, 131; theology
explains M. as the most perfect imitation of Christ because it is a total dedication
of oneself to God, 445; in its significance for the struggle against Satan, in the
Fathers, 387; especially of women, as victory over Satan, 445f.

MARTYRIA: were decorated with biblical scenes selected in accord with the laws governing typology and symbolism, 486 n. 14.

MARTYRS: did not disparage nor despise the flesh as an enemy, 311; the theme of the
Psalms, of God as Protector of the just and pious Israelite, is read in the light of
His even more wonderful protection afforded the M., 469; in the Apocalypse, the
symbolic resurrection of the M. precedes the establishing of the Messianic kingdom,
380; development of the cult of the M., 340; the cult of the M. is the root of the
liturgical cult of the saints, 340; in the 4th and 5th centuries the cult of Mary and
of the confessors is joined to the liturgical commemoration of the M., 340–341;
the concept of the communion of saints and of our veneration of them is determined in a special way in the Mass, 340; the feast of all the M. is a 5th century
precedent for the feast of All Saints, 342.

MARY: the mystery of M., subordinated to the mystery of Christ, is already prepared
for in the O. T., 178; sapiential texts of the O. T. applied to M. by the liturgy,
467f; the prophecy of Gen. 3:15f is interpreted in the light of the doctrine of M.,
the Immaculate Mother of God, 476; the texts from Canticle of Canticles read in

a Christian atmosphere are applied to the love of God for the Church, for individual souls and for M., of which the love of God for Israel was but a pale foreshadowing, 469; liturgical precepts of the O. T. on the presentation of the first-
born in the temple, and M., 472; the prophecy of Isaias in the Advent liturgy, and
M., 473f; the creation as a theme of the Psalms, and its extension to M., in whom
God worked marvels of divine life, 494f; the liturgy reads the Marian texts of the
N. T. in the light of the explicitation of Marian dogmas, 482; patristic non-biblical
typology of M. as Eve, 480–481; and of M. as Judith and as Esther, 481; Marian
feasts and sacred history, mystery of Christ, 178; the Marian feasts emphasize some
aspect of the mystery of Christ, entirely present in every Mass, 178; M. in the
Communicantes of the Mass, 340–341; M. and the actualization in the faithful,
during the liturgical action, of the narrative of Christ's birth, as redemptive power,
483; object of that worship called *hyperdulia*, 136; M., the angels, and the liturgy
of the ill, 357; name of M., along with that of Joseph, introduced in modern times
into the *Proficiscere*, 357 n. 64; M. and the struggle against Satan, 439, 446f; feast
of the Motherhood of M. and its antidemoniacal significance, 448 n. 194; the feast
of M. the Auxiliatrix and its antidemoniacal dimension, 448 n. 194; the struggle
against Satan in recent Marian feasts, 446–448; Mary alone was perfected in the
degree of sanctifying grace and of charity which God had established for her; for
the rest of the faithful it is always a matter of striving for perfection and of growing closer thereto, 648; God, Christ, M., the angels, and the saints sustain the
faithful in their striving for Christian perfection, 649; M. as object of liturgical
meditation, 689; the compositions of the two feasts of the Seven Sorrows of M. as
example of a religious sensibility more subjective than objective, 319 n. 22; the
communion of saints, and first of all with M., is one of the points which the liturgy
presents in a balanced way along with the other basic points of dogma, 666; in
liturgical spirituality the characteristic traits and the light of the objects to be considered (God, Christ, Eucharist, M.), are presented from the liturgy, from the
Bible, and from dogma, hence, from outside the subjects, 667; extraliturgical Marian
devotions, and the liturgy, 671; month of M. as extraliturgical Marian devotion,
and the liturgy, 671; the Little Office of the B. V. M. as witness to Marian devotions
in the Middle Ages, 797; the faith is involved in manners somewhat different in
the Marian feasts of the Assumption, Presentation, Apparition at Lourdes, M. Mediatrix of All Graces, and the Translation of the Holy House of Loreto, 510, 523f,
528f; Assumption, 510, 523f, 528; in the new Mass of the Assumption no mention
is made of the bodily death of M., 525; Immaculate Conception, 524–525, 526f; Apparition at Lourdes, 510, 524; Mediatrix, 509f, 524f, 541; the feast of M., Mediatrix
of All Graces is at present only a theological opinion, even if it is possible that it
may not remain always in this category, 524f, 541; Presentation, 510, 523, 528f;
Translation of the Holy House of Loreto, 510, 524, 528f; conception, sanctification,
espousals, and annunciation of M., according to St. Thomas, 582 n. 35; perpetual
virginity of M. proved from the liturgy by F. A. Zaccaria, 551; Assumption of M.
in the positive-scholastic theologians of the 18th century, 553f; in the visions of
St. Gertrude, 774; M. and the *suppletio* in St. Gertrude, 759; M. and the liturgical
spirituality of St. Gertrude, 766–767. *See*: ASSUMPTION; IMMACULATE CON-
CEPTION.

MASS: and sacrifice of Golgotha, 149; the whole liturgy is ordered to the sanctification
of man and the Christian worship rendered to God in the M., which, therefore, is
the sun and center of the liturgy, 141f, 158–162, 171f; the M. is the realization and
synthetic expression of the whole complexus of the liturgy, 157–179; M., the sun
and center of the supernatural life of the Church, 172f; the fourfold dimension

of the liturgical signs has its highest degree of expression and efficacy in the M., 158–162; the liturgical expression in the anaphoras of the fact that the M. realizes in sum total the mystery of Christ, 162–171; sacrament and sacrifice, 158; presupposing the necessary moral dispositions, the highest unity with God, with Christ, with the angels, with the saints, and with men in the state of grace is realized, in the Mass, 158f; Masses dedicated to Mary bring into relief the position which belongs to Mary in the mystery of Christ, 178; Masses of the angels display some aspect of the mystery of Christ present in every Mass, 178; Byzantine Mass: proclaims repeatedly the presence of the angels at the M., 350f; Masses of the saints display some aspect of the mystery of Christ present in every M., 178; Christ the principal minister of the sacrifice according to patristic tradition, 260; the M. as sacred action in which all the faithful ought to participate actively, even though in a manner hierarchically differentiated, 284–293, 288, 316f, 838–843; how each of the faithful can and must offer the actual sacrifice of the Mass, 152f, 154f; M. and realization of the priesthood of all the faithful, 159; in the M. universal history achieves its fullest significance, 160; the individual concentration of the celebrant and of the faithful is always desirable, but always in a communitarian atmosphere involving the whole of human psychology, 318; M. in the Advent-Epiphany cycle considers the whole mystery of Christ in His epiphanic coming, 176; M. in the Lent-Pentecost cycle considers the whole mystery of Christ under the aspect of redemption, 176; M. of Easter directs the admonitions of Col. 3:1-4 to the faithful present there, in their individual personal situations, 484; the M. of Christmas represents the nativity not as historical event but in its redemptive significance, 483f; the M. of the ill demonstrates the care which the liturgy takes for the welfare of the human body, 314; apostolicity of the essential nucleus of the rites of the M., 561–562; obligation of attending Mass, 653; frequent attendance at Mass and the striving for perfection, 654; more directly didactic character of the fore part of the Mass, 515; communitarian character of the M. in its ancient ceremonies, and the historical vicissitudes thereof to the present time, 284–293; ancient custom of the sole M. as expression of its communitarian nature, 289f; "secret" prayers in the M. since the 4th century, 291f; M. a true sacrifice; liceity of low Mass, time of celebration, principal ceremonies of the M. defended by the positive-scholastics against the Protestants, 552; Christological-Trinitarian structure of the M., 223–230; in regard to the Mass, the liturgical feasts are but an analytic manner of viewing and making psychologically more effective a particular aspect of the single mystery of Christ fully contained in synthesis in every M., 175f; translation of M. into vernacular language long prohibited, 292–293; M. and restoration of infra-human creation to the service of the divine life in the world, 329–334; M. offered on the tombs of the martyrs, 340; M. the place of encounter *par excellence* of the Church militant, suffering, and triumphant, 340; M. and presence of the angels, 349–354; M. and souls in purgatory, 336–339; M. and struggle against Satan, 412–417; M. in the spirituality of St. Gertrude, 741, 768, 774f; the manner of correcting defects in the celebration of M., obligation of priest to celebrate, time of celebration, rites of the M. explained by St. Thomas, 579; Mass and Protestant controversy, 549–552. *See:* EUCHARIST.

MASS OF CHRISM: and its antidemoniacal significance, 410.

MATRIMONY: the fourfold dimension of the sacramental sign of M., 82; as participation in the priesthood of Christ, 146; M. and universal priesthood of the faithful, 144; ecclesial and communitarian dimension of M., 294, 297; like all the sacraments, M. is ordered to the Eucharist, 171; its connatural celebration is had in the Mass or in connection therewith, 174; anomaly of marriage by proxy in view of the law

explained by the Fathers, 592–596; rite of monastic investiture and profession, and the *Exercises* of St. Gertrude, 795.

MONOPHYSITES: importance of the liturgy and of the liturgical argument in the controversy against the M., 613; the M. in consequence of their doctrines, make alterations in the liturgy, 613 n. 88.

MONT-CÉSAR, ABBEY OF: is a center for the liturgical renewal initiated by Dom Lambert Beauduin, xxii.

MORALS AND LITURGY: the moralizational force of the liturgical action in view of the exercise of works of charity toward one's neighbor and the exercise of the moral virtues in the practical life, 142, 704–708; special way the liturgy has of stimulating moral action, 666–667; the moral dispositions of the subject are signified in every liturgical sign, 69f, 72f, 76–85, 89; and the missionary duty of all the faithful, 826f; aspect of moral obligation in the liturgy and the concept of *sacramentum*, 76, 605f; hortatory moral point of view of the interest of the Fathers in the liturgy, 596f; the Mass as the highest of all moral obligational signs in the liturgy, 159–161; morals and the Advent-Epiphany cycle, 176; and the Lent-Pentecost cycle, 176; how the liturgy understands those moral precepts of the O. T. of which it makes use, 460f; morals and catechism, 890; and preaching, 876–880; moral theology and liturgy, 637; moral theology and liturgy in St. Thomas, 585f.

MORTIFICATION: the Bible's exhortations to M. are understood according to the depth of the contemporaries to whom these texts were addressed, 462f; spirit of M. as common means to perfection, 654; Christian M. of the body and of the senses is in view of their true and perpetual vivification, 311; spirit of M.: is necessary even outside the liturgical action proper, 663; private M.: ought to be subordinated and ordered to the liturgy, 663; is one of the themes which the liturgy habitually brings to the attention of the faithful, 689.

MOSES: as historical terminus in the Roman Martyrology for 25th Dec., 327; as theme of sacred salvation history in the *Demonstratio apostolicae traditionis* of Irenaeus, 871; M. and the Exodus as themes of patristic exegesis in the re-evaluations made by modern critics, 458 n. 2; figure of Christ, 479; as a person whose example is proposed for the imitation of the faithful during Lent, by the Mozarabic liturgy, 441; in the baptism of adults in the Roman Ritual, in connection with the angel of baptism, M. is named as one of the patriarchs to whom God assigned an angel, 354.

MOTHER OF A FAMILY: and possibility of liturgical spirituality, 681; example of the Ven. Marie of the Incarnation, 722–729.

MOTIVES OF CREDIBILITY: means, as for example the miracles of Christ, by which we believe that God has revealed certain truths, 534.

MOUNTAIN CLIMBING: blessing of mountain climbing gear in the Roman Ritual, 320.

MOVEMENT, BIBLICAL: its close connection with the liturgical movement, 504; its convergence with the liturgical movement, 902; as pastoral activity, the B. M. must lead to full participation of the faithful in the liturgy, 816; has contributed to a focusing of attention on the modern problem of the catechism, 888; influence of the B. M. on the new German catechism, 892.

MOVEMENT, CATECHETICAL: influence thereof on the new German catechism, 892.

MOVEMENT, CATHOLIC ACTION: among the pastoral activities, must lead the people to the full participation in the liturgy, 816; its convergence toward the center of the modern spiritual renewal, which center is the liturgical movement, 902.

MOVEMENT, CHRISTOLOGICAL-TRINITARIAN: general analysis and synthesis,

191–245; *a-per-in-ad* formula, indicating that every good thing comes to us from the Father (*a Patre*) through the agency of Christ (*per Christum*) in the presence of the Spirit (*in Spiritu*), and in this same way all must return to the Father (*ad Patrem*), 191–192; the Bible considers the Divine Persons first of all in Their relations with the world, in the C.-T. M., 207; recapitulatory formula in the N. T., 198–202; C.-T. M. is a great mystery, but through the N. T. it gives breadth and depth to Christian life, 202; like the Bible, the liturgy too considers the Divine Persons primarily according to the formula of the C.-T. M., 216; in the area of exemplary causality or assimilation, 201; the best explanation of the C.-T. M. is the law of the Sole Liturgist, 183; in the Arian controversy, 204, 208; the formulation *per-in* always supposes the *a-per-in-ad* movement, 220; nevertheless, the abbreviated *per-in* formula has the inherent danger of allowing the faithful to forget the equality of nature expressed in the homoousion, 221; even those prayers which do not name the Holy Spirit in their conclusion always follow the lines of the C.-T. M., 215; in ancient tradition, 203–206; general perspective in the liturgy, 207–246; in the orations, 209–217; in the body of the ancient oration, adoration, petition, and thanksgiving were always in the perspective of the C.-T. M., 213; in the doxologies, 217–223; prior to the Arian strife the doxologies were most often in the *per-in* schema, which is a N. T. structure, 219f; in the sacrifice of the Mass, 223–230; in the anaphora of St. Hippolytus, 225; in the Roman Canon of the Mass, 227–228; in the great final doxology of the Roman Canon, 222; in the sacraments, 230–239; in baptism, 230–234; the ancient reform of baptism was according to the *a-per-in-ad* schema, 233; in the baptismal profession of faith, 231–232; in confirmation, 234–236; the schema of Pauline theology at the root of the theology of confirmation, 234f; in penance, 236–237; in the anointing of the ill, 239; in orders, 237–239; absent in matrimony, 239; in the sacramentals, 239–240; the schema presides over the creation of Christian feasts, 243; the question of the feast of the Most Holy Trinity, 243; in the liturgical cycles, 240–246; from Advent to Epiphany, 243 n. 96; from 1st Sunday of Lent to first Sunday of Passiontide, 240f; from first Sunday of Passiontide to the Ascension, 241–242; as one of the themes that lend balance to liturgical spirituality, 666; one of the themes by which liturgical spirituality is dogmatically concretized, 669; one of the themes which the liturgical action habitually presents to the discursive intelligence, 689, 691.

MOVEMENT, CISTERCIAN: and its influence on devotion during the Middle Ages, 797.

MOVEMENT, ECUMENICAL: as characteristic manifestation of the present era, is oriented to the liturgy, 902; world E. M.: poses the question of the liturgy as one of its basic problems, 831.

MOVEMENT, FRANCISCAN: and its decisive orientation toward devotion to the humanity of Christ, 797.

MOVEMENT, LITURGICAL: and manner of conceiving the liturgy, xxiii f; why the L. M. has not borne all the fruits of which it gave promise, xxiii f; in its first stage the L. M. must interest the young clergy destined for parishes, 848; since 1946 the L. M. has assumed a pastoral intensity, 836f; liturgical pastoral characteristic of the present phase of the L. M., 836f; the L. M. and the question of the universal priesthood of the faithful, 143f; convergence of the various other renewal movements, 902; theological movement, movement of ascetical and mystical knowledge, biblical pastoral movement, Catholic action movement and missionary movement, 504f, 738f, 902; the L. M. has persisted in making known how extraliturgical activity is to be ordered to the liturgy, and not vice versa, 815; the L. M. and the Benedictines, 681–682; the L. M. and the question of the inter-relationships of faith, theology, and liturgy, 509, 543f; the theologian attempts to complete and balance the viewpoints of the positive-scholastic with the more important aspects of Scripture and tradition, 832; the L. M. and the unity between preaching, catechesis, and liturgy, 880; has prompted preachers to make their preaching direct liturgical catechesis, 886–887; not unconcerned with the modern question of the catechism, 888; the new German catechism is important in the history of catechesis itself and in the L. M., 892; the actualities of the L. M. are now under consideration by the orthodox, 835; Orthodox Catholics of the Eastern Rite, and the L. M., 835; Orthodox L. M. and relations with Catholics, 835–836; L. M. in the Protestant communities and relations with Catholics, 834.

MOVEMENT, MISSIONARY: its convergence toward the center of the modern renewal, which center is the liturgical movement, 902.

MOVEMENT, PASTORAL: converges toward the liturgical movement, the center of modern renewal, 902; its decisive influence on the question of the new German catechism, 892.

MOVEMENTS, CORPOREAL: *i.e.*, gestures, etc., as signs in the liturgy, 49f.

MOVEMENT, THEOLOGICAL: its influence on the German catechism, 892.

MOZARABIC LITURGY: and Trinitarian doxologies, 223; and Christological-Trinitarian structure of the Mass, 229f; and the presentation of the mystery of the Trinity in the liturgy after the Arian heresy, 244–245; and Spanish adoptionism, 510; and appeal to its own texts on the part of the Spanish adoptionists, 614 n. 90; the whole mystery of Christ as epiphanic coming of the Lord, in turn as liberation of man from Satan, 444–445; and the triumph of the Cross as triumph over Satan, 444; and the question of the epiclesis of the Holy Spirit in the Mass, 229f; and the Eucharist in the struggle against Satan, 416; and the liturgy of penance as struggle against Satan, 424; and monastic profession as struggle against Satan, 434; and Lent as a special time in the struggle against Satan, 451.

MUSIC: in the liturgy. *See*: ART; SONG (CHANT).

MYRON: consecration of the M. and Christological-Trinitarian dimension, 239; consecration of the M. explained in the East in the patristic age, 592, 593 n. 13; consecration of the M. as *mystérion*, since the 4th century, 604.

MYSTAGOGY: principal mystagogical works in the patristic period, 591–596; M. of St. Maximus the Confessor and other Byzantine mystagogies, 592; mystagogical writings are the principal source for a knowledge of patristic thought on the liturgy, 619.

MYSTÉRION: scriptural origin and development of the concept, 599f; as sign, image, symbol, M. has an analogical relationship with the thing signified, 35f; St. Paul refers the concept of M. only to the sacred history, not extending it to worship, 106; the call of the Gentiles along with the Jews, and M. according to St. Paul, 600; sums up reference to past realities, to the historical life of Christ, to the moral obligation of the faithful, and to the eschatological realities, 607; in the Fathers M. is a representation of sacred, suprasensible things, by means of sensible signs, 30; the concept presents to the ancient mentality something profoundly real, just the opposite of what it does for the modern mentality, 38–39; for the ancients signs are in reference to sacred things in the economy of God in the world, 30; under this term the ancients included the whole of the liturgy, 29; liturgical explanation of the Fathers concentrated on the concept of M., 598–601; M. is the general basis and determining factor of the liturgical theology of the Fathers, 598; since the time of Justin, M. is the symbolic and allegorical dimension of the O. T. in reference to the N., and hence of the historical events of the life of Christ, 600; basic significance in Origen, 601f; for Origen, the primordial M. is Christ, in His concrete

Person, both Man and God, 602; according to Origen the *M.* of the Church is a derivation of the primordial *M.* of Christ, 603; according to Origen, the *M.* of the Scriptures is the Incarnation *sui generis* of the Word, 602; for Origen the rites of worship are the third sphere of meaning in the concept of *M.*, 603; in the Fathers the sign aspect of *M.* prevails over the efficacious aspect, 610; from the 2nd and 3rd century *M.* is the key to the expositive irenic theological vision of the Fathers, 599, 611, 618; acceptance of the concept of *M.* by later patristic writers, 604f; application of the concept of *M.* to the whole of liturgy, in the 4th century, 604f; in the Syrian Monophysites, 604; the concept of *M.* in the liturgies, 606f; merits and deficiencies of the Fathers in the elaboration of this concept, 608f; *M.* is the origin of the Latinized term *mysterium*, 605. *See: MYSTERIUM;* MYSTERY; *SACRAMENTUM;* SACRED (SALVATION) HISTORY.

MYSTERIUM: M., sacramentum, and definition of liturgy, 29f; realist understanding of the concept of *M.* among the ancients, 37; in the Fathers the sign aspect of *M.* prevails over the efficacious aspect, 610; as explanation of the Divine economy in act, 47-48; does not derive from the pagan mysteries but is developed from the concept of sacred history, 106; connected to the general concept of sign, carries with it a twofold antithetical aspect, 36; the drop of water in the chalice is a symbol and hence a *M.*, 45; as framework of the theological and liturgical explanations of the Fathers, 598, 611; *M.* is the key to the whole expositive irenic theological vision of the liturgy in the Fathers, 599; the richness of this concept is found more in the irenic mystagogic literature than in the polemical works of the Fathers, 619; *M.* and *sacramentum* among the Latins, 29f, 605; in the liturgies, 606f; merits and deficiencies of the Fathers in the elaboration of this concept, 608f; preaching as *M.*, 860-864; criteria for establishing to what extent in a specific point of the liturgy there is a *M.*, 608; the sacrament of the word is a *M.*, 882; *M.* and *sacramentum* in St. Thomas, 75-76; *M.* and what the orthodox liturgical movement thinks of *M.* in regard to Catholics, 834-835.

MYSTERY OF CHRIST: M. of C., mystery of the Church, sacred (salvation) history, 13-18; in the Bible the extra-Trinitarian aspect and therefore the relations of the Divine Persons with sacred salvation history, M. of C., are on the primary level, 197; sacred salvation history is the history of God's interventions in the world, all focused and unified in the M. of C., 457, 465; sacred history is the M. of C. in Christ Himself and in His faithful, 485; the liturgy reads the Bible in the light of the supreme principle of the unity of the M. of C., in the progression from the O. T. to the N., and from the present dispensation to the eschatological realities, 456; in the Psalms and in the liturgy, 487-505; in the M. of C. the whole phase of historical preparation of the O. T. tends to the phase of the historical realization of the earthly life of Christ up to the Ascension, 160; the prophecies of the O. T. about the Messias are understood beyond the depth of the contemporaries and on three other levels: on the level of the historical life of Christ, on that of the realization of the M. of C. by means of the liturgy, and on the level of eschatology, 472-473; all the phases of the historical life of Christ up to the parousia form one grand M. of C., 111; the full significance of the M. of C. will be discovered only with the realization of Christ's second coming, 462; the meaning and *raison d'être* of the type in the historical unfolding of the M. of C., sacred history, can be understood only in reference to the antitype, 477; as calling of the Gentiles, together with the Jews, to salvation, 14; in liturgical use of the Bible, the depth of the contemporaries is surpassed by the consideration of the historical realities of Christ in Palestine, of the liturgical realities made present in the Mass, and of the eschatological realities, 464-465; God pours out in Christ the fullness of divine life and thus, in Christ, unites men to Himself, 25; and this takes place from Pentecost to the parousia in the mystery of the Church, 25; M. of C. is by eminent title the celebration of the Paschal mysteries, 270; the Eucharistic mystery is the *anámnesis*, the memorial, not only of the death but also of the resurrection of the Lord, 271; the Eucharistic mystery is the principal manifestation of the Church, according to the Second Vatican Council, 284–285; Paschal mystery: *See*: EASTER; the Paschal mystery witnessed by the Apostles concretizes the whole mystery of history, M. of C., and hence, the mystery of the liturgy, 250–251; God fulfills the M. of C. in us through a regime of signs, the primary and connatural place of encounter between God and man, 39; has an inexhaustible objective richness, and concretizes all the treasures of Divinity and humanity, 248; criteria for establishing to what point in a determinate particular of the liturgy there is a "mystery," 607f; the liturgy is *mysterium, sacramentum*, M. of C., and Paschal mystery, 855; M. of C. concretized in the liturgy, 91–95; the liturgy is prayer and sacral realization of the M. of C. under the signs of sanctification and worship, 826; the liturgy is the privileged place of encounter between God and man, in which, in the concrete actualization of the M. of C., man, through the agency of Christ, in possession of the Spirit, receives every good thing from the Father and makes return to Him, 512; the liturgy makes present *in sacramento*, realizing in individual souls, the whole M. of C., sacred history, 483; the liturgy is the specific manner in which, from Pentecost to parousia, in sanctification and in worship, the M. of C. is actualized in the Church, 157; all this is reaffirmed by the Second Vatican Council, 306–307; in the liturgical action God actualizes in man the M. of C., mystery of the Church: law of objectivity, 101; M. of C. is fulfilled in us in the liturgical action and, by virtue of the *opus operatum*, objectivity is emphasized, 100–101; the liturgical signs actualize in man the M. of C., mystery of the Church and, as instruments of God, they transform man, 102; between the first and second coming of the Lord, the Mass is the center in which, under the veil of signs, all the phases of the M. of C. live and are concentrated, 161; the M. of C., salvific dispensation of the world in Christ, is always expressly recalled in the anaphoras of the Mass, 162–163; concretized primarily in the Mass, *See*: MASS: M. of C. and liturgical cycles, 175–179; in the essential nuclei of the various Roman prefaces expression is made of the diverse aspects of the M. of C. in its historical realization in the earthly life of Christ, 170; in the Advent-Epiphany period the M. of C. is viewed in the concept of the epiphanic coming of the Lord, 473; in the Lent-Pentecost period the O. T. is considered in its prefigurative, typological dimension of the M. of C. as redemption, 474; in the Lent-Pentecost period the M. of C. is viewed in the light of redemption, 473; as redemption, the M. of C. is prepared in the catechumens during Lent, the period *par excellence* of the struggle against Satan, 440; M. of C. and the Marian feasts, feasts of the angels and of the saints, 178–179; liturgical spirituality is biblical and makes us live the Christian life as M. of C., constantly actualizing the biblical realities, 668f; the liturgy is concerned not so much with psychological introspection as with focusing the attention on God and objective realities: Christ, His mystery, redemption, Church, 189; in liturgical spirituality the Paschal triduum and Christmas, M. of C. as redemption and as epiphanic coming, constantly actualized in the liturgy, are the two great beacon lights of the soul, even outside the liturgical action, 696; M. of C. includes also the events of the ascetical and mystical ascension toward perfection, the ultimate seal with which the M. of C. is fulfilled in each of the faithful, 461; for the Fathers, to explain the liturgy is to explain its "mysteries," 604f; presentation of the M. of C. in the spirituality of the Middle Ages, 797; contribution of theology in the 12th and 13th centuries to a better understanding of the M. of C., 873–874; Odo Casel and his theology of the M. of C.: exposition thereof and judgment thereon, 104–112; invitation of Vatican II to professors of theology always to bring to prominence the M. of C. and the history of salvation, 640; views of the orthodox on the Catholic manner of presenting and living the M. of C., 835; preaching the M. of C. in St. Augustine, 871–875; preaching is the oral announcement to the faithful of God's message focused on the M. of C., sacred history, Paschal mystery, made by the Church through the agency of her ministers, 859; content and central object of preaching is the M. of C., sacred history, 865, 867–875; by becoming a liturgical catechesis, preaching will present the liturgy directly as M. of C. always in act, 887; preaching and the M. of C. in the expectations of Vatican II, 858. *See:* CHURCH; CHRIST; *MYSTERION; MYSTERIUM;* EASTER; *SACRAMEN-TUM;* SACRED (SALVATION) HISTORY.

MYSTERY RELIGIONS, PAGAN: 105. *See:* MITHRAS.

MYSTICAL BODY: its will to establish efficacious signs of worship and of sanctification, 98; its totality in the performance of acts of worship, 97; that every member of the M. B. receives grace from God by means of Christ's Humanity, 103; preëminent dignity of the grace of the Church in regard to the M. B., 122–123; each and every member is, by a sacramental character, deputed to the worship of the whole M. B., 139–140; liturgy as the vital, complex action of the whole M. B., Head and members, 512–513; M. B. in St. Gertrude, 769f. *See:* CHURCH; *EK-KLESÍA.*

MYSTICS: mystical aspect and mystical experience in the striving toward perfection, 649; the notion of contemplation and of mystical life, 711f; mystical graces and Christian perfection, 712; mystical experience and esthetic experience, 54f; gnostic-mystical ascension of the soul in the *mystérion* of Origen, 608; M. of the 15th century and theology, 546; mysticism and *gnôsis,* 622; mystical life and liturgical spirituality, 711–739; M. and liturgy: the question of whether or not the liturgy is an apt preparation for mystical contemplation, 713–716; testimony of Cassian, 716–722; testimony of the Ursuline, the Ven. Marie of the Incarnation, 722–729; theoretical solution, 176f, 732f; purifications, according to Cassian, a necessary introduction to the interior sanctuary of perfect prayer, 717–718; prayer of the simple glance, and the liturgical action, 688; mystical life and the recitation and singing of the Psalms, 488f, 492–501; in mystical experience the liturgical action is personalized in the highest degree, 691f; mysticism and liturgy in the Pseudo-Dionysius, 608f; ascetical and mystical instruction, and instruction in the liturgy, 641f; mystical and liturgical life in St. Gertrude: mystical marriage, 744, 748f; mystical life and liturgical life without opposing tensions, 777; mystical graces received by St. Gertrude in the liturgical action or in connection therewith, 779–790.

NARRATIO: as salvation history in the preaching of St. Augustine, 870.

NATURAL: concept of the N. and the supernatural, 391f.

NATURALISM: difficulty of naturalistic mentality in understanding exorcisms, 404f; and of taking into account the realities of the struggle against Satan, 394f, 417; modern N., 404.

NATURE: philosophic, historical, and liturgical consideration of N., 391–396; the use of sensible signs in the liturgy is demanded connaturally by human N., 63–68; corruption of N., 689, 704.

NEOPHYTES: and the Eucharist as an armament against Satan, 413; and biblical texts referred to them, 467.

NEOPLATONISM: and readiness of the ancients to accept the symbolic value of sensible things, 40; disembodied spiritualism of N. contrary to the Christian spirit and, in particular, to the liturgy, 310f, 316; N. of the Fathers, emerges from the eclecticism of their thought, 624; in the concept of *gnôsis* after the Pseudo-Dionysius, 622f; the temptation of N. is real again in our times, 311.

NERI, ST. PHILIP: example of a saint who was frequently subject to the mystical experience of ecstasy, 732.

NE TIMEAS ZACHARIA: Mass, 789.

NEW TESTAMENT: unity of the N. T. with the O. T., 456f; unity of the infrahuman cosmos and of man, to the ends of the kingdom of God in the N. T., 326–329; N. T. and liturgy, 481f.

NOAH: and the deluge as theme of patristic exegesis, and its modern re-evaluation, 458 n. 2.

NOBIS QUOQUE PECCATORIBUS: expresses the union of men with the angels and the blessed, 341 n. 20.

NOMINALISM: and objections against the liturgy in favor of the external works of the apostolate, 820.

NOVENAS: constitute a part of the "pious exercises" recommended by the Second Vatican Council, 671.

NUMBERS: their symbolic value in the liturgy, 60 n. 75.

NUPTIAL CHAMBER: blessing of, 427f.

NUPTIALS, SPIRITUAL *or* MYSTICAL: *See*: BETROTHAL, SPIRITUAL *or* MYSTICAL.

OATH: is the *sacramentum* which was in ancient times a military term and later expresses the Greek concept of *mystérion* in reference to moral obligation, but especially in respect to sacred history, 605.

OBJECTIVISM: and the *opus operatum* in the liturgy, 100f; the law of objectivity, and the liturgy, 183–190; notion, 184f; O. and subjectivism in liturgy, 183–187; O. and subjectivism in spirituality in general, 100f, 658; in liturgical spirituality in particular, 666f.

OBJECTS: as signs in the liturgy, 50.

OBLATIONEM FACERE: equivalent to *Eucharistiam facere*, 318.

OCULI: Mass, 792.

O FELIX CULPA: 585.

OFFERIMUS TIBI: its Gallican introduction into the Mass, 292 n. 31.

OFFERTORY: the offering made by the people at the O. appears during the 3rd century, 288; offering made by the people tends to disappear in the East in the 4th–5th century, 291; disappears in West in Middle Ages, 292; theological dimensions of O. in the Mass for the Dead, 389 n. 37.

OFFICE, DIVINE: Christ the principal celebrant therein, 264; its communitarian and ecclesial nature, 297f; the D. O. recited by persons deputed to it by the Church and in the forms required for its validity, actualizes the prayer of the mystical body, Head and members, by reason of a certain *opus operatum*, apart from whatever may be the worthiness of the one who recites it, 112f; 113 n. 18; in the D. O. the end of worship is more predominant than its didactic end, 515f; the D. O. has an essential connection with the Eucharist, 175; D. O. and the association of infrahuman creation to the praise of God, 322–323; D. O. and the angels, 358f; D. O. and struggle against Satan, 449f; Office of the Dead as supererogatory work in the Middle Ages, 796–797; D. O. and mystical experience, according to Cassian,

PALM SUNDAY: or Second Sunday in Passiontide, and the struggle against Satan, 442f.

PANÉGYRIS: and the single liturgy of cosmic and eternal praise, of Christ, the angels, and the saints in the heavenly Jerusalem, 256, 258, 336, 342, 349. *See*: JERUSALEM, HEAVENLY.

PANGE LINGUA GLORIOSI: hymn, 443–444.

PANGS OF LOVE: as mystical experience in St. Gertrude, 782f.

PANTHEISM: its radical opposition to the great Christian realities, 333.

PARABLES, GOSPEL: of the mustard seed, 482; of the leaven, 482; of those invited to a marriage feast, 328, 375; of the sower, 328, 375; of the wheat and weeds, 328, 482.

PARADISE: of our protoparents: ideal state of mankind in which the primordial unity of the cosmos was in force, 325; restoration of the paradisial state through the redemption, 326, 329; and in particular, through baptism, 481; and through the other sacraments, 481; and through the sacramentals, 85–90, 320f, 331f; biblical typology of P., 481.

PARAPHERNALIA: liturgical, explained by the Fathers in the theological treatises of liturgical interest, 592–596.

PARISH: the liturgical life of the P. ought to be the most efficacious general expression of the communitarian liturgical dimension, 290, 298; the P. a communitarian cell winning or preserving the people for Christ, 811; P., the center of liturgical pastoral, 811, 847; general areas of activity in the parish: preaching, administration of the sacraments, parochial works, personal contacts, 811; forces of disunion in the parish, 847; liturgical movement and revalidation of the P., 847.

PAROUSIA: its prophetic commemoration in the Mass, 111, 160; its meaning of triumph over Satan, 378f. *See*: CHRIST; JERUSALEM, HEAVENLY; SACRED (SALVATION) HISTORY.

PARRESÍA: and preaching, 864.

PARTICIPATION, ACTIVE: communitarian, of the people, parochial, aim of liturgical reform, 838–847; full and conscious, 679; the liturgy wants an A. P. of all the people, but hierarchically structured and differentiated, 842f; psychological efficacy of communitarian A. P., 840f; A. P. and Mass in particular, 284–293, 317f; and sacraments, 293–297; present state of A. P. of the people in the liturgy, 848–852; present state of A. P. not in accord with the liturgical ideal, 827–828 n. 25, 852f; A. P. and the mystics: A. P. and mystic contemplation, 721f, 734f; and ardent prayer, 719; and the prayer of quiet, 729; and suspension of the faculties, 732f.

PASCHAL BANQUET: Jewish, 79.

PASCHAL LETTERS: of the Bishops of Alexandria and their importance for the liturgy and for patristic literature of liturgical theological interest, 595.

PASSION OF CHRIST: signified in the fourfold dimension of the liturgical signs, 69–95; Passiontide and the struggle against Satan, 442f; devotion to the P. in the liturgy, in St. Gertrude, 760, 800f; devotion to the P. in the concrete liturgical celebration, 856–857 n. 4.

PASSIVITY: in mystical experience, 650f; of the higher faculties as mystical experience, 732–733.

PASTORAL: in general, notion, definition, P. as an art, the people the object of P., 804–811; liturgical P.: teaching of the P. aspect of liturgy, xxii; the principles of liturgical P., 804–854; the goal of liturgical P., 783; the liturgy is by its nature the focus, goal, and font of P., 811–822; liturgical P. is based on the principle that the sacrifice of the Mass is the sun and center of the supernatural life of the Church, 172f; psychological efficacy of the liturgy in P., 823f; in P., experience is sovereign,

806–807; in P., liturgical catechesis is communicated in communitarian action, 823f; an obstacle to P. is the deep dissociation which exists today between the people and the liturgy, 850; P. carries the liturgy to the people, 853f; but at the same time it involves an elevation of the people, 811; and an elevating of the people to the liturgy, 851f; in the elevation of the people, four points must be considered, 852f; P. brings the people to Christ and Christ to the people, 806, 807; but P. cannot be classist, 810; P. necessarily bears sacrifices with it, 810–811; P. must be progressive, 851; P. necessarily involves a specific formation of the clergy, 848f; means of liturgical pastoral, 855f; missionary pastoral, 808f, 810f, 824f; liturgical P. and instruction in the liturgy, xxii–xxv; liturgical P. in the teaching of liturgy, 641f.

PATER NOSTER: See: PRAYER, LORD'S.

PATIENCE: as precept and exhortation of the O. T. viewed, in its liturgical usage, primarily in the contemporary depth, 463.

PATRIARCHS: in the intercession of the anaphoras, 341; in the liturgy of the ill, 357.

PEDAGOGY: pedagogic efficacy of the liturgy, 320f, 517f; pedagogic necessity of the catechism, and liturgy, 887–898.

PELAGIANISM: Pelagian controversy, and liturgy, 398 n. 44, 406, 515, 529, 551, 613, 759; P. and exorcisms in general, 398.

PENANCE: fourfold dimension of the sign in the sacrament of P., 80–81; in the sacrament of P. the sanctificational aspect predominates over the aspect of worship, 126; P. as second baptism, 126, 417–421; Christological-Trinitarian dimension of the sacrament of P., 236f; communitarian and ecclesial dimension of the sacramental rite of P. from antiquity to the 6th-7th century, and today, 293f; P. and the Holy Spirit, 24; P. and the angels, 356; P. and the struggle against Satan, 417–421; public P., 417 n. 106, 419, 592; public and private P. in the positive-scholastic theologians, 553 n. 21; rites of public P. explained in patristic liturgical treatises, 592–596; explanation of the liturgical aspect of P. in the theological treatment of P. in St. Thomas, 579. *See*: PENITENTS, RECONCILIATION OF.

PENITENTS, RECONCILIATION OF: in connection with the Mass of Holy Thursday, 174; and Lent as special struggle against Satan, 439f. *See*: PENANCE.

PENTECOST: from P. to the parousia the Church is the agency which communicates the Holy Spirit, 16f; it is in that period, from P. to the parousia, that the mystery of the Church is realized, 25; from P. to the parousia the sacred history of salvation, mystery of Christ, is realized under the veil of liturgical signs, 31, 157, 899f; from P. to parousia the sacramental dispensation is of basic importance, 47f; after P., Christ communicates divine life to men, and men render worship to God in the Church, 61f; the sacrifice of Golgotha reaches out to the mission of the Holy Spirit in P., 111; since P., the Mass is the greatest of the efficacious signs of the encounter between God and man, 158; every Mass contains P., just as it does all the other events of sacred history, 176; P. is, through the Church and the liturgy, the beginning of the realization of the redemption of the faithful, 177; in the last phase of the liturgical cycle, which embraces P., the Holy Spirit occupies the first level of our attention, 242; supplemental date for Christian initiation, 294; Lent-P. cycle and the struggle against Satan, 439f; and prophecies of the O. T., 474f; and historical passages of the N. T., 483f; a period in which genuflection is not made, as subject matter of Syrian liturgical treatise, 604; as a point of reference for deeper recollection, 696; P. and content of preaching, 885f.

PÉNTHOS: or compunction, in the ancient monastic tradition, 659; liturgical action and the exercise of P., 702. *See*: COMPUNCTION.

PEOPLE: as object of pastoral, 808–811; active and communitarian participation of the P. is the aim of liturgical pastoral, 838–847; actual state of the P. today in respect to the liturgy, 827–828 n. 25, 846f; aim of liturgical pastoral is to bring the P. to Christ and Christ to the P. in the liturgy, 851f.

PEOPLE OF GOD: election and formation of the P. of G. in the Psalms and in the liturgy, 495f; P. of G. and the Church, 495f; P. of G. in the Epistle to the Hebrews, 256f; God, in His interventions in the world, intends to form for Himself a People: the law of salvation in community: 276–282; terminology of the P. of G., as employed by Second Vatican Council: *populus Dei*, 59; terminology of the Roman liturgy: *ecclesia tua, familia tua, plebs Dei, populus tuus*, 297; P. of G. royal and priestly, 348; enemies of the P. of G., 498–501. *See*: CHURCH; CHRIST; ISRAEL; PASTORAL.

PERCEPTIO CORPORIS TUI: its introduction into the Mass is of Gallican origin, 292 n. 31.

PER CHRISTUM DOMINUM NOSTRUM: its meaning, 214f.

PER DOMINUM NOSTRUM IESUM CHRISTUM FILIUM TUUM: its meaning, 215f.

PERFECTION, CHRISTIAN: concept, 648–651; various Catholic schools of thought on how to teach and practice the striving toward C. P., 651–661; C. P. and the liturgy, 661–711; ascetic aspect of the striving toward C. P., 683f; purgative way, 650; illuminative way, 650; unitive way, 650; C. P. of being, 649, 662; C. P. of doing, 649, 662.

PERSON: the biblical texts in the liturgical action have reference to the individual persons participating, 483f; the liturgy can and must be personalized by the faithful, 689–694, 719f; the personalization of the liturgy is realized in the highest degree in mystical experience in the liturgical action, 711–738, 719–720; the example of St. Gertrude, 802–803; personal experience, faith and liturgy, 534–541.

PERSONS: as signs in the liturgy, 59f.

PETER: Primacy of Peter and the struggle against Satan, 377f.

PHENOMENOLOGY OF WORSHIP: 64f.

PHILOLOGY: history and criticism in liturgical inquiry, 519f.

PHILOSOPHY: philosophical manner and historical manner, and hence the biblical, traditional, and patristic manner of the consideration of matters by the ordinary and liturgical magisterium, 3–10, 391–396.

PHOTIANISTS: controversies with the PH., and the liturgy, 614.

PHOTIZÓMENOI: category of catechumen pledged to receive baptism at the next Easter, 397–398 n. 42.

PICTURE: *See*: ART.

PLAN OF GOD: for the salvation of man, 330, 428, 456f. *See*: SACRED (SALVATION) HISTORY.

PLATONISM: its influence on the ancients in the understanding of the symbolic value of sensible things, 40f; as a conception of life that disparages the physical body, P. is vigorously rejected by the Church, 310; P. and the semantic evolution of the term *mystérion*, 600f.

PLEASURE, ESTHETIC: and the liturgy, 51–59. *See*: ART.

PNEUMATIKAÌ THYSÍAI: spiritual sacrifices, or sacrifices in the Spirit, 147.

PNEUMATIKÓS: its real significance, 147.

POLEMICS: in revelation and in preaching, 866f; doctrinal P., and liturgy, 515; polemic use of the liturgy, among the Fathers, 611–619; principal patristic works in which a polemic use is made of the liturgy, 596.

POLYTHEISM: utterly opposed to an understanding of the great realities of Christian life and doctrine, 333.

POMPS OF THE DEVIL: 386, 408.

POOR MAN OF YAHWEH, THE: in the Psalms and in the liturgy, the meaning thereof, 501f.

POPE: *See*: ROMAN PONTIFF.

POSITIVE-SCHOLASTIC THEOLOGY: and the liturgy, 546–571; origin of this kind of theology, 546–549; liturgy and theology, in the positive-scholastic theologians, 550–558; insufficient assimilation of liturgical material in the positive-scholastics, 563–568.

POSSESSION, DIABOLIC: in the N. T., 362f, 365f; what is to be thought of it, 389–396. *See*: DEMONS; EXORCISMS; SATAN.

POSTCOMMUNION: fourfold dimension of the liturgical signs in the P., 162.

POST MYSTERIUM: of the Mozarabic liturgy, 229.

POST PRIDIE: of the Mozarabic liturgy, 229, 416.

POST SECRETA: of the Mozarabic liturgy, 229.

POSTURE, PHYSICAL: as signs in the liturgy, 49–50.

POTESTAS: and *imperium* received by the exorcist, for expelling demons, 426.

POVERTY: in St. Francis of Assisi and its significance for the spiritual life, 659.

POWER OF GOD: how the liturgy means those O. T. texts to be understood, which speak of the P. of G., 465–469.

PRAISE: the O. T. develops in a special way the theme that infrahuman creation must be of service to man in praising and adoring God, of whom it is a revelation, 325f; consequence of the divine attributes is the invitation to praise God: theme of the Psalms and in fact of the whole Bible, 502f; the restoration and the transfiguration of infrahuman creation in the liturgy, and hence too in the liturgy of P., are real, 330; in the liturgy of P., the whole of infrahuman creation is associated in the P. of God, 332f; in the Divine Office of P., Christ is present as a physical reality in the operation of His sanctifying power, 267; in the liturgy Christ is always on the primary level, be it in the Sacrifice, be it in sanctification, be it in prayer and in P., 266; Christ completed on earth His liturgy of sanctification and of P., especially on Golgotha, 259; the Divine Office sings P. *donec veniat*, 179; Christ is always the principal celebrant in the Divine Office even as in the sacraments and sacramentals, 264; the presence of Christ in the Church, praying and giving praise, is re-affirmed by the Second Vatican Council, 268; the angels are always present in the Divine Office of P., 358; the prayer of P. of the faithful is united to the prayer of P. of the priest, according to *Mediator Dei*, 152–153; sacrifice of P. as internal act of man totally submissive to God, 155–156; P. alone as imperfect extrinsic character of the sacrifice, 148; sacrifice of P. and of charity toward one's neighbor in Ch. 13 of the Epistle to the Hebrews, 144; prayer of P. in respect to the virtue of religion, 128; in his tract on the virtue of religion St. Thomas treats of vocal praise as a matter directly religious, 580–581; in the liturgy all the literary genres are means of expressing volitions, desires, petitions, thanksgiving, admiration, P., etc., 516; the spirit of adoration, thanksgiving, and P. pervades liturgical spirituality because of the latter's theocentrism, 669; prayer of thanksgiving and of P. and the sense of compunction are permeated by the involvement of the will in simple sentiments of admiration, gratitude, satisfaction in God, 689–690; the liturgy, directed entirely to homage, to P., and to thanksgiving, seems not to favor introspection and the practical resolutions for the amendment of life: yet just the opposite is found, and quite decisively, 690f; the liturgical action in the perspective of the virtue of religion opens into sentiments of humility, reverence, compunction, adoration, with prayer of P., petition, and thanksgiving, 697; the exercise of the theological virtues in the liturgical action involves submission, self-denial, adoration and P. which constitute the general atmosphere of the virtue of religion, 699;

in the exercise of the moral virtues the liturgy focuses attention more on God than on man, and thus, its sentiments are of admiration, reverence, submission, P., adoration, devotion, 702; outside the strictly cultic action of adoration and P., the liturgy does in fact make a deep penetration of the works of moral asceticism in respect to oneself and of apostolic and charitable works in respect to others, 708; the spirit of praise is not sufficient nor does mere participation in the rites suffice for one to be said to have "a liturgical mind," 713 n. 46; the will to praise God in St. Gertrude, 745f, 748; love as unceasing homage of P. and thanksgiving in St. Gertrude, 760f; evangelization precedes the praise of God, 826 n. 24; the P. of God and the life of Christ in community as efficacious means of pastoral liturgy, 824; the life of worship in the parish has great missionary importance because it is the very life of Christ in His people: and since Christ lived to give P. to the Father, the Christian life is principally worship, 828; P. in the eternal liturgy as the goal of the People of God *in via*, 256; in the *Sanctus* we ask God to unite our voice to the P. offered by the angels, 342; every sacramental is a prophetic sign of the cosmic praise of the heavenly Jerusalem, 89; the Apocalypse shows us the *panégyris* of the cosmic and eternal liturgy of all creatures in the adoration and P. of the Lamb and of Him that lives forever, 348–349.

PRAYER: methods of prayer in general, 657; methods of P. and liturgical spirituality in particular, 685–696; according to Cassian, 716–722; various degrees: pure, pure and sincere, burning (ardent), perfect, pure and short, perpetual, according to Cassian, 717; contemplative P., 719; ejaculatory P., 717, 750; burning (ardent) P., 717, 719f, 725; meditative P., 693; mental P., 703; perfect P., 717; most perfect or inflamed P., 720f; P. of quiet, 713, 729, 731; psalmodic P., 693–694.

PRAYERBOOKS: in the Middle Ages, and the spirit of the liturgy, 793.

PRAYER, LORD'S: L. P. as *mystérion* in the Fathers, since the 4th century, 604; L. P. as *mystérion* according to Simeon of Salonika, 30 n. 21; L. P. as *sacramentum* in St. Augustine, 30; L. P. as sacramental since the 13th century, 86 n. 121; L. P. in liturgy of the ill and its antidemoniacal dimension, 423.

PRAYERS, LITURGICAL: their Christological-Trinitarian structure, 209–217; according to the ancient rule, addressed to the Father through Christ, 209f; ancient plan of the liturgical prayers: beginning, body, conclusion — and its later development, 209–217; the fourfold dimension of the sign in liturgical prayer, 23f, 85; P. of the Church actualized in the sacramentals, 88f, 112f, 700; liturgical P. has a dignity superior to that of private P., 120–123, 675–679; *See: OPUS OPERANTIS EC-CLESIAE*; doctrine of this higher dignity, 676f; its dogmatic character, 319; P. of the mystical body of Christ, Head and members, 89, 214; Christ the principal celebrant in liturgical P., 263–264; the aim of the liturgy as worship is not so much to instruct the faithful as to make them pray, 513f, 527f; communitarian and ecclesial character of liturgical P., 297f; tension between communitarian nature of prayer and its necessary personalization and interiorization, 298, 317f, 692f; P. and universal priesthood of the faithful, 143f; extraliturgical P. and liturgical spirituality, 670f; liturgical P. addressed directly to the Trinity, 209; P. and the Holy Spirit, 211 n. 29; personalization of liturgical P.: *See*: PERSON; how the liturgy understands the precept of prayer contained in O. T. texts, 469f; P. and Lent, 439f; P. as means of striving for perfection, 653; vocal prayer and mystical life: the question, 713–716; according to testimony of Cassian, 716–722; according to the testimony of the Ven. Marie of the Incarnation, 722–729; according to the research of Poulain, 731; extraliturgical prayers and spirit of the liturgy in St. Gertrude, 792–803; prayers and liturgy, in St. Thomas, 580; P. of praise: *See*: PRAISE: great Eucharistic prayer of the Mass has Jewish format, 211. *See also*:

PRIESTHOOD, HIERARCHICAL: notion, and difference from the P. common to all the faithful, 151–154; without a H. P. there is no Church and no sacraments, 275f; an aggregate of individuals is transformed by the H. P. so as to constitute a Church, 275–276; H. P. and priesthood of the faithful, 842f; P. of the O. T. a figure of the P. of Christ and of the Christian P., 478; ordination of priest, and Christological-Trinitarian dimension, 237f.

PRIESTHOOD OF CHRIST: in itself, 149f; the whole system of sanctification and of worship in the Church is centered on the P. and worship of Christ, as a participation therein, 24, 142; sacramental character as participation in the P. of Xt., 139–143; orders as a participation *sui generis* in the P. of Xt., 81f; the liturgy as exercise and continuous epiphany on earth of the P. of Xt., 20 n. 2, 266–271; the P. of Xt. according to the Epistle to the Hebrews, 255f; the P. of Xt. in St. Thomas, 582 n. 35.

PRIESTHOOD OF THE FAITHFUL: in the framework of Christian priesthood, 143–154; and the Mass, 151f, 158–162; and the hierarchical priesthood, 842f; priesthood of the O. T. a figure of the P. of Christ and the Christian P., 478.

PRIESTS: ordination of P. and Christological-Trinitarian dimension, 237f; consecration of P. in the O. T. according to St. Thomas, 581.

PRIMACY: of Peter, and the struggle against Satan, 377–378; dogmatic development of the doctrine of the P. of the Pope makes the *Tu es Petrus* easier to understand, 482–483; P. of the Pope and the Photian controversy, 614 n. 91; the conviction of the P. of the Roman Church was well-established in Rome in the 5th-6th century, as may be deduced from the Leonine Sacramentary, 562.

PROFESSION, MONASTIC: as a second baptism, 433; M. P. and the struggle against Satan, 434f; M. P. and the Eucharist, 175.

PROFESSION OF FAITH: baptismal, *See*: CREED.

PROFICISCERE ANIMA CHRISTIANA: its Christological-Trinitarian dimension, 239; and the place of the angels in the liturgy of the ill, 356–357.

PROMISED LAND: entry into the P. L. a figure of baptism in the liturgy, 480; and figure of entry into heaven, 480, 495.

PROPHECIES: how the liturgy understands the O. T. P., 463f, 472–476.

PROPHESYING: and preaching, 864f.

PROSÁGO and *PROSAGOGÉ: to approach* and (to have) *access*, and their cultic religious significance in the N. T., 144.

PROSÉRCHOMAI: to draw near, and its cultic religious significance in the N. T., 144.

PROSPHORAN EPITELEÎN: to complete the offering, terminology of the Mass in tradition, 318.

PROTESTANTISM: misunderstands the true value of the sensible sign in the Christian religion, and the consequences thereof in its whole religious outlook, according to R. Will, 64f; Protestant communitarian dimension and Catholic communitarian dimension, 273–276; ancient tradition contrary to the Protestant mentality of the equalizing of roles in the liturgical action, 289; ancient tradition contrary to the Protestant mentality that asserts the essential self-sufficiency of the individual in the face of other individuals in his relations with God, 290; P. is radically separated from Catholicism through a misunderstanding of the law of incarnation on the part of P., 307; every kind of P. that is logically developed and consistent with itself is deeply antiliturgical, 307; P. is psychologistic in its conception of worship, 274f; the rediscovery of liturgy by P. is a new drawing near to the law of incarnation and hence to Catholicism, 307; anti-Protestant polemic as exaggerated preoccupation of positive-scholastic theology, 553, 555, 557, 563–568; recent P. and concern of recovering a closer union between preaching and liturgy, 880; value of the liturgical movement in relations between Protestants and Catholics, 830–835; modern liturgical rebirth in P., 831; the liturgy in the anti-Protestant controversies, 510, 549–595; P. and Catholic theology in the 16th century, 546–550.

PROVIDENCE: how the liturgy understands the O. T. texts that speak of the P. of God, 493f.

PSALMODY: *See*: PSALMS.

PSALMS: and their reference to the mystery of Christ in the liturgy, 487–505; the consideration of the P. from the point of view of the great biblical themes of the sacred history of salvation, 487–492; their grouping according to these themes, 489f; philological, critical, and historical consideration of the P., 489; how the Fathers considered the P., 490; chanting and reciting the P., and mystical experience, according to Cassian, 717f, 720f; and according to the Ven. Marie of the Incarnation, 724–729; and according to St. Teresa, 467, 729; according to the research conducted by Poulain, 731f; P. and mysticism in St. Gertrude, 779f.

PSYCHOLOGISM: powerlessness of a simple religious P. to arrive at the profundity of the liturgy, 142 n. 39; in the liturgy it is not a matter of heeding proper psychologistic reactions to God's presence, but of going to God, 102, 319; modern P. has enfeebled the once lively sense of the struggle against Satan, 363, 383; Protestant P., in the way of conceiving worship, 274f.

PSYCHOLOGY: liturgy is structured in a regime of sensible signs, as a response to human P., 63f; harmonious actualization of psychological faculties in the liturgy, 316–324; because of the law of the religious psychology of the immediate preparation for prayer, in the liturgy the didactic style does not predominate, 516; the formation of a communitarian religious P. is indispensable for understanding and living the liturgy, 283f, 665; the style of the liturgy is but little conducive to religious introspection, 666f; proper balance of the liturgy in activating the psychological faculties of intelligence, will, and sentiment or emotion, 318f, 668; psychological efficacy of the liturgy as communitarian action, 839; P., and harmonious attunement both internal and external, in the liturgy, 312–316; P. and liturgical pastoral, 711, 851, 853; child P., catechism and liturgy, 887f.

PUER: liturgical biblical appellative of Jesus Christ, equivalent to *Pais*, 211.

PURGATORY: the reality of P. implied in the ancient liturgical practice, 338f; souls in P. and the anaphora of St. Basil, 168–169; defense, by means of the liturgy, of the dogma of P., against the Protestants, 551; communion with the souls of P., 336f.

Q^{e}HAL YAHWEH: Ekklesía toû Theoû, Ecclesia Dei, the holy People of God in the O. T., 59, 279, 336.

QUADRIVIUM: in the Middle Ages, together with the *Trivium*, was a course of studies; its service to the preacher, 594.

QUAM OBLATIONEM: its theological meaning, 229.

QUICUMQUE: or Athanasian Creed, 233.

QUID RETRIBUAM DOMINO: of Gallican origin, an apology in the Mass, 292 n. 31.

QUIET: in mystical experience: mystical grace of Q., 731; praying quiet, 731; jubilant quiet, 731; working quiet, 731.

QUIETISM: whether there is a danger of Q. in the liturgy, 101–102.

QUI VIVIS ET REGNAS: its Christological-Trinitarian significance, 216.

QUOD ORE SUMPSIMUS: under the Gallican influence, an apology introduced into the Mass, 292 n. 31.

QUONIAM IN AETERNUM MISERICORDIA EIUS: 465.

RATIONALISM: and its total failure to understand the liturgy, 558, 561, 565, 570; liberal R., 564.

READING-MEDITATION: as discursive meditation outside the liturgy, 694–696.

READINGS: in the liturgy they are instructions, but with sanctification for their direct end, 514f.

READINGS, BIBLICAL: in the liturgy: not read privately by the priest in antiquity, 286; euchological plan: reading; homily; song; silent prayer; concluding oration of the priest, in a loud voice, 693, 884; the choice of the B. R. in the liturgy determined by the concept of *mystérion*, sacred history, 606f.

REALISM: and liturgy, 103.

RECOLLECTION: of the senses, in the liturgical action, 688.

RECOLLECTION OF GOD'S PRESENCE, PERPETUAL: a moment in which, according to Cassian, the soul frequently renews in itself the awareness of the presence of God, 717.

REDDITIO ORATIONIS: or recitation of the Lord's Prayer from memory, in the rites over the *competentes*, and its antidemoniacal dimension, 402, 403.

REDDITIO SYMBOLI: or recitation of the Creed from memory, in the rites over the *competentes*, and its antidemoniacal dimension, 402, 407; in the literature of the Fathers of liturgical theological interest, 591.

REDEMPTION: as object of the Lent-Pentecost liturgical cycle, 91.

REDITUS AD DEUM: the return to God in Christological-Trinitarian movement, 199, 206, 233. See: *EXITUS A DEO*; MOVEMENT, CHRISTOLOGICAL-TRINITARIAN.

RED SEA: passage through the R. S. a figure of baptism in the biblical typology of the N. T. used in the liturgy, 480.

REFORMS, LITURGICAL: how the question of L. R. is posed, 854; recent successes, value and significance of L. R., xxii f; L. R. of Pius V, 293.

RELICS: veneration of R., and the liturgy, 522; veneration of unauthentic R., 529; appeal to the liturgy in the controversy with Vigilantius about the veneration of R., 612–613; veneration of R. according to St. Thomas, 582 n. 35; depositing of R. in the altar only after the antidemoniacal exorcism in the rite of consecrating an altar, 432.

RELIGARE: of uncertain meaning in the theoretical question of religion, 84 n. 119.

RELIGIO: its meaning, 84 n. 119.

RELIGION: the virtue of R. signified in every liturgical sign, 69f, 73; concept of the virtue of R., 127–133; its general dimension in Christian life, 127f; its relationship to the moral virtues, 129f; and with the theological virtues, 129f, 513f; the virtue of R. as general framework of the exercise of the theological virtues in the liturgical action, 697–702, 817f; theology of the virtue of R. in St. Thomas, 573; theological treatment of the virtue of R., and liturgy, in St. Thomas, 580f.

RELIGIONS, NATURAL: have rites which, in their own way, can be called *sacramenta*, 63.

REMNANT OF ISRAEL: and the law of salvation in community, 279.

RENUNCIATION OF SATAN: in the baptismal rites, 397f, 408f.

RES: of the sacraments, according to St. Augustine, 30–31 n. 22.

RESURRECTION: as phase of God's extraordinary intervention in the world, 7; since the R., the communication of divine life to man is at its maximum, 15; baptism a participation in the R. by reason of word as sign, 47; essential connection of the R. with the Eucharist, 79–80; R. of bodies will signify the greatest sanctification of the same, 87; after the R. of bodies infrahuman creatures will once more be devoted to the total service of divine life in the world, 88–89; R. an object of con-

modern theology, 580; duplex end of the S., sanctification and worship, according to St. Thomas, 575; sacramental character and worship in the theology of St. Thomas, 139, 143, 575; ordering of all the S. to the Eucharist, according to the Pseudo-Dionysius and St. Thomas, 171–172, 575; the S. of the O. T. (circumcision, Paschal lamb, consecration of priests), according to St. Thomas, 581f.

SACRAMENTUM: as sign, 22–25; among the Latins, 605f; see also 529f; in the liturgies, 606f; incarnation and S. in Christ, in the Church, in the liturgy, 62f; S. and oath in baptism, 77; centering of the liturgical explanation of the Fathers on the concept of mystérion, mysterium, S., 598–611; merits of scholasticism and especially of St. Thomas in the elaboration of the concept of S., 610; preaching and S., 860–864. See: MYSTÉRION; MYSTERIUM; MYSTERY OF CHRIST.

SACRED HEART: devotion to S. H., notion, 657; determination of the extent to which the liturgy demands faith in the revelations of the S. H. to St. Margaret Mary Alacoque, 528; the month dedicated to the S. H., and the liturgy, 671; how the liturgy on the feast of the S. H. interprets the texts of Jeremias on the institution of a new and eternal covenant, 476; S. H. and worship of Christ according to St. Thomas, 582 n. 35; the S. H. in St. Gertrude, and the spirit of the liturgy, 798–800.

SACRED PLACES: of the O. T., according to St. Thomas, 581.

SACRED (SALVATION) HISTORY: revelation is presented primarily as S. H., a concept that constitutes the general background of the liturgy: the fact, the great phases of this S. H., their significance in regard to a biblical perspective, theology of history, mystery, mystery of Christ, mystery of the Church, 3–18; unity of the various phases of S. H., 456f; S. H. as object of patristic theology in, for example, Irenaeus, Origen, and Augustine, 869–875; as object of preaching up to the 12th-13th centuries, 870–875; the reality of S. H. as unifying and vivifying center of the Bible, tradition, teaching of the magisterium, theology, preaching, catechism, liturgy, spirituality, 873, 885, 890f; S. H. as unifying factor in the perspective taken by the new German catechism, 892–898; S. H. and the revival of preaching, 876–880; liturgy cannot be understood outside the frame of reference of S. H., which finds its greatest concretization precisely in the liturgy, 3–18, 25, 91–95, 157, 179; and primarily, therefore, in the Mass, 157–179; to the extent that theology is not conceived as explanation of S. H., the liturgy finds no adequate place therein, 588f; S. H. as mystérion, 599f; S. H. and the Psalms, 489–490; S. H. and actualization of faith, of hope, and of charity in the liturgy, 700–701; in the Pseudo-Dionysius' concept of mystérion, and in the tendency depending thereupon, the aspect of S. H. is relegated to a secondary level, 608.

SACRED VESSELS: in the O. T., according to St. Thomas, 581.

SACRIFICE: as sign, 22–23; general concept, 147f; as analogous concept, 148, 155; supreme act of religion and worship, 131, 149; S. and Holy Spirit, 24–25; S's. of Isaac and of Melchisedech, figures of the Eucharistic S., 481; S. and virtue of religion according to St. Thomas, 580f; S. of the O. T. according to St. Thomas, 581f. See: MASS.

SAINTS: object of the worship called dulia, 136; cult, veneration, and intercession of the S., 335–336, 339–343, 522; feast of All Saints, See: ALL SAINTS; communion with the S. in heaven, and the liturgy, 339–343; importance of the S. in the anaphoras, 339, 340–341; development of the cult of S., 340; cult of non-existent S., 529; general significance of the feasts of the S., 178; S. and liturgical meditation, 689; S. and moralizational force of the liturgy, 705; S. and liturgical life in St. Gertrude, 769; liturgy, and defense of the cult or veneration of S., against the Protestants, 551, 555 n. 24; invocation of S. according to St. Thomas, 582 n. 35. See: BLESSED, THE.

SALT: the antidemoniacal significance of the tasting of S. in the baptismal rites, 401; exorcism of S., 401, 430.

SANCTIFICATION: in what sense it is possible to speak of the S. of persons, 86–87; S. and worship in the liturgy, 23–24, 27, 124f; S. and sacramentals, 88, 89f.

SANCTUS: of the Seraphim in Isaias, 345; of the Mass, and union of the heavenly liturgy with that of earth, 226, 342, 352–354.

SATAN: his influence over lower creation after sin, 331; exorcisms to prevent this influence, 331f; the struggle against S. in the N. T., 364f; and in later tradition, 383–389; what is *de fide* in this regard, 381–396; the liturgy of Christian initiation as struggle against Satan, 396–417; the struggle against S. in the principal sacramentals not directly connected with the rites of the seven sacraments, 428–437; the struggle against S. in the temporal and sanctoral cycles, 437–450; expulsion of S. and the kingdom of God, 367–371; struggle against S. in the Apocalypse, 378–379; struggle against S., and the particular judgment, according to Origen, 388; the struggle in general against S., according to the faith, 363f; the lively sense of the truth of this struggle against S. has been lost in modern times, 363; Satanic possession, 363; S. and his satellites in the Psalms that speak of the enemies of the People of God, 498f; S. and the good angels, 348, 357f. *See*: EXORCISM.

SCHOLA CANTORUM: is contrary to the communitarian dimension of the liturgy, if the S. C. executes the chants that pertain to the role of the people, making the people mute spectators, 292.

SCHOLASTICISM: scholastic theology, and the liturgy, in the example of St. Thomas, 572–589.

SCHOOLS OF SPIRITUALITY: in what sense there can be diverse S. of S. in the bosom of Catholicism, 651–660; whether liturgical spirituality is only one among the various S. of S., 675–679; whether liturgical spirituality and Benedictine spirituality are synonymous, 679–683; whether the Church, desiring that the spirit of the liturgy penetrate everywhere, seeks to abolish the various S. of S., 677–678. *See*: SPIRITUALITY, *where the specific schools are noted*.

SCIENCE: concept of S., 627f; S. and *gnôsis*, 628; theology as S., and the relationship between theology and liturgy, 627–631.

SCIENCE, LITURGICAL: nature of L. S. and how L. S. is taught, xx f, 637–643.

SCRIPTURE: and liturgy, 455–505; position of S. in the liturgy in general, 455; fundamental principle according to which the liturgy uses S., 428f; fourfold depth of the single sense of biblical texts, 458–462; deepening of the contemporary perspective in O. T. texts used in the liturgy, 481–486; how the liturgy understands the Psalms, 487–505; vitality of S. viewed in the liturgy, 486; liturgical reading and interpretation of S.: is the traditional biblical catechesis of the Church, 486; liturgical interpretation of S., and art, and paleo-Christian and medieval iconography, 486; interdependence of the biblical question and the liturgical question, 543f; S. can be understood integrally only in the liturgy, 504; the biblical readings in the liturgy are determined by the concept of *mysterium*, sacred (salvation) history, 607f; reading and meditation on S. during Lent in the spirit of the liturgy, 439f; S. and revelation as sacred history, 3–18; biblical character of liturgical spirituality, 669; instruction in S. and initiation to the liturgy, 639; S., sacred history, and *gnôsis*, 619–622; S. as *mystérion* derived from the *mystérion* of Christ in Origen, 63, 601f; personalization of S. in Christian and liturgical reading of the same, 461; *See*: PERSON; biblical movement and liturgical catechesis in the work of Pius Parsch, 837; desire for a closer union between S., preaching, and liturgy, 876–880; S. in positive-scholastic theology, 563f, 567f. *See*: SACRED (SALVATION) HISTORY: PSALMS; CHRIST; TRINITY; PRIESTHOOD;

SIGN; TYPOLOGY; LAW OF SALVATION IN COMMUNITY; CREATION, INFRAHUMAN; MAN; ANGELS; JERUSALEM, HEAVENLY; SATAN.

SCRUTINIA: pre-baptismal and their antidemoniacal significance, 402–410.

SEMINARIES: and liturgy, 543, 637–641, 848f; teaching of liturgy in S., actual status thereof, and observations thereon, 543, 637–641.

SEMI-PELAGIANISM: semi-Pelagian controversy, and liturgy, 515, 529, 551, 613, 759, 832.

SEMI-RATIONALISM: and liturgy, 561.

SENSE, ESTHETIC: and liturgy, 51–59, 320f; E. S. and lack thereof in anyone who would use *Deutschland über alles* as a hymn tune at Mass, 828 n. 35.

SENSES, HUMAN: care and exercise of the S. in liturgy, 318; comparison of the various S. according to their utilization in the liturgy, 60–61; difficulty which the liturgy seems to experience in disposing the subject to the mystical action, and, in the notable and continuous exercise of the external S. which it involves, 712–722, 724f, 732f.

SENSES OF SCRIPTURE: the fourfold depth of the single sense of the biblical texts, the tradition of this point of view, and the resulting practice in the liturgy, 458–486.

SENSUS CATHOLICUS: evolution of dogmas, and liturgy, 533–541.

SENSUS CHRISTI: 92.

SENTIMENT: fostering of S. in the liturgy, 318f; religious S., and liturgy, according to the modernists, 530f. *See*: AFFECTION; LOVE.

SENTIMENTALISM: and preaching, 879.

SEPTUAGINT: Greek version of the O. T., 20 n. 1.

SERAPHIM: and their place in the liturgy, 345, 352, 357. *See*: ANGELS.

SERMON ON THE MOUNT: sheds a necessary light on the precepts and admonitions of the O. T., 471; and this is brought out in the liturgy, 471.

SERPENT: in the desert, typological figure of Christ on the Cross, 479.

SERVERS: in the *Missa lecta*, and communitarian character of the Mass, 291.

SERVICE: of God, and its importance in the spirituality of St. Ignatius of Loyola, 680.

SHADOW *or* FORESHADOWING: and truth, in Origen, of the phases of the sacred history of salvation, 601; as a terminology, passes on a broad scale into the liturgical formularies, 606.

SHEMONEH ESREH: synagogal prayer, 352 n. 44.

SICK: *See*: ILL.

SIGN: and liturgy, 19–95; in general, 32–42; in the liturgy, 42–69; the things signified in the liturgy, according to the fourfold dimension of the liturgical sign, 69–95; St. Thomas knew the fourfold dimension of the liturgical sign, 577–578; ancient mentality and modern mentality in regard to the concept of S., and the influence thereof on the manner of conceiving the liturgy, 35–42; efficacy of the liturgical S., 23, 96–123; why the liturgical S. has its highest and most efficacious expression in the Mass, 157–171; the concept of S. according to the *Summa theologiae* of St. Thomas, 574; the doctrine of St. Thomas on the threefold dimension of the sacramental sign, 574.

SIGN OF THE CROSS: 315, 399, 403–404.

SIGNUM: and the connected concepts of *mystérion, mysterium, figure, symbolum, image*, each of which see in its own place.

SILENCE: moments of silent prayer in the older liturgy and at present, 317, 693–694; moments of silent prayer in the ancient liturgy, 693.

SIN: offense not only against God but also against the Church, 294; S. disrupts cosmic unity, 324f, 328; original S. proved against the Pelagians by means of the liturgy, 551, 613.

SINNER: the penitent S. in the Psalms and in the liturgy, 501.

SION: the holy mountain, the Church, and the heavenly Jerusalem, 497f.

SLEEP: mystical, 733; S. of the faculties, 729f.

SOCIETY: and liturgy: societal character of the liturgy and its structure in sensible signs, 67; S. and the individual, in the liturgy, 272–299. *See*: COMMUNITY; INDIVIDUAL, THE.

SOCINIANS: and liturgy, 551.

SOCIOLOGY: and liturgy, 849–850 n. 65.

SOLA SCRIPTURA: Protestant principle, and effect thereon of the Protestant liturgical movement, 835.

SON: *See*: CHRIST.

SONG (CHANT): is the means *par excellence* to express and create the communitarian sense of active participation in the liturgy, 50; its advantages and dangers for the raising of oneself to God in the liturgical prayer, according to St. Augustine, 56f; literature in respect to the thinking of the Fathers on liturgical S., 56–57; communitarian requirement of liturgical S., 57f; Gregorian Chant, 682; parts of Mass sung by the people and, unfortunately, those of more difficult delivery reserved to the *schola cantorum*, 59, 291; in ancient times, as again at present, parts sung or read *ex officio* by a minister of the Mass were not read privately by the celebrant, 292; popular song and its utter necessity, 293; its harmful restriction, 321; liturgical S., according to St. Thomas, 580f; liturgical S. and mystical experience according to John Cassian, 718, 719f; according to the Ven. Marie of the Incarnation, 726f; according to an investigation conducted by Poulain, 731; according to St. Gertrude, 756, 780, 799; recitation and chanting of the Psalms, and mystical experience, 730f. *See*: ART.

SOUCAS: the laura of S., near Jericho, 703.

SOUL AND BODY: in revelation, 309–312; in the liturgy, 312, 316.

SOULS IN PURGATORY: their communion with the living, in the liturgy, 336–339; sacrifice of the Mass offered for them, and pious works performed for them, 336–339; S. in P. and the unity of the whole cosmos in the mediation of Christ, 666; S. in P. and the total unity of the cosmos in St. Gertrude, 766, 769; devotion to the S. in P. in the Middle Ages, 796–797.

SOURCES: of theology, use of sources in general, and consequences in reference to the use of the liturgy in positive-scholastic theology, 563–571. *See: LOCI THEOLOGICI.*

SPECULATION: speculative aspect of the faith, and the question of the relationship between catechism and liturgy, 889; between preaching and liturgy, 866.

SPHRAGIS: consignatio in the baptismal rites, 399.

SPIRITUALISM: disembodied S. in Orphic, Platonic and Neo-Platonic tradition, and Christian S., 310.

SPIRITUALITY: and liturgy, 647–803; notions of S., 647–651; different schools of S. in the bosom of the Church, 651–660; types of S.: intellectual, voluntarist, and affective, 655f; S. and ascetical mystical character, 660; notions and characteristics of liturgical S., 661–709; its dogmatic character, 668–669; liturgical S. the S. of the Church by a title that does not pertain to the other spiritualities, 677f; whether liturgical S. is the same as Benedictine S., 679–683; liturgical S. and actualization of the psychological faculties, 316–324; liturgical S. centered on the Mass, 157–179; *See*: MASS; liturgical S. and modern aspirations, 738–739; liturgical S. in St. Gertrude, 740–803; whether there are dangers in liturgical S., 709f, 737; relationship between S. and the study of liturgy, 640f; types of S.: apostolic S., 659; Benedictine S., 651, 675, 679f, 682; Carmelite S., 651, 660; Carthusian S., 659; Dominican S.,

651; Franciscan S., 651; Ignatian or Jesuit S., 651, 660, 680; Salesian S., 651; S. for diocesan clergy, 651, 655; S. for the laity, 651, 655.

SPORTS: blessing of the implements of various sporting activities in the Roman Ritual, 320.

STATE OF MAN, PRIMORDIAL: or paradisial state, 325, 344.

STATES OF LIFE: various S. of L. and liturgical spirituality, 680f, 721f.

STELLA MARIS MARIA: antiphon, 754.

STIGMATA: what faith the liturgy demands in the historical fact of the stigmata of St. Francis on his feast day, 510, 524; the invisible S. of St. Gertrude, 790.

STOICISM: 459.

STORMS: antidemoniacal dimension of the entreaties against storms, 432.

STRUGGLE AGAINST SATAN: the S. against Satan is a constant cosmic reality, and is an essential part of revelation, 450; what is *de fide* and what is not *de fide* in the affirmations of the N. T. and of later tradition in regard to the S. against S., 389–396; in the N. T., 364–383; and the mission and work of Christ in the N. T., 367–371; the mission of the Apostles in the N. T., as S. against S., 371–375; the general situation of the Christian and of the world confronted by Satan, after Christ, in the N. T., 372f; the life of the individual Christian as S. against S., in the N. T., 375f; the life of the Church as S. against S., in the N. T., 377–383; tradition after the N. T. and outside the liturgy on the S. against S., 383–389; human body, pagan life, elements of nature, and S. against S., 384f; baptism, martyrdom, monastic life, particular judgment, and S. against S., 387f; and liturgy, 381–451; the liturgies never cease exhorting the faithful to the S. against S., 450–451; theme of revelation which the theologian can discover in depth only in the liturgy, 571; is one of the themes in which the liturgy proposes to the faithful the living of all dogmas in a balanced way, 666; a theme which the liturgy constantly proposes to the discursive intelligence of the faithful in a total synthesis with the other themes of revelation, 689f; in the Psalms the theme of the enemies of the People of God must be transposed so as to understand it as the S. against S., 498f; liturgy of Christian initiation in the S. against S., 396–417; the Eucharist in the perspective of Christian initiation as S. against S., 412–417; confirmation in the perspective of Christian initiation as S. against S., 411f; the blessing of the font and the post-baptismal anointing in the perspective of Christian initiation as S. against S., 409f; the rites over the *competentes* in the perspective of Christian initiation as S. against S., 401–409; the rites over the *audientes* in the perspective of Christian initiation as S. against S., 397–401; the S. against S. in the sacraments other than those of Christian initiation, 417–428; the liturgy of penance as S. against S., 417–421; the liturgy of the ill as S. against S., 421–425; the liturgy of ecclesiastical orders as S. against S.: exorcist, 425f; matrimonial liturgy as S. against S., 427f; S. against S. in the principal sacramental rites not immediately connected with the seven sacraments, 428–437; holy water in the S. against S., 429f; the entreaties against storms, and the S. against S., 432; the consecration of virgins, and the S. against S., 432f; monastic profession and the S. against S., 433f; the liturgy of the dead and the S. against S., 435f; temporal sanctoral cycles and the S. against S., 437–451; Advent-Epiphany season and the S. against S., 437f; Lent as a special time in the S. against S., 439f; liturgy from Passiontide to Ascensiontide and the struggle and triumph of Christ over Satan, 442f; the sanctoral cycle and the S. against S., 445f; martyrdom, especially of women, as victory over Satan, 445f; angels and Mary in the S. against S., 446f; ferial office and the S. against S., 448f; S. against S. hardly mentioned in the works of St. Gertrude, this constituting one of the defects of her writings, 760.

TECHNOLOGY: theology of T., 312 n. 7.

TE DECET LAUS: 218, 220, 222.

TE DEUM: 218, 220, 222, 687.

TE DICIMUS PRAECONIO: 448 n. 194.

TE IURE LAUDANT: antiphon, 764.

TELEÍOSIS: and its Christological meaning, 258.

TELÓNAI: plural, lit., tax collectors; singular: *telónēs*, 388, 390, 425. *See: TELÓNIA; TELONÍA*.

TELÓNIA: plural, lit., customs houses or tax collectors' stations; singular, *telónion*, 358, 412. *See: TELÓNAI; TELONÍA*.

TELONÍA: singular, lit., office (position, status) of tax collector, 390, 425. *See: TELÓNAI; TELÓNIA*.

TEMPLE IN JERUSALEM: Christ, Church, individual souls, Christian temples, heavenly Jerusalem, 497f.

TEMPORALIS DISPENSATIO SALVATIONIS: as salvation history in St. Augustine, 871.

THEANDRISM: in Christ, in the Church, in the liturgy, 301f.

THEOCENTRISM: of the liturgy and of liturgical spirituality, 102, 142, 667, 668; desire for a more theocentric preaching, 877, 879–880.

THEOLOGICAL VIRTUES: and religion, 513f. *See*: FAITH; HOPE; CHARITY; VIRTUES.

THEOLOGY: theoretical notes on the concept of Th., 626–631; Th. as science, 627f; includes also investigation of the historical empirical aspect of the revealed data, 628–631; origin of positive-scholastic Th., 546–550; its ideal of the apologetic proof from the sources, 558f; plan of exposition in positive-scholastic Th., 558f; positive Th. in modern positive-scholasticism, 547, 549f, 558f; positive-scholastic Th. and the catechism, 890f; the *quaestio* method in scholastic Th., 582f; dominant concern in the Th. of St. Thomas, 587f; limitations and specific contribution of positive-scholastic Th., 874f; patristic Th. as *gnôsis*: origin, nature, advantages and defects, 619–625; patristic Th. centered on the sacred (salvation) history, 868–875; pastoral Th., 805f; Th. of modern technology, 312; Th. of labor, 312; symbolic or figurative Th., 589 n. 53, 609f.

THEOLOGY AND LITURGY: theological judgment in liturgical research, 510f, 519f; four principal rules for determining the theological authority of any specific point in the liturgy, 520–529; relationship between general synthetic theology and the liturgy, 542–643; the general question, 542–546; relationship between general synthetic theology and liturgy in the positive-scholastics, 510f, 542–571, 551f, 578 n. 4; and in the theology of St. Thomas, 572–589; comparison from this point of view of positive-scholastic theology and the theology of St. Thomas, 586–589; relationship between theology and liturgy in the Fathers, 590–625; theoretical notes on the question of the relations between general synthetic theology and liturgy, 626–643; investigation of theological aspect of the liturgy, xxii f; nature, necessity, object, division of the theology of the liturgy, xxiv; Th. and L. and their relations with the sacred history of salvation, 588f; Th. and L. in the Middle Ages to the 12th century, 595; liturgical aspect of the individual theological treatises, 635–637.

THEORÍA: its theological significance, 317.

THEURGISM: in the Pseudo-Dionysius, 608.

THYSÍA: as sacrifice, 147.

TIME: present, past, future, in the liturgical signs, 73; T., individuation of actions, and the theory of Odo Casel on the mystery, 104f; the transcending of T. in the liturgy,

90–95, 178–179, 267f; the sacred times in the O. T., according to St. Thomas, 581. *See*: SACRED (SALVATION) HISTORY.

TOTALITY, UNIFIED: [Dom Vagaggini's term in Italian is *unitotalità*; we have rendered it variously as *universality, unified totality, total unity*.] the liturgy and the law of the cosmic universality of the kingdom of God: infrahuman creation, man, angels, saints, souls in purgatory, 308–361; U. T. of the cosmos, and spirit of the liturgy in St. Gertrude, 766–774.

TOUCHES, DIVINE: as mystical experience in St. John of the Cross, 729.

TRADITIO EVANGELII: and its antidemoniacal dimension, 402.

TRADITION: and authority of the liturgy, in the Fathers, 615–619; the liturgy as proof of the apostolicity of the T. of a doctrine according to the positive-scholastic theologians, 56of, 565f; traditional character of the liturgy, 853.

TRADITIO ORATIONIS DOMINICAE: 591; its antidemoniacal dimension, 402–403.

TRADITIO SYMBOLI: 9, 591; its antidemoniacal dimension, 402.

TRANSLATIONS: liturgical, and post-Tridentine prohibition of translating the Missal into the vernacular, 292–293.

TRANSVERBERATION: as mystical experience in St. Gertrude, 782f.

TREATISES: or tracts; theological T. and their relation to the liturgy, 635–637; explanatory T. on the liturgy in the patristic age, 591–596.

TREMENDUM: its relationship with religion and with liturgy, 127, 128.

TRENT: Council of T. and liturgy, 552.

TRINITY: the Christological-Trinitarian movement of revelation and of liturgy, 191–246; worship, sanctification, and T. in the liturgy, 23f; the *a-per-in-ad* schema in the manner of considering the T., 24f, 198–209; the T. in the orations, 209–217; in the doxologies, 217–223; in the Mass, 223–230; in the sacraments, 230–239; in the sacramentals, 239–240; in the liturgical cycles, 240–246; establishment and meaning of the feast of the Most Blessed Trinity, 209, 243–246; indwelling of the Persons of the T. in the soul of the just man, and spirituality, 656; T. and mystical experience, 726; Trinitarian controversies and the liturgy, 551, 612; T. and liturgy in St. Thomas, 585; T. and the concept of preaching, 861; T. and liturgical mystical life in St. Gertrude, 761–763, 787. *See*: MOVEMENT, CHRISTOLOGICAL-TRINITARIAN.

TRISÁGION: 613.

TRIVIUM: course of studies which, in the Middle Ages, along with the *Quadrivium*, was regarded, among else, as of some utility for preaching, the *T.* being the lower branch, consisting of grammar, rhetoric, and logic, while the *Quadrivium* consisted of arithmetic, music, geometry and astronomy, the seven together accounted as the seven liberal arts, 594.

TWO CITIES: doctrine of. *See*: CITY.

TYPOLOGY: biblical, patristic, liturgical T., xxii f n. 10; concept and existence of T. in the Bible, 476–481; specific extent of the typological relationships between O. T. and N. T., 478f; the Fathers and T., 479f; T. in the liturgy, 480f; T. and *gnôsis*, 621f; T. and *mysterium* or *sacramentum*, 606f; difference between T. and Hellenistic allegorism, 459 n. 3, 577.

TYPOS: 36, 38, 476f, 599f.

UNITY, COSMIC: according to revelation and liturgy: infrahuman creation, man, angels, saints, souls in purgatory, 308–361; C. U. of the faithful, of the saints, and of the souls in purgatory, in the anaphora of St. Basil, 168f.

UNITY OF THE TWO TESTAMENTS: and of sacred salvation history as basis for understanding how the liturgy uses the Bible, 456f.

VALIDITY: the liturgy aims not merely at a valid performance of the liturgical actions, but at one which will produce its full individual and social fruit, 841.

VENI SANCTIFICATOR: and its Gallican introduction into the Mass, 292 n. 31.

VIA CRUCIS, or STATIONS OF THE CROSS: and liturgy, 671, 676.

VIATICUM: its antidemoniacal dimension, 424.

VIDI DOMINE FACIE AD FACIEM: responsory, 780.

VIGILS: for the dead, in antiquity, 339; for the martyrs and saints, 340.

VIRGINITY: and universal priesthood of the faithful, 143f, 155; Christological-Trinitarian dimension of the consecration of virgins, 239; consecration of V. and the struggle against Satan, 387, 432f; consecration of V. explained by the Fathers, 591–596; rite of the consecration of V., and the *Exercises* of St. Gertrude, 795.

VIRTUES: treatment of the infused V., and the liturgy, 636; exercise of the moral and theological V. in spirituality in general, 658f; ascetic exercise of the V., and spirit of the liturgy in St. Gertrude, 751–760; relationship between moral V. and religion, 129f; relationship between theological V. and religion, 130f; the theological V. at the service of the virtue of religion, and as actualizing the latter, 130f; the theological V., exercised in the liturgical action in the perspective of the virtue of religion, 697–702; theological V. and preaching, 881. *See:* FAITH; HOPE; CHARITY.

VISIONS: in St. Gertrude, and their significance, 742–748.

WAR: how the liturgy intends and proposes the biblical texts, especially in the Psalms, which speak of the W. against the enemies of God, 498f.

WATER: significance of the drop of water in the wine at the offertory, according to St. Thomas, 579.

WATER, BAPTISMAL: the Christological-Trinitarian sense of the blessing of the baptismal font and of the water, 409f; and the angels, 354f; antidemoniacal dimension of its blessing, 409f.

WATER, HOLY: exorcism over it and the reconsecration of the infrahuman world to the service of the divine life, 332; and the struggle against Satan, 429f.

WEST: symbolic of Satan, 409.

WILL: peculiar manner of the liturgy's engaging of the W., 318f, 516, 668, 690.

WINE: medieval opinion of the consecration of wine in the chalice through mere contact with the consecrated host, 510, 525; opinion of St. Thomas on the mixing of non-consecrated wine with the consecrated in order to increase the quantity of the latter, 579.

WISDOM: Augustinian *sapientia*, 622; W. as ideal of the theology of the Fathers, *See:* GNÔSIS; how the liturgy understands the O. T. texts that speak of the W. of God, 467f.

WOMAN OF THE APOCALYPSE: crowned by twelve stars: and the liturgy, 482.

WORD: (i.e., the spoken word, reading of Scripture), as liturgical sign, 47f; W., sacraments, and liturgy, 880–883; ministry of the W., 882f; its presence always real, 863; operating power of God and of Christ, 863; mystery of Christ completed in the W., 863f; celebration of the W., 504f, 857; W. and sacraments among the Protestants, 861.

WORKS: extraliturgical W., and liturgical spirituality, 672–675; extraliturgical pastoral W., as means ordered to the liturgy and deriving therefrom, 811–821.

WORKS, GOOD: the O. T. texts recommending G. W. are understood first of all in the sense in which they were understood by the contemporaries to whom those texts were addressed, 462f; O. T. texts recommending G. W. understood in the light of the Sermon on the Mount, 471; theme brought habitually to the attention of the liturgical action, 689, 697–698; the theme of G. W. is always much emphasized in the psychological moralizational catechesis of the liturgy, 697–698, 704–705.

WORLD: the "world" under the dominion of Satan, 366.

WORSHIP: notion, 133f; divisions on the basis of the excellence of the one worshiped, 134f; divisions on the basis of the subject worshiping, 136f; latria, 314, 316; dulia, 134, 136; hyperdulia, 134, 136; W. offered to God has its end in reference to the sanctification of souls, 672–673; interior W., 136f; interior W. never excessive, 138; but in exterior W. it is possible to sin either by excess or by defect, 138; social and private W., 69, 74f, 133–139; Christian W., notion, 135f; W. on Golgotha offered to God the Father, 575; eternal and cosmic W. of the heavenly Jerusalem, 72, 75; W. as *aedificatio fidei, spei, et caritatis* in St. Augustine, 700; W. and sanctification in the liturgy, 21, 83, 124f; and its efficient cause, 71; and its exemplary cause, 72; and its final cause, 71–72; and its intrinsic formal cause, 70; and its material cause, 70; images, 582 n. 35; relics and liturgy, 533, 585 n. 35; Jewish W., 135; prayer W., 409; idolatrous W., 576; W. and philosophy, 142; W. and religious psychology, 142; W. and history of religions, 142; prefigurative value of the O. T. W. in respect to Christian W. and heavenly W., 135, 260f, 272f; sacramental characters as habilitation for W., 139–143; W. of the Church as participation of the Church in Christ's W. of God and the Church's W. of Christ, See: CHRIST; theology of W. in the *Summa theologiae* of St. Thomas, 573f; how the notion of W. enters into the definition of liturgy, 19f; phenomenology of W., 64f; in the liturgy as ecclesiastically instituted the present actuality of W. is on the primary level, 83; W. in Christianity and in the pre-Christian religions, 84; the W. included in the sacraments derives from the Eucharist, 172f; it is in sacrifice that religious W. achieves its highest stature, 131, 147, 149; the Mass as supreme W., 158–162; W. in the O. T. according to the *Summa theologiae* of St. Thomas, 581f; W. (veneration) of the saints, and the liturgy, in Perrone, 555 n. 24; W. of Christ, of images, or relics, according to St. Thomas, 582 n. 35.

WOUNDS: of Christ, and worship of Christ, in St. Thomas, 582 n. 35; devotion to the Five Wounds during the Middle Ages, 798f; devotion to the wounds of our Savior, and liturgy, in St. Gertrude, 800f.